BRITISH WRITERS

BRITISH WRITERS

Edited under the auspices of the British Council

IAN SCOTT-KILVERT
General Editor

VOLUME VII

SEAN O'CASEY

TO

POETS OF WORLD WAR II

CHARLES SCRIBNER'S SONS / NEW YORK

Copyright © 1984 The British Council

Library of Congress Cataloging in Publication Data (Revised)

Main entry under title:

British writers.

Includes bibliographies and index.
CONTENTS: v. 1. William Langland to the English Bible—
v. 2. Thomas Middleton to George Farquhar—[etc.]—
v. 7. Sean O'Casey to Poets of World War II.
1. English literature—History and criticism.
2. English literature—Bio-bibliography. 3. Authors,
English—Biography. I. Scott-Kilvert, Ian.
II. Great Britain. British Council.
PR85.B688   820'.9   78-23483
ISBN 0–684–15798–5 (v. 1)   ISBN 0–684–16636–4 (v. 5)
ISBN 0–684–16407–8 (v. 2)   ISBN 0–684–16637–2 (v. 6)
ISBN 0–684–16408–6 (v. 3)   ISBN 0–684–16638–0 (v. 7)
ISBN 0–684–16635–6 (v. 4)

Acknowledgment is gratefully made to those publishers
and individuals who have permitted the use of the following materials in copyright.

"James Joyce"
   From "Chamber Music" and "Alone" from Collected
Poems by James Joyce. Copyright © 1918 by B. W.
Huebsch. Copyright 1927, 1936 by James Joyce. Copyright
renewed 1946 by Nora Joyce. Reprinted by permission of
Viking Penguin Inc. "Chamber Music" reprinted with the
permission also of Jonathan Cape Ltd. Acknowledgment
is also made to The Society of Authors as the literary
representative of the Estate of James Joyce.

"Edith Sitwell"
   From The Collected Poems of Edith Sitwell. Reprinted
by permission of the publisher Vanguard Press, Inc. Copyright © 1968 by Vanguard Press, Inc. Copyright © 1949,
1953, 1954, 1959, 1962, 1963 by Dame Edith Sitwell. Originally published by Macmillan and Company, London,
Ltd. Reproduced by kind permission of David Higham
Associates Ltd.

"T. S. Eliot"
   Excerpts from Collected Poems 1909–1962, Four Quartets,
and The Waste Land: A Facsimile and Transcript of the
Original Drafts, all by T. S. Eliot, are reprinted by per-

mission of Harcourt Brace Jovanovich Inc.; copyright 1936 by Harcourt Brace Jovanovich, Inc.; copyright 1943, © 1963, 1964 by T. S. Eliot; renewed 1971 by Esme Valerie Eliot, copyright © 1971 by Valerie Eliot. Extracts from *Collected Poems 1909–1962* by T. S. Eliot and seven lines from *The Waste Land: A Facsimile and Transcript* edited by Valerie Eliot. Reprinted by permission of Faber and Faber Ltd.

"Aldous Huxley"
Excerpt (12 lines) from "Fifth Philosopher's Song" in *The Collected Poetry of Aldous Huxley*, edited by Donald Watt. Copyright 1920 by Aldous Huxley. Reprinted by permission of Harper and Row, Publishers, Inc. Permission also granted by Chatto and Windus Ltd. Excerpt from "Song of the Poplars," originally published in *The Defeat of Youth* and now included in *The Collected Poems of Aldous Huxley*, edited by Donald Watt, reprinted by permission of Mrs. Laura Huxley and Chatto and Windus Ltd.

"Robert Graves"
Quotations from the poems by Robert Graves are reprinted by his kind permission.

"John Betjeman"
From *Collected Poems* by Sir John Betjeman. Copyright © 1958. Reprintd by permission of John Murray Ltd.

"W. H. Auden"
From *W. H. Auden: Collected Poems*, edited by Edward Mendelson. Copyright © 1976 by Edward Mendelson, William Meredith, and Monroe K. Spears, Executors of the Estate of W. H. Auden. Reprinted by permission of Random House, Inc. Permission also given by Faber and Faber Ltd. Extracts from *The English Auden: Poems, Essays and Dramatic Writings 1927–1939* by W. H. Auden reprinted by permission of Faber and Faber Ltd.

"Louis MacNeice"
From *The Agamemnon of Aeschylus, Goethe's Faust*, translated by Louis MacNeice, and from *The Collected Poems of Louis MacNeice* reprinted by permission of Faber and Faber Ltd.

"Poets of World War II"
Henry Reed: From *A Map of Verona*. Reprinted by kind permission of the author and Jonathan Cape Ltd.
Gavin Ewart: The Editor gratefully thanks Hutchinson Publishers for kind permission to reproduce material from the following poems—"Officers Mess," "Sonnet, 1940," and "When a Beau Goes In.'" From Gavin Ewart's *The Collected Ewart 1933–1980*.
Vernon Scannell: From *New and Collected Poems 1950–1980* by Vernon Scannell. Originally published by Robson Books Ltd. Reprinted by permission of the publisher.
John Bayliss: From *Not Without Glory*. Reprinted by permission of the Woburn Press.
George Fraser: Reprinted from George Fraser's *Return to Oasis*, published by Shepheard-Walwyn Ltd. 1980, by permission of Mrs. George Fraser.
Hamish Henderson: From *Elegies for the Dead in Cyrenaica*. Reprinted by kind permission of the author.
Norman Cameron: From *Collected Poems*. Reprinted by kind permission of the Literary Estate of Norman Cameron and the Hogarth Press.
John Manifold: "Ration Party" and "The Sirens." From *Collected Verse* (1978). Reprinted by courtesy of the University of Queensland Press.
Roy Campbell: From *Collected Poems*. Reprinted by permission of Teresa Campbell.
Roy Fuller: From *Collected Poems 1936–1961*, copyright © 1962, by Roy Fuller. Reprinted by permission of Dufour Editions Inc., Chester Springs, Pennsylvania, and by André Deutsch Ltd., London.
Edward Lowbury: From *Time for Sale* (1961). Reprinted by kind permission of the author.
Bernard Gutteridge: From *The Traveller's Eye*. Reprinted by permission of Routledge and Kegan Paul, London and Boston.
Alan Ross: From *Poems 1942–67*. Reprinted by kind permission of the author.
Charles Causley: From *Collected Poems 1951–1975* by Charles Causley. Copyright © 1951, 1953, 1957, 1961, 1968, 1969, 1970, 1975. Reprinted by permission of David R. Godine, Publisher, Boston.
Sidney Keyes: From *The Collected Poems of Sidney Keyes*, published by Routledge and Kegan Paul Ltd., London and Boston. Reprinted by permission of the publisher.
Keith Douglas: From *The Complete Poems of Keith Douglas*, edited by Desmond Graham. Copyright © Marie J. Douglas 1978. Reprinted by permission of Oxford University Press.
Alun Lewis: From the works *In the Green Tree, Raiders Dawn*, and *Ha! Ha! Among the Trumpets* by Alun Lewis. Reprinted by permission of Allen and Unwin Ltd.

Editorial Staff

List of Subjects in Volume VII

SEAN O'CASEY / *William A. Armstrong*   1

VIRGINIA WOOLF / *Bernard Blackstone*   17

JAMES JOYCE / *J. I. M. Stewart*   41

IVY COMPTON-BURNETT / *R. Glynn Grylls*   59

WYNDHAM LEWIS / *E. W. F. Tomlin*   71

D. H. LAWRENCE / *Alastair Niven*   87

EDITH SITWELL / *John Lehmann*   127

T. S. ELIOT / *M. C. Bradbrook*   143

KATHERINE MANSFIELD / *Ian A. Gordon*   171

JOYCE CARY / *Walter Allen*   185

ALDOUS HUXLEY / *Jocelyn Brooke*   197

J. B. PRIESTLEY / *Kenneth Young*   209

F. R. LEAVIS / *Edward Greenwood*   233

ROBERT GRAVES / *Martin Seymour-Smith*   257

GEORGE ORWELL / *Tom Hopkinson*   273

EVELYN WAUGH / *William Myers*   289

CHRISTOPHER ISHERWOOD / *Francis King*   309

C. P. SNOW / *William Cooper*   321

ANTHONY POWELL / *Bernard Bergonzi*   343

JOHN BETJEMAN / *John Press*   355

W. H. AUDEN / *Richard Hoggart*   379

LOUIS MacNEICE / *John Press*   401

POETS OF WORLD WAR II / *John Press*   421

Introduction

British Writers is designed as a work of reference to complement *American Writers*, the eight-volume set of literary biographies of authors past and present, which was first published in 1974. In the same way as its American counterpart, which first appeared in the form of individual pamphlets published by the University of Minnesota Press, the British collection originates from a series of separate articles entitled *Writers and Their Work*. This series was initiated by the British Council in 1950 as a part of its worldwide program to support the teaching of English language and literature, an activity carried on both in the English-speaking world and in many countries in which English is not the mother tongue.

The articles are intended to appeal to a wide readership, including students in secondary and advanced education, teachers, librarians, scholars, editors, and critics, as well as the general public. Their purpose is to provide an introduction to the work of writers who have made a significant contribution to English literature, to stimulate the reader's enjoyment of the text, and to give students the means to pursue the subject further. The series begins in the fourteenth century and extends to the present day, and is printed in chronological order according to the date of the subject's birth. The articles are far from conforming to a fixed pattern, but speaking generally each begins with a short biographical section, the main body of the text being devoted to a survey of the subject's principal writings and an assessment of the work as a whole. Each article is equipped with a selected bibliography that records the subject's writings in chronological order, in the form both of collected editions and of separate works, including modern and paperback editions. The bibliography concludes with a list of biographical and critical publications, including both books and articles, to guide the reader who is interested in further research. In the case of authors such as Chaucer or Shakespeare, whose writings have in-spired extensive criticism and commentary, the critical section is further subdivided and provides a useful record of the new fields of research that have developed over the past hundred years.

British Writers is not conceived as an encyclopedia of literature, nor is it a series of articles planned so comprehensively as to include every writer of historical importance. Its character is rather that of a critical anthology possessing both the virtues and the limitations of such a grouping. It offers neither the schematized form of the encyclopedia nor the completeness of design of the literary history. On the other hand it is limited neither by the impersonality of the one nor the uniformity of the other. Since each contributor speaks with only one voice out of many, he is principally concerned with explaining his subject as fully as possible rather than with establishing an order of merit or making "placing" comparisons (since each contributor might well "place" differently). The prime task is one of presentation and exposition rather than of assigning critical praise or censure. The contributors to the first volume consist of distinguished literary scholars and critics—later volumes include contributions by poets, novelists, historians, and biographers. Each writes as an enthusiast for his subject, and each sets out to explain what are the qualities that make an author worth reading.

As with its immediate predecessors, Volume VII contains some unavoidable overlapping. Thus the later novels of E. M. Forster and of Ford Madox Ford, which are dealt with in Volume VI, are often considered by critics to belong to the "Modern Movement." On the other hand Volume VII also includes the work of Ivy Compton-Burnett, who, although she continued to write until the 1960's, declared, "I do not feel that I have any real organic knowledge of life later than about 1910." Conversely, while it is convenient to consider World War II as a watershed between Volume VII and what follows, several of the writers included in the present volume have produced some of their best work after 1945. Graham Greene, still an impressively active author, will be included in a supplement to the series. A tidier editorial scheme could only have been devised by unduly contracting Volume VII or expanding its successor.

All the works discussed in this volume were first published in the twentieth century. This fact obliges us to consider briefly the use of the terms *avant-garde, recent, modern,* and *contemporary.* Avant-garde, if it refers to work that is experimental or innovative in its time, is equally applicable in 1908 or 1980. Recent denotes any work produced after a given date. Modern, apart from its commercial or scientific meaning, has also become a critical term with a specific aesthetic and chronological reference, comparable to, say, romantic or regency. The term modern movement is now applied internationally and in all the arts to work of a radically experimental nature produced during the first twenty-five to thirty years of the century. Contemporary, while retaining its obvious sense of present day, has also acquired a critical shade of meaning, so that commentators sometimes distinguish a "modern" writer from a "contemporary" one.

In this critical context the modern writer is one who re-examines the foundations of his art. He is especially concerned with innovations in form, technique, modes of sensibility, vocabulary, linguistic structure, and is correspondingly less concerned with public and social issues; by comparison with the contemporary writer his imaginative world is timeless. The contemporary writer pays less attention to formal or linguistic experiment. His fiction draws its vitality from the world he lives in, from its historical, political, economic, and social character; and he feels himself well qualified to interpret the changing circumstances of his age. In the period under review, James Joyce, T. S. Eliot, and Virginia Woolf are obvious examples of the modern writer; Aldous Huxley, George Orwell, W. H. Auden, C. P. Snow (and at a different level J. B. Priestley) of the contemporary. D. H. Lawrence and Wyndham Lewis, while unquestionably modern in certain respects, have a foot in both camps.

The introduction to Volume VI noted the effect of the continental movements of naturalism and symbolism upon late-Victorian and Edwardian culture. Both forces contributed to the growth of the modern movement, but it was the influence of symbolism,

with its acknowledgment of relative rather than absolute knowledge as the norm of human cognition, and the effects of that acceptance upon artistic and linguistic forms, which played the more important part.

As so often in English cultural life, nothing which could accurately be described as an organized artistic movement took shape. Instead we find the forces of revolt against Victorian and Edwardian literary standards and tastes conspicuously divided, with small groups among the dissenting writers vigorously opposing one another, or writers of undoubted original genius such as Joyce, Lawrence, or Wyndham Lewis working in virtual isolation. The date at which these changes visibly accelerated was 1910. That year also witnessed the end of the notoriously materialistic Edwardian era and the beginning of the Georgian, and coincided with Roger Fry's first post-impressionist exhibition, later styled "the art-quake of 1910." This enterprise scored a spectacular success as an irritant and put the names of such avant-garde painters as Cézanne, Gauguin, Van Gogh, Picasso, and Matisse on the map: it caused an enraged conservative critic to admit that "art has become a viral matter," that is, penetrated the subconscious of the public.

Virginia Woolf, looking back from the 1920's, pinpointed the moment in ironic fashion: "In or about December 1910 human character changed." In other words a decisive change in the artist's perception of it had begun. The apostles of the modern movement in prose and verse alike found the mainstream literature of the day obsolete in its presentation of experience, insular and untrained in technique, flabby in its use of language. These judgments were applied not least to writers who prided themselves on being liberal and up to date in their outlook—John Galsworthy or John Masefield for example.

T. S. Eliot likewise remarked in later life that the situation in English poetry in 1910 was stagnant to a degree which it was difficult for any writer in later years to imagine. Partly the problem was one of language and style. The verbal currency coined by the romantics and the Victorians had become unacceptably worn and dulled. Besides this, Eliot was attacking the assumption that poetry was a mysterious essence, produced by an age-old craft. The poet apprenticed himself to mastering familiar forms of meter and rhyme handed down from the sixteenth century, and then applied this skill to the rendering of twentieth-century experience. Naturally poems would vary in merit, but poetry produced by this formula was instinctively recognizable and required no critical effort from the reader: to apply a conscious scrutiny risked destroying the "beauty" of the poem. The validity of Eliot's attack was later demonstrated by I. A. Richards' famous laboratory experiment in practical criticism, when he tested readers' reactions to a selection of unsigned poems in which verse by Shakespeare and other masters was mingled with inflated and trashy pieces. At its best, the kind of verse Eliot was attacking was represented by the dream-inspired lyrics of Walter de la Mare, the semijournalistic ballads and narratives of Hilaire Belloc, G. K. Chesterton, and Masefield, and the "country week-end" poems of the Georgians. This taste was fostered by a widely shared nostalgia for "the real England," Blake's "green and pleasant land," which was to be found far from the pollution of industry and the spread of suburbia; such nostalgia also sprang from a reaction against the dandified and cosmopolitan spirit of the 1890's and the jingoism of the Boer War period. Poets, it was felt, should be the guardians of this rural heartland, and not a few of them were content to see themselves as minor artists, living under the shadow of the great Victorians, their position similar to that of "Sunday painters."

Eliot and Pound were convinced that any revival of poetry in England demanded a different attitude toward the native tradition. They had no wish to sweep away tradition as such; they had left the United States for Europe expressly to seek out a tradition which they could not find at home. In their poetry and their criticism they strove to make the past alive and new, and thus to transform it into a vital influence on the present rather than a moribund one. Like Henry James, they considered that England, for all the riches of its literature, suffered, by European standards, from insularity and provinciality. They studied French, Provençal, Italian, German, and found both inspiration and technique in foreign models—Far Eastern as well as continental. They believed that the traditional English verse forms, as currently employed, were inadequate to render the sights and sounds, rhythms and impressions of modern life.

Eliot, because of his particular fondness for Jacobean drama and French nineteenth-century poetry, introduced three elements which sharply distinguish his early poetry from that of his Edwardian and Georgian contemporaries. The first was a harshly urban imagery which drew upon the squalor, pollution, and tedium of the modern metropolis—"the fog that rubs its yellow back upon the window panes" —and was addressed to a sophisticated, city-dwelling public. The second was a revolutionary approach to metric and rhythm. In place of an orthodox and sonorous harmony of meter and rhyme, in which words could too often function as "fill-ups" to pad out a stanza, both Eliot and Pound treated the bare image or statement as the metrical unit. Eliot experimented with free verse modelled on Jules Laforgue and irregular blank verse modelled on the Jacobeans; and when he writes in regular quatrains, as in "Sweeney Among the Nightingales," such pieces are highly condensed, allusive, poems in cryptogram. He argued that what gives verse its life is the constant approach to a fixed pattern without quite settling into it. The third element was a deliberate telescoping of expression, a juxtaposition of sharply contrasting ideas and images with the explanatory connections left out. Here too we find a rejection of the conventional reader's expectations. The essence of poetry must not be diluted, nor the sharpness of its impact dulled: the poet should not emulate his Victorian predecessors and often write in a language which the laziest can understand; the reader should work a little for his enjoyment.

Pound never became naturalized, let alone anglicized, as Eliot was to do, but his influence on the second decade of the century as counsellor of poets and impresario of the modern movement, was ubiquitous and amounted almost to a one-man revolution. He launched the imagist group of poets in 1912, advised Yeats on the transformation of his diction and versification in the years 1913–1914, collaborated with Wyndham Lewis in the formation of the Vorticist movement and the founding of *Blast* magazine in 1914, helped Joyce find a publisher for *Dubliners*, sponsored the publication of *A Portrait of the Artist as a Young Man*, "discovered" Eliot when he had written "The Lovesong of J. Alfred Prufrock" and *Preludes*, and later helped him to edit and reshape *The Waste Land*.

M. C. Bradbrook's essay is mainly concerned with Eliot's later major writings, notably *The Waste Land*, *Four Quartets*, his plays, and his criticism. She emphasizes the extent to which Eliot's writings form a closely related whole, the later poems illuminating meanings in the earlier, and his critical judgment being constantly energized by his poetic sensibility. She also devotes a section of the essay to a commentary on the Quinn Manuscript, the original draft of *The Waste Land*, which was only published in 1971.

The leading innovators of the period in fiction—James Joyce, Virginia Woolf, and D. H. Lawrence—all likewise believed that a radical change in the representation of human consciousness was necessary. They shared the conviction that "life," the significant substance of our experience, must be sought in the individual's interior vision, not in the perceptions of man depicted in terms of his external attributes or of his position in society. Each, however, followed this artistic aim by quite different paths.

Joyce's art, which combines elements of realism and symbolism, must be seen against his Irish background. As early as 1900, at the age of eighteen, he was swimming against the tide of the Celtic and nationalist revival, training himself to observe men and women "as we really see them, not as we apprehend them in the world of faery." His earliest fiction, *Dubliners*, was intended "as a chapter in the moral history of my country," "set down in a style of scrupulous meanness." These vignettes are indeed masterpieces of deflation: the symbolist element in his writing is best represented by the last piece, "The Dead," which with the sudden broadening of perspective of its finale, remains one of the greatest short stories ever written. In *A Portrait of the Artist* Joyce proceeds to his next objective, the creation of a character in continuous and magnified close-up: our view is framed by the developing consciousness of the hero, which becomes the setting of the entire book. J.I.M. Stewart's essay traces Joyce's aims as a novelist in his four principal works, discusses the effects achieved in each, and analyzes the transformation which he brought about in his style in pursuit of these artistic purposes.

Of all the moderns considered in this volume, Lawrence's revolt against the values amidst which he had grown up was the most broadly based, the least exclusively literary. His dissent sprang from his vision of the conflict between man and his surroundings (the sheer ugliness of the environment which Victorian enterprise had inflicted upon the nation), between nature and the machine, between the sexes, the classes, the superego and the id. Thus to present life was to him not only a literary problem. In many of his books he draws a distinction between life and an existence which is unworthy of the name: "a thing isn't life just because somebody does it." He wishes to assert the importance of the individual's naive

sense of "at-oneness with the universe." Once he loses this, he becomes a mere social unit, which is, he contends, the fate of the characters in the works of the "materialist" novelists, especially Galsworthy. The reader encounters in all Lawrence's writing a texture of tones that are discordant and yet inseparable—those of the artist, the preacher, and the autobiographer. Lawrence's gift for description, especially of nature, his power to impart the feel and smell and color of living things, is prodigious, and it is in the stories rather than the novels that the reader can most easily enjoy the artistry and block out the message. But to attempt this hinders us from understanding the fact that Lawrence was a pioneer of a new concept of fiction. He develops this idea in a famous letter to Edward Garnett (5 June 1914): "that which is physic (physiological) in humanity is more interesting to me than the old-fashioned human element which causes one to conceive a character in a certain moral scheme . . . and make him consistent. You mustn't look in my novel for the old stable ego of the character." Lawrence was looking for something less conscious or contrived than the surface personality: not What have you made of yourself, but Of what primary substance are you made? This approach obliged him, in a sense, to *live* the text of each novel: his purpose was to catch the immediate flux of experience rather than to execute a planned design. If life offered new material during the period of creation, then this must be included. Such a method of writing naturally produced variable results. *The Rainbow* and *Women in Love* exemplify this technique at its best.

Alastair Niven stresses at the beginning of his essay Lawrence's achievement in keeping pace, more effectively than any other modern writer, with the welter of ideas that transformed society in his lifetime, and justly claims that no English novelist before him had risked such a stretching of language in order to express feelings which are nonverbal. Besides providing a thorough appreciation of the novels, he also surveys Lawrence's extraordinarily diverse achievement as a dramatist, travel writer, letter writer, essayist, and critic.

The most eloquent critical indictment of the "materialist" school of fiction (Wells, Bennett, and Galsworthy), together with an exposition of her own artistic creed is contained in Virginia Woolf's two essays *Mr. Bennett and Mrs. Brown* (1924) and *Modern Fiction* (1925). Her case was that the materialists "write of unimportant things . . . spend immense skill and industry in making the trivial and the transitory appear the true and the enduring. . . . The novel is done to a turn, but the reader lays it down asking, is life like this? Must the novel be like this?" Virginia Woolf asks the same question Lawrence asks—Wherein does "life" consist? and How should the writer represent it? Her approach is to examine an ordinary mind on an ordinary day, "receiving the impressions of an incessant shower of innumerable atoms." For the modern novelist "the accent falls differently from of old, the moment of importance came not here, but there." "Life" is not to be observed by means of lamps artificially arranged as in a photographer's studio: "life is a luminous halo, a semitransparent envelope surrounding us from the beginning of consciousness to the end." This was not merely a critical theory. *Mrs. Dalloway*, *To the Lighthouse*, and *The Waves* are examples of another new fictional genre quite as unfamiliar as those of Joyce or Lawrence. These novels do not offer the interest of the clash of character or the surprises of intricate plotting—on the contrary, they tend to isolate the characters in aesthetic worlds of their own: their appeal lies in the extraordinary delicacy with which the author describes the complexity of experience as apprehended from moment to moment and creates a poetry of mood and sensation.

Bernard Blackstone examines the technical experiments which Virginia Woolf practiced, especially in those novels which are concerned with the flow of time. As regards the isolation of her characters, he contends that Virginia Woolf achieved in her fiction an impressive equilibrium, preserving solitude in the midst of society. He devotes an important section of the essay to her literary criticism. Although Virginia Woolf was never a critic of the stature or influence of Eliot, both played a vital part in the literary history of the century: Eliot through his editorship of the *Criterion* and his partnership in the publishing house Faber and Faber, Virginia Woolf through her foundation of the Hogarth Press. By these means many of the rising generation of poets and novelists were discovered, encouraged, and published. The essay also surveys Virginia Woolf's *Letters* and *Diaries* as invaluable literary chronicles of her times.

At the end of *Mr. Bennett and Mrs. Brown* Virginia Woolf ventured a prophecy: "we are trembling on the verge of one of the great ages of English literature." This was a daring prediction at the time, but events have shown that it was, even then, slight-ly belated. The year 1924 saw the publication of Forster's *A Passage to India*, and the first of Ford Madox Ford's cycle of war novels, *Parade's End*; Lawrence's best work was already behind him. The annus mirabilis had been 1922, when Eliot's *The Waste Land*, Joyce's *Ulysses*, Edith Sitwell and William Walton's *Façade*, Lawrence's *England, My England*, and Katherine Mansfield's *The Garden Party* had all appeared. Virginia Woolf was right to insist on the originality of these works and their superiority to what was to follow. On the other hand the modern movement did not put down deep roots; by the 1930's its impetus had faded, and thereafter the native tradition was to reassert itself.

For the breadth of his interests as a novelist and painter and a critic of literature, aesthetics, and sociology, Wyndham Lewis must certainly rank as one of the seminal intelligences of his time. He has not received his due, partly because of his deliberately assumed isolated and polemical stance, for which the title he chose for his autobiography, *Rude Assignment*, was entirely apt. His books have nourished rather than tempted readers, and his literary personality lacked that treacherous attribute charisma: all these considerations suggest that his time will come. His approach to fiction was diametrically opposite to that of Virginia Woolf; his canvas is loaded to saturation with the visual attributes of his characters, but he is much less interested in their inner sensibilities: "I am for the Great Without, the method of external approach," he explained, and in this genre he created powerful satires of Parisian bohemia in *Tarr* and of the Bloomsbury Group and the Sitwells in *The Apes of God*. Frederick Tomlin gives his subject a philosophical as well as a literary dimension and stresses the need to grasp the breadth and the integrated nature of Wyndham Lewis' writings. There has been no dissipation of energy; the novels, the pamphlets, the wide-ranging critical works reinforce one another. The fact that in his late sixties he should have published such a vigorous analysis of "engaged" literature as *The Writer and the Absolute*, examining the work of his juniors—Jean-Paul Sartre, André Malraux, and Albert Camus—was sufficient evidence of his enduring critical vitality.

World War I profoundly affected the course that English literature was to follow, but this was by no means immediately obvious. With the exception of Wyndham Lewis, most of those who were to become prominent in the modern movement—Pound, Eliot,

Yeats, Joyce, Virginia Woolf, Edith Sitwell, Lawrence, Huxley—for reasons of nationality, sex, or health took no part in active service. On the other hand the avant-garde writing of 1914 had little influence on the work of the young writers who joined up, a number of whom had contributed to Edward Marsh's *Georgian Poetry*. Conversely, the best of their war poetry, the writings of Siegfried Sassoon, Wilfred Owen, and Isaac Rosenberg, made little appeal to spectators of the conflict such as Pound, Eliot, and Yeats (although it was valued by the Sitwells). As for the prose literature inspired by the fighting, with the exception of Ford Madox Ford (already a veteran when he enlisted), no English novelist of the stature of Faulkner or Hemingway emerged, and it was not for a decade that the experience of the front had stabilized sufficiently to enable authors such as Aldington, Blunden, and Graves to complete their memoirs and novels. For Lawrence (who volunteered, but was rejected for service) disillusion with the war set in even earlier than for the soldiers. He viewed the conflict as the ultimate and horrifying union of industrialism and science, the victory of the machine over nature. He regarded the England that he loved as destroyed as early as 1915, and resolved to leave it as soon as circumstances allowed: "as far as I possibly can, I will stand outside this time," he wrote. One reason for these developments was the impassable gulf which grew up between the outlook of civilian and serviceman. Not merely on leave, but long after the war had ended, the combatants felt themselves to belong to another world, to have been plunged into an experience they could neither share nor describe. Graves records that he was still experiencing nightmares of the trenches ten years after the armistice. The major poem by a writer of the modern movement which comments directly upon the war was Pound's *Hugh Selwyn Mauberley* (1920); *The Waste Land* is concerned with the aftermath. Pound is writing of what struck him, above all, as a cultural tragedy—the suicide of the Old World:

> There died a myriad
> And of the best, among them . . .
>
> For two gross of broken statues
> For a few thousand battered books

To the combatants the cause was altogether more personal and intimate. Edward Thomas, asked on leave what he was fighting for, is said to have picked up a pinch of earth and said, "Literally for this." The revolution wrought in poetry by the moderns was undoubtedly a real and a necessary one. The experience of the trenches was another kind of revolution which taught the younger poets, notably Graves, that traditional modes of writing could still serve to express the realities of modern life. When Graves visited Thomas Hardy in 1921, the old poet prophesied that "vers libre could come to nothing in England. All we can do is write on the old themes in the old styles, and try to do a little better than those who went before us." This modest prediction has proved on the whole well founded, and Hardy's own influence in particular has remained remarkably durable to the present day. In due course the native tradition, having absorbed the experience of the war, was to reemerge in the 1930's.

Meanwhile the view most widely shared by writers, however occupied during 1914–1918, was one of disillusionment. This was especially directed at the older generation, who, it was felt, had allowed the war to begin, demanded unlimited sacrifices for it, done well out of it, and bungled its conduct. On this at least the intellectuals and pacifists of Bloomsbury and the ex-combatants could agree. Disenchantment could go no further when in 1929, the year of *All Quiet on the Western Front* and other war classics, the immensely successful play *Journey's End* immortalized the line uttered by a young officer waiting for zero hour, "It all seems a bit silly, doesn't it?"

Although the Sitwells—Edith, Osbert, and Sacheverell—did not play formative parts in the modern movement comparable to those of Eliot and Virginia Woolf, they were certainly in personal and historical terms at the center of the cultural life of London. The capital has never possessed literary cafes and has often lacked literary salons to act as a focus for new and established writers. For domestic reasons the Sitwells had decided when peace had been proclaimed that dullness was the great enemy of English life, and bent their collective efforts to banishing it. During the interwar years their patronage of modern art, music, ballet, new verse and public performances of it, together with their flair for creating publicity, kept them constantly in the news; and Edith and Osbert held court in their respective homes. In the process they engaged in a continuous series of personal duels or jousts, which included Lawrence, Huxley, Wyndham Lewis, Eliot, Gertrude Stein, and critics such as F. R. Leavis, Cyril Connolly, Geoffrey Grigson, and J. C. Squire, and greatly enlivened the literary chronicles of the time.

INTRODUCTION

In literary terms Edith Sitwell's innovations were concerned more with linguistic and metrical changes, matters of style and technique rather than content. The metrical experiments of the *Façade* sequence, for example, resembles a series of musical exercises in technical virtuosity. Edith Sitwell had studied Charles Baudelaire and Arthur Rimbaud, and was especially interested in mingling or transposing different modes of perception—"shrill green," "creaking light," "wooden rain." By such means she wished, like Eliot, to jolt the unadventurous reader. John Lehmann explains these varieties of shock treatment in dealing with her early poetry: he devotes the second half of his essay to Edith Sitwell's altogether graver manner which dominates her later verse. *Gold Coast Customs,* an eloquent attack on the worship of Mammon, is particularly remarkable for having been written before 1929, in other words at a time when the euphoria of the 1920's was still at its height. It foreshadows Edith Sitwell's emergence as the prophetess of human tragedy and suffering which she became in such poems, inspired by World War II, as "Still Falls the Rain," *The Shadow of Cain,* and *The Canticle of the Rose,* the two last being concerned with the implications of the atomic bomb.

Katherine Mansfield was undoubtedly an originator (allowing for a recognizable debt to Anton Chekhov) in the art of the short story, yet she could produce her finest effects while retaining many of the traditional resources of fiction. She shows especial skill in the use of the interior monologue, and her stories are at once beautifully constructed, yet free from the stiffness of development imposed by a linear narrative. She can spring surprises and reveal conflicts of character and motive, while still suggesting that her men, women, and children are behaving spontaneously, not following a track laid down by the design of the tale. Ian Gordon praises the perfect balance of her style, which could borrow from poetry, and yet remained based on a simple and colloquial prose. He draws attention to the failure of the collected editions of her stories to place them in the correct order of composition. This is of great importance in clarifying the fact that her best work dates from her middle twenties, when she turned for her themes to her recollections of life in New Zealand.

Ivy Compton-Burnett's novels must surely strike the literary historian as unclassifiable in whichever age she happened to have been born. They are written to a uniquely consistent pattern. In externals the curtain rises upon a rundown country house at about the end of the nineteenth century; spiritually the milieu is timeless. Her books have affinities in some respects to the domestic comedy of Jane Austen, in others to Victorian melodramatic fiction with its plots involving disputed wills, secret or bigamous marriages, longlost documents, revelations overheard by chance or by eavesdropping. Rosalie Glynn Grylls's essay expertly analyzes the components of Dame Ivy's art, notably the originality of her dialogue in which so often the unexpected part of a statement is taken up by the interlocutor and her adroitness in devising strong situations which lift the novels above the level of conversation pieces. "Dear, dear, the miniature world of the family!" one of her characters exclaims, "all the emotions of mankind seem to find a place in it."

Some critics have regarded Joyce Cary as a novelist who stood apart from the dominant fashions and techniques of his lifetime, and there are obvious resemblances in his fiction to the eighteenth-century picaresque novel and to the larger-than-life characterizations of Charles Dickens. When Cary began to write in the 1920's, the fictional heroes of Virginia Woolf and Aldous Huxley, for example, were somewhat passive figures, "to whom things happen." Cary, by contrast, whether in his novels of African life, his studies of children, or his chronicles of twentieth-century England, has written of personages who are irresistibly driven by their imaginations to mold their own destinies and the life around them. Here he took up an authorial position which was the opposite of Lawrence's. Nobody could accuse Cary's creations of lacking in individuality yet he succeeds in presenting men and women such as Gulley Jimson, probably the most successful portrait of a painter ever realized in fiction, or Sarah Munday, as members of a social fabric who are strengthened rather than dehumanized by their association with it. Walter Allen praises Cary's mastery of the art of impersonation, and sees him as fulfilling the Shakespearean or Keatsian ideal of the artist as "one who continually fills some other body." But he also contends that Cary was well aware of contemporary fictional techniques, and in fact succeeds in grafting on to the trunk of traditional fiction many of the devices introduced by Joyce, Lawrence, and Virginia Woolf.

Like Wyndham Lewis, Huxley was a writer of exceptionally wide interests. His writings on literature and aesthetics do not possess the depth of Lewis' thought, but since his stance toward his readers was of a persuasive and popularizing rather than polemical kind, he was certainly more widely read. He belonged, as did the Stracheys and the Stephens, to one of the intellectual families associated with Bloomsbury. His novels and stories scored an early success, and his urbanity and wit gave him a natural entree to the heart of the London literary scene. His early novels provide a very lively satirical portrait of metropolitan and country house life in the gay 1920's: they have become period pieces of the epoch, much as Evelyn Waugh's did for the following decade; and they abound similarly with sketches of friends and acquaintances drawn in varying degrees from life. But Huxley, unlike Waugh, is limited by his tendency to present his characters not as whole beings, but rather only in terms of their ideas. Jocelyn Brooke draws attention to the pessimism which underlay the light comedy of the early fiction. In the later novels Huxley reveals himself more and more as a didactic author looking for a faith in the bewildering world of the mid-twentieth century. In *Point Counter Point* he stresses the irreconcilable conflict in man between the demands of the flesh and the spirit. In *Brave New World* and *After Many a Summer* he enquires, "is happiness enough, in view of the price we may have to pay for it?" *The Island* is his last attempt at a Utopian formula. Much of the writing of the last third of his life was non-fictional. The final development of his thought in the direction of mysticism and "non-attachment" began with his immigration to California in the late 1930's and produced such treatises as *Ends and Means* and *The Perennial Philosophy*.

The plays of Sean O'Casey had no connection with the modern movement. But his three most famous pieces—*The Shadow of a Gunman, Juno and the Paycock*, and *The Plough and the Stars*—date from the period when the movement was at its height: and since they are concerned with the new Ireland that was emerging from "The Troubles" of those years, they display a "birth of a nation" quality, such as no earlier Irish drama possesses. The present essay reinforces the general judgment that in these dramas O'Casey found a dramatic form and theme, a balance of tragedy and comedy, and a blend of speech at once naturalistic and eloquent which perfectly suited his gifts. In his middle years he used an expressionist technique with a predominantly Marxist slant for the handling of contemporary European problems, and applied a distinctly simplified view to such issues. After World War II he returned to Irish topics, and William Armstrong contends that some of these plays, such as *Cock

A'Doodle Dandy* and *The Bishop's Bonfire*, still comparatively neglected in the theater, could give the world a fresh demonstration of O'Casey's talents.

J. B. Priestley belongs unashamedly to the "materialist" school, as Virginia Woolf dubbed it. During half a century of successful authorship of novels, plays, essays, and travel books, he has established himself as a communicator rather than a literary artist. Although some of his work has inevitably proved ephemeral, the best of his novels, such as *The Good Companions* and *Angel Pavement*, still provide remarkably vivid chronicles of English life between the wars, and other books provide a living history of the intellectual and political preoccupations of his times. As a fellow Yorkshireman, Kenneth Young provides a sympathetic account of Priestley's down-to-earth, no-nonsense attitude to writing. He gives especial praise to that province of Priestley's writing which seems most likely to last, namely the drama, in which he has experimented tirelessly with comedies, farces, melodramas, problem pieces, modern moralities, and plays on the philosophy of time.

Writing near the end of W. H. Auden's life, the late poet George Fraser paired Auden and Graves as the two most fertile, intelligent, and gifted poets then surviving. This is a sound judgment, but Graves has inevitably become best known for his brilliant historical pot-boilers, such as the Claudius books and *Count Belisarius*. His prose should also be known preeminently for *The White Goddess*, his investigation into the origins of poetry and the nature of the Muse—part anthropology, part autobiography, part criticism, and, finally, the testament of a practicing poet. His autobiography, *Goodbye to All That*, remains one of the classic records of World War I.

In his poetry, Graves, as noted elsewhere, is not a technical innovator. Beginning his writing career at the height of the modern movement, he has steadily established himself as a worthy heir to the native tradition, laboring to bring regular forms of rhyme and meter to their perfect expression. He has proved that a poetry of wit, strong linguistic discipline, and intense emotional vitality can still be created by these methods. Some biographical guidance is essential to the understanding of his development as a poet. Martin Seymour-Smith, who published in 1982 the only full-length biography, gives a full sketch of Graves's long career, with its many authorial and personal victories and setbacks, a study of a man who resolved at all times "to avoid a dull, easy life." The last half of the essay provides a particularly lucid appreciation of Graves's approach to poetry and of his achievement.

F. R. Leavis is certainly among the most influential English critics of the present century; the author of this essay describes him as the greatest. But few critics survive merely by virtue of their insights, however brilliant into the creations of other writers. When their work endures, it is because of their power to make general judgments upon the art of letters, and because of their importance in the history of ideas, as could be claimed for Coleridge, Arnold, and Eliot. Leavis criticism combines exceptional powers of close analysis with a firm grasp of the logical character of critical discourse. His writings have always laid a special insistence upon the importance of literature in a social and moral context, upon the writer's duty to guard the health of words and thus the health of human consciousness. The period covered by the present volume has witnessed the rise of the status of literary studies in higher education, and the foundation of chairs of English literature in all British universities. Edward Greenwood's essay touches upon Leavis' career at Cambridge during the early years of the English faculty. He sketches the nature of other intellectual disciplines and influences which were prominent at that time, notably the logico-mathematical, the positivist, and the Marxist, and describes the opposition Leavis encountered in pursuing his own methods and priorities in teaching. He regards *New Bearings in English Poetry, Revaluation,* and *The Great Tradition* as Leavis' major critical productions; he also discusses the achievement of Leavis' famous periodical, *Scrutiny,* and surveys his later books and the evolution of his criticism of Eliot and Lawrence.

At the end of the 1920's history drew a sudden dividing line. Thereafter the events of the next decade took on a lurid clarity which none of those who lived through them can forget. Within months the financial crash of October 1929 had produced a worldwide recession which was to last until the re-armament boom which immediately preceded World War II. The euphoria and the frivolity of the 1920's, the search for pleasure to compensate for the lost years of World War I, were swept away. Britain became a living "waste land," a landscape as Auden described it of "smokeless chimneys, rotting wharves and choked canals," of ghost towns and hunger marches. While the western democracies remained sunk in inertia, the dictatorships seized the initiative, until world affairs took on an apparently irreversible course. Hitler's rise to power was followed by the invasion of Ethiopia, the Spanish Civil War, the annexation of Austria and Czechoslovakia. Writers found themselves obliged to take sides on issues which aroused their passions as no comparable set of events had done since 1918. These developments inspired a literature of exceptional topical urgency.

In England many of the rising generation of poets, novelists, and critics, mostly middle-class and university educated, experienced a feeling of guilt at living comparatively comfortable lives, while their poorer compatriots suffered unemployment and insecurity. They turned for guidance to Marxism, and for hope to the prospect of an alliance with the USSR to ward off the threat of Fascism. Victor Gollancz' Left Book Club rapidly built up a monthly readership of scores of thousands. In his anthology *New Country* (1933), which introduced a number of young authors who have since become famous, Michael Roberts wrote, "Poetry will be revolutionary. The novelist will either write in a way which will show the fatuity of the white-collar class, whose cultural superiority has vanished, or will turn for his subject-matter to the working-class." Charles Madge, echoing Wordsworth's sonnet on Milton, wrote:

> Lenin, would you were living at this hour:
> England has need of you. . . .

However the new and commanding voice in poetry was certainly that of Auden. It is a rare event for a poet in his twenties to articulate so decisively the message of the Zeitgeist. But with *Poems, 1930* and *Look, Stranger* (1936), he produced an impact which could be compared with that of Byron's *Childe Harold* (as a virtuoso of satirical eloquence and of rhyme he has other clear affinities with Byron). Auden succeeded in implicating his readers directly and personally in his verse; he achieved this through his gift of formulating the immediately arresting public question or exhortation:

> What do you think about England, this
> Country of ours where nobody is well?

and also the image of complex and paradoxical feeling

> Lay your sleeping head, my love,
> Human, on my faithless arm

Auden is a poet of many phases and progressions. Richard Hoggart notes that although his art has been formed from elements deeply planted in the English tradition—Middle English, Hardy, Hopkins, Owen —he is nevertheless a socially unrooted poet, who has succeeded in assimilating the influences he absorbed from his residence in America: witness his evolution from an ideologue who in England popularized concepts drawn from Freud, Groddeck, and Marx, to a poetic communicator in America no less dedicated to the doctrines of Kierkegaard and Niebuhr. Hoggart sees Auden as a teacher, a didactic and purposeful writer, but also as a divided man who has continued his search for a belief. At the same time Auden remained open and versatile to a remarkable degree in his poetic technique. The later part of the essay discusses Auden's use of the long verse line in *The Shield of Achilles*, and his success in discovering a new and different audience in America.

"What's nationality these days?" asks the English tramp on a Greek steamer in V. S. Naipaul's *In A Free State*. Writers are often assumed to draw their inspiration from their native roots: but in some instances they write as well without them or by transplanting them. This point is relevant to the work of Christopher Isherwood. "I write," he remarked in an interview, "because I am trying to study my life in retrospect and find out what it is made of." His novels and stories are based to an exceptional degree on autobiography, and this may account for the fact that his writing, like Auden's, was not radically affected by his decision to reside in America. Certainly the effort to study his life in retrospect has led him on the path of the expatriate for most of his career. Judged by artistic standards, his Berlin-based novels and stories comprise his best work. *Mr. Norris Changes Trains* and *Goodbye to Berlin* provide brilliant demonstrations of what he described as E. M. Forster's "art of tea-tabling," that is of toning down the major scenes to a level of anticlimax. By this means he succeeded better than other contemporaries in rendering the menacing quality of life in Germany in the mid-1930's. All the phases in Isherwood's very diverse oeuvre are dealt with in Francis King's essay, but he especially stresses the honesty of observation and the meticulous ear for dialogue which characterize all his best work.

George Orwell's first book, *Down and Out in London and Paris*, was published in 1933, and it epitomizes much of his subsequent career, during which (unlike many of the left-wing writers of the 1930's) he impressed his readers more by example than by exhortation. It was his practice to do at any moment the thing he found most important: this might involve becoming a tramp or a dishwasher, attempting to join the working class in Britain, or enlisting in the Spanish Republican army. Most of his early books consist of straight autobiography, sociologico-literary criticism, and semi-autobiographical fiction. His two spectacularly successful books, *Animal Farm* and *Nineteen Eighty-four*, took the form of a fable and a "dystopian" prophecy, respectively. Like John Bunyan and Jonathan Swift, he was a master of the pamphlet who succeeded in finding in fiction an immensely powerful vehicle for his message. Tom Hopkinson's essay gives a careful assessment of Orwell's limitations as a novelist, in particular his lack of historical perspective; it also pays a strong tribute to the unflinching clarity of his vision and the direct, unvarnished eloquence of his prose.

Evelyn Waugh was four years Auden's senior at Oxford; but four years is a long gap at university, and Waugh was old enough to have experienced the frivolous delights of the 1920's. In any case his stance toward the events of the prewar decade was diametrically opposite to Auden's, though it is worth noting that in later life both men acknowledged a central religious root. Certainly both were very well attuned to the spirit of the time. Waugh's early novels owe something to his work for the media—first as a gossip columnist, later as a foreign correspondent. If Auden's public saw him as part prophet of doom, part entertainer, Waugh's regarded him as wholly the latter. His first two novels were savagely detached satires of the world of "the bright young things" with the hero in each case as a comparatively innocent participant. His fourth, *A Handful of Dust*, its title taken from *The Waste Land*, carried satirically entertaining fiction to the limit, and a perceptive reader might then have become aware that the fires of hell burned beneath the floor. But to most of his public, *Brideshead Revisited* (1945) came as a sudden shock; the inexhaustibly diverting cabaret satirist of the previous fifteen years was seen to have a heart. Evelyn Waugh's art was to pass through other unexpected phases, before he completed the *Sword of Honour* trilogy, which now ranks as the finest fictional record of World War II. William Myers' essay gives a thorough biographical as well as a critical appreciation of Waugh's career, and places it in the context of English history. In his summing up he stresses the sense of perspective which Waugh's religious beliefs gave him: "His awareness of the human condition as fundamentally historical made him intimately responsive to the history of his own times." That factor is especially prominent in his two major postwar works, *Brideshead Revisited* and *Sword of Honour*.

Anthony Powell's literary career falls into two clearly marked divisions. Before 1939 he had established himself as a witty observer of London life, in the area where the smart or would-be smart mingle with the underworld of fashion and the arts. His novels had some affinity to those of Waugh, but dealt with a narrower stratum of English life. Since World War II he has devoted himself to a major fiction cycle, the twelve-volume *A Dance to the Music of Time*. It would be misleading to compare this sequence to the more ambitious ventures of Balzac or Proust in the same genre. Powell's range of observation is largely confined to the upper-middle-class spheres of business, the city, politics, the services, the arts, and the media. But his title is admirably chosen. Across his canvas, which covers more than half a century, the dancers weave in and out of each other's lives, reappearing in unexpected partnerships. Time brings grotesque transformations and Nemesis teaches significant lessons: it is the reward of a design as consistently realized as this one to encompass such effects. In his appreciation Bernard Bergonzi, while acknowledging the limitations of Powell's world, praises his complete mastery of it and his capacity to catch its minutest idiosyncrasies in speech and gesture. He remarks that his subject differs from the majority of modern novelists in showing a general affection for his characters: Powell's vision of humanity recalls the stance of Chaucer, Rabelais, and Shakespeare, in whose works human folly, weakness, and vice are transformed into an unending comic dance.

With his novel sequence *Strangers and Brothers*, C. P. Snow became the first English novelist to embark on an "organic" cycle of this kind: such comparable enterprises as those of Trollope and Galsworthy are more loosely planned. This was also a pioneer venture in the sense of the scientist and man of action creating a history in fiction of his own times. Ford Madox Ford in his Tietjens novels had made the attempt on a smaller scale. Anthony Trollope and Arnold Bennett were men of letters who were obliged to rely upon imagination in describing

the operations of politicians and businessmen: Benjamin Disraeli brought firsthand political experience only to the surface of his novels—much of the rest is myth making. And, unlike the majority of novel-cycles, *Strangers and Brothers* moves on a rising spiral of dramatic interest. The progress of Lewis Eliot's personal rise in the world is matched by the dramas of university life in *The Masters* and *The Affair*, the involvement of atomic scientists in national affairs in *The New Men*, and by the conflicts inseparable from high policy making described in *Corridors of Power*. The limitations of the series are implicit in its material, a certain gray uniformity in this world of scientists, administrators, and politicians, and a lack of descriptive power to feed the senses.

William Cooper writes with the benefit of a long friendship with his subject. He notes that the series is divided into novels of direct experience and observed experience. In the first and smaller category, *Time of Hope*, *Homecomings*, and *Last Things* are concerned with the hero's personal story, his childhood, his two marriages, and his relations with his son; and these volumes contain the most moving chapters in the cycle. Elsewhere the author explains the key to Snow's handling of his material, which consists of "a resonance between what Lewis Eliot sees and what he feels," a link between outward observation and inward experience, these modes of perception being echoed and reexamined from one book to another.

John Betjeman may be compared to Graves as a poet who cannot easily be fitted into any neat literary diagram for his generation, though there are obvious points of sympathy with the work of Waugh. Like Kipling, he has captured a large public which normally reads little poetry: his poems scan, rhyme enjoyably, and are not difficult to grasp, though they contain unsuspected depths of meaning and allusion and repay re-reading. Also like Kipling he often relies upon topical and local references, dear to the British reader but not easy to explain to others. Hardy is an evident influence with respect to his versification, his attachment to the past, his skill in the short poetic narrative, and his feeling for architecture. Betjeman's verse has always been inspired by his awareness of buildings, including some which many find ugly or laughable; and he has made himself the poet of the Gothic revival style, suburbia, and the garden city. The present essay quotes his passionate appeal to the general reader to notice and care for his environment. "Architecture means not a house, nor a single building, nor the glass of Chartres, but your surroundings, our whole over-populated island." John Press gives a detailed account of the strengths and limitations of Betjeman's poetry and stresses its authenticity, its fulfillment of Leslie Stephen's precept that "the poet's ultimate aim should be to touch our hearts by showing his own, and not to exhibit his learning or fine taste." He makes the point that while writers of the stature of Yeats, Eliot, and Lawrence explore the profound currents of thought and emotion in our times, it is the minor writers such as Betjeman who best portray the social habits and customs of our civilization.

Although the first and second world wars were separated by only a quarter of a century, the poetry which they inspired has surprisingly little in common, though we may note the coincidence that the three finest poets of World War II—Sidney Keyes, Keith Douglas, and Alun Lewis—were, like Wilfred Owen and Isaac Rosenberg, killed in action. In the second war, both civilians and combatants, women and men, were involved, if not equally, at least to an important extent, so that no unbridgeable difference in outlook opened between them. Moreover since the war was one of continual movement, no writer served throughout in any one scene of operations, nor could any location be regarded as more significant or typical than another. On the contrary the experience of war was so diverse that the main themes of the poems, as John Press points out in his survey, are often the physical features, social conditions, and historical backgrounds of the different theaters of war in which the poets happened to find themselves.

Some of the survivors wrote of the experience of those years with a force and immediacy which they never surpassed in their later verse; the author quotes in particular F. T. Prince's famous descriptive piece "Soldiers Bathing," and Alan Ross's poems of the war at sea—the only verse in either world war to portray the realities of patrol, rescue, or naval battle. He deals with the work of poets who served in Europe, the Western Desert, East Africa, India, and Burma, but he devotes an important part of his space to the three poets mentioned above. It was Keyes who showed the most brilliant promise of the three, but little of his verse touches directly on the war; he was killed when he was only twenty. Keith Douglas, both in his poems and his prose journal, *Alamein to Zem-Zem*, left behind the most vivid account of battle experience created by any soldier of those years. The poetry of Alun Lewis, who was killed in Burma in 1944, displays a wider, more reflective vision of war, less intensely focussed on the moment of action, keenly aware of the contrast between nature and the battlefield.

The *Writers and Their Work* series was founded by Laurence Brander, then director of publications at the British Council. The first editor was T. O. Beachcroft, himself a distinguished writer of short stories. His successors were the late Bonamy Dobrée, formerly Professor of English Literature at the University of Leeds; Geoffrey Bullough, Professor Emeritus of English Literature, King's College, London, and author of *The Narrative and Dramatic Sources of Shakespeare*; and since 1970 the present writer. To these founders and predecessors *British Writers* is deeply indebted for the design of the series, the planning of its scope, and the distinction of their editorship, and I personally for many years of friendship and advice, and invaluable experience generously shared.

—Ian Scott-Kilvert

Chronological Table

1880   Gladstone's second term as prime minister (1880–1885)
James A. Garfield elected president
Louis Pasteur discovers streptococcus
Browning's *Dramatic Idyls, Second Series*
Disraeli's *Endymion*
Dostoyevsky's *The Brothers Karamazov*
Hardy's *The Trumpet-Major*
James Thomson's *The City of Dreadful Night*
Zola's *Nana*
Death of George Eliot
Death of Gustave Flaubert
Jacob Epstein born
Sean O'Casey born
Lytton Strachey born

1881   Garfield assassinated; Chester A. Arthur succeeds to the presidency
Ibsen's *Ghosts*
Henry James's *The Portrait of a Lady* and *Washington Square*
D. G. Rossetti's *Ballads and Sonnets*
Death of Thomas Carlyle
Death of Benjamin Disraeli
Béla Bartók born
Pablo Picasso born

1882   Triple Alliance formed between German empire, Austrian empire, and Italy
Married Women's Property Act passed in Britain
Britain occupies Egypt and the Sudan
Ibsen's *An Enemy of the People*
Wagner's *Parsifal*
Deaths of Charles Darwin, Ralph Waldo Emerson, Dante Gabriel Rossetti, Anthony Trollope
James Joyce born
Franklin Delano Roosevelt born

Igor Stravinsky born
Virginia (Stephen) Woolf born

1883   Uprising of the Mahdi: Britain evacuates the Sudan
Metropolitan Opera opens
Royal College of Music opens
T. H. Green's *Ethics*
Nietzsche's *Thus Spake Zarathustra* (1883–1891)
Stevenson's *Treasure Island*
Deaths of Edward FitzGerald, Karl Marx, Ivan Turgenev, Richard Wagner
Franz Kafka born
John Maynard Keynes born

1884   Grover Cleveland elected president
The *Oxford English Dictionary* begins publishing
The Fabian Society founded
Hiram Maxim's recoil-operated machine gun invented
Ibsen's *The Wild Duck*
Mark Twain's *Adventures of Huckleberry Finn*
Ivy Compton-Burnett born
Percy Wyndham Lewis born

1885   The Mahdi captures Khartoum: General Gordon killed
Gottlieb Daimler invents an internal combustion engine
Pasteur perfects vaccine for rabies
Marx's *Das Kapital* (vol. II)
Meredith's *Diana of the Crossways*
Maupassant's *Bel-Ami*
Pater's *Marius the Epicurean*
Tolstoy's *The Power of Darkness*
Zola's *Germinal*
Death of Victor Hugo
David Herbert (D. H.) Lawrence born
Sinclair Lewis born
Ezra Pound born

1886 The Canadian Pacific Railway completed
Gold discovered in the Transvaal
The Statue of Liberty dedicated
Linotype first used in the New York *Herald Tribune*
Hardy's *The Mayor of Casterbridge*
Ibsen's *Rosmersholm*
Henry James's *The Bostonians* and *The Princess Casamassima*
Kipling's *Departmental Ditties*
Nietzsche's *Beyond Good and Evil*
Rimbaud's *Les Illuminations*
Stevenson's *The Strange Case of Dr. Jekyll and Mr. Hyde*
Siegfried Sassoon born
Death of Franz Liszt

1887 Hardy's *The Woodlanders*
Verdi's *Otello*
Zola's *La Terre*
Rupert Brooke born
Edith Sitwell born

1888 Benjamin Harrison elected president
Henry James's *The Aspern Papers*
Kipling's *Plain Tales from the Hills*
Rimsky-Korsakov's *Scheherazade*
Strindberg's *Miss Julie*
Death of Matthew Arnold
Death of Edward Lear
Thomas Stearns (T. S.) Eliot born
Thomas Edward (T. E.) Lawrence born
Kathleen Beauchamp (Katherine Mansfield) born
Joyce Cary born
Julian Grenfell born
Eugene O'Neill born

1889 George Eastman produces a celluloid roll film
Henri Bergson's *Time* and *Freewill*
Yeats's *The Wanderings of Oisin*
Death of Robert Browning
Death of Gerard Manley Hopkins
Marc Chagall born
Charles Chaplin born
Adolf Hitler born

1890 Morris founds the Kelmscott Press
Robert Bridges' *Shorter Poems*
Ibsen's *Hedda Gabler*
William James's *The Principles of Psychology*

Henry James's *The Tragic Muse*
Morris' *News From Nowhere*
Tolstoy's *The Kreutzer Sonata*
Ivor Gurney born
Isaac Rosenberg born
Death of John Henry Newman
Death of Vincent Van Gogh
Charles De Gaulle born
Debussy's *L'Après-midi d'un faune*

1891 Gissing's *New Grub Street*
Hardy's *Tess of the d'Urbervilles*
Wilde's *The Picture of Dorian Gray*
Death of Herman Melville
Death of Arthur Rimbaud

1892 Grover Cleveland elected to second term as president
Conan Doyle's *The Adventures of Sherlock Holmes*
Kipling's *Barrack-Room Ballads*
Shaw's *Widowers' Houses*
Toulouse-Lautrec's *At the Moulin de la Galette*
Zola's *La Débâcle*
Wilde's *Lady Windermere's Fan*
Death of Alfred, Lord Tennyson
Death of Walt Whitman

1893 The World's Columbian Exposition opens in Chicago
Munch's *The Scream*
Tchaikovsky's "Pathetic" Symphony
Verdi's *Falstaff*
Wilde's *A Woman of No Importance* and *Salomé*
Death of Guy de Maupassant
Death of Peter Ilyich Tchaikovsky
Wilfred Owen born

1894 Trial and conviction of Alfred Dreyfus
Kipling's *The Jungle Book*
Moore's *Esther Waters*
Marx's *Das Kapital* (vol. III)
Aubrey Beardsley's *The Yellow Book* begins to appear quarterly (1894–1897)
Shaw's *Arms and the Man*
Deaths of Walter Pater, Robert Louis Stevenson, Christina Rossetti
Aldous Huxley born
John Boynton (J. B.) Priestley born

1895 Trial and imprisonment of Oscar Wilde

Roentgen discovers X rays
Marconi sends first wireless telegraph signals
The National Trust founded
Conrad's *Almayer's Folly*
Hardy's *Jude the Obscure*
Wells's *The Time Machine*
Wilde's *The Importance of Being Earnest*
Yeats's *Poems*
Deaths of Friedrich Engels, Louis Pasteur, and Arthur Rimbaud
Robert Graves born
Frank Raymond (F. R.) Leavis born
Charles Sorley born

1896 The Nobel Prizes established
William McKinley elected president
First modern Olympic Games held in Athens
Chekhov's *The Seagull*
Housman's *A Shropshire Lad*
Ibsen's *John Gabriel Borkman*
Puccini's *La Bohème*
Wells's *The Island of Dr. Moreau*
Death of William Morris
Death of Alfred Nobel
Death of Paul Verlaine
Edmund Blunden born
John Dos Passos born
F. Scott Fitzgerald born

1897 The Klondike Gold Rush begins
Conrad's *The Nigger of the "Narcissus"*
Havelock Ellis' *Studies in the Psychology of Sex* begins publication (1897–1936)
Henry James's *The Spoils of Poynton* and *What Maisie Knew*
Kipling's *Captains Courageous*
Rostand's *Cyrano de Bergerac*
Shaw's *Candida* and *The Devil's Disciple*
Wells's *The Invisible Man*
Death of Johannes Brahms
William Faulkner born

1898 Pierre and Marie Curie discover radium
Count von Zeppelin builds an airship
Chekhov's *Uncle Vanya*
Hardy's *Wessex Poems*
Henry James's *The Turn of the Screw*
Moore's *Evelyn Innes*

Shaw's *Caesar and Cleopatra* and *You Never Can Tell*
Wells's *The War of the Worlds*
Wilde's *The Ballad of Reading Gaol*
Death of Lewis Carroll
Death of William Ewart Gladstone
Bertolt Brecht born
René Magritte born

1899 Boer War (1899–1902)
Conrad's *Heart of Darkness* first published (in book form, 1902)
Elgar's *Enigma Variations*
Ernst Haeckel's *The Riddle of the Universe*
Kipling's *Stalky and Co.*
Tolstoy's *Resurrection*
Noel Coward born
Ernest Hemingway born

1900 British Labour party founded
Boxer Rebellion in China
Reginald A. Fessenden transmits speech by wireless
First Zeppelin trial flight
Max Planck presents his first paper on the quantum theory
Conrad's *Lord Jim*
Edward Elgar's *The Dream of Gerontius*
Sigmund Freud's *The Interpretation of Dreams*
William Butler Yeats's *The Shadowy Waters*
Deaths of Friedrich Nietzsche, John Ruskin, and Oscar Wilde

1901–1910 Reign of King Edward VII

1901 William McKinley assassinated; Theodore Roosevelt succeeds to presidency and is elected to office later in the year
First transatlantic wireless telegraph signal transmitted
Chekhov's *Three Sisters*
Freud's *Psychopathology of Everyday Life*
Rudyard Kipling's *Kim*
Thomas Mann's *Buddenbrooks*
Shaw's *Captain Brassbound's Conversion*
August Strindberg's *The Dance of Death*

CHRONOLOGICAL TABLE

Death of Giuseppe Verdi
Death of Henri de Toulouse-Lautrec
Roy Campbell born
André Malraux born
1902 J. M. Barrie's *The Admirable Crichton*
Arnold Bennett's *Anna of the Five Towns*
Cézanne's *Le Lac D'Annecy*
Conrad's *Heart of Darkness*
Henry James's *The Wings of the Dove*
William James's *The Varieties of Religious Experience*
Kipling's *Just So Stories*
Maugham's *Mrs. Cradock*
Times Literary Supplement begins publishing
Deaths of Samuel Butler, Cecil Rhodes, and Émile Zola
1903 At its London congress the Russian Social Democratic Party divides into Mensheviks, led by Plekhanov, and Bolsheviks, led by Lenin
The treaty of Panama places the Canal Zone in U.S. hands for a nominal rent
Motor cars regulated in Britain to a 20-mile-per-hour limit
The Wright brothers make a successful flight in the U.S.
Burlington magazine founded
Samuel Butler's *The Way of All Flesh*
George Gissing's *The Private Papers of Henry Ryecroft*
Thomas Hardy's *The Dynasts*
Henry James's *The Ambassadors*
Shaw's *Man and Superman*
Synge's *Riders to the Sea* produced in Dublin
Yeats's *In the Seven Woods* and *On Baile's Strand*
Death of James McNeill Whistler
Eric Blair (George Orwell) born
Evelyn Waugh born
1904 Russo-Japanese war (1904–1905)
Construction of the Panama Canal begins
The ultraviolet lamp invented
The engineering firm of Rolls Royce founded
Chekhov's *The Cherry Orchard*
Conrad's *Nostromo*

Henry James's *The Golden Bowl*
Kipling's *Traffics and Discoveries*
Georges Rouault's *Head of a Tragic Clown*
G. M. Trevelyan's *England Under the Stuarts*
Puccini's *Madame Butterfly*
First Shaw–Granville Barker season at the Royal Court Theatre
The Abbey Theatre founded in Dublin
Deaths of Anton Chekhov, Leslie Stephen, and Antonín Dvořák
Salvador Dali, Graham Greene, Christopher Isherwood born
1905 Russian sailors on the battleship *Potemkin* mutiny
After riots and a general strike the czar concedes demands by the Duma for legislative powers, a wider franchise, and civil liberties
Albert Einstein publishes his first theory of relativity
The Austin Motor Company founded
Bennett's *Tales of the Five Towns*
Claude Debussy's *La Mer*
E. M. Forster's *Where Angels Fear to Tread*
Richard Strauss's *Salome*
H. G. Wells's *Kipps*
Oscar Wilde's *De Profundis*
Norman Cameron born
Arthur Koestler born
Anthony Powell born
Charles Percy (C. P.) Snow born
1906 Liberals win a landslide victory in the British general election
The Trades Disputes Act legitimizes peaceful picketing in Britain
Captain Dreyfus rehabilitated in France
J. J. Thomson begins research on gamma rays
The U.S. Pure Food and Drug Act passed
Churchill's *Lord Randolph Churchill*
Galsworthy's *The Man of Property*
Kipling's *Puck of Pook's Hill*
Shaw's *The Doctor's Dilemma*
Yeats's *Poems 1899–1905*
Deaths of Pierre Curie, Paul Cézanne, Henrik Ibsen
Samuel Beckett born

John Betjeman born

1907 Exhibition of cubist paintings in Paris

Henry Adams' *The Education of Henry Adams*

Henri Bergson's *Creative Evolution*

Conrad's *The Secret Agent*

Forster's *The Longest Journey*

André Gide's *La Porte étroite*

Shaw's *John Bull's Other Island* and *Major Barbara*

Synge's *The Playboy of the Western World*

Trevelyan's *Garibaldi's Defence of the Roman Republic*

Death of Edvard Grieg

Death of Francis Thompson

Wystan Hugh (W. H.) Auden born

Louis MacNeice born

1908 Herbert Asquith becomes prime minister

David Lloyd George becomes chancellor of the exchequer

William Howard Taft elected president

The Young Turks seize power in Istanbul

Henry Ford's Model T car produced

Bennett's *The Old Wives' Tale*

Pierre Bonnard's *Nude Against the Light*

Georges Braque's *House at L'Estaque*

Chesterton's *The Man Who Was Thursday*

Jacob Epstein's *Figures* erected in London

Forster's *A Room with a View*

Anatole France's *L'Ile des Pingouins*

Henri Matisse's *Bonheur de Vivre*

Edward Elgar's *First Symphony*

Ford Madox Ford founds the *English Review*

1909 The Young Turks depose Sultan Abdul Hamid

The Anglo-Persian Oil Company formed

Louis Bleriot crosses the English Channel from France by monoplane

Admiral Robert Peary reaches the North Pole

Freud lectures at Clark University (Worcester, Mass.) on psychoanalysis

Serge Diaghilev's Ballets Russes opens in Paris

Galsworthy's *Strife*

Hardy's *Time's Laughingstocks*

Claude Monet's *Water Lilies*

Trevelyan's *Garibaldi and the Thousand*

Wells's *Tono-Bungay* first published (book form, 1909)

Deaths of George Meredith, John Millington Synge, and Algernon Charles Swinburne

1910–1936 **Reign of King George V**

1910 The Liberals win the British general election

Marie Curie's *Treatise on Radiography*

Arthur Evans excavates Cnossus

Edouard Manet and the first post-impressionist exhibition in London

Filippo Marinetti publishes "Manifesto of the Futurist Painters"

Norman Angell's *The Great Illusion*

Bennett's *Clayhanger*

Forster's *Howards End*

Galsworthy's *Justice* and *The Silver Box*

Kipling's *Rewards and Fairies*

Rimsky-Korsakov's *Le Coq d'or*

Stravinsky's *The Fire-Bird*

Vaughan Williams' *A Sea Symphony*

Wells's *The History of Mr. Polly*

Wells's *The New Machiavelli* first published (in book form, 1911)

Deaths of William James, Leo Tolstoy, Henri (Le Douanier) Rousseau, and Mark Twain

1911 Lloyd George introduces National Health Insurance Bill

Suffragette riots in Whitehall

Roald Amundsen reaches the South Pole

Bennett's *The Card*

Chagall's *Self Portrait with Seven Fingers*

Conrad's *Under Western Eyes*

D. H. Lawrence's *The White Peacock*

Katherine Mansfield's *In a German Pension*

Edward Marsh edits *Georgian Poetry*

Moore's *Hail and Farewell* (1911–1914)

Strauss's *Der Rosenkavalier*

Stravinsky's *Petrouchka*
Trevelyan's *Garibaldi and the Making of Italy*
Wells's *The New Machiavelli*
Mahler's *Das Lied van der Erde*
William Golding born

1912 Woodrow Wilson elected president
SS *Titanic* sinks on its maiden voyage
Five million Americans go to the movies daily; London has 400 movie theaters
Second post-impressionist exhibition in London
Bennett's and Edward Knoblock's *Milestones*
Constantin Brancusi's *Maiastra*
Wassily Kandinsky's *Black Lines*
D. H. Lawrence's *The Trespasser*
Lawrence Durrell born
Roy Fuller born
F. T. Prince born
Patrick White born

1913 Second Balkan War begins
Henry Ford pioneers factory assembly technique through conveyor belts
Epstein's *Tomb of Oscar Wilde*
New York Armory Show introduces modern art to the world
Alain-Fournier's *Le Grand Meaulnes*
Freud's *Totem and Taboo*
D. H. Lawrence's *Sons and Lovers*
Mann's *Death in Venice*
Proust's *Du Côté de Chez Swann* (first volume of *À la recherche du temps perdu*, 1913–1922)
Ravel's *Daphnis and Chloe*
Edward Lowbury born
Angus Wilson born

1914 The Panama Canal opens (formal dedication on 12 July 1920)
Irish Home Rule Bill passed in the House of Commons
Archduke Franz Ferdinand assassinated at Sarajevo
World War I begins
Battles of the Marne, Masurian Lakes, and Falkland Islands
Joyce's *Dubliners*
Shaw's *Pygmalion* and *Androcles and the Lion*
Yeats's *Responsibilities*

Wyndham Lewis publishes *Blast* magazine and *The Vorticist Manifesto*
Henry Reed born
Dylan Thomas born

1915 The Dardanelles campaign begins
Britain and Germany begin naval and submarine blockades
The *Lusitania* is sunk
Hugo Junkers manufactures the first fighter aircraft
Poison gas used for the first time
First Zeppelin raid in London
Rupert Brooke's *1914: Five Sonnets*
Norman Douglas' *Old Calabria*
D. W. Griffith's *The Birth of a Nation*
Gustave Holst's *The Planets*
D. H. Lawrence's *The Rainbow*
Wyndham Lewis's *The Crowd*
Maugham's *Of Human Bondage*
Pablo Picasso's *Harlequin*
Sibelius' *Fifth Symphony*
Deaths of Rupert Brooke, Julian Grenfell, and Charles Sorley
George Fraser born
Alun Lewis born

1916 Evacuation of Gallipoli and the Dardanelles
Battles of the Somme, Jutland, and Verdun
Britain introduces conscription
The Easter Rebellion in Dublin
Asquith resigns and David Lloyd George becomes prime minister
The Sykes-Picot agreement on the partition of Turkey
First military tanks used
Woodrow Wilson reelected president
Henri Barbusse's *Le Feu*
Griffith's *Intolerance*
Joyce's *Portrait of the Artist as a Young Man*
Jung's *Psychology of the Unconscious*
Moore's *The Brook Kerith*
Edith Sitwell edits *Wheels* (1916–1921)
Wells's *Mr. Britling Sees It Through*
Death of Henry James
Death of Lord Kitchener
Gavin Ewart born
Bernard Gutteridge born
John Manifold born

1917 U.S. enters World War I

Czar Nicholas II abdicates

The Balfour Declaration on a Jewish national home in Palestine

The Bolshevik Revolution

Georges Clemenceau elected prime minster of France

Lenin appointed chief commissar; Trotsky appointed minister of foreign affairs

Conrad's *The Shadow-Line*

Douglas' *South Wind*

Eliot's *Prufrock and Other Observations*

Modigliani's *Nude with Necklace*

Sassoon's *The Old Huntsman*

Prokofiev's *Classical Symphony*

Yeats's *The Wild Swans at Coole*

Death of Edward Thomas

Death of Edgar Degas

Anthony Burgess born

Charles Causley born

John Fitzgerald Kennedy born

1918   Wilson puts forward Fourteen Points for World Peace

Central Powers and Russia sign the Treaty of Brest-Litovsk

Execution of Czar Nicholas II and his family

Kaiser Wilhelm II abdicates

The Armistice signed

Women granted the vote at age thirty in Britain

Rupert Brooke's *Collected Poems*

Gerard Manley Hopkins' *Poems*

Joyce's *Exiles*

Lewis's *Tarr*

Sassoon's *Counter-Attack*

Oswald Spengler's *The Decline of the West*

Lytton Strachey's *Eminent Victorians*

Béla Bartók's *Bluebeard's Castle*

Elgar's *Cello Concerto*

Charlie Chaplin's *Shoulder Arms*

Deaths of Claude Debussy, Wilfred Owen, and Isaac Rosenberg

Muriel Spark born

1919   The Versailles Peace Treaty signed

J. W. Alcock and A. W. Brown make first transatlantic flight

Ross Smith flies from London to Australia

National Socialist party founded in Germany

Benito Mussolini founds the Fascist party in Italy

Sinn Fein Congress adopts declaration of independence in Dublin

Eamon De Valera elected president of Sinn Fein party

Communist Third International founded

Lady Astor elected first woman Member of Parliament

Prohibition in the U.S.

John Maynard Keynes's *The Economic Consequences of the Peace*

Eliot's *Poems*

Maugham's *The Moon and Sixpence*

Shaw's *Heartbreak House*

The Bauhaus school of design, building, and crafts founded by Walter Gropius

Amedeo Modigliani's *Self-Portrait*

Death of Theodore Roosevelt

Death of Pierre Renoir

John Bayliss born

Margot Fonteyn born

Hamish Henderson born

Edmund Hillary born

Doris (Tayler) Lessing born

Iris Murdoch born

Michael Riviere born

1920   The League of Nations established

Warren G. Harding elected president

Senate votes against joining the League and rejects the Treaty of Versailles

The Nineteenth Amendment gives women the right to vote

Warren G. Harding elected president

White Russian forces of Denikin and Kolchak defeated by the Bolsheviks

Karel Čapek's *R.U.R.*

Galsworthy's *In Chancery* and *The Skin Game*

Sinclair Lewis' *Main Street*

Katherine Mansfield's *Bliss*

Matisse's *Odalisques* (1920–1925)

Ezra Pound's *Hugh Selwyn Mauberly*

Paul Valéry's *Le Cimetière Marin*

Yeats's *Michael Robartes and the Dancer*

Keith Douglas born

CHRONOLOGICAL TABLE

Paul Scott born

1921 Britain signs peace with Ireland

First medium-wave radio broadcast in U.S.

The British Broadcasting Corporation founded

Braque's *Still Life with Guitar*

Chaplin's *The Kid*

Aldous Huxley's *Crome Yellow*

Paul Klee's *The Fish*

D. H. Lawrence's *Women in Love*

John McTaggart's *The Nature of Existence*, vol. I (vol. II, 1927)

Moore's *Héloïse and Abélard*

Eugene O'Neill's *The Emperor Jones*

Luigi Pirandello's *Six Characters in Search of an Author*

Shaw's *Back to Methuselah*

Strachey's *Queen Victoria*

1922 Lloyd George's Coalition government succeeded by Bonar Law's Conservative government

Benito Mussolini marches on Rome and forms a government

William Cosgrave elected president of the Irish Free State

The BBC begins broadcasting in London

Lord Carnarvon and Howard Carter discover Tutankhamen's tomb

The PEN club founded in London

The *Criterion* founded with T. S. Eliot as editor

Eliot's *The Waste Land*

A. E. Housman's *Last Poems*

Joyce's *Ulysses*

D. H. Lawrence's *Aaron's Rod* and *England, My England*

Sinclair Lewis's *Babbitt*

O'Neill's *Anna Christie*

Pirandello's *Henry IV*

Edith Sitwell's *Façade*

Virginia Woolf's *Jacob's Room*

Yeats's *The Trembling of the Veil*

Death of Marcel Proust

Kingsley Amis born

Sidney Keyes born

Philip Larkin born

Alan Ross born

Vernon Scannell born

1923 The Union of Soviet Socialist Republics established

French and Belgian troops occupy the Ruhr in consequence of Germany's failure to pay reparations

Mustafa Kemal (Ataturk) proclaims Turkey a republic and is elected president

Warren G. Harding dies; Calvin Coolidge becomes president

Stanley Baldwin succeeds Bonar Law as prime minister

Adolf Hitler's attempted coup in Munich fails

Time magazine begins publishing

E. N. da C. Andrade's *The Structure of the Atom*

Bennett's *Riceyman Steps*

Churchill's *The World Crisis* (1923–1927)

J. E. Flecker's *Hassan* produced

Paul Klee's *Magic Theatre*

Lawrence's *Kangaroo*

Rainer Maria Rilke's *Duino Elegies* and *Sonnets to Orpheus*

Sibelius' *Sixth Symphony*

Picasso's *Seated Woman*

William Walton's *Façade*

Death of Katherine Mansfield

1924 Ramsay Macdonald forms first Labour government, loses general election, and is succeeded by Stanley Baldwin

Calvin Coolidge elected president

Noel Coward's *The Vortex*

Forster's *A Passage to India*

Mann's *The Magic Mountain*

Shaw's *St. Joan*

Sibelius' *Seventh Symphony*

Deaths of Joseph Conrad, Anatole France, Franz Kafka, Giacomo Puccini, Woodrow Wilson, and Lenin

1925 Reza Khan becomes shah of Iran

First surrealist exhibition held in Paris

Alban Berg's *Wozzeck*

Chaplin's *The Gold Rush*

John Dos Passos' *Manhattan Transfer*

Theodore Dreiser's *An American Tragedy*

Sergei Eisenstein's *Battleship Potemkin*

F. Scott Fitzgerald's *The Great Gatsby*

André Gide's *Les Faux Monnayeurs*
Hardy's *Human Shows and Far Phantasies*
Huxley's *Those Barren Leaves*
Kafka's *The Trial*
O'Casey's *Juno and the Paycock*
Virginia Woolf's *Mrs. Dalloway* and *The Common Reader*
Brancusi's *Bird in Space*
Shostakovich's *First Symphony*
Sibelius' *Tapiola*
1926 Ford's *A Man Could Stand Up*
Gide's *Si le grain ne meurt*
Hemingway's *The Sun Also Rises*
Kafka's *The Castle*
D. H. Lawrence's *The Plumed Serpent*
T. E. Lawrence's *Seven Pillars of Wisdom* privately circulated
Maugham's *The Casuarina Tree*
O'Casey's *The Plough and the Stars*
Puccini's *Turandot*
Death of Claude Monet
Death of Rainer Maria Rilke
John Fowles born
1927 General Chiang Kai-shek becomes prime minister in China
Trotsky expelled by the Communist party as a deviationist; Stalin becomes leader of the party and dictator of the USSR
Charles Lindberg flies from New York to Paris
J. W. Dunne's *An Experiment with Time*
Freud's *Autobiography* translated into English
Albert Giacometti's *Observing Head*
Ernest Hemingway's *Men Without Women*
Fritz Lang's *Metropolis*
Wyndham Lewis' *Time and Western Man*
F. W. Murnau's *Sunrise*
Proust's *Le Temps retrouvé* posthumously published
Stravinsky's *Oedipus Rex*
Virginia Woolf's *To the Lighthouse*
1928 The Kellogg-Briand Pact, outlawing war and providing for peaceful settlement of disputes, signed in Paris

by sixty-two nations, including the USSR
Herbert Hoover elected president
Women's suffrage granted at age twenty-one in Britain
Alexander Fleming discovers penicillin
Bertolt Brecht and Kurt Weill's *The Threepenny Opera*
Eisenstein's *October*
Huxley's *Point Counter Point*
Christopher Isherwood's *All the Conspirators*
D. H. Lawrence's *Lady Chatterley's Lover*
Wyndham Lewis' *The Childermass*
Matisse's *Seated Odalisque*
Munch's *Girl on a Sofa*
Shaw's *Intelligent Woman's Guide to Socialism*
Virginia Woolf's *Orlando*
Yeats's *The Tower*
Death of Thomas Hardy
1929 The Labour party wins British general election
Trotsky expelled from USSR
Museum of Modern Art opens in New York
Collapse of U.S. stock exchange begins world economic crisis
Robert Bridges's *The Testament of Beauty*
William Faulkner's *The Sound and the Fury*
Robert Graves's *Goodbye to All That*
Hemingway's *A Farewell to Arms*
Ernst Junger's *The Storm of Steel*
Hugo von Hoffmansthal's *Poems*
Henry Moore's *Reclining Figure*
J. B. Priestley's *The Good Companions*
Erich Maria Remarque's *All Quiet on the Western Front*
Shaw's *The Applecart*
R. C. Sheriff's *Journey's End*
Edith Sitwell's *Gold Coast Customs*
Thomas Wolfe's *Look Homeward, Angel*
Virginia Woolf's *A Room of One's Own*
Yeats's *The Winding Stair*
Second surrealist manifesto; Salvador Dali joins the surrealists

Epstein's *Night and Day*
Mondrian's *Composition with Yellow Blue*
Walton's *Viola Concerto*
John Osborne born

1930 Allied occupation of the Rhineland ends
Mohandas Gandhi opens civil disobedience campaign in India
The *Daily Worker*, journal of the British Communist party, begins publishing
J. W. Reppe makes artificial fabrics from an acetylene base
Auden's *Poems*
Noël Coward's *Private Lives*
Eliot's *Ash Wednesday*
Wyndham Lewis's *The Apes of God*
Maugham's *Cakes and Ale*
Ezra Pound's *XXX Cantos*
Evelyn Waugh's *Vile Bodies*
Von Sternberg's *The Blue Angel* and Milestone's *All Quiet on the Western Front*
Deaths of Robert Bridges, Arthur Conan Doyle, and D. H. Lawrence
Ted Hughes born
Harold Pinter born

1931 The failure of the Credit Anstalt in Austria starts a financial collapse in Central Europe
Britain abandons the gold standard; the pound falls by twenty-five percent
Mutiny in the Royal Navy at Invergordon over pay cuts
Ramsay Macdonald resigns, splits the Cabinet, and is expelled by the Labour party; in the general election the National Government wins by a majority of 500 seats
The statute of Westminster defines dominion status
Ninette de Valois founds the Vic-Wells Ballet (eventually the Royal Ballet)
Chaplin's *City Lights*, René Clair's *Le Million*, and Leontine Sagan's *Mädchen in Uniform*
Coward's *Cavalcade*
Dali's *The Persistence of Memory*
O'Neill's *Mourning Becomes Electra*
Anthony Powell's *Afternoon Men*
Antoine de Saint Exupéry's *Vol de nuit*

Walton's *Belshazzar's Feast*
Virginia Woolf's *The Waves*
Death of Arnold Bennett

1932 Franklin D. Roosevelt elected president
Paul von Hindenburg elected president of Germany; Franz von Papen elected chancellor
Sir Oswald Mosley founds British Union of Fascists
The BBC takes over development of television from J. L. Baird's company
Basic English of 850 words designed as a prospective international language
The Folger Library opens in Washington, D.C.
The Shakespeare Memorial Theatre opens in Stratford upon Avon
Faulkner's *Light in August*
Huxley's *Brave New World*
F. R. Leavis' *New Bearings in English Poetry*
Boris Pasternak's *Second Birth*
Ravel's *Concerto for Left Hand*
Rouault's *Christ Mocked by Soldiers*
Waugh's *Black Mischief*
Yeats's *Words for Music Perhaps*
Death of Lady Augusta Gregory
Death of Lytton Strachey
V. S. Naipaul born

1933 Roosevelt inaugurates the New Deal
Hitler becomes chancellor of Germany
The Reichstag set on fire
Hitler suspends civil liberties and freedom of the press; German trade unions suppressed
George Balanchine and Lincoln Kirstein found the School of American Ballet
André Malraux's *La Condition humaine*
Orwell's *Down and Out in Paris and London*
Gertrude Stein's *The Autobiography of Alice B. Toklas*
Death of John Galsworthy
Death of George Moore

1934 The League Disarmament Conference ends in failure
USSR admitted to the League
Hitler becomes Führer
Civil war in Austria; Engelbert Dollfuss assassinated in attempted Nazi coup
Frédéric Joliot and Irene Joliot-Curie

discover artificial (induced) radio-activity

Einstein's *My Philosophy*

Fitzgerald's *Tender Is the Night*

Graves's *I, Claudius* and *Claudius the God*

Toynbee's *A Study of History* begins publication (1934–1954)

Waugh's *A Handful of Dust*

Deaths of Marie Curie, Frederick Delius, Edward Elgar, and Gustav Holst

1935 Grigori Zinoviev and other Soviet leaders convicted of treason

Stanley Baldwin becomes prime minister in National Government; National Government wins general election in Britain

Italy invades Abyssinia

Germany repudiates disarmament clauses of Treaty of Versailles

Germany reintroduces compulsory military service and outlaws the Jews

Robert Watson-Watt builds first practical radar equipment

Karl Jaspers' *Suffering and Existence*

Ivy Compton-Burnett's *A House and Its Head*

Eliot's *Murder in the Cathedral*

Barbara Hepworth's *Three Forms*

George Gershwin's *Porgy and Bess*

Greene's *England Made Me*

Isherwood's *Mr. Norris Changes Trains*

Malraux's *Le Temps du mépris*

Yeats's *Dramatis Personae*

Klee's *Child Consecrated to Suffering*

Benedict Nicholson's *White Relief*

Death of T. E. Lawrence

Edward Bond born

1936 Edward VIII accedes to the throne in January; abdicates in December

1936–1952 Reign of George VI

1936 German troops occupy the Rhineland

Ninety-nine percent of German electorate vote for Nazi candidates

The Popular Front wins general election in France; Léon Blum becomes prime minister

The Popular Front wins general election in Spain

Spanish Civil War begins

Italian troops occupy Addis Ababa;

Abyssinia annexed by Italy

BBC begins television service from Alexandra Palace

Auden's *Look, Stranger!*

Auden and Isherwood's *The Ascent of F-6*

A. J. Ayer's *Language, Truth and Logic*

Chaplin's *Modern Times*

Greene's *A Gun for Sale*

Huxley's *Eyeless in Gaza*

Keynes's *General Theory of Employment*

F. R. Leavis' *Revaluation*

Mondrian's *Composition in Red and Blue*

Dylan Thomas' *Twenty-five Poems*

Wells's *The Shape of Things to Come* filmed

Deaths of A. E. Housman, Rudyard Kipling, G. K. Chesterton, Maxim Gorky, and Luigi Pirandello

1937 Trial of Karl Radek and other Soviet leaders

Neville Chamberlain succeeds Stanley Baldwin as prime minister

China and Japan at war

Frank Whittle designs jet engine

Picasso's *Guernica*

Shostakovich's *Fifth Symphony*

Magritte's *La Reproduction interdite*

Hemingway's *To Have and Have Not*

Malraux's *L'Espoir*

Orwell's *The Road to Wigan Pier*

Priestley's *Time and the Conways*

Virginia Woolf's *The Years*

Deaths of J. M. Barrie, Ivor Gurney, Ramsay Macdonald, Ernest Rutherford, and Maurice Ravel

Tom Stoppard born

1938 Trial of Nikolai Bukharin and other Soviet political leaders

Austria occupied by German troops and declared part of the Reich

Hitler states his determination to annex Sudetenland from Czechoslovakia

Britain, France, Germany, and Italy sign the Munich agreement

German troops occupy Sudetenland

Edward Hulton founds *Picture Post*

Cyril Connolly's *Enemies of Promise*

Faulkner's *The Unvanquished*

Graham Greene's *Brighton Rock*

Hindemith's *Mathis der Maler*
Jean Renoir's *La Grande Illusion*
Jean-Paul Sartre's *La Nausée*
Yeats's *New Poems*
Anthony Asquith's *Pygmalion* and Walt Disney's *Snow White*
Death of Karel Čapek
Death of Mustafa Kemal (Ataturk)

1939 German troops occupy Bohemia and Moravia; Czechoslovakia incorporated into Third Reich
Madrid surrenders to General Franco; the Spanish Civil War ends
Italy invades Albania
Spain joins Germany, Italy, and Japan in anti-Comintern Pact
Britain and France pledge support to Poland, Romania, and Greece
USSR proposes defensive alliance with Britain; British military mission visits Moscow
USSR and Germany sign nonaggression treaty, secretly providing for partition of Poland between them
Germany invades Poland; Britain, France, and Germany at war
USSR invades Finland
New York World's Fair opens
Eliot's *The Family Reunion*
Isherwood's *Good-bye to Berlin*
Joyce's *Finnegan's Wake* (1922–1939)
MacNeice's *Autumn Journal*
Powell's *What's Become of Waring?*
Deaths of Ford Madox Ford, Sigmund Freud, and William Butler Yeats

1940 Churchill becomes prime minister
Italy declares war on France, Britain, and Greece
General De Gaulle founds Free French Movement
The Battle of Britain and the bombing of London
Roosevelt re-elected for third term
Betjeman's *Old Lights for New Chancels*
Chaplin's *The Great Dictator*
Disney's *Fantasia*
Greene's *The Power and the Glory*
Hemingway's *For Whom the Bell Tolls*
C. P. Snow's *Strangers and Brothers*

(retitled *George Passant* in 1970, when entire sequence of ten novels, published 1940–1970, was entitled *Strangers and Brothers*)

1941 German forces occupy Yugoslavia, Greece, and Crete, and invade USSR
Lend-Lease agreement between U.S. and Britain
President Roosevelt and Winston Churchill sign the Atlantic Charter
Japanese forces attack Pearl Harbor; U.S. declares war on Japan, Germany, Italy; Britain on Japan
Auden's *New Year Letter*
James Burnham's *The Managerial Revolution*
F. Scott Fitzgerald's *The Last Tycoon*
Huxley's *Grey Eminence*
Shostakovich's Seventh Symphony
Tippett's *A Child of Our Time*
Orson Welles's *Citizen Kane*
Virginia Woolf's *Between the Acts*
Deaths of Henri Bergson, James Joyce, Virginia Woolf

1942 Japanese forces capture Singapore, Hong Kong, Bataan, Manila
German forces capture Tobruk
U.S. fleet defeats the Japanese in the Coral Sea, captures Guadalcanal
Battle of El Alamein
Allied forces land in French North Africa
Atom first split at University of Chicago
William Beveridge's *Social Insurance and Allied Services*
Albert Camus's *L'Étranger*
Joyce Cary's *To Be a Pilgrim*
Edith Sitwell's *Street Songs*
Waugh's *Put Out More Flags*

1943 German forces surrender at Stalingrad
German and Italian forces surrender in North Africa
Italy surrenders to Allies and declares war on Germany
Cairo conference between Roosevelt, Churchill, Chiang Kai-shek
Teheran conference between Roosevelt, Churchill, Stalin
Eliot's *Four Quartets*

CHRONOLOGICAL TABLE

Henry Moore's *Madonna and Child*
Sartre's *Les Mouches*
Vaughan-Williams' Fifth Symphony

1944 Allied forces land in Normandy and southern France
Allied forces enter Rome
Attempted assassination of Hitler fails
Liberation of Paris
U.S. forces land in Philippines
German offensive in the Ardennes halted
President Roosevelt reelected for fourth term
Education Act passed in Britain
Pay-As-You-Earn income tax introduced
Beveridge's *Full Employment in a Free Society*
Cary's *The Horse's Mouth*
Huxley's *Time Must Have a Stop*
Maugham's *The Razor's Edge*
Sartre's *Huis Clos*
Edith Sitwell's *Green Song and Other Poems*
Graham Sutherland's *Christ on the Cross*
Trevelyan's *English Social History*

1945 British and Indian forces open offensive in Burma
Yalta conference between Roosevelt, Churchill, Stalin
Mussolini executed by Italian partisans
President Roosevelt dies; succeeded by Harry S. Truman
Hitler commits suicide; German forces surrender
The Potsdam Peace Conference
The United Nations Charter ratified in San Francisco
The Labour Party wins British General Election
Atomic bombs dropped on Hiroshima and Nagasaki
Surrender of Japanese forces ends World War II
Trial of Nazi war criminals opens at Nuremberg
All-India Congress demands British withdrawal from India
De Gaulle elected president of French Provisional Government; resigns the next year
Civil war between Chiang Kai-shek and Mao-Tse-Tung begins in China
Betjeman's *New Bats in Old Belfries*
Britten's *Peter Grimes*
Orwell's *Animal Farm*
Russell's *History of Western Philosophy*
Sartre's *The Age of Reason*
Edith Sitwell's *The Song of the Cold*
Waugh's *Brideshead Revisited*
Deaths of Béla Bartók, Lloyd George, Paul Valéry

1946 Bills to nationalize railways, coal mines, and the Bank of England passed in Britain
Nuremberg Trials concluded
United Nations General Assembly meets in New York as its permanent headquarters
The Arab Council inaugurated in Britain
Frederick Ashton's *Symphonic Variations*
Britten's *The Rape of Lucretia*
David Lean's *Great Expectations*
O'Neill's *The Iceman Cometh*
Roberto Rosselini's *Paisà*
Dylan Thomas' *Deaths and Entrances*
Death of H. G. Wells

1947 President Truman announces program of aid to Greece and Turkey and outlines the "Truman Doctrine"
Independence of India proclaimed; partition between India and Pakistan, and communal strife between Hindus and Moslems follows
General Marshall calls for a European recovery program
First supersonic air flight
Britain's first atomic pile at Harwell comes into operation
Edinburgh festival established
Discovery of the Dead Sea Scrolls in Palestine
Princess Elizabeth marries Philip Mountbatten, duke of Edinburgh
Auden's *Age of Anxiety*
Camus's *La Peste*
Chaplin's *Monsieur Verdoux*
Priestley's *An Inspector Calls*

Edith Sitwell's *The Shadow of Cain*
Waugh's *Scott-King's Modern Europe*

1948 Gandhi assassinated

Czech Communist Party seizes power

Pan-European movement (1948–1958) begins with the formation of the permanent Organization for European Economic Cooperation (OEEC)

Berlin airlift begins as USSR halts road and rail traffic to the city

British mandate in Palestine ends; Israeli provisional government formed

Yugoslavia expelled from Soviet bloc

Columbia Records introduces the long-playing record

Truman re-elected for second term

Greene's *The Heart of the Matter*

Huxley's *Ape and Essence*

Leavis' *The Great Tradition*

Pound's *Cantos*

Priestley's *The Linden Tree*

Waugh's *The Loved One*

Prince Charles born

1949 North Atlantic Treaty Organization established with headquarters in Brussels

Berlin blockade lifted

German Federal Republic recognized; capital established at Bonn

Konrad Adenauer becomes German chancellor

Simone de Beauvoir's *The Second Sex*

Cary's *A Fearful Joy*

Eliot's *The Cocktail Party*

Arthur Miller's *Death of a Salesman*

Orwell's *Nineteen Eighty-four*

1950 North Korean forces invade South Korea

United Nations forces land in South Korea

Wyndham Lewis's *Rude Assignment*

Orwell's *Shooting an Elephant*

Death of George Bernard Shaw

1951 Conservatives win the British general election; Churchill becomes prime minister

Auden's *Nones*

Britten's *Billy Budd*

Greene's *The End of the Affair*

Wyndham Lewis' *Rotting Hill*

Powell's *A Question of Upbringing* (first volume of the *Music of Time,* 1951–1975)

J. D. Salinger's *The Catcher in the Rye*

Stravinsky's *The Rake's Progress*

Vaughan Williams' *The Pilgrim's Progress*

1952– **Reign of Queen Elizabeth II**

1952 Dwight D. Eisenhower elected president

U. S. scientists explode the first hydrogen bomb

Cary's *Prisoner of Grace*

Hemingway's *The Old Man and the Sea*

Huxley's *The Devils of Loudon*

Leavis' *The Common Pursuit*

Dylan Thomas' *Collected Poems*

Waugh's *Men at Arms*

1957 Deaths of Wyndham Lewis and Joyce Cary

1963 Deaths of Aldous Huxley and Louis MacNeice

1964 Deaths of Sean O'Casey and Edith Sitwell

1965 Death of T. S. Eliot

1966 Death of Evelyn Waugh

1969 Death of Ivy Compton-Burnett

1973 Death of W. H. Auden

1978 Death of F. R. Leavis

1980 Death of C. P. Snow

List of Contributors

WALTER ERNEST ALLEN. Novelist and journalist. Literary Editor, the *New Statesman and Nation* (1959–1960); Professor of English Studies, New University of Ulster (1967–1973); Berg Professor of English, New York University (1970–1971); C. P. Miles Professor of English, Virginia Polytechnic Institute (1974–1975). Publications include *Blind Man's Ditch, Dead Man Over All, All in a Lifetime* (all fiction); *The English Novel, Tradition and Dream, The Short Story in English* (all criticism); *As I Walked Down New Grub Street* (memoirs). **Joyce Cary.**

WILLIAM ARMSTRONG. Professor of English Literature, University of Hull (1965–1967), Westfield College, University of London (1967–1974), Birkbeck College, University of London (1974–1980). Assistant Editor, *The Diaries of Samuel Pepys*. Publications include *Elizabethan Private Theatres* and articles on the drama in learned journals. **Sean O'Casey.**

BERNARD BERGONZI. Professor of English (1971–), Pro-Vice-Chancellor (1979–1982), University of Warwick; Visiting Professor, Stanford University (1982). Has written extensively on late-nineteenth-and twentieth-century literature, including studies of H. G. Wells, Gerard Manley Hopkins, T. S. Eliot, and the literature of World War I. Publications include *Reading the Thirties* (1978); *The Situation of the Novel* (2nd edition, 1979); and *The Roman Persuasion* (fiction). **Anthony Powell.**

BERNARD BLACKSTONE. Professor of English Literature, University of Istanbul (1949–1952); Byron Professor of English, University of Athens (1952–1961); Professor of English, University of Bengasi (1961–1965), American University of Beirut (1967–1976), University of Aleppo (1976–1981), University of Rhodesia, Salisbury (1965–1967). Publications include *English Blake; Virginia Woolf: A Commen-*

tary; The Lost Travellers: Variations on a Romantic Theme; and *Byron: A Survey.* **Virginia Woolf.**

MURIEL CLARA BRADBROOK. Professor of English, University of Cambridge (1965–1976). Publications include *Themes and Conventions of Elizabethan Tragedy; The Rise of the Common Player; Shakespeare: The Poet in His World;* and *John Webster.* **T. S. Eliot.**

JOCELYN BROOKE. Novelist and critic. Publications include *The Military Orchid* and *A Mine of Serpents* (autobiographies). **Aldous Huxley.**

WILLIAM COOPER (Harry Summerfield Hoff). Novelist and critic. Adjunct Professor of English Literature, Syracuse University, London Centre (1977–). Publications include sixteen realistic novels; among them a trilogy, *Scenes from Provincial Life, Scenes from Metropolitan Life,* and *Scenes from Married Life,* plus the companion volume *Scenes from Later Life.* Retired from government service in 1977. **C. P. Snow.**

IAN ALISTAIR GORDON, CBE. Professor of English Literature, University of Wellington, New Zealand (1936–1974); Vice-Chancellor University of New Zealand (1947–1952). Honorable Doctor of Letters, universities of Bristol, New Zealand, and Stirling. Publications include *John Skelton, Poet Laureate; John Galt; Undiscovered Country; Katherine Mansfield's Urewera Notebook.* Editor of John Galt's *The Entail, The Provost, The Member, The Last of the Lairds,* and *Short Stories.* **Katherine Mansfield.**

EDWARD BAKER GREENWOOD. Senior Lecturer in English Literature, University of Kent (1966–). Publications include *Tolstoy: The Comprehensive Vision* and articles and reviews in *Essays in Criticism* and other learned journals. **F. R. Leavis.**

R. GLYNN GRYLLS (Rosalie Mander). Biographer and lecturer. Publications include *Mary Shelley*; *Trelawny*; *Portrait of Rossetti*; and *Mrs. Browning*. **Ivy Compton-Burnett.**

RICHARD HOGGART, FRSL. Professor of English, University of Birmingham (1959–1962); Director, Centre for Contemporary Cultural Studies, University of Birmingham (1964–1973); Assistant Director-General, UNESCO (1970–1975); Warden, Goldsmiths' College, University of London (1976–   ); Chairman, Advisory Council for Adult and Continuing Education (1977–   ); Chairman, Broadcasting Research Unit. Publications include *The Uses of Literacy; Speaking to Each Other; Only Connect; An Idea and Its Servants;* and *An English Temper.* **W. H. Auden.**

SIR TOM HOPKINSON, CBE, KBE. Novelist and editor. Editor of *Picture Post* (1940–1950), *Lilliput* (1941–1946), and *Drum* magazine (1958–1960); Director, International Press Institute for Journalism Training in Africa (1963–1966); Senior Fellow in Press Studies, University of Sussex (1967–1969); Visiting Professor of Journalism, University of Minnesota (1968–1969); Director of Centre for Journalism Studies, University College, Cardiff (1970–1975); Chairman, British National Press Awards (1967–1976). Publications include *A Wise Man Foolish, The Man Below, Mist in the Tagus, Down the Long Slide, Love's Apprentice* (all novels); *The Transitory Venus, The Lady and the Cut-Throat* (stories); *In the Fiery Continent* (autobiography); and *Of This Our Time: A Journalist's Story, 1905–1950.* **George Orwell.**

FRANCIS HENRY KING, OBE, FRSL. Novelist and critic. Lecturer in English, the British Council (1942–1964); Drama Critic, the *Sunday Telegraph* (1978–   ); Regular Reviewer, the *Spectator.* President, English PEN; Former Chairman, Society of Authors. Publications include *The Dividing Stream* (Somerset Maugham Award), *The Custom House, The Needle, Act of Darkness* (all novels); *The Japanese Umbrella* (Katherine Mansfield Prize), *Indirect Method* (stories); and *E. M. Forster and His World* and *Florence* (nonfiction). **Christopher Isherwood.**

JOHN FREDERICK LEHMANN, CBE, Hon. D.Litt. Poet, critic, biographer, and editor. Founding Editor of *New Writing* (1936–1950) and *London* magazine (1954). Publications include *Collected Poems; Virginia Woolf and Her World; Edward Lear and His World; Rupert Brooke, His Life and His Legend; English Poets of the First World War;* and *In My Own Time* (autobiography). **Edith Sitwell.**

WILLIAM FRANCIS MYERS. Senior Lecturer in English, University of Leicester (1972–   ). Publications include *Literature and Politics in the Nineteenth Century* (with others); *Dryden;* and *The Teaching of George Eliot* (forthcoming). **Evelyn Waugh.**

ALASTAIR NEIL ROBERTSON NIVEN. Director General, Africa Centre, London (1978–   ); Honorary Lecturer, School of Oriental and African Studies, University of London. Co-editor, the *Journal of Commonwealth Literature.* Editor, the *Commonwealth Writer Overseas.* Publications include *D. H. Lawrence: The Novels; The Yoke of Pity; The Fiction of Mulk Raj Anand;* and many articles on Commonwealth authors. **D. H. Lawrence.**

JOHN PRESS, FRSL. Former Literature Adviser, the British Council. Visiting Professor, University of Paris (1981–1982). Publications include *The Fire and the Fountain; The Chequer'd Shade; Rule and Energy; A Map of Modern English Verse;* and *The Lengthening Shadows.* **John Betjeman; Louis MacNeice; Poets of World War II.**

MARTIN SEYMOUR-SMITH. Poet, biographer, and critic. Publications include *A Guide to Modern World Literature; Reminiscences of Norma* (poems); and *Robert Graves* (Arts Council Prize, 1982). **Robert Graves.**

JOHN INNES MACKINTOSH STEWART. Reader in English Literature, University of Oxford (1969–1973). Publications include *Eight Modern Writers; The Oxford History of English Literature,* vol. XII; *Character and Motive in Shakespeare;* and books on Thomas Hardy, Joseph Conrad, and Rudyard Kipling. **James Joyce.**

ERIC WALTER FREDERICK TOMLIN, CBE, FRSL. Representative and Cultural Counsellor for the British Council in Ankara, Tokyo, and Paris. Visiting Professor of Philosophy, University of Southern California (1960); Professor of English and Philosophy, University of Nice (1972–1974). Publications include

LIST OF CONTRIBUTORS

The Western Philosophers; The Eastern Philosophers; Simone Weil; Living and Knowing; Tokyo Essays; Man, Time and the New Science; The World of St. Boniface; The Crisis of Culture; and an edition with introduction of *Wyndham Lewis.* **Wyndham Lewis.**

Kenneth Young, FRSL. Former Editor, *Yorkshire Post;* Political Adviser, Beaverbrook Newspapers. Publications include *Dryden* (criticism); *Balfour; Baldwin* (biography); *The Greek Passion;* and *Chapel* (history). Editor of *The Journals and Letters of Sir Robert Bruce Lockhart.* **J. B. Priestley.**

BRITISH WRITERS

SEAN O'CASEY

(1880-1964)

William A. Armstrong

I

IRELAND, the Irish character, and Irish civilization are basic themes in Sean O'Casey's finest plays, so the man and his work are best understood if they are related to the period in which he lived, the most momentous in the history of his nation. Following the Anglo-Norman conquest of Ireland in the twelfth century, the Irish made many attempts to shake off the foreign yoke. None came closer to success than one led by Charles Stewart Parnell, who was on the verge of winning Home Rule in 1890 when his party was shattered by internal dissension and the chance was lost. Parnell died in 1891, and thirty years elapsed before Home Rule was at last achieved.

For some years after the death of Parnell, there was a lull in Irish political activity, and the spirit of the nation found expression chiefly in a renaissance of Irish literature. In 1893 Dr. Douglas Hyde founded the Gaelic League to revive the ancient Irish language, to collect myths, legends, and poems, and to make them more widely known by translating them into English with an Irish flavor. In 1898 William Butler Yeats, Lady Augusta Gregory, and others started the Irish Literary Theatre. Between 1899 and 1901 the earliest plays of this movement were performed only a few times by professional English actors in such theaters as were available in Dublin. In 1902, however, Yeats and Lady Gregory joined forces with a talented group of Irish amateur actors headed by Frank Fay and William G. Fay, and established the Irish National Theatre Society. Greatly impressed by their productions, Miss A. E. F. Horniman, an English Quaker, bought the Mechanics' Institute in Dublin in 1904, converted it into a theater, and gave the society free use of it, together with an annual subsidy.

By this time a revival of political as well as literary nationalism was gathering force in Ireland. The Irish Republican Brotherhood was working ardently for separation from England and the creation of an Irish republic. In 1910 the same policy was adopted by the organization known as Sinn Féin ("We Ourselves"). A third political group was the Irish Nationalist party, which held seats in the House of Commons in London and argued that Ireland should have Home Rule but remain within the British Empire. A fourth force emerged in 1910, when the Irish Transport and General Workers' Union was founded by James Larkin and James Connolly, who proceeded to denounce the capitalist members of the Irish Nationalist movement. In 1913 Larkin led a strike known as the "Great Lockout" against those employers who were trying to force their men to leave the Irish Transport and General Workers' Union. On 31 August 1913 the Dublin police made a baton charge on a meeting of strikers, inflicting hundreds of casualties. In November 1913 Larkin went to the United States, and Connolly became the leader of the union. Though it failed in its immediate objectives, the strike lasted until 1914 and revealed the potential power of organized labor.

Yet another power in Irish politics was the Unionist party in Ulster, which was predominantly Protestant and hostile to both the Republican and Home Rule policies. When the British government sponsored a bill for Irish Home Rule in 1912, the Unionists organized a large army known as the Ulster Volunteers to oppose independence. This led the Irish Transport and General Workers' Union to recruit a force known as the Irish Citizen Army in 1913, and Sinn Féin to form an army called the Irish Volunteers in 1914. United under the collective leadership of Padraic Pearse, James Connolly, and others, these two armies proclaimed the establishment of an Irish republic on Easter Sunday 1916 and held the Dublin post office for several days before succumbing to the forces of the British crown. The execution of the leaders of the Easter Rising turned Irish opinion overwhelmingly against the English and toward the separatist policy of Sinn Féin, which in 1919 set up its own legislative assembly, Dáil

Éireann, in defiance of the British Executive in Ireland.

In 1919 David Lloyd George devised a bill that recommended separate parliaments for six of the counties of Ulster and for the remaining twenty-six counties of Ireland. Sinn Féin was bitterly opposed to this plan for the partition of Ireland and intensified its armed conflict with the British Executive. In 1920 a curfew was imposed on Dublin, and the power of the British Executive was reinforced by a special police force recruited from the toughest ex-servicemen of World War I. The Irish nicknamed them the "Black and Tans" because they wore khaki coats, black trousers, and black caps. To combat these forces the Irish Republican Army used guerrilla tactics, with many of its fighters constantly on the run from place to place. These tactics proved so successful that the Dáil Éireann was able to establish its own law courts and police in opposition to those of the crown.

In 1921 the struggle with England ended when Lloyd George made a treaty with certain representatives of the Dáil. It gave Home Rule to a newly constituted Irish Free State, but the latter did not include six of the counties of Ulster, which have remained within the United Kingdom as Northern Ireland. Republican Irishmen regarded the treaty as a great betrayal, and from 1922 until 1923 they engaged in a savage civil war with the protreaty government of the Free State. The government was victorious, but the bitter disagreements of this period still exacerbate Irish politics.

II

FEW Irishmen played a more active part than did Sean O'Casey in the cultural and political movements that have just been described. That he did so is a testimony to the tremendous willpower that enabled him to discover and exercise his genius despite the appalling physical and economic adversities of his early life. The youngest of a large family, O'Casey was born of Irish Protestant parents on 31 March 1880, at 85 Lower Dorset Street, Dublin, and lived in various slums of his native city for his first forty years. During those years, the slums of Dublin were among the worst in Europe: overcrowded, verminous, and disease-ridden.

O'Casey's father died when he was a child, and during his boyhood he suffered from malnutrition and weak eyesight. He had only three years of formal schooling and taught himself to read with the aid of secondhand books. He began work at the age of fourteen for three shillings and sixpence a week. In his teens he read omnivorously and acted parts in plays by Shakespeare and Dion Boucicault that were staged by a small company organized by his brother Archie. During his later teens, the O'Caseys lived in a two-room tenement at 18 Abercorn Road, where he found a friend in the Reverend E. M. Griffin, the Protestant rector of the nearby church of St. Barnabas, "whose sensitive hand," O'Casey later wrote, "was the first to give the clasp of friendship to the author." O'Casey became deeply versed in the idioms and imagery of the Bible, but his highly personal conception of Christianity was conditioned by his reading of Charles Darwin, George Bernard Shaw, and Karl Marx, and would not fit into any denominational mold.

In his early twenties, O'Casey became an ardent disciple of the Gaelic League and the Irish Republican Brotherhood. He acquired a fluent command of Irish, changed his first name from "John" to "Sean," and wrote articles and stories for Gaelic journals. His revolutionary fervor, his contempt for doctrinaire socialism, and his visionary broodings at this time emerge powerfully from Desmond Ryan's fine description of his demeanor and eloquence at a meeting of a Sinn Féin club:

Sean O'Casey sits in silence at the back of the hall during the lecture, a dour and fiery figure swathed in labourer's garb, for he works on the railways just then. His neck and throat are bound in the coils of a thick white muffler, and he looks like a Jacobin of Jacobins as his small, sharp and red-rimmed eyes stab all the beauty and sorrow of the world. He speaks first, and very fluently and eloquently in Irish, then launches out into a violent Republican oration in English, stark and forceful, Biblical in diction with gorgeous tints of rhetoric and bursts of anti-English nationalism of the most uncompromising style. He will have none of the Socialists who have turned in to heckle the lecturer and he rends them savagely and brushes their materialism aside. Yes, he reminds them, when roused by his sharp words they murmur interruptions taunting him with the poverty and degradation of the Dublin workers, there is all that in life. Half to himself he speaks, lowering his voice to an intense whisper, but there is something else: joy. He speaks the word, and his tone gives a meaning to it even as he sinks down into silence on the bench, his fierce small head an angry star over all the others in the rear.

(*Remembering Sion* [1934], p. 82)

Increasingly influenced by Marx, however, O'Casey became convinced that economic enfranchisement was just as important as cultural and political liberation, and his enthusiasm for the Gaelic League and the Republican Brotherhood diminished when he was unable to imbue them with this conviction. He now became a zealous member of the Transport Union and a lifelong admirer of its founder, James Larkin, "a man," he later said, "who would put a flower in a vase as well as a loaf on a plate." When the union formed the Irish Citizen Army, O'Casey was elected secretary of its council, but he resigned this post in 1914 because he was bitterly opposed to the use of uniforms by the Citizen Army and to its increasing collaboration with the Irish Volunteers, who represented for him a shortsighted nationalism tainted with "monetary and commercial interests."

The Easter Rising completed O'Casey's disillusion with Irish republicanism and organized labor. He did not fight in the Rising, though he was imprisoned for a time by English soldiers. He yearned for an independent Ireland, but his sympathies were with the noncombatants during the fighting and continued so in the subsequent struggles between Sinn Féin and the British Executive and between Free Staters and Diehard Republicans. These sympathies were largely generated by his deep affection for his mother, who narrowly escaped being hit by an English bullet during the Rising. O'Casey had often lived on her old-age pension of ten shillings a week, and he never forgot "her gleaming black eyes, her set mouth, forever smitten with a smile; ragged and broken-booted, still looking forward as if she saw freedom and everlasting truth beside her," or the bright flowers she cultivated in biscuit tins on the windowsills of slum tenements. Susan O'Casey must be ranked even higher than big Jim Larkin as an influence on O'Casey's mind and imagination.

During his first forty years, O'Casey completed his apprenticeship as a writer. Most of his early work was prose or verse of a polemical and occasional kind: letters, articles, satirical stories, poems, a lament for Thomas Ashe, a much-censored account of the Irish Citizen Army, and a few one-act plays, most of which have been lost. His style is sometimes pedestrian, sometimes rhetorical. At its best, it has an unusual trenchancy, as when he declares that the Gael "is stronger to suffer than hell can harm," or a ringing eloquence enriched with biblical rhythms and idioms, such as one finds in his tribute to Francis Sheehy-Skeffington as the finest person to die in the Easter Rising. This man was a pacifist who tried to prevent the looting of shops during the fighting and was wrongfully arrested and shot by the British. O'Casey salutes him as "the living antithesis of the Easter Insurrection," as "the soul of revolt against man's inhumanity to man . . . leaving behind a hallowed and inspiring memory of the perfect love that casteth out fear, against which there can be no law."

O'Casey had written a short play in 1911, but he did not become seriously interested in drama as a medium until he became disillusioned with the principal parties in Irish politics. His association with the Abbey Theatre does not seem to have begun until 1919, when he submitted a one-act play to its directors, who rejected it. Two others were likewise rejected, but Lady Gregory and Yeats urged him to write about the slum life that he knew so well and to concentrate on characterization rather than polemics. O'Casey accepted this advice, and its outcome was *The Shadow of a Gunman* (1925), first performed at the Abbey Theatre on 12 April 1923.

III

IN the early years of the Irish dramatic movement, Yeats and Lady Gregory encouraged two types of drama in particular: the play based on heroic myth and the play concerned with Irish peasant life. Most of Yeats's early plays are of the former kind, and John Millington Synge is the finest of the numerous Irish dramatists of peasant life. Like Synge's, O'Casey's imagination functioned best when it was dealing with a time and a place of which he had had firsthand experience. The topical and the local elements in O'Casey's early plays are so strong that some critics belittled him as nothing more than a photographic realist who merely shuffled together for the stage familiar details of life in the Dublin slums during the time of the Troubles. This criticism is invalid, for O'Casey, again like Synge, has the mythmaker's great gift of discerning archetypal characters and situations, of distilling from everyday elements a quintessence of life far superior to the products of any documentary form of realism.

From one aspect, *The Shadow of a Gunman* is a very topical and autobiographical play. Late in 1920, when the struggle between Sinn Féin and the

Black and Tans[1] was raging, O'Casey left 18 Abercorn Road to live with a friend in a tenement at 35
Mountjoy Square, where some of his neighbors
assumed that he was a patriot taking cover. Soon
afterward, Black and Tans raided the house and arrested a man who had been hiding bombs in the
backyard. Correspondingly, the play shows a poet,
Donal Davoren, staying with a friend, Seumas
Shields, in a tenement in "Hilljoy Square, Dublin" in
1920 and being mistaken for a gunman on the run.
"On the Run," incidentally, was the original title of
the play. Most of the other characters derive from
persons known by O'Casey at that time, and the play
realistically portrays such topical matters as the
restrictions of the curfew, the brutality of the Black
and Tans, the quarrels due to overcrowding in the
Dublin slums, and the way in which some of their inhabitants sought justice from the law courts set up by
the Dáil Éireann.

O'Casey, however, imposes a distinctively tragi-
satiric pattern on these characters and events.
Indeed, the play is in some respects an exercise in
self-criticism, showing the superiority of feminine
instinct to masculine rationalizations. The two principal male characters are blighted by egotism. Davoren's aspirations as a poet are genuine and are
symbolized by the jar of flowers on his table. But his
love of beauty is combined with contempt for the
slum-dwellers around him. To them, he says, beauty
is what is for sale in a butcher's shop. Whenever they
interrupt his work, he moans the words of Shelley's
Prometheus: "Ah me! alas, pain, pain, pain ever, for
ever!" Shields is a former patriot who has degener-
ated into fear and selfishness. His self-regarding
religiosity is symbolized by the crucifix and the
statue of the Virgin on the mantelpiece. Outside,
there is savage fighting in the streets, but Shields
makes the most trivial annoyance an excuse for invective against his nation. He, too, has a stock lament: "O, Cathleen ni Houlihan," he groans, "your
way's a thorny way." These words were the refrain
of a popular song of the time. Cathleen ni Houlihan
is the maternal symbol of suffering Ireland in Irish
folklore.

These two egotists are judged in terms of their
reactions to Minnie Powell, a young woman who
lives in the same building and admires Davoren

[1] A large proportion of the Irish police resigned during this time.
Replacements were recruited from England and acquired the name
from the colors of their temporary uniforms.

because she takes him for a dedicated patriot. When
she finds bombs in the tenement, she hides them in
her room to save him. As a result, she is arrested and
soon afterward is killed in an ambush. It is a sign of
moral development in Davoren that his last despair-
ing repetition of the words from Shelley are a reaction to her sacrifice, and no longer seem mock-
heroic. But Shields does not change; he never realizes
that Minnie is an embodiment of Cathleen ni Houlihan, that this slum girl treads just as thorny a path as
the Deirdre of Irish myth or the legendary Countess
Cathleen of Yeats's first play (entitled *Cathleen ni
Houlihan*). The archetypal quality of O'Casey's central character raises his play far above the level of
topical realism.

The Shadow of a Gunman was very popular, and
O'Casey moved to a one-room flat at 422 North Cir-
cular Road, where he had better conditions for
writing than he had known before, though for some
time he continued to work as a laborer. His next full-
length play, *Juno and the Paycock* (1925), first performed at the Abbey Theatre on 3 March 1924, was
even more popular. As S. Cowasjee has tactfully indicated in *Sean O'Casey: The Man Behind the Plays*
(1963, pp. 43–47), most of the main characters in this
tragedy are portraits of people O'Casey knew well.
"Captain" Boyle and Joxer Daly, indeed, are given
the surnames as well as the idiosyncrasies of their
real-life counterparts, whose interminable palavers
provided material that O'Casey jotted down as he
listened to them. This was another method of work
that he had in common with Synge. The charity and
steadfastness of Boyle's wife, Juno, resemble those of
O'Casey's mother, just as the vanity and cultural
pretensions of Mary Boyle resemble those of his
sister Ella, though there is probably an element of
self-criticism in his portrayal of Mary Boyle, for
O'Casey, like her, had been willing to go on strike as
a matter of principle, even though it meant living on
his mother's meager income. The ambushes, bomb-
throwings, savage reprisals, and bitter enmity of
former comrades that occurred during the civil war
of 1921–1922 are vividly reflected in the play. In his
autobiographical volume *Inishfallen, Fare Thee Well*
(1949, p. 124), O'Casey describes how a Captain
Wogen was murdered in a country lane beyond
Finglass. The same locality is mentioned in the play
as the place where Commandant Tancred was shot.

The vanities and violence of the world of men constitute the theme that gives unity to *Juno and the
Paycock*. It is focused by the Boyle family, who live

in a Dublin tenement. The "peacock" of the title is "Captain" Boyle, who shirks any kind of work and spends his time drinking, gossiping, and boasting with his flea-ridden parasite, Joxer Daly. Boyle is a great comic character. There is an exquisite comic sequence in Act II when Boyle, fondly believing that he has inherited a fortune, holds court like one of the kings of old, commanding songs from his guests and eventually reciting some sentimental doggerel of his own composing. But throughout these cosy festivities there is a sinister reminder of the civil war outside in the person of Boyle's son, Johnny, who has lost an arm and had a hip shattered in the fighting. Johnny is subsequently dragged away and shot by his former Republican comrades because he betrayed Commandant Tancred. This political plot shows Ireland preying on herself. It is linked with the main plot by "Captain" Boyle's favorite catchphrase: "The world's in a tarrible state o' chassis." "Chassis"—chaos—descends inexorably on the Boyles. The "Captain" is deserted by his friends when he fails to get the legacy. He casts off his daughter, Mary, when he hears that she has been left with child by her schoolteacher fiancé. The family, like Ireland, is tragically divided. At the end Juno takes her daughter away and leaves Boyle to his drunken philosophizings.

What small hope for humanity there is at the end of this play is due to the courage of its women. O'Casey's criticism of life is again conveyed through the repetition of significant key phrases. The words of Mrs. Tancred's lament are poignantly reechoed by Juno when she, too, is mourning a slain son: "Blessed Virgin . . . take away our hearts o' stone, and give us hearts o' flesh. Take away this murdering hate and give us thine own eternal love." On each occasion these words are addressed to a picture of the Virgin on the wall. The votive lamp beneath this picture acquires a symbolic importance. The guilt-ridden Johnny is anxious to keep it alight; it glows more redly just before he is dragged away; afterward, it goes out. The scene in which Mrs. Madigan delivers the news of his death is like the ritual of an inverted annunciation as Juno stands beneath the picture and the spent lamp. The "chassis" at the end of the play is conveyed by an even more masterly piece of stagecraft. Boyle's creditors have taken his furniture away, and Joxer and he stagger drunkenly into a symbolically empty room and collapse onto a bare floor. Against the vanity and moral bankruptcy of the masculine characters O'Casey elevates the

mother-figure, as when Juno plans to work for Mary and her unborn child. Juno has the wisdom and sympathy of her classical namesake, but she speaks and acts like a Cathleen ni Houlihan. Myth and symbols again unite to give archetypal force to O'Casey's tragic art.

Many critics regard *The Plough and the Stars* (1926) as O'Casey's finest play. It was first performed on 8 February 1926 by the Abbey company, which has acted it far more frequently than any other play in its repertoire. Yet some patriots rioted at its third performance because they regarded it as a calculated denigration of the men who fought in the Easter Rising of 1916. In this play O'Casey certainly concentrates attention on the vanity and fanaticism of men who make a religion out of patriotism and consequently destroy what he regards as finer and more fundamental human relationships.

In Act I the vanity of the patriots is illustrated by their childish delight in picturesque regalia and uniforms. When Flynn, an old laborer, puts on the frilled shirt, top boots, and plumed hat of the Irish National Foresters, he is jeeringly compared to "th' illegitimate son of an illegitimate child of a corporal in th' Mexican army." In the same satiric vein, we are told of how Clitheroe, a bricklayer, was so cocksure of being made a captain in the Citizen Army that he bought a Sam Browne belt and stood at the door showing it off until the streetlamps were put out. But the tragic potentialities of this vanity become plain when Clitheroe abandons his wife, Nora, and marches off on maneuvers as soon as he hears that he has been made a commandant. And in Act II we see how Clitheroe and his fellow officers are hypnotized and dehumanized by the savage rhetoric of a patriotic orator. Most of the orator's lines come from speeches actually made by Padraic Pearse, one of the leaders of the Rising. But O'Casey adds to them the passage in which his orator claims that bloodshed is necessary for national redemption.

The tragic consequences of this fanaticism are powerfully conveyed by devices that fuse the naturalistic and the symbolic in the manner characteristic of O'Casey's early work. The breaking of the links that should bind families together is symbolized in Act II when the adult characters rush out to hear the orator and a baby is abandoned on the public-house floor. Correspondingly, Clitheroe ends his last meeting with his wife by violently thrusting her to the ground. Soon afterward he is killed, her child is stillborn, and she goes mad. The disastrous gamble of the Rising and its result are brilliantly epitomized in the episode at the end of the play where four men play cards beside a coffin containing two dead children.

Paradoxically, O'Casey finds that the bravest people during the Rising were noncombatants, especially women. Nora Clitheroe bravely searches for her husband during the fighting and discovers that it is not genuine courage but the fear of admitting that they are afraid that keeps the uniformed patriots in action. The most heroic character in the play is Bessie Burgess, a bibulous, cantankerous, but fearless old Protestant. She protects the mad Nora and is mortally wounded when she is dragging Nora away from a window while bullets are flying. As she lies dying she sings a few lines about Christ's blood and redemption. The final implication of the play is that true redemption springs from instinctive charity like hers, not from the bloodshed exalted by the patriotic orator in his hyperbole about redemption.

Blending farce, satire, and tragedy, the three plays just examined deploy a remarkable variety of moods and attitudes. O'Casey's command of words, metaphors, and rhythms is equal to the exceptional demands made upon it. In *The Shadow of a Gunman*, Mrs. Grigson's fears for her absent husband are shrewdly blended with her canny speculation, "Do the insurance companies pay if a man is shot after curfew?" The aptly prosaic realism of remarks like this contrasts effectively with O'Casey's racy and impassioned use of Dublin idioms, exemplified by Juno Boyle's characteristic reference to "poor Mrs. Tancred's only son gone West with his body made a collandher of," and by Devine's scathing description of Bentham as "a thin, lanky strip of a Micky Dazzler, with a walkin' stick an' gloves." O'Casey was a master of riposte as well as invective. The intoxicated patriots in *The Plough and the Stars* cap one another's declarations with spontaneous but ominous apothegms:

Clitheroe:	You have a mother, Langon.
Lieut. Langon:	Ireland is greater than a mother.
Capt. Brennan:	You have a wife, Clitheroe.
Clitheroe:	Ireland is greater than a wife.
	(Act II)

This passage shows how effortlessly O'Casey can rise to an incantatory rhythm when necessary. In his greatest triumphs of this kind, he makes the Dublin dialect accommodate the rising and falling rhythms

and the elemental metaphors of the Bible, as in Mrs. Boyle's great lament and invocation in *Juno and the Paycock:*

What was the pain I suffered, Johnny, bringin' you into the world to carry you to your cradle, to the pains I'll suffer carryin' you out o' the world to bring you to your grave! Mother o' God, Mother o' God, have pity on us all! Blessed Virgin, where were you when me darlin' son was riddled with bullets, when me darlin' son was riddled with bullets? Sacred Heart o' Jesus, take away our hearts o' stone, and give us hearts o' flesh. Take away this murderin' hate, an' give us Thine own eternal love!

(Act III)

By 1926, the Abbey Theatre and O'Casey were deeply indebted to each other. The Abbey had enabled him to discover and develop his genius by staging excellent productions of his plays. O'Casey had revived both the artistic and economic fortunes of the theater when both were flagging. But already the relationship was strained. There had been disagreements about the casting of certain roles and about the pungency of certain words and speeches in O'Casey's plays. His candid criticism of some of the plays in the Abbey repertoire had been deeply resented. Nevertheless, when he departed for London on 5 March 1926 he did not intend to leave Dublin for good. He prolonged his stay in London when he fell in love with a beautiful Irish actress, Eileen Carey Reynolds, whom he married in 1927. His wife was known professionally as Eileen Carey. When he completed *The Silver Tassie* (1928) he ignored business advice and offered it to the Abbey Theatre. He was deeply grieved when it was rejected. A year later he had a bitter dispute with the Abbey about the performing rights of *Juno* and *The Plough and the Stars* in Ireland. It was only then that he parted company with the last of the various Irish national movements to which he had given his allegiance and energies, regarding himself henceforth as "a voluntary and settled exile from every creed, from every party, and from every literary clique" in his native land.

IV

WHEN Yeats rejected *The Silver Tassie*, he wrote a letter to O'Casey asserting that it contained "no dominating character or action," that it was "too abstract after the first act," and that the second act was "an interesting technical experiment" but "too long for the material, and after that there is nothing."

This is too severe a criticism of the play. Its hero, Harry Heegan, may not have the stature of a Juno or a Bessie Burgess, but the play certainly has a dominating action, for it offers a sustained illustration of how the brutal processes of war inexorably cut off many common soldiers from the joy of life. O'Casey, moreover, creates a central symbol for his basic theme; it emerges poignantly in the last act when the crippled Harry, sitting in his wheelchair at a dance, squashes the tassie, the silver cup that he won on the football field before his body was shattered in World War I.

The other symbols in the play are not always so convincing and organic as the twisted tassie. Most of them occur in the second act, for there O'Casey abandons naturalism and experiments with various expressionist techniques. Augustus John designed the setting for this act for the first production of the play, which opened at the Apollo Theatre, London, on 11 October 1929. Everything in this battlefield scene—the ruined monastery, the figure of Christ, the howitzer, the gun-wheel—is exaggerated and distorted to indicate the way in which it appears to the common soldier. Correspondingly, when a pompous visitor arrives, he is dressed in part-military, part-civilian costume because he is intended to symbolize the common soldier's awareness of the indifference of both officers and politicians to his hard lot. There is a questionable element of propaganda in these class distinctions, but there is a sure dramatic instinct in the episode in which the soldiers stop the visitor from striking a match on the statue of Christ. Much more than the earlier full-length plays, *The Silver Tassie* is a play with a thesis. And whereas the earlier plays show a rich interaction of the forces making for life and the forces making for death, we have here a continuous and pessimistic emphasis on the death-force.

The Silver Tassie marks a transition in O'Casey's themes and techniques from a predominantly (but not exclusively) naturalistic treatment of Irish problems to a predominantly expressionist treatment of European civilization as it was in the 1930's and 1940's, in *Within the Gates* (1933), *The Star Turns Red* (1940), *Purple Dust* (1940), and *Oak Leaves and Lavender* (1946). O'Casey was acquainted with some of the expressionist plays of August Strindberg, Ernst Toller, and Eugene O'Neill, but he would probably have evolved expressionist techniques even if he had had no knowledge of earlier examples because of the highly experimental bent of his imagination.

Within the Gates illustrates two of the basic themes of expressionist drama in its portrayal of the sufferings caused by the pressures of twentieth-century mass civilization and in its symbolic embodiment of the ideals of a finer civilization as yet unachieved. O'Casey's first version of these themes was a film scenario called "Green Gates." Unable to find a producer for it, he turned it into a play that he called *Within the Gates.* The version published in his *Collected Plays* is shorter than the one published in 1933, but both are too long. The play was first performed at the Royalty Theatre, London, on 7 February 1934, but its run was disappointingly short. It has its origins in what O'Casey had observed in Hyde Park, but it takes the form of an expressionist allegory of the flaws in English civilization during the 1930's. The action is arranged in four symbolic scenes in a park: the first represents morning and spring; the second, afternoon and summer; the third, evening and autumn; the fourth, night and winter. The central character is the Young Woman, whose aspirations toward truth, beauty, and inner peace are persistently frustrated by other type-characters representing organized religion, atheism, secular power, the despair of the unemployed, and the pseudophilosophy of popular orators. She finds happiness shortly before her death by sharing the vital convictions of the Dreamer, whose creed is that God can be worshiped in song, dance, and story. Her final symbolic act is to dance with the Dreamer.

Completed in 1940, *The Star Turns Red* had its first performance at the Unity Theatre, London, on 14 March of that year. It is a crude, black-and-white treatment of a conflict between life-forces and death-forces. The former are workers on strike; the latter are Fascists, whose emblem—a lightning flash inside a circle—was the one actually used by the British Union of Fascists in the 1930's. Red Jim, who leads the strikers, was inspired by O'Casey's memories of Jim Larkin, leader of the Transport Union. O'Casey, however, wanted the play to imply that the conflict of Fascist and Worker was a general issue in contemporary politics, so he does not specify any country in particular as the setting of the play but presents his action and characters continuously on an allegorical level, using a neutral idiom for his dialogue.

O'Casey's purposes are religious as well as

political. The Purple Priest in the play is reactionary and puritanical: he supports the Fascists and approves of their thrashing Julia, the Communist girl who affronts him by wearing a short skirt. The Brown Priest, on the other hand, sides with the workers. When the silver star in the sky turns red after the workers' victory, the Brown Priest sees it as still the star of Christ, "who came as man's pure prince of peace." Though this is the most overtly Marxist of O'Casey's plays, it is significantly un-Marxist in his reconciliation of Christianity and Communism.

Purple Dust was likewise written in 1940, but it did not have its first performance until 1945, at the Playhouse, Liverpool. It contains some penetrating topical satire in its portrayal of two English businessmen, Stokes and Poges, who have settled with their mistresses in an Irish country house, partly to escape from the air raids on England, partly to practice a gimcrack notion of returning to nature. The strongly Marxist impulse in O'Casey's satire at this time is shown by Poges' eagerness to reap large dividends from his shares in a cement company, which will obviously become highly profitable as the bombing of England gets worse. But there is nothing doctrinaire about the robust comedy of the episode in which Stokes and Poges run away in terror when they think a bull has invaded their rustic retreat and the animal in question turns out to be a cow. The life-force in this play is represented by a young Irish Marxist, O'Killigain, who sings a song of liberation when a flood forces Stokes and Poges to flee from the house.

Shortly before the outbreak of World War II, O'Casey and his family took up residence at Totnes, in Devonshire. He came to have a strong affection for Cornwall and Devonshire, which he regarded as essentially Celtic regions. *Oak Leaves and Lavender* has an old Cornish mansion as its setting and makes dramatic use of the local tradition that "whenever death is near, the scent of lavender spreads over the house," as it does in the introductory scene, which portrays the fading graces of eighteenth-century aristocracy. The remainder of the play is supposed to occur during the Battle of Britain in 1941, a period of many air battles and bombings, when eight weeks was the average service life of a fighter pilot, when a Home Guard of part-time soldiers reinforced the standing army, when many civilians were evacuated from the towns to billets in the country, when many young women joined the Land Army to work on farms, when windows were blacked out at night,

when training in the use of gas masks and fire extinguishers was the order of the day.

O'Casey treats this period now humorously, now seriously, but never approaches the tragi-satiric force he achieved in his presentation of a similar theme in *The Plough and the Stars.* The chief agent of humor is a middle-aged Irish butler, Feelim O'Morrigun, who often comments pointedly on red tape and petty regulations, and caustically describes the Home Guard as "old men maneuvring themselves into an early grave," proclaiming that "God must ha' had a rare laugh when he made a serious Englishman." At the same time, Feelim is an efficient air raid warden and a constant source of sympathy and help to those around him.

The serious theme is focused on Feelim's son, Drishogue, a young Marxist who is killed as a fighter pilot in the Royal Air Force. Unfortunately, Drishogue persistently strikes conventional attitudes and declaims journalistic clichés. Describing the Russian people, for instance, he declares, "There must be something great in what the rank and gaudy privilege of the world's power, secular and clerical, is afraid of: but this great people know only a rational fear, for at the top of their resolution is the spearhead of the Red Army." The bookish rhetoric of speeches like this shows O'Casey's powers at a low ebb. His expressionist stagecraft also shows signs of strain and artifice, particularly when he tries to suggest the forward movement of history by having the country house setting change gradually into a factory equipped with machinery. Even so, it is generally agreed that the production that had its first performance at the Lyric Theatre, Hammersmith, on 13 May 1947, fell far short of doing justice to this play.

In *The Unholy Trade* (1952, pp. 174–175), Richard Findlater expresses a widely held opinion when he asserts that as a result of O'Casey's becoming an exile "the holy fire" abated in his work, and that his subsequent plays are "ultimately unsuccessful" because "he was trying to create a new drama in an alien country out of his own head, and he had the imagination but not the intellect to do so." If O'Casey's work had ended with the five plays discussed in this section, it would be hard to gainsay this verdict. None of them attains the unity, intensity, and complexity of his Dublin plays. Expressionism and Marxism lead him to oversimplify character and conflict, and to attempt to create dramatic idioms out of what he has read rather than out of what he has heard. But in the third phase of his work O'Casey reverts to Irish themes and idioms, and his imagination revives in a way altogether remarkable in a writer who was sixty-five years old when he completed *Red Roses for Me* (1942), the play that inaugurates his final manner.

V

LIKE *The Silver Tassie*, *Red Roses for Me* marks an important transition in O'Casey's work as a playwright. First acted at the Embassy Theatre, London, on 26 February 1946, it was written before *Oak Leaves and Lavender*, but it has much closer connections with the first and last phases of his work than any play that he wrote between 1926 and 1947. Like his earliest plays, it is based on his experience of life in Dublin; it is, in fact, the most autobiographical of O'Casey's plays, as a comparison with his memoirs *Pictures in the Hallway* (1942), *Drums Under the Windows* (1945), and *Inishfallen, Fare Thee Well* makes abundantly clear. Ayamonn Breydon, the hero of the play, is closely modeled on O'Casey himself in the days when he was a zealous member of the Transport Union and a firm friend of the rector of St. Barnabas' Church. Like the young O'Casey, Ayamonn has an abortive love affair with a Catholic girl. Ayamonn's mother is a faithful portrait of O'Casey's own mother. The symbolic episode in Act III in which Ayamonn and Finoola lead a joyous dance in the roadway as light breaks through the clouds also has autobiographical origins. The struggle between the strikers and the police in Act IV, in which Ayamonn is killed, has details in common with the Great Lockout of 1913.

In other respects, however, *Red Roses for Me* anticipates the ethos of the final plays. It is more optimistic in tone than the early tragedies and finds hope for mankind not in the mother figure, as do the early plays, but in the militant and enlightened spirit of the younger generation. In Act III, this spirit is evoked by the ritual of the dance and by recollections of mythical and historical heroes of Ireland's past: Goll, Finn MacCool, Brian Boru, and Jonathan Swift. Another anticipation of O'Casey's final mood is the suggestion that the salvation of Ireland will come through a synthesis of the heroic idealism of her past with Christianity and Communism. This is implied by the values represented by Ayamonn and symbolized by the cross of Celtic design that this ardent proletarian fashions out of daffodils for the Easter services of his Protestant church.

Like James Joyce, O'Casey never lost interest in Ireland during his self-imposed exile. Through reading and long conversations with visitors from his native land he kept himself fully informed of current political, social, and cultural developments there. He had news of how the struggle between the Irish Republican Army and the Free States continued long after the establishment of the Irish Free State (now called Eire). He had reports of Eire's having the lowest marriage rate of any country in the civilized world, of the average age at which an Irishman married being thirty-five—and he was not alone in ascribing these facts to an Irish puritanism that makes a fetish of chastity. He also heard of the emigration of tens of thousands of young Irish men and women, and he was not alone in attributing it to poor working conditions and to the puritanical regulation of their leisure pursuits by their bishops and priests. In an authoritative survey, *Ireland Since the Rising* (1966, pp. 240, 235, 234), T. P. Coogan has put on record "the parsimonious, investment-wary attitude of the Irish small-town businessman"; has remarked that until recently the pastoral instructions issued each Lent by the bishops "seemed especially intent on drawing attention to the dangers of ballroom dancing, 'keeping company,' the wearing of shorts by young girls, and mixed cycling clubs"; and has noted that the parish priest who enforces these instructions is still "the traditional figure of authority" in country villages.

Another aspect of Irish puritanism that engaged O'Casey's attention was the Censorship of Publications Board, which was set up in 1929 and banned in Eire on moral grounds many of the works of the best modern writers, including Sigmund Freud, Ernest Hemingway, William Faulkner, Thomas Mann, Jean-Paul Sartre, James Joyce, Graham Greene, Dylan Thomas, George Orwell, and O'Casey himself. He was also aware of the cult of respectability that leads middle-class Irishmen to pay lip service to Gaelic even when they cannot speak it properly, and to preserve various forms of snobbery and ceremony dating from the time of the English ascendancy in Ireland. In his last plays, O'Casey combines satire of these flaws in Irish civilization with an affirmation of a highly personal creed that blends a pagan delight in the free expression of the senses and the imagination with intuitions and ideas drawn from Irish mythology, Christianity, and Marxism. Such is the final form of his basic dramatic theme of conflicting death-forces and life-forces.

This conflict is very apparent in *Cock-a-Doodle Dandy* (1949), a play first performed by the amateur actors of the People's Theatre, Newcastle-on-Tyne, on 10 December 1949. In "O'Casey's Lively Credo," an article published in the *New York Times* (10 November 1958), O'Casey states that many of the satirical portraits and events in the play are based on fact. There are certainly parallels in the social history of Eire to the episodes in which the village businessmen, Marthraun and Mahan, haggle for profits at the expense of their workmen; in which Shanaar, an old humbug, spreads superstition; in which the parish priest of Nyadnanave, Father Domineer, strikes to the ground a man who refuses to obey him; in which Loreleen is assaulted by Catholic zealots merely for having been in a car with a married man; in which Domineer tries to confiscate her copy of Joyce's *Ulysses*; in which the invalid Julia makes a fruitless pilgrimage to Lourdes; in which the young people, Loreleen, Lorna, Marion, and Robin, liberate themselves from puritan superstition, censorship, and violence by emigrating to England, "where life resembles life" more than it does in Nyadnanave.

The pervading spirit of the play, however, is one of myth and fantasy, not naturalism. Its chief embodiment is the Cock, with whose dancing entry and exit the play begins. Crimson-crested and green-winged, the Cock represents those instinctive and creative impulses that men repress at their peril; he is associated with sexual love, laughter, and the arts of music, poetry, and dancing. O'Casey leads us to judge his characters according to their reactions to the Cock. Loreleen is the key character of the play: her crest-like hat associates her with the Cock as soon as she enters. She loves dancing and literature: she reconciles the Dionysian force symbolized by the Cock with Christianity in such passages as the one in which she warns Marthraun and Mahan against "laying up treasures on earth." Those who fear the Cock try to kill him but succeed only in making themselves ridiculous: Father Domineer gets a black eye and a Civic Guard loses his trousers.

In some respects, *The Bishop's Bonfire* (1955) is a rustic tragedy complementary to the rustic comedy of *Cock-a-Doodle Dandy*. In *Time* (14 March 1955), O'Casey described it as "a play about the ferocious chastity of the Irish, a lament for the condition of Ireland, which is an apathetic country now." To hammer home this message, he groups his characters in pairs and gives a preponderance of power to those who repress the natural instincts of Irish youth. Secular power in the village of Ballyoonagh is represented by the wealthy Councillor Reiligan, who combines snobbery with political chicanery. Spiri-

tual power is represented by Father Burren, who makes ruthless use of his authority to compel Reiligan's daughter, Keelin, to marry the aging man of property preferred by her father instead of the laborer she loves. Just as Keelin represents youth thwarted by the social pretensions of her elders, so Foorawn, her sister, represents youth perverted by an ascetic religion, for she has taken a vow of chastity even though Manus Moanroe and she are in love with one another. The force making for life and freedom is, in its secular aspect, Codger Sleehaun, a Dionysian lover of song, drink, and the land; in its religious aspect, Father Boheroe, who tries in vain to break down the barriers between the lovers, warning Foorawn of the "vainglory" of her vow and urging Manus to "fall in love with life."

This morality pattern of character and action is not always in harmony with the fantasy, farce, and melodrama in the play. The statue of St. Tremolo with a horn at its lips is supposed to blow a blast whenever the Catholic faith is affronted, but it does so only at farcical moments, and its silence when the faith is being seriously questioned seems odd and inconsistent. The play ends luridly when Foorawn is shot by Manus and writes a lengthy suicide note to save him from being charged with her murder. This melodramatic climax is unconvincing, though it shows O'Casey's desire to suggest a saving grace in Irish youth as represented in this somewhat oppressive play.

The Bishop's Bonfire was the first of O'Casey's plays after *The Plough and the Stars* to have its first production in Ireland. With Tyrone Guthrie as its director and Cyril Cusack as Codger Sleehaun, it was first performed at the Gaiety Theatre, Dublin, on 28 February 1955. In 1957 there were hopes that this rapprochement between O'Casey and his native land would continue, for the Dublin An Tostal Council invited him to contribute a new play to its International Theatre Festival in 1958 and professed to be highly pleased with the comedy that he offered them, *The Drums of Father Ned* (1960). Unfortunately, the Archbishop of Dublin disliked what he heard about this play, and the festival was canceled. Righteously indignant, O'Casey forbade the professional performance of any of his plays in Ireland.

The Drums of Father Ned was first staged at the Little Theater, Lafayette, Indiana, in 1959. Its theme is in diametric contrast to what happened to the Dublin festival in 1958, because it shows the young men and women of the village of Doonavale transforming its Tostal (spring festival) into a bloodless revolution in which they sweep aside the various forms of political, economic, and clerical tyranny that have held them in bondage and inaugurate a new and happier era. They triumph partly because the old are hidebound and divided against one another. The three businessmen are still squabbling over such old chestnuts as Free State versus Republic, Northern Ireland versus Eire. All three are at odds with the parish priest, Father Fillifogue, because he abominates Communism whereas they want to make big profits by importing timber from a Communist country. The form of the triumph of the young is a Dionysian revel very like that of the *komos* of ancient Greece: they tease, deride, and bewilder their elders as they go in procession around the village, shouting their praises of Angus, the pagan Irish love-god, invading the lord mayor's drawing room to rehearse their songs, and even hoisting their harp banner above the presbytery. The leader of their triumph is the green-eyed and red-haired Father Ned, whose advice always spreads like wildfire among the young people when it is most needed. O'Casey's dedication to the play shows that he sees clear precedents for Father Ned's championship of youth in the moral crusades conducted by certain Irish priests in defiance of their bishops. In the ethos of the play, Father Ned is the symbolic figure who unites what is best in Irish myth and history with what is best in Christianity. At the close, the victorious roll of his drums heralds an Ireland without censorship, governed by youth, not age.

Behind the Green Curtains (1961) was O'Casey's last full-length play. It, too, shows Irish youth liberating itself from various forms of humbug and bigotry, but the victory here is hard won, and the setting is a town, not a village. Much of the play, in fact, is a mordant satire of the intelligentsia of Dublin. Dublin is represented by Senator Chatastray, a wealthy patron of the arts, and by a journalist, a poet, a playwright, and an actor from the Abbey Theatre, who flatter him to his face, accept his help, and sneer at him behind his back. O'Casey's directions concerning the settings for his plays are always significant down to the last detail, and the furnishings of Chatastray's drawing room are a calculated commentary on what passes as respectable in contemporary Irish culture. His green curtains, his paintings of Irish scenes by Paul Henry, his books in Gaelic, and his Abbey Theatre poster are conventional emblems of patriotism, just as his holy picture and his stained-glass window bear witness to his careful conformity to Irish Catholicism. Significantly, there are no flowers in the vase on his table; in O'Casey's plays, flowers are always a life-symbol. Correspondingly, the senator lacks moral courage; he is too timid even to leave Dublin after Catholic bigots have kidnapped him and beaten him up merely for having a young woman resident in his home as a housemaid. By the end of the play, his bright green curtains have come to symbolize the illusions that he is afraid to reject; the window and the view screened off by the curtains symbolize the realities that he dares not contemplate. His housemaid, on the other hand, defies their persecutors and joins two other representatives of the younger generation in a quest for a better life in England.

A remark in "O'Casey's Lively Credo" shows that his final plays were the result of an awareness of the nature and limitations of his own genius that he did not possess when he wrote his middle plays. "Like Joyce," he said, "it is only through an Irish scene that my imagination can weave a way, within the Irish shadows or out in the Irish sunshine . . . if it is to have a full, or at least a fair, chance to play." Though none of his final plays attains the tragic poignancy, or the inspired stagecraft, or the masterly control of quick transitions from the terrible to the farcical displayed in the three Dublin tragedies, it must be added that their requirements in costuming, lighting, scenery, stage effects, dancing, and acting are high indeed; that of them only *The Bishop's Bonfire* has so far been staged by a first-class company; and that a fully informed criticism of them will not be possible until all have been produced in a manner worthy of O'Casey. Happily, he composed his differences with the Irish professional theater in 1964, when he allowed the Abbey Theatre Company to perform *Juno and the Paycock* and *The Plough and the Stars* in Dublin before presenting them at the Aldwych Theatre, London, as part of the quatercentenary celebrations of Shakespeare's birth. Assessing O'Casey in the *Sunday Telegraph* of 20 September 1964, Alan Brien concluded by declaring, "His biggest triumphs on the stage belong to the future not to the present." Time may well confirm this prophecy.

VI

MOST of O'Casey's one-act plays follow the patterns illustrated by his full-length plays. *Nannie's Night Out* (1962) and *Hall of Healing* (1958) are tragi-satiric creations comparable to *Juno and the Pay-cock*. In *Hall of Healing* there is a characteristic transition from the richly idiosyncratic humor of the various characters who are waiting for medical attention in a Dublin parish dispensary to the haunting lament of the mother who comes to tell her husband that he need wait no longer because the child on whose behalf he came is now dead: "Come on Frank, till you see her. She's got all her good looks back again. [*Brokenly*] Oh, me little one'll be runnin' round frightened, lookin' for her mammy, among the spirits of the blest!"

Kathleen Listens In (1962) is in a very different style; it is a satiric fantasy that anticipates some of the themes and techniques of O'Casey's final plays. It shows a young woman, Kathleen O'Houlihan (i.e., Ireland), driven to distraction by the noisy wrangling of characters representative of Free Staters, Diehard Republicans, Gaelic Leaguers, Capitalists, Workers, Farmers, and Orangemen. Being morality plays, *Bedtime Story* and *A Time to Go* (both 1958) have some affinities with *The Bishop's Bonfire*. In *A Time to Go*, the countryman who fears that he has paid too little for a cow and the countrywoman who fears that she has charged too much for it are treated as lunatics and criminals because of their altruism, but they free themselves by making use of miraculous powers to render themselves invisible, and two barren trees symbolically burst into blossom and fruit as they pass by unseen.

In *The End of the Beginning* and *A Pound on Demand* (both 1958), on the other hand, O'Casey creates farce for its own sake as he never does in any of his full-length plays. His virtuosity in this form is seen at its best in *The End of the Beginning*, in which the blundering attempts of two men, one of whom is half-blind, to perform simple household duties produce one of the most brilliant sequences of comic peripeteia to be found in any farce written in English.

VII

AFTER the plays, the most important of O'Casey's writings are the six autobiographical volumes that he published between 1939 and 1954. The reader who turns to them for a considered account of O'Casey's theory and practice as a dramatist will be disappointed, but he will find in them much of the source material of *The Shadow of a Gunman, Nannie's*

Night Out, Juno and the Paycock, The Plough and the Stars, The End of the Beginning, Red Roses for Me, Hall of Healing, Oak Leaves and Lavender, and *A Time to Go*. He will also find in *Inishfallen, Fare Thee Well* (pp. 117–121) an account of O'Casey's lost plays—*The Frost in the Flower, The Harvest Festival, The Crimson in the Tricolour*, and *The Robe of Rosheen*—and discover that O'Casey had seen only two performances of plays at the Abbey Theatre before he submitted a play to its directors, though he had seen many melodramas at the Queen's Theatre, Dublin. The same volume makes it clear that one of the saddest results of his break with the Abbey Theatre was the end of his association with Lady Gregory, who enjoyed more of his confidence and gave him better advice than any other writer he met.

The literary reminiscences in O'Casey's autobiographies, however, are merely part of the pattern that gives unity to the six volumes, that pattern being an interrelated series of struggles: his fight for existence, his fight for an education, his fight for a vocation, his fight for recognition, his fight against criticism, and his fight for a better Ireland. This pattern reveals the child as father to the man; the blow he dealt a sadistic schoolteacher is paralleled by the blow he struck for Ireland when he unhorsed a mounted policeman with a flagpole during a demonstration against England during the Boer War. In this way, the first four autobiographies, *I Knock at the Door* (1939), *Pictures in the Hallway, Drums Under the Windows*, and *Inishfallen, Fare Thee Well*, acquire an epic breadth and depth as they unfold the story of O'Casey's personal struggle against the background of Ireland's struggle for liberation.

Few writers have had better reason for self-pity than O'Casey, but not once does he descend to it in his account of his periods of semistarvation, his ulcerated eyes, his tubercular neck, his comfortless slum life, and his harrowing experiences of the callousness, violence, and madness that poverty brings in its wake. He records these things vividly but objectively, referring to himself in the third person as "Sean" and recapturing whatever grim humor they had, as when he recalls how oddly his appearance consorted with his attempts to advise the leaders of the Irish Volunteers at a time when "his oozing neck, near-sighted eyes, trembling legs, tattered clothes, and broken boots must have been a shuddering sight for Gaelic gods to see." The narrative is also enlivened by sequences in which O'Casey treats topical or historical events and personalities in a spirit of rumbustious and irreverent fantasy, making uninhibited use of pun and parody after the fashion of James Joyce in *Finnegans Wake* (1939).

The last two autobiographies, *Rose and Crown* (1952) and *Sunset and Evening Star* (1954), deal with O'Casey's life and ideas after he settled in England. Though abundantly interesting, they lack the tension and epic breadth of the earlier volumes. They are concerned more with O'Casey's dislikes than his likes, and their tone is sometimes shrill and querulous; but *Sunset and Evening Star* ends with a characteristically vibrant salute to life, written ten years before he died at the age of eighty-four in a Torquay nursing home on 20 September 1964:

Here, with whitened hair, desires failing, strength ebbing out of him, with the sun gone down, and with only the serenity and the calm warning of the evening star left to him, he drank to Life, to all it had been, to what it was, to what it would be. Hurrah!

With this final affirmation of the essential joy of living it is fitting to combine O'Casey's affirmation of his essential Irishness, as expressed in his defense of *The Bishop's Bonfire* in *The Green Crow* (1956):

I know the mind of Ireland because I am within it; I know the heart of Ireland because I am one of its corners; I know the five senses of Ireland because I am within them and they are within me; they bid me look, and when I look, I see; they bid me listen, and when I listen, I hear.

("Bonfire Under a Black Sun," p. 150)

Living intensely in an age of cataclysmic destruction, O'Casey sought a principle of hope and joy, and his quest succeeded most when it was directed by intuitions of Ireland's needs and Ireland's better self.

SELECTED BIBLIOGRAPHY

I. BIBLIOGRAPHY. C. Brandstadter, "Eine O'Casey-Bibliographie," in *Zeitschrift für Anglistik und Amerikanistik*, vol. II, pp. 240–254 (Berlin, 1954), detailed but not always accurate; E. K. Mikhail, *Sean O'Casey: A Bibliography of Criticism* (London, 1971); *The Sean O'Casey Review* (New York, 1974–   ), a bi-annual collection of articles that also publishes an annual bibliography; R. Ayling and M. J. Durkan, *Sean O'Casey: A Bibliography* (London, 1978), comprehensive and invaluable.

II. COLLECTED WORKS. *Collected Plays*, 4 vols. (London, 1949–1951); *Mirror in My House*, 2 vols. (New York, 1956), includes the six vols. of autobiography, repr. as *Autobiographies* (London, 1963).

III. SEPARATE WORKS. *Songs of the Wren, 1st and 2nd Series* (Dublin, 1918), humorous and patriotic lyrics; *More Wren Songs* (Dublin, 1918), poetry; *The Story of Thomas Ashe* and *The Sacrifice of Thomas Ashe* (both Dublin, 1918), biographical panegyrics; *The Story of the Irish Citizen Army* (Dublin–London, 1919), history, written under the pseudonym P. O'Cathasaigh.

Two Plays (London, 1925), contains *Juno and the Paycock* and *The Shadow of a Gunman*; *The Plough and the Stars: A Tragedy in Four Acts* (London, 1926); *The Silver Tassie: A Tragi-Comedy in Four Acts* (London, 1928).

Within the Gates: A Play of Four Scenes in a London Park (London, 1933); *Windfalls: Stories, Poems and Plays* (London, 1934), contains early poems, short stories, and two plays, *The End of the Beginning* and *A Pound on Demand*; *The Flying Wasp: A Laughing Look-over of What Has Been Said About the Things of the Theater by the English Dramatic Critics* (London, 1937), criticism; *I Knock at the Door: Swift Glances Back at Things That Made Me* (London, 1939), autobiography.

The Star Turns Red (London, 1940), drama; *Purple Dust: A Wayward Comedy in Three Acts* (London, 1940); *Red Roses for Me: A Play in Four Acts* (London, 1942); *Pictures in the Hallway* (New York, 1942), autobiography; *Drums Under the Windows* (London, 1945), autobiography; *Oak Leaves and Lavender, or, a World on Wallpaper* (London, 1946), drama; *Cock-a-Doodle Dandy* (London, 1949), drama; *Inishfallen, Fare Thee Well* (New York, 1949), autobiography.

Rose and Crown (London, 1952), autobiography; *Sunset and Evening Star* (New York, 1954), autobiography; *The Bishop's Bonfire: A Sad Play Within the Tune of a Polka* (London, 1955), drama; *The Green Crow* (New York, 1956), miscellaneous, contains parts of *The Flying Wasp*, four stories from *Windfalls*, and some new essays; *Five One-Act Plays* (London, 1958), contains *The End of the Beginning, A Pound on Demand, Hall of Healing, Bedtime Story*, and *A Time to Go*.

The Drums of Father Ned: A Mickrocosm of Ireland (London, 1960), drama; *Behind the Green Curtains* (London, 1961), contains *Figure in the Night, The Moon Shines on Kylenamoe*, and the title play; *Under a Coloured Cap: Articles Merry and Mournful with Comments and a Song* (London, 1963); R. Hogan, ed., *Feathers from the Green Crow: Sean O'Casey 1905–1925* (Columbia, Mo., 1962), contains two previously unpublished plays—*Kathleen Listens In* and *Nannie's Night Out*—some early newspaper articles, *The Sacrifice of Thomas Ashe*, and *The Story of the Irish Citizen Army*; R. Ayling, ed., *Blasts and Benedic-*

tions (London–New York, 1967), contains articles and stories, some previously unpublished; D. Krause, *A Self-Portrait of the Artist as a Man: Sean O'Casey's Letters* (Dublin–London, 1968).

IV. LETTERS. D. Krause, ed., *The Letters of Sean O'Casey*, vol. I: *1910–1941* (London, 1975), very valuable commentary on O'Casey's life and the reception of his plays.

V. BIOGRAPHICAL AND CRITICAL STUDIES. D. Byrne, *The Story of Ireland's National Theatre: The Abbey Theatre, Dublin* (Dublin–Cork, 1929); A. E. Malone, *The Irish Drama* (London, 1929), somewhat disparaging early assessment; D. Ryan, *Remembering Sion* (London, 1934); S. Gwynn, *Irish Literature and Drama in the English Language: A Short History* (London, 1936); K. Wittig, *Sean O'Casey als Dramatiker: Ein Beitrag zum Nachskriegsdrama Irlands* (Leipzig, 1937), valuable pioneer study; L. Robinson, ed., *The Irish Theatre: Lectures Delivered During the Abbey Theatre Festival Held in Dublin in August 1938* (London, 1939); L. Robinson, *Curtain Up: An Autobiography* (London, 1942); L. Robinson, ed., *Lady Gregory's Journals, 1916–1930* (London, 1946), contains important background material about the early plays; E. Bentley, *The Playwright as Thinker: A Study of Drama in Modern Times* (New York, 1946); H. Zaslawski, *Die Werke Sean O'Caseys, unter Besonderer Berücksichtigung seiner zweiten Periode* (Vienna, 1949).

P. Kavanagh, *The Story of the Abbey Theatre* (New York, 1950); J. Koslow, *The Green and the Red: Sean O'Casey, the Man and His Plays* (New York, 1949), rev. ed. titled *Sean O'Casey: The Man and His Plays* (New York, 1966); M. MacLiammóir, *Theatre in Ireland* (Dublin, 1950); L. Robinson, *Ireland's Abbey Theatre: A History, 1899–1951* (London, 1951); R. Findlater, *The Unholy Trade* (London, 1952), contains a lively critique of O'Casey; R. Williams, *Drama from Ibsen to Eliot* (London, 1952), contains hostile criticism; J. C. Trewin, *Dramatists of Today* (London, 1953); J. Gassner, *Form and Idea in Modern Theatre* (New York, 1956); G. Fay, *The Abbey Theatre: Cradle of Genius* (London, 1958); J. Jacquot, ed., *Le Théâtre moderne: Hommes et tendances* (Paris, 1958).

R. Hogan, *The Experiments of Sean O'Casey* (New York, 1960); D. Krause, *Sean O'Casey: The Man and His Work* (London, 1960), still the best all-around study published so far; K. Spinner, *Die alte Dame sagt Nein! Drei Irische Dramatiker: Lennox Robinson, Sean O'Casey, Denis Johnston* (Berne, 1961); A. Lewis, *The Contemporary Theatre: The Significant Playwrights of Our Time* (New York, 1962); H. Oppel, ed., *Das moderne Englische Drama: Interpretationen* (Berlin, 1963); W. A. Armstrong, ed., *Experimental Drama* (London, 1963), contains discussion of O'Casey's last plays; S. Cowasjee, *Sean O'Casey: The Man Behind the Plays* (Edinburgh, 1963), contains some useful biographical research; W. A. Armstrong, ed., *Classic Irish Drama* (London, 1964), contains annotated text of *Cock-a-Doodle Dandy* with introductory study.

G. Fallon, *Sean O'Casey: The Man I Knew* (London, 1965), a controversial study; S. Cowasjee, *O'Casey* (Edinburgh, 1966); S. McCann, ed., *The World of Sean O'Casey* (London, 1966), biographical essays, variable in quality; E. Blythe, *The Abbey Theatre* (Dublin, n.d.), contains useful information about the staging of O'Casey's plays at the Abbey; R. Hogan, *After the Irish Renaissance* (Minneapolis, 1967; London, 1968), contains ch. on O'Casey's plays written after 1926; K. Völker, *Irisches Theater*, vol. II: *Sean O'Casey* (Velber, 1968); R. Ayling, ed., *Sean O'Casey: Modern Judgements* (London, 1969), well-chosen collection of critical essays on the plays, autobiographies, and letters, with lively intro. and useful list of books and articles on O'Casey; M. Malone, *The Plays of Sean O'Casey* (Carbondale, Ill., 1969), well-balanced survey of the plays in relation to their social and political background.

M. B. Margulies, *The Early Life of Sean O'Casey* (London, 1970), offers new facts about O'Casey's early life and an interpretation of them; E. O'Casey, *Sean* (London, 1971), biographical memoirs by his wife; *The Sean O'Casey Review* (New York, 1974–   ), a bi-annual collection of articles on O'Casey; T. Kilroy, ed., *Sean O'Casey: A Collection of Critical Essays* (Englewood Cliffs, N. J., 1974); E. H. Mikhail and J. O'Riordan, eds., *The Sting and the Trinkle: Conversations with Sean O'Casey* (London, 1974), firsthand records of conversations; D. D. Wilson, *Sean O'Casey's Tragi-Comic Vision* (New York, 1976); M. Pauli, *Sean O'Casey: Drama: Poesie: Wirklichkeit* (Berlin, 1977); G. J. Watson, *Irish Identity and the Literary Revival* (New York–London, 1979), considers how efforts to analyze the nature of Irishness influenced O'Casey's work; P. Edwards, *Threshold of a Nation: A Study in English and Irish Drama* (Cambridge, 1979), considers O'Casey's attempts to find a theatrical image for the troubles of Ireland; P. Stapelburg, *Sean O'Casey und das deutschsprachige Theater (1948–1974)* (Berlin, 1979), examines O'Casey's influence on drama in East and West Germany, gives records of stage and radio productions of his plays in German.

H. Hunt, *Sean O'Casey* (Dublin, 1980), a discerning introductory study; *Irish University Review* (Spring 1980), the issue is devoted entirely to O'Casey; R. G. Lowery, ed., *Essays on Sean O'Casey's "Autobiographies"* (London, 1981); B. Atkinson, *Sean O'Casey: From Times Past* (London, 1983); R. G. Lowery, ed., *O'Casey Annual*, no. 1 (Dublin, 1983–   ); R. G. Lowery, ed., *O'Casey's Autobiographies: An Annotated Index* (London, 1983).

LIST OF ARTICLES BY SEAN O'CASEY

"Sound the Loud Trumpet," *The Peasant and Irish Ireland* (25 May 1907); "The Gaelic League in Dublin," *The Peasant and Irish Ireland* (6 July 1907); "Great Northern

Railway, Ireland: Some of Its Works and Pomps: The Charity of Its Officials," *The Irish Worker* (8 June 1912); "The Bonnie Bunch of Roses, O!" *The Irish Worker* (11 January 1913); "Chiefs of the GNRI," I, II, III, *The Irish Worker* (25 January, 8 February, 15 February 1913); "'Euchan' and Ireland: A Challenge to a Verbal Combat," *The Irish Worker* (22 February 1913); "Some Slaves of the GNRI and Others," *The Irish Worker* (1 March 1913); "Guth ar an Ngadre," *Irish Freedom* (March 1913); "Declenda est Larkinism," *The Irish Worker* (10 May 1913); "Faithful Forever," *The Irish Worker* (26 April 1913); "'Irish Freedom' and the 'Irish Nation,'" *The Irish Worker* (10 May 1913); "Tone's Grave," *The Irish Worker* (21 June 1913); "The Gathering," *The Irish Worker* (17 September 1913); "Ecce Nunc," *The Irish Worker* (15 November 1913); "An Open Letter to Workers in the Volunteers," *The Irish Worker* (24 January 1914); "Volunteers and Workers," *The Irish Worker* (21 February 1914); "Irish Workers and Irish Volunteers," *The Irish Worker* (7 March 1914); "The Soul of Davis," *The Irish Worker* (7 March 1914); "A Day in Bodenstown," *The Irish Worker* (27 June 1914); "The Gaelic Movement Today," *Irish Opinion* (23 March 1918).

"The Seamless Coat of Kathleen," *Poblacht Na H-Éireann* (29 March 1922); "Life and Literature," *The Irish Statesman* (22 December 1923); "Gulls and Bobbin Testers," *The Irish Statesman* (6 September 1924); "Irish in the Schools," *The Irish Statesman* (29 November 1924); "The Innocent at Home," *The Irish Statesman* (10 January 1925); Letter on Irish language in schools, *The Irish Statesman* (7 February 1925); "Y.O and 'The Silver Tassie,'" *The Irish Statesman* (4 August 1928); "The Plays of Sean O'Casey: A Reply," *The Nineteenth Century* (September 1928); "Toreador," *Time and Tide* (2 December 1933); "The Public Death of Shakespeare," *Time and Tide* (13 July 1935); "Three Cheers for Noah," *Time and Tide* (10 August 1935); "National Theatre Bunkum," *Time and Tide* (16 October, 7 November, 16 December 1935); "The Dream School," *The Yale Review*, 27 (Summer 1937).

"There Go the Irish," *They Go—the Irish*, L. Daiken, ed. (London, 1944); "No Flowers for Films," *Leader* (19 February 1949); "The Play of Ideas," *New Statesman and Nation* (8 April 1950); "Saintly Sinner, Sing for Us," *New Statesman and Nation* (16 December 1950); "Always the Plow and the Stars," *New York Times Book Review* (25 January 1953); "Jeep Be Jeepers," *New Statesman and Nation* (18 July 1953); "O'Casey's Lively Credo," *New York Times*, International ed. (10 November 1958); "Lettre à Jean Vilar," *Bref*, 43 (1961); "Sean O'Casey Concerning James Joyce," *Massachusetts Review*, 5 (1964).

VIRGINIA WOOLF
(1882-1941)

Bernard Blackstone

LIFE

VIRGINIA WOOLF's lifetime, a mere fifty-nine years, spans two world wars and the collapse of a civilization. Born on 25 January 1882, in the heyday of Victorian and imperial prosperity, she died by her own hand in 1941, as Hitler's bombs rained down on London. The fragility of intelligence and goodness, the frightening strength of evil and stupidity are the themes of her novels: she did not have to seek them anywhere outside the history of her own life and times.

Leslie Stephen, Virginia's father, the eminent Victorian literary critic and agnostic, had two daughters and two sons by his second wife, Julia Duckworth. Vanessa, his elder daughter, showed her talent for painting at an early age and became a leader of the English avant-garde. Virginia was equally committed, to literature. Without much formal education—she went neither to school nor to university—she had the run of her father's vast library and used it to full advantage. Her mother died in 1885 and her beloved half-sister, Stella Duckworth Hills, in 1897, blows from which Virginia never really recovered; after this her sister and various other maternal women figured in her life as substitutes, never with complete success, as is evidenced by the series of nervous breakdowns that pursued her from 1904, the year of her father's death, to her suicide by drowning.

Her childhood and young womanhood were passed in London, with summer holidays at St. Ives in Cornwall. As a novelist she is both a great Londoner, like Charles Dickens and William Makepeace Thackeray, and a great devotee of the sea and its coasts, like Joseph Conrad. After her father's death, she broke away from the respectable Victorian milieu of Kensington and migrated with her sister and two brothers, Thoby and Adrian, to Gordon Square, Bloomsbury. Bloomsbury at the turn of the century was felt to be shabby and disreputable, and the move earned the disapproval of Virginia's half-brothers by her mother's earlier marriage, George and Gerald Duckworth, and of most of their "society" friends. The offense was compounded when the Stephen sisters turned to a thoroughly bohemian way of life and chatted, unchaperoned, into the small hours with the young men their brother Thoby brought back with him from Cambridge. And so the celebrated or notorious Bloomsbury group came into existence.

Virginia Stephen married a member of the group, Leonard Woolf, in 1912. An ex-official of the Ceylon Civil Service and an old friend of Thoby Stephen's at Cambridge, Woolf was a stabilizing presence in her life. Together they founded the Hogarth Press (1917). The amateurish venture was a striking success. Profits, meager to begin with, expanded with the reputation of the press and provided funds for holidays on the Continent, which the Woolfs loved, and the purchase of a country cottage at Rodmell in Sussex—a refuge from the constant round of London parties to which Virginia was being invited, as the fame of her writing spread. Alternating solitude and society, she struggled hard to preserve a precarious equilibrium, frequently punctuated by the episodes of suicidal insanity that generally followed upon the completion of each of her novels.

The mounting pressure of horror from the outer as well as her own inner world assailed her—for she was hypersensitive to suffering—during the years of World War I, in which many of her Cambridge friends were killed or wounded. The period between the wars, in which her major creative and critical work was done, saw the rise of monstrous tyrannies on the Continent. With a Socialist and Jewish husband Virginia could not but be aware of the implications of these for her personal life as well as for European civilization. Could *notre vieille Europe aux anciens parapets* survive a second onslaught? The note of alarm sounds throughout *Jacob's Room* (1922), *Mrs. Dalloway* (1925), *To the Lighthouse* (1927), *The Waves* (1931), *The Years* (1937), and the posthumous *Between the Acts* (1941). She did not live to see the outcome. Walking into the river Ouse at Rodmell, her pockets filled with stones, she drowned on 28 March 1941, unable any longer to cope with her personal problems or "the monstrous agony of the world."

THE WRITER AND THE AGE

In the maelstrom of "movements" that make up the literature of England in our time, we may distinguish two separate and contrary directions: the centrifugal and the centripetal. There is the literature of action—"in the destructive element immerse"; there is the literature of recollection—"be still and know." One current goes with the age; the other opposes it. Yet both are integral to our time: the maelstrom could not exist without them.

That double position accepted, there is no difficulty in pointing out the major figures. On the one hand, James Joyce, D. H. Lawrence, and the novel of violence; on the other, E. M. Forster, Virginia Woolf. In poetry, similar distinctions can be made. There are political overtones, more audible perhaps in the 1930's than today. Stretching a few points, we can sniff religious odors: here, incense and guttering candles; there, dusty hassocks and the cold stone of college chapels. One school, floating in a refined air of mystical agnosticism, looks askance on the sex-cum-blasphemy of the other.

If we ask ourselves in what consists the specific modernity of modern literature, of either the left or the right (as I shall call the two "currents," without political implication), we may find the answer far to seek. Is modern literature everything in "serious" prose and verse written after a particular date, say 1918? Hardly that; for it is notorious that a good deal of highly respected work done since that date might well have been written, as far as its concern with present-day living goes or as far as it shows an awareness of contemporary technique, at any point in the previous half-century. Moreover, a considerable amount of work that does display this awareness was written well before 1918—much of the verse of William Butler Yeats and Gerard Manley Hopkins, most of Forster's prose. We cannot leave this out of account, or we may get a false perspective.

If modernity is not a matter of chronology, what is it? Well, of course chronology comes into the picture. The writer must deal with the events of his time; but if he is a good writer, in his hands they don't stay events—they become experiences. Such a writer is not a mere reporter; he is aware of the significance of what is happening in his age, able to encompass the broad pattern woven of separate events. The journalist cannot see the forest for the trees; the artist grasps the meaning behind phenomena. He is something of a philosopher, a seer, as well as a technician. But the technique comes in too. New wine won't go into old bottles. New ideas, new ways of experience, shatter the old forms. Inevitably, originality of thought and spontaneity of emotion create fresh designs, strange music, new rhythms. With some writers, like Joyce, they even create a new vocabulary. Indeed, if we find a poet using the old forms—the sonnet, the rondeau, blank verse, and so on—we may be suspicious of him—as suspicious as if we caught him aping the idiom of John Milton or Geoffrey Chaucer.

That is the first essential in the modern writer, I think: awareness of what is new and important, and adequate technical response to that awareness. Later we shall see that there is a second "note" of good writing, which I shall call *proportion*. But for the moment let us focus on this aspect, since it provides a useful introduction to our theme in this essay. Virginia Woolf is commonly held to be a difficult writer, which means that she did not use a conventional technique or seek to arouse stock responses in her readers. She was aiming at something new, and we may safely say that she achieved it. What was this something new?

To answer this question fully would entail a discussion of the position of the English novel when Virginia Woolf began to write—around 1915. But in an essay as brief as the present one there is no room for any but positive findings. I would like to make this not a conducted tour but a series of flashes focused now on one, now on another aspect of her art. What has she to offer the reader? What dimension of understanding? What particular insights? In discussing these questions we may find that we are also, in effect, probing into some of the general conditions of the modern novel, for it is futile to consider any writer other than in the context of his or her time. In the case of Virginia Woolf, we shall find especially profitable the distinction that I made first of all, between the two currents of the contemporary maelstrom.

The first characteristic that strikes me is her understanding of human insufficiency. There are affinities here, of course, with the left—with existentialism and the novel of violence; but where the existentialists give up in despair and the Lawrences and Graham Greenes seek their panacea in action—that is, in the movement away from the still center—Virginia Woolf works consistently inward, away from the world of events. Let us begin with an example from her last novel, *Between the Acts*. Here we have a positive statement, that is, a presentation of a moment of sufficiency; but we are shown how that moment can exist only under certain special conditions: in the mind of a child rather than an adult, in the absence of distraction, and exposed to the threat of instant destruction.

Amy was saying something about a feller when Mabel, with her hand on the pram, turned sharply, her sweet swallowed. "Leave off grubbing," she said sharply. "Come along, George."

The little boy had lagged and was grouting in the grass. Then the baby, Caro, thrust her fist over the coverlet and the furry bear was jerked overboard. Amy had to stoop. George grubbed. The flower blazed between the angles of the roots. Membrane after membrane was torn. It blazed a soft yellow, a lambent light under a film of velvet; it filled the caverns behind the eyes with light. All that inner darkness became a hall, leaf smelling, earth smelling, of yellow light. And the tree was beyond the flower; the grass, the flower and the tree were entire. Down on his knees grubbing he held the flower complete. Then there was a roar and a hot breath and a stream of coarse grey hair rushed between him and the flower. Up he leapt, toppling in his fright, and saw coming towards him a terrible peaked eyeless monster moving on legs, brandishing arms.

Little George's moment of sufficiency is flanked by two insufficiencies: the nursemaids with their talk of "fellers" and their sweets, the old man with his Afghan hound and the need to impose himself on his grandson. The vision, which consists in a perfect observation of and identification with that which *is* (in this case the flower, roots, and soil at the foot of a tree), is broken by the intrusion of an adult world. This is the final example in Woolf's work of a repeated pattern. Let us note in passing that there is no condemnation of the nursemaids for being stupid or of Bart for being tyrannical; things are what they

are, and we have moved out of the moral, discriminating world of Dickens and Thackeray. We might call this absence of judgment a note of modernity, indeed of maturity, for Virginia Woolf did not display it from the outset. Her early work, like Forster's, offers value-judgments, particularly in situations directed against organized religion and its ministers. There is, it is true, a survival of this trait in the clergyman of *Between the Acts*, but a balance is preserved with the sympathetic portrait of Lucy fingering her crucifix.

Yet Lucy, however sympathetically drawn, is plainly not a self-sufficient person. She fingers her crucifix; she relies on God. Let us, with George's experience in mind, watch her cutting a loaf of bread:

Why's stale bread, she mused, easier to cut than fresh? And so skipped, sidelong, from yeast to alcohol; so to fermentation; so to inebriation; so to Bacchus; and lay under purple lamps in a vineyard in Italy, as she had done, often.

We see what is happening: George perceives; Lucy muses. George experiences; Lucy reacts. The bread is there, but she does not *see* it. Her thoughts move in a chain; they are slung on the string of memory. Information, morality, nostalgia—all are there, all the debris that chokes the immediate and masks the strange. George's mind is a cavern filled with yellow light, smelling of earth, empty. He labels nothing, moves on to nothing. He experiences bliss. Lucy, in the same situation, would be naming everything she saw and relating it to past or future: "Ah, a worm, there goes a beetle, horrid thing, I must do something about these weeds, how stony this soil is." The screen of concepts would be set between her and reality.

And thus the uniqueness, the joy of the moment, escapes her—as, indeed, Virginia Woolf shows it escaping so many of her characters. Here is Mrs. Ramsay in *To the Lighthouse*, sensing much that is true and good; but she verbalizes it:

When life sank down for a moment, the range of experience seemed limitless. And to everybody there was always this sense of unlimited resources, she supposed; one after another, she, Lily, Augustus Carmichael, must feel, our apparitions, the things you know us by, are simply childish. Beneath it is all dark, it is all spreading, it is unfathomably deep; but now and again we rise to the surface and that is what you see us by.

(I.11)

Words fix her experience. Of course Virginia Woolf knows the danger. Her art, in its development, aims at finding a way out. The very stream-of-consciousness technique that we see at work in Lucy's interior monologue, and that Virginia Woolf derived from Laurence Sterne and Marcel Proust, is a means at least of bringing the evil to the surface, of demonstrating how much we are bound in our mental processes by memories, reactions, obsessions. But need the writer also be found in her art? That, for her, is the question. And so we find her experimenting with technique. Can words, phrases, the very structure of the novel be stripped of their conventional trappings, made to evoke other than stock responses? Can the reader be induced to expect something different or, if not to expect, at least to accept it? Is it possible, above all, to emulate the technique of the painter (we remember her interest in the postimpressionists) and say, "There is what I saw—that is how the thing you call a rose, a jam-jar, or a boat appeared to me, then, at the moment, under those conditions of light, inner and outer"? Can the novel present, as the pictures can, the thusness of each object as it exists in relationship to blue sky, yellow sand, or striped tablecloth?

Let us note how curiously the theme of insufficiency is again asserting itself—this time in the dubious relationship of author and reader. It is the reader, you or I, who now turns back from the immediate experience offered by the novelist. The writer comes bearing gifts and is greeted by a "Timeo Danaos!" ("I fear the Greeks, even though they bring gifts": Vergil, *Aeneid* II. 49). I offer you, says the novelist, a new slant on life, the fresh perception that I have achieved; I doubt if you have been given anything quite like it before. I don't want your new perception, replies the reader; I want Tarzan, or Forsyte, or the mixture as before of Catholicism-and-violence. Go away and leave me in peace. I don't want reality. It bores me and frightens me. In any case, I don't understand you. I can't follow what you are saying.

The reader cannot follow what the writer is saying because she is trying to say it in a different way. Virginia Woolf was, from first to last, intensely conscious of making a different thing out of the novel. The genre had been developed and exploited by men; but she was a woman, and she was sure that a woman novelist had to create her own form. Jane Austen had done it; but the Brontës and George Eliot had stuck too close to the old masculine pattern. The feminine mind, the feminine sensibility, cannot profitably imitate the masculine. A woman novelist has

something new to bring. And so Virginia Woolf experiments ceaselessly in new forms, fresh techniques, always trying to get nearer to an integral expression of life. For truth—her great devotion—is valid here as well as in the realm of ideas, in how a thing is said as well as in what is said. The form of the conventional, commercial novel is not *true*; it is stereotyped, dealing only with certain detached aspects of living (which it exaggerates and distorts) glued together by the crude devices of set descriptions, coincidences, catastrophes, transition passages of mere padding. And all moves on the surface. How, thought Virginia Woolf, how could she find a form that would convey the movement of things under the surface—the free play of thought, emotion, insight?

She learned, of course, from others. Mostly from her contemporaries, from Proust and Joyce and Dorothy Richardson; but also from the older masters in whose work she discerned the same experimental quality, the same focusing on an interior world. There was Sterne, for instance, with his technique of disintegration, his flouting of the time sense and of the connecting link; there was Montaigne, with his delicately poised self-preservation, his irony; there were also the great Russians.

In her first novels we feel rather strongly the influence of Forster. Indeed, these novels are not experimental in form; they are occupied more, after the Forster pattern, in probing the niceties of human relationships. She wants to find out what themes the novel should deal with, what kinds of characters she herself is best fitted to present. *The Voyage Out* (1915) is a fairly straightforward narrative of a young woman, Rachel Vinrace, who is thrust suddenly out of a backwater into the whirl of life, falls in love, and dies. *Night and Day* (1919) is about another young woman, Katharine Hilbery, more self-possessed, more mature, who wonders whether falling in love and marrying may not be a matter of quitting life for a backwater. But in her next novel, *Jacob's Room* (1922), and perhaps even more in the little volume of short stories or sketches *Monday or Tuesday*, which had appeared in the previous year, we find her experimenting: experimenting with the stream-of-consciousness technique, experimenting above all with the disruption of time.

Time is a problem for most modern writers. They feel bound, cramped, by the necessity of keeping to the strict sequence of events: A followed by B, and C following B; they envy the plastic artist his freedom of movement in space, his power of presenting a totality to the eye. Poetry, of course, is freer than prose—poets have always enjoyed a certain license to jump about from present to past and from past to future, to organize their intuitions within a not strictly temporal pattern. But hitherto the novel had been bound. Restricted as it was to the sphere of action, to the telling of a story, it had to present the sequence of cause and effect. The reader wanted to know "what is going to happen now." In particular the Victorian convention (followed by Dickens, Thackeray, and Anthony Trollope) of serial publication prescribed a rigid scheme of "continued in our next" and made development and experiment impossible.

Perhaps the first note of revolt, in England at least, was sounded by Forster. Tentatively in his novels and more boldly in the course of lectures published as *Aspects of the Novel* in 1927, he criticized the time-obsession in fiction. Indeed, he assailed the story, the plot itself, as Virginia Woolf remarks in the review she wrote of his book:

Many are the judgements that we would willingly argue, many are the points over which we would willingly linger, as Mr. Forster passes lightly on his way. That Scott is a story-teller and nothing more; that a story is the lowest of literary organisms; that the novelist's unnatural preoccupation with love is largely a reflection of his own state of mind while he composes—every page has a hint or a suggestion which makes us stop to think or wish to contradict.

("The Art of Fiction")

As a reviewer, she had neither time nor space to debate these points; as a novelist, we find them influencing her increasingly. (The argument about Sir Walter Scott comes at a crucial point in *To the Lighthouse*.) She noted and she pondered. Even within the limits of her review she arrives at certain highly significant conclusions: "In England at any rate the novel is not a work of art. There are none to be stood beside *War and Peace, The Brothers Karamazov*, or *A la Recherche du Temps Perdu.*" She calls upon the critic to be bolder:

He might cut adrift from the eternal tea-table and the plausible and preposterous formulas which are supposed to represent the whole of our human adventure. But then the story might wobble; the plot might crumble; ruin might seize upon the characters. The novel, in short, might become a work of art.

There can be no doubt that Virginia Woolf was stimulated and encouraged by *Aspects of the Novel*, with its first open statement of revolt; but she had already begun to put into practice most of Forster's

hints some six years earlier. *Monday or Tuesday*, however, was a mere collection of sketches. It was in 1925, with *Mrs. Dalloway*, that she first shattered the time-pattern within the space of a full-length novel. Here she made the bold experiment of restricting her scheme to the limits of a single day, a single district of London, a single character in the round (a return to the three unities already signaled in *Ulysses*), while employing the devices of memory and dramatic counterpoint (Septimus Warren Smith's day is linked harmonically with Clarissa Dalloway's, though the two characters never meet) to avoid thinness and monotony. Later, in *To the Lighthouse* (1927), we see her playing other tricks with time. In the first section the action is restricted to one evening, the hours between six o'clock and dinner, and in fact even these few hours are foreshortened to a single moment; for in obedience to Mrs. Ramsay's "Time stand still here!" there is a suspension similar to that imposed by Mr. Weston in T. F. Powys' novel *Mr. Weston's Good Wine* (1927) on the bewildered inhabitants of Folly Down. In the second section, "Time Passes," the human element is withdrawn; the house is left alone to decay. In the third section, memory comes into its own and the present is displaced by the past.

Why, we may ask, this preoccupation with time? Why this ceaseless experimenting with the devices of memory and foreshortening? It is probably not enough to reply that Virginia Woolf found the time sequence inadequate to her intuition of reality, though that is an important point for a writer who attempts, as she does, to give a this-worldly rendering of an other-worldly pattern or a series of patterns or glimpses of patterns. But there is another reason. I think she found the time sequence inadequate also to the simple rendering of character, to the display of her creatures' inner lives. This is most strikingly demonstrated in her next work, the fantasy *Orlando* (1928), in which the life of her heroine, which in *Mrs. Dalloway* and *To the Lighthouse* had been foreshortened to one day, is stretched out to the perspective of four centuries; in which, too, there is a change of sex from masculine to feminine. All this metamorphosis, this complication and explication, is necessary to elucidate that most mysterious entity, the human spirit. "One wanted fifty pairs of eyes to see with," Lily Briscoe had reflected in *To the Lighthouse*. "Fifty pairs of eyes were not enough to get round that one woman with, she thought." Very well, we can hear Virginia Woolf replying, let us see how many pairs of eyes, in four hundred years, are needed to pluck out the heart of Orlando's mystery. Let us show Orlando as first masculine, and then feminine; first in love, and then loved; first jilting, and then jilted; a man of action and a poet, a woman of fashion and a Victorian lady.

In *The Waves* (1931) the process is carried a step further; indeed, to what we can only imagine to be its conclusion, for further development can hardly be expected along a line that had led, as here, to the suppression of plot, dialogue, and exterior description. *The Waves* presents us with six characters who grow up from children to men and women, but who never, in the novel, address one another, never attain an effective relationship; they move in and out of a pattern as in the intricate steps of the ballet. Counterpointed against the changing emotions and sensations of six parallel lifetimes is the process of a solar day. We are presented with a tissue of infinite complexity in which each personality is mirrored in the minds of the other five; and that multiple image is again multiplied in the great glass of the novel, itself a fractional image reflected from the moving pageant of sea and earth and sky that forms the exordium to each of the nine sections of the book. "Mirror on mirror mirrored is all the scene." The undertaking is prodigious, and so, I think, is the effect; but many readers have found the effort of concentration they are called upon to make beyond their powers. More than any other of her books *The Waves* deserves to be labeled "difficult."

With her next novel, *The Years* (1937), she seems to be marking time. There is almost a regression to the early technique of *The Voyage Out* and *Night and Day*. The element of plot returns; there are hints of set descriptions. Time is disrupted, but in no very original manner. We are carried from 1880 to 1891, from 1907 to 1910, and so on, but the result is a series of fragmentary impressions rather than a bold and original perception. It is only with her final (indeed posthumous) novel, *Between the Acts,* that we get a hint of the new direction along which her art is going to develop—a direction that, with its suggestion of a marriage of poetic and prose technique, picks up a note sounded in *Monday or Tuesday* and a thread left hanging in her review of *Aspects of the Novel*:

The assumption that *fiction is more intimately and humbly attached to the service of human beings than the other arts* leads to a further position which Mr. Forster's book again illustrates. It is unnecessary to dwell upon her [fiction's] aesthetic functions because they are so feeble that they can

safely be ignored. Thus, though it is impossible to imagine a book on painting in which not a word should be said about the medium in which a painter works, a wise and brilliant book, like Mr. Forster's, can be written about fiction without saying more than a sentence or two about the medium in which a novelist works. Almost nothing is said about words.

("The Art of Fiction")

THE LAW OF PROPORTIONS

I HAVE italicized a phrase in the last quotation because it serves to introduce the theme of the second part of this essay: What is the relation between fiction and the service of human beings? What is the *moral* task of the artist?

In the very rapid survey we have just made of Virginia Woolf's work there are clearly several gaps. It is hardly credible, for instance, that between 1931 (*The Waves*) and 1937 (*The Years*), or again between 1937 and 1941 (*Between the Acts*), she should have written and published nothing. In fact, these intervals in novel-writing (and there are others) were occupied in reviewing and essay-writing. Virginia Woolf's critical work, collected in the two series of *The Common Reader* (1925 and 1932) and a number of volumes published after her death, is delightful to read and adds a new dimension to our understanding of her. As a critic, she brought a spontaneous delight and a delicate humanism to the understanding of English literature; her taste was catholic, her discernment rapid and assured. Where she could praise, she did so, but not all she wrote was favorable. She disliked whatever was second-rate, middlebrow, and propagandist. She disliked the commercial novel; she disliked the political poetry of the 1930's; she had no patience with cant and pseudoscholarship. She was a highbrow.

Her occasional writing was not entirely taken up with literary criticism. Part of it was devoted to what we can only call invective. There was this side to Virginia Woolf; and indeed it is a corollary of the sensitiveness displayed in her creative work that she should be vulnerable to pity and indignation. She responded to the horrors of war in China, Spain, Abyssinia in a way we can hardly fathom. To her the remote was not tolerable because it was remote, nor the familiar acceptable by its familiarity. Hence *Three Guineas* (1938), hence *A Room of One's Own* (1929). I do not propose to discuss these books. They should, however, be read, and in reading them I recommend that the reader keep in mind two things: how Woolf died and this sentence of Schiller's, "Mit der Dummheit kampfen die Götter selbst vergebens" (With stupidity the gods themselves strive in vain).

It is to her credit as an artist that these sympathies did not blunt her perception, affect her detachment, or upset the balance of her work. They are there, but they are fully absorbed into the stuff of the novel. There are no bits and pieces left over. It is here that her writing differs so radically from that of the "left," the current of action. In speaking of Virginia Woolf's modernity, I suggested awareness of the contemporary situation and adequate expression of that awareness as essential notes; I also suggested a third essential: proportion. It is this note that we must now consider. There is a rightness of balance or perspective that enables a novelist to put first things first, to see in the turmoil of events the point of rest, the still center, that gives meaning and brings understanding. We know how poets mediate this understanding by symbol and allusion, by music and rhythm; but how is the novelist, weighed down by character and plot, to make it felt? This question links our consideration of the importance of technique and the importance of perspective.

The modern vogue of the novel stems undoubtedly from the perplexity of our time. The genre has quite lost its old tang of frivolity. For the Victorians, novels were a species of dissipation, classed with romps and visits to the zoo. Serenely conscious of the stability of their age, they devoted their reading hours to such works as William Paley's *Evidences of Christianity*, to books of travel, or to poetry. They needed no literary picture of their own time: they could see it (they thought) quite clearly for themselves. But for us the novel is a necessity, like modern hospitals or an efficient sanitation system. It performs for us, too, something of the function of a psychotherapist. We hardly feel that we exist unless we find ourselves within the covers of a book. The cinema, on a cruder plane, has the same raison d'être; and as our thoughts and feelings become cruder, other media will no doubt in time entirely replace the serious novel.

The first use of modern writing, I would suggest, is to hold a mirror up to the confusions of the age—or rather, perhaps, a number of mirrors. No single writer is equipped to deal with such chaos: "My soul, like to a ship in a black storm, / Is driven, I know not whither" (John Webster, *The White Devil*, V.vi.

248-249). On all sides the established things are cast down, on all sides a multitude of creeds call for acceptance. Incessantly, violently, we are buffeted by strange winds of doctrine. It is now, however, that the novelists come to our aid. In the camera obscura of the best writers, the raw material of life (so terrifying in its amorphous actuality) is reduced to manageable proportions. We are given a frame, a scale of reference. Certain aspects of chaos are detached and considered apart from the rest: they are thereby provided with a semblance of order. The writer need not distort, need not impose a false symmetry. The act of selection and separation is enough.

In reading the modern novel we pass from one viewpoint to another—from Lawrence to Forster, from Virginia Woolf to T. F. Powys, from Greene to William Golding—as though we walked past a series of windows. All look out upon the same turbulent scene, but each presents us, within the framework of art, with some new aspect of the whole. Lawrence stresses the physical and instinctive, Forster the civilized and the tolerant; Powys shows us the hidden horror of the village, Virginia Woolf the secret places of the heart; Greene presents the conflict of faith and passion, Golding the anatomy of strength in weakness. But through them all (if they do their job properly) there emerges, whatever their religious or political beliefs, a principle that is *the* principle of art and, in consequence, an important aid to satisfactory living: it is the rule of proportion.

The modern writer (let us say it again) is bound to deal with the events of his time. But in this very immediacy, this contemporaneity, lies a pressing danger—a danger to that rule of proportion which the good artist must observe. Approaching the raw material of his age too closely, the writer of talent rather than genius is sucked into the whirlpool and lost—lost, that is, as an artist. As a social writer, as a propagandist, he may continue richly to exist. It requires a powerful mind and an intense individuality—in short, genius—to dominate the dangerous stuff of life. Without genius the window (which I have pictured looking down on the foaming waters of the age) splinters as we press against it—and we fall headlong. The artist is submerged; the politician, the theorist, takes his place. "I am really sorry," said William Blake at the beginning of the last century, "to see my countrymen trouble themselves about politics. If they were wise, the most arbitrary Princes could not hurt them. If they are not wise, the freest government is compell'd to be a Tyranny. Princes appear to me to be fools. Houses of Commons and Houses of Lords appear to me to be fools; they seem to me to be something else beside Human Life."

"They seem to me to be something else beside Human Life"! Exact and pregnant phrase! And what would Blake say, if he were alive today, of the United Nations, of the World Court, of planning and nationalization? Precisely the same, I suspect. For these things *are* something other than human life. They are the frame, and only the frame, within which life may be lived. And, alas, they are too often the frame outside which life must be lived if it is to be *lived* at all. Yet it is with the frame that the men of talent are almost exclusively occupied. We remember H. G. Wells, who began his career with an agreeable flair for writing scientific romances and an observant eye for the oddities of lower-middle-class behavior, but who afterward, toppling into this slough of despond, set himself up as a purveyor of utopias to the world. We have the sad example of Aldous Huxley, whose genuine gifts as satirist and essayist were soon obscured under the mantle of a neo-Brahmin sage. With these, and with many more, the Moloch of abstraction has had its will. Overwhelmed, they either perish in the storm or are whirled away by it.

"In the destructive element immerse": Joseph Conrad's slogan is a true one, and essential to the writer. Yes, we must immerse, but we should not drown or dissolve. We may write about the eagles and the trumpets, about movements, about economic realities; but somewhere we must keep a place for the lovers in their trance of happiness, for the boy chasing a butterfly, for the old man asleep under the chestnut tree. We must observe the law of proportion. This is precisely what Virginia Woolf does. We feel, throughout her novels, the big abstract movements going on: the feminism of *The Years*, monarchy and the war in *Mrs. Dalloway*, the pressure of Europe's coming doom in *Between the Acts*; but these things don't submerge the delicate, exact understanding and handling of the human situation. Her people live; they are not Shavian puppets. The individual is at the center of the stage—and the subtle relations between individuals, what Mrs. Ramsay does *not* say to her husband, what a gesture conveys to Giles Oliver:

The wild child, afloat once more on the tide of the old man's benignity, looked over her coffee cup at Giles, with whom she felt in conspiracy. A thread united them—visible, invisible, like those threads, now seen, now not, that unite trembling grass blades in autumn before the sun rises. She had met him once only, at a cricket match. And then had been spun between them an early morning thread before the twigs and leaves of real friendship emerge. She looked before she drank. Looking was part of drinking. Why waste sensation, she seemed to ask, why waste a single drop that can be pressed out of this ripe, this melting, this adorable world? Then she drank. And the air round her became threaded with sensation. Bartholomew felt it; Giles felt it. Had he been a horse, the thin brown skin would have twitched, as if a fly had settled. Isabella twitched too. Jealousy, anger pierced her skin.

(*Between the Acts*)

It is in order to convey these moments of perception that writers like Proust and Virginia Woolf have forged a new technique of the novel. It is the task of the modern writer to catch these moments amid the increasing hubbub, the diminishing solitude, of modern life. Formerly it was the poets who did it. It was they who explored the secret springs of conduct, who made us see that under the flux of things the great passions still hold sway: love, friendship, hatred, along with birth and death, the rhythm of the seasons, the infinite pathos and splendor of man's destiny:

> O what if gardens where the peacock strays
> With delicate feet upon old terraces,
> Or else all Juno from an urn displays
> Before the indifferent garden deities;
> O what if levelled lawns and gravelled ways
> Where slippered Contemplation finds his ease
> And Childhood a delight for every sense,
> But take our greatness with our violence?
>
> What if the glory of escutcheoned doors,
> And buildings that a haughtier age designed,
> The pacing to and fro on polished floors
> Amid great chambers and long galleries, lined
> With famous portraits of our ancestors;
> What if those things the greatest of mankind
> Consider most to magnify, or to bless,
> But take our greatness with our bitterness?
>
> (W. B. Yeats, *Meditations in Time of Civil War*)

And this is the use of literature in all ages: to show men and women amid the splendor of their environment—and yet, in a moment of passion, of betrayal, of reality, reduced to their essential humanity, to the greatness, the violence, and the bitterness of the lonely heart. In what else is Homer or Shakespeare or Dante great, if not in this? Consider some of the famous lines that color our waking hours and our dreams. The magnificence of Dante's Brunetto Latini, who, though in hell, ran like those who contend for the prize at Verona:

> e parve di costoro
> quegli che vince e non colui che perde.

And John Webster's Duchess, with all her bright world of love shattered about her: "I am Duchess of Malfi still." And, at the supreme height, Shakespeare's Cleopatra as she presses the asp to her breast:

> Dost thou not see my baby at my breast,
> That sucks the nurse asleep?
> *(Antony and Cleopatra*, V.ii)

It is the poets and the great novelists who reduce us to our pure humanity, to the "forked radish," the "unaccommodated man"; and, stripped of the trappings of grandeur and vanity, we see ourselves again as we are: solitary, vulnerable, and transient.

How tremendously helpful this is in a world that tries to persuade us that the important things are religious beliefs, social distinctions, political adherences. Let us listen again to the voice of Blake: "They seem to me to be something else beside Human Life." On all sides, by the radio, the cinema, the daily newspaper, the television we are bludgeoned into disproportion. From a billion loudspeakers, a million silver screens, the Antichrist bellows and gesticulates. It is salutary to be set naked beneath the stars. And it is salutary to see the others, the big imposing men who seek to dominate us, sub specie aeternitatis. Do not let us be worried by them, by their loud voices, their titles, their decorations. "Things are what they are," said Bishop Samuel Butler, "and the consequences of them will be what they will be: why therefore should we wish to be deceived?"

Virginia Woolf's standpoint is, above all, this standpoint of reality. It is for this that she praises the Greeks, that she loves Plato:

> For as the argument mounts from step to step, Protagoras yielding, Socrates pushing on, what matters is not so much the end we reach as our manner of reaching it. That all can feel—the indomitable honesty, the courage, the love of truth which draw Socrates and us in his wake to the summit where, if we too may stand for a moment, it is to enjoy the greatest felicity of which we are capable.

But for her there is not one kind of truth; there are two. There is the truth of the reason and the truth of the imagination. The truth of the reason is preeminently the masculine sphere, while the truth of the imagination is the feminine. Together, these make up what she calls reality. Some individuals combine the male and the female modes of perception more impartially than others; these are the artists, the poets and painters who mediate reality to us. They show us how neither the rational nor the intuitive can get on without the other. Mrs. Ramsay and Mr. Ramsay in *To the Lighthouse* need each other. Mrs. Dalloway, in the earlier novel, because she has married a politician, a sentimentalist, is unhappy: with all his kindness, with all the amenities of her life, she is out of touch with reality. Mr. Ramsay is a philosopher: intolerant, egotistical, eccentric; yet he is a better husband than the impeccable Richard Dalloway, who is a Member of Parliament. Virginia Woolf agrees with Blake: these things are not human life. The Houses of Parliament, the Law Courts, the Mansion House; she gives us her picture of them in *Three Guineas:*

> Your world, then, the world of professional, of public life, seen from this angle undoubtedly looks queer. At first sight it is enormously impressive. Within quite a small space are crowded together St. Paul's, the Bank of England, the Mansion House, the massive if funereal battlements of the Law Courts; and on the other side, Westminster Abbey and the Houses of Parliament. There, we [women] say to ourselves, pausing, in this moment of transition on the bridge, our fathers and brothers have spent their lives. All these hundreds of years they have been mounting those steps, passing in and out of those doors, ascending those pulpits, preaching, money-making, administering justice.
>
> (ch. 1)

And she goes on to show us how absurd it all is, how unreal. Against it she sets, in *A Room of One's Own*, this picture:

> What is meant by "reality"? It would seem to be something very erratic, very undependable—now to be found in a dusty road, now in a scrap of newspaper in the street, now in a daffodil in the sun. It lights up a group in a room and stamps some casual saying. It overwhelms one walking home beneath the stars and makes the silent world more real than the world of speech—and then there it is again in an omnibus in the uproar of Piccadilly.
>
> (ch. 6)

This is, let us note, no aesthetic attitude, no cult of beauty. Reality resides in the scrap of dirty paper as much as in the sunlit daffodil. The thing seen is not important in itself, or rather it is not important what our judgment is of the thing seen. Indeed, we must see it without judgment, without choice, with silent awareness; and then we know reality. This is the message of Virginia Woolf's novels, and it is a rather important message. No one was less of a teacher than she, no one less didactic, yet what she shows us here is of great importance for living. To be taught how to see—is not that a great thing? Because if we can learn to see in this way, there comes (she says it again and again) an extraordinary happiness.

This faculty of seeing directly can exist only in the mind that is concerned for what is, not for what ought to be or will be. That is why Virginia Woolf is antireligious. Belief of any kind blinds and binds. We cannot see what is when we have theories. It does not matter whether the beliefs are religious or political. In an essay called "The Leaning Tower" (originally a paper read to the Workers' Educational Association at Brighton in May 1940, and thus one of the last things she wrote), she discusses those modern writers who seemed to inhabit the leaning tower of Marxist class-consciousness:

If you read current literary journalism you will be able to rattle off a string of names—Day Lewis, Auden, Spender, Isherwood, Louis MacNeice and so on. . . . All those writers . . . are acutely tower conscious; conscious of their middle-class birth; of their expensive educations. Then when we come to the top of the tower how strange the view looks—not altogether upside down, but slanting, sidelong. That too is characteristic of the leaning-tower writers; they do not look any class straight in the face; they look either up, or down, or sidelong. There is no class so settled that they can explore it unconsciously. That perhaps is why they create no characters. Then what do we feel next, raised in imagination on top of the tower? First discomfort; next self-pity for that discomfort; which pity soon turns to anger—to anger against the builder, against society, for making us uncomfortable. Those too seem to be tendencies of the leaning-tower writers. Discomfort; pity for themselves; anger against society. And yet—here is another tendency—how can you altogether abuse a society that is giving you, after all, a very fine view and some sort of security? You cannot abuse that society wholeheartedly while you continue to profit by that society. And so very naturally you abuse society in the person of some retired admiral or spinster or armament manufacturer; and by abusing them hope to escape whipping yourself. The bleat of the scapegoat sounds loud in their work, and the

whimper of the schoolboy crying "Please, Sir, it was the other fellow, not me."

We may regret that Virginia Woolf should devote her talents to castigating these writers of the 1930's, but we are concerned here with the implications rather than with the expediency of her remarks. Religion, political beliefs, moral codes: these things are among the blinders and binders. The writers she mentions were not, in her opinion, interested in what is, but only in their personal responses to what is: they never stood still to experience a situation, but reacted immediately with their stereotyped solutions. Thus the reality of the moment escaped them.

And in her novels it is the same. We can divide her characters, if we will, into those who are open to reality and those who are shut in—enclosed by various manias of faith, hatred, perversion, politics, morality. In the first division we have, to begin with, children. There is George in *Between the Acts*. There are Mrs. Ramsay's children in *To the Lighthouse*:

Then the door sprang open and in they came, fresh as roses, staring, wide awake, as if this coming into the dining-room after breakfast, which they did every day of their lives, was a positive event to them, and so on, with one thing after another, all day long, until she went up to say good-night to them, and found them nested in their cots like birds among cherries and raspberries, still making up stories about some little bit of rubbish—something they had heard, something they had picked up in the garden.

(I. 10)

The quality of eternal freshness, of wonder, surprise, the coming to each day as though it were the first and only day—this note of spontaneity exists in childhood, and is perceived and enjoyed by those who know. "One's children so often gave one's own perceptions a little push forward," thought Mrs. Ramsay. In *Mrs. Dalloway* too: the girl Elizabeth, dismissing the memory of the young men who are already comparing her to poplar trees and hyacinths (the personal, the sentimental, the desirous muddying the clear waters of perception), sees Wren's churches as "shapes of grey paper breasting the stream of the Strand." Jacob Flanders, in *Jacob's Room*, finds his direct vision blocked, like George's in the later novel, by the intruding adult element:

But there, on the very top, is a hollow full of water, with a sandy bottom; with a blob of jelly stuck to the side, and some mussels. A fish darts across. The fringe of yellow-brown seaweed flutters, and out pushes an opal-shelled crab. . . . Jacob was about to jump, holding his bucket in front of him, when he saw, stretched entirely rigid, side by side, their faces very red, an enormous man and woman.

(ch. 1)

And in *The Years* the pervert under the streetlamp wrecks little Rose Pargiter's fantasy.

But not all adults are closed to vision. There are the artists—the poets and painters who really have kept the innocent eye of childhood. These see reality whole from the beginning and express it in its untarnished brightness. Then there are the young men and women who are not artists but, because they are free from prejudice and interested in things as they are, succeed in battling their way toward reality. We have a whole gallery of these sympathetic figures—Jacob Flanders in *Jacob's Room*, Katherine Hilbery in *Night and Day*, Bernard in *The Waves*, and many others. All of them are steeped in the light of Cambridge, the good life that is devotion to truth and unremitting opposition to falsehood and cant, the life of scholarship and beauty. But that light in itself is not enough. It has to be surpassed. Behind truth there is reality; behind the constructs of the mind there lies the realm of pure being itself. It does not do to stay at Cambridge. "Is there not too much brick and mortar for a May night?" thinks Jacob, looking round him at the Great Court of Trinity.

In several of her novels Virginia Woolf gives us the portraits of people who have, in one way or another, "stayed at Cambridge": Ridley Ambrose and William Pepper in *The Voyage Out*, Mr. Ramsay and Charles Tansley in *To the Lighthouse*. And admirable people they are, superior, far superior, to the successful administrators, the Richard Dalloways and Colonel Pargiters, who direct the affairs of the great world from a blank center while the joy of living crumbles away from their wives' hearts little by little in attic rooms. But the "stayers" have become arrested at some point in their development. They have found truth, they are devoted to truth, but they have not pushed on to reality. They are stranded in the realm of the concept.

It is here that the third great class of the elect has its job to do. This is the class of women. The statement, thus flatly made, seems crass and stupid enough. Virginia Woolf is far from seeking to canonize her sex as a whole. What she does imply, throughout the course of her writing, is that the feminine personality is closer to earth, to the simplicity of things, to objects as objects and not as counters to be talked about; and by virtue of this concreteness women manage to achieve an adequacy of response to what is beyond the concrete. The woman's job, mainly, if she is not herself an artist of one sort or another, is to free the male intellect from its conceptual chains, to enrich and fertilize it.

Virginia Woolf has been called a feminist; and of course she was, in several of her writings, especially *A Room of One's Own* and *Three Guineas*. But more truly we might call her an androgynist: she puts the emphasis every time on what a man and a woman have to give to each other, on the mystery of completion, and not on the assertion of separate superiorities. If there is in woman a superiority, it is because *she* is the one to take the first step toward understanding, out of a compassion that is almost the Buddhist karma; more discerning than the male, she lays her light, healing touch on the source of conflict, the knot of refusal-to-be-what-one-is, and it loosens. The theme of Virginia Woolf's novels is often precisely this: the patient effort of the woman toward the reintegration of the man. His resistance is not always overcome. To show things thus would be to falsify; life, in fact, offers few happy endings.

We do not, then, find her placing the emphasis, in the man-woman relationship, on the sexual element; and in this respect she flows against the main current of modern writing. Just as she avoids the portrayal of violent action, so too she largely omits the passional. I don't think she could have given it to us successfully, but in any case it would not have fitted into the world where she is at home as an artist. For this is the world of *freedom*. Passion stultifies, distorts, and corrupts. The people she shows us as married, or thinking of marriage, all envisage the problem in terms of freedom. They are more than ordinarily intelligent persons. They enjoy a vigorous intellectual life of their own, and they want to preserve it inviolate. They don't appear to have very strong physical desires, but they are emotional. They have a lot of affection to give and to receive. They are fascinated and at the same time repelled by the idea of sharing. They see quite clearly the faults of those they love, but love deeply just the same. A movement of uncertainty, of discovery and relief, runs through the novels as a kind of inner action to make up for the lack of external events.

Virginia Woolf's work presents itself, then, as a study of the inner life of individuals as they exist, first of all, in solitude, and then in society; and as a counterpointing of these aspects. Solitude is a constant theme, the native air breathed by her characters when they are most themselves. In *A Room of One's Own* she records the importance of seeing "human beings not always in their relation to each other but in relation to reality; and the sky too, and the trees or whatever it may be in themselves." This is solitude. And since even solitude must have a locus, since one can't be alone without finding somewhere to be alone, her heroes and heroines enjoy their solitariness, as we should expect, among what William Wordsworth called the beautiful and permanent forms of nature. For the point of natural objects is their aloneness. Rocks, plants, rivers have achieved the secret of forming a society without impinging upon one another's privacy.

Virginia Woolf returns again and again to the proud aloofness of natural things. She pictures the tree standing alone in the field through the long summer nights. She sees, in *Orlando*, "those hyacinths—free from taint, dependence, soilure of humanity or care for one's kind." Yet though aloof, they are not inimical to the man or woman who approaches them without arrogance or prejudice. "Hills and trees accept one; human beings reject one," a character in *The Years* muses.

For a novelist, this taste for solitude plainly presents something of a problem. To be effective within the framework of a story, human beings must care for something more than hyacinths and hills: they must care for each other. How does Virginia Woolf solve this problem? In *Three Guineas* she writes: "Inevitably we ask ourselves, is there not something in the conglomeration of people into societies that releases what is most selfish and violent, least rational and humane in the individuals themselves?" These words were written under the (to her) almost unbearable horror of the Spanish Civil War and the growing shadow of Fascism. They represent a real attitude of hers, but not a final or complete one. They do suggest (what cannot be denied) that her scope is limited, that there are aspects of human life she will not touch and situations from which she shrinks back. Her world is a small one, a world of intellectuals and sensitive individuals, of artists and scholars. But it is what she does with that limited world that is important. Can she expand it to contain the great paradoxes of life: love and hate, solitude and society, and the freedom that springs from loving bondage?

And here, I think, she does succeed. By reducing the commitments of her characters to the simplest components—none of Arnold Bennett's bustle or Lawrence's complications for her—she shows us the pattern of lives that, even while harmonizing, preserve their individual melodies. A solitude is kept in the midst of society, sometimes by a deliberate act of withdrawal. Virginia Woolf's view is not far removed from the Blakean doctrine of salvation through art or the Taoist technique of *wei wu wei*. "If one wishes to better the world one must, paradoxically enough, withdraw and spend more and more time fashioning one's sentences to perfection in solitude." These words from the second *Common Reader* refer specifically to the writer, but they apply to every walk of life. Thus Mrs. Ramsay, in *To the Lighthouse*, finds her arduous duties as wife and mother and hostess bearable only if she can, from time to time, sink down to be "a wedge of darkness." "The supreme difficulty of being oneself," as Virginia Woolf calls it elsewhere, becomes insuperable if the world is too much with us. The subtler art of preserving solitude is not by withdrawal, but by fusion. And this, for Virginia Woolf, is the meaning of love. Human beings need one another—not for consolation, for protection, to form a closed circle—but for the joy of sharing. The moment of perception is heightened if it can be held in common:

Some spray in a hedge, or a sunset over a flat winter field, or again the way some old woman sits, arms akimbo, in an omnibus with a basket—these we point at for the other to look at. It is so vast an alleviation to be able to point for another to look at. And then not to talk.

But alas, with how few companions can such detached sharing, such shared detachment, be achieved.

There is always the question of whether it can be achieved at all. And that is why so many of her novels ponder the theme of compatibility or incompatibility. Can one really live with other people, and still be oneself, free to live, free to develop? The question haunts Mrs. Dalloway and Mrs. Ramsay; Katherine Hilbery and Jacob Flanders; Bernard in *The Waves* and Sara in *The Years*. The answer is given in terms of courage and common sense. What has been achieved can be achieved. The problem, we note, is radically a woman's problem. It would hardly occur to a man, unless he possessed a large measure of feminine sensibility. And it implies, radically, that absence of passion which we have already noticed in Virginia Woolf's work. We are here in a very cool, still, twilight region. (Many of her most effective scenes take place at evening.) The air of detachment, of aloneness, takes on an aspect of poignancy in her more elderly characters. I am thinking particularly of Mrs. Dalloway and Mrs. Ramsay. In the case of Mrs. Dalloway the poignancy is stressed: the note of regret, of nostalgia for opportunities that are past, the something lost that time in its swift course will not bring back again. Clarissa Dalloway, indeed, has missed her moment, has made the wrong choice in life's intelligence test, has opted for the successful Richard and not for the scapegrace Peter. But even with Mrs. Ramsay, who has achieved so much, whose life is so rich, there is the note of almost unbearable nostalgia—for what?

For what? That is the question. What is missing from Virginia Woolf's picture? For this note of melancholy tells us that something is missing; it is not a healthy sign. The greatest literature is not sad, though it may be tragic. Behind the brilliant, sensitive world she gives us there is an emptiness. And of course we know at once, in part, why this should be. The sensitivity entails the emptiness. Living in the world between two wars and in the world of war itself, she was unremittingly conscious of the fragility of the civilization that is Western Europe, of the transience of the values that her books so shiningly illustrate. But there is more than this. The lack is not only in her world: it is in herself. It is the lack of what we can only call faith; not the faith that is based on submission to authority or on wishful thinking—she could never have known that—but faith in the reality of her own intuitions, the faith that is really knowledge in its purest form, for there is nothing more certain or immediate to us than our own "feel" of reality. This contact she had, intermittently; the mystic (a word she disliked and for which I would prefer to substitute *poetic*) was strong in her. A dozen passages could be culled from her writing that would worthily stand by the side of Lao Tze's sayings or the gnomic aphorisms of Blake. But her upbringing was against her. Childhood years in an agnostic household, the company of intellectuals as an adult, had not taken the fine point off her spiritual perceptions, but they had effectively blocked the way to a synthesis.

But if the sadness is felt, it is, like the indignation and the pity, absorbed into the stuff of the novels; and the movement inward continues even if it is to a center of which Woolf could not say assuredly, "It is

there." The great artist—and she was a great artist—is used for purposes she may ignore or deny. No one can come away from a reading of these novels without feeling that his experience has been enriched, that he has been taught to see more clearly. There is sensationalism in her novels, the sensationalism of the painter entranced with color and form, of the poet drunk with scents and tastes; but she rises above or rather through sensation to a higher understanding. She is no Walter Pater. Her delight in the moment, the vivid crystal of the here and now, is always escaping into meaning. Just as often, distrustful of metaphysics, she hauls it back. The reality is always more than the sensation, but only in the sensation can reality be known. The ripple of the wave conceals beneath it the world of waters where swim strange, unthinkable shapes of fish and plant. And—if I may stretch my sea metaphor a little further—in the sensationalism of Virginia Woolf there is something one might call "salt," a tincture lacking in Pater and his like. The aesthetes cultivated sensation; she accepts it. The faint smell of decay is absent. They distrusted the intellect; she worships it—in its own place. They withdrew to the ivory tower; she writes *Three Guineas*, preaches feminism. Salt—the tincture of humor, responsibility, reverence for qualities not her own—keeps her writing sweet. Though her world is a limited one, vast perspectives are thrown open. And how wise she was to limit her scope to those intimate relationships that she knew so well.

It is because of this self-limitation, itself stemming from a shrewd assessment of her own resources, that her position in English fiction is, it seems to me, assured. She did supremely well what no one else has attempted to do. She mapped the world of the mind—especially the feminine mind—under certain precise conditions of character and environment. Her work forms a unity, the unity of great poems like T. S. Eliot's *The Waste Land* and *Four Quartets*. Within it we revolve, with Sir Thomas Browne alone in his study, the globe of ourselves:

I could never content my contemplation with those general pieces of wonder, the Flux and Reflux of the Sea, the increase of *Nile*, the conversion of the Needle to the North; and have studied to match and parallel those in the more obvious and neglected pieces of Nature, which without further trouble I can do in the Cosmography of my self; we carry with us the wonders we seek without us: There is all *Africa* and her prodigies in us; we are that bold and adventurous piece of nature, which he that studies wisely learns in a *compendium* what others labour at in a divided piece and endless volume.

(Religio Medici, pt. I, sec. 15)

Virginia Woolf's sphere is neither so bold nor so adventurous, perhaps; but it has its own unity. There, at the mouth of a river in South America, is the little town of Santa Marina. The climate is tropical, but the society might be that of the Cambridge of *Jacob's Room*. A flick of the hand sends the globe spinning to discover a large ramshackle house in the Hebrides—sea, mountains, barren shore are clearly visible, but as we eavesdrop on Charles Tansley and Mr. Bankes in *To the Lighthouse*, we fancy ourselves back again with Katherine Hilbery in Cheyne Walk, in *Night and Day*. It is good conversation: there is no room for stupidity or violence. The women are wise, witty, maternal; the men, whether old or young, wear rather shabby flannels and tweeds and stump up and down the terrace declaiming Tennyson, debating the nature of things. On the outskirts, it is true, certain sinister figures hover: clergymen, "irrelevant forked stakes in the flow and majesty of the summer silent world"; power-lovers and soul-destroyers, the Sir William Bradshawes and the Colonel Pargiters, the Miss Kilmans and the Minnie Marshes.

And beyond these figures of darkness there is the circumambient darkness itself, always felt, always pressing in upon the sphere and threatening to destroy it. There is the darkness deep in the nature of things, the tragedy and waste when Rachel Vinrace dies, her promise unfulfilled (death comes as the end); or when Sally Pargiter is dropped as a baby (death comes as the beginning). These are acts of God. But there are also the acts of men: the clang of war echoes through the early novels, the darkening horror of Fascism dominates the later ones. The colored and fragrant sphere vibrates in the chaos. There it hangs, fragile and iridescent. We tremble for its permanence. But there is no need to fear: this bubble is endowed with a surprising toughness. It will stand wind and weather; it will outlive the eagles and the trumpets. And, watching it, we may find that it focuses, within its little round, essences of human thought and action that escape the net of the blueprint and the interim report. The movement streams inward, toward the still center. But there is a plane of understanding on which the inward is also the outward, and the particular the most valid

representation of the universal. Virginia Woolf's world will survive as the crystal survives under the crushing rock masses. The juggernaut that destroyed its creator has no power over this globe of hers and its inhabitants:

> Forms more real than living man,
> Nurslings of immortality.

ACHIEVEMENT AND INFLUENCE

Since World War II many changes have come over the literary scene. We have seen the rise of the "angry young men" in Britain, of the beatniks in the United States, of the *chosistes* in France, to name only the most prominent among the "new bearings." The "novel of violence" has won hands down over the "be still and know" tradition. Virginia Woolf has had no successor. That fact in itself does not constitute an indictment; there are some writers so great (the greatest, indeed, need not be named) that there is no room in their circle for others. Jonathan Swift was an isolated phenomenon; Sterne had to wait two hundred years for his influence to be felt, and its possibilities are still unexhausted. We are just beginning to wake up to Blake. Byron is due for reassessment.

It must be admitted that Virginia Woolf's stock fell in the postwar years. Simultaneous revolutions may clash, as the Renaissance did with the Reformation, to produce the oddest results in the work of Edmund Spenser or Milton. Virginia Woolf was committed enough, as *Three Guineas* and *A Room of One's Own* show, but her true current, as we have seen, was interior, toward the still center. World War II, with its aftermath, deflected this current and the interest in subtleties of technique that went with it. We have seen its reemergence, perhaps, in a new and fascinating guise, in the interest in Zen. The technical revolution represented so brilliantly by Virginia Woolf has been short-circuited by insistent political and "existential" pressures: angry young men and beatniks write in a strangely outmoded idiom. The voice is Jacob's voice.

This is not to say that Virginia Woolf has been without influence. But her infiltration is pervasive, subtle, and unacknowledged. We can see it most clearly in Alain Robbe-Grillet and his school. Her intelligence was always more French than English in its lucidity, its poise, its irony. And just as we gave John Locke to France and got him back again via Jean-Jacques Rousseau and the *encyclopédistes*, so Virginia Woolf is returning to us quite quietly by way of the *chosistes*. Their admirable insistence on the thing seen, on the object *there* in space uncontaminated by impertinent comment, has long been anticipated in a score of passages in her novels, some of which are quoted in preceding pages, and most clearly, perhaps, in the short story "Solid Objects":

The only thing that moved upon the vast semicircle of the beach was one small black spot. As it came nearer to the ribs and spine of the stranded pilchard boat, it became apparent from a certain tenuity in its blackness that this spot possesssed four legs; and moment by moment it became more unmistakable that it was composed of the persons of two young men. Even thus in outline against the sand there was an unmistakable vitality in them; an indescribable vigour in the approach and withdrawal of the bodies, slight though it was, which proclaimed some violent argument issuing from the tiny mouths of the little round heads. This was corroborated on closer view by the repeated lunging of a walking-stick on the right-hand side. "You meant to tell me . . . You actually believe . . ." thus the walking-stick on the right-hand side next the waves seemed to be asserting as it cut long straight stripes upon the sand.

This is the opening paragraph of a story in which the obsession of an adult mind with solid objects is as convincingly shown as that "inner darkness" of a child's mind which "became a hall, leaf smelling, earth smelling, of yellow light" in the first passage quoted in the present essay.

To go a little further afield: to Patrick White, the Australian novelist who seems to me by far the greatest talent to arise since the death of Virginia Woolf. *Voss* (1957) opens with a domestic interior that brings *Night and Day* directly to mind; there is no imitation, the settings are quite different; as far apart indeed as Cheyne Walk and Sydney, New South Wales, but the accents chime, the technique whereby place becomes an interpreter of grace (or its opposite); and might not this be an aside on Katherine Hilbery?

Already as a little girl she had been softly sceptical, perhaps out of boredom; she was suffocated by the fuzz of faith. She did believe, however, most palpably, in wood, with the reflections in it, and in clear daylight, and in water. She would work fanatically at some mathematical problem, even now, just for the excitement of it, to solve and know. She had read a great deal out of such books as had come her way in that remote colony, until her mind seemed to be complete.

The self-existent life of buildings—particularly of houses—that bulks so large in Woolf, and their reactions to intruding human presences, also crystallizes out:

Not even the presence of the shabby stranger, with his noticeable cheekbones and over-large finger-joints, could destroy the impression of tranquillity, though of course, the young woman realised, it is always like this in houses on Sunday mornings while others are at church. It is therefore but a transitory comfort. Voices, if only in whispers, must break in. Already she herself was threatening to disintegrate into the voices of the past.

And here, finally, is the return to the assurance of the life of things, with a last twist in the paragraph that brings us back to the most characteristic of Virginia Woolf's novels, *The Voyage Out* and *To the Lighthouse*:

All this time Voss was standing his ground. He was, indeed, swaying a little, but the frayed ends of his trouser legs were momentarily lost in the carpet. How much less destructive of the personality are thirst, fever, physical exhaustion, he thought, much less than people. He remembered how, in a mountain gorge, a sandstone boulder had crashed aiming at him, grazing his hand, then bounding away, to the mutilation of trees and death of a young wallaby. Deadly rocks through some perversity inspired him with fresh life. He went on with the breath of life in his lungs. But words, even of benevolence and patronage, even when they fell wide, would leave him half dead.

We may summarize with a new note: on the possibility of a fusion of excellences between the novel of reflection and the novel of action, of the feminine fertilized by the masculine, of a new Conrad arising on a new continent, "nurslings of immortality" made flesh and bone in a new, all-inclusive vision. The ironic yet compassionate expression of the features that animates Virginia Woolf's portrait remains for me, at any rate, "the marble index" of a kind of greatness which, as Nicholas Ferrar remarked of the synthesis he established three centuries ago at Little Gidding, "might prove a pattern in an age that needs patterns."

THE UNCOMMON READER

SET side by side with the novels, Virginia Woolf's literary criticism must always be seen as marginal—an appendix, but one of astonishing resilience and strength, firmly rooted in her personal life, and casting no little light upon her aims and achievements as a novelist. She began her writing career with reviewing, contributing hasty appraisals of third- and fourth-rate books to the *Guardian*, a London weekly newspaper that aimed at readers among the clergy. From this she graduated to the *Times Literary Supplement*, John Middleton Murry's *Athenaeum*, Desmond MacCarthy's *New Statesman*, and even so mundane a periodical as *Vogue*. Most of the *Common Reader* essays took their first flight in these reviews. This was hack work—it brought in the bread and butter, paid for a WC to replace the outdoor privy at Monk's House, bought a second-hand car.

Virginia Woolf went on reviewing books for most of her life. When she achieved fame as a novelist she was free to pick and choose, and refused to write about books that didn't interest her. It was not all grind. Reviewing afforded a measure of relief from the tensions, the "screw," as she called it, of her creative work—the often agonizing intellectual and emotional complexities of *Mrs. Dalloway* or *The Waves*. Then back again she would spin from the "carpentry" of her critical essays with fresh vigor to the anguish, the color, and the flow of her novels. "What a fling I shall have into fiction and freedom when this [the second *Common Reader*] is off!" she writes in her diary on 8 July 1932. But—"at once, an American comes to ask me to consider writing articles for some huge figure."

These are dilemmas that face many artists. Virginia Woolf herself drew a firm line between criticism and reviewing: "Reviews seem to me more and more frivolous. Criticism on the other hand absorbs me more and more," she notes on 18 February 1922. In a letter to Madge Vaughan of December 1904, at the very outset of her career, she admits the tendency of reviewing to corrupt and to stifle: "My real delight in reviewing is to say nasty things; and hitherto I have had to [be] respectful." As late as 31 January 1920, when she had made her mark with *The Voyage Out* and *Night and Day*, she writes in her diary: ". . . I am equally able to write for [J. C.] Squire, Murry or Desmond MacCarthy—a proof of catholicity or immorality, according to your taste."

Friendly voices warned her of the threat to her integrity. And she came to be annoyed by editorial restraints. As early as December 1905 she had complained in a letter to Violet Dickinson that Dame Edith Lyttleton, who ran the Women's Supplement of the *Guardian*, "sticks her broad thumb into the middle of my delicate sentences and improves the moral tone." Bruce Richmond, editor of the *Times Literary Supplement*, coerced her into substituting "obscene" for "lewd" in a review of Henry James's ghost stories. Finally putting her foot down, she declares in September 1920: "I've taken the plunge of refusing my books from the Times, and dictated conditions for the future." She would now review the occasional volume, but only if she thought it worth reviewing; she would write the occasional essay, but only on subjects that interested her.

And what subjects did interest her? She was a catholic critic in the sense that she enjoyed all manner of books and wrote about them with enthusiasm and understanding. Her letters and diaries are full of the sheer delight of reading. After the stress of society, after the exertions of travel, after the clashes of personal relationships, back she slid into the healing world of books, some read for the first time, some for the fifty-first—like a sea creature returning to its element. There she too, like Blake "a mental prince," moved among her peers, and among those who were so devastatingly more than her peers that she was abashed in their presence. "[T]he power to make images . . . ," she notes in her 31 July 1926 diary: "Shakespeare must have had this to an extent which makes my normal state the state of a person blind, deaf, dumb, stone-stockish and fish-blooded. And I have it compared with poor Mrs. Bartholomew [her cook] almost to the extent that she has it compared with me."

Together with her many arrogances Virginia Woolf had her humilities too. Her awe in the presence of Shakespeare comes out most clearly—and to my mind most touchingly—in a diary entry of 9 May 1934 following a visit to Stratford:

I cannot without more labour than my roadrunning mind can compass describe the queer impression of sunny impersonality. Yes, everything seemed to say, this was Shakespeare's, here he sat and walked; but you wont find me not exactly in the flesh. He is serenely absent-present; both at once; radiating round one; yes; in the flowers, in the old hall, in the garden; but never to be pinned down. And we went to the Church, and there was the florid foolish bust, but what I had not reckoned for was the worn simple slab, turned the wrong way, Kind Friend for Jesus' sake forbear—again he seemed to be all air and sun smiling serenely; and yet down there one foot from me lay the little bones that had spread over the world this vast illumination. Yes, and then we walked round the church, and all is simple and a little worn; the river slipping past the stone wall, with a red breadth in it from some flowering tree, and the edge of the turf unspoilt, soft and green and muddy, and two casual nonchalant swans. The church and the school and the house are all roomy spacious places, resonant, sunny today, and in and out [*illegible*]—yes, an impressive place; still living, and then the little bones lying there, which have created: to think of writing The Tempest looking out on that garden; what a rage and storm of thought to have come over my mind.

"[W]hat a rage and storm of thought." From her own dementia, less controlled than Shakespeare's though infinitely less intense, she grasps for this moment at any rate the terror of creating the *Tempest, Lear*, and *Hamlet*. But even more instructive for us as students of Virginia Woolf is the marvelous phrase "one foot from me lay the little bones that had spread over the world this vast illumination." For in this phrase we find the essence of her critical method. First "the little bones": her concern for the immediate, the concrete, the perishable individual; here Shakespeare, elsewhere in her writing the Brontë sisters, Jane Austen, Sir Walter Scott, Daniel Defoe. She makes us aware of many things: of mortality, of "mighty poets in their misery dead," of the incommensurability of the work and its author; of the eternity of the work, of its resonance *in saecula saeculorum*, into the ages of ages, when everything else that remains of an era has vanished. At this point we can say, "She has understood." And if she is big enough to understand Shakespeare, then we shall follow her with confidence in what she has to say about Spenser, Thomas Hardy, Feodor Dostoyevsky.

For writers as diverse as these occupy the pages of the two *Common Reader* volumes and the selections of her critical work published after her death. I have just called her a catholic critic, and so she is in the "categorical" range of her interests. She hops from the Middle Ages to her own time and takes in poets, novelists, and biographers. Writing as a reviewer forced this diversity upon her, but I think a taste for it was part of her equipment. It was part of that concept of freedom for which the Bloomsbury group (which we shall look at) stood. But her freedom had serious limitations, as had the group's. It couldn't

take in writers like Rudyard Kipling, the greatest short-story writer of his time (though Forster, on the fringe of the group, admired him). It couldn't take in genuine religious experience such as T. S. Eliot's, George Herbert's, and Hopkins'. It couldn't take in Lawrence and Joyce, advocates of "normal" sex; and there was little it had to say in favor of the younger demagogues, Stephen Spender, W. H. Auden, and Louis MacNeice.

This critical blindspot operates most unfortunately in the religious field. Oddly enough she can stomach Dante—her diary shows her returning to him again and again for sustenance—but she veers away from George Herbert, Sir Thomas Browne, and the devotional element in John Donne. Here she is firmly Leslie Stephen's daughter. She does not go as far as he does in speaking, grotesquely, of Herbert "skulking behind the Prayer Book"; she feels Herbert's charm and authenticity and regrets she cannot respond to it. She loves the baroque intricacies of Browne's prose, but his piety stumps her. Donne as lover, Renaissance man of all seasons, searcher of human motivations fascinates her, but his activities as dean of St. Paul's, master preacher of his age, God-intoxicated-man leave her cold. This lacuna is a major flaw in her critical equipment.

But what is of supreme interest in the letters and diaries, and in the collection of autobiographical fragments published after her death with the title *Moments of Being* (1978), is the light they throw on her aims as a writer, on the technical problems she came up against in the practice of her art and the strategies she devised to overcome them. "Suppose one thing should open out of another . . . doesn't that give the looseness and lightness I want: doesn't that get closer and yet keep form and speed, and enclose everything, everything?" she writes on 26 January 1920. But, "my doubt is how far it will [include] enclose the human heart." Her doubt and perhaps our doubt. With all the brilliant achievement of the novels, is there not something missing that engages us in Sterne, Fielding, Trollope, Hardy? Has anyone ever loved one of Virginia Woolf's characters? Where is her parallel to Uncle Toby, Mr. Harding, Tess, or Squire Western? Our demand may be, and very probably is, illegitimate. Virginia Woolf was not writing that kind of novel. And yet—the little doubt creeps in.

I have been distracted from the consideration of technique to an aside on emotional values, but with Virginia Woolf, can we draw a line between the two?

Her monologue continues: "My doubt is how far it will enclose the human heart—Am I sufficiently mistress of my dialogue to net it there?" We see how she relates heart to dialogue, emotion to technique. Of course there are other ways: plot, characterization, comment. She will have none of them. This limits her, but also it gives her an immense concentration.

The diaries open up further possibilities. What *shape* is the novel to take? There must be form without formality, freedom that escapes license. "The art must be respected. . . . At the same time the irregular fire must be there," she writes on 18 November 1924. The irregular fire burns up the excrescences: one is left with something like the glowing skeleton of a Victorian house in the blitz.

Constantly pondering form, she thinks also of texture. An early diary entry gives us a glimpse of a discussion on art with Clive Bell and Roger Fry: "Roger asked me if I founded my writing upon texture or upon structure; I connected structure with plot, and therefore said 'texture.' Then we discussed the meaning of structure and texture in painting and in writing" (22 November 1917). The painting side and the writing side of Bloomsbury cross-pollinate; when Virginia Woolf thinks of completing a friend's novel for her, she thinks in pictorial terms: "My brain at once spins to clothe her story for her,—how happiness is to be represented by a green here; a yellow there and so on" (14 January 1920).

"WHO'S AFRAID OF VIRGINIA WOOLF?"

QUITE a lot of people *were*, to judge from the evidence of the diaries and letters and of a wide range of contemporary comment. We have already noted her confession that as a reviewer she delights in saying nasty things about writers mainly unknown to her; now, in the mass of autobiography that has poured from the presses since her death, we see her talent for satire exercised upon her closest friends and acquaintances. This is a Virginia Woolf we should hardly guess at from a reading of the novels and critical essays.

Once again she admits her guilt. "I am alarmed by my own cruelty with my friends," she writes in her diary on 28 March 1929. The cruelty surfaces in the extraordinarily vivid portraits that the diaries and letters give us of the members of that elusive and notorious entity the Bloomsbury group. We may find both instruction and amusement in following what she herself has to say in the letters and diaries about the group's fluctuating fortunes.

The Bloomsbury group, or just "Bloomsbury," was in short the inner circle of friends, relatives, and fellow workers in the arts who gathered around Virginia and Leonard Woolf at Hogarth House, Richmond, where the famous Hogarth Press was established. The genesis of the group was actually much anterior to this period in the Woolfs' careers—may indeed be traced back to the Cambridge Apostles (a prestigious debating society); and the name of course became current only after the Woolfs had moved in 1924 from Richmond to 52 Tavistock Square in the Bloomsbury section of London, close to her sister, Vanessa, and Clive Bell, Vanessa's husband. The nucleus was familial: Virginia and Leonard, Clive and Vanessa and Vanessa's lover, Duncan Grant. Around this nucleus revolved the writers Lytton Strachey and Edward Morgan Forster, the painter and art critic Roger Fry, the economist and Cambridge don John Maynard Keynes. Vanessa, Clive Bell, and Duncan Grant were themselves avant-garde painters and decorators. On the fringe of the group hovered the portentous figure of Thomas Stearns Eliot—portentous but by that very token slightly ridiculous to the ironic Virginia, with his Americanisms, his Anglo-Catholicism, his pedantry—an intimate friend of the Woolfs but decidedly not a habitué of the group.

Bloomsbury was atheistic, cosmopolitan, sexually deviant. This combination aroused a good deal of opposition among the upholders of the status quo; perhaps even more was provoked by the group's exclusiveness and its ascetic ideals of intellectual and artistic integrity. "Lax in morals, priggish in taste" is not a good formula for winning friends. Almost the first reference to Bloomsbury in the diaries is to this intellectual snobbism—as it appeared to the non-elect: "Barbara . . . seems to be ashamed of the unintellectuality of Nick. She wont take him to see her Bloomsbury friends. Bloomsbury, I think, will have one more corpse to its credit; for poor B.'s attainments aren't such as to give her a very secure footing there" (January 1918). Complacent, mildly sadistic. In a conversation with Clive Bell noted in the entry of 14 January 1918, Virginia Woolf discusses "the hypnotism exerted by Bloomsbury over the younger generation": already the group is felt to be a force for good or evil. "In fact the dominion that

'Bloomsbury' exercises over the sane and the insane alike seems to be sufficient to turn the brains of the most robust." Strong words: perhaps not to be taken too seriously.

Virginia has "an amusing talk" with Lytton Strachey on 8 September 1920: "How far has our set justified its promise? Lytton maintains that in ourselves we are as remarkable as the [Samuel] Johnson set, though our works may perish—still we're still at the beginning of our works." Complacency modulating into arrogance. Johnson, Boswell, Garrick, Gibbon, Burke, Reynolds, Goldsmith —can one really dare to compare? But it is interesting evidence that the "Bloomsberries" already saw themselves as a *cenacle*. And "H[arcourt] Brace's catalogue talking of us all by name as the most brilliant group in Gordon Square!" (7 November 1922).

Many detested Bloomsbury. In the eyes of Hubert Henderson, editor of the *Nation and Athenaeum,* the group was a "pest"; Rupert Brooke thought it "corrupt"; Wyndham Lewis lampooned it ferociously in *The Apes of God* (1930). On 13 December 1924, Virginia Woolf records, Edward Sackville-West implored his cousin Vita "to resist the contamination of Bloomsbury, personified in the serpent destroyer, VW." She didn't, and the outcome was *Orlando*. Virginia's affair with Vita and her flirtation with Clive Bell are clear examples of that "ethical code" which "allows poaching" in the preserves of love and friendship (12 March 1922) and gave rise to cries of corruption and contamination. Even Forster, usually counted a member of the group, expresses some dismay: "I don't think these people are little," he confided to his diary, "but they belittle all who come into their power."

Bloomsbury, an early version of the permissive society, was never more permissive than in its penchant for indecency and scatology in the spoken and written word. The indecencies of Virginia Woolf's letters are more sporadic, but they could hardly be nastier. Most of the smut comes in letters to her sister, Vanessa, and one suspects that Virginia Woolf may be keeping her end up, as it were, in the running contest of "I am more liberated than you!" that went on between them.

The diaries are more free than the letters from these blemishes. (I call them blemishes because indecency is tolerable only when it is witty, as in Restoration drama, or contributes an essential part to a larger whole, as in *Ulysses*. Writing about indecency in the first *Common Reader*, Virginia Woolf herself makes a distinction between "the little clod of mud which sticks to the crocus of necessity, and that which is plastered to it out of bravado.") In the diaries she is not called upon to impress or shock; she can simply be herself and develop her own line of thought. The diaries are a gymnasium, a laboratory, a workshop. A gymnasium: Virginia Woolf herself thinks of the diary entries as muscle-flexing in readiness for the novels—practice in form, style, character, atmosphere. They affect the literary essays too: compare, for instance, "On Not Knowing Greek" (in the first *Common Reader*) and the diary entry of 19 August 1918. A laboratory, or, if you like, an analyst's consulting room—where Virginia Woolf herself is both doctor and patient. A workshop: perfecting the diary itself, for she refers to it as "this book," a work of art existing in its own right, to be brought to some sort of perfection. It is a masterpiece, as Quentin Bell rightly claims in the introduction to his biography of Virginia Woolf, and not inferior to *The Waves* or *To the Lighthouse*—though quite different from these: more free, more relaxed, less anguished in the making. Turning to her diary she has no reviewers to fear when the year's stint is done, nor even the dubious approval of her friends to contend with.

The letters and diaries are remarkable for their brilliant gallery of portraits of celebrities and noncelebrities. Many of these, as I have already emphasized, are painted with malice, but by no means all. She can be deeply respectful, even reverential, as in her account of a visit to Hardy at Max Gate on 25 July 1926; she can appreciate the greatness of Eliot while laughing at his mannerisms and remaining puzzled by his piety. Her accounts fascinate by the new light they throw on these great men and by the record of conversations with them on all manner of subjects. We overhear their talk on religion, politics, philosophy, art, and literature.

It is easy to see how some of the published essays in the *Common Reader* and elsewhere grew out of these meetings of minds. And this is another field in which the diaries help us to understand the novelist and the critic. They show conclusively that the "devices" of *Mrs. Dalloway* and the *Common Reader*—Virginia Woolf's use of aspects of the natural world to interweave with and enrich human happenings, her personal commitment to the author she is dealing with and his or her world—are in no sense contrived; they are quite simply the way her sensibility works. Of course in her published work she is more deliberate than she is in her diary entries, but the spontaneity is still there.

Brilliant glimpses of human character and natural phenomena vie for preeminence in her pages. "Human beings have figured less" in her 1919 diary, she notes rather guiltily at the start of the new year, "than the red berries, the suns and the moons risings" (7 January 1920). Is this true, perhaps, of her novels too? One of her discoveries in technique, in "texture," is expressed as a theory of "strata" (1 November 1934): the interweaving of the inner and the outer, the human and the nonhuman worlds, the life of the mind and the life of the senses. Virginia Woolf uses this sort of counterpoint supremely well. But, we may ask, is the stratum of suns and moons and berries and rivers and seas somewhat predominant over the stratum of Eleanor Pargiter and Kitty Malone, of Mr. and Mrs. Ramsay even? This first pair of characters is from *The Years,* where she tries to exploit her technique rather too systematically; the second is from *To the Lighthouse,* where the central section, "Time Passes," isolates the stratum of things-without-man and is considered by some to be her finest achievement.

Yet having said that, it is only fair to add that my observation applies much more to the novels than to the letters and diaries, which is rather odd: one might expect Virginia Woolf's delight in the natural scene to push the human element into the background more decisively here than in the fiction. But no. Side by side with marvels of natural observation like "the churchyard grass running over the old tombstones like green water" in the diary entry of 10 April 1920 and "up in the air across the meadows one sees the handful of grain flung in a semicircle—what birds they are I never know," we may set Mrs. J. C. Squire,

settled into a kind of whitish sediment; a sort of indecency to me in her passive gloating contentment in the arm chair opposite; like some natural function, performing automatically—a jelly fish—without volition, yet with terrifying potentiality. She breaks off into young (reproduces like a vegetable) on the least provocation.

(31 January 1920)

This last vision passes directly into *The Years:* "The men shot [birds], and the women—he looked at his aunt as if she might be breaking into young even there, on that chair—the women broke off into innumerable babies." (The problem of her own child-

lessness racked Virginia throughout her married life.) What a hatred of "the fury and the mire of human veins" is expressed here! Yet for tough, lonely old women, flower sellers or charwomen, she has a lasting admiration.

A bright night; with a fresh breeze. An old beggar woman, blind, sat against a stone wall in Kingsway holding a brown mongrel in her arms and sang aloud. There was a recklessness about her; much in the spirit of London. Defiant—almost gay, clasping her dog as if for warmth. How many Junes has she sat there, in the heart of London? How she came to be there, what scenes she can go through, I can't imagine. O damn it all, I say, why cant I know all that too? Perhaps it was the song at night that seemed strange; she was singing shrilly, but for her own amusement, not begging. Then the fire engines came by—shrill too; with their helmets pale yellow in the moonlight. . . . It was gay, and yet terrible and fearfully vivid.

(8 June 1920)

These human portraits in the letters and the diaries range from old beggar women to flamboyant duchesses and take in the bourgeoisie and the world of business and politics on their way. Virginia Woolf's own servants at Tavistock Square and Monk's House played an important role—often exasperating, always comic—in her life. They too were infected by the libertarian ethos of Bloomsbury and called themselves "the Bloomsbury clique" (12 November 1930): "And today, for the 165th time, Nelly has given notice—won't be dictated to: must do as other girls do. This is the fruit of Bloomsbury" (6 January 1925). Virginia Woolf analyzes their characters and motivations with considerable skill—as indeed she does those of the hundreds of figures, casual callers or intimate friends, who flit through these "fearfully vivid" pages.

The human "insufficiencies" I mentioned earlier most often come under scrutiny, and so do the masks, carapaces, and facades people adopt to conceal them. Of Ka Cox, for instance, she writes: "She has some worm gnawing at her, some passionate desire to impress us" (3 November 1923). Or again:

We have also seen [Richard] Aldington, who calls like a tradesman for orders; a bluff, powerful, rather greasy eyed, nice downright man, who will make his way in the world, which I dont much like people to do. All young men do it. No young women; or in women it is trounced; in men forgiven. It's these reflections I want to enmesh, in writing; or these are among them.

(21 December 1924)

We have already seen her "enmeshing" Mrs. Squire in *The Years*. With such powerful analytical equipment her aims in the novel—to be a social psychologist, or a psychologist of individuals in their gestalts, their circles—are attainable.

Virginia Woolf's character analyses are curiously interwoven with strictures on the London boroughs in which her subjects are resident. She has a feeling for London as a symbolic entity that often reminds us of Blake. Each district possesses its peculiar spiritual character—in every case inferior to that of Bloomsbury! Individuals are assessed in relation to their involvement with their particular gestalt. Can any good thing come out of Hampstead? No: for there the archvillain John Middleton Murry, king of "the Underworld," as she unkindly designates the higher journalism, holds his court. What of South Kensington, her own home of childhood and youth? Rose Macaulay, the poet and novelist, "has lived with the riff raff of South Kensington culture for 15 years, and is rather jealous, spiteful, and uneasy about Bloomsbury" (25 May 1928). Virginia Woolf meets Iolo Williams of the *London Mercury*: "Let me see, there's some failure of sympathy between Chiswick and Bloomsbury, I think, [Williams] said. So we defined Bloomsbury" (24 February 1926). Chelsea fares little better. On a tour of Ireland in 1934 the Woolfs encountered Cyril Connolly and his wife: "They brought the reek of Chelsea with them" (4 May 1934).

Mayfair is suspect for other reasons. It is the home of the aristocracy, and for the aristocracy Virginia Woolf has very mixed feelings. She admires the genuine grande dame or grand seigneur for the same qualities she finds in the old shepherd at Rodmell or the old blind woman in Kingsway: authenticity, spontaneity, indifference to comment, eccentricity, toughness, freedom from cant. The lower-middle and upper-middle classes lack these attributes: they are dull, conformist, timorous, respectable. But there is a false nobility also, a society of arrogant parasites and mindless nincompoops: "The fifth transmitter of a foolish face." So "if I'm Bloomsbury, you're Mayfair" is a defensive riposte to Philip Morrell at Garsington (3 July 1919) after a visit to a pigsty during which Fry and Forster were discussed "most carefully" (23 June 1919). That the pigsty should have been chosen as the venue for a serious literary and aristocratic discussion strikes Virginia Woolf as a lovable aristocratic oddity that should have been unthinkable for the Murrys and the Frank Swinnertons and the Squires. But Morrell's use of "Bloomsbury" as a term of abuse has to be countered.

Virginia Woolf can feel a certain admiration for aristocrats such as Morrell. But on 13 January 1915 she draws a devastating picture of the "aged Countesses and pert young millionairesses" who bully the assistants in Day's lending library:

Days at 4 in the afternoon is the haunt of fashionable ladies, who want to be told what to read. A more despicable set of creatures I never saw. They come in furred like seals and scented like civets, condescend to pull a few novels about on the counter, and then demand languidly whether there is *anything* amusing? . . . The West End of London fills me with aversion; I look into motor cars & see the fat grandees inside, like portly jewels in satin cases.

Conspicuous waste! The glance at *Lear* (fur and civets) opens up a new vein of social satire that we find difficult to associate with Virginia Woolf, despite all her husband's Socialist indoctrination; and indeed she does not pursue it in the novels. But that it is genuinely there and that it caused Virginia some heart-searching is clear from her comments on Knole, the Sackvilles' great Elizabethan house that is the background for *Orlando*. As an example of conspicuous waste Knole would be hard to beat. Virginia is torn between her love as a novelist for the magnificent and the historic and her conscience as a witness of the plight of the London poor. After a seigneurial luncheon alone with his lordship she is led into this moral reflection: "There is Knole, capable of housing all the desperate poor of Judd Street, and with only that one solitary earl in the kernel." Thinking the matter over a little later she comments, as an exercise in self-analysis: "Obviously I did not keep my human values and my aesthetic values distinct." Nor was it ever possible for her to do so.

SELECTED BIBLIOGRAPHY

I. BIBLIOGRAPHY. B. J. Kirkpatrick, *A Bibliography of Virginia Woolf* (London, 1957); R. Majumdar, ed., *Virginia Woolf: An Annotated Bibliography of Criticism* (New York, 1977).

II. COLLECTED WORKS. *Uniform Edition of the Works of Virginia Woolf*, 14 vols. (London, 1929–1952); L. Woolf, ed., *Virginia Woolf: Collected Essays*, 4 vols. (London, 1966–1967).

III. SEPARATE WORKS. *The Voyage Out* (London, 1915),

novel; *The Mark on the Wall* (Richmond, Surrey, 1919), short story; *Kew Gardens* (Richmond, Surrey, 1919), short story; *Night and Day* (London, 1919), novel.

Monday or Tuesday (Richmond, Surrey, 1921), short stories; *Jacob's Room* (London, 1922), novel; *Mr. Bennett and Mrs. Brown* (Richmond, Surrey, 1924), criticism; *The Common Reader* (London, 1925), criticism; *Mrs. Dalloway* (London, 1925), novel; *To the Lighthouse* (London, 1927), novel; *Orlando* (London, 1928), novel; *A Room of One's Own* (London, 1929), essay.

On Being Ill (London, 1930), essay; *Beau Brummell* (New York, 1930), essay; *The Waves* (London, 1931), novel; *A Letter to a Young Poet* (London, 1932), criticism; *The Common Reader: Second Series* (London, 1932), criticism; *Flush: A Biography* (London, 1932), fictionalized biography of Elizabeth Barrett Browning; *Walter Sickert: A Conversation* (London, 1934), essay; *The Years* (London, 1937), novel fragment; *Three Guineas* (London, 1938), essay; *Reviewing* (London, 1939), criticism.

Roger Fry (London, 1940), biography; *Between the Acts* (London, 1941), novel, published posthumously; *The Death of the Moth* (London, 1942), essays, with intro. by L. Woolf; *A Haunted House* (London, 1943), short stories, with preface by L. Woolf; *The Moment and Other Essays* (London, 1947), essays, with preface by L. Woolf.

The Captain's Death-Bed (London, 1950), criticism, with preface by L. Woolf; *Granite and Rainbow* (London, 1958), essays; J. Guiguet, ed., *Contemporary Writers* (London, 1965), contains articles and reviews by Virginia Woolf published from 1905 to 1921; *The London Scene* (London, 1975), essays; L. Ruotolo, ed., *Freshwater. A Comedy* (London, 1976); *Books and Portraits* (London, 1977), further selections from the literary and biographical writings; J. Schulkind, ed., *Moments of Being* (London, 1978), previously unpublished writings; M. Leaska, ed., *The Pargiters* (London, 1978), uncompleted novel-essay portion of *The Years*.

IV. LETTERS AND DIARIES. *A Writer's Diary* (London, 1953); L. Woolf and J. Strachey, eds., *Letters of Virginia Woolf and Lytton Strachey* (London, 1956).

The Letters of Virginia Woolf, vol. I: N. Nicolson and J. Trautmann, eds., *The Flight of the Mind (1888–1912)* (London, 1975); vol. II: N. Nicolson, ed., *The Question of Things Happening (1912–1922)* (1976); vol. III: N. Nicolson and J. Trautmann, eds., *A Change of Perspective (1923–1928)* (1977): vol. IV: N. Nicholson and J. Trautmann, eds., *A Reflection of the Other Person (1929–1931)* (1978); vol. V: N. Nicolson and J. Trautmann, eds., *The Sickle Side of the Moon (1932–1935)* (1979); vol. VI: N. Nicolson and J. Trautmann, eds., *Leave the Letters Till We're Dead (1936–1941)* (1980).

A. O. Bell, ed., *The Diaries of Virginia Woolf*, vol. I: *1915–1919* (London, 1977); vol. II: *1920–1924* (1978); vol. III: *1925–1930* (1980); vol. IV: *1931–1935* (1982).

V. TRANSLATIONS AND INTRODUCTIONS. F. M. Dostoyevsky, *Stavrogin's Confession* (London, 1922), trans., with S. S. Koteliansky; *Talks with Tolstoy* (London, 1923), trans., with S. S. Koteliansky; *Tolstoy's Love Letters* (London, 1923), trans., with S. S. Koteliansky; intro. to J. M. Cameron, *Victorian Photographs* (London, 1926); intro. to L. Sterne, *A Sentimental Journey* (London, 1928); intro. to *Selections from the Works of George Gissing* (London, 1929); intro. to *Recent Paintings by Vanessa Bell* (London, 1930); intro. to M. L. Davies, ed., *Life as We Have Known It, by Co-operative Working Women* (London, 1931; repr. New York, 1975); intro to G. Gissing, *By the Ionian Sea* (London, 1933).

VI. BIOGRAPHICAL AND CRITICAL STUDIES. W. Holtby, *Virginia Woolf* (London, 1932); F. Delattre, *Le Roman psychologique de Virginia Woolf* (Paris, 1932); R. Gruber, *Virginia Woolf* (Leipzig, 1935); L. E. Rillo, *Katherine Mansfield and Virginia Woolf* (Buenos Aires, 1941); D. Daiches, *Virginia Woolf* (London, 1942); E. M. Forster, *Virginia Woolf* (Cambridge, 1942), the Rede Lecture; C. Segura, *The Transcendental and the Transitory in Virginia Woolf's Novels* (Buenos Aires, 1943); J. Bennett, *Virginia Woolf: Her Art as a Novelist* (London, 1945; pprbk. ed., 1975); R. L. Chambers, *The Novels of Virginia Woolf* (London, 1947); B. Blackstone, *Virginia Woolf: A Commentary* (London, 1949).

R. Brower, *The Fields of Light* (New York, 1951; repr. 1962); J. Lehmann, *The Open Night* (London, 1952), contains an appreciation; J. K. Johnstone, *The Bloomsbury Group* (London, 1954); J. Hafley, *The Glass Roof* (New York, 1954); A. Pippett, *The Moth and the Star: A Biography of Virginia Woolf* (Boston, 1955); J. Guiguet, *Virginia Woolf et son oeuvre* (Paris, 1962); D. Brewster, *Virginia Woolf* (London, 1963); R. Freedman, *The Lyrical Novel* (London, 1963); L. Woolf, *An Autobiography of the Years*, vol. III: *Beginning Again, 1911–1918* (London, 1964); vol. IV: *Downhill All the Way, 1919–1939* (1967); vol. V: *The Journey, Not the Arrival, Matters, 1939–1969* (1969); C. Woodring, *Virginia Woolf* (New York, 1966); M. Holroyd, *Lytton Strachey: A Critical Biography*, 2 vols. (London, 1967–1968).

Q. Bell, *Virginia Woolf: A Biography* (New York, 1972); A. V. B. Kelley, *The Novels of Virginia Woolf: Fact and Vision* (Chicago, 1973); A. McLaurin, *Virginia Woolf* (London, 1973); J. Naresmore, *"World Without a Self": Virginia Woolf and the Novel* (London, 1973); J. Lehmann, *Virginia Woolf and Her World* (London, 1975); R. Majumdar and A. McLaurin, eds., *Virginia Woolf: The Critical Heritage* (London, 1975); A. Fleishman, *Virginia Woolf: A Critical Reading* (Baltimore, 1977); H. Marder, *Feminism and Art: The Novels of Virginia Woolf* (London, 1977); I. M. Parsons and G. Spater, *"Marriage of True Minds": An Intimate Portrait of Leonard and Virginia Woolf* (London, 1977); J. Lehmann, *Thrown to the Woolfs* (London, 1978); J. O. Love, *Virginia Woolf: Sources of Madness and Art* (Los Angeles, 1978); R. Poole, *The Unknown Virginia*

Woolf (London, 1978); P. Rose, *Woman of Letters: The Life of Virginia Woolf* (London, 1978); L. Edel, *Bloomsbury: A House of Lions* (London, 1979); M. A. Leaska, *The Novels of Virginia Woolf* (London, 1979); M. Rosenthal, *Virginia Woolf* (London, 1979); B. A. Schlack, *"Continuing Presences": Virginia Woolf's Use of Literary Allusion* (University Park, Pa., 1979).

M. DiBattista, *Virginia Woolf's Major Novels: The Fables of Anon* (New Haven, 1980); R. Freedman, ed., *Virginia Woolf: Revaluation and Continuity* (Los Angeles, 1980); J. Hawthorn, *Virginia Woolf's "Mrs. Dalloway": A Study in Alienation* (Philadelphia, 1980); P. Meiser, *"Absent Father": Virginia Woolf and Walter Pater* (New Haven, 1980); L. A. de Salvo, *Virginia Woolf's First Voyage: A Novel in the Making* (London, 1980); F. Spalding, *Vanessa Bell* (New York, 1983).

JAMES JOYCE

(1882-1941)

J. I. M. Stewart

I

JAMES JOYCE was born on 2 February 1882 in Dublin, where his father was sufficiently prosperous to send him to a fashionable Jesuit boarding school and sufficiently improvident to be virtually penniless a few years later. Partly because of the steady decline in his family's fortunes, and partly because he himself was a little disposed to fudge the evidence, it is difficult to place Joyce tidily in a social class. Virginia Woolf, distressed by the milieu of *Ulysses* (1922), concluded that its author must be "a self-taught working man." Wyndham Lewis (who was educated at Rugby) made fun of Joyce's fictional alter ego, Stephen Dedalus, for his anxiety to appear a gentleman. Perhaps the Joyces became shabby more pronouncedly than they remained genteel. But class consciousness is not important with Joyce, as it is with the other great novelist of the age, D. H. Lawrence. Priest, artist, citizen are Joyce's categories, not gentle and simple.

Nevertheless, what may be called the George Gissing aspect of his youth—the precariousness of his slender degree of privilege, the cultural poverty of life around him—marked him deeply. He grew up arrogant and aloof, contemptuous of all proposals, whether political or artistic, for the regeneration of his country, proud of his precocious knowledge of contemporary continental literature. He renounced the Catholic church, and in 1904 he left Ireland for good, taking with him a young woman named Nora Barnacle, whom he subsequently married. Miss Barnacle was not literary, but a certain pungency attends some of her recorded utterances. "I guess the man's genius," she said of Joyce, "but what a dirty mind he has, hasn't he?" At least she had found a good husband and a devoted father of their two children. To support his family Joyce labored for many years as a teacher of English in Trieste and Zurich; it was only during his later life, when benefactions and his first substantial royalties enabled him to maintain a modest establishment in Paris, that the threat of destitution ceased to hang over him. He appears to have been very sure of his genius. He resisted the discouragements of poverty, neglect, moral censorship, and a grave disease of the eyes. By the time he died in 1941 there was little responsible literary opinion in either Europe or America that failed to acknowledge him as one of the most significant writers of the age. At the same time he attracted much foolish adulation, and his books suffered what they certainly invite, much extravagant exegesis.

II

THE first of Joyce's works to appear in book form was *Chamber Music* (1907), a collection of thirty-six poems. It was completed in 1904 but had to wait three years for a publisher, and in the interval Joyce ceased to feel much regard for it. There is nothing surprising in this. His life's task, if abundantly egotistical, was wholly serious, a presenting of himself and his immediate environment to the world in fictions laying claim to the highest representative significance. With that task, to which he had already addressed himself in the apparently unpublishable *Dubliners* (1914), the poems in *Chamber Music* have nothing to do. They are serious only in a restricted aesthetic sense, which Joyce's genius transcended from the first. He had read Elizabethan lyrics with attention, and his own verses may best be described as consummate imitations of the older poets as they appeared through a fin de siècle haze. They are unchallengeably lyrical; like the best of the Elizabethan, each seems to sigh for its accordant air:

> Who goes amid the green wood
> With springtide all adorning her?

Who goes amid the merry green wood
  To make it merrier?

Who passes in the sunlight
  By ways that know the light footfall?
Who passes in the sweet sunlight
  With mien so virginal?
        (*Chamber Music*, VIII, st. 1–2)

The range is narrow, and one would never guess that these elegant dabblings and paddlings in familiar shallows preluded some of the farthest voyages ever achieved over the wide waters of the word.

Yet of poetry when sufficiently broadly defined all Joyce's work was to be full. From Stephen Dedalus' early turnings-over of words—"a day of dappled seaborne clouds"—on to the last cadence of *Finnegans Wake* (1939):

There's where. First. We pass through grass behush the bush to. Whish! A gull. Gulls. Far calls. Coming, far! End here. Us then. Finn, again! Take. Bussoftlhee, mememormee! Till thousendsthee. Lps. The keys to. Given! A way a lone a last a loved a long the

we hear this poetry plainly; and Joyce's own readings from his work as preserved on phonograph records are astonishing achievements in verbal music. Moreover, his prose is "poetic" in more ways than this. When Stephen is looking out from the Martello tower at the beginning of *Ulysses*, we read:

Woodshadows floated silently by through the morning peace from the stairhead seaward where he gazed. Inshore and farther out the mirror of water whitened, spurned by lightshod hurrying feet. White breast of the dim sea. The twining stresses, two by two. A hand plucking the harpstrings merging their twining chords. Wavewhite wedded words shimmering on the dim tide.

This is consciously presented as poetry; and it is challengingly, not fortuitously, that it comes immediately after a quotation from Yeats. But we are not merely charmed by a cadence. Why—we find ourselves asking—"wavewhite wedded words"? Joyce is concerned with language as *language*; he is never solely concerned with melopoetic effect.

Modern criticism has taught us to recognize in linguistic compressions and ambiguities a range of resources characteristic of poetry proper. At its most effective, Joyce's developed prose was to combine musical suggestion with a hitherto unexampled power to scramble effectively the connotations of words. In *Finnegans Wake* there is a sort of prayer for the River Liffey that runs: "haloed be her eve, her singtime sung, her rill be run, unhemmed as it is uneven!"—thus echoing, enchantingly if profanely, the Lord's Prayer: "Hallowed be Thy Name. Thy kingdom come. Thy will be done in earth. As it is in heaven." It is reasonable to believe that Joyce's peculiar prose has been responsible for a good deal of modern poetry, and for some reinterpretation of older poetry as well. At least it is the work of a writer notably in command of instruments that the present age in particular has considered a large part of the essential endowment of the poet. Yet when Joyce addressed himself, quite simply, to metrical composition, all his largeness and boldness left him.

Pomes Penyeach, the self-consciously depreciatory title of a volume diminutive to the point of affectation, which he published in 1927, shows a mild technical development in consonance with the ideas of the imagists, and is the better—as so much of the century's poetry is the better—from the writer's acquaintance with Ezra Pound. But the poet's properties remain gray, wan, pale, frail, and démodé:

The moon's greygolden meshes make
All night a veil,
The shorelamps in the sleeping lake
Laburnum tendrils trail.
The sly reeds whisper to the night
A name—her name—
And all my soul is a delight,
A swoon of shame.
                    ("Alone")

When these lines were written, *Ulysses* was well under way.

III

Exiles (1918), a play written in 1914 or 1915, is another work of minor interest. Striking as is Joyce's lifelong obsession with Dublin and Dubliners, he was determinedly and from the first a European before he was an Irishman, and in Ibsen he found an international figure who could be held up to point a contrast with the provinciality, as Joyce conceived it, of the Irish literary movement. But *Exiles* is not merely a counterblast, opposing to the theater of Yeats and Synge and Lady Gregory an aggressively naturalistic dramatic convention. It is the work of a writer who has a real if limited temperamental affinity with Ibsen; and it contrives to treat, at once with a bleak painful intensity and a large measure of obscurity, a theme very much from the world of *A Doll's House* and *Hedda Gabler*. We are certainly shown, in one cautious commentator's words, "a puzzling series of dilemmas concerning the limits of freedom, the demands of love, and the possessiveness inherent in marriage." And it seems probable that Joyce proposed to give us something yet closer to Ibsen than this, the spectacle of a harsh ethical absolutism at work in a fatally egotistical personality.

Richard Rowan is an Irish writer who has lived abroad for a number of years with Bertha, a simple and unintellectual girl whom he has been unable or indisposed to marry. They return to Dublin, where an old friend, Robert Hand, is determined that Rowan shall be appointed to a chair of romance literature. But Hand is also determined to seduce Bertha; and presently we find, in a scene of neat theatrical surprise, that Bertha, while passively accepting the successive stages of this advance and even accepting an assignation with Hand, is regularly reporting the developing situation to Rowan. Rowan will not in any degree bind, guide, or support her. He imagines her dead and says to Hand:

I will reproach myself then for having taken all for myself because I would not suffer her to give to another what was hers and not mine to give, because I accepted from her her loyalty and made her life poorer in love. That is my fear. That I stand between her and any moments of life that should be hers, between her and you, between her and anyone, between her and anything. I will not do it. I cannot and I will not. I dare not.

(Act II)

We are shown Bertha presenting again her former passive face to Hand's eventual wooing in his secluded cottage, and then the curtain descends at an ambiguous moment. In the last act Bertha returns to Rowan with an earnest protestation that she has been true to him. But he declares that he now has a deep, deep wound of doubt in his soul, and that this wound tires him. "He stretches himself out wearily along the lounge," and the play closes upon Bertha murmuring a passionate prayer for the return of their earliest days as lovers.

The characters in *Exiles* are very poorly realized. Rowan is represented as a lover but seems not to have the stuff of a lover in him. He constantly demands that he himself be understood, seen for what he is, and so accepted. But he virtually denies that a beloved, or any other person, is knowable. And he never himself contrives to notice this contradiction. We thus feel him to be the projection of a serious but imperfect self-analysis; and this feeling is fatal to any impression of a fullness of dramatic life. A small indication of the extent to which Joyce was here self-absorbed and self-tormented as he worked is the early percolation into the play of talk about Rowan's dead mother and the fact or calumny of his having in some way slighted her. This has no relevance to the action and is a spillover from Joyce's more openly autobiographical writing in the history of Dedalus.

IV

IF the intellectual and emotional pressures that bore upon the young Joyce neither inform his poetry nor fortify his play, they are brought under fruitful artistic control in *Dubliners*. When eventually published in 1914, this volume contained fifteen sketches or short stories, about which Joyce had written thus to a prospective publisher nine years before:

My intention was to write a chapter of the moral history of my country and I chose Dublin for the scene because the city seemed to me the centre of paralysis. I have tried to present it to the indifferent public under four of its aspects: childhood, adolescence, maturity and public life. The stories are arranged in this order. I have written it for the most part in a style of scrupulous meanness and with the conviction that he is a very bold man who dares to alter in the presentment, still more to deform, whatever he has seen and heard.

This is a little manifesto of naturalism; but its most significant phrase is "moral history." And we are not far advanced in *Dubliners* before we realize that Joyce does not differ from other young writers in having as his chief stock-in-trade a set of powerful moral responses before the spectacle of fallen humanity. It is urged upon us that almost every aspect of Dublin life is pitiful or degraded, and that to the effective asserting of this the artist must bend all his cunning. Joyce will allow no half measures. His book is about paralysis—both the word and the thing fascinate a small boy on the first page—and paralysis is uncompromisingly asserted as something to make the flesh creep.

Each one of the stories cries out against the frustration and squalor of the priest-ridden, pub-besotted, culturally decomposing urban lower-middle-class living it depicts. An elderly priest dies in a state of mental and perhaps moral degeneration, and a child to whom he has given some instruction learns from whispering women that the trouble began when he dropped and broke a chalice. Two boys play truant and have a casual encounter with an ineffective pervert. A coarse amorist, to the admiration of a less accomplished friend, gets money out of a servant girl. A drunken clerk is scolded by a bullying employer and humiliated in a public house; he goes home and flogs his son. In another public house a traveler in tea falls down the steps of a lavatory and injures himself. While convalescent he is visited by friends, who talk tediously and ignorantly about ecclesiastical matters, and then endeavor to reform him by taking him to hear a sermon for businessmen. It is recorded by Joyce's brother that lavatory, bedside, and church in this story are designed in a ludicrous correspondence to Dante's Inferno, Purgatorio, and Paradiso.

We may well agree that the style in which such incidents as these are recounted should be "scrupulously mean." And a great part of their effect lies in Joyce's virtuosity here. It is largely a matter of the tact with which a mimetic or semiventriloquial technique is employed. In "Eveline," the story of a very simple girl, we read: "One time there used to be a field there in which they used to play every evening with other people's children. Then a man from Belfast bought the field and built houses in it." And similarly with the adults. The quality of their living is defined in "Two Gallants" by the language:

One said that he had seen Mac an hour before in Westmoreland Street. At this Lenehan said that he had been with Mac the night before in Egan's. The young man who had seen Mac in Westmoreland Street asked was it true that Mac had won a bit over a billiard match. Lenehan did not know: he said that Holohan had stood them drinks in Egan's.

Even an exclamation mark may be made to do this sort of work: "Just as they were naming their poisons who should come in but Higgens!" Higgens, thus acclaimed, is a cipher; he has not appeared before and will not appear again. Such effects would be wearisome if unrelieved; and so the texture of the prose is unobtrusively varied. The first story, that of the priest who broke the chalice, begins in a child's words of one syllable, but presently the priest has a handkerchief that is "inefficacious," and he lies "solemn and copious" in his coffin. Everywhere the description and evocation have a precision and economy and sensitiveness that constitute the reality of the book's style just as the "scrupulous meanness" constitutes its appearance. The style is in fact ironic, contriving to expose what it affects to accept.

A striking use of this technique occurs at the end of "Ivy Day in the Committee Room." We are introduced to a group of canvassers in a Dublin municipal election. They are working only for the money they hope to get from their candidate, whom they despise and distrust and would be quite ready to desert. This, with much more of the degradation of civic and national life that they represent, emerges through the medium of conversation, which eventually turns on Charles Stewart Parnell, the leader of the Irish nationalist movement, who had died shortly after being driven out of political life by opponents who had exploited his involvement in a divorce case. One of those present is persuaded to recite an appropriate poem of his own composition. It begins:

> He is dead. Our Uncrowned King is dead.
> O, Erin, mourn with grief and woe
> For he lies dead whom the fell gang
> Of modern hypocrites laid low.

The verses, which continue in a vein of facile patriotic sentiment and factitious indignation against the treachery that had brought Parnell to ruin, read as if they might have been picked out of a forgotten popular newspaper, but they are a clever fabrication by Joyce himself. And the effect achieved is subtle. The poem is fustian; and its massed clichés and threadbare poeticisms declare it to belong to the same world of impoverished feeling conveyed in the preceding conversations. But that is not quite all. There is a ghost in the poem, the ghost of generous enthusiasms and of strong and sincere attachments to large, impersonal purposes. We respond both ways, as we are later to do to analogous outcrops of romantic clichés in the reveries of Dedalus.

It is in the last and longest story in *Dubliners*, "The Dead," that Joyce's stature as a writer first declares itself unmistakably. Two old ladies and their niece, all obscure figures in the musical life of Dublin, are giving their annual party, and to this their nephew Gabriel Conroy, a schoolmaster with literary tastes, brings his wife, Gretta. The party, which is an undistinguished, rather vulgar, but entirely human affair, is described with a particularity in which the influence of Flaubert may be supposed. Gabriel takes prescriptively a leading part, although his superior education and his sensitiveness prevent his doing it easily, and he makes a speech that we are given in full. This speech, like the poem in "Ivy Day in the Committee Room," is an example of Joyce's deftest double-talk. It is full of trite and exaggerated sentiment, dwelling on spacious days gone beyond recall, absent faces, memories the world will not willingly let die, and so forth; and Gabriel is himself aware of its insincerity as he speaks. But we ourselves are correspondingly aware that it represents a kindly attempt to perform a duty and give innocent pleasure; and our attitude to Gabriel remains sympathetic even while we are being afforded a searching view of him.

After the party Gabriel and his wife drive through the snow to the hotel where they are to spend the night. He is full of desire for her, but she does not respond, and presently he learns that a song heard at the party has reminded her of a boy, Michael Furey, of whom he has never heard, and who died long ago as the result of a passionate vigil he had kept for Gretta when he was already very ill. Gabriel's realization that he has been a stranger to what is thus revealed as the deepest experience of his wife's life now becomes the deepest experience of his:

A shameful consciousness of his own person assailed him. He saw himself as a ludicrous figure, acting as a pennyboy for his aunts, a nervous, well-meaning sentimentalist, orating to vulgarians and idealizing his own clownish lusts. . . .

Generous tears filled Gabriel's eyes. He had never felt like that himself towards any woman, but he knew that such a feeling must be love. The tears gathered more thickly in his eyes and in the partial darkness he imagined he saw the form of a young man standing under a dripping tree. Other forms were near. His soul had approached that region where dwell the vast hosts of the dead. He was conscious of, but could not apprehend, their wayward and flickering existence. His own identity was fading out into a grey impalpable world: the solid world itself, which these dead had one time reared and lived in, was dissolving and dwindling.

A few light taps upon the pane made him turn to the window. It had begun to snow again. He watched sleepily the flakes, silver and dark, falling obliquely against the lamplight. . . . Yes, the newspapers were right: snow was general all over Ireland. It was falling on every part of the dark central plain, on the treeless hills, falling softly upon the Bog of Allen and, farther westward, softly falling into the dark mutinous Shannon waves. It was falling, too, upon every part of the lonely churchyard on the hill where Michael Furey lay buried. It lay thickly drifted on the crooked crosses and headstones, on the spears of the little gate, on the barren thorns. His soul swooned slowly as he heard the snow falling faintly through the universe and faintly falling, like the descent of their last end, upon all the living and the dead.

"The Dead" mingles naturalism and symbolism with a new confidence and richness; tragic ironies play across it subtly and economically; its parts are proportioned to each other strangely but with brilliant effectiveness. And if its artistry looks forward to a great deal in Joyce's subsequent writings, its charity and sympathy are qualities to which he was never to allow so free a play again.

V

A Portrait of the Artist as a Young Man, essentially the story of Joyce's own break with the Catholic church and discovery of his true vocation, was published in 1916, at the end of a process of gestation covering many years. Joyce had begun an autobiographical novel while still in his teens, and he persevered with it until it was 150,000 words long and could be regarded as approximately half finished. About 1908 he decided to rewrite the book on a smaller scale and different method, and it appears probable that the greater part of the original manuscript was then destroyed. The only considerable fragment certainly preserved, which has been published under Joyce's original title of *Stephen Hero* (1944), is rather longer than the whole perfected work but corresponds to only the final third of it.

The technique of *Stephen Hero* is objective, explicit, and ploddingly documentary. It is the only one of Joyce's works self-evidently and at once to rebut Wyndham Lewis' charge that here is a writer stimulated only by ways of doing things, and not by things to be done. It thus has some claim to be considered as a substantive work, with an illuminating place in the development of Joyce's writing, and it certainly possesses the curious interest of closely defining the whole basic structure of Joyce's personality. Nevertheless the mature *Portrait* is of altogether superior artistic significance. Its opening sentence exhibits the new technique: "ONCE upon a time and a very good time it was there was a moocow coming down along the road and this moocow that was coming down along the road met a nicens little boy named baby tuckoo."

Our knowledge of Stephen is now going to come to us mediated through his own developing consciousness. That consciousness is to be the theater of whatever drama the book attempts to present, and at the same time a territory sufficiently broad for the exercise of the vigorous naturalism that Joyce has been learning from continental masters. Yet with a quite bare naturalism he is no longer to be content, and on the second page we come upon him putting unobtrusively into operation a different sort of machinery:

The Vances lived in number seven. They had a different father and mother. They were Eileen's father and mother. When they were grown up he was going to marry Eileen. He hid under the table. His mother said:
—O, Stephen will apologise.
Dante said:
—O, if not, the eagles will come and pull out his eyes—
            Pull out his eyes,
            Apologise,
            Apologise,
            Pull out his eyes.

The whole *Portrait* is an apologia: at the same time its cardinal assertion is that Stephen will *not* apologize; rather he awaits the eagles. Joyce's eyes, moreover, were in actual fact threatened from the first; presently in the *Portrait* Stephen as a schoolboy is going to be unjustly punished as a consequence of defective vision; the master who beats him has just declared twice over that a boy's guilt may be seen in his eyes; the complex of ideas thus established remains with Stephen and is several times resumed in *Ulysses*—in a manner fully intelligible only to a reader equipped with the relevant memories of the *Portrait*.

This technique of weaving elusive symbolic themes percurrently through the strongly realistic fabric of his writing is something that Joyce is to exploit more and more. His prose at length becomes a vast hall of echoes—and one fatally adapted (the toiling inquirer must feel) to the conflicting voices of scholiasts. Eventually Joyce appears to have enjoyed playing up to his commentators. "Eins within a space," we read in *Finnegans Wake*, "and a weary-

wide space it wast, ere wohned a Mookse." The relationship of the mookse to the moocow opens a wide field for conjecture.

The development of young men destined to be artists was already in Britain, as on the Continent, a prolific field of fiction, but this scarcely qualifies the large originality of the *Portrait*, which is as much a landmark in the English novel as is *Joseph Andrews* or *Middlemarch* or *The Way of All Flesh*. We have only to think of the novel's line of representative young men—Roderick Random, Tom Jones, David Copperfield, Arthur Pendennis, Richard Feverel—to realize that Stephen Dedalus is presented to us with a hitherto unexampled intimacy and immediacy. It is true that this is achieved at some cost to the vitality of the book as a whole. Here, as later in parts of *Ulysses*, we are locked up firmly inside Stephen's head; and there are times when we feel like shouting to be let out. What Stephen takes for granted, we have to take for granted too; and as he is aware of other people only as they affect his own interior chemistry, there is often something rather shadowy about the remaining personages in the book. But the picture is always clear and hard in its exhibition of Stephen's successive predicaments. The imaginative and unathletic small boy, hard pressed by the narrow orthodoxies and hovering brutalities of a Jesuit boarding school; his growing realization of his family's drift into squalor, and the pride and arrogance that he progressively summons to his aid; the overwhelming sense of sin into which the severity of Catholic doctrine precipitates him upon the occasion of his untimely sexual initiation; the breaking of his nerve and his phase of anxious and elaborate religious observance; his stumbling but implacable advance, through reverie and through conversation with whatever acquaintances will listen, upon an understanding of the realm of art and his elected place in it; the crisis of his break with church and family, and the exalting moment of revelation and dedication on the strand: all these are vividly realized and rendered experiences.

In the *Portrait* Joyce abandons that aggressively frugal and monotonous prose, pervasive in *Stephen Hero*, out of which he had evolved the highly expressive "scrupulous meanness" of *Dubliners*. Vocabulary, syntax, rhythm are now boldly varied to accentuate the contours of the underlying emotion, and Joyce is thus beginning to deploy his resources as a master of imitative form. *Ulysses*, considered in point of prose style, is to reveal itself quite frankly as a museum displaying, as in a series of showcases, all the old ways of using English and a great many new ones as well. The *Portrait*, although in some degree looking forward to this, renders an overriding impression of unity, since each of the styles reflects one facet of Stephen, who is a highly unified creation. "He chronicled with patience what he saw," we are told, "detaching himself from it and tasting its mortifying flavour in secret."

This Stephen is best represented in some of the conversations—which, as in *Dubliners*, are based upon an ear and intellect so alert as to combine a maximum of significant statement with a minimum of apparent selection. The early scene in which Stephen's father and Mrs. Riordan quarrel over Irish politics during dinner on Christmas day is Joyce's early masterpiece in this kind. When Stephen ceases to be merely a recording intelligence and responds actively to the challenge of a world he finds so largely inimical, the style reaches out at once for weapons and armor, its whole tone becoming an extension of Stephen's most caustic and arrogant condemnations: of Dublin, which has "shrunk with time to a faint mortal odour," of Ireland, "the old sow that eats her farrow," of her church, which is "the scullery-maid of christendom." Stephen himself is "a priest of the eternal imagination," and he speaks in cold exalted phrases consonant with the role.

But there is yet another Stephen in the book, the Stephen who ceaselessly communes with himself on solitary walks about Dublin. It is here—it is in the style Joyce largely employs in rendering Stephen *chez lui*—that the success of the *Portrait* trembles in the balance. The hazard is not the consequence of any simple miscalculation of effect; it is a necessary risk involved in the complexity of what Joyce attempts. There are always two lights at play on Stephen. In the one he is seen as veritably possessing the sanctity and strength he claims—for he has been set aside, not of his own will, to serve the highest. In the other he is only the eldest of Simon Dedalus' neglected children, and his aspirations have the pathos he is to discern in his sister Dilly, when she shyly produces the tattered French grammar she has bought from a stall. Moreover, he is an adolescent as well as an artist; and the emotions of adolescence are often both disturbingly self-indulgent and much in excess of their specific precipitating occasions—expressing themselves in maudlin tags, conventional postures, phrases, and cadences caught up out of books, sometimes hovering agonizingly between

sublimity and absurdity, hysteria and inspiration. It is because of all this that Stephen is represented as outrageously sentimentalizing himself and regularly clothing his poignantly felt nakedness in the faded splendors of a bygone poetic rhetoric:

> He heard the choir of voices in the kitchen echoed and multiplied through an endless reverberation of the choirs of endless generations of children: and heard in all the echoes an echo also of the recurring note of weariness and pain. All seemed weary of life even before entering upon it. And he remembered that Newman had heard this note also in the broken lines of Virgil, "giving utterance, like the voice of Nature herself, to that pain and weariness yet hope of better things which has been the experience of her children in every time."
>
> (ch. 4)

In this kind of writing the key is regularly pitched not to the objective scale of its occasion, but to the dimensions of that occasion as they exist at the moment for the boy. Thus Stephen takes part in some theatricals in the presence of the girl he admires, and the situation excites and disturbs him. So we have:

> He hardly knew where he was walking. Pride and hope and desire like crushed herbs in his heart sent up vapours of maddening incense before the eyes of his mind. He strode down the hill amid the tumult of sudden risen vapours of wounded pride and fallen hope and baffled desire. They streamed upwards before his anguished eyes in dense and maddening fumes and passed away above him till at last the air was clear and cold again.

Before passages like this, or those far more highly wrought pages of the same sort that describe the boy's miserable frequenting of the brothels of the city, one of Joyce's best critics is surely wrong in speaking of "purple passages that have faded considerably." They remain highly expressive, like Juliet's hysteria or Hamlet's rant in Ophelia's grave.

At the book's crisis this boldly heightened writing is employed with great skill. Stephen's coming to his true vocation is by way of successive sensuous impressions, each of which has a sort of trigger action upon forces that have been building themselves up in his mind. The piety that he has evinced since abandoning and repenting his carnal sins has suggested that he is apt for the priesthood, and the question of whether he has indeed a vocation is put to him temperately and wisely by a Jesuit director. His pride and arrogance are brought into play; he is tempted by the thought of secret knowledge and power. He is tempted, too, without clearly knowing it, as an artist: the "vague acts of the priesthood" attract him "by reason of their semblance of reality and of their distance from it." On the threshold of the college the director gives Stephen his hand "as if already to a companion in the spiritual life." But Stephen feels the caress of a mild evening air, sees a group of young men walking with linked arms, hears a drift of music from a concertina. And these impressions are reinforced by memories of his schooldays:

> His lungs dilated and sank as if he were inhaling a warm moist unsustaining air and he smelt again the moist warm air which hung in the bath in Clongowes above the sluggish turfcoloured water.
>
> Some instinct, waking at these memories, stronger than education or piety, quickened within him at every near approach to that life, an instinct subtle and hostile, and armed him against acquiescence.
>
> (ch. 4)

Yet still his mind oscillates. He is entered at the university and celebrates the occasion with comical portentousness in an elaborately harmonious reverie. But this in turn brings to his mind "a proud cadence from Newman":

> Whose feet are as the feet of harts and underneath
> the everlasting arms

and "the pride of that dim image brought back to his mind the dignity of the office he had refused. . . . The oils of ordination would never anoint his body. He had refused." Why? The answer—the positive answer—comes as he walks on the beach. It is, in fact, the secular artist's reply to the "proud cadence" of Newman: "He drew forth a phrase from his treasure and spoke it softly to himself:—A day of dappled seaborne clouds." This is Stephen Dedalus' moment of apocalypse. He realizes that he has apprehended something beautiful. Soon he will be able to write in his diary the final truth about himself: "I desire to press in my arms the loveliness which has not yet come into the world." It is only a shallow irony that would remark that this loveliness is to be represented by Leopold and Molly Bloom in *Ulysses*. Nor need we contemn, in the name of sophisticated restraint, the pitch of the prose in which this moment, a moment at once of final release and final submission, is celebrated:

Where was his boyhood now? Where was the soul that had hung back from her destiny, to brood alone upon the shame of her wounds and in her house of squalor and subterfuge to queen it in faded cerements and in wreaths that withered at the touch? Or where was he?

He was alone. He was unheeded, happy, and near to the wild heart of life. He was alone and young and wilful and wildhearted, alone amid a waste of wild air and brackish waters and the seaharvest of shells and tangle and veiled grey sunlight and gayclad lightclad figures of children and girls and voices childish and girlish in the air.

(ch. 4)

The whole hymn of praise and dedication and pride has still its aspect of precariousness and pathos; it preserves, for all its gorgeousness, the poignancy of the boy's cry in *Stephen Hero*: "Mother . . . I'm young, healthy, happy. What is the crying for?" Stephen, in the last analysis, is singing only as his brothers and sisters have been singing a few pages earlier, when that could be detected in their voices which Newman had heard in the broken lines of Vergil.

VI

In the penultimate section of *Ulysses*, which takes the form of a long catechism, Leopold Bloom is described in bed at the end of the day. He is curled up, we are told, like a child in the womb. And the section concludes thus:

Womb? Weary?
He rests. He has travelled.

With?
Sinbad the Sailor and Tinbad the Tailor and Jinbad the Jailer and Whinbad the Whaler and Ninbad the Nailer and Finbad the Failer and Binbad the Bailer and Pinbad the Pailer and Minbad the Mailer and Hinbad the Hailer and Rinbad the Railer and Dinbad the Kailer and Vinbad the Quailer and Linbad the Yailer and Xinbad the Phthailer.

When?
Going to dark bed there was a square round Sinbad the Sailor roc's auk's egg in the night of the bed of all the auks of the rocs of Darkinbad the Brightdayler.

Where?

Bloom has traveled as the whole crowd of us must travel. But the final question *Where?* is unanswered and ambiguous. If we stress the all-life-in-a-day aspect of *Ulysses*, it is a question about futurity, and there is no answer to it on any premises that Joyce admits. If we think simply of 16 June 1904, then Bloom's journey is from the waking world to the world of dream, and there is a sense in which *Where?* receives its answer in Joyce's next book. Bloom has fallen asleep; we have accompanied him just over the threshold and thereby gained a preliminary glimpse of the vast territory of the unconscious mind into which we are to be conducted in *Finnegans Wake*. The jingle of names (as well as making the statement "Bloom=Everyman=Us") is hypnoidal, and the syntactical obscurity of a *square round Sinbad* and the strange resonance in *Dirkinbad the Brightdayler* expresses the violence done by the unconscious and its queer categories to the logic of waking life.

A positive response to Joyce's writing as a whole depends upon the ability to accept such uses of language as this passage adumbrates. Some readers find it endlessly fascinating. Others declare it boring and assert Joyce to be simply one who, solemn and wide-awake, adds Finbad to Ninbad till the cows come home. There can be no doubt that he became compulsively addicted to letting words fool around, and that his brain was the most elaborately equipped playground for the purpose that has ever left a record of itself in literature. Whether he is to be indicted for progressive artistic irresponsibility makes a hard question not likely to be well answered either by fanatical Joyceans or by those who turn away from his books in disgust and indignation.

The action of the *Portrait* extends over many years, in a manner traditional enough in the novel. *Ulysses* is revolutionary in this regard, being a work of great length in which the entire action is organized, as in a classical play, so as to fall within a single revolution of the sun. Yet it begins precisely as if it were a continuation of the *Portrait*, with the thread taken up after the hero's brief absence from Ireland. In fact, it represents a curious amalgam of just such a sequel with a wholly different project that Joyce had entertained during the period of *Dubliners*. "Ulysses" was to have been the title of a short story descriptive of a day's wandering about Dublin on the part of a certain Mr. Hunter. The ironic association of this personage with the Homeric hero was later enriched through a further association with the Wandering Jew, and from this fusion Leopold Bloom was born. Then Joyce, having hit upon the notion of a loosely organized structural correspondence with the *Odyssey*, perceived that he could begin with a

Telemachia in which the central figure would still be Stephen Dedalus.

But the opening pages, although they have indeed an unforgettable largeness as of great painting, scarcely persuade us that we want to hear much more about Joyce's former hero. Stephen has not been improved by his residence in France. Indeed, we are already more likely to have admired the art of the *Portrait* than the personality of its protagonist. And although that criticism is obviously defective which depreciates the book on the score that Stephen is a prig or a cold fish, it yet remains true that part of a novelist's material, however austere a realist he be, consists in the sympathy of his reader; that he must learn to manipulate this like everything else; and that to miscalculate here is to invite disaster.

In *Ulysses* Stephen is more insufferable than his creator appears disposed to admit. His weariness, his hauteur, his curiously hinted proneness to indulge a dream life in the University of Oxford, his disposition to speak "quietly," "coldly," "bitterly" ("It is a symbol of Irish art. The cracked looking-glass of a servant"), even his dislike of water and presumably of soap: all these are facets of his character that invite fairly enough the jibes of Wyndham Lewis. When presently Stephen is discovered teaching school, we find ourselves disposed to question his declared unfitness for the task, since his mental habit is represented as almost wholly pedantic. This impression is intensified in the succeeding section, which presents us with Stephen's highly allusive and recondite stream of consciousness as he walks on the strand, and which begins thus:

Ineluctable modality of the visible: at least that if no more, thought through my eyes. Signatures of all things I am here to read, seaspawn and seawrack, the nearing tide, that rusty boot. Snotgreen, bluesilver, rust: coloured signs. Limits of the diaphane. But he adds: in bodies. Then he was aware of them bodies before of them coloured. How? By knocking his sconce against them, sure. Go easy. Bald he was and a millionaire, *maestro color di che sanno.* Limit of the diaphane in. Why in? Diaphane, adiaphane.

Part of the obscurity results from Joyce's demand that our consciousness should be steadily at play over the entire surface of his work, so that phrases and associations are intelligible only in the light of others scores or hundreds of pages away. This is a legitimate device, and the extent of its use is a matter of literary tact: the more serious the undertaking, the more vigorous the cooperation we may fairly be expected to bring to it. But so much in Stephen's reverie is resistant to any ready elucidation that we come to wonder whether all this showing off to himself (if it is that) might have been more succinctly accomplished had his creator been less concerned to show off to us.

Certainly Stephen is a Telemachus to whom Ulysses, in the figure of Bloom, comes decidedly to the rescue, so far as the general artistic success of the book is concerned. Whether, within the fable, Bloom ultimately means much to Stephen, or Stephen to Bloom, is a question that has been variously answered by critics. Considered as an action, *Ulysses* ends in obscurity, whether inadvertent or deliberate. But considered as a theater of novel design, constructed mainly for the exhibition of a comic character of striking vitality and verisimilitude, it is an unchallengeable even if dauntingly labored success.

For Lewis, once more always the best devil's advocate when we are judging Joyce—Bloom is a walking cliché; beneath a vast technical elaborateness in the presentation is an orthodox comic figure of the simplest outline. It is certainly true that the lifelikeness of Bloom does not proceed from his being very directly observed from the life. He is a highly evolved literary creation, and his complexity—for he is complex—is literary. Some aspects of him exist only because a body of Anglo-Irish humor existed; others, only because Flaubert's last and unfinished novel, *Bouvard et Pécouchet*, existed. But his principal derivation is surely from the mock-heroic tradition. It has been asserted on eminent authority that the *Odyssey* provided Joyce merely with a scaffolding that a reader may disregard. This is not so. To anyone who has got the hang of the book, Ὀδυσσεὺς πολύτροπος, the much-traveled Ulysses, is sufficiently present to make Bloom seem absurd and diminutive. Yet, as with the best mock-heroic, the reference is capable too of working the other way. Bloom's positive qualities, his representative character, his pathos, all take point from his original.

An elaborate and considered craft is evident too in the medium in which Bloom is presented to us. Joyce had found in Édouard Dujardin's *Les Lauriers sont coupés*, a short novel published in 1887, a technique of internal monologue that in *Ulysses* he develops with immense resource and cunning. Once more he is far from drawing directly on life. Bloom never stops talking to himself—except just occasionally when he talks to someone else—and we are bound to feel that this assiduity in verbalization, although convenient both to his creator and to us who would

make his acquaintance, is something quite outside nature. Yet Joyce achieves with it a vivid and deep illusion. The content of Bloom's mind, his interests, his responses to stimuli, are depicted with deliberation as very much those of any vulgar, curious, kindly man. To give just that with unexampled fullness is largely the idea of the book, and it carries with it the danger of a rather boring lack of particularity. Yet we become convinced that Bloom's mind is not quite like any other mind. It is indeed with his mind as with his hat. On 16 June 1904, many Dubliners must have been wearing a high-grade hat from Plasto's, but only Bloom can have been wearing a high-grade ha. We suspect a misprint (as we often do) but are in the presence of a device. Bloom's internal idiom, too, is consistently and not too obtrusively idiosyncratic. A traditional literary resource—one exploited alike by the creators of Hamlet and Mr. Jingle—has been deftly transferred to a new theater.

Bloom admits us more generously to his intimacy than does almost any other figure in fiction. Yet he is a small man; neither nature nor nurture has given him much; his moral being, which is amebic, and his intellectual interests, which if lively are circumscribed, prove alike unrewarding to exploration on the scale proposed by the book. Bloom thus comes, for all his liveliness and attractiveness, to shoot his bolt with us just as Stephen has done. His environment threatens to swamp him; he ceases to float upon the current of his creator's abounding imaginative vitality and is felt as battling rather desperately against it. It is perhaps by way of redressing a balance here that Joyce offers us finally, and so much at large, the figure of Molly Bloom, the sadly faithless Penelope of the story.

Mrs. Bloom is essentially passive. In the morning, she accepts breakfast in bed from the hands of her husband; in the afternoon, again in bed, she entertains the irresistible Blazes Boylan; in the small hours, in bed still, she indulges herself in the enormous reverie with which the book concludes. The sustained erotic tension of this, which takes about two hours to read, reflects more credit upon Joyce than upon Mr. Boylan. Totally without punctuation (although, for some reason, divided into eight enormous paragraphs), it appears concerned to carry the technique of internal monologue to something near its theoretical limit. And it does achieve, for all its psychological implausibility, an exhibition as of some vast sprawled and monolithic image of female sexuality. Bloom, on the other hand, is throughout in restless motion: he visits the pork butcher, feeds the cat, attends a funeral, pursues his profession as an advertisement tout, has a row in a pub, misconducts himself on a beach, and so on. His most characteristic motion is a wriggle—through inhospitable doors and past averted shoulders. He remains symbolically, if not very impressively, male.

If the Blooms have anything in common it is a retrospective turn of mind. Characters or events in *Dubliners* frequently recur to them. Bloom, engaged on one of his morning duties, recalls how, long ago, he used to jot down on his cuff what his wife said when dressing. "What had Gretta Conroy on?" she had once asked. Bartell d'Arcy, whose singing of "The Lass of Aughrim" called up for Gretta the shade of Michael Furey, has been among Mrs. Bloom's lovers; and so has Lenehan, once the admirer of that Corley who wheedled the gold coin from a servant girl. Mrs. Bloom during her vigil recalls, among numerous other prominent citizens, "Tom Kernan that drunken little barrelly man that bit his tongue off falling down the men's WC drunk in some place or other." Two of the friends who took Kernan to a retreat for businessmen join Bloom at the funeral at Glasnevin; and Bloom reflects that his last visit there was for the funeral of Mrs. Sinico—of whose unfortunate end we have read in a short story called "A Painful Case." Simon Dedalus—another of Mrs. Bloom's bedfellows—is perhaps a little changed, even as his family is further degraded; in some regards an engaging character, he now speaks with a violent foulness and out of a deep venom absent from the *Portrait*.

All this reminiscence reflects Joyce's own mind, which we feel to repose in the Dublin of his youth in a quite extraordinary way. He is nowhere able, or at least disposed, to set out for the past as upon an act of exploration. He has carried the past along with him in his consciousness—as he carried, it is said, its newspapers and tram-tickets along with him in his trunks. It is not indeed wholly true that, as Lewis avers, his thought was "of a conventional and fixed order" that remained unchanged since his early days. *Ulysses* differs from the *Portrait* not merely in elaboration, display, technical variousness, and virtuosity. It mirrors deeper responses to the whole spectacle of enjoying and suffering humanity. But the spectacle itself is confined to the same stage; the old props are trundled on and off; and we are progressively aware of an inflexibly willed, rather desperate resourcefulness as the sustaining principle of the whole. And the resourcefulness is—surely to a hazardous degree—linguistic and stylistic. *Ulysses* is

quite staggeringly full of language. The stuff comes at us in great rollers, breakers, eddies, and tumbles of spume and spray. It is wildly exhilarating. It is also rather buffeting, bruising, exhausting long before the end.

There is evidence that Joyce gave anxious and sustained thought to the form and structure of his work. He certainly let his disciples suppose so; they are fond of expounding the successive episodes in terms of an intricate superimposition of framework upon framework: organs, arts, colors, symbols, and technics. Read, however, without all this instruction, *Ulysses* may strike us as a large-scale improvisation, a hand-to-mouth progression from stunt to stunt— with nearly all the stunts coming off quite brilliantly—but to a final effect of agglomeration before which any summing up, any secure arriving at a right aesthetic total, is singularly hard to achieve.

A curious encyclopedism, such as may be found in certain medieval poets, obsesses the author of *Ulysses*. He seems to feel, for instance, that his book should contain not only his own sort of English—or rather his own sorts of English in their almost inexhaustible variety—but every other sort of English as well; and so he writes one long section, that in which Bloom visits the National Maternity Hospital in Holles Street and meets Stephen, in a succession of parodies tracing the whole evolution of English prose. Some of these are presented out of order; and we are told by the commentators that as this evolution of styles is being appropriately exhibited in a context of development from unfertilized ovum to birth, and as, in an embryo, one or another organ may in fact develop prematurely, there is a particular grace in setting the parodies too in an occasional chronological confusion. Joyce's mind, we must recognize, is as tortuous and pedantic as it is prodigal and—in essentials—poetic. And its prodigality seems to render very uncertain its sense of measure.

Between the longest section of the book, the unparalleled and astounding fantasia of the unconscious, thronged and farced with specters of preternatural vigor and overpowering horror, which opens at "the Mabbot street entrance of nighttown" —between this and the contrasting but equally unexampled long slow earthen pulse of Mrs. Bloom's concluding reverie, there is obviously required some episode of relaxed tension. Joyce provides two such episodes in succession. First, Bloom and Stephen are to be represented as sitting in a cabmen's shelter, exhausted. This exhaustion is to be conveyed, on the governing principle of the book, by recourse to an exhausted, a jejune prose. Joyce therefore contrives what is best described as a sustained cliché of some twenty thousand words. Next the two men—casually thrown together but symbolically regarded as profoundly in search of each other—make their way to Bloom's kitchen. They are isolated individuals, souls struggling toward some obscure self-realization through and against the recalcitrant medium of matter. This recalcitrant medium Joyce evokes overwhelmingly by a yet longer and denser device: an interminable, inexorable catechism, couched almost exclusively in a flat scientific jargon, exhaustively tabulating not only Bloom's present physical environment but also that of the dream-cottage to which he aspires to retire:

What homothetic objects, other than the candlestick, stood on the mantelpiece?
A timepiece of striated Connemara marble, stopped at the hour of 4.46 a.m. on the 21 March 1896, matrimonial gift of Matthew Dillon: a dwarf tree of glacial arborescence under a transparent bellshade, matrimonial gift of Luke and Caroline Doyle: an embalmed owl, matrimonial gift of Alderman John Hooper.

There are more than three hundred such answers to questions, and some of them describe with minute particularity as many as ten or twenty separate objects. Joyce is said to have taken more pride in this part of *Ulysses* than in any other. Certainly it cannot be called idle or even—strangely enough—boring, and there is no reason to suppose that the precise effect it produces could be produced in any other way. Yet this massive accumulation, this enormous stasis, is presented to us at a point where we suppose ourselves to be moving toward the resolution of a fable. What, we ask, is this resolution? The mountain has labored. But where is the mouse?

Stripped and viewed as an action, *Ulysses* reveals itself as being much what it started out to be: a short story in *Dubliners*. We need not suppose that Mr. Hunter's wanderings about Dublin were to have been no more than a small exercise in the picaresque. That was never Joyce's way. Something always happens in his stories—but it is generally a small, muted, problematically or evanescently significant thing. Most characteristically, it is an encounter—an encounter with some circumscribed hinted consequence that is not pursued. And this is the formula of *Ulysses*, the spare skeleton that has been given so much flesh and so many clothes. None of the great

elaborative works of literature—Milton's *Paradise Lost*, Goethe's *Faust*, Mann's *Joseph und seine Brüder*—has made do with quite so little.

Yet this strange book—so *voulu*, so willfully tedious, so dirty, often smelling so queerly of pedagogy and examination papers—is one to which mature readers will return again and again. We revisit it—Edmund Wilson has excellently said—as we revisit a city, a city animated by a complex inexhaustible life. Its material may be "consciously the decay of a mournful province"—the words are Lewis' once more—but it is not itself mournful. And it is not negative. It closes, with passion, on a basic affirmation: "yes I said yes I will Yes."

VII

Ulysses, the record of a single day, exhausts the exploration of the waking mind. *Finnegans Wake*, the formidable work to the elaborating of which Joyce devoted the last fifteen years of his life, is correspondingly the record of a single night; and it proposes to interpret, with an equal exhaustiveness, the nature and content of the mind asleep. To this tremendous proposal Joyce was in part driven by the logic of his own achievement, in part encouraged by the drift of contemporary psychological speculation, and in part lured by the unparalleled opportunities that the fabricating of a dream-language would afford to his remarkable logopoetic faculty.

As if conscious that he had revealed no genius for that sort of large-scale fiction that has significantly a beginning, a middle, and an end, Joyce framed this final work upon a peculiar principle. It begins: "riverrun, past Eve and Adam's, from swerve of shore to bend of bay, brings us by a commodius vicus of recirculation back to Howth Castle and Environs." And it ends: "A way a lone a last a loved a long the."

The last sentence, in fact, runs straight into the first. Ideally, the text should be disposed not in a bound volume but in a single line of type round an enormous wheel. History, Joyce now believed, is such a wheel, and its revolution has been explained by the eighteenth-century Italian philosopher Giambattista Vico. The "commodius vicus of recirculation" introduces us to Vico and his theory, as well as to a pleasant *giro* (round trip) that may be taken round

Dublin bay. Howth Castle and Environs display initial letters preluding the entry of the book's central character, Humphrey Chimpden Earwicker. But as Earwicker is a universal figure, the initials may also stand for "Haveth Childers Everywhere" or "Here Comes Everybody." Eve and Adam's is the popular name for a church on the banks of the Liffey, which is the river that is running in the opening word; but as we are already talking about the stream of history, we are no doubt being invited, incidentally, to consider that stream's first welling-up in the Garden of Eden.

Joyce is said to have declared in a moment of arrogance (which may indeed have been softened by humor) that the demand he made upon his reader was no less than the application of a lifetime. Certainly he now had little regard for anything that can be approximated to lucidity, a fact that becomes apparent as soon as we go on from the first paragraph to the second:

Sir Tristram, violer d'amores, fr'over the short sea, had passencore rearrived from North Armorica on this side the scraggy isthmus of Europe Minor to wielderfight his penisolate war: nor had topsawyer's rocks by the stream Oconee exaggerated themselse to Laurens County's gorgios while they went doublin their mumper all the time: nor avoice frou afire bellowsed mishe mishe to tauftauf thuartpeatrick: not yet, though venissoon after, had a kidscad buttended a bland old isaac: not yet, though all's fair in vanessy, were sosie sesthers wroth with twone nathandjoe. Rot a peck of pa's malt had Jhem or Shen brewed by arclight and rory end to the regginbrow was to be seen ringsome on the aquaface.

"The first impression," Joseph Campbell and Henry Morton Robinson say of this in the volume that they have devoted to a preliminary exegesis of *Finnegans Wake*, "is one of chaos, unrelieved by any landmark of meaning or recognition." But this impression they assert to be totally mistaken, since the passage holds nothing that need shake our faith in Joyce "as a wielder of the most disciplined logic known to modern letters." It is surely abundantly clear, however, that as long as we assert the traditional canons of what constitutes discourse, Joyce *is* producing nonsense. The passage is logical—or claims to be logical—only in the very special sense in which (according to certain psychological theories) the most phantasmagoric dream must be logical; in the sense, that is to say, that its constituting elements are chosen and concatenated not fortuitously but as the designed product of unconscious mental processes in which may be detected the working of intelligible laws. When eventually we discover that Earwicker has a wife and daughter, and that he has reached a phase of sexual involution in which his relations with them are ambiguous, we realize the appropriateness with which the dream-logic calls up both Tristram, who had two Iseults, and Swift ("nathandjoe" being an anagram for Jonathan), who had Stella and Vanessa. If we ask why Vanessa is disguised as "in vanessy" we may find ourselves thinking of "Inverness" and so recalling Macbeth, who, like Earwicker, fell into some moral danger as a consequence of his relations with females.

It will be evident that *Finnegans Wake* offers much scope to the interpreter. The reader's first endeavor, however, should be less with the larger significances that the book is conjectured to embody than with the linguistic technique that it indubitably employs. If one considers, still in the above passage, the phrase "penisolate war," one quickly sees that it is simply "Peninsular War" (the title commonly given by historians to the Napoleonic campaigns in Spain) so distorted as to carry more secondary suggestions than one. For example, if hyphenated as "pen-isolate war" it may call up a whole complex of thoughts about Joyce himself, who certainly fought with a pen—and did so from the isolation of Trieste or Zurich. It was maintained by Freud and his followers that language regularly takes on this ambiguous character—whether in wit or in slips of the tongue or pen—under pressure of conflicting unconscious forces. Psychoanalytic literature, moreover, reports many instances of such obscurely significant disguisings and telescopings of words being remembered from dreams; and it is evident that from this Joyce derived the notion that it should be possible to excavate—or if not to excavate, to invent—a whole dream-language of this sort.

It is certain that *Finnegans Wake* is not, in any simple sense, the product of a psychic automatism. Joyce wrote much of it in comparatively plain language, which he then with great labor elaborated until he had achieved his complex final product. Of some sections of the work early and intermediate versions have been published, and at least some of these have been judged by many readers to be more successful than the later versions evolved from them. Once again we have to question Joyce's sense of measure; he overdoes it, and the eventual effect is of something mechanical or synthetic. But the mere fact that he worked over his text again and again is irrelevant in judging its merits as an artistic evocation of the world of dreams. The more one reads the book, the more one is disposed to acknowledge in it an authentic imaginative correspondence with what we know of unconscious mental life.

But *Finnegans Wake* remains a very hard book. Joyce does nothing to help us. It is only in the penultimate section that we gain anything but the most obscure and fragmentary intimations of what, in any common sense, it is all about. Moreover, to the obscurities of one psychological system Joyce has cheerfully added the obscurities of another. Earwicker, the Dublin publican, dreams obediently on Freud's principles—but when he dreams deeply enough he dreams on Jung's as well, so that his dream becomes anybody's or everybody's dream; universal knowledge, fragmented and distorted, drifts in and out after a fashion that none of the Earwicker family could conceivably compass: and we are presumably being invited to believe that we have penetrated to something like a Great Memory, or collective unconsciousness of the race. Such an exploration must almost necessarily, one supposes, be attended by a large obscurity. But it is sometimes possible to feel that we are in the presence of something much more circumscribed, and that the reduplication of darknesses in *Finnegans Wake* represents simply veil upon veil that Joyce has spun round some personal predicament, some obliquity of the private or domestic life such as had always haunted his writing and that he is now at the last unwilling to exhibit directly either to others or to himself.

Finnegans Wake, then, if enigmatic at a first entrance, is yet largely susceptible of elucidation both as a cunningly contrived and disposed phantasmagoria of near-dreamlike material and as an inexhaustibly subtle, even if at times depressingly dogged, campaign upon the farthest boundaries of language. What is most accessible in it is its often hauntingly beautiful melody, which is perhaps best illustrated by the famous ending of the section originally published under the title "Anna Livia Plurabelle." Anna Livia is the Liffey, and the Liffey is the symbol of the feminine, just as the Hill of Howth is ("Howth Castle and Environs") of the masculine. Here two washerwomen—who as well as being washerwomen are a stone and an elm, death and life—are gossiping about Anna in the gathering dusk. And their gossip—to quote Edmund Wilson—

"is the voice of the river itself, light, rapid, incessant, almost metrical, now monotonously running on one note, now impeded and syncopated, but vivaciously, interminably babbling its indistinct rigmarole story, half-unearthly, half-vulgarly human, of a heroine half-legendary, half-real":

And ho! Hey? What all men. Hot? His tittering daughters of. Whawk.

Can't hear with the waters of. The chittering waters of. Flittering bats, fieldmice bawk talk. Ho! Are you not gone ahome? What Thom Malone? Can't hear with bawk of bats, all thim liffeying waters of. Ho, talk save us! My foos won't moos. I feel as old as yonder elm. A tale told of Shaun or Shem? All Livia's daughtersons. Dark hawks hear us. Night! Night! My ho head halls. I feel as heavy as yonder stone. Tell me of John or Shaun? Who were Shem and Shaun the living sons or daughters of? Night now! Tell me, tell me, tell me, elm! Night night! Telmetale of stem or stone. Beside the rivering waters of, hitherandthithering waters of. Night!

Yet many who have turned to the whole work with excitement after hearing Joyce's own recorded reading of this must have been baffled and disappointed by the indigestible matter they found there. It will never conduce to Joyce's reputation to assert that *Finnegans Wake* is, in any ordinary sense, a readable book. It is not; it is in the main a closed book even to most persons of substantial literary cultivation. But if not readable it may yet be seminal; and it seems possible that, for many generations, its frequentation by a small body of writers and students will indirectly enrich the subsequent stream of English literature.

SELECTED BIBLIOGRAPHY

(Compiled by Jeri Johnson)

I. Bibliography. A. Parker, *James Joyce: A Bibliography of His Writings, Critical Material and Miscellanea* (Boston, 1948), see also W. White, "James Joyce: Addenda to Alan Parker's Bibliography," in *Papers of the Bibliographical Society of America*, 43 (First Quarter 1949), pp. 93–96, and 43 (Fourth Quarter 1949), pp. 401–411, W. White, "Addenda to James Joyce Bibliography, 1950–1953," in *James Joyce Review*, 1, no. 2 (June 1957), pp. 9–25, and W. White "Addenda to James Joyce Bibliography, 1954–1957," in *James Joyce Review*, 1, no. 3 (September 1957), pp. 3–24; J. J. Slocum and H. Cahoon, *A Bibliography of James Joyce: 1882–1941* (New Haven, Conn.–London, 1953), the standard bibliography, listing all publications of Joyce's own work up to 1950, see also A. M. Cohn, "Corrigenda to the Joyce Bibliography (Slocum and Cahoon D 1–2), and a Possible Addendum," in *Papers of the Bibliographical Society of America*, 65 (Third Quarter 1971), pp. 304–307, R. M. Kain, "Supplement to Joyce Bibliography," in *James Joyce Review*, 1, no. 4 (December 1957), pp. 38–40, and A. M. Cohn, "Further Supplement to James Joyce Bibliography, 1950–1957," in *James Joyce Review*, 2, nos. 1 and 2 (Spring–Summer 1958), pp. 40–54; T. E. Connolly, *The Personal Library of James Joyce* [in the Lockwood Memorial Library in the University of Buffalo]: *A Descriptive Bibliography*, University of Buffalo Studies, 22, no. 1 (April 1955), records some marginalia and evidence of use.

R. E. Scholes, *The Cornell Joyce Collection: A Catalogue* (Ithaca, 1961); P. Spielberg, *James Joyce's Manuscripts and Letters at the University of Buffalo: A Catalogue* (Buffalo, 1962); D. Hayman, ed., *A First Draft Version of "Finnegans Wake"* (London, 1963), includes a catalog of the *Finnegans Wake* MSS in the British Museum; the *James Joyce Quarterly* (University of Tulsa), checklists of Joyce criticism, comp. by A. M. Cohn at least annually since 1963, the best listings of material published since the first ed. of Deming's *Bibliography*; R. H. Deming, *A Bibliography of James Joyce Studies* (Lawrence, Kans., 1964; rev. ed., Boston, 1977), the standard annotated checklist of critical material on Joyce complete to December 1973; M. Beebe, P. F. Herring, and A. W. Litz, "Criticism of James Joyce: A Selected Checklist," in *Modern Fiction Studies*, 15 (1969), pp. 105–182.

M. Groden, *James Joyce's Manuscripts: An Index* (New York–London, 1980), the most complete checklist of all extant MSS, typescripts, and proofs of Joyce's works.

II. SELECTED WORKS. *Introducing James Joyce* (London, 1942; repr. 1973), a sel. of Joyce's prose with an intro. by T. S. Eliot; H. Levin, ed., *The Portable James Joyce* (New York, 1947), published in England as *The Essential James Joyce* (London, 1948), contains *Dubliners, A Portrait of the Artist as a Young Man, Exiles, Collected Poems*, "The Holy Office," "Gas from a Burner," and sections from *Ulysses* and *Finnegans Wake*.

III. SEPARATE WORKS PUBLISHED BEFORE 1941. *Note:* In each case the date and place of the first ed. is followed by the same information for the most correct, accepted, or standard ed.

Chamber Music (London, 1907), ed. with notes by W. Y. Tindall (New York, 1954), see *Collected Poems; Dubliners* (London, 1914), ed. by R. Scholes in consultation with R. Ellmann (New York, 1967); *A Portrait of the Artist as a Young Man* (New York, 1916), ed. by R. Ellmann, definitive text corrected from Dublin holograph by C. G. Anderson (New York, 1964), first published serially in the *Egoist* (2 February 1914–1 September 1915); *Exiles* (London, 1918; New York, 1951).

Ulysses (Paris, 1922; New York, 1961), first published serially in the *Little Review* (New York, 1918–1920) and the *Egoist* (London, 1919), but Joyce rev. the text substantially before its final publication in Paris in 1922; many eds. now available, all error-ridden; work on a definitive critical ed. is currently in progress in Germany; *Pomes Penyeach* (Paris, 1927), see *Collected Poems; Collected Poems* (New York, 1936; New York, 1957), includes *Chamber Music, Pomes Penyeach,* and "Ecce Puer"; *Finnegans Wake* (New York–London, 1939), first published in fragments as "Work in Progress" from April 1924, in various pamphlets and periodicals, notably *transition* (Paris).

IV. POSTHUMOUS WORKS. T. Spencer, ed., *Stephen Hero* (New York, 1944), with an intro. by Spencer, rev. with additional MS material and a foreword by J. J. Slocum and H. Cahoon (New York, 1956), further rev. with further manuscript material, and ed. by Slocum and Cahoon (New York, 1963), the surviving part of the first draft of *A Portrait of the Artist; Letters of James Joyce*, S. Gilbert, ed., vol. I (New York, 1957), reiss. with corrections by R. Ellmann (1966); R. Ellmann, ed., vols. II–III (New York, 1966); E. Mason and R. Ellmann, eds., *The Critical Writings of James Joyce* (New York, 1959), includes Joyce's essays "Ibsen's New Drama," "James Clarence Mangan," and "The Day of the Rabblement," book reviews, "The Holy Office," and "Gas from a Burner"; T. E. Connolly, ed., *James Joyce's Scribbledehobble: The Ur-Workbook for "Finnegans Wake"* (Evanston, Ill., 1961), transcript of one of Joyce's largest notebooks in the Wickser Collection at the University of Buffalo Library, with photographs of some pp.; *Daniel Defoe* (Buffalo, 1964), Joyce's lecture at Trieste, Italian text with a trans. and notes by J. Prescott; R. Scholes and R. M. Kain, eds., *The Workshop of Daedalus* (Evanston, Ill., 1965), includes Joyce's *Epiphanies*, his Paris, Pola, and Trieste notebooks, and the autobiographical essay "A Portrait of the Artist," written when he was twenty-one; R. Ellmann, ed., *Giacomo Joyce* (New York, 1968), facs. repro. of a Joyce notebook, written while he was in Trieste, much of which was previously published in Ellmann's *James Joyce*; P. F. Herring, ed., *Joyce's "Ulysses" Notesheets in the British Museum* (Charlottesville, Va., 1972), transcription, annotation, and discussion of the notesheets Joyce compiled in writing *Ulysses; James Joyce: "Ulysses." A Facsimile of the Manuscript*, 2 vols. (New York, 1975), intro. by H. Levin, bibliographical preface by C. Driver, a photo-repro. of the holographic MS now at the Rosenbach Foundation in Philadelphia.

James Joyce: "Ulysses." The Manuscript and First Printing Compared (New York, 1975), ann. by C. Driver, photo-repro. of the text as printed in the *Little Review*, marked to show the differences between it and the Rosenbach MS; issued in a three-vol. set with the above; R. Ellmann, ed., *Selected Letters of James Joyce* (New York, 1975), containing several new letters not published in the three-vol. ed.; P. F. Herring, ed., *Joyce's Notes and Early Drafts for "Ulysses": Selections from the Buffalo Collection* (Charlottesville, Va., 1977), transcription, some photographs; M. Groden, ed., *The James Joyce Archive,*

63 vols. (New York–London, 1978) (index published separately as Groden, ed., *James Joyce's Manuscripts: An Index* (New York, 1980), facs. photo-repro. ed. of Joyce's entire "workshop": all extant and available notes, drafts, MSS, typescripts, and proofs of his work; vol. I: *Chamber Music, Pomes Penyeach, and Occasional Verse;* vols. II–III: *Notes, Criticism, Translations, and Miscellaneous Writings;* vols. IV–VI: *Dubliners;* vols. VII–X: *A Portrait of the Artist as a Young Man;* vol. XI: *Exiles;* vols. XII–XXVII: *Ulysses;* vols. XXVIII–LXIII: *Finnegans Wake.*

V. BIOGRAPHICAL STUDIES. F. Budgen, *James Joyce and the Making of "Ulysses"* (London, 1934), repr. with additional material (London, 1972), about Joyce while he was living in Zurich, best account of him as a friend and writer; H. Gorman, *James Joyce* (New York, 1939; rev. ed., New York, 1948), the first full-length biography of Joyce, written with his help, contains material not available elsewhere; J. F. Byrne, *Silent Years: An Autobiography, with Memoirs of James Joyce and Our Ireland* (New York, 1953), an account of Joyce as a young man by the "Cranly" of *A Portrait of the Artist;* M. Colum and P. Colum, *Our Friend James Joyce* (New York, 1958; ppbk. repr., New York, 1961), describes meetings with Joyce the established writer; S. Joyce, *My Brother's Keeper* (New York, 1958; ppbk. repr., New York, 1964), ed. and with an intro. by R. Ellmann, preface by T. S. Eliot; K. Sullivan, *Joyce Among the Jesuits* (New York, 1958), provides information about Joyce's early education; S. Beach, *Shakespeare and Company* (New York, 1959), includes account of Joyce during his Paris days and the publication of *Ulysses;* R. Ellmann, *James Joyce* (New York, 1959), rev. with additional material (New York–London, 1982), the standard biography; W. Y. Tindall, *The Joyce Country* (University Park, Pa., 1960; ppbk. repr., New York, 1972); S. Joyce, *The Dublin Diary of Stanislaus Joyce* (Ithaca–London, 1962), G. H. Healey, ed., rev. and published as G. H. Healey, ed., *The Complete Dublin Diary of Stanislaus Joyce* (Ithaca, 1971); C. G. Anderson, *James Joyce and His World* (London, 1968), concise account, many pictures; C. P. Curran, *James Joyce Remembered* (New York–London, 1968), Joyce during his Dublin and Paris student days; J. Lidderdale and M. Nicholson, *Dear Miss Weaver: Harriet Shaw Weaver, 1876–1961* (New York–London, 1970), a portrait of the founder of the Egoist Press, which published *A Portrait of the Artist* and *Ulysses,* valuable information on Joyce's early struggles for recognition; S. G. Davies, *James Joyce: A Portrait of the Artist* (London, 1975).

VI. GENERAL CRITICAL STUDIES. E. Pound, "Joyce," in the *Future* (May 1918), pp. 161–163; repr. in T. S. Eliot, ed., *Literary Essays of Ezra Pound* (London, 1954); W. Lewis, *Time and Western Man* (London, 1927), especially "An Analysis of the Mind of James Joyce," pp. 91–130, led to Joyce's collaboration with Stuart Gilbert and a ch. of *Finnegans Wake.*

C. Connolly, "The Position of Joyce," in *Life and Letters,* 2, no. 11 (April 1929), repr. in C. Connolly, *The Condemned Playground* (New York, 1946); E. Wilson, *Axel's Castle: A Study in the Imaginative Literature of 1870–1930* (London, 1931), contains ch. on Joyce; D. Daiches, *The Novel and the Modern World* (Chicago, 1939; rev. ed., 1960), contains chs. on Joyce; E. Wilson, *The Wound and the Bow: Seven Studies in Literature* (New York, 1941; repr. 1959), contains discussion of *Finnegans Wake;* H. Levin, *James Joyce: A Critical Introduction* (Norfolk, Conn., 1941; London, 1944), still one of the best general intros. to Joyce's work; S. Givens, ed., *James Joyce: Two Decades of Criticism* (New York, 1948; rev. ed., 1963), contains a number of important essays, including T. S. Eliot's "Ulysses, Order and Myth" (1923), S. F. Damon's "The Odyssey in Dublin" (1929), and P. Toynbee's "A Study of James Joyce's *Ulysses*" (1947).

W. Y. Tindall, *James Joyce: His Way of Interpreting the Modern World* (New York, 1950); G. Melchiori, "Joyce and the Eighteenth-Century Novelists," in M. Praz, ed., *English Miscellany,* 2 (1951); F. Russell, *Three Studies in Twentieth Century Obscurity* (Aldington, 1954), contains attack on Joyce's later work; H. Kenner, *Dublin's Joyce* (Bloomington, Ind.–London, 1956; repr. Gloucester, Mass., 1969), intelligent and original interpretations of Joyce's work; M. Magalaner and R. M. Kain, eds., *Joyce: The Man, the Work, the Reputation* (New York, 1956), assembles and comments upon a large body of critical material; M. Magalaner, ed., *A James Joyce Miscellany* (New York, 1957), followed by the more important *A James Joyce Miscellany, Second Series* (Carbondale, Ill., 1959) and *Third Series* (Carbondale, 1962), contains wide variety of articles, some of great value; W. T. Noon, S.J., *Joyce and Aquinas* (New Haven, Conn., 1957), sympathetic account of Joyce's use of Aquinas; J. M. Morse, *The Sympathetic Alien: Joyce and Catholicism* (New York, 1959), considers Joyce's use of Aquinas and other patristic writers; W. Y. Tindall, *A Reader's Guide to James Joyce* (New York, 1959), places great emphasis on Joyce's use of symbols; M. J. C. Hodgart and M. Worthington, *Song in the Works of James Joyce* (New York, 1959), contains lists of songs in Joyce's works.

S. L. Goldberg, *The Classical Temper* (London, 1961), Joyce as a novelist, with special attention to *Ulysses;* A. W. Litz, *The Art of James Joyce: Method and Design in "Ulysses" and "Finnegans Wake"* (London, 1961), landmark study in the analysis of Joyce's methods of composition; V. Mercier, *The Irish Comic Tradition* (London, 1962); J. I. M. Stewart, *Eight Modern Writers* (Oxford, 1963); H. Kenner, *Flaubert, Joyce and Beckett: The Stoic Comedians* (London, 1964); J. Prescott, *Exploring James Joyce* (Carbondale, Ill., 1964), essays focusing on Joyce's powers of rev.; A. W. Litz, *James Joyce* (New York, 1966; rev. ed., 1972), short, introductory survey intended for American college students; A. Goldman, *The Joyce Paradox* (London, 1966), an artful discussion of Joyce's methods and philosophy; F. Read, *Pound/Joyce: The Let-*

ters of Ezra Pound to James Joyce, with Pound's Essays on Joyce (New York, 1967), very good, essential to an understanding of the crucial relationship between Pound and Joyce.

R. H. Deming, *James Joyce: The Critical Heritage*, 2 vols. (New York–London, 1970), vol. I: *1907–1927*, vol. II: *1928–1941*, invaluable collection of over 300 articles, some abr., from various viewpoints, very good for a historical perspective on Joyce's reception; H. Cixous, *The Exile of James Joyce*, S. Purcell, trans. (New York, 1972); F. Senn, *New Light on Joyce from the Dublin Symposium* (Bloomington, Ind.–London, 1972), various important articles, especially J. P. Dalton's "The Text of *Ulysses*"; A. Burgess, *Joysprick: An Introduction to the Language of James Joyce* (London–New York, 1973); Z. Bowen, *Musical Allusions in the Works of James Joyce* (Albany, N.Y.–Dublin, 1974); J. Garvin, *James Joyce's Disunited Kingdom and the Irish Dimension* (New York–Dublin, 1976); B. Benstock, *James Joyce: The Undiscover'd Country* (New York–Dublin, 1977); R. Ellmann, *The Consciousness of Joyce* (New York–London, 1977), includes in appendix a complete list of Joyce's Trieste library; C. H. Peake, *James Joyce: The Citizen and the Artist* (London, 1977), especially good on *Ulysses*; H. Kenner, *Joyce's Voices* (Berkeley, Calif.–London, 1978), a stimulating and entertaining rationale for Joyce's varying styles.

D. Manganiello, *Joyce's Politics* (Boston–London, 1980); B. Benstock, ed., *The Seventh of Joyce* (Bloomington, Ind.–Sussex, 1982), includes the best of the papers presented at the Seventh International Joyce Symposium, Zurich, 1979.

VII. CRITICAL STUDIES OF EARLY WORKS. E. Pound, "*Dubliners* and Mr. Joyce," in the *Egoist*, 1 (15 July 1914), repr. in T. S. Eliot, ed., *Literary Essays of Ezra Pound*; M. Magalaner, *Time of Apprenticeship: The Fiction of Young James Joyce* (New York, 1959), reproduces the first version of "The Sisters" and contains interesting notes on the factual bases of Joyce's stories.

T. E. Connolly, ed., *Joyce's "Portrait": Criticisms and Critiques* (New York, 1962; London, 1964), essays by Harry Levin, Dorothy van Ghent, Richard Ellmann, and others; W. E. Morris and C. A. Nault, eds., *Portraits of an Artist: A Casebook* (New York, 1962), wide variety of critical material, with full critical apparatus and bibliography; D. Gifford, with assistance of R. J. Seidman, *Notes for Joyce: "Dubliners" and "Portrait of the Artist"* (New York, 1967; rev. ed., 1982); C. G. Anderson, ed., "*A Portrait of the Artist as a Young Man": Text, Criticism and Notes* (New York, 1968), Viking Critical ed.; W. M. Schutte, ed., *Twentieth Century Interpretations of "A Portrait of the Artist as a Young Man"* (Englewood Cliffs, N.J., 1968), see especially the articles by Wayne Booth, Hugh Kenner, and S. L. Goldberg; J. R. Baker and T. Staley, eds., *James Joyce's "Dubliners": A Critical Handbook* (Belmont, Cal., 1969), contains essays by such critics as Robert Penn Warren and Lionel Trilling; C. Hart, ed.,

James Joyce's "Dubliners": Critical Essays (New York–London, 1969), essays by A. Walton Litz, Fritz Senn, Adaline Glasheen, and others; R. Scholes and A. W. Litz, eds., *James Joyce's "Dubliners": Text, Criticism and Notes* (New York, 1969), Viking Critical ed., standard text and solid criticism.

M. Beja, *Epiphany in the Modern Novel* (Seattle, 1971), especially his discussion of Joyce's epiphanies; M. Beja, ed., *James Joyce, "Dubliners" and "A Portrait of the Artist as a Young Man": A Selection of Critical Essays* (London, 1973), essays by Hugh Kenner, Richard Ellmann, Anthony Burgess, and others; T. F. Staley and B. Benstock, eds., *Approaches to Joyce's "Portrait": Ten Essays* (Pittsburgh, 1976), see especially Hans Walter Gabler's "The Seven Lost Years of *A Portrait of the Artist as a Young Man*."

VIII. CRITICAL STUDIES OF *Ulysses*. E. Pound, "*Ulysses*," in the *Dial*, 72 (June 1922), repr. in T. S. Eliot, ed., *Literary Essays of Ezra Pound*; V. Larbaud, "James Joyce," in *Nouvelle Revue française*, 24 (April 1922), trans. in *Criterion*, 1 (October 1922), the first explanation of the "structure" of *Ulysses*; S. Gilbert, *James Joyce's "Ulysses"* (London, 1930; rev. ed., 1952), written with the help of Joyce, gives an account of the Homeric parallels; C. G. Jung, "*Ulysses*: Ein Monolog," in *Europaische Revue*, 7 (1932), trans. in *Nimbus*, 2 (1953); M. L. Hanley et al., *Word Index to Joyce's "Ulysses"* (Madison, Wis., 1937).

R. M. Kain, *Fabulous Voyager* (Chicago, 1947), Joyce's uses of "facts" (i.e., newspapers, street maps, directories) in the writing of *Ulysses*; W. M. Schutte, *Joyce and Shakespeare: A Study in the Meaning of "Ulysses"* (New Haven, Conn., 1957); R. M. Adams, *Surface and Symbol: The Consistency of James Joyce's "Ulysses"* (New York, 1962); S. Sultan, *The Argument of "Ulysses"* (Columbus, Ohio, 1965), account of the narrative of *Ulysses*; H. Blamires, *The Bloomsday Book* (London, 1966), page-by-page narrative paraphrase, at times wrong; W. Thornton, *Allusions in "Ulysses"* (Chapel Hill, N.C., 1968), most useful.

D. Hayman, "*Ulysses*": *The Mechanics of Meaning* (Englewood Cliffs, N.J., 1970), first to give name to the Arranger as narrative device in *Ulysses*; T. F. Staley and B. Benstock, eds., *Approaches to "Ulysses"* (Pittsburgh, 1970), especially David Hayman's "The Empirical Molly"; R. Ellmann, *Ulysses on the Liffey* (New York, 1972); E. R. Steinberg, *The Stream of Consciousness and Beyond in "Ulysses"* (Pittsburgh, 1973); D. Gifford, with R. J. Seidman, *Notes for Joyce: An Annotation of James Joyce's "Ulysses"* (New York, 1974); C. Hart and D. Hayman, eds., *James Joyce's "Ulysses"* (Berkeley, Calif.–London, 1974), eighteen essays, one for each ch. of *Ulysses*, most of which are excellent; T. F. Staley, ed., "*Ulysses*": *Fifty Years* (Bloomington, Ind.–London, 1974); M. French, *The Book as World: James Joyce's "Ulysses"* (Cambridge, Mass.–London, 1976); M. Seidel, *Epic Geography: James Joyce's "Ulysses"* (Princeton, N.J., 1976), exploration of Joyce's use of Victor Bernard's *Les Pheniciens et l'Odyssée*; M.

Groden, *"Ulysses" in Progress* (Princeton, N.J., 1977), a complete account of the development of the text of *Ulysses;* J. H. Maddox, *Joyce's "Ulysses" and the Assault upon Character* (New Brunswick, N.J., 1978).

E. B. Gose, *The Transformation Process in Joyce's "Ulysses"* (Toronto–Buffalo, N.Y.-London, 1980), Freudian psychoanalytic theory applied to *Ulysses;* H. Kenner, *Ulysses* (London, 1980), interesting and stimulating general introduction to *Ulysses;* J. Gordon, *James Joyce's Metamorphoses* (Dublin–New York, 1981); K. Lawrence, *The Odyssey of Style in "Ulysses"* (Princeton, N.J., 1981), extremely good account of the stylistic "problems" of *Ulysses.*

IX. Critical Studies of *Finnegans Wake.* S. Beckett et al., *Our Exagmination Round His Factification for Incamination of Work in Progress* (Paris, 1929), reiss. with additional material (1961), Joyce said he "stood behind" the twelve authors, presumably directing their work; J. Campbell and H. M. Robinson, *A Skeleton Key to "Finnegans Wake"* (New York–London, 1944; ppbk. ed., New York, 1961), first attempt at page-by-page explication, still very good.

M. J. C. Hodgart, "Shakespeare and *Finnegans Wake,"* in *Cambridge Journal,* 6 (September 1953); J. S. Atherton, *"Finnegans Wake":* The Gist of the Pantomime," in *Accent,* 15 (Winter 1955); A. Glasheen, *"Finnegans Wake* and the Girls from Boston, Mass.," in *Hudson Review,* 7 (Spring 1955); A. Glasheen, *A Census of "Finnegans Wake"* (Evanston, Ill., 1956), followed by *A Second Census of "Finnegans Wake": An Index of the Characters and Their Roles* (Evanston, Ill., 1963), and *A Third Census of "Finnegans Wake"* (Berkeley–Los Angeles–London, 1977), very useful; D. Hayman, "From *Finnegans Wake:* A Sentence in Progress," in *PMLA,* 73, no. 1 (March 1958), a careful study of thirteen stages in Joyce's composition of a sentence.

J. S. Atherton, *The Books at the Wake: A Study of Literary Allusions in James Joyce's "Finnegans Wake"* (New York, 1960; rev. ed., 1974); F. H. Higginson, *"Anna Livia Plurabelle": The Making of a Chapter* (Minneapolis, 1960); F. Senn, "Some Zurich Allusions in *Finnegans Wake,"* in *Analyst,* 19 (December 1960), a thorough account by a native of Zurich; C. Hart, *Structure and Motif in "Finnegans Wake"* (London, 1962); C. Hart, *A Con-*cordance to *"Finnegans Wake"* (Austin, Tex., 1963; rev. ed., 1974); D. Johnston, "The Non-Information of *Finnegans Wake,"* in *Massachusetts Review* (Winter 1964), the entire issue is devoted to writers of twentieth-century Ireland; B. Benstock, *Joyce-Again's Wake: An Analysis of "Finnegans Wake"* (Seattle, 1965; repr. 1975); J. P. Dalton and C. Hart, eds., *Twelve and a Tilly: Essays on the Occasion of the 25th Anniversary of "Finnegans Wake"* (Evanston, Ill.-London, 1966), essays by A. Walton Litz, David Hayman, Richard M. Kain, and others; M. C. Solomon, *Eternal Geometer: The Sexual Universe of "Finnegans Wake"* (Carbondale, Ill., 1969); C. Hart and F. Senn, *A Wake Digest* (Sydney–University Park, Pa.-London, 1969), essays by Hart, Senn, Jack P. Dalton, Adaline Glasheen, and others; W. Y. Tindall, *A Reader's Guide to "Finnegans Wake"* (New York–London, 1969), a report on twenty years of studies at Columbia University.

M. Norris, *The Decentered Universe of "Finnegans Wake": A Structuralist Analysis* (Baltimore–London, 1977); R. McHugh, *Annotations to "Finnegans Wake"* (New York–London, 1980); D. Rose and J. O'Hanlon, *Understanding "Finnegans Wake"* (New York–London, 1982).

X. Special Joyce Journals. *Note:* Several periodicals have been devoted entirely to the task of interpreting Joyce's works. Among them are the following: *James Joyce Review* (New York), ed. E. Epstein, appeared in four quarterly numbers in 1957 and as a single "double number" in 1958, and in 1959, when it ceased publication, several important articles were published in it; the *Analyst,* ed. Robert Mayo, published occasionally by the Department of English, Northwestern University, has devoted many issues entirely to Joyce and published articles, sometimes lengthy ones, by John V. Kelleher, Adaline Glasheen, Fritz Senn, and others; *A Wake Newslitter,* ed. Clive Hart and Fritz Senn, now published in Colchester, England, through the Department of English, University of Essex, first eighteen numbers (March 1962–March 1963), which had no official support, contained articles by Thornton Wilder, M. J. C. Hodgart, Adaline Glasheen, Nathan Halper, the eds., and many others; *James Joyce Quarterly* (University of Tulsa), ed. T. F. Staley, has been appearing since autumn 1963, now the official publication of the James Joyce Society.

IVY COMPTON-BURNETT
(1884-1969)

R. Glynn Grylls

I

Ivy Compton-Burnett was born on 5 June 1884 at Pinner, Middlesex, the daughter of a doctor with a successful homeopathic practice. Her father had five children from his first marriage; Ivy was the eldest of seven by his second wife, so that she was brought up in a large family. She was very close to her two brothers Guy and Noel. Guy died young, and Noel was killed in World War I. Dame Ivy, until the end of her life, kept up with Noel's contemporaries in what had been a brilliant set at King's College, Cambridge. She broke away from the closed circle (*huis clos*) of family life to go to the Royal Holloway College, where she studied classics. She already knew Greek and Latin from having shared her brothers' tutors. She received an honorary degree from the University of Leeds in 1960.

Dame Ivy lived in London from the 1930's on; as she became well known she allowed admirers to call on her at her flat in Cornwall Gardens. She could seem formidable as a hostess, for, once the tributes of chocolates or flowers (which had to be put into water immediately) had been graciously accepted, conversation could be a problem to the uninitiated. She had no interest in current affairs and none of the usual author's vanity in talking about her own books. She enjoyed gossip, particularly about her friends' pecuniary affairs, and was generous in the interest she took in their activities.

Her first book, *Dolores*, which she later preferred to disown, was published at her own expense in 1911. *The Last and the First*, her final book, was posthumously published in 1971, so that it is right to begin the list with *Pastors and Masters* of 1925, as the first of a series.

II

ONE has to tune in to the novels of Ivy Compton-Burnett; there is her authentic note to be caught and certain conventions of time and place, character and dialogue to be accepted. The atmosphere in which her people live and move and have their being (biblical echoes are frequent in her work from early training, not from accepted religious belief) is at once rarefied and down to earth; trivial and yet profound; abstract in that all inessentials have been cut away, and concrete in its everyday setting. On such paradoxes is based the peculiar essence of her work. Her dialogue is simple but subtle, and her characters are ordinary people (that is, they have been brought up in conventional circumstances and are without personal eccentricities) involved in extraordinary situations—cheating, bigamy, suicide, even murder. Their reactions to these are what anybody's would be, mostly bad. We are all criminals, given the chance; our homes all whited sepulchers.

The novels are sui generis: nothing quite like them has come before nor will likely come after. Attempts to find them a literary ancestor or some relation in a modern movement have always proved abortive. Dame Ivy herself would have none of it: she accepted graciously any mention of Jane Austen's name in the same breath as her own, but to Thomas Love Peacock or George Meredith or Henry James, if they were introduced, she extended a polite bow but no sign of recognition. Although Edward Sackville-West was a personal friend and an early admirer of her work, she would have greeted sardonically the *Horizon* article in which he wrote:

the effect of her art recalls the aims of the Cubist Movement in painting, at its inception. Like a Picasso of 1913, a Compton-Burnett novel is not concerned with decoration or with observation of the merely contingent . . . it is constructive, ascetic, low in tone, classical. It inquires into the meanings—the syntactical force—of the things we all say, as the Cubist inquired into the significance of shapes and planes divorced from the incidence of light and the accidents of natural or utilitarian construction.

("An Appraisal," June 1946)

To unsympathetic critics or readers such interpretations will evoke the exasperation expressed by J. B. Priestley writing of "the rockets of praise bursting into a hundred blazing over-statements"; but once attuned to the art of Dame Ivy, one can find everything there: "the syntactical force" and even the elements of de Sade detected by Mario Praz, however unselfconscious about them was the author herself in her complete indifference to any analysis of what she wrote or to possible literary influences.

In approaching the novels we must accept certain conditions as we would at a play. There is a formal painted backcloth that serves many scenes, and actors, made up to look a little larger than life, come forward to speak their lines and often their thoughts in dialogue that is at once natural and highly selected and condensed.

The background to the novels is, in time, the turn of the century or earlier, and, in place, a shabby country house with a run-down estate to be managed. "I do not feel," Dame Ivy once declared, "that I have any real organic knowledge of life later than about 1910," and "I have not been at all deedy."

> The old house in question was large and beautiful and shabby, but only the last to any unusual degree. It had the appeal of a place where lack of means had prevented the addition of new things, and ensured care of the old. The land about it stretched to a fair distance, and in the past had provided its support.
>
> (*A God and His Gifts*, ch. 2)

The household (in two of the novels a school is substituted) is the home of a family whose members seldom escape into a larger world either through having a career or simply moving away. This is a convention but actors must have a stage, and if members of a family never at any time really live on top of each other in this way, equally they cannot get away from their backgrounds and their families, their environment and their heredity. These are things that are there; escape is impossible and kicking against the pricks useless.

The dialogue of the novels is at once simple, with few polysyllables or involved constructions, but complex with allusions, undertones, and dramatic irony. Proverbs and clichés are often quoted in order to turn them inside out to discover their truth:

> "You must take me as I am, as people say. As though that justified their being what they are, when probably nothing could."
>
> (*A Heritage and Its History*, ch. 12)

> "'Know thyself' is a most superfluous direction. We can't avoid it."
>
> "We can only hope that no one else knows," said Dudley.
>
> (*A Family and a Fortune*, ch. 1)

In her conversations Dame Ivy employs a technique for which it is difficult to find a name; diagonal, perhaps, for it is the unexpected part of a question or a statement that is answered. In *Daughters and Sons* the family is discussing the reason for Mrs. Ponsonby's death:

> "I do not know. It would only have taken a slight thing to kill her."
>
> "Then it was not Hetta's speech," said Miss Marcon. "That was not a slight thing."
>
> (ch. 11)

And in *A Family and a Fortune*, the family is discussing pork:

> "It is certainly odd that civilised people should have it on their tables."
>
> "Do uncivilised people have things on their tables?"
>
> (ch. 1)

The talk is cut on the cross, sharply and not to waste, for every thread has its place when it is pieced together.

The way in which conversations are overheard, often by unashamed listening at keyholes or answers to unuttered thoughts, is a convention Dame Ivy imposes. So often in life, after all, we can read the thoughts of other people. Similarly with the revelation of family secrets in public—they would have come out in any case. As Dame Ivy wrote in one of her novels: "Secrets are not often kept. If they were, we should not know there were such things."

Her "artificial" plots involving murder, incest, betrayals of trust (by destroying wills or opening letters) have to be accepted because such drastic situations serve to reveal character. Someone is shown up in a moment of crisis for what he or she really is, which it would take a lifetime of ordinary intercourse to disclose. "People have a way of not coming out well in a temptation. They generally behave quite as ill as they can, don't they?" Dame Ivy remarked in an interview with Kay Dick in the *Times* (London), 30 August 1969.

It is sometimes objected that her backgrounds are unreal because they are out-of-date—there is no servants' hall today—and because social problems are ignored. So they are, in the sense of economic and political problems, but nowhere since Jane Austen has there been a keener sense of personal relations in society.

Dame Ivy's concern is with people; how they react to other people and to outside forces that confront them. The fact that the sphere in which they move is limited does not matter. It is limited in the sense that it is a microcosm. The novels are sometimes said to be based on the elements of Greek tragedy, but this is so only in the sense that the crises, "reversals" (peripeteia in Greek drama), and recognitions (anagnōrises) are inevitably of the stuff of drama, and that Dame Ivy is adept at planting clues which involve dramatic irony.

The characters in the novels are nonrepresentational but realistic, often types or "humors," and yet individuals, so that although they may recur there is something new each time. The dramatis personae may be divided into three groups: first, that of the protagonist, the "tyrant" who exercises power in a household or institution. Then there is a secondary group of friends or local clergy, doctors, or solicitors, who begin by being clearly drawn but are sometimes neglected afterward, with their final fate not recorded: they serve as foils to the primary characters. The third group stands out more clearly than the second, although it seems at first sight further removed from the main scene of action. It consists of employees such as domestic servants or tutors and companions, or groups of young children, all of whom are kept helpless by their subjection. The significance of this grouping was well brought out in the stage productions of *A Heritage and Its History* and *A Family and a Fortune*. Children are not on the wavelength of the crimes and sins committed by their elders, but feel the atmosphere of them and take refuge in their own world or in a nursery world sheltered by a nanny: "They loved her [Bennet, the nurse] not as themselves, and greater love hath no child than this" (*The Present and the Past*, ch. 1).

III

THE dominant theme in Dame Ivy's novels is vanity—the demand for attention, whether admiration or pity—and this is served by the exercise of power, for power is important only when it is acknowledged and self-esteem is thereby satisfied. Power may stem from authority or fame; sometimes it is exercised through sex, that is, as the result of a personal attraction that holds another in thrall, as with the young second wives that widowers, like Duncan Edgeworth in *A House and Its Head* (1935) and Miles Mowbray in *A Father and His Fate* (1957), tend, unsuitably, to marry to bolster their vanity.

The sexual act itself is treated as unimportant, except for what leads up to it and what follows from it. There may be momentous consequences from a moment's indiscretion (Dame Ivy's births often seem to result from instant and immaculate conception), as in *A Heritage and Its History* (1959), where Simon loses his right to the property he loves and would serve well, because of an heir who is really his own child, and the cousins who are in love cannot marry because they find they share a father. Rhoda Challenor, the grandmother, makes a comment that is characteristic of the author when she says about the sexual act: "It has been so much to follow from so little."

Affection that does not provide admiration or minister to the claims of self-pity is not enough. In *Brothers and Sisters* (1929) the widowed Sophia complains at the dinner table: "I don't think I should be left without a little pressing, sitting here, as I am, with my life emptied." And in the posthumous book, *The Last and the First*, Eliza Heriot, a domineering materfamilias, sinks into tears when one of her stepdaughters escapes from her power.

But Dame Ivy recognizes the tragedy attendant on power: the tyrant forfeits the affection of those about him by accepting the responsibility his power brings and its corruption of him. Those who opt out may show a certain charm at first, but it wears thin when they refuse the opportunity to play their part in the world, like the younger brothers—Hugo in *The Mighty and Their Fall* (1961) and Dudley in *A Family and a Fortune* (1939).

The exercise of power is shown at its most direct in the bullying of families by their rulers (fathers and mothers), who impose on them excessive demands of affection and submission and inflict unnecessary economies on the household. Institutions also have their tyrants. In the school setting of *More Women than Men* (1933), the headmistress, Josephine Napier, bullies her staff, her pupils, and their parents, each in a separate way. This is how she deals with an importunate parent:

"Would you recommend my girl to learn the violin?" Josephine placed her hand on the speaker's shoulder.

"I should not, at the moment. I must find what her

talents are, what her health is, in a word, who she is, before I offer an opinion. There are people who will tell me all these things."

"The girls of today are fortunate," said the mother, realising the distance between her child and the person in charge of her. "Will you ask someone to write to me?"

"I *hope* to write you myself," said Josephine, emphasising her second word, and leaving her companion in favour of the state it indicated, as compared with certainty.

(ch. 8)

Most important in its relation to power is money. Dame Ivy is fascinated by the influence exerted by the sudden acquisition of money, the way it corrupts the recipient and those about him. "Riches are a test of character and I am exposed," says Dudley in *A Family and a Fortune*, the novel based most fully on the subject. When the news comes out, no one pays any attention to the exact sum. The tutor, Penrose, congratulates Dudley on "the sudden accession of a quarter of a million to the family."

"It is about a twentieth of a million," said Dudley.
"Well, well, Mr Dudley, putting it in round numbers."
"But surely numbers are not as round as that. What is the good of numbers? I thought they were an exact science."

(ch. 4)

Then, although at first they decently demur, everyone expects to have some benefit for himself or for some cause in which he is interested (still a form of selfishness). *A Family and a Fortune* also provides a study of the ingratitude of relations receiving financial benefits. Matty, the invalid spinster sister, despises the small house allocated to her by the Gavestons at a low rent:

"I think [said Edgar] we might suggest the rent we would ask from a stranger and then see what their not being strangers might cost us."

(ch. 1)

Matty loses no opportunity of making snide remarks. Her niece, Justine, the most patient with her, is wearing a new dress with which she is rather pleased:

"What is the colour?" said Matty, her easy tone revealing her opinion that enough had been said on the matter. "Magenta?"

"No dear," said Blanche [the girl's mother]. "It is a kind of old rose."

(ch. 3)

Could two names given to a color tell more of a story?

Money and its catalytic influence are brought out under other aspects. In *The Mighty and Their Fall*, Hugo's flabbiness of will is revealed when a timely legacy saves him from marrying Lavinia (the fact that she turns out to be his half-niece has not deterred him from consenting to set up house with her). There is also the subtheme of meanness when in *Manservant and Maidservant* (1947) Horace Lamb economizes with his wife's money as a way of saving it. The marriage is summed up:

Horace had married her [Charlotte] for her money, hoping to serve his impoverished estate, and she had married him for love, hoping to fulfil herself. The love had gone and the money remained, so that the advantage lay with Horace, if he could have taken so hopeful a view of his life.

(ch. 1)

Nor does a family come out well from the lack of money; exceptional are the Marlowes, the two sisters and their brother in *Parents and Children* (1941), one of whom says shrewdly:

"Well, the English have no family feelings. That is, none of the kind you mean. They have them, and one of them is that relations must cause no expense."

(ch. 3)

The implications of the theme of power and of other related aspects of Dame Ivy's work have been trenchantly illuminated by Mario Praz in his 1966 essay "I romanzi di Ivy Compton-Burnett":

The universal theme of Miss Compton-Burnett's novels is nothing less than the hell which rages behind the respectable façade of the middle-class households [*case borghesi*] of the latest Victorian period: a theme which the author never indulges in the easy way of cheap effects, falling neither into melodrama nor miracles [*nel teratologico*]. . . . In her novels we find events much more striking than in those of Dickens, but without any sense of improbability. . . .

Oh! there are terrible scourges in this self-satisfied Victorian society, as probably in all societies, but the patina of respectability, which must be safeguarded at all costs, makes them more sinister. . . . But he would be deceived who considered the dominant theme of these novels was sexual passion, so much repressed at this time: the dominant theme of these novels is the lust for power. In all families there are tyrants, victims and witnesses, secret calvaries, buried hatreds [*sorde ostilità*], struggles in order to break the will of another person who, according to the ethos of the epoch, owes a tribute of submission; struggles to secure favor in a will. All this happens between 1885 and 1901; women were wearing the bustle and men the bowler, but they seem to be playing in a much older drama, the Greek or the Elizabethan, in modern dress. . . .

Here this Sybil with lips compressed like a suction plug [*dalle labbra strette da una ventosa di grinze*], as she appears in a portrait, looks an English spinster such as you might meet in an Assisi *pension*. Let us confess that she frightens us. She frightens us more than that poor devil of a Marquis de Sade.

(*Cronache letterarie anglosassoni*, vol. IV)

IV

DAME IVY may not use the terms "exploited" and "oppressed," but she is fully conscious of them. She has compassion for the underdog, whether it is the younger servants bullied by butler and cook, children in the nursery or at school, or those earning their bread in social limbo, the governesses and companions whose gentility handicaps them in their proper claims to consideration and payment. Terence, when he is teaching his cousin, Reuben, in *Elders and Betters* (1941), says:

"My service is of a kind that cannot be paid for in money. And that means it is paid for in that way, but not very well."

At the same time she knows the paradox of pity—how irritating the pitiable can be, whether George, the overcompensated houseboy from the orphanage in *Manservant and Maidservant*, or the companion, Miss Griffin, in *A Family and a Fortune*, turned out in the snow by her employer and rescued by Dudley:

Her short, quick, unequal steps, the steps of someone used to being on her feet, but not to walking out of doors, made no attempt to keep time or pace, and he saw with a pang how she might try the nerves of anyone in daily contact.

(ch. 8)

Often it is the "exploited" who have to be appeased by their employers. In the world of *Elders and Betters* Cook and the housemaid, Ethel, make themselves felt when they arrive. The mistress hastens to explain that the house is not as high as it looks:

"There are only two real storeys to the house; that is, only three floors above the ground floor, if you count the small one you have to yourselves," said Jenney, seeming to resort to complication to cover some truth.

(ch. 1)

The insolence of office is timeless, whether we suffer it today from waitresses and shop assistants who make the customer feel small, or from a butler such as Buttermere in *Men and Wives* (1931). He is told to show Mr. Spon where to wash, and duly indicates the cloakroom:

"The water is hot, sir," said Buttermere, standing by the open door, and producing the impression that for many people he would have turned the tap.

(ch. 19)

Despite her sympathy for the underdog, Dame Ivy finds it difficult not to be irritated by most of her governesses and tutors. Some hold their own by letting indifference (or a small private income) provide them with thicker skins and the ability to work to rule; and some companion-helps are revenged on their bullying employers by earning the confidence of the children, like Patty in *Brothers and Sisters* or Miss Manders in *A Family and a Fortune*, who has the last word on the family secret that is unknown to her employer.

But many wilt under the keen glances of their pupils and the careless ones of their employers (Mr. Penrose in *A Family and a Fortune* can never hold their attention long enough to finish a sentence); or they make things worse for themselves by seeking refuge in a heightened gentility, like Miss Bunyan in *Daughters and Sons* (1937), who thinks it indelicate to have a normal appetite. Miss Hallam in the same book speaks of herself as "the classic governess driven by necessity"; and of Miss Gibson in *A Father and His Fate* someone says:

"She is perhaps hardly educated enough for a governess."
"Well, if she was she would not be one."

(ch. 1)

In private life Dame Ivy was proud of having been educated at home with her brothers. She respected the universities of Oxford and Cambridge, and some of her young men characters gain fellowships and seem to be vaguely admired for this, although they are not shown as leaving home to take them up

(Clement in *A Family and a Fortune*). The studious Gidean Doubleday in *Manservant and Maidservant* regrets: "I paid too much attention to my studies when I was young, and that does lead to people being tutors." It seems to be the same attitude expressed by Bernard Shaw: "Those that can, do; those that can't, teach."

Teachers in schools are no more respected. Mrs. Chattaway's qualifications for teaching English are described in *More Women than Men*: "Her husband had been blamed for leaving her without provision, but with some injustice, as she was qualified for teaching English literature, by being the widow of a man who wrote" (ch. 1).

Dame Ivy has a scorn of "Eng. Lit." as a degree subject, perhaps a soft option to one accustomed to a classical education:

> "What does she teach?" said Zillah.
> "Something to the younger boys."
> "Don't you know what it is?"
> "I know what it is called. The name is *English*."
> "What does she call it?"
> "*English.* I said that was the name."
> "Does not she know what it is?"
> "No, or she would be teaching older boys."
>
> (*A God and His Gifts*, ch. 10)

She put aside any talk of her novels' deliberately following Greek tragedies, and she uses very few literary quotations. Two lines from Christina Rossetti's sonnet "Remember" occur three times:

> Better by far you should forget and smile
> Than that you should remember and be sad

—a stoical outlook that she appreciated, but she made a character in *Men and Wives* add:

> "It is we normal people who have nearly a heart-ache because people do not remember and are not sad."
>
> (ch. 16)

Her historical allusions are all lightly mocking, as if history, like religious observance, was rather absurd:

> "Was Uncle like a man with a mistress in history?"
> "Yes," said Francis, "but when it is not in history, it seems to be different."
> "And the man who was Rosebery's father, was the same?"

> "Yes," said Alice; "but when the mistress is Aunt Miranda, it seems more different still."
>
> (*Mother and Son*, ch. 10)

And on Oedipus blinding himself: "Perhaps fashions have changed. It does not seem that Oedipus was thought to have acted oddly under the circumstances."

Some of her humorous asides may start on the level of the comic social history of Walter C. Sellar and Robert J. Yeatman's *1066 and All That* (1958), but the authentic note comes through at the end. In *Parents and Children* the guilty Ridley takes the center of the stage:

> "You make me feel he is in the pillory, and that you would like to throw rotten eggs at him," said Hope [his stepmother].
> "How did people come by their supplies of eggs in that state," said Isabel. "Did they carry a stock of them, as if they were snuff or tobacco?"
> "Perhaps they were on sale near the pillory," said Daniel, "as buns and nuts are at the Zoo, so that people could be helped to their natural dealings with captive creatures."
>
> (ch. 1)

No type of personality is more completely understood and subtly drawn than that of the writer. She has no use for the silent artist who makes excuses for his incapacity, the lack of a "stronger brain and greater creative force." Mr. Middleton in *A Family and a Fortune* is one of these:

> He had wanted to write, and had been a schoolmaster because of the periods of leisure, but had found that the demands of the other periods exhausted his energy. After his marriage to a woman of means he was still prevented, though he did not give the reason, indeed did not know it. Neither did he state what he wished to write, and this was natural, as he had not yet decided.
>
> (ch. 3)

And she pokes fun as delicately as she did in life, with a half smile and shake of the head, at those who regard novels (particularly if they sell) as a lighter, inferior form of literature—"only" fiction. One of her most delightful heroines, Charity Marcon in *Daughters and Sons*, mocks her own biographical researches:

> "I have been up to London to get the book I am writing, out of the British Museum. I have got a lot of it out, and I shall go up again presently to get some more; and when I have got it all, there will be another book. . . . So many

people were there, getting out their books. It doesn't seem to matter everything's being in books already: I don't mind it at all. There are attendants there on purpose to bring it to you. That is how books are made, and it is difficult to think of any other way. I mean the kind called serious: light books are different. . . ."

(ch. 3)

Dame Ivy had complete understanding of the vanity of the artist. In *A God and His Gifts* (1963), Hereward Egerton, the best-selling novelist, does not want his son, Merton, to follow in his footsteps for fear he might overtake him, and on his side Merton despises his father's success and wants to devote himself to "serious" work. In *Daughters and Sons*, this theme is more deeply explored with John Ponsonby's obsessive jealousy of the success of his daughter, France.

Dame Ivy has pity as well as complete understanding for the scholar whose passionate desire to bring a book to birth leads him to steal one from the bedside of his dying friend, as in *Pastors and Masters*, where Nicholas Herrick succumbs to the temptation.

There is also the attitude of other people to the writer—those who flatter themselves that they could do quite as well if they chose to give their minds to it:

". . . I always feel I could write a novel, if I tried. But I am a bad person for trying, and that is the truth."

"You may be a bad person for achieving. Anyone can try."

(*A God and His Gifts*, ch. 2)

and those who underrate the hard work involved:

"But it must be very beautiful, Jermyn, to go wandering about on the moors, notebook in hand, and jot down any little poetic thoughts—" Dominic made a waving movement with his hand—"that come to the mind with the beauty of everything around. To go roaming hither and thither, with nothing to do but let the fancies crowd through one's brain. If the real business of life had not claimed me, if I had not been vowed upon a somewhat sterner altar, I should have been happy to take my share in the more graceful side of life."

(*Men and Wives*, ch. 6)

V

THE deepest and most satisfactory relationships in the novels are those between equals, their self-esteem balanced: usually brothers who at the end of the

story are reconciled to the loss of wife or fortune so long as their own companionship remains; between siblings; or more rarely, between two women friends. There need be no sexual intercourse involved—"What some people call 'Lesbian,'" Dame Ivy would say, quotation marks poised as delicately as raised eyebrows, and with that gesture of sweeping imaginary crumbs from her skirt which was a literal brush-off of the presumptuous. She was fully cognizant of modern psychoanalytic jargon and mocked it:

Those who always say a thing is something else and tell you what it is. And of course it is that, and we know about it; but it is better not to say what we know.

(*Mother and Son*)

In the same book Emma Greatheart says:

"I know nothing about him except that he is attached to his mother."

"There is no need to know him any better. That is enough in these days."

(ch. 5)

In *Two Worlds and Their Ways* (1949) the schoolmasters who pair off, Oliver Shelley and Oliver Spode, are warned by the headmaster to avoid too conspicuous a friendship:

"I have met the two problems of school [Oliver Shelley tells his family], cheating and this."

(ch. 4)

Dame Ivy's favorite people (they can hardly be called heroines) are middle-aged, intelligent women with a sense of humor and no nonsense about them: for instance, the grandmother, Rhoda Challenor, in *A Heritage and Its History*; the author, Charity Marcon, in *Daughters and Sons*. A woman who nearly makes it but is subtly flawed is Hope Cranmer in *Parents and Children* (1941):

"There is something second-rate going through Hope," said Susan. "She thinks she makes it better by joking about it."

(ch. 5)

Heroes are fewer and appear only in supporting roles, such as the good-natured Sir Roderick Shelley in *Two Worlds and Their Ways* or the sardonic Dr. Anthony Dufferin in *Men and Wives*. Without admiring, Dame Ivy has a soft spot for the intellectual if ineffectual homosexual (although the term is not used) like Sir Felix Bacon in *More Women than Men*.

Children enjoy a special place in the novels, representing an exploited class. She is entirely on their side in *Two Worlds and Their Ways* when they come back with reports of cheating from the boarding school to which Sir Roderick and Lady Shelley have been persuaded to send them. She may be on their side, but she acknowledges their self-centeredness and their lack of sympathetic imagination, although they have plenty of fancy. Neville in *Parents and Children* wants a bow and arrow so as to shoot live birds and refuses to see Faith's objection to this. He offers to have one stuffed for her as a compromise.

Children's relation to animal life is exquisitely shown, a mixture of curiosity and dismay but little pity, in the opening chapter of *The Present and the Past* (1953). The group of three is watching hens pecking to death one of their number who is ill:

"Oh dear, oh dear," said Henry Clare.
His sister glanced in his direction.
"They are pecking the sick one. They are angry because it is ill."
"Perhaps it is because they are anxious," said Megan, looking at the hens in the hope of discerning this feeling.

Tobias, aged three, pushes pieces of cake through the wire, and then eats them himself when they are ignored by the hens. He hopes that his offering will have made the sick one better:

"He did get some," said Toby looking from face to face for reassurance. "Toby gave it to him."
He turned to inspect the position, which was now that the hens, no longer competing for crumbs, had transferred their activity to their disabled companion.

In *Elders and Betters* the children, Theodora and Julius, build a shrine in the garden and take offerings there to propitiate their god, called Sung Hi. No one was more indifferent to anything occult than Dame Ivy, and these devotions represent the way in which primitive man tries to propitiate Fate, or some god, by prayer and sacrifices. Children in their innocence live again this history of the race; it is something she feels the adult should outgrow. To appreciate Dame Ivy's authentic note in handling these scenes, they may be compared with similar episodes in Iris Murdoch's *The Sandcastle* (1957); it is caviar to salmon paste.

Dame Ivy's least favorite characters are firstly bullies, then hypocrites, closely followed by bores. Often the two latter go together, for there is nothing of interest below the surface. Such are the grief-stricken Dominic Spong in *Men and Wives*, who accepts no less than four invitations from condoling friends following his wife's funeral, and Peter Bateman, the unsuccessful family solicitor in *Brothers and Sisters*, "an almost startling example of failure to rise above lack of advantages."

Some of her best-drawn characters are the well-meaning women bores. She succeeds in writing about them without being boring herself—a very demanding art. We long to have another chance of watching them drop their bricks, intensely irritating as we know they are to the other characters: Dulcia in *A House and Its Head* with her second-hand slang—"I'll go bail he will not raise Cain; I undertake to square him"—and Justine in *A Family and a Fortune*. Both are brash young women who make matters worse by their apologies for putting their feet in it:

"Oh, Father, what a crass and senseless speech [exclaims Justine]. Why do I talk about people's want of comprehension? . . . I hope there is one self left behind."
"It is hard on the people, who assist Justine's rise on her dead selves to higher things," said Clement [her brother].
(ch. 7)

Equally clumsy and also plain to look at is Anna in *Elders and Betters*, but she is malevolent as well. She destroys her aunt's will in order to inherit her money, yet demands sympathy because the crime was committed out of love. With money she can marry her cousin, Terence, although she had virtually killed his mother, Jessica Calderon, who died of grief that her sister should have omitted to leave anything to her or her family.

And the most boring function that Dame Ivy can conceive is the parish ladies' working party making garments for the poor or the heathen. It is petticoats for orphans in *A House and Its Head* and embroidered aprons in *Men and Wives*. Mrs. Christy, the culture-vulture before her time—"often there fell to her the happy phrase, the sudden flash of cultural memory"—says:

"Now I think it is such a good thought of Lady Haslam's to have some of the things embroidered. It shows a true sympathy with those less fortunate than ourselves. . . ."

[Polly says she cannot embroider.]

"But my dear you must. You are working for the poor."

"The cutting out of things is more our problem than embroidering them," said Agatha, adjusting her work.

(ch. 15)

Dame Ivy did not care for "do-gooders"—even less for the expression. She considered altruism too often served a person's self-interest and self-esteem, and could be humiliating to those at the receiving end:

"At any time you might act for my good. When people do that, it kills something precious between them."

(*Manservant and Maidservant*)

And subtly she realizes the inherent weakness of affection based on grief or troubles shared:

"You were a friend in need," said Juliet. "That would lead to growing apart. When the need is ended, both sides want a different sort of friend. And one sees the reason."

(*Two Worlds and Their Ways*)

VI

In books so distilled, with no stage directions (few entrances or exits) and rare descriptions, it is surprising to find some characters introduced with full labels to them; for instance:

Christian Stace [the adopted son] was a large, dark man of thirty, looking and seeming more, with a wide face and head, deep set eyes, and the touch of sameness in gesture and voice to the Staces by blood, that grows from a long common life.

(*Brothers and Sisters*, ch. 1)

More usually she hits off her characters in a few phrases that enable the reader to see them for himself. As, for instance, Mrs. Duff in chapter 2 of *The Last and the First*: "a middle-aged woman in undisguisedly working garb, with an inharmonious face and a responsible aspect."

But the features she catalogs do not contribute anything to the part their owners play later in the story, even in cases of unusual beauty, whether the attractions of a young woman like Alison in *A House*

and Its Head ("fair skin and hair, liquid hazel eyes") or the divorced Camilla in *Men and Wives*, or the faded good looks of Lady Haslam in the same book. Such details may have been useful to Dame Ivy to keep the character before her own eyes while writing, for looks were important to her, but she does not make her readers feel their relevance.

Another point on which it is difficult to follow her intentions concerns the names given to characters. She stresses their importance, but nothing seems to arise from it. She does not avoid duplication: there is a lame Reuben aged thirteen in *Elders and Betters* and another Reuben who "at three was puny with a pinched plain face" in *A God and His Gifts*.

When the apple-cheeked housemaid Miriam, in *Manservant and Maidservant*, longs to have had a flower name, Dame Ivy makes points of pathos and irony:

"What kind of name do you like?"

"A name like Rose," said Miriam, with a sort of glow in her voice.

"Well, perhaps you would like to be called a lily as well," said Cook.

Miriam's eyes showed that this was the case.

(ch. 1)

But there seems no reason why in *Two Worlds and Their Ways* she says of the dormant headmaster, Lucius: "His name of Cassidy seemed to have arisen out of himself," or of the solicitors in *A God and His Gifts*: "Messrs Blount and Middleman, names that strike a chill to my soul."

Sometimes there is a literary allusion—one suspects for her own amusement. In *Parents and Children*, Lady Sullivan is called Regan, a name

chosen by her father, a man of country tastes, and, as it must appear, of no others, who had learned from an article on Shakespeare that his women were people of significance, and decided that his daughter should bear the name of one of them, in accordance with his hopes.

(ch. 1)

In her final novel, *The Last and the First*, there is a similar allusion. Dame Ivy says of the mother, Jocasta Grimstone: "Her Christian name had been chosen by a parent with more respect for the classics than knowledge of them"; and of her relations with her son, Hamilton: "she felt to him as a son but had her own view of him as a man and was in no danger of her namesake's history."

VII

A chronological list of Dame Ivy's novels is given in the bibliography. It has not been my intention here to run through these with synopses or to attempt any classification or grading, for each book has its own place. I have tried to show their special quality by references and quotations, and in line with this I propose to indicate an approach to them helpful to the newcomer. But first there must be a word on *Dolores*, written in collaboration with one of her brothers and published in 1911. Fourteen years elapsed before the next, *Pastors and Masters*, which inaugurated the series that appeared at roughly two-year intervals. *The Last and the First* was published posthumously.[1]

Dame Ivy very much disliked any reference to *Dolores* and gave her familiar brush-off to anyone who "thought themselves clever" by knowing about it. For all that a word must be said. It is interesting for what it puts in that the later novels cut out; it is as if the scaffolding had been left up. The opening has this description of a funeral:

It is a daily thing: a silent, unvisited churchyard; bordering the garden of the parsonage; and holding a church whose age and interest spare our words. . . . Let us mark the figure foremost in the sombre throng, that clerical figure of heavy build and with bent head.

So the Reverend Cleveland Hutton is the forerunner of other middle-aged clergy of heavy build to come—the skeptical Oscar Jekyll in *A House and Its Head*, for instance, "a strong, solid man about thirty-eight," whose sermons persuade his parishioners that "faith as deep as his would hardly appear on the surface." There are pointers to the wit ahead too: "Mrs. Hutton was one of the women, to whom masculine failings have a strong excuse in being masculine" (ch. 2). And there is a situation of tragic irony, to be repeated in different contexts later, when the father, for whom the daughter, Dolores, gives up her career to keep house, ungratefully marries a second wife.

The two easiest books to start on are *Pastors and Masters* and *Mother and Son* (1955), one early, one late. Between them come the vintage years of the

longer books with more characters and what happens to them more fully worked out, as in *More Women than Men*, where the background is a school, or *Manservant and Maidservant*, which gives us the household torture chamber par excellence, or *Two Worlds and Their Ways*, where there is a home and school combined.

Pastors and Masters is set in a school that provides the background for the exercise of power by Mr. Merry, the headmaster, who combines the characteristics of the bully and the hypocritical bore. The owner of the establishment is Nicholas Herrick, who gives tone to it on public occasions by appearing in his M.A. gown (which Mr. Merry lacks) and being impressively vague. Both he and his college friend, Richard Bumpus, long to have produced a published book, and at the deathbed of their contemporary "old Crabbe" a manuscript is found. Herrick claims to have written it. The discovery of his fraud is made when the book is read aloud at the request of Emily Herrick, the devoted sister. All the elements of dramatic irony are there, in the moment of revelation with its double entendre:

"It came to me" says Herrick, "as I sat there, the whole thing, the whole book. There it was. I can't explain it."

(ch. 6)

In *Mother and Son* there is a superb opening scene where the domineering mistress of the house, Miranda Hume, interviews a companion. She is a matriarch who ignores her husband, adores her son, Rosebery, and does her duty grudgingly toward the three children—her husband's niece and two nephews—who are in reality his own offspring:

"Good morning, Miss—Burke," she said, referring openly to a paper at her hand, and not concerned with the fact that it was afternoon.

(ch. 1)

The companion is sent away but finds a congenial post in the neighborhood with Miss Greatheart and Miss Wolsey. The latter is about to leave, as she has lost her money and refuses to be dependent on her friend. She takes the post at the Humes' and is very successful there, both with Mrs. Hume and with the father and the son. Rosebery proposes to her. She prefers the father, but he wants to marry Miss Greatheart. In the end the three women refuse the offers of marriage made to them and decide to make their home together.

[1]The unfinished and uncorrected manuscript was found by her biographer, Elizabeth Sprigge, who helped to edit it and wrote the foreword; a critical epilogue was contributed by Charles Burkhart.

There is a subservient tutor, Mr. Pettigrew, and an example of Dame Ivy's supreme artistry occurs in the picture she draws of two cats, animals she disliked in life. The names given to the cats in the two households mark them: Tabbikin, kept to control possible mice and banished to the kitchen, and Plautus, served and adored upstairs. "The difference between the two households stands exposed," says Rosebery.

A conversation about the adored cat provides an example of characteristic diagonal talk:

"Why do you call him 'Plautus'?" said Miss Burke, encouraged by this simple statement of truth.

"Oh, because he *is* Plautus," said Miss Wolsey. "Because the essence of Plautus is in him. How could he be called anything else?"

"Who was Plautus in real life?"

"Who could he have been but the person to give this Plautus his name?"

"He was a Latin writer," said Miss Greatheart, as Miss Burke left a second question unanswered. "I think he wrote plays; not very good ones."

"Why did you call the cat after him?"

"Well, he has not written any good plays either," said Miss Wolsey, holding out her hand to Plautus.

(ch. 3)

The book also provides one of the best examples of the profundities in Dame Ivy's writing that often underlie an apparently trivial observation. When visitors are expected, the hostess discusses how much difference should be made in the normal running of the household:

"Do we use the same china as usual?"

"I am ashamed to say we use a better one. We make a difference for guests, which of course stamps us. And we behave as if we did not, which stamps us further. It shows we do things we are ashamed of. But then I think we ought to be ashamed. . . ."

"Our ordinary china is cracked and mended. But it is old and good. I should think it is rather rare."

"Oh, then we will use it. Cracked and mended, but rather rare! That strikes the exact note. It is like fine old linen carefully darned. I suppose we have not any linen like that?"

(ch. 5)

The artistry in her observation of the ways of a cat is on a par with her perfect understanding of school life. She catches the surface trivialities that cover, and reveal, so much: the importance of having the right, that is, the usual, clothes—new, expensive,

and inconspicuous—as well as relations who are not conspicuous. She shows the shame children feel over such matters when Clemence, in *Two Worlds and Their Ways*, pretends that her badly dressed mother is the governess, and Amy, in *The Last and the First*, tries to explain that Hamilton is not a real uncle but "some sort of relation who lives with us."

The visit home of their school friends in *Two Worlds and Their Ways* is also disastrous for the brother and the sister. The boys are too young for the girls and therefore ignored by them, and both children are ashamed of the luxury of the house and grounds where they live. They would have been no less embarrassed, of course, if these had been small and poverty-stricken. Parents cannot win and Dame Ivy is sorry for them: "Don't be too hard on parents. You may find yourself in their place" (*Elders and Betters*). She has a wise word for them: "Children hate parents who love and do not admire them" (*Brothers and Sisters*), and a penetrating, stern admonition: "Matthew is your son. When you feel you don't understand him, examine into your own heart and you will find the explanation there" (*Men and Wives*).

VII

In her life, Dame Ivy liked pleasantness in those about her. "Nothing goes deeper than manners," she wrote in her last book, "they are involved with the whole of life. It is they that give rise to it and come to depend on it. We should all remember it!" Good manners were expected—and exacted—and good looks were also appreciated in her guests:

"It doesn't follow that people have personality because they are plain."

"Or that they haven't because they are good-looking."

(*Brothers and Sisters*, ch. 2)

She was gracious in welcoming newcomers brought to visit her by established friends. They were expected to contribute to general conversation and not to address each other instead of their hostess. After her two hip operations, she had to forego the luncheons *à quatre* and the Saturday tea parties because her domestic help found them too much: life followed art tragically in her domestic affairs at the end. But many visitors will remember tea—the operative meal in so many of the novels—at the dining-room table in later years, when she liked them to have a hearty meal. Gifts of chocolates and flowers (but not chrysanthemums) were appreciated, and she saw to it that flowers were put in water at once or small plants dug into the bed of soil that ran along the top of her stone balcony.

Dame Ivy's intense interest in trivialities sometimes surprised—even shocked—her visitors; friends appreciated it for one of the paradoxes of her personality as a woman and a writer. At the memorial meeting held on 24 October 1969 (she died on 27 August in London) in Crosby Hall, Chelsea, one of the tributes paid to her memory was sent from New York by Alan Pryce-Jones. In this he recorded their first meeting, when he had the privilege of driving home in her company and that of the late T. S. Eliot and his wife, and looked forward to a literary discussion. However, the conversation consisted entirely of advice, given and received, as to which greengrocers' shops in Gloucester Road provided the best value for money.

Dame Ivy had no author's vanity in the usual sense. If it was very difficult to get her to talk about her methods of work or to discuss literary influences, she had a proper pride in the recognition she received in later years and was always ready to discuss the matter of sales, somewhat resentful of the lack of them in America.

She did not suffer fools or bores gladly, but was tirelessly indulgent to children and ready with generous sympathy to friends in trouble. Mario Praz's use of the term *ventosa* (suction plug) may be an apt description of a mouth immobilized in a photograph; but in real life any first impression of uptightness was quickly dispelled by Dame Ivy's look of lively interest, a twinkle in the eye, and an easy, if not expansive, smile at the absurdity of things. Only when a young reporter who was sent to interview her inquired about her age did the *ventosa* snap closed like a sea anemone about his impertinence.

If Dame Ivy acknowledged no influences, she is also unlikely to prove an influence herself. There are scenes in contemporary novels that recall some of hers; phrases occur in books and articles that are post-Ivy, and she may have helped to eliminate passages of long natural description and the baggage of interlocution ("he said," "she said"), but these are minor matters: in essentials no attempt to imitate her authentic note is likely to be sustained beyond a very faint echo.

SELECTED BIBLIOGRAPHY

I. SEPARATE WORKS. *Dolores* (Edinburgh–London, 1911; repr. 1971); *Pastors and Masters: A Study* (London, 1925); *Brothers and Sisters* (London, 1929); *Men and Wives* (London, 1931); *More Women than Men* (London, 1933); *A House and Its Head* (London–Toronto, 1935); *Daughters and Sons* (London, 1937); *A Family and a Fortune* (London, 1939); *Parents and Children* (London, 1941); *Elders and Betters* (London, 1944); *Manservant and Maidservant* (London, 1947), published in the U.S. as *Bullivant and the Lambs* (New York, 1948); *Two Worlds and Their Ways* (London, 1949); *Darkness and Day* (London, 1951); *The Present and the Past* (London, 1953); *Mother and Son* (London, 1955); *A Father and His Fate* (London, 1957); *A Heritage and Its History* (London, 1959), dramatized version by Julian Mitchell (New York–London, 1966); *The Mighty and Their Fall* (London, 1961); *A God and His Gifts* (London, 1963); *The Last and the First* (London, 1971), published posthumously in uncorrected form.

II. BIOGRAPHICAL AND CRITICAL STUDIES. R. Liddell, *A Treatise on the Novel* (London, 1947), contains a study of I. Compton-Burnett; E. Sackville-West, *Inclinations* (London, 1949); E. Bowen, *Collected Impressions* (London, 1950), contains an essay on I. Compton-Burnett; P. H. Newby, *The Novel, 1945–1950* (London, 1951); P. H. Johnson, *I. Compton-Burnett* (London, 1951); O. Prescott, *In My Opinion: An Inquiry into the Contemporary Novel* (Indianapolis, 1952), contains "Comrades of the Coterie: Henry Green, Compton-Burnett, Bowen, Graham Greene"; R. Liddell, *The Novels of I. Compton-Burnett* (London, 1955); L. Bogan, *Selected Criticism: Prose, Poetry* (New York, 1955), contains an essay on I. Compton-Burnett; R. Frischknecht, *Ivy Compton-Burnett: Kritische Betrachtung ihrer Werke* (Winterthur, 1961); F. R. Karl, *The Contemporary English Novel* (New York, 1962), contains "The Intimate World of Ivy Compton-Burnett"; F. Baldanza, *Ivy Compton-Burnett* (New York, 1964); C. Burkhart, *I. Compton-Burnett* (London, 1965); M. McCarthy, "The Inventions of I. Compton-Burnett," *Encounter*, 27 (November 1966), 19–31; M. Praz, *Cronache letterarie anglosassoni*, 4 vols. (Rome, 1966), vol. IV contains "I romanzi di Ivy Compton-Burnett"; E. Sprigge, *Ivy Compton-Burnett* (London, 1971); H. Spurling, *A Critical Biography of Ivy Compton-Burnett* (London, 1971); C. Burkhart, *The Art of I. Compton-Burnett: A Collection of Critical Essays* (London, 1972); H. Spurling, *The Early Life of I. Compton-Burnett, 1884–1919* (London, 1974); H. Spurling, *Secrets of a Woman's Heart: The Later Life of I. Compton-Burnett* (London, 1974); C. Burkhart, *Herman and Nancy and Ivy: Three Lives in Art* (London, 1977); *Twentieth Century Literature*, vol. XXV, C. Burkhart, ed. (Summer 1979), Hofstra University, issue devoted to I. Compton-Burnett.

WYNDHAM LEWIS

(1884-1957)

E. W. F. Tomlin

I

What is it that men fear beyond everything?
Obviously an open person.
("Enemy Interlude," One-Way Song)

Of the open and the closed society much has been written in our day. The works of Henri Bergson and Carl Popper, to mention no others, have shown this opposition to be the crucial sociological issue of the time. If there is such a thing as a truly "open" society, however, there must be "open" individuals to fill it. For a society is "open" only insofar as such individuals are numerous, active, and held in esteem. Given the imperfections of all human societies, however, the open individual must necessarily be something of a heretic. Like that of Socrates, perhaps the greatest of all "open" individuals, his impact on society will be similar to that of a gadfly. In short, this friend of man will sometimes be obliged to assume the guise of the Enemy.

The many-sided personality who forms the subject of this study may well be described as an "open" individual. In the first place, he was a writer of peculiar integrity. It should be said at the outset that he was also a very distinguished artist. During the whole of his career, he was content to plow a lonely furrow, or, given his versatility, to plow several furrows at once. "The place of honour," he said, "is—outside." Fearless in his expressions of opinion, he was the reverse of those pseudo-Enemies who, seeking to attract attention by attacking a so-called establishment, remain nevertheless "perfectly in tune with the Zeitgeist." Secondly, his mind was always hospitable to a variety of outside influences. As Walter Allen remarked, "A satirist of Lewis's calibre is sustained by an idea of excellence and is its lonely aggressive protagonist," whereas the "micky-taker [debunker] . . . is bound by complicity with his mass-audience" (*Times*, London, 23 February 1967). With his great learning and acquaintance with many cultures, Lewis was among the least provincial of modern English writers. Hence his total indifference to fashion, which "introduces the parochial outlook" (*The Writer and the Absolute*, p. 148). In a period noted for minor orthodoxies or what he called "inferior religions," he steadfastly kept intellectual open house. Thirdly, the fact that "openness" should be associated with a particular organ, the eye, is by no means an accident. Lewis was endowed with a remarkable and disciplined gift of vision. In his literary work, no less than in his painting, the eye played a decisive part. The hallucinatory prose of *Childermass* and the satirical scrutiny of *The Apes of God* reveal an eye at work that impartially surveys the whole hierarchy of experience. Aristotle defined the eye as the organ most closely associated with intellectual knowledge, which "brings to light the many differences between things" (*Metaphysics*, book A.1). It is with an intellectual eye, assessing and appraising, that Lewis chose to view his fellow creatures. If this explains his somewhat limited appeal to his contemporaries, it may likewise explain his capacity to outlast their short-lived idols.

Unless moved by considerations of pure vanity, a creative writer does not desire recognition as such; what he both desires and needs is the appreciation of those of a stature at least equal to his own. He requires worthy judges. Such recognition Lewis was always able to count upon. Despite neglect by the conventional critics, his genius was early hailed by such masters as T. S. Eliot, William Butler Yeats, James Joyce, and Ezra Pound. Not merely did he enjoy the friendship and respect of these men, but with them he exercised a formative influence upon his time. The public for his work has recently shown evidence of marked expansion. Studies and monographs have appeared in Britain and America.[1] He is

[1] One of the first academic figures to recognize his genius was Marshall McLuhan, whom Lewis met during his wartime stay in Toronto; see McLuhan's *Counterblast* (New York, 1969) and the article "Wyndham Lewis: His Theory of Art and Communication" in *Shenandoah* (Summer–Autumn 1953).

the subject of academic theses. Given these signs of wary acceptance, there is all the more need for a brief guide to his overall achievement. What sort of writer was Lewis? How should his work be approached? What are his guiding values? By which books is he likely to be remembered?

First a few words about his life. Percy Wyndham Lewis was born off Amherst, Nova Scotia, on 18 November 1882. Although he was the son of an American who had fought in the Union army during the Civil War, and an Englishwoman of Scotch-Irish descent, he remained a Canadian citizen all his life. He was educated at Rugby, the famous English public school, and, showing artistic talent, he enrolled at the Slade School. Always restless, he traveled extensively in Europe, particularly France, and began to paint and write for a living. By the outbreak of World War I he had become the leading figure in the Vorticist School, written the pioneer novel *Tarr*, and produced an iconoclastic magazine, *Blast*. Apart from journeys abroad, notably to Morocco in 1931, Lewis spent most of his career in London, where until 1939 he inhabited with his wife, Froanna ("Frau Anna"), a studio in Kensington and another home in Notting Hill Gate. In contrast to his active part in World War I, first as an artillery officer and then as a war artist, he lived precariously in Canada and America during World War II. As his sight began to fail he was obliged to abandon painting, but he continued writing doggedly and with remarkable skill and inventiveness until his death. Temperamentally, he was a quiet, unpretentious man, kind to his friends, and a good companion; but he lacked the practical competence of an Eliot, and he could be resentful of supposed slights. His assumption of the role of the Enemy was a means of defending himself against the declining standards of mass civilization.

The body of Lewis' work may be divided into several distinct categories: works of fiction and satire, works of speculative thought, works of socio-literary criticism, and polemics. In the first category may be grouped *Tarr* (1918), *The Wild Body* (1927), *The Apes of God* (1930), *The Enemy of the Stars* (1932), *The Revenge for Love* (1937), *The Vulgar Streak* (1951), *Rotting Hill* (1951), *Self Condemned* (1954) and (almost in a class by themselves) *Childermass, Monstre Gai*, and *Malign Fiesta* (1955–1956). In the second category come the two key volumes *The Art of Being Ruled* (1926) and *Time and Western Man* (1927). In the third category are *The Lion and the Fox* (1927), *Men Without Art* (1934), *The Writer and the Absolute* (1952), and the two autobiographi-

cal works *Blasting and Bombardiering* (1937) and *Rude Assignment* (1950). The fourth category consists of the critical and eristic works, including *The Caliph's Design* (1919), *Paleface* (1929), *The Diabolical Principle and the Dithyrambic Spectator* (1931), *The Doom of Youth* (1932), and others (see bibliography). There is a fifth category, Lewis' poetry—a class of which the sole member is *One-Way Song* (1933).[2]

To suggest that these different genres are of equal importance, or that their author was willing to place them upon the same level, would be an error. Lewis preferred rather to divide his works into the formal and the informal. Of the latter he remarked that "no American President could outdo me in informality." Contrary to what one would suppose, there was no dissipation of energy; each category serves to reinforce the rest. Lewis was obliged to act as his own journalist, his own compère, his own interpreter:

> He has been his own bagman, critic, cop, designer,
> Publisher, agent, char-man and shoe-shiner.
> (*One-Way Song*, 1960 ed., p. 76)

For this reason each of his major works has had its group of defensive outriders.

> I became a "pamphleteer," to start with, in defence of my work as an artist. And I fail to see how an artist who is *outside* the phalansteries, sets, cells or cliques, can to-day exist at all, if he is not prepared to "pamphleteer." . . . The writer or painter is isolated from the general public to an unparalleled extent, at the present time.
> (*The Diabolical Principle*, p. vii)

Thus the novels generated the critical studies, together with such vigorous pamphlets as *Satire and Fiction* (described as Enemy Pamphlet No. 1, this followed the publication of *The Apes of God* in 1930). *The Art of Being Ruled* was the occasion for a whole series of minor works: books on America, on Hitler, on the Jews, on the leftist cult, and on the character of John Bull. *Time and Western Man* was the metaphysical "sun" around which Lewis' entire prose output disposed itself in planetary order. In his early days, Lewis even found the time and energy to edit three spirited reviews—*Blast, The Tyro*, and *The Enemy*—that belong to the history of what F. R. Leavis has called "minority culture." At a time of in-

---

[2]This is not the only poetry Lewis wrote; see also *Rude Assignment*, ch. 22, and A. Munton, ed., *Collected Poems and Plays* (London, 1979).

tellectual slump, such a well-directed stream of commentary and castigation was much needed. Today there is no organized literary life. Moreover, the absence of a homogeneous, educated reading public is far from made good by the existence of several distinct publics not all equally informed. Of the few persons among his peers who succeeded in maintaining the circulation of ideas, Lewis was both the most prolific and the most original. Who else could have written *The Art of Being Ruled*? Eliot called him "the greatest journalist of my time." The description is accurate even with respect to his most serious works—if we bear in mind Pound's definition of literature as "journalism which *stays* news."

We may find it useful here to dwell briefly on certain characteristics of Lewis' work that have tended to bewilder, if not alienate, certain readers. The first is his supposed impersonality. With this characteristic is associated a certain coldness and even inhumanity. To begin by reading his play *The Enemy of the Stars* and to follow it with a novel such as *The Apes of God* is to experience a sensation of having broken irrevocably with the "graces" of traditional drama and fiction. In such works, the solaces or consolations of popular literature are absent. No warm personality meets the reader halfway with a bursting holdall of humor, whimsicality, and good fellowship. Or, as Raymond Rosenthal put it in his introduction to *A Soldier of Humour, and Selected Writings* (1966), "The *costume* of personality, with its cosily familiar trappings of race, national trait, and individual idiosyncracy, are totally absent." As bedside reading, Lewis' books are hardly to be recommended. Taut and astringent, they may be prescribed for those who wish to read themselves awake. They are daylight-creating. The curious paradox is this: although Lewis' books betray an apparent impersonality, the powerful personality of their author is everywhere present. On the purely verbal plane, each sentence is his and not somebody else's. There is a Lewis punch and turn of phrase that no contemporary has come near to imitating. Yet Lewis the man never erupts into his work. He exercises the true creative withdrawal. Significantly, Pierpoint, the only "genuine" character in *The Apes of God* (that is, Lewis himself), never puts in an appearance during 625 pages.

It may indeed be an advantage for a great artist or writer to practice more than one art, for this is a condition of keeping pure a creative imagination otherwise prone to suffer too frequent invasion from the sphere of "personal experience." To devote every-thing to one's art, as the aesthetes claim to do, is to risk devoting to it the wrong things as well as the right. The "show business" of Shakespeare was not waste of energy; it permitted the canalization of an energy unparalleled in literature. That Lewis' creative energies sometimes intermix in unsatisfactory fashion, we shall later suggest; but it is, in general, true to say that his painting, instead of depriving his writing of warmth and color, left his eye free to depict the "colorlessness" or anemia of society. If society has not recognized itself, this would add weight to his accusation that it lacks a capacity for self-examination. Lewis' view of mankind is "impersonal" because of the increasing depersonalization of man himself. For example, in the story "The Rot" (1951), the inhabitants of postwar "Rotting Hill" are not even discontented with their lot. The "indifference" displayed by the workmen who come to repair the ravages of the dry-rot fungi is part of a general indifference to the finer values.

The charge of inhumanity is equally lacking in basis. The literature of engagement, popular in postwar France, gave rise to a type of writer who, anxious to demonstrate his sense of social responsibility, tends to distort his art in the interests of political propaganda. He bends his vision to conform to an absolute situated outside the artistic sphere. Such willful distortion is fatal to professional integrity. Of the Marxian novelist this is particularly true; but it is true likewise of those authors who, like Jean Paul Sartre, write to illustrate a particular philosophical theory. In *The Writer and the Absolute*, Lewis has subjected this literary tendency to a particularly brilliant analysis. Sartre, André Malraux, Albert Camus, and even George Orwell come under his censorious eye. While pretending to display solicitude for man's condition, the attitude of engagement may end by reducing that condition to one of still greater degradation. To descend into the marketplace may be only a step from descending into the farmyard. The writer's true "absolute" is not outside but inside; his absolute is truth, which "is as necessary to everybody as the air we breathe" (p. 4). "Naturally it is much more difficult to explain why this is so," Lewis adds. "There are no lungs, visibly pumping up and down, that correspond to it and illustrate its use." The advantage of the old-fashioned system of patronage was that it usually left the artist to his own devices; glorification of the patron was limited to the terms of the prefatory epistle. The modern patron, whether it be the state or some public corporation or political party, exercises restraint by laying down the conditions under which the artist must work. The effects of such restraint are often damaging, not least to the novelist; it is an ingenuous but common error to suppose that the creative imagination, being exempt from reference to fact, can remain free while the other faculties are enslaved. Under such subtle pressures

> a man will say a thousand things he does not wish to say, mutilate his thought, adulterate his doctrine, compel his will to wear a uniform *against* his will, cause the characters in his books (if a novelist) to behave in a manner that turns them into other characters—to associate with people they would never speak to if allowed to follow their own sweet will.
>
> (*The Writer and the Absolute*, p. 121)

In his novel *The Revenge for Love* (1937), Lewis employs the medium of fiction to illustrate this maleficent process at work. He writes a story about ordinary, decent human beings who, under the influence of fraudulent ideologists, are subtly changed into other people. Like many of Lewis' books, *The Revenge for Love* was in advance of its time by at least a generation: hence the neglect it suffered, and its relevance for us today. (Lewis' account of this neglect is contained in *Rude Assignment*, chapter 37. The character Percy Hardcastle bears an interesting resemblance to Hoederer in Sartre's play *Les Mains sales*, which has a similar theme.) Behind the hard, "pelting" prose is a concern for humanity, or rather for human values, far stronger than that which characterizes either the "existentialist" novels or the Marxist allegories. And no one can deny humanity to the remarkable novel *Self Condemned*, a work in which so many readers made their first discovery of Lewis. When critics repeat the charge of inhuman coldness, they refer perhaps to the absence in Lewis' work of something of which he is temperamentally incapable, namely sentimentality.

The question—What sort of writer is Lewis?—may therefore be answered, if only provisionally, as follows: He is a writer who endeavored to deploy in the service of his art all the forces of intelligence, not merely the "sensitive" or the "aesthetic." Hence the necessity of understanding his mind as a whole. That the human psyche can be divided into two spheres, the intellectual and something vaguely called the "sensibility," he would energetically deny. Nothing whole or integrated can issue from a split-man; part

5 of *The Apes of God* is devoted to a study of that phenomenon.[3] Nor did Lewis hold the view that the artist, being a specialist in the realm of feeling, is entrusted with a mission to compensate his fellows for the cold, abstract world of physical science. The artist is at the center. He is neither an entertainer, nor an amateur psychoanalyst, nor a propagandist—all of whom are specialists in one side of man (including his inside), and all practitioners of some form of hypnosis. The artist's role, by contrast, is that of eye-opener; and in the work of the greatest artists we find a capacity to focus, to integrate, or, in Matthew Arnold's phrase, to see life steadily and see it whole.

The extent to which psychological theories have influenced contemporary writers and critics may be judged from the popularity between the two wars of the idea of the "stream of consciousness." The stream of consciousness was regarded as providing a kind of inexhaustible spring of artistic inspiration. Lewis identified this as merely one aspect of the worship of flux characteristic of so much popular philosophy, and his object in writing *Time and Western Man* was to expose the "time cult" in all its ramifications. The book has never won recognition in philosophical circles (although an exception is *The Nature of Belief*, 1931, by M. C. D'Arcy, S.J.), but it is more orthodox in its defense of the values of intelligence than many works considered academically acceptable. One suspects that its influence, like that of *The Lion and the Fox* (1927), has been more widespread than most people have been prepared to admit. According to Lewis, this "major concept" of our day has led to the "coke-dream" of Surrealism, the exaltation of the naive and the demented, the child cult, the worship of the "dark gods" of sex, the furtive and open excursions into diabolism and sadism, the advocacy of "millennial" politics, and in general to the influence of "the dead hand of the new" so well exposed in *The Demon of Progress in the Arts* (1954). Such manifestations of intellectual anarchy are no less dangerous for having a veneer of sophistication; Lewis' analysis of High Bohemia is valid, at its best, for social groups other than the Bloomsbury satirized in *The Apes of God*.[4]

When Lewis describes the intellect in *The Enemy*

---

[3] It is worthy of remark that Mr. Zagreus observes: "I am afraid that all half-men are right-hand men. The heart is a superfluity" (p. 332).

[4] The time-theme is recurrent in Lewis' work. It is taken up again in the story "Time the Tiger," in *Rotting Hill*, and also in *America and Cosmic Man* (1948), ch. 27.

of the Stars as "the traditional enemy of life," he is using the word "life" to connote the crude biological energy that for so many artists, and also for some modern philosophers, is endowed with quasi-mystical significance. From the days of *Paleface* (1929), with its analysis of the life-worship of Sherwood Anderson and D. H. Lawrence, Lewis regarded this trend of thought as symptomatic of decadence. Like the Bergsonian philosophy (or rather its vulgarization), it involves "capitulation to the material *in struggle against which* the greatest things in the world have been constructed" (*The Art of Being Ruled*, 1926 ed., p. 391).

> Life is in itself not important. Our values make it so; but they are mostly, the important ones, non-human values, although the intenser they are the more they imply a supreme vital connotation. . . . To attach, as the humanitarian does, a mystical value to life *itself*, for its own sake, is as much a treachery to spiritual truth as it is a gesture to "humanity."
>
> (*The Art of Being Ruled*, p. 56)

In maintaining that the "important" values are nonhuman, Lewis does not mean to imply that they are *in*human. His conception of value is based on the traditional view of the intellect as a faculty transcending reason and capable of immediate grasp of value. While the metaphysics of this view are expounded at length in *Time and Western Man*, Lewis is not advancing some aberrant doctrine peculiar to himself. He is returning to the great metaphysical tradition, a tradition preserved in the oriental wisdoms, transmitted to the Western world through Aristotle (who speaks of the "divine intellect"), and present in the scholastic thinkers, only to be driven underground during the last few centuries. Indeed, the assault upon metaphysical thought in our day is one of the clearest, if least understood, manifestations of the time-philosophy. The intellectual intuition has given place to those subrational intuitions which place man's "knowing" faculty in his blood, his animal instincts, or his "unconscious." On this basis, man is allowed to "know" only so long as his knowledge is a kind of ignorance, to "see" only on condition that he is "blind," and to advance only on condition that he does so in somnambulistic fashion.

So thorough and exhaustive is Lewis' analysis that the work of *Time and Western Man* will hardly need to be done afresh; new evidence will merely accumulate in its support. To read the book at nearly sixty years' remove is to appreciate more than ever its ex-traordinary insight into the nature of a movement of thought of which many professional thinkers remained unaware. (The critique of Oswald Spengler's historicism and the analysis of behaviorism are but two examples of masterly interpretation.) Today we are more ready to admit a connection, however devious, between pure speculation in the university or laboratory and what goes on in the public mind: the degree of deviation and vulgarization is itself a matter of profound interest. Not merely did Lewis demonstrate this connection; he detected the operation of forces making for increasing compromise with mass standards and mass emotion, above all a gradual apostasy of the intellectual elite. Such apostasy, as he saw it, followed from the nature of the philosophical ideals to which that elite subscribed. The obsession with time, movement, and change *for their own sakes* involved the wholesale abolition of distinctions, the emulsion of forms, that the intellect had struggled for centuries to establish and uphold. Even the conception of God had undergone subtle transformation, for instead of the Cause of Causes, the God of Emergent Evolution had become the Effect of Effects.

A lengthy treatise could be written—and no doubt is being written—on the Lewis Weltanschauung. It would begin by analyzing the principles of Vorticism, the artistic movement Lewis sponsored just prior to World War I, with its "blasting" of the provincial values of Anglo-Saxon suburban culture.[5] By means of this artistic movement—practically a one-man show—Lewis achieved something very nearly unique. Instead of importing an artistic movement from the Continent twenty or thirty years after its birth, he started one on English soil. Only the Pre-Raphaelites had achieved such a thing as that. The significance of Vorticism lay not so much in what it accomplished (in fact, it was killed by the war) as in the evidence it provided of Lewis' early battles for the recognition of the artist's place in society. To Lewis, the vocation of the artist was to provide an advance-guard for the civilized intelligence. In this sense, the artist and the intellectual—or what Julien Benda has called the *clerc*—are natural allies. Although modern society is not intolerant of the artist, it tolerates him only so long as he is content to re-

---

[5]The chief Vorticist manifestos are *The Caliph's Design* (1919) and the two numbers of *Blast* (1914, 1915). The Vortex symbol was used to imply an "arrest" in the flux, and hence the idea of classic stability.

main eccentric. This is its subtle way of refusing to take him seriously. In such a situation, the role of the intellectual will suffer a similar eclipse. Cut off from the creative forces, the intellectuals will pursue their specializations in increasing isolation, and the growing eccentricity of the artist's vision will be paralleled by the increasing abstraction of the intellectual. Both will tend to withdraw into isolated coteries dedicated to the cultivation of "an elegant sterility or cautious and critical eking out of a little jet of naïvete" (*The Art of Being Ruled*, p. 242). Meanwhile the people fall victim to the apostles of claptrap. Of this serious state of affairs Lewis wrote at length in *Men Without Art* (1934) and *Blasting and Bombardiering* (1937). The final essay in the latter book, entitled "Towards an Artless Society," is the more relevant for us in that we are correspondingly nearer to the consummation he describes. Nor must we be deceived by the spectacle of government subsidies to art, the proliferation of art schools, and so forth. When the state is obliged to step in, the situation must be serious indeed; for we may be witnessing the end of a particular relationship between art and society.

Reference to the state brings us to the other major contribution of Lewis to the defense of civilized values. The key book here is *The Art of Being Ruled*. Like *Time and Western Man, The Art of Being Ruled* has exerted influence in almost every sphere save that in which it might have proved most salutary; but while no work of political theory has acknowledged its merits or even its existence, the argument of the book is of permanent validity. There have been many books concerned with how to exercise power: cynical manuals such as Machiavelli's *The Prince*, breviaries of mystical state worship such as Hegel's *Philosophy of Right*, and the anti-democratic sociological treatises of Vilfredo Pareto. Few books have been concerned with how to cope with power, how to *endure* it. Writing prior to the advent of state socialism, Lewis realized that the danger for our time was that of being ruled out of existence. His diagnosis, like his proposed treatment, was not the conventional one. For this reason it has been either misunderstood or neglected. He fixed his eye on one phenomenon in particular, revolution. In the attitude of mind that advocated revolution for revolution's sake, he detected one more example of the time obsession of his contemporaries. "Extremism," he has said, "is symptomatic of a vacuum"—a point worth bearing in mind in these days of recurrent protest. This blind worship of change is satirized in *One-Way Song*:

Our tri-classed life-express carries oh far more
Back-to-the-engine fares than those face-fore.
Gazing at yesterdays, they squat back-first—
Blindfolded into brand-new futures burst!

(ix)

Admittedly, some of the apostles of this attitude, having quietly or noisily recanted, are today conventional upholders of the status quo. Lewis would argue that this is merely to exchange one form of convention for another; for "revolutionary politics, revolutionary art, and, oh, the revolutionary mind, is the dullest thing on earth" (*The Art of Being Ruled*, p. 23). Admittedly, many people have preached revolution out of sheer acquisitiveness and love of power. Their interest in revolution is by no means disinterested; hence it is easily diverted: "If you take up a thing cynically, you drop it lightly. If *power* is what interests you, when the wind changes you change too" (*The Writer and the Absolute*, p. 40). That such a disinterested advocate of the higher values as Lewis should have been accused of sympathizing with authoritarian forms of government is a sad commentary on the myopia, or perhaps the malevolence, of certain publicists. Lewis' rejoinder late in life forms a useful summing-up of *The Art of Being Ruled* and its outriders, and of much else besides:

My interests, in the first place, have been those of the civilised intelligence—"the politics of the intellect," as I called it. At a time when everyone was for a fanatical *étatisme*, I was not. It seemed to me to promise no good to anybody—to kick out kings and queens and put masters in their place with a hundred times their power.

(*Rude Assignment*, p. 142)

And his own characteristically sardonic statement of his political position could hardly be less sectarian: "partly communist and partly fascist, with a distinct streak of monarchism in my marxism, but at bottom anarchist, with a healthy passion for order" (*The Diabolical Principle*, p. 126).

II

FROM this cursory account of the theoretical basis of Lewis' work, it will be seen that we are dealing with a writer belonging to no recognizable school, with few, if any, disciples, and of transparent honesty.

The artist is relieved of that obligation of the practical man to lie.

(*Time and Western Man*, p. 137)

Except for the Vorticist moment, Lewis was content to remain outside the literary world in a state of "solitary schism," though that world has been uncomfortably aware of the "Enemy without." Given his isolation and the independence of his general standpoint, it is inevitable that he should have been compelled out of self-defense to cultivate the art of satire.[6] Against folly, falsity, and, above all, mediocrity, moral indignation is of itself of little use: what is needed is the satirist's probe, the weapon of deflation. Although he gave a good deal of attention to the function of satire, Lewis' views on this subject are likely to provoke some disagreement. In declaring that "the greatest satire is non-moral," and in arguing that the satirist is concerned to present the "truth of natural science," he seems to leave unexplained the social efficacy of satire. There would be little sense in saying that men resembled behavioristic puppets unless the fact were a matter of reproach. In this respect there is a recognizable change of viewpoint between *The Art of Being Ruled* and *Time and Western Man*. The former accepts man's "instinct towards slavery" and seeks to make the best of it; the latter contends that "people should be compelled to be freer and more individualistic than they naturally desire to be" (*Time and Western Man*, p. 138). What Lewis presumably means (and certain arguments in *Satire and Fiction* confirm this) is that the satirist given to moralizing is an impure satirist; for the moralistic temperament, with its frequent undercurrent of hypocrisy, is among the chief targets of satire: witness Molière's *Tartuffe* and Dickens' Mr. Chadband in *Bleak House*. Some of Lewis' fiction, including parts of *The Apes of God* and lesser works such as *Snooty Baronet* (1932), goes so far toward presenting the "truth of natural science" as almost to pass beyond satire altogether. In witnessing these cold dissections, one observes the operation of satire of the second degree, a kind of satire of satire. There is no *saeva indignatio* ("savage indignation": the Latin original comes from the epitaph Swift composed for his tombstone) against living objects of scorn, merely the helpless rummaging in a charnel house. These people were never alive; even

to dignify them with the names of puppets is to ascribe to them a flexibility they do not possess. The attempt to split split-men still further is a futile occupation. In *The Apes of God* there is an episode that aptly illustrates this divisive process. Mr. Zagreus, the "specialist in genius" who derives all his ideas from Pierpoint, catches sight of the "many gaping life-like garments he was leaving behind in his room. He returned and *battered them out of human shape as far as he could*" (p. 345, italics added). This is the impression with which so much of *The Apes of God* leaves us.

Lewis' satire is more effective when it is allied, as so often, to the comic spirit. Indeed, Lewis' mastery of the comic has been insufficiently stressed. There are passages in *The Apes of God* itself, in *Blasting and Bombardiering* (the accounts of James Joyce and T. E. Hulme, for instance), in *The Vulgar Streak*, in *Rude Assignment*, and even in *America I Presume* (1940) that are as uproarious as anything by the early Evelyn Waugh or by other writers such as Kingsley Amis. This blend of unflinching observation, irony, and lampooning is present in Lewis' earliest work; and it is convenient to introduce the imaginative prose by way of the stories in which the combination is seen in its early perfection, namely *The Wild Body*. Dating from 1909, these stories contain almost the whole of Lewis. Only Lewis the visionary is missing; he emerges first with *Childermass*. Perhaps the most convincing argument for crediting Lewis with not merely talent but genius is the fact of his precocious maturity. Such stories as "Bestre," "The Cornac and His Wife," and "Brotcotnaz" are little masterpieces; and Lewis has provided a valuable commentary on their meaning and construction in the two essays "Inferior Religions" and "The Meaning of the Wild Body":

The root of the comic is to be sought in the sensations resulting from the observations of a *thing* behaving like a person. But from that point of view all men are necessarily comic: for they are all *things*, or physical bodies, behaving as *persons*. . . . The movement or intelligent behaviour of matter, any autonomous movement of matter, is essentially comic.

(*The Wild Body*, p. 247)

Like so many of Lewis' insights, this remark goes to the heart of the matter. That philosophers such as Henri Bergson and Søren Kierkegaard should have reflected deeply, though divergently, on the nature of the comic is significant: for the comic is an integral

[6]"Temperament and circumstances combined to make him a great satirist; satire can be the defence of the sensitive" (T. S. Eliot, "Wyndham Lewis: A Memoir," in *Hudson Review*, Summer 1957).

element in the human situation. Life is a compromise—a compromise between soul and body, nature and spirit; and since all compromises are both provisional and rough-and-ready, there is something inherently comic about an organism engaged in trying to be a person or a "spirit." There is also something pathetic; we know how easily the clown, by the merest gesture, can draw tears as well as laughter. Once the delicate balance of comedy is disturbed, however, the result is either repellent hardness or mawkishness. By depicting some of his characters as complete automata, Lewis may tend to alienate us. Nevertheless, the inhabitants of the Pension Beau Séjour—Francis the wandering musician, Bestre, and above all the Cornac and his wife, impoverished Breton traveling entertainers who bear a savage grudge against their village patrons—are genuine comic characters who arouse pity as well as amusement. A passage from "The Cornac and His Wife" is worthy of quotation as embodying, in addition to comedy, the chief virtues of Lewis' narrative manner:

. . . after my evening meal I strolled over the hill bisected by the main street, and found him in his usual place in a sort of square, one side of which was formed by a stony breton brook, across which went a bridge. Drawn up under the beeches stood the brake. Near it in the open space the troupe had erected the trapeze, lighted several lamps (it was after dark already), and placed three or four benches in a narrow semicircle. When I arrived, a large crowd already pressed around them. "Fournissons les bancs, Messieurs et M'dames! fournissons les bancs, et alors nous commencons!" the proprietor was crying.

But the seats remained unoccupied. A boy in tights, with his coat drawn round him, shivered at one corner of the ring. Into the middle of this the showman several times advanced, exhorting the coy Public to make up its mind and commit itself to the extent of sitting down on one of his seats. Every now and then a couple would. Then he would walk back, and stand near his cart, muttering to himself. His eyebrows were hidden in a dishevelled frond of hair. The only thing he could look at without effort was the ground, and there his eyes were usually directed. When he looked up they were heavy—vacillating painfully beneath the weight of their lids. The action of speech with him resembled that of swallowing: the dreary pipe from which he drew so many distressful sounds seemed to stiffen and swell, and his head to strain forward like a rooster about to crow. His heavy under-lip went in and out in sombre activity, as he articulated. The fine natural resources of his face for inspiring a feeling of gloom in his fellows, one would have judged irresistible on that particular night. The bitterest disgust disfigured it to a high degree.

But *they* watched this despondent and unpromising figure with glee and keen anticipation. . . . When the furious man scowled they gaped delightedly; when he coaxed they became grave and sympathetic. All his movements were followed with minute attention. When he called upon them to occupy their seats, with an expressive gesture, they riveted their eyes on his hand, as though expecting a pack of cards to suddenly appear there. They made no move at all to take their places. Also, as this had already lasted a considerable time, the man who was fuming to entertain them—they just as incomprehensible to him as he was to them from that point of view—allowed the outraged expression that was the expression of his soul to appear more and more in his face. . . .

His cheerless voice, like the moaning bay of solitary dogs, conjured them to occupy the seats.

"Fournissons les bancs!" he exhorted them again and again. Each time he retired to the position he had selected to watch them from, far enough off from them to be able to say that he had withdrawn his influence, and had no further wish to interfere. Then, again, he stalked forward. This time the exhortation was pitched in as formal and matter-of-fact a key as his anatomy would permit, as though this were the first appeal of the evening. Now he seemed to be merely waiting, without discreetly withdrawing—without even troubling to glance in their direction any more, until the audience should have had time to seat themselves—absorbed in briefly rehearsing to himself, just before beginning, the part he was to play. These tactics did not alter things in the least. Finally, he was compelled to take note of his failure. No words more issued from his mouth. He glared stupidly for some moments at the circle of people, and they, blandly alert, gazed back at him.

Then unexpectedly, from outside the periphery of the potential audience, elbowing his way familiarly through the wall of people, burst in the clown. Whether sent for to save the situation, or whether his toilet was just completed, was not revealed.

"B-o-n soir, M'sieurs et M'dames," he chirruped and yodeled, waving his hand, tumbling over his employer's foot. The benches filled as if by magic. But the most surprising thing was the change in the proprietor. No sooner had the clown made his entrance, and, with his assurance of success as the people's favourite, and comic familiarity, told the hangers-back to take their seats, than a brisk dialogue sprang up between him and his melancholy master. It was punctuated with resounding slaps at each fresh impertinence of the clown. The proprietor was astonishing. I rubbed my eyes. This lugubrious personage had woken to the sudden violence of a cheerful automaton. In administering the chastisement his irrepressible friend perpetually invited, he sprang nimbly backwards and forwards as though engaged in a boxing match, while he grinned appreciatively at the clown's wit, as though in spite of himself nearly knocking his teeth out with delighted blows. The audience howled with delight. . . .

(*The Wild Body*, p. 143–147)

The story that presents the eye at its most keenly inquisitive is "Bestre," which is itself the story of an Eye. Bestre is a character whose tyrannical power over his neighbors resides precisely in the power of that organ: "At the passing of an enemy Bestre will pull up his blind with a snap." No wonder the young Lewis, disguised under the sobriquet Kerr-Orr and dubbing himself the Soldier of Humour, would write of his encounters in pre-1914 Brittany: "I learnt a great deal from Bestre. He is one of my masters."[7] The eye is essentially a primitive organ; man observed the world before he could appraise it in speech; the cave painting is the earliest example of creative energy. Such primitive energy surges through all Lewis' work. He has been well described by Eliot as combining "the thought of the modern and the energy of the cave-man." Yet energy by itself is not the same as creativity; it must be transmuted and refined. In Lewis the transformation is a continuous process; one feels the tension in his prose, a straining, cajoling, restless medium, eddying and billowing, yet suggestive of astonishing depths and moving to controlled rhythms. The control is that which distinguishes such writing both from the "folk prose" of popular fiction and from the "idiot-yawp" prose of the school of violence. The Soldier of Humour thus describes himself:

My body is large, white and savage; but all the fierceness has been transformed into *laughter*. . . . I move on a more primitive level than most men, I expose my essential *me* quite coolly, and all men shy a little. This forked, strange-scented, blond-skinned gut-bag, with its two bright rolling marbles with which it sees, bull's-eyes full of mockery and madness, is my stalking-horse. *I hang somewhere in its midst operating it with detachment.*
(*The Wild Body*, pp. 4–5, italics added)

Throughout *One-Way Song*, the method is used in illustration of the method itself:

Swept off your feet, be on the look out for the pattern,
It is the chart that matters—the graph is everything!
In such wild weather you cannot look too closely at 'em—
Cleave to the abstract of this blossoming.
("The Song of the Militant Romance," vii)

Laughter of this kind is therapeutic; it is "the mind sneezing," though "occasionally it takes on the dangerous form of absolute revelation." Finally,

[7]An up-to-date but kindlier Bestre is Mr. Patricks, the "pocket-Selfridge" of Rotting Hill ("Mr. Patricks' Toy Shop," in *Rotting Hill*).

such laughter, which is the laughter of Aristophanes, Chaucer, and Rabelais, remains indifferent to the passage of time: "Laughter does not progress. It is primitive, hard and unchangeable (*The Wild Body*, p. 238).

The most sustained feats of prose in this manner—with laughter in recess, as it were—are those contained in *Childermass* and *The Apes of God*, both works of epic proportions. For the reasons given, *The Apes of God* is hardly a success as a novel; the objection to calling it a failure is that we have no clear idea of how, given its structure, it could succeed. Although it might be possible to compose a mock-epic of Bloomsbury after the manner of Alexander Pope's *The Rape of the Lock* (1712), the task of engaging in this "massacre of the insignificants" was perhaps a thankless one. The "fantastic tricks" of these apes are hardly calculated to "make the angels weep"; all they induce is a passing sneer. It is only when Lewis is satirizing permanent human foibles that his full powers are called into play. The beginning of *The Apes of God*, like most of Lewis' openings, is superb. Rarely has the vanity and pretentiousness of old age been more ruthlessly pilloried than in this scene of a rich dowager at her toilet. Aldous Huxley's attempt at the same theme in *Those Barren Leaves* (1925) is by comparison trivial. It will be observed how the meticulous description of a few movements—the maid at work on the coiffure, "carding" the hair "until the large false-teeth rattled in the horse-like skull," and the laborious seating of the grande dame in her chair—serve to lay bare the secrets of a whole society:

When they were near the rear of the chair, they took a course at a tangent, then tacked, passing around its left arm. They entered the spotlight shot in a shaft computed to be ninety million miles from the solar projector—so stupendously aloft, in its narrow theatre, for this human performance. She lowered her body into its appointed cavity, in the theatrical illumination, ounce by ounce—back first, grappled to Bridget, bull-dog grit all-out—at last riveted as though by suction within its elastic crater, corseted by its mattresses of silk from waist to bottom, one large feeble arm riding the stiff billows of its substantial fluted brim.
(prologue, "Death the Drummer," p. 23)

III

Two years before the publication of *The Apes of God*, an imaginative work of very different quality had begun to take shape in Lewis' mind. This was

Childermass. Its initial impact was slight. Although the finished work was promised almost immediately, the interval between part 1 and its completion was finally protracted to twenty-seven years. Lewis' activities in the intervening period were multifarious: the 1930's and the war years saw a renewed output of painting. His enthusiasm for this potential masterpiece of visionary literature seemed to have waned to the point at which resumption appeared unlikely. Moreover, in the years following World War II, sadly interrupting a prolific period of art criticism, Lewis' sight began to fail. The paint brushes were laid aside. But the pen, moving over huge sheets of paper resting on a drawing board smoothed to the color of amber, produced a series of volumes in which *Childermass* was not merely continued but built into a work surpassing anything its author can originally have conceived. A composite volume containing *Monstre Gai* and *Malign Fiesta* was completed, under the title *The Human Age* (1955–1956). This was perhaps the only great work to come out of the cold war, and the climax of Lewis' literary career.

The action (if it can be called such) of *Childermass* takes place on an arid steppe outside heaven. Humanity, an "emigrant mass," is assembled "in a shimmering obscurity" to undergo examination by an extraordinary figure—half man, half dwarf—called the Bailiff. Following the examination, the individuals are deemed fit or otherwise for admission to the "magnetic city." In the course of the slow unfolding of the scene, the Bailiff's authority is challenged by an obscure figure of which the name Macrob is the only clue to his identity. Finally, there is another group of personages, the Hyperideans, into whose mouth Lewis puts a series of lengthy speeches concerned with the perennial problems that always interested him. To describe adequately the theme of the book is extremely difficult. *Childermass* is a cinerama dream that enjoys no reality outside itself. (When the Bailiff reappears in *One-Way Song* he is another figure, his magic gone, like Mr. Pickwick resurrected in Dickens' *Master Humphrey's Clock*.) In "The Bishop's Fool," Lewis spoke of the kind of writing in which the word melts upon the page. In *Childermass*, by contrast, the words, issuing in molten form from some subterranean foundry ("the intellect has its work-shop underground"), settle and form durable patterns. There are few works in which the sense of stasis is more remarkably achieved. Released from servitude to the time-series,

we are assisting at some archtypal ritual in which nature itself is an active agent:

The western horizon below the ridge, where the camp ends inland, but southward from the highroad, is a mist that seems to thunder. A heavy murmur resembling the rolling of ritualistic drums shakes the atmosphere. It is the outposts or investing belt of Beelzebub, threatening Heaven from that direction, but at a distance of a hundred leagues, composed of his resonant subjects. Occasionally upon a long-winded blast the frittered corpse of a mosquito may be borne. As it strikes the heavenly soil a small sanguine flame bursts up, and is consumed or rescued. A dark ganglion of the bodies of anopheles, mayflies, locusts, ephemerids, will sometimes be hurled down upon the road; a whiff of plague and splenic fever, the diabolic flame, and the nodal obscenity is gone.

(p. 1)

This is the hallucinatory world of Yeats's *Byzantium* and of the "City over the mountains" of Eliot's *The Waste Land*, which "cracks and reforms and bursts in the violet air"; but the effect is achieved by images derived from the several senses, not that of sight alone. The comparison with *Ulysses* is inevitable, though misplaced. Apart from the fact that Joyce's method is often satirized in *Childermass*, Lewis is not concerned to provide an equivalent to the stream of consciousness (which he called a barbarian technique). The stream has been reduced to a trickle—hence the conversational trivialities that abound—and we are shown rather the hard pebbled bed, the "truth of geological science," that supports it. An illusion dear to man is the belief that an impoverished consciousness may be enriched by an uprush of unconscious vitality. As a chthonic creature, man hopes to be born again from the same womb. He wishes to be either pure organism or pure spirit; but he is condemned to be man. To suggest that the metaphysics of the *Childermass* trilogy takes this form is not perhaps fanciful. Pulley and Satters, the two protagonists whose adventures continue throughout the series, remain human beings: "we behave as though we were now what we used to be, in life" (p. 70). They are beings for whom death has effected little change in a consciousness that never enjoyed more than rudimentary vitality. Death is merely a continuation of their dead-and-aliveness. (This applies even to Pulley, who in life was a well-known writer.) They are innocent of thought; and Childermass is the name for the Festival of the Innocents: "You needn't fancy your reason's going.—You haven't got any." To one of the questions in the mock-examination, "State whether in life you were Polytheist, Pantheist, Atheist, Agnostic, Theist or Deist—" Pulley advises his bewildered and uncomprehending companion to write down: "None of these." It is as good an answer as any.

The criticism leveled at *Childermass*, as against the subsequent volumes, is that the whole panoply of supernatural judgment lacks meaning, even acrostic meaning. Where and what is the moral behind it? A careful study of the work shows that the meaning is there; but as a creative artist, Lewis does not break the imaginative spell by obtruding it. He is not writing crude allegory, nor is he preaching a disguised sermon, like Charles Williams or C. S. Lewis. An important clue may be found in the elaborate description of the grotesque court in which the Bailiff conducts his business. The Punch and Judy structure in which he sits is adorned with a variety of occult signs, chief among them being the symbol of the *Maha-Yuga*. Now the *Maha-Yuga* is the name in Vedanta doctrine for a complete cycle of history. Divided into four separate *Yugas*, it implies the successive decline in human righteousness, culminating in the *Kali-Yuga*, in which righteousness reaches its nadir. The representation of the goat-hoof underneath the sign in question, together with the recurrent imagery of the serpent's head (repeated on the Bailiff's banner in *Monstre Gai*), seems to imply that the world brought to judgment has reached its final phase of iniquity. Man is in hell, "without dignity, without tragedy"[8]; and part of his hell is a dim apprehension that the conventional notions of salvation and damnation have been reduced to trivial farce.

Since a good deal of this first volume is occupied with seriocomic badinage on theological and philosophical themes, the reader may be impatient for some action. This is provided in abundance in the next two volumes, in which (among other events) the Third City is subjected to infernal raids on a cosmic scale; emissaries arrive from different regions of the universe; an angelic uprising is suppressed; and we are afforded horrifying glimpses of hell itself. This hell is the more terrible in that it forms a kind of inverted welfare state presided over by Sammael, the Devil, who is portrayed as a puritan intellectual

weary of his long tenure of office and anxious to resign it. In the final volume, *Malign Fiesta*, the impression of nightmare reaches its climax. In contrast to the "good fellowship" hells of modern secular imagination, Dis is shown to be a place of inexorable punishment; and the public may experience no little shock to find the inhabitants of hell behaving as fiendishly to their victims as the inhabitants of earth behave to theirs. Despite the originality and complexity of the theme, the writing is smoother and swifter than that of *Childermass* (the puzzling longueurs are absent), and we put down these extraordinary volumes regretting that the conclusion, "The Trial of Man," was never written.

IV

THE great merit of the *Childermass* series is that its theme grows progressively more articulate. Everything is subordinated to the central imaginative purpose, so that it may be regarded as Lewis' most integrated and proportioned work. What has happened is that Lewis has at last freed himself to be a creative writer. Whereas in his painting he slowly moved away from extreme abstraction, he observed in his writing a contrary discipline: the interest in concrete political and sociological problems, though undiminished, decreasingly invaded his fiction. Where the invasion persists, as in some of the *Rotting Hill* stories, the artistry is impaired. *Self Condemned* (1954), his most impressive performance in straight novel writing, begins to hold the reader the moment the overlong political explanations are put aside. The drama of "the Room," where the impoverished exiled couple learn the meaning of subsistence, remains of permanent significance; and the tragedy that follows the break-up of the primitive community is most movingly done. This note of high seriousness, which is first sounded in *The Revenge for Love* (1937), seems to stem from a deepening insight into human nature, or perhaps from a break in the reticence for which the author was noted. In an early work such as *Tarr*, the characters, though more real than those of *The Apes of God* and *Snooty Baronet*, do not fundamentally excite our interest. Kreisler is made to hang himself because he must somehow be gotten out of the novel; to kill him is a desperate way of making him a "living" character. But Hester's suicide in *Self Condemned* is something

---

[8]Ezra Pound, *Cantos*, xiv. The "Infernal Preliminary" of *Monstre Gai* (vi) underlines this fact clearly. The interpretation I have given had Lewis' approval.

that *she* does almost in spite of the author. The book has by that time taken control: it is in full flight from its creator—a flight beginning with the powerful description of the burning hotel and ending with the "white world" of the hospital; after which Lewis, catching up, ends the story with a university appointment for his Professor and extinguishes our interest.

Lewis' preoccupations with men as automata having no inside and presenting a facade to the world may have been derived in part from his revolt as a painter against the theory and practice of Impressionism. "The ossature is my favourite part of a living animal organism, not its intestines," he writes in *Satire and Fiction*, and in both *Paleface* and the *Dithyrambic Spectator* he praises the kind of art in which hardness and firm outline predominate. In *Men Without Art*, he defends his "external" approach to his characters, especially in *The Apes of God*; but while it is one thing to portray men as "machines governed by mere routine" (for a machine has no "inside"), it is another to maintain that they *are* machines.[9] Lewis seems to have passed through a period of extreme disillusion in which human beings seemed to him to be wholly deprived of what is conventionally called inner life: his posthumously published novel, *The Roaring Queen* (1973), seems to have pushed this notion to its extreme conclusion of negativity. He may have been nearer the truth when, in an early essay, "Tyronic Dialogues," he declared that "the world is in the strictest sense asleep, with rare intervals and spots of awareness. It is almost the sleep of the animal or insect world." And in a curiously interesting passage in *Self Condemned*, he takes up this theme of the essential mystery of human consciousness:

> The polar bear was mad, he was obsessed with being a polar bear; and many men were pretty mad also, incapable of looking at themselves from the outside. No one could imagine why man had abstracted himself and acquired the sanity of consciousness, why he had gone sane in the midst of a madhouse of functional character.
>
> (1983 ed., p. 212)

It is as if Lewis realized that the capacity to look at oneself from the outside can be done only from inside, and that without the cultivation of this inner capacity, human existence would remain what it so

[9]The quotation is from William Hazlitt, writing of Ben Jonson. Lewis defends its application to satire in *Satire and Fiction* (p. 45).

often is, "a nightmare staged in a menagerie" ("Tyronic Dialogues").

If we have repeatedly reverted to Lewis' ideas, it is because a writer's ideas are of fundamental importance. The day is past when it was thought virtuous in an imaginative writer to have nothing particular to say, and rank betrayal for him to presume to think. Once the apostles of form begin to talk about "significant form," they cease to be pure formalists. All great writers are preoccupied ultimately with philosophical issues. It does not necessarily make a man a greater writer to cultivate, like Lewis, his own ideas rather than other people's; but there are epochs, of which the present is one, in which the establishment of an "ideal" background is a condition of being a writer of any stature at all. Background it must be; we do not admire a novel in proportion as it resembles the superficiality of H. G. Wells's *The World of William Clissold* (1926). But a book that fails to illuminate our experience, or at best to add to it, cannot lay claim to artistic merit; and such illumination must derive from an inner source, which is ultimately the author's sense of value—we say "sense," for there need be no explicit formulation. To prophesy concerning literary reputations is proverbially dangerous; but it may be safe to say that the work of Lewis will retain its interest for later generations. The mission of the Enemy is not confined to one life span; it may be of special relevance to epochs in which the Enemy-figure is decreasingly tolerated. As John Holloway wrote in the *Hudson Review* (Summer 1957), his "work was crowned with decisiveness of achievement, and settled into a crystallizing comprehensiveness, only late in life. That is why it makes sense to see him as writing of our own world, of the world a generation later than . . . the others"; and he goes so far as to add, still comparing Lewis with Joyce, Lawrence, Eliot, and Yeats, "for the immediate future I see him as the most directly relevant of all."

Survival other than for the benefit of students of literary history must naturally depend on technical accomplishment of a high order. To maintain that Lewis has restored to English prose something of the vitality associated with the Elizabethans is a commonplace. His deep reading in Elizabethan literature is evident from a work of which much might be written, *The Lion and the Fox*. Thomas Nash is an obvious influence: Lewis has the same gusto, the same gossipy run of words, something of the same humor. But although Lewis' reading in several fields was prodigious—or perhaps because of that—we cannot easily enumerate the influences he underwent; his basic technique in both words and paint seems to have been ready-to-hand at the moment of composition. This is not to say that his work shows no relaxation of tension; some of the smaller pamphlets, such as *The Old Gang and the New Gang* (1933), an attempt to expose the fallacy of "the great blank of the missing generation," betray the impression that their author was impatient to clear them speedily out of the way. The remarkable fact is that Lewis in the course of time so disciplined his creative powers as to be able, once faced with a particular task, to write as if his sole specialty were the genre in question.

In addition to the satirico-comical and visionary talent of which examples have been given, Lewis excels most of his contemporaries in at least three kinds of writing. (It would be tempting to enumerate some of Lewis' other gifts: his genius for striking names, his sense of pageantry, and his remarkable ability to depict Anglican clergymen.) The first is that of invective. In this manner he is never scurrilous, and never merely rhetorical: "the Soldier of Humour is chivalrous, though implacable." The assault on the "Steinstutter" (the prose of Gertrude Stein) in *Time and Western Man*, on the literary cult of "wickedness" in *The Diabolical Principle* and *Men Without Art* (especially the passage on Oscar Wilde), and on upper-class radicalism in *The Revenge for Love* are magnificent denunciations of chicanery, fraud, and falsity. The second might best be described as "sociological analysis"—a technique in which he has had a large number of imitators. Many examples could be given, but a passage from his entertaining account of North African travel (*Filibusters in Barbary*, 1932) is especially worth citing (he is describing the shooting of a typical "desert love" film):

... it occurred to me as I watched these film-cattle that the stage-actor, whose work is done upon a stage, and the film-actor, the backgrounds for whose work are the scenes of everyday, though they have much in common, must differ very widely in important particulars. The stage-actor for instance could at all times be spotted out of the theatre, in his non-public life. Likewise the film-actor, but less so. For on the whole with the latter the actorishness must be of a more insidious sort. His artificiality has to be more intense, since the demands of the *real* everyday background are more exacting. In his professional displays the screen-worker in the nature of things is the last word in *naturalism*, at the opposite pole to a formal art. His actorishness therefore (the stigmata of the trade of Makebelieve

stamped into his features and attitudes) must be rather a distortion of a very common-or-garden norm, rather than the reflections of a transcendant, an abnormal, existence. The Film-man will tend to be a very intense, very slightly heightened Everyman; whereas the Garricks and Irvings would carry about with them in private the impress of successions of great Individuals of the Imagination—separated by all the arts of the formal stage-play from that everyday nature of Everyman, which is the particular province of Film-photography.

(p. 94)

The third form, which is related to the general descriptive capacity, is the rendering of trivial experience with a fidelity that causes a shock of surprised recognition. This might be called the idealization of banality, and it is here that the "external" approach achieves its best results. The effect, as this brief episode in a crowd scene shows, is more revealing than that of the interior monologue:

At his side a man started. He could feel the next body turning upon him. As part of the same system his own trunk revolved, as well, a little. . . . There was another turn of the screw. He allowed himself to be revolved half-left, until a magnified jaw, upon the opposite side, came into action, a half-inch from his profile. As the teeth shattered a luncheon-biscuit, a mild cerulean eye was dragged open by the rumination, into a startled cow's sidelong stare, and slid shut.

(*The Apes of God*, II, pp. 74–75)

Difficult as Lewis may be to classify, he represents the kind of figure who appears every so often, if not perhaps often enough, in the English tradition. There are certain affinities with William Blake. Although no two temperaments appear so different, Blake's social isolation, his struggle for the recognition of his art, his pungent pamphleteering, his "ready-made" genius, and finally his "openness" are characteristics Lewis shares. Admittedly Lewis was not accustomed to meet Isaiah on Rotting Hill as Blake encountered him on South Molton Street. But we can well imagine Blake illustrating the grotesque figures of Hanp and Arghol in *The Enemy of the Stars*; and some of that drama as well as parts of *Childermass* read strangely like the Prophetic Books. Another unclassifiable figure with certain resemblances to Lewis is Samuel Butler (1835–1902); but Lewis possessed something Butler lacked, a capacity to transcend his milieu and likewise to transcend his time. (It is to another Samuel Butler, 1612–1680, that Lewis shows some kinship: *One-Way Song*, "driving its coach-and-four through the strictest of hippical treatises," is in the style of *Hudibras*.) It is this breadth of vision that made Lewis not merely an intellectual (though he was proud to call himself one) but that almost extinct figure, a savant. Finally, with his directness, his hatred of the pliant and the vague (no modernist was less obscure), he may be pronounced an essentially masculine writer; for the power of his imaginative work depends for its stimulus upon what he called "the male chastity of thought."

He worked stolidly, and with the solace of growing renown, until his death in 1957: the affliction of his last years did nothing to curtail the powers of his invention. At the onset of nearly total blindness, he wrote the brave words with which it may be fitting to close: "Pushed into an unlighted room, the door banged for ever, I shall have to light a lamp of aggressive voltage in my mind to keep at bay the night" ("The Sea-Mists of the Winter," in the *Listener*, 10 May 1951).

SELECTED BIBLIOGRAPHY

I. BIBLIOGRAPHY. C. Handley-Reed, ed., *The Art of Wyndham Lewis* (London, 1951), pt. 2: "Chronological Outline," includes a bibliography and valuable notes on Lewis' painting; B. Morrow and B. Lafourcade, *A Bibliography of the Writings of Wyndham Lewis* (Santa Barbara, 1978); O. S. Pound and P. Grover, *Wyndham Lewis—A Descriptive Bibliography* (Folkestone, 1978).

II. COLLECTED LETTERS AND OTHER WORKS. W. K. Rose, ed., The *Letters of Wyndham Lewis* (London, 1962); E. W. F. Tomlin, ed., *Wyndham Lewis: An Anthology of His Prose* (London, 1969), with intro. by Tomlin; A. Munton, ed., *Collected Poems and Plays* (London, 1979).

III. SEPARATE WORKS. *Blast: Review of the Great English Vortex* (London, 1914), review, includes first version of the play *The Enemy of the Stars*; *Blast: No. 2* (London, 1915), review; *The Ideal Giant*; *The Code of a Herdsman*; *Cantelman's Spring Mate* (London, 1917), criticism and stories, privately printed; *Tarr* (London, 1918), novel, first installments published in the *Egoist* (April–November 1917), rev. ed. with added material (London, 1928); *The Caliph's Design: Architects! Where Is Your Vortex?* (London, 1919), art criticism; *Harold Gilman: An Appreciation* (London, 1919), art criticism with L. F. Fergusson.

The Tyro, nos. 1 and 2 (London, 1924), review; *The Art of Being Ruled* (London, 1926), political theory; *The Enemy*, nos. 1 and 2 (London, 1927), review, no. 3 (1929); *The Lion and the Fox: The Role of Hero in the Plays of*

Shakespeare (London, 1927), criticism; *Time and Western Man* (London, 1927), philosophy; *The Wild Body* (London, 1927), essays and stories; *Childermass, Part I* (New York–London, 1928), fiction, planned as a longer work but not immediately proceeded with, see *The Human Age*, below; *Paleface: The Philosophy of the Melting Pot* (London, 1929), sociological criticism.

The Apes of God (London, 1930; New York, 1932), satire; *Satire and Fiction* (London, 1930), pamphlet; *The Diabolical Principle and the Dithyrambic Spectator* (London, 1931), sociological criticism; *Hitler* (London, 1931), political commentary; *The Doom of Youth* (London, 1932), sociological criticism; *The Enemy of the Stars* (London, 1932), drama, rev. ed. of 1914 version; *Filibusters in Barbary* (London, 1932), travel; *Snooty Baronet* (London, 1932), novel; *The Old Gang and the New Gang* (London, 1933), pamphlet; *One-Way Song* (London, 1933), verse; *Men Without Art* (London, 1934), literary criticism; *Left Wings over Europe or How to Make a War About Nothing* (London, 1936), political commentary; *Count Your Dead: They Are Alive!* (London, 1937), political commentary; *Blasting and Bombardiering* (London, 1937), autobiography, new ed. with additional material (London, 1967); *The Revenge for Love* (London, 1937), novel; *The Mysterious Mr Bull* (London, 1938), sociological criticism; *The Jews, Are They Human?* (London, 1939), sociological criticism; *The Hitler Cult and How It Will End* (London, 1939), political commentary.

America I Presume (New York, 1940), sociological criticism; *The Vulgar Streak* (London, 1941), novel; *Anglosaxony* (Toronto, 1940), pamphlet; *America and Cosmic Man* (London, 1948), sociological criticism; *Rude Assignment* (London, 1950), autobiography; *Rotting Hill* (London, 1951), stories; *The Writer and the Absolute* (London, 1952), literary criticism; *Self Condemned* (London, 1954; Santa Barbara, 1983), novel; *The Demon of Progress in the Arts* (London, 1954), art criticism; *Monstre Gai* and *Malign Fiesta* (London, 1955), fiction, see next; *The Human Age*, 3 vols. (London, 1955–1956), comprises *Monstre Gai*, *Malign Fiesta*, and *Childermass*; *The Red Priest* (London, 1956), novel; *The Roaring Queen* (New York–London, 1973), satire, completed in 1936 but withdrawn before publication; *Unlucky for Pringle* (London, 1973), includes unpublished and other stories.

B. Lafourcade, ed., *The Complete Wild Body* (Santa Barbara, 1982); C. J. Fox, ed., *Journey into Barbary* (Santa Barbara, 1983), Morocco writings and drawings.

IV. CRITICAL STUDIES. J. Gawsworth, *Apes, Japes and Hitlerism* (London, 1932), a study and bibliography; H. G. Porteus, *Wyndham Lewis: A Discursive Exposition* (London, 1932); *Twentieth Century Verse* (November–December 1937), issue devoted to Lewis; *Wyndham Lewis the Artist: From "Blast" to Burlington House* (London, 1937); G. Grigson, *A Master of Our Time: A Study of Wyndham Lewis* (London, 1951); *Shenandoah* (Summer–Autumn 1953), Lexington, Va., issue devoted to Lewis; H. Kenner,

Wyndham Lewis (London, 1954); G. Wagner, *Portrait of the Artist as the Enemy* (London, 1957); R. Rosenthal, ed., *A Soldier of Humour and Selected Writings* (London, 1966); *Agenda* (Summer–Autumn 1969), London, issue devoted to Lewis; W. H. Pritchard, *Wyndham Lewis* (New York, 1968); W. Michel, *Wyndham Lewis: Paintings and Drawings* (London, 1971); R. T. Chapman, *Wyndham Lewis: Fictions and Satires* (London, 1973); T. Materer, *Wyndham Lewis the Novelist* (Detroit, 1976); J. Meyers, *The Enemy: A Biography of Wyndham Lewis* (London, 1980); J. Meyers, ed., *Wyndham Lewis: A Revaluation* (London, 1980); T. Kush, *Wyndham Lewis's Pictorial Integer* (Ann Arbor, Mich., 1981), a study of the relationship between Lewis' painting and writing.

D. H. LAWRENCE
(1885-1930)

Alastair Niven

THE WRITER AND THE MAN

No one attending the birth of David Herbert (Richards) Lawrence on 11 September 1885 could have anticipated that this fourth child and third son of a miner in the Nottinghamshire town of Eastwood would become the most frequently studied English novelist of the twentieth century. As this short study of his work emphasizes, he also became a proficient poet and playwright as well as one of the most prolific literary correspondents of modern times, a combative essayist, and a uniquely atmospheric travel writer. His talents extended to book reviewing, translation, philosophical discourse, painting, and teaching, but it was in the powers of his imagination and in his ability to match these with many appropriate aesthetic forms that his true genius lay. It has taken time to recognize Lawrence as a great writer, and in his own lifetime he often resorted to writing short articles in order to earn some of the money that his full-length works never made. His final and subsequently most famous novel, *Lady Chatterley's Lover* (1928), had initially to be privately published in Florence. If this was principally because of its sexual content, it nevertheless summed up the precarious relationship that Lawrence had with the publishing world. His best books were too controversial to be best sellers, the others too elusive to be categorized alongside the fiction of his time. Only since about 1960 has his work attained the reputation that now makes it a pivot of most modern English literature courses in all kinds of educational establishments throughout the world.

Lawrence is not an easy writer to read, but he never meant to be. At a time when the socially realistic novels of John Galsworthy, Arnold Bennett, and H. G. Wells were in vogue, Lawrence wanted to explore beneath the surface of human behavior in an attempt to gauge the forces that may motivate it. In his essay entitled "Morality and the Novel" (1925) he denounces "the smart and smudgily cynical novel, which says it doesn't matter what you do, because one thing is as good as another, anyhow, and 'prostitution' is just as much 'life' as anything else."[1] Lawrence's work is at all times totally concerned with discriminating between levels of existence. The majority of people live half-lives, failing to develop even a tenth of the potential that they retain inwardly without knowing it. Hence the prevalence in his work of images that suggest stunted growth: seeds within husks, fruits within rinds, roots struggling below stones for light and air, but too often only withering and dying. "A thing isn't life," he continues in "Morality and the Novel," "just because somebody does it. This the artist ought to know perfectly well. The ordinary bank clerk buying himself a new straw [hat] isn't 'life' at all: it is just existence, quite all right, like everyday dinners: but not 'life.'" This view shows how out of line Lawrence was with the age that produced Galsworthy's *The Forsyte Saga*, Bennett's *Clayhanger*, and Wells's *Kipps*.

Lawrence's need to explore man's nature below its surface led him into far franker discussions of sex, religion, and psychology than we find in any English novelist before him. He had the advantage over most of his predecessors in having inherited a scientific terminology for these topics to draw upon when he wished, but more normally he creates his own vocabulary, the authentic Lawrentian voice that is so readily recognizable to the practiced reader of his works. One may fairly doubt, however, whether Lawrence contributed to our knowledge any truly original notion about our basic human impulses. The author of "The Woman Who Rode Away" (short story, 1928), "Democracy" (essay, probably written 1917), the Loerke chapters in *Women in Love* (1920), and *The Plumed Serpent* (1926) could verge

---

[1] Quotations and references are from the Penguin editions of Lawrence's writings.

on the bizarre, but from an empirical point of view he more frequently followed initiatives already taken by other intellectuals. This in no way detracts from his radical importance in the development of English literature, for far more effectively than any other contemporary writer he kept pace with the welter of ideas that transformed society in his lifetime and brought them directly into his work. His subsequent reputation depended a great deal upon critics and readers recognizing how, especially in major achievements like *The Rainbow* (1915) and *Women in Love,* he debates many sides of the major issues of the early twentieth century. His work is highly individualized, as all great art must be; it is often eccentric and sometimes reactionary; but the person who has read his way through all of Lawrence has witnessed the transformation of English attitudes to education, morality, science, and culture through the eyes of someone who accepted nothing uncritically and who retained to the end of his life a deep skepticism about the nature of the changes.

Lawrence's writing may be termed "open-ended," even if it is not always open-minded. Though F. R. Leavis effectively linked his moral concern with Jane Austen's and George Eliot's, Lawrence lacks the sense of a confident overview that permeates the work of his nineteenth-century predecessors. Austen and Eliot, in their different ways, do not doubt their own moral perspective. Lawrence, while superficially appearing to be a more dogmatic and authoritarian writer, constantly extends himself to the limits of his understanding, seeming at times to contradict himself. In *Women in Love,* for example, he paints a powerfully seductive portrait of a society harnessed to science in order to serve man's greed, though his intention is to deplore the mechanical life to which it gives birth; at the end of *The Plumed Serpent* he appears to renounce the thesis upon which the novel has been built; he wrote *Lady Chatterley's Lover* three times because his focal point kept shifting. Indeed, in the sexual descriptions of this last novel, as in the pastoral rhapsodies of his first, *The White Peacock* (1911), or in the mystical ceremonies of *The Plumed Serpent,* the resources of language themselves nearly crack under the strain of expressing feelings that are wholly nonverbal in experience. Neither Austen nor Eliot—indeed, no English novelist before Lawrence, with the possible exception of Emily Brontë—had risked such a stretching of language. Lawrence brings to modern prose an instinct to express the nearly inexpressible that previously only some poets had tried. If his work sometimes threatens to collapse into a heap of rhetorical, repetitive, and inflated utterance, it is more because even the prodigiously flexible English language cannot cope with the moments he is seeking to render than because his art has failed.

Many elements in Lawrence's life story found their way into his writing, for he hardly ever wrote about things he had not witnessed or about situations that did not ultimately derive from personal experience. We know him, however, as a novelist, poet, playwright, or essayist, not as an autobiographer. He would plant allusions to his own life in his books—the Beardsall family in *The White Peacock,* for example, take their name from his mother, Lydia Beardsall, who herself became the basis for Mrs. Morel in *Sons and Lovers* (1913) and partly for Lydia Lensky in *The Rainbow.* However, he never allowed his imagination to be dominated by documentary accuracy. Specific details about Lawrence's life can be found in his writing only when he thought them useful to mention, and one wonders, therefore, if their relevance has not been overstressed by many critics.

D. H. Lawrence was brought up in respectable hardship. The atmosphere of Eastwood in the late nineteenth century is best described in his essay "Nottingham and the Mining Country" (1929), in which he rues the social and aesthetic disaster by which old England was made ugly and dehumanized by the spread of industrialism. The theme of erosion obsessed Lawrence all through his writing career—erosion of nature, erosion of humanity:

Now though perhaps nobody knew it, it was ugliness which betrayed the spirit of man in the nineteenth century. The great crime which the moneyed classes and promoters of industry committed in the palmy Victorian days was the condemning of the workers to ugliness, ugliness, ugliness: meanness and formless and ugly surroundings, ugly ideals, ugly religion, ugly hope, ugly love, ugly clothes, ugly furniture, ugly houses, ugly relationships between workers and employers. The human soul needs actual beauty even more than bread.

Lawrence recognized, moreover, that beauty means different things to different people, and that for this reason his parents' marriage had already drifted into a state of implacable resentment when he, the fourth son, was born in 1885. Mrs. Lawrence came originally from a lower-middle-class family in Kent. She had trained as a schoolteacher and continued until her death in 1910 to venerate study and art. Her husband had little formal education and viewed with suspicion anything that was not fundamentally necessary to the practicalities of living. Such a summary, however, has immediately to be qualified, lest it suggest that Lawrence's father was a puritan fundamentalist and his mother an intellectual dabbler. Almost the opposite was true. Lawrence's father had an instinct for comradeship with his workmates that became stronger as he felt more excluded from the life that Mrs. Lawrence created for herself and her children. He knew little more than the Bible, some hymns, and a few robust ballads, whereas she admired all expressions of learning, but she did so with a seriousness more profoundly puritanical than was evident in his love of plain living and easy friendship. Mrs. Lawrence venerated the Protestant ethic of hard work and Nonconformist morality. Pleasure that was not directed toward self-improvement verged on sin. In her son's novels we find this conflict between two almost opposed views of life expressed many times; though it is most obvious in *Sons and Lovers*, it is the issue upon which Rupert Birkin clashes with Gerald Crich in *Women in Love*, and it underlies every crisis in Lawrence's works where reason and will, intellect and passion are at odds. The source of these differences was partly social, or so Lawrence rationalized it at the end of his life in "Nottingham and the Mining Country," where he talks of the "curious close intimacy" between men in a working community and of the instinct for "possession and egoism" in the women left at home. Men disappear in their working lives into the dark womb of the earth, while the women remain on its surface crust, looking outward and beyond, straining for what might be rather than content with what actually is: it is as though our daily existences in an industrial community embody the gulf that has opened up between male and female.

Lawrence's mother idolized her second son, Ernest, who died in 1901. She cared about the education of all her children, however. Lawrence himself attended a local board school, and then from 1898 to 1901 was a student at Nottingham High School. After a brief period as a clerk in a Nottingham factory he became a student teacher in Eastwood, and from 1906 to 1908 he studied at Nottingham University College. It was in these years that he befriended Jessie Chambers, whom he uncharitably represented as the spiritual Miriam in *Sons and Lovers*. The Chambers family lived on a farm called The Haggs, where Lawrence spent many of his spare moments.

For the first time he experienced an environment where love of nature and discussion of serious issues did not have to be indulged defensively. He also came under the influence of William Hopkin, a local bootshop manager who introduced him to the principles of socialism and invited him to attend meetings where he met several Labour leaders. Lawrence always followed political life closely and became increasingly interested in the possibilities of political action in his later novels, but he remained dissatisfied with the values of the British political parties all his life, finding them hierarchical and simplistic.

Jessie Chambers, Alice Dax, Louie Burrows, Hopkin's wife, Sallie, Lawrence's sister Ada—in the years of his young manhood Lawrence was not short of female company. Mrs. Dax is believed to have initiated him sexually, and to Louie Burrows he was briefly and rather unconvincingly engaged. Jessie probably exerted the greatest influence on him because she took the greatest interest in his early attempts at writing, reading his first poems, the earliest draft of his play *A Collier's Friday Night* (published 1934), and the manuscript of *The White Peacock*. In 1908 Lawrence moved to Croydon, just south of London, where for the next four years he taught art, English, and biology at Davidson Road School. He made new friendships—mainly with women—and began tentatively to make contact with the literary world in London. He met Ford Madox Hueffer (later changed to Ford), editor of the *English Review*, Ezra Pound, Edward Garnett; he corresponded with many other writers, gave lectures about some of them, and continually enlarged his reading.

Lawrence's first published work consisted of poems and reviews in the *English Review*. *The White Peacock*, his first novel, was published in January 1911; *The Trespasser*, his second, in May 1912; and *Sons and Lovers*, his masterpiece of self-examination, in May 1913. This rapid production belies the difficulty with which Lawrence perfected his work to his own satisfaction. Each novel and most of his stories and poems went through several drafts. He was, however, a compulsive writer and had been so since the age of nineteen, when he wrote his first poems. For some writers such a prolific output might betoken an inability to relate to the social world, but this was never true of Lawrence. His friendships were sometimes shortlived and quarrelsome, but even in the years when he lived in remote places he enjoyed the fellowship of good company. No modern English writer has had the minutiae of his daily life so frequently observed in the memoirs of the people he met. Though Lawrence left Davidson Road School in 1912 and never again had that kind of regular employment, it would be quite wrong to suppose that he opted out of vigorous social intercourse.

In March 1912 Lawrence met Frieda Weekley, the wife of a Nottingham professor. Only two months later they left England together to visit Germany, where Lawrence was briefly arrested as a spy. Frieda came from a family of minor German nobility called von Richthofen. She was the mother of three children, whom she "abandoned" by going away with Lawrence, but with whom she remained in close contact all her life. It was in every sense an unconventional liaison that shocked contemporary morality, for it not only disrupted the Weekley marriage but it cut across class. When Lawrence and Frieda eventually married in July 1914 they compounded their social unacceptability by going against the current of Anglo-German hostility. The relationship could hardly have been more ill-starred from society's point of view, and this was undoubtedly a major factor in the Lawrences' eventual decision to leave England and live abroad.

By 1914 D. H. Lawrence was an established author, singled out by the elderly Henry James as one of the most promising novelists in England, the friend of many leading intellectuals, and the favored house guest of fashionable patrons. He was at work on his grandest conception, provisionally entitled *The Sisters*, but later to be divided into two quite different works, *The Rainbow* and *Women in Love*. He was flattered by this life and invigorated by his own intellectual capacities. He was, however, wary of being taken over by the Bloomsbury circle, whom he found conceited and soft-centered. He contemplated founding an experimental school with Bertrand Russell, but soon realized how far apart they were emotionally, and the friendship collapsed in cold abuse. He seemed to Russell "a sensitive would-be despot who got angry with the world because it would not instantly obey" (Russell's *Autobiography*, vol. II, 1968, ch. 1). Though Russell's case against Lawrence seems, in the light of Lawrence's complex writings, greatly overstated—"he had no real wish to make the world better, but only to indulge in eloquent soliloquy about how bad it was"—it is only fair to say that many of their contemporaries viewed him in a similar way.

The Lawrences led a peripatetic life during World War I, though regulations prevented them from leaving England. As we shall see in the discussion of his novel *Kangaroo* (1923), Lawrence had the most profound horror at the way the war was conducted. It seemed to him an explosion of all the obscene, violent, destructive, and materialistic characteristics of Western machine-worshiping society, while at the same time he was equally outraged by the loss of young life. He offered himself for war service and was rejected on medical grounds. He and Frieda stayed in London, then in a borrowed house near Padstow, and finally in a house near St. Ives. These were years of conflict with society. When *The Rainbow* was published in 1915 it was abused by the critics and eventually banned as a danger to public morality.

At the end of the war Lawrence at once made plans to leave England, though it was only after Frieda visited her family in Baden-Baden that they left for Italy in November 1919. Here, in various places including Florence, Capri, and Sicily, and with a period of three months in Germany, the Lawrences stayed until February 1922. By the standards of his earlier years this period was not so productive. Lawrence had completed *Women in Love* before he went abroad (it was published in New York in 1920). In Italy he completed *The Lost Girl* (1920) and revised his *Studies in Classic American Literature* (1923); wrote *Aaron's Rod* (1922), drawing on his observations in Florence; composed the poems that became *Birds, Beasts and Flowers* (1923); and produced some of his best short fiction, including "Fanny and Annie," "The Captain's Doll," and "The Fox." None of these works, however, is written on the scale of *Sons and Lovers*, *The Rainbow*, and *Women in Love*. Though there are few signs in this period of Lawrence's imaginative fertility drying up, he was undoubtedly feeling deeply unsettled. At the root of this apprehension was his profound conviction that the war had solved nothing and merely confirmed the wrong course that modern society was taking. He therefore looked around for other societies where alternative options might still be open, or where, perhaps, the people might be confident enough in their own created values not to want to emulate northern Europe and America. Sicily came close to such a society, but the influence of the church was too restricting. Lawrence therefore set sail for Australia, the newest attempt by Western man to start afresh in virginal surroundings; or so he supposed it to be, until he lived there for a few weeks in a house facetiously called "Wyewurk."

From Australia the Lawrences sailed, via New Zealand and Tahiti, to San Francisco, and thence they traveled to Taos in New Mexico. Here a rapacious American *padrona* named Mabel Dodge lived in a state of self-conscious "protection" of the local Indians. Lawrence increasingly resented any form of patronage, but among the descendants of the Aztecs in New Mexico and in Mexico itself he probably came closest to his ideal of discovering a way of life that was still in communion with its own ancestry; this was because the Mexico of the mid-1920's was undergoing a nationalist revival in which it was seriously suggested that the ancient religion of Quetzalcoatl might be a viable alternative to Fascism or to vehement pro-American influences. Lawrence rejoiced in the ruins of the former civilization he saw in Mexico and seriously explored the mystical aspects of the old religion. Out of these experiences came two of his most obscure and symbolic works of fiction, *The Plumed Serpent* and "The Woman Who Rode Away" (1925), but in the end he realized the impossibility of grafting an alien culture onto instincts that had taken centuries to germinate in his own part of the world. He found himself, in other words, as much in touch with the civilization he thought he had rejected, and whose material expressions he would continue to deplore, as the Mexican Indians were in touch with their serpent god.

In 1924 Lawrence made a brief return to Europe, and he finally left Mexico in September 1925, six months after tuberculosis was positively diagnosed as the origin of his continuing physical debilitation. Lawrence had never enjoyed good health, and in his search for other modes of living he always went to warm climates where his condition improved. From 1925 onward, however, his illness prevailed. It affected his creativity. In the last five years of his life he wrote only one novel, *Lady Chatterley's Lover*—though admittedly there are three versions of the book. He wrote some of his best essays, including "Pornography and Obscenity," "A Propos of *Lady Chatterley's Lover*," and "Nottingham and the Mining Country." Poems and stories, the latter including "The Escaped Cock" and "Rawdon's Roof," his philosophical commentary, *Apocalypse* (1931), and many of his best poems also date from these last years. He continued to review books, to write letters, to translate from the Italian, and to see friends. He lived from late 1925 to mid-1928 mainly in Italy and thereafter principally in France, where, at Vence on 2 March 1930, he died at the age of forty-four.

In the last months of his life Lawrence was visited by H. G. Wells, Norman Douglas, Aldous Huxley, Mulk Raj Anand, Mark Gertler, the Aga Khan, and many others. He was very famous but still almost totally unaccepted by the general reader. It took three decades before Lawrence's work automatically appeared on educational syllabi. He remains a controversial figure, not least to the modern feminist movement, which has usually taken issue with him. In 1960 he was the subject of the most publicized literary prosecution in the English courts when Penguin Books successfully defended its unexpurgated edition of *Lady Chatterley's Lover*. Lawrence is now, however, almost certainly the most widely taught twentieth-century writer that England has produced. All his books are in print. A definitive edition of his works is being published by Cambridge University Press. Film versions have been made of *The Trespasser, Sons and Lovers, Women in Love, Lady Chatterley's Lover, The Fox, The Rocking-Horse Winner*, and *The Virgin and the Gypsy*; and in *The Priest of Love* Lawrence's life in Mexico was brought to the screen. An academic journal is devoted to his work. At every point on whatever scale we measure popularity and greatness Lawrence's name appears. More than fifty years after his death he more and more appears as one of the major figures in the history of literature. This account of his work attempts to show why this may be so, and why the questioning and dispute that his name continues to arouse help to justify rather than to undermine his reputation.

THE WHITE PEACOCK

LAWRENCE's first novel is his only one to be told in the first person. *The White Peacock* came out in 1911, a few months after the death of Lawrence's mother, who was nevertheless able to read an advance copy. The new young author revised his work several times before submitting it to the publisher William Heinemann Ltd., and something of this overrefinement can be detected in the more flamboyantly lyrical passages of the novel. Lawrence always liked to reconsider what he had written once the first draft of a novel was complete, but this was usually because he was battling to find an appropriate form to express complex ideas and had even, on occasion, radically changed his views about what he wanted to say. In *The White Peacock* his revisions tend less to the recasting of thought than to a self-conscious decoration of the prose. This is a novel full of adolescent rhapsodizing about love and nature, but it contains many passages that anticipate the mature Lawrence. Its excesses are characteristic of an ambitious writer finding his feet and of someone wanting to harness his exultation in language to his curiosity about human behavior.

Before Lawrence the opportunities for working-class writers to write about working-class life and then to see their work in print were extremely rare. Lawrence therefore made middle-class people the subject of his first novel; in his next book, *The Trespasser*, the social level is less privileged, but the values against which the protagonists react are still essentially middle class; only in *Sons and Lovers* did he find an authentic voice for working-class aspirations. The three central characters in *The White Peacock*—Lettie Beardsall, George Saxton, and Leslie Tempest—are described to us by Lettie's brother Cyril. Lawrence handicaps himself by using an "I" narrator, for after Lettie marries Leslie it becomes difficult to sustain the intimate observation of their relationship, which Cyril's presence beforehand permits. The novel thus loses much of its impetus in its last chapters. Enough has been established by then, however, for us to recognize the error of Lettie's decision to reject the more sensual George. In doing this she denies fundamental needs within herself in order to do what is socially proper and what will bring the surface rewards of position and wealth. This conflict between self-fulfillment and social gratification reflects the more impersonal battleground of society's encroachment upon nature. In *The White Peacock* Lawrence celebrates the beauties of his native countryside with the extravagant enthusiasm of one who fears it may be threatened with destruction by creeping industrialization, a theme he summarizes symbolically by having the archenemy of materialism, the gamekeeper Annable, crushed by a fall of stones in a quarry.

The opening lines of Lawrence's first novel show his characteristic facility in relating the natural world to the human:

I stood watching the shadowy fish slide through the gloom of the mill-pond. They were grey, descendants of the silvery things that had darted away from the monks, in the young days when the valley was lusty. The whole place was gathered in the musing of old age. The thick-piled trees on the far shore were too dark and sober to dally with the sun; the weeds stood crowded and motionless. Not even a little wind flickered the willows of the islets. The water lay softly, intensely still. Only the thin stream falling through the millrace murmured to itself of the tumult of life which had once quickened the valley.

At the start of *The Rainbow* and *Lady Chatterley's Lover*, and at some point in all his novels, Lawrence links the contemporary world with the natural and social history out of which it has evolved. Here at the opening of *The White Peacock* he presents an idyllic scene of unperturbed nature, "gathered in the musing of old age." This is a world once tilled by monks where man has come and gone, but to which he now returns only as an onlooker—or a violator. The natural world throughout this novel has a harmony and self-sufficiency that contrast with the disruptions of the social world.

It is not impossible for man to share in this harmony. The harvest episodes and the scene with George and the narrator bathing in the pond show man and nature in almost rhythmic correspondence. "When I began to swim," Cyril records, "soon the water was buoyant, and I was sensible of nothing but the vigorous poetry of action." This sense of man finding complete freedom in a partnership with nature, as the body is supported here by the upthrust of the water, attracted Lawrence throughout his life. His works may largely be read as an exploration of how such a right balance may be found. The passage continues: "I saw George swimming on his back laughing at me, and in an instant I had flung myself like an impulse after him." Through partnership between human beings something of this absorption within nature may be discovered: certainly an ill-balanced relationship (an unhappy marriage, a dominating lover, a possessive parent) will be no way to achieve it. In *The White Peacock* Cyril's obvious attraction toward the manly George has homosexual undertones that no doubt expressed part of Lawrence's own nature, but they are not the essential point of it.

In novel after novel Lawrence seeks for the establishment of right partnership that will accord with nature. The sexual element is only part of this. Significantly in this passage the narrator speaks of flinging himself after George "like an impulse": not "on an impulse," but as though he has actually *become* a force of nature. For one instant true harmony between men and their natural environment has been created: "our love was perfect for a moment, more perfect than any love known since, either for man or woman." If only this moment could become a continuing reality. That is Lawrence's central urge—to find permanence for those isolated moments of perfect interfusion that we experience perhaps only a few times in our lives, but that, as a consequence, we know could be the character of our existences. In *Lady Chatterley's Lover*, at the end of his career, the insistence on trying to describe the pleasure of orgasm is a further attempt to express this deep conviction, at all stages of his career, that a higher kind of experience is waiting for us if we can only find a means of achieving it.

The only certainty is that all the roads upon which society is traveling are taking men away from the realization of this perfect harmony with nature and with each other. Annable, the keeper in *The White Peacock*, who looks forward to Mellors in *Lady Chatterley's Lover*, believes that all civilization is "the painted fungus of rottenness." He has been humiliated by marriage to a pre-Raphaelite lady—an early indication of Lawrence's antipathy to the destructiveness of gentility—and he has tried to drop out of society by living a "natural" life in the woods. Appealing to Cyril though Annable is, not least for his physical endowments, we are not invited to admire his existence as ideal. This Jacques in Arden has too cynical a view of man's failures: "he scorned religion and all mysticism." Though Lawrence had not yet developed a vocabulary for talking at length about them, he felt deeply that there were mysteries within nature ready for man's discovery. If the novel often retreats into poetic excess—"Here was spring sitting just awake, unloosening her glittering hair and opening her purple eye"—this is mainly because Lawrence strives too anxiously to find a lyrical tone for his quasi-religious motif. In *The Rainbow* he writes more confidently, not because he has greatly developed his sense of man's potential interaction with nature, but because his expression of it has its own personality. It no longer seems enslaved by a Pater-like concept of "beautiful prose." Yet many passages in *The White Peacock* also record Lawrence's wonderful eye for natural detail. Not since Hardy—who stopped writing novels in 1894—had an English novelist written so observantly of country life.

The White Peacock sets a vivid life of social interaction and of family relationships against its eulogy of the natural world. Several episodes indicate the viciousness in man's nature—George flippantly destroying a bee, and the rabbit hunt, for example—but at the core of each main character a crucial weakness exists like a rot: George's narcissism; Leslie's sexual inadequacy (hinted at: the novel of 1911 was still governed by Victorian restraints), for which he compensates by material display; Lettie's lack of courage to be herself; Cyril's detachment; Annable's bitterness. Lawrence's first novel is a study of failure. So, too, is *The Trespasser*, but in this next novel he at least shows elements of triumph in that the main character refuses to compromise with mediocrity. *The White Peacock* shows a natural world vanishing fast and the possibility of private worlds that might have been, but it does not offer the achievement of any world worth having. Lawrence could sow the seeds of his distinction as a novelist in this kind of young man's pessimism, but he could not bring it to fruition.

THE TRESPASSER

The Trespasser (1912) is the shortest of Lawrence's full-length novels. It is also one of his least known. Lawrence moves away from the familiar world of the English Midlands to London and the Isle of Wight. In 1909 he went on a short summer holiday to the Isle of Wight and from that visit he no doubt gained some of the local color for *The Trespasser*, but many of the circumstances of the novel were derived from a brief love affair between one of his Croydon colleagues, Helen Corke, and a music teacher. Helen Corke kept a journal of her relationship with Herbert Macartney during a week they spent together on the Isle of Wight; it was on this and on his conversations with her that Lawrence based the relationship between Siegmund McNair and Helena Verden in *The Trespasser*. Helen Corke re-created her friendship with Macartney in her own novel *Neutral Ground* (1931), and said more about it in her autobiography, *In Our Infancy* (1975). In both works her version significantly differs from Lawrence's. As with *Sons and Lovers*, however, critics have expended much energy on the biographical elements in the book, without always appreciating that Lawrence was writing a work of imagined experience. Its source lay in fact, but the concerns of the novel show a natural development from *The White Peacock*; Lawrence would no doubt have found some other framework to explore the same issues had he not encountered Helen Corke's account of her bizarre romance.

Whereas *The White Peacock* shows a settled

world being disrupted by emotional tensions and by the creeping malaise of modern life, *The Trespasser* begins in a dull suburban house in London. Lawrence sets a substantial part of only one other novel, *Aaron's Rod*, in the capital city, and in both books the main character escapes from it as soon as possible. As Lawrence says at the end of his essay "Dull London" (1928), "the sense of abject futility in it all only deepens the sense of abject dullness, so all there is to do is to go away." Helena's room, where *The Trespasser* begins, has walls "of the dead-green colour of August foliage" and a carpet that lies "like a square of grass in a setting of black loam." These comparisons with nature only highlight the drabness of the room. Siegmund's home is no different, loveless and lightless when we first read of it. Helena and Siegmund escape from their dreary world of mechanical routine to a brief idyll on the Isle of Wight, but they return to London, she in eventual denial of their love, he to his hollow marriage.

Siegmund is the only one of Lawrence's major protagonists to take his own life. He cannot endure a life without Helena, yet to abandon his wife and children is equally inconceivable:

He was bound by an agreement which there was no discrediting to provide for them. Very well, he must provide for them. And then what? Humiliation at home, Helena forsaken, musical comedy night after night. That was insufferable—impossible! Like a man tangled up in a rope, he was not strong enough to free himself.

(ch. 27)

Siegmund therefore hangs himself. His death requires some courage, but the fact that Lawrence never again used such an ending underlines his dissatisfaction with this solution to the novel, and may account for the relatively low estimation of it that most critics have had. In a novelist so passionately interested in seeing how a fulfilled life may be attained, the extinction of life represents a defeat not only for his main character but for his own conception of fiction. Later heroes like Paul Morel in *Sons and Lovers* and Birkin in *Women in Love* overcome their tendency to despair and reach toward a positive view of life, however difficult this may be to sustain.

The Trespasser is not an antifeminist novel—Siegmund's wife, for example, is portrayed with some pity—but it does suggest that between male and female there too often exists an imbalance in the relationship that debilitates both partners. As

Siegmund's acquaintance Hampson puts it, "She can't live without us, but she destroys us." This is not Lawrence's view of what has to happen when men and women conjoin, but his notion of what frequently does happen because the right balance has not been struck, give and take has not been proffered. An assertion of wills must lead to one partner's victory over the other. Since the man normally works closer to the land than the woman, whose role has traditionally been domestic, he is more in tune with the natural forces with which humanity has so often lost touch. In later novels Lawrence shows women breaking out of their expected role and thus showing a capacity to achieve with men the two-way sharing, in harmony with the natural world, that they too frequently resist—Ursula Brangwen in *The Rainbow* is the prime example. Helena in *The Trespasser* goes some way in Ursula's direction, but fatally lacks the final intensity of vision that is needed. Hampson has a point, Lawrence intends us to realize, when he goes on to say: "These deep, interesting women don't want *us*; they want the flowers of the spirit they can gather of us. We, as natural men, are more or less degrading to them and to their love of us; therefore they destroy the natural man in us—that is, us altogether."

The Trespasser shares with *The White Peacock* a vivid realization of the natural world, though in the former Lawrence indulges less in poetic effect for its own sake. Indeed, it tends to be in his analysis of human behavior that his imagery overreaches itself. Self-conscious phrasing—"She was the earth in which his strange flowers grew" or "She felt herself confronting God at home in His white incandescence"—shows how artificial Lawrence could still be. The novel is full of a slightly adolescent religiosity: Siegmund, for example, derives comfort "from the knowledge that life was treating him in the same manner as it had treated the Master, though his compared small and despicable with the Christ-tragedy." At times the urgency of Lawrence's desire to express his sense of there being a mystic reality that makes human ambitions paltry leads him to be nearly incomprehensible:

. . . it only happens we see the iridescence on the wings of a bee. It exists whether or not, bee or no bee. Since the iridescence and the humming of life *are* always, and since it was they who made me, then I am not lost. At least, I do not care. If the spark goes out, the essence of the fire is there in the darkness. What does it matter? Besides, I *have* burned bright; I have laid up a fine cell of honey somewhere—I wonder where?

(ch. 21)

Rationally this passage does not make clear sense: how can "iridescence on the wings of a bee" exist, "bee or no bee"? However, it is necessary to accept, because we encounter many such prose moments in later works, that Lawrence is struggling to express a concept that lies beyond the normal restrictions of language—to convey that there is something deeply interfused in the universe that will continue to exist even if mankind should die out, and that certainly continues when each individual man dies. This creative force can be glimpsed at least representatively in nature—the bee's wings—but man normally makes no attempt to understand what it is or how it may be experienced fully. In *Women in Love* Birkin will reflect on what the world would be like if the human race should cease to exist: "a world empty of people, just uninterrupted grass, and a hare sitting up," an image of a nature still flowing (a favorite Lawrentian word) even if man has failed to live up to it. In *The Trespasser* the novelist reaches for a way of expressing his sense of this other life, beside which human life looks ephemeral and irrelevant. It is worth noting, however, that he has not yet sorted out his scale of values. Siegmund feels increasingly "like a slow bullet winging into the heart of life," as though his human existence has no meaning in the "gorgeous and uncouth" natural world. Later novels are life affirming, with Lawrence seeking to accommodate humanity, not to reject it. *The Trespasser* may have been for him a therapeutic novel, for within it he seems to exorcise the debilitating melancholia and nihilism of the young romantic idealist in order to move, in his next novel, to a more robust and emotionally complex contemplation of the world. Eventually, in *The Rainbow* and *Women in Love,* he came as close as he could to defining the right balance that ought to exist between man's sense of his own worth and his understanding of the life forces that he so often fails to perceive because of his self-obsession.

The Trespasser is full of themes that Lawrence developed more expressively in maturer novels. In itself it is too patchy to be a complete success, though the opening and closing chapters have a severity that shows Lawrence's eagerness not to use language only for poetic effects. The book is another study in stunted growth. In his next novel, *Sons and Lovers,* he developed beyond this because, for the first time, he imagined his own instincts at the center rather than at the periphery of the experiences he was describing.

SONS AND LOVERS

Sons and Lovers is possibly the most widely read serious English novel of the twentieth century. In some respects it renders commentary of any kind absurd. Who, for example, can read the description of Mrs. Morel's death without being reminded of a grief they themselves have experienced? The novel obviously draws on personal recollections so deeply that it seems impertinent to analyze it. Yet our admiration for it results partly from its imaginative intensity and from its masterly control of feeling. Lawrence's narrative never becomes self-indulgent; even in the moments when he tries to be visionary or mystic the prose becomes only slightly overcolored. Personally felt though *Sons and Lovers* is, Lawrence in some ways makes of it his most orthodox novel. It capitalizes on the *Bildungsroman,* a form of fiction that allows the novelist to re-create through the maturing of his protagonist some of his own remembered intensity of experience. *Sons and Lovers* marks a great advance for Lawrence on the two novels he had written before it, but in terms of the evolution of the English novel its main innovations are less a matter of fictional technique than of topic. It is one of the first wholly authentic novels of English working-class life, set mainly in an industrialized as opposed to an agricultural community and written by someone who had grown up within the society he is depicting. It marks Lawrence's arrival as a great novelist, but it may also mark the end of his ability to speak so straightforwardly of working life, for its success provided him with an entrée into other kinds of society to which he had already started to gravitate from the time he began teaching in Croydon.

"Paul Morel [as he initially planned to call *Sons and Lovers*] will be a novel—not a florid prose poem, or a decorated idyll running to seed in idealism: but a restrained, somewhat impersonal novel." This comment, in a letter dated 18 October 1910, shows how self-critical Lawrence could be, for he planned now to write a work wholly different from *The White Peacock* or *The Trespasser,* both of which, we must conclude from the phrasing, dissatisfied him on account of their exaggerated language. *Sons and Lovers,* one must emphasize, is not an autobiography. If it were then there would be no place in it for an incident such as that where Mrs. Morel names her baby son—"She thrust the infant forward to the crimson, throbbing sun, almost with relief." This may be distantly related to an actual happening about which Lawrence's mother talked, but it is realized poetically and symbolically, an initiation rite, a baptism by fire, an exorcism of guilt. It goes far beyond a mere statement of personal history. This is so with every part of the novel.

In the conflict that develops early on in *Sons and Lovers* between Mr. and Mrs. Morel we see dramatized, in an almost emblematic way, two strains in the English national character. This in no way minimizes the powerful clash of temperaments and wills that makes their marriage so tragic and, in the last chapters of the book, so pathetic. It shows *Sons and Lovers* to be not only a novel of private emotions but a study in late-nineteenth-century social life. Mr. Morel displays qualities of unintellectual male-oriented sociability that contrast with his wife's strict Nonconformist morality, high intentions for her children, and possessiveness. Lawrence, in his later books, came to admire the type of man that he believed his father to have been far more than would appear from his portrait of Walter Morel, who is presented initially as unreasonably ill-tempered, then as weak-willed, and finally as an empty husk from whom the kernel of life has been removed. In *Sons and Lovers* the personality of Mrs. Morel dominates all the early chapters and the end of the novel. Lawrence's account of her as magnificently strong-minded, loving but stifling, is one of the chief glories of the book, though his portrait is critical. She sums up much of the imprisoning morality and vaulting intellectual ambition that he increasingly believed to be instilled in the women of industrialized communities.

Paul Morel's growing up and his awakening to the possibilities of the world is the main subject of *Sons and Lovers.* To convey this, Lawrence achieves a synthesis of social realism and metaphor that may be unparalleled in English fiction. There are many instances to exemplify this—Mrs. Morel's expulsion from her house on the night she becomes aware of Paul's conception is one example; Clara's initiation of Paul is another. We find it at all stages of Paul's relationship with Miriam. Here they are, at spring-time, symbolically representing youth and promise, while at the same time tangibly expressing the goodness of nature to which Paul can escape from his industrial home: "Miriam went on her knees before one cluster, took a wild-looking daffodil between her hands, turned up its face of gold to her, and bowed down caressing it with her mouth and cheeks and brow." Her action is sexual yet chaste, loving yet oppressive. It provokes Paul into a cruel denunciation of her possessiveness. "You're always begging things to love you," he says, "as if you were a beggar for love. Even the flowers, you have to fawn on them." The scene thus serves two purposes: to show a pastoral world in which Paul can make contact with pleasures unknown in Bestwood, where he lives, and to use this world for explicitly metaphorical purposes. It is an Eden in which love can be encountered not only as a sexual experience but as something spiritually oppressive, and ultimately life-restricting rather than fulfilling.

Though Miriam is partly based on Jessie Chambers, who was offended by this portrayal of her relationship with Lawrence, she often seems in the novel less a creature of flesh and blood than a "literary" prototype, platonic and allusive. She creates around herself a nunlike and romantic purity, giving herself to Paul more as an act of self-martyrdom than in a spirit of sexual partnership. Her instincts attract her to figures in history and to saints in paintings. She does not like the reality of known experience so much as the chimeras of fiction, and thus she models her relationship with Paul on ideals rather than allowing it to grow out of true instincts. Just as Paul learns to conceal from his mother all his private feelings that do not directly impinge upon her, so he comes to realize how much of his true self has to be held back in his relationship with Miriam.

Like Lettie in *The White Peacock,* Miriam lacks the capacity to grow in harmony with her partner. Paul outstrips her. A modern feminist case against *Sons and Lovers* would center on the manner in which Lawrence presents the women in the novel as only instruments for Paul's awakening to manhood. The charge does not altogether hold true, however. Miriam is inadequate *in her own right.* By the Lawrentian standard she does not permit her repressed sexuality any kind of natural outlet, so that she can give herself only in an act of self-abnegation. She denies the possibilities in her own life as well as in Paul's. Similarly, Paul's mother, though emotionally very affecting for most readers, never knows a life of give and take in equal proportions. She wants to possess or to dominate or to live through the surrogate satisfaction of other people's achievements.

Clara Dawes comes closest to the modern feminist position by making a free choice to return to her husband after initiating Paul into a fuller manhood than Miriam could provide; but Clara's strength contrasts, like Mrs. Morel's and Walter's, with the weakness of her husband. Far from the women of the novel being only staging posts in Paul's progress to adulthood, they loom like intransigent fates who induct him into mysteries only at the threat of extinguishing his personal light. At the end of the novel, when he feels himself "infinitesimal, at the core of nothingness, and yet not nothing," we do not remember Paul as the thwarter of female aspirations. The women of the novel have shown a strength that, alone now, he has to prove he has himself. In his relationships with women, whether as a son or as a lover, Paul has resisted being taken over. It most nearly happens in the natural bond of mother and son, but Miriam and Clara threaten it in different ways. He resists not just to preserve his personal identity but because the right equation cannot be established between a consuming partner, as Lawrence sees each of these women, and a still weak man who has not worked out for himself a conduct of being. The feminist argument has some truth in it if it claims that Lawrence makes the women of *Sons and Lovers* tyrannizing and emasculating, but none at all if the case rests on an accusation that they have no being except to feed Paul Morel's vanity.

In his first two novels Lawrence had tried to deal with sexual feeling in a discreet way. Even in *The Trespasser*, the main subject of which is an adulterous passion, he does not often find a language capable of facing the issues head on. His view of sex sometimes seems more theoretical than intuitive in these early novels, either because of poetic evasions or because of a simple incapacity to talk in a sustained way about sexual feeling. It is therefore astonishing to see how much Lawrence matured as a writer in the few months that separate the final revision of *The Trespasser* in February 1912 and the completion of *Sons and Lovers* in November of the same year. Now when he wants to be poetic the passage does not read as decorative gilding or adolescent extravagance but as a necessary part of the symbolic patterning. Flower imagery is applied with a consciously associative value. Set pieces, like Paul and Miriam beside the ivory-colored roses (in chapter 7) or their lovemaking at the time of the cherry harvest (in chapter 11), are fully integrated into the novel. Naturalistic dialogue is used to explore feeling in a more direct way than perhaps any English novelist had used it before. Here, for example, are Clara and Paul in chapter 13:

> "Do you think it's worth it—the—the sex part?"
> "The act of loving itself?"
> "Yes; is it worth anything to you?"
> "But how can you separate it?" he said. "It's the culmination of everything. All our intimacy culminates then."
> "Not for me," she said. " . . . I feel," she continued slowly, "as if I hadn't got you, as if all of you weren't there, and as if it weren't *me* you were taking——"
> "Who, then?"
> "Something just for yourself. It has been fine, so that I daren't think of it. But is it *me* you want, or is it *It*?"

The passage reads calmly and undramatically, yet it conveys so much that Lawrence struggles to articulate in this novel, but that he had hardly ventured to express in his first two books. What is the relationship of love and sex? Must sexual passion entail possessiveness? Is there a chance of creating a balance between partners? How can the awareness of self in one person be matched by a knowledge of the other person's selfhood? Does the oneness of me necessarily prevent me from seeing the youness of you, and if I see it can I seek it out without wanting to crush it? Are Miriam's self-denial and Paul's self-gratification the only ways in which sexual feeling can express themselves? Lawrence explores personal and sometimes mystical experiences through language that carefully balances ordinary speech with poetic intensification. This, as much as its reputation for emotional honesty, is one of the strengths of this great novel.

Though Lawrence analyzes relationships in *Sons and Lovers* so well, we ought not to forget his success in conveying the detail of late-nineteenth-century working life in both a mining and a farming community. The novel moves freely between the two, partly reminding us of how an industrialized village like Bestwood (Lawrence's own hometown, Eastwood) seems like an ugly gash on the landscape. The miners' lives, the petty class distinctions that grow up even in a poor community, the suspicion of books, the attraction of London, the way in which competitions and scholarships provide almost the only avenue of escape for an intelligent young man, all these come fully alive as we read *Sons and Lovers.* Lawrence's self-analysis and his depiction of the halting way in which youth moves into maturity would have far less density and even credibility if the social background were less effectively realized. In *Sons and Lovers* he wrote probably his most immediately approachable book and the one that readers will bother with, even if they cannot tolerate anything else he wrote. If the ability to remind people of their own lives in a way that makes common experiences seem special is the gift of a major writer, then Lawrence proves himself many times in *Sons and Lovers.*

THE RAINBOW

"I love and adore this new book," Lawrence wrote to Edward Garnett in March 1913. " . . . I think it's great—so new, so really a stratum deeper than I think anybody has ever gone, in a novel." Though he wrote this in the first month of its composition, Lawrence's intention for *The Rainbow* was clear from the start. This was to be a novel not only unlike the three he had written ("It is all analytical—quite unlike *Sons and Lovers,* not a bit visualized," he adds in the same letter) but a new departure for the form of the novel itself. There is immense confidence in the way Lawrence talks of this new book, as though he now felt equipped to tackle something on an altogether larger scale than anything he had attempted before, a novel not drawn from personal experience, as basically both *Sons and Lovers* and *The White Peacock* had been, or from the experience of a friend, as *The Trespasser* was, but concerned with the way in which modern English society had reached its contemporary state. Indeed, more than this, Lawrence took nothing less than the evolution of man as his theme. It shocked him profoundly when *The Rainbow,* published in 1915, met with a disapproving reception and eventual banning on account of its supposed obscenity.

As mentioned earlier, Lawrence conceived *The Rainbow* and *Women in Love* as one novel. Initially he intended calling this work *The Sisters* and subsequently he referred to it as *The Wedding Ring,* a particularly apt title as the central subject of the book was to be the way in which a complete being might be realized, perfectly in union with the chosen partner and at one with a united society. The ring has conventionally been a symbol of union and perfection: in thinking of *The Wedding Ring* as a title for his new work Lawrence intimated his wish to write about the potential perfectibility of man. As he worked further on the novel his bright conception seemed to cloud, and eventually he felt he could no longer sustain the vision in a single book. He thus split *The Sisters* or *The Wedding Ring* into *The Rainbow* and *Women in Love,* linking them principally through the character of Ursula Brangwen, but creating in the second novel almost a modifier of the first. The structure of *Women in Love* is quite different from that of *The Rainbow,* synchronic rather than diachronic (actions happening simultaneously though in different places rather than actions narrated developmentally in a sequence). Though the almost apocalyptic and revelatory images of the first novel carry over into the second, they do so in a less "plotted" way. Whereas the metaphorical patterning of *The Rainbow* seems at times almost in danger of determining the ideas of the novel rather than of expressing already conceived thoughts, there is an even distribution of arguments in *Women in Love* supported by an intricate network of imagery in which no one symbol prevails over the others. *Women in Love* is the more equivocal novel, though in the end the same vision that inspires *The Rainbow* survives the challenges of powerful countervisions. Lawrence seems to have found the imaginative life of *The Rainbow* impossible to maintain into a second volume, for his own intellectual honesty demanded that he be fair to the pervasive forces of materialism, capitalism, and autocracy that his instincts railed against.

The Rainbow thus has a clarity of utterance that is sometimes less evident in *Women in Love.* It is a saga novel, but so unlike contemporary works like Galsworthy's *The Forsyte Saga* or Bennett's *Clayhanger* as to create its own genre within English fiction. The links are with Norse sagas, with the Bible, and with *Paradise Lost* if they are anywhere, but Lawrence's achievement is not seriously comparable with these: names and symbols allude to other literatures, some of the language has a Hebraic resonance; but Lawrence does not depend on any imagination other than his own to express the nature of his vision.

The Rainbow spans three generations of the Brangwen family. A simplified genealogical plan may help us, with the earliest generation married around 1840.

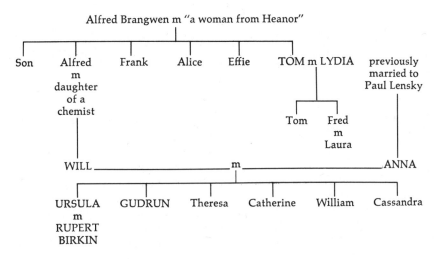

The characters in capital letters in the plan are the principals in *The Rainbow* and *Women in Love*, though Gudrun plays only a minor role in the first novel and Rupert Birkin appears only in the second. Indeed, *Women in Love* concerns the youngest Brangwen generation almost exclusively, Will and Anna having slipped into a passive background and Tom and Lydia being long dead. Though the novels concentrate on the inner lives of these Brangwens, they make their way through a society undergoing such rapid change that this feature itself becomes pivotal to Lawrence's conception. Indeed, the Brangwens in *The Rainbow* have a representational significance, illustrating the movement of solid English farming stock from a wholly agricultural existence to a world in which industrialization and intellectual ambitions have rendered complex and confused their former certainties of belief.

The Rainbow opens with a testament to the lost preindustrial world. Lawrence knew that history cannot be reversed, though lessons may be learned from it. This world is irrecoverable. It may, nevertheless, be lamented. He therefore wrote a prologue to the main novel, though in the guise of an opening chapter, for he wanted the final form of *The Rainbow* to be an organic whole, no part outside the integrated entirety:

In autumn the partridges whirred up, birds in flocks blew like spray across the fallow, rooks appeared on the grey, watery heavens, and flew cawing into the winter. Then the men sat by the fire in the house where the women moved about with surety, and the limbs and the body of the men were impregnated with the day, cattle and earth and vegetation and the sky, the men sat by the fire and their brains were inert, as their blood flowed heavy with the accumulations from the living day.

(I.1)

In a free-flowing, almost impressionistic prose Lawrence establishes an image of pastoral harmony. It is the women who disrupt it:

On them too was the drowse of blood-intimacy, calves sucking and hens running together in droves, and young geese palpitating in the hand while the food was pushed down their throttle. But the women looked out from the heated, blind intercourse of farm-life, to the spoken world beyond. They were aware of the lips and the mind of the world speaking and giving utterance, they heard the sound in the distance, and they strained to listen.

(I.1)

Like Eve, their prototype, the early Brangwen women are not content with their settled existence. They glimpse possibilities of knowledge and material achievement beyond it. Here Lawrence implants in the reader's mind an association—it is no more than that—with the Book of Genesis, and he loosely moves to the Book of Revelations at the end of *Women in Love* when Ursula and Birkin set out to seek a new kind of world; but at no time does he permit his own vision to be molded by the biblical parallels. He is more concerned at the start of *The Rainbow* to evoke a preindustrial world and then to establish within it a conflict of ambitions between the sexes, for this will be the central issue of the novel. The men are content to live this life; the women lust for something more. Lawrence extends the issues upon which the Morel marriage founders in *Sons and Lovers*, but he no longer believes it to be merely a struggle between different kinds of moral perception. The women's behavior is virtually instinctive, as though at some primeval point when the sexes separated out of the initial life-mass they were imbued with a biological hunger for knowledge and advancement. The first sentence of *The Rainbow* begins "The Brangwens had lived for generations of the Marsh Farm," as though they have evolved there from the origins of life.

Throughout *The Rainbow* and *Women in Love* Lawrence insists on the difference between the sexes as more than obviously physical; it is mental, emotional, within the beings of men and women. "The man has his pure freedom, the woman hers," he writes in *Women in Love*. "Each acknowledges the perfection of the polarized sex-circuit. Each admits the different nature in the other." If this is so, however, does it necessarily mean an inalienable gulf between men and women and an irrevocable isolation for each individual? Lawrence seems anxious to resist such a conclusion. His conviction that the sexes can ideally live in balanced harmony with each other, neither claiming possession of the other (though in reality both often do), is the thesis of both *The Rainbow* and *Women in Love*. Each relationship in the novels explores ways in which such equilibrium may be established, testing the claims of each kind of partnership in an earnest search for proof that the ideal is realizable. Tom and Lydia, Will and Anna, perhaps most positively Ursula and Birkin show moments of perfected union, though none of these relationships survives without conflict. Lawrence knew from his own marriage that a measure of struggle and argument between both partners was a natural part of a developing relationship, and that once these ceased the union was threatened with extinction. In the various relationships of *The Rainbow* and *Women in Love*, however, he seeks to distinguish between truly creative conflicts and those that, like war, leave only scars and damage.

Tom Brangwen marries Lydia Lensky. He has grown up mainly among women and has a love of poetry and a resentment of "mechanical stupidity" that separates him from the other Brangwen menfolk of his generation. Lydia is Polish, a stranger in religion and in cast of mind from the community into which she marries. Though Lawrence makes little of her Polishness, using it primarily to convey her "otherness" or the distance that must always exist between her and Tom, he nonetheless makes no mis-

takes historically in talking about her background or her first marriage to a failed radical. The details of *The Rainbow* are always accurate, and the narrative unfolds with a tight control of chronological accuracy.

Tom and Lydia live in struggle with each other but their marriage is ultimately a success in Lawrence's scheme, for it entails a creative kind of self-questioning and a constant move forward. Lydia's daughter, Anna, the child of her marriage to Paul Lensky, grows into a wholly self-sufficient person, inheriting her mother's private instincts but none of her giving nature. Anna is one of Lawrence's most original creations. We follow her from her willful childhood, vexatiously trying to tame the farm geese, to her destructive maturity when she almost voluntarily sloughs her imagination and denies all emotions other than her maternalism. Into her world comes her cousin Will, "a dark enriching influence she had not known before." The potential is there, Lawrence emphasizes, for a fully balanced partnership, he a worker who can make art and beauty shine out of simple wood, she the begetter of children who has yet glimpsed possibilities of a superior life: "Something she had not, something she did not grasp, could not arrive at. There was something beyond her. But why must she start on the journey? She stood so safely on the Pisgah mountain." Anna quite literally cannot make the effort to discover the better world that, imaged by the first appearance of a rainbow in the novel, she has been privileged to glimpse: "She would forfeit it all for the outside things . . . she would throw away the living fruit for the ostensible rind."

There ensues a battle more debilitating than that between the Morels. Will retreats into himself and Anna finds a limited fulfillment in rearing her children. Theirs, however, is a tragedy of wasted opportunity, for both Will and Anna stifle their own growth. A favorite image of Lawrence's is the plant struggling for life above ground only to meet a stone that causes it to twist itself into a half-formed distortion. It can be applied to Will and Anna, who have the capacity to form the kind of balanced relationship that Lawrence seeks to express, but who turn away from this into an existence of destructive conflict and eventual sterility. Even their moments of reconciliation are as though impaired by their self-absorption, opting out of the flow of life.

In their eldest child, Ursula, Lawrence invests the best possibility of creating a new form of life, for she remains always inquiring and, in *The Rainbow* at least, unfettered—"out of nothingness and the undifferentiated mass, to make something of herself!" Her path is partly an intellectual one, partly sexual, but unlike her mother she accepts her destiny as "a traveller on the face of the earth . . . ultimately and finally, she must go on and on, seeking the goal that she knew she did draw nearer to." At times Lawrence seems to echo Charlotte Brontë's imagery in *Jane Eyre* (though in his 1929 essay "Pornography and Obscenity" he calls her novel "slightly obscene" on account of Rochester's need to be emasculated before he is worthy of Jane)—he speaks of Ursula as a bird, an infant crying in the night, a moon-person whose reality is not wholly of this world. Yet her first attempts to make sense of her life are through dedicated service to society. Her days as a schoolteacher show her something of the intractability of human nature, and they allow Lawrence an opportunity to write with scathing accuracy about the English classrooms of his own day, wherein educational ideals almost inevitably fell victim to expediency.

In a perhaps conscious allusion to *Jane Eyre*, Ursula has the opportunity to leave England and go to India. Her relationship with the Polish aristocrat Skrebensky, like Jane's with St. John Rivers, has an almost comic edge to it, for it is wholly out of balance. He is a son of institutional life, restricted by class, by the army, by his code of propriety. She triumphs over him not as Anna triumphs over Will, exulting in being the "Anna Victrix" of chapter 6, but because she is simply too free and too large to be partnered with him for any significant length of time. Skrebensky is a stage in her personal and sexual development, but in the end no more relevant to her fulfillment than her lesbian attraction toward a fellow schoolteacher. Ursula's true consummation comes in *Women in Love*, when it takes almost a mystical and transfiguring form. Lawrence in *The Rainbow* shows the limitations as well as the glories of sexuality.

The Rainbow is five hundred pages long, densely and often poetically written. Occasionally this awareness of its own scale leads to some falseness of vision—the final manifestation of the rainbow, though beautiful in rhythm and tone, surely sacrifices truth to symbol, as though Lawrence felt he must end on a high prophetic note when the argument of the novel calls for an open-ended, speculative, anxious conclusion. The novel cannot be satisfactorily summarized in a few pages, but one can be reasonably certain that nowhere else in English fiction does a writer come so close to embodying in his characters the main tensions of industrialized man or the issues that at once separate and bind the sexes.

WOMEN IN LOVE

In one of his best-argued and most persuasive chapters in *D. H. Lawrence: Novelist* (1955), F. R. Leavis says of *Women in Love*:

> Even a reader who is still far from having grasped the full thematic development must be aware by the time he reaches the end of the book that it contains a presentation of twentieth-century England—of modern civilization—so first-hand and searching in its comprehensiveness as to be beyond the powers of any other novelist he knows of.
> (ch. 4)

Here is the immediate difference between *Women in Love* and *The Rainbow*. Its vigorous contemporaneity contrasts with the more grandiose conception of *The Rainbow*, where Lawrence seems at times to be hampered by the lofty symbolism. Though there is a great deal of explicit social detail in *The Rainbow* it does not convey so specific a sense of period as *Women in Love*, with its café society, its smart observation of clothes and decor, its ear for fashionable nuances, and its foreboding of a threat even to the tarnished civilization that modern man has provided for himself.

At the start of the last section I drew attention to the initial conception whereby Lawrence envisaged *The Rainbow* and *Women in Love* as one novel. Relics of this approach remain in the second novel, even though its basic structure fundamentally differs from the first. Lawrence originally intended a saga of man's history from the marshes (hence the name of the Brangwen farm) out of which life evolved up to the present corruptible moment—and beyond that to a future where he will either have established a viable society quite different from the one he now inhabits, or have ceased to exist at all. The latter proposition is seriously countenanced in *Women in Love*, mainly in what Birkin says, though it may be thought that Gerald Crich's materialistic juggernaut is heading for man's extinction too. Birkin does not want to see the end of the human race, but he does not believe it to be either inconceivable or totally disastrous:

"Let mankind pass away—time it did. The creative utterances will not cease, they will only be there. Humanity doesn't embody the utterance of the incomprehensible any more. Humanity is a dead letter. There will be a new embodiment, in a new way. Let humanity disappear as quick as possible."

(ch. 5)

Lawrence by now had arrived at a religious conviction that he never forsook. It has pantheistic elements, but it is too personally felt and totally uninstitutionalized to be given a recognized conceptual name. He sees in the universe a "primal sympathy—which having been must ever be": Wordsworth's words come close to expressing it. This creative presence informs all nature; man is only a detail, more complex than most but not on this account indispensable to the universe. More than once the novel reminds us of the demise of certain mammals that evolution regarded as expendable. Man may go the way of the dinosaur. If so, the universal force will not die. In a famous image of the novel, there will still be a hare sitting up in an empty field.

Lawrence's romantic vision is presented in some of his most high-sounding but ultimately unsatisfactory prose, for it convinces more by rhetoric and poetic diction than by intelligence. Many times in *Women in Love* we have to be on our guard against Lawrence's compulsive language, for it sometimes argues a point of view contrary to the general direction of the novel. Birkin's speeches on the irrelevance of man to the cosmic scheme exemplify this. Phrases like "Let mankind pass away—time it did" and "Humanity is a dead letter" no doubt express Lawrence's own feelings in certain moods, but they do not satisfactorily indicate the beliefs of the novel, though they come dangerously close to diverting the reader from Lawrence's central conviction that life *is* worth living, that it must survive, and that a world without man would be as good as inert; however dynamic the energies that continued to inform it, a globe devoid of humanity would have no vision to perceive it or consciousness to absorb it. It would be living, but it might as well be dead. Lawrence's faith in man, however monstrously wrong the paths he has taken, never profoundly deserts him. It is a weakness of *Women in Love* that we so often worry that it may be about to do so. This is what Leavis

means when he talks of places in the novel where "Lawrence betrays by an insistent and overemphatic explicitness, running at times to something one can only call jargon, that he is uncertain—uncertain of the value of what he offers; uncertain whether he really holds it."

Women in Love is a novel of ideas, though paradoxically one of its main ideas contends that the world suffers too much from thought and intellect. Indeed, there are points in the book (*pace* the late plays of Samuel Beckett) where Lawrence almost comes to reject language because it is the instrument of cerebral experiences. Birkin expresses this in a passage in which we feel he is not negating the main flow of the novel, as in his speech quoted earlier, but is reaching for a means of saying something that is almost inexpressible. He is speaking to Ursula:

"There is," he said, in a voice of pure abstraction, "a final me which is stark and impersonal and beyond responsibility. So there is a final you. And it is there I would want to meet you—not in the emotional, loving plane—but there beyond, where there is no speech and no terms of agreement. There we are two stark, unknown beings, two utterly strange creatures, I would want to approach you, and you me.—And there could be no obligation, because there is no standard for action there, because no understanding has been reaped from that plane. It is quite inhuman—so there can be no calling to book, in any form whatsoever—because one is outside the pale of all that is accepted, and nothing known applies. One can only follow the impulse, taking that which lies in front, and responsible for nothing, asked for nothing, giving nothing, only each taking according to the primal desire."

(ch. 13)

Here is the kernel not only of *Women in Love* but of all Lawrentian fiction. Characteristically, the truest moments in his prose totally lack rhetoric. This flows naturalistically, like real speech rather than speechmaking. Birkin advocates a meeting of the sexes without the restrictions of morality or custom, the setting up of a new world that quite literally starts afresh. All that language has rationalized and "terms of agreement" defined will be made redundant. It is useless to ask what Lawrence means practically by this: How will such a society be established, where will it operate, how can it preserve privacy? He is writing almost allegorically of the *need* for a better world where the achievements of clever men will not automatically be regarded as the right criteria for human life. He appeals, in other words, for an opportunity whereby the emotional depths in men and women can be allowed to surface. We need not be the slaves of self-restraint.

Ursula aspires to this personal freedom throughout *Women in Love*. "Her spirit was active, her life like a shoot that is growing steadily, but which has not yet come above ground." Within an immensely complex novel Lawrence shows not only Ursula but several other characters striving for personal attainment. Her sister, Gudrun, sees her own salvation within the sophisticated world. Gerald Crich sees it in the triumph of the machine-based society. Both of them wish to discipline their lives, to impose curbs on natural feeling, and to see enforced a set of absolute values that will test people and thus weed out the weak from the strong. Theirs is an antilife belief because it denies nature. We see it most dramatically expressed in the scene where Gudrun exults as Gerald cruelly tries to tame his mare. Eventually Gudrun deserts Gerald for the industrial artist Loerke, who, in the final chapters of the novel, epitomizes the separation of art from life and of reason from instinct.

Lawrence's attitude to Gerald Crich demonstrates his humanity as a novelist. "This is the first and finest state of chaos," says Lawrence of Gerald's beliefs, "pure organic disintegration and pure mechanical organization." Everything that Gerald stands for repels Lawrence, yet his portrait moves us greatly, almost as Milton's Satan makes us weep in pity. Gerald and his father worship the machine, as though it can protect them against a knowledge of death. Terror lies at the center of their beings. They therefore seek power over men, animals, land, and objects, for without it they would topple into the dark abyss. They know no inner life, whereas Ursula and Birkin struggle to release theirs.

Birkin and Gerald are powerfully attracted to each other, and there can be little doubt, if one reads the prologue to *Women in Love* which Lawrence decided to keep back from publication, that the relationship was meant to encompass homosexual feeling. This is presented not with any trace of eroticism, but as one possible means by which men might know each other better. The possibility of love between men (or between women, as suggested in *The Rainbow*) does not appall Lawrence, because he believes it need not exclude the love of men for women. Nor by this is he appealing for bisexuality in men, but for the capacity to love in a brotherly way (this may include touch, hence the wrestling scene, but not homosexual inter-

course) even while one loves a person of the opposite sex. Birkin reaches for a relationship with Gerald at the same time that he moves forward with Ursula: the two relationships need not be mutually exclusive, and it would be absurd to talk of them as promiscuous.

Women in Love, as Leavis implies, presents a picture of contemporary England. Sometimes this can be seen in its satirical portraiture—Bertrand Russell and the famous society hostess Ottoline Morrell are two of the victims, the latter comically parodied in the extravagant Hermione. On a larger scale, however, Lawrence indicts the capitalist ethos of post-Edwardian England. He does not adopt a socialist or radical stance by which to do so, but portrays working-class existence as demeaning and mechanistic. The problem, however, is that he offers no alternative to it. When Ursula and Birkin go off to seek their own fulfillment they have to do so outside any social context. Lawrence himself wandered away from industrialized society in the years following the writing of *Women in Love*, as we shall explore in the next sections of this study, but he failed to realize that this option simply does not exist for most people.

At the end of the novel, literally in its closing lines, the debate about society and personal freedom continues. *Women in Love* is, like most of Lawrence's major fiction, open-ended and uncommitted when it finishes. Ursula and Birkin wander off, uncertain what they will make of the future. Gudrun and Loerke represent all the life-denying forces that, after Lawrence's own death in 1930, were to manifest themselves in Nazism. Gerald has died, crushed by the forces of nature (symbolically represented by a glacier) that he always tried to control. The novel is about exploring life, but not about reaching destinations. English literature has subsequently had other examples of this technique whereby the author does not seek to express certainties or to define absolutes, but *Women in Love* in its own time created a new form of fiction because it did not move toward a settled conclusion or seek to leave a comprehensive overview in the mind of the reader.

In 1925 Lawrence wrote an essay entitled "Reflections on the Death of a Porcupine" in which he describes an incident when he shot a porcupine. The episode illustrates the natural balance of the world: "the whole of creation is established upon the fact that one life devours another life, one cycle of existence can only come into existence through the subjugating of another cycle of existence, then what is the good of trying to pretend that it is not so?" The passage neatly indicates that Lawrence was not a sentimentalist. Nature is rough and it presupposes the superiority of some creatures over others. At the time he wrote the essay, contemporary with *The Plumed Serpent*, Lawrence no doubt assumed that some men were naturally higher in the cycle of existence than others. It provides an interesting retrospective view of *Women in Love*, for in "Reflections on the Death of a Porcupine" he shows that a certain amount of callousness and aggression are endemic to nature. *Women in Love* shares this view but it indicates, often through examples of human mastery over animals (a cuttlefish, a mare, a rabbit), but also through attempts by one man to subjugate another, that the natural balance can easily be overturned by excess—by delight in cruelty, by greed, and by exploitation of others. Though the novel will strike many readers as Lawrence's most intellectual achievement (despite its wish to depose intellectual gods), it resounds with this deep humanity that deplores any kind of behavior that imbalances nature: accept the savagery that must exist within nature as one accepts death as the end of life, but do not add to it. Gerald and Gudrun go too far, Ursula and Birkin draw back. *Women in Love* is less a novel about opposites than about checks and balances.

THE LOST GIRL

It is not uncommon for great writers to reach a point of creative exhaustion following the completion of a major work. This certainly happened to Lawrence, who, after finishing *Women in Love*, seriously contemplated abandoning the writing of fiction, perhaps in favor of speculative essays, more book reviewing, translations (he became fascinated with the Sicilian novelist Giovanni Verga), and poems. He had not recovered from the reception given to *The Rainbow* and seriously questioned the value of writing unappreciated novels. "I feel I don't want to write—still less do I want to publish anything. It is like throwing one's treasures in a bog," he declared in April 1919. It was during this period, when he felt so directionless, that Lawrence wrote *The Lost Girl*, a novel that fundamentally changes its character as it develops. Lawrence starts it as though he were trying to concede ground to critics who resented his lack of

conventionality. In the first half of *The Lost Girl* he does not complicate his realistic portrait of the English lower middle class with sexual radicalism or metaphysics. We might almost be reading a novel by Galsworthy or Bennett. There are, too, strong echoes of Charles Dickens, particularly of *Hard Times*, in the episodes with the traveling vaudevillians, the absurdly named Natcha-Kee-Tawaras. Yet in the second part of the novel Lawrence seems released from these restraints and finds his own voice. The novel moves to Italy, the relationships become more sexually explicit, a longing for nonurbanized living creeps in.

This almost abrupt change of emphasis used to be attributed to a gap in the composition of the novel, it being assumed that the first part was written before 1914, when Lawrence left the manuscript in Germany, and the second half after 1918, when he was able to take it up again. Keith Sagar, however, in his book *D. H. Lawrence: A Calendar of His Works* (1979), has challenged this suggestion and indicates that the whole of *The Lost Girl* was written after the war. If so, it means that the shifts of view within the novel were planned from the outset. Alternatively, and more probably, Lawrence embarked on this novel with the intention of making it more like the kind of fiction his popular contemporaries were writing; but his natural form of self-expression made it impossible for him to complete the book in such a cut-and-dried manner. As he wrote in his 1928 essay on Galsworthy, defending by implication his own tendency not to be straitjacketed by conventions of morality or technique:

If life is a great highway, then it must forge on ahead into the unknown. . . . The tip of the road is always unfinished, in the wilderness. . . . In the three early novels . . . it looked as if Mr. Galsworthy might break through the blind end of the highway with the dynamite of satire, and help us out on to a new lap. But the sex ingredient of his dynamite was damp and muzzy, the explosion gradually fizzled off in sentimentality.

My belief is that Lawrence found his own writing in the middle stages of *The Lost Girl* becoming "damp and muzzy" and that the redirection of the novel was a consequence of his need to preserve his sense of artistic integrity.

Lawrence contemplated several titles for *The Lost Girl*, each one indicating something of its theme. In its earliest form, the one that Sagar says Lawrence began before the war but subsequently scrapped, it was called *The Insurrection of Miss Houghton*. Later on he thought of *Mixed Marriage, Perdition*, and *The Bitter Cherry* as possible titles. The novel concerns Alvina Houghton, a respectably brought up draper's daughter in a town called Woodhouse. She rejects the conventional world in which she is reared by trying several paths of escape—as a nurse in London, a pianist in her father's cinema, and the lover of an inarticulate vaudeville artist called Francesco Marasca, "Cicio." Cicio's surname derives from a kind of cherry, just as "Alvina" relates to the Italian word for "womb" (*alvo*). Lawrence often intended us to pick up hints from the names of his characters, more because of their associations than for what they specifically mean. In *The Lost Girl* the links between the cherry and the womb indicate the strong sexual theme upon which the novel centers. Alvina finds in the dark, magnetic Italian artist a quality of being that is absolutely unknown in damp, repressed Woodhouse. In the last chapters of the book she goes with Cicio to a mountain village in southern Italy, but Lawrence does not provide the banal and sentimental conclusion that a romantic escapist would offer. Life for Alvina becomes harder as Cicio returns to his enclosed world of male comradeship and strong family ties, but she refuses to be crushed by it. At the end of the novel (which, surely taking something from the pre-1914 first version, is set on the eve of the war) Alvina contemplates a future in America, the "New World," with her Italian soul mate.

The English novel has many examples of main characters awakening to a new consciousness of life. Nineteenth-century convention did not altogether disguise the sexual implication in this. Anne Elliot in Austen's *Persuasion*, Jane Eyre in Brontë's novel, Jude the Obscure in Hardy's, all have to come to terms with their own sexuality. Lawrence handles this subject without inhibition, but whereas in Paul Morel and Ursula Brangwen he presents the sexual aspect as only one part of a carefully balanced equation in their personalities—they are as concerned with finding the right kind of society for themselves—in Alvina Houghton's case the flowering of her sexual self is the mainstream of the novel. We understand this early in the book when she goes down her father's mine, an un-Galsworthian interruption among the first chapters:

There was a thickness in the air, a sense of dark, fluid presence in the thick atmosphere, the dark, fluid, viscous voice of the collier making a broad-vowelled, clapping sound in her ear. He seemed to linger near her as if he knew—as if he knew—what? Something forever unknowable and inadmissible, something that belonged purely to the underground: to the slaves who work underground: knowledge humiliated, subjected, but ponderous and inevitable. . . . She felt herself melting out also to become a mere vocal ghost, a presence in the thick atmosphere. Her lungs felt thick and slow, her mind dissolved, she felt she could cling like a bat in the long swoon of the crannied, underworld darkness.

(ch. 4)

This is a totally different way of writing about the mines from that of *Sons and Lovers*. Lawrence hardly seems interested in the work going on or in the economic state of the mine. It exists as a means of exploring Alvina's inner being, the self we have not had revealed in the early, more socially descriptive chapters. Alvina yearns to subjugate her Woodhouse being and become a reborn person. When she meets Cicio, the means of achieving this rebirth, she changes her name and becomes Allaye, as though disposing of one identity to allow the free flow of another. She is "the lost girl" because she loses her own self to release a new person.

Alvina is "lost" in the different sense of being no longer acceptable to the prim society of her upbringing. In his correspondence at the time of writing *The Lost Girl* Lawrence sometimes refers to it as "a rather comic novel." We ought to remember this when we read about the adventures of Mr. Houghton, a man of grandly impractical schemes, of the pinched Miss Pinnegar, the fussy Mr. May, the hysterical Mrs. Tuke, and the theatrical Madame Rochard, who governs the Natcha-Kee-Tawara troupe. Each one is a comic vignette of considerable style. Together they form a Dickensian world that hovers on the edge of caricature, but the satirical humor with which Lawrence endows them helps to temper the passionate relationship of Alvina and Cicio at the center of the book. Since the novel lacks the semiautobiographical pain of *Sons and Lovers* or the marvelous proliferation of ideas that wells beneath the action of *The Rainbow* and *Women in Love*, we need this comic detail to focus the intense main theme.

In *The Lost Girl* Lawrence makes an effective study of English provincial attitudes toward the foreigner. Cicio seems exotic and animal-like in the context of Woodhouse, but ordinary and even sad in his own village of Pescocalascio. He says very little in the novel. His presence is felt more than observed.

Lawrence suggests that Cicio is inscrutable, that he cannot altogether be summarized as Latinate and foreign or be neatly contrasted as Alvina's physical opposite and the instrument of her sexual liberation. He has an "otherness," a mystery resulting not from the author's lack of interest in his subject but from his deliberate intention to create a character who cannot be fully described. In this respect Lawrence, who introduces Cicio quite late in the novel, is experimenting with the possibilities of characterization in fiction. Having begun *The Lost Girl* in a more orthodox way than any of his previous stories, he ends up by trying to portray a character whose nature partly defies rational description or conventional psychological analysis. He takes the attempt further in *The Plumed Serpent*, particularly with Don Cipriano, but this and his next two novels were to be set either entirely or predominantly outside England, as though he was interested in exploring the nature of foreignness itself. *The Lost Girl* is a bridging novel, but in its own right it ought not to be underestimated, for its mixture of comic observation and exoticism makes it one of Lawrence's most easily read and entertaining works of fiction.

AARON'S ROD

And the Lord spake unto Moses, saying . . . And it shall come to pass, that the man's rod, whom I shall choose, shall blossom. . . . And it came to pass, that on the morrow Moses went into the tabernacle of witness; and, behold, the rod of Aaron for the house of Levi was budded, and brought forth buds, and bloomed blossoms, and yielded almonds.

(Numbers 17:1, 5, 8)

Aaron's Rod is a novel about flowering in a strange land. Its main character, Aaron Sisson, lives in the same kind of domestic dullness as Siegmund in *The Trespasser* and, like him, he earns his living by playing in an orchestra. The first chapter dryly describes the bitterness into which Aaron's marriage and home life have sunk: "The acute familiarity of his house, which he had built for his marriage twelve years ago, the changeless pleasantness of it all seemed unthinkable. It prevented his thinking." In *The Trespasser* the hero escapes from this sort of life by committing adultery and then by killing himself. Neither solution pleased Lawrence, for whatever the

strains a marriage might create he did not admire infidelity. The only other major example of it in his work is Lady Chatterley's, though her adultery with Mellors is more a way of attaining a fulfillment that her husband can neither physically nor emotionally supply. As for suicide, we have already seen that Lawrence regarded it as solving nothing. It was an escape *from* life, but not *into* life. In *Aaron's Rod*, however, he begins to examine the possibility that fulfillment may be attained not through sexual means so much as by submission to a dominant person or idea.

Aaron leaves his home and goes to London. Here he encounters Rawdon Lilly, a compulsive philosophizer who befriends him and nurses him back to health when he falls ill. The portrait of Lilly is probably based on John Middleton Murry, the critic and personal friend of Lawrence. Elements of the young Mussolini possibly color the characterization in the Italian chapters of the book, because Lawrence observed at first hand the beginnings of Fascism and heard some of the hectic speeches that accompanied them. Aaron follows Lilly across Europe and at the end of the novel supports such an act of abasement. As Lilly puts it, "there must be one who urges, and one who is impelled." He states this as though it were a natural law like the laws that govern magnetism and gravity.

This thesis of submission of the weak to the strong is a serious attempt by Lawrence to find a way of establishing harmony between human beings. Instead of competition and struggle we should seek for the right balance between people, in sex, in politics, in religion. It fails to convince, however, because Lilly is simply not interesting enough to sustain the role demanded of him by Lawrence. We have to take on trust his charismatic effect upon Aaron. What he actually says and does in the novel is too often bombastic and sometimes confusing. Some critics, therefore, have tried to find a homosexual element in the Aaron-Lilly relationship, but if it is there, as implicitly it may be, it must detract from what Lawrence is centrally asserting, for his point in *Aaron's Rod* is not primarily sexual. He claims that a better balance will be struck in the world if the masses submit to the benevolent will of great leaders. In the early 1920's, when Fascism had not yet been seriously politically tested, this notion appealed to many people; but Lawrence fails to represent it credibly because his embodiment of the leadership impulse lacks intellectual dynamism. Lilly is essentially undistinguished, lacking even the remote otherworldliness of Cicio in *The Lost Girl.*

Though Lawrence led a peripatetic life from 1919 onward, and reflected this in his writing, he did not produce any other work as unrooted as *Aaron's Rod.* Its title and central metaphor betoken wandering, and the novel is wholly concerned with unsettled people. Aaron's companions in London and in Italy are fashionable dilettantes who might as easily have come from the pages of an early Evelyn Waugh novel. Indeed, most of them are based on actual people. Lawrence laughs at them, but without humor. They are butterflies flitting across the surface of Europe, and we can therefore expect little seriousness from them. *Aaron's Rod* is in some ways a tantalizing novel since it raises the specter of deracinated intellectuals abandoning England because it is philistine or because they feel sexually incompatible with its moral climate or simply because they prefer an alternative culture; but it makes little of this theme, even though such a situation was obviously close to Lawrence's own predicament. In his other "travel" novels, *Kangaroo* and *The Plumed Serpent*, he places the wanderer in a context: primeval Australia, Aztec Mexico. In *Aaron's Rod* all the characters seem caught in a vortex relating to nothing outside itself. By setting the novel mainly in London and Florence, Lawrence has the opportunity to create a context for his analysis of leadership and disillusionment, but he avoids it. He provides a civilized setting for his story, only to miss its significance.

Aaron's Rod has never been particularly popular among Lawrence's novels. This may be because it is alone among his works in having no prominent female character. The most characteristically Lawrentian element is therefore missing: the assessment of relationships between the sexes. It was probably a necessary novel for him to have written at the most uncertain period of his life, when he was deciding where his future lay, but it is the closest he came to an aesthetic failure. He wrote it in bits, beginning it in November 1917 and not completing it until June 1921. This shows, for the novel has no coherent imaginative design. It allowed him, however, to experiment with an episodic fictional structure and to try out some ideas that he developed more fully in his next book. *Kangaroo*, an altogether more successful novel, capitalizes on the looseness of form and woolliness of thinking that afflict *Aaron's Rod*, making strengths out of their weakness. If Aaron's rod brings forth any blossoms at all, it is in *Kangaroo*.

KANGAROO

LAWRENCE'S decision to leave England had been intimated in his correspondence and had been detectable, as some of his contemporaries realized, in aspects of *Women in Love, The Lost Girl,* and *Aaron's Rod;* but it was only on 26 February 1922 that he and Frieda embarked at Naples for his first voyage outside Europe. They called briefly at Ceylon, but their destination was intentionally—and perhaps symbolically—as far from Britain as possible. It is perhaps important to remember how comparatively unknown the antipodes were in the early 1920's to most British people: legends of Ned Kelly and Rolf Boldrewood's novels of hardy outdoor life (the most famous of which is *Robbery Under Arms,* 1888) encouraged a notion of Australia as the antithesis of English suburbia. Lawrence hoped to discover there a kind of precivilization where men, learning by the mistakes of the northern European, would in effect have begun again. He was not to find this "ur-society" among Australian men or women, and he did not make contact with aboriginal Australia, as he would surely have wanted to do had he been visiting it now; but he did discover in the landscape of the outback a scale in nature grander than anything he had seen before, and hence, in his estimation, close to the wellsprings of the universe. Trim England, even the wildness of Cornwall, could not compete with the essence of unrestraint that "the pale, white unwritten atmosphere of Australia" had upon Lawrence. It resulted in writing about which it is difficult to talk without evoking a paradox, for it is at once coolly objective and yet wholly passionate:

To be alone, mindless and memoryless between the sea, under the sombre wall-front of Australia. To be alone with a long, wide shore and land, heartless, soulless. As alone and as absent and as present as an aboriginal dark on the sand in the sun. The strange falling-away of everything.

(ch. 17)

Lawrence's descriptions of landscape in *Kangaroo* are among the best he wrote outside his travel books, and even today many native-born Australian writers fall short of them. His account of the humanity that inhabits this preternatural setting does not have the same concentration: instead of achieving a successfully paradoxical style, Lawrence veers confusingly between extremes of emotion. *Kangaroo* is his most autobiographical novel in that he wrote it while experiencing the events from which the novel takes its life. The autobiographical elements in his other novels, including *Sons and Lovers*, are recollections in comparative tranquillity. In *Kangaroo* the writing of the novel often reflects what Lawrence was doing that day, how he felt about Australia, and on what terms he was with his wife, for all but its last chapter was written during the months of June and July 1922, when he and Frieda stayed in New South Wales. The book thus allows us a unique chance to see Lawrence's volatility transmuted into his prose. The shapelessness of the novel, verging occasionally on incoherence, has led the majority of critics to label it a failure, but it is pertinent to wonder whether any other form would have conveyed so much immediacy of reaction. Chapter 8 of *Kangaroo* is called "Volcanic Evidence" and chapter 14 is called "Bits," headings that sum up Lawrence's intention in this novel not to give a fully rounded interpretation of the Australia he visited but something more exploratory, more rough-hewn, and more like the experience of life as we actually feel it.

Richard and Harriet Somers come to Australia as strangers, a point emphasized in the amusing first pages of *Kangaroo* when the "Aussie" workmen speculate whether they might be "Fritzies" or "Bolshies." This is post–World War I society, but the prejudices remain. Indeed, the molding influence of 1914–1918 can scarcely be overstated in connection with this novel. It comes to the fore most obviously in chapter 12, "Nightmare." Here the Somerses recall the indignities of life in England during the war and the reasons for their disillusionment with Western society. "No man who has really consciously lived through this can believe again absolutely in democracy," Lawrence writes. His "Nightmare" chapter is a crucial though very often unregarded analysis of his reasons for leaving England in search of a better society. The people of England had voluntarily subjected themselves to the mass hysteria, as he saw it, of patriotism, to authoritarianism masquerading as democracy. The war for Lawrence was the obscene culmination of industrialization and science—the tyranny of the mechanical over the natural. Though several poets, most famously Wilfred Owen, had alerted the British public to the horrors of trench warfare, a deep-seated revulsion at how the war had been managed, and particularly how the ordinary people had reacted to the chauvinism of their leaders, had not yet set in. Lawrence was in this respect ahead of his contemporaries in making

known his bitterness before it became fashionable to do so:

We hear so much of the bravery and horrors of the front. Brave the men were, all honour to them. It was at home the world was lost. We hear too little of the collapse of the proud human spirit at home, the triumph of sordid, rampant, raging meanness. "The bite of a jackal is blood-poisoning and mortification." And at home stayed all the jackals, middle-aged, male and female jackals. And they bit us all. And blood-poisoning and mortification set in.

(ch.12)

Such writing bears out Lawrence's comment in a letter when midway in creating *Kangaroo*—"the Lord alone knows what anybody will think of it: no love at all, and attempt at revolution." He was describing not just the plot but also the spirit of the book.

Lawrence's own decision to go abroad, dramatized in that of Richard Somers, grew directly out of his conviction that England was dead. As the Somerses leave the coast of England they see it "like a grey, dreary-grey coffin sinking in the sea behind." Lawrence used this image more than once in his fiction, and it presumably captures his funereal feelings as he and Frieda set sail from England in 1919 on the travels that would eventually take them to Australia. In "Nightmare" we trace the source of this bitterness in one of the least known but most trenchant pieces of antiwar writing in modern fiction.

The Australia to which the Somerses come is riddled with political dissension. *Kangaroo* has sometimes been cited as a novel in which Lawrence indicated Fascist tendencies. After the failures of "democracy" in the war, many intellectuals felt the need for tighter political leadership, providing it was based on an ability to heal the dissensions in society. Critics of Lawrence such as Bertrand Russell, who later accused him of setting out on a path leading to Auschwitz, overlook the novelist's constant tendency to self-reappraisal. In *Kangaroo*, and again in *The Plumed Serpent*, Lawrence has by the end reached a point where he is rejecting charismatic autocracy. The novel considers it seriously, and examines too the claims of the trade unions on the left, but at no point can Lawrence seriously be seen as a precursor of the Fascism of the 1930's, with its determination to perfect the machinery of society, or of Soviet-style Communism under Stalin. He poses for his readers a problem of discrimination, for he was genuinely attracted by the notion that mankind would be able to see its way out of its current malaise only if it followed the guidance of a great leader; but he also saw how easily this could lead to perversions of power and to the possibility that people would then surrender the last vestiges of their individualism. If Lawrence saw the seductive side of absolute political movements, he was also a prophet of their evils.

Ben Cooley and Willie Struthers are the two leaders through whom Lawrence debates the merits of individual and mass action. Cooley is the "Kangaroo" of the novel's title, conceived lovingly, associated often with flowers, the phoenix, fire, and Christ, as though filled with goodness and life. Yet this born leader of men closes his mind to views different from his own. His message to the world is one of love and hope for change, but it verges on threat. Somers' disillusionment grows stronger and he finally denies Kangaroo a deathbed reconciliation. The novel ends in doubt and confusion as the Somerses leave Australia. The new country has not offered them the political revelations or the social developments they hoped to find there, though as a time to take stock of each other, to see primeval and petit bourgeois worlds in contact, and to become more positively directed toward spiritual regeneration when political and social impulses have failed them, the Australian weeks have been essential. On his last day Somers reflects that "one of his souls would stand forever out on those rocks beyond the jetty," and so it was for Lawrence, who, in a letter dated 22 June 1922, wrote that "Australia would be a lovely country to lose the world in altogether." At no point in his life, however, could Lawrence make such a remark approvingly. He was too concerned with finding the world to delight in the possibility of losing it.

THE PLUMED SERPENT

LAWRENCE's travels to Mexico took him among stranger human relics than he had ever seen before. If in Sicily he had glimpsed the possibilities of an ancient civilization surviving in an even more ancient physical setting and in Australia witnessed the conjunction of a primeval landscape with vulgar bourgeois encroachments, in Mexico he saw not only scenes of undisturbed beauty but the evidence of a religious revival. Mexico, he believed, was regenerating itself. When Lawrence arrived in 1926 the country was racked by a dispute between church and state that broke out into open conflict; the same year

The Plumed Serpent was published. The expulsion of Christian images from the churches and the revival of dance rites in honor of the ancestral gods actually took place as he describes them in the novel. The religion of Quetzalcoatl (whose name is a compound of Nahuatlan words meaning "plumed serpent") had been a great unifying myth in ancient Mexico. There are different versions of the legend, but undoubtedly Lawrence knew about the religion in detail and was not—as a few critics have supposed him to be doing—weaving a spurious fantasy of his own. He was attracted to the Quetzalcoatl myth because it dealt only in the present, asserting life and rebirth and seeming to deny the finality of death. As Don Ramón puts it in the novel, "There is no Before and After, there is only Now." Its symbol was the phoenix, which Lawrence adopted as his own (it appeared on his grave in France before his ashes were removed to New Mexico). He hoped that in the revival of faith he saw at work in Mexico there might exist a viable formula for mankind as a whole.

Lawrence was forty years old when he wrote *The Plumed Serpent*, the same age as Kate Leslie, its main character. Like her, he was torn between abandoning Europe forever by settling in an unsophisticated community and returning to where he knew his cultural roots would always be. We know from Lawrence's correspondence at the time he first went to Mexico that he felt exactly as Kate does, and that the minor characters at the start of the novel—Owen, Villiers, Mrs. Norris, for example—were based on Mabel Dodge and her associates, with whom Lawrence frequently stayed. The character of the novel changes, however, when he introduces Don Ramón and Don Cipriano, the two main advocates of the Quetzalcoatl revival.

Lawrence does not entirely resolve the problem of how to make Ramón and Cipriano credible as human beings when they spend so much of their time adopting the personae of Aztec deities, Ramón as Quetzalcoatl himself, Cipriano as the war-god Huítzilopochtli. Ramón seems especially remote from real experience, for Lawrence expects him to figure as the repository of an enlightened philosophy—a kindly parent, and, at least with his second wife, Teresa, a loving husband—while at the same time he exacts bloody retribution on those who defy Quetzalcoatl, drives his first wife, Carlota, to her death, and participates in strange ceremonies of invocation to the Morning Star and the wind. He also mouths some of the most repugnant sentiments that Lawrence ever put on paper. Some of these have to do with race, some with the subjection of women to men, some with the need for great individuals to preside over the destiny of the masses. "I would like," Don Ramón says, "to be one of the Initiates of the Earth . . . forming a Natural Aristocracy of the World." Natural Aristocrats, he continues, "can be international, or cosmopolitan, or cosmic. It has always been so. The peoples are no more capable of it than the leaves of the mango tree are capable of attaching themselves to the pine."

This spiritual pride in Ramón does not prevent him from having much of the aura and mystic interest that Rawdon Lilly fatally lacks in *Aaron's Rod.* Though *The Plumed Serpent* may seem faintly absurd to the modern reader, with its elaborate accounts of ritual worship verging on biblical pastiche, it is more likely to be the resonant prophetic tone of the novel rather than the content that alienates people. Lawrence, through Ramón, speaks of the need for a regeneration of mystery in the world: "And a new Hermes should come back to the Mediterranean, and a new Ashtaroth to Tunis; and Mithras again to Persia, and Brahma unbroken to India, and the oldest of dragons to China." In other words, if each community in the world, led by the inspiration of great leaders, could resurrect what is true to its culture, temperament, and climate, then no one religion would be more important than any other, yet all would be part of a global renewal of the spirit. Then, Ramón insists to Cipriano:

"I, First Man of Quetzalcoatl, with you, First Man of Huìtzilopochtli, and perhaps your Wife, First Woman of Itzpapolotl, could we not meet, with pure souls, the other great aristocrats of the world, the First Man of Wotan and the First Woman of Freya, First Lord of Hermes, and the Lady of Astarte, the Best-Born of Brahma, and the Son of the Greatest Dragon?"

(ch. 17)

On the surface this may seem rhetorical and obscure, but it is no more than a plea for the coming together of mankind in common resistance to the age of the machine and the tyranny of materialism. Many of the subcultures of the 1960's and 1970's pleaded for the same ideal through not dissimilar means.

The Plumed Serpent must not be altogether exonerated from criticism, however. There is in the book a peculiar doctrine of blood separatism whereby the races of the world should remain pure from the corruption of intermingling. It also asserts more nakedly than any other Lawrence novel the doctrine of male supremacy. When Kate marries Don Cipriano the ceremony enacts the subjection of woman to man, just as Teresa serenely accepts her servility to Ramón. The very landscape of Mexico, with its phallic cacti and "sperm-like water," is evoked in terms of male sexuality. Ramón and Cipriano share an affinity of spirit that, in the episode where Cipriano is initiated into the role of the war-god, becomes explicitly physical. The general thesis of the novel argues for a positive will to revive our dormant spirituality, and thus it increasingly seems in tune with many people's attitudes today; but within this broad idea many of the particular doctrines in *The Plumed Serpent* remain peculiarly resistible. I suspect that Lawrence came to feel this himself, for the novel loses some of its coherence toward the end. Kate, even in marriage, does not wholly commit herself either to Mexico or to Cipriano. Lawrence likewise becomes less convincing in his presentation of the revivalism as the novel moves to its close. Surely it is he who speaks through Kate in an italicized section on the last page: *What a fraud I am! I know all the time it is I who don't altogether want them. I want myself to myself. But I can fool them so that they shan't find out."*

The Plumed Serpent cannot be easily absorbed as an organic whole. Too many ideas proliferate, some almost contradicting others. There are long passages of ritual incantation. Yet the novel has a vigorous dramatic quality. Sometimes, as in the chapter entitled "The Attack of Jamiltepec" or in the description of the bullfight at the beginning, it arises from the same kind of powerful physical observation that Lawrence so often displays in his travel writings or in such essays as "Reflections on the Death of a Porcupine." It comes, too, from the urgency of his concern for a new world. Though *The Plumed Serpent* is unlikely now to be read with wholehearted seriousness, it would be wrong to dismiss it as some kind of theatrical extravaganza. This is not the world of the Natcha-Kee-Tawaras but an earnest attempt to see what relevance a wholly different culture from our own may have to the kind of society we are still constructing.

LADY CHATTERLEY'S LOVER

For many, *Lady Chatterley's Lover* probably still arouses the sniggers that surrounded it in 1960 when its publishers were taken to court on a charge of purveying obscenity. The novel made D. H. Lawrence a household name but for entirely the wrong reasons. He became identified with "free love," "permissiveness," and "four-letter words," trends in the 1960's that might well have appalled the morally serious Lawrence. As a penalty for his new fame he became erroneously linked with sexual emancipation and frequently trivialized by people who did not understand his work. Even now it needs to be asserted that there are three central themes in *Lady Chatterley's Lover* that make nonsense of the myth that it offers a kind of intellectual's pornography. These themes are fidelity in human relationships, the erosion of old England, and the capacity of the English language to express more than conventional morality wishes it to say. Lawrence had touched on them all in earlier novels, but in *Aaron's Rod, Kangaroo,* and *The Plumed Serpent* his intense concern with the possibilities of reforming society through different kinds of leadership had diverted him from any straightforward discussion of England, its mores, its society, or its language. In his last novel (though he did not know it to be so), Lawrence wrote his most fully English work apart from *Sons and Lovers.* There are no Lydia Lenskys, Loerkes, or Cicios here, no excursions abroad. Altogether abandoning the exotic territories of his previous three novels, Lawrence writes now of an England in which pastoralism and industrialization exist in uneasy conjunction.

There are three versions of *Lady Chatterley's Lover. The First Lady Chatterley*, as William Heinemann Ltd. termed it when publishing it for the first time in England in 1972, is the shortest. Lawrence wrote it between October 1926 and March 1927. His next version, completed in the summer of 1927, is much longer. In its published form it is known as *John Thomas and Lady Jane* (1972). Both these earlier versions of *Lady Chatterley's Lover,* like the familiar third version, were first printed outside of England. *The First Lady Chatterley* was published in America in 1944, and *John Thomas and Lady Jane* appeared in an Italian translation (by Carlo Izzo) in 1954. No version was legally available in Britain before 1960, when the uncut Florence edition of 1928 was republished. This checkered writing and publishing history reflects the self-questioning attitude with which Lawrence approached his subject. He had always been an avid reviser of his own work, but he clearly intended *Lady Chatterley's Lover* not only to be satisfactory in the form it took but to be explicit

in its meaning. The three versions are thus cast in very different ways.

Frieda Lawrence, in her introduction to *The First Lady Chatterley*, expresses her preference for it because, she implies, it is the truest statement of what Lawrence wished to say: "*The First Lady Chatterley* he wrote as she came out of him, out of his own immediate self. In the third version he was also aware of his contemporaries' minds." He kept adjusting the novel, Frieda tells us, because he was frightened that his critics would dismiss the book as mere mysticism (as *The Plumed Serpent* is still sometimes dismissed). He seems not to have bargained for the comparative indifference with which all three versions were treated for thirty years.

The First Lady Chatterley is the gentlest of the three, *John Thomas and Lady Jane* the most detailed, and *Lady Chatterley's Lover* the most polemical. Between the first and the second version Lawrence seems to have worried that the novel would be too dissociated from recognizable daily life. In the second, therefore, he emphasizes the effects of industrialization upon the beauties of England, he peoples the novel with more characters, and he balances pastoral lyricism with some degree of satire. The third version, the one most of us read first, is less changed from version two than version two is from its predecessor, even though it is only now that Lawrence's famous gamekeeper acquires the name Mellors (he is Parkin in the earlier versions). *Lady Chatterley's Lover* does, however, have a franker sexual vocabulary than either of the other versions. In a review in the *Times Literary Supplement* (27 April 1973) the anonymous writer maintains, at the end of an intelligently hostile assessment of the three works, that

there is little point in offering an order of preference between the three versions. Certainly the first, comparatively free from jargon and overt bullying, is the least offensive: lacking the crudely opposed contrasts of *John Thomas and Lady Jane* and more especially of *Lady Chatterley's Lover,* it is more honest in observation, though correspondingly more obscure in purpose. But it does not make enough difference.

The reviewer takes this point of view because he does not regard any version of *Lady Chatterley's Lover* as a major work of art, concluding, indeed, that "much hatred lies within its assumption of tenderness." I believe it does matter, however, which version we like best, for all three attempt different things. My own preference is for the familiar third version because it seems to possess a clarity of statement that, while it may be less "honest" in the sense that it is less fair-minded than the previous drafts, overtly says what Lawrence primarily wanted to get across: namely that contemporary society in the Western industrialized world is based on false values and that until we establish the right kind of relationships between individuals there can be no serious prospect of man fulfilling himself in anything but a mechanical way.

Lady Chatterley's Lover in its final form has the diagrammatic straightforwardness of a fable. Lady Chatterley, Mellors, and Sir Clifford Chatterley have been pared down to prototypes, as though in an allegory. Lawrence had been moving toward this view of character in all his novels since *The Rainbow,* but in his final novel, in its final form, he has come to regard three-dimensional complexities of character as mere accretions. The novelist's task is to be spare, functional, and explicit, as the earliest storytellers were. *Lady Chatterley's Lover,* in this respect, looks forward to the formal experiments of modernism in fiction and back in time, as is appropriate in a novel eulogizing the English past, to the simple structure of primitive storytelling.

Of the three themes mentioned at the start of this discussion of *Lady Chatterley's Lover,* that of fidelity requires most explanation. Is not this a tale of marital infidelity? In a purely legal sense it is, but Lawrence creates in this novel a world so deeply private between Connie Chatterley and Oliver Mellors that it would be virtually sacrilegious to impose judicial restraints upon it. Clifford Chatterley embodies inherited privilege, atrophied power, and sexual denial. He is socially boorish, insensitive to nature, and physically impotent. He has no life in the novel (or in any version of it) other than as the symbolic manifestation of the mechanical will. To insist upon married fidelity between him and Connie would be to assert the superiority of social forms over instinctual behavior. In the serious evaluation of right relationships Lawrence appropriately looks for trueness of feelings, not for conventions approved by a society he believed to be dying.

Connie's life as the lady of Wragby Hall is described early in the novel as "void . . . spectral, not really existing." When she gives herself sexually to Michaelis, a house guest, it means nothing to her, only confirming the emptiness of her being. Lawrence describes the episode with reticence, in ob-

vious contrast to the flowing rhythms with which he later writes of the lovemaking between Connie and Mellors. These early chapters define a world where talk is a substitute for action and where Sir Clifford can seriously intellectualize "this sex thing" as a minor adjunct to "the slow building up of integral personality."

At the conclusion of this conversation we meet Mellors for the first time, "like the sudden rush of a threat out of nowhere." He betokens a new kind of life, isolated from the social world but in obvious harmony with the natural environment, whose right balance it is his duty, as a gamekeeper, to ensure. Though their first encounters are wary, the relationship that develops between Connie and Mellors intensifies to a point where Sir Clifford and his world become extraneous to the needs that the two lovers can fulfill in each other. At the end of the novel Connie is pregnant, awaiting her divorce, and anticipating a future of true personal freedom.

In the *Times Literary Supplement* review already quoted, this ending is reviled as escapism into a "story-book future—for those who are lucky enough to be able to live the forest life. As for the rest, why, their future is none of our concern: they are simply the world which Connie will jettison for her own personal salvation." The implied criticism of Lawrence's scheme has to be faced, and it is best to do so by remembering that though few individuals have the pastoral opportunities of Connie and Mellors, we all have the capacity to form relationships. In getting the private world right we may collectively come closer to a changed society. Having failed in *Kangaroo* and *The Plumed Serpent* to find a practical solution to the malaise in modern society, Lawrence approaches the problem from the other end, through private experience rather than public action.

The family of Chatterley "stood for England and St. George," Lawrence tells us in the first chapter, and "never knew there was a difference." For Lawrence the true England is in the woods and valleys, not in the great houses. Ironically Sir Clifford also sees the woods as a symbol of England, even though his father had cut the trees to supply the war effort. We think back to the crass leadership in the war that Lawrence indicts in *Kangaroo.* Sir Clifford's woods, however, would always be private, untrespassed. They are "property." For Connie and Mellors they are the place where they make love, teeming with natural life and undestroyed beauty. Around them the spread of industrial England blots out more and more of the agricultural landscape. It is as though a black monster has been unleashed, feeding only on England's past:

It was as if dismalness had soaked through and through everything. The utter negation of natural beauty, the utter negation of the gladness of life, the utter absence of the instinct for shapely beauty which every bird and beast has, the utter death of the human intuitive faculty was appalling.

(ch. 11)

Lady Chatterley's Lover is a cry of lamentation for disappearing England. "Ours is essentially a tragic age, so we refuse to take it tragically," Lawrence says in the opening line of the novel. The tragedy is that modern industrialized man has not been the innocent victim of malevolent gods, but has chosen this form of evolution. The only hope for him is that he will see how the process of destruction is not yet complete. The natural world has been contained but not destroyed. When Connie and Mellors place forget-me-nots on each other's sex-parts they express not only the tender intimacy of their love for each other, but their knowledge of a remembered England whose pattern of life was "organic," not "mechanical." In a simple summary this sounds like nostalgic sentimentality, but the import of *Lady Chatterley's Lover* is severe, even brutal. Man must rescue himself or be blotted out. Lawrence hopes, surely, that we will see in Connie and Mellors the same archetypal representation of human possibilities that John Milton intended in the expelled Adam and Eve.

Lawrence, in the third version of the Lady Chatterley story, writes an uncluttered prose that he steers into lyricism when he believes the theme requires it. He is in total command of his language now, with none of the poetic overwriting of his first novels, overurgent didacticism of some passages in *The Rainbow* and *Women in Love*, or confused rhetoric occasionally detectable in the "leadership" novels. *Lady Chatterley's Lover* does not have a single style, but finds at each stage an appropriate correspondence between language and subject. Since some of the novel describes sexual intercourse and explicit responses to sex, Lawrence needs to find an unequivocal language. The best sexual descriptions in the novel achieve a rhythm that conveys the sense of a wholly sensual experience: "And it seemed she was like the sea, nothing but dark waves rising and heaving, heaving with a great swell, so that slowly her whole darkness was in motion, and she was ocean rolling its dark, dumb mass."

At moments such as this Lawrence is extending English prose in an attempt to realize virtually unrealizable sensations. Language can perhaps only be retrospective. When we burn ourselves we feel the pain, and only then do we articulate it. Sexual orgasm likewise lies beyond language, though almost every love poet has tried to recall it in a form of words that may capture the sense of the moment. Lawrence tries to realize the moment itself, to leave out the time gap between experience and recollection. It leads him to adopt the kind of vocabulary that, sparsely used though it is, took the novel into the law courts. He rejoiced in his opportunity to release the English language from some of its prudery—none of the words that caused offense were less than several hundred years old—but he did not really find a way of making them seem less than quaint and archaic. Mellors is a fairly educated man, and his switches into regional speech where sexual words are supposed to sound natural smack too much of a literary device. Lawrence may not have succeeded, therefore, in realizing a new form of English capable of expressing nonlinguistic sensations, but he was defeated more by the limitations of language itself than by his own approach to it.

Lady Chatterley's Lover was written by an ill man who could see almost nothing admirable in the way his society was moving. One might expect in the circumstances a cry of bitter despair, but the novel insists not only that the world is worth saving but that it can still be saved. Lawrence shows himself still interested in the power of the novel as an aesthetic form, experimenting almost dramatically with new methods of presenting character and using English. It is the final major work of fiction in his career, but it shows an artist in full command of his gifts, capable of reviving past strengths that more recent work had obscured, while at the same time inching his talents into new territory. Lawrence died in the midstream of his creative flow, not at the point where the river widens into the dark sea.

LAWRENCE'S OTHER FICTION

THOUGH his ten novels must always be regarded as the basis of his claim to greatness as a writer, Lawrence is also the author of innumerable other works of fiction. Some critics have thought his shorter fiction better art than his full-length works because he necessarily denied himself the elaborations and diversions, the repetitions, and the flights of metaphysical fancy that are integral to his novels. In a short account of these writings it is impossible to mention more than a few of the stories, novellas, and other fictions unless this section is to degenerate into a mere list of titles, for they amount to well over seventy separate creations. None of them lacks interest; some of them are crucial to his development.

Not content to write novels of his own, Lawrence in 1923 spent a considerable amount of time reworking other people's fiction. The most famous outcome of this is *The Boy in the Bush* (1924), a revision of "The House of Ellis," an unpublished novel by M. L. Skinner. He was honest with Mollie Skinner: "You have no constructive power," he told her. He gave the novel (or so we must presume) the qualities that make it an engrossing if lightweight account of a young Australian's growth into manhood in the 1880's. "The only thing was to write it all out again, following your MS almost exactly, but giving a unity, a rhythm, and a little more psychic development than you had done," he told the original author, and she unresistingly accepted his amendments. At the same time Lawrence was translating a novel by the Sicilian writer Giovanni Verga, revising *Dragon of the Apocalypse* by Frederick Carter (published as an essay entitled simply *Apocalypse*, 1931), and continuously reviewing fiction for various London journals.

In his correspondence Lawrence occasionally mentions a book he is currently working on but that never finally saw the light of day or that was later published in another form. Almost every novel he wrote started with a different title. It would be an engaging quiz to ask who wrote the following novels, and by what other names they are known: *Laetitia, The Saga of Siegmund, Paul Morel, The Sisters, The Bitter Cherry, Quetzalcoatl,* and *Tenderness,* for only *Aaron's Rod* and *Kangaroo* seem to have survived under the titles Lawrence first planned for them. One of the novels that never came to anything was to be about Robert Burns, a Lawrentian hero in embryo. It may have been a good thing that Lawrence never took it very far, because he intended to transplant the Scottish poet to a Derbyshire setting. A more determined attempt to write a novel that eventually came to nothing is "Mr. Noon," a vivacious comedy that Lawrence started immediately after completing *The Lost Girl.*

Lawrence's first major story was "The White Stocking" (1907), a prototype of the stories he was to write more maturely in later years, wherein a young wife is torn between decency toward her husband and her natural attraction to a man she meets at a dance. His first published tale was a slight piece entitled "A Prelude," which he had submitted under Jessie Chambers' name for a literary competition in Nottingham. The first story to be printed under his own name was "Goose Fair" (1910).

Lawrence's rapid development as a writer can be seen if we compare these comparatively tenuous early stories with works like "Odour of Chrysanthemums," a tale of grief in a mining community, and "Daughters of the Vicar," in which he explores the social gulf that divides the English middle class from the working class. Only a few months separate all these works, but the intensity of Lawrence's writing has deepened immensely. They were published together in *The Prussian Officer, and Other Stories* (1914), which for many people remains his most satisfactory collection. The title story presents a relationship between an officer and his orderly as concentrated and sensual as any we encounter in the novels. It is tempting in a group of stories such as this to trace the links with other works, but each one has an individual power that bestows on it a separate existence. Though "The Prussian Officer," for example, anticipates something of the Birkin-Crich relationship in *Women in Love,* it has its own kind of violent imagination. We reduce the stories if we see them only as antecedents of larger works.

The same must be said of the stories that appeared in the second collection published during his lifetime, *England, My England, and Other Stories* (1922), of which at least three—the title story, "The Horse Dealer's Daughter," and "Fanny and Annie" —are among the best he wrote. In "England, My England" Lawrence means us to see Egbert, the main character, as a symbol of effete but not altogether impotent English gentility. Lawrence possibly asks too much if he intends us to read the whole plight of this class into one short story, but in the final pages of this loosely constructed tale he manages to conjure up for us the barbarity of war. By contrast "The Horse Dealer's Daughter" creates a private world between a doctor and the girl he rescues from suicide. An intense but not altogether humorless climax brings the two of them to the point of marriage, as though their love has been fanned by the flames of the fire before which they have been drying themselves. Within its own terms the story works well because Lawrence does not deviate from his tight control of atmosphere.

"Fanny and Annie" may serve as a representative example of Lawrence's short-story technique at this middle point in his writing career. It opens with characteristically Lawrentian vocabulary: "Flame-lurid his face as he turned among the throng of flame-lit and dark faces upon the platform. In the light of the furnace she caught sight of his drifting countenance, like a piece of floating fire." A woman returns from a far place where she has been a lady's maid to be met by her first love. The setting is industrial and the theme as much a conflict of attitudes within class as that between the Morels in *Sons and Lovers*, though Fanny does not have Mrs. Morel's different background. This is a coming home to claim her last opportunity to be a wife. She arrives "with her umbrella, her chatelaine, and her little leather case," a mock lady with mock gentility. Harry, by contrast, "had waited—or remained single—all these years." Lawrence carefully balances irony and pathos, for that is the skill of this story. Fanny has to learn humility during the course of it and feels "dragged down to earth, as a bird which some dog has got down in the dust," but the ending leaves it ambiguous as to whether Fanny's final assimilation into her old community is a resignation to the second-rate or a decent alternative to the nonlife she has had as a maid. Lawrence is entirely fair to the Morley villagers in the tale, satirizing them lightly but never dismissively. It is a decent community, proud of its standards, its festivals, its cleanliness. Is not Fanny's return the moment of her release, not least sexually, for Harry has the gruff sexuality of Lawrence's natural man? However we interpret Fanny's history, this story displays Lawrence's technique at its sharpest. Image and theme constantly interrelate so that in only fifteen pages we have met a vivid group of people with the qualified hopes and unexpressed frustrations of countless numbers like them.

In 1923 "The Ladybird," "The Fox," and "The Captain's Doll" were published together. These three novellas were deeply admired by the most influential of Lawrence's critical advocates, F. R. Leavis. In *D. H. Lawrence: Novelist* he wrote:

The inspiration, the *raison d'être*, of *The Captain's Doll* entails the convincing presentment of the Lawrentian themes in an action that shall affect us as belonging, not to a poetic-prophetic Sabbath-world, as *The Ladybird* does, but to the everyday reality in which we live, though, unlike *The Fox*, to a milieu of educated and sophisticated people.

Leavis admired "The Captain's Doll" for its "common sense," but many readers are more likely to be struck by its humor and by the way in which Lawrence appears to be parodying some of his own attitudes toward the relationship of the sexes. "The Fox" is a study in tortured sexual relations, linking the human world with a symbolic value placed on animal behavior. "The Ladybird," in a much more stylized way, explores the kind of territory that *Lady Chatterley's Lover* successfully makes its own, contrasting sexless, almost euphuistic love with true passion.

"St. Mawr" (1925) was described by Leavis as having "a creative and technical originality more remarkable than that of *The Waste Land*, being, as that poem is not, completely achieved, a full and self-sufficient creation. It can hardly strike the admirer as anything but major." "St. Mawr" extends the symbolism of animals much further than the "Rabbit" chapter in *Women in Love* or "The Fox," for St. Mawr is a stallion resentful of the ignoble men who try to master him. The novella suffers from irrelevant Lawrentian diversions about "the secret evil" in men that indulges their greed and death wish, so that Leavis' judgment on it is now likely to seem overstressed for most readers, but it undoubtedly makes a vigorous case against Western civilization. Along with "The Woman Who Rode Away" (1928), an unpleasant but brilliantly sustained tale of female submission to alien gods, it evokes a wholly foreign world that, repellent though it may be to many people, holds total conviction while we read of it.

Lawrence went on writing stories even in the less energetic final years of his life. They include "The Virgin and the Gipsy" (1926; published 1930), which embodies almost definitively the theme of sexual attraction across class and even ethnic barriers, powerfully conveyed through an insinuatingly erotic use of imagery. "Love Among the Haystacks" came out in 1930 (though drafted much earlier); "The Man Who Died" (originally "The Escaped Cock," 1928), "The Man Who Loved Islands" (1927), and several pieces not published until after his death show a writer constantly probing for new ways of expressing his concern for man's future and his fascination with human relationships. These late stories are sometimes too symbolically wrought to seem other than obsessional, but we seldom feel that Lawrence repeats himself. Even when the themes are familiar the imaginative form they take is usually unique.

Some critics claim that the short story and the novella differ from the full-length novel not just in length and scope but in their essential aesthetic being. If this is so, then D. H. Lawrence proves the exception to the rule, for his shorter writings normally parallel themes and concepts in his novels. They are neither less nor more effective at their best, complete achievements in their own right that cast light on the novels only if that is how we want to use them. Though Lawrence maintained close contact with Katherine Mansfield, the main artist of the English short story in the early part of the century, he never imitated her style. Nor did he borrow from the classic continental short-story writers. He found a voice so uniquely his own that one can open almost any page of one of his tales and recognize it as distinctively Lawrentian: urgent prose, with carefully placed emphases and recurring key words; background detail fully creating the intended world yet corresponding to the emotional nature of the protagonists; private moods evoking public themes and metaphysics. It does not always work, but when it does, in a naturalistic tale such as "Odour of Chrysanthemums" or in a ritualistic piece such as "The Woman Who Rode Away," we see in Lawrence a complete master of the shorter narrative.

LAWRENCE AS A TRAVEL WRITER

ALMOST everything Lawrence wrote after *The White Peacock* reflects his personal odyssey. The early novels are full of excursions to English places such as the Isle of Wight (in *The Trespasser*) and Lincoln Cathedral (in *The Rainbow*). In *Women in Love, The Lost Girl,* and *Aaron's Rod,* the novels of his middle period, Lawrence gives increasing emphasis to "abroad." In the early 1920's his correspondence becomes very bitter as he talks about England as a graveyard. There can be little doubt that he regarded the war as a historical disaster that totally failed to arrest the decline of moral wisdom he perceived throughout northern Europe. In 1928 he summed up his true feelings about England in the essay "Dull London." The hostility has gone and he expresses instead a profound distaste for the passionless nature of English society as he saw it. The tone is regretful rather than aggressive:

Of course, England is the easiest country in the world, easy, easy and nice. Everybody is nice, and everybody is easy. The English people on the whole are surely the *nicest*

people in the world, and everybody makes everything so easy for everybody else, that there is almost nothing to resist at all. But this very easiness and this very niceness become at last a nightmare. It is as if the whole air were impregnated with chloroform or some other pervasive anaesthetic, that makes everything easy and nice, and takes the edge off everything, whether nice or nasty. As you inhale the drug of easiness and niceness, your vitality begins to sink. Perhaps not your physical vitality, but something else: the vivid flame of your individual life. England can afford to be so free and individual because no individual flame of life is sharp and vivid. It is just mildly warm and safe. You couldn't burn your fingers at it. Nice, safe, easy: the whole ideal. And yet under all the easiness is a gnawing uneasiness, as in a drug-taker.

Apart from *Kangaroo* and *The Plumed Serpent,* Lawrence's main travel writings are three short books dating from the same period: *Sea and Sardinia* (1921), *Mornings in Mexico* (1927), and *Etruscan Places* (1927; published 1932). He wrote one earlier volume of travel pieces, *Twilight in Italy* (1916), in which there is much Christology and also some first-rate observation of Italian domesticity in which pagan associations are evoked. *Sea and Sardinia* is a more substantial attempt to render what Lawrence was constantly seeking, a society "outside the circuit of civilization," which before he left Europe he instinctively felt would most probably be encountered in the remoter parts of Italy. "The name of Athens hardly moves me," he writes in *Sea and Sardinia,* but on his journey to Sardinia from Palermo he begins to hear the "terrible echo" that calls "from the darkest recesses of my blood." Athens, the ancient seat of reason and learning, leaves him cold, but the territory in which he travels in *Sea and Sardinia,* real places rather than remembered notions, brings him into contact with unspoiled peasant communities where manly virtues still thrive. The Sardinian days are recalled with humor and vitality. There are almost no incursions into philosophical generalization. The result is a book that places Lawrence more straightforwardly as a romantic writer than perhaps anything else he wrote, antirational, marrying instinct and intelligence:

This Sunday morning, seeing the frost among the tangled, still savage bushes of Sardinia, my soul thrilled again. This was not all known. This was not all worked out. Life was not only a process of rediscovering backwards. It is that, also: and it is that intensely. Italy has given me back I know not what of myself, but a very, very great deal. She has found for me so much that was lost: like a restored Osiris. But this morning in the omnibus I realize that, apart from the great rediscovery backwards, which one *must* make before one can be whole at all, there is a move forwards. There are unknown, unworked lands where the salt has not lost its savour. But one must have perfected oneself in the great past first.

(ch. 6)

Perfecting oneself in the great past is the author's dedicated intention in *Mornings in Mexico* and *Etruscan Places.* These sketches, though still in the episodically descriptive manner of the first two books, do not have the same kind of humanity. The interest is more abstract, more abstruse. The readers of *Sea and Sardinia* know the ship's passengers, the bus drivers, the peasants, and the urchins whom we meet in Lawrence's vivid immediate style. He might be in great demand today as a travel commentator, implying social conclusions from anecdotal observations in the way that V. S. Naipaul and Paul Theroux do in their travel books, but in the manner of *Sea and Sardinia* rather than that of the two later books.

Mornings in Mexico ought to be read partly as a companion piece to *The Plumed Serpent,* though it differs in some of the details of ancient rites. The book comprises eight descriptions of Mexican or New Mexican life, the core of which are three essays on Indian dances. Dramatic and vigorous though these undoubtedly are, often discovering a prose rhythm to match the movement of the dance ("Mindless, without effort, under the hot sun, unceasing, yet never perspiring nor even breathing heavily, they dance on and on"), our principal interest in them today may be for the light they throw on the strange doctrines of Lawrence's Mexican novel. Here he defines his attraction to the animistic credo of the Aztec descendants, with their insistence on "the mystic, living will that is in man." The Christian believes in a lost paradise and a future redemption, but in Lawrence's view he despises the present moment. Man feels himself unworthy of God. He is always, in the Western tradition, exorcising his original sin and seeking future grace, so that he has no immediate vitality. This, ultimately, explains the "pervasive anaesthetic" he describes in "Dull London" as a feature of English life: it derives not just from the northern temperament climatically, but from the religious sources of Western man, with their insistence on past error, future need, and present imperfectibility.

Etruscan Places, published posthumously, is incomplete, being six sketches toward an intended cycle of twelve. In 1927 Lawrence visited the four sites he describes in the book. They are Cerveteri, Tarquinia, Vulci, and Volterra. Here he seeks knowledge of a civilization even more ancient and "lost" than that of the Aztecs, for the Etruscans have left nothing behind but paintings, tombs, and the memorabilia of a people doomed to extinction through the colonizing power of brutal Rome (Lawrence's dislike of Roman classicism was as strong as his negative sentiments toward the Greeks). *Etruscan Places* is the work of an art critic rather than a novelist, though even here Lawrence's imagination constantly re-creates the personae of Etruscan life. At this point in his life Lawrence turned to painting as his main form of expression—his last ten years teem with pictures he made himself, pictures about which he wrote, and pictures he went long distances to see. In paintings from the heyday of Etruscan civilization he finds evidence of naturalness and feeling, though these qualities were gradually eroded by rationality, skepticism, and science, Roman qualities that deny "red blood" and "consciousness."

In Lawrence's correspondence, which is now being edited in its entirety for the first time and published by Cambridge University Press, proliferate comments and ideas about the places he visited from his first travels to Germany to his last days in France, supplements not only to his imaginative work but to his travel documentaries. Rootlessness and self-exile have become increasingly familiar to writers in the twentieth century, betokening the breakup of a shared assurance about permanent values in society. Lawrence is a major contributor to the literature of exile and though his travel writings do not especially add to our regard for him as a great writer, they undoubtedly make available details and evidence about him that considerably help our reading of his novels and poetry. In their own right they contain some of his finest prose moments, bringing to life alien landscapes and other cultures. "I am English, and my Englishness is my very vision. But now I must go away, if my soul is sightless for ever. Let it then be blind, rather than commit the vast wickedness of acquiescence," wrote Lawrence in a letter in October 1915. Through his travel writings we can perhaps find the clearest indication of how he avoided the blindness he feared might result from leaving the country of his birth.

D. H. LAWRENCE

LAWRENCE's first published works were some poems selected on his behalf by Jessie Chambers and sent to the *English Review*, where they appeared in November 1902.

> I have opened the window to warm my hands on the sill
> Where the sunlight soaks in the stone: the afternoon
> Is full of dreams, my love, the boys are all still
> In a wistful dream of Lorna Doone.

These opening lines from his first printed poem, "Dreams Old and Nascent," are addressed to Jessie Chambers. If they do not announce the arrival of a great writer, they certainly indicate the young Lawrence's love of plain, natural pleasures. Stillness and warmth, with the same mellowness as the pastoral chapters of *The White Peacock*, flood through the early part of the poem, but then "The surface of dreams is broken" and the poet reaches almost in panic toward "the terror of lifting the innermost I out of the sweep of the impulse of life." We might detect some echoes of Gerard Manley Hopkins and William Butler Yeats in the early Lawrence poems, but he is astonishingly free from other influences. Overwritten and imprecise though he can occasionally be, he nevertheless writes with the confidence that what he has to say matters.

Lawrence wrote poetry all his life. Eight collections were published in his own lifetime: *Love Poems and Others* (1913), *Amores* (1916), *Look! We Have Come Through!* (1917), *New Poems* (1918), *Bay* (1919), *Tortoises* (1921), *Birds, Beasts and Flowers* (1923), and *Pansies* (1929), in addition to the two volumes of his *Collected Poems*, which came out in 1928. Three more volumes were published posthumously: *Nettles* (1930), *Triumph of the Machine* (1930), and *The Ship of Death, and Other Poems* (1933). His writings in this area amounts to an abiding concern for poetic expression, though just as one finds the word "poetic" necessarily coming to mind when talking about so much of his prose, so it is impossible not to read some of his verse without feeling it is only rhetoric or metered prose. This reaction would not have dismayed Lawrence, who regarded divisions among literary genres as arbitrary and banal.

Lawrence's early poems, from 1906 to 1911, are almost entirely autobiographical. Though their lyrical vocabulary is conventionally Georgian, their tone and what he does with the words he chooses show a poet eager to express a personal vision. When he describes a snapdragon

> Strangled, my heart swelled up so full
> As if it would burst its wine-skin in my throat,
> Choke me in my own crimson. I watched her pull
> The gorge of the gaping flower, till the blood did float
>   Over my eyes, and I was blind.

or a water hen

> Oh, water-hen, beside the rushes
> Hide your quaint, unfading blushes,
> Still your quick tail, lie as dead,
> Till the distance folds over his ominous tread.

we see as explicitly as we do in any of the novels how attentive Lawrence was to the details of nature and how sympathetic to the struggle of small creatures before rampant man. These extracts come from "Snap-dragon" and "Cruelty and Love," two of Lawrence's best early poems.

In *Look! We Have Come Through!* Lawrence begins to experiment more drastically with form. Though many of the poems in this collection still rhyme and still retain the combination of ballad clarity and unaffected lyricism that characterizes the earlier work, others flow freely and meanderingly like spoken narratives:

> But why, before
> He waters the horses does he wash his heel?
> Jesus!—his spurs are red with shining blood!
> ("The Young Soldier with Bloody Spurs")[2]

This dramatic, seminaturalistic quality becomes stronger in Lawrence's poetry. The poet's "I" persona speaks up more frequently and the invocations to the life forces in the universe are sounded as though in urgent conversation:

> Come quickly, and vindicate us
> against too much death.
> Come quickly, and stir the rotten globe of the world
>   from within,
> burst it with germination, with world anew.
>   ("Craving for Spring")

Lawrence's poems read well in poetry recitals because of this personalized vigor. Some poems, main-

---

[2]Published in some editions as "A Servant Girl Speaks."

ly in the *Birds, Beasts and Flowers* collection, are therefore standard anthology pieces:

> A snake came to my water-trough
> On a hot, hot day, and I in pyjamas for the heat,
> To drink there.
>
> ("Snake")

The poem, beginning casually, goes through a small moment of horror, "a sort of protest against his withdrawing into that horrid black hole," before leaving the observer with "something to expiate;/ A pettiness."

The animal world can teach man much about the dignity of life or the naturalness of behavior in an unscientific mentality. Always Lawrence admires unconscious instinctive being in the creatures he observes: "Fish, oh Fish/So little matters!" ("Fish"); "She watches with insatiable wistfulness./Untold centuries of watching for something to come." ("Kangaroo"); "Such silence, such suspended transport." ("Mosquito"). These creature-poems are told with humor, for Lawrence sees the comedy in his attempts to outwit an insect, a bat, or a wolf; but beneath them all lies a vast admiration of forms of life that float freely in the world without responsibility or ambition. Lawrence does not sentimentalize his subjects—as his title essay in *Reflections on the Death of a Porcupine* (1925) indicates, he understood the predatory instincts in all living things (even in plants, he might have added)—but he achieves in *Birds, Beasts and Flowers* his twin aim of making observed nature dramatic and symbolic. Each subject lives in his poems individually, but each manifests the dark powers of the universe with which he constantly seeks to make contact.

As one would expect, the poetry that Lawrence wrote in the 1920's (though between 1923 and 1928 he wrote very little) matches the grand exploratory themes of his novels in the same period. It is summed up in "Terra Incognita":

> There are vast realms of consciousness still
> undreamed of
> vast ranges of experience, like the humming of
> unseen harps,
> we know nothing of, within us.
>
> Oh when man has escaped from the barbed-wire
> entanglement
> of his own ideas and his own mechanical devices
> there is a marvellous rich world of contact and sheer
> fluid beauty
> and fearless face-to-face awareness of now-naked
> life.

Urgent, free-flowing verse of this kind can hardly escape an accusation of repetitiousness, even of boring the reader, but at its best (in "Thought" or in "Bavarian Gentians") Lawrence disciplines his language so that his prophetic desperation about mankind carries conviction. His last poems are so strongly shadowed by the possibility of death that even when they lose much poetic concentration in terms of form they still exert a powerful emotional force. "But still I know that life is for delight," he says in "Kissing and Horrid Strife." Here, as in his poems of triumph over death, "The Ship of Death" and "Shadows," he discovers a gravity of diction and calmness of utterance that are deeply affecting. All rhetoric is gone now and only his strict need to go on insisting that life is worth fighting for in a dying world—the world's death, not his own—keeps him from silence:

> then I must know that still,
> I am in the hands of the unknown God,
> he is breaking me down to his own oblivion
> to send me forth on a new morning, a new man.
>
> ("Shadows")

The last poems of Lawrence have this religious sobriety because the mood is intense and the language unstrained. He was a poet capable of greatness only in a few animal poems and in these last pieces on mortality; but in everything he wrote for his poetry collections he expressed himself as though the poem in hand was all that really mattered. We never feel that he is being a dilettante or that his verses are idle compositions on a rest day. They vary wildly in quality but they can never be said to lack conviction or to be less than full of passionate intensity.

LAWRENCE AND THE THEATER

LIKE Henry James, Lawrence was a great novelist who hankered for recognition in the theater but failed even remotely to attain it in his own lifetime. Unlike James, whose work remains largely untouched in the standard repertoire today, Lawrence has since the mid-1960's undergone considerable re-estimation as a dramatist, and at least one of his plays, *The Daughter-in-Law* (1912), was regularly performed in British provincial playhouses in the early 1980's. He wrote eight plays in all, though only three of them were published in his own lifetime: *The*

Widowing of Mrs. Holroyd (1914), *Touch and Go* (1920), and *David* (1926). They span his entire writing career, probably starting with *A Collier's Friday Night* ("written when I was twenty-one, almost before I'd done anything, it is most horribly green") and concluding with his biblical epic, *David*, at the point in his career when he was most obsessed with old religions. His other plays are *The Merry-Go-Round* (probably 1910), *The Married Man* (1912), and *The Fight for Barbara* (also 1912). He also, when in New Mexico in 1924 and 1925, began two other plays, tentatively called "Altitude" and "Noah's Flood," though these are hardly more than fragments.

The theater plays quite a central part in Lawrence's fiction. In *The White Peacock* he writes of George and Meg "shaken with a tumult of wild feeling" at a performance of *Carmen*, as though the combination of music and drama has brought them into contact with a special kind of life: "their eyes were blinded by a spray of tears and that strange quivering laughter which burns with real pain." Siegmund in *The Trespasser* and Aaron in *Aaron's Rod* play in theater orchestras. The Natcha-Kee-Tawara troupe is the catalyst in *The Lost Girl.* Many of the rituals in *The Plumed Serpent* are presented dramatically, with an emphasis on formal speech and patterned action. Lawrence wrote about the theater in *Twilight in Italy* and about dance in *Mornings in Mexico.* He is also known to have taken a practical interest in stage production when teaching at Croydon, was concerned to have the respect of the leading playwright of the day, Bernard Shaw ("one of those delightful people who give one the exquisite pleasure of falling out with him wholesomely," he wrote in 1908), and made efforts, normally without success, to see his own plays staged. On the other hand, he wrote almost nothing on contemporary European theater, even though his lifetime saw the introduction of a regional repertory movement, the rise of German expressionism, the main impact of Henrik Ibsen and Anton Chekhov after their deaths, and a revolution in ways of producing Shakespeare that endorsed precisely those qualities of natural feeling and unmannered simplicity that Lawrence sought for in his own work.

Lawrence's plays were ignored for so long that it has become customary to think of them as diversions, scripts he wrote because he was a compulsive writer taking time off from his more serious work in the novels and essays. Recent productions, however, have suggested a real dramatic ability in these works. They act well and are therefore likely to be seen more frequently. The process by which they have become accepted in the theater has been extraordinarily slow. In his lifetime only two were staged; *The Widowing of Mrs. Holroyd*, initially in an amateur performance and eventually, in 1926, professionally, and *David*, in a 1927 production by the Stage Society. An adaptation of *The Daughter-in-Law* by Walter Greenwood, entitled *My Son's My Son*, was given in London in 1936, but the unadulterated play itself had to wait until 1967, when Peter Gill, a young director who is himself an accomplished playwright, staged it at the Royal Court Theatre.

There followed in 1968 a Lawrence season at the Royal Court when Gill revived *The Daughter-in-Law* alongside *A Collier's Friday Night* (which he had staged without decor for a single performance at the same theater in 1965) and *The Widowing of Mrs. Holroyd* (televised in 1961 but unstaged since 1926). This brilliantly successful season radically altered the standard view of Lawrence as lumpily unstageable. It became apparent that the British theater had an important dramatist of working-class attitudes writing at a time when the bourgeois taste of almost every playgoer prevented his work from being performed. We know that Harley Granville Barker had politely declined to stage *The Widowing of Mrs. Holroyd* in 1911, three years before its publication, at a time when he was attempting (ironically also at the Royal Court) to inject more social realism into the English theater, but it is very strange that between then and the 1960's there was such a total absence of response to Lawrence's plays.

Lawrence's other plays have not been widely performed. Gill staged *The Merry-Go-Round* at the Royal Court in 1973. It is a sleeker play than the earlier trio that he had directed, and on this occasion he "doctored" the text substantially. A production of *The Fight for Barbara* was presented at London's Mermaid Theatre in 1967 as part of a Lawrence evening, but the non-naturalistic elements in this rather stylized play surprised the critics, who received it badly. The Oxford Playhouse staged a first production of *Touch and Go* in 1979. *The Married Man* has not received a recorded performance, nor have the two unfinished pieces. *David*, too, would seem to demand another opportunity to be seen on the stage since Robert Atkins' production in 1927 was mounted without the necessary resources, and at a time when critics and public were less inclined to take Lawrence's religiosity seriously.

Though the priority at the moment must be to see

Lawrence's plays given a chance to establish themselves in the theatrical repertoire, it is already impossible to see or read them without relating them to the novels that were being written at the same time. Indeed, Lawrence perhaps used his plays as a chance to work out some of the issues and characters with which he was struggling simultaneously in his fiction. The most obvious example of this is *Touch and Go*, a play about the relationship between workers and managers that he created while writing *Women in Love*. Though the social debate in this play forms its core, the Lawrentian desire to see "a new freedom, a new life" enshrined in each individual gives it a metaphysical element too. The main male character in *Touch and Go*, Gerald Barlow, sympathetically extends our understanding of men like Gerald Crich.

Lawrence's lasting reputation as a dramatist will probably rest on the first three plays he wrote, for in these he captures the spirit of industrialized livelihood without resorting to sentimentality. In *The Daughter-in-Law* especially, the clash between two generations of women for the possession of Luther Gascoigne is realized through a vigorous use of dialect. The themes of this play, *A Collier's Friday Night*, and *The Widowing of Mrs. Holroyd* echo elements in *Sons and Lovers*, but the dramatic presentation has a muscularity of its own, for in each case Lawrence eschews the poeticizing language and semimystic elaborations that suit passages in his fiction but that would seem theatrically stilted. Indeed, *The Fight for Barbara* and *The Married Man* are unlikely to gain the same kind of place in the theater because they are more artificial and theoretical. *David*, being the story of David, Saul, and Jonathan, makes no attempt at naturalism and might have a hieratic credibility if given a careful production. More probably, though, it will remain principally known on the page, an adjunct to the leadership novels. It is another study in male friendship and the possibilities of autocracy.

If one has a preconception that novelists and poets stray into drama only to the embarrassment of their reputations, then Lawrence proves one wrong. He will almost certainly not now be neglected on the stage as he was for forty years. The case for his drama must not be overstated, however. He always wrote lively, argumentative dialogue in his fiction and he gave careful consideration to the structure of each plot he devised, but though these are dramatic strengths they do not by themselves make for a great playwright. Lawrence's plays lack the tight unfolding of the best naturalistic drama. They flare into life with marvelous intensity on some occasions—the opening section of Act III of *The Daughter-in-Law*, for example, where Minnie and Mrs. Gascoigne talk about their menfolk, or scene 11 of *David*, where Samuel prays for Saul—but the effects are intermittent. "The actual technique of the stage is foreign to me," Lawrence said in 1927, when writing to a possible producer of *David*.

He was partly right, but we ought to remember that the two kinds of plays he handled best, working-class naturalism and stylized religious pastiche, have never been greatly popular in the theater. Though the former has been in vogue for some years now, it may be that Lawrence's regionalism will vitiate his impact, for the Nottinghamshire dialect of the early plays is difficult to reproduce credibly. As for *David*, it requires an epic form of presentation that will always mean it is rarely performed even in the unlikely event of a return to favor of biblical drama. *David* is Lawrence's most ambitious play and in some ways the one he cared about most—he even wrote the music for its original production. His durability in the theater will center, however, on *The Daughter-in-Law* and perhaps on *The Widowing of Mrs. Holroyd*. They will be performed partly out of curiosity value, as minor works of a great novelist, but in their own right they would eventually have achieved some kind of status, even if their author had written nothing else.

LAWRENCE'S ESSAYS AND CORRESPONDENCE

"Essays" is a poor word for these brilliantly varied writings, since "an essay" unhappily implies something formal and academic and highbrow, whereas Lawrence was always intensely personal and spontaneous, with such a horror of pedantry and the university manner that he vastly preferred to be slangy and jaunty. "Non-fictional prose" is worse than "essay," so until somebody coins a better word we must stick to essays, though in Lawrence's case the word is more like a reference number than a description of literary form.

So writes Richard Aldington in his introduction to the 1950 Penguin edition of Lawrence's *Selected Essays*. But the word "essay" derives from the French *essayer*, to try, and in this sense completely justifies its use for Lawrence. His essays are attempts at definition, struggles to articulate complex attitudes to society, literature, sex, religion, education, and philosophy. In almost every one the academic pen can cross out paragraphs as redundant because the point has already been adequately made, but to do this is to bring ruination to a style that relies on underlining and insistence. Against the charge that he is dogmatic, preachy, or rhetorical Lawrence could validly reply, "Who listens to me?" He forces home his points for fear of being ignored. He is ignored less because of the manner in which he speaks —though few of his champions would want to maintain that his essays demonstrate his best prose—than because what he has to say so often seems unpalatable.

Many of Lawrence's essays disappeared from sight during his own lifetime, buried in obscure journals or remaining unpublished. Now, however, virtually everything is in print. Not all of it requires apology or explanation. Essays like "Nottingham and the Mining Country" and "Dull London," to which I have referred in accounts of his imaginative work, are hardly likely to evoke controversy; even though the point of view is distinctively Lawrentian, essays of this kind obviously record a personal response to remembered experience, and it would be as inappropriate to challenge them as to say that Andrew Marvell had no right to speak thus to his coy mistress or that John Keats was wrong to insist that a thing of beauty is a joy forever.

Two of Lawrence's longer treatises, *Pyschoanalysis and the Unconscious* (1921) and its continuation, *Fantasia of the Unconscious* (1922), argue the case for harmony between man and his environment. In them he denounces "the mechanical principle" that he saw prevailing in modern society and that he felt vitiated many of the procedures of Freudian psychoanalysis. These works are best read now as illuminating adjuncts to his novels, particularly to *The Rainbow* and *Women in Love*.

Lawrence is on more vulnerable ground with his literary criticism. His "Study of Thomas Hardy" (1914), for example, contains a number of factual inaccuracies about Hardy's work as well as some silly dismissive statements. On form, however, Lawrence can be crisply perceptive, as he is when pointing out Hardy's main greatness:

His feeling, his instinct, his sensuous understanding is, however, apart from his metaphysic, very great and deep, deeper than that perhaps of any other English novelist. Putting aside his metaphysic, which must always obtrude when he thinks of people, and turning to the earth, to landscape, then he is true to himself.

(*Phoenix: The Posthumous Papers*, ch. 9)

Lawrence felt impassioned about literature, particularly about the novel. He did not care if a writer lacked the limited particularity of an Arnold Bennett providing he was "man alive," that is, fully responsive to the currents that provide life to the body and significance to the universe. When he insists on "blood consciousness" in so many of his works he is basically seeking a metaphor to express this sense of currency, or flow, within living things. "Let us learn from the novel," he says in "Why the Novel Matters"—the same essay in which he talks of "man alive." "In the novel, the characters can do nothing but *live*. If they keep on being good, according to pattern, or bad, according to pattern, or even volatile, according to pattern, they cease to live, and the novel falls dead." This is his charge against Galsworthy, Bennett, even, obscurely, against Dostoyevsky. "A character in a novel has got to live, or it is nothing." Hence Lawrence's verdict on Joseph Conrad ("I can't forgive Conrad . . . for giving in"), on E. M. Forster ("Life is more interesting in its undercurrents than in its obvious; and E. M. does see people, people and nothing but people: *ad nauseam*"), on James Joyce ("utterly without spontaneity or real life"). I glean these last remarks from letters he wrote, for it is often in his correspondence that a chance observation crystallizes something that pages of overstatement in the essays have blurred.

Lawrence wrote several letters a day almost all his life. As the majority of these went to fellow writers, or to publishers, or to editors, they obviously document a living dialogue between him and the literati of his day. He was personally friendly with Aldous Huxley, H. G. Wells, Compton Mackenzie, and Katherine Mansfield, and even when strains came into the relationships he would write an honest view of their work.

Some of Lawrence's literary subjects deviate wildly from the topic apparently planned. His essay on "Pornography and Obscenity," for example, lampoons *Jane Eyre* as "much nearer to pornography than is Boccaccio" only a couple of pages before it goes on excessively about masturbation as "certainly the most dangerous sexual vice that a society can be afflicted with." Juxtaposition of ideas in this way can work only if there is a tight controlling argument, but Lawrence is thinking with his heart, battering us with unsubstantiated generalizations. Within the framework of a novel, even one as extravagantly ritualized as *The Plumed Serpent*, such a technique may carry weight. It fails to do so in many of the essays. It fails partly because Lawrence forgets at these times his central belief that nothing in life should be stationary or fixed, that the flow must always proceed, nothing be totally defined because even the word, liberator of expression though it is, can also be a jailer. As he says of reading books, "once it is *known*, and its meaning is fixed or established, it is dead."

This last statement comes from *Apocalypse*. This was Lawrence's final major work, completed a few weeks before he died. Beginning as an introduction to a book by Frederick Carter, it developed into a free-flowing commentary on the Book of Revelation, imagery from which he had used in *The Rainbow* and to which he now returned in the passionate conviction that beneath what he understood to be a mainly allegorical structure the last book of the Bible held part of the key to an interpretation of life. Some of *Apocalypse* is almost incoherent, some of it pretentiously numerological, but the kernel carries on from where *The Plumed Serpent* drifted unconvincingly to a close. "All religion, instead of being religion of *life*, here and now, became religion of postponed destiny," he writes. In his last and longest essay he once again appeals for a regenerated religion that will inform the life at hand and not the possibly mythical life to come.

Many of Lawrence's essays will strike the reader as idiosyncratic; some of his prolific correspondence is quirky or ill-tempered. Surely, however, we are fortunate to have this extra body of material to throw sudden illumination on the major texts, or simply to enlarge our knowledge of Lawrence's place in the contemporary literary world. A work of art is entire in its own right, and I am not suggesting that *Sons and Lovers* cannot be read independently of "Nottingham and the Mining Country," or that *The Plumed Serpent* will be any the less obscure because one has encountered *Apocalypse*. Even *Lady Chatterley's Lover* does not need the essay "A Propos of *Lady Chatterley's Lover*" that Lawrence wrote as an explanation of the novel's "phallic reality." He meant these essays to be read, however, by anyone who wanted to follow his chain of thought. Sometimes they are too strident to be helpful, but on balance they clarify far more than they cloud. As for his letters, we find in them a record of a major novelist reacting to the world as he experienced it day by day. Often they have a beauty of language as controlled as famous passages in the novels, but these come to us as sudden moments of wonder. Almost alone among his writings Lawrence wrote letters without ever intending to revise them. Here,

very often, we detect the immediate Lawrence, the man of spontaneous feeling who has not fretted for the right phrase or channeled the observation into a distorting theoretical mold. In his letters we can approach the real man, and in the essays we often find the artist with his defenses down. Both are indispensable.

CRITICS ON LAWRENCE: A NOTE

LAWRENCE wrote so trenchantly about other writers and about the art of fiction that it can only be with the greatest trepidation that anyone writes about his work. After his death a number of generally critical reminiscences about him were published by people he liked to consider his friends. The fairest and most pertinent of these is *The Savage Pilgrimage* (1932) by Catherine Carswell. F. R. Leavis pioneered the academic study of Lawrence's work, eventually placing him in a line of great novelists descending from Austen. Leavis' interest in Lawrence was primarily moral. For all its convoluted prose and occasionally weird judgments Leavis' *D. H. Lawrence: Novelist* (1955) remains essential reading. *Thoughts, Words and Creativity* (1976) elaborates upon, but does not greatly add to, the emphases of the earlier book, but it shows how even in old age Leavis regarded Lawrence as the consummate twentieth-century English writer. In recent years there have been many accounts of Lawrence's writing, including "casebook" studies of individual texts. Among the best of the general studies are Keith Sagar's *The Art of D. H. Lawrence* (1966), Frank Kermode's *Lawrence* (1973), an intelligently provocative Freudian critique, and F. B. Pinion's *A D. H. Lawrence Companion* (1978). Émile Delavenay's *D. H. Lawrence: The Man and His Work* (revised 1972) and Harry T. Moore's *The Priest of Love* (1974; revised edition of *The Intelligent Heart: The Story of D. H. Lawrence*, 1955) are the best biographies, with Martin Green's *The Von Richthofen Sisters* (1974) a useful adjunct. I have personally found Sagar's *D. H. Lawrence: A Calendar of His Works* (1979) as invaluable a contribution to the study of a great writer as any produced in recent years. It documents on a day-to-day basis the course of Lawrence's writing, publication schedules, and travels, authenticating evidence that was previously only supposition and discrediting some long-established falsehoods.

D. H. LAWRENCE

SELECTED BIBLIOGRAPHY

I. BIBLIOGRAPHY. E. D. McDonald, *A Bibliography of the Writings of D. H. Lawrence* (Philadelphia, 1925); E. D. McDonald, *A Bibliographical Supplement* (Philadelphia, 1931); L. C. Powell, *The Manuscripts of D. H. Lawrence* (Los Angeles, 1937); E. W. Tedlock, *The Frieda Lawrence Collection of D. H. Lawrence Manuscripts* (Albuquerque, 1948); W. Whyte, *D. H. Lawrence: A Checklist* (Detroit, 1950); M. Beebe and A. Tommasi, "Criticism of D. H. Lawrence: A Selected Checklist with an Index to Studies of Separate Works," in *Modern Fiction Studies*, V, 1 (Spring 1959), 83–98; W. Roberts, *A Bibliography of D. H. Lawrence* (London, 1963), the standard bibliography, includes details of periodical publications; K. Sagar, *The Art of D. H. Lawrence* (Cambridge, 1966), includes a useful chronology at the head of each ch. and information on periodical publications.

II. COLLECTED WORKS. *The Collected Poems of D. H. Lawrence* (London, 1928), vol. I: "Rhyming Poems," vol. II: "Unrhyming Poems"; *The Phoenix Edition of D. H. Lawrence*, 20 vols. (London, 1954–1964); E. D. McDonald, ed., *Phoenix: The Posthumous Papers* (London, 1936), with intro., contains "Study of Thomas Hardy," "The Reality of Peace," "Introduction to These Paintings," "Democracy," "Education of the People," "John Galsworthy," and many essays, reviews, and intros; Penguin ed. (New York–London, 1978), more reliable ed.; *Complete Poems*, 2 vols. (London, 1964); *Complete Plays* (London, 1965); W. Roberts and H. T. Moore, eds., *Phoenix II: Uncollected, Unpublished and Other Prose Works by D. H. Lawrence* (London, 1968, with intro. and notes, includes "The Crown."

A complete edition of Lawrence's works (see LETTERS below) is in progress at Cambridge University Press.

III. SEPARATE WORKS. *The White Peacock* (London, 1911), novel; *The Trespasser* (London, 1912), novel; *Love Poems and Others* (London, 1913); *Sons and Lovers* (London, 1913), novel; *The Widowing of Mrs. Holroyd: A Drama in Three Acts* (New York, 1914); *The Prussian Officer, and Other Stories* (London, 1914), contains "The Prussian Officer," "The Thorn in the Flesh," "Daughters of the Vicar," "A Fragment of Stained Glass," "The Shades of Spring," "The Soiled Rose," "Second Best," "The Shadow in the Rose Garden," "Goose Fair," "The White Stocking," "A Sick Collier," "The Christening," "Odour of Chrysanthemums"; *The Rainbow* (London, 1915), novel; *Twilight in Italy* (London, 1916), travel sketches; *Amores: Poems* (London, 1916); *Look! We Have Come Through!* (London, 1917), verse; *New Poems* (London, 1918); *Bay: A Book of Poems* (London, 1919).

Touch and Go: A Play in Three Acts (London, 1920); *Women in Love* (New York, 1920), novel; *The Lost Girl* (London, 1920), novel; *Movements in European History* (London, 1921), essays written under pseud. Lawrence H. Davison; *Psychoanalysis and the Unconscious* (New York, 1921), essay; *Tortoises* (New York, 1921), verse; *Sea and Sardinia* (New York, 1921), travel; *Aaron's Rod* (New York, 1922), novel; *Fantasia of the Unconscious* (New York, 1922), essay; *England, My England, and Other Stories* (New York, 1922), contains "England, My England," "Tickets, Please," "The Blind Man," "Monkey Nuts," "Wintry Peacock," "You Touched Me," "Samson and Delilah," "The Primrose Path," "The Horse Dealer's Daughter," "Fanny and Annie"; *The Ladybird* (London, 1923), stories, contains "The Ladybird," "The Fox," "The Captain's Doll"; *Studies in Classic American Literature* (New York, 1923), criticism; *Kangaroo* (London, 1923), novel; *Birds, Beasts and Flowers: Poems* (London, 1923); *The Boy in the Bush* (London, 1924), novel written with M. L. Skinner; *St. Mawr: Together with "The Princess"* (London, 1925), stories; *Reflections on the Death of a Porcupine, and Other Essays* (Philadelphia, 1925); *The Plumed Serpent: Quetzalcoatl* (London, 1926), novel; *David: A Play* (London, 1926); *Sun* (London, 1926), story; *Glad Ghosts* (London, 1926), story; *Mornings in Mexico* (London, 1927), travel sketches; *Rawdon's Roof: A Story* (London, 1928); *The Woman Who Rode Away, and Other Stories* (London, 1928), contains "Two Blue Birds," "Sun," "The Woman Who Rode Away," "Smile," "The Border Line," "Jimmy and the Desperate Woman," "The Last Laugh," "In Love," "Glad Ghosts," "None of That"; *Lady Chatterley's Lover* (Florence, 1928), novel; *Sex Locked Out* (London, 1929), essay; *The Paintings of D. H. Lawrence* (London, 1929); *Pansies: Poems* (London, 1929); *My Skirmish with Jolly Roger* (New York, 1929), essay; *Pornography and Obscenity* (London, 1929), essay; *The Escaped Cock* (Paris, 1929), story.

A Propos of "Lady Chatterley's Lover": Being an Essay Extended From "My Skirmish with Jolly Roger" (London, 1930); *Nettles* (London, 1930), verse; *Assorted Articles* (London, 1930); *The Virgin and the Gipsy* (Florence, 1930), story; *Love Among the Haystacks, and Other Pieces* (London, 1930), stories and sketches, contains "Love Among the Haystacks," "A Chapel Among the Mountains," "A Hay Hut Among the Mountains," "Once"; *Triumph of the Machine* (London, 1931), verse; *The Man Who Died* (London, 1931), extended version of *The Escaped Cock*; *Apocalypse* (Florence, 1931), essay; *A Letter from Cornwall* (London, 1931); *Etruscan Places* (London, 1932), sketches; *Last Poems* (Florence, 1932); *The Lovely Lady* (London, 1933), stories, contains "The Lovely Lady," "Rawdon's Roof," "The Rocking-Horse Winner," "Mother and Daughter," "The Blue Moccasins," "Things," "The Overtone," "The Man Who Loved Islands"; *We Need One Another* (New York, 1933), essays; *The Ship of Death, and Other Poems* (London, 1933); *A Collier's Friday Night* (London, 1934), play; *A Modern Lover* (London, 1934), stories, contains "A Modern Lover," "The Old Adam," "Her Turn," "Strike Pay," "The Witch à la Mode," "New Eve and Old Adam," "Mr Noon"; *Foreword to "Women in Love"* (San Francisco, 1936), not originally published with the novel, first included with Modern Library ed.

Fire and Other Poems (San Francisco, 1940); *The First Lady Chatterley* (New York, 1944; London, 1972), first version of *Lady Chatterley's Lover*, 1972 ed. includes intro. by F. Lawrence; A. Arnold, ed., *The Symbolic Meaning* (London, 1962), uncollected versions of *Studies in Classic American Literature; John Thomas and Lady Jane* (London, 1972), second version of *Lady Chatterley's Lover*.

IV. WORKS TRANSLATED BY D. H. LAWRENCE. L. Shestov, *All Things Are Possible* (London, 1920), trans. by S. S. Koteliansky, with collaboration of D. H. Lawrence; I. A. Bunin, *The Gentleman from San Francisco and Other Stories* (London, 1922), trans. by S. S. Koteliansky and L. Woolf, title story co-translated with D. H. Lawrence; G. Verga, *Mastro-Don Gesualdo* (New York, 1923), trans. by D. H. Lawrence; G. Verga, *Little Novels of Sicily* (New York, 1925), trans. by D. H. Lawrence; G. Verga, *Cavalleria Rusticana, and Other Stories* (London, 1928), trans. with intro. by D. H. Lawrence; A. F. Grazzinini, *The Story of Dr. Manente* (Florence, 1929), trans. with intro. by D. H. Lawrence.

V. LETTERS. A. Huxley, ed., *The Letters of D. H. Lawrence* (London, 1932); H. T. Moore, ed., *D. H. Lawrence's Letters to Bertrand Russell* (New York, 1948); H. T. Moore, *The Collected Letters of D. H. Lawrence*, 2 vols. (New York, 1962); J. T. Boulton, ed., *Lawrence in Love: Letters from D. H. L. to Louie Burrows* (Nottingham, 1968); M. Secker, ed., *Letters from D. H. Lawrence to Martin Secker, 1911–1930* (London, 1970); G. J. Zytaruk, ed., *The Quest for Rananim: D. H. Lawrence's Letters to Koteliansky, 1914–1930* (Montreal, 1970); G. M. Lacey, ed., *D. H. Lawrence: Letters to Thomas and Adèle Seltzer* (Santa Barbara, 1976); *The Letters of D. H. Lawrence*, J. T. Boulton, ed., vol. I: *1901–1913* (Cambridge, 1979), G. J. Zytaruk and J. T. Boulton, eds., vol. II: *1913–1916* (1981); in progress are J. T. Boulton and A. Robertson, eds., vol. III: *1916–1921*; W. Roberts and E. Mansfield, vol. IV: *1921–1924*; D. Farmer, ed., vol. V: *1924–1927*; G. M. Lacy, ed., vol. VI: *1927–1928*; K. Sagar and J. T. Boulton, eds., vol. VII: *1928–1930*.

VI. BIOGRAPHICAL AND CRITICAL STUDIES. H. J. Seligmann, *D. H. Lawrence: An American Interpretation* (New York, 1924); F. R. Leavis, *D. H. Lawrence* (Cambridge, 1930); R. West, *D. H. Lawrence* (London, 1930); J. M. Murry: *D. H. Lawrence: Two Essays* (Cambridge, 1930); J. M. Murry, *Son of Woman: The Story of D. H. Lawrence* (London, 1931); A. Lawrence and G. S. Gelder, *Young Lorenzo: Early Life of D. H. Lawrence* (Florence, 1931); C. Carswell, *The Savage Pilgrimage: A Narrative of D. H. Lawrence* (London, 1932); A. Nin, *D. H. Lawrence: An Unprofessional Study* (Paris, 1933; reiss. London, 1961); D. Brett, *Lawrence and Brett: A Friendship* (London, 1933); H. Corke, *Lawrence and "Apocalypse"* (London, 1933); J. M. Murry, *Reminiscences of D. H. Lawrence* (London, 1933)); E. Brewster and A. Brewster, *D. H. Lawrence: Reminiscences and Correspondence* (London, 1934); H. Gregory, *Pilgrim of the Apocalypse: A Critical Study of D. H. Lawrence* (London, 1934); F. Lawrence, *Not I, But the Wind* (New York, 1934); E. T. [Jessie Chambers], *D. H. Lawrence: A Personal Record* (London,

1935); K. Merrild, *A Poet and Two Painters: A Memoir of D. H. Lawrence* (London, 1938).

R. Aldington, *Portrait of a Genius, But . . . : The Life of D. H. Lawrence, 1885–1930* (London, 1950); W. Tiverton, *D. H. Lawrence and Human Existence* (London, 1951); D. Kenmare, *Fire-Bird: A Study of D. H. Lawrence* (London, 1951); V. de S. Pinto, *D. H. Lawrence: Prophet of the Midlands* (Nottingham, 1951); W. Bynner, *Journey with Genius: Recollections and Reflections Concerning the D. H. Lawrences* (New York, 1953); M. Spilka, *The Love Ethic of D. H. Lawrence* (Bloomington, 1955); H. T. Moore, *The Intelligent Heart: The Story of D. H. Lawrence* (London, 1955), reissued with some additional material as *The Priest of Love* (London, 1974); M. Freeman, *D. H. Lawrence: A Basic Study of His Ideas* (Gainesville, 1955); F. R. Leavis, *D. H. Lawrence: Novelist* (London, 1955); G. Hough, *The Dark Sun: A Study of D. H. Lawrence* (London, 1956); E. Nehls, ed., *D. H. Lawrence: A Composite Biography* (Madison, Wis., 1957–1959), vol. I: *1885–1919*, vol. II: *1919–1925*, vol. III: *1925–1930*.

R. L. Drain, *Tradition and D. H. Lawrence* (Groningen, 1960); F. Lawrence, *The Memoirs and Correspondence* (London, 1961), ed. by E. W. Tedlock; A. Beal, *D. H. Lawrence* (Edinburgh, 1961); L. D. Clarke, *Dark Night of the Body: A Study of "The Plumed Serpent"* (Austin, Tex., 1964); G. H. Ford, *Double Measure: A Study of the Novels and Stories of D. H. Lawrence* (New York, 1965); H. M. Daleski, *The Forked Flame: A Study of D. H. Lawrence* (London, 1965); K. Sagar, *The Art of D. H. Lawrence* (Cambridge, 1966); B. Russell, *Autobiography*, vol. II: *1914–1944* (London, 1968); C. Clarke, *River of Dissolution: D. H. Lawrence and English Romanticism* (London, 1969).

R. P. Draper, ed., *D. H. Lawrence: The Critical Heritage* (London, 1970); K. Alldritt, *The Visual Imagination of D. H. Lawrence* (London, 1971); E. Delavenay, *D. H. Lawrence: The Man and His Work—The Formative Years, 1885–1919* (London, 1972), trans., rev., and abridged from the French by K. M. Delavenay (1969), a work of massive research, but not always reliable in its comprehension of Lawrence's language; S. J. Miko, *Toward "Women in Love": The Emergence of Lawrentian Aesthetic* (New Haven, Conn.–London, 1972); H. Coombes, ed., *D. H. Lawrence: A Critical Anthology* (Harmondsworth, 1973); F. Kermode, *Lawrence* (London, 1973); M. Green, *The Von Richthofen Sisters* (London, 1974); S. Sklar, *The Plays of D. H. Lawrence* (London, 1975); M. Black, *The Literature of Fidelity* (London, 1975); F. R. Leavis, *Thought, Words and Creativity: Art and Thought in Lawrence* (London, 1976); F. B. Pinion, *A D. H. Lawrence Companion* (London, 1978); K. Cushman, *D. H. Lawrence at Work: The Emergence of the "Prussian Officer" Stories* (Hassocks, 1978); A. Niven, *D. H. Lawrence: The Novels* (Cambridge, 1978); P. Delany, *D. H. Lawrence's Nightmare: The Writer and His Circle in the Years of the Great War* (New York, 1978); A. Smith, ed., *Lawrence and Women* (London, 1978); A. H. Gomme, ed., *D. H. Law-*

rence (Hassocks–New York, 1978); K. Sagar, *D. H. Lawrence: A Calendar of His Works* (Manchester, 1979); J. Worthen, *D. H. Lawrence and the Idea of the Novel* (New York–London, 1979); C. L. Ross, *The Composition of "The Rainbow" and "Women in Love": A History* (Charlottesville, Va., 1979); G. H. Neville, *A Memoir of D. H. Lawrence: The Betrayal*, C. Baron, ed. (Cambridge, 1981); H. Simpson, *D. H. Lawrence and Feminism* (Croom Helm, 1982).

Note: Further information about Lawrentian criticism is available in K. Sagar, *The Art of D. H. Lawrence,* and from the checklist compiled by M. Beebe and A. Tommasi in *Modern Fiction Studies,* V, 1 (Spring 1959). For an account of the nature and chronology of Lawrence's literary development in the years 1913–1915 that differs in important ways from that put forward in the present essay, the reader is referred to M. Kinkead-Weekes, "The Marble and the Statue: The Exploratory Imagination of D. H. Lawrence," in M. Mack and I. Gregor, eds., *Imagined Worlds* (London, 1968).

EDITH SITWELL

(1887-1964)

John Lehmann

I

IN the course of the history of English literature, there have been very few women to make their name as poets. It would, of course, have been exceptional, not to say scandalous in the conditions of the age, to find a female dramatist in Elizabeth I's reign; but in the subsequent centuries there was increasingly little to prevent a woman devoting herself to the muse, and it is curious and surprising that outstanding poets of the female sex are so rare. Everyone will think at once of Emily Brontë and Christina Rossetti, both of whom belong to the nineteenth century; but in the earlier centuries who besides the duchess of Newcastle and Katherine Phillips are remembered or read today? If such poets even existed, their poems died with them; and yet each of the women whose poetry has survived is an altogether exceptional figure, and her contribution to English poetry both singular and powerful, like an azalea of brilliant white or pure red blossoming in a bank of swamp honeysuckle.

Such a figure, in our own age, is Edith Sitwell. Like Emily Brontë and Christina Rossetti, she came of a remarkable family in which every member has, in the same sudden-flowering generation, displayed uncommon gifts in one branch or another of literary creation; but unlike those two illustrious predecessors, she came to her unique stature as a poet in the English-speaking world today by a long process of development. Edith Sitwell wrote poetry for nearly half a century, and her work went through many phases; it was always unmistakable for the work of anyone else and, in spite of many sharp differences between one phase and another, always showed a basic unity of inspiration; but, as in the case of another great poet of the twentieth century, William Butler Yeats, the sum of her work is greater than its parts. Her early poetry, like Yeats's, would always have been read for its fresh lyricism, its wit and col-

or, if she had never written another word after her first two volumes; but the work of her supreme phase, during World War I and in the years immediately following, was so much more profound and satisfying in its vision of life and displayed such an infinitely subtler control of the technical means that it reflected some of its glory on what went before; while the interest it has for us is enhanced when we see in it the resolution of contrasting themes from the earlier work and can savor it as the full ripening of a mind and artistic personality of extended and persistent growth.

Edith Sitwell also wrote many books of prose, notable among them a biographical study of Alexander Pope (1930) and a novel based on the tragic life story of Jonathan Swift, *I Live Under a Black Sun* (1937). She was also an indefatigable and highly original anthologist, and combined the chosen comments of others with her own obiter dicta in two unique anthology-journals, *A Poet's Notebook* (1943) and *A Notebook on William Shakespeare* (1948). In all these works, or in the introductions to them, she provided a great deal of valuable light on her views of what the lives of poets mean, what poetry is for and how it works; so that the books are not only fascinating in themselves but also important for anyone who wishes fully to appreciate the oeuvre of this remarkable poet. In the present study, necessarily restricted in scope, I shall confine myself to those of her prose works and anthologies which have some connection with poetry; but I hope that what I write may nevertheless stimulate many of my readers to taste the pleasure of such books as *Fanfare for Elizabeth* (1946), *Bath* (1932), and *The English Eccentrics* (1933).

There are no shortcuts to the appreciation of poetry, though there can be many charts, illustrated itineraries, and descriptive milestones. This study, at best, can be no more than one of the latter: to appreciate Edith Sitwell's work one must read it, read it through, and then read it again. And if one believes (as I do) that to hear a poet recite her own work adds something precious to our understanding of it, then one should listen to as many as possible of the many records Edith Sitwell made during her life. She always had a profound interest in music, and her association with William Walton, who wrote the music for the poem sequence *Façade* (1922), and other composers, resulted not merely in a setting to music but, when she recited herself, in a new artistic creation.

Edith Sitwell is a controversial figure in the history of English poetry during the present century. Her eminence is in my opinion certain; but it should not be imagined that the path to that eminence was easy. On the contrary, it was a long and obdurate fight with an often uncomprehending and tardy public opinion, though perhaps some of the opposition may have at times been less purposefully embattled than appeared to the always mettlesomely defensive Sitwellian ardor. Nevertheless, even in the days when her flights of metaphor bewildered those of slower imagination, when she maintained in her poetry that light "creaked" and that rain could "squawk down" "grey as a guinea fowl," she found appreciation in plenty from critics and readers of discriminating and forward-looking taste in the arts. She never belonged to any school, except of her own making; she was deeply influenced by the symbolist movement, but so was the whole of European poetry, and it would be extraordinary indeed if a poet of such sensitive artistic antennae, with such fertile image-making powers, had not responded to that great release of poetic vigor. Above all, she never remained *set*; and though it may appear a paradox that the daughter of an ancient aristocratic family, the avant-garde innovating poet of the highly individual 1920's, should become one of the three or four supreme poetic voices of an age of tragic world upheaval and social leveling, such development could always have been envisaged by those who from the first had understood her willpower and restless energy, and her intense, untrammeled awareness.

II

It is often the case that the imaginative roots of an outstanding creative artist have been nourished by an intensely lived childhood, in which exceptional opportunities existed for the early awakening of aesthetic responses—ample libraries a boy or girl can pick and choose in at will, beautiful pictures at home, an active family devotion to music or the theater, or perhaps the romantic appeal of house and gardens and natural surroundings.

In the last years of her life, Edith Sitwell wrote of her early days in her autobiographical book *Taken Care Of* (1965). She was already a sick woman, and in some ways it is not an entirely reliable record; but long before that, the description that her brother Osbert gives in *The Scarlet Tree* (1946) of the surroundings and exploits of himself, his brother, Sacheverell, and his sister during their childhood and youth reveals that the imaginative experiences were indeed there in abundance, and confirms the impression created by Edith Sitwell's early poetry.

Edith was the eldest child, born in Scarborough on 7 September 1887. Nevertheless, it is clear that her childhood was not easy. Her relationship with her parents was not altogether happy: her extreme sensitiveness, her devotion to books and music and lack of interest in the fashionable pursuits of the *grand monde* that surrounded her family in the ancestral home of Renishaw Hall brought opposition and criticism from her mother that might have reduced an ordinary child to sullen, inhibited acquiescence; with the poet, however, it seems only to have increased her determination to live her own life and to withdraw into her own inner world. "I was fortunate," writes Sir Osbert of Lady Sitwell's visits to him at school,

in being her favourite child, and in thus obtaining much of the love of which my sister was deprived. And though I saw the sufferings of this young creature, it was difficult for me to realize the extent of them; for I was privileged to the degree that she was penalized. Edith still remained in the schoolroom, and so was seldom as yet allowed to come down and see me. Her personality was too strong, her mind too imaginative, her heart too easily touched, to make her a comfortable companion for the conventional. Besides, my Mother saw in her a living embodiment of some past unhappiness of her own. . . .

(*The Scarlet Tree*, p. 135)

Luckily, to counterbalance this frostlike check on her development, a person was soon to come into Edith Sitwell's life who supplied just that adult sympathy and understanding that had been so lacking hitherto, and, with her own musical and literary accomplishments, was an ideal companion to the young girl, in whose mind the buds of poetry were already beginning to form. "Though she was unaware of it," writes Sir Osbert,

help was already on the way, for Helen Rootham, most faithful friend and champion, was due to appear in a few days' time. And she was the first grown-up person to seize the quality—though even then, perhaps, not at first the gifts—of this young girl, with her face of brooding and luminous melancholy, with her lank gold-green hair, and her features, of so distinctive a kind, but which her character, though developing so fast, had not yet fully carved out of the soft matrix of childhood.

Helen Rootham had been engaged in 1903, when Edith was sixteen, and five years later Edith was sent with her new governess to live in Paris to perfect her French; she came back, according to the same witness, a changed being:

In the peace that she now obtained for the first time, no longer fearing every moment that she would be found fault with, able to attend concerts and go to galleries with her governess, and come back home without having to face scenes, all her interests had blossomed in the short interval that had elapsed, and music and poetry burned in her blood like fire. She had become the most exhilarating as well as understanding of companions.

Helen Rootham was not only a pianist of exceptional quality, whose passion for music invaded and transformed the home lives of her new charge and the two brothers from the moment she arrived, but also an extremely sensitive student and interpreter of French literature, whose version of Arthur Rimbaud's *Les illuminations* remains one of the finest translations into English of that difficult poet's work. How important close association with such a personality was in Edith Sitwell's artistic unfolding can surely be seen in all her poetic beginnings and in her constant love of French nineteenth-century poetry, so clearly shown in *A Poet's Notebook*. Edith Sitwell admitted that one of the strongest influences guiding her toward poetry as a life task was a first reading of Baudelaire at the age of seventeen, one of those early revelations in artists' lives the force of which is rarely surpassed in later years. But though France and French literature meant so much, one must not forget another influence, once upon a time the birthright of almost every educated Englishman, that completed the education of a poet who

was eventually to receive European acclaim. "I mention at some length," says Sir Osbert,

the effect, and lingering influence, of Italy on my brother, my sister, and myself, because it provides a clue to the work which later we set ourselves—or which set itself for us—and have since striven, however imperfectly, to accomplish. By this path we came to the classical tradition, through the visual arts, rather than through Greek and Latin. In a sense, as artists, we thus belong to Italy, hardly less than to England, to that old and famous combination of Italian influence and English blood. We breathed in, without being wholly conscious of it, the space and proportion of Italy which for centuries gave grace to Western Europe and even to the Marches. We learnt our lessons in a school that teaches by example and feeling rather than by precept; we came to be able to tell good things from bad, to use our own judgement and not believe anything about the arts that we were merely told. So, though it is with what came to be known as the Modern Movement that our names will be associated, it was partly due to this same upbringing that we were able to perceive genius where it existed in unfamiliar guises, to understand at once—to take three things at random—the force and the fire of a Stravinsky, to see the constructive truth of Modigliani's peasants and the new element that had entered into the theatre with Monsieur Diaghilev's Russian Ballet. The several modern manifestations which we have championed in England, when they needed it, thus owe, through us, something to the past of Italy.

(p. 248)

It would, however, be putting matters into a false perspective to insist too exclusively on Edith Sitwell's direct debt, as an artist, to France or the classical lands of the Mediterranean. She was, above all, deeply rooted in the English tradition, and her *Notebooks* and her anthologies show that the whole of English poetry, from the time of Skelton and Chaucer down to our own century, nourished her poetic spirit. It shows a rare receptivity to differing modes and artistic aims, to know, in one's girlhood, all of Pope's *Rape of the Lock* by heart, and at the same time to have a passion for Swinburne. The influence of both reveals itself in her work to the attentive ear; and it is no surprise to the reader who has become intimate with the full range of her poetry to find how much space she devotes in the three volumes of her anthology, *The Pleasures of Poetry* (1930–1932), to the work of Herrick and of Blake, capturing some of the unequaled country freshness of the former and jewel-like imaginative fire of the latter in her own most brilliant lyrics and songs; to

Shelley in his supreme moments of ethereal conjuration, to the purest instances of romantic image-painting in the work of the Pre-Raphaelites, who found their inspiration in Keats, and to the infinitely subtle technical refinements of Tennyson. It is this extreme richness of the poetic soil that fostered her flowering which makes one feel, in reading Edith Sitwell, that she was, more truly than any other modern poet, the heir of all that had gone before—even to the untraceably ancient nursery rhymes that she learned as a child. The English quality of her poetry is marked, too, by the deep impress of her childhood surroundings: glimpses of the romantic garden of a great English country house appear in the imagery of innumerable poems, but in the alchemy of her imagination it is a garden that has become the natural setting for legend and fairy tale, where King Midas walks among the auriculas and primulas, Pan is dancing among the strawberry beds, and the gardener is

> old as tongues of nightingales
> That in the wide leaves tell a thousand Grecian tales.
> ("The Sleeping Beauty," 44–45)

In such power of transformation, of creating new wonder and significance by the marriage of the familiar with the unexpected symbol already rich in imaginative associations, Edith Sitwell always excelled. The deepest inner experiences and discoveries of her childhood were exploited in this process for her poetry; she never lost them, but, equally, she never ceased to add to them. The acquisitive Ariel of her restless mind continually brought new treasures back to its master spirit of poetry, from the works of mystic philosophers, scientists, and poets of all lands and all ages: anyone who wishes to understand how tireless this activity was should study the notes she added to all her major poems of the 1940's and after.

III

In her introduction to the American edition of *The Canticle of the Rose* (1949), Edith Sitwell wrote of her early poems: "At the time I began to write, a change in the direction, imagery and rhythms in poetry had become necessary, owing to the rhythmical flaccidity, the verbal deadness, the dead and expected patterns, of some of the poetry immediately preceding us." And she went on to describe the shock her innovations caused, and the violent opposition they aroused among the conventional readers (and reviewers) of poetry.

To escape from "the dead and expected patterns": this is the key to Edith Sitwell's poetic endeavors in the 1920's. In *Laughter in the Next Room* (1948) Osbert Sitwell has explained how *Façade* first came to be created:

The idea of *Façade* first entered our minds as the result of certain technical experiments at which my sister had recently been working: experiments in obtaining through the medium of words the rhythm of dance measures such as waltzes, polkas, foxtrots. These exercises were often experimental enquiries into the effect on rhythm, on speed, and on colour of the use of rhymes, assonances, dissonances, placed outwardly, at different places in the line, in most elaborate patterns.

These experiments—which were indeed exercises but also, more often than not, poems of great fascination in their own right—were extremely various, but they all have relationship with one another through the linking quality of the poet's extremely individual imagination, which runs through them all. Both Edith Sitwell and her brother Osbert laid emphasis in their writings on the importance of the rhythmical and textual aspect of the experiments; but the novel choice and association of images, which I have already touched upon, is an equally important ingredient in their originality. Reading them through today, one has the impression that a brilliantly gifted child has taken the fragments of Shelley's "dome of many coloured glass," all the variously strange and lovely things in the world, and all the many facets of experience and emotion, and set them together again in fanciful patterns.

Here is an example of the seemingly effortless music, the transfigured nursery-rhyme world of these early poems:

> Grey as a guinea-fowl is the rain
> Squawking down from the boughs again.
>   'Anne, Anne
>   Go fill the pail',
> Said the old witch who sat on the rail,
> 'Though there is a hole in the bucket,
> Anne, Anne,
> It will fill my pocket;
> The water-drops when they cross my doors
> Will turn to guineas and gold moidores. . . .
> The well-water hops across the floors;
> Whimpering, 'Anne' it cries, implores,
> And the guinea-fowl plumaged rain
> Squawking down from the bougs again,

Cried, 'Anne, Anne go fill the bucket,
There is a hole in the witch's pocket—
And the water-drops like gold moidores,
Obedient girl, will surely be yours.
So, Anne Anne,
Go fill the pail
Of the old witch who sits on the rail.'
("Two Kitchen Songs")

As I indicated earlier, it was just such images as the rain "grey as a guinea-fowl" "squawking down from the boughs" that woke the clamor of dismay that greeted these poems. "The fire was furry as a bear," "the morning light creaks down" "goat's-beard rivers"—later on, in her descriptive notes, Edith Sitwell proposed elucidations to these once so "shocking" conceits; but to a lively imagination they never needed apology. They startle; but it is the business of poetical comparison to startle and, by bringing things together that have never yet met, to refashion thought. And as Shakespeare once thought nothing of bringing a band of most English rustics into "a wood near Athens," so Edith Sitwell, following the impulse of her imagination, discovered that

> The harsh bray and hollow
> Of the pot and the pan
> Seems Midas defying
> The great god Apollo!
> ("Two Kitchen Songs")

In "Green Geese" there is one of the most beautiful examples of this myth-making—or rather myth-changing—power:

> The trees were hissing like green geese. . . .
> The words they tried to say were these:
>
> 'When the great Queen Claude was dead
> They buried her deep in the potting shed.'
>
> The moon smelt sweet as nutmeg-root
> On the ripe peach-trees' leaves and fruit,
>
> And her sandal-wood body leans upright
> To the gardener's fright, through the summer night.

Edith Sitwell wrote in the preface to the 1957 edition of her *Collected Poems*: "In most of the *Bucolic Comedies* [1923] there are no technical experiments, and usually the rhythm is a drone-sound like that of a hive or the wind in the trees." Nevertheless the experiments had begun, were already there in embryo, as the well-known poem "Aubade" shows clearly enough; *Façade* only brought out certain elements of

the art of *Bucolic Comedies* and developed them to an extraordinary degree.[1] The conjunction of images becomes as violent as the clash of symbols, as violent as often the effect of the rhythm and the clanging bells of the internal rhymes and assonances. There are times when the sequence of word pictures, names, and rhymes seems dictated only by the "free association" of a vivid imagination quickened to the highest pitch of excitement and leaping right over the boundaries of sense; and yet, after several readings, especially in mindfulness of the poems that have gone before and the poems that are to come after, the underlying coherence, the unity of spirit behind them, becomes apparent. Her aim of escaping from "the rhythmical flaccidity, the verbal deadness" of contemporary tradition is boldly and brilliantly achieved. What could be less Tennysonian (in the decadent sense of the word) than "Fox Trot"?

> Old
>   Sir
>   Faulk,
> Tall as a stork,
> Before the honeyed fruits of dawn were ripe, would walk,
> And stalk with a gun
> The reynard-coloured sun,
> Among the pheasant-feathered corn the unicorn has torn,
>   forlorn the
> Smock-faced sheep
> Sit
>   And
>   Sleep;
> Periwigged as William and Mary weep . . .
> 'Sally, Mary, Mattie, what's the matter, why cry?'
> The huntsman and the reynard-coloured sun and I sigh.

This was shock-treatment with a vengeance for the sleepy-sickness of poetry; but always one feels a deeper consequence underneath the surface inconsequence (as in the nonsense poems of Edward Lear), and sometimes a note of strange sadness and mystery comes hauntingly through:

> Jumbo asleep!
> Grey leaves, thick-furred

[1] The original version of *Façade* was privately printed by the Favil Press in 1922, a year before the publication of *Bucolic Comedies* (which also contains most of the earlier work); but many of the poems in *Bucolic Comedies* were written or in draft before *Façade* was attempted. The Favil edition contains nine poems under the heading of *Façade*; but the pieces set to music by William Walton included several that were either not in that edition or not under that heading.

As his ears, keep
Conversations blurred.
Thicker than hide
Is the trumpeting water;
Don Pasquito's bride
And his youngest daughter
Watch the leaves
Elephantine grey:
What is it grieves
in the torrid day?
Is it the animal
world that snores
Harsh and inimical
In sleepy pores?—
And why should the spined flowers
Red as a soldier
Make Don Pasquito
Seem still mouldier?
("Lullaby for Jumbo")

In reading *Façade* one should remember that the poems were eventually assembled for William Walton's music and for dramatic presentation: they are wonderfully adapted for their purpose and gain from it as well. It is a stimulating and thrilling experience to be present when they are performed; and the memory of the absurd scandal of the first night has become part of the period flavor that enhances the delight they give—the period of the triumphs of jazz, of Ronald Firbank's novels, of Diaghilev's final conquest of the artistic world of the West.

Edith Sitwell wrote in *Taken Care Of* that the mood in *Façade* is "for the most part of gaiety"; and yet one cannot help noticing how often, through the images, the dark side of life is portrayed.

One of the most interesting things about Edith Sitwell's art is the way in which all aspects of it seem to be present at every stage in her development, while at each stage one particular aspect becomes dominant. At the next stage, in *The Sleeping Beauty* (1924), she turned away from the satirical-fantastic inventions of *Façade* and devoted herself to the exploitation of the elegiac, romantic vein in which she had already begun to work in *Bucolic Comedies*.[2]

²I have in the main followed the order of composition given in *The Canticle of the Rose*; but only the most painstaking research into dates of original publication in magazines or booklets long out of print could establish the order of writing of many of the poems, for Edith Sitwell always assumed the privilege of rewriting her poems and inserting the new versions into later books—often without comment. Even such research, however, cannot be entirely conclusive, because some poems were kept unpublished much longer than others.

The contrast at first sight, between the world of Don Pasquito and Mr. Belaker, "the allegro Negro cocktail-shaker," and "The Soldan's Song," with its Elizabethan and Keatsian echoes, could scarcely be sharper:

When green as a river was the barley,
Green as a river the rye,
I waded deep and began to parley
With a youth whom I heard sigh.
'I seek', said he, 'a lovely lady,
A nymph as bright as a queen,
Like a tree that drips with pearls her shady
Locks of hair were seen;
And all the river became her flocks
Though their wool you cannot shear,
Because of the love of her flowing locks.
The kingly sun like a swain
Came strong, unheeding of her scorn,
Wading in deeps where she has lain,
Sleeping upon her river lawn
And chasing her starry satyr train,
She fled, and changed into a tree—
That lovely fair-haired lady. . . .
And now I seek through the sere summer
Where no trees are shady.'

This romantic period lasted up to the writing of *Gold Coast Customs* at the end of the 1920's; there are moments when the wit of *Façade* reappears, as it were in a different key; and scattered through these poems one comes across many of the poet's favorite images and persons of her legend, such as the

country gentlemen who from their birth,
Like kind red strawberries, root deep in earth
And sleep as in the grave, dream far beyond
The sensual aspects of the hairy sky
That something hides, they have forgotten why!

What is equally interesting is that there are many passages where the mood and the images foretell the supreme phase that was to begin in 1940: if I had not been reading Edith Sitwell's poems for some time, and were asked where the following two stanzas from "Romance" (1933) came in her work, I should find it difficult not to assume they were from one of the long poems in *Green Song* (1944) or *The Song of the Cold* (1945).

And still their love amid this green world grieves:
'The gold light drips like myrrh upon the leaves

And fills with gold those chambers of the South
That were your eyes, that honeycomb your mouth.

And now the undying Worm makes no great stir,
His tight embrace chills not our luxuries
Though the last light perfumes our bones like myrrh
And Time's beat dies.

Some of the poems of this period are among the most lovely that Edith Sitwell ever wrote. In others one feels that her inexhaustible power of verse-spinning has been too little checked by a sense of intellectual form and pattern; such a poem as "Elegy on Dead Fashion" is like some of Shelley's longer poems before the great 1820 volume, full of wonderful passages and flashes of beauty but cloying to the mind and imagination because the note is too unvaried and the riches poured out in too indiscriminate a profusion. There are, however, magical exceptions: the tender, nostalgic poem of transfigured autobiography, "Colonel Fantock," the crystal purity of the songs called "Daphne" and "The Strawberry," and, most famous of all, the rustic elegy "The Little Ghost Who Died for Love," the haunting sadness of which pierces the heart every time one reads it with a fresh pang that survives its reappearances in anthology after anthology:

'Fear not, O maidens, shivering
As bunches of the dew-drenched leaves
In the calm moonlight . . . it is the cold sends quivering
My voice, a little nightingale that grieves.

Now Time beats not, and dead Love is forgotten . . .
The spirit too is dead and dank and rotten,

And I forgot the moment when I ran
Between my lover and the sworded man—

Blinded with terror lest I lose his heart.
The sworded man dropped, and I saw depart

Love and my lover and my life . . . he fled
And I was strung and hung upon the tree.
It is so cold now that my heart is dead
And drops through time . . . night is too dark to see

Him still. . . . But it is spring: upon the fruit-boughs of
    your lips,
Young maids, the dew like India's splendour drips;
Pass by among the strawberry beds, and pluck the
    berries
Cooled by the silver moon: pluck boughs of cherries
That seem the lovely lucent coral bough
(From streams of starry milk those branches grow)
That Cassiopeia feeds with her faint light,
Like AEthiopa ever jewelled bright.'

The poem rises to an unforgettable climax when the village girl who was hanged in 1708, for shielding her lover in the duel, prophesies a doom hanging over the world for its corruption:

'. . . so I sank me down,
Poor Deborah in my long cloak of brown.
Though cockcrow marches, crying of false dawns,
Shall bury my dark voice, yet still it mourns
Among the ruins—for it is not I
But this old world, is sick and soon must die!'

In her next phase Edith Sitwell was to write again of this corruption and doom, but in accents from which nostalgia and sadness were completely banished. In the long poem *Gold Coast Customs*, she used again the strong rhythms, the clashing rhymes and assonances of *Façade*, but for an effect far removed from the wit and gaiety of that sequence: the banging, insistent drumbeat that runs through it, the hard, explosive consonants, the vivid images of horror, create an almost unbearable atmosphere of savagery, loathsomeness, and spiritual death. The contrast between *Gold Coast Customs* and such poems as "The Soldan's Song" and "The Little Ghost Who Died for Love" is a revelation of the range of Edith Sitwell's poetic powers. "In this poem," Edith Sitwell wrote,

the bottom of the world has fallen out. . . . We see everything reduced to the primal need—the "rich man Judas, brother Cain," and the epitome of his civilization, Lady Bamburgher, are at one with the slum-ignorance and the blackness and superstition of the African swamp. The beating of their fevered hearts and pulses is no more than the beating of the drums that heralded the Customs, as they were called, in Ashantee, a hundred years ago, when, at the death of any rich or important person, slaves and poor persons were killed so that the bones of the dead might be washed with human blood. So the spiritual dead-in-life cry for a sacrifice—that of the starved.

The poem is characteristic of all Edith Sitwell's longer works, in that it has no precise plot as Shakespeare's *Venus and Adonis* or Coleridge's "The Ancient Mariner" has a plot or sequence of events; there is rather the statement of various themes, their repetition and intermingling in a manner that is more reminiscent of music: structure is there, but it is the structure of images, ideas, and emotions that are gradually developed, contrasted, and resolved in a deeply moving prophetic cry—as Shelley's themes in the "Ode to the West Wind" are resolved. The poet employs considerable skill in a montage of Lady Bamburgher's parties and the heartless nightmare of the African rites, so that each appears as a metaphor of the other; and underlying them both one senses a third parallel theme, of personal betrayal and love disgraced. The tremendous strength of the imaginative realization appears at once:

> One fantee wave
> Is grave and tall
> As brave Ashantee's
> Thick mud wall.
> Munza rattles his bones in the dust,
> Lurking in murk because he must.
>
> Striped black and white
> Is the squealing light;
> The dust brays white in the market-place,
> Dead powder spread on a black skull's face.
>
> Like monkey-skin
> Is the sea—one sin
> Like a weasel is nailed to bleach on the rocks
> Where the eyeless mud screeched fawning, mocks
>
> At a negro that wipes
> His knife . . . dug there,
> A bugbear bellowing
> Bone dared rear—
> A bugbear bone that bellows white
> As the ventriloquist sound of light,
>
> It rears at his head-dress of felted black hair
> The one humanity clinging there—
> His eyeless face whitened like black and white bones
> And his beard of rusty
> Brown grass cones.

Immediately after, Lady Bamburgher, image of a corrupt civilization, of "something rotten in the state of Denmark," and more particularly of a moneyed ruling class glorying in a callous indifference at a moment when suffering is at its most intense in the world, is introduced:

> Here, tier on tier
> Like a black box rear
> In the flapping slum
> Beside Death's docks.
> I did not know this meaner Death
> Meant this: that the bunches of nerves still dance
> And caper among these slums, and prance.
>
> 'Mariners, put your bones to bed!'
> But at Lady Bamburgher's parties each head,
> Grinning, knew it had left its bones

> In the mud with the white skulls . . . only the grin
> Is left, strings of nerves, and the drum-taut skin.

This atmosphere of macabre horror and cruelty is sustained through nearly sixty stanzas in which the rhythm is varied with the utmost mastery, so that in spite of the terrible compulsion of the underlying drumbeat the mind is never wearied. Only occasionally does the poet allow the vision of what is lost, of a fulfillment of longing, to break in:

> O far horizons and bright blue wine
> And majesty of the seas that shine,
> Bull-bellowing waves that ever fall
> Round the god-like feet and the goddess tall!
> A great yellow flower
> With the silence shy
> To the wind from the islands
> Sighs 'I die.'

It is impossible in this remarkable poem not to be reminded at times, in spite of all surface dissimilarities, of the author of *Atalanta in Calydon*; and to remember that Edith Sitwell herself confessed to an early passion for Swinburne. Equally, however, Yeats was surely right when he wrote in 1930 to Wyndham Lewis that, reading *Gold Coast Customs*, he

felt that something absent from all literature was back again, and in a form rare in the literature of all generations, passion ennobled by intensity, by endurance, by wisdom. We had it in one man once. He lies in St Patrick's now under the greatest epitaph in all history.[3]

(A. Wade, ed., *Letters of W. B. Yeats*, 1955)

In the great climax, Edith Sitwell, having earlier in the poem spoken prophetically of "the thick sick smoke of London burning," spoke prophetically again, as much of her own coming development, the next supreme phase of her art, as of changes in the outside world:

> Yet the time will come
> To the heart's dark slum
> When the rich man's gold and the rich man's wheat
> Will grow in the street, that the starved may eat—
> And the sea of the rich will give up its dead—
> And the last blood and fire from my side will be shed.
> For the fires of God go marching on.

[3]Yeats was referring to Jonathan Swift, whose epitaph reads: "Jacet . . . ubi saeva indignatio ulterius cor lacerare nequit" (He lies . . . where fierce indignation can no longer tear his heart).

IV

In *Laughter in the Next Room*, Sir Osbert Sitwell says of his sister's life during the 1930's:

Alas, after 1929 began the long and mortal illness of our old friend Helen Rootham. And in the next decade, until Helen's death in 1938, the concern my sister felt for her, and the necessity she found herself under to earn money, compelled her to turn away from the natural expression of her being, towards prose: for some ten years she was obliged to abandon poetry. Also her close attendance upon the invalid often prevented her from going with us to Italy.

It is safe to guess that these years were a time of great spiritual trial and suffering in the life of the poet, a time when the world turned its most hideous face and despair was not far off; the novel (her only novel) that she published in 1937, *I Live Under a Black Sun*, is evidence of this. And yet, compared with *Gold Coast Customs*, the novel seems to have strange sunbursts, interstices of light among dark clouds, that suggest that now she was gradually making her way back to delight and faith—a new faith deeper than any she had known before.

In January 1942 Edith Sitwell's first volume of poetry for more than a decade, *Street Songs*, was published; and this was followed two years later by *Green Song*. The two volumes contain only about three dozen poems, and yet their appearance was one of the three or four most important literary events of the war years. *Street Songs* opens with three poems that were immediately felt to express the deepest emotions of that time of darkness and endurance, transmuted by an imagination that used symbols with consummate mastery. The bitter irony of "Serenade," with its transposition of Marlowe's "Come live with me and be my love," into the terms of Europe at war, where the lover must be unfaithful because he is "the cannon's mate" and "death's cold puts the passion out," and the only serenade is "the wolfish howls the starving made," is matched by the nightmare symbolism of "Lullaby," where there is nothing left in the world but the monster "the Babioun," which sings to the abandoned child on a desecrated earth:

> 'Do, do, do, do—
> Thy mother's hied to the vaster race:
> The Pterodactyl made its nest
> And laid a steel egg in her breast—
> Under the Judas-coloured sun.
> She'll work no more, nor dance, nor moan,

> And I am come to take her place
> Do, do.'

These two terrible poems are contrasted with "Still Falls the Rain," one of the most memorable of all Edith Sitwell's poems, written of the air raids on Britain in 1940 and moving with a deep pulse of funereal solemnity that is a triumph of skill in rhythmic art and the music that can be created from words:

> Still falls the Rain—
> Dark as the world of man, black as our loss—
> Blind as the nineteen hundred and forty nails
> Upon the cross.

> Still falls the Rain. . . .

In this great achievement the poet openly declared her Christian faith, and conceived the falling of the bombs as a rain that is at the same time the falling of blood from Christ's side; a rain that thus becomes a symbol of punishment and suffering and redemption through that suffering. In the last line Christ speaks: "Still do I love, still shed my innocent light, my Blood, for thee."

In the extreme tension of emotion held within their art, in their technical virtuosity and the force of their imagery, these three poems proclaimed that Edith Sitwell had returned to poetry with her powers undiminished, indeed enhanced. What was perhaps more significant, she seemed able to approach her tremendous theme—at a time when complaints were loud that no war poetry worthy of the cataclysm was being written—through symbols that needed no special intimacy with the esoteric fancy characteristic even of *Gold Coast Customs*, but could be apprehended directly and universally. How valuable a gain this was can be seen most clearly from "An Old Woman," the last poem in *Street Songs* and at the same time the first complete realization of the new mode of Sibylline utterance to which the other poems showed her feeling her way:

> Wise is the earth, consoling grief and glory,
> The golden heroes proud as pomp of waves—
> Great is the earth embracing them, their graves,
> And great is the earth's story.
> For though the soundless wrinkles fall like snow
> On many a golden cheek, and creeds grow old
> And change—man's heart, that sun,
> Outlives all terrors shaking the old night:
> The world's huge fevers burn and shine, turn cold,
> Yet the heavenly bodies and young lovers burn and shine,
> The golden lovers walk in the holy fields
> Where the Abraham-bearded sun, the father of all things,

Is shouting of ripeness, and the whole world of dews and
    splendours are singing
To the cradles of earth, of men, beasts, harvests,
    swinging
In the peace of God's heart. And I, the primeval clay
That has known earth's grief and harvest's happiness,
Seeing mankind's dark seed-time, come to bless,
Forgive and bless all men like the holy light.

The unprecedented series of long odes in the grand manner, of which "An Old Woman" is the first example, is continued in *Green Song* and *The Song of the Cold* with increasing artistic assurance and skill. Underlying their structure is an iambic line of five beats, the traditional form of English recitative poetry; but this is occasionally increased to six or even seven or eight beats, and at rare intervals reduced to four or three; rhyme—or rather end rhyming, for her lines are full of subtle hints of internal rhyming and assonance—is discarded, but her medium is far removed from the free verse of our time, which has come to mean little more than prose statement on which an additional system of sense-pauses is imposed by division into lines. There is rhythmic life and shape in every one of these poems, of the most supple and breathing sort, and they seem to evolve organically, and differently in every instance, out of the heart of the poem's conception. The long, flowing lines with their apparent ease and simplicity, their movement as of a swan floating on a softly gliding river that can suddenly turn to a majestic drumming of wings across the sky as the bird rises into flight, are the culmination of Edith Sitwell's lifetime of devoted apprenticeship to her art. She was always intensely aware of the importance of music and texture in the making of verse, as her studies of other poets' technique showed more than once; in these odes she handles sound and texture to create poetic effects of the most astonishing variety and complexity; to find any comparable achievement one must look beyond her beloved Walt Whitman to the later work of Blake, such as *The Book of Thel* (1789). It is difficult to get an impression of the flexibility of this instrument in her hands from a short quotation, but here are the opening lines of "Invocation" (from *Green Song*), a passage remarkable for its range of mood and tempo:

I who was once a golden woman like those who walk
In the dark heavens—but am now grown old
And sit by the fire, and see the fire grow cold,
Watch the dark fields for a rebirth of faith and wonder.

The turning of Ixion's wheel the day
Ceased not, yet sounds no more the beat of the heart
But only the sound of the ultimate darkness falling
And of the Blind Samson at the Fair, shaking the pillars of
    the world and emptily calling.

For the gardeners cried for rain, but the high priests
    howled
For a darker rain to cool the delirium of gold
And wash the sore of the world, the heart of Dives,
Raise wheat for the hunger that lies in the soul of the
    poor—
Then came the thunderous darkness.

In this phase of her art Edith Sitwell used symbols of the widest range, from Christian and classical history and legend, from the Old Testament and even beyond—from the primitive prehistory and shadowy beliefs and customs on which civilization was gradually built; and she married these with the more ancient and universal symbols of animal and flower and corn, gold and precious metal, sea and sun and stars. It is by such means that she managed to convey, in these odes, such an extraordinary sense of depth in time and space, of wisdom ripening in eternal contemplation from a mountaintop vantage point. The "golden woman grown old," symbol for the poet-philosopher who through long personal suffering and identification with the sufferings of others has reached a vision beyond the accidents of history, is inspired to see that all created things are sacred; that if death and darkness are necessary to the order of the universe, there is also eternal renewal, of the spiritual as well as of the physical world; and that behind the evil and terror of the world there is divine forgiveness and charity. The heart of the poet's vision, of her thought, would seem to be the quite simple idea—simple, yet so often lost sight of, and seldom so beautifully expressed, an idea that unites her with the great Christian mystics and the English mystical poets of the seventeenth century—that as the world of nature is transformed and re-created again and again by the action of the sun, so Love transforms and conquers all our sufferings, all the passing triumphs of its opposite, so that "all in the end is harvest." Of all the poems of this period, "Eurydice" has perhaps the most exultant declaration of this faith:

Fire on the hearth! Fire in the heavens! Fire in the hearts
    of men!
I who was welded into bright gold in the earth by
    Death

Salute you! All the weight of Death in all the world
Yet does not equal Love—the great compassion
For the fallen dust and all fallen creatures, quickening
As is the Sun in the void firmament.
It shines like fire. O bright gold of the heat of the Sun
Of Love across dark fields—burning away rough
   husks of Death
Till all is fire, and bringing all to harvest!

It would be easy to assume that such a philosophy of reconciliation and peace-in-love might lead the poet to an underestimate of the real and terrible tragedies and horrors of the world. With Edith Sitwell the very opposite is the case. The poems that followed "An Old Woman," "Harvest," "Invocation," and "Eurydice" present the problem of evil with extraordinary imaginative power. In reading *The Song of the Cold* and the three poems on the age of the atom bomb, "Dirge for the New Sunrise," "The Shadow of Cain," and "The Canticle of the Rose," one has the feeling that the poet has a presentiment of a terrifying crisis and cataclysm in the history of man. In her symbolism the heart, the heat of the blood, has always represented good; and cold—"the ultimate cold within the heart of man"—evil; and Dives and Lazarus, the craving for riches and the destitute, sore-covered human condition (never, it is interesting to observe, the lust for power and the humble misery of powerlessness) are always opposed to one another. And now Dives seems to be about to triumph and his gold to banish the other gold, the gold of the ear of corn that is life:

We did not heed the Cloud in the Heavens shaped
   like the hand
Of Man. . . . But there came a roar as if the Sun and
   Earth had come together—

The Sun descending and the Earth ascending
To take its place above . . . the Primal Matter
Was broken, the womb from which all life began.
Then to the murdered Sun a totem pole of dust arose
   in memory of Man.

The cataclysm of the Sun down-pouring
Seemed the roar
Of those vermilion Suns the drops of the blood
That bellowing like Mastodons at war
Rush down the length of the world—away—away—

The violence of torrents, cataracts, maelstroms,
   rains
That went before the Flood—
These covered the earth from the freshets of our
   brothers' veins;

And with them, the forked lightnings of the gold
From the split mountains,
Blasting their rivals, the young foolish wheat-ears
Amid those terrible rains.

"The Shadow of Cain," quoted above, has been well called by Sir Kenneth Clark "this craggy, mysterious, philosophic poem," and its conclusion, in the dialogue between Dives and Lazarus, "the poet's deepest and most passionate statement of her concern with original sin." And what is most remarkable about it is that, as she approached the awe-inspiring manifestations of evil and destruction, as in "Still Falls the Rain," her instinct was not to despair but to call upon the most powerful symbols of love she knew, the symbols of Christianity: "He walks again on the Seas of Blood, He comes in the terrible Rain" is the last line of the poem.

The years since the conclusion of World War II have been a time of vast political and economic transformation, affecting the circumstances of almost every human being alive. Yet the volcanic shift in the balance of power among nations and empires has not affected them more than the change in the spiritual climate in which they live. This has been so swift, so revolutionary that it appears, not unnaturally, to have had a numbing effect on the higher faculties of man. The war, in the end, found its voices in the work of many poets and novelists; but the peace, the victory, the defeat, the bewilderment in defeat and the heartbreaking disappointment in victory, the apocalyptic manifestation of atomic power—the poets seemed too long to have been too dazed to speak of them. There is only one exception of the highest order during those crucial years that one can think of: Edith Sitwell. And because she felt herself equal to, and dared to face, this challenge in her art, she is of such supreme importance today. The three great poems of the atom bomb lifted man to the level of the drama of our time. And I can think of nothing else, either poem or novel or painting, that has done so with anything approaching the same power and visionary insight.

I have remarked before on the fact that, though each phase of Edith Sitwell's poetry seems distinctly marked off from those that preceded it, the more carefully one studies them the more closely one sees that they are related. They are like a continuing argument between the two poles of her inspiration, between romance and satire, affirmation and irony; now one gains the ascendancy, now the other, in method as in content. In her poems from "Still Falls the Rain" to "The Canticle of the Rose" they seemed to find a resolution with a larger synthesis: the depth of tenderness and compassion, the understanding of human desolation that so poignantly informed "The Little Ghost Who Died for Love" are there, and at the same time the savage mockery of *Gold Coast Customs*, the dreamlike incantations of *The Sleeping Beauty*, and the hard drumbeat of rhythms first evolved in *Nursery Rhymes*.

During the last years of her life, Edith Sitwell entered on a new phase in her career, which had really begun with the immensely successful lecture tours of America undertaken with her brother Osbert after the war. She became more and more a public figure, famous above all for her witty, oracular comments in television interviews. She was awarded the Foyle Poetry Prize in 1958, and in 1959 she gave a memorable recital of her poems at the Edinburgh Festival. On the occasion of her seventy-fifth birthday in 1962 a celebration concert was given for her at the Royal Festival Hall, which was especially remarkable for the enthusiasm of a younger generation, present in large numbers in the packed auditorium.

Her *Collected Poems* had come out in 1957, a volume that contains more than four hundred pages of poetry. In a long appreciative review in the Sunday *Times* (28 July 1957), Cyril Connolly wrote: "When we come to compare the collected poems of Dame Edith Sitwell with those of Yeats, Mr Eliot or Professor Auden, it will be found that hers have the purest poetical content of them all." She was writing poetry to the last, but some of it seemed, even to her most devoted admirers, rather to repeat what she had already achieved in the glittering period that produced "Eurydice" and "The Shadow of Cain" than to break new ground. Even so, in two of her last published volumes, *Gardeners and Astronomers* (1953) and *The Outcasts* (1962), it is difficult not to feel that new impulses were stirring, that she was beginning to feel her way toward new modes of expression. Such poems as "The Death of Prometheus" are more savagely bitter than anything she had written since *Gold Coast Customs*; others, such as "La Bella Bona Roba" and "The Yellow Girl," are of a greater lyrical purity and technical perfection than she had shown since *Troy Park* (1925). And it seems, to the present author at least, that the far-reaching significance of her "planetary system" in such later poems as "Sailor, What of the Isles?" still remains to be unraveled.

V

A few words remain to be said, in conclusion, about those prose works of Edith Sitwell that have most bearing on her poetry.

The biography *Alexander Pope*, which was published in 1930, is remarkable for the deep intuitive sympathy she shows for the unhappy, complex genius of Twickenham, whose astonishing achievement it was to fix the canons of English poetry for almost a century. At first sight, it might seem paradoxical that a poet such as Edith Sitwell, who dissolved conventional verse forms into innumerable new and beautiful shapes of her own devising and allowed herself the greatest freedom of experimentation in metaphor and image, should be drawn to such a close and devoted study of the arch-priest of inflexible rule: the gulf, one is inclined to say, between *The Rape of the Lock* (1712) and *The Shadow of Cain* (1947) is unbridgeable. As one reads *Alexander Pope*, however, one divines that her admiration rested on a deeper and more significant community of spirit: the heroic tenacity with which Pope triumphed over suffering and denigration, the tremendous force of intellect that he packed into his work, and the extremely subtlety of his poetic ear. "This man," she wrote in her introduction, "who was one of the greatest poets England has produced, whose sense of texture in poetry was so excessively delicate that it has never been surpassed, and, I think, has scarcely been equalled"; and later in the book she analyzed the refinements of his verse at length, and in her own incomparable manner. She conceived the book, it is clear, as a defense of an unjustly unpopular master, and as part of her battle against the state of poetry as she found it when she began to write. She established her challenge in the introduction:

I do not know why the unhappy Pope's underlying beauty of character and kindness have not been more commented upon, since his life's record is one of loyalty to his friends, unchanging love where that love was not betrayed, financial generosity, and where that generosity was extended, the most extraordinary delicacy and kindness. Was this man filled with nothing but hatred and malice? His letters to his friends are among the most touching letters that any great man has written: his devotion to his parents and to his old nurse was beautiful and flawless; it lasted through their lives and after their deaths, unchanged and undimmed. Those whom he loved, he saw only with the eyes of love. . . .

Alexander Pope is one of the most important prose works by Edith Sitwell. It tells one almost as much about the author as about Pope, and has in abundance the special fascination of all biographies written by one great poet about another.

For the hero of her other outstanding prose work, she chose one of Pope's closest friends, the other towering figure of English literature in the first half of the eighteenth century, Swift. *I Live Under a Black Sun* is cast in the form of a novel, and as a novel, it must be admitted, it has many faults; and yet it is so astonishingly transmuted by the fire of poetic genius that sweeps through it that it must be called a masterpiece. She took the story of Swift's relations with Stella and Vanessa and told it as if it had happened in our time; so that, in the strangest way, the setting of World War I and the appurtenances of modern life, cars, trains, and police stations, are superimposed upon the England and Ireland of the eighteenth century. This curious device does not entirely come off; and yet its failure scarcely matters at all. For what matters in the book is what matters in Edith Sitwell's poetry: her passionate vision of the beauty of natural life, of the joys and terrors of love, of the suffering in poverty and war—in the toils of the man-made machine of civilization—of the simple and good in heart; and of the awful presence of madness that stands behind those too fine in mind and spirit to endure unscathed the grim reverses of life. *I Live Under a Black Sun* has the power of a Websterian tragedy, and the beauty of her language brings the prose to the very frontiers of poetry.

It is also interesting to find in it ideas and images that had already shown themselves as dominant in her early poetry, and many, too, that anticipate the later poetry: "the Priests of Baal crying to an unhearing God for rain" and "the Potter's Field, the Field of Blood," for instance. The great chapter on the beggars recalls again and again the black vision of *Gold Coast Customs*; and there are passages of general description that have the unmistakable ring of the great odes of *The Song of the Cold* that were to come a few years later, such as the opening of chapter 2:

Under the hot gold rays of the rough fruitful sun, the wisdom and lore of the countryside sprang from the growth and ripening and dying of the seasons, from the peaceful rhythms of their life, rising and toiling and sowing and reaping in the holy fields, loving and giving birth, growing old and sinking into sleep. This was the life they knew in the countrysides before the dawn of the day that was to change and maim the rhythm of the seasons and of all pulses.

Through the long darkness, lulled by the maternal night, the earth lay, gigantic in its slumber, breathing in a gentle sleep, and from the world of growing things a sweet breath arose, the sound that comes before the dawn. A sigh, a breath among the leaves, and the sound was gone.

Then rose the guiltless light, over the quiet countrysides, and over the cities where men have created and known fear. It filled with peace the faces of the blind from life, the man-made chasms between man and man; all men were brothers in spite of the differences of creed and speech and colour, united and made equal by the holy light. . . .

To read *I Live Under a Black Sun* after the poetry is to experience again the remarkable consistency of Edith Sitwell's inspiration. For anyone who wishes to explore that further, *A Poet's Notebook* and *A Notebook on William Shakespeare* are fascinating material—fascinating and stimulating to mind and imagination in the highest degree as well. These two books are striking testimony to the range of her reading, of her search for those moments of illumination among the great artists and critics who could help her to define—and enlarge—her own ideas about the nature and function of poetry. Her favorite authors are marked by their reappearances—Blake, Coleridge, Shelley, Baudelaire, Wagner, Schopenhauer, Whitman, Cocteau among the foremost; but her own notes to the quotations, the sparks they struck off her mind, add immensely to the interest of *A Poet's Notebook*. Commenting on a remark of Schopenhauer's she wrote:

The poet accomplishes his designs instinctively, but at the same time with knowledge. In him, knowledge has become instinct, and during the conception of the poem knowledge works in him as if it were nature alone.

When the work is almost completed, when the inspiration has pronounced its will, then, and only then, does the knowledge become conscious knowledge once again.

The difference between the poet and the person who is not a poet, although he may (and no doubt does) write reams of verse, lies partly in the fact that the poet has this instinctive knowledge.

("Notes on Technical Matters")

The method by which Edith Sitwell worked in compiling her *Notebooks* is the true method of poetry applied in a different sphere: she brought together the discoveries of minds working far separate so that they cast light upon one another and a new discovery is made in the conjunction. This process produces its most striking results in *A Notebook on William Shakespeare* (1948), where she quotes from authors as different as Nietzsche, Baudelaire, and Meister Eckhart in her examination of the plays. This *Notebook* is full of treasures of observation and inspired perception, and there are pages, particularly on the tragedies, that seem to me to take their place with the finest Shakespearean criticism of our time. What is above all important, however, is her fundamental conception of Shakespeare's stature. In nothing was Edith Sitwell's own stature more clearly revealed than in her sense of Shakespeare as a poet so far above all other poets that he is almost a power of nature, so that as it were unconsciously he is able, in the pattern of his plays and in the movement and imagery of his verse, to reveal meaning below meaning to those who have ears to hear, to the very central mysteries of life. In her summing up of the tragedies she says:

> Sometimes the gigantic phrases, thrown up by passion, have the character of those geological phenomena, brought about in the lapse of cosmical time, by the sun's heat, by the retained internal heat of the earth,—or they seem part of the earth, fulgurites, rocky substances fused or vitrifed by lightning, as in *Timon of Athens*. Or, as in *King Lear*, the words seem thunderbolts, hurled from the heart of heaven. *King Lear, Timon of Athens*, seem the works of a god who is compact of earth and fire, of whom it might be said that he is a fifth element.

> ("Some General Notes on the Tragedies")

Only one who was a great poet herself could have written that.

SELECTED BIBLIOGRAPHY

I. BIBLIOGRAPHY. T. Balston, *Sitwelliana 1915–1927: Being a Handlist of Works of Edith, Osbert, and Sacheverell Sitwell* (London, 1928); R. Fifoot, *A Bibliography of Edith, Osbert, and Sacheverell Sitwell* (London, 1963).

II. COLLECTED AND SELECTED WORKS. *Collected Poems* (London, 1930); *Selected Poems* (London, 1936), includes an introductory essay; *The Canticle of the Rose* (New York–London, 1949), selected poems, 1920–1947; *Façade and Other Poems, 1920–1935* (London, 1950), with an introductory essay by Jack Lindsay; *Selected Poems* (London, 1952), a selection by the author; *Collected Poems* (London, 1957); *Edith Sitwell* (London, 1960); *Selected Poems* (London, 1965); J. Lehmann and D. Parker, eds., *Edith Sitwell: Selected Letters* (London, 1970).

III. SEPARATE WORKS. *The Mother* (Oxford, 1915), verse; E. Sitwell, ed., *Wheels: An Anthology of Verse* (Oxford, 1916–1921), published in seven parts, the final parts bearing a London imprint; *Twentieth Century Harlequinade and Other Poems* (Oxford, 1916), written with Osbert Sitwell; *Clowns' Houses* (London, 1918), verse.

The Wooden Pegasus (Oxford, 1920), verse; *The Children's Tales—From the Russian Ballet* (London, 1920), with illus. by I. de B. Lockyer, reiss. as *The Russian Ballet Gift Book* (London, 1922); *Façade* (London, 1922), verse; *Bucolic Comedies* (London, 1923), verse; *The Sleeping Beauty* (London, 1924); *Poetry and Criticism* (London, 1925), essay; *Poor Young People* (London, 1925), written with Osbert and Sacheverell Sitwell, anthology; *Troy Park* (London, 1925), verse; *Elegy on Dead Fashion* (London, 1926), verse, with illus. by T. Lowinsky; *Rustic Elegies* (London, 1927), verse; *Five Poems* (London, 1928), verse; *Popular Song* (London, 1929), verse, illus. with designs by Edward Bawden; *Gold Coast Customs* (London, 1929), verse.

Alexander Pope (London, 1930), biography; *The Pleasures of Poetry*, 3 vols. (London, 1930–1932), anthologies; *Epithalamium* (London, 1931), verse; *In Spring* (London, 1931), verse, with wood engravings by E. Garrick; *Jane Barston* (London, 1931), verse, with drawings by R. A. Davies; *Bath* (London, 1932), topography; *The English Eccentrics* (London, 1933; new and enl. ed., 1958), biography; *Five Variations on a Theme* (London, 1933), verse; *Aspects of Modern Poetry* (London, 1934), criticism; *Victoria of England* (London, 1936), biography; *The King of China's Daughter* (Dublin, 1937), a Cuala Press broadside; *I Live Under a Black Sun* (London, 1937), novel based on the life of Jonathan Swift; *Trio, Dissertations on Some Aspects of National Genius* (London, 1937), written with Osbert and Sacheverell Sitwell, delivered as the Northcliff Lectures at the University of London, includes "Three Eras of Modern Poetry" by Edith Sitwell.

Edith Sitwell's Anthology (London, 1940), anthology; *Poems New and Old* (London, 1940), verse; *Look! The Sun* (London, 1941), anthology of verse primarily for children; *English Women* (London, 1942), essay in "Britain in Pictures" series; *Street Songs* (London, 1942), verse; *A Poet's Notebook* (London, 1943), belles-lettres; *Green Song, & Other Poems* (London, 1944); *Planet and Glow-worm: A Book for the Sleepless* (London, 1944), anthology; *The Song of the Cold* (London, 1945), verse; *Fanfare for Elizabeth* (London, 1946), a study of the childhood of Elizabeth I; *The Shadow of Cain* (London, 1947), verse; *A Notebook on William Shakespeare* (London, 1948), criticism.

A Book of the Winter (London, 1950), anthology; *Poor Men's Music* (1950), verse; *The American Genius* (London, 1951), anthology of poetry and some prose; *A Book of Flowers* (London, 1952), anthology; *Gardeners and Astronomers* (London, 1953), verse; *The Outcasts* (London, 1962), verse; *The Queens and the Hive* (London,

1962), a study of Elizabeth I's relations with Mary Tudor, Mary, Queen of Scots, and Catherine de Medici; *Music and Ceremonies* (New York, 1963), verse; *Taken Care Of* (London, 1965), autobiography.

IV. BIOGRAPHICAL AND CRITICAL STUDIES. R. L. Mégroz, *The Three Sitwells* (London, 1927); D. Powell, "Edith Sitwell," in *Life and Letters* (March 1931); Osbert Sitwell, *Left Hand! Right Hand!* (London, 1945), autobiography; Osbert Sitwell, *The Scarlett Tree* (London, 1946); C. M. Bowra, *Edith Sitwell* (Monaco, 1947); J. G. Villa, ed., *A Celebration for Edith Sitwell* (New York, 1948); A. Ross, *Poetry, 1945–50* (London, 1951); M. W. Joyce, *Triad of Genius* (London, 1953), part I: "Edith and Osbert Sitwell"; G. Singleton, *Edith Sitwell: The Hymn to Life* (London, 1960); M. C. Sandt, *A Critique of Dame Edith Sitwell's Three Poems of the Atomic Age* (New York, 1962); E. F. Salter, *The Last Years of a Rebel: A Memoir of Edith Sitwell* (London, 1967); J. Lindsay, *Meetings with Poets* (London, 1968); J. Lehmann, *A Nest of Tigers: Edith, Osbert and Sacheverell Sitwell in Their Times* (London, 1968); J. Pearson, *Façades* (London, 1978); V. Glendinning, *Edith Sitwell* (London, 1983).

T. S. ELIOT

(1888-1965)

M. C. Bradbrook

INTRODUCTION

WHEN T. S. Eliot celebrated his sixtieth birthday on 26 September 1948, tributes that he received from the country of his birth and the country of his adoption, from Europe, and indeed from all over the world made it plain that he was very generally acknowledged as the greatest living poet of the English language. Nevertheless, his poetry at first provoked strong disagreement, and the reviews of his later work, especially his dramas, show that his continued development and intellectual growth could still give rise to new misunderstanding.

Eliot's literary career illustrates in a striking manner the controlling force of the poetic impulse. He was born in St. Louis, Missouri, where his father held an important position in the business world. But he was descended on both sides from New England families of the early settlements: his ancestor Andrew Eliot went to Massachusetts from the Somerset village of East Coker in 1670, and his mother was a descendant of Isaac Stearns, who went out in 1630 as one of the original settlers of the Massachusetts Bay Colony. Among his forebears, T. S. Eliot numbered many distinguished scholars, clergymen, and men of letters; in his early poems there are a number of sketches, not always entirely dutiful, of Boston relatives and of that Puritan society, earnestly intellectual and highly exclusive, which still in some measure survives, although it no longer centers on the city of Boston. In *Four Quartets* (1943), Eliot has described both East Coker, the village from which his family emigrated more than three hundred years ago, and, in "The Dry Salvages," the Massachusetts coast that he knew in his childhood.

Eliot's family tradition connected him with Harvard, where he received his education. At Harvard there is now a collection of material relating to Eliot's early life, together with much of his juvenilia. He spent four undergraduate years at this university, being especially interested in the study of philosophy. In 1910 he went to the Sorbonne, to read literature and philosophy, subsequently returning to Harvard for further study. Afterward he studied in Germany and at Oxford. During World War I he stayed in England, working first as a schoolmaster, then as a banker, and finally as an editor and publisher. It was during this period that his poetic work began to appear in various magazines, and between 1917 and 1920 in small volumes. But it was in 1922, with the publication of *The Waste Land*, that Eliot assumed that commanding position in English poetry which he ever after retained. In 1927 he became a British subject and announced in the preface to a book of essays that he was now a classicist in literature, a royalist in politics, and an Anglo-Catholic in religion, a statement that caused some disturbance in literary circles, where none of these tenets was very prominently advocated.

During the next decade he published some important poetry, wrote and lectured on a wide variety of subjects connected with literature and society, and, through his editing of the *Criterion*, a quarterly magazine, exercised considerable influence on the literary world. During the war he published what many people consider his greatest poem, *Four Quartets*, and then turned quite deliberately to the stage; but the *Criterion* had ceased publication in 1939, and Eliot tended to write less criticism than formerly. His authority and reputation had, however, grown steadily, and while in the early 1920's he was known chiefly to the young and enthusiastic students of the universities and to the younger literary generation in London, he became gradually accepted during the course of the next decade by the more traditional and conservative guardians of literary reputations. He is now treated with the greatest respect by even the crustier old gentlemen of the clubs and academies, and accorded the reverence (which he would have found somewhat embarrassing) of literary ladies and provincial clerics. He received from King George VI the Order of Merit; that most rare and coveted of honors, the Nobel Prize for Literature, in 1948; and the highest American civilian honor, the Medal of Freedom, in 1964. His double task was the interpretation of the age to itself, "holding the Mirror up to Nature," as the greatest poet of all proclaimed, and maintaining the standards of strict literary excellence, "purifying the dialect of the tribe," as he himself, quoting Stéphane Mallarmé, declared his aim to be. As Eliot said of another poet, in his own work the reader will find "a record of the spiritual struggles of a man of intellectual power and emotional intensity who gave much toil to perfecting his verses. As such, it should be a document of interest to all who are curious to understand their fellow men."

THE POET OF THE WASTE LAND

ELIOT's early poetry, published during World War I, depicts in ironic and epigrammatic terseness the little anxieties, social embarrassments, and unacknowledged vacuity of polite society in Boston and London. The world he displays is the world of Henry James's novels, where frustrated society ladies breathe their invitations and deprecations by a faint nuance, where corrupt financiers and decayed nobility drive their social bargains, where the final reckoning discloses only that "I have measured out my life with coffee spoons."

In "T. S. Eliot" (*Abinger Harvest*, 1936), E. M. Forster described the relief with which he discovered a little volume of Eliot during a period of convalescence in Cairo:

For what, in that world of gigantic horror, was tolerable except the slight gestures of dissent? He who measured himself against the war, who drew himself to his full height, as it were, and said to Armadillo-Armageddon "Avaunt!" collapsed at once into a pinch of dust. But he who could turn aside to complain of ladies and drawing rooms preserved a tiny drop of our self-respect, he carried on the human heritage.

Yet behind the hesitancies, the ironic wit of a young man trying to protect himself against *faux pas* in the society of the Old World, behind the futilities and the boredom of the middle-aged unsuccessful Prufrock, or the middle-aged unsuccessful lady of

"Portrait of a Lady," with its reminiscence of Henry James in the very title, Eliot would occasionally show a glimpse of horror or of glory. In a single phrase—joined with some sardonic self-depreciatory gesture—he can call up a vision of lyric beauty, alien but poignantly felt. This very simple device, the juxtaposition of the lovely and the squalid, or the passionate and the trivial, so that they make their own comment on one another, is the basis of his poetic structure:

I grow old . . . I grow old . . .
I shall wear the bottoms of my trousers rolled.

Shall I part my hair behind? Do I dare to eat a peach?
I shall wear white flannel trousers, and walk upon the beach.
I have heard the mermaids singing, each to each.

I do not think that they will sing to me.

I have seen them riding seaward on the waves
Combing the white hair of the waves blown back
When the wind blows the water white and black.

We have lingered in the chambers of the sea
By sea-girls wreathed with seaweed red and brown
Till human voices wake us, and we drown.
("The Love Song of J. Alfred Prufrock")

Here are not only echoes of John Keats's "magic casements opening on the foam/Of perilous seas," of the chambers of the sea where the forsaken Merman of Matthew Arnold lingered—the situation, it will be noted, is reversed—but the fresh stiff drive of a lively off-shore breeze. This seascape may be compared with those of "Mr Apollinax" and "Gerontion," "Marina," the last poem of *Ash-Wednesday* (1930), and "The Dry Salvages," the third of the *Four Quartets*. Eliot has a few strong and central symbols, as he has a few strong and central themes, and the sea as the source of primal life and energy is one of the most important. Hence even in the lovely fourth movement of *The Waste Land*, "Death by Water"—a passage adapted from the French of his poem "Dans le Restaurant"—Phlebas, the drowned Phoenician sailor, appears as one who has lived a full, simple natural life and died a clean death. In the land of drought, Death by Water holds more beauty than terror; for both the present scene and the recollections are of beauty:

Gentile or Jew,
O you who turn the wheel and look to windward,
Consider Phlebas, who was once handsome and tall as you.

144

T. S. ELIOT

To the generation that wasted its youth in that earlier war, the shock of discovering the instability of their world was more severe than anything the generation of 1939 had to meet. Political and religious skepticism, already an intellectual fashion, was strengthened by general disillusion, and the temper in England during the war years and the following decade was one of cynicism, irony, and a protective, defensive toughness of mind. A. E. Housman, Lytton Strachey, Aldous Huxley, and the Sitwells were the fashionable reading of the intellectuals; the poetry of John Donne and other difficult seventeenth-century poets enjoyed a vogue that was partly created by the critical writings of Eliot himself. Social conventions were by general consent taboo: and while it could be considered by serious critics a virtue in Eliot to achieve "a complete severance between his poetry and *all* beliefs," it was held that experience should be as wide, unrestricted, and uninhibited as possible. The juvenile naughtiness of the neurotic 1920's takes on in retrospect a certain pathos. It was the reaction from a shattering experience and the refuge of those who did not wish to remember, because they could not attempt to organize or control their memories of the war years. Eliot's early poetry, with its subtle deflation of feelings ("Conversation Galante"), its shocking juxtapositions in the manner of Donne ("Whispers of Immortality" and "Mr Eliot's Sunday Morning Service"), is summed up in the Sweeney poems, "Sweeney Erect" and "Sweeney Among the Nightingales." The lovely world of Renaissance art, classic legend, and natural beauty is superimposed on the squalors of tavern and brothel. There is no comment, no explanation, and no attempt to connect the two. Instead the sharp hard lines of the verse, the alternation of magnificence and familiarity in the words, and the startling incongruity of the images are left to make their own effect. The reader has to complete the work within his own experience. Here is to be seen one of Eliot's principal poetic weapons—his use of *implication*, of statements that carry a weight far beyond their ostensive meaning. These "re-echo, thus, in your mind" by their evocative resonance inviting legitimate variation of response. For Eliot always wrote with a very strong sense of his readers. He made demands on them without which the poems are incomplete. It is no use approaching Eliot in a state of wise passiveness. You have to use your wits.

This method of ironic implication is clearly of the greatest value in an age when there are in fact no longer any generally accepted standards of belief the poet may take for granted. It enables the poet to escape or evade the kind of direct statement with which his reader may not agree—and which the poet himself will not feel capable of providing. For Eliot never claimed to speak with authority, as his later admirers suggest. He declared that some of his earlier essays "in spite of, and partly because of, their defects preserve in cryptogram certain notions which if expressed directly would be destined to immediate obloquy, followed by perpetual oblivion."

In this ironic disclaimer may be read something of the difficulties that the contemporary climate of opinion imposed on a lyric poet. The Sweeney poems are in a sense poems in cryptogram, but each reader is invited to provide his own solution. This does not mean that they are ambiguous. They are merely condensed. The single scene, the grand vista opened by an evocative phrase, the impartial and controlled movement of the verse impose a direction even while they decline to state it:

> Gloomy Orion and the Dog
> Are veiled; and hushed the shrunken seas;
> The person in the Spanish cape
> Tries to sit on Sweeney's knees.
>
> Slips and pulls the table cloth
> Overturns a coffee-cup. . . .
>
> The host with someone indistinct
> Converses at the door apart,
> The nightingales are singing near
> The Convent of the Sacred Heart,
>
> And sang within the bloody wood,
> When Agamemnon cried aloud,
> And let their liquid siftings fall
> To stain the stiff dishonoured shroud.
> ("Sweeney Among the Nightingales")

The lovely song and the birds' droppings, the squalid intrigue in the tavern and the murder of a king, are not merely contrasted in ironic equivalence. They are somehow seen as having at least so necessary a relation as to be inseparable. Here is the source of the gratitude his contemporaries feel toward Eliot. He has interpreted the chaos of their world, so that it no longer presents itself as chaotic:

> *Erhebung* without motion, concentration
> Without elimination, both a new world
> And the old made explicit, understood

In the completion of its partial ecstasy
The resolution of its partial horror.
                                ("Burnt Norton," II)

While the Sweeney poems sum up Eliot's achievement at this time, there are two others that point forward to his later work. These are "La Figlia che Piange" and "Gerontion." It has been said, on good authority, that "La Figlia che Piange" is written about a statue of a weeping girl that the poet hoped to see in Italy but never located. Even the word of Eliot himself would not convince me that a poem beginning

Stand on the highest pavement of the stair—
Lean on a garden urn—
Weave, weave the sunlight in your hair—
Clasp your flowers to you with a pained surprise—
Fling them to the ground and turn
With a fugitive resentment in your eyes:
But weave, weave the sunlight in your hair.

had very much to do with marble. The curious shifts between second and third person in the address, the hint of a Henry James situation at the end of the second stanza, and the summing up, "I should have lost a gesture and a pose," indicate clearly that the very substance of the poem is the relation between life and art—particularly between those moments when life falls into the ordered pattern of art; but the beautiful movement, the alternation of longing and control, conveys most poignantly a human situation that re-echoes through all the poetry down to *The Family Reunion* (1939). "Gerontion," "the old man," whose soliloquy stands at the head of the *Poems* of 1919, is a dramatic figure not unlike Tiresias, the old blind seer of *The Waste Land*. Both are voices rather than persons—the voices of representative Man, as he contemplates a decaying civilization, and the pitiable fragments of humanity that inhabit this "decayed house." Mr. Silvero, Hakagawa, Madame de Tornquist, and Fräulein von Kulp are only names, but the mixture of nationalities, the suggestions of various kinds of international hocus-pocus, artistic, or occult, accords with the description of the "owner of the house," the Jew

Spawned in some estaminet of Antwerp,
Blistered in Brussels, patched and peeled in London.

All, including Gerontion, are displaced, homeless persons, whose spiritual desolation is symbolized in the traditional religious metaphor of drought. There is no apparent sequence of thought or logical arrangement in the poem, only the broken fragmentary recollections and meditations of the old man, as he recalls those heroic deaths in battle, suggestive of Homeric war, that he did not share:

I was neither at the hot gates[1]
Nor fought in the warm rain
Nor knee deep in the salt marsh, heaving a cutlass,
Bitten by flies, fought.

In the meditation that follows, not only contemporary society but the inner world of the individual is seen to be crumbling:

These with a thousand small deliberations
Protract the profit of their chill delirium,
Excite the membrane, when the sense has cooled,
With pungent sauces, multiply variety
In a wilderness of mirrors.

By a technique not unlike that of the early Russian films, Eliot gives a series of "shots" that when put together form a single sequence. The unity lies in the mood and tone, the flat, listless accents of the old man whose vision may have the inconsequence of a dream, because, as Eliot says in the quotation from Shakespeare that heads the poem,

Thou has nor youth nor age,
But as it were an after dinner sleep,
Dreaming of both.

The poem is full of echoes of Shakespeare and of other Elizabethan dramatists. These literary echoes have often caused apprehension in the minds of readers, who feel that without an ability to recognize such allusions, they may lose the point of the poem. This fear is, I think, without foundation. A successful poem does not rely upon anything but itself for the essential core of its meaning. Eliot's use of literary allusions is part of his technique of implication. As in the Sweeney poem he could evoke the majesty of Greek tragedy in the images of Agamemnon and the nightingales, could summon up a whole train of associations in contrast to what the rest of the poem suggests, so, in his many echoes of the French symbolists, Donne, and the metaphysical poets, Dante and the poets of the *dolce stil nuovo*, which

[1]Thermopylae.

occur throughout *The Waste Land*, he sets his vision of desolation and spiritual drought in implicit contrast with the visionary worlds of the elder poets, his masters. Sometimes the contrasts are ironic, as the echoes of Shakespeare's *Antony and Cleopatra* in the second movement of *The Waste Land*, which describes the boudoir of a neurotic fine lady of the present day and her rasping quarrel with an almost silent figure, her husband or her lover. Sometimes literature consoles and supports by reminding a distraught generation that it is not alone—in recognizing the right words for the present situations, it marks the first step toward control; to accept such a definition in terms of another time and another place marks also the first step toward integration. Eliot used the words of the *Inferno* to describe the city crowd that "flowed up the hill and down King William Street" because only a Dante could define for him the depth of their desolation. The poet accepts the personal suffering that such a vision entails, and the two utterances that give it most clearly are the cry of Arnaut Daniel from his purgatorial flames, "Sovegna vos" (Be mindful), which is not uttered but recalled:

Poi s'acose nel foco che gli affina
(*Purgatorio* 26, 147)

Then he hid himself in the fire that refines them

and St. Augustine on the drowned Phoenician sailor. Each marks a renunciation, and each had echoed through Eliot's poetry for some time. There are indeed many familiar figures who appear momentarily—the old German princess; the damp and depressed figure of Lil, as described in the public-house scene; the typist, who might have been one of Sweeney's girl friends, and the three Thames daughters, her sisters; Mme. Sosostris, the famous clairvoyant; and Mr. Eugenides, the Smyrna merchant. All are seen through the blind eyes of old Tiresias, the seer, who has "foresuffered all"; for as Eliot says: "The poem is what he sees." The lesser characters are not clearly distinguished; they melt into each other, for they are phantoms inhabiting an unreal city. Such is Eliot's vision of the postwar world, a land by no means fit for heroes to live in, and that in any case most of his friends did not live to inhabit. It is a cosmic vision, seen on a small scale. While Joyce took seven hundred pages to describe a single day in the life of Dublin, Eliot concentrated his vision in

four hundred lines. The whole poem, but especially its last lines, employs the technique of ironic juxtaposition, which has already been described, in a deeper and more tragic manner. The "wild and whirling words" of a mind unstrung, clutching desperately at the fragmentary and disintegrating remains of the world of literature, shored against its ruin, are suddenly broken in upon by the tolling magnificence of the Sanskrit benediction:

Datta. Dayadhvam. Damyata.
Shantih shantih shantih

The contemporary public was of course bewildered by *The Waste Land*, but after half a century of exposition there should be little difficulty for the reader who has been given the right line of approach, and who has at his disposal a large number of commentaries, some of which ascribe to the poem depths of significance its author modestly disclaimed. The quickest means of reaching its meaning is probably to listen to a reading by someone who is familiar with the work or, better still, to hear Eliot's own recorded reading, made for the Library of Congress.

The form of the poem has received a good deal of attention: it is divided into five movements, and each movement has a certain completeness in itself. The musical analogy has been much stressed by critics, the different recurring themes of drought and rain, sterility and violation, ruin and social trivialities being compared with musical themes. While the analogy is a useful one, it should be used with caution. It may suggest to the reader the kind of attention he should give and the kind of design he should look for, but it must not be pressed further.

Nor should the poem be read as a vision of despair. It has been called Eliot's *Inferno*, but even in the *Inferno* there are gleams that recall another world. Here in the first movement the vision of beauty and love is not completely shut out:

—Yet when we came back, late, from the Hyacinth garden
Your arms full, and your hair wet, I could not
Speak, and my eyes failed, I was neither
Living nor dead, and I knew nothing,
Looking into the heart of light, the silence.
Oed' und leer das Meer.

Again, in the final movement, in "the awful daring of a moment's surrender/Which an age of prudence can never retract" and in the picture of guided happiness:

> The boat responded
> Gaily, to the hand expert with sail and oar
> The sea was calm, your heart would have responded
> Gaily. . . .

there is a momentary escape from the kingdoms of sterility and drought. Moreover, though the world depicted is one of disorder and decay, the poem contains within itself a subtle and implicit order that makes the vision bearable, if only just bearable. It has several times been pointed out that those recurrent images which are repeated throughout the poem "release markedly different shades of feeling according to their special contexts." The subtle variation between the different images of the river, for instance, or the fading of Philomel to a mere entablature in the second movement, contrasted with the violent emphasis of the third movement on the seduction of the typist, implies some order, some principle of organization within this apparently haphazard scheme of things. The repetition with modifications of the same image cannot yield any *statement* to set against the many gestures of weariness, confusion, and despair; perhaps their pattern is as arbitrary as that of the suits of a pack of cards, and indeed the symbols of the Tarot pack are in the first section identified with most of the leading symbols of the poem. Yet arbitrary as the pack of cards may be, its conventions are orderly.

As the vision of the Hyacinth girl conferred eternity upon a moment, so at the end of *The Waste Land* there is a strange sense of expectancy, of quiet, that recalls Cleopatra's line:

> My desolation does begin to make
> A better life.

Nothing explicit warrants this feeling, except possibly the mysterious Sanskrit benediction, but it can be felt through the rhythm, which becomes stronger, more emphatic, as though a pulse were beginning to beat after the hurried staccato movement of the "nightmare" passage at the beginning of the last movement. The words of the thunder, "give, sympathize, control," have been fulfilled for the reader in the poem itself. The sincerity and penetration with which it renders the vision of desolation console and demand response; while the power to project such a vision in the form of words, to objectify and realize it, implies the highest measure of control.

If it is not his greatest poem, *The Waste Land* is certainly Eliot's most influential poem. The generation that grew up in the later 1920's took it to themselves, absorbed it so that it became part of their habit of mind. As Auden said in his verses for Eliot's sixtieth birthday:

> it was you
> Who, not speechless with shock but finding the right
> Language for thirst and fear, did most to
> Prevent a panic.

Moreover, the depth and violence of the contrasts in the poem, the sense that the poet is wrestling with the problems of his outer and inner world is stronger here than in the later poetry. Even in The *Four Quartets* we do not feel that "Spinoza and the smell of the cooking" (to use Eliot's formula) have been brought into relation with each other. It is the smell of the cooking that tends to disappear. The later poems are concerned more exclusively with inner experience.

THE WASTE LAND

The mysterious Quinn Manuscript—the original draft of T. S. Eliot's *The Waste Land*, with nine satellite poems—was published just fifty years after its completion in the latter part of 1921. It had long been known that Ezra Pound drastically edited this first draft, cutting down to 433 lines what, because of its concentration, he termed "the longest poem in the Englisch langwidge." The version that first appeared in the first number of the *Criterion* (October 1922) represented about two thirds of the draft.

What has been recovered and printed is:

(a) a single typescript of section I, "The Burial of the Dead";
(b) a typescript, with one carbon copy added, of the next two sections, both extensively annotated by Pound, and section II annotated by Vivien Eliot also;
(c) manuscripts of the last two sections, with typed copies made on Pound's typewriter;
(d) nine satellite poems, some manuscript, others typed.

Eliot told John Quinn, a New York lawyer and collector of literary manuscripts, that for much of the typescript "no manuscript, except scattered lines, ever existed"; he composed on the typewriter. The last two sections were probably written at Margate in October and at Lausanne in December 1921; later he said the poem had been written "mostly at Lausanne" (*Transcript*, p. xxii).[2] Following a complete breakdown, he was there on leave from his employment as confidential clerk in the foreign department of Lloyd's Bank in the City.

In a broadcast to introduce the new edition, given on 7 November 1971, Valerie Eliot confirmed that the passage in Eliot's essay on Pascal (1928) referred to the composition of *The Waste Land*:

it is a commonplace that some forms of illness are extremely favourable, not only to religious illumination, but to artistic and literary composition. A piece of writing meditated, apparently without progress, for months or years, may suddenly take shape and word; and in this state long passages may be produced which require little or no retouch. I have no good word to say for the cultivation of automatic writing as the model of literary composition; I doubt whether these moments *can* be cultivated by the writer; but he to whom this happens assuredly has the sense of being a vehicle rather than a maker. . . . You may call it communication with the Divine, or you may call it a temporary crystallization of the mind.

(*Selected Essays*, enl. ed., p. 405)

Eliot had mentioned the poem two years earlier in a letter to Quinn; the struggle is described by Conrad Aiken, a friend from Eliot's Harvard days, who, in spite of some inconsistencies about dates, has no doubt recalled the essentials:

In the winter of 1921–2 I was in London, living in Bayswater, and Eliot and myself lunched together two or three times a week in the City, near his bank . . . he always had with him his pocket edition of Dante . . . discussing also the then-just-beginning possibility of *The Criterion*, through the generosity of Lady Rothermere. And it was at one of these meetings, in midwinter, that he told me one day, and with visible concern, that although every evening he went home to his flat hoping that he could start writing again, and with every confidence that the material was *there* and waiting, night after night the hope proved illusory: the sharpened pencil lay unused by the untouched sheet of paper.

("A Reviewer's ABC," in T. S. Eliot, *"The Waste Land": A Casebook*, pp. 91–92)

[2]V. Eliot, ed., *The Waste Land: A Facsimile and Transcript* (London, 1971). The Quinn Manuscript was sold to the New York Public Library in April 1958, but its whereabouts were announced only in 1968.

When told of this at second-hand, an analyst said, "all that's stopping him is his fear of putting anything down that's short of perfection. He thinks he's God." The foreseeable result was that, when told of it, Eliot became speechless with rage:

The *intrusion*, quite simply, was one that was intolerable. But ever since I have been entirely convinced that it did the trick, it broke the log jam. A month or two later he went to Switzerland, and there wrote *The Waste Land*.

Eliot may still have been affected by his father's death in January 1919, for he had hoped to justify his desertion of America—which had estranged his father—by publishing; *The Sacred Wood* (1920) had been inscribed to his father's memory.[3] A sensitive and overdriven man, with a desperately sick wife, shifting from one home to another and with no funds to meet the expenses of illness, Eliot's scrupulous conscience may well have inhibited his writing. The lifting of inhibitions associated with general disturbance may have contributed, with the effects of a good holiday, to bring about a release; whatever the cause, by Christmas Eve Pound was writing enthusiastically of "the Poem," now evidently in shape, for he says, "The thing runs from April to Shantih without a break," and gives advice on the "superfluities." On his way home, Eliot in early January stopped in Paris to see Pound; perhaps this was when the last part was typed.

One fact is immediately clear: the "missing links" are not links. Their elimination did not make the poem less, but rather more, coherent; the excision did not cut out logic, copulatives, or argument, but deleted subsidiary episodes, weaker versions of the pub scene, the typist's seduction, and the death of Phlebas. Their recovery makes the work seem less unified, less integrated. "I think it was just as structureless, only in a more futile way, in the longer version" was a characteristic sally of Eliot.

Certain traces of release and of the lifting of inhibitions are suggested in the structure of the drafts. Sections I, III, and IV are introduced by long narratives, which all turn out to be false starts, of an autobiographical or quasi-autobiographical character. These were the parts that Pound cut out, and their presence would have certainly turned the single poem into a series.

[3]Compare his determination to finish his philosophical thesis for Harvard, to meet his obligations: "this return at least I owed to Harvard."

Section II, heavily worked over in collaboration, also trails a satellite entitled "The Death of the Duchess"—possibly an already discarded false start to the boudoir scene that replaced it. Moreover, section IV also trails a satellite entitled "Dirge," so that this section is really a triad of one lengthy sequence and two brief ones.

Then suddenly, and as it would seem subliminally ordered, the final section "came." Even here there are some discarded opening lines, themselves highly elucidative, which Mrs. Eliot would date very early from the handwriting.

> After the turning of the inspired days,
> And the praying and the silence and the crying
> And the inevitable ending of a thousand ways
> And frosty vigil kept in withered gardens
> After the life and death of lonely places
> After the judges and the advocates and wardens
> And the torchlight red on sweaty faces. . . .
> (*Transcript*, p. 109)

The several internal censors, judges, and advocates and wardens have been dethroned, but the speaker is identified with Jesus, the Hanged Man. The original title, "He do the Police in different Voices" (applied to reading newsprint in Dickens' *Our Mutual Friend*) would be applicable to some of the excised stories; the riotous scene in Boston might have fed a newspaper column, the heroic deaths of the fishermen certainly would; and the Lady Fresca must have featured in gossip columns. Eliot's failure at once to recognize the weakness of these lines is a strong proof of his disturbance. The last section, the one that was "given," had at first no title at all; but Pound added "O.K. from here on, I think" above the opening line.

In August 1923 Eliot wrote to Ford Madox Ford that there were about thirty "good" lines in *The Waste Land* and "the rest is ephemeral"; later he explained that these were the twenty-nine lines of the water-dripping song in the last section. He also told Bertrand Russell at this time that section V was not only the best part but "the only part that justifies the whole, at all" (*Transcript*, p. 129).

It is not uncommon for a writer to find the shaping impulse of his work revealed only when he completes it. Here the special power of release that impelled the work forward was also a unifying power. The poem grew into unity.

After Pound had brought Eliot to Quinn's notice, he financed the little booklet that Eliot wrote in 1917

in praise of Pound to introduce *Lustra* to the American public; he placed Pound, at Eliot's suggestion, as Paris correspondent of the *Dial*. Acting as Eliot's attorney, he placed Eliot's *Poems* of 1919 and placed *The Waste Land* with Boni and Liveright, the New York publishers. Since the poem had already been accepted by the *Dial* and was also to appear in the *Criterion*, this involved some delicate negotiation. In gratitude, Eliot gave Quinn the original draft of *The Waste Land* together with a small collection of unpublished poems, for which Quinn insisted on making payment. These manuscripts were dispatched in October 1922 and acknowledged by Quinn in February 1923.

Eliot wrote to Quinn in September 1922: "I am quite overwhelmed by your letter [an eleven-page letter of fatherly advice], by all you have done for me, the results that have been effected and by your endless kindness. . . ." Pound had written to Quinn that Eliot's new poem is "about enough to make the rest of us shut up shop" and, more soberly to his former professor at Philadelphia, "Eliot's *Waste Land* is I think the justification of the 'movement,' of our modern experiment, since 1900" (*Letters*, p. 248).

LATER POETRY

"THE Hollow Men" (1925) marks the sharpest break in Eliot's poetry; it may be looked on as a kind of prologue or antechamber to *Ash-Wednesday*. They have in common a new kind of image, a new kind of rhythm, and a new mood.

The world depicted in "The Hollow Men" is a gray, phantasmal country, featureless and nameless—"death's dream kingdom." The London of *The Waste Land* had been as vividly realized as Charles Baudelaire's Paris, but now the outer world is left behind. Some lines from *Four Quartets* seem best to sum up the experience conveyed in "The Hollow Men," and its relation to *The Waste Land*:

> . . . the strained time-ridden faces
> Distracted from distraction by distraction
> Filled with fancies and empty of meaning
> Tumid apathy with no concentration
> Men and bits of paper, whirled by the cold wind
> That blows before and after time. . . .
> Driven on the wind that sweeps the gloomy hills of
>   London,
> Hampstead and Clerkenwell, Campden and Putney,

Highgate, Primrose and Ludgate. Not here
Not here the darkness, in this twittering world.

Descend lower, descend only
Into the world of perpetual solitude,
World not world, but that which is not world,
Internal darkness, deprivation
And destitution of all property,
Desiccation of the world of sense,
Evacuation of the world of fancy,
Inoperancy of the world of spirit. . . .

("Burnt Norton," III)

"The Hollow Men" marks the dead center in Eliot's poetry: it records the experience of utter destitution where there are no forms, not even the forms of nightmare. The "hollow men" who are also the "stuffed men," that is, scarecrows, straw dummies, whisper together only with the voice of the wind over dry grass. This image is taken from the last movement of *The Waste Land*, the approach to the Chapel Perilous, but it is very differently used. The stone images, the "cactus land," and the "beach of the tumid river" on which the hollow men gather in the twilight of death's kingdom (an image taken from the *Purgatorio* II. 100–102) are unredeemed by any vision of beauty. That has been left behind in the world of the living:

Eyes I dare not meet in dreams
In death's dream kingdom
These do not appear:
There, the eyes are
Sunlight on a broken column
There, is a tree swinging
And voices are
In the wind's singing
More distant and more solemn
Than a fading star.

(II)

There is a distant, barely expressed hope that the eyes, like Beatrice's "*occhi santi*," may reappear

As the perpetual star
Multifoliate rose
Of death's twilight kingdom
The hope only
Of empty men.

(IV)

but the poem ends with a broken disconnected attempt at phrases from the Lord's Prayer and with the empty jingle of a child's nursery rhyme.

From the passages that have just been quoted it will be seen that the rhythm of "The Hollow Men" depends on short, nerveless lines, with occasional, rather haphazard rhyming. The effect conveyed is one of peculiar exhaustion, flatness, and remoteness. The voice moves in a thin and mechanical way through the repetition of phrases and of words ("death's dream kingdom," contrasted with "death's twilight kingdom" and "death's other kingdom"). This mood seems to be described dramatically in the speeches of Harry in *The Family Reunion*, when he recalls to Mary, and later to Agatha, some phases of his wanderings.

Compared with "The Hollow Men," *Ash-Wednesday* shows a movement toward recovery, a turning toward life. Whereas "The Hollow Men" would seem to be a personal poem, recording the effects of some disaster at the moment when the shock was most severe, *Ash-Wednesday* depicts reemergence into a new and strange world, which can be described only by formal and highly stylized images, so that the effect is still rather remote. Eliot was clearly at this time most strongly under the influence of Dante's poetry. He wrote a monograph on Dante (reprinted in his *Selected Essays*), which provides incidentally the best comment on his own poetry. Speaking of the Divine Pageant at the end of the *Purgatorio*—the scene in which Dante for the first time reencounters Beatrice—he says:

It belongs to the world of what I call the *high dream*, and the modern world seems capable only of the *low dream*. I arrived at accepting it, myself, only with some difficulty. There were at least two prejudices, one against Pre-Raphaelite imagery, which was natural to one of my generation, and perhaps affects generations younger than mine. The other prejudice—which affects this end of the *Purgatorio* and the whole of the *Paradiso*—is the prejudice that poetry not only must be found *through* suffering but can find its material only *in* suffering. Everything else was cheerfulness, optimism, and hopefulness; and these words stood for a great deal of what one hated in the nineteenth century. It took me many years to recognize that the states of improvement and beatitude which Dante describes are still further from what the world can conceive as cheerfulness, than are his states of damnation.

This passage not only directly recalls the lines from *Ash-Wednesday*, IV, where the Lady is restored, a vision sheathed with white light:

. . . Redeem
The time. Redeem

151

The unread vision in the higher dream
While jewelled unicorns draw by the gilded hearse

but it also points to the lines in the opening poem:

Consequently I rejoice, having to construct something
Upon which to rejoice

to the image of the purgatorial stairs in *Ash-Wednesday*, III (originally published under the title "Al Som de l'Escalina," a phrase from the speech of Arnaut Daniel), and of course to the quotation that comes almost at the end of the poem, "In la sua voluntade è nostra pace":

Suffer us not to mock ourselves with falsehood
Teach us to care and not to care
Teach us to sit still
Even among these rocks,
Our peace in His will. . . .

These lines embody the theme of the whole poem: "Teach us to care and not to care" suggests the mingled impulses of regret, renunciation, and redirection of the will that are interwoven throughout the sequence. The poem is strictly formal and makes use of the traditional formulas of the church as well as the more personal symbols drawn from Dante and from Eliot's own earlier work. Rarefied and elusive and deeply personal as it is, though its power has always been recognized, the quality of its themes and style has made it something of a connoisseur's piece among Eliot's writings.

About the same time as *Ash-Wednesday*, Eliot wrote a number of single poems, published in the series *Ariel Poems* or in magazines. "The Journey of the Magi" and "A Song for Simeon" may be compared with "Gerontion" as dramatic lyrics presenting a picture of a whole life, seen from the end by an old man looking back and meditating on its significance; with the difference that the significance is now found in the Incarnation. But the poems are Songs of Experience and not religious verse, in the sense that George Herbert or Henry Vaughan wrote religious verse; that is to say, the references are oblique and implicit. There are touches of irony—especially in "The Journey of the Magi," where the petty humiliations and discomforts of the journey stick in the mind of the Old Man and seem far clearer to him than the mysterious conclusion, which he does not understand.

The most important of the *Ariel Poems* is "Marina," the dramatic monologue of old King Pericles, the hero of Shakespeare's play of that name, who meditates on the recovery of his daughter, miraculously returned from the dead, like the Lady of *Ash-Wednesday*. This poem, one of Eliot's most beautiful and moving, is prefaced by a line from Seneca's *Hercules Furens*, the cry of the hero as he emerges from the darkness of Hell to the light of day:

Quis hic locus, quae regio, quae mundi plaga?

What place is this, what kingdom,
what shore of the world?

The sense of wonder, of the gradual return of life restored to a mind numbed by sorrow, is presented in images of tenderness, in a hesitant, delicate movement of the verse, that seem to capture the moment of the old king's awakening from his trance:

What seas what shore what grey rocks and what islands
What water lapping the bow
And scent of pine and the woodthrush singing through
    the fog
What images return
O my daughter. . . .

What is this face, less clear and clearer
The pulse in the arm, less strong and stronger—
Given or lent? more distant than stars and nearer than
    the eye.

The moment of beatitude and of recognition, which is the complementary and opposite experience to that of "The Hollow Men," is given in terms of a landscape such as we have already seen in the last poem of *Ash-Wednesday* and are to meet again in "The Dry Salvages"—the misty coast with granite rocks and islands, which is part of the landscape of the poet's childhood. Here, in this poem, as the images of life return, the threatening shapes of what was thought to be life "become unsubstantial" and are seen to be a form of death. The poem transmits an extraordinarily intimate and deeply felt state of being, in accents of remote and unearthly serenity.

Two other poems rely on Shakespeare for their background, the two jointly entitled "Coriolan" —"Triumphal March" and "Difficulties of a Statesman." These brilliant ironic monologues of the new political regime are given first from the mob's point of view and second from the politician's—the unwilling politician confronted with a "situation of great delicacy and difficulty." In the anxious period of the early 1930's, before Hitler had really got going, these two poems provided a remarkable forecast of the political scene as it was to unfold itself. In "Coriolan" Eliot projected the helplessness of the statesmen and of the crowd alike, swept toward war and conscious only dimly and in a lost, unfocused way of what they had abandoned or betrayed. The language and rhythm of these poems show a greater variety than the preceding ones; there are free colloquialisms, such apparently unpoetic material as the catalogue of armaments in "Triumphal March," yet also the dramatic flexibility of the speaking voice and occasional lines of grand and reverberating weightiness:

Stone, bronze, stone, steel, stone, oakleaves, horses' heels
Over the paving.

In these two poems the two leading speakers of Eliot's drama seem to emerge—the Hero and the Chorus. Neither is exempt from satire; neither is wholly satirically drawn. The worried politician, trying to reconcile the conflicting interests of various parties, and the humble spectators of the triumphal procession, whose "Please, will you give us a light?" is given such unexpected depths of implication by the repetiton of the last word

Light
Light

were to be followed by the more fully dramatic studies of *The Rock* (1934) and *Murder in the Cathedral* (1935). Eliot set a fashion for verse drama in the middle 1930's that was followed by W. H. Auden, Stephen Spender, Louis MacNeice, and others whose attempt to write drama, and political drama especially, produced some lively occasional verse but nothing that is highly likely to survive. Eliot himself eschewed political drama, though there are implications of a political kind in *The Rock* and *Murder in the Cathedral*, in the speeches of the Tempters and the Knights in particular. During this period Eliot also wrote a number of books and articles on social and religious questions, such as *After Strange Gods* (1934) and *The Idea of Christian Society* (1939). His second drama, *The Family Reunion*, appeared in 1939. It is probable that in turning to the

stage he was not merely working out his own bent but was putting into practice the ideas he expressed in *The Use of Poetry and the Use of Criticism* in 1933:

The most useful poetry, socially, would be one which could cut across all the present stratifications of public taste—stratifications which are perhaps a sign of social disintegration. The ideal medium for poetry, to my mind, and the most direct means of social "usefulness" for poetry is the theatre. In a play of Shakespeare you get several levels of significance. For the simplist auditors there is the plot, for the more thoughtful the character and conflict of character, for the more literary the words and phrasing, for the more musically sensitive the rhythm, and for auditors of more sensitiveness and understanding a meaning which reveals itself gradually.

This passage indicates those aspects of the drama that Eliot himself was likely to find most congenial, and the last phrase suggests that method of implication and gradual exploring of the full significance of an image that has been described already as one of the leading features of his style. In *Ash-Wednesday* he had further deepened his power to explore and unfold traditional liturgical symbols. His reliance on the liturgy, the creeds, the great public affirmations is a sign of coordination between the public and the private worlds. In the plays he uses historic or mythological material. Finally, in his last and, by general agreement, his greatest poem, *Four Quartets*, which was worked out slowly between 1935 and 1942, he achieves both a new depth and a new clarity. This work (like *Ash-Wednesday* and *The Waste Land*) consists of a number of poems complete in themselves yet also forming a unity. Each single poem is divided into five movements, and each is also named from a place: Burnt Norton—an old house in Gloucestershire, at Aston-sub-Edge under the lip of the Cotswold Hills; East Coker—the Somerset village from which Eliot's family originally came; The Dry Salvages, named from three small islands off the coast of Cape Ann; and Little Gidding, a village in Huntingdonshire where, in the early seventeenth century, Nicholas Ferrar retired with his family to live a life of ordered devotion in his "Protestant nunnery." It was to be known and loved by George Herbert, to give shelter to the defeated King Charles after Naseby, and to remain as perhaps the most perfect example of that exquisite blend of piety, learning, decency, and comeliness of life which distinguished the religious life of the seventeenth century at its best.

In these poems, Eliot meditates upon a wide diversity of material: his personal experiences as they have shaped themselves into a pattern; the pattern of history, including the beginning of the war and the London blitz; the difficulties of a poet and the nature of language. Such diversity is far greater than that of *The Waste Land*, yet it is as strictly organized as *Ash-Wednesday*. The method is again *solvitur ambulando* (solution is found in performance). Phrases are repeated from poem to poem: experiences that are recognizably related, if not the same, reappear in different contexts. There are numerous echoes of the early poems, which do not have the effect of repetition, but rather of older partial statements reintegrated and completed. There is a kind of finality and mastery about the work; the ease and boldness of the transitions are coupled with a manner still tentative and exploratory, especially in the first poem. By the time the last poem is finished, the symbols have been fully unfolded, and the accent is one of assurance and power. In spite of the apparent lack of progression, by the restatement and redefinition of the symbols "a meaning reveals itself gradually," which is then seen to have been latent, though unrecognized, in the earlier parts. This particular use of implication is assisted by various formal devices, some of which are in the nature of scaffolding and are relatively unimportant. For instance, each of the poems is concerned with one of the four elements—"Burnt Norton" with air, "East Coker" with earth, "The Dry Salvages" with water, and "Little Gidding" with fire. The four elements are brought together at the beginning of the second movement of "Little Gidding," where they are seen to be symbols of multiple meaning. The water and fire are not only those of the raids on London—firemen's or bomber's elements—they are the water of baptism and the fire of purgatory, the water that is a symbol of natural life (as in *The Waste Land*) and the fire that is a symbol both of destruction and of renewal. In medieval interpretations of poetry, each statement could have three, four, or sometimes even seven meanings—Dante, for instance, offers the interpretations of his own poems in this way in the *Vita nuova*. Each of Eliot's poems moves on several planes simultaneously, and can be both topical and timeless in its implications. Commentaries on the meaning of the *Four Quartets* are almost as plentiful as commentaries on *The Waste Land*, and almost as divergent; but the best of all has been provided by Eliot himself:

Trying to learn to use words, and every attempt
Is a wholly new start, and a different kind of failure
Because one has only learnt to get the better of words,
For the thing one no longer has to say, or the way in which
One is no longer disposed to say it. . . .

Home is where one starts from. As we grow older
The world becomes stranger, the pattern more
    complicated
Of dead and living. Not the intense moment
Isolated, with no before and after,
But a lifetime burning in every moment,
And not the lifetime of one man only
But of the old stones that cannot be deciphered. . . .
                              ("East Coker," V)

It seems, as one becomes older,
That the past has another pattern, and ceases to be a mere
    sequence— . . .
The moments of happiness—not the sense of well-being,
Fruition, fulfilment, security or affection,
Or even a very good dinner, but the sudden illumination—
We had the experience but missed the meaning,
And approach to the meaning restores the experience
In a different form, beyond any meaning
We can assign to happiness.
                              ("The Dry Salvages," II)

We shall not cease from exploration
And the end of our exploring
Will be to arrive where we started
And know the place for the first time.
                              ("Little Gidding," V)

"The intense moment" (which is also called "the moment of the rose" and "the moment of the yew tree'") had been present in *The Waste Land* as part of an emerging but still implicit order; in all the subsequent poetry, it is present as remembered experience to be recovered only through "approach to the meaning." The struggle to renounce "the infirm glory of the positive hour" without denying its glory creates the tension of *Ash-Wednesday*. By these movements only we have existed, Eliot says in *The Waste Land*. In *The Family Reunion* Agatha looks back to the moment when

I only looked through the little door
When the sun was shining on the rose-garden
                              (II.2)

yet in a sense she no longer lives by it, and has even rejected it.

There are hours when there seems to be no past or future,
Only a present moment of pointed light
When you want to burn. When you stretch out your hand
To the flames. They only come once,
Thank God, that kind. Perhaps there is another kind,
I believe, across a whole Thibet of broken stones,
That lie, fang up, a lifetime's march.

(II.2)

However different the experience in these different contexts, it is the same *quality* of experience that is presented in each; and it is the reconciliation of these moments of illumination with the pattern of daily living that is the theme of the later works in general and of the *Four Quartets* in particular:

I can only say, *there* we have been; but I cannot say where
And I cannot say, how long, for that is to place it in time.

("Burnt Norton," II)

"The point of the intersection of the timeless with time" is the theme of the dramas, and is stated most explicitly in the choruses to *The Rock.* Throughout Eliot's poetry these words reecho, but not with the meanings they would have in prose or in philosophic discourse. The words are there to be explored, as in the passage on different sorts of time in the first movement of "The Dry Salvages" or the passage from the second movement quoted above, or that in the fifth movement, which concludes:

For most of us, there is only the unattended
Moment, the moment in and out of time,
The distraction fit, lost in a shaft of sunlight, . . .
          These are only hints and guesses,
Hints followed by guesses; and the rest
Is prayer, observance, discipline, thought and action.
The hint half guessed, the gift half understood, is
    Incarnation.

What Eliot is trying to say cannot be paraphrased, reduced to a prose equivalent, or made into a message. For it is in the relationship of all the different fields of experience that are brought together in the poem that its full significance lies, and these different fields of experience cannot be related by any instrument less delicate, fine, and complex than Eliot's own language. The variety of styles in *Four Quartets* ranges from epigrammatic brilliance to such beautiful lyric interludes as the sestines of "The Dry Salvages," or the fourth movement of "Little Gidding,"

in which the nature of fire is finally defined as the flame of that Third Person of the Trinity to Whom Love is appropriated as His title:

Who then devised the torment? Love.
Love is the unfamiliar name
Behind the hands that wove
The intolerable shirt of flame
Which human power cannot remove.
    We only live, only suspire
    Consumed by either fire or fire.

In this use of a very simple and elemental symbol—which had moreover been one of the leading symbols of his own earlier poetry—Eliot seems to provide that satisfying and perfected embodiment of a long-sought truth that gives at once the impression of recognition and of discovery. Eliot himself said elsewhere: "A man who is capable of experience finds himself in a different world in every decade of his life; as he sees it with different eyes, the material of his art is continually renewed." In his essay on "Tradition and the Individual Talent," he observed that the production of a new work of art makes "something happen simultaneously to all the works of art that preceded it. The existing monuments form an ideal order among themselves which is modified by the introduction of the new (the really new) work of art among them." Whether or not this is true of European literature as a whole, it is certainly true of Eliot's own work, which forms a closely related whole. The later work has modified, illuminated, and developed the significance of the earlier work: the strict sense of pattern that can be felt in *Four Quartets* can also be felt throughout the body of the poetry. "East Coker" opens with the motto of Mary Stuart reversed: "In my beginning is my end," and concludes with the motto itself: "In my end is my beginning." In the "contrapuntal" juxtaposition of themes, the use of implication and irony, Eliot controlled and related an unusually wide range of experience; and by the precision and conscious artistry of his style he was able to subdue and unify it. Toward the end of the last poem in *Four Quartets* he writes:

And every phrase

And sentence that is right (where every word is at home,
Taking its place to support the others,
The word neither diffident nor ostentatious,
An easy commerce of the old and the new,

The common word exact without vulgarity,
The formal word precise but not pedantic,
The complete consort dancing together)
Every phrase and every sentence is an end and a beginning,
Every poem an epitaph.

Such a trained and disciplined way of writing is not common in English; and Eliot might have given the impression, in his less happy moments, of keeping too tight a rein. But in these later poems the commerce of old and new is indeed more easy and familiar; the transitions subtler and more gracious; so that such bold modifications of language as appear in describing the last of the four seasons in accents of the fourth Evangelist become perfectly natural:

> Midwinter spring is its own season
> Sempiternal though sodden towards sundown,
> Suspended in time, between pole and tropic,
> When the short day is brightest, with frost and fire,
> The brief sun flames the ice, on pond and ditches,
> In a windless cold that is the heart's heat,
> Reflecting in a watery mirror
> A glare that is blindness in the early afternoon.
>
> ("Little Gidding," I)

This landscape, at once the country around Little Gidding and that landscape of the heart where the flames reappear after the long march "across a whole Thibet of broken stones," recalls, with the matter-of-fact conclusion about "the early afternoon," that the poet is talking of a physical journey, though the spring he sees—the hedgerow blanched with snow as with blossom—is "not in time's covenant." This use of everyday things to mirror the sublime, as well as the formal ordering of the whole poem, is reminiscent of Dante in a deeper, though less obvious, way than the structure of *Ash-Wednesday*. Eliot uses his personal symbols to give that kind of relationship between one realm of discourse and another, which in Dante is provided both by the formal structure of the journey and also by the Thomistic structure of belief. Very rarely in the poems does Eliot make use of religious terminology, although anyone acquainted with devotional writing will recognize the background of such passages as that on the virtue of detachment ("Little Gidding," III) or the dark night of the soul ("East Coker," III), which is also a description of how things felt at the beginning of the war:

> O dark dark. They all go into the dark,
> The vacant interstellar spaces, the vacant into the
>   vacant. . . .

> As, in a theatre,
> The lights are extinguished, for the scene to be changed
> With a hollow rumble of wings, with a movement of
>   darkness on darkness,
> And we know that the hills and the trees, the distant
>   panorama
> And the bold imposing façade are all being rolled
>   away—

The autobiographical passage in which the poet encounters the shade of the dead master at the end of a night's fire-watching is written in a modified terza rima, and the shade is more like Dante's than anyone else's. Here surely Eliot is speaking directly in the ironic account of the gifts reserved for age. But the "I" of the poem is perhaps no more to be identified with the poet speaking in his own person than are the passages in the first person in *The Waste Land*, spoken through the lips of Tiresias. The speakers in the early dramatic monologues were often subjected to implicit satire. In "The Hollow Men" the "I" has become a "we"—for in the sheer pain of that poem the sense of personality has lapsed. Eliot's growing interest in the drama had been exercised on material very similar to that which is the basis of *Four Quartets*. Several rather severe warnings were in any case issued by Eliot against the personal interpretation of his writing. "Honest criticism and sensitive appreciation is directed not upon the poet but the poetry," he observed in "Tradition and the Individual Talent," and, a little later, "Poetry is not a turning loose of emotion but an escape from emotion; it is not the expression of personality but an escape from personality. But of course only those who have personality and emotions know what it is to want to escape from these things."

Yet *Four Quartets* remains a poem of inner experience. The house of Burnt Norton is empty and deserted, and only the vision of children seen in the garden suggests the possible existence of other human forms. In "East Coker" the ghosts of the village merrymakers are seen dancing in a field at midnight; in "The Dry Salvages" the fishermen setting and hauling, the travelers and the women

> who have seen their sons or husbands
> Setting forth, and not returning

are more substantial; and in the final movement appears Eliot's old enemy, the Fortune Teller, dealer in past and future. "Little Gidding" is filled with a sense of historic characters—Milton, Charles I, the Ferrars, Julian of Norwich, whose words are quoted. The "familiar compound ghost" who appears at the end of the air raid speaks only when the poet, "assuming a double part," hails him; his words are mordant, sympathetic, instructive; the accent by no means unfamiliar; the effect at once of an echo and a messenger.

THE DRAMATIST

ELIOT'S interest in the drama long preceded his experiments in dramatic form, and so his early essays on dramatic theory can be applied only with some caution to the consideration of his plays. But we have Eliot's own word that he had from the first wished to write plays, as well as the fragmentary *Sweeney Agonistes* (1932) by way of witness.

The essays "Rhetoric and Poetic Drama," "Four Elizabethan Dramatists," and the "Dialogue on Dramatic Poetry," which are all reprinted in Eliot's *Selected Essays*, were written during the 1920's. In the first of these essays, which should be taken in conjunction with the essay on Ben Jonson, Eliot is concerned to defend rhetoric and the "artificial" style in drama. Jonson's rhetoric is "the careful precise filling in of a strong and simple outline, and at no point does it overflow the outline . . . there is a definite artistic emotion which demands expansion at that length." Characters are seen not in terms of individual roles, recalling figures of real life, but in "their combination into a whole. And these figures are not personifications of passions: separately, they have not even that reality, they are constituents." He might be describing the Tempters and the Knights of his first play, *Murder in the Cathedral*, or the uncles and aunts who form the chorus of *The Family Reunion*. Eliot sees Jonson as the follower of Christopher Marlowe, whose tragic "farce" he succeeds with "something falling under the category of burlesque or farce."

In the essay "Four Elizabethan Dramatists" Eliot defends convention and regrets only that the Elizabethans were not more consistent in their use of it. He praises the impersonal art of the ballet:

The difference between a great dancer and a merely competent dancer is in the vital flame, that impersonal, and, if you like, inhuman force which transpires between each of the great dancer's movements. . . . No artist produces great art by a deliberate attempt to express his personality. He expresses his personality indirectly through concentrating upon a task which is a task in the same sense as the making of an efficient engine or the turning of a jug or a table-leg.

In "A Dialogue of Dramatic Poetry" Eliot again suggests that drama should approximate to the formality of the ballet, that verse drama is preferable to prose because "if we want to express the permanent and the universal we tend to express ourselves in verse." Poetry and drama are not separable elements in such a play. The most successful of Elizabethan dramatists are the most successful poets.

Eliot's own attempt to create a new drama began with the rhythms of the music hall. The jazz songs in *Sweeney Agonistes*, the simple caricatures who form the dramatis personae, and the lurid story of murder combine into a tragic farce.

The world of *Sweeney Agonistes* is rather like the world of Graham Greene's early novels or Harold Pinter's plays. The gangsters, toughs, prostitutes, and dumb businessmen are all pursued by hidden fear. This fear is suggested by the ominous pounding rhythms and the heavy repetitions and echoes. The movement is a very simple echoing chime of two or three voices. It starts:

> *Dusty.* How about Pereira?
> *Doris.* What about Pereira?
> I don't care.
> *Dusty.* You don't care!
> Who pays the rent?
> *Doris* Yes he pays the rent
> *Dusty.* Well some men don't and some men do
> Some men don't and you know who
> *Doris.* You can have Pereira
> *Dusty.* What about Pereira?
> *Doris.* He's no gentleman, Pereira:
> You can't trust him!
> *Dusty.* Well that's true.

The sinister echoes are continued when Doris cuts the cards and draws the coffin (two of spades), and when Sweeney later breaks into the party with his story of the man who "did a girl in" and kept her body in a bath:

> Nobody came
> And nobody went
> But he took in the milk and he paid the rent.

The play ends with a nightmare chorus in a rapid triple rhythm: "When you're alone in the middle of the

night and you wake in a sweat and a hell of a fright";
and a slow crescendo of knocks on the door, which
presumably herald the arrival of the dangerous
Pereira.[4]

This little fragment could never have been extended into a play of any length; the rhythm is too violent
and the caricature too broad. But it is the first work
to introduce Eliot's dramatic style—a very free,
heavily stressed irregular verse, with emphatic
rhymes and an almost unvaried accent of ominous
foreboding. The piece is prefaced by the words of
Orestes: "You don't see them, you don't—but I see
them: they are hunting me down, I must move on."

Eliot has said that there is nothing more dramatic
than a ghost, and all his plays have a potent flavor of
the supernatural. His first piece of dramatic writing,
a pageant called *The Rock*, was written for the
Building Fund of London diocese. The choruses
alone are reprinted in his *Collected Poems* and, while
they are of interest as technical exercises, their chief
significance is to show how wide the difference is between an adequate statement of Eliot's philosophical
themes and his genuine poetry. These choruses are
necessarily very much more simplified in rhythm
and in language than his lyric poetry. They are
designed to fulfill that social function of drama
which he described in *The Use of Poetry and the Use
of Criticism*. The whole work is built on the theme of
religion and society. There are a few epigrammatic
lines, satiric and admonitory:

In the land of lobelias and tennis flannels
The rabbit shall burrow and the thorn revisit,
The nettle shall flourish on the gravel court,
    And the wind shall say: "Here were decent godless people:
    Their only monument the asphalt road
    And a thousand lost golf balls."

This is the world of "Coriolan," with the chorus of
unemployed as background, the world of the slump
and of the rise of the dictatorships in Europe. *The
Rock* is frankly propaganda and has the merits and
limits of propaganda. The seventh chorus, "In the
beginning God created the world," contains in an
early form some of the themes of *Four Quartets*; and
the influence of biblical rhythms, especially those
parts of the Bible that form part of the public services
of the church, anticipates the use of these rhythms in
the later plays.

---

[4]An unpublished final scene was given at the Globe Theatre on 13
June 1965, in a program entitled "Homage to T. S. Eliot."

Murder in the Cathedral, The Family Reunion,
and *The Cocktail Party* (1950) form a closely related
group; all retain something of the pageant, or the
ballet, and are built on a contrast between the Hero
and the Chorus, between the man who sees and the
rest who are blind. Eliot is a dramatist in a very
special and limited sense; but he recognized and used
his limitations, so that his particular form of drama,
though very restricted, is coherent, self-consistent,
and extremely actable. Like the plays of Ben Jonson,
these dramas are two-dimensional but not superficial. They are plays of the surface, but the implications go far below the surface. The characters exist
only in relation to each other: they fit in with each
other and are constituent parts, distorted to scale, of
the main theme. The action is of the slightest. A
single moment of choice, the Kierkegaardian choice,
is set before the main character; the rest of the play
leads up to and leads away from this moment. There
are no subplots, minor interests, or digressions. The
moment of choice is the same for all. There is often
actual repetition from one of these plays to another.
As Eliot observed in *Four Quartets*:

You say I am repeating
Something I have said before. I shall say it again.
("East Coker," III)

The main theme is the relation of "the moment in
time" to "the moment out of time"—the moment of decision for Thomas of Canterbury, the moment of recognition for Harry Monchensey, the moment of blind
choice for Celia. In all three plays the central character has literally to choose between life and death
—their own deaths for Thomas and Celia. Harry,
the hero of *The Family Reunion*, who is based on the
Orestes figure that had haunted Eliot so long, makes
the choice that kills his mother and goes forward to
an unknown future. The choice lies between two
kinds of action; the result is in each case a resolution
of the dilemma. These plays are not tragedies; they
are the kinds of plays that are written when the tragic
experience—necessarily a temporary, though an inevitable, state for each individual—has been left
behind. Eliot's tragedy, had he written one, would
have belonged to the period of "The Hollow Men."

The plays reflect, then, in simplified but nonetheless genuine form, the same experience as *Four
Quartets*, scored for brass rather than strings.
Murder in the Cathedral is quite popular. *The Family Reunion*, which would appear to be too personal,

too imperfectly projected (to contain, in short, the kind of difficulties Eliot attributed to *Hamlet*), does in fact act extremely well. *The Cocktail Party* is technically the most developed of the three; in this play, Eliot seems to have succeeded in finding the appropriate formula (the "objective correlative," to use his own phrase) for which he has been looking.

The assassination of Thomas à Becket is an important event in English history; the story of the *Oresteia* is one of the great myths common to Europe; the nervous breakdown, legacy of World War II, was for some years a determining factor of the social scene, a kind of modern equivalent of the Black Death. Eliot has firmly rooted his plays in these external grounds, but they are essentially plays of inner experience.

> . . . people to whom nothing has ever happened
> Cannot understand the unimportance of events
>
> (I.1)

says Harry in *The Family Reunion*, and the Fourth Tempter describes to Thomas a time when

> men will not hate you
> Enough to defame or to execrate you,
> But pondering the qualities that you lacked
> Will only try to find the historical fact.
>
> (I)

The choice made by Thomas is not "for the lifetime of one man only." It is seen as part of the pattern of timeless moments: seen as such for a moment only, for as Thomas says (echoing a line from "Burnt Norton"): "Human kind cannot bear very much reality." But in the light of such moments the common man lives out his life.

In *Murder in the Cathedral*, there are three levels of character: Thomas, who speaks with the full consciousness of the Hero; the Tempters; and the Chorus of the poor women of Canterbury, who sense the "supernatural evil" that is descending upon the place but who try to live out their humble lives as unobtrusively as possible:

> We do not wish anything to happen.
> Seven years we have lived quietly,
> Succeeded in avoiding notice,
> Living and partly living.
>
> (I)

As the "small folk who live among small things" they are rather unwillingly faithful, compelled to wait and bear witness, conscious at the end of the guilt of their weakness:

> Forgive us, O Lord, we acknowledge ourselves as type
> of the common man,
> Of the men and women who shut the door and sit by the
> fire. . . .
>
> (II)

Thomas knows that in returning he is choosing his death, and in the scene with the Four Tempters he makes his decision to stay. He rejects the bribes of power—even the spiritual power offered by the choice of martyrdom that the Fourth Tempter proffers:

> The last temptation is the greatest treason:
> To do the right deed for the wrong reason.
>
> (I)

The figures of the Tempters are paralleled by the Four Knights, who, after they have murdered Thomas, come forward with good watertight explanations of the necessity and high-mindedness of the act. They, like the Tempters, are given a modern colloquial idiom, and they speak in the phrases of the modern politician. They come from the land of lobelias and tennis flannels as well as from Aquitaine, and the ingenuity of the final plea—that Thomas was deliberately courting death and was therefore really responsible for what happened ("I think, with these facts before you, you will unhesitatingly render a verdict of Suicide while of Unsound Mind")—does not even sound particularly farfetched in the light of totalitarian practices.

Satire, epigram, and social caricature alternate with the poetic choruses in which the sense of supernatural evil is given in verse of a free and irregular sort, based on the biblical rhythms, dropping sometimes into biblical phrases, at other times colloquial, and always highly repetitive. The ritualistic quality of the speech, the stylized characters, and the very limited action contrast sharply with the complex language (the play has long passages in prose, including a sermon from the Archbishop). The sardonic note suggested in the title (which might be that of a detective story) is maintained to the last in the treatment of the Knights, who may be reminiscent in some ways of the comic devils of morality plays but are in others rather like a music-hall turn. In one production, one of the Tempters carried a golf club, with which he made practice shots in the intervals of his speech.

The Family Reunion does not employ Christian terminology, nor does *The Cocktail Party*. This certainly does not mean that they are allegories and that as one reviewer of the latter play remarked, "We see that the doctor *is* a priest, that his patients *are* the church. . . ." The use of a modern secular setting enables Eliot to relate his material more exactly and closely; the satire is less superficial, the integration more complete. In *The Cocktail Party* there is a very noticeable return to the rhythms of *Sweeney Agonistes*:

Julia.   But how did he come here?
Edward.   *I* don't know.
Julia.   *You* don't know! And what's his name?
        Did I hear him say his name was Riley?
Edward.   I don't know his name.
Julia.   You don't know his *name?*
Edward.   I tell you I've no idea who he is
        Or how he got here.

                          (I.1)

The bright conversation that opens this play might sound as if it were being merely too faithful to the banalities of social chatter were it not for this extremely ominous rhythm, which sounds its echoing chime all round the circle of the symmetrically grouped characters. In *The Family Reunion*, there is a chorus of four uncles and aunts who are used for similar purpose; they are stupid people, who do not understand what is wrong with Harry, and who are torn reluctantly away from their clubs and vicarage tea parties to participate in the drama of the Eumenides.

The hero of *The Family Reunion* is haunted by a crime, and he dwells in a shadowy and terrifying world until he returns to his home. Here the guilt is lifted from him by the revelation of the past—not his own past but that of his father and mother. His father's desire to murder his mother has been projected into a belief that he himself had murdered his wife:

Harry.   Perhaps my life has only been a dream
        Dreamt through me by the minds of others.
          Perhaps
        I only dreamt I pushed her.
Agatha.   So I had supposed. What of it?
        What we have written is not a story of detection,

Of crime and punishment, but of sin and
    expiation.
It is possible . . .
You are the consciousness of your unhappy
    family,
Its bird sent flying through the purgatorial
    flame. . . .

                          (II.2)

The suffering of Harry, and in a lesser degree of Mary, the woman who had loved him but had not been noticed ("It's just ordinary hopelessness"), and Agatha, who had loved and renounced his father, form the core of the play. Here the play is closest to the lyric poems, and sometimes more moving in its simplicity. The social setting and the blind dominating figure of the mother are there to contrast with this core of suffering. They are not related to it. Thus the play moves on two levels—the social and the supernatural—like the two worlds of *The Waste Land*.

In *The Cocktail Party* the two worlds are more closely related. It begins with an unsuccessful party and ends with a successful one. In the interval the trivialities of social exchange have all been explored and their implications fully brought to light. The four main characters have reached three different solutions: the solution of work and social success; the solution of accepting the limits of "the human condition" and maintaining the common routine, learning to avoid excessive expectation; and the other solution of a difficult vocation and a violent death.

The minor characters, who had at first seemed so tiresome—the interfering old woman, the helpful man of the world—turn out to be in benevolent league with the doctor who effects the cures, and all work together for good.

In a sense these plays are not at all realistic. It has been said that Agatha would not be likely to be elected the principal of a women's college, but I do not think anyone who was would fit in very comfortably to *The Family Reunion*. It has been said that Celia would not be sent straight out to a difficult country by any religious order, but her sudden exit and her violent death are not to be read on the level of "historical fact." There are on the other hand some scenes of quite excruciating realism, such as the quarrel between Lavinia and Edward, a full-length study of the scene suggested in *The Waste Land*, II. But this is a scene that has internal significance; it is not a mere event. There is a good deal of mordant humor that is sometimes taken amiss by inattentive readers—a tone of mock dignity and assumed gravity, which Sir Henry Harcourt-Reilly shares with Agatha and the First Priest of *Murder in the Cathedral.* It is a tone that belongs to Eliot himself:

Julia.   Oh, Henry!
            Lavinia is much more observant than you think.
            I believe that she has forced you to a show-down.
Reilly. You state the position correctly, Julia.

(II)

The epigrammatic comments recall the earliest poems. The central scene, that in which Celia states her case and makes her choice, belongs to a different mode. But this scene reflects back on her earlier scene with Edward, her lover. In this play the past is altered by the present, and a technique of retrospective illumination enables even the frivolities of the opening lines to be recalled quite naturally at the close.

After *The Cocktail Party*, Eliot's main dramatic impulse spent itself, although in the following decade *The Confidential Clerk* (1954), *The Elder Statesman* (1959), and two lectures, *Poetry and Drama* (1951) and *The Three Voices of Poetry* (1953), extended his theory and practice of drama. The first lecture treats of the nature of dramatic writing, and of the relation between author and audience. Eliot thinks that "the chief effect of style and rhythm in dramatic speech, whether in prose or verse, should be unconscious"; therefore there should be no disturbing transitions from one to the other:

> We should aim at a form of verse in which everything can be said that has to be said. . . . But if our verse is to have so wide a range that it can say anything that has to be said, it follows that it will not be "poetry" all the time. It will only be "poetry" when the dramatic situation has reached such a point of intensity that poetry becomes the natural utterance, because then it is the only language in which the emotions can be expressed at all.

In the second part of the lecture, Eliot describes his own experiments, the search for a form that would establish communications between the three collaborators in dramatic art—authors, actors, and audience: "In the theatre, the problem of communication presents itself immediately. . . . You are aiming to write lines which will have an immediate effect upon an unknown and unprepared audience, to be interpreted to that audience by unknown actors, re-

hearsed by an unknown producer." Eliot makes it clear that he is not satisfied with any of his own experiments and critically examines their shortcomings. Yet he captured an audience not confined to poetry readers: both *The Cocktail Party* and *The Confidential Clerk* succeeded in the West End and on Broadway. In *The Three Voices of Poetry*, Eliot notes the slight shock thereby produced among those of his admirers who prefer to be among the sweet, selected few: "It may be that from the beginning I aspired unconsciously to the theatre or as the critics might say, with more asperity, to Shaftesbury Avenue."

The three voices of poetry, as distinguished by Eliot, are that of the poet talking to himself; that of the poet talking to an audience; and that of the poet speaking through another character—or meditative, rhetorical, and dramatic poetry. The comparative simplicity and directness of vocabulary, syntax, and content that he demands for the third voice are certainly exemplified in his own work. The story of *The Confidential Clerk* may be based on the *Ion*, but at a London theater I have sat behind what appeared to be the mothers' meeting of some suburban church and heard them commend act III as being "almost like a whodunit." Eliot would probably have approved. The central theme of the drama, which seems to be a search for identity, the hero's need to establish a true self, is clothed in a fantastic tale of mistaken identity involving three babies (one of them, like Betsy Trotwood Copperfield, not being forthcoming), designed to appeal to simple tastes. The moments of poetry in this play are very few; for the most part it is merely verse. Eliot sacrificed the finer qualities of his writing to the needs of communication. One moment of poetry occurs when the hero and his supposed father approach each other through their common experience as frustrated artists; another is that in which the hero and a young woman are led by the power of music to that enkindled sympathy in which mind begins to play in and out of mind. But the moment of inspiration and the moment of love are alike renounced at the end of the play, in a scene where all the characters get their wishes, only to find that the fulfillment of a wish, since choice means elimination, involves a kind of death as well as a rebirth. The Cumaean Sybil from Teddington who effects this is the hero's long-lost mother: but she has deliberately forfeited her claim to him, and he in turn now renounces all relationships:

Let my mother rest in peace. As for a father—
I have the idea of a father.
It's only just come to me. I should like a father
Whom I had never known and couldn't know now,
Because he would have died before I was born
Or before I could remember; whom I could get to know
Only by reports, by documents. . . .

Perhaps some light is cast upon this Father when the former confidential clerk says to the hero, whom he has taken under his protection and who replaces his own dead son, "You'll be thinking of reading for orders"; for Colby, like Celia, has awakened to his vocation.

Perhaps also it is not a coincidence that there are echoes of the two climaxes of this play in *The Three Voices of Poetry*—especially in view of Eliot's determination to say in that lecture something he had *not* said before. Sir Claude describes the "secret moment" of the artist:

That state of utter exhaustion and peace
Which comes in dying to give something life. . . .

and in the lecture Eliot describes the satisfactory imposition of form upon the psychic material that has struggled to find it, in terms significantly new: "a moment of utter exhaustion, of appeasement, of absolution and of something very near annihilation which is in itself indescribable." Yet a poem is handed over to the unknown audience to shape and reform for themselves, and this "seems to me the consummation of the process begun in solitude without thought of the audience, the long process of gestation of the poem, because it marks the final separation of the poem from the author. Let the author rest in peace."

If a classical model is to be found for *The Elder Statesman, Oedipus at Colonus* would serve. Hiding private failure behind public success, the hero learns to live with his ghosts—himself little more than a ghost. Cherished by his Antigone, rejected by his son, he dies under a beech tree, having exorcised the shadows of moral turpitude—inward fears, though outwardly represented by two figures from his past.

This work stands to ordinary plays rather as oratorio to opera: it lacks the dimension of outward action. The language has that sententious finality usually associated with a chorus. Exploration of the connection between private and public worlds may justify the dramatic form: the only concession to a popular audience is a variation on the comic landlady. This is an attempt to transpose themes from poetry of the first voice into poetry of the third voice. As a perceptive critic observed, it is more effective when read than when acted; a personal note of confession and of valediction is heard in the last lines:

Age and decrepitude can have no terrors for me,
Loss and vicisitude cannot appal me,
Not even death can dismay or amaze me,
Fixed in the certainty of love unchanging.

Since the late 1950's, a revival of drama has paradoxically produced the most vigorous writing of the period by exploiting the physical conditions of the living theater, using flat writing as part of a collaborative production. However far removed from Eliot, Samuel Beckett, Edward Albee, Harold Pinter, and their contemporaries are exploring possibilities that he as a critic was the first to point out. In *The Birthday Party*, Pinter by the very title resembles Eliot; this comedy of menace, in which the hero is kidnapped by a pair of diabolic guardians, seems like a shadow-image of Eliot's play of redemption. But unlike Eliot's work, it has little validity on the written page and exists for production.

THE CRITIC AND MAN OF LETTERS

HAD he not become the most famous poet of his time, Eliot would have been known as its most distinguished critic. This statement must be qualified by adding that it is really impossible to distinguish the poet and the critic; for his criticism springs from his poetic sensibility, and his poetry is best explained in terms of his criticism. Among English critics the most memorable are those who have also been creative artists—Philip Sidney, Ben Jonson, John Dryden, Samuel Johnson, Samuel Taylor Coleridge, and Matthew Arnold. Indeed Eliot once ventured upon the statement that he thought "the *only* critics worth reading [were] the critics who practised and practised well, the art of which they wrote." This extreme view he does not attempt seriously to sustain; but his definition of the function of criticism, as of the perfect critic, assumes that "the two directions of sensibility are complementary; and as sensibility is rare, unpopular and desirable, it is to be expected that the critic and the creative artist should frequently be the same person" ("The Perfect Critic").

Eliot's conception of the true critic is that he should be impersonal, instructed, and without either the unfulfilled creative impulses that make some criticism an imperfect form of creation or the desire to use literature as a substitute for other things, for example, religion. The first type of "imperfect critic" is exhibited by Eliot in the person of Arthur Symons: "the reading sometimes fecundates his emotions to produce something new which is not criticism, but is not the expulsion, the ejection, the birth of creativeness." The second type of "imperfect critic" is discerned in Matthew Arnold: "The total effect of Arnold's philosophy is to set up Culture in the place of Religion and to leave Religion to be laid waste by the anarchy of feeling."

The task of the critic is defined in the words of Rémy de Gourmont: "Ériger en lois ses impressions personelles, c'est le grand effort d'un homme s'il est sincère" (To build a code of law from personal experience is the supreme objective of the clear-sighted man). Taking for granted that the critic is a man of natural sensibility, the impressions of his reading will "tend to become articulate in a generalized statement of literary beauty" since "perceptions do not, in a really appreciative mind, accumulate as a mass, but form themselves into a structure; and criticism is the statement in language of this structure: it is a development of sensibility."

The work of a good critic will therefore appear cold and impersonal to the reader in search of a stimulus; for it is not the business of the critic to stimulate, but to put the reader in possession of the necessary facts—not, of course, simply external facts, but the presentation of the work of art itself, by commentary or reading, which is one of the subtlest forms of interpretation: "But in matters of great importance the critic must not coerce and he must not make judgements of better and worse. He must simply elucidate; the reader will form the correct judgement for himself."

In "Tradition and the Individual Talent," the process of poetic creation itself is described as "a continual self-sacrifice, a continual extinction of personality," and the poet is compared with a catalytic agent, whose part in a chemical reaction is simply to induce the reaction and not to participate. Later, as we have seen, this moment of creation was redefined.

It follows that the emotional critic is almost necessarily a bad critic; and while scholars or dealers in facts cannot corrupt, "the real corruptors are those who supply opinion or fancy; and Goethe and Coleridge are not guiltless—for what is Coleridge's *Hamlet*: is it an honest inquiry as far as the data permit, or is it an attempt to present Coleridge in an attractive costume?"

Reserve, self-suppression, and the search for structural principles by submission to experience are not only the virtues of the critic, they are the most striking features of Eliot's early poetry. His method of juxtaposing two scenes, or two worlds, and leaving them to make their comment on each other, his reliance on implication and what he himself called the contrapuntal method has been described earlier: it is the exact equivalent of his advocacy of the Socratic, or maieutic method, in criticism. The ironic concentration of his poetic style is likewise paralleled by the terse, epigrammatic, and almost equally concentrated style of his prose. He himself described it in an ironic little poem:

> How unpleasant to meet Mr Eliot!
> With his features of clerical cut,
> And his brow so grim,
> And his mouth so prim,
> And his conversation, so nicely
> Restricted to What Precisely
> And If and Perhaps and But.
> ("Lines for Cuscuscaraway . . .")

Eliot's style is indeed stripped and neutral, though not without powerful resources of tone and inflection. It works much in terms of negatives, qualifications, and restrictions:

> It is not so easy to see propriety in an image which divests a snake of *winter weeds*. . . .
> ("John Dryden," *Selected Essays*)

> We are baffled by the attempt to translate the quality indicated by the dim and antiquated term wit, into the equally unsatisfactory nomenclature of our own times. . . .
> ("Andrew Marvell," *Selected Essays*)

Precisely this lack of a general critical terminology was responsible for much of his nervous stiffness and defensive irony, and the "pontifical" tone for which Eliot was later to apologize. Like the poet, the critic of the early 1920's found himself in a wasteland and had little on which he could rely in the way of equipment. Eliot was indebted principally to the French critics of the late nineteenth and early twentieth centuries, and perhaps also to the critical prefaces of Henry James. He was engaged upon an exploration of the principles of criticism as well as an examination in detail of the work of those poets to whom he as a poet was most particularly indebted. His general theory of literature is set forth in "The Perfect Critic," "Imperfect Critics," "Tradition and the Individual Talent," and "The Function of Criticism." The first three appeared in *The Sacred Wood* (1920) and the last in *Selected Essays* (1932). These brief works exercised an influence out of all proportion to their scale; and the Cambridge school of criticism, as it has come to be called (without perhaps very much justification), is based largely on the early critical writings of T. S. Eliot and of I. A. Richards, which also form the basis of the "new criticism" in America.

Eliot's work on individual writers was even more influential in redirecting the taste of the day. Based on his experience as a poet, he attempted to "reopen old communications" and "to bring back the poet to life—the great, the perennial task of criticism." In a definition of the twofold function of criticism he remarked that there are two theoretical limits of criticism, at one of which we attempt to answer the question "What is poetry?" and at the other, "Is this a good poem?" He goes on: "No theoretical ingenuity will suffice to answer the second question because no theory can amount to much which is not founded upon a direct experience of good poetry; but on the other hand our direct experience of poetry involves a good deal of generalizing activity" (*The Use of Poetry and the Use of Criticism*, p. 16).

In Eliot's writings on individual poets, the precise quality of their work is shown by carefully placed and exactly chosen quotation. The quotations are made to do the critic's work, and the reader is made to work on them. They are more than happy quotations in the usual sense: frequently they constitute the critic's main statement. In this way they recall the use of quotation in Eliot's poetry. The reader is obliged to work over these particular lines, to respond actively to them, to relate them to all his past experience of the writer under discussion. Hence the strength with which Eliot's quotations stamp themselves on the mind of the reader and the frequency with which they pass into general circulation.

His earliest critical essays, *The Sacred Wood* and *Homage to John Dryden* (1924), contain, besides the essays on general subjects, the studies of Ben Jonson, Christopher Marlowe, and Philip Massinger, the metaphysical poets, Andrew Marvell, and John Dryden. In these, Eliot set the fashion for a whole decade. The complex, ironic, and skeptical poetry of Donne and of Marvell was very much to the taste of the age; while the poetry of rhetorical writers, who maintained a surface approach but implied the depths they did not directly explore, was almost equally suited to a generation that avoided all fundamental questions, denied the validity of metaphysics, and found refuge in a bright and brittle disillusionment. The Elizabethan poets and the metaphysical poets—Donne, Herbert, Herbert of Cherbury, Marvell, and the rest—were of course among the strongest shaping influences on Eliot's own poetry. His revaluation of their work indicates what he learned from them; the famous passage about "wit" in the essay on Andrew Marvell might have been written of his own verse:

Wit is not erudition; it is sometimes stifled by erudition, as in much of Milton. It is not cynicism, though it has a kind of toughness which may be confused with cynicism by the tender-minded. It is confused with erudition because it belongs to an educated mind, rich in generations of experience; and it is confused with cynicism because it implies a constant inspection and criticism of experience. It involves, probably, a recognition, implicit in the expression of every experience, of other kinds of experience which are possible.

The contrasts with poetry of the nineteenth century, such as William Morris' *Song of Hylas*, or that between Dryden and Milton, served not only to define the quality of the poets from whom Eliot learned so much but also to define those qualities of which he disapproved. His attitude toward Milton has become notorious; in a lecture given before the British Academy in 1947, Eliot achieved a delicate and diplomatic recantation on the grounds that while Milton was a bad influence in the 1920's, when the need was for flexibility, variety, and experiment, he had now ceased to be a bad influence for young practitioners, who were rather in need of restraint:

It was one of our tenets that verse should have the virtues of prose, that diction should become assimilated to cultivated contemporary speech, before aspiring to the elevation of poetry. Another tenet was that the subject-matter and the imagery of poetry should be extended to topics and objects related to the life of a modern man or woman: that we were to seek the non-poetic, to seek even material refractory to transmutation into poetry, and words and phrases which had not been used in poetry before. And the study of Milton could be of no help: it was only a hindrance.

We cannot in literature, any more than in the rest of life, live in a perpetual state of revolution. . . . Poetry should help, not only to refine the language of the time, but to prevent it from changing too rapidly: a development of language at too great a speed would be a development in the sense of a progressive deterioration, and that is our danger to-day.

It cannot be denied that when Eliot uttered these words, the attitude of the aged and distinguished academicians who formed the audience was rather reminiscent of the Inquisition listening to the recantation of a dangerous and influential heretic. One of them even cried out (although the whole performance was being broadcast), "A little louder, please!" But Eliot never recanted on the subject of the nineteenth-century poets. It is true that he edited an anthology of Kipling, with an introduction in which he paid tribute to Kipling's technical powers. But Matthew Arnold and the Pre-Raphaelites remain unreprieved.

One or two of Eliot's critical phrases have attained a popularity that, he says, was "astonishing to their author." The "dissociation of sensibility" he described as setting in with Milton and Dryden is one of them. In the later seventeenth century, the peculiar unification of thought and feeling he discerned in Donne and Marvell was broken up:

A thought to Donne was an experience: it modified his sensibility. When a poet's mind is perfectly equipped for its work, it is constantly amalgamating disparate experience: the ordinary man's experience is chaotic, irregular, fragmentary. The latter falls in love, or reads Spinoza, and these two experiences have nothing to do with each other, or with the noise of the typewriter or the smell of cooking; in the mind of the poet these experiences are always forming new wholes.

It is the forming of new wholes, the *relating* of experience, that Eliot learned from the Elizabethans and from the metaphysicals, and this was what he particularly valued in their work. His account of the poetic experience is clearly based on the great definition by Coleridge of the Poetic Imagination from the fourteenth chapter of *Biographia Literaria.* Eliot quotes this passage in his essay on Marvell. The poet who is least represented in this phase of Eliot's criticism is Shakespeare himself. The essay on *Hamlet* is a document more revealing of Eliot's own difficulties than of Shakespeare's: it might stand, for instance, in part at least, as a commentary on *Sweeney Agonistes.*

During the later 1920's Eliot published a number of essays, but the little monograph on Dante (1929) marks the next phase in his critical development. It coincides with the change in his poetic style already described. At this time he also wrote an essay comparing Dante and Donne, to the great advantage of the former. The poetry of Dante remained the greatest single discernible influence in the writing of Eliot, and his interest in medieval literature, like his earlier interest in the seventeenth century, promoted a general taste for the period. Later contributions took the more informal mode of public lectures, in one of which, *The Frontiers of Criticism* (1956), he summed up the merits and defects of his own earlier "work-shop criticism." In his last work, a study of George Herbert, Eliot took a point of view opposite to that of "Tradition and the Individual Talent," for he saw Herbert's poetry as "a personal record," and, some may feel, a record with a certain likeness to Eliot's own.

CONCLUSION

ELIOT's death on 4 January 1965 seemed to come as the end of the long farewell that gave to his last play its deeply personal poignancy: "He has gone too far to return to us." In his line of traditional and civilized poetry, he has left no successor. His unique position of authority, comparable only with that of Samuel Johnson, derived from a variety of causes. In the first place, the particular consistency and coherence of his writing made it a structural whole; indeed in his later work, the interest of its place in the whole sometimes predominated over the effect of the particular part. The risk of overdetermination has not always been avoided, although a constant development of theme can also be followed, the early themes of the City and the Garden giving way to those of identity and relationship, communication and solitude.

The range of Eliot's output and literary concerns also conferred authority; during the decade and a half that he edited the *Criterion,* this quarterly journal was one of the most influential literary publications of its time, and in its editorials appeared some of Eliot's best occasional writing, trenchant and invigorating. The publishing firm of which he was a director, Faber and Faber, specialized in poetry, and the work of many younger poets appeared under its imprint.

But Eliot did not enjoy the atmosphere of academies, literary societies, or intellectual good causes, and some of his tastes were even unliterary. He published an extremely lively book of comic verse about cats, written originally for children, but designed to appeal to all who appreciate the naturally lawless behavior, intellectual superiority, and strong business instincts of cats. "Old Possum"—Pound's nickname for Eliot—remained an elusive jester, whose taste for practical jokes was known in private, but whose peculiar (and rather American) brand of irony was liable to be misunderstood in public. The Broadway success of *Cats* would have invited Eliot's satiric wit.

The title of one book describes him as *The Invisible Poet*. In the last few years, when his health became precarious, Eliot tended to withdraw more and more from the literary scene; yet at the same time, relaxing the impersonality of his earlier position, he gradually conceded some elements of an intellectual autobiography. His mischeivous confession, that the notes to *The Waste Land* were originally supplied to fill out the bulk of a slender volume, was perhaps a half-truth combining ironic self-deflation with mockery of his more pedantic followers. But publication of his forty-eight-year-old Harvard thesis, *Knowledge and Experience in the Philosophy of F. H. Bradley*, as a "curiosity of biographical interest" provided a new and much more extended commentary on the poem. As philosophy, the work of the man whom Bertrand Russell described as "my best pupil at Harvard" shows little trace of Russell's influence; it is written in terminology that philosophers no longer employ and that Eliot confessed in 1964 he was no longer able to think in—"Indeed, I do not pretend to understand it." Originally composed only because "Harvard had made it possible for me to go to Oxford for a year; this return at least I owed to Harvard," its sustained argument confirms that the cryptic style of Eliot's other early prose was assumed for a purpose. Parts of the conclusion reveal something of the poet behind the philosopher; this constitutes its interest:

If you will find the mechanical anywhere, you will find it in the workings of mind; and to inspect living mind, you must look nowhere but in the world outside.

(p. 154)

Our first step is to discover what experience is not, and why it is essentially indefinable.

(p. 157)

The world, as we have seen, exists only as it is found in . . . experiences so mad and strange that they will be boiled away before you boil them down to one heterogeneous mass.

(p. 168)

In 1968, the long-lost first draft of *The Waste Land* came to light in New York, and proved, as was known, much longer than the final version. The drowned sailor began as a fisherman from the coasts of Eliot's boyhood, lost in the northern ice; other passages suggest *Sweeney Agonistes* in their tone of ironic jest. Pound's advice to cut the work seems to have made it more consistent and more powerful, as well as more classical. It is clear also from Martin Browne's account of collaboration with Eliot that even at the end of his career he was ready to take advice from his friends, for the plays were many times redrafted and their significance altered.

Now that his achievement is completed, those who have lived with Eliot's work, and felt it changing and growing while remaining a unity, can absorb its final form. The power to grow and change will remain with it, however, as it develops within the minds of its readers, at those deeper levels where "words, after speech, reach/Into the silence."

On the red stone that commemorates Eliot at East Coker, where he lies buried, are carved only the words "Remember Thomas Stearns Eliot, Poet," the dates of birth and death, and the two phrases "In my beginning is my end" and "In my end is my beginning."

SELECTED BIBLIOGRAPHY

I. BIBLIOGRAPHY. D. Gallup, *T. S. Eliot: A Bibliography* (London, 1925; rev. ed., 1969), a complete and accurate record, including contributions to periodicals and translations into foreign languages; M. Martin, *A Half Century of Eliot Criticism: An Annotated Bibliography of Books and Articles in English, 1916–1965* (Lewisburg, Pa., 1972); M. Frank, H. P. Frank, K. P. S. Joachum, eds., *A Supplementary Bibliography to Mildred Martin* (Edmonton, 1978).

II. COLLECTED WORKS. *Ara Vos Prec* (London, 1920), lim. ed., includes contents of *Prufrock*, *Poems*, and additional poems including "Gerontion"; *Poems 1909–1925*

(London, 1925), includes contents of *Ara Vos Prec, The Waste Land*, and "The Hollow Men"; *Collected Poems 1909–1935* (London, 1936), includes the contents of *Poems 1909–1925*, together with *Ash-Wednesday, Ariel Poems,* "Unfinished Poems," "Minor Poems," Choruses from *The Rock*, and "Burnt Norton"; *The Complete Poems and Plays* (New York, 1952); *Collected Plays* (London, 1962); *Collected Poems 1909–1962* (London, 1963); *Complete Poems and Plays* (London, 1969).

III. Selected Works. *Selected Essays 1917–1932* (London, 1932), enl. ed. (London, 1951) omitting dates from title, contains essays from *The Sacred Wood, For Lancelot Andrewes*, and other sources; *Essays Ancient and Modern* (London, 1936), supersedes *For Lancelot Andrewes*, omitting some essays Eliot did not wish to preserve, and incorporates additional ones including prefaces to Pascal's *Pensées* and Tennyson's *In Memoriam; The Waste Land and Other Poems* (London, 1940), selections from *Collected Poems 1909–1935; Later Poems 1925–1935* (London, 1941), selections from *Collected Poems 1909–1935;* J. Hayward, ed., *Selected Prose* (London, 1953; pprbk. repr., 1963); *On Poetry and Poets* (London, 1957), contains essays, lectures, and addresses from various sources written and separately printed with one exception after 1932; *Selected Poems* (London, 1961); *To Criticize the Critic* (London, 1965), lectures and essays from various periods collected by Eliot but published posthumously; *Poems Written in Early Youth* (London, 1967), reiss. of ed. collected by J. Hayward and privately printed (1950) under supervision of Eliot; F. Kermode, ed., *Selected Prose* (London, 1975).

IV. Separate Works. *Prufrock and Other Observations* (London, 1917), verse; *Ezra Pound: His Metric and Poetry* (New York, 1917), criticism, pub. anonymously; *Poems* (Richmond, Surrey, 1919), hand-printed by Leonard and Virginia Woolf at the original Hogarth Press; *The Sacred Wood: Essays on Poetry and Criticism* (London, 1920), contains essays and reviews originally contributed to the *Times Literary Supplement*, the *Athenaeum*, the *Egoist* (of which Eliot was assistant ed. 1917–1919); *The Waste Land* (New York, 1922), verse, first printed in first no. of the *Criterion* (October 1922); first English ed. (Richmond, Surrey, 1923), hand-printed by Leonard and Virginia Woolf (lim. ed., London, 1962); first French ed., *Poemes 1910–1930*, P. Leyris, trans. (Paris, 1947), contains additional notes by J. Hayward, facs. and transcript of original drafts including annotations of Ezra Pound, ed. by V. Eliot, original MSS, in the Berg collection of the New York Public Library, obtained in 1968 as part of the collection of John Quinn, to whom Eliot sent it in 1922; *Homage to John Dryden: Three Essays on Poetry of the Seventeenth Century* (London, 1924), contains "John Dryden," "The Metaphysical Poets," "Andrew Marvell"; *Journey of the Magi* (London, 1927), no. 8 of publisher's series of *Ariel Poems* (single poems issued as pamphlets), subsequently including "A Song for Simeon," no. 16 (1928), "Animula,"

no. 23 (1929), "Marina," no. 29 (1930), "Triumphal March," no. 35 (1931), "The Cultivation of Christmas Trees," new series (1954); *For Lancelot Andrewes: Essays on Style and Order* (London, 1928), criticism, permanently out of print, see *Essays Ancient and Modern* above; *Dante* (London, 1929), criticism.

Ash-Wednesday (London, 1930), verse, signed lim. ed. of 600 copies pub. simultaneously in New York and London preceded regular ed. by five days; *Anabasis: A Poem by St. J. Perse with a Translation by T. S. Eliot* (London, 1930; rev. eds., New York, 1938, 1949); *Thoughts After Lambeth* (London, 1931), pamphlet containing observations on ecclesiastical policy discussed at Lambeth Conference; *John Dryden: The Poet, the Dramatist, the Critic* (New York, 1932), criticism; *Sweeney Agonistes; Fragments of an Aristophanic Melodrama* (London, 1932), poetic drama; *The Use of Poetry and the Use of Criticism: Studies in the Relation of Criticism to Poetry in England* (London, 1933), essays originally delivered as lectures during Eliot's tenure as Charles Eliot Norton Professor of Poetry, 1932–1933, at Harvard; *After Strange Gods: A Primer of Modern Heresy* (London, 1934), Page-Barbour Lectures delivered at the University of Virginia, 1933; *The Rock: A Pageant Play* (London, 1934), verse libretto, "Written for Performance at Sadler's Wells Theatre 28 May–9 June 1934, on behalf of the Forty-Five Churches Fund of the Diocese of London"; *Elizabethan Essays* (London, 1934), collected essays on Elizabethan and Jacobean drama, all previously published except essay on John Marston, later added to *Selected Essays* (London, 1951); *Murder in the Cathedral* (London, 1935; rev. eds., 1936, 1937, 1938), poetic drama, film script (London, 1951), contains considerable additions, ed. with notes and intro. by N. Coghill (London, 1965); *The Family Reunion* (London, 1939), poetic drama; *Old Possum's Book of Practical Cats* (London, 1939), verse biographies of fanciful cats written for children and published under pseudonym coined by Ezra Pound; *The Idea of Christian Society* (London, 1939), sociology.

The Music of Poetry (London, 1942), 3rd W. P. Ker Memorial Lecture delivered at the University of Glasgow, 24 February 1942; *The Classics and the Man of Letters* (London, 1942), presidential address delivered to the Classical Association, 15 April 1942; *Reunion by Destruction* (London, 1943), "Reflections on a Scheme for Church Union in South India, addressed to the Laity"; *Four Quartets* (New York, 1943; London, 1944; lim. ed., 1961), each Quartet previously published separately: "Burnt Norton" in *Collected Poems 1909–1935*, "East Coker" (London, 1940), "The Dry Salvages" (London, 1941), "Little Gidding" (London, 1942), French version, *Quatre Quattuors*, P. Leyris, trans. (Paris, 1950), contains notes by J. Hayward; *What Is a Classic?* (London, 1945), address delivered to the Vergil Society, 16 October 1944; *Milton* (London, 1947), Master Mind Lecture for 1947 delivered to the British Academy; *Notes Towards the Definition of Culture* (London, 1948), sociology.

The Cocktail Party (London, 1950; pprbk. repr., 1958), poetic drama; *Poetry and Drama* (Cambridge, Mass., 1951), 1st Theodore Spencer Memorial Lecture, delivered at Harvard, 21 November 1950; *An Address to Members of the London Library* (London, 1952), presidential address, lim. to 500 copies; *American Literature and the American Language* (St. Louis, 1953), centenary address at Washington University; *The Three Voices of Poetry* (London, 1953), 11th annual lecture of the National Book League; *The Confidential Clerk* (London, 1954; 2nd ed., 1967), poetic drama; *Goethe as Sage* (Hamburg, 1955), German and English text of lecture delivered at Hamburg on receiving the Hanseatic Goethe Prize, 1954; *The Frontiers of Criticism* (Minneapolis, 1956), Gidea-Seymour Memorial Lecture at the University of Minnesota, 1956; *Essays on Elizabethan Drama* (New York, 1956), new selection of essays on Elizabethan and Jacobean drama; *The Elder Statesman* (London, 1959), poetic drama; *George Herbert* (London, 1962), essay; *Knowledge and Experience in the Philosophy of F. H. Bradley* (London, 1964), dissertation completed in 1916, published "only as a curiosity of biographical interest"; V. Eliot, ed., *The Waste Land: A Facsimile and Transcript* (London, 1971).

Note: Eliot made contributions of prose and verse to over a hundred books or pamphlets by other writers; his contributions in prose or verse to periodicals (including numerous book reviews, broadcast lectures, and the "commentaries" written for the *Criterion* during his editorship, 1922–1939) number close to six hundred. The majority of these contributions have not been reprinted or collected. In addition, Eliot edited and introduced Ezra Pound's *Selected Poems* (London, 1928), Marianne Moore's *Selected Poems* (London, 1935), *A Choice of Kipling's Verse* (London, 1941), *A Selection of Joyce's Prose* (London, 1942), and *Ezra Pound's Literary Essays* (London, 1953).

V. BIOGRAPHICAL AND CRITICAL STUDIES. E. Pound, "The Love Song of J. Alfred Prufrock," in *Poetry* (Chicago), 10 (1917), the first understanding criticism of Eliot's work to appear in print; B. Dobrée, *The Lamp and the Lute* (Oxford, 1929), contains a critical essay on Eliot's early work, 2nd ed. (London, 1964) includes additional essay on his last two plays; E. Wilson, *Axel's Castle* (New York, 1931), contains first important critical estimate of Eliot's work; T. MacGreevy, *Thomas Stearns Eliot* (London, 1931), a short study but the first book entirely devoted to Eliot's work; F. R. Leavis, *New Bearings in English Poetry* (London, 1932), contains a penetrating critique; A. Oras, *The Critical Ideas of T. S. Eliot* (Tartu [Dorpat], 1932), comprehensive survey in English by an Estonian critic; W. Lewis, *Men Without Art* (London, 1934), contains a long critique by one of Eliot's earliest and most intelligent critics; F. O. Matthiessen, *The Achievement of T. S. Eliot* (London, 1935; rev. enl. ed., 1947), the most comprehensive and important study of the interwar years, 3rd ed. (1958) includes additional ch. on Eliot's later

work and an appreciation of Matthiessen, both by C. L. Barber; M. Praz, "T. S. Eliot and Dante," in *Southern Review*, II, iii (1937); *Harvard Advocate*, 125, 3 (1938), contains tributes by such leading American poets and critics as Conrad Aiken, R. P. Blackmur, Richard Eberhart, Archibald Macleish, F. O. Matthiessen, Wallace Stevens, Allen Tate, Robert Penn Warren, William Carlos Williams.

M. Bodkin, *The Quest for Salvation in an Ancient and a Modern Play* (London, 1941), analogizes the *Oresteia* and *The Family Reunion*; F. R. Leavis, "T. S. Eliot's Later Poetry," in *Education and the University* (London, 1943); R. Preston, *Four Quartets Rehearsed: A Commentary* (London, 1946), an essay in interpretation; B. Rajan, ed., *T. S. Eliot: A Study of His Writings by Several Hands* (London, 1947), contains 8 critical essays by Cleanth Brooks, E. E. Duncan Jones, H. Gardner, M. C. Bradbrook, and others, and a bibliographical checklist; L. Unger, ed., *T. S. Eliot: A Selected Critique* (New York, 1948), 31 extracts from important critical studies, contains an extensive checklist of books and articles in English about Eliot's work up to 1948, the year in which he received the Nobel Prize; R. March and Tambimuttu, *T. S. Eliot: A Symposium* (London, 1948), a tribute to Eliot on his 60th birthday, contains 47 contributions, including poems, essays, and personal reminiscences; F. Wilson, *Six Essays on the Development of T. S. Eliot* (London, 1949), an excellent introduction to Eliot's poems and poetic dramas; E. Drew, *T. S. Eliot: The Design of His Poetry* (New York, 1949), a Jungian interpretation; K. Smidt, *Poetry and Belief in the Works of T. S. Eliot* (Oslo, 1949; rev. ed., London, 1961), a study of the philosophic affiliations of Eliot's thought.

G. Williamson, *A Reader's Guide to T. S. Eliot* (New York, 1953); K. Nott, *The Emperor's Clothes* (London, 1953), contains a spirited attack on Eliot's orthodoxy; G. Smith, Jr., *T. S. Eliot's Poetry and Plays* (Chicago, 1956), an exhaustive study of Eliot's literary sources; A. Alvarez, *The Shaping Spirit* (London, 1958); N. Braybrooke, ed., *T. S. Eliot: A Symposium* (London, 1958), contributions by some fifty authors in honor of Eliot's 70th birthday; V. Buckley, *Poetry and Morality: Studies on the Criticism of M. Arnold, T. S. Eliot and F. R. Leavis* (London, 1959).

H. Kenner, *The Invisible Poet: T. S. Eliot* (London, 1960); D. E. Jones, *The Plays of T. S. Eliot* (London, 1960); L. Unger, *T. S. Eliot* (Minneapolis, 1961); D. W. Harding, *Experience into Words* (London, 1963); M. C. Bradbrook, *English Dramatic Form* (London, 1965), contains a ch. on Eliot's drama; H. Howarth, *Notes on Some Figures Behind T. S. Eliot* (London, 1965); L. Unger, *T. S. Eliot: Moments and Patterns* (Minneapolis, 1966); H. L. Gardner, *T. S. Eliot and the English Poetic Tradition* (Nottingham, 1966), the Byron Lecture, Nottingham, 1965; A. Tate, ed., *T. S. Eliot, The Man and His Work* (London, 1967), a collection of 26 essays, including personal recollections of I. A. Richards, Herbert Read, Stephen Spender, Ezra Pound, Frank Morley, E. Martin Browne, Robert Speight, originally published in the *Sewanee Review;* C. B. Cox and A. P. Hinchcliffe, eds., *T. S. Eliot: "The Waste Land." A Casebook* (London, 1968); E. M. Browne, *The Making of T. S. Eliot's Plays* (London, 1969), an account of the composition and production of the plays based on recollections of their director and his private memoranda and letters; F. R. Leavis, *English Literature in Our Time and the University* (London, 1969), the Clark Lectures, 1967.

G. Martin, ed., *Eliot in Perspective: A Symposium* (London, 1970), essays by F. W. Bateson, Donald Davie, and others; R. Kojecky, *T. S. Eliot's Social Criticism* (London, 1971), an account of Eliot's membership in the Moot, with new work by Eliot; G. Patterson, *T. S. Eliot: Poems in the Making* (Manchester, 1971); H. Kenner, *The Pound Era* (London, 1972), considers Eliot in relation to modernism; J. D. Margolis, *T. S. Eliot's Intellectual Development, 1922-1939* (Chicago, 1972); A. Serpieri, *T. S. Eliot; Le strutture profonde* (Bologna, 1973), the best account of Eliot's transformational activity; S. Sullivan, ed., *Critics on T. S. Eliot* (London, 1973); D. Ward, *"Between Two Worlds": A Reading of T. S. Eliot's Poetry and Plays* (London, 1973); F. R. Leavis, *The Living Principle* (London, 1975), the last third is a long essay on *Four Quartets;* E. Schneider, *T. S. Eliot: The Pattern in the Carpet* (London, 1975); B. Rajan, *The Overwhelming Question: A Study of the Poetry of T. S. Eliot* (Toronto, 1976); S. Spender, *T. S. Eliot* (New York-London, 1976); D. A. Traversi, *T. S. Eliot: The Longer Poems* (London, 1976); H. Freed, *T. S. Eliot: Aesthetics and History* (London, 1977); L. Gordon, *Eliot's Early Years* (Oxford, 1977); D. Newton-De Molina, ed., *The Literary Criticism of T. S. Eliot: New Essays* (Atlantic Highlands, N. J., 1977); J. E. Miller, *T. S. Eliot's Personal Waste Land: Exorcism of the Demons* (Philadelphia, 1977); B. Bergonzi, *T. S. Eliot* (London, 1978), Masters of World Literature series; H. Gardner, *The Composition of "Four Quartets"* (Oxford, 1978); M. L. Rosenthal, *Eliot, Yeats and Pound: Sailing into the Unknown* (Oxford, 1978); B. Southam, ed., *Gerontion, Ash Wednesday and Other Shorter Poems: A Casebook* (London, 1978); A. D. Moody, *T. S. Eliot, Poet* (Cambridge, 1979); B. Lee, *Theory and Personality: The Theory of T. S. Eliot's Criticism* (London, 1979); C. J. Thomas, *Poetic Tradition and T. S. Eliot's Talent* (London, 1979).

N. Frye, *T. S. Eliot: An Introduction* (Chicago, 1981); P. Gray, *T. S. Eliot's Intellectual and Poetic Development, 1909-1922* (Brighton, 1981); E. Lobb, *T. S. Eliot and the Romantic Critical Tradition* (London, 1981); M. Grant, ed., *T. S. Eliot, The Critical Heritage,* 2 vols. (London, 1982), the first vol., which ends with 1930, is of special interest.

Note: The John Hayward collection bequeathed to King's College, Cambridge, in 1965 contains an almost complete assemblage of printed works by and about Eliot as well as an extensive group of MSS and typescripts. Those who wish to consult unpublished material should write to T. S. Eliot's Literary Executrix, c/o Faber and Faber Ltd., London.

LIST OF COLLECTED ESSAYS

(The titles in italics indicate the volumes in which the essay is contained; essays marked with an asterisk were added to the enlarged edition of *Selected Essays,* 1951.)

"The Age of Dryden," *The Use of Poetry and the Use of Criticism;* "The Aims of Education," *To Criticize the Critic;* "American Literature and the American Language," *To Criticize the Critic;* "Andrew Marvell," *Homage to John Dryden, Selected Essays;* "Apology for the Countess of Pembroke," *The Use of Poetry and the Use of Criticism;* "Arnold and Pater," *Selected Essays;* "Beaudelaire," *Selected Essays, Selected Prose;* "Beaudelaire in Our Time," *For Lancelot Andrewes, Essays Ancient and Modern;* "Ben Jonson," *The Sacred Wood, Selected Essays, Elizabethan Essays;* "Blake," *The Sacred Wood, Selected Essays;* "Byron," *On Poetry and Poets;* "Catholicism and International Order," *Essays Ancient and Modern;* "Charles Whibley," *Selected Essays;* "Christopher Marlowe," *The Sacred Wood, Selected Essays, Elizabethan Essays;* "The Classics and the Man of Letters," *Selected Prose;* "Cyril Tourneur," *Selected Essays, Elizabethan Essays.*

"Dante" (1920), *The Sacred Wood;* "Dante" (1929), *Selected Essays;* "A Dialogue on Dramatic Poetry," *Selected Essays;* "Euripides and Professor Murray," *The Sacred Wood, Selected Essays;* "Ezra Pound, His Metric and Poetry," *To Criticize the Critic;* "Four Elizabethan Dramatists," *Selected Essays, Elizabethan Essays;* "Francis Herbert Bradley," *For Lancelot Andrewes, Selected Essays, Essays Ancient and Modern;* "From Poe to Valéry," *To Criticize the Critic;* "The Frontiers of Criticism," *On Poetry and Poets;* "The Function of Criticism," *Selected Essays.*

"Goethe as Sage," *On Poetry and Poets;* "Hamlet," *The Sacred Wood, Selected Essays, Elizabethan Essays, Selected Prose;* "The Humanism of Irving Babbitt," *For Lancelot Andrewes, Selected Essays, Essays Ancient and Modern;* "Imperfect Critics," *The Sacred Wood;* *"In Memoriam" [by Tennyson], Essays Ancient and Modern;* "John Bramhall," *For Lancelot Andrewes, Selected Essays, Essays Ancient and Modern;* "John Dryden," *Homage to John Dryden, Selected Essays;* "John Ford," *Selected Essays, Elizabethan Essays;* "John Marston," *Elizabethan Essays;* "Johnson as Critic and Poet," *On Poetry and Poets.*

"Lancelot Andrewes," *For Lancelot Andrewes, Selected Essays, Essays Ancient and Modern;* "The Literature of Politics," *To Criticize the Critics;* "Marie Lloyd," *Selected Essays;* "Matthew Arnold," *The Use of Poetry and the Use of Criticism;* "The Metaphysical Poets," *Homage to John Dryden, Selected Essays, Selected Prose;* "Milton" (I and II), *Selected Prose, On Poetry and Poets;* *"Modern Education and the Classics," Essays Ancient and Modern;* "The Modern Mind," *The Use of Poetry and the Use of Criticism;* "The Music of Poetry," *Selected Prose, On Poetry and Poets;* "Niccolò Machiavelli," *For Lancelot Andrewes;* "A Note on Richard Crashaw," *For Lancelot Andrewes.*

"The Pensées of Pascal," Essays Ancient and Modern, Selected Prose; "The Perfect Critic," *The Sacred Wood;* "Philip Massinger," *The Sacred Wood, Selected Essays, Elizabethan Essays;* "Poetry and Drama," *Selected Prose, On Poetry and Poets;* "The Possibility of a Poetic Drama," *The Sacred Wood;* "Reflections on Vers Libre," *To Criticize the Critic;* "Religion and Literature," *Essays Ancient and Modern, Selected Prose;* "Rhetoric and Poetic Drama," *The Sacred Wood, Selected Essays;* "Rudyard Kipling," *On Poetry and Poets;* "Second Thoughts About Humanism," *Selected Essays;* "Seneca in Elizabethan Translation," *Selected Essays;* "Shakespeare and the Stoicism of Seneca," *Selected Essays, Elizabethan Essays;* "Shelley and Keats," *The Use of Poetry and the Use of Criticism;* "Sir John Davies," *On Poetry and Poets;* "The Social Function of Poetry," *On Poetry and Poets;* "Swinburne as Poet," *The Sacred Wood, Selected Essays.*

"Thomas Heywood," *Selected Essays, Elizabethan Essays;* "Thomas Middleton," *For Lancelot Andrewes, Selected Essays, Elizabethan Essays;* "Thoughts After Lambeth," *Selected Essays;* "The Three Voices of Poetry," *On Poetry and Poets;* "To Criticize the Critics," *To Criticize the Critics;* "Tradition and the Individual Talent," *The Sacred Wood, Selected Essays, Selected Prose;* "Virgil and the Christian World," *On Poetry and Poets;* "What Dante Means to Me," *To Criticize the Critic;* "What Is a Classic?" *On Poetry and Poets;* "What Is Minor Poetry?" *On Poetry and Poets;* "Wordsworth and Coleridge," *The Use of Poetry and the Use of Criticism;* "Yeats," *On Poetry and Poets.*

KATHERINE MANSFIELD

(1888-1923)

Ian A. Gordon

I

FOR some centuries now the Englishman has been a considerable traveler. War, adventure, commercial instincts, empire building, the selfless missionary spirit, a profound faith in the English way of life (and at times a profound distaste for it), sometimes mere curiosity have all sent generations of Englishmen beyond the seas. Most of these wrote nothing except letters to their families; many of them not even that. But from all these centuries of foreign adventures English literature has profited, emerging always with fresh experiences and on occasion with new insight. Two main themes can be detected in this literature of life overseas. The first, and more obvious, is the undisguised and uninhibited delight in expanded horizons that gives freshness and gusto to writers otherwise as different as Tobias Smollett, Frederick Marryat, and Graham Greene. The second appears in more introspective writers, who—placed in a foreign setting—turn their eyes resolutely homeward: Robert Louis Stevenson in Samoa remembering Edinburgh with affection, James Joyce in Switzerland fascinated though appalled by his native Dublin, the usually unsentimental Rudyard Kipling recalling his Devonshire schooldays. The theme of exile with its elegiac undertones is seldom far from the thoughts of the apparently confident Englishman on his journeys.

To this second group belongs Katherine Mansfield, though her affinity to these manifest exiles has seldom been recognized. It is, however, the key to a full understanding of her writing. She was a third-generation New Zealander who received her childhood education in her own country. After further schooling in London, she went back unwillingly to New Zealand with the single-minded intention of returning with all speed to the literary capital. Wearing down her family's resistance, she was back in London within a couple of years. The remainder of her life was spent there and in the south of England, with longer and longer periods on the Continent as her health deteriorated. She did not return to New Zealand and for some years felt little but her adolescent contempt for the narrow round of colonial life in its early-twentieth-century capital of seventy thousand inhabitants. But events caught up with her. The glittering prizes came her way only when they had ceased to matter. Life, if it never singed her wings, certainly burned her fingers, not once but several times. A reunion with her brother, shortly afterward killed in World War I, completed her enlightenment, and in her middle twenties, a mature and experienced—almost too experienced—woman, she came to recognize that a New Zealander can be as much of an exile in England as an Englishman on an island in the Pacific. From the moment of that discovery the note of elegy entered her work, and she turned for her themes to her origins. All of her best work dates from this point.

The editions of her writings do not make it easy to follow this development. Her earliest volume, *In a German Pension* (1911), was brought out by an obscure publisher and, attracting little attention, went out of print. After her death in 1923, when her reputation was probably reaching its highest point, this resentful and ill-natured volume was reprinted, in 1926, somewhat to the disturbance of readers who were then familiar only with her finished and sensitive work in New Zealand stories like "The Garden Party." Meanwhile the publication in 1924 of *Something Childish, and Other Stories* (in America entitled *The Little Girl*), which contains a mixture of stories of various dates, from some written shortly before her death at the age of thirty-four to one written when she was nineteen, had further confused any but the most careful reader bent on following the pattern of her development, whether in technique or in theme. The collected edition of her work casts no further light. It merely reprints, still as separate entities, each of her separately published volumes; most of the stories are undated, and the dates on others are demonstrably false. In any subsequent edition, one hopes that the stories will be printed in the order of composition, or at least that this information will be made available in a brief but accurate appendix.

It is not that the precise date of composition of any one story matters in itself. But it is important before making a critical judgment on a story to know where it fits into her work. The chronological sequence is important for another reason. Katherine Mansfield, to a degree almost unparalleled in English fiction, put her own experiences into her stories. She wrote of nothing that did not directly happen to her, even when she appeared to be at her most imaginative and fanciful. Her stories, read in their order of composition, gain force and significance, and are illuminated at all points, by the events of her own history. Her whole work read in this manner emerges as a kind of *recherche du temps perdu*, a remembrance of things past in a distant dominion.

II

KATHLEEN BEAUCHAMP was born in 1888 in Wellington, New Zealand. Her father, Harold (later Sir Harold) Beauchamp, was a merchant who combined a shy sensitivity at home with a ruthless drive in his business affairs. She grew up in a family group of two older sisters and a younger brother, with a grandmother and unmarried aunts among the adult members. From the village school she went via the Girls' High School to a private school for young ladies, and then (the family ambition and fortunes still rising) to four years at Queen's College, Harley Street, London. Returning to Wellington in 1906, her head filled with Oscar Wilde and the glamour of the literary life, she sulked and refused to play the part of the accomplished middle-class daughter back from finishing school. She undertook a strenuous six-week camping trip in rough and sometimes primitive conditions and showed her new independence by taking courses in bookkeeping and typing in the Wellington Technical College. The family capitulated. With an allowance from her father (which continued throughout her life) she left for London in 1908 to establish herself as a writer. She was nineteen. She had published a few sketches. All she re-

quired was experience. The process was not pleasant. Within a short time she was in retreat, seeking one refuge after another. What she could not know at the time, and came to recognize only after years of despair, was that when she left her own country at the age of nineteen she had already experienced all that she required. The material for her finest work lay in the family group she had abandoned and in the colonial town she had so contemptuously left behind.

Within a year of her arrival in London she was pregnant. She married George Bowden, although he was not the father of her child, left him abruptly, and was packed off to Bavaria by her mother, who was on a hurried visit to England. The child was miscarried, and so the incident was closed. But all of this lay behind the snarling ill humor of her stories of this period. They were first printed in periodicals during 1910, after her return from Bavaria, and (if one excepts "The Modern Soul") form the first seven stories in her 1911 volume, *In a German Pension*. The Germans are observed with loathing. But the Germans are not the real target. What she is depicting is the grossness of the male, guzzling and drinking, pressing his unwanted attentions on the young girl in "At Lehmann's" and on the middle-aged wife in "Frau Brechenmacher Attends a Wedding." Katherine Mansfield's own situation at the time, the pregnant girl surrounded by curious middle-aged matrons, is underlined in "Frau Fischer." For all their German background and variety of characters, these stories are almost autobiography.

Back in London by early 1910, she found temporary refuge with Ida Baker, a friend from her Queen's College days who was to become her guardian angel thereafter. She placed her Bavarian stories with A. R. Orage's the *New Age* and shortly after embarked on a new love affair. The results were almost but not quite as disastrous as the first, and the young man faded from the picture. She began on more stories, some based on her Bavarian memories, two of them—"The Journey to Bruges" and "A Truthful Adventure"—springing from a brief visit to Belgium. The *New Age* published both stories (they did not appear in book form until 1924) and a Bavarian one, "A Birthday." These stories of 1911, though five of them are printed in *In a German Pension*, show a mellower spirit than the 1910 stories. There is a certain genial and kindly humor in "The Advanced Lady"; and love, in "The Swing of the Pendulum," in spite of the intrusion of a predatory male, leads to a conclusion acceptable to the central woman character. But nothing shows the change of attitude so clearly as "A Birthday." The theme is the birth of a child, and the father, Andreas Binzer, is shown as (being a male, inevitably) selfish, but sensitive, nervous, and finally overjoyed. There is nothing of the disgust with childbirth so clearly enunciated in "At Lehmann's" of the previous year.

What caused the change? Partly, one can only suspect, the happier love affair during 1911. But there is a deeper reason. In "A Birthday," Katherine Mansfield is for the first time drawing on her own family. In spite of the German names, "A Birthday" is set in Wellington and Andreas Binzer is a preliminary sketch for the mostly true-to-life picture of her father that was to dominate so many of her later stories. In "A Birthday" there is a harbor, there are ferns in a glass case, there is a gully, the wind shakes the window sashes: the scene is Wellington, so accurately depicted that one can today identify even the streets and the actual house in the story.

III

A few months after the publication of her first book, Katherine Mansfield moved on to her final love affair. This time it was permanent. The story of her meeting John Middleton Murry in 1912 and of their life together (they could not marry until 1918, when her husband divorced her) has been fully recorded by Murry and by Katherine Mansfield in her published letters. Henceforth, she had a center to work from, and her early disastrous affairs, though they continued to provide a few themes for stories, sank below the horizon. But it is not mere gossip-mongering to record them. Without a knowledge of them the critic must read her early stories as mere literary exercises. They are more than that. They are a first beginning at the recording of experiences often little transmuted in the telling.

During the next two years Katherine Mansfield wrote stories for the two journals that Murry successively edited, *Rhythm* and the *Blue Review*. Most of these are based on New Zealand material. They fall into two groups. First, three tales of violence, all involving murder—the sort of thing that English readers readily associate with a rough colonial background. The best known of these is "The Woman at the Store." The second group begins

where "A Birthday" left off. The New Zealand Burnell family begins to emerge, though they are not yet given a name: the little daydreaming girl in "How Pearl Button Was Kidnapped" (at first glance a mere fairy tale); the bullying father, the tender grandmother, the mother, and the family of little girls in "New Dresses" and "The Little Girl."

Early 1914 saw the collapse of Murry's journals. During the year that followed, Katherine Mansfield wrote two of her best stories to date, "Something Childish but Very Natural," a love story that is evidently her and Murry's love-in-a-cottage situation projected back to a couple of youngsters, and "An Indiscreet Journey," based on a visit she paid to Paris in early 1915 to renew acquaintance with an old admirer. To these months also belongs "The Little Governess," a longer story on several of her recurring themes—the young woman alone in the world, the predatory male, the unsympathetic foreign official. Katherine Mansfield had known them all. The story represents a technical advance. For the first time she is inside her character. We are at the beginning of that sensitive feeling for characters portrayed through their own fleeting thoughts that lies at the basis of all her mature work.

IV

IN 1915 occurred one of the several crises that determined her life. Her brother arrived from New Zealand on his way to the army. The exchange of old memories led to the writing of two short New Zealand sketches, "The Apple Tree"[1] and "The Wind Blows." Before the end of the year her brother was dead. When the first shock was over, she knew what lay before her—the *recherche du temps perdu*:

I want to write recollections of my own country. Yes, I want to write about my own country till I exhaust my store. Not only because it is a sacred debt that I pay to my country because my brother and I were born there, but also because in my thoughts I range with him over all the remembered places.

She was ill, and she and Murry moved for a time to the south of France. There at Bandol she completed in early 1916 her first major story, "The Aloe," a recollection of New Zealand. It was not published in

---

[1]In *The Scrapbook* (1939); not included in *Collected Stories* (1945).

its original form until 1930. She laid it aside for revision. Emotion and nostalgia were not enough. Technique required an intellectual effort that demanded more time and cooler reflection. The revision was published as "Prelude" in 1918. It is the story that set the standard and established the pattern for all her later work. The Burnell family are evoked in their early days, the little girls still small children, Stanley Burnell at the opening of his prosperous career, the whole told "in a kind of special prose" (the phrase is her own) that is one of the secrets of her originality.

During the two years following "The Aloe" she was increasingly oppressed by illness. She had seldom been completely in health since her first arrival in London. By the end of 1917 her illness was diagnosed as tuberculosis and in early 1918 she was back in Bandol again. The year between the two visits to Bandol saw her returning on ten occasions to the *New Age*, but not with New Zealand stories. While "Prelude" was maturing in her mind as her major work, she was content to publish only lighter stuff, perceptive but not very deeply felt. "Mr. Reginald Peacock's Day," with its simpering hero, and "A Dill Pickle," the story of the meeting of two disillusioned lovers, are typical of the group. The best of these is "Feuille d'Album," an adolescent love story, remarkable because it is her first full use of the interior monologue. In 1917 that meant being in the forefront of technical experiment.

Her writing of 1918 includes two New Zealand stories, "Sun and Moon," on the surface an allegory but in fact a Burnell family story of the "Prelude" group, and the unfinished "A Married Man's Story," an interior narrative in a Wellington setting. Her best two stories of the year are "Bliss," with its innocently happy wife who recognizes in a moment of horrified insight her successful rival, and the polished "Je ne parle pas français." This last represents a return to old experiences, handled with a technical competence that is approaching its peak. She revives her old memories of the woman on her own, abandoned in Europe by her lover. The situation of her earlier experience was reinforced by the circumstances in which she was writing. Murry was in London— where he had to earn a living. Katherine Mansfield, ill and alone in Bandol (except for the faithful Ida Baker), bombarding him with urgent and not always fair accusations of neglect, felt as abandoned as Mouse, who is finally deserted by her lover in Paris, in the caustic but effective ending of "Je ne parle pas français."

By spring 1918 she was in London again. She was married to Murry in May. Illness prevented much writing, and in later 1918 it had to be the Continent again for the winter. "The Man Without a Temperament," with its theme of a sick wife and coldly patient husband, is her comment on the period. It is of peculiar significance that its original title was "The Exile." The summer was spent back in England. After arranging for the publication of a volume of her stories of the last few years—they were published as *Bliss, and Other Stories* in late 1920 and included the subtle and evocative "Prelude"—she left again for the south of France. It was the final break with England, to which she was henceforth but a fleeting visitor. If she had to be an exile, it might as well be where her failing health had some expectations.

V

FROM then on, for a space of less than two years, Katherine Mansfield worked with the concentrated fury of a woman who has only a little time left. She had been publishing since she was nineteen. She was now thirty-two. The critics had ignored her first book in 1911. Her second, *Bliss*, was acclaimed on all sides. But she was dissatisfied with it: "A great part of my Constable book is *trivial*."[2] This is a harsh judgment. But in view of what she planned—and what she achieved in these remarkable two years—it was true.

The writing of these two final years was to yield a total almost as great as all the work of her previous career. It was done in two bursts of fertile activity, the first at Menton in the south of France during the winter of 1920–1921, and the second from the middle of 1921 till the middle of 1922, when she was with her husband in Switzerland and later was undergoing treatment in Paris. The last half-year of her life (she died on 9 January 1923) understandably produced nothing that has survived.

At Menton she wrote six stories. With her reputation rising rapidly, she found that the solider literary journals were now waiting for her, and all six were published variously in the *Athenaeum*, the *Nation*, and the *London Mercury*. Three are on her leitmotiv of the woman on her own in an unfriendly world. The central situations in "The Lady's Maid," "Miss

[2]Constable & Co. were Katherine Mansfield's publishers.

Brill," and "Life of Ma Parker" are variations on this theme, with the lonely woman now slipping into middle age. "The Daughters of the Late Colonel" is a magnificently envisaged story of two women devastated by the death of their father. In life he took everything from them, and his disappearance leaves them without a reason for existing. Constantia, the younger of the sisters, is based on Ida Baker, who (as revealed in *Letters*, 1951) drove Katherine Mansfield to alternate fits of exasperation and gratitude. Both aspects are present in Constantia. "The Young Girl," a slight but sensitive sketch of adolescence, and "The Stranger" complete the group written at Menton. "The Stranger" is a New Zealand story. Stanley Burnell (what matter if he is now called John Hammond, who had been Andreas Binzer?) waits on the Auckland waterfront for the liner bringing home his wife. Burnell is aging, as so many of Katherine Mansfield's characters are at this time, but he is the same man, bustling in public, sensitive and vulnerable in his private relations. His wife has been delayed at the bedside of a dying passenger, and Burnell jealously resents the intrusion: "They would never be alone together again."

When Katherine Mansfield moved to Switzerland, the pressure of work mounted: 1921 was the busiest year of her life. Stories poured from her pen, finished and ready for the publisher, sometimes within an evening, though the themes had often been dormant for years. This is the great year of the Burnell family sequence, lovingly remembered at various periods of their lives. "Sixpence" (excluded from *The Garden Party* volume of 1922 as "sentimental") shows Burnell punishing his small son and then relenting. The father-image has ceased being merely a big bully. In "An Ideal Family" he is sympathetically conceived (now "old Mr. Neave") as an old, failing man, swamped by his three daughters and his son, who has taken over the business. In "Her First Ball," daughter and son are young people, brought face to face with the cynicism of middle age. "The Voyage" recounts an earlier memory, the heroine a mere child with her beloved grandmother. The series culminated toward the end of the year with the magnificent perception of "At the Bay," where the children are youngsters at the family's seaside cottage, and "The Garden Party" (they are now the Sheridans), where the girls and their brother are almost grown up, and they meet for the first time the horror of death—and life—on the other side of the street. Katherine Mansfield in these sensitively felt stories is not merely recording experience. She is expressing a view of life on a basis of recorded memories.

All of this group and the six Menton stories were published in *The Garden Party, and Other Stories*. They do not exhaust its contents. Along with some earlier work there is the love story "Mr. and Mrs. Dove," delicately poised between mockery and sentiment, and a vicious delineation of a brittle woman rejecting the love of a devoted husband, "Marriage à la Mode," written perhaps in contrition to make peace with herself for having written "The Man Without a Temperament." *The Garden Party* evoked a chorus of praise on both sides of the Atlantic. By the end of the following year it had been reprinted once in England and seven times in America. If Katherine Mansfield wanted either popular fame or critical reputation, they both were hers now.

VI

It was too late to matter. Her illness was progressing, but she pushed ahead with her writing. Between the end of 1921 and the middle of 1922, when she ceased writing, she wrote sufficient stories for her final volume, *The Dove's Nest*, published in 1923, a few months after her death. It contains several stories on the relationship of husband and wife—"A Cup of Tea," "Honeymoon," "Widowed," "All Serene!"—and one on her recurring theme of the lonely woman, here deserted even by her pet bird, "The Canary." But the strength of the volume lies once again in the stories of her own town, preeminently in the classic re-creation of childhood "The Doll's House." The childhood is Katherine Mansfield's, the family is the now familiar Burnell group, the scene is an authentic Wellington suburb, where the creek and the house she describes are still discernible. But, like all her best New Zealand stories, it transcends mere locality. Her accurate rendering of background is only part of her larger accuracy in the rendering of life. To this final group of Wellington memories recalled belongs "Taking the Veil," with its adolescent daydreams, and, among the unfinished stories in the book, "A Bad Idea," "A Man and His Dog" (which is an appendix to "Prelude"), and "Susannah."

Two stories, both among the last things she wrote, bring the series to a close and complete the theme on which the death of her brother had launched her, the final repayment of the "sacred debt." The first is "Six Years After"—the title is self-explanatory for anyone with a knowledge of her life history—in which Stanley Burnell (he is now simply "Daddy") and his wife start on a voyage. For him the bustle of shipboard is enough. For his wife the memory of the dead son makes the experience of the journey intolerable. "Six Years After" provides a clue to "The Fly," which was assessed by that masterly critic of the short story E. J. O'Brien as one of the fifteen finest short stories ever written, "as inevitable as the passage of time." "The Fly," written in early 1922, when she knew that the finish was not far off, is often asserted to be her indictment of life. It is, rather, her clear-eyed admission that life goes on. Two old men, retired businessman and boss (both, aspects of Burnell), linger over the memory of the boss's son, killed "six years ago" in the war. When the old man goes, the boss plays with a fly ink-soaked on the blotting-paper, until the fly finally gives up the struggle:

> The boss lifted the corpse on the end of the paper-knife and flung it into the waste-paper basket. But such a grinding feeling of wretchedness seized him that he felt positively frightened. He started forward and pressed the bell for Macey.
>
> "Bring me some fresh blotting-paper," he said sternly, "and look sharp about it." And while the old dog padded away he fell to wondering what it was he had been thinking about before. What was it? It was . . . He took out his handkerchief and passed it inside his collar. For the life of him he could not remember.

This may be an indictment of life, but it is much more an admission that the dead pass on, and the living must live their own life. "The Fly" is full of symbolism that the author may not herself have recognized. The spirit of her dead brother, which had driven her on to such urgent activity, was finally at rest. The debt was paid.

VII

MUCH of the above could not have been written in the years immediately following her death, and criticism of Katherine Mansfield has tended to fasten on what could be judged solely from her published stories—her prose style, insight, technique. All of these are important both for an appreciation of her work and in view of the great influence she had on the art of the short story. She had the same kind of directive influence on the art of the short story as James Joyce had on the novel. After Joyce and Katherine Mansfield neither the novel nor the short story can ever be quite the same again. They beat a track to a higher point from which others can scan a wider horizon.

Criticism of her published stories, however, is powerfully reinforced and given a deeper significance by a knowledge of the sources of her material. Such a knowledge has become increasingly possible with the publication of Katherine Mansfield's own background writing—her *Journal* in 1927, her *Letters* in 1928, and in 1951 the full text of her letters to her husband. The importance of the New Zealand themes (for example) is clear enough to any careful reader of her later stories. But when we turn to her *Journal* of that period and find her haunted night after night with dreams that she is on shipboard sailing back to her own country, we do not need to be psychoanalysts to see the connection between "The Garden Party" and "The Doll's House" and the recurring dream pattern.

Until quite recently Katherine Mansfield's *Journal* and *Letters* have been the best commentary on her stories. But they are sometimes fragmentary and leave unexplained considerable passages in her own history. Biographical studies, which should expand and supplement her own account, have been largely hampered by the 12,000-mile separation between the two parts of her life and also because so many of her associates who are still alive have been chary of discussion. Ruth Mantz's study of 1933, although the author visited New Zealand, is slight, is based on partial evidence, and leaves her subject with all her major stories still to write. Sylvia Berkman's study of 1951 is a much more impressive piece of work, based on an accurate knowledge of the printed materials, of which there were many more available than in 1933, but had the bad luck to be written and published before the full text of the letters was available.

Antony Alpers, who published a biography in 1953, used the 1951 edition of the letters, and, as a New Zealander with substantial residence in England, he was in a position to both overcome the difficulties that earlier biographers had encountered and follow the pattern of her development. He was able to persuade several people to give accounts who had hitherto kept silence, notably Ida Baker, the French poet and novelist Francis Carco, and George

Bowden, Katherine Mansfield's first husband. His information on her father was faulty, however, and he portrayed him in a bad light. Since 1953 others have dug into bank accounts, family and school archives, and Katherine Mansfield's own manuscripts and have corrected the record in significant detail. Meanwhile, Ida Baker has published her memoirs, and numerous firsthand accounts of the London literary scene of Katherine Mansfield's time have appeared. Alpers published a completely rewritten version of his biography in 1980. It is as near to a standard biography as we are likely to see.

VIII

THE material of Katherine Mansfield's stories, based so directly on her own experiences, is in the central tradition of the English novel, the affairs of every day heightened by sensitivity and good writing. Her range is even more restricted than Jane Austen's few families in a country village. For her, one family and a few relationships were enough to express a universality of experience. Essentially the stress is on character and the subtle interrelationships of people in small groups, bound together by bonds of emotion. To express these she concentrates her writing, discarding the heavy lumber of narration and descriptive background. In the end she has not more than half a dozen themes. First, there is the woman alone in the world, as she had been in her younger days. As Katherine Mansfield grew older, so did this character age, a girl in "The Tiredness of Rosabel," a woman in "Life of Ma Parker" and "The Canary." Second, there are the stories of the man and woman for whom a happy relationship seems impossible because the woman is the victim of a predatory or an indifferent male, as in "The Little Governess," "This Flower," "The Man Without a Temperament," and "Je ne parle pas français."

In a small group of stories, the situation is reversed. In "The Black Cap," "The Escape," and the bitter "Marriage à la Mode," it is the husband who is loving and trusting and the wife who deserts him. Indeed, in Katherine Mansfield, a happy marriage relationship is apparent only in those stories that she based on her parents—Stanley and Linda, under these and other names, face life with confidence and together, in the pages of "Prelude," "At the Bay," and "The Garden Party," and can clearly survive the marital crises depicted in "The Stranger" and "Six Years After."

Her other major theme is children in their relationships with one another and with the adults in the family. The child-father bond is subtly drawn in a series of magnificent studies, starting with the resentment of the young child against the omnipotence of the parent in "Sixpence," "A Suburban Fairy Tale," and "New Dresses"; through relief at his departure from the house and indifference toward him, expressed most clearly in "At the Bay"; to a recognition, in "The Little Girl," that he is "Poor father! Not so big, after all"; and finally to a growing sympathy for him and, as child and parent grow older, a recognition of his adult problems, in "An Ideal Family." This sequence is rounded off with the warning conveyed in "The Daughters of the Late Colonel," where the daughter-father bond has persisted until life without the parent becomes impossible.

All of these relationships may be found in other writers. But in the delineation of children together Katherine Mansfield stands alone. Her lifelong discipline in entering into the mind of her subject ("I have just finished a story with a canary for a hero, and almost feel I have lived in a cage and pecked a piece of chickweed myself") is nowhere more essential than when the writer enters the mind of a child. If an adult writer portrays the mind of an adult character, only the most percipient critic can detect where the character is not fully realized and is "contaminated" by the writer's own personality. Because of this, the delineation of adult character and the impact of adult on adult is, by comparison, easier. The writer may "contaminate" his character with something of himself and still create on paper a credible personality. But the least "contamination" by the adult writer's personality of the character of a child he is creating on paper shows up immediately. Few children are drawn in literature without some adult perception showing through. The author's feeling of adult condescension or regret for his own lost childhood usually comes across. The very titles of books like *The Golden Age* or *When We Were Very Young* imply an adult assessment. But Mansfield portrays children as children, seen through their own eyes and the eyes of other children. Kezia and Lottie and Isabel Burnell and the Trout boys, Pip and Rags (and their dog, a uniquely children's dog), in "Prelude" and "At the Bay," with the unforgettable Lil and Our Else in "The Doll's House," are creations that stand by themselves in English writing.

IX

THE technique of the stories of Katherine Mansfield's maturity lies partly in their construction and partly in her lyrical use of language. Straightforward chronological narration is seldom favored, but rather an alternation of time present and time past (and sometimes time future), with scenes juxtaposed to heighten the emotional effect. In "The Daughters of the Late Colonel" the two tenses of the story (past, the happiness of life with father; present, the desolation of life without him) are implicit from the opening sentence, every apparently simple word of which has been written and placed with craftsmanlike care: "The week after was one of the busiest weeks of their lives."

The remainder of the story is an expansion of the implications of these opening words, in scenes alternating between present and past, with occasional shuddering glances into the empty future. The story opens with the two women anxiously discussing the disposition of their dead father's effects; it slips back a few days (Nurse Andrews will stay on for a week as guest); a few days further back, to the death of Father; forward to the present—the visit of the clergyman; back to the past—the scene at the funeral; forward to the present, and the problem again of Father's things: should his watch go to their brother, Benny, or to Cyril, the grandson? The question has the effect of sending the story to the past again—a former visit by Cyril; and this merges into Cyril's visit to his grandfather, the old man presented not as a memory but living and grimly in action. The story finally returns (through an interior monologue by one of the sisters) and remains in the bleak present. This manner of presenting a story is familiar enough today. Virginia Woolf and Joyce, to name but two major figures, have made it a commonplace in the novel. But "The Daughters of the Late Colonel" was written in 1920. *Ulysses* did not appear till 1922, and *Mrs. Dalloway* was published in 1925. Katherine Mansfield's handling of time and of interior monologue is her own.

Writing in her *Journal* of another story she is quite explicit about her method of construction: "What I feel the story needs so particularly is a very subtle variation of 'tense' from the present to the past and back again—and softness, lightness, and the feeling that all is in bud, with a play of humour over the character."

This play of time backward and forward is done with great narrative skill. She discards the clumsy mechanism of scene-shifting of the typical novel of the nineteenth and early twentieth centuries, and recaptures a narrative economy in transition from scene to scene that English fiction had lost since Jane Austen. In the story just mentioned, Cyril has written a note of condolence to his two aunts:

> Dear boy! What a blow his sweet, sympathetic little note had been! Of course, they quite understood; but it was most unfortunate.
> "It would have been such a point having him," said Josephine.
> "And he would have enjoyed it so," said Constantia, not thinking what she was saying.
> However, as soon as he got back he was coming to tea with his aunties. Cyril to tea was one of their rare treats.
> "Now, Cyril, you mustn't be frightened of our cakes. Your Auntie Con and I bought them at Buszard's this morning. We know what a man's appetite is."
>
> ("The Daughters of the Late Colonel," viii)

This skillfully written passage starts in the present, glimpses an unattainable future that is already past, shifts to the real future, and then, without a word of transition, introduces a long scene from the past.

The "subtle variation of 'tense'" is a notable feature of all Katherine Mansfield's later stories. It is often used with peculiar appropriateness as one of her means of quietly unfolding character. In "At the Bay" and "Prelude" Stanley Burnell and his mother live in the bustling present; his wife, Linda, dreams in her steamer chair beneath the manuka tree in a timeless past; Kezia and the children occupy the eternal present of childhood; and Beryl, the unmarried girl, lives in a continually imagined future.

X

THE second part of the passage quoted from her *Journal* emphasizes the care with which Katherine Mansfield contrived the feeling of each situation and character. Whether her people are the little girls of "The Doll's House" or schoolboys (like Hennie in "The Young Girl") or selfish young men and women (like the hero of "A Dill Pickle" and the heroine of "Revelations") or the older men and women of stories like "The Fly" and "The Voyage," the author never allows herself to come onstage as a presenter of whose intrusion we are conscious. She sinks herself inside each of her characters, thinking or speaking in their tone of voice. "Prelude" opens with the family disputing for space in the buggy:

There was not an inch of room for Lottie and Kezia in the buggy. When Pat swung them on top of the luggage they wobbled; the grandmother's lap was full and Linda Burnell could not possibly have held a lump of a child on hers for any distance.

That "lump of a child" is not Katherine Mansfield's comment. It is Linda's unexpressed thought, beautifully worked into the structure of a sentence that in its opening words had the simple function of carrying the narrative and now carries the tone of voice of one of the central characters.

This sense of always being inside the character is one of Katherine Mansfield's greatest contributions to the craft of fiction. Her interior monologues are, for contemporary readers, readily recognizable, though there is nothing mechanical or obvious about her use of them. In addition to examples already mentioned, "The Little Governess," "Feuille d'Album," "Taking the Veil," and "The Doll's House" (to cite stories both before and after she achieved her mature technique) all contain characters who are revealed through their own thoughts. But the innerness of her character-drawing goes beyond the interior monologue. In her best stories the world is always seen through the eyes of one of her characters. Where she describes scenery, it is not merely the background of a situation. It is conveyed to the reader emotionally, and uniquely, as only the person in the story can feel it. Episode vii of "At the Bay" is introduced by such a scene:

Over there on the weed-hung rocks that looked at low tide like shaggy beasts come down to the water to drink, the sunlight seemed to spin like a silver coin dropped into each of the small rock pools. They danced, they quivered, and minute ripples laved the porous shores. Looking down, bending over, each pool was like a lake with pink and blue houses clustered on the shores; and oh! the vast mountainous country behind those houses—the ravines, the passes, the dangerous creeks and fearful tracks that led to the water's edge.

The rocks like great beasts, the pool clustered round with "houses" backed by mountains, the sense of fear and danger—this is not the confident and factual downward-looking view of the adult; it is the viewpoint of a small child seeing objects larger than

herself, rendered even larger and more fearful by her fancy. The reader has in this manner been introduced to Kezia, the daydreaming little girl, though he must read another full page before she appears in person. But she is there already. We have approached the beach through her eyes.

Subtler still is Katherine Mansfield's remarkable (one might even dare to say unique) ability to shift the point of view (and so introduce several characters) within the confines of a single sentence. The opening of "Prelude" has already shown a narrative sentence shaping itself into the color of a person's thoughts. In "The Daughters of the Late Colonel" the two sisters ring for the maid: "And proud young Kate, the enchanted princess, came in to see what the old tabbies wanted now." Here within less than twenty words we shift from the point of view of the two sisters, awed and obscurely envious of the girl's dazzling youth, to the viewpoint of the maid, haughtily resentful of her elderly mistresses' having once again rung the bell. Not a word need be added. Not a word could be dropped. And yet it is all there.

XI

SEVERAL critics have pointed out the poetic qualities of Katherine Mansfield's writing. The American critic Conrad Aiken as early as 1921 in a review of *Bliss, and Other Stories* made the essential point. Katherine Mansfield writes a short story with the resources and the intention of lyrical poetry. Her stories should not be (and were not written to be) read as narratives in the ordinary sense, although considerable narrative movement is implied in the majority of them. She conveys, as a lyric poet conveys, the feeling of human situations, and her stories have all the unity and shapeliness and the concentrated diction of implied emotion that characterize the well-wrought lyric. As with the lyric, her stories yield their full meaning only on rereading, when the reader can link up the implications of phrase upon phrase that are not always apparent on the first run-through. And like the lyrics of a poet the stories illuminate each other. An early critic, G. S. Street, writing in the *London Mercury* in 1921, confessed how he found his clue to the apparently fragmentary "Bliss" when he reread the conclusion of "The Daughters of the Late Colonel." This illumination of one story by another is particularly evident in the

New Zealand family sequence, which, when read *as* a sequence, not in the order of composition but in the internal time-order of the family's own history, is one of the most sensitive and finely conceived writings of our time.

Each separate part, even each separate phrase and word, of her best stories contributes to the final emotional impression of the whole. In "Mr. and Mrs. Dove," the hero is young, insecure, impressionable, and romantic. How well this is captured in a few lines, as Reggie walks toward the house of the girl he is in love with:

"And where are you going, if your mother may ask?" asked the mater.

It was over at last, but Reggie did not slow down until he was out of sight of the house and half-way to Colonel Proctor's. Then only he noticed what a top-hole afternoon it was. It had been raining all the morning, later summer rain, warm, heavy, quick, and now the sky was clear, except for a long tail of little clouds, like ducklings, sailing over the forest. There was just enough wind to shake the last drops off the trees; one warm star splashed on his hand. Ping!—another drummed on his hat. The empty road gleamed, and the hedges smelled of briar, and how big and bright the hollyhocks glowed in the cottage gardens.
("Mr. and Mrs. Dove," in *The Garden Party*, p. 120)

This is admirably done. It is not so much the articulation of the narrative as the implications of the words used that convey the impression of the very ordinary young man ("mater" and "top-hole") who with a sense of release enjoys sensuously the sights and sounds and smells of the fresh afternoon. The fanciful duckling image, the sailing image, the "gleam" of the road, and the "one warm star splashed on his hand": the whole summer afternoon and his sense of elation are compressed into poetic language implicit with emotive overtones, the achievement of the aim Katherine Mansfield had, years earlier, set before her: "Perhaps not in poetry. Nor perhaps in prose. Almost certainly in a kind of *special prose*." One of her greatest achievements lay in this, the creation of a prose style that could borrow from poetry but nevertheless remain prose, firmly based on a simple and even colloquial movement.

XII

SINCE the language—one might almost say the diction—of Katherine Mansfield's writing, with its subtle evocation of mood and scene and its poetical use of overtones, is such an important part of her meaning, it is important for the English—or, for that matter, any—reader to remember that certain of her words are used in a sense peculiar to New Zealand and not current in England. In her letters these words and phrases are freely used. There she talks of "swags" of strawberries; a good issue of a journal is "a perfect corker"; depressed by the winter weather of Italy she "had a rare tangi over this climate"; she will do better reviews and send two "bonzers." "Corker" and "bonzer" are both New Zealand slang words corresponding roughly to the current English "smasher"; "swag" is the swagman's bundle; and "tangi"—the word is Maori—is standard New Zealand usage for a general lamentation.

In the stories also there is an occasional New Zealand colloquialism, but only where it is appropriate—among small children, or on the lips of a workman:

"Say, cross my heart straight-dinkum."
The little girls said it.
("At the Bay," in *Collected Stories*, p. 216)

But when they reached the top of the hill and began to go down the other side the harbour disappeared, and although they were still in the town they were quite lost. Other carts rattled past. Everybody knew the storeman.
"Night, Fred."
"Night O," he shouted.
("Prelude," in *Collected Stories*, p. 16)

New Zealand words or usages of a more general nature are introduced to evoke the local scene. The "piece of loose iron" that bangs on the roof in several stories tells the reader snug under slates or tiles that the early colonial houses were roofed with corrugated iron, invariably referred to simply as "iron." The "creek" that runs through "Prelude" is a little stream, not an arm of the sea as it would be in British English. The "bush-covered hills" at the opening of "At the Bay" are covered with heavy forest, not small bushes. Perhaps no word of Katherine Mansfield's, with her insistence on the importance of half-tones and quarter-tones, is so likely to convey the wrong tone as the "paddocks" that surround the houses of her characters. "Paddock" in British usage implies horses, with an undertone of hunting or at least a pony club. Nothing could be further from Katherine Mansfield's meaning. "Paddock" in New Zealand is simply the normal word for field—a grassy meadow into which Kezia and the children can run.

On occasion the setting of the scene in New Zealand is done obliquely, without the use of local language, and yet with quiet precision. In "Prelude" toward the end of the day Kezia waits in the empty house:

Kezia liked to stand so before the window. She liked the feeling of the cold shining glass against her hot palms, and she liked to watch the funny white tops that came on her fingers when she pressed them hard against the pane. As she stood there, the day flickered out and the dark came.

This is not the close of an English day with its slow twilight and its imperceptible gradation to night. It is the quick oncoming of night that Katherine Mansfield remembered from the latitude of her childhood.

XIII

THIS essay has been confined to Katherine Mansfield's life-story so far as it seems to be of importance for an understanding of her work and a critical examination of the literary quality of her stories. There has been considerable writing on her (since the publication of her *Journal*), on her mysticism, her "secret," her isolated "purity," which would make her a vaguely symbolic and saintly figure. It cannot be denied that chapter and verse can be found for much of this kind of thing in the later entries in her *Journal.* It is well to remember that in her final year she was a very sick woman, facing death with only the rags of a Christian faith and ready to grasp at dubious philosophic alternatives; she was, too, throughout her whole life in many ways (though never in her craft) naive. She had the intellectual gaps of the self-educated woman that she was. The final scenes of faith-healing under the guidance of a crazy Russian while she formulated a spiritual creed can hardly be the basis for a fair judgment either of her real quality or of her view of life. Katherine Mansfield the writer had laid down her pen many months before that melancholy final passage.

There is nothing vague or nebulous—or naive—about her writings. She is assured in her craft, and knowledgeable even to the placing of a comma. She writes with precision, knowing the effect she intends and achieving it in all her best work with an accuracy and an inexplicable rightness in prose expression that is perhaps in the end the only real secret that died with her.

XIV

THE disparity between the assured professionalism of the short stories and the otherworldliness that emerges from the *Journal* is something that I have always found difficult to reconcile. Yet there, published in the *Journal* of 1927 and the expanded definitive edition of 1954, are her own comments on life and letters, clearly a primary—if not indeed *the* primary—source for both biographer and critic. It is up to each to effect his own reconciliation of the two Katherine Mansfields or to ignore the wraith of the *Journal* and focus attention on the meticulous craft of the storyteller.

There the matter might have rested. But after the death in 1957 of John Middleton Murry there came on the market a large collection of Katherine Mansfield's notebooks and manuscripts. These were bought by the New Zealand government for the Alexander Turnbull Library, Wellington. They consist of four diaries (for 1914, 1915, 1920, and 1922), which (like most other people's diaries) peter out somewhere between February and March, some thirty notebooks filled with story fragments, ideas for stories varying from a few words to several pages, quotations, personal observations, notes on her reading, lists of household expenses kept in meticulous detail, accurately kept income and expenditure accounts (she was very much, as it appears, the banker's daughter), and some hundred single sheets onto which are copied poems, vignettes, a section of her abortive novel "Maata," an unfinished play, and some finished stories copied out ready for the printer. It is a remarkable record of a writer at work.

A close comparison of this heterogeneous mass of material with the books published after her death has revealed some interesting facts. From this untidy heap of material Murry created the *Journal* of 1927; from some of the leftover pieces he created *The Scrapbook* of 1939; and working over it once again a decade later he created the definitive *Journal* of 1954. Murry was a brilliant editor, and his most brilliant work was the synthesis of his wife's loose papers in what became—justifiably—recognized as a minor classic.

But synthesis it was. Katherine Mansfield did not keep a journal in any usual sense of the word. She bought occasionally a pocket diary and for a few weeks made brief entries. In her working notebooks, among the drafts of stories and notes on possible situations and characters, she made from time to time a personal entry or observation. Something like half of the published *Journal* consists of passages that were in no recognized sense journal material; indeed one or two of them are demonstrably story fragments, fiction, not personal records. The editor has interpolated these pieces, often at precise dates, even where his own penciled notes on the source material reveal that he has doubts about the date. He regularly salvages passages of poetry (by herself and others) that she had copied out—sometimes on a single undatable sheet—and inserts them at appropriate places, to expand and illuminate a diary entry that originally stood in isolation. Occasionally a passage from one notebook is run together, without indication, with a passage from another notebook of different date. The omissions, even in the "definitive" edition, are considerable. The working writer, the businesswoman—the banker's daughter—drop out of sight. There is nothing in the published versions of the *Journal* that is not by Katherine Mansfield. But by selection and by maneuvering the raw material, particularly by the juxtaposition of passages originally unconnected and by printing diary entries continuous with scraps of story-drafting without indication of the change in his material, the editor has created something that was not in the manuscripts and notebooks, a persona, an idealized picture of his dead wife.

It is a curious business so to dismember a book that many readers have come to cherish. And one must be fair. Murry is absolutely scrupulous in his own penciled annotations on the Mansfield manuscripts. He indicates his omissions, and sometimes even writes in his reasons for the omission. He handled the actual documents like a scholar. He published what he decided to transcribe as a creative editor. He was, after all, writing a memorial portrait, not a biography.

But whatever the literary value of the published *Journal*, its value to biographers and critics is severely limited by the editorial method. Any further biographical or critical work on Katherine Mansfield will have to be based on the notebooks and not on the *Journal*, which no longer can retain the status of a primary document. The Katherine Mansfield of the *Journal* is an intense and over-rarefied spirit, conjured up by piety and affection. From the notebooks, as a full edition will show, she emerges as what must be a truer and certainly a more interesting figure, the writer in the workshop with her nose to the grindstone.

There was, as one had always suspected, only one

Katherine Mansfield. She is not as pleasant a creature as the persona. She is more businesslike, ruthless on occasion, and sometimes quite cold-blooded. Further confirmation of this emerged some years ago, when her three surviving sisters were asked for their memories of her in a radio interview. The text was published in 1963 (see the bibliography). One sister said, "I think she was very selfish at times," and the second responded, "She was completely self-centered, she was ruthless." This is not the Katherine Mansfield of the legend; but it is the Katherine Mansfield of the notebooks, a single-minded writer—and a more credible human being.

SELECTED BIBLIOGRAPHY

I. Bibliography. R. E. Mantz, *The Critical Bibliography of Katherine Mansfield* (London, 1931), some inaccuracies corrected in Berkman's 1951 study, listed below.

II. Collected Works. *Collected Stories* (London, 1945); D. M. Davin, ed., *Selected Stories* (London, 1953); I. A. Gordon, ed., *Undiscovered Country: The New Zealand Stories of Katherine Mansfield* (London, 1974).

III. Separate Works. *In a German Pension* (London, 1911), stories, repr. (New York, 1926); *Prelude* (Richmond, Eng., 1918), story; *Je ne parle pas français* (London, 1918), story; *Bliss, and Other Stories* (London, 1920); *The Garden Party, and Other Stories* (New York–London, 1922); *The Dove's Nest, and Other Stories* (New York–London, 1923); *Poems* (London, 1923; New York, 1924); *Something Childish, and Other Stories* (London, 1924), published in U.S. as *The Little Girl*; J. M. Murry, ed., *Journal* (London, 1927), autobiography, rev. and enl. ed. (1954); *The Aloe* (London, 1930), story, original form of *Prelude* of 1918; J. M. Murry, ed., *Novels and Novelists* (London, 1930), reviews contributed to the *Athenaeum* 1919–1920; J. M. Murry, ed., *The Scrapbook of Katherine Mansfield* (London, 1939), miscellany; I. A. Gordon, ed., *The Urewera Notebook of Katherine Mansfield* (Wellington, N.Z.–London, 1978), a fully annotated ed. of her 1907 travel diary; M. Scott, ed., "Katherine Mansfield: The Unpublished Manuscripts," in *Turnbull Library Record* (January 1940–November 1962; n.s. March 1967– , Wellington, N.Z.), a continuing series of transcripts from the library's MSS holdings, seven parts published to date, most recent one in 1979.

IV. Letters. J. M. Murry, ed., *Letters*, 2 vols. (London, 1928); J. M. Murry, ed., *Letters to John Middleton Murry, 1913–1922* (London, 1951), contains full texts of letters given partially in earlier ed. of letters; "Forty-six Letters by Katherine Mansfield" (to Anne Estelle Rice and Sydney and Violet Schiff), *Adam International Review*, no. 300 (1965).

Note: An edition of Mansfield's letters, including hundreds of unpublished ones, is in progress at Oxford University Press under the editorship of Margaret Scott, assisted by Vincent O'Sullivan.

V. BIOGRAPHICAL AND CRITICAL STUDIES. J. W. N. Sullivan, "The Story-Writing Genius," *Athenaeum* (April 1920); C. Aiken, "The Short Story as Poetry," *Freeman* (May 1921); M. Armstrong, "The Art of Katherine Mansfield," *Fortnightly Review*, 113:484 n.s. (March 1923); G. S. Hubbell, "Katherine Mansfield and Kezia," *Sewanee Review* (July–September 1927); E. Wagenknecht, "Katherine Mansfield," *English Journal* (April 1928).

R. E. Mantz and J. M. Murry, *The Life of Katherine Mansfield* (London, 1933), chiefly her early years; F. Carco, *Souvenirs sur Katherine Mansfield* (Paris, 1934), recollections by a writer on whom Katherine Mansfield based a character in several of her French stories; E. Schneider, "Katherine Mansfield and Checkhov," *Modern Language Notes* (June 1935); A. Maurois, *Poets and Prophets: Portraits and Criticism* (London, 1936); W. A. Sewell, *Katherine Mansfield: A Critical Essay* (Auckland, N.Z., 1936); W. Cather, *Not Under Forty* (London, 1936); J. M. Murry, *Between Two Worlds: An Autobiography* (London, 1936); H. Beauchamp, *Reminiscences and Recollections* (New Plymouth, N.Z., 1937), contains ch. on Katherine Mansfield by G. H. Scholefield; W. Orton, *The Last Romantic* (London, 1937); A. D. M. Hoare, *Some Studies in the Modern Novel* (London, 1938); D. Daiches, *The Novel in the Modern World* (Chicago, 1939).

H. E. Bates, *The Modern Short Story* (London, 1941); I. A. Gordon, "Katherine Mansfield, New Zealander," *New Zealand New Writing* (1943, Wellington, N.Z.); L. E. Rillo, *Katherine Mansfield and Virginia Woolf* (Buenos Aires, 1944); V. S. Pritchett, "Review of *Collected Stories*," *New Statesman and Nation* (February 1946); "Katherine Mansfield's Stories," *Times Literary Supplement* (March 1946); P. Lawlor, *The Mystery of Maata* (Wellington, N.Z., 1946); J. M. Murry, *Katherine Mansfield and Other Literary Portraits* (London, 1949).

S. Berkman, *Katherine Mansfield: A Critical Study* (New Haven, Conn., 1951), excellent study, contains a detailed life, with information from one of Katherine Mansfield's sisters, good bibliographical notes; A. Alpers, *Katherine Mansfield: A Biography* (New York, 1953), at the time of its publication the fullest biography, with new material from Katherine Mansfield's associates, but contains errors on Sir Harold Beauchamp that were corrected in 1980 ed. (see below); I. A. Gordon, "The Editing of Katherine Mansfield's Journal and Scrapbook," *Landfall* (March 1959, Christchurch, N.Z.).

B. Brophy, "Katherine Mansfield," *London* (December 1962); O. Leeming, "Katherine Mansfield and Her Family," *New Zealand Listener* (29 March and 11 April 1963, Wellington, N.Z.), text of radio interview with Katherine Mansfield's sisters, revealing and important; C. A. M. Mortelier, "Origine et développment d'une legende:

Katherine Mansfield en France," *Études Anglaises* IV (1970), excellent survey of French critical opinion; I. Baker, *Katherine Mansfield: The Memories of LM* (London, 1971), the memoirs of Katherine Mansfield's schoolfellow at Queen's College and lifetime companion; I. A. Gordon, "The Banker and the Banker's Daughter," *New Zealand Listener* (27 November 1972, Wellington, N.Z.), concerned with Sir Harold Beauchamp's lifelong financial support of Katherine Mansfield; V. O'Sullivan, "The Magnetic Chain: Notes and Approaches to K.M.," *Landfall* (June 1975, Christchurch, N.Z.); I. A. Gordon, "Warmth and Hydrangeas: Katherine Mansfield's Wellington Years," *New Zealand Listener* (8 May 1976), sheds new light on the years 1907–1908 with documentation of Katherine Mansfield's enrollment in a technical college for commercial subjects; A. Alpers, *Katherine Mansfield* (London, 1980), a completely rewritten version of the 1953 biography, with fuller documentation and correction of misapprehensions contained in the first version; now the standard biography.

LIST OF SHORT STORIES

(The title in italics refers to the volume in which the story first appeared. Stories marked with an asterisk were published as unfinished stories in *The Dove's Nest*.)

"About Pat," *Scrapbook*; "The Advanced Lady," *In a German Pension*; *"All Serene!" *The Dove's Nest*; "The Aloe," see "Prelude"; "The Apple Tree," *Scrapbook*; "At Lehmann's," *In a German Pension*; "At Putnam's Pier," *Scrapbook*; "At the Bay," *The Garden Party*; "Baby Jean," *Scrapbook*; *"A Bad Idea," *The Dove's Nest*; "Bains Turcs," *Something Childish*; "Bank Holiday," *The Garden Party*; "The Baron," *In a German Pension*; "A Birthday," *In a German Pension*; "The Black Cap," *Something Childish*; "A Blaze," *In a German Pension*; "Bliss," *Bliss*; "By Moonlight," *Scrapbook*; "The Canary," *The Dove's Nest*; "Carnation," *Something Childish*; "Cassandra," *Scrapbook*; "The Child-Who-Was-Tired," *In a German Pension*; "A Cup of Tea," *The Dove's Nest*.

*"Daphne," *The Dove's Nest*; "The Dark Hollow," *Scrapbook*; "The Daughters of the Late Colonel," *The Garden Party*; "A Dill Pickle," *Bliss*; "The Doll's House," *The Dove's Nest*; "The Dressmaker," *Scrapbook*; "The Escape," *Bliss*; "Father and the Girls," *The Dove's Nest*; "Feuille d'Album," *Bliss*; "The Fly," *The Dove's Nest*; "Frau Brechenmacher Attends a Wedding," *In a German Pension*; "Frau Fischer," *In a German Pension*.

"The Garden Party," *The Garden Party*; "Germans at Meat," *In a German Pension*; "Her First Ball," *The Garden Party*; *"Honesty," *The Dove's Nest*; "Honeymoon," *The Dove's Nest*; "How Pearl Button Was Kidnapped," *Something Childish*; "An Ideal Family," *The Garden Party*; "An

Indiscreet Journey," *Something Childish;* "Je ne parle pas français," *Bliss;* "The Journey to Bruges," *Something Childish;* "Kezia and Tui," *Scrapbook.*

"The Lady's Maid," *The Garden Party;* "Last Words to Youth," *Scrapbook;* "Late at Night," *Something Childish;* "Life Is Not Gay," *Scrapbook;* "Life of Ma Parker," *The Garden Party;* "The Little Girl," *Something Childish;* "The Little Governess," *Bliss;* "The Lost Battle," *Scrapbook;* "Love-Lies-Bleeding," *Scrapbook;* "The Luft Bad," *In a German Pension;* *"A Man and His Dog," *The Dove's Nest;* "The Man Without a Temperament," *Bliss;* "Marriage à la Mode," *The Garden Party;* *"A Married Man's Story," *The Dove's Nest;* "Millie," *The Garden Party;* "Miss Brill," *The Garden Party;* "Mr. and Mrs. Dove," *The Garden Party;* "Mr. and Mrs. Williams," *The Dove's Nest;* "Mr. Reginald Peacock's Day," *Bliss;* "The Modern Soul," *In a German Pension;* "New Dresses," *Something Childish.*

"Pension Séguin," *Something Childish;* "The Pessimist," *Scrapbook;* "Pictures," *Bliss;* "Poison," *Something Childish;* "Prelude" ("The Aloe," rev.), *Bliss;* "Psychology," *Bliss;* "The Quarrel," *Scrapbook;* "Revelations," *Bliss;* "Rose Eagle," *Scrapbook;* "The Scholarship," *Scrapbook;* *"Second Violin," *The Dove's Nest;* "See-Saw," *Some-*

thing *Childish;* "Sewing-Class," *Scrapbook;* "The Sheridans," *Scrapbook;* "The Singing Lesson," *The Garden Party;* "The Sister of the Baroness," *In a German Pension;* *"Six Years After," *The Dove's Nest;* "Sixpence," *Something Childish;* "Sleeping House," *Scrapbook;* "Something Childish but Very Natural," *Something Childish;* "Spring Pictures," *Something Childish;* "Strange Visitor," *Scrapbook;* "The Stranger," *The Garden Party;* "A Suburban Fairy Tale," *Something Childish;* *"Such a Sweet Old Lady," *The Dove's Nest;* "Sun and Moon," *Bliss;* *"Susannah," *The Dove's Nest;* "The Swing of the Pendulum," *In a German Pension.*

"Taking the Veil," *The Dove's Nest;* "Tea on the Train," *Scrapbook;* "There Is No Answer," *Scrapbook;* "This Flower," *Something Childish;* "The Tiredness of Rosabel," *Something Childish;* "The Toothache Sunday," *Scrapbook;* "A Truthful Adventure," *Something Childish;* "Two Tuppenny Ones, Please," *Something Childish;* "Violet," *Something Childish;* "The Voyage," *The Garden Party;* *"The Weak Heart," *The Dove's Nest;* *"Widowed," *The Dove's Nest;* "The Wind Blows," *Bliss;* "The Woman at the Store," *Something Childish;* "The Wrong House," *Something Childish;* "The Young Girl," *The Garden Party.*

JOYCE CARY
(1888-1957)

Walter Allen

IN a famous passage in the *Biographia Literaria* (1817), Samuel Taylor Coleridge isolates two opposed modes of the creative activity in their purest and most comprehensive expression:

While Shakespeare darts himself forth, and passes into all forms of character and passion, the one Proteus of the fire and flood, Milton attracts all forms and things to himself, into the unity of his own ideal. All things and modes of action shape themselves anew in the being of Milton; while Shakespeare becomes all things, yet for ever remaining himself.

Coleridge is not making a value judgment; he is contrasting the objective imagination with the subjective—we might say, the extrovert as artist with the introvert.

Few poets and novelists are so completely of their type as William Shakespeare and John Milton; between the two extremes are infinite gradations. Yet if one looks at English fiction since the 1930's in the light of Coleridge's distinction, it is apparent that it has been predominantly Miltonic, subjective, introvert; so much so that the Shakespearean, objective, extroverted writer stands out with the novelty of the exceptional. He appears old-fashioned, or at least out of step with his time. The neat generalizations we evolve to sum up contemporary writing do not seem to apply to him. And this, perhaps, is the first thing that strikes us when we contemplate the novelist Joyce Cary against the background of his contemporaries. We are immediately aware of his *difference*, and the first difference is that preeminently he is "the one Proteus" of the English novel of his time. Like the poet as seen by John Keats, he appears to have "no identity—he is continually in for and filling some other Body." So in turn, it seems without the slightest difficulty and with the greatest air of conviction, he becomes an African warrior, an African clerk from the mission school, an Irish landowner, an evacuee Cockney delinquent boy, a middle-aged domestic servant in prison for theft, a crotchety old lawyer, a painter of genius, the wife of a Radical politician. He is, to put it at the lowest, a superb impersonator, a truly protean actor. This in itself is much; but what gives him a value beyond this is the fact that his novels, taken together, are the expression of a view of life interesting and important in its own right, a view of life so considered and coherent as to be a whole system of belief. His novels are self-contained entities. Cary is as much "outside" his work as Gustave Flaubert was, so his system of belief is never explicitly stated in his novels; but it can be derived from them, and it is the substratum of their being.

Standing apart from what are usually judged the main tendencies of his time in fiction, Cary also stands apart from the majority of contemporary English novelists in the circumstances of his life. He came to the writing of fiction relatively late; his first novel, *Aissa Saved*, did not appear until 1932, when he was forty-four. He was born in Londonderry, in Northern Ireland, in 1888, of a family originally from Devon; he returned to both locales in his novels. He was an art student in Paris before going up to Oxford, and after Oxford he served in the Balkan War of 1912–1913 with a British Red Cross unit, an experience described in the posthumously published *Memoir of the Bobotes* (1964). In 1913 he joined the Nigerian Political Service, serving in the World War I campaigns against the Germans in West Africa, until he resumed his duties as magistrate and executive officer in a remote region of Nigeria. It was not until his retirement in 1920 to Oxford, where he lived until his death in 1957, that he began to write. He came to literature, then, after a career unlike that of most novelists, a career spent among primitive peoples and largely concerned with government and administration.

He published fifteen novels—a sixteenth, put together by other hands, and another, unfinished work appeared posthumously; two narrative poems, *Marching Soldier* (1945) and *The Drunken Sailor* (1947); *Art and Reality* (1958), a volume of criticism based on the Clark Lectures he delivered at Cambridge in 1956; two works of political philosophy, *Power in Men* (1939) and *The Process of Real Freedom* (1943); and two studies of African problems, *The Case for African Freedom* (1941) and *Britain and West Africa* (1946). In *The Case for African Freedom* Cary describes himself as a man who

after ten years of active, thoughtless and various experience in the world, began, rather late in youth, to ask what it amounted to; to dig up all his foundations, to find out exactly what they were; who discovered then, as you might expect, that some of them were mud, some were hollow caves of air, others sand; and who then slowly and painfully rebuilt them, as far as he could manage the task, as a coherent whole, on which to found a new life and a new mind.

It was from this transvaluation of values following a life largely removed from literary preoccupations that Cary's fiction sprang.

II

ARTISTIC development in the usual sense is absent from Cary's novels. One reason lies in his method of work. "I do not," he said, "write one novel at a time. The process is more like collecting. . . . I have a great number of . . . manuscripts in every stage of development." Yet a general movement may be traced through his work, a movement from the treatment of the comparatively simple theme to that of the much more complex; and in retrospect, his novels seem to fall into four main groups, which may be loosely characterized as the African novels: *Aissa Saved, An American Visitor* (1933), *The African Witch* (1936), and *Mister Johnson* (1939); the novels of childhood: *Charley Is My Darling* (1940) and *A House of Children* (1941); the novels *Herself Surprised* (1941), *To Be a Pilgrim* (1942), and *The Horse's Mouth* (1944), which relate the history of their time through the individual stories of three characters whose lives to some extent are intertwined; and the novels written after those: *The Moonlight* (1946), *A Fearful Joy* (1949), and the Chester Nimmo trilogy, comprising *Prisoner of Grace* (1952), in which Cary appears

again as the historian of the past seventy years of English life as seen through significant characters, *Except the Lord* (1953), and *Not Honour More* (1955). The classification is admittedly very rough; and the list omits *Castle Corner* (1938), which was published during what one thinks of as Cary's African period and which seems to me a brilliant failure, despite the huge gallery of characters and the extraordinary vividness of its description of Anglo-Irish life and the rise of colonial imperialism in the 1890's. *Castle Corner* is an early attempt at the novel of contemporary or near-contemporary history that Cary wrote so successfully a few years later.

All these novels, despite their great variety of scenes, actions, and characters, are of a piece; only Cary could have written them. Each is a metaphorical statement, a statement expressed through images of human beings in action, of Cary's underlying beliefs about the nature of man and the universe, of his philosophy. But the word "philosophy" may well bring us up short. A man may have the profoundest, most comprehensive, and wisest views on the nature of things and still, when he attempts fiction, be a very poor novelist. Novelists and philosophers follow different modes of apprehending reality; that is why novelist-philosophers are so rare. Normally nothing is so much beside the point in the discussion of a novel as its author's beliefs, for many great novels have been written by men whose beliefs have been superficial, absurd, and even ignoble. And the validity of Cary's beliefs is not the first thing that concerns us here. What is important now is that his characters, along with the technical means he uses in order to render them in action, all originate in his beliefs about the nature of man. He has stated these beliefs explicitly in his political philosophy; they may equally well be deduced from his fiction.

The characters of every novelist or dramatist, no matter how protean his imagination, bear a family resemblance to one another. This is true even of Shakespeare's. Cary's characters too are plainly products of the same man's imagination. Black or white, rich or poor, male or female, they have certain outstanding qualities in common. Aissa, in *Aissa Saved*; Bewsher and Obai, in *An American Visitor*; Rackham, Judy Coote, Louis Aledai, Schlemm, in *The African Witch*; Jarvis, in *Castle Corner*; Mr. Johnson, in the novel of that name; Charley, in *Charley Is My Darling*; Pinto, Delia, Anketel, in *A House of Children*; Sara Monday and Rozzie, in *Herself Surprised*; Wilcher, in *To Be a Pilgrim*; Jimson, in *The Horse's Mouth*; Aunt Rose and Harry Dawburn, in *The Moonlight*; Tabitha Baskett, Lord Gollan, and Bonser, in *A Fearful Joy*; Nimmo, in *Prisoner of Grace*; empire-builders, warriors, clerks, drunken tutors, children, cooks, barmaids, lawyers, painters, spinsters, wives, mistresses, politicians, all the characters that seem typical of Cary are in the grip of what can only be called the creative imagination. Wilcher is in some ways an exception, but he recognizes its power in others, as when he says of his sister Lucy and her husband, Brown, the hellfire-and-damnation evangelist from the working class:

They were both people of power; life ran in them with a primitive force and innocence. They were close to its springs as children are close, so that its experiences, its loves, its wonders, its furies, its mysterious altruism, came to them as children, like mysteries, and gave them neither peace nor time to fall into sloth or decadence.

(*To Be a Pilgrim*, p. 99)[1]

The creative imagination: Cary is its novelist and its celebrant. His characters are impelled by fantasies personal in the deepest sense, unique to each one of them, which must be translated into action. Life about them is, as it were, so much raw material that must be shaped according to their fantasies, which are never seen as fantasies because they are so fundamental to the characters who are moved by them. And the shaping fantasy, creative imagination, is something belonging to man by virtue of his being man. Cary's *Power in Men* begins:

The weakest child has power and will. Its acts are its own. It can be commanded, but it need not obey. It originates each least movement. It is an independent source of energy which grows with its life and ends only with its death.
This power is creative. . . .
This creative power is free. . . .

He goes on: "Liberty is creation in the act. It is therefore eternal and indestructible." And elsewhere, in his broadcast conversation with Lord David Cecil, published in the *Adam International Review* as "The Novelist at Work" (1950), he spoke of "this world which is condemned to be free; which is condemned to be free and condemned to live by its imagination." And the creative action of the imagination is unceasing, continuous, each man "trying to create a universe which suits his feelings." Inevi-

tably, since each man is unique and his shaping fantasy unique, his fantasies clash with those of his fellows and, often, with the established order of society, the generally accepted scheme of things. For the individual the consequences may be tragic; equally, from the standpoint of society, they may be comic. In Cary's novels the comic and the tragic are different sides of the one coin.

An important part of Cary's main theme is the creative imagination of the individual in action, in conflict with the imaginations of others or with authority. To begin with, in his African novels, he dramatized this conflict as the conflict between races and colors; between modes of being alien, and more or less incomprehensible, to each other. We are shown in these novels primitive peoples confronted with a new and almost wholly unintelligible civilization, taking what they want from the white man's religion and way of life and making of it a new thing, satisfying to them but quite baffling to the white administrators and missionaries. One thinks especially of the mission scenes in these novels: the native who has "got" Christianity does not become as a result any more like his white Christian mentors; indeed, his interpretation of Christianity may appear to them as a blasphemous parody. But the "Christianized" native is in conflict not only with his saddened white teachers, but also with his fellows who are still pagan and with those who are Moslem. The African world described, then, is one in which everyone is at cross-purposes with everyone else. Inevitably, the tragic and the comic are inextricably mingled.

As renderings and interpretations of primitive psychology, these novels are among the best we have in English, and an index of Cary's success in them is the fact that the white characters are revealed as no less essentially strange than the black. Cary enters the minds of both with an impartial gusto and sympathy, as E. M. Forster, for example, in *A Passage to India* (1924), does not enter the minds of his English characters. The resident magistrate Rudbeck, in *Mister Johnson*, is just as much caught by compulsive fantasy, the fantasy of himself as a builder of roads—there are all sorts of good reasons for building roads, but in his case they are all rationalizations of an overmastering desire to build roads for the sake of building roads—as is the infinitely comic, infinitely pathetic Johnson himself, the clerk from the mission school who identifies himself with the white man's way of life and, full of lordly exuberance and expansiveness, combines the ingenuousness of a child with the myth-making mind of a poet—to his

[1]Quotations from the works are from the *Carfax Edition* (London, 1951–1967).

ultimate catastrophe, death at the hands of the white man's justice.

It was perhaps a natural step for Cary to take, to pass from the representation of primitives to the representation of children. It was wholly typical of him that when he did so he should write in rapid succession two novels depicting children placed in utterly dissimilar circumstances. The first is *Charley Is My Darling.* The second, *A House of Children,* is avowedly autobiographical in origin: it is presented as the author's memories of his early boyhood among a large upper-middle-class family living on the northwest coast of Ireland during the 1890's. There is no attempt to re-create childhood in itself; what are admirably caught are the changes, the growth, the discontinuities, even the regressions of childhood when looked back upon from adult life, and, above all, the sudden sense of glory that, however intermittently, illuminates every childhood at some time. It is an enchanting novel.

Most of the characters of *Charley Is My Darling* are London slum children evacuated to Devon in the early days of World War II. Charley Brown, a boy of fifteen, as much as any character in Cary's world suffers from that "hunger of the imagination," in Dr. Johnson's tremendous phrase, "which preys incessantly on life." His imagination, in response to the life about him, is constantly setting him ideals of behavior he must try to live up to; and it is from sheer exuberance of imagination working in unfamiliar circumstances that he drifts into what I suppose must be called juvenile delinquency. The end of the novel is near-tragedy, poignantly so; but it is reached through episodes of comedy that, though often tender and moving, become progressively wilder, almost to the point of farce. Yet, wild as the comedy is, we do not doubt either the reality of the characters or the truth of the situations they find themselves in. One reason lies in the particular methods Cary has evolved for rendering character in action, methods rooted in his philosophy.

III

As a novelist Cary is generally spoken of as being much more traditional than most of the major novelists of our time. This does not mean that he practiced his art precisely as the eighteenth-century novelists or the Victorians did theirs. Inasmuch as he renders human beings as unique individuals caught in their own fantasies, and often at the extremes of individuality, as Jimson is in *The Horse's Mouth,* it is understandable that he should draw characters in the minute particulars of eccentricity such as we find in Charles Dickens. Again, in the furious pace of his comedy, in his later novels especially, as in his high spirits, he has an obvious kinship with Tobias Smollett. Then, the first-person narration of *Herself Surprised,* and the overtones of the device, hark back to Daniel Defoe's *Moll Flanders* (1721). Yet *The Horse's Mouth* could scarcely have been written by someone who had not absorbed into his own artistic being the "laboratory" work of James Joyce; and if there are affinities with Defoe, Smollett, and Dickens, those with D. H. Lawrence are hardly less plain.

Indeed, one of Cary's most considerable achievements is his success in grafting onto the trunk of our traditional fiction, with its stress on story, action, and broadly conceived character, technical devices first used in the experimental novels of this century, particularly by Joyce, Lawrence, and Virginia Woolf, in their various ways. In classic English fiction for the most part—there are obvious exceptions, Samuel Richardson and Laurence Sterne the most conspicuous—the action of the novel is, as it were, completed before the reader picks up the book and reads. The action lies in the past, and the novelist's role is that of reporter of events already over; as he reports his closed sequence of events he feels himself free to comment as he wishes on the action, to generalize and moralize on it, even to advise the reader which characters to admire, which to deplore. The reader is therefore at a distance from the characters of classic fiction: the author is in between. With Joyce and Woolf, and in a different way with Lawrence, this is not so; their aim was precisely to break down the old barriers between reader and character. The methods differ with each writer, but always the reader is taken right inside the minds of the characters: plunged into the stream of consciousness of Mr. Bloom, given the freedom of Mrs. Bloom's drifting unspoken soliloquies; made to feel the very sense of outrage and defilement Aaron feels when his pocket is picked in *Aaron's Rod;* invited to share the sensibility and fine discriminations of Mrs. Ramsay as she contemplates her husband, children, and guests, and the lighthouse they may or may not visit. These novelists were intent on rendering the moment of consciousness in itself; in their different ways they give us close-ups of consciousness; and as we read them we find ourselves for much of the time—occasionally the author has to provide us with the equivalents of stage directions—in what may be called a continuous present.

We experience much the same thing when we read Cary: while reading, we are at the cutting-edge of the present. None among recent novelists has been more successful in pinning down the sense of life at the actual moment of being lived. This is true even of his first-person novels, which, as fictitious autobiography, must be retrospective. Take the following passage from *A House of Children:*

We shrieked together in joyful terror. We were growing drunk with expectation, which was increasing all the time. For in us children it was a pure passion and never checked itself for reason. It burned on its own fuel, so that its size had no relation to its source; we were often in a fever for something so trifling that we had forgotten it before it arrived. All one day one would live in the sense of something to come; it would be with one during lessons, bathing, digging, meals, until at last, getting into bed, one would notice it particularly and say: "But what am I expecting?" Then one would discover that it had been doughnuts for tea, already eaten, but without any sense of fulfilment. The expectation had flowed over the fact as time runs over the apple flowers before one can grasp the spring. But with us, it was like an eddy on a strong tide. A specific anticipation was no more than a fresh bubble in the stream of our hope, rushing towards fulfilment. . . . We were not the pathetic deceived infants of the story-books, entering step by step the prison shades of grown-up disillusionment, we were confident of happiness because we had had it before. Our several expectations were sometimes not realised, but that was usually because our whole expectation was being renewed every hour. We didn't notice the disappointments because our minds were full of something else, something new, something interesting.

(ch. 6)

The passage expresses a truth about the nature of children; but its immediate relevance is as a key to Cary. For Cary, to be alive is to be in a state of continuous creation, and this is why he must seek always to snare the moment of living itself. But simultaneously he has to do something else, something that on the face of it should defeat the aim of snaring the moment in itself. I have said that his novels are metaphorical statements of his system of beliefs. These metaphorical statements have to be generalized. Two quotations will show how he does this. The first is from *Mister Johnson;* the hero is giving a highly successful party:

Johnson walks through the crowd in his best white suit, new patent leathers, and a pearl-grey hat, exactly like Gollup's, on the side of his head. His face shines with sweat and his mouth is spread perpetually in an enormous grin. Every moment he shouts out some joke, some greeting, takes a step with the dancers, miming their leaps, throws a ball for the juggler or, all by himself, makes a little song and dance expressing some impulse of delight, pride or hospitable affection for mankind.

It is, incidentally, a good example of the way Cary's empathetic imagination works, his ability to feel himself into his characters in their changing moods and emotions, physical behavior, gesture. Indeed, it is just Johnson's gestures that Cary is at pains to imitate; they are in a sense the generalization itself.

The second quotation is from *Charley Is My Darling.* It describes the end of that momentous day when Charley takes his gang to the cinema, an excursion involving the theft of both a car and a handbag. The gang is splitting up for the night. Ginger goes first; "Good night Liz," he says.

Lizzie does not answer. They watch Ginger stroll into the shadow of the tall house, towards the back door. They hear it open and shut, and they still stand looking towards the house. Liz sighs suddenly. "Poor Gingurr. I wish I'd said good night to him."

"I dunno." Charley turns away.

"E's all right," Harry says. "E can go in wen e likes and no one says a word to im."

"Funny ow e got stuck in the cafee—e was shy."

"Ginger—e aint shy."

"I like Gingurr—I do wish I'd said good night to him," Liz sighs again. "Poor Gingurr."

As usual with this expression of pity she seems to be expressing an emotion much wider and much more deeply felt than a passing sympathy with the object mentioned. Children use the same tone, when, on the loss of a doll or a boat, they say: "Poor doll, poor boat." They do not pity the doll or the boat so much as wonder, sometimes with curiosity, sometimes fear, at the circumstances within which dolls and boats can be so helplessly smashed.

(ch. 22)

When such vivid descriptions of character in action are combined with the swift, glancing generalization, the accuracy and insight of which we always accept, we see the character as with a double vision. There is the black Johnson, the girl Lizzie, caught while in motion as by a film camera, and there is the generalization like a shadow behind the character, but the shadow not precisely of the character itself, rather of all the children, of all sketchily westernized blacks like Johnson; so that in the behavior of the specific character, acutely defined though it is, is the behavior, the development and experience, of the whole class of beings to which the specific character belongs.

Generalization is part of Cary's way of creating character and giving it significance. Yet we never feel his generalizations as shocking intrusions on the action as we do the moral judgments of William Makepeace Thackeray or, at times, George Eliot. In the two quotations above, what "carries" the generalizations is the use of the historic present tense. Now, almost by definition, the historic present, so often employed by French novelists, rarely succeeds in English; ninety-nine times out of a hundred it seems artificial, unnatural. It does not in Cary, partly, I think, because of the speed of his narrative. He is like a radio commentator of genius who rapidly, almost breathlessly, describes what he sees and interpolates his comment on the action at the very moment of the action, so that comment and generalization become part of the description, part of the total rendering of the scene. Comment, as it were, appears as a spontaneous response.

Cary uses the historic present tense, or a modification of it, in *Mister Johnson, Charley Is My Darling*, and *A Fearful Joy*. The last is especially interesting in this respect because of the complexity of the subject matter to which the device is applied. By comparison, the earlier novels were novels of a simple situation; in *A Fearful Joy* Cary's role is that of the novelist as historian of his own times. He interprets the history of England during the past sixty years as it impinges on his heroine, Tabitha Baskett. A girl in the 1890's, she is seduced by an engaging scoundrel named Bonser, a young man who lives by his wits and deserts her when she is pregnant. She falls under the protection of a businessman who is one of the patrons of the literary and artistic movement of the time. On his death she marries a new-rich millionaire, an engineer whose ambition is to make an airplane that will fly. When he dies, she meets Bonser again; they marry and together keep a seaside hotel and then a roadhouse in the Midlands. Through her children she experiences further social change, so that by the end of the novel she contains the social history of sixty years.

A Fearful Joy is a presentation of change, of the ceaseless striving for novelty that Cary sees as one outcome of the creative imagination. It is not until we have finished the novel and pondered over it that we realize that the change described is largely the result of changes in mechanical transport. For Tabitha herself the fact of change is something known only after the event, when its reality is brought home to her by other people, as in the following passage set in the year 1900, after her protector, Sturge, the impresario of the Aesthetic movement, has died:

And this new age is present to everybody's imagination as something quite clearly divided from the old, not only by the magic figures 00 on the calendar, but by war and the death of the old queen. . . .

Everyone expects newness in art, law, politics, morals; and history itself is renewed from day to day. Enterprising young men, looking for a new field of exploration, have already discovered the 'nineties, and Sturge's obituaries, written, as always of the dead, with an historical bias, have placed him and his clique as important figures of that epoch. Boole at forty-seven is a living relic of antiquity. When, therefore, he cries to all comers, "Let me introduce you to Mrs Bonser, the Mrs Bonser of *The Bankside, chère amie* of Bunsurge," glances directed at Tabitha are full of approval as well as curiosity. She is soon surrounded by men.

"How do you do, Mrs Bonser. Did you really know Beardsley?"

"No, I'm afraid I only met him once." Tabitha's voice shows that she does not value Beardsley very highly.

"Mrs Bonser, excuse me—." An eager youth accosts her. "I've been *so* longing to meet you. I'm engaged on a thesis about the aesthetic movement."

"But was it really a movement?" Tabitha looks with sad enquiry at the enthusiast. "Was it really important?"

"Enormously important. One of our great revolutions, it brought down the Victorian bastille." And delighted by the very idea of this destruction, he draws a picture of heroes going out to war against a tyranny; of Morris routing the money grubbers, Pater and Symons undermining a philistine morality, Sturge and Boole releasing imprisoned souls from dark oubliettes.

"But Mr Sturge was a churchman," Tabitha says; "and he greatly admired the old queen."

"Now that *is* a most interesting point."

(ch. 53)

Tabitha has no historical bias, which is the result of the creative imagination working on the past; she is the innocent, uncomprehending present to which things happen unawares. She is, as it were, always at the present moment of time: open the novel wherever you like and it is today; and tomorrow—the next page—is also today. What is caught is the flow of time itself, and this gives a compelling immediacy to Tabitha's experiences. The effect of the novel is of a series of cartoons drawn with great vigor and speed, the characters, apart from Tabitha and Bonser, sketched in boldly rather than developed in detail. Thus to exhibit changing social history in fiction, the social history of a complex period, is an intellectual feat. If *A Fearful Joy* is less successful than the earlier *To Be a Pilgrim* and *The Horse's Mouth*, it is, I think, because Tabitha is less interesting in her own right than Wilcher and Jimson; it is her role to be passive, and she is not, as they are, transfigured by any abiding values for which she may stand. It is Bonser, her first seducer, last husband, and only love, who steals the book whenever he appears. A blackmailer, a fraud, a womanizer, a drunkard, he remains one of Cary's most lavishly comic creations, for he is redeemed—and the reader's moral judgment inhibited—by his vitality, his sheer delight in living. It is Tabitha's love for him that is the fearful joy of the title. It is the essence of the characters one thinks of as typically Cary's that they enhance life. In a note to his poem *The Drunken Sailor*, Cary writes: "There is nothing sure, nothing dependable, but the spirit of life itself and its invincible desperation which, among the cruelty of circumstance that is the form and effect of its real being, begets for ever in newness and innocence eternal delight." Bonser is a manifestation of the invincible desperation of life and so, despite his rogueries, holds Tabitha always in thrall. "He brought me to life again," she thinks after his death; "it was like a resurrection of the dead." And in the last analysis his rogueries are beside the point.

IV

CARY has another way of achieving the sense of the creative moment itself with the almost simultaneous generalization upon it: the use of first-person narration. It is here that his ability to feel himself into character, so that he becomes the character telling the story, is seen at its fullest. He uses first-person narration in the related novels *Herself Surprised, To Be a Pilgrim*, and *The Horse's Mouth*, and in the later Chester Nimmo trilogy. *Herself Surprised* is the first novel, as Cary said,

of a trilogy which was designed to show three characters, not only in themselves but as seen by each other. The object was to get a three-dimensional depth and force of character. One character was to speak in each book and describe the other two as seen by that person. Sara, the woman in a woman's world, was to see Wilcher and Jimson in that world, in relation to her own life and her own fortunes. She was to recall their history and the history of the times, as part of her own history. In practice this scheme, for technical reasons, did not come off.

(preface)

The result was not a trilogy in the sense of John Galsworthy's *The Forsyte Saga* (1906) or Ford Madox Ford's Tietjens books (a tetralogy, 1924–1928), but rather three novels the stories of which touch at certain points, the link between them all being the character of Sara Monday, the narrator of *Herself Surprised*. The three novels, then, compose a group rather than a sequence.

They compose, in my view, Cary's finest work. It is, to say the least, a feat of extraordinary virtuosity that in successive novels he should have assumed so completely such diverse personalities as Sara Monday, Wilcher, and Gully Jimson. *Herself Surprised*, the story of Sara and her associations with Jimson and Wilcher, is one of the most delightful of modern novels, as Sara is one of the most delightful of modern heroines. She recalls, in the warmth and simplicity of her feelings and in the innocence of her sensuality, Jean Renoir's nudes. She is writing her story in prison, in a state of repentance. Like Moll Flanders in the novel by Defoe, which *Herself Surprised* often reminds us of, she thinks of her life as a moral object-lesson. A cook, she has married her employer's son and become a wealthy woman; then, after his death, she becomes the mistress first of Jimson and later, as his housekeeper, of the elderly lawyer Wilcher, whose property she has been convicted of stealing. She is woman in the twin role of mother and mistress; despite her good intentions and her early religious education, she is incapable of resisting the demands that man, the male child, makes on her. If she cannot square her behavior with her sincerely held religious beliefs, it is because they cannot in the nature of things be squared. In her own eyes she is a sinner, but to the reader her life is a hymn of praise to creation and the Creator.

Along with *Mister Johnson* and *A House of Children*, *Herself Surprised* seems to me the most perfect of Cary's novels. But perfection in art commonly goes with a relative simplicity in theme and treatment. Cary noted that he "cut out history and art in Sara's book" because "when I let Sara talk about art and history I found that she lost something of her quality and force; the essential Sara was diluted." Compared with the two later novels of the group, Sara's book is on a small scale. If hers is Cary's most perfect novel, *To Be a Pilgrim* and *The Horse's Mouth* are his richest in complexity and his most authoritative as expressions of his attitude to life. The authority in each comes from the strength and freshness, the three-dimensional solidity, of the main character, the narrator.

It is difficult to know which to admire more as a creative triumph, Wilcher in *To Be a Pilgrim* or Jimson in *The Horse's Mouth*. On the face of it, Jimson is the more striking, for here Cary achieves the almost impossible, a convincing representation of artistic genius. Jimson as we meet him is an old and battered man just out of prison, a man for whom the visible world exists in an almost overpowering intensity, which he transmits to the reader in a completely idiosyncratic idiom of speech—extravagant, rhetorical, slangy, as though he were the child at once of James Joyce and William Blake. Blake, indeed, is his great exemplar, the Prophetic Books the nearest thing to his Bible. Like Blake, he is a visionary painter whose work is wildly unfashionable; but he lives wholly for his painting, and, though always stricken with poverty and engaged in ingenious and near-criminal schemes for obtaining money, he never loses his integrity as a painter.

We see the world as Jimson sees it. Through him, indeed, Cary creates a whole world, eccentric perhaps, but still a genuine image of the real one. *The Horse's Mouth* is certainly Cary's most sustained effort at comedy, and to match the speed and vigor of the writing and its author's ability to keep it going, one would have to go back as far as Smollett's *Peregrine Pickle* (1751). At times Jimson's adventures are ludicrous, almost to the point of slapstick farce, though we must remember that it is Jimson himself, not a stickler for fact, who is narrating them. But the extravagance of the comedy does not make for unreality: it is an expression of the whole man, and of the whole man's continual creation of the world he lives in. In spirit, *The Horse's Mouth* is Cary's most eighteenth-century novel: Jimson is really the rogue hero, looking for a fine wall to paint on, as the eighteenth-century rogue hero looked for a wealthy woman to gull. The comedy depends for its effect on its mounting intensity and duration, and space forbids quotation; otherwise one would delight in transcribing the wonderful account of Jimson's occupancy of Sir William Beeder's flat and his wrecking

and stripping of it in order to paint the mural of the raising of Lazarus that Sir William has not commissioned; and the masterly climax of the novel, in which Jimson and his young disciples furiously paint a wall of a building that the local authorities are even then busy demolishing as unsafe.

Striking as Jimson is, the character of Wilcher seems to me in essentials the greater feat, as I find *To Be a Pilgrim* more profound and on a vaster scale than *The Horse's Mouth*. Wilcher is a true original: there is no other character like him in the range of English fiction. He is an old man aware that he is regarded by the young as a fogy. He has played second fiddle all his life, ministering as a lawyer to his elder brothers and sisters, men and women more vital than himself, men and women of action. He is pedantic and fussy, personally a little ridiculous, and he knows it:

We were sailing in his cranky little boat, a pursuit which causes me acute misery. For wet, especially in the seat, always gave me rheumatism; the motion of a boat, even on a calm day, made me ill; the necessity of continually getting up and moving across to the other side of the boat, and ducking my head under the boom, at the risk of my hat, broke up every conversation and exasperated me extremely; and, finally, I could conceive nothing more stupid than to proceed by zigzags, from nowhere to nowhere, for the sake of wasting a fine afternoon. Neither, if I may mention such a point, though it is probably unimportant, have I ever been able to understand why there was no accommodation provided on small yachts, for things like sticks and umbrellas; whereas land conveyances, such as gigs and even governess carts, always have a basket designed for their proper storage and protection.

(p. 245)

Moreover, as we see him in the journal he is writing—and the novel is really his journal—he is a little cracked, an old man on the verge of senility, an old man whose emotional life has been so repressed that it is now breaking out in ungovernable tendencies toward indecent exposure, so that he has to be kept under restraint by his family. At the same time—and this is perfectly clear throughout—he is a man of real intellect and a man of real religious faith.

In *To Be a Pilgrim*, Cary handles three stories at once. In his journal Wilcher is concerned with his own immediate problem of how to escape the restraint he is under and run away to rejoin and marry his housekeeper-mistress, Sara, who feels only pity for the comic, inhibited, fierce old man. He is also concerned, first in a spirit of hostile scrutiny, with the lives of his niece, a doctor, who is looking after him, and her husband, and a nephew, who is struggling to bring the family estate at Tolbrook into cultivation again; and then, at the same time, he is consciously reliving his past, exploring his relations with his parents, brothers, and sisters in order to discover the sources of their strength and his failure. It is here that the novel becomes a magnificent evocation of English history from the 1890's to 1939 from the standpoints of political liberalism and religious Nonconformity—the Protestant position at its most intransigent. Wilcher's brother Edward has been a Liberal politician of daring and distinction; his brother Bill, a soldier; his sister Lucy, the wife of an itinerant evangelist. All were people of force and power; Wilcher himself is not, but he is a man of imagination; and as he relives his experiences in his journal he brings his family to life again in all its strength and sense of obligation.

Technically, the organization of *To Be a Pilgrim* is brilliantly skillful. The three stories are told in such a way that each is set off and given added significance by the others; and all are bound together, fused into one, by the darting generalizations, the constant reinterpretation of experience, of Wilcher. By the end of the novel we have realized that the house at Tolbrook, with Ann, Wilcher's doctor-niece, writing her father's biography in what was his study, and Robert, her husband, using the threshing machine in the great saloon, surrounded by the Adam paneling, under the Angelica Kaufmann ceiling, is a symbol of England itself; a more successful one, it seems to me, because more comprehensive, than Forster's similar identification of a house with England in *Howards End* (1910).

This brings us to what is fundamental to both *To Be a Pilgrim* and *The Horse's Mouth*. Here the title of the former is highly relevant; it is from John Bunyan's great hymn "To Be a Pilgrim":

> Who would true valour see
> Let him come hither;
> One here will constant be,
> Come wind, come weather.
> There's no discouragement
> Shall make him once relent
> His first avowed intent
> To be a pilgrim.

Bunyan, with his direct intuition of the presence of God, his assurance that all power is from him, and his insistence that no one and nothing, neither priest nor ritual, should be allowed to come between him and God, stands as an archetype of the English Protestant or Nonconformist. When the great nineteenth-century Nonconformist newspaper editor W. T. Stead referred to God as "the Senior Partner," from whom he got his instructions direct, he was expressing a conviction similar to Bunyan's. Gully Jimson's references to God are even more familiar than Stead's, but he is no less directly God-inspired, and it is the knowledge of this that is ultimately the sanction of his behavior.

The Protestant or Nonconformist tradition, though its manifestations change from generation to generation, has been one of the most potent and formative in English life, in politics no less than in religion. Cary's system of beliefs is central to that tradition, and in his fiction, in *To Be a Pilgrim* and *The Horse's Mouth* above all, he has restated it for our time. D. H. Lawrence, who was brought up in religious dissent and remained essentially in dissent all his life, used to say, according to Aldous Huxley, "I don't feel it *here*," pressing his hands to his solar plexus. In the last analysis, all Protestantism, Nonconformity, begins with the hands pressed on the solar plexus and the "I don't feel it *here*"; for, in the last analysis, his own existence, his own deepest feelings, are all that any man can be sure of. Often the Nonconformist will appear a hypocrite, as he did to Henry Fielding and Smollett and Dickens, and often he will appear mad, as Blake himself did. Both are the consequences of his awareness that he is "condemned to freedom" and that responsibility is his and no one else's. The burden that he feels called on to bear, simply by being a man, is such as to be endurable only so long as he has faith. Their characters' abiding faith is what gives *To Be a Pilgrim* and *The Horse's Mouth* the special dimension in which they have their being.

It is the quality of Jimson's faith, his unquestioning certainty that he must live and paint according to the light of his intuitions, without regard to the cost in material success, that makes him so much more than a mere eccentric and gives his vision of society, as we see it through his eyes, its value. Jimson shows us an aspect of English working-class life that has rarely had adequate recognition—that perpetual and fructifying ferment of Nonconformity, religious and political, among the relatively self-educated. We see it at work among Jimson's friends, Mr. Plant the philosopher, Mr. Ollier the postman, members of tiny societies meeting in back rooms to discuss or reform the universe. They are cranks, but cranks in the tradition of George Fox and Bunyan, Blake, Robert Owen, and Keir Hardie. They are not cranks to Jimson; and though the reader may see in him the eternal irresponsible artist, the artist who decides that art is enough for a man to live by, without acquiring other loyalties, to Mr. Plant and his friends Jimson is perfectly normal, for they know that religion takes men in diverse ways and that painting is as natural and proper a mode of religious experience and expression as any other.

In *To Be a Pilgrim*, Wilcher's intuitions are intermittent. Temperamentally, he is a conservative, inclined to take the letter for the spirit. Much of the time he is the pettifogger his sister accuses him of being. Faith comes to him through the living example of others. But he too is a pilgrim. Early in the novel he asks himself: "Why do I ever forget that the glory of my land is also the secret of life, to see at every sunrise, a new horizon? Why do I ever forget that every day is a new landfall in a foreign land, among strangers?" And at the very end, in a wonderful apostrophe of England, he takes up this note again:

The truth must be confessed, that I am an old fossil, and that I have deceived myself about my abilities. I thought I could be an adventurer like Lucy and Edward, a missionary. I shouted the pilgrim's cry, democracy, liberty, and so forth, but I was a pilgrim only by race. England took me with her on a few stages of her journey. Because she could not help it. She, poor thing, was born upon the road, and lives in such a dust of travel that she never knows where she is.

"Where away England, steersman answer me?
We cannot tell. For we are all at sea."

She is the wandering Dutchman, the pilgrim and scapegoat of the world. Which flings its sins upon her as the old world heaped its sins upon the friars. Her lot is that of all courage, all enterprise; to be hated and abused by the parasite. But, and this has been one of the exasperating things in my life, she isn't even aware of this hatred and jealousy which surrounds her and, in the same moment, seeks and dreads her ruin. She doesn't notice it because she looks forward to the road. Because she is free. She stands always before all possibility, and this is the youth of the spirit. It is the life of the faithful who say, "I am ready. Anywhere at any time."

(ch. 155)

In the end, then, the Nonconformist, Protestant spirit, which is one aspect of the creative imagination that eternally shapes things anew, is equated with the spirit of England herself.

In the novels that follow, *The Moonlight*, *A Fearful Joy*, and the works of the Chester Nimmo trilogy, *Prisoner of Grace*, *Except the Lord*, and *Not Honour*

More, Cary dramatizes themes that form part of the whole of *To Be a Pilgrim*. *A Fearful Joy* has already been discussed. *The Moonlight* takes up the problem of the clash of generations and the changing position of women during sixty years. The novel is told in the third person, but three stories are kept going at once and the lives of the daughters of an upper-class Victorian family are re-created in depth. *The Moonlight* is memorable as a study of the change in women's attitudes to sex and romantic love and as a study also of what Cary has called "the injustice risked by everyone who accepts responsibility for government": Rose, who accepts responsibility for her sisters and takes on the role almost of father and mother combined, is in the end hated by them all and poisoned by Ella, the weakest of them and the most rebellious, the one she has been at most pains to protect. This novel is also distinguished by a much-increased visual intensity in Cary's style, as though, having in the previous book assumed the character of Jimson, he had afterward retained his painter's eye.

In *Prisoner of Grace*, Cary went back to an examination of the working of the creative imagination, this time in politics; and the creative imagination is shown as synonymous with the religious imagination. Chester Nimmo, a Radical politician, begins his career during the Boer War as a pacifist; in 1914, a cabinet minister, he is the leader of the militant section of the British government. His principles appear to change, but his self-assurance never does. Whatever he does is right because he regards himself as divinely inspired; his political intuitions, however convenient they may be to him personally, he attributes to God. This confidence of inspiration gives him his authority: he is in a state of grace. It is his wife, Nina, narrator of the story, who is the prisoner of grace. She is an unwilling prisoner: of a higher social position than Nimmo, she had been forced to marry him by her aunt, the young politician's patron, when discovered pregnant by her cousin Jim Latter. But however much she may love Latter and however much she may criticize Nimmo and his actions—for her values are not political—she cannot escape him; she always, as Lawrence might have put it, recognizes and responds to the god in him. And she knows that he is not a hypocrite, whatever he may seem: he is simply immersed in the political life.

As a study of the politician in action, *Prisoner of Grace* is masterly, and when one compares it with other political novels in English, even with Benjamin Disraeli's, one sees that it is unique in its profundity.

It is as though we have for the first time the truth about the quintessential politician, the man for whom politics is a way of life and a vocation in the same dedicated sense as art may be for the artist or religion for the priest. Nimmo himself is a creation of tremendous power; as with Jimson, one feels that one is in the presence of a force of nature. And Cary quite triumphantly overcomes the obvious difficulties that faced him in this novel. We know very well what the actual history of the decades before and after World War I was; but in the most uncanny way Cary seems to supplement it. We know very well who the great historic figures of the times were—Henry Campbell-Bannerman, Arthur Balfour, David Lloyd George, Herbert Asquith, Winston Churchill; it is a proof of his author's achievement that Nimmo, as a fictitious character, is still thoroughly convincing when we recall them.

The second book of the Chester Nimmo trilogy, *Except the Lord*, is presented in the form of Nimmo's autobiography, written when he is an old man. It does not, however, reproduce the events described in *Prisoner of Grace*, but recounts Nimmo's story before he met Nina. It shows Cary at his gravest and most austere. The exuberance is severely curbed, and comedy is almost entirely absent. It is a very packed novel, a slice of working-class social history in the Devon of the last decades of the nineteenth century; and it has many memorable characters, notably Nimmo's father, an old soldier who combines farm labor with his vocation as pastor of a small Nonconformist sect preaching the imminence of the Second Coming, and Nimmo's sister Georgina, one of Cary's most striking representations of children, a *farouche* child whose sense of responsibility and love for her family are expressed through a sort of baffled, indignant criticism of them. But packed though the novel is, and rich in the quality of felt life, everything is subordinated to the theme of the religious nature of man as manifest in the direct intercourse of man with God, which is fundamental to Nonconformity. *Except the Lord* is Cary's most explicit rendering of the Nonconformist, Protestant spirit; and it is this very explicitness and directness that give the novel its power and authority.

The third novel of the trilogy, *Not Honour More*, is written in the form of a confession on the eve of execution, from the point of view of Jim Latter, Nina Nimmo's lover and, later, her husband. The action takes place against the background of the General Strike of 1926, though the public events described cannot be separated from the personal. As Andrew Wright has said, "*Not Honour More* established, this time catastrophically, the connection between public and private politics." Just as Nimmo is a representation of the inspired politician, so Latter may stand for his opposite, the soldier and administrator for whom order and duty are everything. Eternal opposites, they are also enemies, and the resolution of the enmity between them is necessarily tragic.

In these last novels of Cary the comic note is increasingly muted, and somberness is intensified almost to darkness. Brilliant though these books are, one gets the impression that their author was less and less interested in fiction, more and more concerned with the philosophy underlying it. This greater explicitness is achieved at the expense of some elements, at least, of his art. And this impression seems to be borne out by his posthumous novel *The Captive and the Free*, his gravest novel and a notable study of the God-possessed man, even though we cannot know whether Cary himself would have accepted the version we have, since it was assembled—most skillfully—by his literary executor, Winifred Davin.

V

OUR approach to contemporary writers differs from our approach to writers of the past. We are too close to our contemporaries, not only in time but in feelings, assumptions, fears, and hopes, to be able to see them clearly and whole. We share a world with them, and, in a way the writers of the past are not, they are part of ourselves. So to ask of a contemporary whether he will be read in the future or what his stature will be in the eyes of posterity is to ask the wrong questions, questions that in any case cannot be answered. The proper question is: Is he good for us now, and in what way?

We shall not demand of him qualities he does not profess to have; nor, if we are wise, shall we use him as a means by which to denigrate his fellows in the art he practices: one of the great virtues of art is its variety, and what we value in any artist is the sense we have of his uniqueness, the strong impression that the imaginary world he creates is special to him, the expression of one individual mind. So, where Cary is concerned, I do not grumble because his novels in the main lack the particular aesthetic quality of form that we find in the work of novelists in the tradition of Jane Austen and Henry James, much as I appreciate it in those novelists; it is in fact doubtful whether it is ever in the power of the extrovert novelist to give us this.

For myself, I value first in Cary the emphatic power of his genius, the protean nature that enabled him, in his African novels, for example, most vividly to bring forth the clash not so much of colors but the modes of being underneath the difference of colors. Then, accompanying the empathetic imagination, is his exuberance of creation—not a common quality in the English novel today—which seems to reproduce, no less, the "daedal dance" of life itself. This exuberance cannot be separated from the comprehensiveness of his vision, which enabled him to bring into his fiction a larger area of English life than, probably, any of his contemporaries.

But fundamental to everything else is the nature of his vision. Cary has been described by a wit as the Protestant answer to Graham Greene. It would be as true to say that he is the English retort to the Existentialist writers, whether Christian or atheist; though it arises from sources very different from theirs, his view of life in its implications is just as Existential. But it is a very English Existentialism, and if, as I think is true, England and the English cannot be understood except by reference to the working of the Protestant, Nonconformist spirit, then a reading of Cary, of all twentieth-century novelists, is essential to an understanding of the English. His great value is that he used all the resources of his art and talent to reinterpret in fiction an enduring tradition in English life and feeling, one without which England and the English would be very different from what they are.

SELECTED BIBLIOGRAPHY

I. COLLECTED WORKS. *The Carfax Edition of the Novels of Joyce Cary* (London, 1951–1967).

II. SEPARATE WORKS. *Aissa Saved* (London, 1932), novel; *An American Visitor* (London, 1933), novel; *The African Witch* (London, 1936), novel; *Castle Corner* (London, 1938), novel; *Mister Johnson* (London, 1939), novel; *Power in Men* (London, 1939), political science; *Charley Is My Darling* (London, 1940), novel; *A House of Children* (London, 1941), novel; *The Case for African Freedom* (London, 1941; rev. ed., 1944), political science; *Herself Surprised* (London, 1941), novel; *To Be a Pilgrim* (London, 1942), novel; *The Process of Real Freedom* (London, 1943), political science; *The Horse's Mouth* (London, 1944), novel; *Marching Soldier* (London, 1945), poem; *The Moonlight* (London, 1946), novel; *Britain and West Africa* (London, 1946), political science; *The Drunken Sailor* (London, 1947), poem; *A Fearful Joy* (London, 1949), novel.

Prisoner of Grace (London, 1952), novel; *Except the Lord* (London, 1953), novel; *Not Honour More* (London, 1955), novel; *Art and Reality* (Cambridge, 1958), criticism, the Clark Lectures, Cambridge, 1956; *The Captive and the Free* (London, 1959), novel, assembled and published by W. Davin after Cary's death; *Spring Song and Other Stories* (London, 1960); *Memoir of the Babotes* (London, 1964), autobiography, an account with illus. by the author of his experiences as a stretcher-bearer in the Balkan War of 1912–1913; A. G. Bishop, ed., *Cock Jarvis* (London, 1974), an unfinished novel with foreword by Walter Allen.

III. CRITICAL STUDIES. H. Reed, *The Novel Since 1939* (London, 1940), includes brief criticism of Cary's work; *Adam International Review*, nos. 212–213 (November–December 1950), devoted to Cary and containing articles by him on the novel, his broadcast conversation with Lord David Cecil, and some critical estimates; P. H. Newby, *The Novel, 1945–50* (London, 1951), includes brief criticism of Cary's work; A. Kettle, *An Introduction to the English Novel*, vol. II (London, 1951); A. Wright, *Joyce Cary: A Preface to His Novels* (London, 1958); R. Bloom, *The Indeterminate World: A Study of the Novels of Joyce Cary* (Philadelphia, 1962; London, 1963); M. M. Mahood, *Joyce Cary's Africa* (London, 1964); G. L. Larsen, *The Dark Descent: Social Change and Moral Responsibility in the Novels of Joyce Cary* (London, 1965); W. van O'Connor, *Joyce Cary* (London, 1966); J. Wolkenfeld, *Joyce Cary: The Developing Style* (New York–London, 1968); M. Foster, *Joyce Cary* (London, 1969).

ALDOUS HUXLEY

(1894-1963)

Jocelyn Brooke

ANY comparison between Aldous Huxley and H. G. Wells must seem, at first glance, impossibly arbitrary and far-fetched: for surely no two writers—considered merely as writers—could be more dissimilar. Yet such a comparison is, I think, not only justified but, as a matter of literary history, almost unavoidable.

For those who came to maturity during the first two decades of the present century, the most potent intellectual influence was probably that of Wells; it was an influence that might be resisted but could hardly be ignored by any up-to-date young man of the period. Wells was not only the first and greatest of the scientific popularizers; he was also a prophet and a revolutionary, and his perky, disrespectful attitude to "respectable" institutions, combined with an immensely readable style, seemed to his younger contemporaries to typify the intellectual climate of the time.

How different, it may well be objected, was the case of Huxley: aloof, fastidious, and, by contrast with Wells's bouncing optimism, profoundly a pessimist; upper-class both by birth and disposition, whereas Wells was plebeian and proud of it; preoccupied largely with problems of pure aesthetics and, latterly, with mysticism, for both of which Wells would have felt little but an amused contempt. Yet, viewed in a wider context, the similarities between the two men can be seen to outweigh their differences: for Huxley was also a popularizer, not only of aesthetic and philosophic ideas, but also (like Wells) of scientific ones; he too—though in a somewhat different sense—was both a revolutionary and a prophetic writer; and, most notably, he was, like Wells before him, the "typical" writer of his generation, and a major influence upon the young intelligentsia of his time.

His importance, in this last respect, can hardly be exaggerated, though there is a very natural tendency among the youngest generation to underestimate it.

For those who, like the writer of the present essay, were growing up during the 1920's, Aldous Huxley seemed unquestionably the most stimulating and exciting writer of the day: his style in itself was a novelty—highly wrought yet extremely readable, deriving from unfamiliar models, and providing a refreshing contrast to that of such older writers as John Galsworthy, Arnold Bennett, and Wells himself. Huxley was gay, sophisticated, and (for those days) agreeably shocking; but more important for his young readers was the impact of an alert, penetrating, and widely ranging intelligence. By comparison, most other contemporary writers seemed stuffy, unenlightened, and old-fashioned.

The effect was intoxicating: like the great Knockespotch, that imaginary genius described in *Crome Yellow* (1921), Huxley had "delivered us from the dreary tyranny of the realistic novel"; like Knockespotch, again, he preferred to study the human mind, not "bogged in a social plenum," but "freely and sportively bombinating":

"Oh those Tales—those Tales! [exclaims the eloquent Mr. Scogan]. How shall I describe them? Fabulous characters shoot across his pages like gaily dressed performers on the trapeze. There are extraordinary adventures and still more extraordinary speculations. Intelligences and emotions, relieved of all the imbecile preoccupations of civilised life, move in intricate and subtle dances, crossing and recrossing. . . . An immense erudition and an immense fancy go hand in hand. . . . The verbal surface of his writing is rich and fantastically diversified. The wit is incessant."

(ch. 14)

This description, one felt at the time, could well have been applied to the tales of Huxley himself. The combination of wit and erudition is an uncommon one in English fiction, and one has to go back to Thomas Love Peacock (by whom Huxley was much influenced) to find a comparable example. Huxley's

197

erudition was, even in his earlier works, encyclopedic; yet he wore his learning lightly, with an offhand, man-of-the-world air that was entirely dis-
arming. He was often, in those days, accused of intellectual snobbery, and it is true that he was
capable, on occasion, of referring to such comparatively recondite figures as, say, Crébillon *fils* or
Notker Balbulus with an air of casual omniscience
that somewhat suggested the style of the contemporary gossip writer ("Lady So-and-so, who *of
course* . . ."). The trick, one suspects, was consciously employed, partly from a sense of mischief, partly
from an amiable desire to flatter his readers. In the
essay *Vulgarity in Literature* (1930), he remarks of
Paul Morand that he "has a wonderfully airy, easy
way of implying that he has looked into everything—absolutely everything, from God and the
Quantum Theory to the slums of Baku (the world's
most classy slums—didn't you know it?)." Here, one
feels, Huxley is having a sly dig not only at Morand
but at himself.

If Huxley had written nothing after 1925, it is
probable that he would be remembered today merely as a brilliant and somewhat eccentric minor writer
comparable in stature, say, with Ronald Firbank.
Judged by those early works, his subsequent development is astonishing: not only was he one of the
most prolific of living English writers (his published
works number between fifty and sixty volumes); he
was also one of the most versatile. Novels, poetry,
drama, travel books, short stories, biography,
essays—there is almost no literary form that he did
not, at one time or another, attempt. His writings,
moreover, cover an enormous range not only of
form but of subject matter: apart from his purely
creative work, he wrote learnedly and perceptively
about painting, music, science, philosophy, religion,
and a dozen other topics. Yet, considering the
breadth of his interests and the magnitude of his output, his work, examined as a whole, has a surprising
homogeneity; nor, despite the temptations that
could beset a successful author, did he ever seriously
compromise his intellectual integrity. Though a best-
seller, he remains, paradoxically, an essentially unpopular writer.

His development falls roughly into three phases.
The earlier stories and novels are mainly satirical
and (like the historical studies of Lytton Strachey)
are largely concerned with the debunking of accepted ideas and standards. Like T. S. Eliot, James
Joyce, Wyndham Lewis, and others of his own or a
slightly earlier generation, he was profoundly affected by the progressive breakdown of nineteenth-
century ideals that had culminated in World War I,
and his predicament is reflected in these early
volumes, in which the surface gaiety serves only to
emphasize his underlying pessimism. Religion, conventional morality, romantic love—all are subjected
to a cynical and ruthless mockery. The world of *Antic Hay* (1923) has much in common with that of
Eliot's *The Waste Land* (which had appeared in the
previous year); it is a world of "broken images,"
where "the dead tree gives no shelter, the cricket no
relief." Only in the realm of pure art (it is implied)
can one hope, perhaps, to discover some kind of
established order to set against the prevailing anarchy. Yet the fin de siècle doctrine of art for art's sake
could never have proved finally satisfying to a man
of Huxley's lively and speculative intelligence; and
there is soon apparent a growing preoccupation not
only with the more advanced theories of modern science, but also with psychology, ethics, and
philosophy.

This second phase may be said to have begun with
the publication of *Proper Studies* (1927), the first of
his books to be explicitly serious in intention.
Thenceforward, though he continued to write novels
and short stories, he assumed a more responsible
role—that of the teacher, the professional philosopher—and one can no longer regard him as primarily
a novelist, whose chief purpose is to entertain. During the 1930's he developed an increasing interest in
politics and, more particularly, in the contemporary
cult of pacifism; at the same time, he began to turn
his attention to the Eastern mystics, and the third
and final stage in his development can already be in-
ferred from the works of this period.

Though by temperament a skeptic, Huxley always, one imagines, recognized within himself the
need for some kind of religious approach to the
universe; moreover, throughout his career as a
writer, he showed a recurrent interest in the
phenomena of mysticism. Others among his contemporaries, though sharing his initial skepticism,
subsequently became converted to one form or
another of the Christian faith; Huxley, with greater
intellectual resistance, refused to abandon his empirical attitude in such matters, and the approach to
his later philosophical position was cautious in the
extreme. His prolonged study of the mystics convinced him that the mystical experience itself—the
individual's direct union with the Godhead—is an
objective fact that can be experimentally verified;
and his last works are almost all concerned, directly

or indirectly, with an attempt to synthesize the existing evidence into a comprehensive system, to which he gave the name "the Perennial Philosophy."

One can say, then, that Huxley progressed from a purely aesthetic, through a politico-ethical, to a predominantly religious point of view. This, of course, is a drastic simplification. In reality, his development was far more complex—for, as I shall try to show in this essay, most of the beliefs that he embraced in his maturity are latent in his earliest published works.

Aldous Leonard Huxley was born at Godalming, Surrey, on 26 July 1894, a son of Leonard Huxley (editor of the *Cornhill* magazine) and grandson of T. H. Huxley, the illustrious scientist; Sir Julian Huxley, the biologist, was his brother. His mother was an Arnold, and he was thus connected on both the paternal and maternal sides with that distinguished intellectual aristocracy which was so dominant a force in late-nineteenth-century England. He was educated at Eton and at Balliol College, Oxford; after leaving the university, he taught for a while at Eton (an incongruous interlude to which he refers, disrespectfully, in *Antic Hay*), but soon decided to devote himself to writing. He married comparatively early, to Maria Nys in 1919,[1] and spent much of his time during the 1920's in France and Italy. He traveled widely, not only in Europe but in the East and in America, and lived in California for many years before his death there on 22 November 1963.

His first published work was a small volume of poems; and this is perhaps a good moment to note that Huxley, though less known as a poet than as a prose writer, was an extremely accomplished writer of verse. These early poems are chiefly remarkable today for being so wholly unlike the average product of the contemporary Georgian school.[2] Huxley, like Eliot before him, had plainly been much influenced by the French symbolists; his third collection of verse, *The Defeat of Youth* (1918), is an admirable translation of Stéphane Mallarmé's *L'Après-midi d'un faune*. Sometimes there are echoes of a rather eighteen-ninetyish romanticism:

> Shepherd, to yon tall poplars tune your flute:
> Let them pierce, keenly, subtly shrill,
> The slow blue rumour of the hill;

> Let the grass cry with an anguish of evening gold,
> And the great sky be mute.
>
>   ("Song of Poplars")

Many of these early poems are, however, satirical or epigrammatic; and in the volume called *Leda* (1920) the more memorable pieces, apart from the title poem (an ambitious and on the whole successful work in rhymed couplets), are of a similar character—for example, the "Fifth Philosopher's Song":

> A million million spermatozoa,
>   All of them alive:
> Out of their cataclysm but one poor Noah
>   Dare hope to survive.

> And among that billion minus one
>   Might have chanced to be
> Shakespeare, another Newton, a new Donne—
>   But the One was Me.

> Shame to have ousted your betters thus,
>   Taking ark while the others remained outside!
> Better for all of us, froward Homunculus,
>   If you'd quietly died!

A third volume, *The Cicadas* (1931), shows the same verbal felicity, but with a leaning toward more serious (and more formal) verse. Two or three of the poems there reprinted appeared originally in the novel *Those Barren Leaves* (1925), where, significantly, they were attributed to one of the leading characters, Francis Chelifer, who has more than a little in common with Huxley himself.

Huxley's first prose work, *Limbo*, appeared in 1920, the same year as *Leda*; this is a collection of stories, one of which—"Farcical History of Richard Greenow"—is in fact a short novel or long tale and occupies almost half the volume. This story is one of Huxley's most hilarious and successful essays in ironic comedy; the hero is a "spiritual hermaphrodite," a Jekyll-and-Hyde personality in whom are combined an overfastidious intellectual and a vastly successful lady novelist. Rereading it today, one is still astonished by its intellectual maturity and by the richness of Huxley's comic invention. Among the other six stories in the book, all extremely accomplished, may be mentioned "Happily Ever After," in which one of Huxley's chief preoccupations becomes for the first time apparent. Guy Lambourne, the hero of the story, is the prototype of many subsequent Huxley heroes—the young lover who is tortured by an irreconcilable conflict between romantic passion and physical sexuality. In later

---

[1] Huxley's first wife died of cancer in 1955; the next year he married his second wife, Laura Archera, an Italian concert violinist and psychotherapist.

[2] So called in reference to the series of anthologies, *Georgian Poetry*, edited by the late Sir Edward Marsh.

works this dichotomy will become almost obsessional, for Huxley had much of Jonathan Swift's hatred for bodily functions, combined with a lively appreciation of the pleasures to be obtained therefrom.

In 1921 appeared Huxley's first novel, *Crome Yellow*, and with it he established his reputation. In many ways it remains—on a purely aesthetic level—his most successful achievement. Like *Limbo*, it is an extraordinarily mature production for a young man still in his twenties, yet it has, too, all the freshness and spontaneity one associates with an "early" work. It is Huxley's gayest and happiest book; the graver, more responsible attitude of his later years can already be detected, as it were, in embryo, but the novel as a whole is a thoroughly light-hearted affair, enormously readable and, in parts, extremely amusing.

The structure of *Crome Yellow* owes much to Thomas Peacock: a number of people are gathered together at a house party; there is plenty of incident—the characters dance, go swimming, attend a garden fete, fall in love; but above all they talk—brilliantly, wittily, and almost without stopping. The book is a conversation piece in which the characters, though sharply drawn and clearly differentiated, are employed primarily as vehicles for the prolific and highly imaginative ideas of their creator. It is a useful device that Huxley was to adopt again in subsequent books, though seldom quite so successfully as he employs it here. The danger of such a method is that the action of the novel—and the characters themselves—will be swamped by the stream of conversation; in *Chrome Yellow*, however, the balance is almost perfectly maintained, and Mr. Scogan, for example, though irrepressibly eloquent, is never allowed to become a bore.

In *Chrome Yellow* Huxley presents a gallery of characters many of whom will be resuscitated, with slight variations (and under different names), in his later novels. For instance, there is Denis, the "hero" (it is difficult to refer to Huxley's very unheroic heroes without the ironic qualification of quotation marks), the typically Huxleyan young man, burdened (as he complains) by "twenty tons of ratiocination," romantically in love yet sexually inhibited and profoundly convinced of the futility of life and of himself. There is Mary Bracegirdle, with her bobbed hair like "a bell of elastic gold about her cheeks," the too-intelligent ingenue whose practical experience of sex is so sadly disproportionate to her

theoretical knowledge of it. In sharp contrast is Anne—uninhibited, hedonistic, sexually sophisticated—in whom one recognizes the forerunner of Mrs. Viveash and Lucy Tantamount, the femmes fatales who play so prominent a part in the more mature works.

In *Chrome Yellow*, as I have already hinted, one can detect the germs of several ideas that will be developed in later books: a good example is Mr. Scogan's prophetic description of a scientific Utopia:

"An impersonal generation will take the place of Nature's hideous system. In vast state incubators, rows upon rows of gravid bottles will supply the world with the population it requires. The family system will disappear; society, sapped at its very base, will have to find new foundations; and Eros, beautifully and irresponsibly free, will flit like a gay butterfly from flower to flower through a sunlit world."

(ch. 5)

This passage contains, in essence, an idea that Huxley developed and elaborated eleven years later in *Brave New World*. Mr. Scogan himself, despite his loquacity, is one of Huxley's best-conceived characters, and the scene in which he impersonates Madame Sesostris, the Sorceress of Ecbatana, is one of the most richly comic episodes in a novel that, apart from its other merits, is certainly among the funniest in modern English fiction. *Crome Yellow* derives, as I have pointed out, from Peacock; one guesses, too, that Huxley was also influenced at this period by Norman Douglas' *South Wind*, and perhaps to a lesser extent by the novels of Ronald Firbank.

Crome Yellow was followed, in 1922, by *Mortal Coils*, another volume of short stories. During the subsequent decade the short (or long-short) story accounted for a considerable proportion of Huxley's output, and it will be convenient at this point to consider his achievement in the form.

In the opinion of many critics, these shorter pieces are Huxley's most successful contribution to fiction. In his novels he is too apt to use the form merely as a vehicle for the presentation of his own ideas; in the short stories he shows a greater respect for his medium and, whereas his novels tended to become longer, more serious, and more diffuse, his shorter tales retained much of the gaiety and compactness of form that one finds in *Chrome Yellow*. Among a large output may be mentioned "Nuns at Luncheon" (*Mortal Coils*, 1922), "Little Mexican" (in the volume of that name, 1924), and "The Claxtons" (*Brief Candles*, 1930)—all admirably written in Huxley's best comic vein. The title story in *Two or Three Graces* (1926) is also noteworthy, partly as a fascinating character study of a woman afflicted by *bovarysme* and partly for its portrait of D. H. Lawrence ("Kingham"), which may be compared instructively with the very different version of Lawrence in *Point Counter Point* (1928).

During this period Huxley established himself as a master of the short essay, a form that has tended to decline sharply in popularity during the last fifty years or so. His first collection, *On the Margin* (1923), consisted mainly of pieces contributed to weekly reviews. This was followed at intervals by half a dozen other volumes, among which may be mentioned *Proper Studies*, Huxley's first serious excursion into the realm of sociology and philosophy, and *Do What You Will* (1929), especially memorable for the perceptive essay on Charles Baudelaire. Among other miscellaneous writings of this period are the two excellent travel books, *Jesting Pilate* (1926) and *Beyond the Mexique Bay* (1934), besides *The World of Light* (1931), a satirical comedy about spiritualism. The drama is not a form at which one would have expected Huxley to excel, yet *The World of Light* is not only highly entertaining to read, but also extremely good theater, as the present writer, who saw the original production at the Royalty Theatre in 1931, is able to testify. ("The Gioconda Smile," in the volume *Mortal Coils*, has also been successfully dramatized.)

Huxley's second novel, *Antic Hay*, appeared in 1923 and created a considerable sensation, owing to its frank and detailed treatment of sexual matters. Today, this would hardly arouse comment, but at that time *Antic Hay* acquired an undeserved reputation for "obscenity," and several of the more respectable libraries refused to stock it. It is a considerably longer and more ambitious work than *Crome Yellow* and, though it has much of the high spirits of the previous book, is more serious in intention. The scene is set mainly in London, and the characters are drawn largely from the artistic and intellectual coteries of the time; many of them are thinly disguised portraits of real persons, among others the composer Philip Heseltine (known as Peter Warlock), who is easily recognizable in the character of Coleman. In structure the book is loose and episodic, though the story plays a more important part than in *Crome Yellow*; conversations are fre-

quent and often prolonged, but here they are for the most part subordinated to the narrative. The hero, Theodore Gumbril, is an older, more worldly version of Denis in *Crome Yellow*, and serves to illustrate once again the predicament of the modern intellectual torn between his youthful idealism and the inconvenient promptings of *l'homme moyen sensuel* (the average sensual man). The book is an odd mixture of broad farce and a kind of ironic realism, but one feels at times that the two elements are not perfectly fused: thus, the episode of Gumbril's "patent smallclothes" and his farcical disguise as the Rabelaisian "Complete Man," though extremely funny in themselves, strike one as curiously out of key with the more serious passages.

Yet *Antic Hay*, if it lacks the structural perfection of *Crome Yellow*, is in many respects a more important book. Of all Huxley's novels, it is the one that is most "alive": the characters are presented more vividly and their relation to their background is more authentic than in any previous or subsequent work. Mr. Mercaptan, Mrs. Viveash, Lypiatt, Shearwater—they remain in the memory as living entities, not as mere mouthpieces for Huxley's erudite and witty disquisitions. In this novel, too—in spite of its predominantly comic theme—it is noticeable that Huxley strikes a more emotional note than is usual with him: there are passages in which he betrays a feeling of romantic nostalgia (though tempered by a habitual irony) that one seldom finds elsewhere in his work. It should be noted, too, that in *Antic Hay* he is already beginning to employ a technique that in his next few books becomes increasingly important—the technique of describing one form of experience in terms of another and of uniting a number of apparently diverse phenomena into a logical and self-contained unity. In the following passage Gumbril is lying in bed with his (platonic) mistress, Emily:

Very gently, he began caressing her shoulder, her long slender arm, drawing his finger tips lightly and slowly over her smooth skin; slowly from her neck, over her shoulder, lingeringly round the elbow to her hand. Again, again: he was learning her arm. The form of it was part of the knowledge, now, of his finger tips; his fingers knew it as they knew a piece of music, as they knew Mozart's Twelfth Sonata, for example. And the themes that crowd so quickly one after another at the beginning of the first movement played themselves aerially, glitteringly in his mind; they became a part of the enchantment.

(ch. 13)

Love in terms of music—music in terms of love: it is a typically Huxleyan transposition of terms, and is greatly elaborated in the next two novels. One may add that *Antic Hay*, like *Crome Yellow*, sometimes strikes a prophetic note—as, for instance, in the passage in chapter 22 where Gumbril is soliloquizing after luncheon to the somnolent Mrs. Viveash: "'I have a premonition,' he went on, 'that one of these days I may become a saint. An unsuccessful flickering sort of saint, like a candle beginning to go out."

Without disrespect to Huxley, I think one can infer from Gumbril's flippant words a faint adumbration of his creator's future progress toward the philosophy of nonattachment.

Those Barren Leaves, the next novel, was published in 1925. Here, as in *Crome Yellow*, Huxley adopts the Peacockian device of the house party. The background, in this case, is a villa on the Italian Riviera, but the characters have a good deal in common with those of the earlier book. Thus, the would-be sophisticated Mary Bracegirdle reappears as Irene, the niece of the hostess, Mrs. Aldwinkle (who, like the hostess of *Crome Yellow*, is largely a comic character); Mr. Scogan is replaced by Mr. Cardan, no less loquacious, cultured, and concupiscent than his predecessor; the romantic Ivor of *Crome Yellow* becomes Calamy, the handsome young philanderer; and so on. In this novel, as in *Antic Hay*, Huxley introduces a number of grotesque episodes, but here they are more closely integrated with the rest of the book. For example, the story of Mr. Cardan's betrothal to a lunatic heiress and her subsequent death from food poisoning is, if sufficiently fantastic, at least more plausible than Gumbril's pneumatic trousers, and the whole episode is a vividly imagined essay in the farcical-macabre.

Again, love plays a considerable part; here, however, a new element enters, foreshadowing the direction in which Huxley is moving. In *Antic Hay*, his attitude to sexual relations is one of almost Proustian pessimism: sexuality, he seems to imply, is inherently squalid and disgusting, but it is unavoidable. The philosopher, therefore, must accept it with a shrug and make the best of it. In *Those Barren Leaves*, however, he makes the young lover, Calamy, willingly renounce his affair with a fellow guest and retire to a mountaintop where, significantly, he spends his time in philosophic meditation.

"And what [asks the skeptical Mr. Cardan] will happen at the end of three months' chaste meditation when some lovely young temptation comes toddling down this road . . . ? What will happen to your explorations of the inward universe then, may I ask? . . . Perhaps you'll find that you can explore simultaneously both the temptation and the interior universe."

Calamy shook his head. "Alas, I'm afraid that's not practicable."

(Conclusions, ch. 4)

I mentioned Proust in another connection, and it is noticeable that in *Those Barren Leaves* Huxley shows signs of Proustian influences, not so much in the matter of style (though this indeed is more elaborate than in the earlier books) as in his delineation of character: Mrs. Aldwinkle, for instance, with her proprietary attitude to her "view," and to Italy in general, owes much to Mme. Verdurin; and Miss Thriplow's reminiscences, prompted by the smell of a bay leaf, also have a suggestive Proustian flavor.

If *Those Barren Leaves* owes something to Proust, its successor, *Point Counter Point*, is even more heavily indebted to another French writer, Andre Gide, from whose novel *Les Faux-monnayeurs* Huxley has frankly borrowed a number of technical devices. *Point Counter Point* is one of Huxley's longest and most ambitious novels and, I should say, the most perfectly constructed—though the intricacy of its form entails a certain loss of spontaneity; admirable though it is, it lacks some of the force and vitality of *Crome Yellow* and *Antic Hay*.

The title provides a clue to Huxley's intention, which is to present, by a method analogous to counterpoint in music, a kind of multiple vision of life, in which the diverse aspects of experience can be observed simultaneously. (The technique has already been hinted at, as I have pointed out, in earlier novels.) The method is best described in the words of one of the characters, Philip Quarles. Quarles is a novelist and keeps a journal in which he discusses, at considerable length, the novelist's technique (this device of the novelist-within-a-novel is borrowed from *Les Faux-monnayeurs*):

The musicalization of fiction. Not in the symbolist way, by subordinating sense to sound. . . . But on a large scale, in the construction. Meditate on Beethoven. The changes of moods, the abrupt transitions. (Majesty alternating with a joke, for example, in the first movement of the B flat major Quartet. . . .) . . . A theme is stated, then developed, pushed out of shape, imperceptibly deformed, until, though still recognizably the same, it has become quite different. . . . All you need is a sufficiency of characters and parallel, contrapuntal plots. While Jones is murdering a wife, Smith is wheeling the perambulator in the park.

(ch. 22)

Point Counter Point is precisely the kind of novel that Quarles contemplated writing. The contrapuntal method resolves itself, in practice, into a system of elaborate and judicious "cutting," comparable to the technique of the cinema; many other writers have employed it subsequently (Graham Greene, for example), but seldom on so large a scale or so successfully as Huxley.

So far as its moral and philosophical implications are concerned, *Point Counter Point* seems to indicate a partial regression to Huxley's earlier pessimism; the promise (implied in the closing pages of *Those Barren Leaves*) of a possible escape from the "wearisome condition of humanity" is not fulfilled, and Huxley's habitual cynicism takes on a harsher, more ferocious quality. A new preoccupation with violence is noticeable—the murder of Webley the fascist, for example (one of Huxley's few attempts at melodrama and a not wholly successful one); death and suffering, in one form or another, pervade the book—for example, old Bidlake's duodenal ulcer and the death of Quarles's little boy. With few exceptions, the characters are even more unsympathetic than Huxley's previous creations: Webley the fascist, Spandrell the ineffectual diabolist, Lucy Tantamount, a typically Huxleyan femme fatale, though less perfectly characterized than some of her predecessors.

The most vividly drawn character in the book—and in many ways the most significant—is Spandrell, a modern incarnation of Baudelaire (whose personality Huxley had always found fascinating). The Baudelairean situation is reproduced almost exactly—the child's adoration for the widowed mother, the mother's remarriage to an elderly army officer, the boy's revulsion and his subsequent cult for debauchery and the "artificial paradises" of drugs and alcohol. Yet Spandrell is more than a mere echo of Baudelaire, for he represents (in a fictitious and, of course, exaggerated form) an aspect of Huxley himself to which I have already drawn attention —the perpetually recurring conflict between sensuality and asceticism. In Spandrell's case the conflict is presented in its most extreme and perverse form. Debauchery has become, as it were, a moral compulsion, a prolonged and unremitting protest against the mother's defection; Spandrell is filled with a passionate hatred not only for all moral values but even for, among other things, the beauties of nature. This is well illustrated in the following passage (Spandrell has taken out an elderly and ill-favored prostitute for a day in the country):

"Lovely, lovely," was Connie's refrain. The place, the day reminded her, she said, of her childhood in the country. She sighed.

"And you wish you'd been a good girl," said Spandrell sarcastically. "'The roses round the door make me love mother more,' I know, I know." . . .

"Oh, the foxgloves!" cried Connie, who hadn't even been listening. She ran toward them, grotesquely unsteady on her high heels. Spandrell followed her.

"Pleasingly phallic," he said, fingering one of the spikes of unopened buds. And he went on to develop the conceit profusely.

"Oh, be quiet, be quiet," cried Connie. "How can you say such things?" She was outraged, wounded. "How can you—here?"

"In God's country," he mocked. "How can I?" And raising his stick he suddenly began to lay about him right and left, slash, slash, breaking one of the tall proud plants at every stroke. The ground was strewn with murdered flowers.

"Stop, stop!" She caught at his arm. Silently laughing, Spandrell wrenched himself away from her and went on beating down the plants. . . .

"Down with them," he shouted, "down with them." . . . Connie was in tears.

"How could you?" she said. "How could you do it?"

. . . "Serves them right," he said. "Do you think I'm going to sit still and let myself be insulted? The insolence of the brutes! Ah, there's another!" He stepped across the glade to where one last tall foxglove stood as though hiding among the hazel saplings. One stroke was enough. The broken plant fell almost noiselessly.

(ch. 29)

As in the other novels, many of the characters in *Point Counter Point* are drawn from living models—notably Mark Rampion, a full-length portrait of D. H. Lawrence. It is significant that the previous sketch of Lawrence in *Two or Three Graces* is extremely unsympathetic, not to say malicious; Rampion, on the other hand, is drawn with great sympathy, even with affection, and one feels that he is the only character in the book of whom Huxley almost wholly approves. The contrast between the two portraits is probably due to the fact that in the intervening period Huxley had become increasingly sympathetic to Lawrence's ideas. One would have supposed the two men to be poles apart—and in many respects they were; yet a strong friendship united them during the latter years of Lawrence's life, and Huxley, though never quite prepared to accept Lawrence's philosophy in its entirety, was certainly profoundly influenced by it. Himself (as he often confessed) a prisoner of the intellect, debarred by his temperament from a complete and satisfying participation in the life of the senses, Huxley doubtless saw in Lawrence's "philosophy of the blood" a possible means of escape from his own predicament. After Lawrence's death, however, he seems finally to have rejected (if somewhat reluctantly) the instinctual approach to life, and in his subsequent works the Lawrentian influence became less and less noticeable. (It should be mentioned, however, that Huxley's introduction to Lawrence's letters[3] is one of the fairest and most balanced assessments of Lawrence and his work.)

Point Counter Point suffers from its overelaborate construction; some of the old gaiety has gone, and in the quality of the prose itself one notes a tendency to overfacility, a lack of tautness, and an increasing use of certain rather irritating mannerisms. Yet there can be little doubt that, technically speaking, *Point Counter Point* is Huxley's most considerable achievement in fiction. The interest of his subsequent novels is mainly one of content rather than of form: henceforward he concentrated less upon problems of pure technique and tended more and more to use the novel merely as a convenient medium for the expression of his ideas. I propose, therefore, to deal with the remaining novels rather more briefly.

Brave New World (1932) is a "novel of the future," and might be described as the reverse of the Wellsian medal. "Homo *au naturel*—" remarks Mr. Mercaptan in *Antic Hay*, "*ça pue*. And as for Homo à la H. G. Wells—*ça ne pue pas assez*." Huxley's Utopia, like that of Wells, "doesn't stink enough," and besides being hygienically odorless it is in other respects modeled largely on its Wellsian prototype; the difference between *Men Like Gods* (1923) and *Brave New World* lies chiefly in the point of view of the two writers. For Huxley the Wellsian Utopia, far from being a desirable state of affairs, represents the triumph of all that he most fears and dislikes, for it is a world in which humanity has been dehumanized, a world in which scientific progress has been produced, so to speak, to the *n*th degree. Mr. Scogan's

prophecy in *Crome Yellow* has been more than fulfilled: babies are incubated in bottles and a system of strictly scientific conditioning ensures that each individual shall perform automatically his allotted function within the community. It is a totalitarian and quasi-theocratic world; its gods are Karl Marx and Henry Ford—the latter referred to on pious occasions as Our Ford (or occasionally as Our Freud). In an artificially inseminated society, the most obscene word is "mother" and hygiene has become the ultimate moral value (the children are taught such variants of old-fashioned nursery rhymes as "Streptocock-Gee to Banbury T, to see a fine bathroom and W.C.").

The theme is developed with inexorable logic and with much of Huxley's characteristically ironic humor. The end, however, is tragic—the story culminates with the suicide (in a lighthouse in Surrey) of a "savage" imported from one of the few remaining native reservations, where life remains on a purely primitive (and pre-Fordian) level. *Brave New World*, if stylistically inferior to his previous novels, is one of Huxley's most spirited performances. Its main weakness lies, I think, in the fact that Huxley argues from an arbitrarily chosen set of premises and ignores a number of present tendencies that are quite as likely to influence the future as the ones with which he chooses to deal. Thus—as he himself admitted in a new preface to the book—there is no mention of nuclear fission, which had, as he says, "been a popular topic of conversation for years before the book was written." *Brave New World* may profitably be compared with George Orwell's *1984*, which, allowing for the fact that it was written nearly twenty years later, seems a far more plausible (and even more depressing) vision of the future than Huxley's.

The same year saw the publication of *Texts and Pretexts*, a personal anthology in which the verse extracts are interspersed with notes and short essays by Huxley himself. Besides testifying to his wide knowledge of English and French literature, the book also shows Huxley in one of his happiest roles—that of literary critic and "interpreter."

Brave New World is Huxley's nearest approach to popular fiction and probably served to introduce him to a far wider public. In his next novel, *Eyeless in Gaza* (1936), he reverts to an earlier and more characteristic manner. The first section describes the leading character looking at an album of photographs; his memory shifts to and fro over the past, as

[3]*The Letters of D. H. Lawrence* (London, 1932).

each photograph evokes a different scene or episode; thereafter the novel shifts backward and forward in time, the successive chapters being arranged unchronologically—thus, from 1933 we jump to 1934, thence back to 1933, then to 1902, and so on. The method probably owes something to Christopher Isherwood's *The Memorial* (1932), which is constructed on a very similar plan; and politics plays a far larger part in this book than in the previous novels—a fact that again suggests that Huxley may have been affected by politically minded writers of a younger generation.

The world of *Eyeless in Gaza* is still, very largely, the world of *Point Counter Point*, and the same kinds of characters and situations recur; there is, however, an increasing interest not only in politics (more especially in the political aspects of pacifism) but in the doctrines of mystical philosophy. Huxley's final convictions are as yet only implicit; but the philosophical outlook implied in *Eyeless in Gaza* is already very different from that of *Point Counter Point*. It is interesting to note that the further Huxley progressed toward his ultimate goal of nonattachment, the more preoccupied he seemed to become with the more unpleasant aspects of the human body. One would have expected the reverse to happen; yet in this novel and its successors there are a number of passages in which his "nastiness" seemed, to many readers, almost gratuitously offensive. In his earlier books one could attribute such lapses to mere youthful high spirits and a desire to shock bourgeois sensibilities; recurring in his maturity, they are perplexing, and one can only assume that the progressive heightening of his spiritual vision in some way intensified, retrospectively, his old Swiftian loathing for the body and its functions. The only good life, he seems to imply, is the spiritual life; but we are "born under one law, to another bound," and since we are condemned to live in a world of lust and excretion, of enemas and halitosis, we should do well not to forget the fact.

Many of the political and philosophic ideas in *Eyeless in Gaza* are further elaborated, in a more systematic form, in *Ends and Means* (1937), a long essay that appeared in the following year. Here Huxley's main thesis is that, in political as in individual behavior, the means condition the end and that therefore the much-invoked dictum "the end justifies the means" is demonstrably fallacious; the point is surely an important one and Huxley's elucidation of it is a valuable contribution to political thought.

Ends and Means cannot, however, be regarded as a mere political tract for the times: it is, among other things (as Huxley says), a kind of "cookbook" of reform and supplies an extremely comprehensive survey of the contemporary intellectual scene. The ideal goal of human effort has, as he says, been a matter of general agreement for the last thirty centuries: "From Isaiah to Karl Marx the prophets have spoken with one voice. In the Golden Age to which they look forward there will be liberty, peace, justice, and brotherly love." The trouble is—as Huxley sees it—that there has been no such general agreement about the means by which this ideal is to be attained: "Here unanimity and certainty give place to utter confusion, to the clash of contradictory opinions, dogmatically held and acted upon with the violence of fanaticism." Huxley's own solution of the problem (insofar as he attempts a solution) is in essence a religious one—the doctrine of complete nonattachment. Whether or not one agrees with Huxley's conclusions is hardly a matter of great importance; the chief value of *Ends and Means* lies in the attempt to evolve some kind of synthesis from the political, ethical, and religious confusions of our age. And, as Huxley modestly remarks in his closing words, "even the fragmentary outline of a synthesis is better than no synthesis at all."

After Many a Summer (1939) is a comedy of longevity set in Hollywood: a scientist, attempting to prolong human life by artificial means, is confronted by an actual bicentenarian who has anticipated his own discoveries a century and a half before. Much of the novel is in Huxley's best comic manner, but the philosophic divagations are inserted somewhat arbitrarily and tend to destroy the balance of the book. The same might be said of *Time Must Have a Stop* (1944), perhaps the least successful of Huxley's novels; in it he attempts the difficult feat of describing the mental processes of a man already dead, but the experiment can hardly be said to succeed.

Apart from fiction, Huxley's most substantial work to appear during World War II was *Grey Eminence* (1941), a detailed and scholarly biography of Father Joseph, the confidential adviser of Cardinal Richelieu. This is a model of its kind and makes one wish that Huxley's excursions into historiography had been more frequent. His researches into the life and times of Father Joseph may well have drawn his attention to the events related in *The Devils of Loudon* (1952). This is a detailed psychological study of an extraordinary case of demonic possession in seventeenth-century France. It is of great interest, but here again—as so often in his later work—Huxley seems overpreoccupied with the more unpleasant physiological aspects of his subject. There is, for instance, a description of the monstrous enemas employed as aids to exorcism that recalls certain comparable passages in *Eyeless in Gaza* and would seem to suggest that for Huxley the subject had a recurrent and somewhat morbid fascination.

During the last twenty years or so of Huxley's life, his output was hardly less prolific than formerly, and the works of this period show a remarkable diversity. Essays and belles lettres on the whole predominated over fiction, but three novels were published after 1945, and it will be convenient to consider these together. *Ape and Essence* (1948) is a short book, hardly more than a novella. It is a post-atomic vision of the future, and though the theme may seem to justify Huxley's melodramatic treatment of it, the most gloating relish with which he piles on the horrors somewhat diminishes the total impact of the story. *The Genius and the Goddess* (1955) explores a situation that Huxley had more than once dealt with before: the frequent combination of intellectual preeminence with a total inability to cope with the emotional (and, as often as not, the purely practical) demands of life. Henry Maartens is a physicist of genius, married to a beautiful wife who runs his life for him. The story is told by his younger assistant, Rivers, to the narrator, a novelist. Rivers had become the lover of Maartens' wife, Katy, at a moment when Maartens was dangerously ill; the young man is tortured by guilt at having betrayed his adored master, yet his act restores to Katy what Huxley calls the quality of "grace," and she is thus enabled, by a kind of psychosomatic miracle, to save her husband's life. The situation, with its neat reversal of ethical cause and effect, has a typically Huxleyan irony. "*Le Cocu Miraculé.* What a subject for a French farce!" comments the narrator; but, as Rivers points out, Oedipus or Lear could equally well be conceived in farcical terms.

In *Island* (1962) Huxley returns once again to the theme of Utopia. A remote island, Pala, is populated by a community whose principles of government are founded, basically, upon Tantric Buddhism and an uninhibited but rational attitude to sex. In contrast with *Brave New World*, this later Utopian fantasy portrays a way of life many aspects of which, it may be supposed, its author would have found congenial.

But Huxley, though he may have preferred the world of Pala to that of *Brave New World*, came to realize that such earthly paradises must prove finally helpless against the assault of industrialism and modern scientific techniques. This novel is, even for Huxley—who had never taken a very hopeful view of the future—a profoundly pessimistic one.

The more significant of Huxley's later writings were nonfictional. In 1945 appeared *The Perennial Philosophy*, a kind of anthology with an extensive running commentary, drawn from the writings of the mystics. Huxley's purpose was to extract from the manifold aspects of the subject a kind of highest common denominator, a system of philosophy that would include yet transcend the various methods by which men have sought to attain direct communication with God. As Huxley himself admitted, the mystical experience is, and must remain, finally incommunicable; many will dispute the validity of the mystic's claims, but whether one agrees or disagrees with Huxley's conclusions may be largely a matter of temperament. On the other hand, there can be no doubt whatsoever about the intellectual integrity of Huxley himself. His conversion (if one can use the word in this context) involved no intellectual surrender, no sudden act of faith; it was the result, rather, of a prolonged and critical investigation of the available evidence conducted with the caution and objectivity of a scientist.

The Perennial Philosophy was followed by two studies dealing with the effects of mescaline and lysergic acid (LSD): *The Doors of Perception* (1954) and *Heaven and Hell* (1956). Huxley maintains that the hallucinatory states produced by these drugs are hardly to be distinguished from the beatific vision of the mystics. This leads him to some interesting speculations as to the relationship between mind and body. Mescaline, for example, is allied to adrenochrome, which, it is thought, may occur spontaneously in the human organism. "In other words," writes Huxley, "each one of us may be capable of manufacturing a chemical, minute doses of which are known to cause profound changes in consciousness." The mystical state, therefore, may prove to be a mere function of the adrenal glands.

Adonis and the Alphabet (1956) is a volume of essays, all of which show that Huxley was a master of this form. The essay has become unpopular in an age of mass communications, but it was always well suited to the didactic strain in Huxley that he perhaps inherited from his grandfather. In this volume the title piece may be singled out as particularly characteristic. It describes a visit to Syria and Lebanon and relates the myth of Adonis to that unknown Phoenician who "about thirty-five centuries ago . . . invented, or at least perfected, the ABC." Here Huxley is in his best vein, and the witty, erudite writing recalls the lighthearted mood of such early travel books as *Jesting Pilate* and *Beyond the Mexique Bay.*

Brave New World Revisited (1958) is a long essay in which Huxley reconsiders his prophetic novel of 1932. He points out that many of his predictions came true very much sooner than he expected and the outlook gives little cause for optimism; yet it is our duty, he says, to resist the forces that menace our freedom, even though we may be (and probably are) fighting a losing battle.

It is a far cry from *Limbo* to *The Perennial Philosophy*, yet Huxley's works, considered as a whole, reveal a remarkably consistent pattern of development. His earliest books, apparently so slight and even frivolous, contain the germs of his later and more serious productions. This internal cohesion is the more surprising in view of Huxley's enormous range of interests; one could instance many modern writers whose work has the same kind of unity, but for the most part they are writers whose ideas operate within far narrower limits or who have some specific ax to grind. Huxley never ground an ax in his life—unless his unremitting and disinterested search for truth may be so described; yet, despite the homogeneity of his writings, he remains a strangely paradoxical figure: an intellectual who profoundly distrusted the intellect, a sensualist with a deep-seated loathing for bodily functions, a naturally religious man who remained an impenitent rationalist.

SELECTED BIBLIOGRAPHY

I. BIBLIOGRAPHY. H. R. Duval, *Aldous Huxley: A Bibliography* (New York, 1939); C. J. Eschelbach and J. L. Schober, *Aldous Huxley: A Bibliography 1916–1959* (Berkeley, Calif., 1961).

II. COLLECTED WORKS. *Twice Seven: Fourteen Collected Stories* (London, 1944); *The Collected Edition* (London, 1946–1960); *Collected Short Stories* (London, 1957); *Collected Essays* (New York, 1959); D. Watt, ed., *The Collected Poetry of Aldous Huxley* (London, 1969); *Collected Works* (London, 1970–).

III. SELECTED WORKS. *Selected Poems* (Oxford, 1925); *Essays New and Old* (London, 1926); *Rotunda* (London, 1932), a general selection; *Stories, Essays and Poems* (London, 1937); *Verses and a Comedy* (London, 1946); M. Philipson, ed., *On Art and Artists* (London, 1960); H. Raymond, ed., *Selected Essays* (London, 1961); C. J. Rolo, ed., *The World of Aldous Huxley: An Omnibus of His Fiction and Nonfiction Over Three Decades* (New York, 1957); G. Smith, ed., *Letters of Aldous Huxley* (London, 1969).

IV. SEPARATE WORKS. *The Burning Wheel* (Oxford, 1916), verse; *Jonah* (Oxford, 1917), verse; *The Defeat of Youth and Other Poems* (Oxford, 1918).

Leda and Other Poems (London, 1920); *Limbo* (London, 1920), short stories; *Crome Yellow* (London, 1921), novel; *Mortal Coils* (London, 1922), short stories; *Antic Hay* (London, 1923), novel; *On the Margin* (London, 1923), essays; *The Discovery* (London, 1924), drama, adaptation of F. Sheridan's play; *Little Mexican* (London, 1924), short stories; *Along the Road* (London, 1925), travel; *Those Barren Leaves* (London, 1925), novel; *Jesting Pilate* (London, 1926), travel; *Two or Three Graces* (London, 1926), short stories; *Proper Studies* (London, 1927), essays; *Point Counter Point* (London, 1928), novel; *Arabia Infelix* (London, 1929), verse; *Do What You Will* (London, 1929), essays; *Holy Face, and Other Essays* (London, 1929).

Brief Candles (London, 1930), short stories; *This Way to Paradise* (London, 1930), dramatization of *Point Counter Point* by C. Dixon, preface by Huxley; *Vulgarity in Literature* (London, 1930), criticism; *The Cicadas and Other Poems* (London, 1931); *Music at Night* (New York, 1931), essays; *The World of Light* (London, 1931), drama; *Brave New World* (London, 1932), novel; *Texts and Pretexts* (London, 1932), anthology; *Thomas Henry Huxley as a Man of Letters* (London, 1932), criticism; *Beyond the Mexique Bay* (London, 1934), travel; *Eyeless in Gaza* (London, 1936), novel; *The Olive Tree* (London, 1936), essays; *What Are You Going to Do About It? The Case for Constructive Peace* (London, 1936), commentary; *Ends and Means* (London, 1937), commentary; *The Elder Pieter Breugel* (New York, 1938), art criticism; *The Most Agreeable Vice* (Los Angeles, 1938); *After Many a Summer* (London, 1939), novel.

Words and Their Meanings (Los Angeles, 1940); *Grey Eminence* (London, 1941), biography; *The Art of Seeing* (London, 1942), essay; *Time Must Have a Stop* (London, 1944), novel; *The Perennial Philosophy* (New York, 1945), commentary; *Science, Liberty and Peace* (New York, 1946), commentary; *Ape and Essence* (New York, 1948), novel; *The Gioconda Smile* (London, 1948), drama, adapted from a story in *Mortal Coils*; *Food and People* (London, 1949), with Sir John Russell; *The Prisons* (London, 1949), criticism.

Themes and Variations (London, 1950), essays; *The Devils of Loudon* (London, 1952), biography; *Joyce the Artificer: Two Studies of Joyce's Method* (London, 1952), with S. Gilbert; *The Doors of Perception* (London, 1954), essay; *The Genius and the Goddess* (London, 1955), novel;

Adonis and the Alphabet (London, 1956), essays; *Heaven and Hell* (London, 1956), essay, sequel to *Doors of Perception; Brave New World Revisited* (New York–London, 1958), essay.

On Art and Artists (London, 1960), anthology; *Island* (London, 1962), novel; *Literature and Science* (London, 1963), essay; *The Crows of Pearblossom* (London, 1967), children's story.

V. Translations and Introductions. R. de Gourmont, *A Virgin Heart* (New York, 1921), trans. from French by Huxley; C. P. de Crébillon, *The Opportunities of a Night* (London, 1925), trans. by E. Sutton, intro. by Huxley; *The Autobiography and Memoirs of Benjamin Robert Haydon* (London, 1926), intro. by Huxley; J. H. Burns, *A Vision of Education* (London, 1929), intro. by Huxley; *The Letters of D. H. Lawrence* (London, 1932), intro. by Huxley; A. Huxley, ed., *An Encyclopedia of Pacifism* (London, 1937); *The Song of God: Bhagavad-Gita* (Hollywood, 1944), trans. by S. Prabhavanda and C. Isherwood, intro. by Huxley.

VI. Biographical and Critical Studies. G. Vann, *On Being Human: St. Thomas and Mr. Aldous Huxley* (London, 1933); A. J. Henderson, *Aldous Huxley* (London, 1935); A. Gérard, *À la rencontre de Aldous Huxley* (Paris, 1947); S. Chatterjee, *Aldous Huxley: A Study* (Calcutta, 1955); J. Atkins, *Aldous Huxley: A Literary Study* (London, 1956).

S. Ghose, *Aldous Huxley: A Cynical Salvationist* (London, 1962); J. Huxley, ed., *Aldous Huxley, 1894–1963: A Memorial Volume* (London, 1965); S. J. Greenblatt, *Three Modern Satirists: Waugh, Orwell and Huxley* (London, 1965); R. W. Clark, *The Huxleys* (London, 1968); P. Bowering, *Aldous Huxley: A Study of the Major Novels* (London, 1968); L. A. Huxley, *This Timeless Moment: A Personal View of Aldous Huxley* (New York, 1968); J. Meckier, *Aldous Huxley: Satire and Structure* (London, 1969); D. P. Scales, *Aldous Huxley and French Literature* (London, 1969).

C. M. Holmes, *Aldous Huxley and the Way to Reality* (Bloomington, Ind., 1970); L. Brander, *Aldous Huxley: A Critical Study* (London, 1970); G. Woodcock, *Dawn and the Darkest Hour: A Study of Aldous Huxley* (London, 1972); K. May, *Aldous Huxley* (London, 1972); P. Firchow, *Aldous Huxley, Satirist and Novelist* (Minneapolis, 1972); S. Bedford, *Aldous Huxley*, 2 vols. (London, 1974, 1979); R. E. Kuehn, ed., *Aldous Huxley: A Collection of Critical Essays* (Englewood Cliffs, N. J., 1974).

C. S. Ferns, *Aldous Huxley, Novelist* (London, 1980); K. Gandhi, *Aldous Huxley* (London, 1981).

J. B. PRIESTLEY

(1894-   )

Kenneth Young

INTRODUCTION

J. B. Priestley is the most frequently performed living English dramatist across five continents. His novels, from *The Good Companions* (1929) to a late major composition, *The Image Men* (1968), are enjoyed by millions who know nothing of English concert parties in the 1920's nor of the modernistic universities and advertising agencies of more recent times. From him too have come long, shrewd studies such as *Literature and Western Man* (1960); descriptive works full of original perceptions; essays both appreciative and polemical; studies of humor and theater, and, latterly, spectacular reexpositions of the eras of the Prince Regent and Queen Victoria. It was he who popularized the studies of time by J. W. Dunne[1] in the 1930's. He has added at least two words—"admass" and "nomadmass"—to the language, and condemned with some effect such words as the literary-trendy "committed," though apparently he has accepted "the Establishment."

Why all this hopping about from novels to plays to autobiographical-descriptive books? "Possibly," he wrote, because of "a fundamental lack of what I appeared superficially to have in abundance—self-confidence." Certainly he was never the "Jolly Jack" of legend, nor later the soured cantankerous ex-radical. He can be blunt, tender, apocalyptic; mostly his style is humorous and lively.

His ratings in critical rather than individual esteem have gone up and down as in a political opinion poll. He was lauded as a bright young essayist in the 1920's and widely praised for his early novels; his further success in the London theater of the 1930's was all too much for some famous but pettifogging critics, but mostly he has not been bothered by his

detractors. His early wartime broadcasts, talking essays, brought him national fame, though some thought them "socialistic." Evidently they were too popular for his literary reputation, for this reached a new low in the early postwar years, when ironically, some of his best work was appearing—the play *The Linden Tree* (1948), the novel *Bright Day* (1946). Today, however, younger critics are treating Priestley's wide range of work with the seriousness it deserves; three discriminating books on it have appeared since the early 1950's.

Not a genius, he says, of himself, but a man with many talents, "fertile but careless." He has told us much of himself in *Midnight on the Desert* (1937) and *Rain upon Godshill* (1939), both subtitled "Chapters of Autobiography," in *Margin Released* (1962), in many an essay, in *Delight* (1949), and in sections of the brilliantly reported *English Journey* (1934); and there are tendrils of his own life in both plays and novels.

He has been reticent about three matters in which he was personally involved. First, World War I: his own appalling experiences in the trenches are described only briefly in *Margin Released* and very obliquely in *The Town Major of Miraucourt* (1930), though he subsequently regretted not writing a sort of *War and Peace*. There are, however, repeated references to the *results* of the war. The world before and after it is the crux of much of his writing and is the whole inspiration of one of his best novels, *Bright Day*.

Second, his three postwar years at Cambridge are seldom mentioned, though he was apparently successful enough in his examinations for his teachers to suggest that he should stay on to lecture and coach. Cambridge nevertheless seems to stir little in his creative mind; it has never been a background for his fiction.

In *Instead of the Trees* (1977), which is sadly subtitled "A Final Chapter of Autobiography," he writes

---

[1]Dunne was the author of *An Experiment in Time* (London, 1927), in which he proposed a serial theory of time; the concept is that time is not irrevocable.

of Cambridge, "I never felt at home in the place and never looked back on my three years there with the faintest glimmer of sentiment," even though his present wife was born and educated in Cambridge. Certainly he is grateful for those years and for the friends he made there, such as the poets Davison, Bullett, and Kendon. But he never felt really happy there, and not even "cosily at home." Already in 1919 "the girls were not only invading men's rooms but were dropping their skirts before they had hardly closed the doors."

The rest of the book is concerned with dreams and with long, interesting speculations about the nature of heaven. He is still worrying about his alleged brusqueness in company and puts much of that down to his face:

It has always been treacherous. It expresses far more than I really feel. . . . I can look furious when I am no more than mildly annoyed. All that staring, glowering, frowning, glaring, merely mean that it is up to its tricks again, well out of my control.

It is a sort of apologia for having been "tactless, overbearing, insensitive, disappointing, alienating people who might have become my friends." He recognizes his luck and says that it is time, before it is too late, "that I give the world more smiles and far fewer howls and begin thanking God on my knees."

A third subject he has avoided is that of his own personal life, though he has been thrice married; on this one can only congratulate him and add, however, that in his fiction the treatment of sexual affairs has moved, in consonance with the times, toward a greater frankness, such as he shows in *The Image Men.*

Priestley is above all the teller of a tale. He is a writer of gusto and attack; he does not expend indulgent pages upon an evanescence or upon exploring the inner refinements of a soul or subtilizing a character to extinction. *L'attaque, toujours l'attaque.* He is no Dostoyevsky agonizing in a tormented world. He has no vivid vision, such as C. S. Lewis', of the immanence of evil in human kind, though of human capability for cruelty, frustration, and sheer nastiness he is not in doubt. He says he is not a Christian, so his perpetual awareness of the mystery of human existence has led him toward the speculations of C. D. Ouspensky, to studies of dreams; and what hope of immortality there may be comes to him in the thoughts of John William Dunne rather than from the New Testament.

On earth, he believes—or used to—that most bad things are remediable, though he has today no faith that they will be remedied by any of the mass "isms." His socialism is of the thoroughly English variety, springing from his disgust with the way the poor were forced to exist, particularly during the 1930's, and in *Rain upon Godshill* there is a blazing, rather wild attack on "the faked financial crisis of 1931," on plutocracy, on the "right people" occupying all the key positions. But even at that time he distrusted the Labour party's "trade union basis"; and later on, in *Margin Released,* he denied being "one of the starry-eyed do-gooders." That is a charge from which he may easily be absolved, except for his part in starting the Campaign for Nuclear Disarmament, which, after Priestley left it, was clearly discernible as a subversive organization. Here, for a limited period, his humanitarianism conquered his reason.

But has he not always speculated, tentatively and fearfully, that even those he would regard as right-thinking would not always prefer the better to the worse? It is the theme of his play *They Came to a City* (1944). In his beatific city, the characters who have viewed it report, life didn't have to be "a dog-fight round a dustbin." But some reject Utopia. It is not the sort of place many of the characters he himself has created would want to call home.

Priestley made his individual mark during several generations that did not lack giants—Shaw, Wells, Hardy, and Bennett; he dominated the theater in the age of Noel Coward, Somerset Maugham, and Sean O'Casey.

LIFE

JOHN BOYNTON PRIESTLEY was born in 1894 in the wool-dominated town of Bradford, son of a schoolmaster who was the first to introduce school meals in an elementary school, and of an Irish mother named Hoult who died not long after his birth. Both parents had a working-class ancestry. Educated in Bradford, he showed no desire for universities, drifted into a wool merchant's office, and enjoyed the remarkably rich life such a city then offered: family parties (his father had remarried), friends he made through his taste for art and music—for Bradford, like Manchester, had its Jewish and German immigrants (the composer Frederick Delius was born there) who lovingly pursued the arts. Priestley played the piano reasonably well. He stowed himself into the cheaper seats at theaters, he visited music halls (then in their final age of glory and not well viewed by his Baptist father), he attended arts clubs and playgoers' societies; and above all, in his little room, surrounded by what books he could afford from his exiguous pay, he read and wrote and even had articles printed in local papers, including a local Labour weekly.

For he wanted to write, though he was, as he humorously recalls, "ready to conduct symphony orchestras and do a little great acting from time to time." It was a glorious, unforgettable period of Priestley's life, the more poignantly evoked in his subsequent writing because it was all ended for good by "the murderous imbecility" of World War I: "I will swear that . . . all the great golden afternoons when a man might plan an epic, and even begin it, came to an end in August 1914."

Priestley served from his twentieth to twenty-fifth year in the Duke of Wellington's West Riding Regiment and then in the Devonshire Regiment, part of the time as a subaltern in the trenches in France; most of the friends he made were killed, even before the slaughter of the Somme battle in 1916, as though they were animals in a messy abattoir. He himself was invalided home when a mortar bomb fell on his trench and "the world blew up." He was therefore not at Passchendaele, "where [Field Marshal Earl] Haig, who ought to have gone up there himself or gone home, was slicing my whole generation into sausage meat held above a swill bucket."

His bitterness remained as late as 1962, when he wrote in *Margin Released* that the army should have "turned on Haig." "Even without the negotiated peace we ought to have had in 1916, [which the Tory leader Lord Lansdowne proposed], we could have saved half a million British lives if we had handed the whole mess over to a few men from Imperial Chemicals, Lever Brothers or Lyons and Co." Priestley emerged from the war "with a chip on [his] shoulder," and, he adds with raw bitterness, "a big, heavy chip, probably a friend's thigh-bone." He was released from the army in the spring of 1919 and went to Cambridge (Trinity Hall) on an inadequate grant. Before long he had a wife from the West Riding who was expecting a child. Having taken his degree he left, aged twenty-eight, to free-lance in London. His capital: £50. He wrote reviews, short stories, and critical and general essays, for which there was then a considerable call in papers of all kinds. He received help from J. C. Squire, editor of the *London Mercury*, and Robert Lynd, literary editor of the *Daily News*, a gentle, ingenuous essayist whose worth today is regrettably forgotten.

Priestley prospered sufficiently to maintain a child and a wife who was soon to die. He read manuscripts for John Lane's publishing firm, The Bodley Head, and wrote for, among others, the *Bookman, Spectator, Saturday Review* (later to be amalgamated with the *New Statesman*), and some daily newspapers. He brought out books: *The English Comic Characters* (1925), one on George Meredith, and another on Thomas Love Peacock. Some of his essays were collected in book form, but tastes were changing and "the intellectual young" no longer much read the sometimes too bland essayists; instead they sought meaning in the disjointed, allusive Ezra Pound, in the fine-spun novels of Virginia Woolf and E. M. Forster, while war-horror novels and poems made them a pacifist, socialist generation. G. B. Shaw, H. G. Wells, Arnold Bennett, Hilaire Belloc, James Barrie, H. M. Tomlinson were still, however, active figures with a large following, some of them, too, socialists of Victorian provenance. Priestley met and described them in *Margin Released* and elsewhere.

He became a close friend of the highly successful novelist Hugh Walpole, who was perceptive—and generous—enough to collaborate with the young Priestley in a novel called *Farthing Hall* (1929), so that Priestley should have a share in the royalties that the name Walpole then ensured. Priestley never forgot his kindness. Before that he had written the pleasant, fantastic *Adam in Moonshine* (1927); his gift for the slightly satirical extravaganza—the sort of thing a much later writer, Simon Raven, did in *The Sabre Squadron*—never left him, as may be noted in *It's an Old Country* (1967), when the "well-round-the-bend" Lady Ellowstone gives her dinner party. In 1927 the beginning novelist also published *Benighted*, which became the successful thriller film *The Old Dark House* (1932).

He then began the long narrative novel *The Good Companions*, which made his name in 1929 and in that autumn was selling several thousand copies a day; it has never ceased to sell. He swiftly followed it with a totally different though equally long novel, *Angel Pavement* (1930), which sold no less well: "This giant jackpot, this golden gusher," he called his sales of these two books.

Success—but it was not enough. The conquering novelist, like some jousting medieval knight, would take on all comers. The theater, too, must fall to his powerful lance. He became a playwright and was victorious again. "If Bernard Shaw is headmaster," wrote J. C. Trewin on the 1930's, "Priestley is one of the senior prefects." He even went into management and at one time had several plays running simultaneously in London. Not all were financially successful, but some were; and some, coolly received in London, were acclaimed abroad.

During the 1930's he spent much time in the United States, both scriptwriting in Hollywood, which benefited pocket and experience, and in Arizona, from which sprang *Midnight on the Desert* (1937). There he first glimpsed the sheer horror that he felt against much town life in the United States and depicted in *Journey Down a Rainbow* (published in 1955, in collaboration with his third wife, Jacquetta Hawkes). Another kind of horror emerged in his on-the-spot study *English Journey*. Here the most powerful passages are those that describe the areas of bad unemployment, and they gain by the contrast he makes with the reasonably prosperous parts of the country.

Time was already at his heels in such plays as *Time and the Conways* (1937) and *I Have Been Here Before* (1937), and in *Midnight on the Desert*. But time of a more mundane nature was catching up with him. World War II, the imminence of which he had often forecast in his blasts against the Chamberlain government's policies, broke out in September 1939. He, so to speak, "introduced" that war when he began serial readings on the BBC of his novel *Let the People Sing*, a few hours after Chamberlain's "state of war" broadcast. The novel's title has a certain irony; it is in fact a music hall comedy-romance.

Priestley was now forty-five, so not liable for active military service, and his main contribution was the sensible, intuitive broadcast series "Postscripts," which he gave every Sunday after the nine o'clock news. He now thinks that these were "ridiculously overpraised," but some still read most movingly. He wrote two or three works on such obvious propagandist themes as *British Women Go to War* (1943); a pleasing spy thriller, *Black-out in Gretley* (1942); and an excellent novel, *Daylight on Saturday* (1943), focusing on human relations inside an aircraft factory.

The war over, he entered one of his best periods, in the novel, the drama, and topical, polemical contributions to periodicals. Some years later he branched out into new media, writing a libretto for Sir Arthur Bliss's opera *The Olympians* (1949); a play or two for television; a codramatization with one of the newer novelists, Iris Murdoch, of her novel *A Severed Head*; serious studies of time theories and of past history and literature; and yet more experimental stage shows. He even ran for Parlia-

ment as an Independent, waged war against postwar governmental policies, and in 1968–1969 wrote what the present writer and Priestley himself are inclined to think his best novel, the two volumes titled *The Image Men*.

NONFICTION

PRIESTLEY's early essays, of which there is a fair selection in *Essays of Five Decades* (1968), he himself has dubbed "anachronistic." They were written in the 1920's to divert the comfortable reader, who was not yet willing to devote all his weekly reading to grim economic or political themes and was happy to allow his attention to wander to trivia treated with some fancifulness. Such were "First Snow," "The Flower Show," and "On the Moors." They have a period charm. But then we come to *Delight*, in which he develops his essay-writing gifts into an almost apothegmatic French style recalling moments of happiness, or fortunate resolutions of frustrations, or simple discoveries—on quietly malicious chairmen; on giving advice: "I, who manage my own affairs with as much care and steady attention and skill as—let us say—a drunken Irish tenor"; on "frightening senior civil servants"; on "graceful fountains, exquisite fountains, beautiful fountains"—yes, delights.

The later essays, however, are as tough as old boots, polemical, devastating in their logic, often sharply observant in a subtle, intuitive fashion. Those collected in *Thoughts in the Wilderness* (1957) have made Priestley a direct influence on many intelligent readers. Long before most of us, he was against "bigness"—in vast organizations, states, entertainment, and housing projects. He was almost the first to observe that in England it is not politicians of opposite parties who are, except in public, against one another, but all of them who are against us. On quite another theme he notes that in England over thirty or so years "the visual appreciation of things has increased while the literary sense is decaying."

He may set out from a personal reaction and end in a profundity. In "Something Else," for instance, he begins with the dissatisfaction and ache of disappointment that many (and not merely the elderly) so often feel about something they had expected to enjoy: a dinner party with friends, a visit to the theater where great performers are at work, a beautifully played concert. And yet, and yet "something else" is missing. The reason?

We lack, we Something Elsers, the unifying force of a strong religious faith. Where the central-heating furnace ought to be in the basement is a dark, cold, empty space. Our lives have no sacred common ground. Some essential links, even within ourselves as well as with others, are missing. We cannot see one another as subjects of the same invisible kingdom.

(p. 92)

Or perhaps it is that "the patterns," fixed so long for enjoyment, "are becoming worn."

Perhaps our friends ought to come and act for us or paint us. Perhaps we ought to crowd round the stage and exchange speeches with Dame Edith [Evans] or Sir Ralph [Richardson]. Perhaps Bertrand Russell ought to help the Sadler's Wells Ballet, and Arnold Toynbee appear with the Philharmonia Orchestra. Perhaps we ought to rehearse our dinner parties and extemporise our stage performances. Perhaps novels ought to be a mixture of printed pages and recordings . . . I don't know. But I know there could be, must be, Something Else.

(p. 93)

He is acute too on deep changes in society that often go unnoted. People and particularly politicians in most of the West live in yesterday's world. Thus a politician

will talk to us about our traditions, even if those traditions no longer have any inner validity and force and are in fact only part of the great show that amuses the idle-minded mob. He will still praise the love of liberty of people who would cheerfully exchange their last glimpses of freedom for a new car, a refrigerator, and a fourteen-inch television screen. . . . He will orate about our Christian community to men and women who are living in the most blankly secular and material society the world has known since Hadrian's Rome. He will praise the spiritual values of people . . . who have believed for years that all they can hope for is a better spring mattress in the execution chamber.

Priestley has a withering dislike of high-pressure advertising and salesmanship not merely because most goods sold in this way are unnecessary, but because he sees these processes producing a society as uniform in the West as it is in the East, where "Communism only offers a grimmer variation of this society" with propaganda and the secret police playing the role of advertising and salesman. He writes of the "twin ideals of our time, organization and quantity" producing a nightmare vision of the future "with billions of people, all numbered and registered with not a gleam of genius anywhere. . . . Everything is becoming part of a huge idle show."

He continues to ask of his country, "Where are we going?" and too often is shouted down by those who think "we are half way to Paradise." He refuses to accept that production and yet more production is the answer:

a consumer race with donkeys chasing an electric carrot. This enables you to build up and enjoy a civilization in which innumerable men with anxiety neuroses sit cursing in new and larger cars that cannot move, just because innumerable other men, with stomach ulcers, are also out in their new and larger cars. . . . Much of this elaborate folly is the result of thinking in terms of figures, statistics, abstractions, and not in terms of human beings and their age-old primary satisfactions, for which three visits a week to a psycho-analyst are a poor substitute.

Well, human beings *may* just win out but "our age may be drawing on a spiritual cultural capital, accumulated by past generations," and that cannot last forever. When it is gone the "old middle class," with its core of "vigilant, combative, radical, and enthusiastic persons," will have gone, too, and we shall be left with

small groups enjoying the exercise of power, and a great mass, no longer haunted by the images of any bows of burning gold and arrows of desire, content to be ordered about and moulded so long as it feels materially secure, comfortable, and not too bored for lack of amusement.

There is much more of his nonfictional writing worth attention, particularly *Man and Time* (1964) and *English Humour* (1976), where he defines his subjects as "thinking in fun while feeling in earnest." Outstanding, however, is *English Journey*, "being," he writes as part of his title, "a rambling but truthful account of what one man saw and heard and felt and thought during a journey through England during the autumn of the year 1933." It is not all as grim as might be expected in that time of unemployment and the dole. He portrays some of his characters as humorously as in the novels. He notes that in the Cotswolds, though the men on the land are not well paid, they can live: "people looked comfortable. The children were noticeably in good shape." Staying in hotels, he observes the veneration of steak: "When an ordinary English waiter mentions any other dish, he is a realist and his very tone of voice tells you what that dish really is—muck. But when he mentions Steak, his voice is low, hushed, reverent."

Soon, however, he is among the pitiful and the sordid. In his hometown, Bradford, he attends a reunion dinner of his old regiment and discovers that many of the "pals" could not even afford the modest tavern dinner; even though offered free places, they were ashamed to come because their clothes were not good enough. "They ought to have known that they would have been welcome in their sorriest rags."

In Liverpool he talks to some of the deprived mélange of races who have made the city their home, and hears: "Now that boy looks English enough, doesn't he? But as a matter of fact, he's half Chinese. Yes, and he's all Chinese inside. He has dreams, that boy, and they're all Oriental dreams. Queer isn't it?"

In Lancashire where the cotton trade is in severe decline, he bursts out:

What is the use of England—and England in this connection of course, means the City, Fleet Street, and the West End clubs—congratulating herself upon having pulled through yet once again, when there is no plan for Lancashire. Since when did Lancashire cease to be a part of England? . . . No man can walk about these towns, the Cinderellas in the baronial household of Victorian England, towns meant to work in and not to live in and now even robbed of their work, without feeling that there is a terrible lack of direction and leadership in our affairs.

(pp. 226–227)

The distress in Lancashire is but a prologue to the abomination of desolation he finds in Durham and Northumberland—"If T. S. Eliot ever wants to write a poem about a real wasteland instead of a metaphysical one, he should come here." Jarrow is

a derelict town. . . . There is no escape anywhere in Jarrow from its prevailing misery, for it is entirely a working-class town. One little street may be rather more wretched than another, but to the outsider they all look alike. One out of every two shops appeared to be permanently closed. Wherever we went there were men hanging about, not scores of them but hundreds and thousands of them. The whole town looked as if it had entered a perpetual penniless bleak Sabbath. The men wore the drawn masks of prisoners of war.

(p. 249)

His other outstanding work of nonfiction is the long *Literature and Western Man,* in which he surveys what Europe, Russia, and America have created and enjoyed in their writing from the Renaissance onward. His judgments are sometimes controversial but never less than thought-provoking. The book, however, is written not so much as a literary history but because of his conviction that "ours is an age of supreme crisis when the most desperate decisions have to be made," and that this study "might help us to understand ourselves."

To his theme he brings both sense and sensibility. But it is surprising, for example, that the time scheme should have been framed so as to omit Chaucer, who was as much a Western man as Rabelais and Shakespeare. But his brief chapter on Spain and Cervantes is masterly. Not only does he claim that *Don Quixote* is "the best novel in the world," but he sees its author as "the magical ironist of the relativeness of reality, of truth at war with illusion," pointing forward, "beyond where his faith and hope could reach" to Miguel de Unamuno, Proust, Pirandello, Mann, and Joyce.

We sweep swiftly through the centuries. To Priestley the "high" eighteenth-century writers were less proclassical than antimedieval; Swift is "that mutilated giant"; Sterne's "cheap" tricks in *Tristram Shandy* he finds "embarrassing," though he was "a humorist of genius." Under the skill of Priestley the novelist, the writers come to life as vividly as characters in his novels.

I doubt whether certain obiter dicta—such as that "the Classical depends upon the conscious mind, the Romantic upon the unconscious"—are adequate anymore; certainly they are not new. The thought is to be found in most pedestrian histories of literature, and many of us have heard too much about "the explosion of Rousseau's unconscious" having created romanticism to believe it anymore.

There is, however, little to fault and much to praise in his chapter on Goethe and Heine. But John Wesley, surely, and the Evangelicals would have been worth a passing note. Later in the book it is at least worth pondering over his contention that the Aesthetic movement from Théophile Gautier to Oscar Wilde was not fundamentally aesthetic but social, the urge to shock bourgeois sensibilities being stronger than the urge to create.

Is it correct, however, to say that to Thomas Macaulay the Reform Bill of 1832 was "the entrance to the Promised Land"? Rather, surely, he saw it as a necessary concession to avoid England's being infected by a European epidemic of revolution. But three cheers at any rate for Priestley's suggestion that Thomas Carlyle should be reread, at least in selection, because he compels us to see the "age and all its triumphs dwindling and shrivelling" and because "we are further in, not out of the wood that Carlyle describes so vividly."

Partly because of his own novelistic methods,

Priestley may not be completely just in remarking that Gustave Flaubert "remained the slave of his method." Of a descendant of Flaubert, Henry James, he is fair in saying that he brought to fiction, much in need of them, "adult and exquisitely civilized standards"; nevertheless, he is properly critical of James's "tiptoeing along interminable airless corridors" and of the "complacency and supercilious self-righteousness" of some of his disciples. A major novelist, yes, but not, Priestley believes, "a supreme master."

In part 5, he writes of those he calls "The Moderns," of whom he believes many intelligent readers are wary. No wonder! Look at the "arrogant intolerance" of critics, reviewers, and lecturers on Literature who, like bad-tempered customs officers on a bad day, insist on dividing literature from Literature. This "absolutist" attitude insists that a serious writer "ought to be difficult, hard to read." Though he is very understanding of how that came about, it did create the false dichotomy between "highbrow" and "lowbrow" that "did no good service to literature." Proust, Joyce, Valéry, Eliot, Virginia Woolf, Hesse, Mann, Kafka "have their own genius and depth," but "it would be absurd to pretend that they have the old broad appeal on many different levels, beginning with anybody who wants a book to read."

With this important proviso, however, Priestley treats the "highbrow" writers fairly—Eliot, for instance, "has created for himself a poetic instrument, which, though low in tone and rather narrow in compass for a major poet, he uses with wonderful skill"; Kafka "within the limits he set for himself is a master"; and he sees clearly into the being of D. H. Lawrence:

The poetic half of him is wonderful. . . . The prophetic side of him is far less satisfactory. . . . He knew in his blood and bones that our society was hurrying to disaster but had not the temperament, the time and patience . . . to discover for himself, coolly and analytically, what exactly was wrong.
(p. 424)

But then who has?

Priestley spends too much time on Willa Cather and L. H. Myers, and none at all (barring a passing reference) on Ford Madox Ford, a major if uneven novelist, or Wyndham Lewis, whose work as both artist and writer is highly relevant to his theme of

that curious *malaise* of modern Western Man. Too many things are going wrong at the same time. . . . Patterns of living that had existed for thousands of years are destroyed within a generation. Deep dissatisfactions, really belonging to Man's inner world, are projected on to the outer world, except by a few profoundly intuitive men of genius who now begin to prophesy disaster.

In his Conclusion he once more identifies religion as the hope of the future:

Religion alone can carry the load, defend us against the dehumanising collectives, restore true personality. And it is doubtful if our society can last much longer without religion, for either it will destroy itself by some final idiot war or, at peace but hurrying in the wrong direction, it will soon largely cease to be composed of persons.
(p. 444)

It is fine to have a religion and a church:

But I have no religion, most of my friends have no religion, very few of the major modern writers we have been considering have had any religion; and what is certain is that our society has none. No matter what it professes, it is now not merely irreligious but powerfully anti-religious. And if we all joined a Christian Church tomorrow, the fundamental situation would be unchanged, because no Church existing today has the power—and we could not give it this power by joining it—to undo what has been done. . . . So we have no religion and, inside or outside literature, man feels homeless, helpless and in despair.

We must wait. . . . but, just as a first step, we can at least believe that Man lives, under God, in a great mystery, which is what we found the original masters of our literature, Shakespeare and Rabelais, Cervantes and Montaigne, proclaiming at the very start of this journey of Western Man. And if we openly declare what is wrong with us, what is our deepest need, then perhaps the despair and death will by degrees disappear from our modern arts.
(pp. 445–446)

THE NOVELS

PRIESTLEY has explained that he found it much harder to write a novel than to fill the same number of pages with critical essays and reviews. He was not a born novelist, able instinctively to "maintain an even flow of narration," but he had lots of ideas and could not resist the challenge. Eventually he found the writing of fiction "more exciting."

As we saw, he had had some not unsuccessful practice at fiction before he produced *The Good Companions*, the first of his major novels, which is often referred to as picaresque but technically is not.

The *pícaro* was a rogue engaged on roguish journey-ings. These characters journey but cannot be called rogues. Jess Oakroyd, Miss Trant, Inigo Jollifant are, as David Hughes points out, rebelling from their different backgrounds; they join up with a third-rate touring concert party and meet a variety of people "on the road"; they have fun and make the newly constituted concert party, "The Good Companions," a success; then, in the third part of this 640-page novel, they split up and move into new lives, a few pleasant—or at any rate success-ful—more, questionably happy, and one or two dubiously so. The ending is in fact tinged with melancholy about the uncertainty of life:

In this place . . . perfection is not to be found, neither in men nor in the lot they are offered, to say nothing of the tales we tell of them, these hints and guesses, words in the air and gesticulating shadows, these stumbling chronicles of a dream of life.

No, *The Good Companions*, a fine story, is very bittersweet. If it resembles other novels at all, it is those of William Makepeace Thackeray, and the Victorian style is emphasized by the jocose chapter subheadings (removed from the paperback edition), such as "In Which Colonel Trant's Daughter Goes into Action, Sticks to Her Guns, and May Be Considered Victorious."

With minor characters Priestley had already developed what musicians call "attack"—they are immediately there before us—helped by his use of descriptive voice-noises identifying the speaker ("chum-ha," goes the headmaster), which we find in almost all his novels.

Hard on the heels of this most successful novel came another, *Angel Pavement*, no less success-ful—but extraordinarily different, both in technique and subject. It has one of the most impressive pro-logues of all Priestley's fiction—a Baltic steamship gliding up the Thames in the late afternoon and docking at Hay's Wharf, bearing the chief character, the *diabolus ex machina* of the coming story, the foreign Mr. Golspie, looking like a quiet buccaneer, casually drinking the captain's vodka and smoking his cigars (and casually, too, smuggling in 250 of his own). So pleased is he with his feeling of cunning and strength that "he could have shaken hands with him-self." He is coming to trade cheap veneers and inlays: a massive man, with a high bald forehead, "cheer-fully brutal," entering this rich London—"double

whiskies in crimson-shaded bars; smoking hot steaks and chops; glitter and velvet of the music hall; know-ing gossip, the fine reek of Havanas, round a club fender and fat leather chairs; pretty girls"—to make a killing.

That is Golspie's London; but it is not that of the rest of the characters who live, as members of the lower middle class, among the chilly, hostile streets or, up one class level, in a flat in Wimbledon or at a boring ladies' hostel. *Angel Pavement* is in part a novel of place; the very title is the name of a small street (as is Arnold Bennett's *Riceyman Steps*), where is to be found the small firm of Twigg and Der-singham, in which many of the chief characters work and which Golspie is now to galvanize with his vi-sions of cut-price veneer supplies, and eventually to ruin.

Upon this basic theme hang, like clothes on a line, the varied but seldom happy adventures of the main characters, and since each adventure is quite absorb-ing, the critic David Hughes is right to note that "small adjustments of attention are necessary all the time." There is the weak, amiable Dersingham, the proprietor of the office—surely a first sketch for Mr. Alison of *Bright Day* or Mr. Cornelius in the play *Cornelius* (1935); his chief clerk, Smeeth, modestly comfortable but hating and eventually exploding about his wife's friends, thrilling to a Brahms sym-phony at the Queen's Hall, utterly alienated from his children ("who would have been understood at a glance by a host of youths and girls in New York, Paris and Berlin"), and fearful of being fired, as he eventually is.

The most dramatic story in the novel concerns the humble, spotty-faced clerk, Turgis, living in lonely digs, who is briefly, to his astonishment and on a whim, taken up by Golspie's beautiful, bored daugh-ter, Lena, who soon casts him off with casual cruel-ty. Maddened, Turgis wheedles his way into her apartment, strangles her, and goes home to gas himself—only to find he lacks a shilling for the meter. Here is a sordid, tragic situation portrayed by Priestley with vivid and convincing power. Turgis' loneliness, agony, and pathos are truly felt and conveyed.

Yet Lena is not dead; and there is a general conces-sion to a "happy ending," or at least hints of new and less illusioned restarts—Turgis out with an admiring girlfriend; Miss Matfield, left at Victoria Station after Golspie has promised her a weekend in Brigh-ton, back in her hostel denying that life there is really so horrid—and anyway "it's our own fault if it gets us down." Smeeth and his wife are reconciled to fate, and he is going to seek a better job and make more money.

Nevertheless that little segment of life which was lived in the veneer firm in Angel Pavement is utterly destroyed, and there goes the destroyer, Golspie, his pockets relined, drifting down the Thames, where he had begun his marauding raid, off to seek another small fortune in South America. He observes to a fellow spirit that Londoners are "half dead, most of 'em. . . . No dash. No guts . . . ; I was sorry for the poor devils—some of em." Then he goes below—for a "piece of steak nicely done." He, indeed, could be termed a *pícaro*. Neo-Golspies recur in Priestley's novels, rogues still, but less destructive.

During the 1930's Priestley took on another challenge, plunging into writing, producing, and scripting plays, and wrote nothing that could be called a major novel, though *Faraway* (1932), *Wonder Hero* (1933), and *The Doomsday Men* (1938) are never less than readable. *They Walk in the City* (1936), which he himself later thought of as "a Hash," ending in melodrama "and not even good melodrama," is in fact much more what is now called a documentary than a novel. It is *Angel Pavement* without its genuine novelistic grip. He pictures hard-faced London, "a stone and brick forest nearly thirty miles long," where "eight million people eat and drink and sleep, wander among seven thousand miles of streets, pay their insurance money, send for the doctor, and die." Priestley gazes into small hotels that seem, with their strict rules pinned on bedroom doors, to regard customers "as potential criminals"; "the only flavour these inhuman boxes have is that of their occupants' accumulated misery." As before, however, the city itself enchants him—"a faintly luminous haze, now silver, now old gold, over everything. . . . Cockaigne made out of faint sunlight and vapour and smoke."

Topical references abound; indeed the accidental involvement of the lost young couple who are the chief characters in a Communist demonstration and a Black Shirt counterdemonstration serves once more to separate those whose constant separations are the plot's main machinery.

Let the People Sing (1939) might be called the adventures of an out-of-work comedian, Timmy Tiverton, who, contemplating suicide, has an IRA bomb planted on him; he throws it from a bus, and it blows up a statue and a fountain. Fearing that his story of the planting of the bomb will not be be-

lieved, Tiverton takes flight—and so does the story—into a world of eccentrics, namely a touring concert party traveling in a van and including a musical, Freudian foreign professor (who is on the run for different reasons); they arrive in a country town, where they become involved with the county, triumph over pettifogging officials, and, backed by a local bigwig, the plethoric Sir George ("found in some moon-haunted stratosphere of high spirits"), put on their show.

The happy ending is preordained; so are a pair of young lovers at last united; so is Tiverton happy with an old stage love and a contract to play a chain of provincial towns. Priestley tells the tale with verve, humor, and memorable descriptions of, for instance, "a sagging oldish man with a face like a boiled suet pudding that had been wedged into a bowler-hat too small for it"; or of Lady Foxfield, "a soldierly-looking woman with big craggy features that had been heavily powdered, so that she looked not unlike a whitewashed Sergeant-Major." The dialogue is a joy, lively, often pungent, touching when required.

We are not short, either, of what gradually were becoming Priestley trademarks: music playing (here Schubert and Mozart); music hall songs (Sir George, Timmy, and the professor singing and playing "You can't give father any cockles/You can't give mother any gin"); and the sleepy English (ready to die, not ready to live, but now perhaps "not taking so many orders without question, asking for some fun of their own").

Excellent wartime entertainment came in the spy thriller *Black-out in Gretley*, narrated in the first person by the somewhat soured counterespionage agent Humphrey Weyland, who is perhaps not unrelated to certain Graham Greene characters. Priestley enjoys himself here in drawing women—"exquisite, long-necked, sweet-smelling, downy rats." Who are goodies and who baddies in the story, and whence would come the dénouement, are not obvious until late—surely a tribute to Priestley's skill in this, for him, unique genre. And once more we find the trademark—the English "slow patience, their lack of fire and fury . . . were they half-dead or simply better people than any I'd known before?"

One other wartime novel—unaccountably passed over by at least two of his recent critics—is worth reading: *Daylight on Saturday* (1943), in which he explores the relations of men and women working long hours in an aircraft factory, whence they emerge in winter into daylight only on Saturday afternoons; hence the title. Priestley had visited many such factories and, while avoiding technicalities for security reasons, let his imagination play on what working in them was like:

> You washed and dressed, goose-fleshed, in the dark, hurried down the lane for the bus, shivered in the bus, with everybody round you yawning and muttering and grumbling (except the determined bright ones, the worst of all, who made silly jokes all the time). . . . And none of it, of course, except the noise and the light and the sheer length of time, was quite real. . . . It was in a way like a long, roaring, glaring dream. It was a bit like having a temperature.
>
> (ch. 3)

The plot reveals the tensions among the managerial staff, caused largely by class differences. Blandford, the engineering director and an upper-middle-class Tory, explains to a colleague:

> "Now my class, Angleby, may be stupid about some things—their taste in literature, for example, is appalling—but they are wonderfully quick at allying themselves with any new power. Instead of fighting it, as so many of their kind abroad have tried to do, they get to know it, they dine and wine it, they marry it, and finally control it. . . . Fundamentally this new industry is quite undemocratic, as I said before, for all the Joint Production Committees and Works Councils in the world can't really bridge the terrific gulf between the few people who are outside the machine and the unthinking crowd that is inside it. This industry already has its own aristocracy. But of course it's not *quite* the real thing."
>
> (ch. 9)

Elrick, no less clever an engineer, but rough, "red," and domestically harassed, is his natural antagonist and indeed the character of chief interest. His death (from a machinery accident) ends the book on a tragic note, even though Priestley again somehow makes a dash for a happier future.

Particularly attractive is Priestley's sharply etched portrait gallery of personalities, important and less so, their interrelationships, their dalliances, hopes, and fears, even ambitions: Miss Barrows, one of the secretaries "so busy raising herself in the social scale that she was altogether too refined and dignified to live . . . dosed herself with liquid paraffin and slowly ploughed her way across the world's great literature as if it were an enormous heavy-clay field"; Cleeton, foreman and kindly "old fashioned radical"; Miss Shipton, the welfare officer wearing enormous spec-

tacles with crimson rims, in love with a married schoolmaster; Ogmore, the foreman who "worshipped Russia"; the remote Stonier, who goes mad; the useful Sammy Hamp, "a little wreck of a man in his fifties"; and many others.

The novel has all the atmosphere of the time and place—rationing; visits from ENSA, the touring performers who entertained camps and factories; the influence of war news on the workers (if bad, boredom sets in; if good, increase in productivity); and overall the jingling, canned music while they work. It reveals much of what Britons really felt in a bleak war in vital though unglamorous occupations.

With Priestley himself (see *Margin Released*), I agree that this novel "does not deserve to be forgotten"; again with Priestley I agree that his 1945 novel, *Three Men in New Suits*, is too "hasty topical," despite one or two agreeable though insufficiently developed characters such as Uncle Rodney.

Emerging from the war (and a good deal of play writing), Priestley girded his novelistic loins once more and wrote *Bright Day*, which, until *The Image Men*, was his own favorite. It is technically a departure, for he uses such devices as the time-shift and the *progression d'effet*, which Ford Madox Ford, Joseph Conrad, and James had learned from Flaubert and Turgenev. Yet there is no unevenness, the narrative flows, everywhere there is precision.

Here is Dawson, the well-reputed film scriptwriter, recently returned from years on "the Coast," (Hollywood), hastily reworking a script—was Priestley thinking of his own rush to rewrite the Charles Laughton film *Jamaica Inn?*—in a luxurious hotel on the Cornish coast in the weeks immediately following the end of the war in 1945, and recalling, often almost compulsively, the Alison family and the wool men of his early years as a somewhat gauche but ambitious youthful clerk in Bruddesford before World War I. Sometimes during his narrative—done, like *Black-out in Gretley*, in the first person—he actually meets personages from those days, such as Lord and Lady Harndean, who are staying in the Cornish hotel, so stiltedly prewar—and learns from them the truth of situations he had misjudged in those early years. Others he has known and been half in love with, such as Bridget Alison, reappear, but now, like himself, changed and middle-aged. Sometimes we are plunged for pages into his pre-1914 life in Bruddesford—Priestley's "clouds of glory"—and then brought back to the present and his relations with the beautiful film star Elizabeth or with an urgent film mogul who cannot comprehend his refusal to accept splendid terms to return to Hollywood.

It is a wonderfully atmospheric book. The narrator, however (presumably Priestley himself), resolutely rejects mere nostalgia, though not such more obvious contrasts as those between Eleanor Nixey circa 1912, with "fine eyes, creamy skin, and a superb proud neck," and Eleanor Nixey, alias Lady Harndean, circa 1945, "an elderly lady, still fairly erect, but moving slowly and using a stick," yet with "those same eyes."

Here Dawson takes off:

I experienced a sensation so profoundly disturbing that it seemed as if my spine contracted and shivered. What I perceived then, in a blinding flash of revelation, was that the real Eleanor Nixey was neither the handsome young woman I had been remembering nor the elderly woman I saw before me, both of whom were nothing but distorted fleeting reflections in time, that the real Eleanor Nixey was somewhere behind all these appearances and fragmentary distortions, existing outside change and time; and that what was true of her was of course true of us all.

Something like this experience had probably been Priestley's and may have started his time explorations, which, particularly in his plays, preoccupied him from the 1930's onward.

Another theme reappears, the blessedness of the meek: for example, Mervin, who has renounced money and power to paint in a Yorkshire cottage, or the contemplative, unaggressive Jock, devoted to looking after his sick sister, who is to win the Victoria Cross and die. It is he with his quiet insight who, when asked whether a war would not be lunacy, replies, "Collectively people don't mind lunacy, they often find it easier than sanity and more of a relief."

Indeed Priestley's passing observations often have a subtle insight. Commenting on the change in actors' personal styles from the flamboyant performers of his youth who "played at being actors all the time," Dawson observes that now they have suppressed "these signs and badges of their profession, and go about looking like lawyers and dentists and the wives and daughters of deacons." The result? "What cannot come out has turned and worked its way inward, often subtly corrupting the mind and heart."

There is heart-twisting poignancy in the book; but what lingers is the sour smell of success. To Dawson his own success is Dead Sea fruit; as his film-star girlfriend divines, he is "all muddled and churned up." Though it would be quite incorrect to equate Dawson with Priestley, the reader can scarcely doubt that the author was himself depressed and torn by decisions to come. It was something more, we feel, than Britons generally being physically and mentally worn-out and disliking the Americans, "energetic and helpful, generous and rich—and hardly any of us poor half-starved Europeans can stand 'em." It wasn't even that those who had pinned their hopes on a Labour government were speedily disillusioned, nor, as yet, that Priestley understood that the victory as far as Britain was concerned was hollow, and that the old country, even in the watered-down form of the 1930's, was gone forever. It was rather that the author, no less than Dawson, was in the process of a radical, middle-aged (he was fifty-two) change of life and was uncertain of his personal future, as of the direction of his life and work.

Dawson himself makes a tentative dash out of the past and out of his indecision in the last few pages of the book when he meets Mrs. Childs, now a widow, whom he had known when she was a child. She is on the committee of a group of young stage and cinema people who want films to "show how real people behaved in a real world." Will Dawson join them? If he did, perhaps in the group he "might soon find the same rich warm world" as in Bruddesford long ago. The last line in the book is "Something good might come out of it." *Bright Day*—even its title—holds out hope, as do all of Priestley's novels (though not his plays), but more cautiously than the rest.

Whatever morbidity, or what the Anglo-Saxons called wanhope, there may be in *Bright Day* (and some of his plays), it has vanished in his next full-length novel, *Festival at Farbridge* (1951), the longest he had written. It jumps with fun and suspense, and is jam-full of those entertaining characters he excels at creating, often in a page or two. The story tells how the rather dim little Midlands town of Farbridge, with its prewar characters living in a dreary, ramshackle, postwar Britain, was enthused, reluctantly and despite downright opposition, into putting on its own Festival of Britain show with music, plays, dance bands, and a fireworks display.

The chief hustler, though a stranger to the town, is the temporarily unemployed naval commodore Horace Tribe (an honorary South American rank, he explains), who "looked something between a clever old actor and a rather raffish admiral." A con man, perhaps, but benevolent and humane where the other con man, Golspie in *Angel Pavement*, was malign. He is a Priestleyan ancestor of Professor Cosmo Saltana of *The Image Men* and probably of the stage illusionist Uncle Nick of *Lost Empires* (1965). Is not, too, Tribe's chubby little ally, the ex-Conservative agent Captain Mobbs, a foretaste of the chubby, but much cleverer Tuby, companion and fellow conspirator of Saltana in *The Image Men?*

The Commodore teams up with the pretty and clever young secretary Laura Casey and a huge, handsome, rich, but shy young man, Theodore Jenks, a colonial who, surprisingly, had a Chinese grandmother. He fulfills two functions for Priestley: apart from being useful in helping promote the Festival, he is destined, despite many setbacks and misunderstandings, to provide, with Laura, the main love interest. He is also Priestley's mouthpiece, as an outsider, on the state and people of England five years after the war's end. For example, Theodore becomes Priestley as he wonders whether mass listening to radio—television then had scarcely started—is a good thing:

We might be piping it out to people who are really more civilized without it. . . . Perhaps they're missing something—an opportunity to think, to make discoveries about themselves. . . . Most people now seem to think you can go on adding things to life without taking anything away, without anything dropping out. But can you?

One of the most entertaining characters is the bulky, hard-headed supporter of the Festival team, Seth Hull, the local hotel-keeper, a proper description for whom is the North Country word "brussen": he is tough, determined, and not above a bit of blackmail when necessary (as with the craven editor of the local weekly). But one recalls with pleasure a whole string of personages: the unfortunate Major Bulfoss, MP; the mayor, with his strange buzzing delivery, "He was very glad that it had fallen— *Pzzz*—to his lot to preside at a gathering—*Pzzz*—of this kind . . . ; and the mysterious Grace, who comes and goes in the Commodore's life and finally—for this, too, is a book without unhappy endings— stays. The novel contains some excellent set pieces. One is the hilarious parody of the BBC "Next Question Please" program, a traveling team that visits Farbridge and, packed by a pro-Festival claque, is an element in the narrative but would have been there somehow, one suspects, even if Priestley hadn't

thought of a tie-up: the short parsonical-looking chairman, "gravely delighted with himself," the professional countryman Dan Cobbley, the radio-show plumber George Bray, "with a hectoring style and a cockney accent"—British listeners know them all.

They also know—indeed Priestley has written about the type in an earlier essay—Leonard Mortory, "very distinguished critic who also lectures at Cambridge," and has written *Disavowals, Rejections,* and *Exclusions.* The Festival's chosen highbrow speaker, he decides on "The Novel" as his subject but is wasting no time, he explains, on "most so-called great novelists . . . Fielding, Sterne, Dickens and Thackeray."

As much fun are the exploits of the not-so-young young leading man Patrick Gorebarry, who precedes his appearance in a contemporary romantic play in verse, *Why Should the Nightingale?*, by going on a day-long carouse. But black coffee revives him:

He roamed about in a strange but fascinating way, as if he had discovered some new and more flexible style of acting. Sometimes he hesitated or muttered odd words or phrases that could not be properly heard; and at other times his magnificent voice rang out like a trumpet or went curving down into melancholy and defeat like a muted violin, so that as she listened she would feel her eyes hot with tears. What a wonderful thing such acting was! . . . Some of his speeches . . . were . . . faintly silly, but now and then, when he was most vivid and challenging, he would bring out passages of great beauty, which Laura could not help feeling she had heard somewhere before.

(pt. III, ch. 3)

No wonder; for Gorebarry has inserted bits and pieces from *Hamlet, Henry IV, Richard III*—much to the distress of his fellow actors, waiting for cues.

With all this gallimaufry of character and by-plots, Priestley has achieved a miracle of interweaving and narrative flow. It cannot be denied that occasionally one sees a flat stretch approaching, but it never quite arrives. It is one of his best novels: no wonder he felt "stung" by its disappointing reception.

In the next few years he wrote a good many novels, few worth instant dismissal—particularly *Sir Michael and Sir George* (1964), but he was scarcely in top form again until *Lost Empires* (1965). This is the story of a painter, Herncastle, told by himself, though with the author's prologue and epilogue, who in old age has become sufficiently renowned to have a book written on his work. The bulk of the novel, however, concerns Herncastle's youthful pre-1914 career on and off the music-hall stage as assistant to his famous uncle, Ollanton, the illusionist—"tallish, thin and very dark, with a hooked nose and a slight cast in his eyes, that I think he cultivated"—and with a passion for champagne.

Lost Empires (departed music halls, not colonies) is a backstage story of variety performers, their lives, their "digs," their amours, their misunderstandings, and, yes, their tragedies. There is sexual passion—a good deal more explicitly described than before—and plenty of swear words. There are some grotesque moments, such as the choosing of dwarfs for the show, and nasty scenes, including wife-beating, attempted voyeurism, and murder that leads to a most thrilling, unique—and illegal—illusionist's triumph.

Throughout, the dominating character is Ollanton, the magician, a proud, cynical, often brutal man obsessed with his craft:

I thought too how odd it was that he should be so tirelessly concerned with stage magic when, because of some deep flaw in his nature, he couldn't enjoy, couldn't even recognize, the magical element in life, all the enchantments of love and art to which, I was sure, he was blind and deaf.

So comments Herncastle-Priestley. Such is Ollanton's obsessive pride that he damned the war "because he saw it as another, bigger, more impressive and demanding performer, a rival top of the bill."

Another notable personage is Inspector Crabb of Scotland Yard—policemen generally rather intrigue Priestley, appearing often in his fiction and plays. Crabb fails in the murder case, not because he doesn't know who the murderer is, but because, on very humanistic grounds, Ollanton spirits him away; but Crabb is very much there in the latter part of the novel—"doesn't look like a crab but he behaves like one—moves sideways, then suddenly it's a pinch." As Priestley makes him say: "I've enough suspicion in me to choke a horse." The novel's tone is less sour than that of *Bright Day*, yet darkened with regret: regret for the idiocy of war, for the passing years.

It's an Old Country is a slighter work, picturing England as "a meaningless society" in the eyes of another overseas innocent (not unlike Theodore), Tom Adamson, a well-to-do lecturer from an Aus-

tralian university in search (the novel of search is an ancient genus) of the father he does not remember. Like many (too many?) of Priestley's novels, it all works out well in the end, too often in women's-magazine prose ("They stared at each other in tender amazement") and with wedding bells ringing all over—but there are many compensations, such as the cocktail party ("the individual voice, never heard elsewhere, high and harsh, and jeering pitilessly, of some collective monster they had created"); wise old Dr. Firmius, planning in his basement the teaching of "culture and wisdom" to "rescue men and women in their forties—often a desperate age—from emptiness and despair"; one of his best sketches of "experimental"—and awful—theater; a few mad aristocrats; the image of false infatuation with the Countess Helga, who might have come out of Edmund Spenser's *Faerie Queene*; the retired major-general, who, probably like the author, doesn't like London anymore ("begins to look like Constantinople or Calcutta"), and his grandson "pigging it" with a "couple of dirty little trollops," to which Adamson responds that such exist in Australia too—"slopping around in the university . . . they look awful, they're both cocky and ignorant, they're lazy. . . ." Yet "among themselves they've done more in ten years to destroy the power of social position and money than the rest of us have done in the last hundred years."

In *The Image Men*, amounting in all to 300,000 words, Priestley, aged seventy-four, summoned every ounce of his writing experience, his unblunted sensibility, and his gift for character sketching to the task of writing a long, sustained comedy; without doubt it is his masterpiece. Mildly satirical, its sphere is new universities, new subjects such as sociology, the modern arts of self or company projection—public relations, advertising, newspapers, and the craft (not to say craftiness) of government.

The pivots of the action are two sharply contrasted characters working together. One is another avatar of our old friends Golspie, the Commodore, and Ollanton, now presented as Professor Cosmo Saltana, English by birth but with some Spanish ancestry, who has spent years teaching philosophy in South American universities: tall, thin, deep-set dark greenish eyes, and black hair streaked with white—a mesmeric, commanding man. His partner, Dr. Owen Tuby, chubby, bespectacled, balding, who has taught English in the Far East for some years, has a voice that "could talk a woman into anything"; even his landlady is after him. Both have returned from their distant parts and failed to find jobs in England. In fact, they have temporarily no money to meet their bills in Robinson's "good old-fashioned" hotel in London, where they are "paying through [their] noses to sit in the sodden ruins of an Empire."

Chance and their ungentlemanly natures allow them to peep at a distressed lady's papers, left briefly in the hotel lounge, and give them a heaven-sent opportunity to take over the affairs of a wealthy American sociological foundation that wishes to set up an establishment in England. The two become sociologists and invent the Institute of Social Imagistics—"the selection, creation, projection of suitable and helpful images"—and they manage to attach it to the new University of Brockshire in the West Country. The lady, Elfreda, becomes their valued friend.

So the tale begins. It is a tale with as varied characters as any Priestley has created; yet few of them go off on their own tangents, as happens in *The Good Companions* and *Festival at Farbridge.* They are firmly within the orbit of Saltana and Tuby, who alone are permitted divagations, often of an amatory kind, which, in this permissive age, are somewhat freely described beyond the bedroom door.

Memorable are such sketches as those of the vice-chancellor and his erring wife, Isobel: the delicious Dr. Hazel Honeyfield; the awful broadcasting professor, Cally: and the pompous Sir Leopold Namp. Petronella, the young, naughty Duchess of Brockshire, is a delightful invention. The dealings with the students' confederation, the smooth and phony Major Grandison, and the newspaper magnate Birtle provide some hilarious moments of satire. After various dramas, our two "heroes"—and their benefactress, Elfreda, who is, I suppose, the heroine—leave the university for London, the background for the second half, where the Institute of Social Imagistics is reestablished on a commercial basis.

The narrative need not be detailed here, though certainly the story reaches new heights (of impudence?) with Saltana and Tuby advising both government and opposition leaders on ways to present their images. It must, however, be said that Priestley does in fact make out a most convincing case for the institute's methods, investing Saltana and Tuby with ingenuity and subtlety.

It might be mentioned here that a large part in many of Priestley's novels, notably *Festival at Farbridge* and *The Image Men,* is played by drink and, to a lesser extent, good food or, indeed, any food, bad, good, or, usually, indifferent, to which Priestley was always sensitive. They are not drinking men, say Saltana and Tuby—just "convivial and clubable"; but the amount they are recorded as consuming would make most of us both incoherent and impotent, which clearly neither of them is. (Priestley defended himself in his "Something Else" essay by alleging that "we middle-class English are steadily pickling ourselves"; even so, "there are men among us doing important jobs, and doing them well too, who have not been strictly sober for years.")

Quite the most startling creation is the film sexpot Miss Meldy Glebe and her astounding entourage, installed in the whole of the top floor of a new American hotel in London, entirely decorated in English "period" style—her suite is called "Wars of the Roses": "an insane mixture of 1968, 1568 and 1267," full of electronic devices, Tudor beams, suits of armor, and battle-axes; two waiters dressed "as if they had just been brought back from the Forest of Arden, even though one was a Maltese or Cypriot and the other a Central European wearing thick glasses."

She appears with Tuby on a TV interview show where Tuby, smiling and smoking his pipe, makes the sneering interviewer look bad-tempered and oafish—and an ignorant fool. "He will," Tuby gently inquires, "have heard of such psychologists of images as Pleyel, Broadwood, and Steinway's analysis of the underlying sexual element?" The interviewer: "I agree with some of it of course."

"But they're all pianos," cried Meldy. "I know because I worked in a music shop one time. How can they be all pianos, Dr. Tuby?"

"Because I had to think of some names very quickly, Meldy," said Tuby, smiling. "And they were the first I thought of. So if I was going to talk a little solemn nonsense—"

"Miss Glebe, Dr. Tuby," Murch [the interviewer] broke in desperately, "thank you for coming along—."

(vol. II, ch. 5)

Priestley's observing eye tracks across some of the public acres of the crude, uncivilized nastinesses defacing English life in the early 1960's. Once more he presents two men long abroad to deplore the deteriorated and banalized England. But he deepens his theme by having these observers engulf themselves in the very putridities they deplore and then shape them to their own ends. Their aim is money, then freedom. They are not without an element of nihilism.

Having profited greatly from the imagistic ideas bought by both government and opposition, they hope, cynically, that "it won't confuse the viewing floating voters." Only reflective readers will see them as the opportunist black-marketeers of a civilization in decay, for Priestley has given such life and sparkle to his novel that it ripples along, scarcely a sentence without flavor or revelation.

Where then is the "freedom" to which these successful scavengers of decay, Romans picking over the shards of fallen Greece, aspire? Here comes a touch of restitution and of good works with a particularly Priestleyan tinge. Saltana explains:

"Tuby and I want to create a university—or simply a college, we don't care which—entirely for people over forty. No degree factory here. . . . Many people past forty, already looking down the hill towards the cemetery, have a desperate need to learn, to understand, to enjoy, to enrich the spirit, to live before they die. They may have money, position, prestige and authority, but they find themselves asking, So what, so what? And we want to offer them an answer."

It has to be on an island, in the best tradition of Coleridge and many other writers, but no balmy tropics or hideouts in the Mediterranean. Instead, hard-headed to the end, they choose the Isle of Man (between the Lancashire coast and Ulster) because the income tax is only twenty percent, there is no surtax, and the island's "fungus growth from Blackpool and Margate" can be avoided at both northern and southern ends. And the composition of the course? Even more Priestleyan: there will be "a broadly-based scientist or two, a first class art-historian, one good historian . . . a lively depth psychologist, preferably a Jungian, if only to provoke argument, a resident string quartet," and Tuby and Lois for literature.

Shortly before this Elfreda, now Saltana's intended, happily contemplating the dinner and the wine in "this flickering mid-Victorian room," has been wafted into one of those moments when in a flash she knows that "life is a dream," as did Priestley at the end of *The Good Companions*. In another sense, Priestley's Isle of Man college is life in a dream.

THE PLAYS

MANY believe that the best of Priestley is in his plays, which he began writing in 1932. Ivor Brown, a most perceptive critic, thought so; so did Frank Swinnerton in *The Georgian Literary Scene* (1938). The trouble is that "the content and form of his plays can only be properly evaluated in the context of rehearsal and performance . . . a context not always by any means available." So writes Gareth Lloyd Evans in *J. B. Priestley, the Dramatist* (1964); and so must we all say who were not able to follow Priestley's dramatic progress in the theater from the early 1930's to the 1950's. There have been, of course, many revivals on stage and adaptations for television and radio; some of his plays have become standbys for amateurs across the world. Nevertheless, in the main, later writers must rely on the text, not their theater memories; and, as Priestley himself remarked in the introduction to volume II of *The Plays*, with a comedy "inflections and timing are all-important." Only "if properly produced [do] they come alive."

Priestley has written in many styles, both conventional and experimental, and on a remarkable variety of themes—his extraordinary versatility is a tribute to both his energy and his imagination. But instead of grouping them together as, for example, "time" plays, broad comedy, and even tragedy, it will be most convenient here to deal with them chronologically, particularly since these group categorizations tend to blunt the uniqueness of impact that each play possesses.

After a fruitful collaboration with the "play-doctor" Edward Knoblock (who had also assisted Arnold Bennett) in dramatizing *The Good Companions*, Priestley wrote *Dangerous Corner* (1932); he later dismissed it as "an ingenious box of tricks," but it remains one of his most popular plays. The story revolves around the question of how, before the play begins, did Martin, a relative or intimate of the characters on the stage, die with a bullet in his head? With a good deal of suspense, tension, and as many swift twists as a detective story, the truth finally emerges; so does the truth of the group's interrelationships, though perhaps, as Olwen says, "the *real* truth is something so deep you can't get at it this way. . . . It isn't *civilized*." Another character, Stanton, agrees: "I think telling the truth is about as healthy as skidding at sixty round a corner," which prompts the play's title. For all the frenetically gay dancing as the final curtain falls, there is a bleakness about the last act, when all "this rotten stuff" has come out, and the slightly tipsy Robert observes that his illusions have helped him to live. He has no faith, "just this damned farmyard to live in."

It is a very nineteen-twentyish sort of play, bittersweet, with nineteen-twentyish, comfortably off, middle-class brittle characters—the sort with whom, in however different a way, the early Coward or Maugham might have toyed. Most of the events occur before the play begins and are, as in the best Greek drama, only reported to the audience: how very clever, then, that Priestley keeps us on the edge of our seats for so long.

Laburnum Grove (1934), which Priestley calls "an immoral comedy," remains no less popular than *Dangerous Corner* but belongs to quite another genre. Its central character is Radfern, a suburban, lower-middle-class paterfamilias who grows tomatoes and supports a scrounging brother-in-law; his twenty-year-old daughter, Elsie, who wants to marry Harold (who "has nothing in him"); and his wife, Dorothy: all very commonplace, until Radfern nonchalantly reveals (though not yet to his wife) that he is a forger and counterfeiter, in short, a crook. But is he telling the truth or simply trying to scare off his brother-in law and Elsie's Harold? The arrival of a Scotland Yard inspector "on routine enquiries" clears out the hangers-on effectively and confirms that the amiable Radfern is indeed a forger; the dialogue between the inspector, who hasn't yet quite enough facts to arrest Radfern, and his quarry, is a splendid bit of cool swordplay allowing Radfern to whisk his wife and daughter off for a long tour of the Far East: hence "immoral," for crime *does* pay.

Eden End (1934) bears no resemblance to these first two plays, though it has affinities with later novels and plays such as *The Linden Tree* and *Bright Day*. It is set in the pre–World War I period—1912. "Eden End" is a doctor's house in, presumably, a Yorkshire village. The elderly doctor lives with his younger daughter, Lilian, and Sarah, his old Yorkshire servant of many years. His wife is dead. His son, Wilfred, a very young man, is on leave from West Africa and is taken up with the musical shows he has seen in London—when the curtain rises he is trying to pick out tunes on the piano from *Gipsy Love*—and a local barmaid.

The action begins with the unexpected return after eight years of the doctor's elder daughter, Stella, who was to have been a great actress but has spent dull and uncomfortable years trekking the world in a stock company. The newly succeeded local squire, Geoffrey, an old friend of the family who has been paying attention (if not court) to Lilian, is now immediately taken up with Stella, whom he admired long ago. Mortified, Lilian, who has discovered that her sister has been married but is now separated, summons her brother-in-law, a casual, pleasant, ne'er-do-well actor, and the family finds itself amid bitter home truths from which no happiness emerges: Stella goes off with her husband to try the stage once more. But Geoffrey does *not* after all fall into Lilian's arms; he takes off for New Zealand. Lilian is left alone with her father, who has, we are told, not long to live, and the ever faithful Sarah.

No great climax, no happy ending, and little hope —this is life, is the play's message. Despite a highly amusing drunken scene, it is a sad, autumnal play (though its writer was barely in his forties and at the height of his powers), showing nostalgia punctured and hopes dashed. It has moments of genuine pathos, and much of Priestley's own lingering regret for the happy prewar days—the theme that haunted him— before families were broken up and the slaughter of 1914–1918 began.

Cornelius: A Business Affair in Three Transactions harks back to *Angel Pavement*. It concerns the collapse of a small firm under its rather weak owner, the trivial affairs of his office staff, and the growing insanity of Cornelius' partner. It is a sad though not quite hopeless drama, for Cornelius, ruined, throws away his revolver and looks toward an old dream—"we decided to take the track into the clouds—to find—among those heights—the lost city of the Incas." There followed *Bees on the Boat Deck* (1936), a curious farcical political satire for which the author retains a considerable fondness; read, it does not seize us, and was probably carried off by the extraordinarily powerful cast, among them Kay Hammond, Ralph Richardson, Laurence Olivier, and Raymond Huntley. At this period, as J. C. Trewin says, there were all too few good dramatists for the plethora of fine performers.

Time and the Conways returns yet more powerfully to the family theme. The first and last acts are set in 1919; the middle one takes us on to 1937 itself and contains many moving ironies, for we see what Mrs. Conway, a bright but rather feckless mother, and her children have made of their lives: how, for instance, the prettiest daughter, Hazel, has married the gauche ugly duckling she spurned, who has become a rich but vengeful man, while the kindest of

224

the daughters, Carol, is dead. The only son, Alan, still a plodding clerk, has become the calm, quiet man of wisdom. Him alone time has not hurt, because he has an almost mystical vision of it that he passes on to his sister, the disillusioned Kay—once "the modern working woman, a cigarette and a whiskey and soda"—who has come to believe that "there's a great devil in the universe and we call it Time." To this Alan replies:

"No, Time's only a kind of dream, Kay. If it wasn't, it would have to destroy everything—the whole universe —and then remake it again every tenth of a second. But Time doesn't destroy anything. It merely moves us on—in this life—from one peep-hole to the next."

The Conways when young are not really gone forever:

they're real and existing. . . . We're seeing another bit of the view—a bad bit, if you like—but the whole landscape's still there . . . we're only a cross-section of our real selves. What we really are is the whole stretch of ourselves, all our time, and when we come to the end of this life, all those selves, all our time, will be us—the real you, the real me. And then perhaps we'll find ourselves in another time, which is only another kind of dream. . . . You know, I believe half our trouble now is because we think Time's ticking our lives away. That's why we snatch and grab and hurt each other.
(Act II)

Alan's answer is comforting—if it can be believed —and is of course part of Priestley's interest in the time theories of the 1930's. The play has other virtues: a certain wit in Mrs. Conway's speeches, an argument about the rights and wrongs of strike-breaking, and a curious statement about progress, that peoples have learned their lesson about war and have high hopes of the League of Nations—ironical to us, perhaps ironical even in 1937, when Priestley wrote it. The whole point and quality of the play are in the third act, as Priestley rightly pointed out, "when we know so much more about the characters than they know themselves."

In 1937 also appeared *I Have Been Here Before* (the déjà vu), where time plays a yet more prominent though quite different part. Here a foreigner, Dr. Görtler, is a far more thrusting sage than Alan in what is a queer, tight circle in a remote inn in the Yorkshire Dales. It is a play of unhappiness between a husband and wife, of the interdependence of people, and, once again, of "something malicious . . .

corrupt . . . cruel . . . at the heart of life," something the rich businessman Ormund feels within him "waiting to blot out the whole bloody business." Görtler has a hard time persuading Ormund of the "magic" of imagination and of the recurrence of events in the lives of people until at last they take off to a new plane; you may be, he tells Ormund, "in the unusual and interesting position of a man who is moving out on a new time track, like a man who is suddenly born into a strange new world." The ending is tentatively hopeful. Nevertheless, over many of Priestley's plays of this period there hangs a profound, almost deathly gloom that is stronger than the philosophic good hope.

Before returning to rake over again the gloomier hinterland of his imagination and the strange and now rather dated theories of salvation—rather more cogently, convincingly, and better expressed in the Christian "I believe in the Holy Ghost . . . the forgiveness of sins, the resurrection of the body, and the life everlasting"—Priestley indulged himself and entranced audiences with a broad Yorkshire comedy.

When We Are Married (1938) depends for its effects on a situation no longer taken so seriously: the horror of discovering after twenty years of marriage that you were not properly married at all. The plot, which Priestley himself calls "nonsensical," depends on chance and is resolved by a minor legality, but it gives Priestley an opportunity to display some of the riper characters—petty businessmen, councillors— whom he knew in his youth. It might be termed a "revenge comedy" with husbands and wives, believing that they are not married, venting their spleen and dissatisfaction. It is often exciting and usually unexpected in its action; it presents in some sense the essence of the oddities and curiosities of West Riding characters of a certain period; their dialogue is full of carefully observed and remembered "meat."

Then, also in 1938, came *Music at Night* (published 1947), a strange but impressive play called "experimental" by Priestley. Set throughout in the large music room of the sort of society lady who used to put on private musical soirées (and had the money to do so), its characters are a collection of politicians, businessmen, bright young things, a gossip writer, a demimondaine, a poet, a composer, and a quartet of musicians. The dialogue begins as smart, cutting, bitchy. But then the play develops into almost the stage equivalent of a stream-of-consciousness novel, such as those written in this Georgian period by

Dorothy Richardson, Virginia Woolf, James Joyce, and others. By means of surely difficult stage directions, such as "Ann hurries back to her chair, where she must get back into her frock"—indeed the whole spectacle is a field day for the lighting and music departments—we see the characters delving into their pasts (with relevant personages thence appearing). Here again we have the magic theme ("If you no longer feel that magic is at work, bringing you miracles, then really you are dead"). Once more nostalgia is shown up ("nice sweet slow wistful thoughts, because our bellies are full"); here is the "farmyard" image of life ("everybody'll sleep with anybody and nobody'll care and it won't matter—just like one big farmyard").

The play wanders, as its conception demands, into poetry, prosaic perhaps on paper—but that is where the actor is the key. This is an extraordinary phenomenon. We see the balloon of the characters being pricked and deflated, and the whole turning in Act III from joy to horror, and into almost Eliotian phraseology—"we are all guilty creatures. But we can beg forgiveness." Toward the end of the play there occurs this dialogue, or antiphone:

PETER (ecstatically): I remember from the time when the world grew cold and the ice came. . . .

KATH. (ecstatically): I remember from the time of the great flood. . . .

MRS. A. (same): I remember from the time of the baking of bricks and the shaping of pottery. . . .

CHILHAM (same): I remember from the time of the first canals. . . .

SIR J. (same): I remember from the time of the first forging. . . .

ANN (same): Remembering and remembering, not in any one time or place. . . .

LADY S. (same): But in all times and places since there were men and women. . . .

KATH. (same): Always going on and on, young men growing old, finding love or losing it. . . .

SIR J.: And the guilt of one is the guilt of all and one cannot suffer without all suffering. . . .

(Act III)

Johnson over Jordan (1939) offers us the experiences of a man recently dead (a subject that in 1923 had been successfully treated in Sutton Vane's *Outward Bound*) and an evocation of his life: in short, it is a sort of dramatic biography and, since Priestley himself referred to it as "entirely and deeply subjective," perhaps more autobiographical than his other work. It is another experimental drama, much

needed on the English stage in the 1930's, when most successful drama (except by foreign writers such as Elmer Rice, Pirandello, Karel Čapek) was firmly stuck within the proscenium picture-frame—*Storm in a Teacup, Dear Octopus, French Without Tears,* and even the brilliant plays of James Bridie.

After his death Johnson passes unwittingly into a state of purgatory, which some have compared with the Tibetan Bardo.[2] Here memories of his former business life come to taunt him, and in Act II, where his conscience beats him to the ground and into the belief that he is in Hell, the masked Figure tells him that "it was yourself reproaching yourself." He wishes to return home to make recompense. But there is no going back, for "in that world you are really dead," says the Figure. However, since he is only "an average sort of fool," he may stay a little while in "the Inn at the End of the World." There, in Act III, the most moving part of the play, the happier parts of his life are, as it were, played back to him.

One of Priestley's favorite words is "rum": this is now dated slang meaning "odd," "strange," "queer," though with a slightly comfortable ring about it—"odd," but not deeply disturbing. It is repeatedly used in this play. "Rum" undoubtedly is the concatenation of pictures from the past that Johnson glimpses—a long-dead county cricketer, Hansel and Gretel (with Humperdinck's music), a pantomime clown, his brother killed in World War I, his old books, Don Quixote, a coach driven by Sam Weller, someone he has saved from suicide. Finally the mood changes and becomes almost unbearably poignant:

JILL (his still living wife): Who am I, Robert?

JOHNSON (slowly at first but with mounting excitement): You are Jill, my wife. And you are Jill, the mother of my children. And you are Jill, the girl I saw for the first time at a dance nearly thirty years ago. And you are Jill, the girl who had not yet been to that dance, who had never seen me, who dreamed perhaps of a lover and a husband very different from me. You are all those, and something more as well, something even more than the Jill who went with me on that wedding journey to Switzerland, so young, so happy. You are the essential Jill whom I was for ever finding, losing, then finding again. You are my love, the wonder and terror and delight of my heart.

(Act III)

Then she disappears, to his terrible distress, and the Figure tells him it is time to go; but Jill's voice is

[2]A state of limbo comparable to purgatory.

heard talking to their daughter: "I suddenly saw—quite clearly—everything's all right—really all right—*now*. . . ."

Goodbye, goodbye, and Johnson stands alone:

I have been a foolish, greedy and ignorant man;
Yet I have had my time beneath the sun and stars;
I have known the returning strength and sweetness of the season,
Blossom on the branch and the ripening of fruit . . .
Farewell, all good things!

THE FIGURE (gravely): Robert Johnson, it is time now.
(Johnson puts on his overcoat and hat and picks up his bag.)

JOHNSON: For Thine is the kingdom, the power and the glory . . . and God bless Jill and Freda and Richard . . . and all my friends—and—and—everybody . . . for ever and ever . . . Amen . . .

He puts on his hat and is now ready to go. He looks up at the Figure, doubtfully.

JOHNSON (hesitantly): Is it—a long way?
THE FIGURE (suddenly smiling like an angel): I don't know, Robert.
JOHNSON (awkwardly): No . . . well . . . good-bye. . . .

As majestic music begins, Johnson looks "very small, forlorn," shivers a little, and turns up his coat collar. The blue light intensifies and we see the glitter of stars in space, and against them

the curve of the world's rim. As the brass blares out triumphantly and the drums roll and the cymbals clash, Johnson, wearing his bowler hat and carrying his bag, slowly turns and walks towards that blue space and the shinging constellations, and the curtain comes down and the play is done.

(Act III)

This is not just another guess about the nature of life-after-death; much less does it involve such time theories as those of *I Have Been Here Before*. What moves us most deeply is the pathos of parting forever from loved ones and cherished memories; the now never-to-be redeemed wrongs done and things left undone (for instance, not having talked often enough to the children); the now unavailing regrets. But perhaps Priestley's overriding purpose is to reconcile himself and us to the fact of death and to soften a little its apparent harsh finality with a hope. In that he does not succeed. It is the bleakness of parting and the sadness that remain with us when the

curtain comes down. The conviction grows upon us, at least as readers, that there is nothing quite so powerful in the novels as in this play and its predecessor.

We may pass over his *Goodnight, Children* (1942), a squib on the BBC, "really excellent vintage nonsense," as Priestley tells us James Bridie called it; and come to the immensely popular *They Came to a City*, which again plunges us into life-after-death, with some of the old lingering sadness but with a different purpose—to make us think of a better life *before* death and more particularly to look at the reactions of varied characters toward the new Jerusalem, the Utopia, which we never view—perhaps an irony here?—and about which we hear in only a generalized way from those characters who have penetrated it. It was very much an era, midwar, when the thoughts of many turned to planning the avoidance of the shudderings of war and the unemployment of the previous decade. Priestley's City seems to be all sweetness and light. As one character reports: "Here, they start every morning feeling as we only feel for about half an hour every two years, half lit at somebody's birthday party," and as another puts it:

Where men and women don't work for machines and money, but machines and money work for men and women—where greed and envy and hate have no place—where want and disease and fear have vanished for ever—where nobody carries a whip and nobody rattles a chain. Where men have at last stopped mumbling and gnawing and scratching in dark caves and have come out into the sunlight.

(Act II)

Such expectations are far from those of some other characters: the financier has found the City frustrating—he couldn't find a post office and has been mocked; Sir George merely wants to get back to golf; others are angry or fearful or bored. The suspense in the first act is well sustained, but it is the perkiness of the contrasting dialogue, particularly of the shrewd cockney characters, that appeals to the playgoer. Also, the playgoer of that time enjoyed seeing the upper classes portrayed as blinkered buffoons. One cannot, however, disagree with Priestley's own verdict: "It is not one of my own favorites."

Desert Highway (1944) is a play about a tank and its crew lost in the desert fighting in Syria in the earlier part of World War II—absorbing enough but not intended as a major contribution to the drama.

An Inspector Calls (1947) is a return to the "revelation" style, the ripping off of masks, of his first play, *Dangerous Corner*, with the addition of a maguslike police inspector relentlessly pursuing the truth, and there is also a time-shift element. Just when the audience is tiring of discoveries, the whole action is given a violent twist and everything becomes exciting again. It has been produced all over the world and made into a film (1954).

Next came *Ever Since Paradise* (1950), an experimental play in the purely theatrical sense. It is a comedy about love and marriage with excellent neo-Shavian dialogue and a happy ending. Each set of three couples is both observer (addressing the audience) and participator in the plot, which is underlined by appropriate piano music (there are two grand pianos onstage). This is a play of light ironies that, Priestley says, should be produced to have "the air of a gay charade."

The Linden Tree is in part a return to the mood of *Eden End*. A professor of history at a civic university, aged sixty-five, is about to be retired by a brash new vice-chancellor, "a high-pressure educationalist." Professor Linden resists, not so much because he does not want to retire but because he wants to stem the new trend in teaching, which he regards as vocational at best and merely expedient at worst. He stands firm. Yes, Burmanley (Manchester? Leeds?) is shabby, boring, dismal—this is the immediate postwar world of rationing—but he believes that a better time is coming:

. . . we're trying to do something that is as extraordinary and wonderful as it's difficult—to have a revolution for once without the Terror, without looting mobs and secret police, sudden arrests, mass suicides and executions, without setting in motion that vast pendulum of violence which can decimate three generations before it comes to a standstill. We're fighting in the last ditch of our civilization. . . .

(II.i)

His fond family, met for his sixty-fifth birthday, think differently. They have been plotting with their mother to get him away. His smart but kindly son, Rex, who has made a fortune selling stocks and shares, but who is humorous or cynical enough to describe himself as "a de luxe model Spiv" in the City, offers his mother and father a comfortable home in his country house in Hampshire.

Rex's philosophy is simple: "gather ye rosebuds," because he does not doubt that the ultimate choice is

between a lot of Trade Union officials giving themselves jobs and titles or Tory Big Business screaming to get back into the trough. All the same racket. . . . We can't last. And anyhow when the atom bombs and rockets really start falling, whichever side sends 'em, it's about ten to one we'll be on the receiving end here. . . . I'll take what's coming. But before then I propose to enjoy myself.

(I.ii)

His daughter Marion, who has married a rich French aristocrat, offers them a quiet, country life in France—"away from this messy and slovenly and drab" country—and hopes that, like her, they will find "the Faith" and a love for the land. His daughter Jean, a hospital doctor, astringent and science-bound, is not so sure about their leaving, partly because she has hopes of England becoming a "properly planned community" on the lines of her father's socialist aspirations, partly because she is preoccupied   and annoyed with herself about it—with an unhappy love affair.

But stay the professor will—even though his wife of many years drives off sadly and regretfully—to be looked after by his loyal, music-loving youngest daughter, Dinah, eighteen, and Mrs. Cotton, a cockney who, as someone says, has never quite come out of the blitz. The professor insists that "I don't want to walk away from real life, give it up as a bad job."

The penultimate scene begins to the gramophone accompaniment of the Elgar cello concerto—"a kind of long farewell," the professor remarks, "to his world before the war of 1914 . . . smiling Edwardian afternoons—Maclaren and Ranji batting at Lords, then Richter or Nikisch at the Queen's Hall—all gone, lost for ever." It is a recurrent mood in Priestley's writing and here presented without any time-theory consolations—once more autumnal, trembling on the verge of winter.

The play has other virtues—the professor's tutorials are full of wisdom, Priestleyan wisdom; the playwright, too, has caught on to postwar slang—"bulsh," "he's had it," "skoal," the word "spiv" itself, so often coupled in the dreary postwar months with "drone"; and Priestley has really understood such provincial students as the snotty (literally) Fawcett and the pathetically unkempt Edith Westmore.

No one would suggest that *Home Is Tomorrow* (1949) has the intensity of *Johnson over Jordan* or the entertaining twists and turns of *Ever Since Paradise*, but to dismiss it as "lacklustre," as does one writer, is going too far, even if, as Priestley recounts, "it was a

228

thumping flop." The play is about an English official, Sir Edward Fortrose, and his erring wife, Jill, whom he continues to love despite her wanton ways, and the unrequited love for him of his secretary, who shares his ideals. But this is involved with the United Nations—Fortrose is chief administrator of a tropical island, Corobana, where, assisted by a Czech, a Frenchman, and a Chinese, he seeks on behalf of the UN to transform the island from its "undeveloped" state into a civilized, going concern.

But international big businessmen interfere because the island contains, it is believed, great stocks of the valuable beryllium; they fan a native revolution and at the end of the play Fortrose, the donnish idealist, is shot dead on stage. His wife, Jill, has always thought the whole thing (the UN)

pretentious and damn silly. All this stuff about internationalism and a world society—it's nothing but empty talk—busybody nonsense . . . sterile, arid, lifeless. . . . What they're trying to make here will never be really alive. Only an imitation of something half-dead somewhere else. Surbiton in the tropics. No more dignified Indians and jolly lazy blacks and picturesque riffraff, enjoying their life in their own way. Instead—committees of pimply clerks and anaemic schoolteachers droning on about Education and Culture and the United Nations and Internationalism and Peace. . . .

Fortrose's opposite view is put far less strongly and less convincingly by Priestley. Perhaps he had already realized that the United Nations contained a great number of totally ruthless people who do not hesitate at murder. Melniz, the Czech on Fortrose's staff, urges that the only thing to do about the revolutionary leader—"this reactionary, this counter-revolutionary swine, this tool of big capitalism—is to liquidate him"; and his gentle Chinese colleague agrees. Fortrose firmly demurs. "Liberal sentimental man—play the game—eh?" sneers the Czech.

Thirty-five years after the play, most of us have to admit that Jill was right. In short, we cannot today read *Home Is Tomorrow* without bearing much later *Home Is Tomorrow* without bearing much later events in mind. But we can still enjoy the drama—the so-French Frenchman Riberac; the divided mind and heart of the local employee, Rosa; Fortrose's forthright attack on marriage regarded as "farm-yard-and-swell-time ideas of sex" rather than in his view as "a sort of strange door . . . leading to the other side of things, the enchanted place. . . . You see

it sometimes in the corner of a picture . . . in a line of verse."

A year later came *Summer Day's Dream* (1950), which may be described as a postatomic pastoral, or a rather late example of the "soil, sweat, and beer" school of the late nineteenth century. After Britain has been devastated by atom bombs, the survivors have developed a new, placid way of life based on tilling the land by horse plow and cultivating the fruits of the earth—presumably the soil has not been entirely poisoned—that they barter with neighbors. They live quite happily without telephones and radios, or even much transport. There are still local supplies of electricity (made by "a couple of wind vanes up on the down"). Nothing is organized from a center. There is time for poetry, music, conversation, and books.

Into this little idyllic community, complete with both another maguslike figure, Margaret, and Stephen reminiscing about the Great War, enter three members of the new master race—an American man, a Russian woman, and an Indian scientist, all totally and exclusively involved in the grim, nerve-racking world of high technology. Here indeed is one-worldism, internationalism—mentioned in *Home Is Tomorrow*—in full frenzied operation; but it is really an extrapolation of Priestley's old horrors so vividly described before the war in essays and *Midnight on the Desert*. We gather that the play written in 1950 is set in the 1970's. The atomic cataclysm has not yet happened; but certainly the pressures Priestley feared have not decreased.

The nub of the play is the temptation the three visitors experience from this idyllic pastoral life. Even the frosty-faced Russian Irina, Communist-subjugated, blossoms and falls in love with the handsome Chris. They depart reluctantly with the young country girl's words in their ears: "All right—go places and get some action. But don't try and make other people run away from themselves. Don't choke them with your dust."

No one can pass final judgment on this infinitely fertile writer while he is still alive. He has stimulated political, sociological, and literary thought; entertained us mightily with his Bayeux tapestry (not every thread perfect) of novels; made us laugh and cry and wonder with his plays, some of which are still being played all over the world, many years after they were first produced, and so have earned the right to the title of modern classics.

SELECTED BIBLIOGRAPHY

I. COLLECTED WORKS. *The Works of J. B. Priestley*, 28 vols. (London, 1931), the Presentation ed.; *The Plays*, vol. I (London, 1948), published in U.S. as *Seven Plays* (New York, 1950), vol. II (London, 1949; New York, 1950), vol. III (London, 1950; New York, 1952).

II. SELECTED WORKS. *Self-Selected Essays* (London, 1932); *Four in Hand* (London, 1934), contains *Adam in Moonshine*, *Laburnum Grove*, *The Roundabout*, and some nonfiction pieces; *Going Up* (London, 1950), stories and sketches; *The Priestley Companion* (Harmondsworth, 1951), intro. by I. Brown; *Essays of Five Decades* (Boston, 1968).

III. SELECTED PLAYS. *Two Time Plays* (London, 1937), contains *Time and the Conways* and *I Have Been Here Before*; *Three Plays* (London, 1943), contains *Music at Night*, *The Long Mirror*, and *They Came to a City*; *Four Plays* (London, 1944), contains all of *Three Plays* and adds *Desert Highway*; *Three Comedies* (London, 1945), contains *Goodnight, Children*, *The Golden Fleece*, and *How Are They at Home?*; *Three Time Plays* (London, 1947), contains *Two Time Plays* and adds *Dangerous Corner*.

IV. SEPARATE WORKS. *The Chapman of Rhymes* (London, 1918), verse; *Brief Diversions* (Cambridge, 1922), miscellany; *Papers from Lilliput* (Cambridge, 1922), sketches; *I for One* (London, 1923), essays; *Figures in Modern Literature* (London, 1924), criticism; *The English Comic Characters* (London, 1925), criticism; *Essays of Today and Yesterday* (London, 1926); *George Meredith* (London, 1926), criticism; *Talking* (London, 1926), essays; *Adam in Moonshine* (London, 1927), novel; *Benighted* (London, 1927), novel, published in U.S. as *The Old Dark House* (New York, 1928); *The English Novel* (London, 1927), criticism; *Open House* (London, 1927), essays; *Thomas Love Peacock* (London, 1927), criticism; *Apes and Angels* (London, 1928), essays; *Too Many People* (New York–London, 1928); *The Balconinny* (London, 1929), essays; *English Humour* (London, 1929), criticism; *Farthing Hall* (London, 1929), novel, with H. Walpole; *The Good Companions* (New York–London, 1929), novel, dramatized with E. Knoblock (1935).

Angel Pavement (New York–London, 1930), novel; *The Town Major of Miracourt* (London, 1930), novel; *Dangerous Corner* (London, 1932), drama; *Faraway* (London, 1932), novel; *Albert Goes Through* (London, 1933), story; *I'll Tell You Everything* (New York, 1933), mystery novel, with G. Bullett; *The Roundabout* (London, 1933), drama; *Wonder Hero* (London, 1933), novel; *Eden End* (London, 1934), drama; *English Journey* (London, 1934), description; *Laburnum Grove* (London, 1934), drama; *Cornelius* (London, 1935), drama; *Duet in Floodlight* (London, 1935), drama; *Bees on the Boat Deck* (London, 1936), drama; *Spring Tide* (London, 1936), drama, originally published as by G. Billam and P. Goldsmith, the latter a pseudonym for Priestley; *They Walk in the City* (New York–London, 1936), novel; *I Have Been Here Before* (London, 1937), drama; *Midnight on the Desert* (New York–London, 1937), autobiography; *Mystery of Greenfingers* (London, 1937), drama; *People at Sea* (London, 1937), drama; *Time and the Conways* (London, 1937), drama; *The Doomsday Men* (London, 1938), novel; *When We Are Married* (London, 1938), drama; *First Mercury Story Book* (London, 1939); *Johnson over Jordan* (London, 1939), drama; *Let the People Sing* (London, 1939), novel; *Rain upon Godshill* (London, 1939), autobiography.

Britain Speaks (New York–London, 1940), radio broadcasts; *Postscripts* (London, 1940), radio broadcasts; *Out of the People* (London, 1941), commentary; *Black-out in Gretley* (New York–London, 1942), story; *Britain at War* (New York, 1942); *Goodnight, Children* (London, 1942), drama; *British Women Go to War* (London, 1943), sociology; *Daylight on Saturday* (London, 1943), novel; *Manpower* (London, 1944), written for the Ministry of Labour on wartime use of manpower; *Desert Highway* (London, 1944), drama; *Here Are Your Answers* (London, 1944), pamphlet; *They Came to a City* (London, 1944), drama; *How Are They at Home?* (London, 1945), drama; *Letter to a Returning Serviceman* (London, 1945), essay; *Three Men in New Suits* (London, 1945), novel; *Bright Day* (New York–London, 1946), novel; *Ever Since Paradise* (London, 1946), drama; *Russian Journey* (London, 1946), travel; *The Secret Dream* (London, 1946), essay; *The Arts Under Socialism* (London, 1947), lecture; *An Inspector Calls* (London, 1947), drama; *Jenny Villiers* (London, 1947), drama; *The Long Mirror* (London, 1947), drama; *Music at Night* (London, 1947), drama; *The Rose and Crown* (London, 1947), drama; *Theatre Outlook* (London, 1947), criticism; *The Golden Fleece* (London, 1948), drama; *The High Toby* (London, 1948), drama; *The Linden Tree* (London, 1948), drama; *Delight* (London, 1949), essays; *Home Is Tomorrow* (London, 1949), drama; *The Olympians* (London, 1949), opera libretto.

Bright Shadow (London, 1950), drama; *Summer Day's Dream* (London, 1950), drama; *Festival at Farbridge* (London, 1951), novel, published in U.S. as *Festival*; *Dragon's Mouth* (London, 1952), dramatic quartet, with J. Hawkes; *Mother's Day* (London, 1953), drama; *The Other Place* (London, 1953), stories; *Private Rooms* (London, 1953), one-act play; *Treasure on Pelican* (London, 1953), drama; *Try It Again* (London, 1953), one-act play; *A Glass of Bitter* (London, 1954), one-act play; *Low Notes on a High Level* (London, 1954), fiction; *The Magicians* (London, 1954), novel; *Journey Down a Rainbow* (London, 1955), travel, with J. Hawkes; *All About Ourselves* (London, 1965), essays; *Mr. Kettle and Mrs. Moon* (London, 1956), drama; *The Writer in a Changing Society* (Aldington, 1956), essay; *The Art of the Dramatist* (London, 1957), essay; *Thoughts in the Wilderness* (London, 1957), essays; *The Glass Cage* (London, 1958), drama; *Topside, or the Future of England* (London, 1958), essay; *The Story of*

Theatre (London, 1959), published in U.S. as *The Wonderful World of Theatre* (New York, 1959).

Literature and Western Man (London, 1960), criticism; *William Hazlitt* (London, 1960), essay; *Charles Dickens: A Pictorial Biography* (London, 1961); *Saturn over the Water* (London, 1961), novel; *The Thirty-First of June* (London, 1961), novel; *Margin Released* (London, 1962), literary reminiscences; *The Shapes of Sleep* (London, 1962), novel; *A Severed Head* (London, 1963), drama, with I. Murdock; *Man and Time* (New York–London, 1964), essay; *Sir Michael and Sir George* (London, 1964), novel; *Lost Empires* (London, 1965), novel; *The Moments and Other Pieces* (London, 1966), essays; *Salt Is Leaving* (London, 1966), suspense novel; *It's an Old Country* (London, 1967), novel; *The Image Men* (London, 1968), novel, vol. I: *Out of Town*, vol. II: *London End*; *Trumpets over the Sea* (London, 1968), essay; *The Prince of Pleasure* (London, 1969), social history.

Anton Chekhov (London, 1970), criticism; *The Edwardians* (London, 1970), social history; *Over the Long High Wall* (London, 1972), essay; *Victoria's Heyday* (London, 1972), social history; *The English* (London, 1973), social history; *Outcries and Asides* (London, 1974), essays; *A Visit to New Zealand* (London, 1974), travel; *Particular Pleasures* (London, 1975), essays; *English Humour* (London, 1976), essay; *Lost and Found: The English Way of Life* (London, 1976), essay; *Instead of the Trees* (London, 1977), autobiography.

V. BIOGRAPHICAL AND CRITICAL STUDIES. R. Pogson, *J. B. Priestley and the Theatre* (Clevedon, 1947); E. Gillett, *Introduction to J. B. Priestley* (London, 1956); D. Hughes, *J. B. Priestley: An Informal Study* (London, 1958); L. Löb, *Mensch und Gesellschaft bei J. B. Priestley* (Berne, 1962); G. Lloyd-Evans, *J. B. Priestley, the Dramatist* (London, 1964); S. Cooper, *J. B. Priestley: Portrait of an Author* (London, 1970).

F. R. LEAVIS
(1895-1978)

Edward Greenwood

FRANK RAYMOND LEAVIS was born in Cambridge on 14 July 1895, and educated at the Perse School and Emmanuel College, Cambridge. He served in World War I in an ambulance unit as a stretcher bearer, carrying, it is said, a pocket Milton all through the ordeal. It was no doubt his having lived through those times that made it impossible for him to endorse the sublime simplicity of Leon Trotsky's reference to the "2nd of August, 1914, when the maddened power of bourgeois culture let loose upon the world the blood and fire of an imperialistic war." In "T. S. Eliot as Critic," in *"Anna Karenina" and Other Essays* (1967), Leavis speaks of "those early years after the great hiatus," when he "struggled to achieve the beginnings of articulate thought about literature." He first read history and then English as an undergraduate, becoming a student in the newly founded English School for the second part of the Tripos. (Cambridge honors degrees were known as the Tripos from the three-legged stool on which candidates for the degrees originally sat. They followed the original two-part pattern of the B.A. degree in mathematics. It was possible to read in two different subjects for each part.)

The figures who "really counted" in the achieving of his "articulate thought about literature" were George Santayana (despite this, "not fundamentally congenial") and Matthew Arnold. To them was added Eliot's own influence as a critic. Leavis bought Eliot's first volume of essays, *The Sacred Wood*, in 1920. Along with the works of these writers went the influence of the writing in Ford Madox Ford's (or Hueffer's) *English Review*, to which Leavis had subscribed as a schoolboy back in 1912, and in which he had made his first acquaintance with D. H. Lawrence's writing in "The Prussian Officer." Leavis was impressed by Ford's acceptance of the view that in the "irreversible new conditions" of modern industrial civilization the concern for "the higher cultural values" must be restricted to a small minority, while at the same time that concern must concede nothing "to the preciousness, fatuity or spirit of Aestheticism." That same view was to be a cornerstone of the enterprise of Leavis' own periodical, *Scrutiny*. It was no wonder then that Leavis was outraged when Brother George Every suggested in his *Poetry and Personal Responsibility* that "the error of the *Scrutiny* writers was to look for the intelligentsia in the same place where aesthetes were recruited in the days of the Yellow Book and the Rhymers' Club."

Leavis was stimulated by such teachers in the new English School as Mansfield D. Forbes and I. A. Richards, who is discussed at greater length in the second section of this essay. He wrote a doctoral thesis on the periodical literature of the eighteenth century, with particular reference to Joseph Addison's *Spectator*, and this further contributed to his lifelong concern with the way in which the ethos of a periodical can both reflect and mold the cultural aspirations of a wider public. His wife, Q. D. Leavis, was to carry on this interest in the social relations between literature and its public in her classic study (which grew out of a doctoral thesis) *Fiction and the Reading Public* (1932).

Leavis also greatly admired the periodical *Calendar of Modern Letters*, edited by Edgell Rickword. It ran from 1925 to mid-1927, and though retrospectively Leavis was to see its failure "to win the interest and loyalty of a sufficient public to keep it alive" as an index of cultural decline, its concern with the maintenance of critical standards was to be an important inspiration of his own editing. The *Calendar* ran a series of intelligent deflations of what it saw as the exaggerated reputations of such contemporary figures as H. G. Wells, J. M. Barrie, G. K. Chesterton, and John Galsworthy (the Galsworthy critique was written by D. H. Lawrence); these articles were later collected by Rickword under the title *Scru-*

tinies. Leavis was to call the periodical he founded in 1932 *Scrutiny,* and in the following year he published a selection of material from *Calendar* with an appreciative preface under the title *Towards Standards of Criticism.*

By 1925 Leavis was teaching English literature at Emmanuel College, Cambridge. D. W. Harding, who was later to be a fellow editor of *Scrutiny,* recalled his dynamism as a teacher when, looking back fifty years in a broadcast symposium in 1975, he said:

He was really superb. I remember the feelings with which this other man and I would come away. We would be partly exhilarated, and partly a bit subdued and rueful, perhaps. Exhilarated because of the new insights and the fine discriminations he had made, and sobered because he kept such extremely high standards in insight and one just realised how unskilled one was as a reader. At the same time, there was no feeling that he belittled you in any way—if you had difficulties or raised objections, then he met you on those. He could scrap what he was going to say and just meet you on whatever you were interested in.

In 1929 Leavis married Queenie Roth, and the next few years brought a wonderful harvest of critical work culminating in the annus mirabilis of 1932, when Leavis published *New Bearings in English Poetry,* his wife published *Fiction and the Reading Public,* and the quarterly periodical *Scrutiny* was founded. In view of the not wholly unjustified accusation that *Scrutiny* in its later years was hostile to contemporary literature, it is worth stressing that the young Leavis was in the vanguard in this matter. He incurred the displeasure of the university authorities and the English faculty by lecturing on James Joyce's *Ulysses* to his classes in the mid-1920's. Leavis recalls in "Letter to the *Times Literary Supplement* May 3rd 1963"[1] "conventional academics" saying of him at the time of Lawrence's death in 1930, "We don't like the kind of book he lends undergraduates." At this time the faculty librarian sanctioned the withholding of D. H. Lawrence's and T. F. Powys' works from undergraduates who wanted to borrow them or read them in the library. As to the teaching of contemporary work in the 1930's, Muriel Bradbrook recalls Leavis' interest in the poetry of I. A. Richards' pupil, the ex-student of mathematics William Empson. She says, "It cannot be very often that undergraduates are taught the poetry of a fellow undergraduate, but

[1]Reprinted in Leavis' *Letters in Criticism,* J. Tasker, ed. (London, 1974), p. 98.

we were taught about some of Empson's poems by Leavis."

Leavis had enemies among the English faculty, however, and all this brilliance and the *Scrutiny* project did not enable him to obtain, as in all justice it should have, a permanent faculty post. At last, in 1936 (the year in which *Revaluation* appeared), he was made a lecturer at the age of forty-one, after having been a probationary (or assistant) lecturer since 1927, and after having seen a younger candidate given precedence over him. All this was a source of great bitterness to him, both at the time and in later years. Leavis had moved from Emmanuel to Downing College in 1929 and was elected a fellow there in 1936 after the faculty had made him a lecturer.

Revaluation, although it contains material from *Scrutiny* articles, has unity as a book in mapping out a new history of English poetry, as René Wellek recognized at the time, when he wrote: "It seems the first consistent attempt to rewrite the history of English poetry from the twentieth-century point of view." It is not annalistic but critical history, history concerned with making firsthand judgments distinguishing the first-rate from the second-rate. It does not make the mistake of F. W. Bateson in his *English Poetry and the English Language* (1935), which was to suppose that critical judgment can find its validation in a combination of assertions about social and linguistic history. In reviewing Bateson's book, Leavis found that Bateson's view of language involved excessive reliance on a too simple "denotation"/"connotation" dichotomy and a too naive view of the nature of critical judgment. The two critics were to clash again on the subject of literary history when Bateson attacked Leavis' reading of Andrew Marvell's poem "A Dialogue Between the Soul and Body," in an article in *Essays in Criticism* in January 1953. Leavis pointed out that the historical context in which Bateson proposed to anchor the reading of the poem was something much less determinate than the poem itself, to whose complexities his reading was manifestly inadequate: "the most essential kind of knowledge can come only from an intelligent frequentation of the poetry."

The Great Tradition, published in 1948, did for the English novel what *Revaluation* had done for English poetry: it provided literary history that possessed an essential focus or center of interest. *The Common Pursuit* (1952) collected many of Leavis' best articles from *Scrutiny. D. H. Lawrence: Novelist* (1955) showed a falling off for those who could not see Lawrence as so flawless a writer as Leavis did, and had a significantly greater amount of pure quotation and exclamatory praise as opposed to the close analytic criticism that is Leavis' distinction. There was then a twelve-year gap in books before "Anna Karenina" and Other Essays inaugurated a rich spate of works (some, notably Dickens the Novelist [1970], joint productions with his wife) written during Leavis' seventies. The Dickens book and the engagement with Lawrence's text in Thought, Words and Creativity (1976) and with Eliot's Four Quartets in The Living Principle (1975) showed a welcome return to Leavis' true strength, the discussion of particular examples of prose and poetry, after the in some ways less satisfactory engagement with more general matters of wider cultural health in such works as English Literature in Our Time and the University (1969) and, especially, Nor Shall My Sword (1972). The latter contains Leavis' attack of 1962 on C. P. Snow, which introduces the interesting idea of the "third realm" as a name for the mode of existence of works of literature. They are not merely private, like a dream, nor public in the sense of something that can be tripped over, but exist only in human minds as a work of collaborative reconstruction. Much in the lecture and the book, however, is too personal in the wrong sense of the word and lacks the fuller disinterestedness of Leavis at his best. If humanity has the creativeness Leavis attributes to it, there is no need, perhaps, to strike such a note of despair at the state of institutions such as the university.

Leavis was appointed reader in English at Cambridge in 1960 and held this post until his retirement from the faculty in 1962. He was appointed visiting professor of English at the University of York from 1965 to 1968 and subsequently held visiting professorships at the University of Wales and the University of Bristol. He was awarded doctorates of literature by the universities of Leeds, York, Queen's Belfast, Delhi, and Aberdeen. He was made a Companion of Honour in the New Year's list for 1978. He died on 14 April 1978 at the age of eighty-two.

THE SIGNIFICANCE OF LEAVIS' CRITICISM

To try to bring out what is special about Leavis' approach to literary criticism, I will begin by quoting from the preface of Towards Standards in Criticism: "Literary criticism provides the test for life and con-

creteness; where it degenerates, the instruments of thought degenerate too, and thinking, released from the testing and energizing contact with the full, living consciousness, is debilitated, and betrayed to the academic, the abstract and the verbal." Behind this statement lies a famous passage in Ezra Pound's How to Read, which Leavis quoted and endorsed in his own "How to Teach Reading" (1932), later reprinted as an appendix to Education and the University (1943). Pound wrote that literature

has to do with the clarity of "any and every" thought and opinion. It has to do with maintaining the very cleanliness of the tools, the health of the very matter of thought itself. Save the rare and very limited instances of invention in the plastic arts, or in mathematics, the individual cannot think or communicate his thought, the governor and legislator cannot act effectively or frame his laws, without words, and the solidity and validity of these words is in the care of the damned and despised literati. When their work goes rotten—by that I do not mean when they express indecorous thoughts—but when their very medium, the very essence of their work, the application of word to thing goes rotten, i.e. becomes slushy and inexact, or excessive or bloated, the whole machinery of social and of individual thought and order goes to pot.

The view as to the intimate relation between the health of language and the health of consciousness that underlines both passages has, of course, been held by figures as diverse as John Ruskin, Matthew Arnold, R. G. Collingwood, Ludwig Wittgenstein, Kenneth Burke, and George Orwell. But there is one especially important point that a close reading of the Leavis passage brings out. That is the answer to the question which puzzles many who have only a peripheral acquaintance with Leavis' work as the work of one among many writers on literature, the Lewises, Tillyards, Fryes, Trillings, Kermodes, and Blooms—namely, "What is all this fuss about one teacher of English, and one in an English provincial backwater at that?" Leaving aside the question as to whether Cambridge was a provincial backwater (though I think many would still endorse Leavis' remark that "the British university as represented by Oxford and Cambridge has a distinct and strongly positive organic life, rooted in history"), the contention that "literary criticism provides the test for life and concreteness" shows that literary criticism had a meaning for Leavis quite different from that which it had for any of the writers on literature mentioned above. It becomes, in short, the central organon for humanistic studies.

There is an admirable definition of the poet's task by William Hazlitt. He calls it that of "unravelling the real web of associations, which have been woven round any subject by nature, and the unavoidable conditions of humanity." But the poet is moved by such associations to picture such webs rather than to unravel them. The unraveling, or explication, of such wholes, the refining and articulation of first-hand perceptions of them into delicate and relevant commentary is surely the task of the critic, and one that, incidentally, should obviate the standard and misleading move to fob him off as a failed creator or as a parasite on other men's works. Aristotle, with his habitual common sense, remarked, "It is a thing very difficult, if not impossible, for a man to be a good judge of what he himself cannot do"; but Aristotle, it should be remembered, divided doing, or *praxis*, into two parts: making things and performing actions. The passage just quoted, from the *Politics* 1340b, is on judging *musical* performance. But as regards made things, whether shoes or poems, Aristotle, like Plato, thought that the "user," not the maker, was the best judge. When Bateson suggests in *Essays in Critical Dissent* (1972) that it would be a good thing for critics to give "public evidence of their creative metal" by publishing examples of their poetic efforts, and remarks in his grudging survey of Leavis' work in the *Sewanee Review* (1977) on "the curious absence in the typical *Scrutiny* critic of creative talent," his assumption has a gratuitous irrelevance about it. The notion that a critic must compose a poem as a sort of implicit guarantee that he can be trusted to talk about poetry is little short of grotesque. If we can't tell that from the discourse itself, no amount of imitating Tennyson or Auden will help us.

It is certainly true that Leavis is an exception to the rule that all the major critics from John Dryden to T. S. Eliot have written criticism as a counterpart to their creative efforts. In Dryden and Eliot in particular there is a constant atmosphere of the workshop. Samuel Johnson's criticism reflects (as Leavis' essays on him well bring out) both the strength and limitations of Augustan assumptions. William Wordsworth's criticism is an apology for his own work, and much of Samuel Taylor Coleridge's is a defense of those divagations into the abstractions of German philosophy that he had come to love. Arnold's criticism conspicuously demands from poetry what he is regretfully aware he cannot himself give as a poet. But it could be claimed that this complete lack of any bias as a practitioner, this putting of his whole energy into an encounter with the text, into the full realization of what is before him, is the very thing that enables Leavis to attain that "peculiar completeness of response" which he believes is the critic's task to achieve and to develop into commentary.

If there is sometimes animus in Leavis (and the account of his career shows that he had some warrant for resentment against the Cambridge English faculty), that animus is, as Christopher Ricks pointed out in the BBC broadcast symposium in 1975, closely linked to an animation inseparable from the intensity of conviction with which he tries to communicate his insights. Leavis' prose style has often been criticized by those whose ideal of prose is a kind of compound of Walter Pater, Logan Pearsall Smith, and Lord David Cecil; but he developed a prose style no doubt partly related to his spoken idiom with pupils and partly adapted (Ricks suggests) from Henry James (who imitated oral patterns), in whose style qualification and nuance involve an increment rather than a loss of energy. Criticism was ideally, for Leavis, a collaborative dialogue, and much of his life's work as a critic actually took the form of oral as well as written communication, in lectures, supervisions, and seminars. He ended the introduction to *Revaluation* with the words: "The debt that I wish to acknowledge is to those with whom I have, during the past dozen years, discussed literature as a 'teacher': if I have learnt anything about the methods of profitable discussion I have learnt it in collaboration with them." At the same time, on more than one occasion he expresses his dislike of the suggestion of that "authoritative telling" associated with teaching. In *English Literature in Our Time and the University* he writes:

The peculiar nature of the study of English worth pursuing at university level entails its being in the most essential regards, though a special study, not what "specialist" suggests. A genuine teacher doesn't find himself holding back his subtlest insight and his most adventurous thought because they are not suitable for communication to first- or second-year men. He tests and develops, in "teaching" his perceptions, his understanding, and his thought, and with good men may do so very fruitfully. For what we call teaching is, if genuine, a matter of enlisting and fostering collaboration; the teacher in English has, in what I have pointed to in the distinction between "special" and "specialist," a peculiar advantage—or a given kind of advantage in a peculiarly rewarding form. The qualifications of a teacher are given in these observations. He is one who has the kinds of interest in literature that go with finding pleasure and profit in discussing it with intelligent young students.

("The Present and the Past: Eliot's Demonstration")

Such discussion will of course have no truck with the notion of literature for literature's sake or the chimera of "purely literary values." There is no "significant form" in literature providing an "aesthetic emotion" to be exclaimed about in a way unrelated to one's other concerns and mode of life. Form in a work of literature can, for Leavis, "only be a matter of significance such as can be intelligently and profitably discussed." Literary values are bound up with moral and spiritual ones, and it is oddly enough this very fact that may lead to the puzzling phenomenon of "the peculiar hatred any intelligent conception of the importance of English may expect to encounter in a university English School." Leavis would entirely endorse his master Santayana's condemnation of "holding a single interest free from all others" as only making the aesthetic sphere contemptible in the end; and he would agree with Santayana that "art being a part of life, the criticism of art is a part of morals." In addition to this, Leavis is strongly attracted to the view that it is good for those engaged in the political and social affairs of a nation to be affected by a climate touched by a vital literary culture.

I have spoken of Leavis' concern with putting his whole energy into an encounter with the text, and it would be as well to have a concrete example of his work in front of us before engaging further with the problems raised by his critical work as a whole. I therefore quote from pages 108–110 of *The Living Principle* parts of the analysis of a speech from Cyril Tourneur's *The Revenger's Tragedy*. This has the advantage for purposes of economy that Leavis is analyzing one passage, not comparing two:

> Does the silkworm expend her yellow labours
> For thee? For thee does she undo herself?
> Are lordships sold to maintain ladyships
> For the poor benefit of a bewitching minute?
> Why does yon fellow falsify highways,
> And lays his life between the judge's lips
> To refine such a one? Keeps horse and men
> To beat their valours for her?

The key word in the first line is "expend." In touch with "spin," it acts with its force of "spend" on the "yellow," turning it to gold, and so, while adding directly to the sug-

gestion of wealth and luxury, bringing out by a contrasting co-presence in the one word the soft yellowness of the silk. To refer to silk, emblem of luxurious leisure, as "labours" is in itself a telescoping of conflicting associations. Here, then, in this slow, packed, self-pondering line (owing to the complex organization of meaning the reader finds he cannot skim easily over the words, or slip through them in a euphonious glide) we have the type of the complexity that gives the whole passage that rich effect of life and body. It relates closely to the theme of the play, but there is a vitality that is immediately apparent in the isolated extract, and we are concerned here with taking note of its obvious manifestations. . . .

The nature of the imagery involved in

> . . . lays his life between the judge's lips

might perhaps not be easy to define, but it is certainly an instance in which effectiveness is not mainly visual. The sense of being at the mercy of another's will and word is focused in a sensation of extreme physical precariousness, a sensation of lying helpless, on the point of being ejected at a breath into the abyss. In "refine" we probably have another instance of a double meaning. In the first place "refine" would mean "make fine" or "elegant" (the speaker is addressing the skull of his dead mistress). But the gold image, coming through by way of "sold" (and the more effectively for never having been explicit), seems also to be felt here, with the suggestion that nothing can refine this dross. In this way the structure of the last sentence is explained: horse and men are represented by their "valours," their "refined" worths, which are beaten for "such a one," and so the contrast of the opening question is clinched—"her yellow labours for *thee*?"

(2, "Judgment and Analysis")

THE PROBLEM SITUATION

In order to understand Leavis' work it is necessary to grasp the problematic situation that he faced at the outset of his critical career and to touch further on the difficulties with the Cambridge English faculty already mentioned. First of all we must remind ourselves how recent is the notion that the literature of the vernacular tongue can be made the center of a humanistic education. Here E. M. W. Tillyard's *The Muse Unchained*, D. J. Palmer's *The Rise of English Studies*, and John Gross's *The Rise and Fall of the Man of Letters* are all useful. When Matthew Arnold in the 1880's somewhat shakily defended the importance of literature in education as against T. H. Huxley's claims for the preeminence of science, even Arnold went only so far as to say that the vernacular literature should be taught along with the classical literature of Greece and Rome. It was Huxley himself who suggested that the vernacular literature might stand alone as the vehicle of humanistic culture at a time when so many and varied educational demands were being made: though it must be confessed that Huxley's own emphasis on the "how" of teaching fell forbiddingly on literature as philologically illustrative of the science of language, an idea that others were to build into the Oxford English school when it was eventually founded.

It was perhaps the Cambridge philosopher Henry Sidgwick who first grasped philosophically the idea that the literature of the vernacular tongue could be made central to humanistic education. Because of this, Q. D. Leavis was later to associate Sidgwick with his friend, the critic and historian of ideas Leslie Stephen, in a kind of Cambridge tradition to which she felt that the work of her husband, herself, and their colleagues at *Scrutiny* could be linked; at the same time she wished to dissociate them from the other Cambridge tradition, connected with the Bloomsbury of Stephen's daughter Virginia Woolf and her friend Desmond MacCarthy (then the chief reviewer of the *Sunday Times* and an influential figure in literary journalism), and from the academicism of ex-classicists such as Tillyard. Q. D. Leavis writes:

We believe with Stephen that criticism is not a mystic rapture but a process of the intelligence. No doubt the environment of Clerk Maxwell and Henry Sidgwick was peculiarly favourable to the development of such an attitude to literature, but we recollect that Arnold and Coleridge also practised this method when they were most effectual.

("Leslie Stephen: Cambridge Critic")[2]

In "Henry Sidgwick's Cambridge," which appeared in *Scrutiny* for 1947 and includes a good brief account of Sidgwick's pioneering work for women's education, Q. D. Leavis recurs to Sidgwick as wanting "to pitch the Classics overboard" in favor of the study of English literature "in association with other modern literatures," which is exactly F. R. Leavis' own program in his *Education and the University*.

Sidgwick had written in the 1890's about English literature as a subject for study, but its establishment did not come until 1918. The process is described in E. M. W. Tillyard's *The Muse Unchained* (1958). He tells how, as a result of meetings at Professor E. M.

Chadwick's house in 1916, an English Tripos in two parts was proposed. Chadwick envisaged students would probably combine only one part of this with classics, law, history, or a modern language. The first examinations in the new Tripos were held in the Easter term of 1919. All this despite the fact, mentioned by Basil Willey in his *Cambridge and Other Memories* (1968), that the philosopher J. M. E. McTaggart had said, "a Professorship of such a subject would not only be useless but positively harmful to the University." At the end of the 1920's modifications made it possible, in Tillyard's words, "to get a degree in English since Chaucer, with certain additions"; and this became more common than the combined degree.

Two men who soon came to the fore in the new school were Mansfield D. Forbes, a teacher of genius who wrote nothing, and the more widely known I. A. Richards. Leavis dedicated *English Literature in Our Time and the University* (1969) to the memory of Henry Chadwick (who had been instrumental in getting the study of English literature separated from the study of Old English—contrary to the state of things at Oxford) and of Forbes. Forbes himself emerges from the introduction to that book as a kind of proto-Leavis, with something of Leavis' effect. Leavis writes:

Of course, he incidentally reinforced some conceits and exposed his influence to the charge of inspiring and equipping ambitious stupidities and stark insensibilities to posture as something else. But what "teacher" can be insured against this kind of hazard? Where does safety lie unless in nullity? We didn't need Nietzsche to tell us to live dangerously; there is no other way of living. Forbes, himself a vital force of intelligence, had, in the strong disinterested way, the courage of life and, it follows, the impulse and the power to stir intelligence into active life in others.

When he was asked to comment on Edna St. Vincent Millay's sonnet "What's this of death, from you who will never die?" Forbes's idiosyncratic vivacity produced the following:

This is a studied orgasm from a "Shakespeare-R. Brooke" complex, as piece 7 from a "Marvell–Wordsworth–Drinkwater, etc., stark-simplicity" complex. Hollow at first reading; resoundingly hollow at second. A sort of thermos vacuum, "the very thing" for a dignified picnic in this sort of Two-Seater Sonnet. The *"Heroic" Hectoring* of line 1, the hearty *quasi*-stoical button-holing of the unimpeachably-equipped beloved, *the magisterial finger-wagging* of

[2]Published in *Scrutiny*, VII, no. 4 (March 1939), p. 407.

"I tell you this"!! Via such conduits magnanimity may soon be laid on as an indispensable, if not obligatory, modern convenience.

These remarks were called up by a very famous experiment. I. A. Richards distributed unsigned and undated poems, a mixture of Shakespeare, Donne, and other masters, with pieces of inflated and sentimental trash, and then collected and published selections from the "protocol" reports on them by students and members of faculty in part 1 of his book *Practical Criticism.* The significance of Richards' experiment for criticism has been well described by the best of the writers in *Scrutiny* after Leavis himself, D. W. Harding. Harding writes:

It is . . . possible to show that differences of opinion in literary matters frequently arise from errors of approach which even those who make them can be brought to recognize. With people who assert that they know what they like, the one hope is to demonstrate to them that in point of fact they *don't,* that according to standards they themselves recognize elsewhere their judgment here is mistaken. As these inconsistencies are faced and abandoned, the possibility of agreement with other people grows greater.

("I. A. Richards")[3]

Even if in the end we find irreducible differences of taste (and even then the procedure will have established *something*), Harding believes, as Leavis himself does, that much common territory can be discovered in this quasi-Socratic dialectical way before the stage of irreducible difference is reached. What are needed are not grandiose theories or rhapsodies about the adventures of one's soul among masterpieces, or, for that matter, the dry, purely external application of technical equipment from, say, linguistics, but "fully illustrated discussions of actual instances." These discussions will offer starting points for further investigations. They will "draw attention to serious possibilities of misreading and misjudging" and show that "the adequate reading of poetry is a discipline and not a relaxation," without, of course, giving the notion of "discipline" connotations of the mechanical. It is on these assumptions that Leavis tried to argue for the criticism of literature as being the central humanistic discipline. Leavis himself later praised Richards for conferring the benefit of liberation "from the thought-frustrating spell of 'form,' 'pure sound value,' prosody, and the

³Published in *Scrutiny,* I, no. 4 (March 1933), p. 334.

other time-honoured quasi-critical futilities," but he had no time for Richards' pseudoscientific psychological and semantic ambitions.

We have seen something of the opposition to the inauguration of English studies at Cambridge. With typical acerbity Leavis was later to characterize many of the early faculty powers (Forbes and Richards excepted) as "unchecked mediocrities." One suspects that Leavis had the classicist (and Miltonist) E. M. W. Tillyard particularly in mind. Yet Basil Willey, who was taught by Tillyard, can write of him as though he, too, in those heady early days was a sort of proto-Leavis: "From the start his method was to direct our attention to particular texts and passages, to make us taste their diverse qualities, comparing and distinguishing. In our essays we were to avoid mere gossip, metaphysical vapourings and woolly mysticism." But whatever the rifts that were to develop within the faculty and give rise to so much bad blood and to a fascinating tangle for some fair-minded future historian to unravel (if that should turn out to be possible), there were at the end of the 1920's and the beginning of the 1930's three main tendencies that made the argument for literary criticism as the central humanistic discipline difficult to accept. These were, first, the strong Cambridge tradition that found its expression in the work of Alfred North Whitehead and Bertrand Russell (and something of a sanction, as I shall show, in the views of G. H. Hardy), according to which the essential nature of what constitutes a discipline is best exemplified by mathematics and logic; second, the rise of Positivism, with its central contention that only the method of natural science gives us knowledge; and third, the growing influence, particularly in the 1930's, of a somewhat reductionist form of Marxism.

I shall illustrate the notion of the primacy of the logico-mathematical from G. H. Hardy's famous book *A Mathematician's Apology.* Although this book was not published until 1940, Hardy had had a distinguished career as a fellow of Trinity (Russell's college also) since 1900, and it is difficult to believe that Leavis was not acquainted directly or indirectly with the ethos it represents. Hardy reveals himself in the book as strongly anti-utilitarian and as appreciative of aesthetic qualities in mathematics. Nevertheless there is a note of philistinism in the way he regards literary criticism. In the very first paragraph we find the standard cliché "Exposition, criticism, appreciation, is work for second-rate minds." This view makes it impossible to do justice to the central task of the humanities, which is "to unravel the web of associations" constituted not just by works of literature in the narrow sense of poems and plays and novels, but by works of history, biography, autobiography, and philosophy as well. It is significant that the only opponent of the case Hardy can conjure up (this in the Cambridge of *Scrutiny*) is A. E. Housman, who had an established reputation safely associated with classics. This is surely indicative of the status that the English studies pursued in his own university must have had in Hardy's eyes. Hardy then goes on: "As W. J. Turner has said so truly, it is only the 'highbrows' (in the unpleasant sense), who do not admire the 'real swells,'" by which Turner presumably meant what for him were the "great names" of literature, Shakespeare and Dickens, whom he apparently wished to emphasize were non-highbrows. When Hardy comes to consider poetry, he emphasizes that its interest lies not at all in ideas but solely in "the beauty of the verbal pattern." So much for Matthew Arnold's emphasis in his essays "The Study of Poetry" and "Wordsworth" on the importance of "moral ideas" in the poetry that repays frequentation. Hardy insists, like Russell, on pattern, interconnectedness, and generality as "external" sources of "intense emotional satisfaction." Even a person who is in many respects the utter antithesis of Hardy and Russell, Simone Weil, can express this Platonistic reverence for mathematics as the discipline of disciplines when she writes: "Unless one has exercised one's mind seriously at the gymnastic of mathematics one is incapable of precise thought, which amounts to saying that one is good for nothing."[4]

The sense that many distinguished minds accepted logico-mathematical procedures as the paradigm for what constitutes a discipline must have disturbed Leavis. He was struck by Santayana's observation in *Winds of Doctrine* that Russell's intellect was "at its best in subjects remote from human life," namely formal logic and mathematics, but faltered when it had to cope with concrete issues of life and mind. He endorses D. H. Lawrence's judgment: "What ails Russell is, in matters of life and emotion, the inexperience of youth. . . . It isn't that life has been too much for him, but too little." As late as 1967 we find Leavis saying, "'English' suffers by reason of its extreme remoteness as an academic study and disci-

pline from Mathematics: how produce and enforce the standards that determine genuine qualification?" The need is particularly pressing because creative literature itself affords an example of what Leavis in *The Great Tradition* calls "knowledge alive with understanding"—disciplined thinking that calls for apprehension by powers that are perhaps the antithesis of the mathematical.

The second tendency Leavis had to oppose was that of Positivism. The Positivists saw the method of natural science as the only source of empirical knowledge. This method consisted of the use of observation to verify or falsify whatever hypothesis was in question. The Positivists were so taken with this notion that they thought they could use it to mark the distinction between not just the scientific and the nonscientific but the meaningful and meaningless, as in A. J. Ayer's famous book *Language, Truth and Logic*, published in 1936. But the case for the view that only science can give us empirical knowledge and that all the rest is merely psychologically conditioned chat had already been wittily put in a short paper delivered in 1925 in Cambridge by the mathematical philosopher Frank Ramsey, friend of John Maynard Keynes, Russell, and Wittgenstein, and brother of Arthur, the future archbishop of Canterbury. Ramsey's paper was reprinted as the epilogue to his book *The Foundations of Mathematics*, published in 1931. It poses the basic question in its very title, "What Is There to Discuss?" Ramsey's Positivist answer is very brief, which was fortunate as the papers delivered were limited to five minutes by a rule of the society that gathered to hear them. It is, in effect, "Nothing!" Ramsey proclaims the Positivist credo, "There is nothing to know except science." Ethical and aesthetic disagreements (the very center of humanistic disputes) become merely a subject for psychological investigation as to their causes. No arguments in such subjects can be rationally vindicated. They take the absurd form of A saying, "I went to Grantchester this afternoon" and B saying, "No, I didn't," and each thinking he has contradicted the other. For Ramsey, in literary-critical disputes, men are still at the stage of using such formally feeble arguments as "Who drives fat oxen must himself be fat." Ramsey's psychological subjectivism was adopted by F. L. Lucas, a member of the Cambridge English faculty, who cited Ramsey's paper with approval in his book *Literature and Psychology* (1951). Lucas oddly combines the view that disagreements as to the "pleasure-value" of

---

[4]Quoted in S. Pétrement, *Simone Weil: A Life*, R. Rosenthal, trans. (London–Oxford, 1976), p. 212.

literature are irresolvable matters of temperament with the conviction that the "influence-value" of literature on conduct is objectively determinable: If persons read Charles Baudelaire constantly and keep Joyce's *Ulysses* under their pillows, it is unwise to marry them.

What told against the Positivist view for Leavis was presumably reflection on his experience. Hadn't the writings of Eliot and others, combined with his own reading of English poetry, shown him that the acquisition, articulation, and stabilization of literary preferences cannot be summed up in dismissive words about comparing notes on feelings? One talks about a poem, say, as something objectively there, not, it is true, in the same sense as a chair or a Cambridge college, not trippable over or pointable to in the way such physical things are, but nevertheless something with an existence of its own, even if it depends on our minds for "realizing" its significance. However difficult it might be to some (and repellent to others) to speak of "analysis" and "discipline" in this area, however inviting of misunderstanding on the part of friends and dismissal on the part of entrenched foes, it was necessary to do something to vindicate his insight. He put his problem in clear words in the preface to *Education and the University*, in which he summed up his intention to formulate a discipline not of scholarly industry and academic method (as in *Literaturwissenchaft*), but of intelligence and sensibility: "I was preoccupied with finding out how to talk to the point about poems, novels and plays, and how to promote intelligent and profitable discussion of them." The main enemies to be combated were the prestige of generality and misplaced demands for precise definition of terms. The wish for generality and definition come together in the aspiration to discover or lay down general norms from which the merits (or demerits) of literary works can be deduced. Leavis sees this way of trying to introduce "discipline" into this area as entirely misplaced. Norms can only lend a bogus objectivism to what vindicates itself on the level of phenomenological description.

René Welleck's failure to see this danger in the critically appreciative letter to *Scrutiny* on *Revaluation*, in which he asks Leavis to spell out the norms by which he measures every poet, prompted Leavis to reply:

By the critic of poetry I understand the complete reader: the ideal critic in the ideal reader. The reading demanded by poetry is of a different kind from the reading demanded by philosophy. I should not find it easy to define the difference satisfactorily, but Dr Wellek knows what it is and could give at least as good an account of it as I could. Philosophy, we say, is "abstract" (thus Dr Wellek asks me to defend my position "more abstractly") and poetry "concrete." Words in poetry invite us, not to "think about" and judge but to "feel into" or "become"—to realize a complex experience that is given in the words. They demand not merely a fuller bodied response, but a completer responsiveness—a kind of responsiveness that is incompatible with the judicial, one-eye-on-the-standard approach suggested by Dr Wellek's phrase: "your 'norm' with which you measure every poet." The critic—the reader of poetry—is indeed concerned with evaluation, but to figure him as measuring with a norm which he brings up to the object and applies from the outside is to misrepresent the process. The critic's aim is, first, to realize as sensitively and completely as possible this or that which claims his attention; and a certain valuing is implicit in the realizing. . . .

In making value-judgements (and judgements as to significance), implicitly or explicitly, he does so out of that completeness of possession and with that fullness of response. He doesn't ask, "How does this accord with these specifications of goodness in poetry?"; he aims to make fully conscious and articulate the immediate sense of value that "places" the poem.

("Literary Criticism and Philosophy: A Reply")[5]

Leavis is careful to insist that the type of analysis of poetry proposed should be completely dissociated from all notions of "murdering to dissect." There is no purely external "apparatus" that can be handed over, so that in a kind of Baconian "levelling of wits" any fool can use it. There can be nothing in the nature of "proof" or "laboratory demonstration." Even "the best critical terms and concepts . . . will be inadequate to the varied complexities with which the critic has to deal," for the critic is concerned with the particular use of assonance, say, not with subsuming an instance under the general classification "assonance" in order to deduce some further value property—"a certain valuing is implicit in the realizing." Leavis developed an extraordinary skill at naming the nexus of associations called up in his mind by a particular passage of poetry and at articulating an appropriate network of reflection around it. His constant concern was "the appropriate directing of attention upon poetry," so that the poetry is "apperceived" or taken into the mind in such a way as to connect up with a matrix of relevant connections.

[5]Published in *Scrutiny*, VI, no. 1 (June 1937), pp. 60–62. Reprinted in *The Common Pursuit* (London, 1952).

Perhaps the best account of the process is to be found in the essays entitled "Judgment and Analysis: Notes in the Analysis of Poetry," originally published in *Scrutiny* for 1945 and reprinted in *The Living Principle*. Just as the poet in his poem presents us with a situation in such a way that his "presenting involves an *attitude towards*, an element of disinterested valuation of what is presented," so the critic performs a second valuational act or "placing" on this already existent and artistically objectified primary one. This second act is an analysis of the critic's own experience of the poem and in performing it the critic must, in Leavis' words, "while keeping it alive and immediately present as experience, treat it in some sense as an object." We are not just making autobiographical remarks about our feelings, then, as Ramsey supposed, but are performing the complex act of talking about objects to which those feelings are directed—objects that, however, do not exist independently of those feelings and objects which have themselves been created originally out of a combination of presentations and implicit valuations by the poets themselves. Leavis, then, is a Formalist insofar as all his discussions (at their best) are tied to the particular tone and texture of actual works; but he is a moralist in that there is a substantive concern with human attitudes constantly present in those discussions.

In fact it can reasonably be claimed that what Leavis provided was a way of grappling with moral problems without commitment to discredited substantive ideologies on the one hand, and without the vacuousness of the meta-ethical approaches that had begun to engross moral philosophy itself on the other. In short, Leavis' approach filled the gap left for the ethical sensibility by Positivists like Ramsey and Ayer. That sensibility was given free play in the rich pastures of imaginative literature, a storehouse of nontrivial examples of morally perplexing situations with implicit valuations already built into the way they were actually presented. At the same time, Leavis' own tough-mindedness, his iconoclasm toward the grandiose ambitions of the literary historians of the past, and toward any hint of religious and metaphysical bombinations *about* literature as opposed to an engagement *with* literature, meant that his practice had a curious parallel to that of the Positivists, with their deflation of empty edification in morals and pretentious metaphysics in speculation. Leavis, too, importantly shared the Positivist skepticism about the transcendental claims of

religion. In the 1945–1955 period the (in some ways opposed, in some ways parallel) twin influences of Positivism and of Leavis' criticism met in a hard-headed concern to force people to spell out the values of whatever claims they were making in the presence of particular examples. Leavis' influence was certainly at its height in that postwar decade.

The third tendency Leavis had to oppose was the Marxism that was growing more and more popular among intellectuals in the 1930's. Leavis' reaction against it is well exemplified in his essay on Trotsky's *Literature and Revolution*. This was entitled "'Under Which King, Bezonian?'" and appeared as an editorial to the third number of the first volume of *Scrutiny* in December 1932. The title is a happy allusion to the impudent braggadocio of Pistol, when, in Act V, scene iv, of *Henry IV Part Two*, he teases Shallow (who claims authority as a Justice under the King, not knowing that Henry IV has died) with the challenge: "Under which king, Bezonian? Speak or die."

Leavis opens by saying: "It would be very innocent of us to be surprised by the frequency with which we are asked to 'show our colours.'" If the elusive Santayana himself can resort to such a formulation, what can we expect from the devotees of orthodoxy? As far as Marxism is concerned, Leavis is very witty about the problem of discovering "what precisely orthodoxy is." Even the Cambridge economist Maurice Dobb, "whom Mr Eliot singles out for commendation," is not "very lucid." But on one thing Leavis is clear: "the dogma of the priority of economic conditions" must be rejected as hostile to the whole ethos of the *Scrutiny* enterprise, an enterprise incompatible with the notion that the free intelligence of man is wholly determined by material forces beyond its grasp, indeed the living falsification of such a notion. Whether Karl Marx himself constantly held such a view is, of course, moot. A recent commentator on Marx and literature, S. Prawer, recognizes that Marx seems to hold such a position in his famous preface to *A Contribution to the Critique of Political Economy*; but Friedrich Engels, in his equally famous letter to Joseph Bloch, replaced the notion of one-way causality by a notion of dialectical interaction that is less offensive at the price of being even more vacuous.

Leavis sees Trotsky himself, "the Marxist excommunicate," as "a cultivated as well as an unusually intelligent man" who recognizes that there is much more to "culture" than something merely class-conditioned. Indeed, despite "the familiar air of scientific rigour" where scientific rigor of the kind we associate with physics and mathematics is impossible, Trotsky recognizes that it is the autonomous striving toward a truly human culture that makes man the being he is. Man is neither a mere epiphenomenon of economic forces nor an aspirer to pure science and nothing else. But an advocate of a truly human culture like Trotsky, who can "cheerfully contemplate fifty years of revolutionary warfare," is, for Leavis, tainted by the shallow optimism we associate with H. G. Wells at his worst. Leavis shares Trotsky's view that "the development of Art is the highest test of the vitality and significance of each epoch," but he is much less confident that the gigantic industrialized societies of the future, as conceived by Trotsky, will produce art of the quality left us by those creative minorities within the agrarian societies of the past, which did not lose fructifying contact with the agricultural rhythms that were the material base of their lives. Leavis' deploring of the readiness of writers to line up in rival camps as having more to do with ego and with chic than with thinking, and his cutting irony at "the ready development of antagonisms among those whose differences are inessential," have lost nothing of their force and relevance. Though he may be guilty of idealizing the past, he may be correct in undercutting Marxism by suggesting that it could itself be an epiphenomenon of the situation it purports to be uniquely able to explain:

Class of the kind that can justify talk about "class-culture" has long been extinct. (And, it might be added, when there was such "class-culture" it was much more than merely of the class.) The process of civilization that produced, among other things, the Marxian dogma, and makes it plausible, has made the cultural difference between the "classes" inessential.

Leavis saw the function of *Scrutiny* in this connection as being to insist on the importance of its own task of providing a platform for the kind of "disinterested" criticism of literature, the intense engagement without bias that was not able to find an outlet elsewhere. Any further, "more immediate engaging upon the world of practice" he felt to lie within the world of education, rather than with any grandiose schemes for economic and political revolution in society at large.

It ought to be emphasized that it was not just Marxist demands for "showing one's colours" that

Leavis rejected. The 1940's and early 1950's also saw a revival of what might be called neo-Christianity. The C. S. Lewis–Charles Williams circle at Oxford developed their distinctive version of neo-Christian apologetic. Elsewhere the now Anglican Eliot's poetry, particularly *Ash Wednesday* and *Four Quartets*, played its role. W. H. Auden had been converted to a sort of Kierkegaardian Christianity from his flirtation with Marx and Freud. I am old enough to remember coming across Brother George Every's little book *Poetry and Personal Responsibility*, a Student Christian Movement publication, being sold on a stall at a school discussion on religion around 1949–1950. Ronald Hayman is perhaps right to call Leavis' attack on this book "of little interest today," and to regret the inclusion of Leavis' review of it in *The Common Pursuit* (1952) at the expense of better material. Nevertheless, insofar as the moral substance of ideologies (as opposed to their scientific pretensions) is concerned, Christianity is infinitely more important than Marxism, which insofar as it makes moral judgments (whatever Marx's overt disclaimers about doing so) can even be regarded as a Christian heresy. It remains of interest, therefore, to see what Leavis' literary-critical stance vis-à-vis Christian claims is. Brother George Every had fallen into a not unnatural (though, in the case of Leavis, rather a crass) mistake. He had assumed that because Leavis did not commit himself in the abstract to a substantive ideological position he must be an aesthete, or, in Marxist parlance, a Formalist. He did not see that if we are to call Leavis a Formalist, it must be with the qualification that his Formalism can encompass a consideration of the ethical content internal to (or "realized" in) the works of art he is discussing, and is no pure Formalism of patterns and textures. Indeed Leavis' criticism of the work of Charles Williams, a poet and critic enjoying something of a vogue in certain circles at that time, and praised by Every, is essentially an ethical one:

If you approach as a literary critic, unstiffened by the determination to "discriminate Christianly," or if you approach merely with ordinary sensitiveness and good sense, you can hardly fail to see that Williams' preoccupation with the "horror of evil" is evidence of an arrest at the schoolboy (and -girl) stage rather than of spiritual maturity, and that his dealings in "myth," mystery, the occult and the supernatural belong essentially to the ethos of the thriller. To pass off his writings as spiritually edifying is to promote the opposite of spiritual health.

("The Logic of Christian Discrimination")

Leavis' dismissal of "attitudinizing and gesturing" about causes that one feels important will never lose its timelessness; nor will his warning that those who propagate the idea that "to feel vaguely excited and impressed is to have grappled with serious problems" will damage the doctrine they purport to be defending. The "critical examination" performed even in the cause of some doctrine must bear internally within itself evidence of the rightness and delicacy of the critic's responses to the work he is examining. When that delicacy is absent, no asseveration of orthodoxy, of whatever kind, can make up for it.

LEAVIS' NEW HISTORY OF ENGLISH POETRY

THE art of poetry centrally engaged the interest of the early Leavis. Later his emphasis was to shift to prose fiction. As we have seen in our account of his later dispute with Bateson, he had come to reject literary history in the old sense, what we might call "expository" history. He objected to Oliver Elton's *Survey of English Literature*, for example, because "there is not a paragraph of criticism in all the six volumes." The only kind of literary history possible for Leavis now was "critical" history. This history would involve characterizing judgments of particular examples. It would not have the objectivity of dates recordable in annals, but rather that of descriptions of the reactions of sensibility to specific passages or works offered for corroborative assent or dissent. In Leavis' case it was a sensibility newly alerted by T. S. Eliot to the possibilities of poetic expression inherent in the English language. The seminal works *New Bearings in English Poetry* (1932) and *Revaluation* (1936) are literary history of this "critical" kind.

Leavis' reaction against literary history in the old sense has a strong affinity with Friedrich Nietzsche's reaction in his essay "The Use and Abuse of History" against the idea that a neutralist academic objectivity is possible in history proper. Such inert history is, for Nietzsche, the enemy of life. When we contemplate the "classic" and the "rare" in the past, it is in order to hearten us for equivalent achievement in the present, not in order to escape to some fortress of safe classicism from which we can scorn all living growth. A purely "internal culture" unrelated to the "external barbarism" around us is no good, and only makes us more firmly a part of that "external barbarism" ourselves. A true objectivity with regard to the achievements of the past is reached only by an intimate personal engagement with the content and form of the works themselves, not by a "historicist" preoccupation with their sources and antecedents in the history of the life and times of their authors. Moreover, declares Nietzsche: "You can explain the past only by what is most powerful in the present."

These words might well have been made the motto of *New Bearings in English Poetry* and *Revaluation*. In both books it is conspicuously the influence of Eliot that figures as the example of "what is most powerful in the present" and underwrites the whole approach. What might well be called Leavis' "sober Nietzscheanism" ("We didn't need Nietzsche to tell us to live dangerously; there is no other way of living") is nicely brought out in the later essay "Eliot's Axe to Grind," in *English Literature in Our Time and the University* (1969). In it Leavis defends the value of Eliot's criticism of the metaphysical poets against J. B. Leishman's claim that it was vitiated because Eliot had an "axe to grind" and worked from too limited a knowledge of the poets. For Leavis this is somewhat like saying that Shakespeare did not know enough about classical antiquity to write Roman plays. He retorts that Eliot "knew enough for his purpose." We might compare Nietzsche's remark, "The knowledge of the past is desired only for the service of the future and the present, not to weaken the present or undermine a living future." Eliot, for Leavis, does not give us "inert" knowledge about the seventeenth century that we can passively take over, as if it were "certified factual knowledge." He invites collaborative assent (or dissent) to observations that arise from what might paradoxically be called an "interested disinterestedness," as opposed to the purely scholarly and, as Leavis sees it, less challenging "disinterestedness" of a Leishman. Leavis does not think Eliot's formula of "felt thought" has worn well as a characterization of Donne, but he defends the notion of "the dissociation of sensibility" as sensitizing us to the important distinction between the ability to turn our interests "into poetry" and "merely [to] meditate on them poetically," in Eliot's phrase.

The distinction is central for Leavis. He is ruthless in spotting "the will to poetry" masquerading as the real thing, as in Edith Sitwell's writing "emotionally, and with characteristic afflatus, about Christ." One only wishes that Leavis himself had had the energy to go on sorting out the examples of "the will to poetry" from the genuine article in more recent writers. And it is not always just the false afflatus that he condemns. The sort of "objectivist" poetry that trusts to the negative virtues of avoiding such afflatus was also touched on by Leavis in his review of Pound's *Active Anthology* in 1933, when he wrote that "the inadequate conception of 'technique'" was the most charitable explanation of "the inclusion, for instance, of so much nullity by Mr Louis Zukofsky." Leavis was also unconvinced by the claims made for the dry poetry of Marianne Moore.

Both *New Bearings* and *Revaluation* raise difficult issues that now need surveying. Discounting the point as to whether Leavis exaggerates his own part in getting Eliot's poetic achievement (and the nature of the modern poetic achievement in general) recognized, there is, first, the question as to whether his account of the nature of that achievement in *New Bearings* is sufficiently coherent. Second, there is the often repeated contention that Leavis' methods are adapted only to doing justice to the short poem of some intellectual complexity. Third, there is the issue of whether some of Leavis' own rewriting of literary history, in particular his assessment of John Milton, and his view of Alexander Pope as a continuer of metaphysical wit, are not by now, naturally enough, in need of some revaluation themselves.

Leavis begins *New Bearings* by arguing that "contemporary intelligence" goes into fields other than poetry. Perhaps Leavis has mathematics, natural science, and economics in mind. Poetry since the nineteenth century has been seen as a dream escape composed by one who is "the idle singer of an empty day." Indeed, Eliot's particular achievement has resulted from his gift for putting the full and free play of his intelligence at the service of his poetry, so that all his interests as a mature adult can enter that poetry through a working together, or synergy, of his interest in experience and his interest in words. Leavis, it is too seldom noticed, is not completely dismissive of "a poetry of withdrawal" and does make fine discriminations between examples of it. He is particularly good on the fruitfulness of the tension between Yeats's worldly shrewdness and energy and his attraction to reverie, and on the link between enchantment and disenchantment in Walter de la Mare. Thomas Hardy's work does not belong to the poetry of daydreams, but Leavis shrewdly sees the "modern thought" that engrossed him as comfort-

ingly Victorian in its certitudes rather than really modern, even if those certitudes were bleakly pessimistic. Eliot's "modernism" involves the invention of techniques "that shall be adequate to the ways of feeling, or modes of experience, of adult sensitive moderns." I want now to consider the coherence of Leavis' account of this "modernism."

He proposes a multiplicity of criteria for it. The first is the defiance of "the traditional canon of seriousness." The second is the revolt against the notion of the intrinsically "poetical." The third is a use of "audacities of transition and psychological notation, such as are forbidden to the novelist" and that enable the poet to project himself into "a comprehensive and representative human consciousness." The fourth is the closeness of the poet's work to the idiom of "his own speech," perhaps the most ambiguously troublesome criterion of all. The fifth (perhaps bound up with the third) is the use of a disjointed allusiveness arising from the complexity of an educated man's relation to the past. The sixth is the use of "musical" as opposed to "narrative" organization. Leavis never makes it sufficiently clear whether any one of these six criteria is a sufficient condition for the presence of a "modernity" with a kinship to Eliot's distinctive achievement. He may, indeed, intend to suggest that Eliot's distinctiveness lies in the fact that his work embodies all six criteria. As far as Leavis' rewriting of the history of English poetry in the light of his strong reaction to Eliot's achievement goes (and this applies very much to *Revaluation* as well as to *New Bearings*), it is the fourth criterion concerning idiom or diction, namely the demand for the closeness of the poet's work to the idiom of "his own speech," that is both the most important and gives the most trouble.

The trouble arises because Leavis does not seem enough aware of the fact that he oscillates between a rather narrow interpretation of his fourth criterion (namely that the "poetic voice" should be demonstrably close to that of the poet's conversation with his contemporaries, "language such as men do use," in Ben Jonson's words) and a rather wider interpretation of it, which sanctions a past poet's use of a "lofty and formal decorum" that no modern poet could use, but that a modern reader "should have no difficulty in living into." The first interpretation is precise, but exclusive. The second interpretation is flexible enough to include passages in *Paradise Lost* and *The Prelude*, which one assumes that the first would exclude. Leavis is using the first interpretation when he claims that the "staple idiom and movement" of Eliot's own poetry "derive immediately from modern speech," and when he writes in *Revaluation* that Donne gives us the "utterance, movement and intonation" of "the talking voice" and that his satire III has "a natural speaking stress and intonation" and shows a remarkable "mimetic flexibility," which in "a consummately managed verse" can "exploit the strength of spoken English." He is using the second interpretation when in the essay on Pope in *Revaluation* he speaks of the poet's decorum as "natural because it was sanctioned by contemporary convention."

Of course Leavis is right to protest in *The Common Pursuit* against Tillyard's travestying his views into the claim that the "language of small talk is the basis of all good poetry." But for Leavis to go on to say that he never complained that "Milton did not write *Paradise Lost* in the style of Shakespeare," or (however different this is) "in a conversational style" or the "tone of ordinary speech," as he does in his reply to Tillyard in *The Common Pursuit*, in the essay "In Defence of Milton," is to be disingenuous. Of course, Leavis never made precisely those claims, but they are not (unlike the remark about small talk) unwarranted distortions of the contrast in *Revaluation* between the "Shakespearean life" of parts of *Comus* and "the laboured, pedantic artifice" of *Paradise Lost*, with its remoteness "from any English that was ever spoken" and its "wearying deadness," even when it is at its most brilliant, "to the ear that appreciates Shakespeare." On the wider interpretation of Leavis' fourth criterion it could be claimed that *Paradise Lost* has a decorum which may indeed not have been very far from the living voice of John Milton, and which, though (to borrow Leavis' own phrasing from his essay on Pope) "so lofty and formal" that no modern poet could adopt it successfully, is nevertheless of a type that a modern reader "should have no difficulty in living into."

The questions raised by the debate about Milton's style are too complex to examine in detail in a study devoted to Leavis himself, but it is necessary to say something about them. The controversy, as Christopher Ricks has pointed out in his book *Milton's Grand Style*, is a triangular one. There is, on the one hand, Leavis' clash with C. S. Lewis, who claims to see Milton's verse as Leavis does but to reject Leavis' criteria—in short, to admire the very same qualities in the poetry that Leavis dislikes. Then there is the position of Ricks himself, who, rightly I think, sees

Paradise Lost as having more variety than either Leavis or Lewis allows, and who, sharing Leavis' demand that poetry should not employ an empty eloquence that disarms attention, but should, on the contrary, call for the closest scrutiny, claims that much of *Paradise Lost* asks for and rewards the most minute attention. What can certainly be claimed for Leavis is that he allows no one to assent to the value of Milton merely conventionally, on the grounds of inert tradition.

One of the puzzling elements in Leavis' rejection of Milton is Leavis' own turning away from a Puritan moral ethos of "decency" (with an almost Lawrentian concern to celebrate the primal mysteries of sexual love) to endorse the interest of the work of a court wit like Thomas Carew, with its affirmation of libertine sensuousness. This is hard to square with Leavis' later asseveration, "I don't believe in any 'literary values,' and you won't find me talking about them; the judgments the literary critic is concerned with are judgments about life." Leavis finds the great literary exemplar of Puritanism (perhaps he ought more precisely to be called a sectary, as R. L. Greaves suggests) in John Bunyan, perhaps because of the more experiential quality of Bunyan's expression of his religious interests, what Greaves calls the Lutheran concern with the wrath/grace dichotomy, as opposed to the Calvinist concern with "the divine will and omnipotence." In Luther's commentary on *Galatians*, which we know from *Grace Abounding* that Bunyan read and was influenced by, there is a passage (quoted by Greaves) which states that "true Christian divinity . . . commandeth us not to search out the nature of God," and adds that there is "nothing more dangerous than to wander with curious speculations in heaven, and there to search out God in his incomprehensible power, wisdom and Majesty." Milton, in his portrayal of Satan's fall and of God the Father (particularly the latter's speech in book III of *Paradise Lost*), boldly ignored Luther's warning and embarked on "things unattempted yet in prose or rhyme." Nevertheless, Leavis' contention that Milton was "ludicrously unqualified" to undertake a poetic theodicy, in that he possessed "character rather than intelligence," raises more complex issues than the critic seems prepared to consider and makes one wonder how far Leavis himself had really pondered the nature of such an enterprise in terms of the expectations and beliefs of a seventeenth-century Christian. Leavis' view that Milton was tactless and clumsy in the way he handled his material seems, for example, difficult to reconcile with the fact that an intelligent contemporary of Milton's (and one whom Leavis greatly admired), Andrew Marvell, could write in "On Mr. Milton's *Paradise Lost*":

Thou hast not missed one thought that could be fit.
And all that was improper dost omit.

A further reason for Leavis' inability to do justice to *Paradise Lost* may lie in the fact that the kind of intense local scrutiny that works for a lyric by Donne or George Herbert may not be appropriate for a poem of such length. The notion that "the whole organism is present in the part" in longer works is a matter of faith rather than vindicated assumption. True, it seems to work with much of the "organic" Shakespeare (any of whose great tragedies Leavis sees as "an incomparably better whole than *Paradise Lost*"). But isn't the drama, as a genre, traditionally and by definition more tightly knit than the epic? We shall meet this problem again in connection with the criticism of the novel. One feels that Leavis' repugnance to the theological material intrinsic to the poem may lie behind his unwillingness to concede that he has not done justice to the narrative and ideological problems involved in the architectonic of *Paradise Lost*, an architectonic beside which modern long poems such as Pound's *Cantos* and William Carlos Williams' *Paterson* emerge as collections of single passages rather than unified poems. Sometimes one wonders if some of the hostility aroused by a classicizing critic like Tillyard was not displaced onto Milton himself. At one point in *The Common Pursuit* Leavis turns round and defends "that unique heroic figure," with whom he is nevertheless so deeply out of sympathy, against his defender, Tillyard.

One figure with whom Leavis is importantly engaged in *New Bearings* and later is Gerard Manley Hopkins. Later studies of Hopkins have tended to stress his links with his own period, and the artifice of his language as opposed to its closeness to spoken idiom. We know from his letters that Hopkins greatly admired the irregular rhythm of Milton's *Samson Agonistes*, a work that Leavis had always regarded as overrated. Nevertheless, the late publication of Hopkins' poetry (it did not appear until 1918) meant that Leavis' account was one of the earliest original and important contributions to its appreciation. Leavis emphasized its contrast with the dream world of many of the Victorians, and also with the cult of mellifluous musicality associated with Alfred Ten-nyson. Hopkins' neglect and the misunderstandings of Bridges could with some justice be attributed to the too narrow neoclassicism fostered by that sense of superiority given by the cultivation of Latin and Greek, that "trade in classic niceties" which Leavis always saw as an enemy. Hopkins' view that "the poetical language of an age should be the current language heightened," and his rejection of archaisms, was exactly the view Leavis championed in his evaluation of Eliot's distinctive achievement. At the same time, Hopkins' linguistic experiments were not the mere exuberance of a Robert Browning, but put to the service, notably in "The Wreck of the *Deutschland*," of delicate moral apprehensions. There are also two excellent essays on Hopkins in *The Common Pursuit*. Leavis' lecture to the Hopkins Society in 1971 makes some qualifications. In it he says that he never found "The Windhover" successful (there is no indication in *New Bearings* that he thought it a failure, and it is commended in *The Common Pursuit*), and he reiterates his praise for the un-Swinburnian, basically "traditional" art of "The Wreck of the *Deutschland*." He claims Eliot to be "very much the greater poet" but finds that Hopkins, as man and personality, rouses his "respect, admiration and affection," perhaps because, as he says in his conclusion, "Hopkins, in a wholly unpejorative sense, was simple," a judgment some might indeed make of Leavis himself.

On Shakespeare Leavis did not offer a great deal in quantity, and admirers (or ex-admirers?) of Leavis' work have even spoken of "*Scrutiny*'s failure with Shakespeare." Nevertheless the work he has given us here makes up for its sparseness by its quality. There is a fine analysis of a Macbeth soliloquy in *Education and the University* and, in *The Common Pursuit*, a suggestive interpretation of *Othello* (which, however, probably overreacts against the romanticizing of Othello's character), a thoughtful look at *Measure for Measure*, and a helpful piece on the late plays. Leavis also gives us, in the essay "Tragedy and the 'Medium,'" an excellent essay on tragedy that stresses the element of exaltation aroused by certain tragedies and the concomitant "escape from all attitudes of self-assertion," coupled with a recognition of positive value that avoids pessimism on the one hand and optimism on the other. The essay is yet another illustration of what I have called Leavis' sober Nietzscheanism. Among modern poets, Yeats (whom he nevertheless assiduously read) does not receive his due in terms of analysis, despite Leavis' excellent account of the "Byzantium" poems and his recognition of the poet's greatness, particularly in *The Tower*. However, the Leavisian approach rightly challenges that kind of pure exegesis which assumes proprietorial rights, so to speak, over the poet and from which both Yeats and William Blake have suffered. Leavis' refusal to accord greatness to Auden, his unwillingness to concede more than a clever intelligence and a fluency with words and concepts, is very much a matter of controversy.

THE NOVEL: THE GREAT TRADITION

In "How to Teach Reading," first published as a reply to Pound's pamphlet *How to Read* and reprinted as an appendix to *Education and the University*, Leavis admits that all the exemplifying in the pamphlet "has been from poetry," but goes on to claim that "prose demands the same approach" while conceding that it "admits it far less readily." Novels raise once again the problem of the failure of the Leavisian approach to deal as happily with questions of architectonic as it does with that of "local life"; indeed, they compound it, as a long poem is not supposed to fall beneath a certain minimum distinction of style even in "flat" passages, while, as Leavis acknowledges, "a page of a novel that is as a whole significant may appear undistinguished or even poor." Nevertheless Leavis goes on to say:

> Yet though the devising and applying of a critical technique may be found difficult in the case of prose-literature it should not . . . be impossible. Out of a School of English that provided the training suggested here might come, not only a real literary criticism of Shakespeare, but a beginning in the criticism of the novel.

A rueful note appended in 1943 adds:

> I leave those light-hearted sentences about the "criticism of the novel" as they stood. Actually, nothing helpful in respect of that problem can be said briefly. I hope to bring out before long in collaboration with Q. D. Leavis a book that deals with the grounds and methods of the critical study of novels.
>
> ("The Problem of Prose")

This work, like the article on Joseph Conrad entitled "Conrad, the Soul and the Universe," announced in *The Great Tradition*, remains one of the great un-written works of criticism. But at least *The Great Tradition* includes some penetrating reflections on the nature of Conrad's work. What it certainly does not do is demonstrate that "the grounds and methods of the critical study of novels" are the same as those of the critical study of complex lyric poems. A lyric poem can be held in the mind and so surveyed as a complete, self-contained whole. One sometimes wonders whether Leavis' reference to Lawrence's novels as "dramatic poems" in *D. H. Lawrence: Novelist* is not an attempt to stake the struggle on a name; but, in any case, it involves a recognition of the *difference* between Lawrence's novels and, for the most part, the novels dealt with in *The Great Tradition*.

In *The Great Tradition* itself, as John Killham has pointed out in an article in the *British Journal of Aesthetics* for January 1965, the term "concreteness" does not always very happily fit the "patterned," more "fabular" novel of the type of Charles Dickens' *Hard Times*. He sees Leavis as equivocating on the term. Sometimes it evokes verisimilitude, as when applied to the portrayal of Gwendolen Harleth in George Eliot's *Daniel Deronda*, and sometimes it evokes a "realism" of moral insight on the part of the author that is compatible with a fabular violation of verisimilitude. Leavis, for Killham, oscillates between the notion of "felt life" as connectible with the author's life experience and ultimately rooted in his personal problems, and the more Horatian notion of it as the artist's gift for transporting his readers into "well-imagined situations." The term "realization" also lends itself to ambiguities here in the analysis of both prose and poetry. In the essay "Reality and Sincerity" Leavis had even hazarded the view that "it is a case in which we know from the art what the man was like" after discussing Hardy's "After a Journey," a remark that seems particularly ironic in the light of the revelations of the second volume of Robert Gittings' biography of Hardy. Killham indeed questions the coherence of Leavis' claims for the study of English literature, a question bound to arise if we regard his approach as a discipline. After claiming that in *Education and the University*, the earlier book, "one finds rehearsed the whole argument of *The Great Tradition*, complete with self-contradictions," Killham writes:

> we are told on the one hand that: "What we are concerned with in analysis are always matters of complex verbal organization," and on the other that not merely the train-

ing of the sensibility but "the equipping of the student against the snares of 'technique'" is the aim of literary education. It is hard to see, on the face of it, that these ends are not mutually exclusive.

Killham sees it as an objection to Leavis that he uses the term "concreteness" so indiscriminately that it becomes "nothing more than an index of its user's own sensibility." I would say, on the contrary, that the Leavisian approach is defensible here. Killham himself seems to be hoping for some bypassing or short-circuiting of the individual sensibility by the critical method adopted. He is guilty of an ignoratio elenchi, or refutation of a view not actually advanced by his opponent. It is Leavis' very contention that in this area we have to combine the apparently dichotomous notions of discipline and personal sensibility. It is not self-contradictory to suppose that we can at the same time train the sensibility and warn against the snares of technique. If the use of a term reveals the sensibility of the user (rather than being purely neutral and external to it), that is the very thing the Leavisian approach is after. But though I would reject Killham's case against this approach, I do think his essay brings out some of the particular difficulties of that approach as far as the art of the novel is concerned.

Leo Tolstoy, surely one of Leavis' touchstones, wrote in his diary: "There is a novelist's poetry: (1) in the interest of the arrangement of occurrences . . . (2) in the presentation of manners on an historic background . . . (3) in the beauty and gaiety of a situation . . . (4) in people's characters." This novelist's "poetry" calls for a distinctive approach, an approach that cannot dispense with a concern for probability, the management of the passage of time, the portrayal of manners, the situating of a diversity of characters, the sense of where to begin and end a narrative and subnarrative, the use of illuminating incident, the nature of convincing character psychology, all the kinds of thing dealt with in a book like, say, Edith Wharton's *The Writing of Fiction*. In fact a work like *The Great Tradition* has to deal with them too, and does not and cannot contain the type of analysis with which Leavis approached lyric poems such as Hardy's "After a Journey" or Arnold's sonnet on Shakespeare. It is here that there is something of the incoherence that Killham discerned. Leavis, in parallel with L. C. Knights's rejection of the "character" approach to Shakespeare, disclaims a concern with the creation of "delightful characters"

for its own sake and with irrelevant "chaotic liveliness." So far, so good; but there are further overtones of a theoretical rejection of "character" with which the actual practice in *The Great Tradition* conflicts.

Edith Wharton once remarked that the distinction between the novel and the short story turns on the fact that "the *test* of the novel is that its people should be *alive*" because "no subject in itself, however fruitful, appears to be able to keep the novel alive; only the characters in it can." The novel was called "a system of biographies" by the Russian poet Osip Mandelstam. Whatever the theoretical disclaimers at the outset, there is much in *The Great Tradition* that is, in fact, perfectly compatible with both these remarks. Leavis, like any naturally engaged reader of George Eliot's *Middlemarch*, has moments when he would like to break Rosamond Vincy's graceful neck. He finds George Eliot's "sheer informedness about society" impressive as "knowledge alive with understanding" and compares her "profound psychological analysis" with that of Tolstoy. Leavis even suspects that "an actual historical person" lies behind Conrad's portrayal of Peter Ivanych in *Under Western Eyes*, and yet there is no indication that such a suspicion points to a flaw in the "art" of the book; rather the comment seems to register as a tribute to Conrad's powers of character portrayal. Leavis much prefers the early Henry James novels (notably *The Bostonians* and *The Portrait of a Lady*) to the later James, and acknowledges that these books possess "overt attractions that might seem to qualify them for popularity," by which one assumes that he means convincing characters and striking scenes. Even though it is true that he speaks of the vitality of *The Portrait of a Lady* as having nothing of "irrelevant 'life'" about it, as being "wholly of art," yet within that art he sees James as achieving some remarkable "psychological analysis," particularly in *The Bostonians*.

The novel is the art form that least lends itself to the "dehumanization of art" spoken of by José Ortega y Gasset, who also, by the way, thought that character and atmosphere were of primary importance within it. It is not surprising, then, that explicitly denaturalizing and dehumanizing schools of criticism, notably Structuralism, should find "character" particularly difficult to deal with. Jonathan Culler, a recent sympathetic if critical expositor of Structuralism, puts the issue as follows on p. 230 of his *Structuralist Poetics:*

Character is the major aspect of the novel to which structuralism has paid least attention. . . . Stress on the interpersonal and conventional systems which traverse the individual, which make him a space in which forces and events meet rather than an individuated essence, leads to a rejection of the prevalent conception of character in the novel: that the most successful and "living" characters are richly delineated autonomous wholes, clearly distinguished from others by physical and psychological characteristics.

It is to its honor that, for all his caveats about the "character" approach, the whole thrust of Leavis' criticism leads to the rejection of the denaturalization and dehumanization of one of the greatest forms and forces for moral exploration and understanding invented by man, and one unknown to classical antiquity—the novel. *The Great Tradition* emphasizes how important for humanity's moral development the right understanding and prizing of that invention are.

The standard objection to *The Great Tradition* on its appearance was that it was too narrow, too uncatholic. The objection was wittily anticipated by Leavis himself when, on the opening page, he (rightly) prophesied that people would attribute to him the view that "except Jane Austen, George Eliot, James, and Conrad, there are no novelists in English worth reading." I read the book as an undergraduate at Oxford in the early 1950's, when the English syllabus still ended in 1832 (except for an optional paper), and when it was possible to take the examination papers without doing a single essay on a novelist (as, in fact, I did), though, of course, one was expected to read some. My tutor, F. W. Bateson, held the view that the novel (except as a vehicle of satire) was intrinsically inferior to poetry as a genre; he later gave this view witty expression in a lecture entitled "The Novel's Original Sin" (printed in his *Essays in Critical Dissent*), a discussion in which one finds something of the classicist's looking down on the novel as a form, combined with an odd echo of the old Evangelical objection to fiction as lying and time-wasting—in short, an "addiction." For me (and I suspect for many others) *The Great Tradition* did not close doors (as C. S. Lewis has accused the Leavis-type criticism of doing), but opened them. It guided me to a diversity of riches I don't think I would have discovered for myself, while at the same time giving me some sort of bearings among that diversity. The kind of concern with Eliot, James, and Conrad that has entered so much published criticism

in the more than three decades since the book was published, and the way in which these authors have figured in fiction courses taught in new universities, surely owes an incalculable amount to *The Great Tradition*.

The positive achievement is a magnificent one and can never be taken away from Leavis. To take one instance: George Eliot's defects had commonly been related to overintellectualism. With great finesse Leavis brought out in his analysis of her work how they were really bound up with a kind of overemotionalism. But, of course, there are reservations to be made about Leavis as a critic of prose fiction. He was undoubtedly too dismissive of both Marcel Proust and Thomas Mann. One suspects he was too much influenced by the fact that the first was taken up by Clive Bell and Bloomsbury, and that both were treated somewhat critically by D. H. Lawrence. He never engaged at any length with Feodor Dostoyevsky or Anton Chekhov. He is unsatisfactory on many aspects of Bunyan (his essay on *The Pilgrim's Progress* in "*Anna Karenina*" *and Other Essays* is disappointing and plays down the difficulties raised by Bunyan's religious fanaticism), on American literature outside James, on Dickens, and on Lawrence himself, in the latter case because of overpartisanship.

The case of Dickens is an interesting one. In *The Great Tradition* he is frankly dismissed as no more than "a great entertainer" who "had for the most part no profounder responsibility as a creative artist than this description suggests" except in one work, *Hard Times*. He would be good family reading if the habit of family reading still persisted, but "the adult mind doesn't as a rule find in Dickens a challenge to an unusual and sustained seriousness." *Hard Times* is exempted because its fable embodies a moral indictment of the "Benthamism" that Leavis sees as the enemy of life in our own time as well as during the nineteenth century. Yet with the appearance of *Dickens the Novelist* in 1970, a work of joint authorship with Q. D. Leavis, who made distinguished contributions to it, all this was modified. Of course it is perfectly legitimate that critics should change their minds (the German novelist Robert Musil once said that he had done so several times about Rainer Maria Rilke and was still undecided), but at least they should explicitly acknowledge the fact. It was disingenuous, to say the least, to write a preface to *Dickens the Novelist* that referred disparagingly to those who "tell us with the familiar easy assurance that Dickens of course was a genius, but that his line was entertainment" without at least acknowledging that this was the very same view that *Fiction and the Reading Public* and *The Great Tradition* had endorsed.

The preface argues that those critics whose account of Dickens' art would deny ·him "marked intellectual powers—a capacity, for example, to read and understand Bentham"—are mistaken. And one of the useful strands of the Dickens book is Q. D. Leavis' insistence that the reactions of the Victorians themselves (for example, those of Dickens' friend and biographer, John Forster) are often a better guide to the understanding of Dickens than the psychological jargon of modern biographers and critics. Yet surely the fact that there is no account of Dickens' having studied Bentham in Forster is evidence against rather than for the Leavis case. Moreover, the Benthamite *Saturday Review* critics (who included the admired Leslie Stephen) were contemptuous of Dickens' understanding of social matters and of his sentimental philanthropy. However, it could be claimed, more tenuously, that Dickens had sensed the underlying spirit of Benthamism and that the very contempt of these critics, in their Benthamite mood, evidences this. In any case *Dickens the Novelist* is a book no responsible reader of Dickens can afford to ignore. It shows that Dickens was "the great entertainer," yes, but also that he combined this facility with an imaginative exploration of the problems of his age that could be comprehensible to his contemporaries without, at its best, sacrificing subtlety. Take the Meagles family in *Little Dorrit*: "It is quite unjust to assume that Dickens 'endorses' simple-mindedly Mr Meagles's sermon to Tattycoram," writes Q. D. Leavis, defending the novel against R. Garis' attack. F. R. Leavis makes a strong case for the view that "the usual easy and confident denial of any profundity of thought to Dickens is absurd and shameful" in a subtle analysis of *Little Dorrit* in which the reality of Little Dorrit (as opposed to the "contrived unreality" of Little Nell) is skillfully defended; and Q. D. Leavis makes a superb defense of the portrayal of Pip in *Great Expectations* against naive charges of snobbery. Her account of the nature of the relationship between Dickens and Tolstoy in the essay on *David Copperfield* is interesting, but the suggestion that the portrayal of the David–Dora relationship influenced the Prince Andrew–Lise relationship in *War and Peace* is unconvincing.

LEAVIS, LAWRENCE, AND ELIOT

IN many ways Leavis' engagement with Lawrence did harm to both. It encouraged Leavis to overindulge that sectarian certainty of righteousness which, tempered by his other qualities of flexibility and perceptiveness, gives an exhilarating astringency to his work, but which, left to luxuriate alone, too much encouraged Leavis to allow mere assertion to replace analysis of the type discussed earlier in this survey. At the same time it has allowed those who dislike Lawrence to find support for their dislike in the sometimes injudicious tone of his admirer. The admiration was not always injudicious. The essay on Lawrence, written in the same year as Lawrence's death (1930) and printed in *For Continuity* (1933), is a most creditable piece of work about a recent author, despite Leavis' later reservations about it. Lawrence's preoccupation with the primitive is criticized as fostering "in him a certain inhumanity," and *The Rainbow* and *Women in Love* are singled out as remarkable, but nevertheless flawed, works that buy "a strange intensity" at the price of a limited range. At this stage Lawrence's discursive works, such as *Fantasia of the Unconscious*, were to be considered at all only because of his artistic achievements in other works, a far cry from the way they are wholeheartedly endorsed in *Thought, Words and Creativity*. But in the essay "D. H. Lawrence and Professor Irving Babbitt," written in 1932 and also included in *For Continuity*, a new note is already heard. We are at the beginning of that use of Lawrence as a touchstone for bringing out the deficiencies of T. S. Eliot and, in particular, the failure of Eliot's periodical, *Criterion*, for which Lawrence has been "an opportunity and a test." The theme of Eliot's deficiencies is to become a more and more insistent one in Leavis' later books. When Leavis, with his wife and other collaborators, embarked on the production of their own journal, *Scrutiny*, one of the most important critical periodicals in English of the twentieth century, the fate of the *Criterion* stood as an awful warning to them.

The first number of *Scrutiny* appeared in May 1932, and the journal ran as a quarterly until October 1953. Two substantial anthologies of it were made: Eric Bentley's *The Importance of "Scrutiny,"* published in 1948 and reprinted in 1964, and Leavis' own *A Selection from "Scrutiny,"* in two volumes, published by Cambridge University Press in 1968. None of the contributors or editors were paid, and the periodical worked only because of their devotion, that of the editorial board (from 1934 F. R. Leavis, L. C. Knights, Denys Thompson, and D. W. Harding), and particularly of Q. D. Leavis and F. R. Leavis. Because of demand, the set was reprinted by the Cambridge University Press in 1963. As I have said, *Calendar of Modern Letters* was a significant inspiration for the enterprise. Little in the way of poetry or fiction was included, but, as was consonant with Leavis' concern to link literature with other concerns, the range of subjects covered was much wider than literature proper. Articles on philosophy, politics, education, sociology, and psychology were published. James Smith, Martin Turnell, and Dennis Enright contributed work on Italian, French, and German culture. D. W. Harding, one of the most distinguished contributors, was later to become professor of psychology at the University of London. Much of Leavis' own published work originally appeared in the periodical. At first *Scrutiny* was quite abreast of the contemporary scene, but some have felt, perhaps justly, that earlier figures like Joyce, Yeats, Mann, and Proust were never adequately encompassed, and that in the 1940's the immediately contemporary began to be too dismissively dealt with. Yet even here it might be claimed that this course was far better than the attempt to "keep up," which so often leads to a shallow facility. An editor, like a critic, must be allowed his economies.

There is, unfortunately, a not unwarranted suspicion that Leavis' growing exaltation of Lawrence at Eliot's expense was not entirely disinterested, for we now know that Eliot, on the strength of his admiration for Leavis' pamphlet *Mass Civilization and Minority Culture* (1930), had commissioned a piece for the *Criterion* that he had then decided not to use—a most delicate situation. Ronald Hayman says that the substance of the piece appeared in *Scrutiny* for September 1932 under the title "What's Wrong with Criticism?" It is not unreasonable to suppose that Leavis' rejection by the poet whose innovative work he had so strongly championed must have cut deeply. As late as 1976, in the March issue of *New Universities Quarterly*, a rankling resentment against the poet can be detected underlying Leavis' strange account of a visit by Eliot to see him in Cambridge in 1940 or 1941. Leavis prefaces it by saying that "although we rarely met and rarely corresponded, Eliot and I knew each other well. The knowledge was a matter of finding each other so very uncon-

genial as to generate a great deal of awareness—on my side, certainly diagnostic." Leavis ends by making the extraordinary claim that he (Leavis) was "a major focus of the guilt feelings expressed in *The Family Reunion*, the most revealingly personal of his works."

I have suggested that it might be the case that some of Leavis' hostility toward Milton is directed not so much against Milton (its ostensible object) as against some of Milton's classically trained apologists. The view that Leavis' criticism of Lawrence is, both in its praise of Lawrence and in some of its attacks on Lawrence's critics, not disinterested in the same way that the criticism of Jonathan Swift or Pope in *The Common Pursuit* is disinterested, can, I think, be advanced with even more confidence. *D. H. Lawrence: Novelist*, for all its undoubted usefulness to the sympathetic reader of Lawrence (to the unsympathetic reader it will only act as a further irritant), marks the beginning of a decline in Leavis' work as a strictly literary critic (his real forte), a decline only partially redeemed by his interesting essay on *Anna Karenina* and his long analysis of Eliot's *Four Quartets* in *The Living Principle*. Leavis occasionally makes concessions about weaknesses in Lawrence, or speaks of the special difficulties Lawrence had, but these concessions and qualifications have curiously little effect on a too continuous acclamation (sometimes insufficiently supported by analysis) of Lawrence's consummate artistry, moral insight, and lack of defects as both man and writer. The claim that Lawrence's best works are "dramatic poems" sometimes seems part of a bid to capture assent, by means of persuasive nomenclature, to the view that the novel can be approached as poetry. Leavis oscillates between the view that Lawrence's works are continuous with those of George Eliot and Tolstoy, and have nothing in them that will disconcert admirers of those two novelists, and the view that Lawrence undertook radical departures from their vision, scope, and mode of presentation. I feel an uneasy strain between the simultaneous acclamation of Lawrence's creative-exploratory quality and his quality of convincingness and verisimilitude: for example, Hermione, in *Women in Love*, is praised as "triumphantly a character," and the dialogue in that book is called "convincingly dramatic in every respect."

The difficulties raised by Lawrence's intriguing mixture of realism and symbolism (for all Leavis' repudiation of the latter term, he uses it) are never really faced. For example, is Gerald Crich's father sufficiently convincing as an actual mine owner (in the way Hermione is convincing as a society hostess) to carry Lawrence's poignant indictment of industrial society, an indictment Gerald himself is also somewhat unconvincingly used to sustain? But perhaps the most baffling part of *D. H. Lawrence: Novelist* is the sixth chapter, which presents what Michael Tanner has justly called a "grotesquely high" estimate of *St. Mawr*. Leavis claims that *St. Mawr* presents "a creative and technical originality more remarkable" than that of Eliot's *The Waste Land*. This part of the book in particular is more remarkable for assertion and will (oddly enough, characteristics against which both Leavis and Lawrence protest) than for analysis. Once again one feels that hostility to Eliot, and to the Bloomsbury with which Leavis now associated him, is the real motive behind many of the remarks, not a disinterested critical engagement with Lawrence's text.

In the appendix to *D. H. Lawrence: Novelist*, Leavis calls the twentieth century in English literature "the age of D. H. Lawrence and T. S. Eliot"; and if we thought the balance in Leavis' work had swung too much to a preoccupation with Lawrence, Leavis certainly redressed this fault with his account of *Four Quartets* in *The Living Principle* (1975), an account that Christopher Ricks rightly called "the most sustained piece of criticism that he has ever produced, of a single work of poetry or of prose." It is impossible to deal in a short compass with these deeply engaged prose reflections on poems, which, if uneven, contain passages that constitute some of the finest poetic meditations on the form in the twentieth century. Both Eliot's poetry and Leavis' reflections on it call for constant frequentation. Perhaps the main point I can make about Leavis' reflections on it here is to say that they are critiques in which he, for the first time, unequivocally operates with a discursive criterion, by which I mean a criterion applied to the contents of a poem irrespective of their formal embodiment. Whereas previously Leavis had been concerned with ideas only insofar as they were poetically realized, he now questions Eliot's ideas in themselves, independently of any poetic realization of them. This is perhaps particularly evident when Leavis claims that there can be no really coherent presentation of a transcendent reality, and that "time is an essential constituent of reality" and cannot truly be said to be unreal in the way that the "Bradleyan" Eliot asserts it to be. Leavis' critique is salutary and important as showing

that, contrary to Stéphane Mallarmé's often quoted and pernicious dictum, poetry *is* made with ideas as well as with words, and that this is the case even with so apparently "musical" and "non-discursive" a work as the *Four Quartets*. The depth of the outrage Eliot's ideas offer to Leavis' own beliefs, the sense Leavis has that his answers to the questions Eliot poses "are not Eliot's," are what provoked Leavis' clear dissent from the discursive and paraphrasable "wisdom" Eliot's lines offer, indeed his seeing of much of it as unwisdom.

VALEDICTION

I had originally thought of ending this survey of Leavis' work with a portrayal of the Leavis of such later books as *English Literature in Our Time and the University* (1967) and *Nor Shall My Sword* (1972); as a kind of would-be prophet or *salvator mundi* figure, like Lawrence's Birkin in *Women in Love*, but one unredeemed, alas, by the dramatic testing and ironic scrutiny through which Lawrence "places" Birkin; and one, moreover, subject to an illusory view of institutions (such as the "University," or, for that matter, "English Literature") that his hero, Lawrence, would have treated with irreverent insouciance and dispatched to the lumber room of outmoded ideals and belated postures. But to end an account of the greatest literary critic of the twentieth century on such a note would be ungracious. We shall have to contend with many winds of doctrine blowing from the camps of various embattled orthodoxies, and one or another of them may perhaps, in the end, sweep us off our feet; but the critical work of Leavis at his best, despite what his enemies say, is no such orthodoxy among others, but a source of energy and strength and insight enabling us to investigate the attitudes underlying any orthodoxy (or heterodoxy) through a close engagement with the style in which those attitudes present themselves. Leavis' own energy of mind found an adequate and complex vehicle in a supple and scrupulously self-qualifying style that was for far too long subject to belle-lettristic detraction. If Leavis has "troubled" some, then we may say with René Char that "*ce qui vient au monde pour ne rien troubler ne mérite ni égards ni patience*" (whoever comes into the world to trouble nothing merits neither respect nor patience). One wants to retort to cavilings about praise of

Leavis in the way that E. M. Forster retorted to Eliot's cavilings about his praise of Lawrence on Lawrence's death: "There are occasions when I would rather feel like a fly than a spider."

There is a fine passage by Henrik Von Wright on a great philosopher with whom Leavis himself had a somewhat equivocal relationship, Wittgenstein. Indeed, Leavis' interesting "Memories of Wittgenstein," published in *Human World* for February 1973, are not, perhaps, free of a certain undercurrent of feeling that Wittgenstein was a kind of rival. The "Memories" certainly bring out incidentally how intensely "local," how Cambridge, a man Leavis was as opposed to the "agoraphobic," almost "displaced" philosopher. I should like to conclude by quoting this passage because it seems to me to apply just as strikingly to Leavis himself if we substitute his name for that of Wittgenstein:

To learn from Wittgenstein without coming to adopt his form of expression and catch-words and even to imitate his tone of voice, his mien and gestures, was almost impossible. The danger was that the thoughts should degenerate into a jargon. The teaching of great men often has a simplicity and naturalness which makes the difficult appear easy to grasp. Their disciples usually become, therefore, insignificant epigones. The historic significance of such men does not manifest itself in their disciples but through influences of a more indirect, subtle and, often, unexpected kind.

SELECTED BIBLIOGRAPHY

I. BIBLIOGRAPHY. D. F. Mackenzie and M.-P. Allum, *F. R. Leavis. A Check List 1924–64* (London, 1966).

II. SEPARATE WORKS. *Mass Civilization and Minority Culture* (London, 1930); *D. H. Lawrence* (London, 1930); *New Bearings in English Poetry* (London, 1932), contains "Poetry and the Modern World," "The Situation at the End of the War," "T. S. Eliot," "Ezra Pound," and "Gerard Manley Hopkins"; *How to Teach Reading: A Primer for Ezra Pound* (London, 1932); *For Continuity* (London, 1933), contains "Marxism and Cultural Continuity," "Mass Civilization and Minority Culture," "The Literary Mind," "What's Wrong with Criticism," "Babbitt Buys the World," "Arnold Bennett: American Version," "John Dos Passos," "D. H. Lawrence," "D. H. Lawrence and Professor Irving Babbitt," "'Under Which King, Bezonian?'" "Restatements for Critics," "This Poetical Renascence," and "Joyce and 'The Revolution of the Word'"; *Culture and Environment* (London, 1933), with D. Thompson; *Revaluation: Tradition and Development in English Poetry* (London, 1936), contains "The Line of Wit," "Milton's

Verse," "Pope," "The Augustan Tradition," "Wordsworth," "Shelley," and "Keats."

Education and the University: A Sketch for an English School (London, 1943), contains "The Idea of a University," "A Sketch for an English School," "Literary Studies," and appendices: "T. S. Eliot's Later Poetry" and "How to Teach Reading"; *The Great Tradition: George Eliot, Henry James, Joseph Conrad* (London, 1948), contains "The Great Tradition," "George Eliot," "Henry James," "Joseph Conrad," "*Hard Times*: An Analytic Note," and appendix: "*Daniel Deronda*: A Conversation by Henry James"; *Mill on Bentham and Coleridge. With an Introduction* (London, 1950); *The Common Pursuit* (London, 1952), contains "Mr. Eliot and Milton," "In Defence of Milton," "Gerard Manley Hopkins," "The Letters of Gerard Manley Hopkins," "The Irony of Swift," "*The Dunciad*," "Johnson and Augustanism," "Johnson as Poet," "Tragedy and the Medium," "Diabolic Intellect and the Noble Hero," "*Measure for Measure*," "The Criticism of Shakespeare's Late Plays," "Literature and Society," "Sociology and Literature," "Bunyan Through Modern Eyes," "Literary Criticism and Philosophy," "The Wild Untutored Phoenix," "Mr. Eliot, Mr. Wyndham Lewis and Lawrence," "The Logic of Christian Discrimination," "Keynes, Lawrence and Cambridge," "E. M. Forster," "Approaches to T. S. Eliot," and "The Progress of Poetry"; introduction and two interpolations in M. Bewley, *The Complex Fate* (London, 1952); *D. H. Lawrence: Novelist* (London, 1955), contains "Lawrence and Art: The Lesser Novels," "Lawrence and Class: *The Daughters of the Vicar*," "Lawrence and Tradition: *The Rainbow*," "Women in Love," "*The Captain's Doll*," "*St. Mawr*," "*The Tales*," "Note: *Being an Artist*," and appendix: "Mr. Eliot and Lawrence."

Two Cultures: The Significance of C. P. Snow (London, 1962), contains the 1962 Richmond Lecture, with an essay by M. Yudkin on Snow's 1959 Rede Lecture; "*Anna Karenina*" *and Other Essays* (London, 1967), contains "Anna Karenina," "Johnson as Critic," "The Pilgrim's Progress," "Adam Bede," "The Europeans," "What Maisie Knew," "The Shadow-Line," "The Secret Sharer," "*Pudd'nhead Wilson*," "The Americanness of American Literature," "*The Complex Fate*," "Pound in His Letters," "'Lawrence Scholarship' and Lawrence," "T. S. Eliot as Critic," "Towards Standards of Criticism," and "The Orthodoxy of Enlightenment"; *Lectures in America* (London, 1969), with Q. D. Leavis, contains "Luddites? or There Is Only One Culture," "Eliot's Classical Standing," "Yeats: The Problem and the Challenge" by Leavis, and "A Fresh Approach to Wuthering Heights" by Q. D. Leavis; *English Literature in Our Time and the University* (London, 1969), the Clark Lectures, contains "Literature and the University: The Wrong Question," "The Present and the Past: Eliot's Demonstration," "Eliot's 'Axe to Grind,' and the Nature of Great Criticism," "Why *Four Quartets* Matters in a Technologico-Benthamite Age," "The Necessary Opposite, Lawrence: Illustration—The Opposed Critics on *Hamlet*," "Summing-Up: 'Monstrous Unrealism' and the Alternative,'" and appendices: "The Function of the University," "Rilke on Vacuity," and "Research in English."

Dickens the Novelist (London, 1970), with Q. D. Leavis, contains "The First Major Novel: *Dombey and Son*," "*Hard Times*: The World of Bentham," "Dickens and Blake: *Little Dorrit*" by Leavis, and "Dickens and Tolstoy: The Case for a Serious View of *David Copperfield*," "*Bleak House*: A Chancery World," "How We Must Read *Great Expectations*," "The Dickens Illustrations: Their Function" by Q. D. Leavis; *Nor Shall My Sword: Discourses on Pluralism, Compassion and Social Hope* (London, 1972), contains the introduction: "Life Is a Necessary Word," "Two Cultures? The Significance of Lord Snow," "Luddites? or There is Only One Culture," "'English,' Unrest and Continuity," "'Literarism Versus Scientism': The Misconception and the Menace," "Pluralism, Compassion and Social Hope," and "Elites, Oligarchies and an Educated Public"; J. Tasker, ed., *Letters in Criticism* (London, 1974), a collection of letters written by Leavis to newspapers and periodicals 1932–1973; *The Living Principle: "English" as a Discipline of Thought* (London, 1975), contains "Thought, Language and Objectivity," "Judgment and Analysis," "Thought and Emotional Quality," "Imagery and Movement," "Reality and Sincerity," "Prose," "*Antony and Cleopatra* and *All for Love*," and "*Four Quartets*"; *Thought, Words and Creativity* (London, 1976), contains analyses of D. H. Lawrence's *The Plumed Serpent, Women in Love, The Captain's Doll*, and *The Rainbow*; *Reading out Poetry and Eugenio Montale: A Tribute, Together with the Proceedings of a Commemorative Symposium on Leavis* (Belfast, 1979).

G. Singh, ed., *The Critic as Anti-Philosopher: Essays and Papers* (London, 1982).

III. Works Edited by Leavis. *Towards Standards of Criticism: Selections from the Calendar of Modern Letters, 1925–27* (London, 1933), ed. with intro. by Leavis; *Determinations* (London, 1934), ed. with intro. by Leavis, contains J. Smith's "On Metaphysical Poetry," W. Empson's "Marvell's Garden," D. W. Harding's "A Note on Nostalgia," F. R. Leavis' "The Irony of Swift," L. C. Knights's "Notes on Comedy," J. Speirs's "Burns," W. A. Edwards' "John Webster," R. Bottrall's "XXX Cantos of Ezra Pound," D. Thompson's "Our Debt to Lamb," D. W. Harding's "I. A. Richards," M. Oakeshott's "The New Bentham," and J. L. Russell's "The Scientific Best-Seller".

IV. Uncollected Essays and Reviews. "Dr. Richards, Bentham and Coleridge," in *Scrutiny*, III (March 1935), review of I. A. Richards' *Coleridge on Imagination*; "Mr. Auden's Talent," in *Scrutiny*, V (December 1936), review of W. H. Auden's *Look Stranger* and Auden and C. Isherwood's *The Ascent of F-6*; "Revaluations (XI): Arnold as Critic," in *Scrutiny*, VII (December 1938); "Hart Crane from This Side," in *Scrutiny*, VII (March 1939), review of *The Collected Poems of Hart Crane*; "Revaluations (XIII): Coleridge in Criticism," in *Scrutiny*, IX (June 1940); "Hardy the Poet," in *Southern Review*, VI (1940–1941); "James as Critic," intro. to M. Shapira, ed., *Henry James: Selected Literary Criticism* (London, 1963); "Justifying One's Valuation of Rilke," in *Human World*, no. 7 (May 1972), lecture at Bristol University; "Memories of Wittgenstein," in *Human World*, no. 10 (February 1973); "'Believing in' the University," in *Human World*, nos. 15–16 (May–August 1974); "Mutually Necessary," in *New Universities Quarterly* (March 1976).

V. Biographical and Critical Studies. M. McLuhan, "Poetic v. Rhetorical Exegesis: The Case for Leavis Against Richards and Empson," in *Sewanee Review* (April 1933); L. Trilling, *A Gathering of Fugitives* (London, 1957), contains "Dr. Leavis and the Moral Tradition"; W. W. Robson, "Mr. Leavis on Literary Studies," in *Universities Quarterly*, XI (February 1957); D. Davie, "F. R. Leavis's *How to Teach Reading*," in *Essays in Criticism* (July 1957); V. Buckley, *Poetry and Morality: Studies on the Criticism of Matthew Arnold, T. S. Eliot, F. R. Leavis* (London, 1959); R. Williams, *Culture and Society, 1780–1950* (London, 1959); R. Williams, R. J. Kaufmann, and A. Jones, "Our Debt to Dr. Leavis—A Symposium," in *Critical Quarterly* (Autumn 1959).

B. Bergonzi, "Criticism and the Milton Controversy," in F. Kermode, ed., *The Living Milton* (London, 1960); J. Holloway, "The 'New Establishment' in Criticism," in *The Charted Mirror: Literary and Critical Essays* (London, 1960); G. Steiner, "Men and Ideas: F. R. Leavis," in *Encounter* (May 1962), repr. in both Steiner's *Language and Silence* (London, 1967) and D. Lodge, ed., *Twentieth Century Literary Criticism* (London, 1972); C. D. Narasimhaiah, *F. R. Leavis: Some Aspects of His Work* (Mysore, 1963); C. Ricks, *Milton's Grand Style* (London, 1963); R. Wellek, "The Literary Criticism of F. R. Leavis," in C. Camden, ed., *Literary Views: Critical and Historical* (Chicago, 1964); J. Killham, "The Use of 'Concreteness' as an Evaluative Term in F. R. Leavis's *The Great Tradition*," in *British Journal of Aesthetics* (January 1965); W. W. Robson, "Mr. Leavis on Literary Studies," in *Critical Essays* (London, 1966); J. Casey, *The Language of Criticism* (London, 1966); J. M. Newton, "Scrutiny's Failure with Shakespeare," in *Cambridge Quarterly*, I, no. 2 (Spring 1966); J. Gross, *The Rise and Fall of the Man of Letters* (London, 1969).

I. Robinson, *The Survival of English: Essays in Criticism of Language* (London, 1972); C. James, *The Metropolitan Critic* (London, 1974); P. French, ed., "Leavis at 80—What Has His Influence Been?" in *Listener* (24 July 1975), a symposium with contributions from D. W. Harding, L. C. Knights, M. C. Bradbrook, and others; "F. R. Leavis; b. 1895: Stability and Growth," in *Universities Quarterly*, XXX, no. 1 (Winter 1975), contributions by M. Tanner, A. Gomme, M. Black, F. Inclis, D. Holbrook, and others; R. Hayman, *Leavis* (London, 1976); C. Ricks, "But Yes," in

Essays in Criticism (October 1976), review of Leavis' *The Living Principle*; F. W. Bateson, "The Scrutiny Phenomenon," in *Sewanee Review*, 85 (1977); D. Davie, *The Poet in the Imaginary Museum* (London, 1977), contains an article prompted by Leavis' *"Anna Karenina" and Other Essays*; R. Boyers, *F. R. Leavis: Judgment and the Discipline of Thought* (Columbia, Mo.–London, 1978); R. P. Bilan, *The Literary Criticism of F. R. Leavis* (Cambridge, 1979); F. Mulhern, *The Moment of "Scrutiny"* (London, 1979).

P. French, ed., *Three Honest Men: Edmund Wilson, F. R. Leavis, Lionel Trilling* (Manchester, 1980); W. Walsh, *R. R. Leavis* (London, 1980); P. J. M. Robertson, *The Leavises on Fiction* (New York–London, 1981); M. C. Bradbrook, *The Collected Papers*, vol. II: *Women and Literature, 1779–1882* (Brighton, 1982), contains the papers "My Cambridge" and "Queenie Leavis: The Dynamics of Rejection."

Note: F. R. Leavis was closely associated with the founding of *Scrutiny* in 1932 and joined the editorial board toward the end of that year. The journal was published continuously throughout World War II; the seventy-sixth, and final, issue, with a valedictory by Leavis, appeared in October 1953. A photographic reprint of the complete set, with an index and a retrospective essay by Leavis, was published by Cambridge University Press in 1963. Eric Bentley edited a volume of selections from *Scrutiny* entitled *The Importance of "Scrutiny,"* which was published in 1948 and reprinted in paperback in 1964. Leavis' two-volume paperback edition of *A Selection from "Scrutiny"* was published by Cambridge University Press in 1968.

ROBERT GRAVES

(1895-   )

Martin Seymour-Smith

I

To poets, Robert Graves is mainly known as a poet. This, of course, is what he wishes. To the intelligent general reading public (and even today, when he has become an international celebrity, it is on this, not on his fellow poets or even on lovers of poetry generally, that he depends for a living), he is also known as one of the most versatile English prose writers of our time. He has done distinguished work in prose as a provocative and lively historical novelist, as a humorous and polemical pamphleteer, as a close critic of poetry and a general poetic theorist, as a mythographer, as a translator, as a writer in the Old and New Testaments, as a playwright (though his plays have never been performed), as an essayist, and as a biographer and autobiographer. The value of his work in prose is uneven; but he has seldom written a paragraph or a sentence that is not crisp and workmanlike or put forward an idea that does not in some way provoke discussion. Even where, as in his Clark Lectures, he appears a cranky, cantankerous, and careless writer, he is more worth reading than most "safe" writers on his range of subjects. All his writing carries the flavor of a most original personality, a personality not superficially at all endearing, but with a lingering tart appeal, like the flavor of quinces.

Though it is his prose that displays Graves's versatility, and some of the more agreeable oddities and eccentricities of his interests and his character, it is his poetry that is likely to prove lastingly important. Nevertheless, since Graves's prose provides the most useful "background reading" for the study of his poetry, it is logical to begin a sketch of this sort with a study of it. Three of Graves's books have a peculiarly direct relevance to his poetry. One is his early autobiography, largely concerned with his school days and his war experiences, but also dealing with his troubled personal life in the 1920's, *Goodbye to All That*. This gives the reader of Graves a no-

tion of the sort of raw material, in stress and joy, out of which at least the earlier poems came. Another early book, *Poetic Unreason* (1925), relates Graves's reaction as a poet to dreams, shell shock, and a Freudian theory of the workings of the subconscious mind that he derived from the anthropologist and psychoanalyst W. H. R. Rivers. His most ambitious prose book, *The White Goddess* (1948), written during World War II, generalizes this historical and psychological material and his personal life in the 1930's, very ambitiously, into a myth about the nature of poetic inspiration. It should be read after reading these early prose books, and after reading the poems. Taken by itself, especially for young poets, it can be heady and dangerous stuff.

Goodbye to All That (1929) is one of the best autobiographical books written about the period of the war years. But it has a wider range than the war. It is a portrait, also, of a class, an age, the disillusionment of a generation. Its main relevance to our purposes here, however, is the light it throws on Graves's own character.

Graves's father, Alfred Percival Graves, was a well-known Irish poet and songwriter whose knowledge of folk poetry and instinctively true ear Graves inherited. Born on 24 July 1895 in Wimbledon, he was descended on his mother's side from the German historian Leopold von Ranke, and much that is most oddly individual in his writing might be explained as arising from a combination of Celtic mysticism and love of "nonsense" with a dour, methodical Prussian rationalism. Though very few writers of our time have used the English language with a more chaste sense of a specifically "English" tradition, Graves's character is by no means a typically English one—in fact he has no English blood at all. He could never, for instance, be described as a sentimental, a tolerant, or an easygoing man. There is something more rugged and more wild in him than we find in most English writers. There is a hauteur and an arrogance about him that strike us today either as foreign or as harking back to the eighteenth-century aristocrat. But his arrogance is seldom humorless.

Graves's boyhood was the conventional one of a youth of his class. He went to a good public school. He was strong, but clumsy and awkward, and not a good mixer; by learning to box, he achieved a certain position at school, but he was never popular. A sense of awkwardness and clumsiness in his relationship to his own body has remained with him all his life, and also the inaptitude for facile gregariousness. When World War I broke out, his boxing helped him to overcome the bad impression made on his commanding officer by his heavy and untidy appearance. Before the war, he had published a few early poems in such magazines as the *Spectator*; they were more or less in his father's tradition, drawing on the world of chivalry, romance, and nursery rhyme. It is significant that most of his juvenilia was experimental—he experimented with assonance, the Welsh *englyn* form, and a host of other complicated Welsh meters and rhyme schemes—but always within the limits of tradition. He was a gallant soldier but found, like many of the surviving soldier poets of his generation, that the war had left him with a trauma. He wrote "realistic" poems of trench warfare, more or less like his friend Siegfried Sassoon's, but without the bitter satiric edge. He did not draw a pacifist moral from his experiences; he helped, indeed, to persuade Sassoon—who had wished to refuse to serve, as a protest against aimless slaughter—to go back to the trenches. The year 1918 found him in a bad psychological state, and the ghost of World War I was never permanently exorcised, although its effect was diminished by the writing of his autobiography ten years later. In his old age, after he had stopped writing (1975), it returned to haunt him with guilt and fear.

He went to Oxford, where, however, he lived not in college but in the country, for the sake of his health. He had a special dispensation to do a B.Litt. on a literary theme instead of the ordinary B.A. He married, had four children, and lived quietly in a cottage. The marriage broke up after some years, and Graves then began an association with the American poet Laura Riding,[1] who had a revolution-

ary effect on his attitude to poetry, although there is little he learned from her that he had not already anticipated in inchoate early work. It was during his association with her that he wrote many of his most notable poems. He and Laura Riding parted in 1940, and Graves later married again and had four more children. Apart from an uncongenial spell of teaching in Egypt in the 1920's (in a post obtained for him by his friend T. E. Lawrence), he has lived all his life by writing. Since 1930 he has resided in Mallorca, except during the years of the Spanish Civil War and World War II.

Such, in brief, is Graves's personal history. It is more directly relevant to his poetry than many personal histories of poets are. Two facts are fundamental. World War I gave Graves a personal shock from which, at a deep level, he never quite recovered. It destroyed, as the title of his autobiography suggests, his belief in the existence of traditional, stable values in European and English society. It gave him a sense of isolation and insecurity. It left him with images of pain and horror that bit deep into his mind. At the same time it left him with a soldier's pride and a soldier's admiration for dour, staunch, disciplined courage. War, as in *Count Belisarius* or *Sergeant Lamb*, is a subject with which Graves feels at home. He has the World War I veteran's admiration for the soldier as such, and dislike of the "frock" or politician; his dislike of metaphysics, of abstract theorizing, is partly a feeling from the same source.

The second fundamental fact is that relationships with women have had a primary importance in Graves's life, and that they have always been difficult relationships. It is obvious, also, that one main theme running through all his mature poems is what may be called unhappy love, or perhaps merely romantic love (for it is part of the notion of romantic love that it should end unhappily). We can seek a source of this unhappiness when we gather from Graves's autobiography that his nature is extremely squeamish as well as passionate about the physical expression of love. He says in *Goodbye to All That*: "I have never . . . engaged in unnatural vice" or "slept with a prostitute."[2] His love poems are passionate, and they have sometimes a passionate salacity, but they are never—in Thomas Carew's or John Donne's sense, say—truly sensuous. It is not that he regards

---

[1]Born in New York in 1901, she first wrote under the name Laura Riding Gottschalk, her name by her first marriage. From the mid-1920's until 1940 she signed herself Laura Riding. Since then she has signed what little she has published Laura (Riding) Jackson, her name by her second marriage to an American farmer, Schuyler Jackson, who died in 1968.

[2]The sentence reads: "I have never mastered any musical instrument, starved, committed civil murder, found buried treasure, engaged in unnatural vice, slept with a prostitute, or seen a corpse which has died a natural death."

the body as an inadequate house for the spirit, but that he is never able to escape from his old feeling of awkwardness and clumsiness. There is, too, a streak in him of simple puritanism, combined with public-school or old-soldier hardness: a streak of resentfulness at being bound to the body by sexual need. The external shock of World War I and these internal tensions dictate the immediately recognizable texture of Graves's poems.

II

GRAVES is one of the most successful of modern historical novelists; yet of the type of imagination whose ability is to follow out action for its own sake, to make an imaginary train of consequences from a postulated situation and character—of the inventive type of imagination, in short—he has little or none. The action of a "modern" novel of his like *Antigua, Penny, Puce* (1936), or of a "futuristic" novel like *Seven Days in the New Crete* (1949), is trivial or fantastic in itself and throws no light at all on the complexities of human behavior. This is really because Graves is interested not in ordinary human behavior for its own sake, but only in human behavior when it conforms to, or illustrates, some poetic or predetermined pattern. Thus in his historical novels, where the reader's attention is held—and sustained by a series of shocks—by Graves's interpretation, and sometimes manipulation, of happenings he has not had to invent, he always chooses as his heroes men who have had the inner force to mold events, to set patterns of behavior, to make history: Jesus of Nazareth, Belisarius, or a mythical hero, like Jason of *The Golden Fleece*. His heroes are always either godlike men, like Belisarius or Jason, or in a special sense they are literally gods, like Claudius and Jesus.

The two Claudius novels, *I, Claudius* and *Claudius the God and His Wife Messalina* (both 1934), remain Graves's most successful and psychologically acute achievement in the field of full-length fiction. He had discovered a theme exactly suited to his needs and his talents: the eccentric, bewildered, but always active and positive character of Claudius—hitherto written off by most historians as a half-crazy nonentity—set against the violent, pleasure-loving, and superstitious background of first-century Rome. He wrote *I, Claudius* with great urgency and under financial pressure. Asked once if while writing it he knew it was going to be a best seller, he replied: "I knew it bloody well had to be!" The only two other prose works he has written with the same sense of urgency are *The Shout* (1929), a brilliant story of the supernatural, and his most important work of poetical theory, *The White Goddess*. But, though he took two years to write *The White Goddess*, he had no illusion that it would be a best seller. It was, like his poems, not part of his livelihood but one of his tributes to the Muse.

Graves's attitude toward the craft of fiction is expressed wittily in his poem "The Devil's Advice to Story-tellers":

> Lest men suspect your tale to be untrue,
> Keep probability—some say—in view.
> But my advice to story-tellers is:
> Weigh out no gross of probabilities,
> Nor yet make diligent transcription of
> Known instances of virtue, crime, or love. . . .
> Assemble first all casual bits and scraps
> That may shake down into a world perhaps. . . .
> Sigh then, or frown, but leave (as in despair)
> Motive and end and moral in the air;
> Nice contradiction between fact and fact
> Will make the whole read human and exact.

Actual written history, with its jumble of "casual bits and scraps," does (in the Earl of Clarendon or Bishop Burnet, say) read "human and exact" in this way; a classically constructed novel like *Adolphe* or *Pride and Prejudice* does not; it has a unity of theme and development that is, in one sense, an abstraction from the untidiness of life. Graves does not like reading novels; in fact he reads very little. Splendid craftsman as he is in prose, it is only in poetry that he sees a place for rigorous and classical "art"; and he has been studiously discreet about the enormous amount of art that goes into his verse.

The younger Graves was a humorous and polemical writer of great distinction. His two little pamphlets of the 1920's, *Lars Porsena, or the Future of Swearing and Improper Language*, and *Mrs. Fisher, or the Future of Humour*, can still be read with great pleasure. What gives them their lasting quality is that, underneath the high jinks, there is a serious concern—resembling that of an acute amateur sociologist—with popular canons of what is obscene and what is funny. There is a double layer of sardonic irony: popular notions of obscenity, and ways of avoiding it, often seem to Graves themselves obscene; popular notions of what is funny seem to him funny. The joke, as in the ferocious *Pamphlet Against Anthologies* (1928), written with Laura Riding, is on the reader, or on an obtuseness that the reader must be shaken out of. As a serious critic of poetry, Graves is at his best (as in *A Survey of Modernist Poetry*, 1927, again written with Laura Riding) in close analysis. Their famous analysis of a Shakespeare sonnet in 1927 gave William Empson the clue for his method in *Seven Types of Ambiguity* (1930). In dealing with the character and achievements of individual poets, Graves is, however, too often carried away by a deep personal prejudice that has been seen by some commentators as revealing nothing more nor less than jealousy. In what he has to say in his weakest and most arrogant work of criticism, the Clark Lectures, printed in *The Crowning Privilege* (1955), about poets so diverse as Pope, Wordsworth, Tennyson, Yeats, Pound, Eliot, Auden, and Thomas, it is obvious that he is not even beginning to attempt a fair estimate of the poet but giving vent—often in a pungently amusing way—to an instinctive, strong dislike of the man. However, it must be remembered that these lectures were intended to provoke—and they succeeded in this. For the reader, however, *The Crowning Privilege* is frustrating: Graves's unorthodox attitude is in itself interesting and frequently valuable, but he fails to support it by arguments worthy of his critical intellect. His later criticism, much of which stemmed from his years as professor of poetry at Oxford, remains entertaining, but it is increasingly diffuse and does not equal his poetic achievement.

His earlier critical work is less contentious but equally provocative intellectually. *On English Poetry* (1922) was written, characteristically, more with a view to clarifying its author's own difficulties as a practicing poet than with the intention of putting forward a new theory of poetry. It consists of a series of notes, some of them much influenced by W. H. R. Rivers, on the psychological processes by which poems come into being, and on such purely technical matters as how to deal with the letter *s*. It anticipates, though, most of his later concerns: he cannot be understood without a knowledge of it.

Poetic Unreason, which served Graves as the thesis by which he obtained his degree of bachelor of literature, represents a more important stage in his critical development, one that he not long afterward rejected as wrongheaded and even mischief-making. Again, it is a reflection of the practical experiments he was making at the time; one section deals exclusively with the way in which he rewrote a poem according to his newly found Freudian principles. The theory expounded is that the poet's audience may be "hypnotized," their subconscious minds held, by the use of Freudian manipulation. Although he has since regretted this theory as artificial and tending to lead to "manufactured" poetry (his suppression of nearly all of his poems of this period may be attributed to this), the magnitude of the step from here to *The White Goddess* is less apparent to the follower of his development than it is to Graves himself. The basic change of view, however, is important: poetry cannot, by its own nature, be "made." The shift in thought is from a rationalistic to a more ambiguous attitude: Freud's theories were useful because they seemed to be scientifically true, but the Goddess is worshiped, above all, for her own sake.

A Survey of Modernist Poetry is a defense of the reaction from the traditionalism of the Georgian poets of the 1920's, but it is by no means full of praise for the exponents of the new poetry. Only Gerard Manley Hopkins (who had recently been "discovered") and E. E. Cummings are defended with anything approaching warmth. The chief purpose of the book was not to show that modernist poetry was necessarily good because it was new, but to show that it made sense; a poet was entitled to do anything so long as he wasn't merely showing off. Three lines of Pound's (each consisting of one word, together making up a poem) are taken as an example of a poem that doesn't make enough sense. The extensive use of ellipsis, so fashionable in the poetry of the 1950's and 1960's, is here decisively rejected. The most influential section of the book is an irrefutable demonstration, by means of a brilliant analysis of Shakespeare's sonnet 129, of how much is distorted and lost by modernization of spelling and punctuation. One of Graves's tutors at Oxford, Percy Simpson, author of *Shakespearean Punctuation*, provided the inspiration and the ammunition; the critical method was Graves's. There are errors in his analysis, as has been well demonstrated, but it nonetheless laid one of the foundations of the New Criticism.

A Pamphlet Against Anthologies is a spirited and often malicious attack on the practice of misrepresenting a poet by arbitrary, insufficient, or irresponsible selection from his work, and on the profitable "anthology poem" that is its result. T. S. Eliot had conducted a similar though briefer and less sharp attack some years prior to this, and Graves was aware of it. Graves criticized Eliot, but always respected him.

Graves's essays in *Epilogue*, a critical miscellany whose three volumes he and Laura Riding edited and published in Mallorca between 1932 and 1936, represent his best criticism, and are certainly superior in scholarship (though even this cannot be said to be of a high standard) and argument to those in *The Crowning Privilege*. They were written under the direct supervision of Laura Riding.

The Common Asphodel (1949) collects most of these essays, in a thoroughly revised form, together with almost entirely rewritten and sometimes rearranged extracts from the books mentioned above. There are also a number of new essays, including a characteristically eccentric and erroneous one on the sources of *The Tempest*.

The critical strength of *The Common Asphodel*[3] as compared with the lack of care often displayed in *The Crowning Privilege* led many to hope that Graves would some day devote his energies to a comprehensive and close survey of English poetry; but he always refused to do this.

Graves's single most important work of prose, in relation to his poetry, is certainly the famous book *The White Goddess*, which he began writing in 1944 and published in 1948. An enlarged and revised edition was published in 1952. It must, perhaps, ultimately be judged as Graves's personal poetic testament and not as the "historical grammar of poetic myth," which is its description on the title page. Graves has several times complained that his White Goddess is not "Mr. Graves's White Goddess," as many critics have described her, but that familiar and traditional figure, the Muse, the religious invocation of whom is the true function of all poetry. Some critics, however, like Empson, who have recognized this, have complained that she is an excessively primitive and bloody-minded Muse.

Roughly, what Graves believes is that true poetry sprang from a matriarchal society, in which a Queen, who was the temporary incarnation of the Goddess, took to herself periodically a King, who had to be sacrificed before his strength decayed, to preserve the fertility of the land. The Muse is the female principle and represents something more fundamental than the male principle: she is the Mother who bears man, the Lover who awakens him to manhood, the Old Hag who puts pennies on his dead eyes. She is a threefold process of Birth, Copulation, and Death, or of Creation, Fulfillment, and Destruction. She is at once the Goddess of Life and Joy, and of Pain and Death, and it is impious and fatal to reject her in any of her manifestations. When a matriarchal society becomes a man-dominated society, Apollo (originally a contemptible little mouse-god) usurps the place of the Muse; poetry gives way to rhetoric. In reading both Graves's poems and *The White Goddess* itself, only a few readers will be tempted to dismiss this idea as absurd in a metaphorical sense, though there is, alas, no evidence that there ever did exist a "matriarchal" society.

Graves's ideas on the subject, which are markedly Victorian, resemble those of Johann Jakob Bachofen's *Das Mutterrect* (1861), which has been thoroughly discredited. Characteristically, Graves has since somewhat modified his ideas about the White Goddess. A psychologist could say that his attitude had become less overtly masochistic. He has asserted that an even more important figure, whom he calls the Black Goddess, lies behind the White Goddess. This figure is gentler, and is nonsexual in aspect. (His poem of 1963 "The Black Goddess" is quoted and discussed in a later section, which deals with later developments in his poetic thought.)

But it is obvious that Graves's picture of the Muse at the time he wrote *The White Goddess* is almost exclusively based on his personal experiences with and attitudes toward women. He tended to overemphasize the cruelty of the Goddess at the expense of her gentleness (his worship, like all worship in the strictly pagan sense appreciated by anthopologists, has fairly obvious latent elements of fear and disgust). Once, when asked for an example of a gentle aspect of the Muse, he frowned for some time and then named a woman character in his rehandling of the story of Jason, *The Golden Fleece* (1944). This character, though certainly gentle in speech, nevertheless causes somebody to be chased down a gorge and stoned to death. In Graves's conception of the Muse, there is, in fact, an element of morbidity. In a later poem he tried to deal with this, but not altogether convincingly. He says, in effect, that he will allow the woman he loves to flog his feet—but not because he is a "fetishist," only because he loves her. This has seemed to some critics—in particular to the late Herbert Read—to represent a rather large and perhaps even a disingenuous claim. Graves's

[3]It must be admitted, however, that one early essay included in this collection, on Shakespeare's sonnets, represents Graves at his most wayward, inaccurate, and irresponsible.

two Penguin volumes on *The Greek Myths* (1955) can be read as a sort of extended series of footnotes to *The White Goddess*, and the same idea of the dominance of the Goddess lies behind his rehandling of the book of Genesis and his novel *King Jesus* (1946).

Whatever judgment scholars may make on its fundamental soundness, *The White Goddess* is a breathtaking work. The bewildering and labyrinthine pursuit of successive clues (the book, which began its life as a projected history of English poetry, was originally to be called "The Roebuck in the Thicket") leaves the reader as breathless as Graves was while writing it. It is not a book to dip into; it is essential to follow the chase from cover to cover. Read in this way, there are few books in the English language more full than *The White Goddess* of profitable asides, fascinating lore, and poetic wisdom. It will take its place beside Robert Burton's *The Anatomy of Melancholy* (1621) as an eccentric classic of English literature. Further, like another masterpiece of a very different sort, Wyndham Lewis' *Time and Western Man* (1927), it expounds—couched in Graves's unfamiliar, often inimitable terms—many of the "new ideas" that have stimulated the last three generations of writers, and other "new ideas" that are still waiting to fructify.

After 1957 Graves as a prose writer abandoned the historical novel and turned his attention more fully to translation, humor (for some time in the 1950's he was a regular contributor of short humorous pieces to the *New Yorker* and to *Punch*), and commentary. A projected novel about Tonga in the nineteenth century was abandoned, and a "realist" modern novel, partly inspired by a reading of Graham Greene's *The End of the Affair*, which Graves regarded as very poor, was perhaps happily left unfinished.

His most learned, objective, noneccentric, and detailed book was written in collaboration with Joshua Podro and published in 1953. *The Nazarene Gospel Restored*, a meticulous examination of the life of Jesus from a Jewish point of view, aroused violent controversy when it appeared—but its thesis anticipated, by over a decade, more recent findings; the book was admired by the distinguished theologian Reinhold Niebuhr. T. S. Eliot, then a director of the publishing house Faber and Faber, told Graves that he might have published it had it been "a drier book."

Apart from *Hebrew Myths* (1964)—written in collaboration with Rafael Patai, and a characteristic exercise in Gravesian interpretation of myths—Graves's prose of his last creative years added little to his stature as a prose writer. But, as he has said, he writes prose for a living. If his later prose has been more obviously hack-work, this has been because of the relatively greater ease with which he can command the market. His translations have been uniformly workmanlike: Lucan's *Pharsalia* (1956), Suetonius' *The Twelve Caesars* (1957), and Homer's *Iliad* (1960) are among them. The strain of writing creative prose for a living was largely eliminated, and he was able—for the first time in his life—to concentrate exclusively on writing poetry. In fact, he produced a far greater number of poems each year in the 1960's than he was ever able to do previously, when he seldom wrote poems except "in between" his historical novels. He also suppressed fewer of his current poems.

In 1961, in succession to W. H. Auden, he was elected professor of poetry at Oxford, where he was a success with undergraduates and graduates alike. His lectures show some interesting developments or relaxations in his critical thought. Previously known to praise only three or four contemporary poets over a period of thirty years, Graves during the 1960's introduced or allowed himself to be quoted in recommendation of at least eight contemporaries, most of them young. Yet his view of some of the poets of the past whom he once admired had changed, as his lectures show. He retains his antipathy to Vergil and his enthusiasm for John Skelton, but becomes much more severely critical of both Thomas Wyatt and John Donne. Again, as in the Clark Lectures, this is spoken criticism, and his arguments are not as detailed as one could wish. In fact, for the most interesting developments in his thought, which are often reflected, but only partially so, in the lectures, we have to turn to his most recent poetry—and this, of course, cannot be understood without a prior knowledge of his progress as a poet since the 1920's.

III

ONE of the most difficult things to accept in Graves's work is the apparent contradiction between a religious and a rational attitude. One of the statements he never makes about the White Goddess is that she *exists* in the sense in which theologians discuss the question: *An Deus sit?* (in theological terms: Where and how in time and space does God exist?). As a mythographer, he has always tended to euhemeristic interpretations; and he likes to reduce myths to misinterpretations of ancient icons, recording rituals or ceremonies that priests of a later generation—either through ignorance or to make old traditions fit into the pattern of a new, heretical Father God religion—more or less plausibly misread. At one level, he is completely a rationalist; at another he can say of the White Goddess—in a phrase he has at least twice used in conversation with other poets—"Unworthy as I am, I am her man!" The friction between his religious and rational attitudes has provided Graves with some of his most successful poems, yet it has proved to be the point at which he has failed to resolve and clarify his thought, although his most recent poems, as will be seen, deal with the question much more overtly. His attitude toward "life"—as exemplified, for instance, in "The Devil's Advice to Story-tellers"—and his notion of poetry as something "above" and altogether better than "existence," might lead to the supposition that his final position is that of a mystic. But this is not so: he is fundamentally as much opposed to any kind of overt transcendentalism as he is to "scientific humanism." However, if there has been a shift either way in his thought, it has been toward mysticism, as is shown by his enthusiastic introduction (1964) to a lurid and essentially vulgar book about Sufism. When he became old he did indeed sometimes give the impression of believing in magic; but those who knew him best recognized that this was the result of exhaustion and not truly characteristic of Graves.

The sense of painful separateness from those about him, and from his own actions and even his own body, that has already been alluded to—it would now fashionably be described as a profound sense of alienation from self—is apparent, though at first in an unrealized form, in all of Graves's poetry from at least 1920; even when, in his own words, he was "strongly moved by poetic urgencies" but "attempted to identify them with the impulse of romance." At this stage, the "pseudo-adult experience" of four years of trench warfare caused him to melodramatize his sense of unreality:

> A song? What laughter or what song
>   Can this house remember?
> Do flowers and butterflies belong
>   To a blind December?
>   ("The Haunted House")

This feeling of foreboding is the underlying tone of all but the lightest of his poems of the early 1920's, when he was newly married, living in a cottage near Oxford with his wife, and writing his earliest critical works, *On English Poetry* and *Poetic Unreason.* Though he wished to write romantic poetry of a happy sort, "with the love-theme," so he declared, "went the old fear-theme, sharpened rather than blunted by the experiences of peace." And the fear-theme perhaps saved him as a poet; for, he tells us, "everything worth preserving that I wrote between 1922 and 1926 was written in spite of . . . my new theories."

What were these new theories? Graves in the early 1920's was at first concerned, like many of the poets of his generation, with the pleasurable, quaint, and consoling aspects of poetry, the music of words, the beauties of nature, the humors of rustic life. Then he realized that his concentration on ways of capturing and holding the reader's attention had led him to neglect the significance of the *content* of poetry; and so he embarked on a protracted study of Freudian psychology. As we have seen, he had learned a great deal about psychological theory from W. H. R. Rivers, who treated many of his friends for shell shock, and, under Rivers' influence he became interested in dream images, with their powerful latent content, as a means of hypnotizing the reader of poetry. The deeper seriousness about poetry that he had derived from the study of psychology was reinforced by his meeting with Laura Riding in 1926. Since few critics take Laura Riding's poetry or influence on Graves seriously, it is important to record that their meeting was not accidental. Graves wrote to her after having read some of her poems. From the time of this meeting onward, he made a policy of suppressing whatever early poems he felt "misrepresented his poetic seriousness at the time." There are poems in *The Pier-Glass* (published in 1921, before he knew Laura Riding or knew of her work) which show that in the earlier 1920's he had already anticipated his later manner and begun to become engrossed with the themes that, after 1926, were to occupy him profitably for the next fifteen years. However, the part played by Laura Riding in his development as a poet cannot possibly be overemphasized, and it is a serious defect in most studies of his work that it is minimized. Others, who have not written on Graves—including W. H. Auden and Philip Larkin—are aware of her importance as a poet in her own right.

The concern of the premonitory poems in *The Pier-Glass*, which are written in a spirit of physical and emotional rather than intellectual unease, is with the search for a cure for a sickness from which both the poet and his time are suffering:

> Mouth open, he was lying, this sick man,
> And sinking all the while; how had he come
> To sink?

The sick man, in this poem, "Down," tries to get up, but is hopelessly thrust back again:

> Falling, falling! Day closed up behind him.
> Now stunned by the violent subterrene flow
> Of rivers, whirling dam to hiss below
> On the flame-axis of this terrible earth;
> Toppling upon their waterfall, O spirit. . . .

Such a poem expresses a profoundly unhappy state of mind, something deeper than mere war neurosis, or shell shock: a perpetual half-life of dread and terror on the verge of total destruction; existence as an experience of being killed and then brought back to life to be killed again. Graves is describing here (without quite knowing that he is doing so) the hell of those who have the capacity to awake but who choose to remain asleep. He is also anticipating a central theme of his later work: the necessary symbolic death of any poet, who must be torn to pieces like Orpheus and float down the river before he can find peace. But the death, or hell, of "Down" is peculiarly unbearable in that it seems perpetual, not a prologue to any moment of peace.

Another poem of this period, "Mermaid, Dragon, Fiend," represents a step forward from this neurotic misery, toward a new conception of love, and also something like a farewell to the traditional symbols of romantic poetry and the Georgian desire for escape:

> Mermaids will not be denied
> The last bubbles of our shame,
> The dragon flaunts an unpierced hide,
> The true fiend governs in God's name.

Graves does not, here, reject mermaid, dragon, and fiend as idle tales. Rather, he realizes that

> They have neither tail nor fin,
> But are the deadlier for that cause.

The reality of the world of fancy is as a projection of the actual evils of life. Dragons are the products of man's despair, symbols of his continual defeat, or partial victories breeding new wars, in an unending struggle. "God," the good that the world imagines it worships, is in reality merely the desires of the world, which are "the true fiend." But for the confusion that apparently lies at the heart of reality we should have no rage for order; but for the war in our hearts, no idol of peace. The traditional ways of escape are part of the total mechanism of the trap. The last line, with its strong rhythm equating "the true fiend" and "in God's name," emphatically rejects known values and systems as useless for salvation; salvation, as the world understands it, is an illusory byproduct of universal damnedness. But there is more hope in the first two lines of the stanza,

> Mermaids will not be denied
> The last bubbles of our shame,

Mermaids remain symbols of beauty, even if they drown us. The way to salvation may be through a love that knows that, of its own nature, it is bound to perish. If it is vain for love to "abjure the mermaid grot," then it is a true poet's obligation to explore it. This acceptance of the cost of love represents the decisive turning-point in Graves's development as a poet. For the next fifteen years, his poems can be read as various explorations of the way of salvation through love and its accepted losses, against the background of a public world whose confusions and dangers are a perpetual threat:

> Neither ends nor begins,
> Rambling, limitless, hated well,
> This Town of Hell
> Where between sleep and sleep I dwell.
> ("In Procession")

IV

THOUGH after 1926 Robert Graves consciously rejected all the public values of modern civilization as irrelevant to his own task and vocation, and though his settling down in Mallorca (in 1930)—then remote, unruined, and not a favorite haunt of summer tourists—was a symbol of this rejection, he did not retreat from the world in the manner of an ascetic or a mystic. He remained concerned with the public, external world—in a sense not only with the social world, but with the mere physical world also, and with his own body as part of it—as a "brute fact" with which he must come to terms. Between 1930 and 1934, particularly, many of his poems are concerned not directly with the love theme but with the proper attitude of the poet, possessed by that theme, toward "the world." As he wrote in 1938, "To manifest poetic faith by a close and energetic study of the disgusting, the contemptible, and the evil is not very far in the direction of poetic serenity, but it has been the behaviour most natural to a man of my physical and literary inheritance."

Graves has consistently displayed faith in his capacity as a poet to transform his natural world so that it can be seen truly, but no longer "hated well." If one gives up the illusion that it is a possible Paradise—or contains possible paradises—need it, nevertheless, be the "Town of Hell"? The content of Graves's poems at this period is, in the best sense, human and domestic reality. There is not in him, for all his glumness, that pessimistic and antihuman bias so strong in such notable contemporaries as T. S. Eliot and Aldous Huxley. If Graves stops to meditate in the manner of a medieval Manichee on the loathsomeness of fleshly existence, he always smells the supper burning; and his appetite even for a charred supper is enough to turn the Manichee's stomach. He manifests this spirit very boldly in "Certain Mercies," a subtle poem which crystallizes a great deal that is central in his attitude toward the rewards and punishments of physical existence:

> Now must all satisfaction
> Become mere mitigation
> Of an accepted curse?
>
> Must we henceforth be grateful
> That the guards, though spiteful,
> Are slow of foot and wit?
>
> That by night we may spread
> Over the plank bed
> A thin coverlet?
>
> That the rusty water
> In the unclean pitcher
> Our thirst quenches? . . .
>
> That each new indignity
> Defeats only the body,
> Pampering the spirit
> With obscure, proud merit?

This is a poem of nagging resentfulness about the material conditions of existence, but it contains no suggestion that its author desires to abandon the defeated body and seek refuge in the spirit. There is a dogged determination to go on eating, drinking, and sleeping, even while grumbling that the food and the drink and the bed are only just tolerable. The curse of existence is accepted (the prison in this poem is, of course, the human body, and "the guards" are the penalties we suffer for neglect or misuse of the body), but it is accepted as a personal curse, redeemable only by a personal salvation. Conditions in the prison—how far we can learn to be contented or at one with our physically limited existence—depend on the self, which has the freedom of a small cell. Graves's insistence on remaining physically engaged with circumstances is nowhere expressed more forcibly than here. The characteristic linguistic subtlety and complexity of the final stanza, in which the spirit is "pampered" with "merit," should on no account be missed.

Besides a disgusted, defiant clinging to physical existence, in some other poems of this period a new, more ironically benevolent attitude toward the physical world is beginning to manifest itself. The world ceases to be nightmarish and becomes, instead, childishly and touchingly silly:

> Children, if you dare to think
> Of the greatness, rareness, muchness,
> Fewness of this precious only
> Endless world in which you say
> You live, you think of things like this:
> Blocks of slate enclosing dappled
> Red and green, enclosing tawny
> Yellow nets, enclosing white
> And black acres of dominoes,
> Where a neat brown paper parcel
> Tempts you to untie the string.
> In the parcel a small island,
> On the island a large tree,
> On the tree a husky fruit.
> Strip the husk and cut the rind off:
> In the centre you will see
> Blocks of slate enclosed by dappled
> Red and green, enclosed by tawny
> Yellow nets, enclosed by white
> And black acres of dominoes,
> Where the same brown paper parcel—
> Children, leave the string untied!
> ("Warning to Children")

All purely speculative thought, Graves means, can result only in such an eternal recurrence of meaningless though not unattractive nonsense. He says elsewhere:

> We are also tending
> To be less philosophical,
> We talk through hats more personally,
> With madness more divine.
> ("To Be Less Philosophical")

All speculative or abstract thought, all thought not focused on a central personal concern, is for Graves—as for a very different man and thinker, Kierkegaard, a writer whom Graves loathes, and whom once (with unconscious irony) he dismissed in conversation by pointing out that his name meant "churchyard"—a turning away from reality, an evasion of the issue. And yet, at the same time, to lose oneself in speculation is not to dull one's anxieties but to risk plunging into the chaotic terror of an early poem like "Down."

All this comes out very clearly in one of Graves's most powerful poems of this period, "The Cool Web," a poem close to the heart of the meaning of all his work, so typical of him in rhythm, diction, multiple layers of meaning, and the personal flavor of its symbolism that it deserves close examination:

> Children are dumb to say how hot the day is,
> How hot the scent is of the summer rose,
> How dreadful the black wastes of evening sky,
> How dreadful the tall soldiers drumming by.
>
> But we have speech, to blunt the angry day,
> And speech, to dull the rose's cruel scent,
> We spell away the overhanging night,
> We spell away the soldiers and the fright.
>
> There's a cool web of language winds us in,
> Retreat from too much joy, or too much fear:
> We grow sea-green at last and coldly die
> In brininess and volubility.
>
> But if we let our tongues lose self-possession,
> Throwing off language and its watery clasp
> Before our death, instead of when death comes,
> Facing the wide glare of the children's day,
> Facing the rose, the dark sky and the drums,
> We shall go mad no doubt and die that way.

What this poem is about is obviously a contrast between the innocent, dangerous, and agonizing immediacy of experience and language as a means of making sense of that immediacy, of controlling it, of keeping it at a safe distance, and therefore of making

it to a certain extent seem unreal. Somewhere between inarticulate innocence and the chaos of madness, of "letting go"—the chaos of total recall—lies the frightening terrain of the poet. The metaphors for language, a net and the sea, are peculiarly interesting. Language *is* a "web," it is a network of relationships that, for men, holds together a multitude of things that—like fish caught in a net—would otherwise swim apart. But *we* are partly the fish; it is language that holds us together, inherited words and concepts that prevent us from achieving a savage independence, that enable society, when it wants us, to haul us in. But language is not only a network of logical relationships, it is also all the emotive connotations that words carry. It is what holds together not only individual societies but that vaguer, larger, profounder thing, human society. In that sense it is the sea, what we swim in, where we move and live and have our being. At some level, compared to the heat of the day and the scent of the rose and the drumming of the soldiers, which are "real" though symbolic in the poem, the sea and the net (or the sea *as* a net) are "unreal," or metaphorical: and that suggests the precariousness of the poet's achievement and his situation.

The act of "spelling away the soldiers and the fright" represents the employment of every possible valid—that is, truly felt and self-demonstrable—"poetic" response, in the controlling of experience. The old fear-theme is still present, but it is handled in a much wider way. Graves is dealing here with the very modern theme of the apparent gratuitousness of what Albert Camus would have called the absurdity of existence, a gratuitousness that our use of language, if it is sufficiently sensitive, can help us to handle; but a gratuitousness that is primary, where our use of language is a secondary response to it. Graves finds himself in the same predicament as Kierkegaard: "The attempt to infer existence from thought is a contradiction. The thought takes existence away from the real and thinks it by abrogating its actuality, and translating it into the sphere of the impossible." But where Kierkegaard—and his many modern descendants on the Right and the Left—finds a refuge only in a blind faith or a lucid nihilism, a faith that blasphemes its nature when it seeks to find reasons for itself, and a nihilism that blasphemes *its* nature when it bothers to postulate itself or to become concerned abut the human condition, Graves is satisfied with his trust in poetry. We must have faith in what is progressively revealed to us by our experience. His lack of nihilism often made this essentially modernist poet seem curiously old-fashioned and led to his being labeled as Georgian, until the 1960's.

We find this paradox cropping up again and again in Graves's work. He believes that the truth of poetry is timeless and that history and historical action are "local," possessing only a relative truth: in a sense, of course, *all* "ordinary" experience is historical and therefore, for Graves, local and relative. Nevertheless, he thinks of the observation of that local truth as a prime necessity of poetic practice: it is only through the "local," so to speak, that we can approach the timeless. The poet, for him, in relation to society in general is rather like the soldiers in his historical poem "The Cuirassiers of the Frontier." They care nothing for the empire, nothing for the church. They care for their duty and their honor:

> In Peter's church there is no faith or truth,
> Nor justice anywhere in palace or court.
> That we continue watchful on the rampart
> Concerns no priest. A gaping silken dragon,
> Puffed by the wind, suffices us for God.
> We, not the City, are the Empire's soil:
> A rotten tree lives only in its rind.

The despair of such poems as "Thief":

> you shall steal
> . . . the excuse for life itself
> From a boat steered toward battles not your own,

is relieved by Graves's faith in the practical means he had chosen, in his poetic method. Only the means are true. And with no unifying philosophy, he stubbornly refuses to give up hope of resolving his paradox, contrasting, and attempting to reconcile, his groping, intuitive poetic self with his "divided human self," shrewd and superficial:

> He in a new confusion of his understanding,
> I in a new understanding of my confusion.
> ("In Broken Images")

V

THE "new understanding of my confusion" flowered notably during the years from 1938 to 1947, years overlapping World War II a little on both sides. For most of his time, during these years, Graves was living quietly in a South Devon farmhouse and was establishing his new family.

During these years, he completed his most significant work in poetry and *The White Goddess.* His poems from 1938 to 1947 are richer and more intense than those of the preceding period from 1926 onward, itself a rich one. The various themes that had previously preoccupied him, often producing a mood of despair, are fused into a more harmonious unity; and there is a resurgence in his lyrical poems of tender and gentle feelings, not dissimilar to the feelings expressed in a few of his earliest poems but expressed with a greater tautness of language and carrying a deeper significance.

Graves's love poems, up to about 1938, tend to deal not so much with love as with "aspects of love." They are deliberately one-sided. (There are very few exceptions to this generalization. The most notable of them is "The Terraced Valley," which is among the finest "metaphysical" poems of our time.) Up to 1938, in every love poem he would tend to pursue a single theme: a disgust in accepting the need for a physical expression of love; a feeling of awe and reverence too strong to permit sexual desire to come into his picture; an acceptance of lust, considered abstractedly and sometimes humorously. His earlier love poems do not have the confident serenity, the strength, the realism and the subtlety, the human tenderness of the poems of this period.

Such lines as these, for instance, from one of them, "To Sleep," have the urgency of real life because they are prompted by real life. Furthermore, they arise from a tenderness of domestic circumstance that Graves had not previously experienced. They are not "manufactured":

> Now that I love you, as not before,
> Now you can be and say, as not before:
> The mind clears and the heart true-mirrors you
> Where at my side an early watch you keep
> And all self-bruising heads loll into sleep.

Yet, "true to life" as it is, such a stanza has a depth lacking in everyday experience not only because—like everything Graves wrote in later life—it is technically impeccable but because it is the answer to many years of despair.

It would be unjust to attempt to illustrate the merits of Graves's *Poems 1938–1945,* the volume that contains most of the group of poems under discussion, by isolated fragments of quotation. The story they tell is indescribable except in their own terms. The mechanics—the wit, the many levels of meaning, the beauty and confidence of phrase—are merely incidental to the experience and the truthfulness with which it is recorded. These are happy poems in the best sense; they convey hope, without offering it or indulging in sentimentality. As Edwin Muir wrote at the time, "No one writes quite like this now." These poems are memorable, lucid, grateful, but never oversimplified. In such lines as these, for instance, we remember, when we read them, Graves's early passion for Skelton, and we realize how few poets of our time are capable of this depth of tenderness:

> Have you not read
> The words in my head,
> And I made part
> Of your own heart?
> We have been such as draw
> The losing straw—
> You of your gentleness,
> I of my rashness,
> Both of despair—
> Yet still might share
> This happy will:
> To love despite and still.
> Never let us deny
> The thing's necessity,
> But O, refuse
> To choose
> Where chance may seem to give
> Loves in alternative.
> ("Despite and Still")

Here is conveyed, as beautifully and exactly as anywhere in English poetry, the desperate tenderness of the lover, unable to express his belief in the transcendence of love except in physical terms. Here, at its origin, is the expression of Graves's predicament:

> Never let us deny
> The thing's necessity.

Yet it is at this point that we must (in a figure appropriate to Graves's outlook) stop and "sweat it out." To go further, to attempt to get really beyond "the thing's necessity," would be to abandon the essential earthly and earthy state, which is what we have been given and all that we, here, may rightly know.

The poems of the 1950's represented in *Poems and Satires, 1951* and *Poems, 1953* and those included in *The Crowning Privilege*, a volume also containing Graves's Clark Lectures and a miscellany of essays, seemed to be marking time, characteristically refusing to commit themselves to what had not yet been revealed. They showed signs of a new emotional disturbance, not yet fully resolved into a new serenity of outlook:

> And how can I, in the same breath,
>   Though warned against the cheat,
> Vilely deliver love to death
>   Wrapped in a rumpled sheet?
>
> Yet, if from delicacy of pride
>   We choose to hold apart,
> Will no blue hag appear to ride
>   Hell's wager in each heart?
>   ("Questions in a Wood")

Occasionally, he attempted to present the total myth. But such a poem as "Dethronement" is too much like an attempt to versify the theory of *The White Goddess* and lacks his usual authority. Graves's poems of the 1950's were, curiously enough, best where they avoided direct reference to the Goddess and the common doom of all poets: where they described instead the nature of that doom, where they forgot (perhaps) the Goddess and remembered the doom. They were best where they were gloomiest.

VI

AFTER *Poems, 1953*, Graves published nine collections of new poems, if we include the comparatively large number of previously unpublished poems in *Collected Poems 1959* and *Collected Poems 1965* (and exclude privately printed volumes whose contents were taken over into trade editions). At the beginning of the 1964 volume *Man Does, Woman Is*, he writes that it "closes a three-book sequence dramatizing the vicissitudes of poetic love. Because such love walks on a knife-edge between two different fates, Parts XV and XVI . . . supply alternative endings to the sequence." But in commenting on the poems in *Poems 1965–1968*, he writes, of some of those that preceded it, "I . . . deceived myself into thinking that this particular poetic battle had ended."

The first thing to say about Graves's last poems is that they are, if anything, more technically impeccable than ever. Graves has never been a real technical innovator in the sense that, say, William Carlos Williams or even Laura Riding was—Williams in his use of ellipsis and "natural" rhythms and Laura Riding in her astonishing and certainly unique use of nonmetrical rhythms; Graves's verse has rather represented the carrying of traditional English technique to its most perfect expression, but with less use of an overtly rhetorical effect, as in Yeats, to bolster it and give it fluency. Consider "A Time of Waiting":

The moment comes when my sound senses
Warn me to keep the pot at a quiet simmer,
Conclude no rash decisions, enter into
No random friendships, check the runaway tongue
And fix my mind in a close caul of doubt—
Which is more difficult, maybe, than to face
Night-long assaults of lurking furies.

The pool lies almost empty; I watch it nursed
By a thin stream. Such idle intervals
Are from waning moon to the new—a moon always
Holds the cords of my heart. Then patience, hands;
Dabble your nerveless finger in the shallows;
A time shall come when she has need of them.

A study of the use of vowel sounds in this shows the extreme amount of conscious artistry that Graves puts into the final drafts of his poems, and tends to give the lie to those who accuse him of too extensively "fiddling about" with his work. The sense is never interfered with for the sake of the sound; rather, the poet has faith in the fact that the "right" sound, when found, will correct, or at least sharpen, the sense. As Graves himself has said, the writing of poetry is partly a matter of progressively peeling off layers of self-obtuseness, until the writer can reveal the truth—the real sense that a certain part of him does not want to see. Part of this process is physical: the poet relies upon his sensuous appreciation of rhythm, diction, and sound to uncover, in a semi-intuitive manner, the finer points of his meaning. When he sits down to write a poem—or a poem in the Gravesian sense—he does not know *exactly* what he wants to say. This is progressively revealed to him as he works away at his blurred first draft.

But what of the content of these poems, and of the "two fates" between which the poetic lover walks on a knife-edge? This has attracted much less attention.

One of the fates, that of despair, of a hell where communication is impossible, is most aptly illus-

trated in the poem "I Will Write," with its tragic conclusion:

He had done for her all that a man could,
And, some might say, more than a man should,
Then was ever a flame so recklessly blown out
Or a last goodbye so negligent as this?
"I will write to you," she muttered briefly,
Tilting her cheek for a polite kiss;
Then walked away, not even turned about
                    . . .
Long letters written and mailed in her own head—
There are no mails in a city of the dead.

Graves has recognized a world that is dead because of the dominance of physical love—a world killed by its own inhabitants' exclusive concentration on the consummation of physical desire, by their impossible insistence upon possession of each other.

"Are you patient, still," he asks Orpheus, whose scarred face his lover has stroked and called beautiful,

                    . . . when again she has eaten
Food of the dead, seven red pomegranate seeds,
And once more warmed the serpent at her thighs
For a new progress through new wards of hell?
                    ("Food of the Dead")

It is from such lines as these that we can begin to understand Graves's motives in his attacks on Wyatt and Donne: whether justifiably or not, he sees in them too much of that patience of which, by stern implication, he warns Orpheus (and of course himself). There is a hint of the new world he is coming to describe in some of the poems that deal with what might be called the "physical" fate. One poem begins:

However artfully you transformed yourself
Into bitch, vixen, tigress,
I knew the woman behind.
                    ("The Ample Garden")

The woman behind is the Black Goddess, who, in Graves's mind now, lies behind the crueller White Goddess. It is necessary, however, to be faithful to this more physical manifestation, in every one of her three aspects, in order to pass beyond it and to reach the more peaceful domains of the Black Goddess.

The second fate of poetic love is, of course, to consort with the Black Goddess. The poems deal more with the possibilities of this state than with the state

269

itself. Here is the poem actually entitled "The Black Goddess":

> Silence, words into foolishness fading,
> Silence prolonged, of thought so secret
> We hush the sheep-bells and the loud cicada.
>
> And your black agate eyes, wide open, mirror
> The released firebird beating his way
> Down a whirled avenue of blues and yellows.
>
> Should I not weep? Profuse the berries of love,
> The speckled fish, the filberts and white ivy
> Which you, with a half-smile, bestow
> On your delectable broad land of promise
> For me, who never before went gay in plumes.

What kind of world is this which Graves now explores? Clearly it is one in which the lover is freed from the trap of physical desire—but what does he gain from this freedom? The short answer is: practical understanding and wisdom. Physical separation, for example, is no longer a cause of anguish:

> Lovers in time of absence need not signal
> With call and answering call:
> By sleight of providence each sends the other
> A clear, more than coincidental answer
> To every still unformulated puzzle,
> Or a smile at a joke harboured, not yet made,
> Or power to be already wise and unafraid.
>
>   ("In Time of Absence")

The world he is trying to describe is the real world that exists beneath and in spite of the illusory one we imagine we inhabit. The idea (in literature as opposed to philosophy) of the world as an illusion will be most immediately familiar to those who have read or seen Jean Genet's play *The Balcony*, or many of the plays and novels of Luigi Pirandello. But Graves (like the French novelist and critic Nathalie Sarraute, in her own different way), is not concerned merely to expose the ordinary world as a barren illusion: he wishes to explore the history and geography of the true world—a world made possible only by a deliberate, though not orthodoxly saintly or in any sense dogmatic, sacrifice of the so-called values and the aspirations of the ordinary world.

This, it will surely be seen, is a predictable path to pursue for a man who has never fully accepted the necessity of his body or "the blood sports of desire," as he calls them in "The Green Castle," a poem that describes—in what is, for Graves, an unusually

allegorical form—the progress of the soul. The "celestial" heavens, the second three of seven, "Are awkward of approach: Mind is the prudent rider; body, the ass."

"The seventh heaven" is "most unlike those others" and is entered only "by a trance of love": as Graves continues as a poet, it is of this seventh heaven, and of the black hell of aware alienation from it, that he writes, as in "The Utter Rim":

> But if that Cerberus, my mind, should be
> Flung to earth by the very opiate
> That frees my senses for undared adventure,
> Waving them wide-eyed past me to explore
> Limitless hells of disintegrity,
> Endless, undifferentiatable fate
> Scrolled out beyond the utter rim of nowhere,
> Scrolled out . . . . . .
>   who on return fail to surrender
> Their memory trophies, random wisps of horror
> Trailed from my shins or tangled in my hair?

It is true that Graves uses more rhetoric in these poems than ever before, and there is a corresponding loss of tension; it will be the critics of the future who will determine whether his latest work is his best. So far it has met with respect but with less detailed examination than this earlier work. The general view now, since Graves's writing of his last poem in 1975, is that the output of the years 1950 to 1975 is considerably more diffuse, despite its technical mastery and lapidary skill. But there are at least a dozen triumphant exceptions.

And surely, with such unforgettable fragments as "The Narrow Sea,"

> With you for mast and sail and flag,
> And anchor never known to drag,
> Death's narrow but oppressive sea
> Looks not unnavigable to me.

he has reached a technical perfection that has not been surpassed in the language.

SELECTED BIBLIOGRAPHY

I. Bibliography. F. H. Higginson, *A Bibliography of the Work of Robert Graves* (London, 1966), a useful preliminary study, lists journals and anthologies containing critical articles on Graves's work.

II. Collected Works. *Collected Poems* (London, 1938); *Collected Poems 1914–1947* (London, 1948); *Collected Poems 1959* (London, 1959); *Collected Poems 1965* (London, 1965); *Collected Short Stories* (London, 1965); *Poems 1965–1968* (London, 1968); *Collected Poems* (London, 1975), now the standard ed.

III. Selected Works. *No More Ghosts: Selected Poems* (London, 1940); *Selected Poems* (London, 1943); *Poems Selected by Himself* (London, 1957), pprbk. ed.; *Poems About Love* (London, 1969).

IV. Separate Works. *Over the Brazier* (London, 1916), verse; *Fairies and Fusiliers* (London, 1917), verse; *Country Sentiment* (London, 1920), verse; *The Pier-Glass* (London, 1921), verse; *On English Poetry* (London, 1922), criticism; *The Feather Bed* (London, 1923), verse; *Whipperginny* (London, 1923), verse; *Mock Beggar Hall* (London, 1924), sketches; *The Meaning of Dreams* (London, 1924), commentary; *Contemporary Techniques in Poetry* (London, 1923), criticism; *John Kemp's Wager* (London, 1925), pageant play; *Welchman's Hose* (London, 1925), verse; *Poetic Unreason* (London, 1925), criticism; *Twenty Three Poems* (London, 1925), verse; *My Head! My Head!* (London, 1925), novel, "the history of Elisha and the Shunamite Woman; with the history of Moses as Elisha related it, and her questions put to him"; *Another Future of Poetry* (London, 1926), criticism; *Impenetrability, or the Proper Habit of English* (London, 1926), essay, one of the bases for *The Reader over Your Shoulder*, see below; R. Graves, ed., *Skelton: Selected Poems* (London, 1927); *Poems 1914–1926* (London, 1927); *Poems 1914–1927* (London, 1927), "with nine additional poems: 1927"; *The Less Familiar Nursery Rhymes* (London, 1927), anthology; *The English Ballad* (London, 1927), critical survey, rev. and extended into *English and Scottish Ballads* (London, 1957), see below; *Lawrence and the Arabs* (London, 1927), biography; *Lars Porsena, or the Future of Swearing and Improper Language* (London, 1927), essay; *The Rediscovery of "Loving Mad Tom"* (London, 1927), essay, discusses the ballad "Tom o' Bedlam" and suggests Shakespeare as the author, later rev. and repr. in *The Common Asphodel*; *Mrs Fisher, or the Future of Humour* (London, 1928), essay; *The Shout* (London, 1929), story; *Goodbye to All That* (London, 1929; rev. pprbk. ed., 1957), autobiography; *Poems* (London, 1929).

But It Still Goes On: An Accumulation (London, 1930), miscellany, contains repr. of *The Shout* and other material as well as autobiography; *Ten Poems More* (London, 1930); *Poems 1926–1930* (London, 1931); *To Whom Else* (London, 1931), verse; *The Real David Copperfield* (London, 1933), novel, Dickens' *David Copperfield* treated as falsified autobiography and rewritten as Graves considers Dickens would have written it if he had told the truth; *Poems 1930–1933* (London, 1933); *I, Claudius* (London, 1934; pprbk. ed., 1943), novel; *Claudius the God and His Wife Messalina* (London, 1934; pprbk. ed., 1941), novel,

sequel to *I, Claudius*; *Antigua, Penny, Puce* (London, 1936), novel; *Count Belisarius* (London, 1938), novel; *Sergeant Lamb of the Ninth* (London, 1940; pprbk. ed., 1961), novel; *The Story of Marie Powell, Wife to Mr Milton* (London, 1943), novel; *The Golden Fleece* (London, 1944), novel; *King Jesus* (London, 1946; New York, 1981), novel; *Poems 1938–1945* (London, 1946); *The White Goddess* (London, 1948; enl., rev. ed., 1952), "A historical grammar of poetic myth"; *The Common Asphodel* (London, 1949), criticism, everything Graves wished to preserve collected and rev., some material having been written in collaboration with Laura Riding, who has repudiated Graves's rev. of her original work; *Seven Days in the New Crete* (London, 1949), futuristic novel.

The Isles of Unwisdom (London, 1950), novel; *Occupation: Writer* (London, 1951), miscellany, repr. all of *But It Still Goes On* that Graves wished to preserve and adds uncollected essays, short stories, and poems; *Poems and Satires, 1951* (London, 1951); *Poems, 1953* (London, 1953); *The Greek Myths*, 2 vols. (London, 1955), examines and explains the whole field of Greek mythology with the aid of distinguished assistants, repr. with rev. intro. (London, 1958); *Homer's Daughter* (London, 1955; Chicago, 1982), novel; *The Crowning Privilege* (London, 1955), criticism, includes the Clark Lectures, essays on poetry, and sixteen new poems; *Adam's Rib, and Other Anomalous Elements in the Hebrew Creation Myth: A New View* (London, 1955); *!Catacrok!* (London, 1956), repr. pieces from *Punch*, the *New Yorker*, and other periodicals, mainly humorous; *They Hanged My Saintly Billy* (London, 1957; pprbk. ed., 1962), novel, fictional reconstruction of the Palmer poisoning case; *English and Scottish Ballads* (London, 1957); *Steps: Stories, Talks, Essays, Poems, Studies in History* (London, 1958).

The Penny Fiddle (London, 1960), verse for children, no new poems but a selection of poems the author thought suitable for children; *More Poems* (London, 1961); *Myths of Ancient Greece* (London, 1961), for children, illus. by J. Kiddel-Monroe; *The More Deserving Cases: Marlborough* (London, 1962), verse, signed lim. ed. containing poems omitted by Graves from all eds. of his *Collected Poems*; *Oxford Addresses on Poetry* (London, 1962); *New Poems 1962* (London, 1962); *The Siege and Fall of Troy* (London, 1962), for children; *Ann at Highwood Hall: Poems for Children* (London, 1964), new poems for children, illus. by E. Ardizzone; *Man Does, Woman Is* (London, 1964), verse; *Majorca Observed* (London, 1965), illus. by P. Hogarth; *Love Respelt* (lim. ed., London, 1965), verse, thirty-three poems in MS; *Mammon and the Black Goddess* (London, 1965), criticism; *Seventeen Poems Missing from "Love Respelt"* (lim. ed., London, 1967); *Colpohon to "Love Respelt"* (lim. ed., London, 1967); *Two Wise Children* (London, 1967), for children, illus. by R. Pinto; *The Poor Boy Who Followed His Star* (London, 1968), a story and three poems for children, illus. by A. Meyer-

Wallace; *The Crane Bag and Other Disputed Subjects* (London, 1969), essays, lectures, and articles; *Beyond Giving* (lim. ed., London, 1969), verse.

They Hanged My Saintly Billy (Chicago–London, 1980), with illus.; *An Ancient Castle* (New York–London, 1981), verse for children, with illus.

V. WORKS WRITTEN IN COLLABORATION. *A Survey of Modernist Poetry* (London, 1927), criticism, with L. Riding; *A Pamphlet Against Anthologies* (London, 1928), with L. Riding; *Epilogue*, 3 vols. (Mallorca, 1932–1936), critical miscellany, ed. by Graves and L. Riding; R. Graves, ed., *T. E. Lawrence to His Biographers* (London, 1938), with B. H. Liddell-Hart, letters of Lawrence to his biographers with their comments on them; *The Long Week-End: A Social History of Great Britain 1918–1939* (London, 1940), with A. Hodge; *The Reader over Your Shoulder: A Handbook for Writers of English Prose* (London, 1943; abr. ed., 1947; New York, 1979), with A. Hodge; *The Nazarene Gospel Restored* (London, 1953), with J. Podro, a new look at the story of Jesus Christ from a Jewish point of view, written "to convert the Church of England to Christianity"; *The Nazarene Gospel* (London, 1955), repr. part 3 of the longer work, the Gospel as rewritten by Graves and Podro; *Jesus in Rome* (London, 1957), with J. Podro; *Hebrew Myths* (London, 1964), with R. Patai.

VI. TRANSLATIONS. G. Sand, *Winter in Majorca* (London, 1957), trans. with full commentary of *Un hiver à Majorque*, reconstructs the story of Sand's love affair with Chopin; Lucan, *Pharsalia: Dramatic Episodes of the Civil War* (pprbk. ed., London, 1956); Suetonius, *The Twelve Caesars* (pprbk. ed., London, 1957); Homer, *The Anger of Achilles* (London, 1960), trans. of the *Iliad*; *The Rubaiyyat of Omar Khayaam: A New Translation with Critical Commentaries* (London, 1967), with O. Ali-Shah, aroused great controversy during which Graves found few supporters.

VII. BIOGRAPHICAL AND CRITICAL STUDIES. D. J. Enright, *Robert Graves and the Decline of Modernism* (Singapore, 1961), inaugural lecture by the Johore Professor of English at the University of Malaya, 17 November 1960; D. Day, *Swifter than Reason: The Poetry and Criticism of Robert Graves* (London, 1964), interesting on early poetry but marred by factual and critical errors, mainly about Graves's association with L. Riding, a view expressed by Graves and quoted by author but ignored; G. Stade, *Robert Graves* (London, 1967), an introductory essay; D. G. Hoffman, *Barbarous Knowledge: Myth in the Poetry of Yeats, Graves and Muir* (London, 1967); M. Kirkham, *The Poetry of Robert Graves* (London, 1969), a solemnly academic approach; M. Seymour-Smith, *Robert Graves: His Life and Work* (London, 1982), the authorized biography, contains much criticism.

GEORGE ORWELL

(1903-1950)

Tom Hopkinson

I

GEORGE ORWELL's reputation as a writer rests largely on his novels, but his gifts are not those of a novelist, and, if the novel had not happened to be the prevailing literary form during the twenty years when he was writing, he would probably never have been attracted to it. Orwell had little imagination, little understanding of human relationships; his sympathy was with humanity in general rather than with individual human beings. His gifts were an inspired common sense and a power of steady thought; a wary refusal to be taken in by attitudes and catchwords; the courage of the lonely man who is not afraid of being lonely and has learned, in his loneliness, to regard himself with some detachment. These, however, would have made Orwell no more than an unusual citizen in the tradition of English individuality, a tradition which, happily, still survives despite the pressure exerted by both the main political parties—a pressure toward convention and conformity from the Right, and pressure toward leveling and uniformity from the Left. Orwell's distinction is that these gifts in his case were supported by a talent for writing nervous, flexible, and lucid prose: so deeply indeed was writing a part of Orwell's nature that qualities are manifest in his work which did not reveal themselves in his life.

Orwell, for example, was a good talker in a somewhat didactic manner, but no one, I think, would have called him witty. His writings, however, particularly his essays, are full of wit, and his masterpiece, *Animal Farm* (1945), is a river, or at least a sparkling brook, of witty observation and lively, vigorous expression.

These gifts of Orwell's implied—as gifts do—their certain defects. His common sense could degenerate into pawkiness. His habit of lucid thought led him at times to brush the other person's, or the other side's, arguments out of his way, disposing of opposition not by reasoning but with a kind of comprehensive sideswipe: "In spite of his [Swift's] enormously greater powers, his implied position is very similar to that of innumerable silly-clever Conservatives of our own day—people like Sir Alan Herbert, Professor G. M. Young, Lord Elton, the Tory Reform Committee, or the long line of Catholic apologists from W. H. Mallock onwards. . . ."[1] His wariness sometimes became suspicion—as when he fancied a leading London publisher was persecuting him by trying to prevent *Animal Farm* from being published. And his lonely courage involved a concentration on himself that had two unsatisfactory results.

First, all his novels are alike. They are all tales of solitary characters, each in one way or another an expression of Orwell himself, seen against backgrounds that are taken from his own experience. These solitary characters seek to make contact with others but are usually rebuffed, slighted, or betrayed. The backgrounds are vividly drawn, often with a painful grittiness which implies that the author is doing his utmost to be fair about what was really an intolerable situation. But the essence of the novels is that they are unforgiving, and the author's own anger conveys a sense of discomfort to the reader, who feels he is being nagged at for something which is only very indirectly his fault and resents that an author of such uncommon talents should care so little whether he conveys enjoyment to his readers.

Second, Orwell's concentration on himself leads him to see the outside world as an enlarged projection of his own personal problems. He was, from childhood—indeed from infancy—hampered by lack of money, and he came to see the world as a succession of money rackets. He was by birth and up-

[1]From "Politics vs. Literature: An Examination of *Gulliver's Travels*," in *Shooting an Elephant, and Other Essays* (London, 1950).

bringing—or, rather, through an upbringing strangely ill-suited to his birth—acutely sensitive to class distinctions, and he supposed everyone else to be as painfully affected by them as he was himself. Because they had conditioned his own life, he regarded them not as temporary phenomena doomed to disappearance, but as part of the basic order of human existence, at least in the British Isles.

Moreover, in his work he tends to dwell on relatively unimportant subdivisions of society, as when, in *A Clergyman's Daughter* (1935), he makes the grim headmistresss class her pupils in three categories—those who may be ill-treated to any extent, those with whom some care should be exercised, and those who must on no account be touched and whose work must always be described as excellent—according to how promptly the parents pay their bills.

Orwell's strength and weakness relate to a single source; he was without historical perspective. He saw the world of his day with peculiar intensity because he saw extremely little of its past and tended to regard the future as simply a continuation and extension of the particular present that he knew. In his essay "Wells, Hitler, and the World State" (in *Critical Essays*, 1946), Orwell derides H. G. Wells for having completely misunderstood Hitler and the course that World War II would take because his mind was stuck in the early 1900's, so that he was still slaying paper dragons at a time when real ones were ravaging the world. But in his last book, *Nineteen Eighty-Four* (1949), Orwell shows that his own mind was similarly stuck, so that his picture of the future resembles the present—but in a more stupid, oppressive, miserable, dirty, and ill-fed form.

This concentration on the present, this belief that the historic moment is *now*, led Orwell—backed by his uncommon courage—to do at any point in life the thing that seemed to him most important. If fear of poverty is the enemy, the thing to do is to face it, reducing oneself to the lowest state, learning what happens when the last coat is pawned, the last franc is spent, the bugs on the wall are massing in battalions, and one's temperature indicates pneumonia. If on the Spanish Civil War hangs the hope of human freedom, then the inevitable step is to take part: the fact that one may be an incompetent soldier, and that one will certainly come under the suspicion of authority for the rest of one's life for having done so, can be neither here nor there.

This direct connection between what he felt to be the situation and his own response to it is Orwell's strength—a manner of acting that truly deserves the word "magnificent," deserving it all the more because Orwell was not naturally a man of action. On the contrary, his contacts with the physical world were ineffective: if he painted a room, the walls were smeared; if he cleaned a lamp, it caught fire; even the cigarettes he rolled continually fell to pieces. But his concentration on the present moment is his weakness too, because though this particular moment is historic, it is no more so than any other moment. Every hour is both man's finest and his feeblest.

Orwell's preoccupation with the present acted as a handicap to his understanding of the past and his perception of the future. And his preoccupation with his own experience and his own duty, besides being a source of strength, served also as a limitation since it prevented his enlarging that experience by a sympathetic understanding of others. He could endure the company of a derelict in the next hospital bed by conscious effort, but the moment conscious effort was relaxed, his fellow human beings appeared odious and detestable. And the closer they were, the more odious they usually appeared. Orwell was a writer and a highbrow, but "The modern English literary world, at any rate the high-brow section of it, is a sort of poisonous jungle where only weeds can flourish." Orwell was a Socialist, but

the typical Socialist . . . is either a youthful snob-Bolshevik who in five years' time will quite probably have made a wealthy marriage and been converted to Roman Catholicism; or, still more typically, a prim little man with a white-collar job, usually a secret teetotaller and often with vegetarian leanings, with a suspicion of nonconformity behind him, and, above all, with a social position which he has no intention of forfeiting.

In the second part of *The Road to Wigan Pier* (1937), from which these extracts are taken, Orwell seems able to loathe his fellow men for such varied reasons as that they are bald, or hairy; their clothes are good, or bad; they have an accent, they have none, or, if they had one, they have given it up; they smell—or else, having abandoned the honest simplicity of a working life, they have ceased to do so.

·If one were forced, after a study of Orwell's gifts and limitations, to say in what form of literature he could deploy them best, one would suggest in Swiftian satire against mankind, or in the recording of frustrating personal experience. Certainly if one had given such an answer, its truth would have been amply proved. Orwell, besides novels and essays, wrote two admirable records of misfortune—*Down and Out in Paris and London* (1933) and *Homage to Catalonia* (1938), his picture of the Spanish Civil War—as well as one satire, *Animal Farm*.

Masterpieces are never the result of happy chance but are always the full flowering of a nature; this is true even when, as is often the case with poets, they are written in youth, before contact with life. Concerning the few, the very few, writers who produce a masterpiece, there is always one question of supreme interest: How did he come to do it? We can seek the answer in two places: in Orwell's books and in his life. Each of his books contains a section of autobiography; we can therefore follow the progress of his life and examine his production as a writer at the same time.

II

ORWELL was born Eric Arthur Blair at Motihari, in Bengal, on 23 January 1903. His father was a minor official in the Indian Customs who retired on a small pension when his only son was a few years old. There were also two daughters, one older than the boy and one younger. Orwell later placed his family with typical precision as belonging to "the lower-upper-middle class," and he clearly felt this as a misfortune, though in fact the combination of a sparse upbringing with a reverence for intellectual values which distinguishes this class has produced a quite disproportionate number of notable men and women. It does not as a rule produce characters of grace and charm, but it does produce characters—and Orwell himself was among them.

From the first, as he remembers in *Such, Such Were the Joys* (1953), human relationships were not easy for him:

Looking back on my own childhood, after the infant years were over, I do not believe that I ever felt love for any mature person, except my mother, and even her I did not trust, in the sense that shyness made me conceal most of my real feelings from her. . . . I merely disliked my own father, whom I had barely seen before I was eight and who appeared to me simply as a gruff-voiced elderly man forever saying "Don't."

A fashionable preparatory school on the south coast was chosen for the small boy. There his parents managed to keep him, at considerable sacrifice—and, Orwell adds, at reduced fees because the headmaster hoped he would win a scholarship. This school, in which the other boys were so much better off than he was and in which prestige attached only to those gifts and qualities he did not have, set in his mind, he believed, a pattern of failure and depression:

I had no money, I was weak, I was ugly, I was unpopular, I had a chronic cough, I was cowardly, I smelt. . . . The conviction that it was *not possible* for me to be a success went deep enough to influence my actions till far into adult life. Until I was thirty I always planned my life on the assumption not only that any major undertaking was bound to fail, but that I could only expect to live a few years longer.

Despite this conviction of failure, Orwell was awarded at the age of thirteen not one but two scholarships. He chose the more distinguished, to Eton, and was there from 1917 to 1921. Of this time he later wrote: "I did no work there and learned very little, and I don't feel that Eton has been much of a formative influence in my life." There is, in my opinion, a non sequitur in those few lines. The fact that Orwell did little work at Eton may have been the result of his school's influence rather than evidence that it had none. Many young Englishmen do no work at their universities, but acquire a broadening of outlook and a confidence in the power of the mind to solve complex problems, an ability which is far more valuable than academic learning. Orwell certainly acquired these gifts from somewhere: Eton, in its tolerant attitude toward the individual and its appreciation of intellectual freedom, is much more like a university than a school and probably deserves more credit than he gave it. Most other schools would have expelled a boy who, holding a scholarship, chose to do no work.

When the time came to leave Eton, the natural course for Orwell would have been to go to Cambridge, to which he could almost certainly have won a scholarship. He did not do so, and it is clear that he resented the fact and felt that those who did gained an easy advantage over him.[2] Instead, he was advised by one of his tutors to break free from a way of life he found so painful, that of a poor boy among those richer than himself, and take a job abroad. By

[2] In *Keep the Aspidistra Flying* (1936) the hero, Gordon Comstock, has a manuscript rejected and ruminates, "'The Editor regrets!' Why be so bloody mealy-mouthed about it? Why not say outright, 'We don't want your bloody poems. We only take poems from chaps we were at Cambridge with. You proletarians keep your distance'?"

the time he was forty he would have saved money and earned the right to a good pension; he could then choose his own way of life. A post in the Indian Imperial Police was open. Orwell took it and spent the years 1922–1927 in Burma.

He embodied this experience in *Burmese Days*, which was published in New York in 1934. It is a moving story of frustration and humiliation—the humiliation, associated with social snubs, being rather more pressing than the frustration, which derived from the difficult and painful official relationship between the English and the Burmese.

Malcolm Muggeridge, who knew Orwell and was living in India at the time Orwell was in Burma, wrote:

The ordinarily-accepted view is that Orwell was deeply revolted by what was expected of him as a member of the Burma Police Force, and that his subsequent political views were to some extent a consequence of the great revulsion of feeling thereby induced in him. Personally, I consider that this is an over-simplification. It is perfectly true that Orwell was revolted by . . . police duties in Burma, . . . and, indeed, to a certain extent by authority as such; but it is also true that there was a Kiplingesque side to his character which made him romanticize the Raj and its mystique.

In this connexion, it is significant that one of the most vivid descriptive passages in *Burmese Days* is of the hunting expedition that Flory (the "hero") went on with Elizabeth. Another is of the attack on a small handful of Englishmen in their club by an enraged Burmese mob. Flory was the hero of this occasion. . . .

("Essay on *Burmese Days*," in *World Review*, June 1950, pp. 45–48)

In Burma Orwell also wrote, or found material for writing, his essay "Shooting an Elephant," which was to rank as a classic within his lifetime and gives an example of his prose style at its most lucid and precise. An elephant runs amok, and Orwell, as the British official of the district, has to take action. Carrying a borrowed rifle, he follows the beast to the fields, where it is standing peacefully, recovered now from its attack of madness:

As soon as I saw the elephant I knew with perfect certainty that I ought not to shoot him. It is a serious matter to shoot a working elephant—it is comparable to destroying a huge and costly piece of machinery. . . .

However, the pressure of the crowd's will, all determined to witness a shooting, is too strong, and Orwell fires:

In that instant, in too short a time, one would have thought, even for the bullet to get there, a mysterious, terrible change had come over the elephant. He neither stirred nor fell, but every line of his body had altered. He looked suddenly stricken, shrunken, immensely old, as though the frightful impact of the bullet had paralysed him without knocking him down. At last, after what seemed a long time—it might have been five seconds, I dare say—he sagged flabbily to his knees. His mouth slobbered. An enormous senility seemed to have settled upon him. One could have imagined him thousands of years old. I fired again into the same spot.

To this period also probably belongs the short essay "A Hanging," which appeared in the *Adelphi* in 1931. Into these six-and-a-half pages Orwell has concentrated his falcon's power of observation and his living sympathy with mankind, but they are under the control of an artist's impartiality and detachment.

Between victim and executioners Orwell takes no side; he understands the Superintendent's grim responsibility equally with the victim's agony:

We stood waiting, five yards away. The warders had formed in a rough circle around the gallows, and then, when the noose was fixed, the prisoner began crying out to his god. It was a high, reiterated cry of "Ram! Ram! Ram! Ram!" not urgent and fearful like a prayer or cry for help, but steady, rhythmical, almost like the tolling of a bell. The dog answered the sound with a whine. The hangman still standing on the gallows, produced a small cotton bag like a flour bag and drew it down over the prisoner's face. But the sound muffled by the cloth, still persisted, over and over again: "Ram! Ram! Ram! Ram!"

Finally, when all is over, comes the jocular relief that dissolves even racial barriers; this too Orwell accepts without moral indignation: "We all had a drink together, native and European alike, quite amicably. The dead man was a hundred yards away."

Because of the detachment that is so often lacking in his novels, the result—in spite of its tiny scale—is a complete work of art. No more on the subject need ever be said.

III

IN 1927 Orwell came home, ostensibly on leave:

I was already half determined to throw up the job, and one snuff of English air decided me. I was not going back to be part of that evil despotism. But I wanted much more than merely to escape my job.

("How I Became a Socialist," in *The Road to Wigan Pier*)

Either because he saw the situation more clearly than others, or else for reasons of his own temperament, Orwell felt deep guilt over his experience in Burma. His conviction that the British ought to withdraw from the country would be regarded as outrageous when voiced by him in 1934—but it is worth recalling that, little more than ten years later, it had become the official policy of the British government. This guilt was one of the reasons Orwell gave for the next, most extraordinary, change in his life.

He went to Paris, ostensibly in order to write books and articles; but no one wants the books and articles of an unknown writer in a foreign country and it is clear that his real motive must have been different. Orwell went to Paris in order to plunge himself into the destructive element he had been brought up to dread; to experience failure in its most painful form; to rub shoulders with mankind at its lowest and dirtiest; to commit an act of public defiance against the money values of our world, and particularly of those wealthier than himself, by whom he had been surrounded and, he felt, humiliated at his schools.

Besides guilt over his Burmese experience ("For five years I had been part of an oppressive system. . . . I was conscious of an immense weight of guilt that I had got to expiate"), Orwell records the desire, which many men feel, to test himself in hardship. There is, he says:

a feeling of relief, almost of pleasure, at knowing yourself at last genuinely down and out. You have talked so often of going to the dogs—and well, here are the dogs, and you have reached them, and you can stand it. It takes off a lot of anxiety.

Another reason that he sometimes gave was the actual difficulty in the years 1927–1928 of finding any kind of job. It is certainly true that, in the late 1920's, thousands of young men in Orwell's position (and hundreds of thousands in worse ones) struggled in vain to find any kind of work. But I think the pressure was indirect: not that Orwell himself literally could not obtain paid employment, but rather that by identifying himself with the underdogs of every given moment, he deliberately sought to equate the suffering of his life with theirs.

There are two further reasons for his down-and-out life that were not stated by Orwell but that ought, I think, to come into the reckoning. First, Orwell's impression of working-class life (it appears particularly strongly in *Nineteen Eighty-Four*) was as a kind of warm feather bed into which one could sink, abandoning all pretensions. His own family, he seemed to feel, had only recently and with great difficulty hauled itself up into the middle classes. The enterprise of a grandparent, the foothold gained by his father as a minor official, his own sufferings at school, and the sacrifices made by parents and sisters to keep him there had led only to this: a police job that was more than he could stomach. Since the whole upward fight had been in vain, the sensible thing to do was to relax and go down. The resulting hardship would be well compensated for by peace of mind.

Second, there is the reason that governs so much of a writer's life, though it is a reason which he must often conceal from himself: the hope that out of this dramatic, even desperate, change of circumstance would come a book. Orwell could not say to himself, "I will fall through the bottom of society and live the life of a complete outcast. Then I will write my experiences," for this would have given too journalistic a color to his project. What he quite naturally did was to invite the experience for other reasons and make a record of it when the experience was complete.

Down and Out in Paris and London, Orwell's first book, was published in January 1933. It is a remarkable and fascinating work, somewhat scrappy, but containing a succession of curious portraits and a flow of practical comments on the outcast's life. The first words set the note:

The Rue du Coq d'Or, seven in the morning. A succession of furious choking yells from the street. Madame Monce, who kept the little hotel opposite mine, had come out onto the pavement to address a lodger on the third floor. Her bare feet were stuck into sabots and her grey hair was streaming down.

Madame Monce: "Salope! Salope! How many times have I told you not to squash bugs on the wallpaper? Do you think you've bought the hotel, eh? Why can't you throw them out of the window like everyone else? *Putain! Salope!*"

The woman on the third floor: "Vache."

For eighteen months Orwell endured abysmal poverty in Paris rather than apply to friends who could, and would, gladly have helped him. His best days during this period were when he succeeded in getting a job as a dishwasher in a large Paris hotel. Then, quite suddenly, in a manner he does not explain, Orwell felt free to ask help of an English friend, who at once sent him five pounds and the promise of a job. Back in London, he learned that the job could not begin for a month and, once again, the mysterious barrier fell: "Sooner or later I should have to go to B. for more money, but it seemed hardly decent to do so yet, and in the meantime I must exist in some hole-and-corner way."

So there begins an English workhouse and doss-house life to supplement his recent French experience, in which a cup of tea, a slice of bread and butter, and shelter for the night are the deepest concerns of life. This life is described in as matter-of-fact a way as if Orwell were writing a tramp's handbook or doss-house guide; and it ends as suddenly as his Paris life, when Orwell feels free to apply again to B. and borrow a few pounds more.

Down and Out in Paris and London did not sell well, but it received high praise from the critics and must have established Orwell in his own eyes as a writer. It is notable that, from the start, his work was noticed and praised by leading critics. In 1934, when the first book had been followed by *A Clergyman's Daughter* and *Burmese Days*, Compton Mackenzie wrote: "No realistic writer during the last five years has produced three volumes which can compare in directness, vigour, courage, and vitality, with these three volumes from the pen of Mr George Orwell." However, until the great popular success of *Animal Farm* eleven years later, this critical approval was not translated into cash. Over the ten years 1930–1940, Orwell himself, in the sort of calculation he was fond of making, reckoned his literary earnings at not quite three pounds a week.

IV

BETWEEN 1929 and 1935 Orwell kept himself afloat with difficulty as a private tutor and a teacher in cheap private schools—of which *A Clergyman's Daughter* gives a horrifying picture—as well as by books and journalism.

A Clergyman's Daughter is a book Orwell himself came to dislike heartily. He ceased to include it in his list of published works and is said to have bought and destroyed any copies he could find. It has a dif-

ferent flavor from any of his other works: first, because of its theme and teaching, which appears to be that faith is what matters, regardless of whether one can believe in the faith or not; second, because its central character is a woman. Orwell identifies himself with a clergyman's daughter who shrinks from and has a horror of sex, manifested in a ceaselessly nagging conscience; and there can be no doubt—when one recalls the two painful seduction scenes in *Keep the Aspidistra Flying* and *Nineteen Eighty-Four*—that this corresponded to a strong side of his own nature. Indeed it would be possible to regard the novel as in essence the story of an attempt on the part of one who feels fear and loathing for the world to make contact with it. This contact is so painful that it can be brought about only through loss of memory, involving the loss of everything else as well, including reputation. Finally, the one seeking to make contact abandons the attempt and retreats into the shelter of a faith—any faith, no matter what, being better than exposure to life without protection.

In construction the book follows the picaresque convention, being simply a series of adventures in which the heroine moves about from place to place while different things happen to her. Orwell was thus able to use his own experiences of hop-picking in Kent, of London doss-houses, and of the worst kind of private school to provide gloomily impressive backgrounds and give his work the reforming message that he seldom failed to introduce.

There is one quite extraordinary scene, vivid and disastrous as a glimpse into a corner of hell, in which the clergyman's daughter finds herself homeless in Trafalgar Square on a freezing night with a handful of characters as lost as but more desperate than herself. Their talk forms a kind of litany of the damned, with the defrocked parson, the woman whose husband has locked her out, the louse-ridden old tramp, the lads from the north singing round the pubs for a living—and, every now and then, the policeman coming to move them all on just as they are beginning to experience an illusion of warmth.

Orwell's next book, *Keep the Aspidistra Flying*, published in 1936, is essentially the same mixture of a gloomy setting—implying angry criticism of the way life is organized—with an analysis of the values around which that life is built. This time the theme is money.

Gordon Comstock, a solitary young man of literary leanings, gives up an opportunity in an advertising firm and takes a job as a bookshop assistant at two pounds a week in order to have time for writing. Inevitably, his poverty so dominates his thoughts that he cannot get on with his literary work—a fact he never faces, living in a kind of envious haze of all who have inherited or achieved a more workable adjustment to life than he has. Most of the miseries of Comstock's life spring directly from his own confusion: he regards himself as at war with money and respect for money, yet suffers deeply when a waiter is insolent because he is poor.

"In love" with a girl called Rosemary, he does his best to pass his humiliations on to her and reproaches her for not bringing into his life the warmth and comfort he lacks; but his manner of bringing about the desired fulfillment is to ask complainingly, "Are you *ever* going to sleep with me?" or else to make love to her on the ground in a copse in outer suburbia. When for a sufficient reason she rejects him, he ascribes the rejection to his poverty.

The book ends on a more positive note. Rosemary is about to have a baby; the couple decide to marry; and Comstock discovers the commonplace pleasures of owning some furniture and a place to put it, and the commonplace virtues of paying one's way, raising a family, and putting the best face on life one can. It is from this that the book takes its title, with that almost indestructible potted plant, the aspidistra, as a symbol of middle-class endurance and sense of personal responsibility. These virtues, Orwell seems to say, are constantly sneered at, but the sneerers themselves would often be in a poor way unless these same virtues were at work, making their world at least reasonably orderly and solid.

Keep the Aspidistra Flying was not a success, but Orwell was pleased by the number of young men who wrote to tell him that his hero's experience—taking a girl out for the day on a few shillings and wondering the whole time whether the money would last out—had often enough been their own.

In making his central figure a bookseller's assistant, Orwell once again was using his own experience. For about eighteen months, between 1932 and 1934, he worked as an assistant in a Hampstead bookshop, and was also at this time writing for various magazines, in particular the *Adelphi*, edited by his friend Sir Richard Rees. However, Orwell had always detested London, and when he married in 1936 he moved to Hertfordshire. His wife was Eileen O'Shaughnessy, described by Rees, who knew her well, as "a charming and intelligent women." The cottage they took together was also the village shop, the idea being that Orwell should write in the mornings and see to the shop in the afternoons. As a business venture it was not a success—the profit from the store was a bare one pound a week—but this was clearly a happy period in his life. "Outside my work," he once wrote, "the thing I care most about is gardening, especially vegetable gardening. . . . My wife's tastes fit in almost perfectly with my own."

During this time, however, he also became active as a Socialist, and his publisher, Victor Gollancz, who had founded and was running the Left Book Club, invited him to make a journey through one of the depressed areas of Britain, setting down what he saw. The result was *The Road to Wigan Pier* (1937), which takes its title from a North Country joke. "Pier" suggests the seaside, holidays, gaiety. Wigan is a somewhat forbidding inland town whose pier is a derelict wharf on a canal.

The Road to Wigan Pier is Orwell's worst book. It is made up from his habitual blend of immediate impressions with past personal experience, but in this case the blend is particularly uneasy. The first section gives his impression of life in the depressed area and is, in a curious way, misconceived. It is clear that Orwell largely failed to make the close contact with the working class which was the purpose of his journey. John Beavan, who was later editor of the *Daily Herald*, had lived in Wigan for years on the low pay then earned by a reporter on a local paper, and wrote of it:

> He attacked the class barrier at its thickest and highest point. He tried to get into the manual working class and into a very special section of it—the miners. He chose, moreover, a sub-section of the miners—those out of work; and he chose a sub-section of the unemployed: those who lived in the worst slums.
> (*"The Road to Wigan Pier,"* in *World Review*, June 1950, pp. 48–51)

Had the choice been a more reasonable one, Beavan adds, Orwell

would have been accepted and he would have learned something from the inside of the worker's enormous zest for life, the richness of his humour, the breadth of his ambitions, and the simple philosophy which sustains him so long in adversity. But the barrier here was too low. There was no expiation to be found along this easy path.

In the early part of the book Orwell shows an exaggerated, sometimes an undignified, humility toward the working class. "If there is one man to whom I do feel myself inferior, it is a coalminer," he writes. But the artist has no business feeling himself inferior to his subject matter, and the guilt Orwell expresses over his expensive education and middle-class background serves rather to embarrass the reader than to win sympathy for those whose life Orwell is describing.

In the second part there is much that is interesting about the writer's own life, but again Orwell seems to misconceive the way in which good relations between classes come into being and are, on the whole, maintained—that is, by each person accepting as naturally as he can the position in which he finds himself, while being ready to accept changes that are for the general benefit.

Because he lacked historical sense and could not allow for the element of time that dominates every human calculation, Orwell wanted an immediate resolution of all class differences. This was to be obtained by himself and other middle-class people identifying themselves with the manual worker—not merely with his political aspirations but with his choice of pictures and his taste in food:

It is no use clapping a proletarian on the back and telling him that he is as good a man as I am; if I want real contact with him, I have got to make an effort for which very likely I am unprepared. For to get outside the class-racket I have got to suppress not merely my snobbishness, but most of my other tastes and prejudices as well. I have got to alter myself so completely that in the end I shall hardly be recognizable as the same person. What is involved is not merely the amelioration of working-class conditions, nor an avoidance of the more stupid forms of snobbery, but a complete abandonment of the upper-class and middle-class attitude to life.

In other words, what Orwell is asking for is not "real contact" but identification. Though in argument the book is often misguided (and marred by resentful criticism of the Labour party, the middle classes, the working man who has made money, and many other dummy figures put up to be knocked over), it was a natural reaction from a man of sympathy and courage to the sight at close quarters of honest, capable men living on a pittance in enforced idleness because their country's financial system could not see how to make profit from their labor.

The Road to Wigan Pier was published as a "choice"(the term used for an officially recommended book) of the Left Book Club, which had at that time tens of thousands of members and some influence. It appeared with a foreword by Victor Gollancz, who on behalf of himself and his fellow selectors, John Strachey and Harold Laski, criticized strongly the work he was recommending and recorded that he had "marked well over a hundred minor passages about which I thought I should like to argue with Mr Orwell in this Foreword." However, by the time the book came out, early in 1937, it was too late for its publisher to argue with its author. Orwell had already gone to Spain.

V

IT was Orwell's way, as we have seen, to do at any moment the thing he found most important. In the early part of 1936 it seemed most important to investigate firsthand the life of a depressed area; by Christmas, it was to observe the Spanish Civil War. In each case the backing of a publisher was needed; and since Orwell had now changed publishers, it was the firm of Secker and Warburg that supported his Spanish journey. However, if one wished to see anything when one got to Spain, political contacts were as necessary as money: Orwell's chief connections in England were with the Independent Labour party, a rather forlorn offshoot of the Labour party. The ILP lined up not with the Spanish Communists but with a much smaller group known as the POUM (Partido Obrero de Unificación Marxista), which had Anarchist affiliations. Orwell went with a group that included Bob Smillie (the grandson of a noted miners' leader) and some former gunmen of the Irish Republican Army. Because of his different contacts, his experiences were quite different from those of most foreigners, who went to Spain under Communist auspices and who, if they fought at all, probably joined the International Brigades.

Orwell's behavior when he reached Spain was as typical of him as the manner in which he went. In *Homage to Catalonia*, written after he returned in 1938, he recalled:

I had come to Spain with some notion of writing newspaper articles but I had joined the militia almost immediately, because at that time and in that atmosphere it seemed the only conceivable thing to do.

After a brief parody of training, decked in uniforms so various that Orwell says they should have been called "multiforms," and armed with such weapons as rusty Mausers stamped "1896," he and his fellow militiamen found themselves at the front:

And quite half the so-called men were children—but I mean literally children, of sixteen years old at the very most. Yet they were all happy and excited at the prospect of getting to the front at last.

Fortunately the fighting lines were too far apart for either side to make much contact.

Later, near Huesca, his unit was involved in serious fighting, and it was there at five o'clock one May morning that Orwell was hit. The bullet, according to the Spanish doctors, missed severing Orwell's windpipe and carotid artery "by about a millimetre," passing right through his throat. For two months after this he could not speak above a whisper; then the other vocal chord "compensated" for the one that had been paralyzed. His voice, always flat, had from then on a strange cracked quality of which he was probably unaware.

The wound put an end to Orwell's fighting, but it did not prevent his experiencing the true horror of the war—the ferocious internal dissensions and, in particular, the ruthlessness and treachery of the Communists, which ended by destroying the government side's resistance and paving the way for Franco's victory. It was Orwell's bitter experience to be recovering from a wound in Barcelona when his party, the POUM, was denounced by the Communists, its offices seized, and its leaders imprisoned or liquidated. Militiamen on leave were prevented from returning to the front lest they lower the morale of fellow soldiers fighting, ill-armed and quarter-trained, by letting them know they were accused by men at home (nominally their allies) of being "Fascist spies" and "traitors." Orwell and his wife, who was with him, both took serious risks to help certain of his friends, before themselves escaping across the border into France.

However, the confusion and treachery that it was his lot to meet in Spain exercised an entirely clarifying and strengthening effect on Orwell. Much of his painful concern over class and money values had now been shrugged off in the face of grimmer troubles. There are also glimpses throughout *Homage to Catalonia* of a new capacity to make contact with his fellow men; true, these are only slight encounters—an Italian militiaman met for a moment in the barracks, an officer who shakes his hand when Orwell risks his liberty on behalf of a fellow member of the POUM. But they are real:

This war, in which I played so ineffectual a part, has left me with memories which are mostly evil, and yet I do not wish that I had missed it. . . . Curiously enough, the whole experience has left me with not less but more belief in the decency of human beings.

The reason for this is clear. It is that Orwell had now a more firmly based confidence in his own essential decency and courage.

Homage to Catalonia is a first-rate piece of reporting—vivid, dramatic, remorselessly objective—but an objective picture of the Spanish Civil War had no attraction for the supporters of either side. Those of the Right preferred stories about the desecration of dead nuns' bodies; those of the Left demanded a heroic picture of unity and courage. Of the fifteen hundred copies printed, no more than nine hundred had been sold by the time of Orwell's death; and in America the book was not published until 1952. Its reputation has increased so much that it is now rightly regarded as one of his finest books.

VI

Returning home, Orwell lived quietly in Hertfordshire for the two years before World War II broke out, except for one winter he spent in Morocco, probably because his wound and the hardships he had undergone in Spain had aggravated the lung trouble from which he suffered all his life. The novel he published during 1939—*Coming Up for Air*—was the first book of his to meet with some success, and went into several editions. Once more it is the story of a "solitary," but in this case the solitary is a fat, good-natured man with a ripe and easy humor. George Bowling, a middle-aged insurance salesman, wins a few pounds on a horse and succeeds in concealing it from his wife. He decides to spend the money on a visit to the little country town where he was brought up, which has remained for him the symbol of idyllic peace and rural beauty. He gets there only to find that it has been submerged in the hellish "development" that destroyed so much more of Britain during the twenty years between the wars than the enemy attacks did later and that has continued at an accelerated pace since the last war ended.

The book is written with dash and some enjoyment. Though the insurance man's life is dreary, he is not a dreary character himself. Not until George reaches his hometown does Orwell's passion for "rubbing the reader's nose in it" overcome him and us. When George looks down on Little Binfield, he sees at a glance the hateful transformation that has overtaken his birthplace. So do we. But then for page after page the reader is obliged to accompany George round the town, while he sees what has happened to the old marketplace, the old High Street, the old horse trough, the teashop, the corn merchant's, the churchyard, and, finally, to the girl he once loved and to the most cherished memory of his childhood, the pool where the great fish used to lie.

The book is incidentally memorable for a vivid picture of the effects of bombing, soon to become painfully familiar to millions of Britons, and probably a memory of something Orwell had seen in Spain. The bomb on Lower Binfield (it has fallen by accident in peacetime) sheers away the front of a house, leaving its contents exposed but strangely undisturbed, as intimate and complete as a doll's house with the door open.

This bomb is the open statement of an undercurrent that runs through the book and that had been running through Orwell's writing for some time—a warning of the imminence of war. "I have known since about 1931," he wrote in a war diary of 1940, "that the future must be catastrophic. . . . Since 1934 I have known war between England and Germany was coming, and since 1936 I have known it with complete certainty. I could feel it in my belly."

Before we come to the war and the two books of Orwell's that grew out of it, we should take note again of his essays. Orwell wrote four books of essays: *Inside the Whale* (1940), *Critical Essays* (1946), and two volumes that appeared after his death, *Shooting an Elephant* (1950) and *England Your England* (1953). The latter appeared in the American edition as *Such, Such Were the Joys*, this being the title of an autobiographical essay about his preparatory school life that was left out of the English edition because of possible libel proceedings.

He also wrote *The Lion and the Unicorn* (1941), a sociological tract in the form of a long essay, as well as the text for a picture book, *The English People* (1947), that is descriptive rather than illuminating.

Many of the essays in these books are slight, but there are some that show Orwell's unique qualities to advantage. Because of his sympathy with the lives of ordinary men and women, he chose subjects other writers overlooked; two of the most famous deal with the so-called comics then read by schoolboys and the humorous postcards seen in newsagents' shops at the seaside. His own ambivalent attitude to the empire helped him to write penetratingly, if incompletely, about Kipling; and he makes certain points about Dickens with clarity and force. A delightful humor gleams out at times; of Gandhi's insistence that to take animal food is a sin, even if life is in danger, even if the life is that of a wife or child, Orwell comments, "there must be some limit to what we will do in order to remain alive, and the limit is well on this side of chicken broth."

To many readers a chief interest of the essays will be that they contain the seeds of much of Orwell's other work. "Politics and the English Language" foreshadows his invention of "Newspeak" in *Nineteen Eighty-Four*, and his study of Swift in "Politics vs. Literature" points in the direction of *Animal Farm*.

Once war began, Orwell made repeated efforts to join the army. When these failed, he volunteered for the Home Guard, became a sergeant, and took his duties very seriously, though he was never really at home in his dealings with the physical universe. In the autumn of 1941, by which time the life of an independent writer had become almost impossible, he joined the Indian service of the BBC. Throwing himself into this work with devotion, he insisted on delivering almost all the talks to Malaya, his special field of action, himself.

For the whole period of the war, Orwell consistently overworked; moreover, the conditions of the time affected him far more seriously than they would a person of normal health. Most London offices had their windows largely bricked-up against bombardment, so that one worked always by artificial light in airless rooms. It was common to work far into the night, and not unusual to remain all night, lie down for a few hours on a camp bed, and start the day again. Such conditions were harmful enough for anyone whose lungs had been affected, but in Orwell's case there was another source of weakness. In the last year of the war, Orwell's wife died, collapsing after a quite minor operation. To a friend who visited him, he remarked that this was probably due to lack of strength; both of them, he said, had consistently gone without their rations or part of their rations, "so that there should be more for other people."

VII

In May 1945, the month war with Germany ended, *Animal Farm* was published. By far Orwell's finest book, it did not have an easy passage into print. It had been written between November 1943 and February 1944—"the only one of my books I really sweated over," Orwell said of it. Certainly it is the only one of his books that shows not the least sign of having been sweated over, flowing absolutely clear from start to finish, as though the author had needed to do nothing but copy it out. Four publishers refused it on the ground that at that time it was not possible to print a book attacking a military ally. As events turned out, however, the book's appearance could not have been better timed and it was quickly a best-seller; in America its success was even greater than in Britain.

Animal Farm is a ninety-page satire on Stalinist dictatorship. The animals on a farm unite against their master, Jones. They are successful in getting rid of the tyrant and in managing the practical work of the farm, but they are disastrously unsuccessful in something they had never regarded as a problem—their dealings with each other. The revolution is hardly complete before differences appear: "The pigs did not actually work, but directed and supervised the others. With their superior knowledge it was natural that they should assume the leadership." With the leadership they also assume the buckets of milk yielded by the cows and the apples from the orchard.

"Comrades!" [cried Squealer.] "You do not imagine, I hope, that we pigs are doing this in a spirit of selfishness and privilege? Many of us actually dislike milk and apples. . . . Milk and apples (this has been proved by Science, comrades) contain substances absolutely necessary to the well-being of a pig. We pigs are brain-workers. The whole management and organisation of this farm depend on us. . . . It is for *your* sake that we drink that milk and eat those apples. Do you know what would happen if we pigs failed in our duty? Jones would come back! . . . Surely, comrades,"

cried Squealer almost pleadingly, skipping from side to side and whisking his tail, "surely there is no one among you who wants to see Jones come back?"

Once there is no longer any danger of Jones's return, a new threat must be found to keep the other animals working their hardest, contented in submission to the pigs. The new threat is himself a pig, Snowball, who believes that the proper strategy is to "send out more and more pigeons and stir up rebellion among the animals on the other farms." This is opposed by the pigs' leader, Napoleon, backed by Squealer, who insists that "what the animals must do was to procure firearms and train themselves in the use of them." Long after Snowball has been driven into exile, his name serves as a slogan of hatred: his machinations are held responsible for every failure on the farm, and every animal suspected of disaffection is denounced as an emissary of Snowball:

a goose came forward and confessed to having secreted six ears of corn during the last year's harvest and eaten them in the night. Then a sheep confessed to having urinated in the drinking pool—urged to do this, so she said, by Snowball. . . .

At last the farm is established as a going concern, but the animals are surprised to find that—except for the pigs and their protectors, the watchdogs—life is exactly as hard and painful as it always was. Even their sense of pride as animals is destroyed when, on returning from the fields one evening, they find that the pigs have taken to walking on two legs and carrying whips; meantime, the basic principle of the revolution, "All Animals Are Equal," inscribed on the barn wall after the expulsion of Jones, has been given a qualifying clause: "But Some Animals Are More Equal than Others."

Animal Farm is conceived and written in the classic tradition of satire, the tradition of receding planes, which gives it precisely the depth of every reader. Like *Gulliver's Travels* or *Aesop's Fables*, it makes a delightful children's story. It is manifestly an attack on Stalinism. It can be read as a lament for the fate of revolutions. But it is also a profound and moving commentary on the circumstances of human life: each of us is forced to combine with others in order "to get things done," but must compromise with his own truth and honesty in every combination that he makes. It may be of interest here to mention that *Animal Farm*, like *Nineteen Eighty-Four*, was one of the books used for English instruction in the training of African journalists at the centers in Nairobi and Lagos run by the International Press Institute. *Animal Farm* exercised just the same magic in Africa that it does in Britain and America, and more than one student told me that he was convinced Orwell must have known and been writing about the African state from which he had come.

One question that arises is: How was Orwell, a somewhat irritable man whose writings tended to overemphasize the gloomy aspects of every subject and experience he treated, able in this one book to achieve such admirable good humor and detachment, which at once raises his satire to a higher plane? Disillusion with Communism was a common complaint among Orwell's generation, that is, among those of Orwell's generation whose minds had been at any time receptive. But as a rule this disillusion was expressed in a form either violent or peevish; Orwell himself had contributed to a symposium called *The Betrayal of the Left* (1941), published before the Nazi attack on the USSR caused a swing back in many minds (though not in Orwell's) in favor of the Soviet system.

Part of the answer lies, I think, in Orwell's Spanish experience, which had purged his mind of much personal rancor, enabling him to see events of the day with a new detachment. A friend of Orwell's and a fellow author, T. R. Fyvel, has made the ingenious suggestion that part of the answer also may lie in his having chosen to write about animals rather than human beings. Orwell actively liked animals. "Most of the good memories of my childhood, and up to the age of about twenty," he wrote, "are in some way connected with animals."

Besides money and an international reputation, Orwell achieved with *Animal Farm* something he had been seeking all his life—contact with ordinary people, to whom for the first time he really got across. A mere succès d'estime would never have satisfied him. "I would far rather have written 'Come Where the Booze Is Cheaper' or, 'Two Lovely Black Eyes,'" he declared once in the *Tribune* (the left-wing London magazine of which he was literary editor), "than, say, *The Blessed Damozel* or *Love in a Valley.*"

For two more years Orwell, now a successful author and an established journalist, worked on in London. Then in 1947 he left for the remote island of Jura, off the west coast of Scotland. He was tired. He wished to get on with the writing of *Nineteen Eighty-Four;* and he was anxious, if one takes his own state-ments seriously, to get away, with his adopted son, from possible atomic war. My own impression of Orwell, from the evidence of his life and work and from some personal knowledge, is that if he had expected atomic war, he would certainly have remained in London.

From the point of view of scenery, Jura was delightful, but as a place of recovery for a consumptive he could scarcely have chosen worse. The house was twenty-five miles from the island's only shop, eight of them almost impassable by car. Conditions were primitive and in damp weather the house dripped. Before long he was obliged to go into a hospital near Glasgow; after his release he had to continue making periodic visits to be medically checked, and from Jura every journey was an undertaking.

By 1949 Orwell was ordered by his doctor to go south. He entered a sanatorium in Gloucestershire, from which friends who visited him regularly urged him to come up to London; he was removed before long to University College Hospital. Meantime, by an immense effort, he had succeeded in finishing *Nineteen Eighty-Four:* "It wouldn't have been so gloomy," he said, "if I hadn't been so ill."

Nineteen Eighty-Four, as its title implies, is Orwell's version of the future awaiting mankind. The scene is England, now known as "Airstrip One," which forms part of "Oceania." A ceaseless, pointless war goes rumbling on, a war in which Oceania is in alliance with Eastasia against Eurasia—at least that is the statement put out by the Ministry of Truth. However, nobody any longer feels certain about anything; it is fairly clear that only four years previously Oceania had been in alliance with Eurasia against the common enemy, Eastasia, and by the end of the book the situation has switched back. Though the war is unending, and the population continually stimulated by news of overwhelming victory or sensational defeat, nothing actually happens. An occasional rocket falls. A few prisoners are escorted through the streets. Life becomes steadily a little grimmer, a little meaner; the houses become dirtier and more overcrowded, the food worse. A daily Two Minutes' Hate, directed against the mythical Goldstein (a Trotsky or Snowball figure), distracts people from their sufferings. Everything is controlled by the Party, which is itself controlled by the secret Inner Party; the Party's three slogans are "War Is Peace," "Freedom Is Slavery," and "Ignorance Is Strength."

All apparatus of government is concentrated into four ministries. The Ministry of Truth concerns itself with education, news, the arts—all boiling down in practice to propaganda. The Ministry of Love maintains law and order, largely through the dreaded Thought Police. The Ministry of Plenty keeps everyone down to the barest necessities of life, continually announcing increases in rations that are actually reductions. The Ministry of Peace is occupied with the conduct of the war.

Orwell's central character, Winston Smith, works in the Ministry of Truth, where his job is largely the rewriting of history to suit the shifts of Party policy and removing from previous records the names of persons who have since been "vaporized." In secret revolt against the Party and his own miserable life, Winston Smith keeps a diary in which his private thoughts and feelings are recorded—not an easy matter when there is a telescreen in every room through which the smallest action may be observed. He also permits himself the folly of being attracted to Julia, a girl in another department of his ministry.

One day as he is passing her in the office corridor (it was in an office corridor that Comstock met Rosemary in *Keep the Aspidistra Flying*), she passes him a scrap of paper on which is written "I love you." They succeed in spending a day together, and make love in the open (again like Rosemary and Comstock). From that time on they arrange meetings, usually in a room that he rents above a junk shop. Here they plan conspiracy against the Party and, believing on very little evidence that a fellow member of their staff—a senior called O'Brien—is also a revolutionary, they confide in him. O'Brien proves to be a pillar of the existing order, and Winston is imprisoned, beaten, and tortured until all resistance is burned out of him, and he finally betrays Julia, who has already betrayed him.

The weakness of *Nineteen Eighty-Four* is a double one. Orwell, sick and dispirited, imagined nothing new. His world of 1984 is the wartime world of 1944, but dirtier and more cruel, and with all the endurance and nobility that mankind shows in times of stress mysteriously drained away. Everyone, by 1984, is to be a coward, a spy, and a betrayer.

Even technically, the world has not moved on. The war of 1984 is fought with the weapons of 1944, rockets and tommy guns; all that has happened is that they are now less effective than they used to be, and the horror that distorts life in the future is merely the horror that hung over existence in the author's lifetime. Totalitarianism, with its ceaseless witch-hunts, its secret police—whose charges are never formulated and can therefore never be answered—

covers the whole world instead of only a large part of it, and all alleviating aspects have been removed.

The book's second weakness is another expression of the first. By amputating courage and self-sacrifice from his human beings, Orwell has removed any real tension from his story. The only challenge to totalitarianism must derive from the individual's assertion of personal values and beliefs against mass standards, and from the upholding of human love against artificially stimulated hate. This Winston Smith is incapable of doing: he is a feeble creature in himself and can draw no strength from his relationship with Julia, since what he feels for her is not love; it is not even lust, but merely a tepid mixture of attraction and contempt.

Though these two failures undermine the interest of the book, it has importance for our age as a warning: this is what happens if the state is allowed to become all-powerful. It also contains one notable invention that has contributed words and phrases to our common speech. This is Newspeak, the version of the English language approved by the Party:

The purpose of Newspeak was not only to provide a medium of expression for the world-view and mental habits proper to the devotees of Ingsoc [English Socialism] but to make all other modes of thought impossible. It was intended that when Newspeak had been adopted once and for all and Oldspeak forgotten, a heretical thought—that is, a thought diverging from the principles of Ingsoc—should be literally unthinkable, at least so far as thought is dependent on words. . . . To give a single example. The word *free* still existed in Newspeak, but it could only be used in such statements as "This dog is free from lice" or "This field is free from weeds." It could not be used in its old sense of "politically free" or "intellectually free," since political and intellectual freedom no longer existed even as concepts, and were therefore of necessity nameless.

During the last months of his life Orwell married again. His second wife was Sonia Brownell, whom he had known for some years and who, as editorial assistant on the magazine *Horizon*, had been involved in the publication of some of his essays. With her Orwell discussed his plans for future work: he intended to make a complete break from his former polemical, propagandist way of writing and to concentrate on the treatment of human relationships. He had actually roughed out a story in the new manner, but it was destined never to be completed.

George Orwell died on 23 January 1950, a few minutes following a tubercular hemorrhage. He was not yet forty-seven.

SELECTED BIBLIOGRAPHY

I. Bibliography. I. R. Willison, *George Orwell: Some Materials for a Bibliography* (London, 1953); Z. G. Zeke and W. White, "George Orwell: A Selected Bibliography," in *Bulletin of Bibliography*, 23, no. 5 (May–August 1961); Z. G. Zeke and W. White, "Orwelliana," in *Bulletin of Bibliography*, 23, nos. 6–7 (September–December 1961 and January–April 1962); I. R. Willison and I. Angus, "George Orwell: Bibliographical Addenda," in *Bulletin of Bibliography*, 24, no. 8 (September–December 1965); J. Meyers, "George Orwell: A Bibliography," in *Bulletin of Bibliography*, 31, no. 3 (July–September 1974).

II. Collected Works. *The Uniform Edition* (London, 1948–1960); *The Orwell Reader: Fiction, Essays, and Reportage by George Orwell* (New York, 1956); *Selected Essays* (London, 1957); G. Bott, ed., *Selected Writings* (New York, 1958); *Collected Essays* (London, 1961); S. Orwell and I. Angus, eds., *The Collected Essays, Journalism and Letters of George Orwell* (New York–London, 1968), vol. I: *An Age Like This, 1920–1940*, vol. II: *My Country, Right or Left, 1940–1943*, vol. III: *As I Please, 1943–1945*; vol. IV: *In Front of Your Nose, 1945–1950*.

III. Separate Works. *Down and Out in Paris and London* (London, 1933), autobiography; *Burmese Days* (New York, 1934), novel; *A Clergyman's Daughter* (London, 1935), novel; *Keep the Aspidistra Flying* (London, 1936), novel; *The Road to Wigan Pier* (London, 1937), sociology; *Homage to Catalonia* (London, 1938), history; *Coming Up for Air* (London, 1939), novel.

Inside the Whale, and Other Essays (London, 1940), contains "Inside the Whale," "Charles Dickens," "Boys' Weeklies"; *The Lion and the Unicorn: Socialism and the English Genius* (London, 1941), pamphlet; *Animal Farm: A Fairy Story* (London, 1945), satire; *James Burnham and the Managerial Revolution* (London, 1946), pamphlet; *Critical Essays* (London, 1946), contains "Charles Dickens," "Boys' Weeklies," "Wells, Hitler, and the World State," "The Art of Donald McGill," "Rudyard Kipling," "W. B. Yeats," "Benefit of Clergy: Some Notes on Salvador Dali," "Arthur Koestler," "Raffles and Miss Blandish," "In Defence of P. G. Wodehouse"; *The English People* (London, 1947), essay, in the "Britain in Pictures" series; *Nineteen Eight-Four: A Novel* (London, 1949).

Shooting an Elephant, and Other Essays (London, 1950), contains "Shooting an Elephant," "A Hanging," "How the Poor Die," "Lear, Tolstoy and the Fool," "Politics vs. Literature: An Examination of *Gulliver's Travels*," "Politics and the English Language," "Reflections on Gandhi," "The Prevention of Literature," "Second Thoughts on James Burnham," "I Write as I Please," "Confessions of a Book Reviewer," "Books vs. Cigarettes," "Good Bad Books," "Nonsense Poetry," "Riding Down from Bangor," "The Sporting Spirit," "Decline of the English Murder," "Some Thoughts on the Common Toad," "A Good Word for the Vicar of Bray"; *Such, Such Were the Joys* (New York, 1953), contains "Such, Such Were the Joys," autobiography, and the following essays: "Why I Write," "Writers and Leviathan," "North and South," "Notes on Nationalism," "Anti-Semitism in Britain," "Poetry and the Microphone," "Inside the Whale," "Marrakech," "Looking Back on the Spanish War," "Down the Mine," "England Your England"; *England Your England, and Other Essays* (London, 1953), the English edition of *Such, Such Were the Joys*, without the autobiography.

Note: Orwell contributed to V. Gollancz, ed. *The Betrayal of the Left* (London, 1941), an examination and refutation of Communist policy from 1939 to January 1941, and to *Talking to India* (London, 1942), a series of broadcasts. He wrote an introduction to Jack London's *Love of Life and Other Stories* (London, 1941) and to the first two vols. of selections from *British Pamphleteers* (London, 1948). The Orwell archive at University College, London, contains, among other things, letters and unpublished Ph.D. theses on Orwell. A wartime diary by Orwell appeared in a special number of *World Review* (June 1950) that also contains a number of personal and critical tributes to him.

IV. Biographical and Critical Studies. J. Atkins, *George Orwell: A Literary Study* (London, 1954; new ed., 1971); L. Brander, *George Orwell* (London, 1954); C. Hollis, *A Study of George Orwell: The Man and His Works* (London, 1956).

R. Heppenstall, *Four Absentees* (London, 1960), reminiscences of Orwell and others; R. Rees, *George Orwell: Fugitive from the Camp of Victory* (London, 1961); R. J. Voorhees, *The Paradox of George Orwell* (Lafayette, Ind., 1961); J. Strachey, *The Strangled Cry, and Other Unparliamentary Papers* (London, 1963), contains an essay on Orwell; S. J. Greenblatt, *Three Modern Satirists: Waugh, Orwell and Huxley* (New Haven, Conn., 1965); R. A. Lee, *Orwell's Fiction* (Notre Dame, 1965); E. M. Thomas, *Orwell* (Edinburgh, 1965); G. Woodcock, *The Crystal Spirit: A Study of George Orwell* (Boston, 1966); B. T. Oxley, *George Orwell* (London, 1967); J. Calder, *Chronicles of Conscience: A Study of George Orwell and Arthur Koestler* (London, 1968); K. Alldritt, *The Making of George Orwell: An Essay in Literary History* (London, 1969).

M. Gross, ed., *The World of George Orwell* (London, 1971); S. Hynes, ed., *Twentieth Century Interpretations of "1984": A Collection of Critical Essays* (Englewood Cliffs, N. J., 1971); R. Williams, *Orwell* (London, 1971); D. L. Kubal, *Outside the Whale: George Orwell's Art and Politics* (Notre Dame, 1972); P. Stansky and W. Abrahams, *George Orwell. The Transformation* (London, 1972); P. Stansky and W. Abrahams, *The Unknown Orwell* (London, 1972); H. Ringbom, *George Orwell as Essayist: A Stylistic Study* (Åbo, 1973); J. Buddicom, *Eric and Us: A Remembrance of George Orwell* (London, 1974); A. Sandison, *The Last Man in Europe: An Essay on George Orwell* (New York–London, 1974); R. Williams, ed.,

George Orwell: A Collection of Critical Essays (Englewood Cliffs, N. J., 1974), in the "Twentieth-Century Views" series; Alex Zwerdling, *Orwell and the Left* (New Haven, Conn., 1974); J. Meyers, *A Reader's Guide to George Orwell* (London, 1975); C. Small, *The Road to Miniluv: George Orwell, the State and God* (London, 1975); J. Meyers, ed., *George Orwell: The Critical Heritage* (London, 1975); W. Steinhoff, *The Road to "1984"* (London, 1975), published in the U.S. as *George Orwell and the Origins of "1984"* (Ann Arbor, Mich., 1975), includes a bibliography; A. Burgess, *Nineteen Eighty-Five* (London, 1978), the first half is a searching criticism of *Nineteen Eighty-Four* and the second consists of Burgess' own predictions.

B. Crick, *George Orwell: A Life* (London, 1980); L. Smyer, *Orwell's Development as a Psychological Novelist* (St. Louis, 1980); T. R. Fyvel, *George Orwell: A Personal Memoir* (New York, 1982).

EVELYN WAUGH

(1903-1966)

William Myers

EVELYN WAUGH seems always to have realized that as a writer and probably as a man he needed a lot of attention. "How badly I write when there is no audience to arrange my thoughts for," he noted in his diary (18 April 1926).[1] With his first two novels he secured just such an audience, and for the rest of his life he was a public figure, continually invited to make pronouncements on a vast range of topics, which he willingly, if somewhat cantankerously, did. Nor did he keep his views out of his novels. Fiction, he maintained, is an "exercise in the use of language"; an author can expect his readers to want the same effects as he does, and, prompted by his material, he can "throw out a number of personal opinions and theories" for their consideration (*Spectator*, 6 November 1942). From the beginning, therefore, Waugh was a didactic writer.

His first novel, *Decline and Fall* (1928), tells the story of a young innocent, Paul Pennyfeather, who is unjustly sent down from Oxford and finds himself teaching at Llanabba Castle, a ludicrous Welsh boarding school. There he meets the exquisite Margot Beste-Chetwynde, the mother of a favorite pupil. They are on the point of being married when he is arrested for organizing the international prostitution racket that is the source of her considerable wealth, and sent to prison. However, his death is faked, and he returns to Oxford to start his life anew. Margot marries a retired politician, Lord Metroland—but takes as a lover the very Alastair Digby-Vane-Trumpington whose drunken party first set Paul off on his adventures. Waugh structures this absurd story around a series of comic characters who keep reappearing. The novel opens and closes with descriptions of a drunken undergraduate party. The central figure at the first is Alastair—handsome, decent, not very bright; the second is dominated by Margot's son, Peter (now Lord Pastmaster), an intelligent, attractive young man who lost his innocence too soon. (When we first meet him, his favorite books are a children's story and a pioneering study in sexual psychopathology.) Without compromising the novel's effortless amorality, these opening and closing scenes provide the framework of a genuine fall from innocent freshness to worldly-wise knowledge.

Vile Bodies (1930) is structurally less satisfactory. It tells the story of Adam Fenwick-Symes's engagement to Nina Blount. In a succession of parties, hangovers, and fatal motorcar races (Adam is temporarily a gossip columnist), they keep getting and losing the thousand pounds that will enable them to marry. Finally, to pay a hotel bill, Adam "sells" Nina to a man called Ginger. Later he and Nina spend an adulterous Christmas together, but war breaks out, and Adam finally gets possession of his (now worthless) money on the field of battle. In spite of its weak ending *Vile Bodies* shares many memorable qualities with *Decline and Fall*, including an economy of statement and incident reminiscent of the furniture and buildings of the interwar years—a style Waugh mocks but which his technique reflects. Much of his reputation for heartlessness comes from this economical style. Lady Circumference's brief remarks in *Decline and Fall* about the trivial injury, cruel decay, and painful death of her son, Tangent, are typical. So are the passing references to Adam's money in *Vile Bodies*.

Another of Waugh's devices is to use flagrantly inappropriate language. The descriptions of the Welsh bandsmen in *Decline and Fall*, for example, are staggeringly offensive: "On seeing the Doctor they halted and edged back, those behind squinting and moulting over their companions' shoulders" (1.8).

[1] All quotations are from Penguin Books editions, as the most generally available, except for quotations from the travel books, which are from first editions. References are to the dates of entries in the *Diaries*, to page numbers of the *Letters* and travel books, and to part and chapter numbers of other works.

Equally characteristic is the slangy exchange between Adam and Ginger over Nina's "sale." Waugh's incidents and characters are quite as outrageous as his vocabulary. In *Decline and Fall*, a pederastic public school man, Captain Grimes, is forced into bigamous marriage with the headmaster's hideous daughter and has to fake suicide to escape. Later a prison chaplain has his head sawn off by a madman.

Not all this extravagance succeeds. The stories of Philbrick the mad butler in *Decline and Fall* and the ludicrous scenario of a film about John Wesley in *Vile Bodies* are overdone, but Waugh's grotesquerie generally pleases. So does his celebration of glamour, laced as it is with high eroticism. The future Margot Metroland's first appearance—"two lizard-skin feet, silk legs, chinchilla body, a tight little black hat, pinned with platinum and diamonds, and the high invariable voice that may be heard in any Ritz Hotel from New York to Budapest" (*Decline and Fall* 1.8)—is justly celebrated.

Astonishingly, much of the material of these early novels has a basis in personal experience. As an undergraduate, Waugh at first lived a relatively respectable life, like Paul Pennyfeather. He then joined a fashionable set, more decadent than Alastair Trumpington's, and came down with a poor degree and a taste for drunken parties. He taught in two schools; in one he formed a faintly amorous attachment to two boys, models for Peter Beste-Chetwynde; in the other he met the original Captain Grimes, and himself attempted the farcical suicide he attributes to the latter. Later he worked briefly on the *Daily Express*. More significantly, his relations with his first wife, whom he married in 1928 and from whom he was divorced a year later, were very like those between Adam and Nina. All of Waugh's later books were to be similarly based on his experiences.

But there is an even more personal element in his writings. They are full of private jokes and portraits of friends and acquaintances. Waugh wrote for two kinds of reader—the public and a group of initiates, not all friends but all in his social circle. Some of these jokes are relatively trivial. He introduces the names of his Oxford tutor, C. R. M. F. Cruttwell, and the critic Cyril Connolly, for example, into deliberately undignified contexts. More seriously, in *Black Mischief* (1932), he gives his own nickname, Boaz, to the leader of fashion among "cosmopolitan blacks . . . and . . . the decayed Arab intelligentsia" (ch. 5); Boaz ends up murdering the young emperor

and being himself murdered. There are similarly ambiguous allusions to friends. The amoral Basil Seal of *Black Mischief, Put Out More Flags* (1942), and *Basil Seal Rides Again* (1963) is recognizably the one-time husband of Waugh's close friend Nancy Mitford. Sebastian Flyte in *Brideshead Revisited* (1945) is partly based on the great friend of Waugh's youth, Alastair Graham (his mother is the original Lady Circumference). And both Harold Acton and Brian Howard contribute to the ambivalent figures of Ambrose Silk in *Put Out More Flags* and Anthony Blanche in *Brideshead Revisited*. There is little doubt that Waugh and his friends realized that in time this side of his work would become known to the public, and that the effects he achieved by thus weaving personal allusions into books designed for general consumption would cease to be a merely private pleasure. That, however, was for the future.

What struck the readers of his first two novels was their bright, modern surface. Waugh builds his narrative out of short sequences of externally observed incidents and snatches of dialogue that expose, excite, and conceal with the impersonality of the film or the gossip column. Thus the first four chapters of *Vile Bodies* are constructed around the secret that the mousy Miss Brown, who urges the bright young things to finish their party at her house, is in fact the prime minister's daughter. Waugh reveals this important detail at exactly the right moment. The ensuing scandal brings down the government, an unforeseeable event mysteriously anticipated by the Jesuit Father Rothschild. Meanwhile a customs officer burns Adam's manuscript autobiography as obscene, his friend Agatha Runcible—later to die after a car crash and a hospital drinking party—is strip-searched, and the appalling evangelist Mrs. Melrose Ape arrives in England with the chorus girls she dresses as angels at her revivalist meetings. Margot Metroland later appraises them "one by one, with an expert eye" (ch. 6). The adroitness with which Waugh edits this material makes the first six chapters of *Vile Bodies* one of the funniest tours de force in English fiction.

A no less subtle ingredient of these first two novels, however, is their recognition of human vulnerability. Paul Pennyfeather is a generally colorless character, but he becomes touchingly alive once he is attracted to Margot. Margot herself is allowed her moments of vulnerability too—in a reference to her as a "romantic young heiress who had walked entranced among the cut yews, and had been wooed, how phlegmatically, in the odour of honeysuckle" (2.1) and when she visits Paul in prison. The most serious character in *Decline and Fall*, however, is Margot's son, Peter, capably greeting his mother's degenerate guests while she lies in her room fragrantly sedated, yet unable to stop admiring himself before Paul's wedding, and turning white when Paul is arrested. His final scene with Paul, in which he keeps referring to Margot's marriage to the recently ennobled Lord Metroland, is especially well written. "You know you ought never to have got mixed up with me and the Metroland," he tells Paul (epilogue): it is painful to hear Peter referring to his mother so crudely. In *Vile Bodies* Peter bitterly tells his stepfather to "go to hell" when the latter draws attention to Alastair's hat on the hall table (ch. 5). The lovers in *Vile Bodies* also have their moments of vulnerability: Adam when he dances by himself in Margot's hall, Nina when she nervously admits to being a virgin. Touches such as these are crucial to Waugh's art. Thus the entire history of Margot's first marriage is encapsulated in the two words "how phlegmatically."

Waugh is less adroit, however, in "throwing out" his "personal opinions and theories" in the two early novels. Like T. S. Eliot's *The Waste Land*, a poem Waugh greatly admired, both *Decline and Fall* and *Vile Bodies* present a series of fragmented images of English society in decay. In addition (and unlike Eliot) Waugh tries to give explicit expression to some of the values against which modernity offends. He uses Professor Silenus in *Decline and Fall* and Father Rothschild in *Vile Bodies* for this purpose, but the key speeches of both are inchoate and shallow, and are dressed up in pretentious symbolism: Silenus compares "life" to "the big wheel at Luna Park" (3.7); Father Rothschild speaks of the "almost fatal hunger for permanence" shown by divorce (ch. 8).

The world of *Vile Bodies* is a kind of vorticist nightmare: "I thought we were all driving round and round in a motor race and none of us could stop," says the dying Agatha Runcible (ch. 12). *Vile Bodies* ends literally in nightmare—an invented world war—an indication, perhaps, that fashionable modernity on its own was insufficient to sustain Waugh's art. He himself hated *Vile Bodies*, which he had to complete while his marriage was breaking up. He told Harold Acton that he felt "chained" to it: "It is a welter of sex and snobbery" (*Letters*, p. 37). To Henry Yorke he wrote: "It all seems to shrivel up & rot internally and I am relying on a sort of cumula-tive futility for any effect it may have" (*Letters*, p. 39).

Waugh's imagination, however, had resources other than the contemporary scene, resources ultimately attributable to his roots in a traditionally minded upper-middle-class home. He was the son of a publisher and writer, Arthur Waugh. Before the drunken orgies and homosexual romances of his undergraduate days, he had had an excellent education at a High Anglican boarding school, which gave him a thorough grounding in the classics and encouraged his talents as a draftsman, and from which he won a history scholarship to Oxford. He was naturally religious; even in his dissolute post-Oxford days he thought about ordination. He was also a natural craftsman. In one of his early travel books, *Ninety-Two Days* (1934), he compares the writer's desire to reduce the amorphous experience of life into communicable form with the carpenter's itch to shape a piece of rough timber. More surprisingly for a young man of his generation, he was a connoisseur of Victorian painting and furniture. In 1926 he published *P.R.B., An Essay on the Pre-Raphaelite Brotherhood 1847–1854*, and in 1928 his first book, *Rossetti*, on the Victorian painter and poet. In all his books his descriptions of buildings are careful and technically accurate.

Granted this interest in traditional craftsmanship and the Victorian period, the influence of Victorian novelists on his work is to be expected, notably that of Charles Dickens, whom Waugh often ridicules but whom he also calls "the most daemonic of the masters" in *The Ordeal of Gilbert Pinfold* (1957). The headmaster's daughter in *Decline and Fall* is reminiscent of Fanny Squeers in Dickens' *Nicholas Nickleby*, and the fantasies of Philbrick are told with a Dickensian relish. Another Victorian influence is William Makepeace Thackeray. Like Waugh, Thackeray was of middle-class origins and made his reputation writing about the lives of the very well-to-do—city merchants and a decaying nobility. Thackeray's view of the social scene was cynically detached; he highlighted the artificiality of his texts and was a gifted parodist. From him Waugh learned the art of casually introducing characters from earlier novels as background figures in later ones. This gives the reader a sense of privileged familiarity with the author's world and provides the writer with an invaluable shorthand for making moral points or achieving comic effects.

Important as these mid-Victorian influences are,

however, Waugh is better understood as a novelist of the age immediately following it. The world of the mid-Victorian novel is insular, commercial, and optimistic. From about 1870 English culture became increasingly imperialist, pessimistic, and inclined to decadence. (Waugh parodies Decadent works like Aubrey Beardsley's *Under the Hill* in *Decline and Fall*, 1928.) The novelists of this "age of imperialism"—the seventy-year period from about 1870 to 1940—were less insular than their Victorian predecessors. Foreigners were no longer "comic" Frenchmen, "heavy" Germans, and "brash" Americans, but Chinese, Indians, Arabs, and black Africans—by turns exotic, savage, possessed of the ancient wisdom or the ancient terrors of "primitive" man, or informed with cultural traditions at least as venerable as those of Europe.

Victorian confidence in the rightness of Western science and Western religion was undercut by these new cultural perspectives. Yet it fell to many of the most intelligent of the British, educated first at boarding schools and then at Oxford, Cambridge, or the military academies, to govern where they were emotionally, intellectually, and sometimes even morally least secure. The fiction of this time returns repeatedly to stories of isolated individuals stumbling against the limitations of their class-based and race-based beliefs, and then staking out for themselves a new area of order, psychological and political, against a background of incipient anarchy and personal disintegration. In Britain itself, of course, this territory of order was secured institutionally, in schools, country houses, London society, the armed services, and possibly the Church of England. But Waugh and his generation were unable to identify themselves wholly with the blander assumptions and professed self-confidence of this English world. Waugh himself was too conservative and pessimistic, too fearful of the consequences of anarchy, to wish to see it overthrown as some of his contemporaries did. On the other hand he was not afraid to observe it with the satirical detachment of a disillusioned initiate.

This certainly is the stance of the travel books and his two historical works, the biography *Edmund Campion: Jesuit and Martyr* (1935) and *Helena* (1950), the postwar novel about the emperor Constantine's mother, reputed discoverer of the cross on which Christ was crucified. Taken together, these works offer a full account of "imperialist" geography, history, and psychology, as interpreted by a writer who openly admitted his fascination with "distant lands and barbarous places, and in particular . . . the borderlands of conflicting cultures and states of development" (*Ninety-Two Days*, p. 13). For Waugh and many of his contemporaries, travel was a way of putting both their own characters and Western culture to the test. It also had overtones of sexual license and personal liberation. Waugh was a habitué of foreign brothels and was excited by perversion, slavery, primitive nudity, and the sexual implications of racial dominance.

Indeed it was precisely because travel liberated such feelings in himself that it also confirmed his commitment to law, order, and "civilization." "Civilization . . . is under constant assault," he writes in *Robbery Under Law* (1939); we are all "potential recruits for anarchy." The "positive work" required of the conservative, therefore, is to keep that anarchy at bay. In *Helena* the future emperor Constantius sees the great wall protecting the imperial frontiers in just these terms, as "a single great girdle round the civilized world; inside, peace, decency, the law, the altars of the Gods, industry, the arts, order; outside, wild beasts and savages, forest and swamp, bloody mumbo-jumbo, men like wolf-packs" (ch. 3).

Precisely because he felt the attractions of "bloody mumbo-jumbo" so strongly in himself, Waugh was able to despise the racialist attitudes of those of his countrymen who pretended they did not. "What," he wonders in his first travel book, *Labels* (1930), "gives the Anglo-Saxons, alone among the colonists of the world [their] ungenerous feeling of superiority over their neighbours?" (p. 187). Of the Arabs in Port Said he writes: "Their intensely human joviality and inquisitiveness, their animal-like capacity for waking-up and sleeping in the dust, their unembarrassed religious observances, their courtesy to strangers, their uncontrolled fecundity, the dignity of their old men, make an interesting contrast with the wrangling and resentment of northern slums" (p. 86).

While writing *Labels* Waugh had come to believe that the superficiality and triviality of contemporary attitudes were such as to vitiate almost entirely Western claims to cultural superiority over most other peoples. What particularly dismayed him was the sense of history characteristic of his generation:

It consists of a vague knowledge of . . . social, religious, and political institutions, of drama, of the biographies of the chief characters of each century, of . . . scraps of diaries and correspondence and family history. . . . This sense of the Past . . . colours our outlook on our own age. We wonder . . . how . . . this absurd little jumble of antagonising forces, of negro rhythm and psycho-analysis, of mechanical invention and decaying industry, of infinitely expanding means of communication and infinitely receding substance of the communicable, of liberty and inertia, how will this ever cool down and crystallise out?

(p. 40)

The world, in other words, is opaque and chaotic; reason and order are necessary illusions. This is a common "imperialist" view, but Waugh was not to hold it for long. Before the publication of *Labels*, he had become a Roman Catholic, an event of the first importance in his life and for his art, the implications of which require separate consideration.

The church that Waugh joined in 1930 was in many respects itself an imperialist institution. In 1870 papal authority had been reinforced by the First Vatican Council's definition of papal infallibility. Throughout the next seventy years, Catholic missionary activity expanded steadily. Everywhere Waugh traveled he encountered Catholic priests imposing their little patches of ecclesiastical law and order alongside the functionaries of secular empires. Catholicism also fitted happily into Waugh's sense of the Mediterranean as the historical center of civilization. (He refers to it in *The Ordeal of Gilbert Pinfold* as that "splendid enclosure which held all the world's history and half the happiest memories of his own life" [ch. 6].)

More parochially, English Catholicism appealed to Waugh's sense of social class. Most of his fellow Catholics in England were Irish and working class or lower middle class. But there were Catholics also among the most ancient and socially superior families in the country, families that had held onto the old faith during the dark days of Tudor persecution. In addition, a number of distinguished Englishmen had become Catholics in the nineteenth century. There was much in English Catholicism, therefore, to appeal to the worldling and the snob in Waugh.

The real appeal of the church, however, was that it apparently solved the problem of historical and moral insecurity expressed in *Labels*. Here were an eternal empire and certitudes that commanded profounder assent than the provisional pragmatism of beleaguered conservatism. Nor was the faith anti-intellectual: anyone familiar with traditional Catholic thought can recognize allusions in Waugh's work

(sometimes ironic, sometimes serious) to highly recondite ideas. Besides, it was not in his nature to become a tamely conformist Catholic. Some of his clerical characters, notably in *Helena*, are as unattractive as they are typical, and the *Letters* and *Diaries* contain many tart references to churchmen and church affairs, including a less than overawed account of his private audience with the pope in 1945.

Nevertheless, Catholicism gave Waugh a sense that at bottom things were simple. Helena roundly declares her preference for facts over ideas; in *Remote People* (1931) Waugh contends that theology is "the science of simplification by which nebulous and elusive ideas become formalised and made intelligible and exact" (p. 88); at "the root of all Catholic apologetics," he writes in *Edmund Campion*, lies "the claim . . . that the Faith is absolutely satisfactory to the mind, enlisting all knowledge and all reason in its cause; that it is completely compelling to any who give it an 'indifferent and quiet audience'" (ch. 3).

Waugh realized, however, that that word "any" had dangerous implications for traditional conservatism: in the end Christianity leaves no room for human hierarchies. In the nineteenth century Cardinal Newman, in his *Apologia*, had claimed that the illiterate peasant or naked savage had ways of grasping the truth as rational as the philosopher's, and that in any case "a lazy, ragged, filthy, story-telling beggar woman . . . had a prospect of heaven, such as was absolutely closed to an accomplished statesman, or lawyer, or noble, be he ever so just, upright, generous, honourable, and conscientious, unless he had also some portion of the divine Christian graces."

Christianity thus pulls down the walls of the empire and obliterates distinctions of race and class. In *Helena*, Waugh writes:

A Thracian or a Teuton might stop a fellow countryman in the streets, embrace him and speak of home in his own language. Not so Helena and the Christians. The intimate family circle of which she was a member bore no mark of kinship. The barrow-man . . . in the gutter, . . . the lawyer or the lawyer's clerk, might each and all be one with the Empress Dowager in the Mystical Body. And the abounding heathen might in any hour become one with them.

(ch. 8)

The church is not a substitute for human empires, against which it is in any case powerless. *Helena* is full of ironic indications that all the folly, corruption, and self-importance of Roman imperial politics will reappear in later empires, the victory of Christianity notwithstanding. Similarly in *Edmund Campion* worldly success follows the self-aggrandizing "new men" of Tudor England; the Catholics, of "good" family or of none, are rendered powerless. This comprehensive dismissal of all political effort has, of course, conservative implications. If "no form of government is ordained of God as better than any other" (*Robbery Under Law*, pp. 16–17), there are no grounds in principle for radical political change. Is it possible, then, after all, that Catholicism makes no difference? Critics have been tempted to draw such a conclusion on the strength of Waugh's next two novels, *Black Mischief* (1932) and *A Handful of Dust* (1934). Only a careful reading shows them to be wrong.

Black Mischief is set in Azania, a fictitious African island peopled by Arabs and Africans. It boasts an ancient, heretical Christian church and a new ruling dynasty, founded by Amurath, the son of a slave, who was in turn succeeded by his daughter and her son, Seth. But when the novel opens, Seth's throne is in danger because education in the West has left him insecure and incompetent. He is saved by a white mercenary called Connolly, the rival claimant (who is actually Seth's father) being killed and eaten by mountain tribesmen. But Seth falls under the influence of Basil Seal, whom he knew as an undergraduate. Basil makes love to the British minister's daughter, Prudence, and negotiates cynical commercial deals with various parties. He quarrels with Connolly over the issue of boots to the army, which are eventually eaten by the soldiers; Seth backs Basil and alienates the Nestorian patriarch and the old black nobility by campaigning for the introduction of birth control into Azania. A long-forgotten son of Amurath (kept naked and in chains for decades by Nestorian monks) is wheeled out and crowned. Two English ladies campaigning against cruelty to animals have to be rescued during the ensuing disturbances, as a prelude to the flight by air of the entire British legation. But their plane crashes. Basil meanwhile tries to save Seth but finds that he has been murdered, and that he himself has inadvertently dined on the remains of Prudence. Unabashed, he returns to London. Britain and France take over Azania, Connolly is exiled (largely on account of his African wife, Black Bitch), and the sole beneficiary of all this turmoil seems to be the charming and sublimely selfish Armenian trader Mr. Youkoumian.

In language as in plot, *Black Mischief* seems at first to be a thoroughly offensive book. In a Port Said brothel Basil discusses the monetary systems of the world with a Dutch South African while four native dancing girls huddle together "in the corner like chimpanzees" (ch. 3). Later Connolly's black wife lifts "her dress and wipes her hands on her knickers" before accepting an invitation to dine at the French legation (ch. 5). We are even asked to believe that the Azanians are capable of assuming that the visiting English ladies are in *favor* of cruelty to animals: "Ladies and gentlemen, we must be Modern," declares Viscount Boaz at the banquet in their honor, "we must be refined in our Cruelty to Animals. That is the message of the New Age" (ch. 6). The joke seems to be that the primitive, animal-like Azanians are ludicrously inept in their attempts to assimilate Western culture. Seth's only comment on the Wanda's method of disposing of his father, for example, is that they are "barbarous . . . totally out of touch with modern thought. . . . They need education. . . . We might start them with Montessori methods" (ch. 1).

The novel seemed particularly offensive to Waugh's fellow Catholics. The *Tablet*, a Catholic weekly, objected to Prudence's affair with Basil; his eating her "stewed to pulp among peppers and aromatic roots" (ch. 7); a scene in which Alastair Trumpington and his wife, Sonia, entertain their friends in a bed on which their dog keeps making a mess; the birth control pageant; the ridicule of the two humane ladies; and Waugh's treatment of the Nestorian monastery, with its venerated cross "which had fallen from heaven quite unexpectedly during Good Friday luncheon some years back" (ch. 6). In his own defense Waugh maintained that he was attacking the corruptions of a heretical and schismatic church, not his own. This argument is a little disingenuous since the Nestorian church has a great deal in common with European Catholicism, including "muscular Christians" eager "to have a whack at the modernists and Jews" (ch. 6).

It is not just European Christianity but the whole of Western society that is gruesomely mirrored in the world of Azania. The Earl of Ngumo, who arrives late and drunk at Seth's victory ball demanding "some gin and some women and some raw camel's meat for my men outside" (ch. 4), is obviously a caricature, and not just of a cannibal chief but of a Tory backwoods peer as well. As such, however, he and other characters like him in the novel, notably

Boaz, the Youkoumians, and the British minister, help to resolve some of the difficulties it raises. They belong to the world of farce, not of satire. Accordingly Waugh's second line of defense is that the novel's characters are not "real people" at all (*Letters*, p. 73). He is no more attacking ecclesiastical corruption or African primitivism or the diplomatic service in this novel than he was attacking boarding schools and British prisons in *Decline and Fall*. Finally, to those who accuse him of racism, he can point to the barren absurdity of life in the French and British legations compared to the natural fecundity and vigor of the Azanians. It is Seth's European education, not his African blood, that has left him "strapped down to mean dimensions" (ch. 1).

None of these arguments, however, has more than limited force. Seth might have been more comfortable in the naked intimacy of a mud hut, but Azanian life remains unutterably cruel. (Waugh was disgusted by the brutalities he encountered on his visit to Abyssinia for the imperial coronation in 1930.) Nor are all the novel's characters as unreal as the humane ladies and Prudence's parents. Seth is real enough; so is the wildly romantic Prudence during her seedy little affair with Basil. This makes it quite impossible to compare her death with that of the prison chaplain in *Decline and Fall*, whose unreality is unquestionable. The cannibal scene is thus irreducibly serious.

We can come to terms with it, however, if we read the text as an arrangement of Waugh's thoughts for the audience that had read and relished his two earlier novels, an audience he clearly expects to be seduced by the "corker" Basil Seal, to delight in the stealing of Lady Seal's emeralds, to relish Basil's sadistically terrifying the ladies in the besieged legation, and to feel relieved and justified when he proves unexpectedly loyal to Seth. But that audience has then to face the fact that Basil eats Prudence and emerges unscathed from the experience. This is the point at which Waugh in effect challenges the reader. In *Black Mischief* Waugh hardly alludes to his new faith, but he knows that the novel will be read as the work of a notorious man-about-town, divorcé, and Catholic convert, and he therefore offers the reader in the person of Basil an embodiment of a universality that perversely reflects that of the church. Basil moves freely on both sides of the imperial frontier, and in a horrifying parody of the Eucharist he obliterates distinctions between the primitive and the civilized on which secular imperialism is based. Im-

plicitly Waugh says to his readers: "You liberals, colonialists, and decent agnostic pragmatists—you laugh at my jokes, and are excited like me by wealth, sex, barbarity, and power—but can you face the implications, for society and for yourselves, of identifying with Basil Seal and recognizing him as Everyman? If you cannot, then perhaps I have resources you lack. However, I leave it to you to find out what they are."

Waugh's next novel, *A Handful of Dust*, makes essentially the same points by exactly opposite means. It too mingles an English upper-class world with that of a primitive people, but in proportions that reverse those of *Black Mischief*. Like Basil, its hero, Tony Last, is the only character to unite the two worlds; but unlike Basil he is naive, honorable, and innocent, the creature, not the maker, of circumstance. Yet he is a universal figure, too, in his fashion. What sort of world is it, the reader asks, in which such decency can end up as wretchedly as Tony does? And the answer, of course, is, the same sort of world as that in which a man like Basil Seal can flourish, a world comprehensively in need of redemption.

When the novel opens, Tony Last's life seems perfect. He is married to Brenda; has a son, John Andrew, and an ugly neo-Gothic country house called Hetton; and loves all three. But Brenda takes a lover, a worthless young man called John Beaver. She spends an increasingly large amount of time in a flat she has rented in London, and during one of her absences her son is killed in a riding accident. A family friend, Bruce Scott-Menzies, brings her the news. Momentarily she thinks he is referring to Beaver, and when she realizes that he means John Andrew she says "Thank God" and bursts into tears. After the boy's funeral, she leaves Tony and they agree on a divorce for which Tony is to provide the evidence. After a disastrous trip to Brighton, on which he and his supposed mistress are accompanied by her little girl, Tony learns that Brenda, at Beaver's instigation, is demanding such heavy alimony that he will have to sell Hetton; so he calls off the divorce and sails to Latin America with an absurd explorer, Dr. Messinger, in search of a mythical lost city. He has a futile shipboard romance with a young Catholic girl, and the expedition goes fatally wrong. The final stages of the novel alternate between Tony's fever-dreams in the jungle and Brenda's deprivations in London after Beaver deserts her. Brenda at least ends up married to Bruce Scott-Menzies, now an M.P., whereas Tony is imprisoned by a madman, Mr. Todd, who forces him to read Dickens aloud for the remainder of his days.

The novel takes its title from Eliot's poem *The Waste Land*, certain features of which reappear in it. Thus *The Waste Land* represents the decay of ancient fertility myths into such degenerate forms as telling fortunes with Tarot cards; the fortune-teller in *A Handful of Dust* reads the soles of her clients' feet. *The Waste Land* looks behind the medieval Arthurian story-cycle to the Celtic rituals from which it derives. *A Handful of Dust* gives us a degraded modern version of the same material: Tony is King Arthur, Brenda Guinevere, and Beaver her lover, Lancelot. (The rooms in Hetton are named after the characters in Tennyson's heavily Victorian version of the same story.) And just as Eliot's poem contrasts the "Unreal City" of London with the great cities of legend—Jerusalem, Athens, Alexandria, Vienna: all "fallen," all finally unreal—so Waugh's novel ends with Tony, like a knight searching for the Holy Grail, vainly seeking his mythical city and finding nothing but his own special hell on earth.

This sustained body of literary allusion gives *A Handful of Dust* a greater range of ironic implication than Waugh was ever again to attempt. It is in parts exceptionally funny. The vicar of Tony's church had originally written his sermons while serving in India, and he mindlessly repeats them each Sunday at Hetton to hilarious effect; but his wordy fatuities about the unity of the servants of a far-flung empire have a cruel bearing on the appalling isolation that is Tony's ultimate fate. At least as funny are the absurdities of Tony's supposedly adulterous weekend with Milly and her horrid daughter. The final section is brilliantly edited. The text cuts between Tony's sufferings in the jungle and the loneliness of Brenda in London (or alternatively between Bruce Scott-Menzies asking fatuous questions in the Commons about Japanese pork pies and the explorers' Indian guides gorging themselves on pig meat after a hunt). Finally, in a phantasmagoric fever-dream Tony blends the worlds of London, the jungle, and his dream city (a fantastically elaborated Hetton) only to wake in the hands of Mr. Todd, and to the knowledge he has gained "in the forest where time is different. There is no City" (ch. 6).

Two points remain. Clearly this story of marital betrayal bears closely on Waugh's personal experience. Putting it on public record, however indirectly, was a new instance of his willingness to outface his public. It is remarkable for its generosity toward Brenda. The moment when she discovers that Beaver is alive and John Andrew is dead is handled with great delicacy. Once she has made her terrible remark, she weeps helplessly, pressing her forehead against the gilt back of a hard little empire chair. Her behavior is clearly compulsive. Later she is for a time impoverished and demoralized, but her real punishment has been to see her situation for what it is from the beginning. Nor is this handled with any vindictiveness. Waugh gives Brenda the dignity of self-knowledge. "I was never one for making myself expensive," she says in chapter 3 when Beaver lets her see herself home. Wit of this kind is a sign of grace in Waugh, though not quite the grace that sanctifies. In all his later writing (with one exception in *Brideshead Revisited*) he remained uncensoriously compassionate in his attitude to faithless women. For a humiliated cuckold, the stance was a fundamentally honorable one.

Far more problematical is the treatment of Tony. The Mr. Todd sequence was originally published in the United States as a short story before work on the novel began. Consequently an American serialization of *A Handful of Dust* has a different ending, in which Tony returns to London, is reunited with Brenda, and cynically takes over her flat in London in order to prosecute his own infidelities. The novelist Henry Yorke felt the English version too "fantastic. . . . The first part is . . . a real picture of people one has met and may at any moment meet again." With his own recent travels in South America in mind (he actually met the original Mr. Todd in 1933), Waugh replied that for him savages were just such people: "the Amazon stuff had to be there" (*Letters*, p. 88). The American version is certainly more urbane, but its effect is cynically to restore, not subvert, civilization. Waugh's scheme, however, was to show "Gothic man in the hands of savages—first Mrs Beaver [John's mother] etc. then the real ones." Even when Tony's happy cousins inherit Hetton, the vixens on their silver-fox farm keep having their brushes bitten off; barbarism can never really be kept at bay. What Tony learns but fails to understand is that, in the words of the Epistle to the Hebrews: "we have not here a permanent city but we seek that which is to come" (13:14, Douai). Waugh's strength as a novelist is that, precisely as a sophisticated inhabitant of the city of man, he was prepared to face all the consequences of its being, in the end, an illusion.

While writing these two novels and for several years thereafter, Waugh lived a restless, self-indulgent life. He made three journeys to Ethiopia and others to Latin America, Morocco, and Europe. His friends included the Roman Catholic Lygon sisters, the fashionable and attractive Diana Guinness (later the wife of the Fascist leader Sir Oswald Mosely), and Lady Diana Cooper, wife of a Conservative Member of Parliament. The *Letters* and *Diaries* record (and jokingly exaggerate) a life of calculated promiscuity and serious repentance. In 1931 he fell in love with "Baby" Jungman, but she was a Catholic and he was divorced; this incident is reflected in Tony Last's shipboard romance. Later Waugh discovered that his first marriage was invalid in church law, and when this was confirmed in 1936 he married another Catholic, Laura Herbert. While house-hunting in the West Country and immediately after their marriage, he was at work on his fifth novel, *Scoop* (1938).

Compared with its predecessors, *Scoop* is a minor work. Combining the formulas of *Decline and Fall* and *Black Mischief*, it tells the story of William Boot, the naive young writer of nature notes for the *Daily Beast*, who is sent to report a war in the African state of Ishmaelia in place of John Courtney Boot, a successful writer. When William Boot returns after pulling off an enormous scoop, it is John Courtney Boot who is knighted and William's uncle, Theodore, who is feasted and rewarded by the press baron Lord Copper. Like Paul Pennyfeather, William is back where he started. Based on Waugh's undistinguished record as a war correspondent in Abyssinia, the novel joyfully seizes on the absurdity of "cablese" (the grotesque abbreviations and neologisms that journalists resorted to when cabling their stories), the ignorance of newspaper proprietors, and the irresponsibility of newspapermen.

The book is largely farcical; no one suffers. William Boot's sexual initiation, for example, is neither touching like Paul's nor sad like Prudence's. The vitality of the book derives from its extravagance of incident, character, and language. The denouement is effected by an absurdly athletic millionaire and parachutist of mixed racial origins who has modestly assumed the name of the former British prime minister, Mr. Baldwin. He is an impishly successful reworking of the Father Rothschild figure in *Vile Bodies*. The most famous incident in the book is the performance of Mrs. Julia Stitch (based on Lady Diana Cooper) in driving her car safely into the gentlemen's lavatory in Sloane Street.

Some excellent comedy concerns Boot Magna Hall, from which William writes his nature notes,

"Lush Places." All his relations are ill-mannered, unmarried, and self-absorbed. Their house is decaying in a riot of fertility. This bears out the view of the *Daily Beast*'s foreign editor, who regards the country as a jungle "where you never [know] from one minute to the next that you might not be tossed by a bull or pitch-forked by a yokel or rolled over and broken up by a pack of hounds" (1.2). Magna thus matches the other wildernesses in the novel, Fleet Street and Ishmaelia. But the blending of tropical and English disorder in *Scoop* carries none of the solemn implications of such fusions in earlier novels.

Nevertheless, even in this most cheerful book a somber note is sounded. As usual there are a number of insolently offensive references to blacks in the novel: "The black-backed, pink-palmed, fin-like hands beneath the violet cuffs flapped and slapped" (1.4). Ishmaelia is governed by an unprincipled black family called Jackson, all inappropriately named after eminent British liberals (Garnett, Huxley, Gollancz, Earl Russell). But the Communists imprison the Jacksons and threaten Mr. Baldwin's and Western interests. They are led by a "short and brisk and self-possessed" man, "soot-black in face, with piercing boot-button eyes" (2.2) called Benito, the only seriously competent man in the whole novel. He controls the journalists like a headmistress subduing schoolgirls ("What's that blackamoor got to be superior about?" mutters one). In Mr. Baldwin's operatic counterrevolution, however, Benito is unceremoniously killed.

Married, settled, and starting a family, Waugh had hardly worked his way into his new role of opinionated country gentleman when war broke out in 1939. He at once abandoned the novel he was writing and talked his way into the Royal Marines. He was later transferred to the Commandos and participated in a futile assault on Dakar by the Free French forces and later in the retreat from Crete. Sailing home from Cairo via the Cape he found time to write one more novel about "Metroland," the world that up to now had been his imaginative base. The dedication of *Put Out More Flags* describes the novel's protagonists as "no longer contemporary" and "disturbed in their habits by the rough intrusion of current history." Many old characters make virtually valedictory appearances: Alastair and Sonia, Peter Pastmaster and his mother, Lady Seal and her booby friend Sir Joseph. New characters appear, notably Poppet Green, Communist and sculptress, much preoccupied with the departure to America of the poets Parsnip and Pimpernell (W. H. Auden and

Christopher Isherwood), and a homosexual dilettante, Ambrose Silk.

The central character, once again, is Basil Seal, the chief preoccupation of his mother, Lady Seal, his sister, Barbara Sothill, and his mistress, Angela Lyne. Barbara, we are told, married Freddie, who is "gifted with that sly, sharp instinct for self-preservation that passes for wisdom among the rich" (1.1), because she loved his exquisite house; in her eyes Hitler is just a mean-minded ascetic whose heart is bent on its destruction. She and Basil are of a kind: when they kiss "Narcissus [greets] Narcissus from the watery depths" of their equally clear blue eyes (2.2). Indeed, a knowing evacuee child thinks Barbara fancies Basil. This child is one of a singularly repellent family, the Connollys, refugees from the city whom Barbara has the duty of billeting on her neighbors. Taking this job over from her, Basil imposes the Connollys on the most respectable local families until bribed to remove them. Faced with the prospect of having them in her home, one pretty young wife stares at Basil "like a rabbit before the headlights of a car" (1.9). This he finds delicious, and he makes love to her instead. His relations with Angela, the "golden daughter of fortune" (1.3), are equally without moral bearings. Angela's passion for Basil is her curse: only death will part them; and with the war, that possibility does arise. But it is Cedric, her husband, who dies. Angela is in many ways a splendid person. Driven literally to drink by her infatuation and teetering on the edge of social humiliation, she stages an impressive social recovery at Peter Pastmaster's wedding. But her neglect of her aesthetically sensitive husband and her lively, lonely son is chilling. So is the joylessness of her union with Basil.

Then there is Ambrose, the great love of whose life, a half-Jewish Brownshirt, is now in a concentration camp. In his honor Ambrose writes a limp novella, which Basil persuades him to edit so that it reads like a hymn of praise to Nazi youth. Basil then reports the matter to Colonel Plum, for whom he works in the Ministry of Information. To escape internment Ambrose flees to Ireland (where he goes melancholy-mad); his publisher is comfortably ensconced in prison for the duration; and Basil, who was denied the promotion he was scheming to obtain, joins Peter and Alastair in the newly formed Commandos. "There's only one serious occupation for a chap now," he says, "that's killing Germans. I have an idea I shall rather enjoy it" (epilogue).

And that of course is the problem. Some critics have found *Put Out More Flags* too optimistic. But the booby Sir Joseph, Lady Seal's confidant, sees "a new spirit on every side" in the closing scene. He is right in one respect: the premiership has passed to Churchill and the "phoney war" is over. But we have just left Alastair and Peter boyishly plotting to go to war, and Basil relishing the thought of killing people. In the book as a whole the two recurring themes are immaturity and savagery: the Ministry of Information is an officially sanctioned Azania in the middle of London; the Connellys are a domestic species of savage. The novel ends with the central characters still absorbed in their money, their prospects, and their fantasies. Cedric is dead, and the one character who knows what the war is really about—Ambrose —because his beloved is among "the prisoners rolled away to slavery" in Europe (2.1), is prevented by his "singularity" from doing anything at all. Barbaric emotions, Waugh wrote in 1939, invade the territory of civilized man by assuming "the livery of the defence"; they "pass through the lines . . . [and] there is always a Fifth Column . . . ready to receive them. . . . That is how the civilized man is undone." In *Put Out More Flags*, the moral defenses of London at war are betrayed in just such a fashion. The novel does not contradict but anticipates the pessimism of Waugh's later work.

The words just quoted are from *Work Suspended* (1942, 1.4), the novel Waugh abandoned when war broke out. Its chief character, John Plant, is a writer of detective fiction who, following his father's death, fails to finish a novel. In the story as we have it, Plant's defenses are threatened in three ways. Having spent his professional life preserving his privacy by writing in the most impersonal genre he knows and avoiding all confidences (he even lies about himself in the Moroccan brothel he patronizes), he is betrayed into emotion when he verbalizes his grief for his father. Later he falls in love with the pregnant wife of a friend, her complete emotional openness further weakening his defenses. At the same time he has to cope with Atwater, whose atrocious driving killed the elder Plant and whose lonely, innocent, egotistic vulgarity—he is a brilliant comic characterization—completely overwhelms Plant's gentlemanly aloofness. Emotional, artistic, and class barriers are thus all under pressure.

A startling departure, not only for Plant but also for Waugh, whose technique hitherto had been flawlessly impersonal, is that *Work Suspended* is a first-person narrative. This in itself is almost a betrayal of the insolent refusal to explain that makes Waugh's such a powerful but suppressed presence in the prewar novels. Now Plant and, insofar as he is Waugh's surrogate, Waugh himself are lured into the treacherous area of explanation, justification, and self-betrayal. In all the novels after *Put Out More Flags* there is a central character whose point of view invites comparisons with that of the author, where the earlier novels prohibited them; and in most of the later fiction, too, that central character is like an imperial city under siege to the forces, divine and human, by which civilized man is undone.

By 1944 Waugh was ready at last to produce another major work. The previous year had been a bad one. He had aroused fiercely negative feelings in his subordinates and superiors and had been forced to resign from the Commandos. The authorities were probably well pleased when he sought special leave from regimental duties to write what was to become his most celebrated novel, *Brideshead Revisited*.

Like *Work Suspended*, *Brideshead Revisited* is a first-person narrative, written purportedly by an architectural painter, Charles Ryder. At the beginning of book 2, Ryder describes artistic inspiration as an unexpected flooding of consciousness by "the memorials and pledges of the vital hours of a lifetime," and he likens such moments to those "epochs of history" in which an unknown race for a brief generation or two stupefies the world by bringing "to birth and nurture a teeming brood of genius" (2.1). The novel itself represents just such an explosion in Waugh's career. It teems with an abundance of new characters, incidents, settings, and even meals. Above all it teems with words, elaborately developed metaphors and descriptions. Most surprisingly of all, it teems with speeches, not just of paragraph length, but flowing on, page after page. Some speeches are comic—as in the case of Charles Ryder's cunning, selfish, mad old father; some sinister—as in the case of the homosexual Anthony Blanche; and some hysterical—as in the case of Julia Flyte, when she is brutally reminded of her position in the eyes of the Catholic church as the faithless wife of a divorced man. The economy of the earlier novels has been abandoned, and Waugh puts on a virtuoso display as a stylist, which he counterpoints with a series of comically unglamorous characters: Hooper, an ungainly wartime officer in Charles Ryder's company; Charles's prosy cousin Jasper; Mr. Samgrass, a syco-

phantic don; Rex Mottram, a political upstart from Canada who marries Julia Flyte; and Celia, Charles's ambitious, well-born, adulterous wife. It is as if Atwater's absurd insensitivity in *Work Suspended* had released an entire tribe of equally repugnant, comic, and vulnerable characters in Waugh's imagination.

But language assumes the livery of the defense and undoes the civilized man. Its abundance in this novel is inextricably involved in a series of interrelated failures and betrayals. The central betrayal, both symbolic and actual, is that of Brideshead itself, ancestral home of the Flytes, which is violated and degraded when requisitioned by the army during the war. Other fine houses are actually pulled down in the course of the narrative, something Charles Ryder sees as "just another jungle closing in" (2.1). But Brideshead is not only the Flytes' home; it would have become Charles's if he had married Julia: barbed wire in the dry, litter-filled fountain therefore symbolizes the betrayal and failure of a grand passion. And it is not just the house and the lovers that have been betrayed, but the family by its own members. The eldest son, Brideshead, a logic-chopping religious fanatic, marries a spiteful, respectable widow who is past childbearing; his younger brother, Sebastian, the beautiful, pagan friend of Charles's youth—"forerunner" of his passion for Julia—ends up a hanger-on in a Moroccan religious house, a lonely, alcoholic homosexual. Of the two Flyte daughters, one gives up her religion to marry Rex Mottram and then returns to it rather than marry the love of her life; the other, the effervescent, affectionate Cordelia, successfully prevents herself from falling in love by devoting herself to good works. And finally art is betrayed—and not just Charles's. Brideshead itself is full of aesthetic resonances—of Troilus and Cressida, of classical comedy, of Pre-Raphaelite painting. All are swept away at the novel's end. In Cordelia's words (she quotes from the Vulgate translation of the Book of Lamentations): "*Quomodo sedet sola civitas*"— "How doth the city sit solitary." Brideshead is Tony Last's dream city, derelict and abandoned to the barbarians.

Words, however, are above all the betrayers of those who utter them. "Thank God I think I am beginning to acquire a style," Waugh wrote in his diary (21 March 1944) as he was working on the novel. When it was published, however, there were elements of malice, curiosity, amusement, and dismay in its reception. The style Waugh had acquired seemed too ornate; the scenes of sexual passion between Charles and Julia were thought ill-judged; the deathbed repentance of Lord Marchmain was parodied; and the novel was believed to reveal aspects of Waugh's own youthful involvements and his moral seduction by the English upper class. Waugh was sensitive to such criticisms and constantly revised the novel in their light, but the charges against it remain to be answered. They are in essence that it is simultaneously too worldly and too religious.

Central to both aspects of the problem is the figure of Lady Marchmain. Nancy Mitford asked Waugh if he was on Lady Marchmain's side. He replied that he was not, but that God was. Nevertheless, the deathbed repentance of her husband looks very much like a posthumous victory for her and all she stands for—the remorseless manipulation of others by means of beauty, charm, and wealth, which presents itself as sincere religious faith and practice but in fact is egocentric, snobbish, and consumed with a hatred of sexuality and life. The portrait of Lady Marchmain can thus be read as an unwitting revelation of what Waugh's Catholicism really was, and it was indeed meant to be read as a kind of literary temptation for the unbelieving reader, an excuse for rejecting God. "I sometimes think," says Cordelia, "when people wanted to hate God, they hated Mummy . . . she was saintly but she wasn't a saint" (1.8). In any case, Lady Marchmain's world is overthrown in the closing stages of the novel. The reopening of the family chapel for the troops is represented as the goal toward which two ambitious aesthetic projects —Brideshead itself, and the working out of the "fierce little human tragedy" that constitutes the novel—have been moving. Yet it is a grossly democratic and aesthetically vulgar goal, from which Lady Marchmain herself would have shrunk.

Replacing the great and terrible chant of Holy Week, "*Quomodo sedet sola civitas*," are the brazen cries of army bugles, "Pick-em-up, pick-em-up, hot potatoes" (epilogue)—all so that Catholic Hoopers can have their mass while Britain is at war. For as Waugh told Nancy Mitford, *Brideshead Revisited* is "about God" (*Letters*, p. 196). In a notorious passage Charles reads Mr. Samgrass' edition of Lady Marchmain's brother's writings—all of her brothers had died in World War I—and reflects bitterly on how such men had to be sacrificed like "garlanded victims . . . to make a world for Hooper . . . so that things might be safe for the travelling salesman, with his

polygonal pince-nez, his fat wet hand-shake, his grinning dentures" (1.5). Mr. Samgrass sees Lady Marchmain's brothers in pagan terms. Charles, however, goes on to wonder if the rest of the family might not also be marked out for destruction "by other ways than war." And of course they are, but only so that the purposes of a Christian God might be fulfilled, purposes that include the saving of their souls, Charles's conversion, and the relighting of "a beaten-copper lamp of deplorable design" (epilogue) before the tabernacle at Brideshead in time of war. Unlike Lady Marchmain, the God of *Brideshead Revisited* has little use for charm, nor is he put off by grinning dentures as Charles is.

But if God thus overrides human notions of beauty and propriety, a novel "about" him must necessarily declare its own unsatisfactoriness. It is in these terms that the deathbed repentance has to be seen. Critics have traditionally argued that a simple change of mind is an unsatisfactory way of ending a story. Lord Marchmain's repentance, Julia's contrition, and Charles's conversion constitute a kind of ill-designed sanctuary lamp in the very text of the novel. Perhaps the nonbelieving reader can "save" *Brideshead Revisited* from this in-built fault in design by seeing in it an ultimate irony consistent with the novel's other formal complexities. But if the offense it causes is too serious to be outweighed by mere considerations of form, then a reader holding such views is entirely justified in regarding the novel as morally and aesthetically flawed. This, of course, need not worry the Catholic reader, since, outside the city of man, artistic notions of success have no meaning anyway: that is the point the novel has all along been seeking to make.

After writing *Brideshead Revisited*, Waugh accompanied Randolph Churchill (the wartime prime minister's son, to whom *Put Out More Flags* is dedicated) on a mission to the partisan forces in Yugoslavia. Like all his other wartime activities, it was not entirely successful. With that episode his career as a soldier came to an end, and he returned to civilian life. A Labour government was in office, "Metroland" had vanished forever, and Waugh had difficulty in settling down. His family continued to grow. He and Laura had had four children by 1944 (one died) and were to have three more, but Waugh proved a remote and eccentric father, not least because he deliberately adopted the manners and attitudes of an unpredictably irascible old man. This was the time when his offensiveness to strangers, particularly Americans and journalists, both by letter and face to face, became notorious. Some of his least tolerable behavior is triumphantly recorded in his diary.

His disgust with the postwar world was given prompt expression in two short works of fiction. After the stylistic and thematic elaborations of *Brideshead Revisited*, Waugh returned to a purely comic mode in *Scott-King's Modern Europe* (1947), though in a new manner. His innocent central character is no longer the pliable youth of earlier novels but an aging classics schoolmaster, who is invited to Neutralia for celebrations commemorating an obscure sixteenth-century Neutralian poet. (Waugh himself had accepted a similar invitation to Spain.) Scott-King finds himself first the victim of a ludicrous political intrigue, then a refugee who has to disguise himself as a nun, and ends up a bewildered inmate of "No. 64 Jewish Illicit Immigrants Camp Palestine." The story is light farce, the tone one of wry fatalism, but Scott-King's final refusal to change from the teaching of classics to economic history, because "it would be very wicked indeed to do anything to fit a boy for the modern world," makes its point.

The comedy of *Scott-King's Modern Europe* is almost benign; not so that of Waugh's next work of fiction, *The Loved One* (1948). It is the story of Denis Barlow, a young English writer in Hollywood who is reduced to working in an animal cemetery. Denis meets a dedicated morticians' make-up artist called Aimée Thanatogenos (a name that means "the loved one of the people of death") when he goes to arrange the funeral of an expatriate English scriptwriter who has committed suicide. Aimée works at the famous burial park Whispering Glades (based on Forest Lawn in Hollywood) and is half in love with the chief embalmer, Mr. Joyboy. Wooed by Denis with scraps of famous English love-poetry that she takes to be his own, she eventually breaks with him when she discovers his shameful place of work. Amid great publicity in the morticians' social world, she and Mr. Joyboy become engaged, but guilt and a drunken advice-columnist drive her to suicide in Whispering Glades itself. This sacrilege threatens Mr. Joyboy's career. Denis, whose plans to set up as an interdenominational minister have shocked the English community into paying his fare home, then milks Mr. Joyboy of his savings before agreeing to dispose of Aimée's body at his own disreputable workplace. He returns to England in style, leaving behind

"something that had long irked him, his young heart." In its place he carries back "the artist's load, a great, shapeless lump of experience."

This chilling little phrase establishes a significant link between character and writer: the exchange is one that the reader is expected to imagine Waugh himself as having made. In Hollywood, which he visited in 1947, Waugh found an abundance of that modern world he had represented in Neutralia with comparative lightheartedness. It was uncivilized in a way that invited treatment such as he had given distant places in the prewar novels. But California money, California guilelessness, California insensitivity, California paganism—a world in which corpses are painted to look like whores—is too absurd and unnatural, too divorced from traditions of any kind, for the tonal shifts into compassion and seriousness that so enrich *Black Mischief* and *A Handful of Dust*. The only points at which the text touches seriousness, therefore, are when it is uncompromisingly heartless. But for all its scandalous indifference to the taboos surrounding death and mourning, *The Loved One* is an ebullient book. Denis Barlow's hardness of heart is a condition of his art. He and Waugh have a secret they cannot share with the human souls they rub along with in day-to-day living—the rare, classic periods of artistic inspiration.

It is not really surprising, therefore, that Waugh's most uninhibitedly happy fiction, *Helena*, should follow two such apparently disenchanted books as *Scott-King's Modern Europe* and *The Loved One*. This is not a generally well-regarded book, though Waugh was fond of it. It needs to be read sympathetically as a joke about serious subjects. It was followed by another travel book, *Holy Places* (1952).

In some ways, then, the late 1940's and the early 1950's were a satisfying time for Waugh, particularly as a writer. This is the period of his most buoyant and engaging letter writing. In public he entered into a spirited foray against modern art, and thoroughly outwitted the historian Hugh Trevor-Roper (now Lord Dacre) in a correspondence in the *New Statesman* in 1953–1954. In private his letters to Nancy Mitford and other friends maintained a constantly high standard. Waugh was a passionate, uncalculating letter writer, intemperate at times, a vicious gossip, but also, on occasion, vulnerable. By the mid-1950's, however, things started to go badly for him. He had all along intended to turn his wartime experiences to artistic advantage. His plan was to write a series of novels based on the experiences of a central character, but with each volume also focusing on a second major figure. From the start he felt uneasy with the scheme. The first volume did not satisfy him while he was writing it. In 1953 he published a bleak tale of the future, *Love Among the Ruins*, the story of an arsonist who works for the Euthanasia Department of the Welfare State and whose mistress has a lovely flowing beard; Waugh illustrated the story himself. It has some sprightly gibes at favorite targets, but it lacks the energy and verve of *The Loved One*. Waugh then had a breakdown. He was drinking too much and taking uncontrolled doses of a mixture of drugs that had been prescribed for him at various times. While on a cruise to recover his health he began hearing voices and imagined that he was the victim of a monstrous and wicked conspiracy. He recovered, and the second of the war novels, *Officers and Gentlemen*, came out in 1955, but for a time it seemed that he would be unable to continue the series. What he did next, however, was in many ways one of the most significant and courageous acts of his life: he turned his experience of madness into a novel, *The Ordeal of Gilbert Pinfold*.

At one level, *The Ordeal of Gilbert Pinfold* is virtually plotless. Mr. Pinfold is a Catholic novelist living in the country with his wife and large family. His memory starts failing him; he is drinking too much and dosing himself indiscriminately with drugs. After a BBC radio interview set up by a man called Angel, Mr. Pinfold goes on a cruise for his health and on board ship is beset by hallucinations. His behavior embarrasses his fellow passengers. He discovers that there is a family called Angel on board, attributes the voices he has been hearing to a plot by the Angels and the BBC to control his mind, and leaves the ship. The voices pursue him; he sends alarming letters to his wife and receives an urgent summons home, which he obeys. The voices try to persuade him to keep quiet about his experiences, but he decides to tell his wife. His local doctor attributes the experiences to the drugs Mr. Pinfold has been taking—but Mr. Pinfold rejects this simple-minded diagnosis: "he had endured a great ordeal, and unaided, had emerged the victor" (ch. 8). So he sets briskly to work to write the narrative account *The Ordeal of Gilbert Pinfold*.

Uncomplicated as this basic narrative is, however, the novel about his madness is the most intensely plotted of all Waugh's works, a breathtaking account of how inspiration and craftsmanship interact in the mind of a gifted writer. The characters whose voices surround Mr. Pinfold on board ship have the autonomous, self-generating power of the imagination. They are brilliantly inventive, accusing Mr. Pinfold of being a Jew, a homosexual, a social climber, and a snob; they threaten to horsewhip him or to hand him over to a Spanish boarding party (Spain is supposed to be threatening to seize Gibraltar by force). Alternatively they offer him a deliciously nubile young virgin for his pleasure. But these disorganized "inspirations" have to be sorted out and made consistent with one another and integrated with the day-to-day, nonhallucinatory life aboard ship. Otherwise Mr. Pinfold's madness will become apparent to him. Sometimes the solution to these "technical" problems is generated by the voices themselves. Sometimes we see the crafty consciousness of Mr. Pinfold himself working out suitable explanations of what is happening to him. His victory, therefore, is not exclusively located in the crucial decision to tell his wife about the voices. The unfolding of the hallucination, its articulation and development, are themselves achievements of a mind with its twin powers of inspiration and organization working at full stretch.

The excitement of reading the book is thus in part the excitement of suspense. Mr. Pinfold's fantasies get themselves into impossible situations. At one point, for example, he hears a Spanish corvette pull alongside the SS *Caliban*. He bursts from his cabin, fully dressed in tweed and brandishing his blackthorn, only to find the ship in perfect order and no other vessel in sight: "He had been dauntless a minute before in the face of his enemies. Now he was struck with real fear. . . . He was possessed from outside himself with atavistic panic. 'O let me not be mad, not mad, sweet heaven,' he cried" (ch. 5). We are convinced that he will be unable to explain *this* away and the spell will be broken. But no. His cry is a quotation from Shakespeare's *King Lear*; it puts him in mind of one of the voices he had heard earlier, that of a sadistic woman he had named Goneril after Lear's vicious eldest daughter. All he has to do is to "hear" Goneril laughing at him and an explanation of the entire "Spanish" incident is at hand: it was all a trick to break his spirit.

Equally brilliant is the resolution of the defloration episode. Here we see Mr. Pinfold in a state of intense and ludicrous sexual expectation. A delightful and obedient virgin is being disrobed for his pleasure, but she fails to come to him. Again he leaves his cabin; the corridor is empty, but he can hear the voices still, mingled with a sleeping passenger's snores. It is crucial, of course, that the device of the hoax should not be repeated. So Mr. Pinfold gets cross. He refuses to chase the girl around the ship and returns to his bunk to wait for her in his pyjamas. Then he hears her weeping; she has heard the other passenger's snores and mistaken them for Mr. Pinfold's, who, she thinks, has rejected her. "It was Glover snoring," says Mr. Pinfold, and though nobody hears him, he is safely restored to his nightmare (ch. 6).

An important element in the novel's comedy is that of parody. When he "discovers" that Angel is on board, Mr. Pinfold feels "as though he had come to the end of an ingenious, old-fashioned detective novel which he had read rather inattentively" (ch. 7), but the genre most enthusiastically imitated is that of the boy's adventure story, in which vigorous, boarding-school-educated young Britishers battle heroically against the scheming, caddish, and usually foreign enemies of the empire. Mr. Pinfold's consciousness thus locates itself in two worlds: the deluded, ridiculous, and morally reductive world of imperialist fantasy, and that other world—Mediterranean, classical, and Catholic—in which his true self lives and moves and has its being. His superficial madness and underlying resources are thus a statement about historical as well as psychological situations and possibilities. In addition, of course, there is the openly autobiographical element in the book. Waugh faces the unbelieving, liberal reader and acknowledges the extent to which his representations of a mad world, in Azania or California, are simultaneously representations of the chaos in his own mind. His defense of himself, however, as a man, an artist, and a Catholic, is precisely that his capacity to admit the presence in his own soul of the madness and vice he observes also in the world is the measure of the strength he derives from his art and his faith.

For this reason the first chapter of the novel is among the most important of his writings. It is remarkable for its combination of frankness, astuteness, and vivid phrasing:

He looked at the world *sub specie aeternitatis* and he found it flat as a map; except when, rather often, personal annoyance intruded. Then he would come tumbling from his exalted point of observation. Shocked by a bad bottle of wine, an impertinent stranger, or a fault in syntax, his mind like a cinema camera trucked furiously forward to confront the offending object close up with a glaring lens.

(ch. 1)

Even those who only saw Waugh interviewed on television can vouch for the unnerving accuracy of this description. What surprised those who did not know him better was the sensitively understated portrait of Mrs. Pinfold. This tribute to Laura Waugh is perhaps the most effective demonstration in the book of Mr. Pinfold's—and of Waugh's—underlying soundness of mind and heart.

However, for the very reason that it treats of both the author's everyday irascibility and actual madness with an audacious cold-heartedness as uncompromising as the treatment of California attitudes to death in *The Loved One*, *The Ordeal of Gilbert Pinfold* is ultimately protective of its author: the man who originally experienced these disorders is different from the man who assimilates them and puts them on display. Thus the novel considerably enriches the public persona Waugh had created for himself, but it also limits and controls those elements of explanation and justification by which an author's personal privacy is ultimately betrayed.

There was a real possibility that after *The Ordeal of Gilbert Pinfold* Waugh's career as a novelist had come to an end. Disliking the first volume of the wartime series, he found in writing the second that material he had planned to use in two books was needed to complete one. Then the project went dead, and he turned to nonfiction instead, producing in 1959 the official biography of his friend Msgr. Ronald Knox, wit, preacher, detective novelist, linguist, and translator of the Bible. This was followed by his last travel book, *A Tourist in Africa* (1960). Eventually, however, the third and last novel of the wartime series, *Unconditional Surrender*, was published in 1961. Waugh then set about revising his earlier novels, particularly *Brideshead Revisited*, and in 1964 started work on turning the war trilogy into a single continuous work which was published in 1965 under the title of *Sword of Honour*. This final version of the wartime novels is the most authoritative, but the original versions of the three novels continue to circulate widely. In the following discussion, therefore, references are to the trilogy in its original and not its final version, unless otherwise indicated.

The great difference between the *Sword of Hon-*

our novels and *The Ordeal of Gilbert Pinfold* is that the trilogy is drawn into the treacherous territory of explanation and justification. It is true that it is also less overtly autobiographical. The hero, Guy Crouchback, shares Waugh's opinions but has a different personality. However, the distinguishing characteristic of the trilogy is its insistent development of a comprehensive and Catholic view of the moral life and of history. For Waugh such explicitness was undoubtedly riskier than the ironically crafted self-portrayal of *The Ordeal of Gilbert Pinfold.*

This is not to suggest that he abandoned his technique of skillfully pointing his text with small clues about his larger intentions and meanings. Indeed some of the most important changes in the final *Sword of Honour* version of the trilogy relate to such moments. In the first volume, *Men at Arms*, for example, Guy hears some gossip about the sole survivor of an illustrious old Catholic family who was left childless when his wife abandoned him for another man. Years later, however, after her remarriage, she had an affair with her first husband, to whom in church law she was still married. A child was conceived, and, the wife's second marriage being childless also, this son by the first husband succeeded in time to the second husband's title. Moreover by marrying a Catholic he ensured the continuance of an ancient family under a new name but in the old faith. The man Guy is talking to calls this providential. Guy, however, cannot believe that Divine Providence concerns itself with the perpetuation of the English Catholic aristocracy. But of course it does, comes the reply: "And with sparrows too, we are taught" (1.10). The immediate effect of this conversation is to stir Guy to seek out his own former wife—the only woman he may lawfully sleep with because he too is a Catholic—but his scheme is a failure. Virginia is rightly disgusted by the implications of such a seduction, and that apparently is that.

In the second volume, *Officers and Gentlemen,* Virginia has an affair with a vulgar sexual braggart named Trimmer, a former ladies' hairdresser, and in the third, *Unconditional Surrender,* she becomes pregnant by him. She and Guy meet. Guy agrees to marry her and to acknowledge Trimmer's child as his own. Of her own volition Virginia becomes a Catholic and, after the baby's birth, is killed in an air raid. Guy is thus free to marry again, and in the original version he has two sons by his second marriage. Some readers have interpreted these later children as the reward of Guy's generosity, which weakens the

point Waugh wished to make. Consequently, in *Sword of Honour,* Guy has no children by his second wife, and the providential pattern outlined in *Men at Arms* is thus almost exactly reversed. The sole heir of an ancient Catholic name is the bastard son of a ladies' hairdresser—but a Catholic nonetheless.

This indicates clearly enough the lesson Guy learns in the course of the war, namely the worthlessness of all merely human conceptions of honor, and in particular the ultimate insignificance of the traditional English idea of the gentleman. The eclipse of gentlemanliness as a value and a significant fact of English social life is symbolized by the rise of Trimmer. An officer but not a gentleman, he becomes involved in an absurd foray into occupied France, set up in the first place as a publicity stunt by Ian Kilbannock, a Scottish peer and former sporting journalist. By thus cynically establishing Trimmer as a popular hero, Kilbannock connives at the extinction of his own class, and in this his behavior is representative. Paralleling the rise of Trimmer is the self-inflicted disgrace of Ivor Clair, the handsome, decadent embodiment of the ideal of the gifted gentleman-amateur. In all three novels the wealthy and privileged reveal themselves to be completely without a sense of history or a sense of values. Even the glamorous Julia Stitch is prepared to ruin Guy's career to protect Ivor's reputation and is too self-preoccupied to forward the identity disc of a dead soldier to the proper authorities as Guy requests her to.

What dismays Guy above all as the war proceeds is the complete indifference of all around him to its purposes and conduct. No one recognizes how the opportunistic alliances of the Western Powers deprive them of their moral standing as belligerents. This issue comes into focus in *Unconditional Surrender* with the appearance of a ruthlessly ambitious young American officer known as "Loot" and a group of upper-class Communists, including Sir Ralph Brompton and Frank de Souza, a gifted Jewish fellow officer of Guy's. Both are involved in furthering the cause of the Communist partisans in Yugoslavia, where against much opposition Guy works hard to relieve a party of Jewish refugees. Waugh evidently regards Loot and de Souza as embodiments of the powers destined to inherit the earth when the war is over.

Over and against all these self-preoccupied or conspiratorial representatives of a decaying past and a valueless present stand the Catholic characters, and it is with them that Waugh's difficulties begin. There are fewer "bad" and "sad" Catholics in the trilogy than in *Brideshead Revisited.* Nearly all the minor Catholic characters are overtly sympathetic—notably Guy's sister, Angela Box-Bender, and her lively, eager son, Tony, both of them a puzzle to Angela's non-Catholic husband, Arthur, a Conservative M.P. One of the minor motifs in the narrative is the news that trickles through about Tony after he is taken prisoner early in the war. In the end, to his father's dismay, he decides to become a monk. The Catholic background to the trilogy is thus less troubled than that in *Brideshead Revisited,* and, if less glamorous, it is socially rather more select. In a minor way, Waugh may be fairly accused of painting too selective and favorable a picture of English Catholicism in these novels.

More serious are the problems raised by the exceptional goodness of Guy's father, the conversion of Virginia, and Guy himself: Mr. Crouchback because he is didactic as well as holy, Virginia because her conversion seems gratuitous and her death too convenient, and Guy because he seems to be too often, and somewhat priggishly, in the right. All this has suggested to some readers that Waugh glamorizes Catholicism in the trilogy by making it socially superior, sanctifies social superiority by making it Catholic, and sentimentalizes both by having Guy forgive Virginia and Virginia die a Catholic.

Some of these charges are undoubtedly sound. The account of Mr. Crouchback's difficulties with the management of the hotel where he lives after the sale of his home confuses vice with vulgarity and virtue with old-world good manners. On the other hand, to anyone familiar with old men and women who spend a lot of time in prayer, his ruminative gentleness seems almost commonplace. The real difficulty is his willingness to talk uninhibitedly with Guy about "the spiritual life." Father and son are interested in much more than the rightness and coherence of Catholicism in principle; they are concerned most of all with salvation as a practical experience of the consciousness and the will. "The Mystical Body"—the church—"doesn't strike attitudes," Mr. Crouchback writes to Guy. "It accepts suffering and injustice. It is ready to forgive at the first hint of compunction" (*Unconditional Surrender,* prologue). At his father's funeral Guy realizes that his sense of God's presence in the world has been too passive, that God "commanded all men to *ask*" (2.3), and he prays to be shown what to do. Like Lord Marchmain, Guy changes his mind, but he lacks the tact of Marchmain. Instead of making a sign, he works out his salvation discursively, in his head.

To understand his position, however, it is necessary also to attend to the clues in the narrative itself as well as to explicit argument. Sometimes these clues take the form of silences—the absence of explanation. In Virginia's case, for example, there is the matter of her feelings about Trimmer's baby. After the birth, she packs him off to the country to be looked after by others. We are not told why. However, in one laconic sentence we learn that she expects to be killed by a flying bomb, as indeed she is. Later some Catholic acquaintances remark that her death may be regarded as providential, since her future was not to be counted on. Be that as it may, her indifference to the child saves its life. Is that providential too? The reader is left with the task of drawing his own conclusions.

There is a comparable challenge in the remark of Box-Bender's with which *Unconditional Surrender* concludes: "Yes . . . things have turned out very conveniently for Guy." To the extent that Guy was joyless and alone in 1939 and (childless or not) is happily married and among friends in 1951, this is true enough. But Box-Bender's remark also voices the complaint that critics of the text are most likely to make against it: that Waugh has made things too easy for Catholicism and for God. A consideration of this problem requires a careful examination of the first and last stages of Guy's story.

The account of the trilogy that has been given so far has failed to indicate the range and inventiveness of its comedy, from the wild excesses of Ben Ritchie-Hook, Guy's alarmingly ferocious, one-eyed commanding officer in *Men at Arms,* to the comic set piece in *Officers and Gentlemen* in which Guy and Tommy Blackhouse (Virginia's second husband) are entertained at dinner by a mad Scottish laird. *Unconditional Surrender,* however, is more somber than its predecessors. At its close Ben Ritchie-Hook gets himself stupidly killed in a tragic replay of his farcical invasion of enemy territory with Guy in *Men at Arms.* This is an indication of how carefully organized the entire narrative in fact is. Wild and extraneous as much of the farce in the trilogy may seem, it is generally integral to a grand design, and of no character is this more true than that of Apthorpe, the central secondary character in *Men at Arms.*

Apthorpe is a great comic creation. He is also a remarkably well-observed study of a recognizable type—innocent, pathetically self-absorbed, and boastful. In spite of his claims to extensive and arduous experiences in the African bush, it is Apthorpe who is taken ill in West Africa. With the best of intentions Guy smuggles a bottle of whiskey into the hospital, and Apthorpe dies as a result, leaving Guy the solemn duty of delivering a grotesque collection of tropical gear to Apthorpe's equally grotesque friend "Chatty" Corner. Because of the sheer absurdity of much of *Men at Arms* we do not take any of this very seriously. In *Unconditional Surrender*, however, Guy's interventions have no less disastrous results. He nearly gets a priest arrested by the partisans when he has mass said for the repose of Virginia's soul, while his efforts on behalf of the Jews have even more serious consequences when his particular friends, the Kanyis, are tried and apparently executed by a people's court for being in possession of some American illustrated magazines that he had given them as a parting gift.

The Kanyis' tragedy is all the more significant because it is Mrs. Kanyi who enables Guy to take the last and decisive step in his spiritual life—to repent of his sins. At the beginning of *Men at Arms*, he welcomes the German-Soviet pact because it enables him to see the war in moral terms and so find a purpose in life. Hence his horror when the Soviet Union enters the war on the side of the Allies: "I don't think I'm interested in victory now," he tells his father in *Unconditional Surrender* (prologue). "Then you've no business to be a soldier," Mr. Crouchback replies, by which he means that a Christian may fight only if he believes in what he is fighting for. The clear implication is that Guy's whole military career is a sin, but Guy himself lacks the spiritual insight to see this: *Men at Arms* opens with his making a singularly shallow and arid confession. At the end of *Unconditional Surrender*, however, Mrs. Kanyi remarks that even "good men thought their private honour would be satisfied by war," and Guy answers, "God forgive me. I was one of them" (3.4). If things turn out conveniently for Guy, it is here, when he is given the grace to confess his sins and beg forgiveness in the presence of a Jewish woman whom inadvertently he is going to send to her death. This is the moment when he realizes at last that history is the territory not of vindication but of trust, where, in his father's words, "Quantitative judgements don't apply" (*Unconditional Surrender*, prologue). Convenience of this kind is beyond Box-Bender's imagining.

Things did not, however, turn out conveniently for Evelyn Waugh. In the closing years of his life he was enraged by changes in the Roman Catholic Church: the great chant "*Quomodo sedet sola civitas*" was replaced by the "Pick-em-up, pick-em-up, hot potatoes" of the Divine Office sung in English. His friends died, his children grew up, his health deteriorated. In 1963 he published his last short story, *Basil Seal Rides Again*. He was not a great short-story writer: his work is chilling without the implicit qualifications possible in an expansive text; but *Basil Seal Rides Again* has a special interest in the final glimpses it gives us of the Metroland characters. Peter Pastmaster flourishes; Ambrose Silk has been given the Order of Merit; and Margot Metroland spends her days watching television in a darkened room. It is all rather joyless. The 1960's seemed to vindicate Waugh's past forebodings and present fears. There were some compensations, however. Some of his letters to and about his children at this time are engaging and affectionate, and in 1964 he published *A Little Learning*, the first volume of a projected autobiography. But he made no progress with the second volume, and church affairs cut him to the quick. "The Vatican Council has knocked the guts out of me," he wrote; he clung "to the Faith doggedly without joy" (*Letters*, pp. 638–639). He died on Easter Sunday 1966, after hearing mass in the old rite. Like Virginia Crouchback, he was not tried beyond his limits.

He left behind a body of work of immense importance. It is grounded in endlessly inventive comic powers, in a love of craftsmanship and reason, in an astringent economy of expression, and in an appetite for the pleasures of art, friendship, and love. But his most significant gift was the sense of history that his religion gave him. His versions of the past may be fanciful and prejudiced, but his awareness of the human condition as fundamentally historical made him intimately responsive to the history of his own times. He caught up into his comic gift the myths and ideologies of the post-Victorian world and gave them a dramatic significance for an audience whose attention he had captured with his first two novels. This is why his work will last: whether one agrees with him or not, his writings are among the most vivid instances in this century of the way in which English literature receives and preserves the impressions of time.

SELECTED BIBLIOGRAPHY

I. Bibliography. R. M. Davis, P. A. Doyle, H. Kosok, C. E. Linck, Jr., *Evelyn Waugh: A Checklist of Primary and Secondary Material* (Troy, N.Y., 1972); R. M. Davis,

A Catalog of the Evelyn Waugh Collection at the Humanities Research Center, University of Texas at Austin (Troy, N.Y., 1981).

II. SELECTED WORKS. M. Davie, ed., *The Diaries of Evelyn Waugh* (Boston–London, 1976); D. Gallagher, *Evelyn Waugh: A Little Order* (London, 1977), essays and reviews; M. Amory, ed., *The Letters of Evelyn Waugh* (London, 1980).

III. SEPARATE WORKS. *P.R.B., An Essay on the Pre-Raphaelite Brotherhood 1847–1854* (London, 1926); *Rossetti, His Life and Works* (London, 1928), biography; *Decline and Fall, An Illustrated Novelette* (London, 1928; rev. ed., 1962), novel.

Vile Bodies (London, 1930; rev. ed., 1965), novel; *Labels: A Mediterranean Journey* (London, 1930), travel, new ed. with intro. by K. Amis (London, 1974), published in U.S. as *A Bachelor Abroad* (New York, 1930); *Remote People* (London, 1931), travel, published in U.S. as *They Were Still Dancing* (New York, 1932); *Black Mischief* (London, 1932; rev. ed., 1962), novel; *Ninety-Two Days: The Account of a Tropical Journey Through British Guiana and Part of Brazil* (London, 1934), travel; *A Handful of Dust* (London, 1934; rev. ed. with variant ending, 1964), novel; *Edmund Campion: Jesuit and Martyr* (London, 1935), biography; *Mr. Loveday's Little Outing, and Other Sad Stories* (London, 1936), short stories; *Waugh in Abyssinia* (London, 1936), travel; *Scoop, A Novel About Journalists* (London, 1938; rev. ed., 1964); *Robbery Under Law, the Mexican Object-Lesson* (London, 1939), travel, published in U.S. as *Mexico: An Object-Lesson* (Boston, 1939).

Put Out More Flags (London, 1942; rev. ed., 1967), novel; *Work Suspended* (London, 1942), novel, rev. and repr. with *Scott-King's Modern Europe* in the collection *Work Suspended, and Other Stories Written Before the Second World War* (London, 1949); *Brideshead Revisited: The Sacred and Profane Memories of Captain Charles Ryder* (London, 1945; uniform ed., 1949; rev. ed., 1960), novel; *When the Going Was Good* (London, 1946), repr. of parts of some prewar travel books; *Scott-King's Modern Europe* (London, 1947), novel; *Wine in Peace and War* (London, 1947), essay; *The Loved One: An Anglo-American Tragedy* (London, 1948; rev. ed., 1965), novel.

Helena (London, 1950), novel; *Men at Arms* (London, 1952), novel, rev. version forms first part of *Sword of Honour*; *The Holy Places* (London, 1952), travel; *Love Among the Ruins: A Romance of the Near Future* (London, 1953), story; *Tactical Exercise* (Boston, 1954), stories, includes *Work Suspended, Love Among the Ruins*, etc.; *Officers and Gentlemen* (London, 1955), novel, rev. version forms second part of *Sword of Honour*; *The Ordeal of Gilbert Pinfold* (London, 1957), novel; *The Life of the Right Reverend Ronald Knox, Fellow of Trinity College, Oxford, and Pronotary Apostolic to His Holiness Pope Pius XII* (London, 1959), biography.

A Tourist in Africa (London, 1960), travel; *Unconditional Surrender* (London, 1961), novel, published in U.S. as *The End of the Battle* (Boston, 1962), rev. version forms third part of *Sword of Honour; Basil Seal Rides Again, or The Rake's Regress* (London, 1963), short story; *A Little Learning* (London, 1964), autobiography; *Sword of Honour* (London, 1965), novel, one-vol. version of *Men at Arms, Officers and Gentlemen,* and *Unconditional Surrender*; "Charles Ryder's Schooldays," in *Times Literary Supplement* (5 March 1982), pp. 255–258, included in *Work Suspended* (Harmondsworth, 1982), Penguin ed., literary fragment.

IV. BIOGRAPHICAL AND CRITICAL STUDIES. Arthur Waugh, *One Man's Road, Being a Picture of Life in a Passing Generation* (London, 1931); D. S. Savage, "The Innocence of Evelyn Waugh," in B. Rajan, ed., *Focus Four: The Novelist as Thinker* (London, 1947); H. Acton, *Memoirs of an Aesthete* (London, 1948); G. Mikes, "Evelyn Waugh," in *Eight Humorists* (London, 1954); S. Marcus, "Evelyn Waugh and the Art of Entertainment," in *Partisan Review,* 23 (Summer 1956); S. O'Faolain, *The Vanishing Hero: Studies in Novelists of the Twenties* (London, 1956); A. A. De Vitis, *Roman Holiday: The Catholic Novels of Evelyn Waugh* (New York, 1956); H. Breit, *The Writer Observed* (Cleveland, 1957); F. J. Stopp, *Evelyn Waugh, Portrait of an Artist* (London, 1958).

A. E. Dyson, "Evelyn Waugh and the Mysteriously Disappearing Hero," in *Critical Quarterly,* 2 (Spring 1960), repr. in *The Crazy Fabric: Essays in Irony* (London, 1965); P. Green, "Du Côte de chez Waugh," in *Review of English Literature,* 2 (1961); G. Martin, "Novelists of Three Decades: Evelyn Waugh, Graham Greene, C. P. Snow," in *The Pelican Guide to English Literature,* vol. VII: B. Fox, ed., *The Modern Age* (London, 1961); R. Wasson, "*A Handful of Dust:* Critique of Victorianism," in *Modern Fiction Studies,* 7 (1961–1962); Alec Waugh, *The Early Years of Alec Waugh* (London, 1962); B. Bergonzi, "Evelyn Waugh's Gentleman," in *Critical Quarterly,* 5 (Spring 1963); J. Jebb, interviewer, "The Art of Fiction 30. Evelyn Waugh," in *Paris Review,* 8 (Summer–Fall 1963); M. Bradbury, *Evelyn Waugh* (London, 1964); K. Allsop, "Pinfold at Home," in *Scan* (1965); S. J. Greenblatt, *The Modern Satirists: Waugh, Orwell, and Huxley* (New Haven, Conn., 1965); A. Kernan, *The Plot of Satire* (New Haven, Conn., 1965); J. M. Cameron, "A Post-Waugh Insight," in *Commonweal,* 83 (October 1966); R. Delasanta and M. L. Avanzo, "Truth and Beauty in *Brideshead Revisited,*" in *Modern Fiction Studies,* 11 (1965–1966); P. Hinchcliffe, "Fathers and Children in the Novels of Evelyn Waugh," in *University of Toronto Quarterly,* 35 (1966); F. Donaldson, *Evelyn Waugh: Portrait of a Country Neighbor* (London, 1967); Alec Waugh, *My Brother Evelyn and Other Profiles* (London, 1967); P. A. Doyle, *Evelyn Waugh* (Grand Rapids, Mich., 1969).

T. Eagleton, *Exiles and Emigrés* (London, 1970); H.

Acton, *More Memoirs of an Aesthete* (London, 1970); D. Lodge, *Evelyn Waugh* (New York, 1971); W. J. Cook, *Masks, Modes, and Morals: The Art of Evelyn Waugh* (Rutherford, N.J., 1971); D. Price-Jones, ed., *Evelyn Waugh and His World* (London, 1973); J. St. John, *To the War with Waugh* (London, 1974); B. W. Wilson, "Sword of Honour: The Last Crusade," in *English*, 23 (Autumn 1974); G. D. Phillips, *Evelyn Waugh's Officers, Gentlemen, and Rogues: The Fact Behind His Fiction* (Chicago, 1975); D. P. Farr, "The Novelist's Coup: Style as Satiric Norm in *Scoop*," in *Connecticut Review*, 8 (April 1975); C. Sykes, *Evelyn Waugh: A Biography* (London, 1975); Dom H. van Zeller, "The Agreeable Mr. Waugh," in the *Critic*, 13 (Fall 1976); M. Stannard, "Davie's Lamp," in *New Review*, 3 (December 1976); Y. Tosser, *Le Sens de l'absurde dans l'oeuvre d'Evelyn Waugh* (Lille, 1977); W. Myers, "Potential Recruits: Evelyn Waugh and the Reader of *Black Mischief*," in *Renaissance and Modern Studies*, 21 (1977), repr. in *The 1930s: A Challenge to Orthodoxy*, ed. J. Lucas (Brighton, 1978); J. Meckier, "Evelyn Waugh," in *Contemporary Literature*, 18 (Winter 1977); A. Powell, *Messengers of Day* (London, 1978); S. G. Auty, "Language and Charm in *Brideshead Revisited*," in *Dutch Quarterly Review*, 6 (August 1978); M. Stannard, "*Work Suspended*, Waugh's Climacteric," in *Essays in Criticism*, 28 (October 1978); J. Meckier, "Cycle, Symbol, and Parody in Evelyn Waugh's *Decline and Fall*," in *Contemporary Literature*, 20 (Winter 1979).

P. Fussell, *Abroad* (New York–Oxford, 1980); R. Davis, *Evelyn Waugh, Writer* (Norman, Okla., 1980); J. Heath, *The Picturesque Prison. Evelyn Waugh and His Writing* (London, 1982); R. Johnstone, *The Will to Believe: Novelists of the Nineteen-Thirties* (Oxford, 1982); M. Stannard, "Debunking the Jungle: The Context of Evelyn Waugh's Travel Books 1930–39," in *Prose Studies*, 5 (1982), repr. in *The Art of Travel*, ed. P. Dodd (London, 1982); I. Littlewood, *The Writings of Evelyn Waugh* (Oxford, 1983).

Note: Several important articles on Waugh have been published in *Evelyn Waugh Newsletter* (Garden City, N.Y., Spring 1967–   ). Other articles will appear in M. Stannard, ed., *The Critical Heritage*, in progress.

CHRISTOPHER ISHERWOOD
(1904-   )

Francis King

I

"WITH me, everything starts with autobiography," Christopher Isherwood has declared. Possessed of an insight into character, an incisiveness of style, and an architectural sense all far superior to his powers of invention, he belongs essentially to what might be called the "suppose-if" category of novelists. For such novelists the process of creation begins with something that they themselves have either experienced or observed at close quarters. Taking this foundation of reality, they then proceed to build on it imaginatively by a series of "suppose-ifs"—suppose if I had done that and not this, suppose if so-and-so had said this and not that. There should be a word for writing of this kind, poised halfway between fact and fiction. Perhaps "faction" would do. When Isherwood has stayed closest to reality, as in the Berlin stories of his prewar period or *A Single Man* (1964) of his postwar one, he has been at his best; when he has strayed furthest from it, as in *The World in the Evening* (1954), he has been at his least convincing.

Since his life story is, to such a large extent, the story of each of his fictions in turn, a summary of it is an essential preliminary to any critical study. Both life and literary career are decisively cut in two by World War II—which he was bitterly criticized at the time for escaping by his departure for America in 1939. Born at High Lane, Cheshire, on 26 August 1904, of upper-middle-class parents (it is essential to know this to appreciate the early fiction), he was only ten when his father was killed in France in the fighting around Ypres. He has denied that this event had any particularly traumatic effect on him—"I think I would have been just as happy as an orphan" —but the character of the typical mother's boy that recurs in his early books suggests the contrary. After attending a public school, he went to Cambridge, which he left without graduating. There followed an unsatisfactory period when he tried to study medicine. In 1928 Isherwood published his first novel and from then onward he lived mostly out of England—notably in Berlin—while he built up a reputation as probably the most gifted novelist of his generation.

With his departure for the United States this reputation began to slump, and it was not until several years after the war that it revived again. This was undoubtedly due in some part to a feeling, however unjust, that he had abandoned his country at a time of need, but also to the fact that expatriation seemed at first to have a deleterious effect on his talent, virtually silencing him for five or six years and then causing him to produce the basically unsatisfactory *The World in the Evening.* For part of the war he worked as a conscientious objector with the American Friends Service. In 1946 he became a U.S. citizen; and soon he had acquired not only American nationality but an American accent, manner, and style of dress. Settling in Santa Monica, California, he divided his time between working on films, lecturing at the University of California, and writing books.

Two additional facts about him need to be given, since both are crucial to an understanding of his work. The first is an increasing interest in Indian mysticism: among his works are *An Approach to Vedanta* (1963) and *Ramakrishna and His Disciples* (1968), a biography of a famous nineteenth-century Indian mystic. The second is his homosexuality, about which he has become increasingly outspoken with the relaxation of the taboos that used to hedge the subject. In his treatment of his own homosexuality and homosexuality in general he has displayed a crusading courage—"In taking up the cause of one minority, that of homosexuals against the dictatorship of heterosexuals, I have spoken out for all minorities," he has said.

CHRISTOPHER ISHERWOOD

WHEN Isherwood published his first novel, *All The Conspirators* (1928), at the age of twenty-four, it sold only three hundred copies. Yet to read it now is to be astonished, despite the obvious debts to James Joyce, Virginia Woolf, and E. M. Forster, by its air of assurance. In an introduction to a 1939 reissue of the novel, the English critic Cyril Connolly describes it as "a key . . . to the twenties." Some qualification to this extravagant claim is necessary. There are whole areas of life in the 1920's—poverty, unemployment, political upheaval, the emancipation of women among them—that the book never touches and was never intended to touch; but as a key to the attitudes of the upper-middle-class young of the time it is invaluable. Like the young of today, the young of Isherwood's novel are in a state of protest. But, as Isherwood himself has pointed out, whereas the protest today is against society, then it was against the family. Isherwood has described the book as "a minor engagement in what Shelley calls 'the great war between old and young'" and the battle cry of its author as having been "My Generation—right or wrong!"

What is both saddening and surprising about the book is the basic timidity and impotence of the young, despite all the vehemence with which they denounce their elders. The hero, Philip, like the Isherwood of the time, is a would-be writer. Tied to a mother who stifles him with her domineering love, he makes repeated attempts to break free of her. But he fails, partly because he does not have the courage and initiative to venture out into a world in which he must learn to support himself and partly, and more subtly, because deep within himself this maternal domination is something that he actually enjoys and craves. No less weak are his closest friend, Allen; his sister, Joan; and the hearty young man, Victor, who is Allen's rival for Joan's love. All of them know what they want; and all suffer from a paralysis of the will that prevents them from taking it. Eventually, because of that paralysis of will, we suspect (though the book does not follow them that far) that they will each of them get immovably stuck, with all progress or development denied them.

In his autobiographical *Lions and Shadows* (1938), subtitled *An Education in the Twenties*, Isherwood describes the way in which he revised *All the Conspirators*, often in obedience to suggestions from his friend the novelist Edward Upward, and so made it even less intelligible (though that was not, of course, his intention) to the readers of the day. Stage directions, like "he said," "she replied," "they both laughed," and so forth, were cut to a minimum; and any big dramatic scene—the book was to end with Allen's murder of Victor—became instead "an indecisive, undignified scramble." Isherwood and his friends at that period had a phrase for this kind of treatment, of which they felt that E. M. Forster was the master: "tea-tabling." As Upward put it: "The whole of Forster's technique is based on the tea-table: instead of trying to screw all his scenes up to the highest possible pitch, he tones them down until they sound like mothers'-meeting gossip. . . . In fact, there's actually *less* emphasis laid on the big scenes than on the unimportant ones." This judgment is no less applicable to *All the Conspirators* and to much of Isherwood's later work.

Isherwood's brilliant debut was followed four years later by *The Memorial* (1932)—which had for its author the private title "War and Peace," since its subject is not the actual events of World War I but the effect of that war on those who lived on after it. Here, again, there is a bitter antagonism between a widowed mother and her son. But the most memorable character, among a host of memorable ones, is the shell-shocked, homosexual ex-airman Edward Blake, who bungles his suicide attempt as he bungles so much else; who lives with a woman with whom he is incapable of making love; who travels about the world but finds no resting place; and who, at the end of the book, is in Berlin with a mercenary German boy lover. In the closing scene, he and the boy talk about the war:

> "It must have been terrible."
> "It was awful," said Edward.
> "You know," said Franz, very serious and evidently repeating something he had heard said by his elders: "that War . . . it ought never to have happened."

This overt statement of an unexceptionable thesis is the one moment when Isherwood's artistry fails him. Until these final words, everything has been subtly implied, never stated. We have seen the characters in a state of emotional, moral, or financial bankruptcy because of the war; we have seen how an established order has started to disintegrate, with nothing to replace it. We can draw the necessary conclusion for ourselves; it does not have to be thrust at us.

Technically, like *All the Conspirators*, the book is

a highly interesting one. The style has less youthful trickiness and more gravity and depth; but it, too, is remarkably concise, so that, when one has reached the last page, one has the satisfying feeling of having read a book far more substantial than its actual eighty thousand or so words. Isherwood had planned to write "an epic disguised as a drawing-room comedy," and, against all odds, that was what he succeeded in doing. The time scheme of the book is particularly interesting. The worst thing about epics, Isherwood decided, is that their beginnings are so dull. Why not, therefore, plunge into the middle, go backward, and then go forward once more? That way, the reader "comes on the dullness half-way through, when he is more interested in the characters; the fish holds its tail in its mouth." The idea works.

The four years that Isherwood spent in Berlin from 1929 were extremely important to him, both because it was then that he was first able fully to explore his sexual nature and because they gave him the novella *Sally Bowles* (1937), which was to have worldwide success as a play (*I Am a Camera*), as a film of that play, as a musical (*Cabaret*), and as a film of that musical. Yet of all his Berlin stories this work is, ironically, the least considerable. Far weightier, though not much longer, is the masterly *Mr. Norris Changes Trains* (1935). That on its publication this book should have been regarded by many intelligent and civilized people as shocking and even pornographic now seems barely credible.

In all the Berlin stories, with the exception of *Mr. Norris Changes Trains*, the hero-narrator appears as "Christopher Isherwood"—"Chris" to Sally Bowles, the expatriate English girl with ambitions to be both a demimondaine and a singer, "Herr Issyvoo" to the Germans. Isherwood describes this fictional persona as "a convenient ventriloquist's dummy, nothing more," but we need not take that disclaimer too seriously; the ventriloquist's dummy (to whom I shall refer in this study as "Isherwood," with quotation marks around his name) and the author have much in common. In *Mr. Norris Changes Trains*, the hero-narrator is given the name of William Bradshaw. Like Isherwood at that period, Bradshaw is a young would-be writer of left-wing sympathies who supports himself in Berlin, in a state of semipoverty, by giving English lessons. His feelings for the Germans are ambiguous, being compounded in equal measure of love and hate, admiration and disgust. On the train taking him to Berlin, he falls in with a

fellow Englishman in his fifties, a man who can most charitably be described as an adventurer and most accurately as a crook. This is Mr. Norris. A gentleman by birth, he has often been reduced to the ungentlemanly expedients of blackmail, fraud, and theft to keep himself in the luxury to which he has long been accustomed. "A queerly cut fringe of dark-grey hair . . . compact, thick and heavy" soon makes it clear to Bradshaw that his train companion is wearing a wig. But his baldness is not the only thing that Mr. Norris has to conceal; his sexual tastes are decidely unorthodox. Through Norris, Bradshaw meets Baron von Pregnitz, a rich pederast who invites them to his luxurious country villa and who, it soon becomes clear, is being blackmailed by Mr. Norris and his sinister secretary-companion, Schmidt. Parallel with this frieze illustrating the moral twilight of the Weimar Republic, Isherwood paints another of the political ferment of the time. Norris proclaims himself to be a Communist, addresses meetings of, not surprisingly, somewhat bewildered Communist workers, and introduces his young protégé to one of the Communist leaders. But in fact he is a traitor to the Communist movement, selling its secrets to the French intelligence service.

The other Berlin stories also deal with this period when, humiliated by the Treaty of Versailles, disgusted by the lack of discipline of the Weimar Republic, and disillusioned by years of economic chaos, many Germans were preparing to give an enthusiastic welcome to Hitler and the Nazis. Though fragmentary—Isherwood had originally hoped to write a huge episodic novel of pre-Hitler Berlin entitled "The Lost," but the hope was never realized—they are surprisingly wide in their range. On the one hand, there are the poor, living in their near-slums, perpetually anxious about work and money, succumbing to illness from overcrowding and malnutrition, and dreaming of an illusory escape to another life in another country. On the other hand, there are the rich, often Jews, who can afford to employ a struggling would-be writer from England as tutor, inviting him to their luxury town flats or their splendid seaside or country houses, but who sense that at any moment a new wind, whether Nazi or Communist, will sweep them and their wealth away.

In his essay "Mr. Norris and I" (1956) Isherwood writes, "what repels me about *Mr. Norris* is its heartlessness," going on to describe the book as "a heartless fairy-story about a real city in which human beings were suffering the miseries of political violence and near-starvation." This accusation of heartlessness could be leveled by a hostile critic against all the Berlin stories, and the reason must, I think, be found in the Bradshaw/"Isherwood" persona itself. This young foreigner "who passed gaily through these scenes of desolation, misinterpreting them to suit his childish fantasy" (the words are Isherwood's) is at once innocent and knowing, sensitive and immune. He perches on the edge of the steaming Berlin caldron, while the others, whether English or German, thrash about in agony in its waters. He is far more self-contained and self-protective than Isherwood can possibly have been in real life, to judge from all one knows about him. His immunity extends even to sex. Others, like Sally Bowles, attract men or are attracted by them; others, like Mr. Norris or Baron von Pregnitz, pursue their less orthodox obsessions, often with disastrous results to themselves or their loved ones. The young narrator looks on, smiles, says some words of sympathy or encouragement, scribbles in his notebook. Hindsight now makes it clear why Isherwood made Bradshaw/"Isherwood" a man without apparent sexual drive. He was too honest to adopt the usual homosexual novelist's device of substituting girl for boy; and at that period it was extremely difficult and even dangerous to tell the truth.

There are, nonetheless, many moments in the German stories when "Isherwood's" shell of detachment cracks. The most moving of these is when he goes to visit his former landlady in the sanatorium from which it seems unlikely that she will ever emerge. Her son, Otto, is with him. When the time comes for the two young men to leave, Frau Nowack, previously composed, breaks down: "Clasping her hands over her breast, she uttered short yelping coughs like a desperate injured animal. . . . Two sisters gently tried to lead her away, but at once she began to struggle furiously. She wouldn't go with them." In seeming menace, the patients gather closer and closer around the bus that is to take away the visitors, and briefly "Isherwood" has an absurd dread that they are going to launch an attack—"clawing us from our seats, dragging us hungrily down." Then they draw back. It is a masterly scene, written with the force of an agonized compassion.

The last work that Isherwood published before he emigrated to America was the autobiographical *Lions and Shadows*, subtitled *An Education in the Twenties*. Just as his fiction has always contained a high proportion of fact, so this factual account contains, on his own admission, a high proportion of fiction. "Read it as a novel," he advises the reader in his preface; and it is perfectly feasible to do so, since it has the necessary pace, qualities of surprise, and architectural unity. Many of Isherwood's friends of the period, who have since achieved fame themselves—Stephen Spender, W. H. Auden, and Upward are the most important—appear caricatured under other names. One interesting feature of the book is that Isherwood's mother, obviously the most important person, for good or ill, in his life at that period, never appears at all—when he has to mention her, she becomes "my female relative" or "my relatives" or "my family." (With typical frankness, Isherwood has himself commented on this omission.) It is as though, at the period in question, she still exerted such authority over him that he felt that even to write of her could be dangerous. Another curious feature is the account of how, while students, he and Upward invented for themselves a private fantasy world, to which they gave the name "The Other Town," and later "Mortmere." They peopled this world with imaginary characters; devised bizarre eccentricities, vices, and misadventures for them; and, to categorize them, invented a number of words and phrases not to be found in any dictionary. Isherwood and his friend Auden, both separately and in collaboration, were often to indulge in such private allusions and jokes in their later published writings, as though reverting to this undergraduate game.

Isherwood's works written in collaboration with Auden were *Journey to a War* (1939), an account of the war in China, and three plays strongly influenced by German Expressionist drama—*The Dog Beneath the Skin* (1935), *The Ascent of F6* (1936), and *On the Frontier* (1938). Isherwood worked only on the plotting and part of the prose of the plays and did not (as is sometimes thought) write any of the verse. The plot of *The Ascent of F6*, the best of the plays and the one most worth reviving, has a particular psychological interest. When, after tremendous hardships and struggles, its mountaineer hero at last reaches the summit of the hitherto unscaled peak, F6, that he has set out to conquer, it is revealed to be his mother. Whether consciously or not, Isherwood had perhaps here found a symbol for his own success under the spur of his dominating mother's ambition for him, and for his guilty feeling that he could never win her wholehearted approbation and yet must go on striving to do so.

III

AFTER his departure for the United States shortly before the war, there followed a period of some six years when Isherwood wrote very little. One critic has talked of "the dark night" of his soul. Certainly he felt dissatisfied, disorientated, and creatively depleted. His leaving England had provoked some bitter comment; the novelist Evelyn Waugh had even made him and his fellow exile the poet Auden characters in his novel *Put Out More Flags* (1942), under the names of Parsnip and Pimpernell, having them quit the country, not for the safety of the New World, but for that of neutral Ireland. That two people who had so energetically fulminated against Fascism in Germany, Italy, and Spain should have opted out of the struggle against Fascism when it was on the point of coming to open warfare was calculated to arouse mockery and indignation among many people in the England of that time, and Waugh's contemptuous satire was expressive of a common, if ugly, attitude.

The first work of fiction to break the silence was *Prater Violet* (1945), written in America but looking back to a period when Isherwood was still resident in England. Though extremely brief, an extended short story rather than a novel, it succeeds, like *Sally Bowles* and *Mr. Norris Changes Trains*, in compressing a great deal into its narrow compass. Here again "Isherwood," at once knowing and innocent, sympathetic and detached, is the person chosen to tell the story. Living with his mother and brother as he struggles to complete a novel, he receives an unexpected telephone call asking him to write the script of a film set in Old Vienna. He has been approached because of a ludicrous misunderstanding: the studio has mistaken his knowledge of Germany for a knowledge of Austria. Chosen to direct the film is a famous Austrian director, Friedrich Bergmann, whose family has stayed on in Vienna during his absence. Young "Isherwood" and Bergmann (the character was based on the director Berthold Viertel) at once establish a close rapport, as between a wayward and affectionate son and a sympathetic and occasionally irascible father. This "Isherwood," like the hero of *All the Conspirators*, is a mother's boy. Bergmann at once perceives this, telling him that the typical mother's boy "is unable to cut himself free, sternly, from the bourgeois dream of the Mother. That fatal and comforting dream. He wants to crawl back into the economic safety of the womb. He hates the paternal revolutionary tradition, which reminds him of his duty as its son." At this moment, as at many others in the book, it is as though it were not Bergmann speaking to "Isherwood" but Isherwood communing with his inmost self.

While Bergmann is engaged on making his light, frothy musical, Austria is all at once racked by the political dissension that eventually brought defeat to the Socialists and the Fascist Engelbert Dollfuss to supreme power. Bergmann is plunged into gloom, as he waits anxiously for news of his country and his family. The contrast between the triviality of his film and the seriousness of real events is all but unbearable to him. But he eventually pulls himself together when it seems likely that the studio will replace him with another director, and *Prater Violet* (the title of the film as well as the story) is a huge success.

The tone of the whole book is, for the most part, humorously ironic. By the time that he came to write it, we know that Isherwood had put in a great deal of work in Hollywood film studios and had long since become familiar with the industry. But with great adroitness he thought himself back to a period when he was still able to view it with the amazed and bewildered eyes of innocence. Everything is new, strange, and startling to his "Isherwood"; and he succeeds in making everything new, strange, and startling to us.

Using that old technique of "tea-tabling"—of domesticating drama and even tragedy—Isherwood gives a certain absurdity to Bergmann's anguish over the fate of his film, his family, his country, and, finally, Europe. But that anguish is nonetheless real and is made real to us. Seeing Bergmann for the first time, "Isherwood" thinks: "The name, the voice, the features were inessential, I knew that face. It was the face of a political situation, an epoch. The face of Central Europe." Bergmann therefore—intelligent, ironical, cultivated, sometimes solemn, and sometimes playful—is a symbol of the race to which he belongs, the area on the map of Europe that he inhabits, and the period in which he lives. That he is not only a symbol but also a three-dimensional person in his own right is a measure of Isherwood's artistry.

The brilliant surface of the book suddenly deepens and darkens for the last ten pages. "Isherwood," the detached and nonchalant observer of the agonies of others, suddenly reveals his own. First he puts to himself the question "What makes you go on living?"

CHRISTOPHER ISHERWOOD

and then comes up with the answer that life for him has been a supine process of doing, in succession, whatever people have recommended to him. Among the things recommended has been Love; and he then meditates on his affair with someone called J. Isherwood still shrinks in this book from total frankness about himself and so the sex of J is left indeterminate, with Isherwood avoiding any use of "he" or "she," "him" or "her." The prose is, not unnaturally, oddly gauche in consequence of this absence of personal pronouns; but that very gaucheness, as of someone stammering out an embarrassed confession, makes it extremely moving.

Finally, Isherwood writes of the fears that assail him: of death, war, illness, and other more trivial, childish things. How is one to escape from a life lived in perpetual fear of something or other? Briefly, he has a vision of "the way that leads to safety": it is like "the high far glimpse of a goat-track through the mountains between clouds." But he cannot go that way. "I could never do it," he tells himself. "Rather the fear I know, the loneliness I know. . . . For to take the other way would mean that I should lose myself, I should no longer be a person. I should no longer be Christopher Isherwood." The passage is a strangely enigmatic one, since it is never entirely certain from the text alone whether the self-annihilation to which he is referring is that of the suicide or of the mystic. In the light of his increasing interest in Vedanta, the latter seems certain.

Almost ten years were to pass before Isherwood published another novel, and, since in the 1930's he had been such a fluent writer, many of his admirers began to assume that his career as a novelist had come to an end. (He was working assiduously on his religious books during this period.) When he at last published *The World in the Evening*, it was not wholly reassuring. The hero, Stephen Monk, a wealthy, rootless, handsome Anglo-American, is the sort of person of whom one comments, "He has never really grown up." In the habit of running away from any unmanageable situation, he retreats to his suburban Philadelphia birthplace and his Quaker foster-mother after he surprises his second wife, Jane, being unfaithful to him at a Hollywood party. Running away yet again from the suffocating goodness and worthiness of his foster-mother and her circle, he has a motor accident in which a truck breaks his thigh, and he is then back with his foster-mother, immobilized for the next ten weeks. This enforced idleness forces him to review his past life, with all its inadequacies and betrayals, and so lay the foundation for something better.

Religious people would say that the accident that starts this process of self-redemption was an act of God; students of Freud would say that not God but Stephen's subconscious had intervened. Isherwood probably intended both. At least one reviewer has described the theme as being "the making of a saint"; and though that may be an exaggeration—perhaps the theme is merely the making of a mature human being—there is no doubt of Isherwood's religious preoccupation. Unfortunately this whole process by which Stephen begins to grow up as he lies in bed, reads his dead first wife's letters, and talks to his foster-mother, his homosexual doctor, his doctor's boyfriend, and a German woman refugee, is curiously artificial and unconvincing. When in *Crime and Punishment* we read of how a callow young Russian officer becomes Father Zossima, we do not for a moment question the conversion; but Isherwood's Stephen, like Somerset Maugham's Larry in *The Razor's Edge* (1944), is always more credible in his unregenerate days.

Stephen's first wife, Elizabeth Rydal, an English novelist, is dead at the opening of the book. As in the case of Stephen's foster-mother—a garrulous, seemingly muddle-headed, seemingly ingenuous spinster—there exists in her a strong element of goodness, even saintliness. Elizabeth knows that her husband has been unfaithful both with the young man whom they regard as their adopted son and with the woman whom he eventually makes his second wife; herself a chronic invalid, she knows too that she has not long to live. But she has learned the total acceptance that Stephen himself finds so difficult to learn. The character of this woman—based, one would guess, on that of Katherine Mansfield, a writer whom we know Isherwood has always admired—is revealed with admirable subtlety, whether through Stephen's memories of her or through her letters. The letters themselves are clever pastiches of the kind of letters that Katherine Mansfield wrote and of the kind of journals that Virginia Woolf (another writer whom Isherwood greatly admired) kept. At first we think that they are the product of a first-rate writer and a second-rate human being; then, gradually, with great adroitness, Isherwood shows us that they are, in fact, the product of a first-rate human being and a second-rate writer.

There are many other things to admire—descriptions of life and scenery in the Canary Islands, the account of Stephen's sexual betrayal of Elizabeth with the "adopted son," the character of the stoical, almost grim German refugee awaiting news of her lover, a prisoner in a concentration camp—but a curious miasma of unease seeps through the book. This may be because Isherwood was not sufficiently familiar with American life and the American idiom by the time that he came to write it. It may also be that, as a homosexual, Isherwood did not feel at home in handling Stephen's relationships with his two wives—certainly the relationship with the "adopted son" is physically more convincing. Because this unease keeps obtruding, because Stephen's declaration at the end of the book, "I really do forgive myself from the bottom of my heart" (as though self-forgiveness might not be another and even more insidious kind of self-indulgence than his egotism in the past), strikes all too glib a note, and because the relationship between the homosexual doctor and his boyfriend is handled in so embarrassingly skittish and arch a manner, what was no doubt intended as the "big" book of Isherwood's creative maturity seems both smaller and less mature than his early book *The Memorial*.

Down There on a Visit (1962) is a more satisfactory work, since it returns in three of its four episodes, with total self-confidence, to Isherwood's European, prewar past; and in the fourth episode, set in California in the 1940's, the American scene and idiom have been perfectly assimilated. The first section, "Mr. Lancaster," is the shortest and most fragile. It might also be regarded as a preface to the Berlin stories, set as it is in the year 1928 and describing Isherwood's first introduction to the country in which he was later to make his home. The Mr. Lancaster of the title is a distant family conection, a pompous and prurient businessman working with a shipping firm in Germany, who, when on leave, calls unexpectedly on "Isherwood" to visit him. The young man, who has just published his first novel, travels across the North Sea on one of the ships belonging to Mr. Lancaster's firm. The crew is described with characteristic crispness and vividness. Face to face with his host and benefactor, "Isherwood" feels for him only hatred and contempt. Mr. Lancaster is a fantasist, a man whom loneliness has driven to live "too long inside his sounding-box, listening to his own reverberations, his epic song of himself." But the heartless and amused young man sees not the pathos but only the absurdity. Lancaster has a German adolescent, Waldemar, working for

him as an office boy. This boy, who takes "Isherwood" swimming and later introduces him to a youthful orgy of "slippery sounds of nakedness, of Turkish cigarettes, cushion-dust, crude perfume and healthy sweat," appears in each of the subsequent episodes. "Isherwood" goes sailing with his host and, too terrified to defy him openly, gets his revenge by half-deliberately causing the outboard engine to fall into the water. Later, when he is once more back with his loving mother and faithful friends, he learns of the mysterious death of Mr. Lancaster by his own hand. As so often in life, the suicide has had no prior build-up or warning. Possibly, Isherwood speculates, Mr. Lancaster invited him so surprisingly to be his guest in a desperate last attempt to establish contact with the outside world. The attempt failed; he was submerged by despair, just as the outboard motor was submerged by the muddy waters. The story has an inconsequentiality and perfunctoriness about it, as though it belonged to a memoir, in which the author is obliged to set down things exactly as they happened, rather than to fiction, in which he may give them artistic shape. But it is precisely this seemingly inconsequentiality and perfunctoriness that make the whole incident (it is little more) so lifelike.

The next episode, "Ambrose," has more substance and architectural unity and is the best of the four. Five years have passed; it is now 1933, and the young "Isherwood" is traveling to Greece with Waldemar, whom he has met again in Berlin. Waldemar has been promised a job with an eccentric Englishman, the Ambrose of the title (based on the English archaeologist Francis Turville-Petre), who is living on a wild little Greek island off the coast of the larger, densely cultivated island of Euboea. Ambrose (who has been at Cambridge with "Isherwood") asks him to stay on the island too. There, in what to many people would seem a hell of discomfort, squalor, and intellectual and moral degradation, Ambrose attempts to rule a little kingdom of misfits and parasites. The Greek boys whom poverty has brought to the island spend their time exploiting their master or quarreling among themselves. The adults sit around all day drinking or recovering from their hangovers. Yet what to most other people would be hell is heaven to Ambrose. "Isherwood" eventually leaves the island, knowing that he does not belong there; but, after this odd and devastating experience, he is haunted by the feeling that he does not belong anywhere else either.

Waldemar reappears in the third section, which bears his name for its title. It is now 1938, the period of near-war before the war actually breaks out. Waldemar arrives in England in the company of an English girl, a Communist from a well-to-do upper-middle-class family, whose lover he has become. The girl has difficulty with the English immigration authorities, who are reluctant to admit a non-Jewish German with no money to support himself. Later, she has further difficulties with her family (Isherwood is here reverting to his old theme of the war between the generations), who disapprove of her openly living with a man who is not her husband. The relationship between the two becomes increasingly difficult and stormy, and finally Waldemar decides to go home. He is not a Nazi, he has no sympathy with the Nazis; but if war is to come, then he feels that his place is in his own country. Interspersed with this account of Waldemar and his English girlfriend are diary entries (one guesses that they derive from actual diaries kept by Isherwood at the time) about the crisis that was ended, though only temporarily, by Chamberlain's flight to Germany and the Munich agreement. These catch the ominous atmosphere of the period with great fidelity, even if their relevance to the story of the German boy and the English girl is not always wholly clear. This section concludes with "Isherwood" reaching a decision the exact opposite of Waldemar's: he will quit his homeland for exile.

The last section, "Paul," is for the most part set in America during the war. "Isherwood," now the disciple of an English expatriate guru named Augustus (a character based on the philosopher Gerald Heard) and working in a film studio, is introduced to a male prostitute called Paul. Paul shows a surprising desire to give up his worldly existence to study religion and, to this end, persuades "Isherwood" to introduce him to Augustus. But though he is totally sincere in this wish and though it is clear, by the end of the story, that he has probably progressed further along the path of enlightenment than "Isherwood" himself will ever do, he is so far removed from the usual convert in behavior, speech, and attitude that he inevitably excites suspicion and even hatred. Eventually he turns to opium to provide him with the vision that he seeks. Such a life—at first gregarious, mercenary, and destructive, then lonely, impoverished, and drug-dependent—would strike most "normal" people as hell. But, as in the case of Ambrose, the hell of others provides Paul with his glimpse of heaven.

Paul accuses "Isherwood" of being "down here on a visit"—a perpetual tourist, gaping at the hells of others but never himself condemned to their torments; and this idea provides both the title of the book and whatever unity it possesses other than that derived from the appearance of Waldemar and "Isherwood" in all four sections. (Isherwood's viewing of himself as a temporary visitor to hell has already occurred in *Prater Violet,* where the film director, Bergmann, tells the young "Isherwood" that he is "the good Virgil who has come to guide me"—an allusion to Vergil's guiding of Dante through the Inferno.) But despite the fact that each of the sections is about people shut up in hells of their own making, with the author as spectator, the book remains scrappy and lacking in cohesion. One feels that, having in his desk drawer a number of fragments—notes, letters, diary entries, the beginnings and ends of stories—Isherwood has set about weaving them into a single fabric. The book is not an organic growth but a skillful assembly.

Two years later Isherwood published *A Single Man* (1964), in my view his finest novel, even though it is not his most popular. Here, the narrator (George) is describing not the hell of others, but the hell in which he himself is living. Superficially his life as a lecturer at a California university is happy and successful; he is popular with his students, he has enough money to spare, and, though he has now reached late middle age, his health is good. But he is also a bachelor and a homosexual whose former lover, killed in a car crash, has become a perpetually haunting memory to him. Unlike *Down There on a Visit*, with its lack of cohesion, this is a novel severely ruled by the classical unities. It begins with the hero waking up alone in his "tightly planned little house" and ends with his going to bed, again alone, in it. What happens in the meantime—a lecture on an Aldous Huxley novel to his students, a visit to a woman dying of cancer, a frustrating flirtation with one of his male students in a seafront bar—does nothing to change his life, and if he wakes up the next morning (it is possible, as he is well aware, that he may not do so) the succeeding day is unlikely to be much different. But as he moves through these events, now comic, now tragic, now pathetic, now embarrassing, he is revealing to us everything about himself and about the predicament of a middle-aged, middle-class homosexual of that time and social status and place. There is no reason, children apart, why a homosexual's life should be any more sterile than a heterosexual's; but the hell in which George lives is a desert and it is significant that his final action of the day should be a totally arid one—masturbation. The book is bleak in its vision of stoicism in the face of bereavement, loneliness, imminent old age, and eventual death; but it is redeemed from being depressing by its ever present humor (the account of George's lecture on a Huxley novel is very funny) and by the vigor and freshness of its writing. George may himself be world-weary and discouraged; his creator never appears to be so.

In his last novel to date, *A Meeting by the River* (1967), Isherwood writes yet again—and writes more convincingly than ever before—of the first steps a man takes on the road to spiritual enlightenment. The younger of two brothers, Oliver, leaves his work with the Red Cross in Munich to become the disciple of an expatriate Hindu swami resident in the city. The swami dies, in circumstances that suggest that he himself has chosen the exact moment for his departure, and Oliver then travels to India, partly in order to transport the swami's ashes for committal to the Ganges and partly in order to take his final monastic vows at the head monastery of the order. Oliver's elder brother, Patrick, decides to stop off at the monastery on his way to Thailand, where he is involved in the shooting of a film, in order to try to dissuade Oliver from the irrevocable step he has in mind. The brothers have always been very close to each other; but it is hate, as much as love, that has caused their closeness. At first Patrick does everything in his power to weaken Oliver's resolve: he mocks him, questions his motives, and, most devastatingly of all, forces Oliver to recognize in himself both the ability to impose his will on others and the ambition to do so. But the book concludes with Oliver's acceptance of his role as swami, Patrick's acceptance of Oliver's decision, and the brothers' acceptance of each other.

The story is told through the medium of letters—many of them written by Patrick to his wife, his mother, and the young man with whom he has been having an affair—and of Oliver's journals. That letters and journals should be almost identical in style at first strikes the reader as a failure of technique. But this similarity reinforces the view of Patrick and Oliver as, in some sense, two conflicting halves of the same person, perhaps even as two conflicting halves of their creator. Patrick is worldly, sly, tough, bisexual; Oliver is unworldly, straightforward, sensitive, in love with his brother's wife.

With the almost offhand effortlessness that we have learned to expect from him, Isherwood gives, through Patrick's eyes, a brilliant picture both of the monastery and of India—a country, as he sees it, of "a kind of nauseating enchantment." Oliver's spiritual odyssey, described step by step, is no less vivid. Like Patrick, we smile from time to time at the near-absurdity of his conduct and question his motives or his wisdom; but, again like Patrick, we eventually come to see that he has taken the course that is right for him, if not for everyone else. The final reconciliation between the two brothers, halves of the same identity—they embrace each other after the ceremony of initiation—is perfectly convincing.

The next of Isherwood's books to appear was *Kathleen and Frank* (1971), a long memoir—some might say too long, despite its quality—of his father and mother, based on their letters to each other and on his mother's diary. Meeting in 1895, Frank and Kathleen were married in 1903 after Frank, a regular officer in the army, had returned from the Boer War. Both were highly observant people and both wrote in a vigorous and vivid, if wholly unliterary, manner. Through them we view many of the major events of the Edwardian age; share the preoccupations and attitudes of the upper middle classes of the time; and, very movingly, see how two strongwilled, not always easy people came to adjust to each other in marriage. Tragedy came with the war, in which Frank was killed in 1915. Kathleen lived on until 1960, dying at the age of ninety-one in full possession of her by then formidable powers.

One realizes—and he himself confesses this—that this exploration of the lives of his parents was for Isherwood an act of both reparation and reconciliation, akin to the embrace between the two brothers at the close of *A Meeting by the River*. The young Isherwood had rebelled against the image of a herofather and all that he had seemed to represent: patriotism, the public-school system, a rigid sexual morality, a no less rigid class structure. Later, reading his father's letters, he had come to see that here was a man who was not the symbol of oppression and reaction he had supposed him to be, but a gentle, intelligent, often admirable human being. Similarly, the young Isherwood and his mother had often argued and even quarreled furiously—it was his revolt against her domination, his determination not to acquiesce in the role of mother's boy, that had been largely instrumental in propelling him to Germany at the end of the 1920's and to America at the end of the 1930's, thus (as he himself put it) "separating himself from Mother and Motherland at one stroke." But now, reading her letters and diaries and pursuing her ghost in memory, he saw that her constant opposition had, so far from depriving him of resolution, merely served to strengthen it. Indeed, perhaps even his marvelous readability derived from a desire to seduce her into enjoying what might otherwise, if judged merely by its subject matter, have disgusted and shocked her. Writing the book, Isherwood began to see the extent to which heredity made him and his brother, on the one hand, and their parents, on the other, merge into each other, to make almost a single entity.

When writers age and, though possessed of a professionalism far sharper than they commanded in the past, nonetheless find that they are running out of imaginative steam, they sometimes attempt stylistic improvements of their earlier works. In *Christopher and His Kind* (1976), Isherwood set himself a parallel task: not to rewrite his early work better but to rewrite it more truthfully.

The defect in the characterization of the narrator-hero of the Berlin fiction is that where his sexuality should be, there is merely an unfilled hole. It is easy to see the reason for this lacuna. In prewar times it would have required a high degree of courage for Isherwood to present him as a homosexual; and to adopt the kind of transposition practiced by other homosexual novelists would have appeared a cheat to a writer who was so honest. Now, in the interest of truth rather than art, Isherwood set about putting the record straight. "To Christopher Berlin meant Boys," he declares early on; and so, to a large extent, did Amsterdam, Copenhagen, Paris, London, New York, Los Angeles, and San Francisco.

In this relentless self-exposure, there is an admirable truthfulness; but just as André Gide produced his journal of his journal and could no doubt have produced yet another journal of *that* journal and so on ad infinitum, it is difficult to see why the process should ever cease for a writer as obsessive as Isherwood. The effect of this particular stage of his confessions is rather as if a choreographer were to take one behind the scenes after a magical performance of one of his ballets. The scenery looks tatty. Worse, the dancers look much smaller and less attractive than from out in front; they stink from all the physical effort, and their costumes are stained with grime and sweat. It is interesting to see how an illusion was created; but in that demonstration, the illusion is destroyed.

Nevertheless Isherwood's account of his love affair with a German boy, Heinz, and his efforts to get him foreign nationality so that he can avoid the draft is told with unobtrusive artistry. There is something touching about all the silliness and triviality so faithfully recorded; something repugnant too—as Isherwood has far too much self-knowledge not to be aware—in the picture of this simple-minded boy being treated as though he were some kind of curio. The book also contains memorable passages of reminiscence about Isherwood's writer friends.

My Guru and His Disciple (1980) is a less satisfactory memoir. When Isherwood arrived in the United States in 1939, he was taken by his friend Gerald Heard to meet an Indian monk, Swami Prabhavananda, who was head of a center in Hollywood for the study and practice of Hindu philosophy. For over thirty years, the swami and Isherwood, so unlike each other, remained friends, even collaborating on translations of the *Bhagavad-Gita* (1944) and other Hindu texts. Indeed, so strong was the influence of this mentor that for a time Isherwood contemplated becoming a monk himself. The swami clearly had both wisdom and wit. When Isherwood asked him whether he could lead a spiritual life while having a sexual relationship with a young man, he received the answer: "You must try to see him as the young Lord Krishna." It is when the book concentrates on this sly, skittish, enigmatic figure that it is most interesting. Elsewhere it is too often scrappy and thin-textured.

IV

ISHERWOOD has paid literary tribute to E. M. Forster, Virginia Woolf, Katherine Mansfield, Ford Madox Ford, and Aldous Huxley. But, at least as far as narrative technique is concerned, the older writer to whom he is closest is Somerset Maugham. Although Isherwood has a marvelous ability, denied to Maugham, to produce one startling yet illuminating image after another, the style of both novelists is notable not for poetic grandeur, but for the more modest virtues of lucidity, simplicity, and an almost conversational relaxation. More importantly, both novelists have made use of a persona—the Ashenden of many of Maugham's stories, the "Isherwood," Bradshaw, or George of most of Isherwood's. These personas have never been entirely identical with the actual personalities of their projectors. Maugham was capable of a passion, irrationality, and vindictiveness alien to his always tolerant, rational, and benevolently amused Ashenden. Isherwood describes how in the past his friends regarded him as "part despot, part diplomat," ascribed to him an overpowering will, and remarked on his ruthlessness. None of these are qualities that one would associate with the "Isherwood" of the stories. In Isherwood's case, however, one has the sense that, with each book, persona and real person have been more and more nearly superimposed on each other, until in *A Single Man* the identification has become almost complete. One of the reasons for this tendency to speak less and less through the "ventriloquist's dummy" with the passing of the years may have been the increasing frankness with which Isherwood has felt himself able to refer to his homosexuality without giving offense.

Maugham was a writer who, by deliberately visiting out-of-the-way places and cultivating out-of-the-way people, perpetually sought to extend his range. Isherwood's range, on the other hand, has tended to narrow with the years, covering a far wider spectrum in an early work like *The Memorial* than in a later one like *A Single Man*. This narrowing is probably a reflection of a narrowing in his own life after his decision to settle in California. The main characters of the later books rarely want for money. They either have private means or else they earn their living by writing or teaching. Many are either bisexual or homosexual. There are, of course, novelists the breadth of whose literary range has been in inverse proportion to the narrowness of their lives; but these have been writers who have not depended, to the extent that Isherwood has, on their personal experiences.

This increasing narrowness may in part account for the fact that, regarded in the 1930's as a potentially major novelist, Isherwood has ended up as a minor one—albeit of great accomplishment. Another reason for what some people would regard as a decline may be Isherwood's increasing interest in Vedanta. Vedanta, like other Eastern religions, teaches the necessity for detachment from all worldly desires and preoccupations and the elimination of self. It is, however, precisely in worldly desires and preoccupations and in the differences, attractions, and conflicts among individual selves that the novelist has usually sought his material.

But though few people would now claim Isherwood for the first rank of modern novelists, he stands out in the second rank. The world he creates is a solipsistic circle: he himself is its center, his perceptions its radii, his consciousness its circumference. What makes this world, admittedly confined, fascinating to the reader is the tone of voice—humane, totally truthful, ironic, benevolent—that its creator employs to describe it. It is chiefly this unique tone of voice that gives Isherwood his distinction as one of the most entertaining and likable of novelists at work in the English language today.

SELECTED BIBLIOGRAPHY

I. BIBLIOGRAPHY. *Christopher Isherwood: A Bibliography, 1923–1967* (Los Angeles, 1968); R. W. Funk, *Christopher Isherwood: A Reference Guide* (Boston, 1979).

II. COLLECTED WORKS. *The Berlin Stories: The Last of Mr. Norris—Goodbye to Berlin* (New York, 1954), adapted as a play and film entitled *I Am a Camera* by J. Van Druten; *The Ascent of F6, and On the Frontier* (London, 1958), plays, with W. H. Auden; G. Hulson, *An Isherwood Selection* (London, 1979).

III. SEPARATE WORKS. *All the Conspirators: A Novel* (London, 1928); *The Memorial: Portrait of a Family* (London, 1932), novel; *Mr. Norris Changes Trains* (London, 1935; new ed., 1937), novel; *The Dog Beneath the Skin: Or, Where Is Francis?* (New York–London, 1935), play, with W. H. Auden; *The Ascent of F6* (London, 1936; New York, 1937), play, with W. H. Auden; *Sally Bowles* (London, 1937), novella; *Lions and Shadows: An Education in the Twenties* (London, 1938), autobiography; *On the Frontier* (London, 1938), play, with W. H. Auden; *Journey to a War* (London, 1939), stories, with W. H. Auden; *Prater Violet* (New York, 1945), story; *The Condor and the Cows* (London, 1949), travel; *The World in the Evening* (London, 1954), novel; *Down There on a Visit* (London, 1962), novel; *An Approach to Vedanta* (Hollywood, 1963), religion; *A Single Man* (New York, 1964), novel; *Exhumations: Stories, Articles, Verses* (London, 1966); *A Meeting by the River* (London, 1967), novel; *Ramakrishna and His Disciples* (London, 1968), religious biography; *Kathleen and Frank* (London, 1971), biography; *Christopher and His Kind: 1929–1939* (New York, 1976; London, 1977), autobiography; *My Guru and His Disciple* (New York–London, 1980), on Swami Prabhavananda.

IV. TRANSLATIONS. *Intimate Journals* (London, 1930), trans. of Baudelaire's *Journaux intimes*; *A Penny for the Poor* (London, 1937), trans. of Brecht's *Dreigroschenroman*, reiss. as *Threepenny Novel* (London, 1958; 2nd ed., 1960); *Bhagavad-Gītā* (London, 1944), with Swami Prabhavananda, trans. from the *Bhagavadgītā* of the Mahābhārata; *Shankara's Crest-Jewel of Discrimination* (London, 1947), with Swami Prabhavananda, trans. from S. Acharya's *Vivekachudamani*; *How to Know God* (London, 1953) with Swami Prabhavananda, trans. of the Yoga aphorisms of Patanjali, includes new commentary.

V. WORKS EDITED OR CONTAINING CONTRIBUTIONS BY ISHERWOOD. *Vedanta for the Western World* (Hollywood, 1945), ed. by C. Isherwood; *Vedanta for Modern Man* (New York, 1951), ed. by C. Isherwood; *Great English Short Stories* (New York, 1957), ed. with foreword and intro. by C. Isherwood; *What Religion Is, in the Words of Swami Vivekānanda* (London, 1962), with biographical intro. by C. Isherwood; Swami Prabhavananda, *Religion in Practice* (London, 1968), intro. by C. Isherwood.

VI. BIOGRAPHICAL AND CRITICAL STUDIES. A. Wilson, "The New and Old Isherwood," in *Encounter* (August 1954), pp. 63–68; S. Poss, "A Conversation on Tape," in *London* (June 1961), pp. 41–58; S. Hampshire, "Isherwood's Hell," in *Encounter* (November 1962), pp. 80–88; F. Kermode, "The Interpretation of the Times," in *Puzzles and Epiphanies* (London, 1962); J. Whitehead, "Christophananda Isherwood at Sixty," in *London* (July 1965), pp. 90–100; C. G. Heilbrun, *Christopher Isherwood* (New York, 1970); A. Wilde, *Christopher Isherwood* (New York, 1971); B. Finney, "Christopher Isherwood: A Profile," in *New Review* (August 1975), pp.17–24; J. Fryer, *Isherwood: A Biography* (London, 1977; New York, 1978); P. Piazza, *Christopher Isherwood: Myth and Anti-Myth* (New York, 1978); B. Finney, *Christopher Isherwood: A Critical Biography* (London, 1979); C. J. Summers, *Christopher Isherwood* (New York, 1980).

C. P. SNOW

(1905-1980)

William Cooper

LIFE

C. P. SNOW is a novelist of unique experience. At a period of history when the world of literature and the world of science and technology are sharply separated from each other, he has come to hold a key position in both simultaneously. A novelist by vocation, he is also a scientific administrator and man of affairs.

Snow was born on 15 October 1905, the second of four sons in a lower-middle-class family living in Leicester. The city, whose existence is based on the hosiery and boot-and-shoe trades, has always been relatively prosperous: the family—his father had a minor job in a boot-and-shoe firm—was relatively unprosperous. The effect of such a situation on an intelligent and affectionate young boy is touchingly described at the beginning of his novel *Time of Hope* (1949). Nevertheless Snow's was a family strongly rooted in a stable, flourishing part of industrialized society; and consequently Snow's tone when writing about society, both the part of it in which he was born and the parts that he got to know later, has always been deep-seatedly confident.

He was educated as a scientist. He went to Alderman Newton's Grammar School, where, at the stage of entering the sixth form, he specialized in science. As the school at that time had no arts sixth, he had no option; though he says now that, when committing himself to a career to which he was not unequivocally drawn, he thought that he would be able to "break through" later to what he really wanted to do.

After leaving the school, Snow returned there as a laboratory assistant while working for a university scholarship. In those days it was much less easy than it is nowadays to get a free university education. He won a scholarship that took him to Leicester University College—whose students took London degrees—where he got a first class honors in chemistry of such brilliance that he was awarded a grant to stay on and do research. He chose to work in the field of infrared spectroscopy, which attracted him because of its susceptibility to theoretical study in terms of the currently developing quantum mechanics. He took a master's degree in physics in 1928 and was awarded a scholarship that enabled him to go to Cambridge, where he entered Christ's College as a research student.

At Cambridge the quality of his research was such that in 1930 his college elected him to a fellowship, which meant that he might hope to find a permanent place in a university: among scientists he was beginning to be spoken of, like Arthur Miles in *The Search* (1934), as a bright young man. His future career in scientific research looked as though it were settled. In the last few years, however, he had grown more certain, rather than less, that his future career lay elsewhere; so he turned to literature. He had begun to think of "breaking through." He writes: "I was educated as a scientist, as Miles was: but I never had his single-minded passion, and in fact knew my own ultimate vocation from the time I was about eighteen" (prefatory note to the reissue of *The Search*, 1958).

The ultimate vocation he knew as his own was that of a novelist. As a beginning he wrote two novels, a detective story and a Wellsian work of scientific imagination. They served the dual purpose of enabling him to get his hand in as a writer, and, because they were in an easily recognizable, uncontroversial mode, of getting him ready publication.

In 1933 he came to a turning-point. It is impossible to sustain simultaneously a career as a research scientist and a career as a novelist. Original research and creative art both draw on the same source of psychic energy. Though they may exist together for a time, in the end one of them has to go. Snow's turning-point, a piece of research that went wrong through oversight, was externally rather like that in Arthur Miles's scientific career, though different, of course, internally. Snow went away and wrote *The Search*, his first serious novel. In effect, the "break through" was complete. From then on he did no more research. However, he continued to teach science in the university, and was appointed to a college tutorship in 1934.

Yet *The Search*, though it made a reputation for Snow as a novelist, did not represent what he finally meant to write. In the prefatory note to the 1958 edition of *The Search* he says: "It was a false start. I wanted to say something about people first and foremost, and then people-in-society, in a quite different way, and at a quite different level from anything in this book."

On 1 January 1935 Snow had the original idea—he records that the idea was quite sharp—for the chain of novels that is commonly known as the Lewis Eliot series and that has finally been given the title temporarily borne by the first book in the series, *Strangers and Brothers*. It is clear now that whereas *The Search* was a study of individual character against a background of society, *Strangers and Brothers* is a study, at once more penetrating and more revealing, of individual character acting upon society and reacting to it. By 1939 Snow had laid down the general pattern of the series and had written the first volume. Then war broke out. He put writing aside, and did not resume until 1945.

During the autumn of 1939, Snow had been asked by a committee of the Royal Society to assist in devising the best way of organizing university scientists for the war. In 1940 the function of this committee was formally taken over by the Ministry of Labour, and Snow became a civil servant. He was thus brought into public affairs. During the war his chief role was to exercise personal judgement on how individual scientists might be best employed, in research, in government research establishments or industry, or as technical officers in the Armed Forces; and to plan how the number of scientists and engineers in the country might be increased. In the course of this work he formed a friendship with the chairman of English Electric Company, which led to his being invited in 1944 to join the board of directors.

When the war was over Snow was invited to become a civil service commissioner with special responsibility for scientific appointments. Although this represented a change from acting as an employment agency to acting as an employer, the same techniques of human and scientific judgement were re-

quired—assisted, in Snow's case, by a wide-ranging interest in scientific and engineering research, together with a remarkable memory for the professional records of individual scientists. Since he was now free to start writing novels again, he accepted only a part-time appointment. For all his activities in public affairs and industry, he intended to make certain of reserving some of his time for his creative work.

Snow's role in affairs from 1945 to 1960 was considerable, yet not easy to define. He participated in all the major appointments of scientists to the government service; and he acted as an essential point of reference in questions of official policy relating to scientific manpower and technological education. But one may presume that his major contribution, less formal and more permeating, was to bridge the gap between scientists, whose professional training tends not to encourage them in making human judgements, and men of affairs, whose professional training may leave them something short of adequate when making scientific judgements. For his services to the country in public affairs a knighthood was conferred on him in 1957. But the time came when he felt he must free himself altogether from his formal commitments to official life, and in 1960 he retired from the Civil Service.

However when the Labour party came to power in the General Election of October 1964, the Prime Minister, Mr. Harold Wilson, invited Snow to join his government as Parliamentary Secretary to the newly-created Ministry of Technology, and Snow accepted on the understanding that he would be committed full-time to political life for only a limited period. In order that he might hold ministerial office without having been elected a Member of Parliament, he was raised to the House of Lords with a life peerage. He acted as Parliamentary Secretary to the Ministry of Technology during its first formative year and a half, resigning office in March 1966. Since then he has kept in touch with political life as a moderately active member of the House of Lords.

Between 1947 and 1970 Snow completed the eleven novels which comprise the *Strangers and Brothers* cycle. It is quite different from a chronicle-sequence or a *roman fleuve*. In content it is essentially a personal story—the story of a man's life, through which is revealed his psychological and his moral structure—yet by extension and implication it is an enquiry into the psychological and moral structure of a large fraction of the society of our times. As the volumes appeared, its form was disclosed as massive and intricate, yet fundamentally simple. In concept it has been seminal: several other serious writers have taken up this kind of novel cycle as an essential form.[1] *Strangers and Brothers* must inevitably be regarded as a key work of the decades in which it was written.

In addition to his two main activities as novelist and administrator, Snow has many others, public and private. He married Pamela Hansford Johnson, the novelist, in 1950, and they have a son. He has travelled widely in the United States and the Soviet Union, and has received many honours in both countries. He writes for English and American journals and periodicals, frequently on the theme for which his unique position in the literary and scientific worlds especially fits him. Seeing the scientific and non-scientific worlds becoming even more sharply separated, he devotes himself to the task of bringing them together. The range of what he writes in this context is very wide: from *Science and Government* (1961, the Godkin Lectures at Harvard University, 1960), in which he dilates on the situation of government where major scientific/technical decisions have to be made by a handful of men who may well not have firsthand experience of either their basis or their consequences; to *Variety of Men* (1967), a serious-minded *jeu d'esprit*—if such a phrase is permissible—in which making a writer's observations, many of which have appeared nowhere else, he portrays nine men as widely different as Rutherford and Lloyd George. It is in activities such as these that Snow has come strongly to influence current thought about the nature and future of our culture.

EARLY NOVELS

Death Under Sail (1932) was Snow's first novel. It is a detective story about a murder on a sailing-boat in the middle of the Norfolk Broads; it conforms to the conventions, and the plot is admirably organized. But what singles it out from other novels in the genre is the fact that the plot grows out of the characters rather than the characters out of the plot. They are presented as interesting persons outside the puzzle;

[1]Examples of interest are Anthony Powell's *The Music of Time* and Doris Lessing's *Martha Quest* series.

and though the author treats them with uncommon psychological understanding, something is always left, as it would be in a serious novel, for the reader's speculation.

It is, of course, very much a young man's book and very much of the early thirties—it sparkles with high spirits, and the importance of *amour* and sophistication are taken with delightful romantic gravity—and yet the sureness of his style and, even more notably, the sureness of his literary tact, signalize a writer who, having decided what he intended to do, has exactly done it. *Death Under Sail* was an odd but nevertheless remarkable beginning.

New Lives for Old (1933) was published anonymously. It is about the discovery of a hormone which will effect the rejuvenation of human beings, and the time is what was then the future—the story begins in about 1950 and ends just over thirty years later. The consequences of the discovery are the moral and economic deterioration of the Western world.

At the time, Snow was doing research and among scientists was being spoken of as a bright young man: it seemed possible that the publication of this book might lead to his being spoken of as too bright. *Death Under Sail* had not done any damage of this kind, possibly because the majority of scientists (a) did not take detective stories seriously, and (b) liked reading them in their spare time. Actually, it can now be seen that publication of *New Lives for Old* under his own name would not have made any difference to Snow's career.

New Lives for Old is inferior to H. G. Wells's early achievements in this genre. It opens, as they do, in matter-of-fact realism, but remains there, with no touch of that Wellsian inflation of manner necessary to bring off such a story completely. Also, where Wells was writing out of unalloyed optimism, Snow's vision is darker, and his psychological insight, especially into the sexual natures of men and women, is too disturbingly truthful to find a comfortable place in fantasticated history.

Incidentally, the book contains an interesting reference to "consciousness," which was preoccupying Snow during that period, " . . . consciousness of motive, awareness of one's emotions and those of the people around one, perception of the reasons behind the actions that human beings do." It is this particular preoccupation that is the clue to the investigatory element in all Snow's later novels.

The Search (1934) is the first novel Snow wrote

outside a specific genre. It is the story of a young scientist, Arthur Miles, told in the first person, from his boyhood to maturity: he makes his way, by means of scholarships, from lower-middle-class origins to a position of distinction in the scientific world.[2] *The Search* is the only novel about being a scientist to be written by a man who, at the time of writing, was more distinguished as a scientist than as a novelist; and it gives the most authentic answers to some of the questions that preoccupy most non-scientists a half-century later—What is it like to be a scientist? What is it like to do experiments, to make a discovery?

The Search also illuminates the question of whether the pursuit of scientific truth and the pursuit of a career in science conflict or accord with each other, or can be, in the end, the same thing. Arthur Miles, at the height of early success in research, becomes involved in the politics of getting a research institute founded; and, while so doing, overlooks an important detail in the current research on which his reputation depends. His career as a scientist collapses, and he is forced to ask himself the most searching questions of all.

The main point about the novel, however, is that it creates for the reader not "a scientist," but a whole individual who happens to be a scientist. And instead of handing the reader the answers to his questions, it enables him, by putting him in possession of the whole individual, to disentangle the answers—if they exist—for himself.

THE SEQUENCE STRANGERS AND BROTHERS

MASSIVE and intricate, the novel-sequence *Strangers and Brothers* is fundamentally simple in design. It traces the life-story of the narrator, Lewis Eliot, in terms of alternation between what Snow himself calls "direct experience" and "observed experience." The titles of the novels in the sequence can be set out on the page to illustrate this:

Time of Hope 1914–1933

    George Passant 1925–1933
    The Conscience of the Rich
    1927–1936

    The Light and the Dark
    1935–1943
    The Masters 1937
    The New Men 1939–1946

Homecomings 1938–1948

    The Affair 1953–1954
    Corridors of Power 1955–1959
    The Sleep of Reason 1963–1964

Last Things 1964–1968

The books in the column on the left are those in which Lewis Eliot tells his own story: they are predominantly "direct experience."[3] In those on the right, Lewis, in the role more of observer than participant,[4] tells the story of friends: they are predominantly "observed experience."

The design of the sequence is continuously cyclical. With *Time of Hope* (1949), Lewis Eliot first of all tells his own story over a certain period of time and then, in the next five novels, the stories in turn of some of his friends during more or less the same period. (The dates following the title of a novel above are those of the period which the novel covers.) With *Homecomings* (1956), Lewis begins a second similar cycle over a later period. And *Last Things* (1970), again a novel of "direct experience," draws the whole work together.

Each novel, though its place in the sequence is clear, is designed so that it can stand alone, a self-contained story which anyone can fully understand without having read any of the other books. Yet each book gains, as Snow in planning the series intended that each book might gain, by being read in conjunction with the books that precede it—and that follow it. *Strangers and Brothers* is based on the concept that the present moment of time is indissolubly a part of the past and of the future: it can be taken on its own, complete as it is in itself; but only when it is shown to have embedded in it signs of what has gone before, and what is to come, does it signify fully.

Time of Hope is the first novel of "direct experience." Lewis Eliot tells his own life story, beginning in 1914, when he was nine years old, and ending in 1933, shortly after George Passant's trial and just before the marriage of Charles March in *The Conscience of the Rich* (1958).

While being a novel of self-revelation, *Time of*

---

[2]The extent to which *The Search* is autobiographical is commented upon by the author in the prefatory note to the reissue of the novel in 1958.

[3]There is a resemblance, in this role, to that of Henry James's "foreground observer."

[4]Predominantly—for a novelist completely to segregate observed and direct experience is scarcely possible; and if he did succeed in doing so, the result would seem peculiarly sterile.

Hope is, more subtly, a novel of self-discovery. Later, in telling the story of George Passant, Lewis sees a man whose potentialities are brought to nothing by a peculiarity of nature so intrinsic as to be irremediable—even by the effort of intelligence and will. Telling the story of his own life, Lewis discovers a different kind of flaw, a particular strand in his nature which, apart from whether it is responsible for causing him unhappiness or not, affronts his moral apprehensions. Brought near to failure in his career, after a brilliant start, and brought to ruin in his marriage through his own choice, he finds himself, in self-discovery, stating the nature of a moral struggle which he intends shall occupy the next part of his life. Intelligence and will in this struggle *can* avail. There *is* hope.

It is in love, which Lewis sees as the profoundest relationship between human beings, that he discovers himself. First in his love for his mother, and then in his love for his wife, he realizes that there is something gravely wrong from his side. His mother, vain and imperious, yet passionately anxious for his future success in life, loves him without restraint—and he is unable to respond equally. The possessiveness of her love provokes him to evasion: when her emotions flow towards him, he absents himself. She dies without his being able to tell her that his own ambitions match her dreams for him.

After his mother's death, his ambitions flare up beyond anything his friends had expected of him. From a clerking job in a local government office, he decides to work for the Bar. And he begins with remarkable success. He is a very clever young man and outward-turning by nature: he makes many friends, for he is affectionate and sympathetic—provided his innermost reserve is not menaced, he can respond with emotion more freely flowing than most men's. And in his detachment he has a knack for handling other men shrewdly. Yet, by the time he is twenty-eight and practising at the Bar, he knows that, judged by the standard of his talents and his first ambitions, he has not come off. His career has been eroded by his marriage.

For eight years Lewis has been in love with a girl called Sheila Knight. She has the gift of beauty. And she is incapable of sustained feeling. In the depths of her nature she is remote and splintered, so that her emotions seem to arise, jerkily and fleetingly, from unconnected sources. In desperation, for the sake of making herself feel at all, she turns cruelly on anyone who is devoted to her. Having failed to love, she lets Lewis marry her. Now, for the first time, Lewis is not evading, absenting himself. His innermost reserve is thrown open to another human being, to another human being who can neither give nor demand anything in return. He loves her without restraint *because* she can neither give nor demand anything in return. And so he discovers what is wrong with him. The bar to his innermost reserve is vanity, vanity so strong that it can be broken down not by another's love but only by his own suffering.

As *Time of Hope* ends, the central problem for Lewis Eliot is at last stated. He has discovered what is wrong, and that, in itself, gives him some hope. He also knows what he must do, if he is ever going to have the profoundest relationship with another human being.

When *George Passant* (1940)[5] begins, George is twenty-six years old and six years Lewis's senior, a qualified clerk in the most solid firm of solicitors in Lewis's native provincial town. In the mid-1920's he is giving evening lectures on law at the local Institute of Arts and Technology, which Lewis formerly attended; and by force of his personality he is the focus of a group of young people who look to him for guidance in both their careers and their lives. This is far from the popular 1950's conception of the 1920's, as whimsical, riotous, modishly decadent. For George's friends in the provinces they are years of hard work and hard, dazzling hopes.

The story of George Passant, a story of "observed experience," is tragic, tragic in its sense of human loss. He is a remarkable man gifted with formidable intelligence and striking personality, a man of probity, integrity, and loyalty. He has the makings of a great man. At the end of the novel, in 1933, he is seen escaping by the skin of his teeth from the criminal charge of fraud—squalid, petty fraud. How could it have happened? Where was the flaw?

George Passant is an idealist, with the idealist's capacity for creating a private world, a cosmos, from his own fantasies. The elements on which his cosmos is founded are freedom and hope. Living among what Lewis calls "the ragtag and bobtail of the lower middle-classes," he has gathered round him young people of promise, to whom he means to bring freedom from constraining habits and conventions of thought, and hope for wider horizons and

---

[5] In his recension of the whole work after completing it with *Last Things*, Snow gave it—according to his long-standing intention—the title *Strangers and Brothers*; and to the first-written novel of the series, which had originally borne that title, he gave the title *George Passant*.

more brilliant careers. "The world seemed on the march," says Lewis. "We wanted to join in." George translates his cosmos into a reality. He welds his young people into a group which migrates at weekends to an isolated farm on the outskirts of the town, to experience there a foretaste, or perhaps only a simulacrum, of the intellectual and social freedom that he desires for them. In the group are some attractive girls.

Now, George Passant has a strongly sensual nature. At first his sensuality is completely separated from his idealism. But then there comes into his group a very different kind of young man, Jack Cotery, dashing and engaging, labile, something of an amorist. Jack is morally blind; and he goes straight to the core of moral blindness in George—for George, despite his stature of mind and of personality, is vulnerable to his own desires; just as his idealistic cosmos cuts him off from the world of ordinary men, so this blindness cuts him off from true perception of his own motives. Jack Cotery's world of ordinary men happens to operate on the edge of sharp practice: his insight into George's motives is artlessly cynical.

George Passant begins with a trivial scandal in which George saves Jack Cotery from a minor misfortune; it ends with a major scandal in which George, as a result of Jack's activities, stands in danger of utter ruin.

For two reasons this novel may be felt to be the most "difficult" of the sequence. The first reason is the psychological rarity of George Passant himself: the reader may find himself without previous experience of anyone like him. On the other hand, though George is far removed from the author in temperament, he is the most triumphantly realized character in the sequence. The other reason is that in meeting the analytical problem presented by George's temperament, Snow has left the book rather bare of those familiar incidentals that help the reader along. Even so, the book has an extraordinary atmosphere, pervading, almost claustrophobic. For this, and above all for sheer originality of theme, *George Passant* has a claim to be regarded as the most remarkable novel of the entire sequence.

The Conscience of the Rich comes third in the sequence, although it was not published till 1958. It is about Lewis's friend, Charles March. It begins in London, in 1927, when Charles and Lewis, about the same age, are pupils at the Bar, though they have entered different chambers. Lewis, who is attracted to Charles as much by his warmth of heart, his pa-

tience, and his delicacy of feeling as by his incisive mind, is astonished by the cold, angry voice in which Charles invites him to his house. He soon discovers the meaning of it: the invitation has forced Charles to disclose that he is the son of a rich, aristocratic Anglo-Jewish family. And Charles suffers from conflicting emotions about being Jewish and about being rich.

Lewis is introduced to Mr. March, Charles's father, an active, lively man, comically fluid in change of mood yet essentially pertinacious, who retired at the age of thirty-three from competitive existence as owner of the family bank, and who now lives, with undisguised pleasure and apprehension, entirely for his children. "I want something for you," he says to Charles. "I wish I could know that you'll get something that I've always wanted for you." Even so early in the story, Lewis foresees that though Charles may arrive at some sort of harmony with his Jewish origins, he can only arrive at tragic disharmony with his father; for in the depths of his nature, Charles is equally self-centered.

Possessive love is the principal theme of this novel, though there are several others. Charles is forbidden by his conscience to take advantage of the opportunities given him by his wealth. He might easily become an adornment to fashionable society, equally easily carve out a brilliant personal success at the Bar with the help of his family connections. He will do neither. After a violent quarrel with his father, who retaliates by trying to keep him financially dependent, he embarks, humbly, like any poverty-stricken student, on training for the medical profession—a profession which promises only that he will be *useful* to the human beings about him.

In this revolt, he has the encouragement of Ann Jessel, the girl he is going to marry. Unlike the man whom Charles's sister, Katherine, marries, causing Mr. March further misery, Ann is both Jewish and moderately rich. She, however, is suffering a conflict of conscience parallel to Charles's: like many non-Jewish rich young men and women of her time, she is in revolt against the disastrous trend of history which her own class appears to her to be accelerating, and she has become a Communist. At the end of the book she finds herself in a position to wreck the career of Mr. March's most beloved and revered elder brother.

There is no chance of Charles and his father ever coming to terms. The possessive love of parents for children is "a darkness of the heart." Yet, like George Passant, in the preceding novel, the two men, in the midst of their suffering, are strengthened by hope, hope for the future.

The Light and the Dark (1947) is about Roy Calvert, who appeared as a boy in *George Passant*[6] and who is now a young graduate of the Cambridge college of which Lewis Eliot, when the story begins in 1935, has been a Fellow for about a year.[7] He is the most gifted man that the College has produced for many years past. Already, at twenty-five, he has won an international reputation as an Oriental-ist—his specialty is deciphering and interpreting fragments of ancient texts. He is extremely hand-some and attractive: he is debonair and humorous: everything he does, or so it seems, is done with ele-gance and ease. The Master makes him his protégé. The Master's daughter falls in love with him. Yet in the background there are continual rumours about an extraordinary and tormented private life: drink, women, wild dissipation—it is a side that the College does not see, but somehow knows. The rumours are true.

Lewis, in the depths of his despair over Sheila, is drawn to Roy, and, with insight sharpened by his own suffering, he pierces to the secret of Roy's misery. It is no accident, he feels, that Roy has chosen to devote himself to restoring texts relating to the Manichean heresy, a religion in which man's spirit is part of the light and his flesh part of the dark: the battle sways from side to side—"the most subtle and complex representation of sexual guilt," Lewis comments. Roy in his own life mirrors this struggle between the light and the dark.

But the source of the struggle, Lewis discovers, lies in the depths of Roy's temperament: he is prey to in-escapable melancholia. As he fights against it, he fluctuates between a sparkling, energetic composure and a black, hopeless lethargy from which he can liberate himself only by some act of maniac wild-ness, usually of a self-destructive nature. Lewis comes to understand Roy's temperament before he himself does, realizing that the cyclical fluctuation between high spirits and complete despair, with a destructive act as the releasing mechanism, will go on as long as he lives. Time after time, in crisis after crisis, Lewis tries to mitigate the misery and shield

[6]He is the unwitting cause of the minor scandal from which George Passant defends Jack Cotery. He is a cousin of Lewis's wife, Sheila.

[7]Lewis's election to a fellowship is an event that Snow has seen fit, deliberately and tantalizingly, not to recount directly: we are told that it resulted from the activities of Katherine March's husband, Francis Getliffe.

his friend from the consequences of the outbursts. All the time his fear is growing that one day Roy will see the truth clearly and kill himself.

Against the background of European events lead-ing to World War II, Lewis watches Roy trying to escape from himself by seeking for some kind of outer authority: seeking it through trying to believe in God, through an extraordinary flirtation with the Nazis in Berlin, through a commonplace marriage to a shallow, attractive girl who will not seek to know him too deeply. All these things fail him. He gives up his wartime intelligence job and becomes a bomber pilot because Lewis, Lewis of all people, has let him know that at this stage of the war a bomber pilot stands the highest statistical chance of being killed.

It is a sombre story; yet paradoxically the effect of the book is not sombre at all, because it is constantly lit up by the bright and flashing aspect of Roy Calvert, the most hero-like, the most romantic of all Snow's figures.

This novel, which is for some readers, because of its attractive and vivid surface, the most haunting and the most "easy" book of the sequence, has never-theless a central difficulty, the converse of the second novel's. George Passant is sometimes found hard to comprehend and appreciate because he is drawn in exceptional depth and complexity; though Roy Cal-vert dominates this book and shines over it, too much about him is left untold and unguessable.

The Masters (1951) is the story not of one man but of a group of men—the Fellows of Lewis's Cam-bridge college, engaged during the year 1937 in elec-ting a new Master. Although there are only thirteen Fellows involved, thirteen academic persons locked away in an ancient institution, the novel is about men's love of power and their equivocal needs to in-dulge and subdue it. Throughout the rituals of the dining hall and the combination room, the collogu-ings in seventeenth-century rooms, the to-ings and fro-ings across cobbled courts, runs the motive force of political intrigue, as urgent and unassuageable as anywhere in the macrocosm outside.

Although every man plays an individual role as an elector, three men are the prime movers in the story—Brown, Chrystal, and Jago. Jago is one of the candidates for the Mastership; the other two are the main persons in his supporting caucus. Chrystal, the Dean, is the typical man of power, active and masterful, loving the feel of power—and given to near-adoration for men who win his respect. Yet it is Brown, the apparently contented, harmonious, fat man, who really dominates the proceedings: tactful, adroit, sensitive to shades of feeling and of mood, fluid yet stable, tolerant, unhurried, and outwardly benign, he is the born politician. Brown has chosen Jago, and he draws his friend Chrystal in with him. His task is not easy because Jago is an unusual man. In fact it is the unusual things about him, which sometimes put people off, which appeal to the side of Arthur Brown that is hidden; Jago's impulsiveness, his quick temper, his passionate pride and remorse, his insight and his frankness, in particular his "nakedness to life"—they are things which Arthur Brown has envied or things in his own nature which he has by force of will had to subjugate.

The alternative candidate is a scientist named Crawford, an able man, an excellent administrator, a successful participant in scientific affairs, bland, impassive, conceited—and impersonal. His supporting caucus is run by Francis Getliffe, also a scientist, who regards him as the candidate any reasonable man would vote for.

In January the Fellows have had the news that the old Master is dying; in December the thirteen men enter the College chapel to elect one of their number Master. The new Master is elected by a majority of seven to six. After months have been spent in discussion and caucus-forming, the one who turns the scale has changed sides during the last twenty-four hours.

The Masters is the most "comfortable" novel in the sequence. The singleness and the familiarity of the theme give the reader something comparatively easy to catch on to. At the same time, the framework of events imposes a unity of time, place, and cast of characters as integral as that of, say, *Death Under Sail*. And also the book abounds with those touches of apparently inessential detail which were missing from *George Passant*, which here, selected and handled consummately, evoke a friendly, almost cosy warmth.

The New Men (1954) is about the emergence of atomic scientists into the affairs of the nation between 1939 and 1945. Lewis Eliot tells the story of a group of atomic scientists who are working in a government research establishment especially created for them at a place in Warwickshire called Barford.[8]

At the beginning of the war, Lewis, like many

other dons, has gone into the Civil Service, and through chance personal connections he is posted to a department of government that is very small but close to the scientific conduct of the war. It is his departmental Minister, with whom Lewis works intimately, who is entrusted with the task of getting Barford going and keeping an eye on what becomes of it. Thus Lewis sees from the outside how, from the prewar discovery of nuclear fission, the scientists of Barford move step by step, as purely professional men, to the manufacture of an atomic bomb. He also sees, because one of the scientists is his brother, Martin, their affairs from the inside: he sees them move, in their moral outlook, step by step from optimism and single-mindedness to violent agitation and remorse. The new men start out with the moral responsibility of scientists, a moral responsibility to scientific truth and nothing else. They end at variance with each other and with their own consciences: when they learn that, against their wishes, the bomb has been dropped on Hiroshima, they discover a moral responsibility towards the rest of mankind. The new men have emerged into the world of power, and they are confronted with the price they have to pay for it.

These are the events through which Lewis lives, yet at the heart of *The New Men* there is a second theme: an exploration of brotherly love. In 1939 Martin is at Lewis's College, doing nuclear research, and Lewis induces him to ask—for what, to Lewis, appears as Martin's own good—to be posted to Barford. Lewis has to do it subtly, because Martin himself is a cautious, subtle young man, far-sighted and calculating, hiding his own romantic hopes under a kind of stoicism. Thus begins the interplay of wills and possessive love between the two brothers. At Barford, set on the track by Lewis, Martin makes the moves necessary for getting on, first by attaching himself to Luke, a better scientist than himself, and finally putting himself in a position—through breaking down a Communist at Barford whom Luke had decided not to investigate—to profit by Luke's mistake and to get offered the Chief Superintendency of the establishment. His final moves are not Lewis's moves for him, and Lewis is shocked, even repelled. They quarrel bitterly. Only when Martin makes his last throw does Lewis fully realize that Martin's moves are also moves in assertion of independence, of freedom from Lewis's planning for him.

As between Mr. March and Charles, between

---

[8]Though Barford exists as a village in Warwickshire, there was no counterpart to the research establishment in real life. The most talented atomic scientists in this country were sent over to North America to join in the American and Canadian atomic energy projects.

Lewis's own mother and himself, the interplay of wills and possessive love can end only in conflict of the one and destruction of the other. Martin's last throw makes it plain that he has changed from a younger brother to an independent man. Lewis knows well enough the fate of filial love by now.

"At the springs of my nature I had some kind of pride or vanity which not only made me careless of myself but also prevented me going into the deepest human relation on equal terms." That is how Lewis Eliot states his cardinal discovery about his own nature when, at the beginning of *Homecomings*, he takes up again his own life-story five years after the point where he left off at the end of *Time of Hope.*

Homecomings takes Lewis from 1938 to 1948. At the beginning he is still a Cambridge don, and he has added to his professional activities by becoming a consultant to an eminent industrialist. Yet his marriage to Sheila, at the core of his existence, makes his existence sterile. The suffering she has caused him, which, though he despised it, at least broke down the bar of vanity to his heart, has lost its power. And Sheila has deteriorated still further: she has even given up the bursts of cruelty that once brought her feelings to life.

Yet, though Lewis feels only sorry for her, he is still, as he always was, apprehensive of what he may find when he goes home to her. In an atmosphere of growing coldness and dread, she spends most of her time alone. Then one day he is called home, to find that she has been able to bear it no longer: she has killed herself. Stricken with sorrow and remorse, Lewis realizes that he is freed. He is freed to try and find a second, true love: he is freed to *try* to overcome the flaw at the springs of his own nature.

Numbly he spends a year—the war has now begun—concentrating on his work as a civil servant in Whitehall, and then he meets Margaret Davidson. She is twenty-four, clever and strong-minded, daughter of a Bloomsbury family, and also a civil servant. She is attractive, piquantly shy and careless. Lewis is drawn to her immediately; and she is drawn to him. Her natural insight into people's natures happens to be sharpest and deepest at just such places as the one where Lewis's flaw is hidden. They recognize each other, and she comprehends, as soon as he tells her about Sheila, the moral struggle of which he stands on the verge. They fall in love, become lovers, and then find that to achieve true love, a desolating battle lies ahead of them.

While Lewis becomes steadily more successful in

Whitehall,[9] playing an increasing part in the inner workings of the world of power,[10] his struggle to bring himself into the kind of relationship with Margaret that will satisfy him morally swings to and fro. At one point, realizing that Lewis is refusing her his confidence—he has concealed from her that Sheila's death was suicide—she decides that she is unable to sustain a one-sided relationship in which she offers trust totally and Lewis offers nothing. She gives up and marries someone else.

Lewis finds no consolation. When they meet some years later, they find that their love for each other has not changed. Margaret now acts differently. Partly because she is, in love, completely committed to him; and partly because love, for her, is linked with moral striving, she gets a divorce and marries him. Lewis realizes now that the stronger impulse for achieving his regeneration cannot come from her: it must come from himself.

Homecomings ends with Lewis finding that stronger impulse in himself. Their child, whom Lewis loves without constraint, falls desperately ill, and Lewis discovers that in his anguish he is shutting Margaret out. At last he sees how to remove the bar from his heart. He longs to go alone to see his child, but triumphantly he cries to Margaret—and his tone tells her what depths in his nature the cry comes from—"Come with me!" The book ends with their coming home.

The setting of *The Affair* (1960) is the same as that of *The Masters*, this time the year being 1953. The story relates how the Fellows of the College deal with the situation in which one of their number, a young physicist called Howard, is accused of scientific fraud. Lewis Eliot is drawn into the affair first when his brother, Martin, who has returned to the College after resigning from Barford (*The New Men*), asks his advice privately, and later when he is called in to act professionally in the legal complications that arise.

In sixteen years the College has changed a good deal. In particular it has lost some of its inbred air: it has grown in size and, correspondingly, in impersonality; and the activities of the Fellows outside

[9]He is able to bring in George Passant as his assistant. It is interesting to note that although in the first novel George was a difficult character, strange and hard to understand, the latent effect of the earlier book makes him reappear now with the familiarness of an old friend.
[10]Among all the "external" scenes in the sequence, those set in official life rank very high.

academic life are beginning to integrate College affairs with those of the external world. The cosiness is gone. Arthur Brown, still running the College—since running the College is what he loves most, he has come to terms with Crawford, the new Master—still gives little claret-parties in his rooms for his friends, where they talk over their plans; yet somehow there is a feeling that the best days are over. After these meetings the young Fellows go home and take heed of what their wives have to say. Willy-nilly College life has acquired more than a tinge of life at some such place as Barford.

Whereas *The Masters* was a study in politics, *The Affair* is a study in justice, actually justice tied down and regulated by a "fine-structure" of politics, again with the College microcosm symbolizing the macrocosm. Before the story begins, Howard's case has already been considered by a Court composed of the four senior members of the College—the Master, Brown, Nightingale, and Winslow. He has been found guilty and ejected from the College. But further evidence is brought to light by another young scientist, no friend of Howard's, indicating that the first judgement may have been wrong, that what appears to be a fraud may have been committed by Howard's senior colleague, a most distinguished scientist who is now dead. Howard may have been misjudged; yet there is strong resistance among the Fellows to reopening his case, partly because of renewing the possibility of public scandal, but mostly because Howard is a cold-natured young roughneck with near-Communist opinions.

In the setup as a whole there is a marked resemblance, as one of the Fellows remarks, to that of the Dreyfus case. (This is why the novel is called *The Affair*.) After much argument and heart-searching, a majority of Fellows demands that the case shall be reopened. The Court of Seniors duly reaches the same conclusion as before. The majority, unconvinced, now threatens to take the case outside the College. At this, Brown and his party agree to a hearing with legal advisers—Lewis Eliot advises for Howard, whose case now has the support of Martin and of Francis Getliffe—and the last part of the novel is occupied with the legal proceedings.

In the meantime, throughout the novel, there is preparation for the next magisterial election, when Crawford retires, in which the two most likely candidates for the Mastership are Getliffe and Arthur Brown—unless their behaviour over the affair loses them supporters. At the legal hearing Howard is finally exonerated. But the College resolutely refuses to have him back in more than a token sense. "The only comfort," observes Crawford, "is that sensible men usually come to sensible conclusions."

From politics in microcosm it seemed inevitable that Lewis Eliot would finally come to politics in macrocosm, and in that line *Corridors of Power* (1964) stands as the climax to the series of novels of "observed experience." It is about Westminster and Whitehall, the seat of government and the seat of high affairs; the place where in full view the politicians are seen publicly to hammer out the country's great decisions, and the place where, behind the doors of "closed politics," the politicians, the civil servants, and (in this novel) the scientists and the industrialists constantly parley, sound out each other's intentions, judge the strength of each other's hands. The phrase "corridors of power"—which first appeared in *Homecomings* and has since made its way into the currency of everyday English speech—poetically evokes the exact physical reality of the places and the men who inhabit them, simultaneously with the mystery of where power is actually located.

In *The New Men*, to which *Corridors of Power* comes nearest in general ambience, there was a theme secondary to the main scientific-political argument, a theme torn from the flesh of Lewis himself, namely his relationship with his brother, Martin. In *Corridors of Power* there is no such secondary theme. Instead, torn from the flesh of Lewis, of all the men and women in the novel—and in real life of most men and women in our times—is the primary political argument of the story itself: How are we to avoid world thermonuclear war?

The story Lewis narrates begins in the spring of 1955, England having a Conservative government and a general election in prospect—and the disastrous invasion of Suez just beyond the horizon. It ends four years later. It is the story of Roger Quaife, a youngish Conservative MP, a man of manifest talent and political insight, who becomes Minister for a department whose central concern is the country's defence. He is a man of unusual personal quality; along with the alternations of ruthless simplicity and subtlety characteristic of a political boss, he has a deep-running streak of idealism and a capacity for responding to impulse that make him suddenly attractive, touched with a sort of glamour. In public he speaks much of the time with the voice of his party, of the Conservative official world; but then he "talks in his own voice," and that voice sounds from the heart as well as the head.

Quaife believes that, above all, thermonuclear war is to be avoided, and to that end the country should take steps to divest itself—partly out of plain recognition of its dependence on America—of its thermonuclear arms. This becomes the sole end to which he decides to devote his power as a politician. He succeeds in gathering allies: scientists, civil servants, and industrialists. He realizes that such allies hold to him only loosely; and, more seriously, that he may be going against the grain of public feeling at the time. But he believes that time is short and that now is his chance. The risk to his career is grave; he has the opportunity to slide out—and refuses to take it.

It is an exciting story, the most steadily exciting of the series. The theme is compelling and moving in its own right. Its singleness makes for each successive incident—each meeting in Whitehall or in Westminster, each dinner party in a London house or in the country, each encounter at the opera in Covent Garden, by the lake in St. James's Park, at the American embassy, in a Fulham public-house—contributing directly to the drama that springs up when Quaife, after preliminary skirmishing and testing, takes Lewis first into his confidence and then into his friendship, and which crashes down when, the vote having been counted after his culminating speech in favour of his White Paper, he hears the chant opening up from the Opposition: "Resign, resign!"

Corridors of Power is the most steadily exciting story in the series: it is also one of the most diverse. In the corridors of power there are all manner of men, and of women: Quaife's wife, bold, brilliant, aristocratic; his mistress, superficially diffident and severe but ardently devoted; the grand political hostess with her riches, her confidence, and her love not only of impressing but of being impressed.

Yet behind his story throbs Lewis's intention to resolve the mystery of where, in the highest affairs of state, power is actually located. That is what *Corridors of Power* is about. And there is no mystery, really, nor ambiguity. As Lewis unfolds his story we see power shifting continually from man to man, from one group of men to another, from place to place. No one is sure that he has it: all want it.

El sueño de la razón produce monstruos (The sleep of reason gives birth to monsters). So runs Goya's inscription under one of his etchings. The monstrous thing at the centre of *The Sleep of Reason* (1968) is

murder, a particularly horrifying murder. Two young women, lesbian lovers, kidnap a young boy, torture him, and kill him. They live in Lewis Eliot's native town, and one of them is a niece of George Passant. She has been on the fringe of George's group of young people and has stirred to the sound of his passionate speeches about freedom: "What is to tie me down except myself? It is for me to will what I shall accept. Why should I obey conventions which I didn't make?" On George's youthful lips they were declarations full of hope; in Cora Passant's imagination thirty years later, they have been infected by existentialist notions of ultimate freedom, of "going to the limit."

The novel opens quietly, domestically, in 1963. Lewis takes his sixteen-year-old son, Charles, a spirited youth who has had an education very different from his father's, back to the town for a first visit to his grandfather. What was once the College where George taught has been transmogrified into a new university, where Lewis, as in *The Masters*, has a task to discharge as a member of the University Court. His moves are suddenly complicated by his being stricken with illness, a detached retina; but after an operation he recovers. Then the quiet of domestic life is broken by the sound of approaching tempest. The body of a missing boy is found, beaten to death; the police have traced and are questioning Cora Passant and her woman-friend.

Lewis goes to see George, who, alternating between reviving his old declarations of belief and frigidly disowning the behaviour of its current practitioners, says that he relies on Lewis to do whatever can be done. Lewis, despite the risk to his public reputation by association, decides to plunge. There is a quarrel, at once revealing and prophetic, between him and his son, who considers the choice sentimental. Ashamed of being reminded of days when he himself was rapacious and at the same time calculating the odds, Lewis, recognizing already the innate independence, pride, and secret ambitiousness in his son's nature, says: "My God, if you can be that cold, what sort of life are you going to have?" Charles replies: "I shall take more risks than you ever did. But I shall know what I'm taking them for." The two young women are arrested and accused of murder, and Lewis and his brother, Martin, arrange to attend the trial.

The last third of the novel is taken up with the trial. In *George Passant* it was George who was on trial; in this novel it is his niece; but in both trials what is ultimately up for judgement is freedom as George—and many other people—conceive it, freedom for an individual to develop all his potentialities in terms of action. In George's trial the issue is abstract, located in the future, illumined with hope. In Cora's trial the issue is located in the here and now, a powerful component of what is coming to be called the permissive society. The evidence in the trial, particularly the psychological evidence of the young women's states of mind, covers fascinatingly and dramatically the arguments for and against.

Folie à deux, transference of fantasy into action, abnormality of mind and impaired responsibility, the excitement of feeling freer than anyone around them, the fantasy about being lords of life and death: the tale is horrifying and sensational, and cannot be dissociated either from the nature of the society in which it is rooted or from the particular ideological preoccupations it throws light on, "glorifying unreason, wanting to let the instinctual forces loose." Briefly and uncynically, Martin, paraphrasing Lincoln Steffens' "I have seen the future. And it works," says at the end of the trial: "I have seen freedom. And it rots."

The novel returns to domestic quiet as the tempest ends. Nevertheless it is a quiet from which some of the deepest of human experiences spring: death, of Lewis's father; birth, of Martin's first grandchild; and the beginning of independent existence, of young Charles as for the first time he leaves home for a year's travel.

The title of the final novel in the series, *Last Things*, might lead one to expect not so much a novel like the others—exploring the natures of a certain number of chosen human beings as they travel through time and accumulate the experience of daily living with each other, with society, and above all with themselves—so much as static Proustian lucubrations on the termination of earthly existence. Not so. *Last Things* is just as much a novel as any of the others. "It might have seemed an end," Lewis thinks as he sees his son, Charles, finally go out into the world for his career. "But not to me, and not, perhaps, to him. He might know already, what had taken me so much longer to learn, that we make ends and shapes and patterns in our minds, but that we didn't live our lives like that. We couldn't do so, because the force inherent in our lives was stronger and more untidy than anything we could tell ourselves about it."

The book is patterned by plot, shaped by changing relationships between characters. At the core of it is the relationship between Lewis and his son, and it ends with a turn that is final. Yet the strength and the untidiness of the force inherent in our lives is there, as it were carrying the novel on into the unwritten future. Many, very many of the people in the earlier novels come in, and go out again. Some of them die; some of their children come in, just as young Charles has.

Last Things begins, like *The Sleep of Reason*, in a domestic mood, with the affairs in later 1964 of Martin Eliot's son, Pat, an appealing, good-for-nothing young man, the disturber and yet ultimately the joy of his shrewd and cautious father's heart. Pat has married Muriel, Roy Calvert's daughter, a clever young woman, cool and determined, who gets rid of him after they have had a child. On the plane of story-telling, *Last Things* is mainly, perhaps surprisingly, about young people. Muriel and Charles and some of their Cambridge friends go in for being revolutionaries, organizing a cell that takes part in protests and demonstrations and which, in a headstrong confusion of liberal idealism with action for its own sake reminiscent of *The Possessed*, finally gets into trouble before it peters out.

But what of death, hell, heaven, and judgment? Lewis' lucubrations on eschatology enter and become a central feature of the novel, in a most original and striking manner. Lewis suffers a recurrence of detached retina, and during the operation his heart stops; it has to be artificially re-started. Whether or not he can be said to return from the dead, the experience is traumatic. His first reaction to the news of what has happened to him is to feel "frozen with dread." But then, during the next week or so, the feeling is astoundingly reversed, almost to anti-dread: joy, peculiar liberation from self, a new view of that self in the uniqueness of its final solitude and in the common, erring nature of its relationships with other human beings. Seemingly new horizons appear wide-open before his eyes. He has faced death; heaven and hell are here in one's own life; and the judgement on oneself can be passed by oneself— "Be merciful!" a clergyman friend exhorts him.

Meanwhile Lewis's love for his son goes through its most crucial phase, though "love," he feels, is a word that confuses the issue, which, for all its powerful elements of love and affection, is rooted in the interplay of wills and possessiveness. Young Charles, with his unusual cleverness and maturity, with his independence, his secret ambitions, his pride, is menaced by the worldly distinction of his father—both he and his father recognize it: "It was not the penalties he wanted to escape from but the advantages. There were times when I seemed omnipresent. Anyone of strong nature would have preferred to be born obscure." And so in darker moments Lewis muses on Dostoyevsky's question: *Who has not wished his father dead?* The answer is: Not Charles; and yet . . . Somehow they reach a sort of solution, surprising in its actual form and yet predictable in its nature. Quietly Lewis watches Charles go off to take risks greater than he ever did.

And so the last of the series is written, the *roman fleuve* flows out of sight—but flows on. "It might have seemed an end." In a sense it is. Yet: "What I had imagined was nothing like the here and now, the continuous creation, the thrust of looking for the next moment which belonged to oneself and spread beyond the limits of oneself. When one is as alone as one can get, there's still no end."

THEMATIC MATERIAL AND DESIGN

THE title *Strangers and Brothers* states at once the deepest theme of the sequence as a whole—that all men, locked away in the isolation of their own selves, are lonely, strangers to each other; while in the similarity and resonance between them, in their joys, their aspirations, and their sufferings, they are all brothers. And every man exists in his own dynamic equilibrium between the two, sometimes more stranger than brother, sometimes more brother than stranger.

What are men, solitarily, in themselves and how, in their common experiences, are they brothers: These are the two main questions Snow sets out to investigate; experimentally, with techniques like those of a scientist, making hypotheses about the natures of his characters and testing them against the way those characters behave, suggesting theories about how in general their actions arise, yet concerning himself always with individual acts and their causes. And these are the two main questions whose answers, so far as they are to be found, Snow conveys to the reader by means of the techniques of art, adopting a tone of evocation and revelation, so that the reader, as well as being told the answers, *knows* them—he becomes aware that he is a stranger and a brother himself.

Apropos the investigatory element in his work, Snow wrote,[11] in the early days of his career as a writer, that he wanted to examine "how much of what we *are* is due to accidents of our class and time, and how much is due to something innate and unalterable within ourselves?"

It is clear that to do this he had to portray the society in which his characters were embedded and to study the moral and political health of that society. In *Strangers and Brothers* the extent of the society under examination is as broad as Balzac's,[12] ranging from the provincial lower middle class to the cosmopolitan aristocracy; it includes the worlds of government, the university, and industry. And in the end, the period of time encompassed half a century. The sounding of the moral and political health of society is generally implicit, made plain to the reader through the behaviour of the characters as seen by Lewis Eliot; for example, the form in which the particular turns of conscience of Charles March and Ann express themselves—for all Charles's and Ann's striving after goodness, a form cruelly destructive—illuminates the defects and decadence of upper-class Anglo-Jewish society in the 1930's.

All the same, where the question is posed in general terms, *Strangers and Brothers* gives the answer that men seem to be *less* what they *are* due to accidents of class and time than to things innate and unalterable within themselves. Lewis Eliot's is a dark view of life. Nevertheless, *Strangers and Brothers* is about individuals grappling with their fate rather than having it either imposed on them by random external events or imposed on them at birth as a foregone conclusion.[13] The crisis in each book of the sequence is essentially tragic, and yet not unrelievedly tragic; because somehow Snow irradiates it with a belief in the ultimate fortitude of the human race, with a belief that in the acceptance of the essential tragic nature of their own situation men are nevertheless borne up, rightly, by hope for what lies ahead. Their situation is tragic, but their fibres are alive with hope—this concept is the key to Lewis Eliot's own moral attitude to life.

[11]Letter to his publisher in 1938.

[12]Snow, like Balzac, reveals character against the background of society; but the structure of *Strangers and Brothers*, unlike that of *La Comédie humaine*, is built upon the underlying personal theme or themes.

[13]This theme of constant struggle gives dramatic suspense throughout the whole sequence beyond narrative suspense in any particular member.

At the same time, the tragic nature of the human situation, as seen by Lewis Eliot, is relieved at levels nearer to the surface. First of all, there is a characteristic down-to-earthness about the author. For example, the possessive love of parents for children is a "darkness of the heart," yet Snow presents it as so much the lot of all of us that we no more expect it to break the lives of his characters than it breaks our own lives. Secondly, there is an ironic nerve of comedy always in play. It is important not to miss this: at the height of his sufferings, Mr. March is still clowning, Roy Calvert playing monkey-tricks on pompous people, Lewis himself being outmaneuvred by his slatternly landlady. And, thirdly, the tragic stories are invested with a peculiar kind of glamour that springs partly from the subduedly romantic way in which Lewis, with his "residue of identification with those outside, pushing their noses against the window," sees life—the glamour of midnight visits of intrigue in a College, of the tormented bohemian ways of a dazzling scholar, of secret confabulations in the corridors of power—and partly by the role played in precipitating the crises of the stories by scandal, which has, in its capacity for drawing everybody cosily and sensationally, an alluringness not far removed from glamour.[14]

The central story of the sequence, the story of Lewis Eliot, is strong and simple; through it are interwoven the stories of his friends. The social relationship of the various characters to each other is intricate; but it is the intricate relationship of their experience with Lewis's experience that enables Snow to build up a novel of remarkable psychological as well as social solidity. Yet this intricacy in thematic relationship is not aimed merely at producing solidity in the architectural sense; its function is to provide means for the kind of revealing and evoking that is at the heart of Snow's technique as an artist. The clue to this function is given in a note written by Snow himself, in the prefatory note to *The Conscience of the Rich*, about the design of *Strangers and Brothers*:

Obviously, the entire work tells the stories of a number of people through a period of time: that does not need saying. Obviously, through the entire work there is an attempt to give some insights into society: those have been better understood than I expected when I began. Nevertheless,

the inner design has always lain elsewhere—at any rate for me, and I cannot speak for anyone else. It consists of a resonance between what Lewis Eliot sees and what he feels. Some of the more important emotional themes he observes through others' experience, and then finds them enter into his own. The theme of possessive love is introduced through Mr. March's relation to his son: this theme reappears in *The New Men* in Lewis's own experience, through his relation to his brother, and again, still more directly, in *Homecomings*.

The clue is: "It consists of a resonance between what Lewis Eliot sees and what he feels." Resonance, the phenomenon of something that vibrates being able to stir and magnify a similar vibration in something that has been previously *attuned*, gives *Strangers and Brothers* its power, through evocation and revelation, over one's emotions and one's imagination.

There are resonances of many kinds and on many levels. Now that the sequence is complete, the extent to which the author has planned to use different kinds of resonance is fully apparent. In George Passant's story, for instance, Lewis observes, among other things, the love of power impelling a man whose character is flawed; in Charles March's story, the love of a parent who wants certain things for his son. In *Time of Hope* both these themes had appeared, resonating in Lewis's own experience: in *Homecomings* they resonate again; and in *Last Things* yet again, finally but differently, after his strange and arresting confrontation with death—they resonate now in a more coolly-accepted way that amounts almost to harmony.

There is some similarity, in this use of resonance, with *A la recherche du temps perdu*, where Proust examines the theme of obsessional jealousy in Swann, before coming to it in Marcel. What Snow does is to extend it in a *cyclical* fashion. This is original; no other writer has done it. *Time of Hope* is about what Lewis is feeling during the period covered by the succeeding five novels, in which he records, on a much wider canvas, what he is seeing—there being a resonance between the two. *Homecomings* begins a similar cycle, exploring a still greater depth of personal experience and still wider range of social observations: there is a similar internal resonance within this second cycle—plus a further external resonance between it and the first cycle. In *Last Things*, while the possibility of further experiences is left open, as in life itself, a synthesis of all the resonances is achieved.

[14]In the use of scandal, Snow has obviously learned a good deal from Ibsen.

C. P. SNOW

STYLE

I answered sullenly. The present moment, the existent moment—as we sat there, in the sultry darkness, we could neither deal with it nor let it be. We could not show each other the kindness we should have shown strangers: far less could we allow those words to come out which, with the knowledge and touch of intimacy, we were certain could give the other a night's peace. If she could have said to me, it doesn't matter, leave it, some day you'll be better and we'll start again—if I could have said to her, I will try to give you all you want, marry me and somehow we shall come through—But we could not speak so, it was as though our throats were sewn up.

We stayed, our hands touching, not tired so much as stupefied while the time passed: time not racing hallucinatorily by, as when one is drunk, but just pressing on us with something like the headaching pressure of the thundery air in which we sat. Sometimes we talked, almost with interest, almost as though we were going out for the first time, for the first meal together, about a play that ought to be seen or a book she had just read. After another bout of silence, she said in a different tone: "Before we started I asked what you wanted from me."

(*Homecomings*, ch. 26)

Two things strike one immediately: the first, how simple the literary style appears to be; the second, how much, in a matter of 230 words, happens to have been said. The two things are directly related. The words chosen are those which say most.

For the most important and serious things he has to say in this passage, Snow has chosen to write mainly in simple, common words,[15] words that we all use all the time—especially at moments when we are struggling to express something difficult. His underlying aesthetic theory is clear. The simple common words, because we use them all the time, often using the same word for different purposes, are the words which have come to acquire separately the most elaborate nexus of allusions;[16] and therefore, strung together, they can make the most subtle and pregnant of sentences. Furthermore, because they are simple and common, they do not distract in a "literary" sense; because they are familiar, one feels naked to their meaning. "If I could have said to her, I will try to give you all you want, marry me and somehow we shall come through"—that is how, in

this complex situation of conflicting love, one might have said it to oneself; reading it, nothing comes between one and the author's meaning. The style has fitted perfectly what the author had to say.

While appearing simple, the style is, of course, strong and subtly poetic. (Snow relies little on adverbs—there are only two in the above passage.) Common words are interspersed with uncommon ones, carefully chosen for their effect on more than one level: in the first two lines of the extract, "sullen" and "sultry" ring on a poetic level, and in so doing they bind together more strongly the mood of the characters with the atmosphere of the place in which they are sitting. Polysyllabic words, when they are used, make their special impression: in the third sentence, "intimacy" stands out; struck by it, one remembers the characters have been intimate as lovers. Even more markedly, Snow makes the most of literary images: at the end of the last sentence of the first paragraph, the tension built up by the sentences linked with dashes is clinched—as it could not have been clinched by the statement "But we could not speak so"—by the remarkable image "it was as though our throats were sewn up."

To illustrate Snow's total range in verbal texture, one has to go further than one extract. It is significant that Snow varies his verbal texture according to what he is writing about. In general, he presents scene and narrative most simply. For comment, especially the kind of extended comment with which he sometimes ends a chapter, his verbal texture usually becomes denser, richer, more elaborate. For example:

As to many of us, when young, the labile, the shifting, the ambivalent, the Lebedevs and Fyodor Karamazovs, had given me an intimation of the depth and wonder of life.
(*Homecomings*, ch. 28)

Both structurally and syntactically, Snow's style is also more complex and more calculated than it seems. For example, the second paragraph of the longer quotation is constructed to lead suspensefully from the static "We stayed, our hands touching," through the disturbing "headaching pressure of the thundery air" and the desultory strain of "Sometimes we talked, almost with interest," to the climax of what it was that she said in a different tone.

Going into it still further, it is important to note —since it seems to be so frequently missed, presumably because the depths are so movingly stirred by

---

[15]Over 80 percent of the words are monosyllables; less than 15 percent have two syllables; and less than 4 percent have three or more.

[16]Compare the nexus of allusions associated respectively with the words "give" and "hallucinatorily."

fundamental issues—that the surface of Snow's work constantly ripples with humour. It is an idiosyncratic humour, sophisticated and ironic, closer to wit in the seventeenth-century sense than to wordplay in the twentieth—there is negligible appearance of the latter, as exemplified either by the algebraic inventiveness of P. G. Wodehouse or by the punning illumination of James Joyce. Instead, it is the humor-inherent in slyly observing the goings-on of human beings when they are unaware of themselves—in the seventeenth-century sense, for example, in the comment on the young Guevarras in *Last Things* happily quaffing Coco-Cola, "the liquid emblem of capitalism"; or on young Charles, expatiating on living in Belgravia being as quiet as living in a small country-town, "I didn't have the presence of mind to enquire whether he had ever lived in a country-town, small or otherwise." And, on a more ironic level, the young scientist Leonard Getliffe saying someone would never be really first-rate, would probably never make the Royal Society, "as though that were the lowest limit of man's endeavour"; or the politician and the academics at their council, "They thought they were using him: he thought he could use some of them. That made for general harmony." It is interesting to see that it is in the later novels, where the underlying themes become, as it were, more cosmic, that the surface ripples of humour become freer and more constant.

However, to sum up, the main point about Snow's style is that it has been developed firstly to give *absolute conviction on the plane of immediate fact*, though it has been developed so flexibly that it can also be used for both narrative and analytical purposes. It has a compelling tone which arises not only, or even mainly, from knowledge, but from the author's total involvement in what he is doing. To read it is to believe it. The fact that Snow has such a wide experience and understanding of life in England naturally gives what he writes a peculiar authority; his style, simple, unaffected, and moving, is such as to make what he writes immediately recognizable as plain truth.

LATE NOVELS

WITH the sequence ended, Snow published *The Malcontents* (1972). It is a novel about seven young men and women aged twenty-two or so, most of them at university; clever, thoughtful, and ener-getic—what Snow often refers to elsewhere as "the intelligent young." And the theme is the question: What do men live by? That question, and—as it strikes the young people—its answer in terms of action now, in 1970. A common response binds the seven together as allies and friends into a cell which they call "the core."

The setting is a bustling, modern provincial city, where, because of its light industry and its prosperousness, there is an unusually large influx of brown-skinned immigrants, mostly Asian. It is the cause of getting decent treatment for the latter that provides "the core" with an opening for action now. One of them, son of a docker, has tracked down, near to his own backstreet lodgings, an example of West Indian families being rackrented as they might have been in a nineteenth-century slum. The sub-landlord is West Indian, but the chain of property-ownership leads ultimately to the owner of the whole street, an influential Tory Member of Parliament, member of the Shadow Cabinet (there being a Labour Government at the time) and one who is proved to have interests in South Africa.

"The core" has its counterparts, anti-racialist cells in universities other than those the seven go to, and they have contacts with the press and radio and with anti-racialist Members of Parliament. At the best-judged moment, the news of the discovery is to be fed into the network, where it will build up—they plan—into a national scandal with major political consequences for the Right-Wing Establishment.

When all the members of "the core" are together during the Christmas vacation, the solicitor father of the central young man hears, from talk among his legal friends, that the plan has been leaked in advance to ill-disposed people, thence to official security organisations—to the police and probably to MI5. The seven meet immediately in the backstreet lodgings; then later for a strange, slightly hysterical party in the rooms of a classy young man who "experiments" with marijuana and LSD. Their first preoccupation, with which they deal expeditiously, is: Can they act before the official world acts against them? Their second, with which they wrestle all night, is: Who has betrayed them? Towards the end of the party, one of them falls out of the high open window and is picked up dead. The police are called in.

The accident provokes a turning-point in the story, not only in precipitating the revelation of who betrayed the rest and why, but also in ending the active future of "the core." More importantly, though, it provokes a turning-point for each of the seven, in discovering how to live, despite the disaster which has befallen "the core," decently and hopefully with society, and perhaps more importantly still, decently and hopefully with himself or herself. And that does not imply passivity for any of them. They *are* "the intelligent young." They cannot, *will* not let life pass as it is: they mean to make changes.

In Their Wisdom (1974) is a long, single novel of remarkable intricacy, remarkable density; yet the structure is nevertheless constantly definable, the texture constantly lucid. The main plot is about a disputed will. A rich old man, eccentric and wilful, is dead: his estranged daughter—estranged on his side rather than on hers—who lives in near-poverty is disinherited in favour of the son of a woman who has acted as the old man's secretary-companion-nurse during his last years. Did the mother exert "undue influence" in the English legal sense on the old man? The daughter disputes the will not of her own accord, but under the bullying of a Napoleonic property-dealer who is in a remote sense her employer.

The dispute goes through the stately English legal processes. It is heard in Court (first climax), when the will is reversed in favour of the estranged daughter. The son and his mother then give notice of Appeal: all the lawyers and counsel advise both sides to agree on a compromise settled out of Court; but the son decides wilfully to risk everything by going ahead with the final legal step, the Appeal (second climax). His decision leads to the hearing of the Appeal in Court, where the first judgement is reversed (third and final climax). So, as so often in life, the undeserving prosper—incidentally Snow has some interesting things to say about luck. Between the climaxes in the main plot there are skilfully interspersed climaxes in the sub-plots: in one of them the disinherited daughter marries a peer, a solitary, high-minded man as poverty-stricken as herself, and their lives are suddenly visited unexpectedly by physical joy; and after the third climax the book ends with a thrilling account of a surgical operation on the brain of an elderly Nobel scientist, also a peer, in which he is cured of Parkinson's disease.

It is no secret that Snow's title for the novel was *The Onlookers*. Who, then, are the onlookers, and what are they looking on? They are three elderly men, all men of substance, of experience, and of differing forms of wisdom: they are peers, working members of the House of Lords. One, a former Conservative Cabinet Minister: another, "historian by trade, inquisitive by vocation," a peer for his lifetime only and of relatively lowly social origins: the third the Nobel scientist. While the case of the disputed will rolls on, each of these three, either connected with the case or drawn into it, stands in the background, commenting not only on the case but also on the state of the English nation and the future of the kind of society in which it lives. (The period is 1972–1974.) Their attitude is subject to deep forebodings—tinged with a sense of personal responsibility, since the society now falling into such disarray is one they played some part, themselves, in forming. Yet even so, in the wisdom of looking back they know how narrow were the limits of choice in action that the course of events allowed them.

Yet Snow would not be the writer he is if the message of the book were not ultimately shot through with *hope*. Hope in what? Not, alas not, simply in a re-organisation of society under a different set of rules. Snow seems to be conveying that he finds human nature too flawed, the element in human beings of the intractable, too ineradicable for hope to reside in such mechanical solutions. He looks to a deeper level. Ultimately hope resides in an enhanced feeling of *their common humanity* in single individuals. A deeper level, more abstract and perhaps more difficult to comprehend? Snow does not leave it there, at the abstract level; but in a masterly stroke demonstrates it precisely as it were in the flesh, at the successful end of the brain-operation, when it flashes instantaneously between the surgeons, nurses, technicians, and spectators. A deeply moving moment, a moment when the reader shares the feeling and the hope.

With his sixteenth novel, *A Coat of Varnish* (1979), Snow takes up again the genre of his first, the detective-story. With what a difference! Early in the book a murder takes place, a brutal murder in Belgravia (an upper-class quarter of London), of an old lady, a former "beauty" and widow of a Marquess. It is shocking, unspeakable—to her friends and to the neighbours almost unthinkable. And yet . . . below the surface, as they are suddenly forced to recognise, things are not so unthinkable. One of the characters, a rabbinical American scholar, recognises this nakedly. "Civilisation is hideously fragile," he observes. "There's not much between us and the horrors underneath. Just a coat of varnish, wouldn't you say?"

The detection is entirely in the hands of the police,

led by a youngish Detective Chief Superintendent called Frank Briers, who has formerly been on friendly professional terms with an elderly Lewis Eliot–like resident of Belgravia called Humphrey Leigh, now retired from a career in Security. The incidental sub-plots are woven between a succession of interrogations, whose course is determined partly according to police procedure; yet partly—in typically Snovian fashion—according to the man Briers *is*. The two men are at first separated by Briers' professional caginess; but gradually they come to terms under which they can usefully collaborate, and their friendship springs up again, Briers' energetic optimism finding a countervalent in Leigh's "dark stoicism."

It is early settled that the old lady must have been murdered by someone she knows. So the lives of the people she knew, most of whom live nearby, come under the scrutiny of Briers and Leigh. Their lives, the way they live; set in the time and the place they live in—upper-class Belgravia, 1976. We see the men and women they *are*, their relationship with each other, their jobs, their incomes, what they feel about the world, about politics, about money, about their future. The picture of their reality is thus total.

The problem of selecting those bits of information which will add up to a total picture of reality, and then of conveying them lucidly and readably—that is one of the major technical problems for the realistic novelist. The uninspired solution is to deal with each element of reality separately and completely, to spend a protracted passage in turn on, say, a character's physical appearance, his philosophical beliefs, his sexual nature, his response to another character, the room in which he is sitting, the weather outside. Snow's solution is to make each paragraph a mélange of partial contributions to the different elements, of bits of information about first one and then another, melting into each other. There is nothing unusual in principle about this solution—many realistic writers adopt it to be a greater or less degree. In *A Coat of Varnish* Snow adopts it to a much greater degree than most other writers, with the skill of utter confidence. His writing may be said to be dense, not in the sense that it is in the least opaque or turgid, but in the sense that, while remaining completely lucid and readable, it conveys an extraordinary density of selected bits of information. It is all done without calling attention to itself—many a reader may well not notice it. Just so. Technique in its highest manifestation conceals itself.

OTHER WORKS

AT first sight Snow's book *Trollope* (1975) looks like what is commonly known as a "coffee-table book" —large pages, relatively few of them, attractively illustrated. It is nevertheless a work of entirely serious intent. It is apparent that while the author has read Trollope with scholarly attention and has thoughtfully weighed up the relationship between Trollope's art and his life, he approaches Trollope as a fellow-novelist rather than as a professional scholar or critic. Furthermore—and here lies the particular value of the book—one feels that Snow must have, although he does not say so, a good deal in common with Trollope, both in temperament and in experience of living in the world of men. This leads him to observations of a particular order, which are often illuminating and sometimes moving.

The crux of the book is Snow's case that Trollope possessed to an extraordinary degree the combination of insight (looking into them deeply and sympathetically from the *outside*), and empathy (looking outwards from the *inside*, *as* them) for the actual men and women from whom he created the characters in his novels. This degree of combined insight and empathy, for which Snow uses the single word "percipience" because it is a single, unified gift, is extraordinary in its breadth as well as its depth, and in the variety of men and women with whom it works. It is Trollope's great gift; and on it essentially, since he shares to a lesser degree some of the novelist's other gifts, depends what one thinks of Trollope. For Snow the gift clearly is supreme.

That is the crux of the book. The general plan follows the chronology of Trollope's life, with interpolations dealing with his art. His appallingly neglected boyhood and young manhood, and his building for himself a resistant outer personality; his career in the Civil Service, with its success and (in his eyes) final failure; his harmonious married life and disappointments in his family; his double attitude, combining confidence and humility, to his literary career. This, with Snow's own analysis of, and original insights into, Trollope's art, makes the book a most attractive and valuable lead-in to anyone who does not know Trollope's novels and can only add to the appreciation of anyone who does.

Stendhal, Balzac, Dickens, Dostoyevsky, Tolstoy, Galdós, Henry James, and Proust—these are the subjects of *The Realists* (1978), Snow's choice of the world's greatest realistic novelists. To each of them he devotes an essay in which he examines their novels with the professional eye of a realistic novelist, and at the same time sketches their lives with the pen of a realistic novelist. "As the coolest-headed of them said himself," Snow observes, "briskly dismissing the opinion of outsiders (meaning those who were not creative), a writer's life is not just connected with his work, it cannot be separated from it. I believe that to be utterly true."

Nobody should be surprised by any serious artist's making the greatest claims for the art-form he has himself chosen—if he has devoted the whole of his life and talent to working in that art-form, one would be foolish to expect anything else. In his preface, Snow writes cogently, yet himself "cool-headedly," about his own chosen art-form at its peak, thus:

In the great realistic novels, there is a presiding, unconcealed, interpreting intelligence. They are all of them concerned with the actual social setting in which their personages exist. The concrete world, the world of physical fact, the shapes of society are essential to the art. The people have to be projected, not only as novelists, major and minor, have tried to project them, but also examined with the writer's psychological resources and with cognitive intelligence. Both those components are features of realism. It is interesting, and sometimes significant, to see how often intuitive wisdom and cognitive thought have converged, and have anticipated later discoveries brought about by more strictly rational processes. [And later:] Most of all, in these novels the lessons about individual human beings are some of the deepest, and the most complete, ever written. Owing to various trends in twentieth century literature and thought, many of the realists' discoveries still haven't been accepted into the general consensus. All of them said things of startling originality. Some of these statements haven't proved valid; but a good many now seem incontestably true. In the midst of his fugues of psychological imagining, Dostoievsky shot out insights about multiple motives and hidden purposes which no one had thought of before or can challenge since. Much earlier, Stendhal, with absolute lucidity, made findings about intermittences of emotion, and about his famous crystallisations, which should be part of anyone's psychological equipment.

The foregoing quotation gives a key to the eight studies; in the sense that it both declares what Snow believes about the realistic novel, and illustrates what above all he is looking for—and finds—in the world's greatest realistic novelists, in their work and their lives. So far as his actual choice of writers goes, it is obvious that Dickens is not a realistic novelist: he is included, "with a touch of chauvinism," Snow

admits, because he is one of the greatest of English geniuses. On the other hand, Galdós will probably be for many English and American readers—as indeed he was for Snow until late in life—a fascinating discovery.

When Snow died in 1980, he left behind the first draft of *The Physicists* (1981), a book to which he intended to add much more material in the second half. The present writer, first associated in 1931 as a physics undergraduate at Cambridge with Snow, then a physics Research Fellow at the same College, was called upon to help in turning the draft into a publishable form; which, although it could be little more than half of what Snow's final version would have been, contained so much fresh and irreplaceable material as to make it a valuable book in its own right.

The eponymous physicists are the originators of what is loosely known as "modern physics," that is to say, the physics which came into being with the discovery of sub-atomic particles, beginning with electrons, then protons, neutrons, and so on—the discovery still continues. And a double aim underlies Snow's writing the book: to elucidate for the layman the science which, in not much over a generation, changed the world; and to capture the flavour of the lives, often through his own personal reminiscences, of the scientists themselves. (After reading the book one may speculate privately: Can a *scientist's* discoveries and his life be separated?)

Since Snow had lived through The Golden Age of physics—roughly 1919–1939—his first draft of the book was written chiefly from his singularly accurate and retentive memory. In *The Physicists* all the great figures of that Age, Rutherford, Bohr, Einstein, Dirac, appear in person, their colleagues, peers, and successors: there are comments on their temperaments and experiences, photographs of them, and illustrated theoretical interpolations to explain their contributions to the art of science.

The Golden Age of discoveries went some way towards changing the world; but it was the concomitant Dark Age of exploiting those discoveries in the cause of human slaughter which produced the change that has most preoccupied society ever since—and that in Snow's book comes in for his moral examination as a humanist. (It is a symptom of the darkness of the age that the term "liberal humanist" has had its original moral connotation reversed in some quarters.) And the book concludes with appendices in which one of Snow's most remarkable speeches about science and scientists, a speech delivered to the American Association for the Advancement of Science in 1960, is printed: it is entitled "The Moral Un-neutrality of Science."

BASIC ATTITUDE

WHEN Snow expresses his view on what is happening nowadays in the world in general, two main theses are discernible. The first arises from his concern over the widening, in the Western world, of the gap between science and literature: his thesis is that this widening is in any case intellectually and socially undesirable, and that in the case of a country in the particular situation of Britain, it could in a short time be catastrophic. He argues that the splintering of a culture into an increasing number of fragments, between which communication becomes less and less possible, inevitably leads to attrition and decay. A country as small as Britain cannot afford fragmentation of any kind. Its economic future depends on keeping ahead in technological innovation, and any split which hives off part of its intellectual and social potential into non-comprehension of, if not opposition to, scientific studies and activities is likely to be disastrous more quickly than it would be for a larger, richer country, which is not compelled to make absolutely the most of its available talent.

The second thesis is that the widening of the gap between science and literature in the Western world obscures the existence of the major gap in the whole world today, namely, that between the countries which are technologically advanced and the rest—a major gap because it is a more deep-seated cause of possible world conflict than any other. The prime social task of the advanced countries, for the sake of their own continued peaceful existence if no one else's, is to reduce the gap. This can be done only by helping the less advanced countries to industrialize themselves as rapidly as possible. And this in turn can be done only if the advanced countries are confident in their own culture, confident in the results of their own industrialization.

The split in Western culture between the scientific and the non-scientific parts has its root superficially in the incapacity of the non-scientific part to comprehend the scientific, but more deeply in the incapacity of the non-scientific part to adjust itself to—let alone have confidence in—the conditions of life in industrialized society. Before the potentially

tragic consequences of the culture's being so divided, Snow's attitude is the reverse of acquiescent. In this, as well as in his novels, he is totally involved. *"Though the individual condition is tragic, the social condition need not be."*[17] Lewis Eliot's view of human nature, like Snow's view, is a dark one. Yet some things in the tragic human condition can be affected, as his own condition is affected in *Time of Hope* and more particularly *Homecomings* by the exercise of will, and in *Last Things* by the realization of death, his own death, as an agent in liberating the spirit from self; and this gives him hope. Thus Snow views what is happening nowadays in the world in general. The split in the culture alarms him, and the gap between the rich, advanced nations and the poverty-stricken, backward ones troubles him both practically and morally. But both gaps can be reduced by men of goodwill if they set themselves to do it. There is no reason why the human *social* condition should be tragic. It can be affected by human action. The *is* hope for the future.

SELECTED BIBLIOGRAPHY

I. BIBLIOGRAPHY. R. Greacen, *The World of C. P. Snow* (London, 1962), with bibliography by B. Stone.

II. SELECTED WORKS. S. Weintraub, ed., *C. P. Snow: A Spectrum. Science—Criticism—Fiction* (New York, 1963).

III. SCIENTIFIC PAPERS. *Proceedings of the Royal Society, 1928–1929, 1930–1932, 1935,* papers on molecular structure; *The Cambridge Library of Modern Science,* ed. C. P. Snow (Cambridge, 1931–   ).

IV. SEPARATE WORKS. *Death Under Sail* (London, 1932; rev. ed., 1959), novel; *New Lives for Old* (London, 1933), novel, published anonymously; *The Search* (London, 1934; rev. ed., 1958), novel; *Strangers and Brothers* (London, 1940), novel, retitled in 1970 *George Passant* when original title was applied to entire sequence that includes the following ten novels: *The Light and the Dark, Time of Hope, The Masters, The New Men, Homecomings, The Conscience of the Rich, The Affair, Corridors of Power, The Sleep of Reason, Last Reasons* (see below); *The Light and the Dark* (London, 1947), novel; *Time of Hope* (London, 1949), novel.

The Masters (New York–London, 1951), novel; *The New Men* (New York–London, 1954), novel; *Homecomings* (New York–London, 1956), novel; *The Conscience of the Rich* (New York–London, 1958), novel; *Two Cultures*

---

[17]A recurrent theme in Snow's speeches and conversations; it first appeared in the Rede Lecture at Cambridge University in 1959.

and the Scientific Revolution (Cambridge, 1959), essay, given as the Rede Lecture at Cambridge University, expanded ed. titled The Two Cultures: And a Second Look (Cambridge, 1964).

The Affair (London, 1960), novel; Science and Government (Cambridge, Mass., 1961), the Godkin Lectures, Harvard University, 1960; A Postscript to Science and Government (London, 1962); Magnaminity: Rectorial Address (London, 1962), given at St. Andrews University, 1962; Corridors of Power (London, 1964), novel; Variety of Men (London, 1967), biography; The Sleep of Reason (London, 1968), novel; The State of Siege (New York, 1969), essay, the John Findley Green Foundation lectures.

Last Things (London, 1970), novel; Public Affairs (New York, 1971); The Malcontents (London, 1972), novel; In Their Wisdom (London, 1974), novel; Trollope, His Life and Art (London, 1975), biography; The Realists (London, 1978), essays; A Coat of Varnish (London, 1979), novel; The Physicists (London, 1981), science and biography.

V. CRITICAL STUDIES. Walter Allen, Reading a Novel, 2nd ed. (London, 1956), includes essay on The Masters; Pamela Hansford Johnson, "Three Novelists and the Drawing of Character," in English Association, Essays and Studies, III (1950), 82–99; Walter Allen, The Novel (London, 1955); L. Trilling, "The Novel, Living or Dead," in A Gathering of Fugitives (London, 1957); F. R. Karl, C. P. Snow: The Politics of Conscience (Carbondale, Ill., 1963); G. Petelin and J. Simkin, Čarl'z Persi Snou, pisatel i čelovek (Rostov-na-Donu, USSR, 1963); J. Thale, C. P. Snow (Edinburgh–London, 1964); R. G. Davis, C. P. Snow, Columbia Essays on Modern Writers, no. 8 (New York–London, 1965); R. Rabinovitz, The Reaction Against Experiment in the English Novel, 1950–1960 (New York–London, 1967).

ANTHONY POWELL

(1905-   )

Bernard Bergonzi

I

SOME novelists achieve an instant fame with their first book and spend the rest of their lives failing to live up to that early promise. Anthony Powell's reputation has developed in quite the opposite way, in a slow and deliberate fashion, from fairly obscure beginnings to a point where he is now widely regarded as one of the finest living English novelists. Powell was born on 21 December 1905 and educated at Eton and Oxford, and he published his first novel, *Afternoon Men*, in 1931. It did not arouse much interest and was followed by four more novels between 1932 and 1939. During World War II Powell served in the army and wrote no more fiction, but he made a study of the seventeenth-century antiquarian John Aubrey, and brought out a biography of Aubrey in 1948 and an edition of Aubrey's *Brief Lives* the following year. Then, in 1951, he published *A Question of Upbringing*, the first volume of *The Music of Time*, the long novel sequence on which his reputation largely rests. The whole work, comprising twelve volumes, was completed in 1975.

Afternoon Men can be placed with Evelyn Waugh's *Decline and Fall* (1928) as one of the few outstanding first novels to appear in England during the 1920's and 1930's. Both Powell and Waugh were satirically interested in the London circles, partly fashionable and partly artistic, that had been more cheerfully described and exposed in the early novels of Aldous Huxley. Yet Waugh is more cruel, hysterical, and gay; Powell is a detached but sympathetic observer, delineating human folly with the calm of an anthropological field worker. *Afternoon Men* is pitched in a uniformly minor key; it is a comic masterpiece that avoids extravagance and achieves its effects by a relentless, laconic wit and a stylized manner that looks like artlessness. The danger is that apparent flatness can be mistaken for the real thing, and *Afternoon Men* has never had the recognition it deserves. In this novel Powell first established the fictional territory that he has made peculiarly his own, where several social groups overlap and intersect: writers, artists, journalists, and film makers; professional people with vaguely bohemian tastes; undisguised layabouts; and members of the lesser aristocracy. As Walter Allen has said, Powell's world can be located geographically and spiritually at the point where Mayfair meets Soho. Atwater, the dim but likable hero of *Afternoon Men*, works in a museum, and the serious side of the story concerns his unsuccessful love affair with Susan Nunnery, who leaves him for a wealthier man; but the comic aspect arises from Atwater's friendship with the painters Pringle and Barlow and their eccentric associates.

Afternoon Men already contains the essence of Powell's fictional method. There is, first, his preoccupation with style as a mode of mediating and re-creating experience; he is not a "stylist" in the sense of writing poetic prose or seeking colorful verbal effects, but in the novels of the thirties and again in *The Music of Time* Powell achieves a stylistic manner that matches his particular subject matter. The process is apparent in the opening pages of *Afternoon Men*, where the syntax conveys a sense of experience fragmented into countless disparate units that are only barely connected (the scene is a London drinking club):

Atwater did not answer. He read a newspaper that someone had left on the table. He read the comic strip and later the column headed "Titled Woman in Motor Tragedy." He was a weedy-looking young man with straw-coloured hair and rather long legs, who had failed twice for the Foreign Office. He sometimes wore tortoiseshell-rimmed spectacles to correct a slight squint, and through influence had recently got a job in a museum. His father was a retired civil servant who lived in Essex, where he and his wife kept a chicken farm.

"How long has this place been open?" said Pringle.

"Not long. Everybody comes here."
"Do they?"
"Mostly."

(I. 1, "Montage")

This clipped, laconic style occurs throughout *Afternoon Men* and Powell's second novel, *Venusberg* (1932), both works which dwell on the absurdity of human attempts to form genuine relationships. Later in the thirties Powell's style changed; the sentences became longer and the syntax more elaborate, and in *The Music of Time* he writes in a way quite unlike *Afternoon Men*: a complicated, leisurely, reflective, and analytical manner that unsympathetic readers have found merely long-winded. Yet whereas the style of Powell's first two novels had effectively rendered the comic disparity and randomness of experience as it unfolds moment by moment, in *The Music of Time* Powell is attempting to make aesthetic sense of a lifetime of vanished experiences, to understand them and draw out the significances that were hidden at the time. Powell seems no more convinced in the sequence than he was in the early novels that order and coherence are actually part of reality, but he is prepared to allow that they may appear in the verbal patterning that the novelist imposes on his material, so that style is a necessary principle of order.

The other major aspect of Powell's method that is already quite apparent in *Afternoon Men* is his preoccupation with anecdote and gossip. To some extent such an interest is an essential part of any novelist's equipment, for he is nothing if he is not both a collector and a teller of stories. But Powell's sense of anecdote is remarkably well developed. Thus in *Afternoon Men* one of the unifying motifs in the story consists of recurring references to an absent friend of the principal characters, who never appears but is often spoken of:

". . . William has had a letter from Undershaft. He's in New York, living with an Annamite and playing the piano."
"Is he making any money?"
"Doing very well, he says."

(I.1, "Montage")

In Powell's view of life such anecdotal allusions are a way of bringing the various strands together, and if the stories are already familiar to those recounting them, they provide a welcome sense of assurance in a world without fixed points of reference:

Pringle had been in pretty good form all day. Barlow said:
"What's come over him? It's like when one of the critics said there was a quality of originality about his treatment of water."
"When he rang up Pauline de Chabran at Claridge's?" said Atwater.
"The week he told Mrs. Beamish her parties were the worst in Europe."
"But he's never been to one."
"That was what made her so angry," said Barlow.

(II. 26, "Perihelion")

The anecdotal method is used in a far more extensive but not essentially different way in *The Music of Time*, which is, among other things, a vast, expanding collection of anecdotes about the innumerable people who move in and out of the life of the narrator, Nicholas Jenkins, from childhood to middle age. Some are as brief and fragmentary as those in *Afternoon Men*, while others are very long and circumstantial, like Nicholas Jenkins' childhood memory of the dramatic events one Sunday in the summer of 1914, involving his father's cook, Albert, a female servant called Billson, and the visiting General Conyers, which takes up the first seventy pages of *The Kindly Ones* (*The Music of Time*, vol. VI). This superb piece of writing, one of the great achievements of the whole sequence, contains within itself fragments of small-scale anecdote: "Bertha Conyers has such an amusing way of putting things," my mother would say. "But I really don't believe all her stories, especially the one about Mrs Asquith and the man who asked her if she danced the tango.'"

Although *The Music of Time* is Powell's major achievement, *Afternoon Men* is, within its far smaller compass, his most sustainedly brilliant book and remains an endlessly rewarding piece of comic fiction. If it anatomizes a between-wars world of futility and boredom, it does so with calm geniality and with no sense of moral indignation or metaphysical anguish. In Powell's vision of reality, the comic form remains a permanent assertion of human value, however shabby the behavior it renders. Although Powell's sense of the absurd is unsurpassed, it is always closer to the purely comic than to the existential. Consider, for instance, the loveless sexual union of Atwater and a girl called Lola, where Powell makes a deliberate and effective departure from the laconic stylistic norm of *Afternoon Men*:

Slowly, but very deliberately, the brooding edifice of seduction, creaking and incongruous, came into being, a vast Heath Robinson mechanism, dually controlled by them and lumbering gloomily down vistas of triteness. With a sort of heavy-fisted dexterity the mutually adapted emotions of each of them became synchronised, until the unavoidable anti-climax was at hand. Later they dined at a restaurant quite near the flat.

(II. 9, "Perehelion")

Or there is the even more startling shift of style when one of the lesser characters, a sad, unsuccessful young journalist called Fotheringham, suddenly launches into a long, wordy tirade about "this mad, chaotic armageddon, this frenzied, febrile striving which we, you and I, know life to be," which turns into a page-long sentence of ever-increasing syntactical complexity, until Fotheringham finally loses the thread of what he is trying to say. Devoted admirers of *Afternoon Men* have their favorite episodes; one of my own is the section in which Pringle, who has been entertaining a party of friends in his cottage near the sea, has a row with his girl and decides to commit suicide. He leaves a note announcing his intention of not returning from bathing. A few hours later, after his friends have been in much distress, he is discovered in fisherman's clothes, looking round the cottage for the note. He explains that he changed his mind and was picked up by some fishermen. A little later, when one of the fishermen comes to claim his clothes, an argument arises between Pringle and his friends about how much he should give the man for saving him; ten shillings seems too little, and a pound too much, so he compromises with fifteen shillings. The man simply says "Tar" ("Thanks") when handed the money, and Pringle observes, "That was obviously the right sum."

Venusberg, Powell's next novel, is stylistically similar to *Afternoon Men,* and its hero, Lushington, is another likable, ineffectual young man. The book describes his adventures in a small Baltic capital where he is sent as a journalist; he has an unhappy love affair with the wife of a professor and runs into a variety of exotic local characters. There are a number of entertaining scenes, but the novel is for the most part slight and overepisodic, with little of the comic brilliance of *Afternoon Men.* It ends on a note of sudden, arbitrary violence and death that is rather beyond Powell's abilities to make convincing.

His third novel, *From a View to a Death* (1933), is a good deal more interesting. It is set in an English village, a society of declining county families who are disturbed by the advent of an ambitious and social-climbing young artist called Zouch, a vulgar and unattractive figure who nevertheless has a degree of energy and drive that is lacking in the society he is trying to penetrate. Zouch has, in fact, some slight affinity with Stendhal's Julien Sorel, and like Julien comes to an abrupt and violent end; certainly Stendhal has always been an author much admired by Powell, and figures of boundless will power are endlessly fascinating to him. In *From a View to a Death* the prose is less economical and more explicit than in *Afternoon Men,* and the novel as a whole has greater solidity and less sharpness. It displays a recognizable segment of English society in some depth, whereas the first two novels concentrated on the antics and collisions of individual characters; to this extent Powell is already looking forward to the method of *The Music of Time.* Although parts of the book are as funny as anything that Powell has written, its total impact is by no means wholly comic; the novel is pervaded by an atmosphere of lassitude and frustration that recalls other, more socially committed writings of the 1930's. It seems that in this novel Powell was trying to convey his own sense of what W. H. Auden, in an exactly contemporary work, *The Orators,* called "this England of ours where no-one is really well," where even a richly grotesque character like Major Fosdick, who likes dressing up in women's clothes in the privacy of his study, is not merely a comic figure but a sign of the malaise of his class.

Yet if in *From a View to a Death* Powell, like many other English writers of his time, reflected on the condition of society, in his next novel he turned away to the pursuit of pure farce. *Agents and Patients* (1936) is, to my mind, the weakest of Powell's prewar novels, and the one where he most directly invites comparison, to his disadvantage, with the early Evelyn Waugh. *Agents and Patients* is about two hard-up adventurers, Maltravers, a film writer, and Chipchase, an art critic and amateur psychoanalyst. They devote themselves to financially exploiting a rich, Candide-like young man called Blore-Smith, who at the start of the novel has more money than sense, though by the end he has acquired wisdom the hard way. The story moves in a brisk, picaresque fashion across Europe and contains some lively passages set in a German film studio, no doubt embodying some of Powell's own experiences as a scriptwriter in the 1930's.

After a three-year interval Powell published his last prewar novel, *What's Become of Waring?* (1939). It takes its title from a poem by Robert Browning and describes the attempt to discover a popular author called T. T. Waring, who has never been seen in the flesh by his publisher and who is one day reported to be dead. Powell works out this quite fruitful idea in an unusually tightly plotted work that is full of entertaining incident, though lacking in real inventiveness. In the perspective of Powell's later work, *What's Become of Waring?* is particularly interesting for its evident anticipation of the manner of *The Music of Time*. The story is told in the first person by an unnamed young publisher who shares one of Powell's abiding interests: he is trying to write a book called *Stendhal: And Some Thoughts on Violence*. In his account of the hunt for the semimythical Waring, he is reminiscent of Nicholas Jenkins; he too has a cool, unobtrusive, but sharply observant, way of noting the oddities of human behavior in a style that is more elaborate than anything Powell had so far attempted. His account of an old acquaintance, General Pimley, is characteristic:

A man in shirt-sleeves whom I recognised as General Pimley was mowing the lawn. He was much as I remembered him, slight and wizened, with a dome-shaped head across the brow of which ran three heavily marked lines that give him the worried humorous expression of an actor wearing a false forehead. When he saw us he hunched his shoulders and swung forward ape-like over the mower. His posture and the fact that he had removed his collar and tie heightened the illusion that he was a sad clown about to perform a tumbling act to entertain a not very appreciative audience.

(ch. 3)

Nicholas Jenkins, also, is given to similarly elaborate theatrical metaphors and similes, and to observing human life as a seriocomic spectacle or series of performances; on a later and more formal occasion, General Pimley, this time wearing an opera hat and black overcoat, is said to look like an "immensely distinguished conjuror." On the last page of *What's Become of Waring?* the narrator sets down his thoughts during a sleepless night; he broods restlessly on the nature of power and on the different ways in which the characters of the story have pursued it. And here we have a direct and striking anticipation of *The Music of Time*, a work in which many people

have a taste for power and live by the exercise of the will: Widmerpool, Sillery, Sir Magnus Donners, J. G. Quiggin, Alf Warminster, Tuffy Weedon, Idwal Kedward, a famous British field marshal. At the time when he concluded *What's Become of Waring?* Powell seemed ready to go on to *The Music of Time* or some similar work. But World War II intervened, and it was twelve years before he returned to writing fiction.

II

In an interview in *Summary* (Autumn 1970), Powell describes the spirit in which he made a study of John Aubrey during the war years:

I thought that I wouldn't be able to write a novel immediately after the war if I survived, and therefore did start making notes on John Aubrey, the seventeenth-century antiquary, with the idea of writing a book on Aubrey. During my leaves I did quite a lot of work on that, and at the end of the war I produced this book which was simply a question of plugging away at a lot of historical material—and then I found that somehow did the trick, and one was in a mood to write a novel again.

Powell's transitional study of Aubrey is very relevant to *The Music of Time*, where the anecdotal method and the endless interest in the oddities of human behavior and character indicate a cast of mind akin to Aubrey's own. Indeed, Powell has referred to Aubrey's "presentation of life as a picture crowded with odd figures, occupying themselves in unexpected and inexplicable pursuits," words that could appropriately be applied to *The Music of Time*.

In the same interview Powell discussed the genesis of his sequence:

After the war I thought a good deal about my writing—about writing novels in general—and I came to the conclusion that as I had already written the 80,000 sort of novel now I was going to settle down to do something much longer—generally approach the thing more thoroughly. If you wrote a lot more novels, each one separate, you would be losing a lot from the ideas you put into them by not connecting those ideas, if you see what I mean. And therefore I thought one would do best to settle down to write one really long novel. I hadn't then decided that it would necessarily be twelve volumes, but I did think it would be a great number of volumes, and that one would, so to speak, pick up in that way all you lose by ending a book and starting again with a lot of entirely new characters.

A Question of Upbringing opens with a long, detailed description of a group of workmen warming themselves round a coke brazier, with snow falling on them. This image releases in Jenkins' mind a number of potent suggestions; he thinks of the ancient world—"legionaries in sheepskin warming themselves at a brazier: mountain altars where offerings glow between wintry pillars; centaurs with torches cantering beside a frozen sea"—and then, by further association, of a painting by Poussin called *A Dance to the Music of Time,*

in which the Seasons, hand in hand and facing outward, tread in rhythm to the notes of the lyre that the winged and naked greybeard plays. The image of Time brought thoughts of mortality: of human beings, facing outward like the Seasons, moving hand in hand in intricate measure: stepping slowly, methodically, sometimes a trifle awkwardly, in evolutions that take recognisable shape: or breaking into seemingly meaningless gyrations, while partners disappear only to reappear again, once more giving pattern to the spectacle: unable to control the melody, unable, perhaps, to control the steps of the dance. Classical associations made me think, too, of days at school, where so many forces, hitherto unfamiliar, had become in due course uncompromisingly clear.

(ch. 1)

It is characteristic of Jenkins that experience presents itself to him in strongly visual terms, either in recalling actual, familiar works of art, or as formal tableaux of characters that suggest both painting and theatrical performance. There is a striking instance in *The Kindly Ones* in which Sir Magnus Donners, to gratify some private taste of his own, induces his guests to dress up as figures representing the Seven Deadly Sins; the resulting spectacle offers full scope to Jenkins' narrative gifts. The dance so graphically imagined at the beginning of *A Question of Upbringing* is a comprehensive emblem of the action of Powell's long novel, where a large number of characters do indeed weave in and out of each other's lives, disappearing and reappearing in unexpected ways. Or at least it is true of the earlier volumes of *The Music of Time*, where Jenkins is a young man making his way in the world, moving through the complex, interrelated circles of fashionable and bohemian life in London, and steadily enlarging his

groups of acquaintances. But in the later volumes, the number of the dancers has been much reduced, by old age or other intrusions of mortality, and above all by war. In the iconography of modern art and literature, the dance is an image of freedom from time, change, and decay; as Powell's novel moves toward its conclusion, and Jenkins becomes middle-aged, the carefree absorption of the dancers has become vulnerable to the depredations of history and mortality, so that the dance seems less adequate as a structural principle.

Powell intended the twelve volumes of *The Music of Time* to fall into four constituent trilogies. The first of them is composed of *A Question of Upbringing, A Buyer's Market* (1952), and *The Acceptance World* (1955). In *A Question of Upbringing* we first meet Nicholas Jenkins in 1921 as a schoolboy at Eton and then move on to his days as an undergraduate at Oxford (neither institution is named, but both are clearly identifiable); in this novel we meet three school-fellows of Nicholas who are to remain central characters in much of *The Music of Time*: Charles Stringham, witty, elegant, self-assured, though with an underlying melancholia that later turns him into an alcoholic; the raffish, womanizing Peter Templer, whom Stringham warns, "If you're not careful you will suffer the awful fate of the man who always knows the right clothes to wear and the right shop to buy them at," a phrase that exactly sums up Templer's worldliness, though it does not anticipate the far grimmer fate that will descend on Templer during World War II. And there is, above all, Widmerpool, one of the great characters of modern fiction, whom we encounter in the opening chapter: Jenkins is returning from a walk on a winter afternoon when an ungainly boy lumbers past in sweater and running shoes, returning from a solitary run. It is Widmerpool, who already is notorious at the school as an oddity; but it was at this point, Jenkins says, that "Widmerpool, fairly heavily built, thick lips and metal-rimmed spectacles giving his face as usual an aggrieved expression, first took coherent form in my mind." Widmerpool is at this point no more than a figure of fun: "That boy will be the death of me," remarks Stringham; but twenty years later his words come literally true.

In *A Buyer's Market* Jenkins wanders through London society in the late 1920's. He and Widmerpool are both in love with Barbara Goring, a pretty but irresponsible girl who subjects Widmerpool to a spectacular humiliation at a dance. Remarking,

"Why are you so sour tonight? You need some sweetening," she picks up a heavy sugar bowl, meaning to sprinkle a few grains over him. But the top falls off, and Widmerpool is covered in a cascade of sugar. It is one of the few overtly farcical pieces of action in *The Music of Time*, and the absurdity is heightened by the slow-motion description and Powell's habitual sense of the visually grotesque:

Widmerpool's rather sparse hair had been liberally greased with a dressing—the sweetish smell of which I remembered as somewhat disagreeable when applied in France—this lubricant retaining the grains of sugar, which, as they adhered thickly to his skull, gave him the appearance of having turned white with shock at a single stroke; which, judging by what could be seen of his expression, he might very well in reality have done underneath the glittering incrustations that enveloped his head and shoulders.

(ch. 1)

But it takes more than such a debacle to depress Widmerpool's energies for long. *The Acceptance World* carries the story on into the early 1930's, when the carefree twenties give way to a phase of leftist politics and social commitment. Nicholas remains as detached as ever, but he is for a time involved with St. John Clarke, an elderly novelist who has taken up Marxism late in life, and an Oxford acquaintance, J. G. Quiggin, an able literary critic and left-wing activist who frequently asserts his humble origins and is a forerunner of the angry young men of the 1950's. Widmerpool is rising in the "acceptance world" of credit finance, and Nicholas has his first serious love affair, with Templer's cousin Jean Duport.

The second trilogy comprises *At Lady Molly's* (1957), *Casanova's Chinese Restaurant* (1960), and *The Kindly Ones* (1962), and covers the middle and late 1930's. It is a period of consolidation in Nicholas Jenkins' life: he establishes a modest reputation for himself as a novelist and marries Lady Isobel Tolland, whose many relations bring a whole host of new acquaintances into his life. Isobel's brother is the "red earl," Erridge, or Lord Warminster, known as "Alf" to his intimates, a marvelously drawn aristocratic eccentric and one of Powell's many characters who aspire to live by the power of the will, though in practice his political aspirations come to nothing. As Nicholas marries, so do several other characters, not always successfully, and the theme of marriage is dominant in *Casanova's Chinese Restaurant*. In *At Lady Molly's* even the self-absorbed Widmerpool

had contemplated marrying Mrs. Mildred Haycock, a sophisticated widow with two children, several years older than himself; he circumspectly asks Jenkins whether his fiancée might not expect him to sleep with her before the marriage:

"In fact my fiancée—Mildred, that is—might even expect such a suggestion?"
"Well, yes, from what you say."
"Might even regard it as *usage du monde*?"
"Quite possible."
Then Widmerpool sniggered. For some reason I was conscious of embarrassment, even of annoyance. The problem could be treated, as it were, clinically, or humorously; a combination of the two approaches was distasteful. I had the impression that the question of how he should behave worried him more on account of the figure he cut in the eyes of Mrs. Haycock than because his passion could not be curbed.

(ch. 2)

This passage shows how the laconic dialogue of *Afternoon Men* has come to carry a wide range of social nuance, while Nicholas' own cool reflection illustrates his capacity for precisely delineating human folly and self-deception. Widmerpool makes the experiment, which is not a success, and the engagement is shortly broken off. It is worth noting, incidentally, that though Nicholas has no difficulty in seeing through Widmerpool, he continues to like him, or at least to find his company perfectly supportable, unlike many others of their acquaintance.

Casanova's Chinese Restaurant is a more somber work than any of the preceding volumes. The rise of Fascism in Europe and the civil war in Spain cast a shadow, while English society is shaken by the crisis over the abdication of Edward VIII. Powell gives little space to direct discussion of these events, but he shows his characters as clearly responding to the public issues of the time. At the same time their lives are noticeably less carefree than in the earlier volumes. The embittered music critic Maclintick commits suicide, while another new friend of Nicholas, the composer Moreland, and his wife have a baby who dies. Nicholas' wife has a miscarriage, and marriages seem to be falling apart on all sides. His own married life seems to be stable and happy, though he says very little about it, and Powell has been criticized for this reticence, for making his narrator tell us so much about other people's lives and so little about his own. Yet there is an important passage in which Nicholas dwells on the impossibility of giving a convincing account of marriage from the inside:

A future marriage, or a past one, may be investigated and explained in terms of writing by one of its parties, but it is doubtful whether an existing marriage can ever be described directly in the first person and convey a sense of reality. Even those who suggest some of the substance of married life best, stylise heavily, losing the subtlety of the relationship at the price of a few accurately recorded, but isolated, aspects. To think at all objectively about one's own marriage is impossible, while a balanced view of other people's marriage is almost equally hard to achieve with so much information available, so little to be believed. Objectivity is not, of course, everything in writing; but even casting objectivity aside, the difficulties of presenting marriage are inordinate. Its forms are at once so varied, yet so constant, providing a kaleidoscope, the colours of which are always changing, always the same. The moods of a love affair, the contradictions of friendship, the jealousy of business partners, the fellow feeling of opposed commanders in total war, these are all in their way to be charted. Marriage, partaking of such—and a thousand more—dual antagonisms and participations, finally defies definition.

(ch. 2)

The Kindly Ones begins with an extended memory from Nicholas' childhood of the eve of war in 1914; it returns to the present reality of 1939 and the death of his Uncle Giles, a rather disreputable figure who had made a variety of mysterious but portentous appearances in Nicholas' early life; a few days later, World War II breaks out, bringing to an end both a phase of history and the early manhood of the narrator.

III

THE third trilogy, made up of *The Valley of Bones* (1964), *The Soldier's Art* (1966), and *The Military Philosophers* (1968), covers the six years of war and the narrator's military service, first as a rather over-age subaltern with a Welsh regiment stationed in Northern Ireland, then as an officer with the Intelligence Corps in London engaged in liaison duties with the allied armies. Nicholas continues to make new friends, though at nothing like the rate of his early life, and several old and familiar faces disappear. His wife's aunt, Lady Molly Jeavons, his sister-in-law, Priscilla, and her husband, Chips Lovell, are killed in the bombing of London. Stringham dies as a prisoner of the Japanese, having been sent to the Far East by Widmerpool, now his military superior, and Peter Templer is killed in mysterious circumstances on a secret mission in German-occupied Europe. On the other hand, Widmerpool rises steadily in the military hierarchy. Nicholas becomes a father, and we leave him after the Victory Service in St. Paul's in 1945. *Books Do Furnish a Room* (1971), the first volume of the final trilogy, covers the years from 1945 to 1947. Nicholas Jenkins picks up the threads of civilian life by writing a book on Robert Burton, author of *The Anatomy of Melancholy*—an evident parallel to Powell's own study of John Aubrey—and contributing to a small literary magazine called *Fission*. Powell brings together many figures in the chronicle who have survived the war, in some cases going back to Jenkins' childhood; Widmerpool is prominent as a Labour M.P. and at the end of the book has achieved minor office in the Attlee government. He is married to Charles Stringham's niece, Pamela, a beautiful, neurotic, and consistently destructive girl. For the first time his customary ebullience is somewhat dented, and he shows an unaccustomed capacity for suffering. The book is both serenely comic and gently elegiac. It catches a particular moment in recent history: a short-lived phase of literary activity and aspiration in a London that still showed all the physical destruction and decay of six years of war.

This bare outline of *The Music of Time* will not convey anything of its true flavor, particularly of its intricacy and multiplicity of anecdote, and the immense range of characters, major and minor, that must run into several hundred. The appeal of Powell's work is of a remarkably simple kind: to our love of storytelling and gossip and anecdote. It provokes, and partially assuages, an intense but uncommitted curiosity about humanity, and a traditionally English interest in "characters" and eccentrics. It is possible for addicted readers of *The Music of Time*, eagerly awaiting the appearance of the next volume, to become caught up in the antics and interrelations (particularly the sexual alliances and severances) of Powell's characters just as if, in the time-honored phrase, "they were real people." This, one imagines, is precisely how innumerable Victorian readers felt about the work of the great novelists of their age as they published their books in monthly parts.

Powell writes, admittedly, of a fairly small world, even though it is densely populated; his vision of it is in the central tradition of English social comedy that derives from Jane Austen. He is totally intimate with this world and yet is invariably detached enough to catch with dazzling accuracy the minutest aspect of its manners. As Lionel Trilling has written, "one of the things which makes for substantiality of character in the novel is precisely the notation of manners, that is to say, of class traits modified by personality." Consider for instance in *A Question of Upbringing*, the appearance of Stringham's stepfather, the "polo-playing sailor" Buster Foxe, first observed cleaning a cigarette-holder with the end of a matchstick:

He was tall, and at once struck me as surprisingly young; with the slightly drawn expression that one recognises in later life as the face of a man who does himself pretty well, while not ceasing to take plenty of exercise. His turn-out was emphatically excellent, and he diffused waves of personality, strong, chilling gusts of icy air, a protective element that threatened to freeze into rigidity all who came through the door, before they could approach him nearer.
  "Hallo, you fellows," he said, without looking up from his cigarette-holder, at which he appeared to be sneering, as if this object were not nearly valuable enough to presume to belong to him.

(ch. 2)

In *The Kindly Ones* there is a fine instance of Nicholas Jenkins' awareness of the typical in the idiosyncratic when he describes Sir Magnus Donners' method of shaking hands,

giving, when he reached me, that curious pump-handle motion to his handshake, terminated by a sudden upward jerk (as if suddenly shutting off from the main valuable current of good will, of which not a volt too much must be expended), a form of greeting common to many persons with a long habit of public life.

(ch. 2)

The segment of English society that Powell writes about is one in which, in a loose sense, everyone knows everyone else, where Oxford, Cambridge, the public schools all have connections with the principal London focuses of intellectual, professional, and business life, to form a fairly coherent network. This is less so today than it was in the 1920's and 1930's; nevertheless, it is still true that a surprising number of English people in different walks of life know each other, or at least know of each other, and links are preserved between disparate circles by a network of friends or relations, or friends of friends. Although *The Music of Time* is full of chance meet-

ings and the discovery of coincidental links between previously unrelated people, none of them seems to strain credulity, since they are typical of the stratum of English life Powell has made his own, where novelistic possibilities lie all around. Not that they can be realized without some degree of effort and difficulty; as Nicholas observes in *The Acceptance World* of his own novel-writing activities: "Intricacies of social life make English habits unyielding to simplification, while understatement and irony—in which all classes of this island converse—upset the normal emphasis of reported speech." In his fascinated awareness of these intricacies, his constant sense of the gap between aspiration and achievement, and between appearance and reality, Powell is in the mainstream of English social comedy, where our perception of the world requires a perpetual mild, ironic adjustment. One critic, James Hall, has written about the "polite surprise" that Nicholas is always displaying at some fresh manifestation of absurdity or unpredictability in his surroundings. For Powell, he suggests, life "is a series of small shocks to be met with slightly raised eyebrows and the instantaneous question of how it all fits. Above everything else, Nick wants to know within a safe margin of error where he is at any given moment." This is, I think, an important observation. Although Powell offers us a plentitude of character comparable to one of the great Victorians', his fictional universe, unlike theirs, is not at all solid or stable; we are constantly aware of its inherent fragility and of the uncertainty of Nicholas' relation to it, of his need to know "where he is at any given moment." Hence the importance of style, which in *The Music of Time* is a tentacular, analytical, leisurely style, as a means of preserving the narrator's poise and equilibrium. The device is cumulatively successful; as the sequence develops we feel more and more that the one trustworthy point of reference in an endlessly shifting world is the cool, tentative intelligence of Nicholas Jenkins.

Unlike Evelyn Waugh, Powell is not a mythologizer, and there is nothing in his fiction comparable to the romantic image of the doomed gentleman that we find recurring in such novels by Waugh as *A Handful of Dust, Brideshead Revisited*, and *Sword of Honour*. Although Powell is acutely interested in the past, he does not lament it; change and even decay are seen as inevitable and something to be endured with as good a grace as possible, since, whatever happens, life goes on. There are certainly traces of nostalgia in Nicholas' make-up, usually evoked by paintings or buildings, but he never allows them to dominate him. In his attitude to the past, Powell both recalls and differs from Proust. Superficially, of course, *The Music of Time* is very indebted to Proust's great novel: in its title, its verbal organization, and the kind of life it describes. Indeed, there might be a case for calling it a deliberate "imitation" of *À la Recherche du temps perdu*. Nevertheless, the differences are crucial: unlike Proust's Marcel, Nicholas Jenkins is only occasionally introspective, and he is far more interested in other people than himself. Nor is Powell much concerned with time itself as an intractable or delusive element; the chronology of *The Music of Time* is straightforward, and, to quote James Hall again, "time moves onward as persistently in Nick's story as in Arnold Bennett, and the changes it brings, rather than the possibility of reliving lost experience, interest him."

Another critic, Arthur Mizener, has acutely described *The Music of Time* as the work of "an enormously intelligent but completely untheoretical mind." It is true that Powell has never resorted to the abstract sustaining principles of other writers of extended fiction: history for Tolstoy, time for Proust, or tradition for Waugh. Indeed, he has an English distaste for ideas, and his reliance on anecdote rather than theme can produce a random, even disorienting effect. Nevertheless, Powell has a clear sense of history, even if he lacks a definite or fixed attitude to it. Powell's novel, it can now be confidently asserted, is a great work of social comedy, but it undoubtedly describes a shabby and dispirited society, and one's delight in his characters is sometimes tempered by a feeling akin to Matthew Arnold's outburst at the Shelley circle: "What a set!" In the first two trilogies Powell is writing about a world still suffering from the physically and morally traumatic effects of World War I, and in a quiet and unembittered way he is continuing the anatomy of a society in decline embarked on by Ford Madox Ford in his *Parade's End* tetralogy (1924–1928). Indeed, a critic has written an essay on *The Music of Time* called "Chronicle of a Declining Establishment." But it is easy to overemphasize this aspect of Powell's work and to miss the necessary nuances of tone in the story as Nicholas Jenkins tells it. *The Music of Time* is essentially a comedy, and Powell has no time for myths of catastrophe. Nevertheless, he does, perhaps, allow himself a few convictions about life, of a kind suggested by Mizener, who has pointed to the contrast between Widmerpool and Stringham as "a major contrast of twentieth-century natures." For Powell, Widmerpool represents in an unusually pure form the power of the will: he is insensitive, pompous, socially inept, and monstrously selfish; yet he possesses an almost demonic energy and an unstoppable urge to succeed. At intervals Nicholas reflects with reluctant admiration on Widmerpool's prowess, as when he instantly summons a taxi at a moment of crisis: "A cab seemed to rise out of the earth at that moment. Perhaps all action, even summoning a taxi when none is there, is basically a matter of the will." Against Widmerpool and all that he stands for is set the graceful and attractive but doomed Stringham. Here is how he is described in *A Question of Upbringing*, in one of Powell's characteristic art-historical images:

> He was tall and dark, and looked like one of those stiff, sad young men in ruffs, whose long legs take up so much room in sixteenth-century portraits: or perhaps a younger—and far slighter—version of Veronese's Alexander receiving the children of Darius after the Battle of Issus: with the same high forehead and suggestion of hair thinning a bit at the temples. His features certainly seemed to belong to that epoch of painting: the faces in Elizabethan miniatures, lively, obstinate, generous, not very happy, and quite relentless. He was an excellent mimic, and, although he suffered from prolonged fits of melancholy, he talked a lot when one of these splenetic fits was not upon him: and ragged with extraordinary violence when excited.
> (ch. 1)

In the early stages of the novel sequence the elegant Stringham seems an immeasurably superior person to the gross and pompous Widmerpool. But by degrees their relative positions change, as Stringham is undermined by his own weaknesses, becoming for a time an alcoholic and having to be looked after by a former governess, Miss Weedon; while Widmerpool continues inexorably to exert his iron will, despite incidental humiliations. The crucial change in their relationship comes in *The Acceptance World*, where Jenkins and Widmerpool take the drunken Stringham home, and Widmerpool succeeds in getting him into bed by sheer physical force. Mizener has suggested that Powell sees the twentieth century "as a world nearly transformed by Widmerpools though still haunted by Stringhams." This is a reasonable comment to make on the early volumes of the sequence, even though it makes Powell seem too consciously elegiac a writer, in the manner of Waugh.

Nicholas Jenkins' attitude to Widmerpool is not, in fact, simple; as I have suggested, much as he deplores Widmerpool's behavior, he always tolerates him and even finds him fascinating: the cool observer and the man who lives by the will seem, indeed, to have a secret affinity for each other, and this, rather than the early contrast between Widmerpool and Stringham, may prove to be the deeper pattern of the whole sequence. Powell is unlike other twentieth-century novelists in having a general affection and even respect for all his characters, no matter how tiresome or obnoxious they may appear in their actions: no one is condemned for being "antilife" or morally corrupt or a social upstart. We are all sinners, he seems to imply, and should not judge one another; and, although Powell displays a quintessentially secular caste of mind, he regards his creations with an exemplary religious compassion. Underlying the marvelously observed and recorded social comedy of a particular culture and phase of history, there is something more fundamental: the basic human comedy, where, as in Chaucer and Rabelais and Shakespeare, folly and weakness and vice are transformed into an unending comic dance.

IV

THE last three volumes of Powell's sequence, published between 1971 and 1975, bear the revised general title *A Dance to the Music of Time*. Powell evidently wants to insist that the whole work is to be regarded as a dance, however much the dancers decrease in number in the last phase, and however difficult it is to keep up with the music. Yet in these volumes—*Books Do Furnish A Room, Temporary Kings*, and *Hearing Secret Harmonies*—Powell's way of treating time changes noticeably. For one thing, time is greatly foreshortened. The first nine volumes cover about a quarter of a century; from 1921, when Nicholas Jenkins is a schoolboy, to 1945, when he leaves the army at the end of World War II. The treatment of the intervening period is, as all readers know, leisurely and detailed, a true *roman fleuve*, flowing steadily on, relating Jenkins' own growth and development with changes in the social and public worlds he inhabits. The last three volumes cover, again, roughly twenty-five years, from 1946, at the beginning of *Books Do Furnish a Room*, to about 1971, at the end of *Hearing Secret Har-*

monies. (Powell is reluctant to give dates, and the references to contemporary events offer only approximate and sometimes contradictory pointers to chronology.) Here the treatment is not continuous, but episodic and selective; the three volumes describe events at ten- or twelve-year intervals: London literary life just after the war in 1946 and 1947; a cultural congress in Venice about 1958; the English scene of the late 1960's and early 1970's, marked by the appearance of the new universities, vogues among the young and would-be young for libertarianism and occultism, and, in higher places, rumors of treason concerning men in public life. The effect is of a series of separate stills, rather than a steadily unfolding film.

If many of the original dancers have died, or in other ways disappeared, others take their place: the critic, editor, and television personality Lindsay "Books-Do-Furnish-a-Room" Bagshaw; the novelist Ada Leintwardine, later wife to J. G. Quiggin; another novelist, the talented but eccentric X. Trapnel; the enigmatic American scholar Russell Gwinnett; the sometime publisher, film-producer, and motor-racing enthusiast Louis Glober; the tyrannical young diabolist Scorpio Murtlock. Powell's inventiveness in matters of character is still apparent and rewarding; the dominant figure in these volumes, though, is the beautiful and demonic Pamela Widmerpool, formerly Pamela Flitton, niece of Charles Stringham. She is one of Powell's most impressive embodiments of the will, and, if anything, is too large a figure for this late phase of the sequence, tending to disturb the balance of the work. Arguably, she needs separate treatment, in a different way from the original participants in the dance, just as Nicholas does. The people we know when we are young and growing up, or even in early adult life, may mean more to us, or affect us more deeply, than the new acquaintances we make in middle age, however likable we find the latter. And because of the long intervals at which we encounter Powell's new characters, given the very selective fictional treatment of the postwar years, we remain less involved with them; apart, perhaps, from the toweringly malign Pamela.

Some familiar figures remain, or reappear after long absences as men and women in their sixties, seventies, and eighties. And there is still Widmerpool, whom Powell increasingly presents as the central character of the sequence, while showing his ultimate decline to pathetic outrageousness and folly. In my view Widmerpool was never the same after the disappearance of Stringham, who had for several volumes been his necessary, if ineffectual, foil. The last years of Widmerpool are interesting, dramatic even, but not altogether credible. After ten years in Parliament as a fellow-traveling Labour M.P., he loses his seat in 1955, becomes a life peer, and then falls under a cloud because of the excessive closeness of his business and cultural contacts with an East European country. Betrayal of official secrets is suspected, but nothing is proved. In the last part of his public life, Lord Widmerpool is chancellor of a new university. By now he is a man of the far libertarian Left, a follower of the radical young, a Marcuse-like guru. In the end he collapses and dies after an early morning run ordered by the younger, more ruthless guru Scorpio Murtlock. The parallel with Widmerpool's first appearance, in *A Question of Upbringing,* as an ungainly schoolboy running through the mist is somewhat overemphatic.

Powell had to face formidable problems in concluding the sequence. The attitude to time inevitably changes as the events presented come closer to the moment of writing. For most of *A Dance to the Music of Time* Nicholas describes what he remembers. Any of us can misremember past events and have to be corrected by others; but subjectively our memories are self-authenticating. As readers of Powell we are convinced by what Nicholas remembers. But as the author draws closer to the present day (itself a moving point over the twenty-five years it took to write the sequence) memory has to give place to fresh observation and fresh invention. As we know from his fiction of the 1930's, Powell could observe very accurately indeed. But in *Hearing Secret Harmonies* he does not observe, or know, enough; he is not sufficiently convincing in his presentation of Widmerpool's bizarre final phase, in the harsh, alien settings of swinging England; the treatment remains external and perfunctory. Powell could effectively satirize the Old Left of the 1930's in *The Acceptance World,* but the New Left of the 1960's is much harder for him to get right.

At the same time there is more plot in these later volumes. For the greater part of the sequence, one had been caught up with the *fleuve,* the flow of events, whether sluggish or torrential; the remote past could suddenly and unexpectedly affect the present, just as it does in life, but without the need for evident authorial manipulation and invention. In the last part of *A Dance to the Music of Time,* though, Powell is busily at work, weaving plots and intrigues, notably those surrounding the mysterious, never properly realized figure of Russell Gwinnett. And at the end Powell is much concerned to enforce recapitulations in order to round off the whole work; not only in the *a capo* removal of Widmerpool, but in the deliberate parallel between Murtlock's occultist band and the followers of Dr. Trelawney in *The Kindly Ones.* There is a clash between the demands of observation and the pressures of plot-making and plot-concluding.

When Powell began work on the sequence in the late 1940's, he did not know how it was going to end, though he knew it would take twelve volumes to complete. This openness to contingency was courageous and admirable; but the future, when it arrived, proved intractable. Perhaps he would have done better to have ended the work with the ninth volume, at the end of the war, the climacteric that marked the maturity of Jenkins' generation and destroyed many of them. That would have been a natural closure provided by history, so much more powerful a plot-maker than any human author. Yet curiosity has always been a dominant element in Powell's art; inevitably he wanted to know what happened next to Widmerpool and the other survivors. And so do we, and despite all artistic imperfections we are glad to know. Most novels end unsatisfactorily, for reasons lately explored by theorists of fictional form. Insofar as this is true of *A Dance to the Music of Time,* the largeness of scale makes the final unsatisfactoriness more evident. But the achievement is prodigious, and one does not really wish it any shorter.

Since the completion of *A Dance to the Music of Time* Powell has published a sequence of memoirs in four volumes, *To Keep the Ball Rolling,* and a short novel, *O, How the Wheel Becomes It!* The latter is a story of literary life, telling how the personality and work of a minor writer who died during World War II unexpectedly become an irksome burden in the 1980's to an elderly man of letters who had known him in the 1920's and 1930's. It is a very slight piece of fiction; the leisurely, convoluted descriptive manner and the concern with time may recall Powell's *roman fleuve,* but the general impression it makes is closer to his novels of the 1930's, such as *From a View to a Death* or *What's Become of Waring?*

The memoirs are full of anecdotal interest and reveal the origins in Powell's personal experience of many of the characters and situations in his fiction, but they lack the richness and surprises of *A Dance to the Music of Time.*

SELECTED BIBLIOGRAPHY

I. Separate Works. *Afternoon Men* (London, 1931; new ed., 1952), novel; *Venusberg* (London, 1932; new ed., 1955), novel; *From a View to a Death* (London, 1933), novel; *Agents and Patients* (London, 1936; new ed., 1955), novel; *What's Become of Waring?* (London, 1939; new ed., 1953), novel; *John Aubrey and His Friends* (London, 1948; rev. ed. 1963), biography; *Brief Lives, and Other Selected Writings by John Aubrey* (London, 1949), biography, ed. with intro. by Powell; *A Question of Upbringing* (London, 1951); *A Buyer's Market* (London, 1952); *The Acceptance World* (London, 1955); *At Lady Molly's* (London, 1957); *Casanova's Chinese Restaurant* (London, 1960); *The Kindly Ones* (London, 1962); *The Valley of Bones* (London, 1964); *The Soldier's Art* (London, 1966); *The Military Philosophers* (London, 1968); *Books Do Furnish a Room* (London, 1971), the preceding ten novels form part of the sequence *The Music of Time*; *The Garden God, and The Rest I'll Whistle* (London, 1971), plays; *Temporary Kings* (London, 1973); *Hearing Secret Harmonies* (London, 1975), the preceding two novels complete *The Music of Time*; *To Keep the Ball Rolling: The Memoirs of Anthony Powell* (London, 1976–1982), vol. I: *Infants of the Spring* (1976), vol. II: *Messengers of Day* (1978), vol. III: *Faces in My Time* (1980), vol. IV: *The Strangers All Are Gone* (1982).

II. Biographical and Critical Studies. "From a Chase to a View," in *Times Literary Supplement* (15 February 1951); A. Brownjohn, "The Social Comedy of Anthony Powell," in *Gemini* (Summer 1957); "A Who's Who of *The Music of Time*," in *Time and Tide* (2, 9 July 1960); J. Brooke, "From Wauchop to Widmerpool," in *London* magazine (September 1960); "Taken from Life," in *Twentieth Century* (July 1961), interview; F. Kermode, *Puzzles and Epiphanies: Essays and Reviews 1958–1961* (London, 1962); J. Hall, *The Tragic Comedians: Seven Modern British Novelists* (Bloomington, Ind., 1963); W. Allen, *Tradition and Dream: The English and American Novel from the Twenties to Our Time* (London, 1964); G. S. Fraser, *The Modern Writer and His World* (London, 1964; rev. ed., 1970), rev. ed. contains most material on Powell; A. Mizener, *The Sense of Life in the Modern Novel* (London, 1965); V. S. Pritchett, *The Working Novelist* (London, 1965); J. Symons, *Critical Occasions* (London, 1965); J. J. Zigerell, "Anthony Powell's *Music of Time*: Chronicle of a Declining Establishment," in *Twentieth Century Literature* (October 1966); K. W. Gransden, "Taste of the Old Time," in *Encounter* (December 1966); M. Glazebrook, "The Art of Horace Isbister, E. Bosworth Deacon and Ralph Barnaby," in *London* magazine (November 1967); R. K. Morris, *The Novels of Anthony Powell* (Pittsburgh, 1968); W. H. Pritchard, "Anthony Powell's Serious Comedy," in *Massachussetts Review* (Autumn 1969); S. Wall, "Aspects of the Novel, 1930–1960," in B. Bergonzi, ed., *Sphere History of Literature in the English Language* (London, 1970–), vol. VII: *The Twentieth Century*; "Anthony Powell: A Symposium," in *Summary* (Autumn 1970); J. Russell, *Anthony Powell: A Quintet, Sextet and War* (Bloomington, Ind., 1971); A. Brownjohn, "Anthony Powell: A Profile," in *New Review* (September 1974); J. Tucker, *The Novels of Anthony Powell* (London, 1976); W. H. Pritchard, *Seeing Through Everything: English Writers, 1918–1940* (London, 1977); H. Spurling, *Handbook to Anthony Powell's "Music of Time"* (London, 1977); K. McSweeney, "The End of *A Dance to the Music of Time*," in *South Atlantic Quarterly*, 76, 1 (Winter 1977), pp. 44–57; R. Bader, *Anthony Powell's "Music of Time" as a Cyclic Novel of Generations*, Swiss Studies in English 101 (Bern, 1980).

JOHN BETJEMAN
(1906-   )

John Press

INTRODUCTION

JOHN SPARROW's preface to John Betjeman's *Selected Poems* (1948) reminds us that at one time Betjeman was in danger of becoming an eccentric, modish poet, admired only by a little circle of devotees who took a sophisticated pleasure in the cult of Victoriana that had sprung up in the Oxford of the 1920's: "It looked indeed as if Mr. Betjeman was fated to end his days as the Laureate of the suburbs and the Gothic Revival." Today Sir John (he was knighted in 1969) is more widely known than any other living English poet. His appointment to the laureateship in 1972 was acclaimed by millions of people who probably scarcely knew the name and had never read a page of any other contemporary poet. This was partly because he had by then become a popular figure on television, where his prowess on TV panels and his programs on architecture and topography had won him an enormous audience. The first edition of his *Collected Poems* (1958) reputedly sold more than a hundred thousand copies and enjoyed a success unparalleled since his publishers brought out Lord Byron's *Don Juan* in Regency England. He is a friend of the royal family and a pillar of what may be loosely called the literary and artistic establishment, a Companion of Literature, a former Royal Fine Art Commissioner, a holder of honorary doctorates from several universities. Despite the jealousies and feuds of the literary world, the majority of his fellow poets welcomed his succession to the laureateship. Like one of his most illustrious predecessors, Lord Tennyson, he appeals to a very wide public and manages to voice the aspirations of many ordinary people while retaining the respect of his fellow practitioners, even if some of them are a little scornful of his showmanship and a trifle weary of reading about his teddy bear, Archibald, which fulfills much the same role as Winston Churchill's cigars.

It is clear that Betjeman is an extraordinary character who has, over the years since he first delighted his friends at Oxford, enjoyed a remarkable career. Although it is not easy to disentangle the achievement of the artist from the trappings of his personality, the purpose of this essay is to trace his progress as a writer in prose and in verse, and to illustrate the range and variety of his work.

LIFE

JOHN BETJEMAN, who was born on 28 August 1906, was the only child of Ernest Betjeman, the head of a prosperous family business that made furnishings and other domestic objects for expensive shops, and Mabel Bessie Dawson. We can reconstruct Betjeman's early life not only from his autobiography in verse, *Summoned by Bells* (1960), but from a score of short poems that refer to incidents of his childhood. Those who believe that the first few years of our lives determine our natures and our destinies can find in Betjeman's poems a wealth of material to support their thesis. We learn of his love for his parents, his gentle, devout mother and his stone-deaf father, with whom his relations were later to become strained. Betjeman soon learned to distinguish the subtle, deadly gradations of class, hierarchy, and snobbery that animated the quietly opulent North London Edwardian suburbs in which he was bred. He caught the ineradicable terror of death and of damnation from a Calvinist nursery maid. Perhaps his most poignant evocation of his childhood world is to be found in these stanzas from "St Saviour's, Aberdeen Park, Highbury, London, N":

These were the streets my parents knew when they loved
and won—
The brougham that crunched the gravel, the laurel-
girt paths that wind,

355

Geranium-beds for the lawn, Venetian blinds for
                                        the sun,
A separate tradesman's entrance, straw in the mews
                                        behind,
Just in the four-mile radius where hackney carriages run,
    Solid Italianate houses for the solid commercial mind.

These were the streets they knew; and I, by descent,
                                        belong
    To these tall neglected houses divided into flats.
Only the church remains, where carriages used to
                                        throng
    And my mother stepped out in flounces and my
                                father stepped out in spats
To shadowy stained-glass matins or gas-lit evensong
    And back in a country quiet with doffing of chimney
                                        hats.

Great red church of my parents, cruciform crossing they
                                        knew—
    Over these same encaustics they and their parents
                                        trod
Bound through a red-brick transept for a once familiar
                                        pew
    Where the organ set them singing and the sermon let
                                        them nod
And up this coloured brickwork the same long shadows
                                        grew
    As these in the stencilled chancel where I kneel in the
                                presence of God.

From an early age Betjeman longed to be a poet. At his preparatory school in Highgate, one of the masters was T. S. Eliot. Betjeman had already written a great many poems and believed that they were as good as those of the early-nineteenth-century poet Thomas Campbell:

> And so I bound my verse into a book,
> *The Best of Betjeman*, and handed it
> To one who, I was told, liked poetry—
> The American master, Mr. Eliot.
>   (*Summoned by Bells*, ch. 3)

His adolescent years were darkened by his unhappiness at his public school, Marlborough, where vicious bullying was rampant. One of the masters, H. L. O. Flecker, a brother of the poet James Elroy Flecker, read aloud and mocked a poem on a city church written by Betjeman when he was fifteen, an incident that left Betjeman with a lifelong hatred and fear of destructive criticism. He was also made unhappy by the deterioration of his relationship with his father, who wished to be taken for a country gentleman, and who tried in vain to instill into his son his own enthusiasm for shooting and fishing.

Oxford was a delight after Marlborough. Maurice Bowra, later Warden of Wadham and at that time a young don, tells us in his *Memories* (1966) that he immediately recognized the originality of Betjeman's mind and his extraordinary familiarity with the bypaths of the Victorian age. Bowra also admired such poems as "Death in Leamington," "The Arrest of Oscar Wilde at the Cadogan Hotel," and "Hymn." Betjeman ran up large bills for expensive architectural books that he hoped his father would pay, mixed with undergraduates who provided material for the early novels of Evelyn Waugh, and neglected the work he should have been doing for his degree in English. His tutor, C. S. Lewis, ignorant or contemptuous of Betjeman's genuine learning in his own chosen fields, had little sympathy with his literary aspirations. When Betjeman, after more than one attempt, failed to pass a ludicrously easy qualifying examination called Divinity Moderations, he was obliged to leave Oxford without taking his Finals. Lewis dourly remarked, "You'd have only got a Third," but to Betjeman exile from Oxford was a blow:

> I'd seen myself a don,
> Reading old poets in the library,
> Attending chapel in an M.A. gown
> And sipping vintage port by candlelight.
>   (*Summoned by Bells*, ch. 9)

Most of his references to Oxford are affectionate, but the portraits of dons in *An Oxford University Chest* (1938) are sharply satirical, and "May Day Song for North Oxford" contains an ironical allusion to his old tutor:

> Oh! well-bound Wells and Bridges! Oh! earnest ethical
>   search
> For the wide high-table λογος of St. C. S. Lewis's Church.

Betjeman also makes a slightly barbed comment in the acknowledgments to his Shell Guide *Devon* (1936): "For mental inspiration the Editor had only to think of Mr. C. S. LEWIS, tweed-clad and jolly, to get busy with his pen."

After a hilarious interlude again reminiscent of Waugh, in which Betjeman got a job at a school by pretending to be a devotee of cricket, he obtained a post on the *Architectural Review*, thanks to the influence of Maurice Bowra. The salary was £300 a year, which Betjeman regarded as a pittance, although it compared favorably with the salaries of young professional men at that period. In 1933 he married Penelope, daughter of Field-Marshal Sir Philip (later Lord) Chetwode, Commander-in-Chief, India. According to Bowra, Lady Chetwode produced a remark worthy of Oscar Wilde's Lady Bracknell when, in the early days of Betjeman's friendship with her daughter, she said, "We ask people like that to our houses, but we don't marry them."

Despite his father's pleas and his own sense of guilt at his failure to carry on the family business, Betjeman continued to live by his pen. During World War II he worked for a time as United Kingdom Press Attaché in Dublin, and also served in the Admiralty and in the Books Department of the British Council, which was then housed in temporary hutments in Blenheim Palace, near Oxford. After the war he resumed his career as a journalist and, as the influence of television increased, became one of the most accomplished masters of the new medium. The growth of his fame as a television performer accompanied his rise in a more august world. A guest at Windsor Castle, a Commander of the British Empire, a Governor of the Oxford Anglican study center, Pusey House, Betjeman is more warmly admired by the court, by fashionable society, and by academics than any laureate since Tennyson. Nor has he lost the respect and affection of his peers. On his seventy-fifth birthday a group of his fellow poets called at his home to present him with the gift of a book in which were printed poems they had written in his honor.

Yet, despite his renown as a public entertainer and the presence of autobiographical elements in his writings, Betjeman has contrived to remain a private figure, the very opposite of the confessional writer who bares his inner life to the public gaze. His loyalty to old friends and his kindness and generosity to the humble and obscure are, like his family life, largely unknown and unpublicized. Instead of lingering any longer on biographical details, we should now turn to consider the prose writings that stretch from *Ghastly Good Taste* (1933) to *A Nip in the Air* (1974).

PROSE WORKS

ANYBODY who has seen Betjeman on the television screen can hardly fail to be enchanted, whether he is discoursing on baronial Gothic in Australia, an English country house, or the Metropolitan Railway.

He communicates to his audience a wealth of fascinating information with no trace of pedantry or condescension. His zest, exuberance, and gaiety are irresistible. Tom Driberg's article "A Walk with Mr. Betjeman," which appeared in the *New Statesman* (6 January 1961), conveys something of the quality of Betjeman's conversation. Betjeman took Driberg on a brief tour of the City of London on foot—"As you haven't brought a bicycle we shall have to walk"—and proceeded to pour out a stream of lively and perceptive comments on the buildings old and new that passed before their eyes. Betjeman's marvelous knowledge of London's social and architectural history continually illuminated the view of the churches, monuments, shops, and public buildings. He rejoiced in Blackfriars Station, one of whose façades is adorned with heavily rusticated pilasters, into which are cut the names of the principal stations once served by the South Eastern and Chatham Railway: Beckenham and Baden-Baden, Walmer and Wiesbaden, Westgate-on-Sea and St. Petersburg. "Mr. Betjeman," Driberg assures us, "once went in and asked for a ticket to St. Petersburg: the clerk referred him to Victoria (Continental) without a flicker of surprise."

Even on the printed page the ease and warmth of Betjeman's conversational style carry the reader along, holding his attention from start to finish, giving him a sense of listening to an intimate, friendly voice talking in a relaxed tone. Betjeman's prose works are almost all topographical essays or guides to certain aspects of English architecture. It would be unrewarding to attempt a summary of these works, especially as they advance no formal thesis and put forward no systematic aesthetic doctrine. Betjeman is not primarily an art historian, nor does he pretend to be a detached observer, recording in a tone of dry neutrality the evolution of architecture in Britain. He is a partisan, passionately involved in his theme, celebrating what he loves, excoriating what he detests. It is significant that the title of his most substantial book should be *First and Last Loves* (1952).

It may be useful to trace briefly the growth of his aesthetic taste and to indicate the values that have guided his writing on architecture over the last forty years. The second edition of *Ghastly Good Taste*, which appeared in 1970, contains an introduction by the author entitled "An Aesthetic Apologia," the story of Betjeman's intellectual and artistic development from boyhood to the eve of his marriage in 1933. Even before going to Marlborough Betjeman had developed a voracious, undiscriminating appetite for old buildings, particularly for anything that was, or purported to be, medieval or Tudor. At Marlborough he learned to love eighteenth-century buildings and Victorian art and poetry, although at this stage he did not take Victorian architecture seriously, and before going up to Oxford he had come to dislike Gothic. During his time at Oxford he was invited to stay at a number of eighteenth-century Irish houses, an experience which led him to believe that Ireland was the most beautiful country in the world and gave him a lasting admiration for the virtues of the Anglo-Irish ruling classes. Another factor that permanently influenced his taste was his reading of A. E. Richardson's *Monumental Classic Architecture in Great Britain and Ireland* (1914).

During the general strike of 1926 he tried to help the strikers, waiting in vain at Didcot to carry messages for the National Union of Railwaymen. He was at this period a follower of Conrad Noel, the "Red Vicar" of Thaxted in Essex, who wanted to restore medieval joy and simplicity to the lives of twentieth-century men and women. Betjeman's work at the *Architectural Review* brought him into contact with elderly architects, survivors of the Victorian and the Edwardian eras, as well as with the apostles of modernism. Since then his study of architecture has become more exact and profound; he has come to appreciate Gothic; his knowledge of Victorian architecture has grown more extensive and more discriminating. The body of his work testifies to his familiarity with countless villages, small towns, ports, churches, railway stations, public houses, theaters, canals, gardens, bridges, barns, shops, gas stations, and streetlamps in every part of the country.

It is a more complex task to summarize the artistic and spiritual principles that have informed his essays and other architectural writings since the early 1930's. Popular and superficial accounts of Betjeman portray him as an idolater of the past, with a special fondness for Victorian buildings even when they are third-rate; as a compulsive protester who leaps into action whenever any kind of ancient relic is threatened with destruction. It is alleged that he is out of touch with the realities of contemporary life; that he takes little interest in the housing of the masses; that his attacks on bureaucracy are vitiated by his failure to understand the necessity of large-scale governmental planning in town and countryside. He is, in this view, a romantic individualist steeped in nostalgia for the hierarchical society of earlier ages, a sophisticated modern version of a Victorian aesthete.

Such a portrait of Betjeman is a mere caricature. His favorite architectural period is not the Victorian age but the first quarter of the nineteenth century. Nor does he praise indiscriminately the work of Victorian architects and the vanished streets of London. In *Victorian and Edwardian London from Old Photographs* (1971) he describes a photograph of Hampstead Road taken in 1904:

But when I look at the noisy muddle . . . as depicted in the photograph and see the faceless efficiency of overpass and underpass churning in its clouds of diesel through the impersonal slabs which are there now, I realize we have only changed one sort of bad for another sort of bad.

It is untrue that he cares little for the needs of ordinary people in a modern industrial society. He remarks in *English Cities and Small Towns* (1943) that "to someone who likes people as well as buildings, the industrial towns are the hope and life of England." In the same essay he declares that "only by planning on a national scale will we preserve the hundreds of beautiful old cities of England," although he goes on to warn his readers that "a single year of over-enthusiastic 'post-war reconstruction' may destroy the lot." As long ago as 1937, in *Antiquarian Prejudice*, a pamphlet reprinted in *First and Last Loves*, he was arguing in favor of well-planned prefabricated houses:

I see no hope for the majority until they are made here. Lord Nuffield had a wonderful opportunity to make them at his pressed-steel works at Oxford. He missed it, and many of his workers are housed in some of the worst speculative estates to be seen.

It is this same concern for the quality of human life that led him to denounce the proposal to build motorways through various residential districts of London.

Betjeman has always responded to architecture as the visible manifestation of the spiritual life of a society. When, in *Vintage London* (1942), he laments the passing of old London, it is the inhabitants of that vanished city whom he celebrates. Every year, he says, old London lessens, "as more and more of its members are carried with all the pomp of a long subscription to the Burial Society to that most Victorian sight of all London—the windy Carrara-covered cemetery." He observes elsewhere that a modern crematorium is the appropriate resting place for those who spend so many hours in an Odeon cinema. Architecture is for him not only the reflection of a society's political and economic structure but an outward and visible sign of an inward and spiritual grace, or lack of grace. Or, as Francis Thompson wrote:

Our towns are copied fragments from our breast:
And all man's Babylons strive but to impart
The grandeurs of his Babylonian heart.
("Correlated Greatness," 12–14)

Betjeman's approach to the visual arts is diametrically opposed to that of Roger Fry, who remarked in a letter written in 1920: "It's all the same to me if I represent a Christ or a saucepan, since it's the form and not the object itself that interests me." Betjeman wants to preserve old buildings for a variety of reasons, but mainly because of their human associations, which are indeed inseparable from their aesthetic power and beauty. He would echo an observation made by Thomas Hardy in a paper he prepared in 1906 to be read before the Society for the Protection of Ancient Buildings:

I think that the damage done to the sentiment of association by replacement, by the rupture of continuity, is mainly why our loss is so tragic. To protect a building against renewal in fresh materials is more of a social—I may say a humane—duty than an aesthetic one.

It is clear from a study of his work that, in his writings about architecture, Betjeman is almost invariably a passionate advocate of certain moral and cultural values. The opening paragraph of *Antiquarian Prejudice*, originally delivered as a lecture to the Group Theatre, succinctly conveys the spirit of his entire work in this field:

I come to you fresh from Evensong and with my outlook widened. Architecture has a wider meaning than that which is commonly given to it. For architecture means not a house, or a single building or a church, or Sir Herbert Baker, or the glass at Chartres, but your surroundings, not a town or a street, but our whole over-populated island. It is concerned with where we eat, work, sleep, play, congregate, escape. It is our background, alas, often too permanent.

He has unceasingly attacked those speculators and bureaucrats whose rapacity and unimaginative insensibility have devastated Britain more wantonly and irreparably than the raids of the Nazi bombers. In *Vintage London* he observes that "non-vintage London of to-day extends over most of Britain," and places the blame squarely where it belongs: "The speculative builder is abetted by the contractor, who is abetted by the Building Society, which is abetted by the Banks; and these sinister agents have their central organisations in London."

Betjeman's loathing for the speculative builder is fierce enough to satisfy the most ardent Marxist. Indeed he detests our society for its worship of money. The prefatory essay in his collection of architectural essays, *First and Last Loves*, denounces the perverted values by which we live:

We accept the collapse of the fabrics of our old churches, the thieving of lead and objects from them, the commandeering and butchering of our scenery by the services, the despoiling of landscaped parks and the abandonment to a fate worse than the workhouse of our country houses, because we are convinced we must save money.

Nor does he spare bureaucrats, civil or ecclesiastical, who advance good reasons for allying themselves with the vandals. He describes in the *Spectator* (16 July and 27 August 1954) the incivility he encountered at the hands of the town clerk of Fulham when he went to inspect The Grange, an old building threatened with destruction; and he waxes satirical over an archdeacon who referred to a splendid old church as a heavy drain on the financial resources of the diocese, and indicates his low view of the Anglican hierarchy: "Bishops are becoming the slaves of finance. They do not realise that a beautiful church is a more lasting witness to the Faith than they are."

We are witnessing, says Betjeman in *First and Last Loves*, the apotheosis of suburban man, whose yearning for culture is little more than an expression of restlessness and no more fruitful than the proliferation of government housing schemes:

By looking only at well-laid out municipal estates and averting one's eyes from the acres of unimaginative modern housing, by forgetting those terrible pipe-dreams come true of thick-necked brutes with flashy cars, elderly blondes and television sets—those modernistic, Egyptian, beaux-arts and other façades of the new factories outside every large town, by ignoring all these and much more, it is possible to live in a fool's paradise of imagined culture, a sort of Welwyn Garden City of the mind.

No wonder he calls this prefatory essay "Love Is Dead" and quotes the Collect for Quinquagesima from the Book of Common Prayer, thus linking the restoration of artistic health with the gift of love:

O Lord, who hast taught us that all our doings without charity are nothing worth; Send thy Holy Ghost, and pour into our hearts that most excellent gift of charity, the very bond of peace and of all virtues, without which whosoever liveth is counted dead before thee. Grant this for thine only Son Jesus Christ's sake.

Betjeman writes admirable prose that is always beguilingly readable and that at times commands an effective polemical force. His range is wide: he can describe with mocking and merciless accuracy a landscape devastated by greed and insensitivity; he can portray with a wealth of loving detail a vanished way of life; he can evoke the harmonious pattern of the English countryside, where man has enriched the bounty of nature; he can bring before our eyes the architectural richness and uniqueness of our cathedrals. Two passages of some length may convey something of Betjeman's gifts as a prose writer. The first, taken from his Rede Lecture at Cambridge, *The English Town in the Last Hundred Years* (1956), is a good example of Betjeman's powers of persuasion, his ability to describe with deadly precision the spoliation of the countryside by ignorance, misguided progressiveness, greed, and the unchecked ravages of technology:

Those old thatched cottages of the water colours have been condemned by Medical Officers of Health who know as much about architecture as I know about whooping cough. These cottages have been destroyed instead of enlarged and modernized, as they could have been for less than the cost of a new council house, because people who do not care for what is old sincerely believe that only what is new is worth having. In the old farm buildings, the fine barns have been replaced by Dutch barns or patched with concrete and sheets of corrugated iron. Hedges are fast disappearing and giving way to concrete posts supporting chain-link fencing. Elms have been felled for fear one of their branches will fall on a ratepayer, and no trees have been planted in their stead. Where the village smithy stood is now a garage with a front like a modernistic chimney-piece magnified forty times and the tin signs set out along the road for a hundred yards in either direction. Poles and wires are everywhere: Post Office wires on one side of the road, the thicker wires of the Central Electricity Board on the other; and a transformer like a monkey up a stick is given the most prominent skyline in sight in the village.

The second passage, from the *Collins Guide to English Parish Churches* (1958), reveals Betjeman in a quieter, more appreciative vein, although the gentle-

ness of tone is reinforced by a few tartly satirical observations. He is celebrating with glowing but unsentimental romanticism the diverse character of the parish churches he knows so intimately and loves so much:

The Parish Churches of England are even more varied than the landscape. The tall town church, smelling of furniture polish and hot-waterpipes, a shadow of the medieval marvel it once was, so assiduously have Victorian and even later restorers renewed everything old; the little weather-beaten hamlet church standing in a farmyard down a narrow lane, bat-droppings over the pews and one service a month; the church of a once prosperous village, a relic of the 15th-century wool trade, whose soaring splendour of stone and glass subsequent generations have had neither the energy nor the money to destroy; the suburban church with Northamptonshire-style steeple rising unexpectedly above slate roofs of London and calling with mid-Victorian bells to the ghosts of merchant carriage folk for whom it was built; the tin chapel-of-ease on the edge of the industrial estate; the High, the Low, the Central churches, the alive and the dead ones, the churches that are easy to pray in and those that are not, the churches whose architecture brings you to your knees, the churches whose decorations affront the sight—all these come within the wide embrace of our Anglican Church, whose arms extend beyond the seas to many fabrics more.

Although he is never pedantic or oversolemn, Betjeman is a consistently serious writer whose books and essays on architecture display firm moral and social principles no less than a penetrating and highly individual aesthetic perceptiveness. He may have taken a youthful pleasure in affronting the duller Oxford dons by praising the more hideous examples of Victorian objets d'art, but he soon developed a mature understanding and love of Victorian architecture and did much to open our eyes to its merits. His writings are less weighty and scholarly than the major works of Kenneth Clark, John Summerson, and H. S. Goodhart-Rendel, to name only three architectural historians whom Betjeman himself praises for their labors as pioneers in the appreciation of Victorian building. Nevertheless, he has probably done more than any other single person to bring about the decisive change in our attitude to the Victorian achievement in the visual arts.

Nor is he merely one of those figures who acquire a modish reputation by influencing the taste of the day. He is in the direct line of descent from such Victorian sages as John Ruskin and William Morris, whose love of the arts was linked with their desire for the regeneration of society. Betjeman lacks Morris' prophetic vision of a world in which men live as brothers, just as he seldom attains the magnificence of Ruskin's finest prose. Yet, in a more modest and wittier spirit, he has fought the same battles. "We must lift [people's] eyes from the privet hedge to the hills," he declares in his Rede Lecture, and he goes on to say that "for the . . . important missionary work of opening people's eyes we have the film and television." As long ago as 1933 he expressed certain fundamental beliefs about architecture and society, in the final paragraph of *Ghastly Good Taste*:

Architecture can only be made alive again by a new order and another Christendom. I repeat that I do not know what form that Christendom will take, for I am not an economist. It is unlikely that it will be capitalism. Whatever it is, this generation will not see it.

The whole body of his prose is animated by his desire to further the coming of that Christendom.

POETRY: THEMES AND CHARACTER

ALTHOUGH Betjeman's prose writings are more substantial than is often supposed, he is first and foremost a poet. While his books and essays have expressed strongly held convictions, and even his gifts as a public entertainer have been employed to open people's eyes to their surroundings, Betjemen has said that his prose has been "primarily a means of earning money in order to buy the free time in which to write poetry." He may, in ironical self-deprecation, have referred to himself as "the Ella Wheeler Wilcox[1] *de nos jours*," but his sense of vocation has always been strong. His declaration in *Summoned by Bells* rings true:

> For myself,
> I knew as soon as I could read and write
> That I must be a poet. Even today,
> When all the way from Cambridge[2] comes a wind
> To blow the lamps out every time they're lit,
> I know that I must light mine up again.
>
> (ch. 2)

It is a mark of his originality and authenticity as a poet that he has always remained indifferent to

[1]Ella Wheeler Wilcox (1850–1919) was an American writer of doggerel that sold in vast quantities.
[1]Referring to a school of criticism there, considered by many to be overcensorious.

changes in poetic fashion and to dominant critical shibboleths. Just as he ignored the doctrines of Roger Fry in the field of the visual arts, so he remained unaffected by the modernist movement in poetry, which was all the rage in his undergraduate days. The heritage of symbolism, the revolution inaugurated by T. S. Eliot and Ezra Pound, and even the discovery of Gerard Manley Hopkins seem to have influenced him not at all. He resembles the mythical figure who prefers Dekker, Hawker, and Flecker to Rilke, Kafka, and Lorca. From the very start he has written unashamedly about the themes that evoke his love, his interest, his hatred, and his amusement, and, like William Wordsworth's true poet, he has created the taste that now enjoys him.

His preface to *Old Lights for New Chancels* (1940) lists a few of the subjects that awaken in him the desire to compose a poem: "I love suburbs and gaslights and Pont Street and Gothic Revival churches and mineral railways, provincial towns and Garden cities." Nor is he taking a perverse, mocking pleasure when he depicts scenes regarded by many as ugly, quaint, or risible: "I see no harm in trying to describe overbuilt Surrey in verse. But when I do so I am not being satirical but topographical." The part played by topography in Betjeman's poetry is so important that we must pause to consider its nature and significance. As an architectural historian, Betjeman delights in portraying with the utmost precision the minutest details of places and buildings, just as he relishes the subtlest inflections of accents and modes of speech, and the intricate gradations of class and social hierarchies in English life. W. H. Auden's introduction to *Slick but Not Streamlined* (1947), a selection of Betjeman's verse and prose, analyzes what he calls *topophilia*:

Topophilia differs from the farmer's love of his home soil and the litterateur's fussy regional patriotism in that it is not possessive or limited to any one locality; the practised topophil can operate in a district he has never visited before. On the other hand, it has little in common with nature love. Wild or unhumanised nature holds no charms for the average topophil because it is lacking in history. . . . At the same time, though history manifested by objects is essential, the quantity of the history and the quality of the object are irrelevant; a branch railroad is as valuable as a Roman wall, a neo-Tudor teashop as interesting as a Gothic cathedral.

Betjeman's love of landscape and in particular of the Cornish coast has become more apparent since Auden wrote these words, but in general this account of topophilia throws valuable light on Betjeman's poetry.

There is one aspect of Betjeman's topophilia and of his fondness for exact description that has not received much attention from his readers. We may approach it by considering certain qualities in the work of Tennyson, who is in many ways closer than any other poet to Betjeman. In a broadcast colloquium on Tennyson early in 1973 Betjeman referred to him as holding "a very vague faith such as is mine." Both find in the sea and in their childhoods an immensely rich source of emotional power and resonance, and both are at times overwhelmed by an instinctive terror of death and a stifling horror aroused by the contemplation of eternity. Some of Betjeman's blank verse has a Tennysonian movement that may reflect more basic affinities. The following passage from Tennyson's *The Princess* (1847), quoted by Betjeman in his 1940 preface, clearly anticipates certain features of his own descriptive verse:

> and on the pavement lay
> Carved stones of the Abbey-ruin in the park,
> Huge Ammonites, and the first bones of Time;
> And on the tables every clime and age
> Jumbled together; celts and calumets,
> Claymore and snowshoe, toys in lave, fans
> Of sandal, amber, ancient rosaries,
> Laborious orient ivy sphere in sphere,
> The cursed Malayan crease, and battle clubs
> From the isles of palm. . . .

In his study *Tennyson* (1972) Christopher Ricks follows Humphry House in conjecturing that Tennyson's minutely precise descriptions of external things stabilized his mind and allayed his restlessness. Ricks carries this speculation one stage further:

> The same might be said of Tennyson's insistence upon accuracy in his poems (accuracy scientific, historical, reminiscential) . . . when [Harold] Nicolson speaks of Tennyson's "maddening accuracy" it should be retorted that it may have maddened Nicholson but it helped to keep Tennyson sane.

It is probable that Betjeman's loving reconstruction of some historical incident and his concern for period detail spring from a similar emotional need.

At a time when most young poets were striving to emulate Hopkins or Eliot, Betjeman was turning toward remote and unfashionable poetic models. His 1940 preface describes the kind of verse that has, from the beginning of his career, nourished his imagination:

> In the eighteenth century Dr. Watts, Swift, Robert Lloyd, Thomson, Dyer, Shenstone, Mickle, Cowper and Burns are easily among my favourites, not for their finer flights, but for their topographical atmosphere. In the nineteenth century Crabbe, Praed, Hood, Clare, Ebenezer Elliott, Capt. Kennish, Neale, Tennyson, Charles Tennyson Turner, Clough, William Barnes, Meredith, William Morris and a score or so more. I find great pleasure in what is termed minor poetry, in long epics which never get into anthologies; topographical descriptions in verse published locally.

Compared with the enigmatic hints of Eliot, and the superb oracular revelations of William Butler Yeats about the creative process, Betjeman's account in the *Spectator* (8 October 1954) of how he writes poems is unpretentiously straightforward:

> First there is the thrilling or terrifying recollection of a place, a person or a mood which hammers inside the head saying "Go on! Go on! It is your duty to make a poem out of it." Then a line or a phrase suggests itself. Next comes the selection of a metre. I am a traditionalist in metres and have made few experiments. The rhythms of Tennyson, Crabbe, Hawker, Dowson, Hardy, James Elroy Flecker, Moore and Hymns A & M[3] are generally buzzing about in my brain and I choose one from these which seems to me to suit the theme.

He jots down rough drafts on cigarette packets or old letters before writing them on foolscap, but the aural element remains dominant: "Then I start reciting the lines aloud, either driving a car or on solitary walks, until the sound of the words satisfies me."

The names mentioned by Betjeman in the two passages quoted above by no means exhaust the poets who have influenced him. Reminiscences of Frederick Locker Lampson, Father Prout, Charles Dibdin, William Allingham, Henry Wadsworth Longfellow, and Henry Newbolt may be detected in his verse. The model for some of his poems is almost certainly Rudyard Kipling, with whom he shares one or two basic attitudes: a robust patriotism; a mistrust of politicians, bureaucrats, and progressive intellectuals; an extraordinary sensitiveness to pain and an understanding of loneliness fostered by experiences of bullying in childhood and youth that left a searing

---

[3]*Hymns Ancient and Modern* (1861), a widely used Anglican hymnbook.

mark; a fondness for controlled irony that sometimes bursts out into a scalding jet of fury. John Sparrow's review of his *Collected Poems* (1958) in the *Times Literary Supplement* (12 December 1958) remarks on the affinities in tone and movement between Betjeman's verse and certain poems by John Meade Falkner, who is better known as a novelist then as a poet:

> Post pugnam pausa fiet;[4]
>   Lord, we have made our choice;
> In the stillness of autumn quiet,
>   We have heard the still, small voice.
> We have sung *Oh where shall Wisdom?*[5]
>   Thick paper, folio, Boyce.

And, from another poem:

> On the fly-leaves of these old prayer-books
>   The childish writings fade,
> Which show that once they were their books
>   In the days when prayer was made
> For other kings and princesses,
>   William and Adelaide. . . .
>
> Is the almond-blossom bitter?
>   Is the grasshopper heavy to bear?
> Christ make me happier, fitter
>   To go to my own over there:
> Jerusalem the Golden,
>   What bliss beyond compare!

It is significant that Philip Larkin, one of Betjeman's most fervent admirers, has included in his *Oxford Book of Twentieth-Century English Verse* (1973) the two poems by Falkner, "After Trinity" and "Christmas," from which these extracts are respectively drawn.

It would be inappropriate in a brief essay to devote much space to the elements of parody, pastiche, and allusion in Betjeman's poetry, and only a patient researcher endowed with an encyclopedic knowledge of recondite poets of the eighteenth and nineteenth centuries could hope to track down all the references and echoes interwoven in the texture of Betjeman's verse. Yet this kind of device is so pervasive in the body of his poetic work and affords such pleasure that we must glance for a moment at the way in which it operates.

Some poems are direct parodies of hymns or of

famous Victorian poems. "Dorset" is a smoothly elegant imitation of Hardy's "Friends Beyond"; "Love in a Valley" reproduces the meter, though not the spirit, of George Meredith's "Love in the Valley"; "Huxley Hall" is based on Tennyson's "Locksley Hall" and is markedly inferior to its model. In many poems Betjeman is not so much imitating directly as fashioning a pastiche of minor poetry of the late nineteenth century. Or, to reverse the comparison, we may feel that a poem of that period appears to anticipate certain features of his style. He himself, in *A Pictorial History of English Architecture* (1972), quotes, without revealing the source, a ballad on Bedford Park, a late-Victorian garden suburb built by Norman Shaw, one of Betjeman's favorite architects. The following stanza glitters and sparkles like a vintage Betjeman 1931:

> With red and blue and sagest green
>   Were walls and dado dyed,
> Friezes of Morris' there were seen
>   And oaken wainscot wide;
> Now he who loves aesthetic cheer
>   And does not mind the damp
> May come and read Rossetti here
>   By a Japanese-y lamp.

It is sometimes difficult to know whether Betjeman is deliberately borrowing, and relishing the pleasure of counterpointing one idiom against another, or whether he has so thoroughly absorbed an earlier poet's work into his own sensibility that no question of conscious imitation arises. John Sparrow says that we often enjoy Betjeman for his "auditory associations, from hearing, as it were, a new song set to an old tune; sometimes the tune and pattern are his own, as in 'Wantage Bells.'" He quotes a stanza from this poem:

> Wall flowers are bright in their beds
>   And their scent all pervading,
> Withered are primroses' heads
>   And the hyacinth fading
> But flowers by the score
> Multitudes more
> Weed flowers and seed flowers and mead flowers our
>   paths are invading.

A similar tune and pattern occur in a translation by Catherine Winkworth of a German hymn that Betjeman may well have known, since it is to be found in *Hymns Ancient and Modern:*

---

[4]"After the battle there shall be rest."
[5]An anthem by William Boyce (1710–1779)

Praise to the Lord, the Almighty, the King of Creation;
O my soul praise him for he is thy health and salvation.
   All ye who hear,
   Now to His temple draw near,
Joining in glad adoration.

Good poets have the power to assimilate and to renew the material they have borrowed. We notice here the skill Betjeman has employed to surpass the original. The tune is far more elaborate and delicate, the poem moves with an enchanting lyrical grace, the sensuous quality of the bells ringing out among the blossoms is conveyed with perfect sureness of touch. The hymn is a decent piece of devotional verse, whereas Betjeman's canticle of praise attains the condition of poetry.

Before examining his poems in detail we should briefly consider the question of Betjeman's development. Some major artists appear to grow ever more complex and enigmatic, and it is possible to divide their work into clearly defined periods that mark certain dramatic changes in their growth. Shakespeare, Beethoven, Van Gogh, and Yeats are obvious examples of such artists. In the course of the twentieth century this observation about the careers of some major artists has hardened into the dogma that all genuine artists develop in this way, and that they stand convicted of artistic immaturity, almost of moral turpitude, if they fail to remake their style and themselves as frequently as possible. Modernistic critical theory and the desire of public-relations men to keep the market active have combined to inflate this theory of artistic development into an unquestioned axiom. Yet it does not work even for all major artists: in the field of English poetry, Alexander Pope, Wordsworth, Samuel Taylor Coleridge, and Tennyson do not conform to the prescribed pattern. As for poets of slightly lesser stature, though still of the finest quality, the names of George Herbert, Andrew Marvell, Thomas Gray, and Christina Rossetti may serve to show how constricting and presumptuous it is for critics to subject the natural growth of artists to some arbitrary theory of development.

Betjeman is an example of a writer whose career shows no spectacular development, no sudden leap into a new dimension. His poetry has indeed grown steadily more assured, subtle, and moving as his experience of life and the range of his emotions have widened and deepened. The man and the artist have gained in wisdom and maturity, but the subject matter and formal pattern of the poetry have undergone no dramatic transformation. Betjeman continues to take delight in the themes that have always aroused his interest, and his poems still fall into a few categories that can be readily defined: satirical and light verse; narrative and anecdotal poems, often set in the nineteenth century and based on a historical event; personal poems about childhood, love, and death; topographical poems, especially those in which he portrays landscapes, townscapes, or seascapes with figures. Nor has he felt the impulse to discover a new poetic language or to make formal innovations, but has been content to inherit the idiom of his predecessors, inventing a few more tunes and composing variations on familiar themes. It will be convenient to look at Betjeman's poetry chronologically, to observe the changes in mood and emphasis from volume to volume, to notice how his mastery of tone, texture, meter, and rhythm has increased over the years. We can, should the need arise, follow the thread of certain strands in his work from one volume to another and thus trace the emergence of recurrent motifs. We may then be in a position to judge the significance of his poetry and to determine the nature of his achievement.

THE SHORTER POEMS

Mount Zion (1931) was published by a friend of Betjeman's who owned a small firm. Its typography, illustrations, and pink-and-green paper mark it clearly as a book designed to be savored by a small circle of initiates. The poems are prefaced by an illustration of Sezincote, a beautiful house in Gloucestershire where fashionable undergraduates of Oxford in the 1920's were regularly entertained. The volume bears a dedication typical of the spirit in which the whole enterprise is conceived:

MRS ARTHUR DUGDALE
therefore, the hostess of Sezincote, I run risk
of alienating
by dedicating to her this precious
hyper-sophisticated book.

We can trace in this first volume many of the preoccupations and attitudes that recur throughout Betjeman's career: the element of parody ("Hymn"); the satirical portrait of businessmen ("The City"); the delight in making affectionate fun of a small town or a suburb portrayed with loving detail ("Camberley" and "Westgate-on-Sea"); the recollection of a vanished way of life, obliterated by death ("Croydon"); the slightly macabre description of a deathbed ("Death in Leamington"). This latter poem characteristically relates the decay of a building to the physical dissolution of an old lady:

> Do you know that the stucco is peeling?
>   Do you know that the heart will stop?
> From those yellow Italianate arches
>   Do you hear the plaster drop?

Despite the obvious weaknesses of this first volume, the exuberance and sense of fun still retain the power to amuse the reader. "The 'Varsity Students' Rag" satirizes the snobbish mindlessness that animated undergraduates of the period who were both wealthy and rowdy. One does not need a detailed knowledge of the area around Piccadilly in the late 1920's to appreciate the following stanza:

> *We* had a rag at Monico's. *We* had a rag at the Troc.,
> And the one we had at the Berkeley gave the customers
>   quite a shock.
> *Then* we went to the Popular, and after that—oh my!
> I *wish* you'd seen the rag we had in the Grill Room at the
>   Cri.

Equally high-spirited, and more accomplished, is "Competition," one of the nine poems from *Mount Zion* omitted from the *Collected Poems*. It recounts the eagerness of the Independent Calvinistic Methodist Chapel (1810), the Wesley Memorial Church (1860), and the Mount Carmel Baptists (Strict) (1875) to surpass one another in the splendor and modernity of their ecclesiastical furnishings:

> The Gothic is bursting over the way
>   With Evangelical Song,
> For the pinnacled Wesley Memorial Church
>   Is over a hundred strong,
> And what is a New Jerusalem
>   Gas-lit and yellow-wall'd
> To a semi-circular pitchpine sea
>   With electric-light install'd?

Continual Dew (1937), although aimed at a slightly wider audience than *Mount Zion*, may still be regarded as precious and hyper-sophisticated in its typography and general appearance, with a surrealistic jacket by McKnight Kauffer and imitation gilt clasps such as one used to find on prayer books. It contains some of the poems from *Mount Zion* and a number of new poems. The subtitle, *A Little Book of Bourgeois Verse*, is a piece of self-mockery, but what of the main title? It is drawn from the Prayer for the Clergy and People, which is said in the Anglican order for Morning Prayer and for Evening Prayer:

> Almighty and everlasting God, who alone workest great marvels; Send down upon our Bishops, and Curates, and all Congregations committed to their charge, the healthful Spirit of thy grace; and that they may truly please thee, pour upon them the continual dew of thy blessing.

It is difficult to fathom Betjeman's religious beliefs at this stage of his career, because his poems so often take refuge in an evasive irony. The subtitle of his first volume is *In Touch with the Infinite* and we are puzzled to know how seriously we should take it. And how are we meant to respond to a poem called "Suicide on Junction Road Station after Abstention from Evening Communion in North London"? The jauntiness of the rhythm is at odds with the subject of the poem, and the final rhetorical question invites a ribald answer:

> Six on the upside! six on the down side!
>   One gaslight in the Booking Hall
> And a thousand sins on this lonely station—
>   What shall I do with them all?

In general, the volume marks an advance on *Mount Zion*, in both technical assurance and emotional maturity. Many of the poems are, indeed, little more than highly entertaining pieces of skillful pastiche. Even the deservedly famous "The Arrest of Oscar Wilde at the Cadogan Hotel" is a thoroughly self-indulgent performance, perhaps appropriately so in that its protagonist exhibited similar traits. The arrest of Wilde by two plainclothes policemen is presented as a mixture of melodrama and farce, and Betjeman cleverly avoids committing himself by adopting an ambiguous tone, deliberately playing up the absurd elements in the scene in order to conceal his own response to the tragedy of Wilde's downfall:

> "Mr Woilde, we 'ave come for tew take yew
>   Where felons and criminals dwell:
> We must ask yew tew leave with us quoietly
>   For this *is* the Cadogan Hotel."

He rose, and he put down *The Yellow Book.*
He staggered—and, terrible-eyed,
He brushed past the palms on the staircase
And was helped to a hansom outside.

One of the poems in the collection, "Slough," has enjoyed a certain notoriety ever since it appeared:

Come, friendly bombs, and fall on Slough
It isn't fit for humans now,
There isn't grass to graze a cow
Swarm over, Death!

Betjeman's satirical and comic verses, which are dotted here and there throughout the *Collected Poems,* are the poems by which he is best known to the large majority of his readers. His satire is aimed at a wide variety of targets: profiteers, vulgar businessmen, progressives, hypocrites of every persuasion, bureaucrats, planners, brewers who modernize unpretentious inns. We have seen that some of his satirical prose is highly effective, and it is therefore disappointing that his verse satire is comparatively feeble. Many facets of contemporary life arouse his keen dislike, and at times his irritation becomes intense; but he lacks the qualifications of a major satirical poet. The great masters of satire, such as Juvenal and Jonathan Swift, exude an overpowering loathing of humanity, portraying men as monsters of cruelty and greed, depicting women as maenads given over to the pursuit of vicious luxury. Betjeman is incapable of viewing his fellow creatures as odious vermin, however nasty and stupid they sometimes appear to be. His natural kindness reinforces his Christian belief in the capacity of men to be redeemed, just as his awareness of mortality reminds him that we are all deserving of compassion because we are moving toward death. He cannot, therefore, follow the example of Yeats and study hatred with great diligence. It is impossible to believe that Betjeman genuinely wished Slough to be destroyed: one feels that he would have found that it went against the grain to exult in the destruction of Sodom and Gomorrah.

Even the neatest of his satirical poems are deficient in the touch of savagery, the clinching power, that lend such virulent force to G. K. Chesterton's "Antichrist" or Kipling's "Gehazi." The figures he attacks in "Group Life: Letchworth," "The Planster's Vision," "The Town Clerk's Views," "Huxley Hall," and "The Dear Old Village" are men of straw. Two

of his early satires, "Bristol and Clifton" and "In Westminster Abbey," were taken by some to be anti-Christian poems, whereas they are orthodox Christian attacks on certain aspects of Anglican formalism and obtuseness. Their impact, however, is so feeble that their purport is largely irrelevant.

The galumphing comic poems, which have been described as *New Statesman* competition poems, lack the redeeming features of the satires and are scarcely worthy of mention. They afford a harmless pleasure, but they are small beer. Betjeman himself is more aware of the weaknesses inherent in his comic and satirical poems than are the anthologists who continue to reprint them. Referring specifically to "Slough," "In Westminster Abbey," and "How to Get On in Society," he has remarked that "they now seem to me merely comic verse and competent magazine writing, topical and tiresome."

Many of his good poems, of course, are enchantingly funny and exhibit delightful flashes of satire, but the wit and satire are subordinated to the main design and mood of the poem. Betjeman is at his most characteristic and moving when he is dwelling with loving particularity on a landscape or on a quirk of human nature, when he is remembering his childhood or contemplating the way in which past and present mingle. Irritation and frustration may spur him into satirical verse, but he is stirred to write genuine poetry only when affection and compassion arouse the lyrical impulse.

This is true of "Love in a Valley" and "Death of King George V," the two poems in *Continual Dew* that unmistakably suggest that the period of Betjeman's juvenilia was drawing to its close. "Love in a Valley" takes us for the first time into Betjeman country—the physical landscape of the Home Counties, where the prosperous upper middle classes have built their comfortable retreats:

Deep down the drive go the cushioned rhododendrons,
Deep down, sand deep, drives the heather root,
Deep the spliced timber barked around the summer-house,
Light lies the tennis-court, plantain underfoot.

We are also being introduced to Betjeman country in a metaphorical sense, to the world of amatory relations where Pam and Miss J. Hunter Dunn await us. In "Love in a Valley" it is the girl who speaks:

Take me, Lieutenant, to that Surrey homestead!
Red comes the winter and your rakish car.

And the poem ends, unexpectedly, on a muted note:

Leaded are the windows lozenging the crimson,
    Drained dark the pines in resin-scented rain.

Portable Lieutenant! they carry you to China
    And me to lonely shopping in a brilliant arcade;
Firm hand, fond hand, switch the giddy engine!
    So for us a last time is bright light made.

In "Death of King George V," based on the *Daily Express* headline "New King Arrives in His Capital by Air," the perception that Edward VIII's accession marked the passing of an epoch is crystallized in a complex, vivid image:

Old men who never cheated, never doubted,
    Communicated monthly, sit and stare
At the new suburb stretched beyond the run-way
    Where a young man lands hatless from the air.

Further evidence of Betjeman's increasing mastery of his medium is to be discerned in "The Heart of Thomas Hardy," a poem composed at this period and included in *Collected Poems*, though not previously published in book form. The tone is ambivalent, the concept behind it odd to the point of eccentricity; but the handling of the tricky meter is exceptionally skillful, and one image is memorably grotesque:

Weighted down with a Conscience, now for the first time
                                                    fleshly
Taking form as a growth hung from the feet like a
                                            sponge-bag.
There, in the heart of the nimbus, twittered the heart of
                                                    Hardy.

Old Lights for New Chancels reinforces the impression made by the more successful poems in *Continual Dew*. The title of "A Shropshire Lad" suggests that we are in the pastoral world of A. E. Housman, but the lad is Captain Webb, who was born at Dawley in an industrial district of that county, and the poem, which, the author tells us, *"should be recited with a Midland accent,"* is a mock-serious ghost story that moves to one of Betjeman's most captivating tunes:

The gas was on in the Institute,
    The flare was up in the gym,
A man was running a mineral line,
    A lass was singing a hymn,

When Captain Webb the Dawley man,
    Captain Webb from Dawley,
Came swimming along in the old canal
    That carried the bricks to Lawley.
Swimming along—
Swimming along—
Swimming along from Severn,
And paying a call at Dawley bank while swimming along
                                                    to Heaven.

Three or four poems strike a more somber, wistful note than anything in the first two volumes. "Oxford: Sudden Illness at the Bus-Stop" is the first of many poems about North Oxford, dons and their wives, sickness, and the intimations of mortality; "Holy Trinity, Sloane Street" conjures up the atmosphere of early-twentieth-century Anglican ritualism in Chelsea; "On a Portrait of a Deaf Man," an elegy for Betjeman's father, plunges into that macabre preoccupation with the physical horror of death that Betjeman's faith seems powerless to exorcize.

The collection bears the subtitle *Verses Topographical and Amatory* (there is also a section labeled "Miscellaneous"). Betjeman's amatory poems, although not among his finest achievements, have attracted much interest and praise. They certainly possess a unique flavor. One of the most celebrated appears in this 1940 volume, and its title, "Pot Pourri from a Surrey Garden," not only indicates the geographical setting but contains an oblique joke, since it is also the title of a late-Victorian book by Mrs. C. W. Earle, a diary with sections on gardening and cooking, dedicated to her sister, Lady Constance Lytton. Betjeman, in this poem as in later poems, portrays himself as a Gulliver among the female Brobdingnagians: the emphasis is on the commanding strength of the girl, whose physical prowess and dominating character constitute a major part of her erotic fascination:

See the strength of her arm, as firm and hairy as Hendren's;
    See the size of her thighs, the pout of her lips as, cross,
And full of a pent-up strength, she swipes at the
                                            rhododendrons.

The reference to Hendren, a famous cricketer of the interwar years, the deliberately outrageous rhyming, the dwelling on the formidable charms of the "great big mountainous sports girl" all pile on the slightly perverse romantic agony, which culminates in marriage celebrated in a Victorian Gothic church whose decoration is as cunningly elaborate as the poet's metrical pattern and extravagant rhymes:

Over the redolent pinewoods, in at the bathroom casement,
   One fine Saturday, Windlesham bells shall call:
Up the Butterfield aisle rich with Gothic enlacement,
   Licensed now for embracement,
     Pam and I, as the organ
   Thunders over you all.

It is amusing but perhaps irrelevant to wonder whether Betjeman is deliberately or unconsciously drawing on memories of *Dorothy: A Country Story* (1880) by A. J. Munby, who secretly married a servant girl, and whose journal was published in 1972. The heroine of this poem springs from a much lower class than Pam, but physically and psychologically they are sisters under the rippling muscles:

Oh, what a notable lass is our Dolly, the pride of the dairy!
   Stalwart and tall as a man, strong as a heifer to work:
Built for beauty, indeed, but certainly built for labour—
   Witness her muscular arm, witness the grip of her
              hand.

Such Amazonian figures reappear in several poems in this and in subsequent volumes. We have Myfanwy, who is "Strong and willowy, strong to pillow me," and who is apostrophized as "my silken Myfanwy,/Ringleader, tom-boy, and chum to the weak." "A Subaltern's Love-Song" celebrates the charms of Miss J. Hunter Dunn, who vanquishes the subaltern at tennis and becomes engaged to him after they have sat in the parking lot at Camberley during the golf club dance. Betjeman has told us that this poem records his feelings for a superintendent in the Ministry of Information canteen during the war, and although Betjeman has never been a subaltern he may have felt like one in his youth when he was seeking the hand of a field-marshal's daughter. "The Olympic Girl" portrays yet another formidable young woman, a "Fair tigress of the tennis courts." The most accomplished poem in this category is "The Licorice Fields at Pontefract," which begins as an irreverent parody of Yeats's "Down by the Sally-Garden":

In the licorice fields at Pontefract
   My love and I did meet

Yet, in the final stanza, which once again casts the poet in the role of the weak male dominated by the powerful woman, the sophisticated self-mockery is consumed in a sudden flare of eroticism. This embracement is certainly unlicensed:

She cast her blazing eyes on me
   And plucked a licorice leaf;
I was her captive slave and she
   My red-haired robber chief.
Oh love! for love I could not speak,
It left me winded, wilting, weak
And held in brown arms strong and bare
And wound with flaming ropes of hair.

Elsewhere, notably in "Senex" and still more in "Late-Flowering Lust," sexual desire is linked with the horror of physical decay, with a vision of two skeletons:

Dark sockets look on emptiness
   Which once was loving-eyed,
The mouth that opens for a kiss
   Has got no tongue inside.

One poem in *Old Lights for New Chancels*, "Trebetherick," hints at reserves of lyrical delicacy and power that may have astonished some admirers of Betjeman:

But when a storm was at its height,
   And feathery slate was black in rain,
And tamarisks were hung with light
   And golden sand was brown again,
Spring tide and blizzard would unite
   And sea came flooding up the lane.

This lyrical vein runs through *New Bats in Old Belfries* (1945) and reappears in some of the half-dozen poems published for the first time in *Selected Poems*. The opening lines of "Before the Anaesthetic; or, A Real Fright" reveal Betjeman's accomplishment as a landscape artist:

Intolerably sad, profound
St Giles's bells are ringing round,
They bring the slanting summer rain
To tap the chestnut boughs again
Whose shadowy cave of rainy leaves
The gusty belfry-song receives.

The sea, particularly the Cornish coast, and memories of childhood are among the most potent sources of poetry for Betjeman. Two poems in blank verse, "Sunday Afternoon Service in St. Enodoc

Church, Cornwall" and "North Coast Recollections," spring from the confluence of these two sources and exemplify the poet's mastery of an exacting medium. The echoes of eighteenth- and nineteenth-century writers may appear to detract from Betjeman's originality, but at the same time they form an essential part of the pleasure that the poems yield. One of the finest passages of "Sunday Afternoon Service" is the long paragraph that concludes the poem, too long to quote in full. A brief extract may suggest something of its quality but cannot do justice to the poet's command of syntax, tone, and change of pace, which have traditionally been the hallmark of poetic intelligence:

> Where deep cliffs loom enormous, where cascade
> Mesembryanthemum and stone-crop down,
> Where the gull looks no larger than a lark
> Hung midway twixt the cliff-top and the sand,
> Sun-shadowed valleys roll along the sea.
> Forced by the backwash, see the nearest wave
> Rise to a wall of huge, translucent green
> And crumble into spray along the top
> Blown seaward by the land-breeze.

The closing lines of "North Coast Recollections" attain an equally firm amplitude, although they are less concerned with the minute particulars of the seascape than with its emotional resonance:

> Then pealing out across the estuary
> The Padstow bells rang up for practice-night
> An undersong to birds and dripping shrubs.
> The full Atlantic at September spring
> Flooded a final tide-mark up the sand,
> And ocean sank to silence under bells,
> And the next breaker was a lesser one
> Then lesser still. Atlantic, bells and birds
> Were layer on interchanging layers of sound.

Yet, despite Betjeman's deft craftsmanship as a writer of blank verse, he is at his best and most characteristic when his lyrical impulse is quickened by the challenge of rhyme schemes and stanzaic patterns. The more intricate the tune, the more nimbly and inventively his imagination dances, the more daringly he fuses a variety of emotions into a poetic unity. In "Henley-on-Thames" the pastoral idyll is saved from sinking into an inertly sentimental reverie by the solidity of the two stalwart young women, members of the Auxiliary Territorial Service, and also by the lithe movement of the verse:

> When shall I see the Thames again?
> The prow-promoted gems again,
>   As beefy ATS
>   Without their hats
> Come shooting through the bridge?
>   And "cheerioh" and "cheeri-bye"
>   Across the waste of waters die,
>   And low the mists of evening lie
> And lightly skims the midge.

Betjeman was wise to abandon the use of blank verse until he required it for the special purpose of writing his autobiography. His metrical skill attains a full maturity in *New Bats in Old Belfries* in a dozen haunting poems.

The publication of *A Few Late Chrysanthemums* (1954) dispelled any lingering suspicions that Betjeman was not a serious artist. The good poems come so thick and fast that any appraisal of the volume runs the risk of degenerating into a laudatory catalog. It may be more helpful to devote some detailed attention to one poem and to refer to a few others, rather than attempt a summary of the whole collection.

"Middlesex" brings together many of the strands we have traced in the prose and in the earlier poems: Betjeman's ability to be funny, tender, and lyrical simultaneously; his delight in recording minutiae of class distinctions and social habits; his nostalgia for the vanished world of his childhood and of vintage London; his complex response to the collocation of past and present; his sense of mortality and of the pathos of human life vividly recalled to our eyes and hearts by the image of the great London cemeteries.

The poem opens with two stanzas devoted to a description of Elaine's return, presumably from work in Central London, to her suburban home. Just as Eliot in *The Waste Land* contrasts the love stories of the legendary Iseult and Queen Elizabeth I with the seduction of the typist, so Betjeman ironically depicts a modern girl whose name is Tennysonian but whose way of life is lower middle class:

> Gaily into Ruislip Gardens
>   Runs the red electric train,
> With a thousand Ta's and Pardon's
>   Daintily alights Elaine;
> Hurries down the concrete station
> With a frown of concentration,
> Out into the outskirt's edges
> Where a few surviving hedges
> Keep alive our lost Elysium—rural Middlesex again.

Well cut Windsmoor flapping lightly,
    Jacqmar scarf of mauve and green
Hiding hair which, Friday nightly,
    Delicately drowns in Drene;
Fair Elaine the bobby-soxer,
Fresh-complexioned with Innoxa,
Gains the garden—father's hobby—
Hangs her Windsmoor in the lobby,
Settles down to sandwich supper and the television screen.

The irony is affectionate; the description of her home life is gently satirical; the brand names of the clothes, shampoo, and cosmetic are recounted with a humorous relish, almost as if they constitute a Homeric roll call. Then the poem changes mood and direction, as the third stanza pivots away from the built-up suburb of the 1950's to the lost Elysium of Betjeman's childhood:

    Gentle Brent, I used to know you
        Wandering Wembley-wards at will,
    Now what change your waters show you
        In the meadowlands you fill!
    Recollect the elm-trees misty
    And the footpaths climbing twisty
    Under cedar-shaded palings,
    Low laburnum-leaned-on railings,
Out of Northolt on and upward to the heights of Harrow hill.

In the final stanza Betjeman fills his landscape with figures from *The Diary of a Nobody* (1892), a late-Victorian work of fiction by George and Weedon Grossmith. The last four lines transport us to a remote world where archaic licensing laws provide for the needs of *bona fide* travelers, and where the "cockney anglers, cockney shooters" stand out in their sharp, quirky individuality against the blurred masses of our consumer society. The long amplitude of the concluding line evokes what Betjeman has called "that most Victorian sight of all London—the windy Carrara-covered cemetery." Elaine, unlike Murray Posh and Lupin Pooter, will end up in the crematorium, delivered there in a Cooperative funeral van:

    Parish of enormous hayfields
        Perivale stood all alone,
    And from Greenford scent of mayfields
        Most enticingly was blown
    Over market gardens tidy,
    Taverns for the *bona fide*,
    Cockney anglers, cockney shooters,
    Murray Poshes, Lupin Pooters

Long in Kensal Green and Highgate silent under soot and
    stone.

We may resent Betjeman's air of kindly condescension toward Elaine, and argue that she is in no way inferior to the characters affectionately portrayed by the Grossmiths. The poem can be read as an example of Betjeman's nostalgia for the days when sweated labor, cheap domestic help, and the laws of a rigidly hierarchical society kept his parents in comfort and the workers in their proper station. "The Metropolitan Railway," another poem that juxtaposes past and present, lacks the element of mild snobbery and patrician irony that tinges "Middlesex." The irony in "The Metropolitan Railway" is tender, and is directed against a married couple of his own class whose youthful dreams have faded since Edwardian days. Again we find ourselves in "autumn-scented Middlesex," but only for a moment: the emotional heart of the poem is Baker Street Station, with its "many-branched electrolier" under which perhaps "your parents" met one evening at six-fifteen and caught the train to that lost Elysium. When the poem returns to the present day we learn of the desolation the years have made and see the dark side of fair Elaine's world for the survivors of Edwardian England:

    Cancer has killed him. Heart is killing her.
        The trees are down. An Odeon flashes fire
    Where stood their villa by the murmuring fir.

A third poem that counterpoises the vanished and vanquished world of the past against the vulgar present is "The Old Liberals." The opening lines conjure up an interior that is gracious yet a shade pedantic and eccentric, the ghostly relic of an epoch when Robert Bridges compiled his hymns at Yattendon and the dreams of William Morris still lingered on among the dwindling groups of his disciples:

Pale green of the *English Hymnal*! Yattendon hymns
    Played on the *hautbois* by a lady dress'd in blue
    Her white-hair'd father accompanying her thereto
On tenor or bass-recorder.

Betjeman knows that such people are defeated, and in lamenting their fate he is mourning a part of his youth, a lost dream of England, banished by a harsher, uglier world:

Where are the wains with garlanded swathes a-swaying?
Where are the swains to wend through the lanes-a-maying?

Where are the blithe and jocund to ted the hay?
Where are the free folk of England? Where are they?

Ask of the Abingdon bus with full load creeping
Down into denser suburbs.

Betjeman divided *A Few Late Chrysanthemums* into three sections, "Medium," "Gloom," and "Light." His article in the *Spectator* (8 October 1954), which contains an answer to certain of his readers who regretted the presence of so much encircling gloom, provides a valuable gloss on his temperamental endowment and on his emotional development since his days at Oxford:

In those days my purest pleasure was the exploration of suburbs and provincial towns and my impurest pleasure the pursuit of the brawny athletic girl. When most of the poems in my latest book were written, I was the self-pitying victim of remorse, guilt and terror of death. Much as I dislike trying to conform to Christian morality . . . the only practical way to face the dreaded lonely journey into Eternity seems to me the Christian one. I therefore try to believe that Christ was God, made man and gives Eternal Life, and that I may be confirmed in this belief by clinging to the sacraments and by prayer. . . . For there is no doubt that fear of death (a manifestation of the lack of faith I deeply desire), remorse and a sense of man's short time on earth and an impatience with so-called "progress," did inform many of the poems in my latest volume. Since then I have grown a little more cheerful and thankful and hope to produce some poems expressing the joys of being alive.

Betjeman has for many years combined a genuine Anglican piety with a gnawing uncertainty about the truth of Christianity, and it is arguable that this fruitful ambivalence gives many of his poems a keen poignancy and a finely poised delicacy that a more robust assurance would blunt and coarsen. His beloved Thomas Hardy disbelieved in the Christmas story yet hoped that it might be true; Betjeman affirms his faith in it while fearing that it may be false. Even in "Christmas," one of his most serene and unaffected expressions of Christian devotion, the last three stanzas, which proclaim the wonders of the Incarnation, ask three times the question "And is it true?" and answer in the conditional tense: "For if it is . . ."

Betjeman's output of lyrical poems since *A Few Late Chrysanthemums* has been steady though not prolific. *Collected Poems* (1958), which brought him so remarkable and unexpected a measure of popular applause, contains most of the contents of *Mount Zion* and of *Continental Dew*, almost every poem from the subsequent volumes, one from *Poems in the Porch* (1954), a pamphlet in verse about church matters, and nineteen hitherto uncollected poems. The third edition (1970) incorporates eight poems from earlier books added to the 1962 edition and the contents of *High and Low* (1966), while the 1979 edition contains all the poems from *A Nip in the Air* (1974).

Many of the poems written between 1954 and 1966 record the poet's deepening awareness of change and decay, mortality, and the passing of the old order. In "Good-bye" and "Five o'Clock Shadow" the physical horror of death is apprehended so fiercely that the artistic distancing and impersonality that an achieved poem requires are distorted and overwhelmed. Much more successful are the poems in which the recollection of beloved scenes and of past happiness counterpoises the lamentation and the fear. Yet in such poems the dominant note is still one of sadness, of regret that the modern world is more brutal and ugly than the one it has superseded. In "Monody on the Death of Aldersgate Street Station" the remembrance of church bells in the City cannot avert the desecration of London, and the closing of Aldersgate Street Station symbolizes both the destruction of vintage London and the declining powers of the poet and his coevals:

Snow falls in the buffet of Aldersgate station,
Toiling and doomed from Moorgate Street puffs the train,
For us of the steam and the gas-light, the lost generation,
The new white cliffs of the City are built in vain.

Even the ostensibly lighter poems may take a sinister turn. "Winthrop Mackworth Redivivus," written in the meter of Winthrop Mackworth Praed's most scintillating poem, "Goodnight to the Season," starts off in a vein of highly entertaining satire that dissects with deadly accuracy the foibles of a silly, snobbish woman:

And plants for indoors are the fashion—
Or so the *News Chronicle* said—
So I've ventured some housekeeping cash on
A cactus which seems to be dead.
An artist with whom we're acquainted
Has stippled the dining-room stove
And the walls are alternately painted
Off-yellow and festival mauve.

Yet we learn in the fourth stanza that the woman's daughter, Matilda, appears to harbor the delusion that she is a horse. The jokey tone of the poem merely intensifies the desolation of a household where the parents, who pride themselves on being cultured and highly rational, resort in vain to psychoanalysis and to a riding school, in the hope of healing their daughter's spiritual unease, and wonder, in despair, whether the church might be called in to exorcize something—the poverty-stricken vagueness of the word evokes the hollow uncertainty of the speaker.

In some of the Cornish poems with which *High and Low* opens, an affirmative faith dissipates for a moment the melancholy reflections. "Winter Seascape" ends with the poet's surveying "a huge consoling sea"; in "Old Friends" his sadness at the thought of vanished friends is lightened by a sense that we may enjoy communion with the dead:

> As I reach our hill, I am part of a sea unseen—
> The oppression lifts.

But "Tregardock," perhaps the finest poem in the collection, moves from a quietly menacing exordium toward a climax in which the poet anatomizes with exultant savagery the cowardice that makes him resist the lure of self-destruction:

> The dunlin do not move, each bird
> Is stationary on the sand
> As if a spirit in it heard
> The final end of sea and land.
>
> And I on my volcano edge
> Exposed to ridicule and hate
> Still do not dare to leap the ledge
> And smash to pieces on the slate.

Two of Betjeman's most powerful later works in *Collected Poems* revert to his preoccupation with death and eternity. "N.W.5 & N.6" evokes memories of his childhood and of the way in which a nurserymaid's talk of damnation, "world without end," communicated to the child, as the church bells rang out through the late evening sky,

> . . . her fear
> And guilt at endlessness. I caught them too,
> Hating to think of sphere succeeding sphere
> Into eternity and God's dread will
> I caught her terror then. I have it still.

"Felixstowe; or, The Last of Her Order," one of many poems in which Betjeman conveys his sym-

pathy for the old and the lonely, is a monologue by the last survivor of "The Little Sisters of the Hanging Pyx," an order founded in 1894. As so often in Betjeman, the changing moods of the sea awaken a flood of emotion, and the minute external particulars of Felixstowe—"the cushioned scabious," "a cakeshop's tempting scones," "the red brick twilight of St John's"—are dwelled on lingeringly in the hope that they may allay a turbulent uncertainty and fear. The final avowal of faith, with its emphasis on safety, its repeated claim that inner peace has been attained, suggests the desperate need of the speaker for comfort and reassurance:

> Safe from the vain world's silly sympathising,
> Safe with the Love that I was born to know,
> Safe from the surging of the lonely sea
> My heart finds rest, my heart finds rest in Thee.

The whole body of Betjeman's poetry charts the oscillation between the terror experienced by the child in North London and the faith that as death draws near clings to belief in God.

A Nip in the Air, though not his finest collection, demonstrates that Betjeman has lost neither his idiosyncratic view of the world nor his ability to delight readers. The best of the poems written to celebrate royal occasions is "A Ballad of the Investiture 1969," and it may be significant that it is not, strictly speaking, an occasional poem, because it was written several years after the poet had dined in Trinity College, Cambridge, with the prince of Wales, who as he left issued a command: "I want a poem out of you on my investiture in Wales." What the prince belatedly received was "a kind of rhyming letter" in which vignettes of landscapes glimpsed on the railway journey to Wales blend with observations on the ceremony at Caernarvon:

> The railway crossed the river Dee
> Where Mary called the cattle home,
> The wide marsh widened into sea,
> The white sea whitened into foam
> . . .
> Wet banners flap. The sea mist clears.
> Colours are backed by silver stone.
> Moustached hereditary peers
> Are ranged in rows behind the throne.

The poem "14 November, 1973" illustrates some of the difficulties that may confront a poet laureate in an age when the royal family and their publi rituals are judged in part by their success in enthralling the television audience. The opening lines of this short poem on Princess Anne's wedding sound indeed like an enthusiastic television commentary:

> Hundreds of birds in the air
> And millions of leaves on the pavement.

But the poem ends with a reversion to an older mode, an apostrophe to the princess such as Tennyson might have addressed to Princess Alexandra of Denmark on her marriage to the future Edward VII:

> Glow, white lily in London,
> You are high in our hearts today!

The satirical poems are deft but disappointing, although "The Newest Bath Guide" successfully mingles the ingredients that have so often before yielded a delicious, unique flavor—pleasure in the recollection of old ways and ancient buildings, regret at the passing of traditional manners and customs, satirical contempt for the mediocre architecture and town planning inflicted on our cities by bureaucratic committees and speculative builders. Betjeman's verdict is uncompromisingly hostile:

> Now houses are "units" and people are digits
> And Bath has been planned into quarters for midgets.
> Official designs are aggressively neuter,
> The Puritan work of an eyeless computer.

"Shattered Image" represents a new departure for Betjeman. It is a poem in blank verse about a public relations man named Rex, who, while facing trial on a charge of committing a sexual offense against a minor, meditates suicide as he sits in his tasteful flat in Alvarez Cloister (a nice malicious touch, since A. Alvarez, who wrote a study of suicide, *The Savage God*, has often written disparagingly about Betjeman). Rex turns for help to a Roman Catholic priest; two friends, one of whom is a solicitor; and his boss. All offer conventional sympathy and wash their hands of the whole nasty business. The affable, stony-hearted boss suggests a pleasant way out:

> Instead of letting me ask you to resign
> *You* send a note to *me*, in which you say
> That resignation is your own idea
> And unconnected with your work for us.

The blank verse of the poem reflects a world that is emotionally blank, one in which there is no response to Rex's anguish—no strong moral condemnation, no understanding, no compassion, but merely a mouthing of platitudes inspired by a wish to get rid of an embarrassment. Betjeman employs the resources of his art to portray what is null and void.

Whereas in the past the sound of church bells has for Betjeman been ambivalent, their message in this volume is one of desolation and mortality. The church bells ring out our destiny in "Loneliness":

> The tasteful crematorium door
> Shuts out for some the furnace roar;
> But church-bells open on the blast
> Our loneliness, so long and vast.

And in "On Leaving Wantage 1972" it is to the clashing out of church bells that Betjeman and his wife leave their home:

> From this wide vale, where all our married lives
> We two have lived, we now are whirled away
> Momently clinging to the things we knew—
> Friends, footpaths, hedges, house and animals—
> Till, borne along like twigs and bits of straw,
> We sink below the sliding stream of time.

It is a mark of Betjeman's artistry that it can encompass the beautifully controlled plangency of those lines as well as the hollow deadness of the blank verse in "Shattered Image." Further proof that his hand has not lost its metrical cunning can be found in "Fruit," one of the three or four poems in this volume that rank among his most accomplished and moving achievements:

> Now with the threat growing still greater within me,
> The Church dead that was hopelessly over-restored,
> The fruit picked from these yellowing Worcestershire
> orchards
> What is left to me, Lord?
>
> To wait until next year's bloom at the end of the garden
> Foams to the Malvern Hills, like an inland sea,
> And to know that its fruit, dropping in autumn stillness,
> May have outlived me.

SUMMONED BY BELLS

BETJEMAN's long autobiographical poem, *Summoned by Bells*, stands apart from the rest of his work. This account of his life from early childhood down to his departure from Oxford is written in a medium he had hitherto essayed in only three poems. His prefatory note explains the reason for his choice of blank verse: "The author has gone as near prose as he dare. He chose blank verse, for all but the more hilarious moments, because he found it best suited to brevity and the rapid changes of mood and subject." Evelyn Waugh's acerbic comment in his diary on *Summoned by Bells* is characteristically bitter and unfair:

John demonstrates how much more difficult it is to write blank verse than jingles and raises the question: *why* did he not go into his father's workshop? It would be far more honourable and useful to make expensive ashtrays than to appear on television and just as lucrative.

Yet Waugh displays his habitual acuteness in perceiving that the subtle constraints of blank verse are less welcome to Betjeman's poetic sensibility than the challenges of rhyme and metrical patterns. It is a readable, enjoyable poem that affords us an interesting account of the poet's childhood and adolescence, of his growing estrangement from his father, of his first gropings toward religious faith, of his "sense of guilt increasing with the years." The most memorable passages are those describing the hideous bullyings organized with ritual cruelty at Marlborough, and those that recount his lifelong perplexity about the central doctrine of Christianity:

> What seemed to me a greater question then
> Tugged and still tugs. Is Christ the Son of God? . . .
> Some know for all their lives that Christ is God,
> Some start upon that arduous love affair
> In clouds of doubt and argument; and some
> (My closest friends) seem not to want His love—
> And why this is I wish to God I knew.
>
> (ch. 9)

Summoned by Bells suffers from the fact that it appears to be covering familiar ground, because the autobiographical element in the collected poems is so strong and vivid. Yet the verse autobiography contains a great deal of fresh material and goes into detail about a number of matters that are merely glanced at in the remainder of Betjeman's work. It is a measure of the book's merits and limitations that, although admirers of Betjeman will value it for its intrinsic quality as well as for the light it sheds on the man and the poet, *Summoned by Bells* is not a volume that one would recommend to anybody unacquainted with the author's shorter poems.

CONCLUSION

BETJEMAN's achievement remains a matter for discussion, which can speedily degenerate into acrimonious debate. Some of his severe critics hold him up to scorn as a cult figure promoted to an undeservedly high status by smart journalists, and cite his career as an example of the way in which the upper-middle-class network of metropolitan London promulgates a false set of cultural values. In this view Betjeman is nothing more than a twentieth-century Praed or Thomas Moore, a licensed jester of the establishment who has contrived to flatter the prejudices of sophisticated readers and, at the same time, to catch the eyes and ears of television viewers who wish to be thought sophisticated. This would in itself be a feat demanding at the very least a remarkable degree of sheer cleverness and virtuosity; but it would invalidate his claims to be regarded as a serious artist.

Those who are tempted to dismiss Betjeman in such a cavalier fashion may pause and recall that he has never lacked admirers among fine critics and poets of widely different generations and tastes. In 1958 Edmund Wilson remarked that, apart from Auden and Dylan Thomas, Betjeman was the most interesting English poet since T. S. Eliot. W. H. Auden's preface to *Slick but Not Streamlined* celebrates the skill and originality of the poet to whom he dedicated *The Age of Anxiety*. More recently, Philip Larkin has written a brilliant introduction to the 1971 American edition of Betjeman's *Collected Poems* in which he makes very large claims about Betjeman's place in the history of twentieth-century poetry, claims reinforced by the amount of space allotted to him in Larkin's own anthology, *The Oxford Book of Twentieth-Century English Verse*.

We need not accept Larkin's extremely high estimate of Betjeman. In particular we may view with skepticism his belief that Betjeman's poetic stature and significance are comparable to Eliot's. Larkin ingeniously supports his argument by quoting from Eliot's *Notes Towards the Definition of Culture* (1948) a passage that lists the properties of our "whole way of life": "Derby Day, Henley Regatta, Cowes, the twelfth of August, a cup final, the pin table, the dartboard, Wensleydale cheese, boiled cabbage cut in sections, beetroot in vinegar, nineteenth-century Gothic churches, and the music of Elgar." As Larkin observes, "if this passage reminds us of anyone's poetry, it is Betjeman's rather than Eliot's or anyone else's." Yet we do not habitually

turn to the major poets if we want to inform ourselves about the properties, the accidents, of a
civilization. Tennyson, Matthew Arnold, and Hopkins reveal to us profound truths about the mind and
heart of Victorian England, but we must go elsewhere, to minor writers and journalists, for detailed
accounts of Victorian social habits, furnishings, and
fashions. Yeats, Eliot, and D. H. Lawrence interpret
to us the profound currents of thought and emotion
during the first half of our century, yet they tell us little about the appurtenances of our civilization.

Betjeman does not, for all his variety and his keen-
ness of social observation, give us a powerful and
comprehensive vision of society or a sustained argument about the nature of man. While it is not true
that he is indifferent or unsympathetic to the poor,
he shows little understanding of the political and
social aspirations that animate large numbers of
working people. Even his religious preoccupations
are individualistic: he broods intensely on his own
death and the deaths of his friends; he longs for
salvation after death for himself and those he loves,
rather than for the redemption of all mankind, the
renewal of the creation.

Yet these very limitations, this fidelity to his
temperament and to his experience, this refusal to
pretend, give his poems a rare grace and authenticity. He is, moreover, a lyrical poet of singular purity
whose mastery of the singing line and melodic flow
enables him to compose a variety of enchanting
tunes. In "Ireland with Emily," his finest tribute to
the country that has fascinated him since his Oxford
days, he describes with an exuberant wit the decaying beauty of a ruined abbey:

> There in pinnacled protection,
>   One extinguished family waits
> A Church of Ireland resurrection
>   By the broken, rusty gates.
> Sheepswool, straw and droppings cover
> Graves of spinster, rake and lover,
> Whose fantastic mausoleum
> Sings its own seablown Te Deum,
>   In and out the slipping slates.

He can suggest, with equal felicity, a very different
ambience in which the lower-middle-class mother of
five drags her way round the crowded stores and
waits on line for rationed goods:

> But her place is empty in the queue at the International,
>   The greengrocer's queue lacks one,

So does the crowd at MacFisheries. There is no one to go
                                            to Freeman's
    To ask if the shoes are done.

The command of meter and rhythm in that poem,
"Variation on a Theme by T. W. Rolleston," is surpassed in the superb elegy for Walter Ramsden of
Pembroke College, Oxford, which moves to one of
Betjeman's most cunning tunes. He conveys within a
tiny compass the sadness of the three old Fellows of
the College who survive Walter Ramsden and who
recall the distant summers and the long-dead rowing
men returning to celebrate their feats on the river.
The observation of detail, the evocation of mood,
the control of tone are masterly:

> They remember, as the coffin to its final obsequations
>   Leaves the gates,
> Buzz of bees in window boxes on their summer ministrations,
>   Kitchen din,
>   Cups and plates,
> And the getting of bump suppers[6] for the long-dead
>   generations
>
>   Coming in,
>   From Eights.

Despite Betjeman's metrical adroitness he has not
felt the need to make the kind of radical innovation
in poetic technique that has distinguished the work
of Pound, Eliot, and Lawrence. Those who reproach
him for his innate conservatism will find it salutary
to reflect on the words put by Anton Chekhov into
Treplev's mouth in *The Seagull* (1896): "I have come
more and more to believe that it is not a question of
new and old forms, but that what matters is that a
man should write without thinking about forms at
all, write because it springs freely from his soul." As
Leslie Stephen remarks in his essay "Gray and His
School," "the ultimate aim of the poet should be to
touch our hearts by showing his own, and not to exhibit his learning, or his fine taste, or his skill in
mimicking the notes of his predecessors." No contemporary poet has displayed more skill than Betjeman in composing variations on traditional
themes, yet his best poetry fulfills the conditions laid
down by Stephen.

One of Betjeman's finest though comparatively
unfamiliar poems, "The Cottage Hospital," is worth

[6]To celebrate the achievement of a number of "bumps" in Eights
Week, when the college eight-oared boats race in single file up the
narrow river, any boat touching the stern of the competitor ahead
taking its place on the following day.

quoting in full to demonstrate his power to touch our hearts. It is a fair criticism of much of his work to say that its appeal is limited to those who share its cultural background (although most good poets yield more pleasure if we are prepared to attune ourselves to their range of knowledge and sensibility). "The Cottage Hospital" makes no such demands upon its readers, even if it is mildly useful to know that a cottage hospital normally serves a rural district. We need to bring nothing to the poem, whose theme is universal, except an alert intelligence and a candid heart. Betjeman's poems usually employ a traditional narrative or logical order, unlike poetry of the modernist movement, which relies on the logic of images, the auditory imagination, the quasi-musical progression. In this poem Betjeman adopts some of the devices of symbolism: there is no logical connection between the fly trapped in the spider's web and the poet's death as envisaged in the final stanza; and we are left to discern for ourselves the links between the sets of images, to respond to the poem's emotional development. "The Cottage Hospital" abounds in felicitous touches. The adjective "fizzing," usually associated with the opening of champagne or ginger-beer bottles, takes on a grim association when applied to the auditory and the visual aspects of the buzzing fly's hopeless struggle. "Inflexible nurses' feet" brilliantly mimes not only the tap of heels on the parquet but also the attitude of the nurses, whose impersonal sympathy must seem like indifference to the dying man, an indifference no less cruel than that displayed by everything in the garden to the dying insect. Yet the drift toward self-pity is halted. Betjeman does not dwell exclusively on the horror of physical dissolution, but recognizes that during his death agony the cycle of natural growth will continue, that in every generation children play on, unmindful of the suffering around them, and that in the midst of death we are in life:

> At the end of a long-walled garden
> in a red provincial town,
> A brick path led to a mulberry—
> scanty grass at its feet.
> I lay under blackening branches
> where the mulberry leaves hung down
> Sheltering ruby fruit globes
> from a Sunday-tea-time heat.
> Apple and plum espaliers
> basked upon bricks of brown;
> The air was swimming with insects,
> and children played in the street.

> Out of this bright intentness
> into the mulberry shade
> *Musca domestica* (housefly)
> swung from the August light
> Slap into slithery rigging
> by the waiting spider made
> Which spun the lithe elastic
> till the fly was shrouded tight.
> Down came the hairy talons
> and horrible poison blade
> And none of the garden noticed
> that fizzing, hopeless flight.

> Say in what Cottage Hospital
> whose pale green walls resound
> With the tap upon polished parquet
> of inflexible nurses' feet
> Shall I myself be lying
> when they range the screens around?
> And say shall I groan in dying,
> as I twist the sweaty sheet?
> Or gasp for breath uncrying,
> as I feel my senses drown'd
> While the air is swimming with insects
> and children play in the street?

SELECTED BIBLIOGRAPHY

I. BIBLIOGRAPHY. M. L. Stapleton, *Sir John Betjeman: A Bibliography of Writings by and About Him* (London, 1974), with an essay by R. J. Mills.

II. COLLECTED WORKS. *Slick But Not Streamlined* (New York, 1947), verse and prose, sel. and with intro. by W. H. Auden; *Selected Poems* (London, 1948), sel. and with preface by J. Sparrow; *Collected Poems* (London, 1958; 2nd ed., 1962; 3rd enl. ed., 1970; 4th enl. ed., 1979), 1st ed. comp. and with intro. by the earl of Birkenhead; *Selected Poems* (London, 1958), in Pocket Poets series; *A Ring of Bells* (London, 1962), poems for children, sel. and with intro. by I. Slade; *Collected Poems* (Boston, 1971), enl. ed. with preface by P. Larkin; *The Best of Betjeman* (London, 1978), verse and prose, sel. by J. Guest; *Uncollected Poems* (London, 1982).

III. SEPARATE WORKS. *Mount Zion; or, In Touch with the Infinite* (London, 1931; facs. repr. 1975), verse, pub. without date but copy in Bodleian Library, Oxford, marked as having been received 19 December 1931; *Ghastly Good Taste* (London, 1933), architecture, rev. and with new intro. by author (London, 1970); *Antiquarian Prejudice* (London, 1937), architecture, a Hogarth Pamphlet, repr. in *First and Last Loves* (London, 1952); *Continual Dew: A Little Book of Bourgeois Verse* (London, 1937); *Sir John Piers* (Mullingar, 1938), verse pamphlet, published under the pseudonym Epsilon, repr. in *Old Lights for New*

Chancels (London, 1940) and *Collected Poems* (London, 1958); *An Oxford University Chest* (London, 1938; facs. repr. 1970), architecture and social history.

Old Lights for New Chancels: Verses Topographical and Amatory (London, 1940); *Vintage London* (London, 1942), topography; *English Cities and Small Towns* (London, 1943), architecture, in Britain in Pictures series; *John Piper* (London, 1944), art criticism, illus. monograph in Penguin Modern Painters series; *New Bats in Old Belfries* (London, 1945), verse.

First and Last Loves (London, 1952), architecture, selected essays; *A Few Late Chrysanthemums* (London, 1954), verse; *Poems in the Porch* (London, 1954), verse pamphlet, illus. by J. Piper, with author's note: "These verses do not pretend to be poetry. They were written for speaking on the wireless, and went out over the Western Region"; the poem "Diary of a Church Mouse" repr. in *Collected Poems*; *The English Town in the Last Hundred Years* (Cambridge, 1956), architecture, the Rede Lecture, delivered at the Senate House, Cambridge, 9 May 1956.

Summoned by Bells (London, 1960), verse autobiography; *Ground Plan to Skyline* (London, 1960), architecture, published under the pseudonym Richard M. Farran, but Bodleian Library possesses letter from Betjeman acknowledging his authorship; *High and Low* (London, 1966), verse.

A Pictorial History of English Architecture (London, 1972), architecture; *London's Historic Railway Stations* (London, 1972), architecture; *West Country Churches* (London, 1973), architecture; *A Nip in the Air* (London, 1974), verse; *Archie and the Strict Baptists* (London, 1977), short story; *Church Poems* (London, 1981), illus. by J. Piper.

IV. Works Edited or Containing Contributions by Betjeman. *Cornwall Illustrated* (London, 1934; enl. ed., 1964), topography, a Shell Guide; *Devon* (London, 1936; rev. eds., 1939, 1955), topography, a Shell Guide; *English, Scottish and Welsh Landscape, 1700–ca. 1860* (London, 1944), verse anthology, with G. Taylor; *Murray's Buckinghamshire Architectural Guide* (London, 1948), architecture, with J. Piper; *Shropshire* (London, 1951), topography, with J. Piper, a Shell Guide; *Gala Day* (London, 1953), topographical miscellany, photographs by I. Bidermanas, text by various hands, contains two short uncollected poems by Betjeman; *English Love Poems* (London, 1957), verse anthology, with G. Taylor; *Collins Guide to English Parish Churches* (London, 1958), architecture, ed. and with long intro. by Betjeman; *Altar and Pew: Church of England Verses* (London, 1959), anthology, ed. and with intro. by Betjeman, in Pocket Poets series; C. T. Turner, *A Hundred Sonnets* (London, 1960), sel. and with intro. by Betjeman and Sir Charles Tennyson; *English Churches* (London, 1964), architecture, ed. by B. Clarke and Betjeman, text by Clarke, illus. mainly chosen by Betjeman; *Victorian and Edwardian London from Old Photographs* (London, 1969), topography, intro. and commentary by Betjeman; *Victorian and Edwardian Oxford from Old Photographs* (London, 1971), topography, sel. by Betjeman and D. Vaisey, intro. by Betjeman; *Victorian and Edwardian Brighton from Old Photographs* (London, 1972), topography, sel. by Betjeman and J. S. Gray, intro. by Betjeman; C. Burkhart, ed., *The Art of Ivy Compton Burnett* (London, 1972), symposium, contains Betjeman's short review of *A Father and His Fate*, repr. from the *Daily Telegraph* (16 August 1957).

V. Biographical and Critical Studies. D. Stanford, *John Betjeman: A Study* (London, 1961), contains valuable material and interesting photographs; J. Brooke, *Ronald Firbank and John Betjeman* (London, 1962), in Writers and Their Work series; L. Sieveking, *John Betjeman and Dorset* (London, 1963), an account by the producer of Betjeman's early broadcasting of "Dorset" and "Westgate-on-Sea"; J. Sparrow, *Independent Essays* (London, 1963), contains essay on Betjeman expanded from preface to *Selected Poems* (1948) and incorporating material from an unsigned review in the *Times Literary Supplement* (12 December 1958); C. M. Bowra, *Memories, 1898–1939* (London, 1966), recalls Betjeman at Oxford and in the early 1930's; P. Larkin, "It Could Only Happen In England," in *Cornhill* magazine, no. 1069 (Autumn 1971), written as the preface to 3rd enl. ed. of *Collected Poems* and containing material from Larkin's review of *Collected Poems* (1958) in *Listen*, VIII, ii (Spring 1959); P. Taylor-Martin, *John Betjeman: His Life and Work* (London, 1983).

W. H. AUDEN
(1907-1973)

Richard Hoggart

THE WANDERER

MANY of us who began our adult reading during the 1930's in England will always think of W. H. Auden with a particular warmth, with the family sense we reserve for those writers who place their fingers on the pulse of a crucial period, whose writings are interwoven with our own intellectual and imaginative maturing. We may differ in our judgments of his later work, but we agree in remaining grateful that at such a time he spoke about our common situation with intelligence and breadth, with urgency and energy and wit; that he spoke—to use a word he would probably have found congenial—memorably. Auden's middle-class and private jokes were as puzzling to some of us as they were to foreigners; but we responded to his high spirits and confidence, his novelist's interest in the details of social life, the exciting concreteness with which he captured salient features of the gray England of the raw suburbs and housing estates, the arterial roads and chromium-and-plastic cafés. With due scaling-down we can say of him what he said of Freud:

> To us he is no more a person
> now but a whole climate of opinion.
> ("In Memory of Sigmund Freud,"
> 67–68)[1]

We are not likely to forget the apt releasing force of such poems as "Dover," "Musée des Beaux Arts," "Sir, No Man's Enemy," and "A Shilling Life," or his vivid vigorous openings, or many scattered passages, such as:

What do you think about England, this country of ours where nobody is well?

[1] Unless noted otherwise, quotations are from E. Mendelson, ed., *Collected Poems* (New York–London, 1976).

or,

> The vows, the tears, the slight emotional signals
> Are here eternal and unremarkable gestures
> Like ploughing or soldiers' songs:
>   ("Dover," 28–30)

or,

> May with its light behaving
> Stirs vessel, eye, and limb,
> The singular and sad
> Are willing to recover.
>   ("May," 1–4)

Yet, though Auden has held a high and special place in English poetic experience since the 1930's, it is easy to feel some force in the argument that his illuminations are sometimes no more than heterogeneous surface insights, and his technical skill more often showy than profound. Auden does occasionally employ certain fashionable clichés of tone and feeling; and he has been overrated in some literary circles. Just as surely, he has been underrated in others. Both attitudes tell something about contemporary cultural conditions in Britain. They tell less about the merits of Auden himself.

Auden remained intellectually and technically open and fluid (these are not polite euphemisms for "fickle") to a degree that is not evident in any of those who were once known with him as "the poets of the thirties." His technical fluidity may be seen in his exercises in various poetic forms, especially after 1940. He practiced, for instance, in terza rima, the villanelle, the sestina, and the ballade. From this point of view the long poems *New Year Letter* (1941), *The Sea and the Mirror* (1945), *For the Time Being* (1945), and *The Age of Anxiety* (1948) are all aspects of the same formal search.

Yet this technical openness probably derives in

part from a more radical quality, from an intellectual quixotry and eclecticism. Auden was something of an intellectual jackdaw, picking up bright pebbles of ideas so as to fit them into exciting conceptual patterns. He was evidently aware of this tendency and of one related to it; that is, of his inadequate submission to the "this-ness," the immediate sensuous stuff, of life. More than once he refers with admiration to Rainer Maria Rilke's "acceptance," or insists that one must "bless what there is for being," or that "every poem is rooted in imaginative awe." "One must be passive to conceive the truth," he says in "Kairos and Logos"; and a fine metaphorical passage by Caliban in *The Sea and the Mirror* ("The shy humiliations . . .") treats the same theme.

We can probably carry this same line of argument even further. For the intellectual unsteadiness seems to be a function of a yet deeper force: of a profound desire to come to ordered moral terms with life, and of a profound difficulty in doing so. *The Double Man* was the American title of *New Year Letter.* It is not one of Auden's best poems, though it has some moving lyric passages; it is nevertheless the fullest exposition of his philosophical problems. The American title was a peculiarly apt image for Auden's position at the time, and might still apply, though with less stress. Throughout his career, but with special force in the period before he became a professed Christian, Auden seems to have been an unusually divided man: searching for a belief toward which he could be truly humble, and finding humility difficult; questioning constantly the tensions within his own nature as both a fallen man and a creative artist. For Auden is primarily a purposive and moral writer. He is in the best sense a teacher, one who loves to influence others; on his weaker side he can be a somewhat gawky prose moralizer. For him—the characteristic assertion indicates both a limitation and the source of much of his strength—"Art is not enough."

Thus we may think of Auden in terms of one of his favorite images—that of the Wanderer, the man on a Quest. His poetry abounds in journeys over hills and across plains, in ascents of mountains and voyages across seas. The image appears in his very early adaptation of a Middle English poem, "Sawles Warde":

> But ever that man goes
> Through place-keepers, through forest trees,
> A stranger to strangers over undried sea. . . .
> ("The Wanderer," 7–9)

Variations occur throughout the 1930's: in the Airman of *The Orators,* in poems such as "Reader to Rider," and in the central characters of the plays *The Dog Beneath the Skin* and *The Ascent of F6.* Later, the same figure appears in the group of Quest sonnets printed in one volume with *New Year Letter,* in *The Sea and the Mirror,* in *The Age of Anxiety,* and in the libretto of *The Rake's Progress.* It is the theme of Auden's one full-length book of criticism, *The Enchaféd Flood* (1951), in which the sea and the desert are considered as complex images of man's spiritual wanderings. Less sustained instances occur throughout all Auden's work, from the early "mad driver pulling on his gloves" to "A Change of Air" (in *About the House*).

In Auden's final decade the Wanderer figure was not quite so prominent. Before then we might have been justified in saying, with many qualifications, that Auden was himself the Wanderer, the Wanderer pursuing the questions outlined above—of the "double man" and, especially, of the double man as an artist.

Any one of a hundred passages could exemplify the first kind of question. The quotation below has been deliberately chosen at random from the *Collected Shorter Poems* so as to indicate the frequency of the theme:

> In my own person I am forced to know
> How much must be forgotten out of love,
> How much must be forgiven, even love.
> ("Canzone," 46–48)

The second question is raised most strikingly in Auden's elegies on other writers, as in these lines on Henry James:

> All will be judged. Master of nuance and scruple,
> Pray for me and for all writers living or dead;
> Because there are many whose works
> Are in better taste than their lives; because there is no end
> To the vanity of our calling: make intercession
> For the treason of all clerks.
>
> Because the darkness is never so distant,
> And there is never much time for the arrogant
> Spirit to flutter its wings . . .
> ("At the Grave of Henry James," 55–60)

Yet it is important to notice that the Quest is not undertaken for its own sake. That would be a romantic delusion, and Auden never had much patience with the self-regarding romantic personality.

The Quest is for order, for pattern and meaning, in life.

The constant interaction of all the qualities we have briefly outlined—Auden's great technical skill (in particular his fine ear and sense of timing); his remarkably acute eye for revealing detail; his intellectual responsiveness, liveliness, and range; his search for spiritual order—all these combine to produce Auden's characteristic tones and themes:

> The earth turns over; our side feels the cold;
> And life sinks choking in the wells of trees:
> The ticking heart comes to a standstill, killed;
> The icing on the pond waits for the boys.
> Among the holly and the gifts I move,
> The carols on the piano, the glowing hearth,
> All our traditional sympathy with birth,
> Put by your challenge to the shifts of Love.
>
> . . .
>
> Language of moderation cannot hide:—
> My sea is empty and its waves are rough;
> Gone from the map the shore where childhood played,
> Tight-fisted as a peasant, eating love;
> Lost in my wake the archipelago,
> Islands of self through which I sailed all day
> Planting a pirate's flag, a generous boy;
> And lost the way to action and to you.
>
> Lost if I steer. Tempest and tide may blow
> Sailor and ship past the illusive reef,
> And I yet land to celebrate with you
> The birth of natural order and true love: . . .
>   ("Through the Looking-Glass," 1–8; 49–60)

1930 TO THE WAR YEARS: THE NEED FOR ORDER

The 1930's in England

Few recent decades in English life have, retrospectively, so boldly defined a character as the 1930's. They seem now like a rising wave after a trough, a wave that preceded disasters.

In domestic affairs the keynote was struck in America, with the Wall Street crash of 1929. From the time this recession reached England until the rearmament boom of the decade's last years, unemployment was an ever-present feature of English life. This was the period of the "Depressed Areas," of what Auden called "the Threadbare Common Man / Begot on Hire-Purchase by Insurance," of "smokeless chimneys, damaged bridges, rotting wharves

and choked canals." It was a period when shabby-genteel clerks could be found selling gimcrack Japanese household sundries from door to door. It was a gray and squalid period, especially for the millions directly affected by unemployment.

Internationally the starting point lies in earlier events, but it may be conveniently taken as Hitler's assumption of the German chancellorship in 1933. Thereafter, as is clear now, there was a giant's march to the explosion of September 1939. The crucial midway stage was the opening of the Spanish Civil War in 1936.

For most young English people with left-wing (or pacifist) interests this was a period of fervent activity, of Popular Front meetings, of milk for Spain and aid for Basque refugees, and of Victor Gollancz's Left Book Club publications. It was marked by a more than usually strong feeling that "the old gang" was appallingly unaware of the changing world situation. It was, in Auden's phrase, a "time of crisis and dismay."

Yet in the apparent simplicity of its issues and in the dramatic or even symbolic quality of its detail (unemployed men standing idle under the lamp posts at street corners; the International Brigades; Guernica) it was a peculiarly heady period. It was in a certain sense enjoyable precisely because of its comparatively clear-cut moral situations and general all-hands-on-deck air. Such a period could call out the best qualities, as well as the more naive enthusiasms, of concerned young Englishmen in all classes, and notably of that traditionally concerned group, the intelligent professional middle class at the universities.

To this class Wystan Hugh Auden belonged. Born in 1907 in York, Auden was the son of a medical officer with wide general and literary interests. His mother was a devout Anglo-Catholic. Subsequently the family moved to the great Midland city of Birmingham, and here no doubt Auden later gained much of his firsthand experience of economic depression. Here too he probably first discovered the unfailing fascination that "the soiled productive cities" had for him, the pull of the great urban sprawls of the commercial Western world (Pittsburgh, Manchester, Detroit, the Ruhr). "My heart has stamped on / The view from Birmingham to Wolverhampton," he said in a light poem he later rejected, and "Tram-lines and slag-heaps, pieces of machinery / That was, and is, my ideal scenery." "Nothing is made in this town," he said of Dover, and the implication was plainly pejorative.

W. H. AUDEN

At Gresham's School, Holt, Auden talked first of becoming an engineer and read technological works, chiefly on mining and geology. But in his early teens, prompted by a friend, he began to write poetry. Thomas Hardy was his first master—an admirably humane man and a magnificently varied and idiosyncratic versifier who yet is rarely so completely successful as to discourage a young practitioner. At Christ Church, Oxford, Auden had reached the stage at which he could one day tell his tutor, with an impressive confidence, that only T. S. Eliot was worth the serious consideration of poetic aspirants. But this was one necessary moment in a poet's development, and there were other influences, notably Anglo-Saxon and Middle English poetry, that continued to fascinate Auden. At Oxford, too, Wilfred Owen and Edward Thomas were admitted to the accepted canon of ancestors for his generation. Auden's friendship with Stephen Spender began (and had about it, typically, something of the English public schools' prefect-to-fag[2] relationship); and his first links were made with others who were to become writers and publicists in what has variously been called the Thirties Group, the Pylon School, and the Auden Group. Incidentally, the members were united more by common assumptions and written influence than by actual meetings. The three best-known poets of the group, Auden, Spender, and C. Day Lewis, did not meet as a trio until the late 1940's, at a cultural conference in Venice.

After a stay in pre-Hitler Berlin there followed for Auden a short period of school teaching, which he seems to have deeply enjoyed. He had, we have already implied, a strong charismatic sense, a good teacher's love and firmness, energy and fidelity. Meanwhile, his first book, *Poems*, had been published in 1930 and had been followed in 1932 by *The Orators*, an acute, fantastic, and vigorous attack on the state of England and the English establishment. In 1935 he married Erika Mann. As the decade progressed he became more and more engaged, not only in his craft as a poet but in the time-consuming borderland where political affairs and the practice of writing mingle. A largely light-hearted visit to Iceland with Louis MacNeice in 1936 was followed by visits to Spain in 1937 and to China and the U.S. with Christopher Isherwood in 1938. A few months before the beginning of World War II Auden settled

[2]An English public-school boy who acts as a servant to an older schoolmate.

in America, and in due time adopted American citizenship.

Politics, Psychology, "Love"

Centring the eye on their essential human element

Some critics suggest that Auden is a peculiarly English poet, and that in leaving England he severed essential roots. The first suggestion is to a large extent true, in both more and less obvious senses. Local and family concerns are very dear to Auden; and his bedside book in New York was a work on the mineralogy of the Lake District. More, the cast of Auden's mind was markedly formed by some of the main elements in the English tradition. His is not a voice from the American Middle West or from Central Europe: "England to me is my own tongue."

Yet does the second suggestion—that Auden weakened his poetry by a physical removal—necessarily follow? Wherever he lived, the bent of Auden's mind, the way he approached the problems that interested him—his particular form of complicated cranky independence as well as his tough gentleness—remained recognizably English. But the nature of these problems had something to do with the decision as to where he might best live. Auden's interest was in people in urban societies, in people living through their perennial moral and metaphysical problems in megalopolitan settings. London or some large English provincial city might have provided such a setting; but England is small and domestically intimate, its cultural life demandingly homely. Auden needed a kind of anonymity within an urban mass, and this New York provided (as well as providing sufficient money and the friendships Auden needed):

> More even than in Europe, here,
> The choice of patterns is made clear
> Which the machine imposes, what
> is possible and what is not,
> To what conditions we must bow
> In building the Just City now.
> (*New Year Letter*, pt. 3)

Auden is a socially unrooted poet who could have been at home in any of the large urban centers of the Western hemisphere. Whatever he might have lost by leaving England was not central to these gifts: in America, he seemed understandably to feel, he was at the chief pressure point of forces that were changing the face of life in the West.

Auden's isolation in a crowd reflects a constant quality of his verse, a quality most plainly indicated in the early figures of the Hawk and the Airman (*The Orators*). The Airman is physically isolated from the messy, close disorder of life below and, more important, able from his post of observation to detect therein some pattern not visible to those immersed in the details of personal involvement. Similarly, Auden's is often an abstracting and generalizing intelligence. In some sense very difficult to define fairly, we may say that he is emotionally detached from much of what he describes, that he has a "clinical" quality.

Though Auden speaks to and for many in his generation, his speech commonly lacks certain kinds of intimacy. There are important areas of experience, particularly those concerned with relations between the sexes, which he either does not touch or touches in a perfunctory or stereotyped or briskly impersonal manner (falling in love, married life, some forms of insecurity, the tragic, gay, and dignified tensions in the day-to-day life of "ordinary" people). At such points he is likely to move into a detached "placing" of detail by the use of successive definite articles:

> The boarding-house food, the boarding-house faces,
> The rain-spoilt picnics in the windswept places,
> The camera lost and the suspicion,
> The failure in the putting competition,
> The silly performance on the pier . . .
> (*The Ascent of F6*, Act I, sc. ii)

A poet's weaknesses are often peculiarly revealing. There are forms of emotional wobble in, say Alfred Tennyson, or of anger and enthusiasm in Robert Browning, or of sensuous indulgence in Dylan Thomas; these weaknesses at once limit the poets and bring them closer to us. In Auden's poetry there are certainly struggles, but they are expressed through a continuous argument with the self rather than through the play of personal emotions. The "I" is there, but is rarely at a loss with itself; it may be exploring its own weaknesses but always does so with an air of control, with the implication that certain areas are sealed off and the limits of the struggle grasped. These are the roots Auden lacks and would have lacked even if he had remained in England.

This quality seems related to the fact that Auden's poems tend to be remembered not so much for their sensuous effects (apart from a few striking exceptions) as for the articulation of their phrasing and the pattern of their moral insights. His poems have little color, smell, or touch. He once said that he tended to think of them as "squares and oblongs"; that is, as geometric shapes rather than as, for example, extended images. The bare shapes are the shapes of his dialectic. Similarly, his epithets usually have a conceptual rather than a sensuous relationship to the nouns they qualify; they comment rather than describe. Where several epithets are used they do not cumulatively describe their noun so much as set up an intellectual friction with the noun and with each other:

> And the active hands must freeze
> Lonely on the separate knees.
> ("Twelve Songs," VI, 7–8)

Auden does not say "green slope" or "grassy slope" but "tolerant enchanted slope"; a lover's head on his arm is caught, beautifully, as a moral rather than a visual pattern:

> Lay your sleeping head, my love,
> Human on my faithless arm.
> ("Lullaby," 1–2)

Again, though Auden's similes are rhetorical, often boldly rhetorical, they usually gain their effect from the yoking of an abstract idea to a vividly concrete fact, from a vivid metaphorical personification of ideas: "Problems like relatives standing," and, "Will Ferdinand be as fond of a Miranda/Familiar as a stocking?" And Auden's geography is almost always economic or political geography; thus his poem about the Chinese port of Macao opens "A weed from Catholic Europe, it took root." Or his landscapes are symbols of human dilemmas.

A varied intelligence, a congenitally pattern-making mind, and a persistent moral drive: all these place the emphases in Auden's work firmly on man rather than nature, and on man-in-the-city rather than man-in-the-fields. It was inevitable that in the 1930's Auden should pursue his psychological and social interests, should be purposively trying to create an order in his experience:

> Our hunting fathers told the story
> Of the sadness of the creatures,
> Pitied the limits and the lack
> Set in their finished features;

Saw in the lion's intolerant look,
Behind the quarry's dying glare,
Love raging for the personal glory
    That reason's gift would add,
                . . .
Who, nurtured in that fine tradition,
    Predicted the result,
Guessed Love by nature suited to
    The intricate ways of guilt . . . ?
("Our Hunting Fathers," 1–8; 11–14)

The bent of Auden's political interests ensured that he was often thought, mistakenly, to be a Marxist. He did find much to admire in Marxist analysis; the argument that "freedom is the recognition of necessity" alone would have won his interest. He did work, incidentally, for left-wing causes ("the expending of powers / On the flat ephemeral pamphlet and the boring meeting"). Of this kind of poem the most representative, whether by Auden or by any of the engaged poets of the 1930's, is "Spain 1937," with its characteristic refrains: "Yesterday all the past," "Tomorrow, perhaps, the future," and "But today the struggle."

But for Auden this activity was inspired chiefly by his urgent search for spiritual order and moral responsibility. At bottom his attitude had more in common with that of some conservative and right-wing intellectuals than with that of the more progressive, "free," and romantically expectant left-wing intellectuals.

And his psychological interest was deeper than his political interest. Why were so many out of love with themselves? How had we become a nation of "aspirins and weak tea"? At this stage Auden was predominantly interested in the plight of the specifically neurotic, of "the lost, the lonely, the unhappy," of "the malcontented who might have been," of the anxious and fear-ridden. The interest remained, but it widened into a concern with a more radical anxiety. In the 1930's Auden's reading of Freud and George Walther Groddeck,[3] notably, encouraged a kind of modern myth-making, since both these writers communicate an unusual imaginative excitement in their presentation of concepts themselves richly suggestive:

Sir, no man's enemy, forgiving all
But will his negative inversion, be prodigal:
Send to us power and light, a sovereign touch

[3]Groddeck (1866–1934) was a German psychotherapist who made a special study of psychosomatic illness.

Curing the intolerable neural itch,
The exhaustion of weaning, the liar's quinsy,
And the distortions of ingrown virginity.
Prohibit sharply the rehearsed response
And gradually correct the coward's stance:

The address to a negatively defined power was an early indication that politics and psychology were only aspects of a more central interest, of Auden's concern with the spiritual dilemmas of individuals beyond the reach of political and psychological reforms. This is, of course, a religious interest; and though it showed itself plainly only toward the end of the decade it had many earlier intimations. Particularly, Auden returns again and again to a single word, "Love"—and uses it elusively:

O Love, the interest itself in thoughtless Heaven,
        (*The English Auden*, pt. 4:
        "Poems 1931–1936," no. VI)

and,

The word is Love
Surely one fearless kiss would cure
The million fevers . . .
        (*Look, Stranger!*, no. XXX)

and,

Birth of a natural order and of Love. . . .
        (*Look, Stranger!*, no. IX)

"Love" seems to have been an undefined but powerful third force, a quality both inside man and affecting man from outside, which at once offered him hope and indicated the perennial and personal nature of his situation. The history of Auden's earlier mental journey is, roughly speaking, that of the gradual discovery of the potentialities of this word's meaning for him—from an unresolved assertion to a rich and complex ambiguity that embraces the idea of Christian love, of conscience, of charity and grace. When that moment was reached Auden was an avowed Christian. The more directly political and psychological interests had fallen into place and the first phase was over. It is easy to exercise hindsight in such matters. In Auden's development the lines are clear and expressed:

Perhaps I always knew what they were saying:
Even the early messengers who walked
Into my life from books
                . . .

Love was the word they never said aloud

. . .

And all the landscape round them pointed to
The calm with which they took complete desertion
As proof that you existed.

It was true. . . .

("The Prophets," 1–3; 7; 18–20)

Public and Private Speech

There is a small body of Auden's very early verse whose qualities are different from those we normally associate with his poetry in the 1930's. These poems are dry and gnomic:

Love by ambition
Of definition
Suffers partition
And cannot go
From yes to no
For no is not love, no is no . . .

("Too Dear, Too Vague," 1–6)

Since the impulse behind these poems is close to that which informs some of Auden's poems of the 1950's, we are reminded once more of the coherence of his intellectual development. But in the 1930's Auden was more characteristically a poet of perceptive epigrammatic verse, of various kinds of conversational meter, and of a number of remarkable lyrics.

The epigrammatic manner clearly took force from Auden's purposively ranging mind and from his insistent rhetorical inclinations. The epigrams usually enshrine memorable social and psychological observation, sometimes not so much crisp as slick, but generally intelligent and pithy:

Steep roads, a tunnel through the downs, are the
approaches;
A ruined pharos overlooks a constructed bay;
The sea-front is almost elegant; all this show
Has, somewhere inland, a vague and dirty root:
Nothing is made in this town.

But the dominant Norman castle floodlit at night
And the trains that fume in the station built on the sea
Testify to the interests of its regular life:
Here live the experts on what the soldiers want
And who the travellers are, . . .

("Dover," 1–10)

Poems such as this are among the more notable instances of the way in which the climate of the 1930's could affect a well-equipped poetic mind. There were other manners of "speaking to the times" that said more for the earnestness of the poet's intentions than for their grasp of poetry's function. We may grant that society was "sick" and that the poets urgently wished to contribute usefully. Yet by the nature of contemporary culture they spoke only to a small minority. How could they speak more widely? Could they in any proper way compete with the truly popular voices?

To this aspect of Auden's work belong the two plays he wrote with Christopher Isherwood and the verse with Louis MacNeice, between 1935 and 1938. In some of their techniques for presenting social problems and for obtaining a sense of urgent participation from the audience they seem to have learned something from the early "epic theater" of the German Marxist playwright Bertolt Brecht. They made use also of hints from German expressionism, from popular songs and variety and music-hall performances. The plays are lively, intelligent, and witty. To those, out of love with a glossy commercial theater, who saw them at Rupert Doone's Group Theatre in London, they must have been unusually exciting. But they have the faults of their originating assumptions. They are lively charades with passages of striking banality and pert "knowingness." Their characters are not merely "types"—that may be true of certain good plays. But they are usually cliché-ridden or idea-ridden types, Freudian or Marxian puppets. Both plays have some good lyrics and choruses, but only *The Ascent of F6* is now worth close attention. In this play the Quest theme, because it is more deeply probed, inspires some scenes much more searching and eloquent than any in *The Dog Beneath the Skin*.

During the 1930's Auden's demotic interests best served his poetry in the practice of the epigrammatic line and of various conversational meters. In the latter he aimed at a laconic and loose-limbed, a dryly ironic or apparently offhand tone of voice. The tone had begun to appear by mid-decade, as in the unbuttoned, in medias res, colloquially reflective opening of "Musée des Beaux Arts":

About suffering they were never wrong,
The Old Masters: how well they understood
Its human position; how it takes place
While someone else is eating or opening a window or
just walking dully along;

. . .

In Brueghel's *Icarus*, for instance: how everything turns
away

Quite leisurely from the disaster; the ploughman may
Have heard the splash, the forsaken cry,
But for him it was not an important failure; the sun
    shone
As it had to. . . .

                ("Musée des Beaux Arts," 1–4; 14–18)

For this manner (especially as it was adopted in his often admirable symbolic sonnets) Auden took much from Rilke. But the most important influence was William Butler Yeats, whose conversational meters Auden most perceptively praised. Yeats's "Easter 1916" begins:

        I have met them at close of day
        Coming with vivid faces
        From counter or desk among grey
        Eighteenth-century houses.

The echo can be plainly heard (though really in no more than a very competent imitation) in Auden's "1st September 1939":

        I sit in one of the dives
        On Fifty-Second Street
        Uncertain and afraid
        As the clever hopes expire . . .

The conversational manner was predominant in *Another Time* (1940). Subsequently, it was influenced by Auden's experience in America, where the rhythms of colloquial speech often seem more flexible than they are in England:

        The sailors come ashore
        Out of their hollow ships,
        Mild-looking middle class boys
        Who read the comic strips;
        One baseball game is more
        To them than fifty Troys.

        They look a bit lost, set down
        In this unamerican place . . .
                ("Fleet Visit," 1–8)

Since this is essentially a relaxed manner it sometimes encouraged Auden's characteristic technical faults, and so became slipshod rather than relaxed, slick instead of laconic, informedly glib rather than finely allusive. At its best its shrewdly loose articulation allowed it to carry very effectively the intelligent, unvatic, contemporary observations Auden often wished to make.

Most of the foregoing comments on Auden's style have a bearing on his social and psychological interests. His lyrics exist much more in their own right, and spring from simpler but very firm poetic roots. This is an aspect of Auden's work that his evident moral drive can easily lead us to underrate. Auden's admirable lyrics have been a continuous feature of his verse, from a fine group in the mid-1930's that includes such poems as "O who can ever praise enough" to "Deftly, Admiral" (*Nones*, 1952). We remember here also the quick and witty choral songs such as "At last the secret is out," the comic and satiric poems such as "O for doors to be open," the nonsense rhyme in *Nones*, and "Willow-Wren and the Stare." The note that seems most characteristic and most impressive in the lyrics is of a kind of stillness; not a passivity nor always the stillness of menace, but a held imaginative stasis where the spirit looks steadily and often tenderly at a still moment of experience. It is all, of course, as much a matter of sound as of sense:

        Dear, though the night is gone,
        Its dream still haunts to-day,
           ("Twelve Songs,"
               no. IV, 1–2)

and,

        Fish in the unruffled lakes
        The swarming colours wear . . .
           ("Twelve Songs," V, 1–2)

and,

        Deftly, admiral, cast your fly
        Into the slow deep hover,
           ("Five Songs,"
               no. I, 1–2)

and,

        Now the leaves are falling fast,
        Nurse's flowers will not last;
        Nurses to the graves are gone,
        And the prams go rolling on.

        Whispering neighbours, left and right,
        Pluck us from the real delight;
        And the active hands must freeze
        Lonely on the separate knees.
           ("Twelve Songs," VI, 1–8)

FROM THE FORTIES TO THE MID-FIFTIES: THE EXPLORATION OF FORMS

"Original Anxiety"

From 1940 to the mid-1950's, Auden moved around the American continent fairly consistently, chiefly as a lecturer and teacher at universities and colleges. Then, from 1956 to 1961, he was professor of poetry at Oxford and so spent some time regularly in England. From 1949 to 1957 he had a spring and summer home on Ischia, an island off Naples. That yielded in 1958 to another spring and summer home in Kirchstetten, lower Austria. He died en route from there to Oxford, where, at Christ Church, he had a "grace and favour" cottage[4] in the last year of his life. But for more than thirty years—from 1939 to 1972—Auden's home base or point of rest was overwhelmingly New York.

The move to America roughly coincided with the clear and frequent appearance in Auden's poetry of a number of new influences. If Freud and Marx were the most striking and typical intellectual influences of the 1930's, then those of the 1940's were Søren Kierkegaard and Reinhold Niebuhr.

The exploration by the Danish "existentialist" theologian Kierkegaard of "original anxiety," the basic insecurity of man that marks both his fallen condition and his possible salvation—this in particular replaced for Auden, as a fruitful area of thought and a seminal metaphor, the psychologists' more scientific analysis of the nature of anxiety. "Psychotherapy will not get much further until it recognizes that the true significance of a neurosis is teleological," Auden now said.

Similarly, Reinhold Niebuhr's analysis of the moral dilemmas and social involvements of man submerged Auden's rather scrappy and qualified interest in Marxism. Niebuhr was, from 1930 to 1960, professor of applied Christianity at Union Theological Seminary, New York; the most accessible exposition of his outlook is in the two volumes of Gifford Lectures, *The Nature and Destiny of Man*. Auden's sense of continuous struggle in the will makes it easy to understand why he should have been drawn to Niebuhr's form of Protestantism—Auden was in fact a Protestant Episcopalian. We may assume that he would have been in sympathy with this statement by Niebuhr: "The Catholic emphasizes the initial act of intellectual assent; the Protestant the continuous process of voluntary assent." Nor was Auden's awareness of society likely to allow him ever to become mystical or contemplative.

Such statements are bound to oversimplify; there are obviously many other interweaving lines of force. But these were the dominant and most revealing forces at this time. Auden quoted Kierkegaard repeatedly, in his poetry and prose; and some of his poems of the 1940's are like versified paragraphs of Niebuhr.

Auden's social and psychological interests remained, but were related now to a central religious root. Man is seen as fallen yet free, and this is his paradox. He is bound by his "creatureliness" yet always tempted to deny the limitations this imposes; he is free to exercise moral choice for good or ill. Hence his "willfulness" in both the senses of "possessing free will" and "prompt to disobey." He works out his destiny here, historically, in time; his consciousness of time informs his awareness of guilt and of possible grace. This awareness marks man's unique situation and is the ground of his anxiety: "Anxiety is the inevitable concomitant of the paradox of freedom and finiteness in which man is involved," said Niebuhr.

Man is unfinished but forever has the possibility of "becoming." By contrast the animals and plants, which appear frequently in Auden's poems as images of unawareness, are perfect, finished, and forever unpromising, unconscious of identity, time, and choice:

> Let them leave language to their lonely betters
> Who count some days and long for certain letters;
> We, too, make noises when we laugh or weep,
> Words are for those with promises to keep.
>
> ("Their Lonely Betters," 13–16)

And elsewhere,

> The hour-glass whispers to the lion's paw,
> The clock-towers tell the gardens day and night,
> How many errors Time has patience for,
> How wrong they are in being always right.
>
> ("Our Bias," 1–4)

So far this description might seem to suggest an anxiety-ridden outlook that could easily become

---

[4] A royal or church residence provided for aged retainers who have served the crown, the church, or some other important institution.

querulous or nagging. Auden is never querulous and rarely nags; his purposiveness and sense of humor both relieve him. "Accept the present in its fullness," he says in a characteristically firm and positive passage. Man is a social creature, and a sign of the individual's growing spiritual maturity is the decision not to try one of the many forms of escape from this commitment, but to stay where he is, soberly and steadily to work out his destiny with the intransigent material of human relations. To work for civility, and to build the Just City—these are favorite phrases of Auden's. The building of the Just City can never be completed, he adds, but could not be even an aspiration were there not outside man an order of which his dream of the Just City is a reflection.

In all this, "Love" is still often invoked by Auden, though now with a more complex sense of its difficulty and also of its ineluctability:

> Let no one say I Love until aware
> What huge resources it will take to nurse
>   One ruining speck, one tiny hair
> That casts a shadow through the universe. . . .
>   ("In Sickness and in Health," 25–28)

Auden's general approach is well illustrated in a vigorous and hortatory poem, "Memorial for the City." The theme is the destruction of traditional European values as they are expressed in the ancient city-architecture of the Continent, and the now more plainly exposed dilemma of fallen man immersed in time:

> The steady eyes of the crow and the camera's candid eye
> See as honestly as they know how, but they lie.
> The crime of life is not time. Even now, in this night
> Among the ruins of the Post-Vergilian city
> Where our past is a chaos of graves and the barbed-wire
>   stretches ahead
> Into our future till it is lost to sight,
> Our grief is not Greek: as we bury our dead
> We know without knowing there is reason for what we
>   bear,
> That our hurt is not a desertion, that we are to pity
> Neither ourselves nor our city;
> Whoever the searchlights catch, whatever the
>   loudspeakers blare,
> We are not to despair.
>   ("Memorial for the City," 24–35)

In a later poem, "The Shield of Achilles," Thetis, the mother of Achilles, looks over the armorer He-

phaestos' shoulder at the decorative scenes on the shield. In the sort of world represented on the shield, there is time and event; but without the sense of sin or the hope of redemption, such a world is, in the most terribly exact sense, meaningless. Auden counterpoints the description of the shield with scenes from similarly "unsaved" worlds:

> A ragged urchin, aimless and alone,
>   Loitered about that vacancy, a bird
> Flew up to safety from his well-aimed stone:
>   That girls are raped, that two boys knife a third,
>   Were axioms to him who'd never heard
> Of any world where promises were kept,
> Or one could weep because another wept.
>   (53–59)

The altered emphasis in Auden's preoccupations often brought with it a greater leanness and firmness of attitude. He seemed less attentive to the rich muddle of life. But we may be disproportionately fascinated, as well as seriously concerned, with the sheer detail of experience. In some ways Auden's approach in the 1940's and early 1950's was more austere than it had been, closer to the kind of promise made in his earlier poems. And in seeking to express this new pattern of interests Auden developed some sinewy and complex verse of great power and interest.

Symbolic Landscape and the Long Line

For a few years after his arrival in America, Auden apparently decided that he would, predominantly, write long poems (poems occupying all or most of one volume) whose structural complexities would embody a variety of materials, tones, and intellectual approaches. Later his collections were of shorter poems, ranging from lyrics to what might be called longish short poems (from sixty to a hundred lines).

But between 1941 and 1948 Auden produced four long poems: *New Year Letter, The Sea and the Mirror, For the Time Being,* and *The Age of Anxiety.* Poetically, the first is the least interesting, though, as we noted earlier, it has some moving lyric passages and is almost everywhere lively; and the Quest sonnets that complete the volume are more than good derivatives from Rilke. The title poem draws to its close, all argument aside, with a joyful invocation to God:

> O Unicorn among the cedars,
>   To whom no magic charm can lead us,

White childhood moving like a sigh
Through the green woods unharmed . . .
                              (pt. 3)

The Sea and the Mirror is subtitled *A Commentary on Shakespeare's "The Tempest,"* and is chiefly about the relations between art, the artist, and society. For each character Auden produces a different verse form, often a highly elaborate one. The result is sometimes merely curious, though the performance is technically brilliant; and some parts (Alonso's address to Ferdinand, Miranda's villanelle) are not only brilliant but more deeply engaging.

For the Time Being, a Christmas oratorio dedicated to the memory of Auden's mother, is more emotionally harmonious than the other long poems, probably because of the greater simplicity and firmness of Auden's theme—of belief in sin and hope for humility. Here, not surprisingly, is to be found the peculiarly "still" lyric note we remarked earlier:

Let number and weight rejoice
In this hour of their translation
Into conscious happiness:
For the whole in every part,
The truth at the proper centre . . .
        ("The Annunciation," pt. 4)

The Age of Anxiety is brilliant, perverse, disjointed, a "baroque eclogue" with all the extraneous ornamentation and deviousness that such a subtitle implies, a structural experiment that does not succeed. Yet even here, in a meter drawn from Anglo-Saxon verse, a few sections achieve an unusual gaunt beauty. A tired clerk in a New York bar nostalgically describes childhood in a city that might just as well have been Birmingham or Dortmund:

. . . how fagged coming home through
The urban evening. Heavy like us
Sank the gas-tanks—it was supper time.
In hot houses helpless babies and
Telephones gabbled untidy cries,
And on embankments black with burnt grass
Shambling freight-trains were shunted away
Past crimson clouds.
        (pt. 2: "The Seven Ages")

Perhaps in the last three of these long poems Auden was tackling his own form of a problem similar to that of T. S. Eliot in *The Waste Land* (though aspects of the same problem in its contemporary form can be seen at least as far back as Robert Browning's *The Ring and the Book*, 1868–1869): how to achieve a form that would embody the detail of social dilemmas, the diverse pressures of moral problems, and the necessary changes of tone, angle, and level of suggestion—in a shape somehow organic to the theme. Auden does not succeed: *For the Time Being* is comparatively harmonious but not really complex; *The Sea and the Mirror* is complex and in a sense unified, but gains its unity chiefly from the assumed background of *The Tempest*.

In his shorter poems Auden continued to use several kinds of conversational meter and seemed still to regard some of this verse as a sort of "public" utterance, though now to a public accepted as small, and sympathetic by predisposition. This is an aspect of what Auden has called "unofficial poetry" and "comic" art:

From now on the only popular art will be comic art—and this will be unpopular with the Management. It is the law which it cannot alter which is the subject of all comic art. . . . Every poet stands alone. [But] this does not mean that he sulks mysteriously in a corner by himself.
        ("Squares and Oblongs," in *Poets at Work*)

Cheerful and debunking comic art can help to preserve self-respect in increasingly "generalized" societies. Against "the lie of Authority" a poet, as one of the few individuals—by profession—in modern society, will propose the idea of the personal life.

Auden seems to have a more deliberate and prescribed purpose in his later use of the conversational voice than he had earlier. He seems to be aiming not at a widely acceptable demotic speech but at a low-temperature verse of intelligent observation and comment:

[We] would in the old grand manner
Have sung from a resonant heart.
But, pawed-at and gossiped-over
By the promiscuous crowd,
Concocted by editors
Into spells to befuddle the crowd,
All words like Peace and Love,
All sane affirmative speech,
Had been soiled, profaned, debased
To a horrid mechanical screech:
No civil style survived
That pandemonium
But the wry, the sotto-voce,
Ironic and monochrome:
        ("We Too Had Known
         Golden Hours," 11–24)

Verse such as this can induce its own cult snob-beries and is no doubt not meant to be of the first im-portance in the body of Auden's work. It is "occa-sional" verse in a valid sense—verse written for and commenting on specific occasions—and within these limits it is usually acute and enjoyable. Inevitably, it retains some of the faults of its kind: it is sometimes slapdash and unmuscular, a versified *New Yorker* journalese that may be observant and intelligent but is too brittle to cut deep.

In his imagery Auden turns instinctively to land-scape: he commonly speaks of "villages of the heart," "our landscape of pain," "suburbs of fear," and so on. We may say roughly that he has two dis-tinctive kinds of natural imagery: that in which land-scape is an illuminating backcloth to some human social activity, and that in which landscape is a sym-bol for an inner dilemma in human personality. Again speaking generally, we may say that the first predominates in Auden's earlier poetry, and the sec-ond later. In the present day the great industrial cities of America might provide the first kind of imagery; and the Apennine backbone of Italy, dropping to its coastal plains, might provide the second. But the scenery common to the Northern and Midland Pen-nines of Auden's childhood and youth continued more than any other to be drawn on for both types of imagery. The lusher scenes of southern England—or the hollyhocks and lawns of Tennyson's rectory gar-dens—had little appeal for him.

In the 1930's Auden was more likely than later to invoke the densely packed, intensively worked-over, huddled, and smoky industrial-revolution landscapes of the Pennines, the grim and uncom-promising little towns of the foothills and valleys or the great black sprawling cities on the plains below. He did write also of the bare, stark uplands then, but was still likely to speak of them, with their aban-doned workings and derelict mines, as illustrations of the same direct social interest: to use them, in short, as backcloths. And of course he loved them in and for themselves:

> Always my boy of wish returns
> To those peat-stained deserted burns
> That feed the Wear and Tyne and Tees.
> (*New Year Letter*, pt. 3)

During the 1950's landscape became for Auden more and more a means of visually symbolizing the spiritual conflicts in man, and to this need the in-volved geometry of the upper hills speaks best. As in so much, Rilke had guided Auden to what he sought here:

One of the constant problems of the poet is how to ex-press abstract ideas in concrete terms. . . . Rilke is almost the first poet since the seventeenth century to find a fresh solution . . . [he] thinks of the human in terms of the non-human . . . one of [his] most characteristic devices is the ex-pression of human life in terms of landscape. It is this kind of imagery which is beginning to appear in English poetry.

Certainly Auden's use of landscape in the 1950's expresses his characteristic urge to wrest meaningful patterns from experience. But it is important to recognize that the landscapes are not being wrenched into the form of symbols. They speak to him—had indeed always spoken to him, though not always receiving his later comprehension—as symbols, as "sacred objects." They spoke to him before he could consciously decipher their language:

> . . . There
> In Rookhope I was first aware;
> Of Self and Not-Self, Death and Dread:
> Audits were entrances which led
> Down to the Outlawed, to the Others.
> The Terrible, the Merciful, the Mothers;
> Alone in the hot day I knelt
> Upon the edge of shafts and felt
> The deep *urmutterfurcht* that drives
> Us into knowledge all our lives . . .
> (*New Year Letter*, pt. 3)

The process is not a fitting of pictures to ideas, but is part of Auden's natural manner of establishing relations with the outside world, of establishing "the relations of man—as a history-making person—to nature":

> Whenever I begin to think
> About the human creature we
> Must nurse to sense and decency,
> An English area comes to mind,
> I see the native of my kind
> As a locality I love . . .

After the war Auden exercised this interest in sym-bolic landscape much more closely, especially in what were described earlier as longish short poems. The sequence began notably with a remarkable poem, "In Praise of Limestone," and was continued in the seven "Bucolics" in *The Shield of Achilles*

(1955). The symbolic landscape and the long line that usually accompanies it combined to make one of the most important and exciting postwar developments in Auden's work.

Auden would muse before a large and varied landscape and seek to evoke from within it his sense that it symbolized an extensive pattern of human dilemmas. In the following passage the people who remain within the gregarious life of the valleys are contrasted with the exceptional few who go elsewhere:

> Adjusted to the local needs of valleys
> Where everything can be touched or reached by walking,
> Their eyes have never looked into infinite space
>
> · · ·
>
> That is why, I suppose,
> The best and worst never stayed here long but sought
> Immoderate soils where the beauty was not so external,
> The light less public and the meaning of life
> Something more than a mad camp. "Come!" cried the
> granite wastes,
> "How evasive is your humour, how accidental
> Your kindest kiss, how permanent is death." (Saints-
> to-be
> Slipped away sighing.) "Come!" purred the clays and
> gravels.
> "On our plains there is room for armies to drill; rivers
> Wait to be tamed and slaves to construct you a tomb
> In the grand manner; soft as the earth is mankind and
> both
> Need to be altered." (Intendant Caesars rose and
> Left, slamming the door.) But the really reckless were
> fetched
> By an older colder voice, the oceanic whisper:
> "I am the solitude that asks and promises nothing;
> That is how I shall set you free. There is no love;
> There are only the various envies, all of them sad."
>
> ("In Praise of Limestone," 32–34; 44–60)

Here Auden is using his long line and verse-sentence, which have themselves some of the qualities of his second kind of landscape. The lines are syllabically counted (13:11 syllables, with elision of all contiguous vowels and through "h"[5]). They have a sinuous, following-through, flexible though connected movement; they follow the ideas suggested by the panorama, varying pitch easily as Auden turns to a new aspect or alters his angle of approach or branches into a side consideration. They hold always to the main thread of the thought, though

[5]The elision of an "h" when it is preceded by a vowel; for example, "the house" becomes "th'ouse."

directed from moment to moment by its sinuosities and qualifications.

The intention differs from that which produced the curt, epigrammatic line of the mid-1930's and probably owes most, insofar as it is indebted to Auden's earlier practice, to the conversational verse of the later 1930's. The long verse-sentence is unusually free from the more obvious demands of line-endings (as, for instance, Auden's laconic sonnets necessarily were not). It is less immediately restricting than the three- or four-beat iambic line of Yeats—though that line was so magnificently varied in Yeats's hands that its apparent limitations turned to real advantage. Auden, we know, immensely admired the Yeatsian line and had sometimes used it. But a longer and more loosely articulated line seemed more natural to him.

Like most of the valuable developments in Auden's verse this line is frequently marred, in this case by jarring and artistically unjustified changes of tone and attitude, and especially by a tiresome overinsistence on remaining too casual. We see the point, in the passage quoted above, about "Intendant Caesars . . . slamming the door" (it echoes an assertion by Josef Goebbels), but the combination is intellectually pert. On the other hand, the verb "fetched" in the same line has a nice ambiguity, drawn from Auden's acquaintance with contemporary American vernacular. To most English readers the verb will mean "brought" or "called away"; to an American it was likely to mean also "emotionally bowled over" (as when jazz enthusiasts said that a solo performer "fetched" them). And this second association—of something slightly hysterical—does add to the ironic texture of the passage.

At its best the long verse-sentence has a beautifully easy spoken note, an attractive mixture of colloquialism and serious observation, of wit and of moral concern—all managed with a verbal and aural skill that hardly any other living poet can approach. The shape and movement of the poem acts out, as it were, the tense dialectic of the poet's will, mind, and heart. In the following passage Auden opens on a typical landscape, limestone hills above the wide plains and their towns. The landscape is both actually and symbolically moving to him:

> If it form the one landscape that we the inconstant ones
> Are consistently homesick for, this is chiefly
> Because it dissolves in water. Mark these rounded slopes
> With their surface fragrance of thyme and, beneath,

A secret system of caves and conduits; hear the springs
   That spurt out everywhere with a chuckle,
Each filling a private pool for its fish and carving
   Its own little ravine whose cliffs entertain
The butterfly and the lizard; examine this region
   Of short distances and definite places . . .

(1–10)

So the complex interplay of human motives for which this landscape speaks begins to be developed. The poem closes on a view in perspective of the statues man makes out of this same rock, and farther back—picking up again the wider panoramic view of the opening—of the rock in its aboriginal landscape:

. . . In so far as we have to look forward
   To death as a fact, no doubt we are right: But if
Sins can be forgiven, if bodies rise from the dead,
   These modifications of matter into
Innocent athletes and gesticulating fountains,
   Made solely for pleasure, make a further point:
The blessed will not care what angle they are regarded
     from,
   Having nothing to hide. Dear, I know nothing of
Either, but when I try to imagine a faultless love
   Or the life to come, what I hear is the murmur
Of underground streams, what I see is a limestone
     landscape.

(84–94)

This kind of poetic activity is altogether less gregarious and less intellectually extensive than that normally associated with Auden's work in the 1930's. But it emerged naturally from the broad lines of his intellectual and poetic development up to that point.

FROM THE MID-FORTIES TO 1973

Lost of course and myself owing a death

Divided Aims: The Game of Knowledge

   . . . Can I learn to suffer
Without saying something ironic or funny
On suffering? . . .

("Prospero to Ariel,"
The Sea and the Mirror)

Auden's work after the war, especially up to *Homage to Clio* (1960), expresses some striking tensions

and divisions; expresses them with unusual directness. The tensions seem to be of three main kinds, each a matter of uncertain relationships: between Auden and his audience, between the artist and the moralizer, and between the artist and the believer.

We noted earlier that Auden was at that time somewhat more "austere" and less "knowing" than he used to be. But the difference is one of degree. He was still very often unsteady in tone and taste; the excellent parts have still to be sifted from much that is merely clever-clever or spry (a poem such as "Homage to Clio" shows this as well as any). To say this is not to be academically portentous or to forget that, then as always, a part of Auden's pertness arises from a deliberate wish to flout all conceptions of artistic decorum. This particular quality is not a tough or quirky comedy so much as something would-be funny. Several kinds of instances could be cited: the raiding of the dictionary for words that are not merely odd but unhelpfully odd; the overworking of pat endings, which had persisted since the early sonnets; the drop into an affectedly colloquial manner; the showy manipulation of conceits; in short, a recurrent bright technical flurry.

These faults seem to arise in part from Auden's unsureness about his exact audience, his lack of relation to a known and fairly homogeneous group whose attitudes he habitually appreciated. He had, we know, a considerable capacity for friendship; and he was not without a good circle of admirers among poets—indeed, he has been a strong influence on American poetry for many years. Yet he was in one sense isolated, and this is partly the result of the move to America we discussed earlier and sought to justify.

We do not now retract that justification. But we need to see as sharply as possible the problems it presented Auden. The difficulty of knowing to just whom he was speaking had sometimes led him to solitary verbal pirouettes or to new versions of the "private joking in panelled rooms" of which he accused himself in the 1930's. At such times the audience seems to be either a very small "in-group" or almost hypothetical—the audience of the brighter weeklies, say, which is not really any of us but is parts of many of us on both sides of the Atlantic and which is intellectually fashionable.

But occasionally Auden could speak steadily as well as wittily and intelligently to an audience composed, we may imagine, of what he called "ironic points of light"; of people whose irony does not preclude charity, who are interested in both poetry

392

and moral ideas, who are on the whole unambitious and who try to steer honestly between righteous indignation, contempt, and self-surrender. No doubt this is a small audience, scattered and hard to find. But it exists, and Auden's career particularly qualified him to seek it:

> O every day in sleep and labour
> Our life and death are with our neighbour,
> And love illuminates again
> The city and the lion's den
> The world's great rage, the travel of young men.
> *(New Year Letter*, pt. 3)

In his vividly metaphorical, alert, and companionable conversational verse and in his landscape poetry Auden could sometimes reach out to the kind of audience he might particularly address. "In Praise of Limestone" is a fine poem and yet a poem severed from local cultures. Its unrooted, engaged intelligence sees, and sees through, the landscape. The later "Whitsunday in Kirchstetten," to which we will return, rediscovers the sense of locality and is companionable in a way that recalls some of the poems of friendship in the early 1930's (such as "Out on the lawn I lie in bed") but is less parochial.

Auden's second area of tension lies in the uneasy relationship between the purposive moralist and the creative artist—the artist who is not concerned to wrest statements from experience directly but works in the intuitive knowledge that, to use Yeats's phrase, "words alone are certain good." We referred to an aspect of this earlier. Since Auden now sees the problem more clearly, the split is not so sharp-edged. It is still there, as the disconcerting unevenness of such a poem as "Memorial for the City" shows. Auden simply will not leave the good verse of the poem's first section to work in its own way, but continues by piling up bright perceptions. He is able to quote with obvious approval "the value of art lies in its effects—not in beauty but in right action"; but he can also refer to "the devil's subtlest temptation, the desire to do good by [your] art." There need be no real contradiction there. Yet for a personality such as Auden's there is likely to be a powerful tension until the exact ways in which each statement may be true have been resolved.

The work of resolution leads directly into what we are calling Auden's third problem. Around this whole area he exercised his mind considerably for many years, and it was entirely typical that he should have devoted his inaugural lecture as professor of poetry at Oxford to aspects of it. The core of the question is the relation of the poet and his work to himself as a man (fallen, free, bound, and willful) and so to God. Its main divisions are: What are the dangers of artistic vocation? What are the justifications?

The theme of the spiritual dangers in the life of an artist has engaged several important contemporary writers, notably Eliot and Thomas Mann. There are striking similarities between the theme of Mann's story *Death in Venice* and the long second part of Caliban's vivid parody of the later Henry James (and also in the whole concept of Prospero) in Auden's *The Sea and the Mirror*. If man's life is a constant struggle in the will, how far is the artist tempted—because he is a sort of creator—to abrogate this responsibility, to get, so to speak, between himself and God? "The artist up to his old game of playing at God with words," quotes Auden from Kierkegaard, and adds a note from the same source about the need to "get out of the poetical into the existential."

Auden had, therefore, to define to his own satisfaction the justification of art. His most typical single phrase from many on the subject asserts that poetry is "a game of knowledge." First, poetry (and all art) is a *game.* It is a form of magic (the naming of "sacred objects") and of fun ("the joke of rhyme"), a release for writer and reader, inspired first not by a desire to do good or acquire fame but by a love of "playing around with words." Also as a game, it is not finally real or serious as "theology and horses" are; it "makes nothing happen." Again like a game, it has fixed rules (patterns, rituals, ceremonies, forms, "necessities"), which the players must obey if they are to enjoy. But pure luck ("the luck of verbal playing") also has a part; something is simply "given" (grace?). "Only your song is an absolute gift," Auden says of the composer, and intends the line to carry the ambiguities of both the idiomatic and the philosophic meanings. The practice of art was for Auden yet another example of the fruitful paradox of freedom and necessity.

Yet poetry is a game of *knowledge.* It is in a certain sense concerned with knowledge, and its magic is meaningful. The knowledge is, though, a product of the play and comes by indirection, as in the serious, absorbed play of a child. Aesthetic patterns and resolutions are not metaphysical patterns and resolutions ("analogy is not identity"), but can analogously point toward them: "And the hard bright light composes / A meaningless moment into an eternal fact." In art's harmony and ritual are mirrored the possibility of a greater order outside man's power; both demand "an acknowledgement that there are relationships which are obligatory and independent of our personality."

So poetry can help to "direct us to ourselves," can "persuade" us to a form of "moral rejoicing," can point through man's "lying nature" to "love and truth." At this stage this was the fullest expression of Auden's continuing urge to irradiate daily human activity with mythical meaning and of his questioning of the relation between art and moral purpose. By the 1960's the dilemma was still not altogether resolved in Auden's personality and could create a jarring unsteadiness. To regret this unsteadiness is not to make aesthetic considerations override all others. For we may say that to the artist, in a special sense, "analogy *must be* identity," that the tense play of ambiguities which make up a poem is indeed part of the poet's "being."

Prose

Of all Auden's varied output during the last dozen years of his life, two main elements demand to be discussed in particular: his prose criticism and his four final volumes of verse (one of them posthumous).

Actually, the earliest volume of prose criticism, *The Enchàfed Flood*, dates back to 1951. It is still interesting and indeed exciting to read; and it showed what were to be over the following twenty or so years the main characteristics of Auden's considerable prose output: his literary criticism is freely ranging, synoptic, paradoxical, aphoristic. It is not much concerned (though it can be occasionally) with close critical analysis of the words on the page; it is much more likely to muse widely on the symbolic and philosophic implications of a work, to deal in parables, recurrent themes, archetypes, myths, patterns.

The Enchafèd Flood, which began as the Page-Barbour lectures at the University of Virginia, is thus closely organized around a number of related themes, those of the romantic symbolism of the sea and of the desert. These were issues to which Auden returned again and again, notably in *The Sea and the Mirror*, *The Age of Anxiety*, the seven "Bucolics," and other landscape poems. He made use of a similar general approach when he delivered the 1967 T. S.

Eliot Memorial Lectures at the University of Kent, Canterbury, which were subsequently published as *Secondary Worlds* (1968). Primary worlds are those of everyday social experience; secondary worlds are those of art: the phrases themselves are from his beloved J. R. R. Tolkien. Here is a typical quotation, typical not only of his manner but of one of his recurrent themes, an aspect of the relations between art and life:

All art is gratuitous [a favorite word], so that one can never say that a certain kind of society must necessarily produce a certain kind of art. On the other hand, when we consider a certain society and the literature which it did actually produce, we can sometimes see reasons why it was possible for such a society to produce it.

Outside of these two "commissioned" volumes, Auden wrote essay after essay for all sorts of different occasions but especially as introductions to collections of other writers' work, as long reviews, and as lectures. His poetry cannot usefully be described as "literary"; there are manifestly literary elements, but they are not a major part of the poems' qualities. But he was certainly a very literary and scholarly man, and the overall impression created by his great bulk of essays is the pendulum swing from literary and historical allusion to general analysis and observation on almost any subject under the sun. The fruit of all this effort, covering about thirty years, is to be found in the more than five hundred pages each of *The Dyer's Hand* (1963) and *Forewords and Afterwords* (1973).

Here we can see in full measure Auden's main qualities as a critic and indeed as a personality, since his own style comes out, necessarily, more directly in his prose than in his poetry. He has a whole range of favorite themes and favorite approaches, ways of dealing with those themes. He also has certain favorite single notions, mild bees in his bonnet, such as the impropriety of publishing a man's letters after his death, or the virtues and the limits of English family life (really, of English upper-middle-class professional family life in the first three or four decades of this century; he never ceased, in spite of all his criticisms, to feel both a nostalgia and a moral admiration for that).

Of his major recurrent themes, one of the two or three most dominant is, once again, the relations between art and life. He talks, at different points in these two volumes, about poems as belonging to a "limitless world of pure joy"; about art as "a mirror in which [we] may become conscious of what [our] own feelings really are; its proper effect, in fact, is disenchanting"; about poetry as "a clarification of life" concerned with two key questions "Who am I?" and "Whom ought I to become?"; and about a poem as "a dialectical struggle between the events the poet wishes to embody and the verbal system." A hundred other similar quotations could be brought forward.

Or one recalls Auden's fondness for observing animals and then for teasing out reflections on the human condition by comparing man—self-aware, having free will, using language—with animals or birds, which have none of these things. Robert Bloom, an American critic, is surely right to call the two essays collected as "Two Bestiaries" in *The Dyer's Hand*, devoted respectively to D. H. Lawrence and Marianne Moore, "masterful, learned and penetrating" and to go on to relate them to Auden's own animal poems: "in them, Auden manifests his own affection for humankind, and his sacred sense of its transcendence over the creatures. And his urgent concern with the nature and exigencies of the human predicament has from the beginning of his career testified to his unending preoccupation with the Good Life."

Yet again, these essays illustrate time after time the perceptiveness, the unusualness, often the quixotry of Auden's powers of general observation. Read only the essay in *The Dyer's Hand* called "The American Scene," which embodies an exceptional range of insights on the texture and nature of American life. Or note the incidental comments scattered throughout his essays, such as this one: "In any modern city, a great deal of our energy has to be expended in *not* seeing, *not* hearing, *not* smelling. An inhabitant of New York who possessed the sensory acuteness of an African Bushman would very soon go mad." And here is a remarkably percipient short paragraph on Rudyard Kipling:

His poems in their quantity, their limitation to one feeling at a time, have the air of brilliant tactical improvisations to overcome sudden unforeseen obstacles, as if, for Kipling, experience were not a seed to cultivate patiently and lovingly, but an unending stream of dangerous feelings to be immediately mastered as they appear.

These two volumes show also, once again and time after time, Auden's love of myth, structure, and pattern. I am not myself a reader or a lover of the "detective story," that characteristically English

form of fiction (which is to be distinguished from the gangster novel, the spy thriller, or the police novel). It was bound to appeal to Auden, and his essay on the genre is, even for one who does not read them, a fascinating exercise in elaborate pattern tracing and symbol identification. Auden never tired of this kind of exercise; here he is in the course of an essay on the brothers Grimm and Hans Christian Andersen:

A fairy story, as distinct from a merry tale, or an animal story, is a serious tale with a human hero and a happy ending. The progression of its hero is the reverse of the tragic hero's: at the beginning he is either socially obscure or despised as being stupid or untalented, lacking in the heroic virtues, but at the end, he has surprised everyone by demonstrating his heroism and winning fame, riches and love.

Or consider the perfectly typical opening of *Secondary Worlds*: "In myth, history and literature, we meet four kinds of human beings, of whom it may be said that their deaths are the most significant event in their lives, the Sacrificial Victim, the Epic Hero, the Tragic Hero and the Martyr." He then proceeds to define them one by one before beginning to play variations on the concepts. Auden's essays, for all their occasional prejudices, opinionations, and admonishings, are on the whole a source of continuous pleasure and insight—into both literature and experience.

Poetry and Companionability

Auden's poetry of the 1960's and 1970's is on the whole more closely contained, more quietly ruminative than before. Technically it is as brilliant as ever, inventive, witty, and extraordinarily skillful. But there is little larger formal experiment. The predominant tones and manners are occasional, domestic, relaxed, and idiomatic rather than more largely thematic or outward-turned.

In the light of all this we can make new glosses on the three divisions in Auden's work we discussed earlier. As for the relation between Auden and his audience: the audience envisaged in this last period is, more often than not, a small group of good friends. Sometimes there is even—though partly with the tongue in the cheek—a prim, keep-your-distance manner toward outsiders. Catching familiar notes in these late poems one realizes sharply that much of Auden's poetry right from the beginning addressed itself to, found its voice in, a small, known, domestic group of friends. It seems at first glance ironic that Auden's reputation in the 1930's should have been so much that of "the conscience of his generation," which seems to imply adopting a much more public intellectual stance. But the reputation was fairly gained; at bottom there is no real contradiction between the two claims.

In talking about the tension between the artist and the moralist in Auden we discussed his description of poetry as "a game of knowledge." The stress later, both in his criticism and in his poetry, was less on the "knowledge" and more on the "game," more on poetry as verbal artifice expressing celebration, awe, or piety before experience. Third, the tension between the artist and the believer seemed less, because poetry had been put in its place as, in the last resort, a side occupation or exercise—enormously worthwhile, of course:

> . . . After all, it's rather a privilege
> amid the affluent traffic
> to serve this unpopular art. . .

but still, as the tone of the above quotation conveys, a marginal matter, secondary to the real questions of faith and the effort to serve God. That life, too, does not demand melodramatic, rhetorical, or histrionic responses. Best, without underestimating the actual melodrama of experience, to work quietly and as well as one can, where we are, trusting in God and his grace. The times may tempt us to do otherwise, and especially tempt writers to assume roles beyond their competence; these voices have to be quietly ignored.

Hence, Auden's last four volumes of verse, which cover the final dozen years of his life, show—like his prose—certain strongly marked and distinctive qualities. The volumes are *About the House* (1966), *City Without Walls* (1969), *Epistle to a Godson* (1972), and the posthumous *Thank You, Fog* (1974). They have common qualities of theme and tone that mark them off fairly decisively from the volumes that preceded them.

It is useful to read them also in conjunction with his commonplace book, *A Certain World* (1971), which, through deploying his favorite extracts from a multitude of writers of many times and nationalities, shows well once again the strange conformations of his idiosyncratic mind. The book is, he said, not an autobiography (he would never have written one of those) but "a map of my planet." Here, too, are all his favorite ideas, but put by other writers:

that poetry makes nothing happen; that it is a form of pure play; that listening to the birds reminds you that man is a creature with "the right to make promises," or—as William Hazlitt is quoted as saying—"man is the only animal that laughs and weeps"; that man is haunted by the difference between what is and what might have been, the exerciser of free will, choice, commitments in speech, and so on.

In these last four volumes of poetry, in general, Auden writes less than he had used to about political or public matters; his poetry still largely lacks the kind of intimacy whose absence from his work, throughout his career, I noted earlier. But this later poetry is much more about personal matters, which is why I used the word "companionability" in the title to this section. I think it is fair to say that most critics do not think as highly of these later volumes as of the earlier ones . I do, and find they give a valuable new dimension to the body of Auden's work.

It is poetry of, first, acceptance; acceptance of creatureliness, of the real world (under God), of the temporal order. It is a poetry of celebration of that natural world, and of harmony and measure before it; it is a humane poetry. One characteristic tone and some of its basic seriousness are caught in the last lines of the last poem of *About the House*:

> . . . about
> catastrophe or how to behave in one
> I know nothing, except what everyone knows—
> if there when Grace dances, I should dance.
> ("Whitsunday in Kirchstetten")

It is therefore poetry that pivots around the idea of a modest, unarrogant acceptance of the self—"my personal city"—and of the body, of home (there are many poems of "place"), and of friendship. Here we need to say more about the role of that small group of friends to which I referred earlier. Look only at the dedications of many of these later poems; they are to living friends, in memoriam for dead friends, to doctors, the local priest (in Austria), relatives, a godchild. It is a small group, and the sense of it was intensified by Auden's renewed Oxford links; the pull of all that held.

All this is admirable, and we should try to take it straight and link it with Auden's continuing preoccupations; in both small and large senses he was coming home. By "small" senses I mean that this poetry could occasionally be that of a rather stiff, mandarin, Oxford man who knew he had been to the best place and who, with his friends, never quite got rid of a sense that the great body of people outside were not quite as nice as *they* were. But then Auden was always very conscious of his privacy and inviolability. He had a right to be like that. What seems to me less justifiable is the tampering with the chronology of the poetry so as to put people off tracing any lines of development (he later allowed chronological printing) and, even more, amending poems written many years ago. Auden justified this by saying: "I have never, consciously at any rate, attempted to revise my former thoughts or feelings, only the language in which they were first expressed when, on further consideration, it seemed to me inaccurate, lifeless, prolix or painful to the ear." I do not think that the full range of his later amendments is caught within the above prescription; some of them do indicate revisions of thoughts and feelings.

The tone is almost always low-keyed (and sometimes high camp). There are irritating oddities and pawkinesses, but overall I would agree with Justin Replogle that throughout this last period Auden can be called almost exclusively a comic poet and that he wrote some of his best poems in this mode. At their best these are seriously playful poems, domestic, conversational, both warm and dry.

As to their craft, they are, to use a favorite word of Auden himself in this connection, elegant "contraptions." They tend to build up a labyrinthine and complex interplay of tones and meanings; thus Richard Johnson, in a particularly subtle book on Auden's poetry—*Man's Place*—can speak of "the coherence of idea, art, organization, and tone" in these later poems.

We noted earlier that after the late 1930's Auden wrote no more very long poems. But what may be said to have taken their place—and he wrote them for more than a decade thereafter—were linked groups, series, or sequences of poems. Again I would agree with Johnson that these are among his most substantial achievements. They include, in *The Shield of Achilles*, the seven "Bucolics," a further development of that landscape poetry to which we have referred earlier, and the seven "Horae Canonicae" in the same volume, a superb sequence. Then, in *About the House*, there are the twelve poems called "Thanksgiving for a Habitat," which are capped, in the same volume, by the fluently tender "Whitsunday in Kirchstetten," from whose last lines I quoted a little earlier in this section. Finally, there are the eight songs from "Mother Courage" in *City Without Walls*.

The harvest of these last years, in short, was a very good and a distinctive one; without it English poetry—and our understanding of Auden's own capacities as a poet—would have been the poorer.

Consistently, through more than forty years of writing, Auden rejected "the soft carpets and big desks" of the successful men of letters and stuck to his explorations with a quite unusual devotion. He made his own mistakes in his own way and, by example and precept, urged "the acceptance by every individual of his aloneness and his responsibility for it, and a willingness continually to re-examine his assumptions." We have suggested that in one sense poetry seemed less absorbing to Auden in his last decade than heretofore. Yet still poetry remained his natural way of speaking; he was always a dedicated poet for whom the practice of poetry was an activity of the moral will. He pursued his honestly persistent inquiries eagerly and hopefully. He could write: "wherever/The sun shines, brooks run, books are written/There will also be this death." But also, just as characteristically, he wrote: "After so many years the light is/Novel still and immensely ambitious."

Meanwhile, Auden's achievement is remarkable: in much pithily epigrammatic verse; in many lovely songs, lyrics, and sonnets; in a flexible, acute, and often comic conversational verse; and in his moral-landscape poetry. He helped considerably to define and make articulate our situation in the 1930's, and also in the 1950's, as this finely rhetorical passage from "The Shield of Achilles" will remind us:

The mass and majesty of this world, all
    That carries weight and always weighs the same
Lay in the hands of others; they were small
    And could not hope for help and no help came:
    What their foes liked to do was done, their shame
Was all the worst could wish; they lost their pride
And died as men before their bodies died.
                          (38–44)

Later, the sense of dramatic menace receded and with it some kinds of urgency in Auden's verse. He now sought different music, other relationships; and in doing so he went back more than ever to his origins:

    Let your last thinks all be thanks:
    praise your parents who gave you
    a Super-ego of strength

that saves you so much bother
digit friends and dear them all,
then pay fair attribution
to your age, to having been
born when you were. In boyhood
you were permitted to meet
beautiful old contraptions . . .

("Lullaby")

Of all this, the result is a considerable body of memorable speech on our times and problems, an example that contributes to the civility Auden so much admired, and a commitment that claims our respect and admiration.

SELECTED BIBLIOGRAPHY

I. BIBLIOGRAPHY. J. P. Clancy, "A W. H. Auden Bibliography, 1924–55," in *Thought*, 30 (Summer 1955), pub. by Fordham University; E. Callan, *An Annotated Check List of the Works of W. H. Auden* (Denver, 1958); B. C. Bloomfield, *W. H. Auden, A Bibliography: The Early Years Through 1955* (Charlottesville, Va., 1964), 2nd ed. (1972), ed. by B. C. Bloomfield and E. Mendelson, extends through 1969.

II. COLLECTED AND SELECTED WORKS. *Selected Poems* (London, 1938); *Some Poems* (London, 1940), small sel. of previously published verse; *Collected Poetry of W. H. Auden* (New York, 1945), published in the U.K. as *Collected Shorter Poems, 1930–1944* (London, 1950), rev. versions of most of Auden's earlier poems, with excisions; *W. H. Auden. A Selection by the Author* (London, 1958), published in the U.S. as *Selected Poetry of W. H. Auden* (New York, 1959; 2nd ed., 1971); *Selected Essays* (London, 1964), criticism; *Collected Shorter Poems, 1927–1957* (London, 1966; New York, 1967), further revs. and excisions of earlier work, arranged chronologically; *Collected Longer Poems* (London, 1968; New York, 1969); E. Mendelson, ed., *Collected Poems* (New York–London, 1976), includes all of *Collected Shorter Poems, 1927–1957* and *Collected Longer Poems*, with some additional poems restored by Auden in later years and with the contents of his later vols. of short poems; Auden's final rev. texts, with many early poems omitted; *The English Auden. Poems, Essays, and Dramatic Writings, 1927–1939* (London, 1977; New York, 1978), repr. the original versions, including all the poems that Auden printed in book form during his lifetime but omitted from his late collections.

III. SEPARATE WORKS. *Poems* (London, 1930; rev. ed., 1932), includes *Paid on Both Sides*, a charade in verse; *The Orators: An English Study* (London, 1932; rev. eds., 1934, 1966), verse and prose, last ed. includes preface by Auden; *The Dance of Death* (London, 1933), verse and prose; *The Dog Beneath the Skin: Or, Where Is Francis?* (London, 1935), drama, verse, and prose, with C. Isherwood; *Look, Stranger!* (London, 1936), verse, pub. in the U.S. as *On the Island* (New York, 1937); *The Ascent of F6* (London, 1936; rev. ed., 1937), drama, verse, and prose, with C. Isherwood; *Spain* (London, 1937), verse, a pamphlet poem; *Letters from Iceland* (London, 1937), travel, verse, and prose, with L. MacNeice; *On the Frontier* (London, 1938), drama, verse, and prose, with C. Isherwood; *Journey to a War* (London, 1939; rev. ed., 1973), travel, with C. Isherwood, includes Auden's sonnet sequence "In Time of War."

Another Time (London, 1940), verse; *New Year Letter* (New York–London, 1941), verse, pub. in U.S. as *The Double Man*, includes the long title poem, the sonnet sequence "The Quest," prologue, and epilogue; *Three Songs for St. Cecilia's Day* (London, 1941); *For the Time Being* (London, 1945), verse, also contains *The Sea and the Mirror: A Commentary on Shakespeare's "The Tempest"*; *The Age of Anxiety: A Baroque Eclogue* (London, 1948), verse.

The Enchafèd Flood, or, The Romantic Iconography of the Sea (London, 1951), criticism, the Page–Barbour Lectures, University of Virginia, 1949; *Nones* (London, 1952), verse; *Mountains* (London, 1954), a Faber Ariel poem; *The Shield of Achilles* (London, 1955), verse; *The Old Man's Road* (New York, 1956), verse.

Homage to Clio (London, 1960), verse; *The Dyer's Hand and Other Essays* (London, 1963), criticism; *About the House* (London, 1966), verse; *Secondary Worlds* (London, 1968), criticism, the T. S. Eliot Memorial Lectures at the University of Kent, 1967; *City Without Walls and Other Poems* (London, 1969), verse.

Academic Graffiti (London, 1971), light verse; *Epistle to a Godson and Other Poems* (London, 1972), verse; *Forewords and Afterwords* (London, 1973), criticism, sel. by E. Mendelson; *Thank You, Fog: Last Poems* (London, 1974), verse.

IV. LIBRETTI. E. Toller, *No More Peace: A Thoughtful Comedy* (London, 1937), trans. by E. Crankshaw, lyrics trans. and adap. by Auden; *The Rake's Progress—An Opera* (London, 1951), music by I. Stravinsky, libretto by Auden and C. Kallman; *The Magic Flute* (London, 1957), music by W. A. Mozart, new English libretto by Auden and C. Kallman; *Elegy for Young Lovers—An Opera* (Mainz, 1961), music by H. W. Henze, libretto by Auden and C. Kallman; *The Bassarids* (London, 1960), music by H. W. Henze, libretto by Auden and C. Kallman, performed at Salzburg; *Love's Labour Lost* (London, 1973), music by N. Nabokov, libretto by Auden and C. Kallman, performed in Brussels; *Paul Bunyan—An Operetta* (London, 1976), music by B. Britten, libretto by Auden, performed at Columbia University, May 1941.

V. EDITED WORKS, INTRODUCTIONS, TRANSLATIONS, AND ANTHOLOGIES. *Oxford Poetry* (London, 1926), anthology, with C. Plumb; *Oxford Poetry* (London, 1927), anthology, with C. Day Lewis; *The Poet's Tongue* (London, 1935), anthology, with J. Garrett; *Poetry* (Chicago), 49 (January

1937), with M. Roberts; *The Oxford Book of Light Verse* (London, 1938), anthology; H. James, *The American Scene* (New York, 1946), intro. by Auden, repr. in *Horizon*, 86 (February 1947); *Tennyson* (London, 1946), sel. from his poems and with intro. by Auden; J. Betjeman, *Slick but Not Streamlined* (New York, 1947), poems and short pieces sel. and with intro. by Auden; *The Portable Greek Reader* (New York, 1948), intro. by Auden; C. Baudelaire, *Intimate Journals* (London, 1949), trans. by C. Isherwood, intro. by Auden.

Selected Prose and Poetry of Poe (New York, 1950), ed. and with intro. by Auden; *Poets of the English Language*, 5 vols. (London, 1952), anthology, with N. H. Pearson; *An Elizabethan Song Book* (New York, 1955), music ed. by N. Greenberg, lyrics ed. by Auden and C. Kallman; *Kierkegaard* (London, 1955), sel. and with intro. by Auden; *The Faber Book of Modern American Verse* (London, 1956), anthology; *The Selected Writings of Sidney Smith* (London, 1957); *The Complete Poems of Cavafy* (New York, 1961), trans by R. Dalvin, intro. by Auden; *Goethe: An Italian Journey, 1786–1788* (London, 1962), trans. and with intro. by Auden and E. Mayer; *A Choice of de la Mare's Verse* (London, 1963), sel. and with intro. by Auden; D. Hammarskjold and L. Sjöberg, *Markings* (London, 1964), foreword by Auden; *The Faber Book of Aphorisms: A Personal Selection* (London, 1964), with L. Kronenberger; *Nineteenth-Century Minor Poets* (London, 1966), ed. by Auden; *The Elder Edda: A Selection* (London, 1969), trans. from the Icelandic by P. B. Taylor and Auden.

G. K. Chesterton: A Selection from His Non-Fictional Prose (London, 1970), sel. by Auden; *A Certain World: A Commonplace Book* (London, 1971), anthology, sel. by Auden; *Selected Poems of Gunnar Ekelöf* (London, 1971), trans. by Auden and L. Sjöberg; *A Choice of Dryden's Verse* (London, 1973), sel. and with intro. by Auden; *George Herbert* (London, 1973), sel. by Auden; Pär Lagerkvist, *Evening Land* (London, 1977), trans. by Auden and L. Sjöberg.

VI. Biographical and Critical Studies. F. R. Leavis, *New Bearings in English Poetry* (London, 1932); S. Spender, *The Destructive Element* (London, 1935), pt. 3 is relevant; M. Roberts, ed., *The Faber Book of Modern Verse* (London, 1936; new ed., 1951), intro. by Roberts describes the social, political, and cultural climate of Auden's time; C. Connolly, *Enemies of Promise* (London, 1938), contains comments on Auden; C. Isherwood, *Lions and Shadows* (London, 1938), contains comments on Auden; L. MacNeice, *Modern Poetry: A Personal Essay* (London, 1938); C. Brooks, *Modern Poetry and the Tradition* (Chapel Hill, N.C., 1939); E. Muir, *The Present Age*

from 1914 (London, 1939), brought up to 1950 with new survey by D. Daiches (1957).

E. Drew, *Directions in Modern Poetry* (New York, 1940); J. G. Southworth, *Sowing the Spring* (Oxford, 1940), a study of the "Auden Group"; R. Jarrell, "Changes of Attitude and Rhetoric in Auden's Poetry," in *Southern Review*, 7 (1941); F. Scarfe, *Auden and After* (London, 1942); S. Spender, *Life and the Poet* (London, 1942); D. S. Savage, *The Personal Principle* (London, 1944); R. Jarrell, "Freud to Paul: The Stages of Auden's Ideology," in *Partisan Review*, 12 (1945); *Poets at Work* (New York, 1948); G. Grigson, ed., *Poetry of the Present* (London, 1949), valuable intro.; F. Scarfe, *Auden* (Monaco, 1949); G. R. Hamilton, *The Tell-Tale Article* (London, 1949).

R. Hoggart, *Auden: An Introductory Essay* (London, 1951); S. Spender, *World Within a World* (London, 1951), contains material on the young Auden; G. S. Fraser, *The Modern Writer and His World* (London, 1953; rev. ed., 1964); J. G. Southworth, *More Modern American Poets* (London, 1954); M. Moore, *Predilections* (New York, 1955); J. Lehmann, *The Whispering Gallery* (London, 1955), contains comments on the young Auden; J. W. Beach, *The Making of the Auden Canon* (Minneapolis, 1957); J. Bayley, *The Romantic Survival* (London, 1957); A. Alvarez, *The Shaping Spirit* (London, 1958); G. S. Fraser, *Vision and Rhetoric* (London, 1959).

R. Hoggart, *W. H. Auden: A Selection* (London, 1961); M. K. Spears, *The Poetry of W. H. Auden: The Disenchanted Island* (New York, 1963); B. Everett, *Auden* (London, 1964); M. K. Spears, ed., *Auden: A Collection of Critical Essays* (Englewood Cliffs, N.J., 1964); J. G. Blair, *The Poetic Art of W. H. Auden* (Princeton, N.J., 1965); H. Greenberg, *Quest for the Necessary: W. H. Auden and the Dilemma of Divided Consciousness* (Cambridge, Mass., 1968); G. Nelson, *Changes of Heart: A Study of the Poetry of W. H. Auden* (London, 1969); J. Replogle, *Auden's Poetry* (London, 1969).

G. W. Bahlke, *The Later Auden* (New Brunswick, N.J., 1970); D. Davison, *W. H. Auden* (London, 1970); J. Fuller, *A Reader's Guide to W. H. Auden* (London, 1970); F. Buell, *W. H. Auden as a Social Poet* (Ithaca, N.Y., 1973); R. Johnson, *Man's Place: An Essay on Auden* (Ithaca, N.Y., 1973); S. Spender, ed., *W. H. Auden: A Tribute* (London, 1975); S. Hynes, *The Auden Generation: Literature and Politics in England in the 1930s* (London, 1976); C. Osborne, *W. H. Auden: The Life of a Poet* (New York, 1979).

E. Mendelson, *W. H. Auden: Nineteen Hundred Seven to Nineteen Hundred Seventy-Three* (New York, 1980); E. Mendelson, *Early Auden* (New York, 1981); G. T. Wright, *W. H. Auden* (rev. ed., New York, 1981).

LOUIS MacNEICE
(1907-1963)

John Press

Louis MacNeice was born in Belfast on 12 September 1907. When Louis was still an infant, his father, John Frederick MacNeice (who later became a bishop), was appointed rector of Carrickfergus. The family, being unable to take immediate possession of the rectory because the retiring incumbent was on his deathbed, moved for a while into a house overlooking the harbor, where the child used to sit watching the sailboats as they moved westward. MacNeice once remarked that most poets have access to a poetic landscape that is the constant background of all their work, and certainly he was haunted throughout his life by memories of childhood scenes. He serves indeed as a perfect illustration of Cyril Connolly's dictum that "the one golden recipe for Art is the ferment of an unhappy childhood working through a noble imagination."

His mother, Elizabeth Clesham, died when he was young, and, despite his father's remarriage, he was often left in the charge of domestic servants, many of whom were unsympathetic to a lonely, sensitive child. Some of his early memories were awesome, but not horrifying. He never forgot the sight of the *Titanic* as she passed down Belfast Lough on her maiden voyage: the image of the doomed ship approaching the iceberg is prominent in a late poem, "Death of an Old Lady," and recurs in *The Administrator* (1964), one of his last plays for radio. Other memories were more disturbing, and some of the mythologies that he wove round the red-brick rectory influenced his dreams until his death. We know from his own account that he was afraid of blindness, of long corridors, of light glancing off a mirror. His loneliness, his mother's illness, the old wives' tales recounted by the servants, his familiarity with the terrifying imagery of the Bible, and his frequent nightmares must have accentuated his predisposition to fear:

When I was five the black dreams came;
Nothing after was quite the same.

Come back early or never come.

The dark was talking to the dead;
The lamp was dark beside my bed.
                              ("Autobiography")

Moreover, as he tells us,

I also had certain early contacts with both mental illness and mental deficiency (these latter may explain the *petrification* images which appear pretty often in my poems, e.g. in *Perseus*). I should add that our house was lit by oil lamps (not enough of them) and so was full of shadows. . . . These circumstances between them must have supplied me with many images of fear, anxiety, loneliness or monotony (to be used very often quite out of a personal context). They may also explain—by reaction—what I now think an excessive preoccupation in my earlier work with things dazzling, high-coloured, quick-moving, hedonistic or up-to-date.

("Experience with Images")[1]

MacNeice recognized the fact that his childhood experiences had left an ineffaceable mark upon him:

I was the rector's son, born to the anglican order,
    Banned for ever from the candles of the Irish poor;
The Chichesters knelt in marble at the ends of a transept
    With ruffs about their necks, their portion sure.
                              ("Carrickfergus," 17–20)

Even in the Chichester transept there was a source of fear: above the huge monument there hung a coat-of-arms that took on the shape of an evil man looking down at the rector's son. And long before Jimmy Porter delivered his tirade against church bells in John Osborne's *Look Back in Anger* (1956), Louis MacNeice saw them as skulls' mouths.

[1]Published in *Orpheus*, II (1949), pp. 129–130.

Yet it would be wrong to suppose that MacNeice gained nothing of positive value from his upbringing. His father was a man of some distinction who played a prominent part in settling a local dock strike and who, in the years before 1914, showed his independence of mind by being a Home Ruler and a pacifist. He later scandalized Belfast by refusing to allow the Union Jack to be hung in perpetuity over the political leader Edward Carson's tomb in St. Patrick's Cathedral. Louis MacNeice also remembered with gratitude that he had grown up in a household where commercial values were not supreme, where he had a good deal of time to himself, and where books were plentiful.

He was educated at Marlborough and then went to Oxford, where he dressed foppishly, grew long sidewhiskers, and cultivated an admiration for Friedrich Nietzsche. His tutor, deceived by MacNeice's apparent neglect of his work, prophesied that he would get a Third, and was confounded when he obtained a First in Mods and in Greats.[2] Over thirty years afterward MacNeice explained that two undergraduates (Quintin Hogg and R. S. Crossman) were pointed out to him as men certain to get Firsts. He thereupon decided that if such dull-looking people could do so, he would emulate them, but "I will lounge my way in like Petronius Arbiter."

Even as an undergraduate he had begun to prefer Aristotle to Plato. Looking back on this youthful preference, he quoted Shelley's lines from "Adonais":

> Life, like a dome of many-coloured glass,
> Stains the white radiance of eternity

and commented, "Aristotle, being among other things a zoologist, never let a transcendental radiance destroy the shapes of the creatures or impose a white-out on everything." His undergraduate days were perhaps, as he put it, "a limbo period spent in slouching," but his abilities and opinions had already started to ripen.

After leaving Oxford he became a lecturer in Classics, first at Birmingham, where he was a prominent member of a remarkably talented circle, and then at Bedford College, London. A youthful marriage contracted in 1930 was dissolved in 1936. The outbreak of war found him in Ireland, and in January 1940 he sailed for the United States to lecture at

Cornell during the spring semester. Characteristically, for he was a man of vivacious, stubborn pugnacity, he chose to come back to England in December 1940. Equally characteristically, he wrote a cool, unsentimental article, printed in *Horizon* (February 1941), about those British writers who had sailed for the United States in the late 1930's and had decided to stay there. A writer, he argued, can best serve his country by writing, and only he can judge where his imagination enjoys its fullest play. MacNeice admitted that although he never felt at home in England he found it more stimulating to live there than in Ireland or elsewhere. He had therefore returned to England but, as an ex-expatriate, he defended those writers who had remained in America: "They have consciences of their own, and the last word must be said by their own instinct as artists."

Soon after his return to England he married Hedli Anderson, for whom W. H. Auden had written some of his early cabaret songs. He began to work for the BBC and remained in its employ until his death over twenty years later. He gave devoted service, and the corporation proved in its turn a generous employer, granting him leave of absence so that he could take temporary posts in South Africa, India, and Greece, where he spent eighteen months in the service of the British Council in Athens from January 1950 to the end of June 1951.

MacNeice wrote and produced a large number of feature programs for the BBC. When recording one of these, *Persons from Porlock*, in the summer of 1963, he insisted on accompanying the engineers down an underground cave, got soaked, and sat about in wet clothes. He contracted a chill, but on 26 August wrote a cheerful letter, enclosed with a note about his forthcoming volume, *The Burning Perch* (1963), which was to be the Poetry Book Society's autumn choice. His chill took a turn for the worse, and he died in a hospital on 3 September.

PROSE WRITINGS

MacNeice was a prolific, versatile, highly professional writer, and it is worth examining his work in other branches of literature before we consider his poetry. He was the author of three works of criticism, a number of lively critical essays, numerous reviews, an autobiography, a score of radio scripts (mostly unpublished), several plays (also mostly un-

[2]Studies of the modern and the classical philosopher-writers.

published), translations of Aeschylus and Goethe, a pseudonymous novel, a children's story, a book on astrology, a booklet on the American army, and two or three volumes that can best be described as gallimaufries. One of these, *Letters from Iceland*, written in collaboration with W. H. Auden and published in 1937, still repays study as a document of the times. It contains some of the silliest bits of facetious writing ever committed by either author, some admirable descriptive prose, a few good poems, Auden's coruscating "Letter to Lord Byron," which unfortunately was never reprinted, and a joint "testament," crammed with personal allusions, cultural chitchat, and bawdy jokes.

Zoo (1938) and *I Crossed the Minch* (1938) are two potboilers. Their ostensible themes are, respectively, the London Zoo and the islands of the Outer Hebrides, but both contain many digressions and autobiographical reminiscences, which are, indeed, the most valuable portions of the books. Two passages from *Zoo* are interesting for the light they throw upon MacNeice's response to the visible world and upon his philosophical outlook:

The pleasure of dappled things, the beauty of adaptation to purpose, the glory of extravagance, classic elegance or romantic nonsense and grotesquerie—all of these we get from the Zoo. We react to these with the same delight as to new potatoes in April speckled with chopped parsley or the lights at night on the Thames of Battersea Power House, or to cars sweeping their shadows from lamp-post to lamp-post down Haverstock Hill or to brewers' drays or to lighthouses and searchlights or to a newly cut lawn or to a hot towel or a friction at the barber's or to Moran's two classic tries at Twickenham in 1937 or to the smell of dusting-powder in a warm bathroom or to the fun of shelling peas into a china bowl or of shuffling one's feet through dead leaves when they are crisp or to the noise of rain or the crackling of a newly lit fire or the jokes of a street-hawker or the silence of snow in moonlight or the purring of a powerful car.

Original Sin won for us a life of progress, pattern of dark and light, the necessity of winning our bread which builds our wits, the tension without which there is no music and the conflict without which there is no harmony.

(pp. 40–41; 239)

MacNeice's other miscellaneous writings need not detain us. His booklet on the American servicemen is sensible, the children's story is unremarkable, and the novel is dull, although it has a promising theme—the attempt of a young intellectual to escape from the futility of life at Oxford, his elopement and marriage with the daughter of the nerve specialist who has certified him as unbalanced, and his return to Oxford as a don, partially reconciled with himself and his environment. *Astrology*, published posthumously in 1964, testifies to its author's lifelong interest in chance, superstition, and the irrational aspects of human nature. When he was a young man MacNeice was adept at telling fortunes by cards, and he never lost his fondness for blarney or his delight in man's credulity.

His critical work, on the other hand, deserves to be studied with some attention. He did not make inflated claims about the value of criticism, as the following passage may suggest:

The best criticism, like the best philosophy, tends to be negative. It is inferior philosophy, like pragmatism, that influences action, and it is a narrow and limited criticism that encourages the production of art. What the artist and the reader need is an Aristotle or a Dr. Johnson.

His own criticism is, within the limits he set himself, acute and illuminating. He believed that a reviewer should not pontificate about poetry in the abstract, but concentrate on singling out specific faults and merits in the individual poems. Even in his full-scale critical works the most valuable portions are those in which MacNeice is speaking as a craftsman and drawing on his knowledge of technique.

Thus in *Modern Poetry: A Personal Essay* (1938) he continually tests abstruse theories of rhythm by reference to specific lines of verse, and suggests that even Gerard Manley Hopkins sometimes allows his passion for elaborate speculation about metrics to distort the movement of his verse. He agrees with G. M. Young that a whole poem written to the pattern of "Put your knife and your fork across your plate" would be intolerable, but argues that in a melodramatic poem about an impending murder the heavy, irregular stresses would produce an admirably sinister effect, if cunningly employed:

The dark is falling and the hour is late:
Put your knife and your fork across your plate.

It is context and normal speech that determine whether or not a particular meter is appropriate. Thus he observes:

"Pussy-cat, Pussy-cat, where have you been?" is a good line rhythmically, but I should not like to write, "Polar

Bear, Polar Bear, where have you been?" For (a) in ordinary speech we say "Pólar Béar" and (b) "bear" is a more important syllable than "-cat" both for sound-value and meaning.

Again, MacNeice remarks that "The Polar Bear prowled on the ice" is a more satisfactory line than "The Polar Bear was prowling on the ice," since the former throws the proper stress on the important words and gives the right effect of weight.

MacNeice always emphasizes the supreme value of rhythmical vitality in poetry. After quoting Vaslav Nijinsky's cryptic utterance "I am going to dance the war," he comments: "In the same way the poet dances his experiences in words." He never abandoned his belief that rhyme, strongly marked rhythmical patterns, artifice, and technical inventiveness were desirable elements of poetry. In a review of Reuben Brower's *The Poetry of Robert Frost* printed in the *New Statesman* (12 July 1963) a few weeks before his death, MacNeice displays an astringent contempt for some fashionable theorizing on these matters:

Thus several reviewers of Thom Gunn's last book seemed to assume that his abandonment of recognizable rhythmical patterns for unrecognizable syllabic ones *automatically* marked an advance and betokened an increase in profundity. Similarly some idiot recently stated that rhyme in English poetry was now a thing of the past.

He quotes with approval Frost's dictum: "I had as soon write free verse as play tennis with the net down," and adds a rider of his own: "A sentence in prose is struck forward like a golf ball; a sentence in verse can be treated like a ball in a squash court. Frost is a master of angles." This recalls the comparison he makes in *Modern Poetry* between poetry and one of his favorite games:

The mere arranging of verse in lines serves the same purpose as the offside rule in rugger and the rule against forward passes; instead of the meaning being passed vertically down the field as it is in prose, each line in verse when it comes to an end passes back to the beginning of the next (and I am not only thinking of typography). This method, as in rugger, gives a sweeping movement, an impression of controlled speed and power—an impression which is enhanced when the verse is on a recognizable rhythmical pattern.

(p. 116)

MacNeice's critical wit, though seldom unkind, is occasionally devastating. After quoting T. S. Eliot's remark about the ordinary man who "falls in love, or reads Spinoza," MacNeice drily observes: "It is typical of Eliot that his ordinary man should read Spinoza." And one of his aphorisms makes abundantly clear the distinction between poetry and propaganda that MacNeice maintained throughout his life: "Others can tell lies more efficiently; no one except the poet can give us poetic truth."

MacNeice's book *The Poetry of W. B. Yeats* (1941) was the first full-length study of the poet to be published after Yeats's death. It was written before any collection of Yeats's letters had appeared, and before the industrious Yeatsian research workers had begun to burrow in the archives preserved by the poet's widow. In a sense, therefore, it is an unscholarly work based on insufficient evidence. Yet it exhibits certain qualities unequaled by later tomes on Yeats: it is by a man who was both a poet and an Irishman and who could look at the published verse and prose of Yeats undistracted by the mass of secondary and often irrelevant documents that all subsequent commentators have felt bound to digest.

MacNeice's chapter on the Irish background remains an admirable introduction to the subject; his discussion of Yeats's political beliefs avoids the uneasy special pleading to which some apologists have been driven. MacNeice acknowledges the distasteful truth that Yeats came to adopt "his own elegant brand of fascism," however tempting it may be to pretend that all he really wanted was a revival of eighteenth-century aristocratic values. Nor does MacNeice burke the fact that Yeats was in some ways a poseur. Yet he has no doubt that, despite his flaws, he was a great poet. It is easy to dismiss MacNeice's view of Yeats as the shallow judgment of a young left-wing poet writing soon after the outbreak of war; but his summing-up is likely to commend itself to all those who, while accepting Yeats as a major poet, are not disposed to revere him as a political guide or as an expounder of esoteric wisdom.

MacNeice occasionally anticipates in a couple of sentences the elaborate disquisitions of more ponderous Yeatsian scholars. Thus he remarks of Yeats's early verse dramas: "Aristotle would not have considered them plays at all. They are pieces of tapestry." Now that Yeats is sometimes spoken of in the same breath as Shakespeare, it is refreshing to read the comments of a man who loved the poetry of Yeats this side of idolatry:

When Yeats was an old man he was not, according to his friends, in the least tortured by fear of death and even welcomed jokes about his own. Being a vain man he was well pleased with himself and with his latter-day fame and even with the publicity of the Senate House. He also drew strength from two new kinds of adventuring—into the world of sense and sensuality on the one hand, and into the magical philosophical world of *A Vision* on the other. His poetry kept pace with these adventures and his poetic energy accumulated.

(ch. 7)

Yeats's later poetry contains an element that is very like humour. When he attempted humour in his plays he usually failed, but in private life he had not only wit and an Irish joy in hyperbole, but a fine supply of animal spirits which made him relish blasphemy, indecency, and malicious personal gossip. . . .

The humour in his later poems seems to be a blend of whimsicality, bravado, canniness and sadism.

(ch. 8)

Whatever the Yeatsian experts may say, MacNeice's book is a stimulating account of a great poet, and a salutary corrective to the adulation that has been lavished upon him.

Varieties of Parable, published in 1965, examines the way in which poets, moralists, and novelists from Edmund Spenser to William Golding have employed the parable as an indispensable mode of communication. This book comprises the Clark Lectures given at Trinity College, Cambridge, in 1961, and, like all MacNeice's criticism, it is refreshingly unpedantic and shrewd, a mixture of robust good sense, unobtrusive scholarship, and keen aesthetic perception. Besides containing a number of acute comments on his chosen authors, it reveals much of MacNeice's own nature and artistic aims, his desire to communicate with his fellow beings, his belief that men live by symbols and learn by parables.

MacNeice's finest prose work is *The Strings Are False* (1965), an unfinished autobiography, mainly written in 1940 and partially revised. It is an extremely honest, intelligent appraisal of himself and his world in childhood, at school, at Oxford, and in Birmingham and London during the 1930's. It speaks directly of the crucial events his poetry glances at obliquely—the death of his mother in his childhood, his mongoloid brother, the collapse of his youthful marriage. His fastidious temperament and his concept of good manners preclude any wallowing in self-pity or in the luxury of confessional outpourings, but he shows us with remarkable skill how he became the man he was and why certain themes recur in his poetry.

DRAMA AND TRANSLATIONS

ALTHOUGH most of MacNeice's dramatic works were in the form of radio scripts, he wrote a number of plays for the stage. "Eureka" remains unpublished and unperformed; "Station Bell," of which all traces seem to have vanished, was given one performance in the 1930's by the University English Club at Birmingham; "Traitors in Our Way," an unpublished drama about treason in a society threatened by communism, was staged by the Group Theatre, Belfast, in 1957; two of his stage plays, *Out of the Picture* (1937) and *One for the Grave* (1968), were published.

Out of the Picture, written for the Group Theatre, London, and performed there in 1937, with production by Rupert Doone, music by Benjamin Britten, and sets and costumes by Robert Medley, is a highly characteristic period piece. The protagonist is a neurotic painter whose picture of Venus is bought by a film star, Clara de Groot. In a confusing sequence of episodes, performed while the radio announces the coming of war, the painter falls in love with Clara, shoots a cabinet minister, and goes to bed with a model called Moll O'Hara, who first gives him a drug that will kill him after two hours, as an act of mercy.

It cannot be described as a successful play. Some of the favorite tricks of the 1930's repertoire are trotted out: surrealist humor, Freudian clichés, a fantastic plot, cardboard characters indulging in buffoonery, satirical attacks on society, and long monologues that mingle farcical parody and hysterical rhetoric. And all these are packed into a ramshackle vehicle whose dramatic machinery makes loud, creaking noises and moves jerkily. MacNeice takes over the radio announcer, beloved of Auden and Christopher Isherwood, and invents one or two symbolic figures, such as a sinister auctioneer, who turns up again in one of his last radio plays, *The Mad Islands* (1964).

MacNeice salvaged a few lyrics from *Out of the Picture* and reprinted them in his *Collected Poems 1925–1948* (1949). There are also some passages that are typical of his youthful preoccupations, notably Venus' speech about those who have gone into the land of death:

> Their heads and their eyes are of stone,
> Being no longer organisms of nature
> But final versions of an artist's vision.

(Act II, sc. i)

We get also some characteristic passages about the sheer pleasure of being alive:

> The dog stares into the fire, beatitude of platitude,
> God be praised that things are as they are,
> That grass is green, that water is wet, that trees are tall,
> (Act I, sc. iii)

and an expression of MacNeice's reverence for courage, uncomplaining endurance, and energy:

> Blessed are the reckless spendthrifts of vitality
> But blessed also are all who last the course,
> Blessed are those who endure as a point of etiquette
> And blessed are the cynics who carry their cross as a gesture.
> (Act II, sc. i)

Another passage seems to anticipate the fire-raids on London that were soon to become a potent image in MacNeice's verse:

> There is nothing to stem the mechanical march of fire.
> Nothing to assuage the malice of the drunken fire.
> FIRE FIRE FIRE FIRE.
> (Act II)

One for the Grave: A Modern Morality Play, written in 1958–1959 and first performed at the Abbey Theatre, Dublin, in 1966, was published in 1968 unrevised, as the author had left it. It is probably MacNeice's most accomplished dramatic work, owing something to the revue technique of *Out of the Picture,* and still more to his experiences in working with the BBC. MacNeice takes the medieval story of Everyman on the brink of death and sets it in a television studio. The revue elements are, he says, "introduced not primarily for their own sake but for satirical purposes, the modern Everyman's world being one which cannot be properly treated *without* satire." He goes on to explain that "the whole device of the Television Studio (where the floor represents the Earth and the production gallery Heaven) is very much more than a gimmick—because it is the fate of the twentieth-century Everyman to live in a world of mass media."

The episodic form of the play is particularly well suited to MacNeice's talents. Some of the episodes recall portions of his own life, notably the encounter between an Edwardian child and his mother "back from her rest cure"; MacNeice employs his favorite image of a mayfly as the symbol of life's brevity and of sexual passion; and two obsessive images recur in

a song about Everyman's journey down the long, long trail a-winding to the land of the tomb

> Where your eyes all turn to blindness
> And the world all turns to stone.

The bitterness, the remorse, the sense of waste are unmistakable in this play, yet a grim wit, a stoical endurance, and a religious acceptance of life precariously survive. Everyman and the Gravedigger who comes to lay him in the tomb pray to the Unknown God, with Everyman repeating the Gravedigger's words:

> I thank Thee for giving me the chance—
> If I failed to use it, forgive me.

The Gravedigger takes away the power of Morty, the Floor Manager, and comforts Everyman:

> *Gravedigger:* But now at this hour of your death—that's right, hold your head up—it's I who call the tune. Everyman, here and now, I salute you in the name of Life.
> *Everyman:* And your name?
> *Gravedigger:* I've just said it. And now, Everyman, relax.

Most of MacNeice's dramatic writing took the shape of radio scripts, a medium in which he labored for over twenty years. Charles Lamb said that his true works lay in the ledgers of the East India Company, and much of MacNeice's literary output is yellowing in the files of the BBC. He believed that his radio scripts contained some of his best writing, and before disputing this verdict we should remember that many of them remain unpublished, including "Prisoner's Progress," which won the Premio Italiano (the foremost award for Italian radio programs) in 1954; but those scripts that have been printed are, for all their ingenuity and skill, unsatisfying and strangely insubstantial.

MacNeice devoted considerable thought to drama in general and to radio drama in particular. In an unpublished lecture delivered at Cambridge in 1959, entitled "Lyric into Drama," he discusses the reasons for the decay of verse in the theater, and suggests that the finest "poetic" effects in the drama of our time have been created by dramatists using the medium of prose. In his introduction to the 1963 edition of his radio play *Christopher Columbus,* which had been first published in 1944, he reverts to this theme, explaining his development as a writer for radio: "In most of my later radio plays (for the same reason I suppose as the more *poetic* of contemporary writers for the theatre) I avoided verse and preferred a kind of sleight-of-hand colloquial dialogue."

Although he continued to write radio scripts, MacNeice admitted that the medium was transitory and limited. The introduction already quoted reads like a valediction to the form on which he had lavished his talents:

Many years later, re-reading both the play itself and my own introduction to it, I feel I am returning to an innocent but quaint and archaic period. The nickname "steam radio" is properly nostalgic: rarely has an up-to-date medium matured, and indeed aged, so rapidly.

There are also more fundamental reasons for the disappointing quality of MacNeice's radio scripts. His introduction to the 1944 edition makes a damaging avowal:

With a literature as old as ours and a contemporary diction so vulgarized, precise and emotive writing comes to depend more and more upon twists—twists of the obvious statement or the hackneyed image. To do this on the printed page requires constant ingenuity and often leads to an appearance of being too clever by half.

The temptation to rely on twists and sleight-of-hand was dangerous to a writer of MacNeice's facility and quickness of wit. The use of radiophonic devices concealed the structural weakness of the writing, and the music—composed for *Christopher Columbus* by William Walton and for *The Dark Tower* (1947) by Benjamin Britten—carried the reader over the thinner patches of the dramas. As MacNeice acknowledged, the music of these composers supplied a dimension that the scripts otherwise lacked.

In *Christopher Columbus* there is no attempt to survey the life of Columbus, or even to portray accurately the complicated dispute between him and the commissioners who opposed his voyage of exploration. MacNeice concentrates on Columbus' fanatical resolve to find the western route to Asia and on the triumphant conclusion of his quest—the discovery of a New World. This is, in many ways, MacNeice's most successful radio script, because he eschews all trickiness and allows his theme to unfold itself in its simplicity and grandeur.

In his introductory note to *The Dark Tower* MacNeice remarks: "Man does after all live by sym-

bols. . . . I have my beliefs and they permeate *The Dark Tower*. But do not ask me what Ism it illustrates or what Solution it offers." *The Dark Tower* resembles *Christopher Columbus* in being a play about a quest. Its hero, Roland, like the hero of Robert Browning's poem "Childe Roland," sets out to challenge a Dragon, who is reputed to live in a Dark Tower. Before the play opens, Roland's brothers have, one by one, undertaken a similar quest and have never returned from their mission.

The Dark Tower is a repository of well-worn symbols from the common stock of the 1930's and from MacNeice's private treasury. There is the Mother who, like the formidable matriarch in Auden and Isherwood's *The Ascent of F-6*, drives on her son to achievement or to vengeance (she appears again in another quest play, *The Mad Islands*, published in 1964 and broadcast two years before). Then we have a Parrot, the voice of negation and defeat, who pops up again in *Autumn Sequel* (1954), and once more we encounter MacNeice's obsession with stone. He felt obliged to write a note about this image, which had baffled his radio audience:

The Child of Stone puzzled many listeners. The Mother in bearing so many children only to send them to their death, can be thought of as thereby bearing a series of deaths. So her logical last child is stone—her own death. This motif has an echo in the stone in the ring.

This stone in the ring plays a crucial part in the unfolding of the action. For when it ceases to burn, thereby signifying that the Mother no longer wants her son Roland to pursue the quest, he throws away the ring, which strikes a stone bearing an inscription:

To Those Who Did Not Go Back—
Whose Bones being Nowhere, their signature is
    for All Men—
Who went to their Death of their Own Free Will
Bequeathing Free Will to Others.

Inspired by this message, he goes on, summons the dragon to come out of the Dark Tower, which has mysteriously arisen from the ground, and blows the challenge call. The voice of the sergeant trumpeter, a cross between a family retainer and a regular noncommissioned officer, repeats the instruction he gave at the opening of the play: "Hold that note at the end." The text then continues: "The trumpet holds it, enriched and endorsed by the orchestra. They come to a full close and that is THE END."

407

The four radio plays published in 1969 under the title *Persons from Porlock* are less ambitious than *The Dark Tower*, but in some ways more satisfactory. *Enter Caesar*, first broadcast in 1946, is an ingenious reconstruction of Roman history from the last days of Sulla to the Ides of March, the day of Julius Caesar's murder. *East of the Sun and West of the Moon* and *They Met on Good Friday*, both first broadcast in 1959, display the variety of MacNeice's talents. The first of these plays is a delightful version of a Norwegian folk tale; the second is "A Sceptical Historical Romance" about the great battle fought on Good Friday A.D. 1014 between the Norsemen and the Irish.

W. H. Auden suggests in his foreword to the volume that radio drama is perhaps the ideal medium for "psychological" drama, and that the title play is a magnificent example of the genre. First broadcast on 30 August 1963, four days before MacNeice's death, it tells the story of Hank, a painter, who is a worldly failure and who becomes an alcoholic after Sarah, the girl he loves, has left him. But she comes back, and Hank, after giving up alcohol, is invited by his old friend Mervyn to resume with him the speleological expeditions that had meant so much to him. Hank dies in an attempt to rescue Mervyn from a flooded cave and, as in *One for the Grave*, various figures from the past appear before the dying man, and an enigmatic figure comes to prepare him for death:

Person: . . . Your friend Mervyn was a man after my heart.
Hank: Was?
Person: Was.
Hank: And me?
Person: Till just the other day I had my doubts about you. You made too many excuses. Still, in the end you behaved well to Sarah.
Hank: I love Sarah.

All his life Hank had been visited by various Persons from Porlock who had interrupted his vision. Coleridge, it will be remembered, was the victim of a man from the Somerset village of Porlock who called on him and shattered the reverie in which he was composing *Kublai Khan.* In the closing lines of the play the Person tells Hank that his swim through the cave will sell his pictures:

Hank: I'm glad it will sell them—if there's anything in them.

Person: Of course there's something in them.
Hank: Thank you. But tell me—before I drop off—why is this going to sell them?
Person: Because they will say he met a noble—well, a noble person from Porlock.

Whatever view one may take of the quality of MacNeice's work for radio, one can only agree with W. H. Auden's observation that a good libretto is likely to survive even the best radio script, and regret that MacNeice never collaborated with Britten, Walton, or some other gifted composer in the writing of an opera. His radio scripts may be revived from time to time, but their probable fate is to lie neglected in the BBC archives or, at best, to achieve the status of cultural exhibits, like the masques of the early seventeenth century.

MacNeice produced various programs of translations from both classical and modern European poets, and was himself the author of two large-scale translations, *The Agamemnon of Aeschylus* (1936) and *Goethe's "Faust"* (1951). It is a commonplace that all translations date, so it is not astonishing that certain features of MacNeice's version of Aeschylus are stamped with the hallmarks of the 1930's—the antimilitarism, the determination to make the speeches sound colloquial, the deliberate avoidance of the loftily heroic. But MacNeice has very largely succeeded in his difficult task. The characters are both credible human beings and ritualistic figures of Greek mythology; they remain men and women who are remote from us in speech and thought but who are no mere resurrected mummies intoning platitudes in wooden verse. The drama is at once a representation of human passions and the working out of a preordained divine pattern. MacNeice unites a contemporary sharpness and directness with a formal dignity that suggests the mode of life in the ancient world. Although the version must be judged as a whole, two brief passages may serve as an index of his skill, the first being part of a chorus, the second an extract from a speech by Clytemnestra:

But the money-changer War, changer of bodies,
Holding his balance in the battle
Home from Troy refined by fire
Sends back to friends the dust
That is heavy with tears, stowing
A man's worth of ashes
In an easily handled jar.

(pp. 27–28)

The man who outraged me lies here,
The darling of each courtesan in Troy,
And here with him is the prisoner clairvoyante,
The fortune-teller that he took to bed,
Who shares his bed as once his bench on shipboard,
A loyal mistress. Both have their deserts.
He lies so; and she who like a swan
Sang her last dying lament
Lies like her lover, and the sight contributes
An appetizer to my own bed's pleasure.

(pp. 62–63)

Aeschylus is notoriously difficult to translate. Walter Headlam's literal prose version of the second passage quoted suggests how hard it is to produce a rendering that is faithful to the original and yet sounds tolerable in English:

Low lies the injurer of me, his wife, the comfort of Chryseus' daughters before Troy, and with him she, the bond-servant and auguress, the divining—concubine, the trusty—bed-fellow, practised—equally in the matter of ship's benches. But the pair have fared after their deserts: this is *his* condition; while *she*, after carolling swan-like her last dying lamentation, she, the lover of him, lies there; she, the trivial by-morsel to my lawful bed, hath only afforded me the luxury of triumph.

(pp. 228–229)

Headlam's version merely helps the reader to construe the Greek original; MacNeice, without departing far from the text of Aeschylus, has given us a passage of acceptable English verse.

In MacNeice's version of *Faust* the twelve thousand lines of the original are cut to eight thousand, yet even so this shortened text is longer than Milton's *Paradise Lost*. The sheer size of the undertaking would have daunted most writers, and probably the most praiseworthy aspect of the venture was the dogged persistence that MacNeice brought to his task. He seems not to have regretted the labors it involved: "It gave me a long and strenuous exercise in the craft of writing and also revealed to me a master who, for all his glaring faults, is a great one."

He made things even more difficult than they might have been by his decision on a technical matter:

I aimed at a line-for-line translation and also (which was made easier by the kinship of German and English) at a prosody equivalent to or, if possible, identical with Goethe's. Some of my friends regretted that I did not turn the whole thing into blank verse or "free verse" but in my

opinion that would have ruined the sense of it. For the rhymes in Goethe are part of the sense and he uses them again and again to clinch his point.

(p. 110)

This recalls the self-imposed penances of another Irish poet, Austin Clarke, who, when asked by Robert Frost what kind of verse he wrote, replied, "I load myself with chains and try to get out of them."

MacNeice's fidelity to the original German leads at times to a grotesque deformation of the English language. At its clumsiest the verse is little better than doggerel, as in this dialogue between Nereus and Thales while they watch spirits fly past in the form of doves:

> *Nereus*   Already over, they pass over
> In oscillation and gyration;
> What reck they of my consternation?
> Ah could they take me with them yonder!
> And yet one single glimpse can cheer
> And last me for another year.
> *Thales*   Hail! Once more hail!
> How I bloom and regale
> On beauties' and truths' penetration!
> Everything live is water's creation!
> Water keeps all things young and vernal!
> Ocean grant us thy rule eternal.
> Clouds—were it not for thee sending them,
> Nor fertile brooks—expending them,
> Rivers—hither and thither bending them,
> And streams—not fully tending them,
> Then what would be mountains, what plains and earth?
> 'Tis thou giv'st livingest life its worth.

This is, admittedly, one of the feeblest passages in the translation, but only on rare occasions does it rise above a pedestrian dullness. One successful portion is Gretchen's song at the spinning wheel:

> My peace is gone,
> My heart is sore,
> I shall find it never
> And never more.
>
> He has left my room
> An empty tomb,
> He has gone and all
> My world is gall.
>
> My poor head
> Is all astray,
> My poor mind
> Fallen away.

This reads like an original lyric, not like the rendering of a foreign text into operatic English. The bulk of MacNeice's version resembles an ambitious but cumbersome libretto that might be tolerable were it set to music by a composer of genius.

It may be that Goethe is untranslatable into English and that MacNeice's venture was foredoomed to fail. One regrets that he did not devote his energies to the translating of Horace, Catullus, Tibullus, Propertius, or Petronius Arbiter: the version of Horace's *Odes* I.4 that he wrote in the mid-1930's demonstrates his brilliance and sureness of touch when translating a congenial poet. He evokes with the utmost delicacy the coming of spring sketched so vividly and economically by Horace:

Winter to Spring: the west wind melts the frozen rancour,
  The windlass drags to sea the thirsty hull;
Byre is no longer welcome to beast or fire to ploughman,
  The field removes the frost-cap from his skull.

And he manages to endow the weighty Horatian commonplaces about the coming of death and the transitoriness of worldly pleasure with a resonance and an evocative melancholy that somehow combine the plangency of modern romantic verse with the clarity and grave precision of classical antiquity:

Equally heavy is the heel of white-faced Death on the
    pauper's
  Shack and the towers of kings, and O my dear
The little sum of life forbids the revelling of lengthy
  Hopes. Night and the fabled dead are near

And the narrow house of nothing past whose lintel
  You will meet no wine like this, no boy to admire
Like Lycidas who today makes all young men a furnace
  And whom tomorrow girls will find a fire.

THE EARLY POETRY

THERE are some poets whose work seems to alter radically at various times throughout their careers, and others whose development, though steady, is so gradual that the superficial reader is scarcely aware of it. MacNeice belongs to this second class; he is, moreover, a poet whose temperament and attitude toward the world do not fundamentally change as he grows older. He constantly recurs to scenes, images, and fears remembered from his childhood; at different stages of his life he writes poems that are variations on one or two basic themes; he persistently celebrates the same human virtues and qualities. Even his characteristic modes of expression do not undergo a dramatic transformation. His technique in many ways becomes more assured, his experiments grow bolder, his range widens, but the curve of his achievement is gradual; and he does not remake himself in the manner of Yeats. It is, therefore, advisable to consider the forces that in his youth formed his poetic nature and to examine the background of poetry in the 1930's, the decade in which he began to gain a reputation.

We have seen that his childhood was in some respects unhappy, and that it was of the kind to stimulate his imagination, but it would be a mistake to overemphasize these early experiences. MacNeice himself, in *Modern Poetry*, gives due weight to other causes when drawing up a list of factors that influenced his poetry:

. . . having been brought up in the north of Ireland, having a father who was a clergyman; the fact that my mother died when I was little; repression from the age of six to nine; inferiority complex on grounds of physique and class-consciousness; lack of a social life until I was grown up; late puberty; ignorance of music (which could have been a substitute for poetry); inability to ride horses or practise successfully most of the sports which satisfy a sense of rhythm; an adolescent liking for the role of "enfant terrible"; shyness in the company of young women until I was twenty; a liking (now dead) for metaphysics; marriage and divorce; Birmingham; an indolent pleasure in gardens and wild landscapes . . . a liking for animals, an interest in dress.

MacNeice became well known as one of the leading "Poets of the Thirties," a term often applied to certain poets of the time who were popularly supposed to form a movement, the most prominent figures reputedly being Auden, C. Day Lewis, Stephen Spender, and MacNeice. It is not easy to disentangle the truth from the legend, but certain facts are well established. There was no school or group, in the continental sense, no working out of a coherent aesthetic doctrine, no manifesto, no organized campaign. Indeed there is no record of all four poets meeting together in the same room during the entire decade. Undoubtedly the members of this alleged cabal were not averse to the publicity they received, and they did what they could to boost one another's reputation. But MacSpaunday, the name bestowed by Roy Campbell on his archetypal left-wing poet, was a misnomer.

It is true that MacNeice was a friend and collaborator of W. H. Auden, that he regarded the ruling classes in Britain as ineffectual and contemptible, that he viewed the rise of Nazism with horror and disgust. Yet he was far from being an orthodox left-wing poet, or even a writer whose poetry had an overt social purpose. It is significant that Michael Roberts omitted him from his two influential anthologies, *New Signatures* (1932) and *New Country* (1933), both of which were designed to hasten the birth of a new social order and the advent of a new Lenin (ambitions later disavowed by Roberts).

MacNeice, by temperament and by conviction, was always hostile to Communism. He was, in politics as in religion, a skeptic who mistrusted lofty idealism and self-righteousness, in no matter what disguise they draped themselves. Nor did he trust any creed that exalted a bureaucratic hierarchy, whether of priests or of politicians, at the expense of the individual. In such poems as "Turf Stacks," "To a Communist," and "The Individualist Speaks," MacNeice explicitly dissociates himself from those who proclaim the millennium: "—But I will escape, with my dog, on the far side of the Fair." Moreover, although he remained all his life a radical, a satirical observer of the established order, and a mocker of shams and pomposities, he was too honest to deny that he enjoyed the pleasures and shared many of the values of upper-middle-class life:

My sympathies are Left. On paper and in my soul. But not in my heart or my guts. . . . With my heart and my guts I lament the passing of class. Of class, property and snobbery. A man for me is still largely characterised by what he buys—by his suits, his books, the meals he gives you, his chair-covers.

(*I Crossed the Minch*, p. 125)

Finally, even in the mid-1930's, when it was fashionable for public-school boys to proclaim their adherence to Communism, MacNeice recognized the equivocal nature of many such conversions:

So many left-wing comrades, at least in England, suffer from the masochism of the puritan. . . . A future of Esperanto, Sunday School treats and homage to the Highest Common Factor. Not that this was Lenin's ideal.
Comradeship is the communist substitute for bourgeois romance; in its extreme form (cp. also fascism and youth-cults in general) it leads to an idealization of homosexuality.

Writing in 1957, MacNeice remarked that even in the early work of Auden, Day Lewis, and Spender, a large proportion of the poems cannot be properly described as "social" or "political." This is still more true of his own early verse. He called his youthful volume, published in 1929, *Blind Fireworks*, because the poems in it "are artificial and yet random; because they go quickly through their antics against an important background." MacNeice came to judge his own juvenilia pretty harshly. The best description of his verse in the late 1920's and early 1930's is to be found in Geoffrey Grigson's *Poetry of the Present* (1949):

Compared with Auden . . . all of MacNeice's fireworks and icicles were alien. Ixion, Pythagoras, Persephone, Orestes, de Sade, Origen—were mixed up in poems of a blatant cleverness. Still, cleverness it was, words were courted; and there in these juvenilia were stretched to tautness criss-crossing wires of form with this spangled acrobat perfoming on them; and the cleverness . . . grew and strengthened itself into a capable and convincing rhetoric, beholden to much, yet chiefly to MacNeice himself. The wires were still silvery and still glittered. The icicles, the ice-cream, the pink and white, the lace and the froth and the fireworks were still there, but underneath the game was the drop, the space, and the knowledge.

What one notices above all in these poems is MacNeice's responsiveness to the brilliance, the glitter of the visible world:

In that Poussin the clouds are like golden tea,
And underneath the limbs flow rhythmically,
The cupids' blue feathers beat musically.
("Poussin")

The yokels tilt their pewters and the foam
Flowers in the sun beside the jewelled water.
Daughter of the South, call the sunbeams home
To nest between your breasts.
("Mayfly")

And the street fountain blown across the square
Rainbow-trellises the air and sunlight blazons
The red butcher's and scrolls of fish on marble slabs.
("Morning Sun")

"Leaving Barra" is both a philosophical poem and a declaration of love, yet when one has forgotten the argument, and the avowal has faded from one's mind, a single image, characteristic of MacNeice, lingers in the memory—"the dazzle on the sea, my darling."

Nevertheless, MacNeice was unable to enjoy unquestioningly the sensuous world or to believe that the mere recording of phenomena was adequate. He had, as we have seen, rejected while still at Oxford the metaphysical assumptions of Plato, and he continued to assert the irreducible diversity of things:

> World is crazier and more of it than we think,
> Incorrigibly plural. I peel and portion
> A tangerine and spit the pips and feel
> The drunkenness of things being various.
>
> ("Snow")

He distrusted all neat philosophical systems, all "the nostrums / Of science art and religion"; he had abandoned his father's Christian beliefs; he regarded the world of scholarship and of museums as an attractive but slightly disreputable escape from reality:

> Museums offer us, running from among the buses,
> A centrally heated refuge, parquet floors and
> sarcophaguses.
>
> ("Museum")

Yet, despite his frequently expressed desire to live in the present, his resolve to cease constructing moral or philosophical codes, his longing to throw off the burden of introspection—"I do not want to be reflective any more"—he was never able to abdicate from the responsibility of being a rational, moral creature. He remained all his life his father's son, often indeed weakening the impact of his poems by his tendency to preach a lay sermon, to expound the necessity of decency, courage, endurance.

Thus in a series of long poems, written between 1933 and 1937, MacNeice wrestles, like a stern Victorian agnostic, with a host of moral and political problems. "The Hebrides" is less an impressionistic picture of a beauty spot than a celebration of human dignity; and his four eclogues are also musings on the condition of man. The closing lines of "An Eclogue for Christmas" sum up what was to be a lifelong preoccupation with the relationship between flux and permanence, the allure of transient phenomena, the possibility of a permanent, divine order:

> A. Let the saxophones and the xylophones
> And the cult of every technical excellence, the miles of
> canvas in the galleries
> And the canvas of the rich man's yacht snapping and
> tacking on the seas

> And the perfection of a grilled steak—
> B. Let all these so ephemeral things
> Be somehow permanent like the swallow's tangent wings:
> Goodbye to you, this day remember is Christmas, this
> morn
> They say, interpret it your own way, Christ is born.

Twenty years later, in *Autumn Sequel*, he was to make the same half-questioning affirmation.

The tension in these early poems springs from MacNeice's intuitive response to physical stimuli and his simultaneous awareness of the need for reflection and moral judgment. He was also profoundly moved by the political events of the time, and watched with a sickening helplessness the senile inability of the Western democracies to preserve the liberties of Europe, or even to understand the nature of the threat to themselves. His "Epilogue to Iceland: For W. H. Auden" expresses his personal loneliness and his sense that human liberty and decency are imperiled throughout the world:

> For the litany of doubt
> From these walls comes breathing out
> Till the room becomes a pit
> Humming with the fear of it
>
> With the fear of loneliness
> And uncommunicableness;
> All the wires are cut, my friends
> Live beyond the severed ends.
>
> So I write these lines for you
> Who have felt the death-wish too,
> But your lust for life prevails—
> Drinking coffee, telling tales.
>
> Our prerogatives as men
> Will be cancelled who knows when;
> Still I drink your health before
> The gun-butt raps upon the door.

All the themes that run through these early poems recur in *Autumn Journal*, published in the spring of 1939. Written in irregular meter, and in a flexible rhyme scheme, the poem is capacious enough to accommodate a mixed assortment of descriptive passages, autobiographical reflections, political rhetoric, memories of a broken marriage, social satire, potted history, philosophical argument, and random jottings about a variety of topics. It still remains a delightfully readable though uneven poem, and the most intelligent record of what it was like to be young, skeptical, radical, and pleasure-loving in England just before World War II. It contains one or two passages of memorable virtuosity, notably section 9, an evocation of ancient Greece and an ironical commentary on the way in which pedants distort the truth about that savage, vital civilization:

> So the humanist in his room with Jacobean panels
>   Chewing his pipe and looking on a lazy quad
> Chops the Ancient World to turn a sermon
>   To the greater glory of God.
> But I can do nothing so useful or so simple;
>   These dead are dead
> And when I should remember the paragons of Hellas
>   I think instead
> Of the crooks, the adventurers, the opportunists,
>   The careless athletes and the fancy boys,
> The hair-splitters, the pedants, the hard-boiled sceptics
>   And the Agora and the noise
> Of the demagogues and the quacks; and the women
>   pouring
>   Libations over graves
> And the trimmers at Delphi and the dummies at
>   Sparta and lastly
>   I think of the slaves.
> And how one can imagine oneself among them
>   I do not know;
> It was all so unimaginably different
>   And all so long ago.

Two of MacNeice's poems written in the 1930's have become popular anthology pieces. Surrealism had little influence on English poetry, and the only good English poet to take seriously this fashionable continental theory was David Gascoyne. But just as the Marx brothers employed modified surrealistic devices in their films, so MacNeice, contemplating the crazy fabric of capitalist Britain, gave vent to his despair and disgust in the high-spirited fantasy of "Bagpipe Music":

> It's no go the Yogi-Man, it's no go Blavatsky,
> All we want is a bank balance and a bit of skirt in a taxi . . .
>
> Willie Murray cut his thumb, couldn't count the damage,
> Took the hide of an Ayrshire cow and used it for a
>   bandage.
> His brother caught three hundred cran when the seas
>   were lavish,
> Threw the bleeders back in the sea and went upon the
>   parish . . .
>
> It's no go the picture palace, it's no go the stadium,
> It's no go the country cot with a pot of pink geraniums,
> It's no go the Government grants, it's no go the elections,
> Sit on your arse for fifty years and hang your hat on a
>   pension.

In "The Sunlight on the Garden," MacNeice shapes his private fears, his sense of coming doom, his delight in the pleasures of the moment into a lyric that, beneath the surface elegance, has a disturbing power:

> The sunlight on the garden
> Hardens and grows cold,
> We cannot cage the minute
> Within its nets of gold;
> When all is told
> We cannot beg for pardon.
>
> Our freedom as free lances
> Advances towards its end;
> The earth compels, upon it
> Sonnets and birds descend;
> And soon, my friend,
> We shall have no time for dances.
>
> The sky was good for flying
> Defying the church bells
> And every evil iron
> Siren and what it tells:
> The earth compels,
> We are dying, Egypt, dying
>
> And not expecting pardon,
> Hardened in heart anew,
> But glad to have sat under
> Thunder and rain with you,
> And grateful too
> For sunlight on the garden.

Many of MacNeice's typical images and themes are here: the sinister ringing of church bells; the noise of sirens, which may be a reference to air-raid warnings but almost certainly is a reminiscence of the foghorns calling from Belfast Lough; the premonition of political disaster; the savoring of transitory happiness, all the sweeter because it passes so quickly. The ingenuity of the rhyming scheme, the verbal dexterity, the rhythmical assurance, even the allusion to *Antony and Cleopatra*, all play their part in making this poem a memorable expression of MacNeice's complex, ironic view of himself and of the world in the shadow of approaching war.

THE WAR YEARS AND THE LATE 1940's

THE coming of war provided MacNeice with a new range of experiences and deeply affected his emotional development. Although his verse undergoes no spectacular change, it gradually alters its character in a variety of ways, becoming less impressionistic and glittering. MacNeice seems now to be more concerned with the congruence of the images in a poem than with their individual brilliance; in the dedicatory lines "To Hedli" he says that he has modified the tone and the texture of his verse

> Because the velvet image,
> Because the lilting measure
> No more convey my meaning.

In an article published in 1949, entitled "Experiences with Images," he attempts to analyze his new method of employing images and the reasons for the changes in his technique. He explains that he sometimes uses "a set of basic images which crossfade into each other," and that he has experimented with a "quasi-musical interlinking of images, with variations on contrasted themes." He has come to value economy and precision of language, and has a particular fondness for the phrase that concentrates a variety of meanings into a narrow compass:

Thus the lines that I am especially proud of in my last book are such lines as these (of the aftermath of war in England):

> The joker that could have been at any moment death
> Has been withdrawn, the cards are what they say
> And none is wild . . .

or (of a tart):

> Mascara scrawls a gloss on a torn leaf

(a line which it took me a long time to find).

The mood of the poems grows more reflective and somber, the wit is darker and harsher:

> After the legshows and the brandies
> And all the pick-me-ups for tired
> Men there is a feeling
> Something more is required.
>
> The lights go down and eyes
> Look up across the room;
> Salome comes in, bearing
> The head of God knows whom.
> ("Night Club")

In many of the poems MacNeice is haunted by Christian symbols, by the ghost of that Christian morality which he has rejected but not exorcised.

The very titles of certain poems—"Didymus" (used for two poems), "Prayer Before Birth," "Prayer in Mid-Passage," "Place of a Skull," "Whit Monday," "Carol"—suggest the cast of his mind. Like Arthur Hugh Clough a century before, he seems hurt and self-reproachful at his inability to accept the Christian faith. In "The Springboard," the protagonist stands

> High above London, naked in the night
> Perched on a board.

He is kept there, "crucified among the budding stars," by his unbelief:

> And yet we know he knows what he must do.
> There above London where the gargoyles grin
> He will dive like a bomber past the broken steeple,
> One man wiping out his own original sin
> And, like ten million others, dying for the people.

The fire-raids on London must have seemed like the fulfillment of his prophecy in *Out of the Picture*. MacNeice senses in the scenes of destruction the operation of a principle that is hostile to human life. In "Brother Fire," contemplating the ravages of war, he draws a comfortless moral:

> Thus were we weaned to knowledge of the Will
> That wills the natural world but wills us dead

—an image that recurs in "Schizophrene," when the child, hearing an "ominous relentless noise," recognizes that "It means a Will that wills all children dead." Characteristically, the child is terrified by church bells and, when she hears the cock crow, identifies herself with St. Peter, for whose denial she wishes to atone:

> But the grey cock still crows and she knows why;
> For she must still deny, deny, deny.

It would be wrong to suppose that all the poems of these years are obsessed by guilt, forebodings, and despair. There are poems celebrating the momentary peace that love may bring when "Time was away and she was here," or that may come as an unlooked-for revelation:

Waking, he found himself in a train, andante,
With wafers of early sunlight blessing the unknown fields.

"The National Gallery" hymns the "pentecost in Trafalgar Square" brought about by the reopening of the gallery after the war; in "Wood," MacNeice depicts his affection for the gentle English countryside; even in ironical surveys of human passions and flaws, such as "Alcohol," "The Libertine," "Epitaph for Liberal Poets," and "Elegy for Minor Poets," a stoical gaiety and a wry resignation counterbalance the bitterness and the pain. Yet the finest poem of this period is "Prayer Before Birth," an anguished protest against the impersonal cruelty of the world. For once MacNeice does not take refuge in evasive irony or allusiveness, but speaks out directly against everything that degrades the spirit of man:

I am not yet born; O hear me,
Let not the man who is beast or who thinks he is God
      come near me.

I am not yet born; O fill me
With strength against those who would freeze my
    humanity, would dragoon me into a lethal automaton,
      would make me a cog in a machine, a thing with
        one face, a thing, and against all those
          who would dissipate my entirety, would
            blow me like thistledown hither and
              thither or hither and thither
                like water held in the
                  hands would spill me.

Let them not make me a stone and let them not spill me.
Otherwise kill me.

THE MIDDLE STRETCH

MacNeice was always attracted by what he calls "This whole delightful world of cliché and refrain," and his poems sometimes rely too heavily on his verbal ingenuity, his gift of the poetic gab. Instead of true originality and genuine distinction of language, we are often fobbed off with paradoxes in the style of Oscar Wilde, tags and proverbs slightly twisted, invented truisms, distorted clichés, ironical borrowings from jazz lyrics, sophisticated parodies of nursery rhymes. Moreover, especially in the longer poems, the moralizing tends to become obtrusive, the prevalence of wise saws and modern instances is fatiguing, the sententiousness grows wearisome. MacNeice's vision of the world is civilized and humane, but after reading "The Kingdom" one is in-

clined to feel that decency, like patriotism, is not enough. Despite the vividness and sparkle of his early poems, an admirer of his poetry, scrutinizing the later work in *Collected Poems 1925–1948*, might well have had doubts about MacNeice's poetic development.

In fact, his verse from about 1949 until the mid-1950's went through a very sticky patch. Even if we were fully acquainted with MacNeice's private life it would be idle to explain this apparent decline in his poetry by reference to his biography. Most artists experience periods of barrenness, akin perhaps to those spells of dryness that are familiar to mystics. The periods sometimes coincide with the onset of middle age; MacNeice himself seems to have been aware that the physiology of a poet is inextricably linked with the development of his art:

        This middle stretch
Of life is bad for poets; a sombre view
Where neither works nor days look innocent
And both seem now too many, now too few.
          ("Day of Renewal," 1–4)

It is possible that the strain of translating *Faust* left MacNeice temporarily exhausted, and that he was unhappily inspired to emulate Goethe by writing long philosophical poems instead of the short lyrics to which his talents were best suited. Whatever the explanation may be, his first two volumes of original verse after the *Collected Poems* were *Ten Burnt Offerings* (1952), a series of medium-length poems, and *Autumn Sequel*, "a rhetorical poem" in twenty-six cantos.

The poems in *Ten Burnt Offerings* are, according to MacNeice, "experiments in dialectical structure." Despite the interest of their themes, their shrewdness of psychological observation, and their skilled craftsmanship, they seldom quicken into poetic vitality: it is disquieting that the liveliest passage in the entire volume is a pastiche—the soliloquy of Lord Byron in Lowland Scots, which begins: "Bards wha hae for Hellas bled."

Autumn Sequel, like the translation of *Faust* and *Ten Burnt Offerings*, was broadcast before publication on the Third Programme. It may be unfair to blame its faults on its origin, for it was not commissioned by the BBC, although, as G. S. Fraser has remarked, the decision to broadcast it can scarcely have taken MacNeice unawares. Described by its author as an attempt to marry myth to "actuality," it portrays various friends of the poet, living and dead, including Dylan Thomas, canonized as Gwilym the Maker and depicted according to the conventions of hagiography.

Ezra Pound has drawn superb sketches of his friends and enemies in *The Cantos*, his vignettes recapturing their exact lineaments. Yeats has transformed his contemporaries into heroic myths, forms more real than living men. The figures in *Autumn Sequel* seem to be neither human beings, idiosyncratic and minutely observed, nor successful mythical creations. As for the Parrot, symbol of flux and of negation, the Mountain that has to be climbed because it is there, the Garden, and the Quest—these are familiar properties, now grown tatty, from MacNeice's theatrical storehouse.

The meter and the rhyming scheme of the prewar *Autumn Journal* are admirably suited to the nature of the material with which MacNeice is dealing. The terza rima of *Autumn Sequel*, though it lends a semblance of unity to the poem, becomes, long before the last canto, monotonous and wearisome: it is a meter that, though well adapted to produce an effect of weight, conciseness, and intensity, does not lend itself to the diffuse, rambling development of loosely associated themes characteristic of *Autumn Sequel*. The poem seldom falls below or rises above a decent competence: it is most satisfying when MacNeice is meditating on his favorite problems or even restating old conclusions, as at the close of Canto XXV, which takes us back to "An Eclogue for Christmas":

> Meanwhile the Plough
> Ploughs its own stars in deeper while the pails
>
> Ring with the new day's milk and one still patient cow
> Still stares beyond to where the skies are warning
> That a new sun is rising and that now,
>
> Take it what way you like, is really Christmas morning.

THE FINAL PHASE

IN the mid-1950's there were many who regarded MacNeice as played out, just as the wits of Dublin and the critical wiseacres had frequently proclaimed between 1900 and 1920 that Yeats was finished. We do not know why a poet's work declines or why, for some poets, there may be a renewal of talent after a period of silence or of desiccation. In his last three volumes, *Visitations* (1957), *Solstices* (1961), and *The Burning Perch* (1963), MacNeice not only recaptures his old vitality but also taps more profound sources of imaginative power than at any time in his career. The poems of this period are less widely known than those written in the 1930's, partly because they have not yet found their way into the anthologies, partly because he was now a somewhat lonely man in his fifties and no longer a leading member of a fashionable group. It seems likely, however, that the work of this last phase will become increasingly admired as time passes.

MacNeice tells us that he was incapable of writing short poems while engaged in composing *Ten Burnt Offerings* and *Autumn Sequel*, and that

> when the lyrical impulse did return, this interval of abstention, it seems to me, had caused certain changes in my lyric-writing. . . . I like to think that my latest short poems are on the whole more concentrated and better organised than my earlier ones, relying more on syntax and bony feature than on bloom or frill or the floating image. I should also like to think that sometimes they achieve a blend of "classical" and "romantic," marrying the element of wit to the sensuous-mystical element.
>
> (*Poetry Book Society's Bulletin,* Spring 1961)

The poems in *Visitations* were the prelude to another flowering of the lyrical impulse in 1959 and 1960: "In particular, in the spring and early summer of 1960 I underwent one of those rare bursts of creativity when the poet is first astonished and then rather alarmed by the way the mill goes on grinding." There was a final spurt of imaginative energy in the three years before his death, which resulted in *The Burning Perch*, a posthumous collection of poems.

In these last volumes there is no startling development, no breakthrough into entirely new territory. Some of the old faults crop up again: the mechanical sprightliness of

> Here come I, old April Fool,
> Between March hare and nuts in May
> ("April Fool")

the jazzing up of a nursery rhyme—"This is the house that Jack built"—in "Château Jackson"; a sophisticated juggling with words and concepts that came all too easily to MacNeice. Many of his standard themes recur. There are poems about the British Museum and about childhood, reminiscences of the fire-raids on London, and satirical reflections on contemporary society in general and metropolitan life in particular. In one of the final poems, "Memoranda to Horace," he reverts once more to the image of a mayfly that had attracted him over thirty years before. One section of "Notes for a Biography" is a virtuoso parody of "Bonny Dundee" that recalls the episode in *I Crossed the Minch* when MacNeice "began to sing various scurrilous songs, improvising words to 'Bonny Dundee.'"

But although much of this terrain is familiar, MacNeice is exploring it in greater depth than ever before. In "Beni Hasan" he contemplates himself and his morality with a fine gravity:

It came to me on the Nile my passport lied
Calling me dark who am grey. In the brown cliff
A row of tombs, of potholes, stared and stared as if
They were the long dead eyes of beasts inside
Time's cage, black eyes on eyes that stared away
Lion-like focused on some different day
On which, on a long term view, it was I, not they, had died.

The old religious preoccupations are now faced with a quiet dignity, a reverence for

Poor Tom o'Bethlehem, only a Mary,
An ox and an ass, a nought and a cross
("The Other Wing")

and an acceptance of agnosticism that has shed the angry unease of the 1930's:

Thank God we do not know; we know
We need the unknown. The unknown is There.
("Jigsaws," V)

He displays a new awareness of his own nature and, in a harsh, astringent poem, "The Habits," acknowledges his lifelong temptation to surrender to those anodynes that may save us from having to bear the pain of reality. He can review his spiritual life as far back as the age of seven, when he was haunted by fears of damnation, and face the truth of what he has become:

He was not Tom or Dick or Harry,
Let alone God, he was merely fifty,
No one and nowhere else, a walking
Question but no more cheap than any
Question or quest is cheap. The sin
Against the Holy Ghost—what is it?
("The Blasphemies")

In the last two volumes there are many poems about bad dreams, nightmarish journeys, and scenes where everything is in flux or the wrong way round. When he assembled the poems in *The Burning Perch*, MacNeice was "taken aback by the high proportion of sombre pieces, ranging from bleak observation to thumbnail nightmares." There are, it is true, poems that seem to attain a Horatian resignation: "But my resignation, as I was not brought up a pagan, is more of a fraud than Horace's."

Perhaps the most original achievements in these final volumes are those poems in *The Burning Perch* that convey a sense of desolation, of something gone awry, as though one were walking down a staircase where a step is missing, or had entered a room where everything is in order except for some terrifying absence or reversal of normality. These poems crackle with an eerie vitality, and are shaken by the kind of savage mirth that informs some of Béla Bartók's later music. A few lines from three of these poems may suggest the nature of the spirit that animates them:

They were introduced in a grave glade
And she frightened him because she was young
And thus too late. Crawly crawly
Went the twigs about their heads. . . .
Crawly crawly
Went the string quartet that was tuning up
In the back of the mind. You two should have met
Long since, he said, or else not now.
The string quartet in the back of the mind
Was all tuned up with nowhere to go.
They were introduced in a green grave.
("The Introduction")

In the third taxi he was alone tra-la
But the tip-up seats were down and there was an extra
Charge of one-and-sixpence and an odd
Scent that reminded him of a trip to Cannes.

As for the fourth taxi, he was alone
Tra-la when he hailed it but the cabby looked
Through him and said: "I can't tra-la well take
So many people, not to speak of the dog."
("The Taxis")

When he came to he knew
Time must have passed because
The asphalt was high with hemlock
Through which he crawled to his crash
Helmet and found it no more
Than his wrinkled hand what it was.

Yet life seemed still going on:
He could hear the signals bounce
Back from the moon and the hens
Fire themselves black in the batteries
And the silence of small blind cats
Debating whether to pounce.
("After the Crash")

There is no reason to suppose that MacNeice had any premonition of his death; but it is appropriate that in one of his last poems, "Charon," he should have described a spectral encounter on the banks of the Thames:

And there was the ferryman just as Virgil
And Dante had seen him. He looked at us coldly
And his eyes were dead and his hands on the oar
Were black with obols and varicose veins
Marbled his calves and he said to us coldly:
If you want to die you will have to pay for it.

CONCLUSION

MacNeice was an unusually complex individual whose character was made up of contradictory elements. He was abundantly sociable, yet fundamentally shy, a man in whom Irish high spirits were blended with Celtic melancholy, an extrovert who talked volubly, while retaining an inner reserve and reticence about his griefs and fears. He described himself in youth as one "whose chief pleasures in life are liking and being liked" and, after remarking that animals are limited because they are specialized, went on: "I shouldn't think it worth it to become even an over-specialized human-being—someone who was only a cricketer, a politician, a stormtrooper, a spiritualist medium, a pianist or a world-authority on any one square inch of subject."

This is why it is pointless to wag a reproving finger at MacNeice for devoting too much of his time to drinking and gossiping with his cronies, and why his faults and virtues, as man and poet, are inseparable. He was, above all, a generous man, who encouraged and helped not only young, up-and-coming writers but those who were elderly and in decline. In 1940 Wyndham Lewis, the old friend and coeval of T. S. Eliot, Ezra Pound, and James Joyce, was living in New York, poor and in distress. It was typical of MacNeice that he should have given financial aid to this distinguished writer of an older generation, whose political views and temperament he could scarcely have found congenial.

MacNeice was always keenly responsive to the delights of the world, including those of sexual love. In a fragment of autobiography, written two or three years before his death, he thanked God for the pleasures of life, not forgetting those offered by the Garden of Adonis; and his love poetry is that of a man who has plunged into the turmoil of passion, gladly accepting its joys and its griefs.

During the course of his memorial address, W. H. Auden referred to MacNeice's enjoyment of "those temporal pleasures which he can no longer share with us, his pleasure in language, in country landscapes, in city streets and parks, in birds, beasts and flowers, in nice clothes, good conversation, good food, good drink, and in what he called 'the tangles.'" To which one might add his pleasure in playing and watching games; he frankly admitted that at times he derived more satisfaction from them than from works of art:

Is it absurd
To have preferred at time a sport to works of art?
Where both show craft, at times I have preferred

The greater measure of chance, that thrill which
sports impart
Because they are not foregone, move in more fluid
borders.
Statues and even plays are finished before they start,

But in a game, as in life, we are under Starter's Orders.
(*Autumn Sequel*, canto XXIII)

Few poets have managed to make poetry out of the enjoyment that they have distilled from the minor pleasures of life. A short list of such poets would include Shakespeare, preeminent in this as in so much else, Ben Jonson, Robert Herrick, Robert Burns, Byron, Alfred Tennyson, and Robert Browning. MacNeice belongs to the select company of those who are able to communicate their delight in the minutiae of daily life, the sense of happiness and well-being that springs from good health, mental alertness, and emotional vitality. It would, however, be wrong to suppose that MacNeice was no more than a graceful celebrator of sensuous pleasures and a painter of surface appearances. Much as he loved the sunlight on the garden and the dazzle on the sea, he was not afraid to explore the colder depths and the dark places of the human spirit. His later poems in particular are marked by a bleak pessimism and a black melancholy: his finest work springs from a fruitful tension between the somber premonitions to which he was prey and the positive qualities of natural energy, intellectual strength, and stoical courage.

During his lifetime MacNeice's poetic reputation had its ups and downs. Even in the 1930's, when he was enthusiastically praised by many readers of his generation, he was assailed by conservative critics, who denounced him as an angry young iconoclast, and was also viewed with disfavor by the censorious judges on the bench of *Scrutiny*. The *Times Literary Supplement*, reviewing in 1949 his *Collected Poems 1925–1948*, weighed him in the balance and found him wanting, a verdict generally endorsed by critical opinion in the late 1940's and early 1950's. It was not until the last few years of his life that he began once again to command widespread admiration and respect.

In a comment on the obituary notice printed in the *Times*, Eliot wrote that MacNeice "had the Irishman's unfailing ear for the music of verse," and spoke of "the grief one must feel at the death of a poet of genius younger than oneself." Whatever MacNeice's rank in our literature may be, he deserves to be honored as a man of letters who practiced his craft with devotion, as a pioneer of radio drama, and as a poet whose sardonic gaiety, brooding sadness, and integrity of mind are reflected in the few dozen lyrics that are his surest title to remembrance.

SELECTED BIBLIOGRAPHY

I. Bibliography. C. M. Armitage and N. Clark, *A Bibliography of the Work of Louis MacNeice* (London, 1973).

II. Collected Works. *Collected Poems 1925–1948* (London, 1949); E. R. Dodds, ed., *Collected Poems* (London, 1966).

III. Selected Works. *Selected Poems* (London, 1940); *Eighty-five Poems* (London, 1950), sel. by MacNeice; W. H. Auden, ed., *Selected Poems* (London, 1964), paperback ed. with brief critical intro.

IV. Separate Works. *Blind Fireworks* (London, 1929), verse; *Roundabout Way* (London, 1932), novel, under pseudonym Louis Malone; *Poems* (London, 1935); *The Agamemnon of Aeschylus* (London, 1936; paperback ed., 1967), verse translation; *Letters from Iceland* (London, 1937; paperback ed., 1967), verse and prose, with W. H. Auden; *Out of the Picture* (London, 1937), verse drama;

The Earth Compels (London, 1938), verse; *I Crossed the Minch* (London, 1938), verse and prose, account of travel in the Outer Hebrides; *Modern Poetry: A Personal Essay* (London, 1938), criticism; *Zoo* (London, 1938), prose, an account of the London Zoo, with autobiographical digressions; *Autumn Journal* (London, 1939), verse, see also *Autumn Sequel* below.

The Last Ditch (Dublin, 1940), verse; *Plant and Phantom* (London, 1941), verse; *The Poetry of W. B. Yeats* (London, 1941; paperback ed., 1967), criticism; *Meet the U.S. Army* (London, 1943), prose, prepared for the Board of Education by the Ministry of Information; *Springboard* (London, 1944), verse; *Christopher Columbus: A Radio Play* (London, 1944; new ed., 1963), verse, with intro. essay on radio drama; *The Dark Tower and Other Radio Scripts* (London, 1947; paperback ed., 1964), verse and prose, with intro. essay on radio drama, latter excludes the additional radio scripts; *Holes in the Sky* (London, 1948), verse.

Goethe's "Faust" (London, 1951; abr. paperback ed., 1965), verse translation, with E. L. Stahl; *Ten Burnt Offerings* (London, 1952), verse; *Autumn Sequel* (London, 1954), verse, sequel to *Autumn Journal*; *The Other Wing* (London, 1954), verse, illus. by M. Ayrton; *The Sixpence That Rolled Away* (London, 1956), children's story, illus. by E. Bawden, repr. with slight textual changes as *The Penny That Rolled Away* (New York, 1954), illus. by M. Bileck; *Visitations* (London, 1957), verse.

Solstices (London, 1961), verse; *The Burning Perch* (London, 1963), verse; *The Mad Islands [and] The Administrator: Two Radio Plays* (London, 1964), prose, with intro. essay on radio drama; *Astrology* (London, 1964), lavishly illus. survey; E. R. Dodds, ed., *The Strings Are False* (London, 1965), autobiography; *Varieties of Parable* (London, 1965), criticism, the Clark Lectures, Cambridge, 1961; *One for the Grave: A Modern Morality Play* (London, 1968), prose; *Persons from Porlock and Other Radio Plays* (London, 1969), prose, with intro. by W. H. Auden, other plays include *Enter Caesar, East of the Sun and West of the Moon*, and *They Met on Good Friday*.

The Revenant: A Song-Cycle for Hedli Anderson (Dublin, 1975).

V. Reviews, Articles, and Essays. "Poetry," in G. Grigson, ed., *The Arts To-day* (London, 1935); "Subject in Modern Poetry," in *Essays and Studies*, XXII (1936); "Traveller's Return," in *Horizon*, III, no. 14 (1941); "Poetry, the Public and the Critic," in *New Statesman* (8 October 1949); "Experience with Images," in *Orpheus*, II (1949); "Lost Generations?" in *London* magazine, IV, no. 4 (April 1957); "When I Was Twenty-One," in *Saturday Book* (1961); "Childhood Memories," in the *Listener* (12 December 1963).

VI. Unpublished Lectures, Manuscripts, and Typescripts. "The Unities in Drama," lecture dated 29 August 1938; "Broken Windows or Thinking Aloud," undated article (1941–1942?); "Lyric into Drama," the Judith

E. Wilson Lecture given at Cambridge, 5 March 1959; various works including the two prose plays "Traitors in Our Way" and "Eureka, Another Part of the Sea: A Play for Television," and a number of radio scripts.

VII. BIOGRAPHICAL AND CRITICAL STUDIES. C. Day Lewis, *A Hope for Poetry* (London, 1934); J. Southworth, *Sowing the Spring* (Oxford, 1940), contains ch. on MacNeice's early poetry; F. Scarfe, *Auden and After* (London, 1942), contains a section on MacNeice's early poetry; "A Poet of Our Time," in *Times Literary Supplement* (28 October 1949), long review of *Collected Poems 1925–1948* that concludes "they show a small talent and a limited achievement, with few signs of possible further development"; G. Grigson, *Poetry of the Present* (London, 1949); A. Thwait, *Essays on Contemporary English Poetry* (Tokyo, 1957), contains a section on MacNeice's poetry;

G. S. Fraser, "Evasive Honesty: The Poetry of Louis MacNeice," in *Vision and Rhetoric* (London, 1959), a generous and perceptive survey.

W. H. Auden, *Louis MacNeice* (London, 1963), privately printed, a memorial address by one of MacNeice's oldest friends: S. Wall, "Louis MacNeice and the Line of Least Resistance," in the *Review*, XI–XII (1964), severely critical review; D. E. S. Maxwell, *Poets of the Thirties* (London, 1969), contains a discussion of MacNeice's poetry; W. McKinnon, *Apollo's Blended Dream: A Study of the Poetry of Louis MacNeice* (London, 1971); D. B. Moore, *The Poetry of Louis MacNeice* (Leicester, 1972); T. Brown and A. Reid, eds., *Time Was Away: The World of Louis MacNeice* (Dublin, 1974); T. Brown, *Louis MacNeice in the B.B.C.* (London, 1980); R. Marsack, *The Cave of Making: The Poetry of Louis MacNeice* (Oxford, 1983).

POETS OF WORLD WAR II

John Press

INTRODUCTION

COUNTLESS books, poems, photographs, and films have imprinted on our memories ineffaceable images of World War I: rat-infested dugouts; fields torn by shells; barbed wire festooned with corpses; men cut down by machine guns as they charged with fixed bayonets; lakes of mud that sucked men under; and brief moments of rest behind the front line in the villages of Flanders or France. World War II presents a different pattern of warfare; one in which mobility largely supersedes the front line and the system of trenches, and tanks and planes become dominant weapons, reinforced by the power of artillery and the courage of trained infantrymen.

C. E. Montague's important work *Disenchantment* (1922) records the process whereby the soldiers who with the noblest ideals and hopes volunteered in 1914 soon became embittered and disillusioned. This did not happen in World War II mainly because only the most naive recruits harbored any illusions that might wither. When Evelyn Waugh's *Put Out More Flags* appeared in 1942, nobody supposed that it would be an undiluted panegyric to the war effort.

During the last two years of World War I many soldiers who were at the end of their tether in the trenches hated their civilian fellow countrymen more than their German fellow sufferers. Siegfried Sassoon's "I'd like to see a Tank come down the stalls," written after a visit to a variety theater in Liverpool in January 1917, anticipates Wilfred Owen's letter of 10 August 1918 to his mother, in which he desires that "the Boche would have the pluck to come right in and make a clean sweep of the pleasure boats, and the promenaders on the Spa, and all the stinking Leeds and Bradford war profiteers now reading *John Bull* on Scarborough Sands."

No member of the armed services would have expressed those sentiments in World War II. Air raids, rationing, shortages, the blackout, conscription of labor, and the absence of husbands and fathers on active service imposed heavy physical and emotional strains on civilians in Britain. Many servicemen enjoying, albeit with a twinge of guilt, the green pastures of Kenya, the pleasures of Egypt, or the imperial grandeur of India might reflect that they were a great deal safer and more comfortable than people in the cities and towns of Britain.

It is significant that whereas some of the best poets of World War I—Julian Grenfell, Edmund Blunden, Siegfried Sassoon, Wilfred Owen, and Herbert Read—were decorated for gallantry, none of the poets discussed in the present essay received a decoration except Norman Cameron, who was made a Member of the Order of the British Empire for work in political intelligence and propaganda. Moreover, barely half these poets were ever in action: this reflects not on their courage but on the way in which the conduct of war had changed since 1918 and on the army's use of manpower.

There is no equivalent in World War II of the trench songs that were composed by anonymous soldiers in World War I. Instead, the ubiquitous radio poured out its message of synthetic good cheer and saccharine comfort. Vera Lynn, the Forces' Sweetheart, assured all servicemen that "There'll be blue birds over/The white cliffs of Dover," and that "We'll meet again." In the Western Desert, however, the Forces' Sweetheart was the Scandinavian Lala Andersen, who sang on the German radio "Lili Marleen," a song admired equally in its German and English versions by the opposing armies. Such musical internationalism, alas, had its limits, as British troops found when they made contact with Yugoslav partisans: to them "Lili Marleen" was taboo because the Germans had sung it when they marched partisans away to execution.

A High Court judge is said once to have advised an incompetent counsel that if he could not present his case logically or chronologically, he might present it alphabetically. It may be expedient to group the poets in this essay geographically, partly because this method enables one to make comparisons between their responses to the same environment. But there is a more cogent reason, which stems from the wartime experiences of many poets. They were moved less by the terror and brutality of war than by the impact on their imaginations of distant lands and unfamiliar civilizations. The main themes of their poems are the physical features, social conditions, and historical backgrounds of the countries where they were stationed.

This essay will first consider the poetry of those whom the fortunes of war dispatched to widely scattered theaters of either battle or comparative peace: Britain, continental Europe, the Middle East, North Africa, East Africa, India, and Burma. It will then look at the work of Alan Ross and Charles Causley, two men who served in the Royal Navy; and finish by surveying the poetry of Sidney Keyes, Keith Douglas, and Alun Lewis, three highly gifted poets who, unlike the others to be discussed, died in active service in North Africa, France, and Burma.

BRITAIN AND EUROPE

DURING the war hundreds of thousands of servicemen spent the years in Britain in barracks, billets, or camps, undergoing training, doing fatigues (labor), polishing boots until they could see their faces reflected in them, polishing the brass collars of antiaircraft guns until they shone so brightly that German planes could see them miles away, being inspected to check that they had not lost their blankets or acquired venereal diseases—all the traditional means of cultivating the military virtues and enforcing military discipline. It is a melancholy fact that only a handful of good poems came out of the armed forces stationed in Britain. There is no satisfactory explanation for this, unless it is that the perils of battle, the extreme loneliness, the posts in distant countries, and the shock of living in an alien civilization may inspire poetry; whereas boredom, discomfort, and a sense of aimlessness produce a dampening effect on the imagination.

Henry Reed (born 22 February 1914), joined the army in 1941 and transferred to the Foreign Office the next year. His few months in the army gave him the material for *Lessons of the War*, his sequence of

three poems—"Naming of Parts," "Judging Distances," and "Unarmed Combat"—that won instant recognition as the definitive comment on one aspect of military life.

All three poems are divided between two voices: that of the noncommissioned officer who is instructing the squad and that of the recruit. The difference in idiom and in sensibility between the two voices appears less and less perceptible as the trilogy unfolds, maybe in order to suggest that the recruit is becoming assimilated to the army and learning the martial virtues. But these nuances are of secondary importance, compared with the central fact that the two voices represent two diametrically opposed principles and responses to the world: the ethos of unquestioning obedience, submission to duty, subordination of the individualistic self to the common purpose imposed from above; and the attitude that values skepticism, irony, the right to judge moral behavior for oneself.

"Naming of Parts" is the richest of the poems, because it moves with a sensuous grace not found in the other two and because Reed sustains throughout its five stanzas a series of witty puns that contrast the different parts of the rifle with the vibrant world of japonica, almond blossom, bees, and branches observed by the recruit as the instructor drones on:

> And this you can see is the bolt. The purpose of this
> Is to open the breech, as you see. We can slide it
> Rapidly backwards and forwards: we call this
> Easing the spring. And rapidly backwards and forwards
> The early bees are assaulting and fumbling the flowers:
>   They call it easing the Spring.
>
>   (19–24)

The fusion of the instructor's demotic syntax and speech rhythm with the recruit's gentle, meditative reflections is a triumph of poetic skill; and the delicate sexuality that pervades "Naming of Parts" lends it a further layer of richness.

A full analysis of the poem and of its companion pieces would reveal how wittily and movingly Reed has demonstrated, without self-pity or even protest, the struggle of the individual to keep alive his humanity, despite the attempt by the army to make him part of an impersonal machine. The final lines of "Unarmed Combat," which can be read as a straightforward acknowledgment that the individual must submit to authority, undermine by their tone and inflection the message they purport to give:

> . . . and we must fight
> Not in the hope of winning but rather of keeping
> Something alive: so that when we meet our end,
> It may be said that we tackled wherever we could,
> That battle-fit we lived, and though defeated,
> Not without glory fought.

Reed, unfortunately, has not published a book of poems since *A Map of Verona* (1946). Gavin Ewart (born 4 February 1916), on the other hand, is a prolific poet, although it is only since 1964 that he has been in full spate. In the war poems section of *The Collected Ewart 1933–1980* (1980) there are only nine works, all displaying various facets of his talent but none so distinctive as the best of his postwar verse, which is often extremely funny and outrageously bawdy, and sometimes genuinely moving. "Officers' Mess" explores the vein of riproaring verse opened up with precocious skill by the schoolboy and undergraduate Ewart between 1933 and 1939:

> And then that new MO came in, the Jewish one, awful
>   fellow,
> And his wife, a nice little bit of stuff, dressed in a
>   flaming yellow.
>
> (5–6)

That is one reaction to the war. Another, more tender and troubled, derives its pathos from the fragility of love menaced by the shadow of separation and of approaching battle, as in the sextet of "Sonnet, 1940":

> And I, before the happy tough battalions
> Engulf me or the frozen seas of Norway,
> Have still my dreams of cities and of dalliance,
> But most of you as standing in a doorway,
> Who might, though I so dissipate my life,
> Be mistress or, fear of the young, a wife.
>
> (9–14)

Ewart wrote another good sonnet, "War Dead," at La Spezia in April 1945, but his most harsh and somber war poem is "When a Beau Goes In," a Beau being the shortened from of Beaufighter, one of the best-known British fighter aircraft. The long, languorous line in stanza 2, with its echoes of Gerard Manley Hopkins and Alfred Tennyson, works against the jerky, jokey short lines and accentuates Ewart's bitterness at the cult of the stiff upper lip in the face of other people's deaths:

> Although its perfectly certain
> The pilot's gone for a Burton[1]
> And the observer too
> It's nothing to do with you
> And if they both should go
> To a land where falls no rain nor hail nor driven
>   snow—
> Here, there or anywhere,
> Do you suppose *they* care?
>
> (9–16)

Behind the exuberant, baroque facade of the riotously lewd jokes that Ewart revels in, there lurk always fury and grief at the raw facts of pain and death.

Ewart is a tough-minded poet, as is Vernon Scannell (born 23 January 1922), who saw hard fighting from El Alamein to Tunis as well as in the invasions of Sicily and Normandy. His war poems are unusual in that they appear in seven collections published between 1957 and 1975 and are as much concerned with World War I as with World War II. Almost all of them dwell on the terror of battle recalled in memory or dream and on those who died in action. Scannell portrays his fellow soldiers as he knew them in all their strong and sometimes coarse physicality. These vigorous poems offer a view of war that is not to be found elsewhere, and they deserve to be more widely known. "Walking Wounded," which has, in addition to the qualities of Scannell's other poems, an extra dimension of visionary strangeness, depicts with almost photographic realism how first

> the ambulances came,
> Stumbling and churning past the broken farm,
> The amputated sign-post and smashed trees,
> Slow wagonloads of bandaged cries. . . .
>
> (12–15)

Then, after a pause, the walking wounded go by, "a humble brotherhood," without splendor. And yet, says Scannell, in lines that confer mythical status on a procession remembered after eighteen years:

> Imagination pauses and returns
> To see them walking still, but multiplied
> In thousands now. And when heroic corpses
> Turn slowly in their decorated sleep
> And every ambulance has disappeared
> The walking wounded still trudge down that lane,
> And when recalled they must bear arms again.
>
> (42–48)

[1]Meaning, in Royal Air Force slang, "to be shot down."

It may appear strange that almost all the poetry written by Royal Air Force pilots and air crew, whose courage and skill were of the highest quality, should be little more than apprentice work: often conventionally romantic, sometimes displaying seeds of promise blighted by early death in action. Scannell in *Not Without Glory* (1976) argues that most pilots and air crew lacked the temperament to devote much time to the kind of solitary meditation that gives birth to poetry. They were, moreover, constantly in action or standing by for action; and for many of them, flying and aerial combat were quasi-mystical experiences that lay beyond the reach of words. He justly singles out for praise a sonnet by John Bayliss (born 4 October 1919) that may serve as an epitaph for all the members of the RAF who died in action. "Reported Missing" tells how two men in a plane with a broken wing, and with their gunner dead, knowing that all is finished, looking at the sea,

> sat in this tattered scarecrow of the sky
> hearing it cough, the great plane catching
> now the first dark clouds upon her wing-base,—
> patching the great tear in evening mockery.
>
> So two men waited, saw the third dead face,
> and wondered when the wind would let them die.
> (9–14)

Tens of thousands of men spent years as prisoners of war. The overcrowding, the sense of anxiety, and the complex of emotions aroused by captivity in a foreign land tended to stifle the poetic impulse. One poet, despite such discouragement, wrote a sonnet of high quality. Having taken part in the defense of Crete in 1941 and having been mentioned in dispatches, Michael Riviere (born 5 January 1919) was captured and sent to Germany. After twice escaping from other camps, he was incarcerated in Colditz (whose epigraph is a line from Sir Philip Sidney: "The poor man's wealth, the prisoner's release") in the summer of 1943; while imprisoned in that fortress, which was especially designed to make escape impossible, he wrote "Oflag Night Piece: Colditz":

> There, where the swifts flicker along the wall
> And the last light catches, there in the high schloss
> (How the town grows dark) all's made impregnable:
> They bless each window with a double cross
> Of iron; weave close banks of wire and train
> Machine guns down on them; and look—at the first star
> Floodlight the startled darkness back again . . .

> All for three hundred prisoners of war:
> Yet now past them and the watch they keep,
> Unheard, invisible, in ones and pairs,
> In groups, in companies—alarms are dumb,
> A sentry loiters, a blind searchlight stares—
> Unchallenged as their memories of home
> The vanishing prisoners escape to sleep.

The level of the sonnet; the gentle irony ("They bless each window with a double cross/Of iron"); the amused reminder that the elaborate precautions are "All for three hundred prisoners of war" may give the poem its distinctive quality, but they do not account for its power to touch the reader's heart. It derives some of its potency from its affinities with two themes in English poetry that have a long history. The first is that of prison literature, beginning with the poetry written by state prisoners of the early Tudors, notably Sir Thomas Wyatt; and continuing with the poetry of Roman Catholics awaiting trial or execution under Elizabeth I. The second is that of invocations to sleep: one thinks particularly of songs and sonnets by Sidney, Samuel Daniel, John Fletcher, John Keats, and Hopkins. Although Riviere's sonnet is in no way an imitation or pastiche and contains no allusion to earlier poems, it quietly takes its place among its ancestors.

THE MIDDLE EAST AND NORTH AFRICA

In the Western Desert and in North Africa, where the British fought the Germans and the Italians, the character of the fighting had no parallel anywhere in either of the two world wars. There was no system of trenches or of other elaborate defensive measures, for this was largely a conflict of tanks that moved rapidly on the offensive over huge tracts of desert, until they were halted and harassed by a counter-offensive. Insofar as war can ever be anything but a loathsome butchery, it was a chivalrous war, fought without rancor by soldiers who respected one another's courage, dash, and tactical skill. Neither side obliterated towns, massacred civilians, or murdered prisoners. In this old-fashioned combat, individual enterprise, unorthodoxy carried to the point of eccentricity, and a cavalier disregard for the niceties of military etiquette flourished exceedingly. The Eighth Army, a gallant fighting force, chased the Germans out of Africa. Lawrence Durrell, not renowned for his conventionality, describes in his introduction to the anthology *Return to Oasis* (1980) the apparition of the poet and critic George Fraser (8 November 1915–3 January 1980):

> I recall George Fraser visiting me in the press department of the Embassy to deliver some poems of his for *Personal Landscape*. I was horrified to see that, though in uniform, he was wearing tennis shoes and a dirty scarf, while his trousers were fastened with string. I asked with concern whether he wasn't reprimanded for such wear and he said that he never had been, probably because his boss was a writer too.

Old soldiers and connoisseurs of military life will be interested to learn that Fraser eventually became a sergeant major.

During the war Alexandria and Cairo housed not only large military forces but a civilian population swollen by refugees from Europe who had sought the comparative safety of Egypt. They were highly sophisticated cities, where every pleasure could be bought and where in 1942 the prevailing frenetic gaiety was tinged with fear, as Rommel's armies marched on victoriously across the Western Desert. Durrell's *Alexandria Quartet* and Olivia Manning's Levant trilogy (*The Danger Tree*, *The Battle Lost and Won*, and *The Sum of Things*) have portrayed indelibly the world of the expatriates and their circle in wartime Egypt. Less melodramatic than Durrell and more kindly than Manning, Fraser in "Egypt" evokes the sultry romanticism of the land:

> The desert slays. But safe from Allah's justice
> Where the broad river of His Mercy lies,
> Where ground for labour, or where scope for lust is,
> The crooked and tall and cunning cities rise.
> The green Nile irrigates a barren region,
> All the coarse palms are ankle-deep in sand;
> No love roots deep, though easy loves are legion:
> The heart's as hot and hungry as the hand.
>
> (13–20)

Those who found themselves in Cairo or Alexandria included a number of English poets: some were civilians, others were members of the forces. Three of the civilians, Durrell, Bernard Spencer, and Robin Fedden, started the poetry magazine *Personal Landscape* in the late autumn of 1941. In the course of its existence it printed work by almost every good poet in the region. The best of the civilian poets, apart from the editors, were Terence Tiller and Ruth Speirs; while the most gifted of the servicemen were Norman Cameron, Fraser, Hamish Henderson, and

F. T. Prince, as well as Keith Douglas and Sidney Keyes, to whom later sections of this essay are devoted.

Hamish Henderson (born 11 November 1919) is best known for his sequence of poems *Elegies for the Dead in Cyrenaica* (1948), an ambitious attempt to portray the war in the desert. Its dedication, "For our own and the others," typifies the spirit in which it was written, one of compassion and guilt toward what Henderson calls in his foreword "that eternally wronged proletariat of levelling death in which all the fallen are comrades." He does not confine himself to a realistic description of the battles, but places them in the perspective of medieval Scottish history—the depopulated Highlands—and Karnak, the subject of the Eighth Elegy. The latter is an impressionistic evocation of a vanished way of life or, rather, of death, for Henderson condemns all that Karnak stood for because it devoted its power and resources to death.

Unfortunately, the scope and high intentions of the poems outrun their linguistic vitality. Occasionally Henderson deploys a vivid image:

> Herons stalk
> over the blood-stained flats. Burning byres
> come to my mind.
>
> (Fifth Elegy, 18–20)

But all too often the elegies degenerate into sequences of ponderous rhetoric that lie inertly on the page; at its worst, as in Interlude ("Opening of an Offensive"), the rhetoric deteriorates into rodomontade garnished with echoes of Hopkins:

> Slake
> the crashing breakers-húrled rúbble of the guns.
> Dithering darkness, we'll wake you! Hélls bélls
> blind you.
>
> (20–23)

The description of the shrill war song is even more flatulent:

> It mounts. Its scream
> tops the valkyrie, tops the colossal
> artillery.
>
> Meaning that many
> German Fascists will not be going home.
>
> (41–44)

The Seventh Elegy, entitled "Seven Good Germans," an allusion to the saying that "the only good German is a dead one," offers succinct biographies of seven who died at El Eleba. It is in many ways the most humane of the elegies, sardonic and unpretentious, shedding more light on the desert war than the booming disquisitions that reverberate through the others. The poem ends with an epitaph on the good Germans, who are linked in the comradeship of the fallen; their requiem is the favorite song of the contending armies in Cyrenaica:

> Seven poor bastards
> dead in African deadland
> (tawny tousled hair under the issue blanket)
> *wie einst Lili*
> dead in African deadland
>
> *einst Lili Marleen.*
> (55–60)

Norman Cameron (1905–1953) served in British political intelligence and propaganda. He was a friend of Robert Graves, who greatly admired his poems. Cameron's work sometimes recalls the flavor of Graves's poetry, although he was far from being a slavish imitator. He is an accomplished poet, capable of writing fine lyrics, beautifully conceived and executed; but the mode he favors is one of formal irony laced with gaiety.

"Green, Green is El Aghir" is not so much a war poem as a celebration of an escape from war into a world of abundance and joy, symbolized by the waters splashing from a fountain with two full-throated faucets at El Aghir. The irregularity of the meter, compounded by the off-rhymes, emphasizes the sense of freedom from constraint felt by all, even by the Arabs who go off with the rest to drink wine:

> And we yelped and leapt from the truck and went at the
> double
> To fill our bidons and bottles and drink and dabble.
> Then, swollen with water, we went to an inn for wine.
> The Arabs came, too, though their faith might have
> stood between:
> "After all," they said, "it's a boisson," without
> contrition.
> (13–17)

"Black Takes White" springs from a later campaign in the Apennines. A party of American blacks, attempting to desert, encounters a party of like-minded Italians. Both groups want to surrender, the impasse being surmounted only because the Italians, being led by an officer, have the whip hand. The reluctant blacks march back with their unsought booty to a heroes' welcome:

> Nobody paused to bother with such trifles
> As where the captors had mislaid their rifles.
> Quickly those fed-up and embarrassed Negroes
> Were praised, promoted, given gongs as heroes,
> And photographs of their victorious battle
> Were published from Long Island to Seattle.

The subtly varied rhythm and the faintly insolent rhymes point the subversive moral of the tale, in which cowardice and mendacity shamelessly mock the pomposity of government propaganda.

John Manifold (born 21 April 1916), an Australian who completed his education at Jesus College, Cambridge, saw military service in the Middle East, West Africa, and France. A convinced Marxist, he writes polemical verse that emphasizes the usefulness of poetry and the need for all to fight unquestioningly for the victory that will bring the triumph of the proletariat one stage nearer. Scannell suggests in *Not Without Glory* that there is much in common between Manifold and Campbell, though neither would greatly relish the comparison. The verse of both men has strong elements of swagger and tough talking; both despise the coward and the sensitive soul who will not fight; Campbell sings the flowering rifle and Manifold the tommy gun, "the clean functional thing." But Campbell, with his cult of the lone wolf, does not share Manifold's admiration for those who find their self-respect only when they surrender their individuality. That is the point of the latter's well-argued sonnet "Recruit"; and in "Ration Party" he again urges the need for sacrifice, exemplified by a fatigue party that bears huge loads up a hill, day after day, a menial, dispiriting task:

> Absurd to think that Liberty, the splendid
> Nude of our dreams, the intercessory saint
> For us to judgement, needs to be defended
>
> By sick fatigue-men brimming with complaint
> And misery, who bear till all is ended
> Every imaginable pattern of constraint.
> (9–14)

In "The Sirens," perhaps the wittiest and most effective of all Manifold's sonnets, the moral of the story is very largely what the reader chooses to make it. Even those who are unsympathetic to the poet's political beliefs, and to the didacticism that marks so much of his verse, can savor the freshness of the language, the ingenious refurbishing of an old legend, the relaxed wit and the stylish versification of the poem:

> Odysseus heard the sirens; they were singing
> Music by Wolf and Weinberger and Morley
> About a region where the swans go winging,
> Vines are in colour, girls are growing surely
>
> Into nubility, and pylons bringing
> Leisure and power to farms that live securely
> Without a landlord. Still, his eyes were stinging
> With salt and sea blink, and the ropes hurt sorely.
>
> Odysseus saw the sirens; they were charming,
> Blonde, with snub breasts and little neat posteriors,
> But could not take his mind off the alarming
>
> Weather report, his mutineers in irons,
> The radio failing; it was bloody serious.
> In twenty minutes he forgot the sirens.

F. T. Prince (born 13 September 1912), a South African who had attended the universities of Oxford and Princeton, had published before the war a volume of poems notable for their technical skill and meditative subtlety. Unlike the works of Henderson and Manifold, "Soldiers Bathing," Prince's best-known poem, does not primarily concern itself with the details of war in the Middle East or with the war's political and social implications. Even in 1941, when the poem first appeared, Prince, a Roman Catholic preoccupied with evil and with the Crucifixion, was already a scholar and a lover of Italian art. The scene is a beach in the Middle East, where Prince was serving in the Intelligence Corps, but the setting could just as well be an imaginary stretch of coast.

The poem opens quietly:

> The sea at evening moves across the sand.
> Under a reddening sky I watch the freedom of a band
> Of soldiers who belong to me. Stripped bare
> For bathing in the sea, they shout and run in the
>   warm air. . . .

Then follows a disquisition on the body and the sweetness of its nakedness when the sea has washed it free of fever, filth, and sweat. Every one of the soldiers

> forgets
> His hatred of the war, its terrible pressure that begets
> A machinery of death and slavery,
> Each being a slave and making slaves of others. . . .
>
>   (15–18)

Contemplation of the naked soldiers awakens in Prince a memory of a Michelangelo cartoon in which bathing soldiers clamber from the water at the sudden incursion of the enemy, and fight, naked as they are:

> —And I think too of the theme another found
> When, shadowing men's bodies on a sinister red ground,
> Another Florentine, Pollaiuolo,
> Painted a naked battle: warriors, straddled, hacked the
>   foe,
> Dug their bare toes into the ground and slew
> The brother-naked man who lay between their feet and
>   drew
> His lips back from his teeth in a grimace.
>
> They were Italians who knew war's sorrow and
>   disgrace
> And showed the thing suspended, stripped: a theme
> Born out of the experience of war's horrible extreme
> Beneath a sky where even the air flows
> With lacrimae Christi. . . .
>
>   (31–42)

There follows a meditation on the relation between Pollaiuollo's painting and the Crucifixion, and on the terror of the great love that is over all we do. It may be that readers must either be attuned to Prince's Christian mysticism or suspend their disbelief, if this section of the poem is not to constitute a stumbling block. No such difficulty arises in the final section: Prince recapitulates all the main themes of the poem, and as he drinks the dusky air—perhaps the sky of Egypt flows with "lacrimae Christi" (tears of Christ)—the reddening sky of the first section is linked with the Crucifixion:

> These dry themselves and dress,
> Combing their hair, forget the fear and the shame of
>   nakedness.
> Because to love is frightening we prefer
> The freedom of our crimes. Yet, as I drink the dusky air,
> I feel a strange delight that fills me full,
> Strange gratitude, as if evil itself were beautiful,
> And kiss the wound in thought, while in the west
> I watch a streak of red that might have issued from
>   Christ's breast.
>
>   (59–66)

EAST AFRICA

DURING World War I East Africa was the scene of heavy fighting between the British and the Germans who, based in German East Africa (now Tanzania), remained undefeated at the armistice. In World War II, although no battles took place in the East African territories, the country was a training ground for the Africanized units of the British army, which were preparing to recover Burma from the Japanese; it was also a naval base for the Eastern Fleet, which sought the safety of Kilindini Harbour, Mombasa, after the Japanese had bombed it out of Singapore, Colombo, and Trincomalee. The East Africa Command was, geographically speaking, the largest in the British army, stretching from Somaliland to Southern Rhodesia (now Zimbabwe) and embracing such widely scattered islands as Madagascar, Mauritius, and the Seychelles.

Most travelers find East Africa overwhelming in its magnificence, whether they first encounter the coast, or the mountains, hills, and valleys up-country. Roy Campbell (2 October 1901–23 April 1957), being a native of South Africa and thus accustomed to something of the same natural splendor, was not bowled over by East Africa when he was posted there after having volunteered for military service when in his late thirties. He had migrated as a young man to England, where he had soon acquired a reputation as a rambunctious satirist, equally happy to castigate the narrow hypocrisy of Afrikaaners or the epicene aesthetes of Bloomsbury. In the late 1920's and early 1930's he wrote some fine lyrics. Unhappily, his loathing of leftist intellectuals and his devotion to an aggressive variant of Roman Catholicism led him to espouse the cause of General Franco and to write *Flowering Rifle* (1939), a long poem whose crude abusiveness and pretentious anthems to the glory of the Roman Catholic Church make distasteful reading.

Having arrived in Nairobi wearing his sergeant's stripes, Campbell looked at the commissioned officers with a somewhat jaundiced eye, as he records in his brief "Snapshot of Nairobi":

> With orange-peel the streets are strewn
> And pips, beyond computing,
> On every shoulder save my own
> That's fractured with saluting.

"Heartbreak Camp," a mordant extravaganza, contains two good stanzas:

> Sir Dysentery Malaria,
> A famous brigadier,
> Commands the whole sub-area,
> And stalking in his rear,
>
> A more ferocious colonel
> Lord Tremens (of the Drunks)
> To whose commands infernal
> We tremble in our bunks.
>
> (21–28)

Yet the poem is spoiled by feeble inversions, forced rhymes, and a slackness that Campbell would not have tolerated at his best.

The collection in which these poems appear, *Talking Bronco* (1946), is something of a ragbag. One can at least be thankful that it marks a return to sanity and decency (with a few lapses) after *Flowering Rifle*. But among pages of wearisome braggadoccio and dreary attacks on left-wing poets and all who fly to the safe retreat of the BBC, there are too few poems of high quality. Among them are the translation from St. John of the Cross, "En Una Noche Oscura," and the "Imitation (and Endorsement) of the Famous Sonnet of Bocage," that homage of one poet to a greater, Luís Vaz de Camoëns. Campbell's own tribute to the author of *The Lusiads* shows that he can still command a sinewy force and gravity infused with lyrical grace. In his sonnet "Luis de Camões," Campbell recognizes his kinship with the Portuguese poet, like himself a common soldier and a Catholic, who had served the cause of Spain; sailed to Mombasa and watched the gaunt mass of Fort Jesus rising above the harbor; followed where duty beckoned; and, bearing his cross, made poetry from his sufferings:

> Camões, alone, of all the lyric race,
> Born in the black aurora of disaster,
> Can look a common soldier in the face:
> I find a comrade where I sought a master;
> For daily, while the stinking crocodiles
> Glide from the mangoes on the swampy shore,
> He shares my awning on the dhow, he smiles,
> And tells me that he lived it all before.
> Through fire and shipwreck, pestilence and loss,
> Led by the ignis fatuus of duty
> To a dog's death—yet of his sorrows king—
> He shouldered high his voluntary Cross,
> Wrestled his hardship into forms of beauty,
> And taught his gorgon destinies to sing.

Roy Fuller (born 11 February 1912) was, like Manifold, a Marxist, but of a very different stamp.

428

Where Manifold is optimistic, confident of victory, enthusiastic about the individual's sacrifice of himself for the common good, a believer in the virtues of the proletariat, Fuller is gloomy, perplexed, doubtful whether the subordination of the individual will advance the coming of the just society, and not particularly enamored of the working classes in the forces or in civilian life. After training as an ordinary seaman in Britain, Fuller was posted to East Africa in mid-1942 as a radar maintenance engineer; he attained the rank of petty officer and in November 1943 returned to Britain, where he worked in the admiralty after getting a commission.

He wrote about thirty poems in East Africa, a slightly larger output than between the outbreak of war in September 1939 and his sailing from Britain in the summer of 1942. The period November 1943 to the end of the war in May 1945 seems to have been comparatively barren, yielding only a half-dozen poems and a sequence of nine sonnets.

The early war poems reflect the hopes and fears of a humane, intelligent man, recently married and the father of a son, caught in the impersonal war machine and the no less impersonal historical process. Most of the poems are worth reading but few rank among his best. "The Middle of a War" deals with a theme that Fuller was to explore more deeply in his postwar verse: the poet gazing at himself, reflecting on what he sees, and making a wry observation:

> My photograph already looks historic.
> The promising youthful face, the matelot's collar. . . .
>
> (1–2)

One phrase, "The ridiculous empires break like biscuits," reminds us, like so many of Fuller's lines, of W. H. Auden, the Auden who wrote "Desire like a police-dog is unfastened." But Fuller's images have a quality of their own, less devastatingly startling and brilliant than Auden's but more in accord with common sense and common usage.

Another good early poem, "Spring 1942," records an incident when a naval chaplain joins a group of enlisted men and sits down among them:

> And under the tobacco smoke:
> "Freedom," he said, and "Good" and "Duty."
> We stared as though a savage spoke.
> The scene took on a singular beauty.
>
> (5–8)

Blank and uncomprehending, dumbfounded by this talk of the great abstractions, the enlisted men make no reply

> And thought: O sick, insatiable
> And constant lust, O death, our future;
> O revolution in the whole
> Of human use of man and nature!
>
> (13–16)

Fuller's posting to East Africa seems to have liberated him from the glum, debilitating atmosphere of wartime Britain. The splendor of the hills and plains, the superb variety of the animals and birds, and the life of the tribesmen seem to have enriched his imagination and bestowed a rhythmical sensuousness on his verse. Not that he succumbed to the picturesque enchantment of the scene: what he found there was a world in which the lions, giraffes, wildebeests, the whole panoply of birds and beasts, live their own lives, unalterably alien to our own and yet symbols of that natural world to which we also belong. The tribesmen are not romantic figures uncorrupted by civilization, but men and women whom the forces of capitalism are wrenching from their homelands, crowding into shantytowns, and offering a pittance to join the armed forces. Even their villages are in pawn to the owner of the *duka* (general store), who is usually descended from one of those Indians shipped over from Bombay forty years earlier to build the railway from Mombasa to Kampala. Fuller can see befor his eyes in dramatic form the working out of capitalism and colonialism in their dying phase.

This sense of the historical process, combined with a powerful and discriminating response to the particularities of the scene, enabled Fuller to write one of the finest series of poems to have come out of World War II. Some of the poems spring directly from Fuller's observation of the landscape up-country. In "The Green Hills of Africa" (how unlike Ernest Hemingway's green hills) the evocation of the village and its inhabitants is exact:

> The girls run up the slope,
> Their oiled and shaven heads like caramels.
> Behind, the village, with its corrugated
> Iron, the wicked habit of the store.
> The villagers cough, the sacking blows from the naked
> Skin of a child, a white scum on his lips.
>
> (11–16)

Having presented the village precisely as it is, Fuller asks us whether we expect to find here gods with healing powers, or subtle ways of life:

> No, there is nothing but the forms and colours,
> And the emotion brought from a world already
> Dying of what starts to infect the hills.
>
> (25–27)

It is instructive to compare Fuller's "The Giraffes" with a poem on a similar theme by Campbell, "Dreaming Spires"—his name for giraffes. Campbell's poem is a sequence of witty fancies about the extravagant absurdities of those animals. Sometimes the fancies move with a lyrical grace:

> The City of Giraffes—a People
> Who live between the earth and skies,
> Each in his lone religious steeple
> Keeping a light-house with his eyes.
>
> (48–51)

Sometimes they are merely ingenious, as though designed to show how clever the poet can be when he sets his mind to it:

> Some animals have all the luck,
> Who hurl their breed in nature's throat—
> Out of a gumtree by a buck,
> Or escalator—by a goat!
>
> (85–88)

Fuller wants to convey the essence of these strange animals who, as he drew nearer, turned,

> An undulation of dappled grey and brown,
> And stood in profile with those curious planes
> Of neck and sloping haunches.
>
> (19–21)

Although Fuller acknowledges that their height is grotesque he does not see them primarily as ludicrous creatures, but rather as animals with whom no communication is possible. The poem's closing lines evoke with controlled tenderness and reverence the otherness of the giraffes:

> So as they put more ground between us I
> Saw evidence that these were animals
> With no desire for intercourse, or no
> Capacity.
>
> Above the falling sun,
> Like visible winds the clouds are streaked and spun,

And cold and dark now bring the image of
Those creatures walking without pain or love.

(24–30)

Another poem, "The Plains," presents in a series of snapshots the array of wildlife before the rains: zebras, gazelles, hyenas, jackals, and, caught in the headlights, a lion:

> Slowly it swung its great
> Maned head, then—loose, suède, yellow—loped away.
>
> (24–25)

As always, contemplation of the natural world leads Fuller to meditate on metaphysical themes. After observing the lion, which is followed by a pair of squint hyenas, Fuller revolves in his mind the course of human history, and archetypal myths; and when four pecking vultures fly away at his approach, he asks himself a fundamental question:

> They left a purple scrap of skin.
> Have I discovered all the plains can show?
> The animals gallop, spring, are beautiful,
> And at the end of every day is night.
>
> (39–42)

Fuller also wrote a small group of poems that touch on the political life of East Africa in the widest sense of the word—the way in which the coming of a war fought for the benefit of white colonial rulers has finally shattered the tribal life of the Africans. In a four-line poem, "Natives Working on the Aerodrome," Fuller gives imaginative form to some ironies of the process whereby the British impose a punishment for the transgression of their law designed to assist the war effort:

> Curls powdered with chalk like a black Roman bust,
> This prisoner, convicted of a lust
> For maize, is whipped to building a great shed
> For bombers; and bears the earth upon his head.

There are a number of poems about the war and the human condition that owe little to the places where they were written. Others derive their imagery from the local scene before moving into the realm of metaphysical speculation. Thus "Autumn 1942" switches from the animals of the plains to

> . . . the news at which I hesitate,
> That glares authentically between the bars
> Of style and lies. . . .
>
> (29–31)

The poem ends with a nightmarish vision of humanity, the kind of vision to which Fuller became increasingly prey as the war dragged on and the news confirmed all his forebodings:

> It half convinces me that some great faculty,
> Like hands, has been eternally lost and all
> Our virtues now are high and horrible
> Ones of a streaming wound which heals in evil.
>
> (37–40)

Fuller wrote a handful of poems about the coastal region, one of which, "The Coast," manages to convey, in thirty-five lines, the ecology, human and natural, of the area. "Crustaceans" might be a commentary on a television nature film, so clearly and specifically does it describe the mass of crabs on the beach. The poem hints at certain affinities between the crabs and human beings; in "The Divided Life Re-Lived," an image from "Crustaceans" reappears as a simile:

> While outside the demon scientists and rulers of the land
> Pile the bomb like busy crabs pile balls of sand.
>
> (23–24)

Perhaps the most poignant of all his wartime poems, "The Petty Officers' Mess," which is also set on the coast, develops Fuller's meditations on history before returning to the opening visit to some captive monkeys:

> The monkeys near the mess (where we all eat
> And dream) I saw tonight select with neat
> And brittle fingers dirty scraps, and fight,
> And then look pensive in the fading light,
> And after pick their feet.
>
> They were secured by straps about their slender
> Waists, and the straps to chains. Most sad and tender,
> They clasp each other and look round with eyes
> Like ours at what their strange captivities
> Invisibly engender.
>
> (46–55)

The wartime poems written after Fuller's return home do not compare in originality and force with the best of his East African poems; this is true even of "Winter in Camp," an ambitious and accomplished sequence of nine sonnets about the slaughterous immensity of the war, the coarseness of the common man, the political inactivity of artists (including Fuller himself), and the contrast between the crude but authentic emotions stirred by the cinema and the illusory world of art.

During the past forty years Fuller has continued to write a large, varied body of verse, much of it concerned with the nature of human society and with metaphysical problems. His poems have evaded the perils of aridity and emotional anemia because he has never ceased to respond with curiosity and zest to the quirks and richness of things animate and inanimate. If he is a man for whom the visible world exists, he owes this partly to the fortunes of war that sent him to Kenya, where he could observe the crustaceans, the dhows, the animals on the plains, and the life that moves to rhythms so different from our own in the green hills of Africa.

Edward Lowbury (born 6 December 1913), who had won the Newdigate prize for poetry when he was an undergraduate at University College, Oxford, was a qualified doctor when he was called up into the Royal Army Medical Corps. During his period of service in East Africa he became acquainted with certain aspects of life that remained a closed book to most of his compatriots: African medicine, the nature of witchcraft, Swahili tales and legends. One of those tales, which an *askari* (African soldier) told him, grew into the poem "The Huntsman." It preserves the laconic simplicity and force of the original, and the short phrases of which the poem is composed heighten the tension, the dramatic plot, and the anxiety that pervade the story.

One is plunged into the action with no preliminary flourishes:

> Kagwa hunted the lion,
>   Through bush and forest went his spear.
> One day he found the skull of a man
>   And said to it, "How did you come here?"
> The skull opened its mouth and said
>   "Talking brought me here."

Lowbury unfolds the tale, departing just enough from the flow of normal English speech to remind the reader that this is a Swahili tale. Kagwa tells his story of the talking skull to the king, who orders two guards to search for the skull, taking with them Kagwa, who is to die if his tale is proved untrue. Eventually they find the skull; despite Kagwa's pleas it says nothing. The poem comes full circle, and it is Kagwa's turn to die:

> The guards said, "Kneel down."
>   They killed him with sword and spear.

Then the skull opened its mouth;
  "Huntsman, how did you come here?"
And the dead man answered
  "Talking brought me here."

(25–30)

Unlike Fuller, who continually reverts to the impact of Europe on the life of East Africa, Lowbury observes that life in all its strangeness, more concerned with what is and has been than with the influence that modern Europe may have on the tribesmen and the coastal inhabitants. If anything, his curiosity is aroused by what Europeans may have to learn from East Africa. Thus, in "Miracle Cure," he restores sight to a twelve-year-old Bantu boy, who cries out:

"I see! I see!"
And as I touched his brow
it seemed an unsuspected power
had passed through my bones
to him—in a blinding
but sight-restoring spark, that gave
new sight also to me.

(38–44)

Something of the same attitude informs "Total Eclipse," about a total eclipse of the sun that Lowbury witnessed in Mombasa. He asks some Africans what has come over the sun and is told:

The Sun goes out because some blow must fall.

(25)

He tries again and gets the same answer:

             "Some blow will fall."
But a hint, this time, of a Dragon which devours
The Sun. . . .

(28–30)

Their explanations, ridiculous and superstitious though they may be, awaken

A twilight consciousness of lost powers,
Forgotten magic, presences
That gave no peace, haunted our sleep and drove us,
When Europe was a child, to acts of frenzy;
And still, for all our cool endeavours, haunt.

(33–37)

When the light returns, the scientific certainty of the astronomers seems irrelevant, because the eclipse has carried a warning of which they are unaware:

It seems we heard pre-echoes, saw
A warning vision of the great Eclipse
In store for the white Sun
In this black continent,
When the Dragon's turn comes, and with a shout
He snatches back the light;
His reason—simply that it's time for one,
Who shone so long unchecked, to be put out.

(42–49)

In "Mua Hills," among Lowbury's strongest and most finely wrought poems, one discovers a total contrast to Fuller's "The Green Hills of Africa." Whereas Fuller anatomizes the decay of tribal life beneath the assault of colonialism and capitalism, Lowbury, while acknowledging the decadence of the tribes—

Black eyes, black heads—Kamba, Kikuyu, Nandi
Sprout like grapes, expert at hanging round
And doing nothing; were they warriors once,
    Now gone to seed?

(8–11)

—lays stress on the unbroken continuity of their traditions symbolized by the dance. In the final stanza he looks back to the middle of the nineteenth century, when explorers from Europe observed the fury of the dance and were mocked when they went home with travelers' tales of great lakes and snowcapped mountains in the heart of Africa:

I catch a glimpse of beaten shield and spear
    Of the ngoma beaten all night long;
Feel something of the astonishment and fear
Of those first hunters from the North who hawked
    Spirit and book, and in exchange took home
Stories which marked them liar if they talked.

(31–36)

As a tailpiece to this section one should recall the brief campaign that wrested control of Madagascar from the Vichy French. Bernard Gutteridge (born 13 March 1916) composed some poems about the episode, one of which, "Patrol: Buonomary," was written on the spot. Like all his work, it is readable and acutely observed; the tone is detached and slightly amused; the versification is elegant. This, one feels, is exactly how it was, with ten small figures "running stumbling over the hill," pursued by British bullets:

And that was all the enemy's resistance.
The pot-bellied children fondled

432

Tommy-guns and Brens; brought bananas; stared.
The chalk road gashed into the distance,
The sea glared.

(6–10)

Gutteridge moved on to Burma, where he fought in the ruthless campaign against the Japanese. Although he planned nothing as ambitious or systematic as Henderson's sequence about the war in Cyrenaica, he executes from time to time an incisive vignette, notable for accuracy and restraint, in a style that springs from a resolution not to over-dramatize or lay too blatant an emphasis on the hideous nature of the fighting. Even so, Gutteridge does not flinch from recording the kind of physical detail that had shocked many of those who read the poems of Sassoon in World War I. In its offhand way Gutteridge's "The Enemy Dead" reveals a great deal about the stark realities of jungle warfare and the frame of mind it engenders in the combatants:

The dead are always searched.
It's not a man, the blood-soaked
Mess of rice and flesh and bones
Whose pockets you flip open.

(1–4)

"Sniper" recounts how ten British soldiers trap one Japanese sniper:

He had killed neatly but we had set
Ten men about him to write death in jags
Cutting and spoiling on his face and broken body.

(12–14)

Gutteridge's work is unusual in that it combines the lucidity of a good military dispatch with the emotional resonance of poetry. Perhaps because of its reticence it has failed to win due recognition, but no other English poet has conveyed so truthfully and concisely the nature of the war in Burma against the Japanese.

THE WAR AT SEA

ALAN Ross (born 6 May 1922) wrote a sequence of poems between 1942 and 1945 about naval warfare in the Arctic. Having served as an ordinary seaman and as an officer, he knew at first hand the life of the messdeck and of the wardroom as well as the roles played in combat by all ranks. His are the only poems of either world war that portray the realities of life in a warship on patrol, the rescue of men after a shipwreck, the technical and moral implications of radar, the nature of an engagement at sea. Ross emulates the accuracy of a good prose reporter without getting bogged down in the prosaic. Instead, most of his poems employ traditional devices such as rhyme, meter, and stanzaic pattern, although he permits himself the freedom to depart from strict forms when he feels the need to do so.

"Messdeck" conveys with overpowering force the claustrophobia and stench in which sailors live:

Bare shoulders
Glisten with oil, tattoo-marks rippling their scales on
Mermaids or girls' thighs as dice are shaken, cards played.
We reach for sleep like a gas, randy for oblivion.

(5–8)

"Destroyers in the Arctic" is a study in grayness, monotony, unreality:

Landfall. Murmansk; but starboard now a lead-coloured
Island, Jan Mayen. Days identical, hoisted like sails,
blurred.

(19–20)

The earlier poems in the sequence are impressionistic, concerned with the outer world and with the trappings of war rather than with the inner reality. "Survivors" depicts the rescue of men from a burning ship and an icy sea. The poem does not merely describe the mechanics of the operation but evokes the exhaustion, the shock to mind and spirit, endured by the victims:

Taken on board as many as lived, who
Had a mind left for living and the ocean,
They open eyes running with surf,
Heavy with grey ghosts of explosion.

The meaning is not yet clear,
Where daybreak died in the smile—
And the mouth remained stiff
And grinning, stupid for a while.

(9–16)

It is not only the guns of the enemy ships that send men to flounder in the icy sea: the guns obey equipment of a subtlety and accuracy hitherto unknown in warfare. "Radar" makes the point that remote control divides the responsibility for killing between those who man the guns, release the depth charges,

433

or fire the torpedoes and those who operate the radar, so all can shrug aside their guilt:

> And destroying the enemy by radar
> We never see what we do.
>
> (11–12)

"J. W. 51B A Convoy," a narrative poem over five hundred lines long, describes how a British force protecting a convoy in the Arctic engaged and drove off a superior German force and brought the convoy safely into port. Ross handles with remarkable skill the various elements of which his poem is made up: the technical details of seamanship and naval warfare that give the poem the authenticity of a documentary film; the life of the lower deck; the horror of a naval battle fought by men trapped within a confined space; the courage and coolness and devotion to duty shown by all ranks during the engagement.

Throughout the poem Ross employs lines of varying length, mainly short, not conforming to any strict metrical pattern; he diversifies the sound of the verse with a scattering of full and half rhyme. This eclectic procedure gives him the flexibility he needs, enabling him to incorporate within the structure of his narrative the stark details of the combat and the familiar trivialities of the daily round.

It is impossible to convey in a brief space the quality of a longish narrative poem whose impact depends in part on the way the story is unfolded while its disparate elements are welded into a unity. Three extracts, however, may indicate Ross's power to handle widely dissimilar aspects of a naval engagement and to find the emotional tone appropriate to the occasion.

There is the dramatic moment when the captain of the *Onslow* signals his destroyers to join him:

> And the destroyers, breaking
> Out of line, heeled over,
> Increasing revolutions, like the spokes
> Of an umbrella being opened,
> Spray icing the look-outs,
> Forming up in line ahead.
>
> (207–212)

The *Onslow* is hit and obliged to retire. Ross gives us a picture of what this means in human terms:

> "A" and "B" Guns unable to fire,
> Radar destroyed, aerials ripped,
> And, forward, the sea stripping
> The Mess decks, spilling over tables,

> Fire and water clinching like boxers
> As the ship listed, sprawling them.
> Tamblin, his earphones awry, like a laurel wreath
> Slipped on a drunken god, gargled to death
> In water with a noise of snoring.
>
> (307–315)

Finally, we turn to the burial at sea, in which Ross employs rhyme and meter with more formal regularity than at any other juncture in the poem:

> Beneath the ice-floes sleeping,
> Embalmed in salt
> The sewn-up bodies slipping
> Into silent vaults.
> The sea of Barents received them,
> Men with no faults
> Of courage, for the weeping
> Would be elsewhere,
> Far from its keeping.
>
> (418–426)

Ross's poems about the war at sea are an impressive achievement. He has gone on to write verse about people, places, and erotic love that is more subtle and sensuous then the poems of his early youth, but he has never surpassed in force and immediacy the poetic testament that he has left of life and death in the waste of Arctic waters.

We move worlds away when we turn from Ross to Charles Causley (born 24 August 1917), who served on the lower deck from 1939 to 1946. Instead of the terse, restrained emotion of Ross's poems we have a warmer, less muted lyricism, a canvas on which brighter colors are more thickly spread. "Chief Petty Officer" shows that Causley can portray things and people as realistically as Ross:

> He is older than the naval side of British history,
> And sits
> More permanent than the spider in the enormous wall.
> . . .
> He has the face of the dinosaur
> That sometimes stares from old Victorian naval
>   photographs:
> That of some elderly lieutenant
> With boots and a celluloid Crippen collar,
> Brass buttons and cruel ambitious eyes of almond.
>
> (1–3; 12–16)

Yet it becomes clear as one reads on that Causley's main concern is not to present a realistic or even satirical portrait of the old monster: what comes over is the warm affection that Causley feels for a dinosaur that has survived.

Causley, though not an overtly learned poet, likes to lace his verse with literary and cultural allusions. The first two lines of "Chief Petty Officer" derive part of their effect from the incongruous comparison between the gross and sinister vulgarian as he squats in the Royal Naval Barracks at Devonport and Leonardo da Vinci's Mona Lisa, who, in Walter Pater's exquisite imagination, is "older than the rocks among which she sits"; while the joke about the CPO's remote origins is sharpened by the sidelong glance at Sir Geoffrey Callender's *The Naval Side of British History* (1924). The phrase in line 15, "a celluloid Crippen collar," with its reference to the famous Edwardian murderer, gives the portrait the kind of period touch so often found in the verse of John Betjeman, a poet whom Causley much admires.

It may be thought regrettable that Causley did not draw a whole gallery of such portraits and that he failed to present a realistic picture of war. His only description of death at sea is coached in highly romantic imagery. "Song of the Dying Gunner A.A.1" begins:

> Oh mother my mouth is full of stars
> As cartridges in the tray
> My blood is a twin-branched scarlet tree
> And it runs all runs away.

It is true that by the end of the poem the dying man has lapsed into the vernacular, but the shift from one poetic convention to another does not come off and the poem is flawed:

> Farewell, Aggie Weston, the Barracks at Guz,
> Hang my tiddley suit on the door
> I'm sewn up neat in a canvas sheet
> And I shan't be home no more.
>
> (13–16)

A note addressed to landlubbers explains that "Guz" is naval slang for Devonport and "Aggie Weston's" is "the familiar term used by sailors to describe the hostels founded in many seaports by Dame Agnes Weston."

One of Causley's favorite modes is the ballad filled with glittering images, owing more to Auden, Betjeman, and A. E. Housman than to the traditional border ballads, and sparkling with gaiety even though the subject is war. It may be objected that his presentation of war does not convince, because it is overstylized and totally disinfected of horror, pain, filth, boredom, and discomfort. Even so, his best poems have such fizz and fire that they stay in the memory much longer than the verse of drabber poets who point out what a wretched business war is. And Causley, though he never sermonizes, reminds us constantly that war is a tragic waste of human life. In "A Ballad for Katharine of Aragon" the death of Causley's childhood friend Jumper Cross, who perished in the Italian snow, has the lyrical force of an aria of Verdi's:

> The olive tree in winter
> Casts her banner down
> And the priest in white and scarlet
> Comes up from the muddy town.
> O never more will Jumper
> Watch the Flying Scot go by
> His funeral knell was a six-inch shell
> Singing across the sky.
>
> (17–24)

"Recruiting Drive" rehearses the story of a young soldier (a cousin of Housman's doomed lads) lured by the butcher-bird's song into joining up and finding death down in the enemy country. The imagery is almost surrealistic, and even at its most restrained it arouses an authentic shiver of terror:

> You must take off your clothes for the doctor
> And stand as straight as a pin,
> His hand of stone on your white breast-bone
> Where the bullets all go in.
>
> (17–20)

Causley wrote a number of poems about his wartime recollections of Freetown, Gibraltar, Sydney, Trincomalee, Kandy, and Colombo. They are skillful evocations, shining with local color, soaked in nostalgic memories, at times degenerating into ecstatic, naive catalogs of remembered places and people. But Causley is not a naive poet, and it is by the poems glanced at above that he claims the admiration of those whose concern is with the truthfully observed and keenly felt poetry of war.

SIDNEY KEYES

Sidney Keyes was born on 27 May 1922; six weeks after his birth his mother died of peritonitis. His father, Captain Reginald Keyes, went to live with his own father, another Sidney Keyes, and the child grew up in his paternal grandfather's house. He was educated at Tonbridge, a well-known public school, where the form master of the History Sixth, Tom Staveley, was a poet who recognized Keyes's poetic gifts and encouraged him to develop them.

An example of his precocious talent is the elegy that Keyes composed for his grandfather in July 1938, the middle stanza of which runs:

> It is a year again since they poured
> The dumb ground into your mouth:
> And yet we know, by some recurring word
> Or look caught unawares, that you still drive
> Our thoughts like the smart cobs of your youth—
> When you and the world were alive.

This is not so much the work of a promising poet as of one who, at sixteen, is already a poet, able to handle with easy mastery the elements of his craft and to deploy in the service of his imagination a command of rhyme, meter, imagery, and rhythm that never failed him.

Keyes was an unusually learned and literary poet. In his introductory memoir to *The Collected Poems of Sidney Keyes* (1945), one of his closest friends at Oxford, Michael Meyer, gives a list of those who most influenced Keyes:

For direction and inspiration, he turned to such visionaries as El Greco, Blake, Holderlin, Schiller, Rilke, Yeats and Sibelius. At the same time, he found his emotional problems most completely resolved in the writings of the nineteenth-century school of haunted countrymen: Wordsworth, Clare, Van Gogh, Hardy and, later, Housman and Edward Thomas.

(p. xiii)

Meyer goes on to note Keyes's love of the macabre: "Donne, Webster, Goya, Beddoes, Dickens, Picasso, Klee, Rouault, Graham Greene; and such as came his way of the early German and Russian films."

Much has been made of Keyes's admiration for Rainer Maria Rilke, whom indeed he praises unreservedly. Writing in January 1943 to Richard Church, he declares his belief that the greatest and most influential poets in the last hundred years are Rilke and William Butler Yeats. In a diary entry of March 1943, after tracing the burgeoning of the death wish implicit in romanticism, he continues: "That's why there had to be a 'Poet of Death' in C.20 [the twentieth century]; and why Rilke is the most important European poet since Goethe and Words-

worth." He was undoubtedly influenced by Rilke, especially by that poet's conception of death as something that we bear within us like a child awaiting birth. In the summer of 1942 he worked on a translation of passages of Rilke's prose and in the autumn of that year he translated an eight-line poem entitled "The Poet."

Yet it is important not to exaggerate the part played by Rilke in the life and the poetry of Sidney Keyes. The overwhelming influence on his early poems is not Rilke but Yeats, and it is likely that Rilke's metaphysical speculations about death merely intensified and deepened the intuitions and discoveries of which Keyes was himself aware. Moreover, Keyes knew that charnel romanticism and the German obsession with the death wish were dangerous models. He referred to "a vaguely bogus atmosphere" in his poems; and in a letter written nine weeks before he was killed he regretted that he had not been born in nineteenth-century Oxfordshire or Wiltshire, "because then I might have been a good pastoral poet, instead of an uncomfortable metaphysical without roots" (Meyer, p. xiii).

It is probable that the decisive influence on his poetry was not Yeats or Rilke, or any visionary artist, but his love for a girl whom he met at Oxford in May 1941. It is also arguable that his finest achievements are not his symbolist poems, of which the two most ambitious are "The Foreign Gate" and "The Wilderness," but the short lyrics on a wide variety of themes, particularly those written from March 1942 onward.

As we have seen, he was already a poet at the age of sixteen, and the first nine poems in his *Collected Poems* were written before he went up to Queen's College, Oxford, in October 1940. He composed the first of his Oxford poems in an examination room, having finished the paper early. "Remember Your Lovers," on the theme of women bereaved in wartime, was a poem that Keyes came to dislike for its "lush sensuality." Even so, it is an effective piece of plangent rhetoric that rises to a resounding climax:

> Young men drunk with death's unquenchable wisdom,
> Remember your lovers who gave you more than love.
> (29–30)

Between November 1940 and the end of April 1941 Keyes wrote only seven poems, the most accomplished being a skillful pastiche of Yeats, "William Yeats in Limbo," and "Advice for a Journey," which begins "The drums mutter for war." This was a barren period for a poet as prolific as Keyes.

During the following six months he wrote over twenty poems, including two that bring out very clearly his preoccupation with pain, "Gilles de Retz" and "Europe's Prisoners," written on 16 and 21 May, respectively. The latter is of interest mainly because it employs Dachau as a symbol of human suffering at a time when even the name was unknown in Britain to all but a handful of people. In "Gilles de Retz," which one may call variations on a theme of pain, there occurs the half-line "Pain is never personal." Events were soon to disprove that philosophical reflection.

Early in May 1941 Keyes met a girl called Milein Cosmann, who had come over to England as a refugee from Nazi Germany. Both she and Renée-Jane Scott, with whom she shared a studio in Oxford, were art students who had been evacuated from London. This is not the place to analyze the tortuous and tortured relationship between Keyes and Milein. It is enough to note that, at first sight, he fell passionately in love with her, and that although she told him she did not reciprocate his feelings he persisted in trying to keep alive a relationship with her until July 1942. He then found some kind of consolation with Renée, while acknowledging that Milein remained the most attractive person he had ever known. He wrote in his diary on 28 July: "I am a damnably self-centered, irresponsible, and often cruel man. But Renée can cure me, if she will."

Within a few days of their first meeting Keyes began to write poems to and about Milein. He continued to find themes and inspiration in literature, notably in Yeats and Rilke, but his own experience of grief now became an element in his poetry. The epitaph on the whole unhappy story is to be found in "North Sea," written in October 1942, one of his most poignant compositions:

> And eastward looking, eastward wondering
> I meet the eyes of Heine's ghost, who saw
> His failure in the grey forsaken waves
> At Rulenstein one autumn. And between
> Rises the shape in more than memory
> Of Düsseldorf, the ringing, river-enfolding
> City that brought such sorrow on us both.
>
> (5–11)

Düsseldorf brought Milein sorrow in that it was the place from which she was exiled; it brought sorrow to Keyes by sending her to England, where he fell in love with her.

During the long vacation of 1941 Keyes wrote a foreword to the anthology *Eight Oxford Poets*, which included poems by himself and by two other poets who were killed in the war, Drummond Allison and Keith Douglas; among the other contributors were Michael Meyer, who later became well known as a translator of Ibsen, and John Heath-Stubbs, one of the best English poets in the twentieth century. In his foreword Keyes announced on behalf of the contributors that "we have little sympathy with the Audenian school of poetry," which was, in his view, too closely concerned with political comment, social observation, modern intellectual concepts, and the employment of colloquial language.

Between September 1941 and the end of the year Keyes wrote over twenty poems, beginning with the much-anthologized "William Wordsworth," partly inspired by Herbert Read's study of the poet. It contains a tribute to Wordsworth's elemental power:

> He was a stormy day, a granite peak
> Spearing the sky; and look, about its base
> Words flower like crocuses in the hanging woods,
> Blank though the dalehead and the bony face.
>
> (11–14)

Of the remainder, the most accomplished are a sonnet, "Pheasant"; a lament and celebration for Glaucus, who was both drowned and glorified: "And cold Aegean voices speak his fame"; and "The Cruel Solstice," the title poem of his posthumous volume, published in 1943. In it he foresees

> A cruel solstice, coming ice and cold
> Thoughts and the darkening of the heart's flame.
>
> (3–4)

In February and March 1942 he worked on an ambitious poem of almost four hundred lines, entitled "The Foreign Gate." Its epigraph comes from Rilke's Sixth Duino Elegy and the whole poem owes much to Rilke, "a pale unlearned poet," while two lines are a direct translation of the first line and a half of the *Duino Elegies*:

> Were I to cry, who in that proud hierarchy
> Of the illustrious would pity me?
>
> (5.12–13)

Although the final section of the poem contains echoes of T. S. Eliot, the predominant influence, according to Meyer, is a poem by Heath-Stubbs, an Oxford contemporary and a great friend whose poetry Keyes passionately admired. Meyer admits that "few of the many literary references have been traced to their ultimate source."

The poem celebrates warrior heroes who have conquered death by sacrificing their lives and thus passing through the foreign gate of death to eternity. Keyes ransacks many lands and epochs for examples of heroes who thus attained peace. Men who died at Dunkirk and Tannenberg blend their voices with those of soldiers who perished at Naseby or in the wars of Rome against Carthage. "Gored Adonis in the myrtle thicket" and Danae make fleeting appearances in section III, which is devoted to the theme of sexual love. Despite some fine resonant passages the poem must be accounted a failure, its diffuse, cloudy symbolism failing to give the reader any sense of poetic coherence. Keyes, however, valued it highly, getting his publisher to delay sending his first volume, *The Iron Laurel*, to the printer until "The Foreign Gate" was completed.

Even as an adolescent Keyes had been aware of the conflict between the forces of death and negation and the power of love. This awareness was proved upon his pulse ever more strongly as the war increased in scale and ferocity, his call-up came ever nearer, and the painful complexity of his feelings for Milein grew more intense. In March 1942 he wrote "War Poet," the theme of which is poets trapped by war:

> I am the man who looked for peace and found
> My own eyes barbed.
> I am the man who groped for words and found
> An arrow in my hand.
>
> (1–4)

More than one commentator has found fault with Keyes for employing the image of an arrow rather than a Bren gun. One might as well censure William Blake for summoning a bow of burning gold, arrows of desire, a spear, chariots of fire, and a sword, on the grounds that, in Blake's day, those weapons of war were obsolete. A poet works through images that kindle his imagination, whether they are contemporary or archaic.

Keyes left Oxford on 8 April, in the middle of term, for Omagh in Northern Ireland, where he reported to the Infantry Training Centre. While stationed there he wrote two fine poems, "Ulster Soldier," in which he expresses his apprehension of "perplexities and terrors," and "The True Heart," a lyrical meditation on sorrow and the end of sorrow:

> Guarded from love and wreck and turbulence
> The sad explorer finds security
> From all distraction but the thin lament
> Of broken shells remembering the sea.
>
> (9–12)

On 8 May he joined the Officer Cadet Training Unit at Dunbar, Scotland. The poet Edmund Blunden, who met him at that period, remarked on his alertness and vigor; and his imaginative energy matched the force with which he mastered his military training. His first poem from Dunbar, called "Dunbar, 1650," unlike most of his work, evokes a particular historical moment in a particular place, and displays some of the characteristics of the Auden school, held in such disfavor by Keyes and his fellow poets at Oxford. Other good poems followed rapidly, displaying an assurance and a disciplined passion that he had hitherto seldom commanded. Two linked poems belong to August, "Dido's Lament for Aeneas" and "Rome Remember." Keyes wrote a number of dramatic monologues, none more rhythmically delicate and emotionally convincing than Dido's speech before her death:

> The smoke blows over the breakers, the high pyre waits.
> His mind was a blank wall throwing echoes,
> Not half so subtle as the coiling flames.
>
> (7–9)

"Rome Remember," whose title comes from the burden of a poem by John Lydgate, is even more impressive, a lament for Carthage and for the city that destroyed her and will in its turn be destroyed by the barbarians from the north:

> O Rome, you city of soldiers, remember the singers
> That cry with dead voices along the African shore.
>
> (8–9)

The blank verse is both firm and flexible, an instrument designed to encompass the entire range of emotions awakened by the theme of imperial triumph and decay.

In late July Keyes had sent a copy of *The Iron Laurel* to Drummond Allison, inscribing on the flyleaf a couplet from George Crabbe:

> Love is like gout; for both diseases spread
> A kind of gloomy pomp about the bed.

He was still enthralled by his infatuation for Milein, and although his growing affection for Renée assuaged the old torment, the few poems he wrote on the theme of love are either nostalgic or uneasy. He contemplated resignation and death more steadily than love.

The finest poems that he wrote between October 1942 and the end of the year explicitly or implicitly weave variations on those twin themes. "Four Postures of Death" confronts them directly; "Moonlight Night on the Port" both mourns those drowned at sea and accepts the likelihood that the poet and his comrades will also drown. "Actaeon's Lament" meditates on a death enshrined in classical legend, while "An Early Death" contemplates the grief of a mother for a son who has died (presumably in war) and the grief of Mary over the crucified Christ. "Poem from the North" opens with three lines that are, for Keyes, unusually firmly rooted in prosaic reality:

> As I passed under the statue of Mr. Gladstone
> The snow came back, dancing down slantwise, whipping
> That righteous face with all the old sky's scorn.

It ends with a menacing vision of a world at war, of a city whose inhabitants are doomed:

> Winter, the hunter's season, will not pity
> The people afraid to be born who crowd the streets
> Or those afraid of death who crouch in bed
> Behind the darkened windows of this city.
> I hear the hunter's horn, the long halloo,
> The cold wind beating at a stone-dead statue.
>
> (17–22)

"William Byrd" is a poem of serenity and hope, qualities not often found in the body of Keyes's work. Byrd was an Elizabethan composer who refused to renounce Roman Catholicism and whose music could not be sung in Anglican cathedrals. It is one of Keyes's most assured dramatic monologues, with a rhythmical delicacy and a verbal poise that lend the poem a rare distinction.

"The Wilderness," Keyes's latest surviving poem except "The Grail," was written between December 1942 and January 1943. He regarded it as one of his "nearest misses." An ambitious poem of 150 lines, it reverts to a theme that had preoccupied him throughout his career as a poet: the journey to the desolate place. He had originally dedicated the poem to "Geoffrey Chaucer, George Darley, T. S. Eliot, the other explorers." Keyes himself believed that he had approached the style of Eliot's *Little Gidding*; and it may well be that this is precisely what is wrong with the poem. It lacks the strong individuality, the lyrical intensity, the poetic coherence that characterize the strongest and most original of his shorter poems.

Keyes embarked for Algiers with his battalion on 13 March 1943. In a letter to Heath-Stubbs dated 6 March he had reviewed his past life and found that "it was all quite worthwhile except for the sex part." But it is reassuring to know that on the voyage out he kept photographs of Milein and of Renée above his bed, "because they are both so beautiful." Although he added in his diary that he never dreamed of them, he wrote to Renée on 27 March describing what he called "a most strange and unlikely dream. I dreamt that *we* were being married and saw the actual ceremony."

Keyes enjoyed his brief stay in Algiers enormously; but all too soon his battalion moved into battle positions in Tunisia, going into action in mid-April. On 29 April Keyes led a patrol into the hills near Sidi Abdallah and, together with his orderly, Harold Smith, lost contact with the rest of the patrol. It was thought that they had been taken prisoner, but on 21 June a unit of the Army Graves Service came upon four graves, two of which bore crosses marked with the names of Sidney Keyes and Harold Smith. The bodies could not be identified, nor has the mystery of Keyes's death ever been solved. Even his personal possessions, which he had left in his billet, disappeared completely in the confusion of the war. It is highly probable that they included the manuscripts of poems.

Keyes saluted Rilke as a "Poet of Death," but he was not a decadent romantic dominated by the death wish. In a letter to Church in January 1943 he remarked that he didn't "even (consciously) follow the present trend towards a new and over-wrought Romanticism" (Meyer, p. xvii). Deeply aware as he was of the significance of death in romantic and postromantic poetry, he viewed with some disdain the persistent presence of the death wish in German poetry, and the predisposition of Germans to make an art of death: "It remains for someone to make an art of love, a much harder task . . . " (Meyer, p. xx). He passionately wanted to live, even into old age, and in a letter to Renée written just before he was killed he announced his determination to "get back *sometime* if it's humanly possible" (Meyer, p. xx).

Very few of Keyes's poems touch directly on the war. Even "Timoshenko," written in September 1942, is a portrait of a remote, historical, almost mythological, figure, only slightly more contemporary than Dido and barely more human than Adonis. Blunden put his finger on an important truth when he wrote of Keyes that "the cruel solstice was to him not war, so much as the larger commotion and dissonance of which war is a partial embodiment." Bearing in mind that qualification, we may recognize in Keyes a war poet of prodigious gifts and lasting achievement, who died in battle a month before his twenty-first birthday.

KEITH DOUGLAS

KEITH DOUGLAS was born on 24 January 1920; when he was eight years old his parents were separated. He remained with his mother, who secured a place for him when he was eleven at Christ's Hospital, a school reserved for poor boys of high academic intelligence. In October 1938 he went up to Merton College, Oxford, where his tutor was Blunden, himself a former pupil at Christ's Hospital.

Douglas had always been a difficult character, and even the kindly Blunden spoke of "an impulsive and obstinate streak which was sometimes the despair of his friends." Less charitable acquaintances found him aggressive and ruthless, unimpeded by conventional good manners or consideration for the susceptibilities of others. His biographer recounts an anecdote of April 1944, when Douglas informed

a "truculent civilian" that if his four-year-old daughter's drawings really were as good as Graham Sutherland's, he should try and retard the child's growth, "she was obviously at her best age and might grow like Daddy."
(D. Graham, *Keith Douglas*, p. 248)

Those unlikeable qualities were the obverse of his characteristic virtues: a directness of approach, a dislike of humbug, a determination to perform the task in hand, and a zest for every kind of adventure. Allied with a determined courage, they fitted him to be a good, pugnacious soldier.

Douglas was fond of women, and his tastes both in Oxford and later in Egypt were catholic and cosmopolitan. Yet although he was neither fickle nor shallow he found it hard to maintain a stable or lasting relationship with women, mainly because they could not meet the exacting emotional demands that he made upon them. He was continually shipwrecked on the wilder shores of love.

The earliest of his poems printed in *Complete Poems*, and entitled "Mummers," bears the date 1934. Like Keyes, Douglas was a precocious poet, writing verse of remarkable maturity even as a schoolboy. His style is more curt than that of Keyes, harder and more aggressive. Perhaps the finest of his early poems is "The Deceased," printed in the Oxford undergraduate periodical *Cherwell* on 15 June 1940:

> He was a reprobate I grant
> and always liquored till his money went.
>
> His hair depended in a noose from
> his pale brow. His eyes were dumb
> . . .
> You who God bless you never sunk so low
> censure and pray for him that he was so.
> (1–4; 7–8)

This slightly mannered, ironical tone recurs throughout Douglas' later poems, although it became less playful and considerably harsher.

Between July 1940 and June 1941, when he was serving in the army in England, Douglas wrote ten poems, most of which confirm his growing maturity. One in particular, "Simplify me when I'm dead," marks his farewell to England. It is an astonishing poem, especially for a man of twenty-one, a poem that contemplates with ironical detachment the poet's imminent mortality. The language is bare and intense, infusing the poem with an energy that is all the more terrifying for being so completely under control:

> Remember me when I am dead
> and simplify me when I'm dead.
>
> As the processes of earth
> strip off the colour and the skin:
> take the brown hair and blue eye
>
> and leave me simpler than at birth,
> when hairless I came howling in
> as the moon entered the cold sky.
> (1–8)

The technical brilliance of the versification and the unobtrusive cunning that links the stanzas with rhymes serve to reinforce the poem's emotional balance and power.

By 25 June 1941 Douglas was on board the ship that was to land him at Suez two months later. After a few weeks in Cairo and a spell in the hospital in Palestine, he joined his regiment, the Sherwood Rangers. This former cavalry regiment was not likely to be congenial to a young man of Douglas' temperament. Their senior officers were mostly rich members of the landed gentry who tended to look down on cocksure young officers like Douglas who had not hunted in prewar England. Indeed, his relations with the commanding officer and other superiors remained at best uneasy and at worst mutually hostile.

This is not the place to describe Douglas' visits to Palestine, Syria, Alexandria, and Cairo, or to follow the intricacies of his relationships with Olga, Renée, Milena, Fortunée, Reman, Marcelle, Pilar, and the girl whom he called the Turkish Delight. It is enough to observe that although some of these were passing fancies, Douglas felt genuine affection for Olga and Milena. His dealings with women, like his widening acquaintance with the life of the Middle East, gave him a greater understanding of the world and of human nature.

Like every British soldier, Douglas observed the contrast between the wretchedness of the poor and the ostentatious wealth of the great landowners. "Egypt," probably written in September 1942, describes a girl "diseased and blind of an eye":

> her beauty, succumbing in a cloud
> of disease, disease, apathy. My God,
> the king of this country must be proud.
> (18–20)

Douglas loathed King Farouk, about whom British troops sang ribald songs, and a year later, in a letter to his mother, referred to him in scatological terms, accusing him of exploiting more *fellahin* (peasants or agricultural laborers) than any of his "great fat oily subjects."

There was, however, an even more dramatic contrast that fascinated Keith Douglas: the one between the glittering, tawdry, pleasure-seeking world of Cairo and the austerity of the desert, where men were locked in mortal combat. Until October 1942 he knew the desert only by repute. When his regi-

ment moved forward in preparation for what was rumored to be a major battle, Douglas was left behind at divisional headquarters in charge of a two-ton Ford truck.

Greedily as he had enjoyed the sensual pleasures of Cairo, Douglas was not the man to skulk in safety while his regiment went into battle. On 23 October he heard the artillery barrage that preceded the El Alamein offensive; four days later he committed a serious breach of military discipline by driving his truck into the battle zone, discovering the whereabouts of the Sherwood Rangers, and presenting himself to Colonel Kellett. The officer greeted his unexpected arrival with admirable suavity: "We're *most* glad to see you—er—as always." Kellett had lost so many officers that his words of welcome were not wholly ironical.

In the days ahead Douglas proved his bravery. Kellett may have disliked him, but he admired Douglas' toughness and courage; he arranged for his unauthorized departure from headquarters to be overlooked and for him to stay with the regiment as it advanced toward North Africa. Douglas fought with such gallantry that he was recommended for a Military Cross, though he did not get one; and on 15 January 1943 he was wounded in action at Zem Zem.

On 25 January he reached No. 1 General Hospital, El Ballah, Palestine, where he spent six fruitful weeks. It was probably there that he began his narrative of the desert fighting published in 1946 under the title *Alamein to Zem Zem*, a vigorous and at times extremely vivid account of the campaign, which contains the germ of some of his war poems. He also wrote a few of his most powerful and accomplished poems at El Ballah.

In February 1943 *Selected Poems of Keith Douglas, J. C. Hall and Norman Nicholson* appeared. Douglas and Hall, who was in England, corresponded between June and August, mainly about Douglas' recent poems, which Hall found unsatisfying compared with his earlier work. Douglas replied in a letter of 10 August, which serves as the best introduction to his war poems that we can hope to have:

> . . . my object (and I don't give a damn about my duty as a poet) is to write true things, significant things in words each of which works for its place in a line. My rhythms, which you find enervated, are carefully chosen to enable the poems to be *read* as significant speech: I see no reason to be either musical or sonorous about things at present. . . . To trust

anyone or to admit any hope of a better world is criminally foolish, as foolish as it is to stop working for it. It sounds silly to say work without hope, but it can be done; it's only a form of insurance; it doesn't mean work hopelessly.

(*Complete Poems*, p. 124)

The first-fruit of Douglas' experience of battle was "Dead Men," which appeared in the March 1943 issue of *Citadel*, a periodical printed in Cairo:

> Tonight the moon inveigles them
> to love: they infer from her gaze
> her tacit encouragement.
> Tonight the white dresses and the jasmine scent
> in the streets. I in another place
> see the white dresses glimmer like moths. Come
>
> to the west, out of that trance, my heart—
>
> (1–7)

It is just possible to read those lines as a romantic invocation of women known and loved in Cairo or in Alexandria, inhabiting the world of Durrell's *Alexandria Quartet*; but the dry vocabulary—"inveigles," "infer," "tacit encouragement"—and the curt rhythm suggest that Douglas is deliberately eschewing romantic lyricism because, as he put it in his letter to Hall, "to write on the themes which have been concerning me lately in lyrical and abstract forms, would be immense bullshitting." And it is difficult to take the operatic invocation, "Come/to the west," as anything but a sardonic gesture, an invitation to a hideous rendezvous, where we shall find

> the dead men, whom the wind
> powders till they are like dolls.
>
> (11–12)

Their bodies may rest undiscovered or a wild dog may have eaten them:

> Then leave the dead in the earth, an organism
> not capable of resurrection, like mines,
> less durable than the metal of a gun,
> a casual meal for a dog, nothing but the bone
> so soon, But tonight no lovers see the lines
> of the moon's face as the lines of cynicism.
>
> (25–30)

"Cairo Jag," like "Dead Men" probably written at El Ballah in February 1943, resumes the themes of that poem more savagely. It opens with a satirical glance at some of the women in Cairo who were the companions of British officers. Douglas appears to despise himself as well as the women in question:

> Shall I get drunk or cut myself a piece of cake,
> a pasty Syrian with a few words of English
> or the Turk who says she is a princess—she dances
> apparently by levitation?

The second stanza modulates from that garish world into the wretched quarters of the Egyptian poor, with the "stenches and the sour smells," which may well be the true habitat of the women of the first stanza, beneath their stink of jasmine. The poem ends with a grim description of the battlefield:

> But by a day's travelling you reach a new world
> the vegetation is of iron
> dead tanks, gun barrels split like celery
> the metal brambles have no flowers or berries
> and there are all sorts of manure, you can imagine
> the dead themselves, their boots, and possessions
> clinging to the ground, a man with no head
> has a packet of chocolate and a souvenir of Tripoli.
>
> (23–30)

Although Douglas wrote other poems at El Ballah in February and March, none has the weight of "Dead Men" and "Cairo Jag"; and the same is true of poems on which he worked during his leave in Tel Aviv after his discharge from the hospital at the end of March. In May and June, after he had rejoined his regiment in Tunisia, he completed two poems, "Aristocrats"[2] and "Vergissmeinnicht," and began work on "How to Kill," which he completed two or three months later.

"Aristocrats" bears as an epigraph the saying attributed by Suetonius to the emperor Vespasian on his deathbed: "I think I am becoming a God." The epigraph sets the tone of the whole poem, helping us to fathom the complex, even contradictory, emotions that were fluctuating in Douglas' imagination as he worked on the poem. During his absence from the regiment, three of its senior officers had fallen in action. Although Douglas had felt no liking for the men and had despised their limitations, their deaths moved him more deeply than he would have thought possible. Mingled with irritation at their stupidity,

---

[2] *Complete Poems* (London, 1978) prints what seems to be a later version of this poem entitled "Sportsmen." The text of "Aristocrats" quoted here is from D. Graham, *Keith Douglas 1920–1944: A Biography* (London, 1974).

other emotions contended for mastery: a sense of comradeship in battle, admiration for their courage and unconcern, amusement at their foibles, compassion at their deaths. "Aristocrats," like all good poems, is more than an expression of emotions, and it has a wider application than any lament for fellow officers. It contains an impersonal recognition that a social order is passing away, the death of three officers of the Sherwood Rangers being a symbol that the old regime was vanishing. Out of these disparate elements Douglas made a poem:

> Peter was unfortunately killed by an 88:
> it took his leg away, he died in the ambulance.
> I saw him crawling on the sand; he said
> It's most unfair, they've shot my foot off.
>
> How can I live among this gentle
> obsolescent breed of heroes, and not weep?
>
> (1-6)

The Sherwood Rangers employed in their radio code a set of sporting terms; the practice exasperated Douglas so much that on one occasion, in the middle of a battle, he communicated a message in a parody of the code and consequently incurred a reprimand for his mild insolence. Now, in the poem's last stanza, Douglas incorporates even this private terminology into the structure of myth and enlists the dead officers of his regiment, with their anachronistic gallantry, into the company of those who fell at Roncesvalles:

> The plains were their cricket pitch
> and in the mountains the tremendous drop fences
> brought down some of the runners. Here then
> under the stones and earth they dispose themselves,
> I think with their famous unconcern.
> It is not gunfire I hear but a hunting horn.
>
> (15-20)

"Vergissmeinnicht," perhaps the most famous of his poems, demonstrates Douglas' mastery of his art: the hard, clear narrative line of the poem, the accuracy of the epithets he uses to describe the German soldier's corpse, the skill of the versification, shifts in the rhyme scheme, and his control of what might have been a welter of disruptive emotions are factors that ensure the poem's success. Douglas comes upon the body of a German in a gunpit; among the dead man's rubbish lies a photograph of his girl on which she has written "Vergissmeinnicht"—forget me

not. Douglas and his companions "see him almost with content," but without denying his satisfaction at the destruction of an enemy, the poet imagines how the girl will weep at the sight of her lover and observes with a measure of compassion how love and death are commingled:

> For here the lover and killer are mingled
> who had one body and one heart.
> And death who had the soldier singled
> has done the lover mortal hurt.

"How to Kill" may owe something to an early poem, "·303," probably written when he was fifteen. He looks through a machine gun's sights and sees men "weep, cough, sprawl in their entrails." Eight years later, in the most subtle and introspective of his poems, Douglas imagines the appearance of a soldier in the crosswires of his dial of glass:

>   I cry
> NOW. Death, like a familiar, hears
>
> and look, has made a man of dust
> of a man of flesh. This sorcery
> I do. Being damned, I am amused
> to see the centre of love diffused
> and the waves of love travel into vacancy.
> How easy it is to make a ghost.
>
> The weightless mosquito touches
> her tiny shadow on the stone,
> and with how like, how infinite
> a lightness, man and shadow meet.
> They fuse. A shadow is a man
> when the mosquito death approaches.
>
> (12-25)

No poem of Douglas' is more disquieting and chill in its apprehension of death and in its metaphysical awareness of damnation.

In September 1943 Douglas was back in Cairo, where he was overcome by various kinds of frustration. In one incident his frustration may have been partially relieved by an altercation with a taxi driver who demanded an exorbitant fare; Douglas broke the taxi's distributor. He enjoyed meeting some of the leading contributors to *Personal Landscape*, Bernard Spencer, Terence Tiller, Lawrence Durrell, and G. S. Fraser, regaling them with tales of burning tanks and roasting bodies. But Douglas was soon to bid farewell to Egypt and to his friends: his regiment embarked for Britain on 17 November. He left copies of most of his war poems with the editors of *Personal Landscape*, among them his last poem on Cairo life, "Behaviour of Fish in an Egyptian Tea Garden." The fish are men with predatory intent toward the white stone who, with red lips and carmine fingernails, sits in the sea floor of the afternoon, slyly eating ice cream. Douglas sustains the underwater image and its attendant metaphors throughout all seven stanzas of his gently satirical and relaxed poem.

The Sherwood Rangers discovered on their return home that they were to train for the invasion of Europe. During his six months in England Douglas met his last love, Betty Jesse, an intelligent, attractive young woman who worked for Nicholson and Watson, the firm that had agreed to publish a collection of Douglas' poems. Piqued by his arrogance and cynicism, she told him, half-seriously, that he was her "bête noire." This prompted him to begin a poem entitled "Bête Noire," of which we have fragments; and to write a note on a drawing for the jacket of "Bête Noire," the title for his projected volume of poems. The "Bête Noire" fragments resume the themes of certain earlier poems and, had Douglas been able to complete it, he might have achieved a masterly summing up of his life and art. But he knew it was a poem he couldn't realize.

What he could write was "To Kristin Yingcheng Olga Milena," a masterly valediction to those "Women of four countries" whom he had loved, even though he labels them "four poisons for the subtle senses." His last poem, "On a Return from Egypt," regrets that he has had to leave unpicked the lilies of ambition:

> but time, time is all I lacked
> to find them, as the great collectors before me.
> (17–18)

Envisaging what awaited him in Europe, Douglas ends his poem with a confession:

> I fear what I shall find.

Like Keyes fifteen months before, Douglas was about to embark on a journey from which he was certain he would not return. There are other parallels between the two poets: both accepted Rilke's notion that a man carries his death within him; and although Keyes was more completely under the influence of Rilke than was Douglas, the latter had read a number of Rilke's poems in German as well as in an English translation by Ruth Speirs. Dissimilar as they were in their approach to women, Douglas and Keyes had both endured the stresses of love and exploited the conflict of love and death.

At the end of May 1944 Douglas took communion at an altar set up beside his tank by Leslie Skinner, the regimental padre, and attended evensong in the small village church at Sway in the New Forest. The regiment sailed for France on 5 June at midnight; on 6 June Douglas commanded a tank troop in the assault on the Normandy beaches, and on 8 June he was with his regiment when it entered Bayeux. The next day, in a skirmish near the village of St. Pierre, he was killed by mortar fire.

ALUN LEWIS

ALUN LEWIS, who was born on 1 July 1915 at Aberdare in Glamorgan, Wales, differed sharply from Keyes and Douglas in his upbringing, education, and emotional life. The members of his family had followed a variety of callings: his grandfather worked as a miner for fifty years; his father, at one time a schoolmaster, became the director of education for Aberdare; one uncle was professor of Celtic studies at Aberystwyth and another was a Congregational minister. Although Lewis committed himself to no political or social cause, he was aware of belonging to a community, and his sense of detachment as a poet was always balanced by a feeling of sympathy with his fellowmen, whether they were British private soldiers or Indian peasants.

Whereas Douglas and Keyes moved on from English public schools to Oxford, Lewis, after winning a scholarship locally at Cowbridge Grammar School, became a student at the University College of Wales at Aberystwyth, where he gained first-class honors in history before obtaining an M.A. at Manchester.

In 1941 he married Gweno Ellis, a teacher of German, thus securing the kind of loving and stable relationship denied to Douglas and to Keyes; but his constant postings in Britain and his embarkation for India made any settled life together impossible. He celebrated their love in "Postscript: for Gweno":

> If I should go away,
> Beloved, do not say
> "He has forgotten me."

For you abide,
A singing rib within my dreaming side;
You always stay,
And in the mad tormented valley
Where blood and hunger rally
and Death the wild beast is uncaught, untamed,
Our soul withstands the terror
And has its quiet honour
Among the glittering stars your voices named.

There is nothing so directly passionate as this lyric in the poetry of Douglas or of Keyes or, indeed, in the poetry of any other war poet.

Despite his early pacifism Lewis volunteered for military service in 1940, becoming a postal clerk with the Royal Engineers and gaining a commission as an infantry officer the following year. In 1942 his regiment was converted to tanks, and in 1943 Lewis embarked for India. His early poems appeared in March 1942 under the title *Raiders' Dawn*, and included work that went back to his days as a private. Some of his poems convey with remarkable fidelity the mood of the British army after all British forces had been driven out of Europe in June 1940, not to return until June 1944. Several hundred thousand troops stationed in camps or in barracks underwent training designed to make them ready to resist a German invasion and, eventually, to land in Europe as a liberating army. Units moved from place to place within Britain for no apparent reason, enduring the wretchedness that is always the lot of those serving in the ranks: boredom, discomfort, petty restrictions, the crushing weight of the military machine that is indifferent or hostile to individuality. Many soldiers knew that their wives and children were exposed to the dangers of air raids and to the wearisome routine of blackouts and rationing.

Lewis found in those conditions material for poetry that was both honest and imaginative. His best-known poem of army life, "All Day It Has Rained," presents with rare sympathy the sense of weariness and resignation, tinged with nostalgic longing, that afflicts men under canvas on a Sunday in England. The varying lengths of the lines, combined with the unemphatic rhymes, give the poem an air of relaxed formality, just as the monotony of the rain combines with the twilight to anesthetize any bitterness or pain that might arouse the soldiers from their lassitude:

And we stretched out, unbuttoning our braces,
Smoking a Woodbine, darning dirty socks,

Reading the Sunday papers—I saw a fox
And mentioned it in the note I scribbled home;—
And we talked of girls, and dropping bombs on Rome,
And thought of the quiet dead and the loud celebrities
Exhorting us to slaughter, and the herded refugees;
—Yet thought softly, morosely of them, and as indifferently
As of ourselves or those whom we
For years loved, and will again
Tomorrow maybe love; but now it is the rain
Possesses us entirely, the twilight and the rain.

(13–24)

The poem veers away from its theme when Lewis reflects on Edward Thomas, a poet whom he greatly admired, and who fell in action in 1917 at Arras. The trite observation that Thomas brooded on death and poetry does nothing for the poem or for our understanding of Thomas.

On the other hand, "To Edward Thomas" is a finely conceived and executed tribute to the poet of World War I. It contains a rich and expertly controlled passage about the view that greeted Lewis when he visited the Edward Thomas memorial stone above Steep in Hampshire:

I sat and watched the dusky berried ridge
Of yew-trees, deepened by oblique dark shafts,
Throw back the flame of red and gold and russet
That leapt from beech and ash to birch and chestnut
Along the downward arc of the hill's shoulder. . . .

(17–21)

In the last section of the poem, Lewis meditates on Thomas and on the voice, "soft and neutral as the sky," and growing ever clearer

Till suddenly, at Arras, you possessed that hinted land.

(54)

Lewis portrays the realities of army life without hysteria or evasion in "After Dunkirk":

. . . the rough immediate life of camp
And barracks where the phallic bugle rules
The regimented orchestra of love;
The subterfuges of democracy, the stench
Of breath in crowded tents, the grousing queues,
And bawdy songs incessantly resung
And dull relaxing in the dirty bar.

(30–36)

He was aware that he could not passively accept the dehumanizing effect of such an existence; nor could he accustom himself to the debased standards of his fellows, as he declares in "The Soldier":

> But leisurely my fellow soldiers stroll among the trees.
> The cheapest dance-song utters all they feel.
>
> (13–14)

Lewis is not preening himself on his superiority, but expressing his sadness at the emotional poverty of so many lives.

When Lewis was posted to India he was both unhappy at the prospect of leaving his wife and their unborn child and resolved to come to grips with whatever he found overseas. His approaching departure, embarkation, and voyage form the subject of various poems. "Goodbye" is a sadder, less ecstatic poem than "Postscript: for Gweno," but it is more complex and mature in that it faces the cares of everyday life and the fears that are inseparable from it. It is a poem capable of dealing with both the emerald that the soldier gives his wife and the patches she has sewn on his battle dress:

> Yet when all's done you'll keep the emerald
> I placed upon your finger in the street;
> And I will keep the patches that you sewed
> On my old battledress tonight, my sweet.
>
> (29–32)

The voyage to India moved Lewis to write several good poems: "The Departure"; "On Embarkation"; "A Troopship in the Tropics"; "Port of Call: Brazil"; "Song." "A Troopship in the Tropics" gives a vivid picture of life aboard the ship where five thousand people are crammed into squalid quarters:

> The smell of oranges and excrement
> Moves among those who write uneasy letters. . . .
>
> (13–14)

The sharp precision of those two lines may serve as a reminder that Lewis was a short-story writer as well as a poet. His first collection of short stories appeared in 1943, and more stories were published after his death. Indeed some critics have maintained that he was basically a prose writer rather than a poet, and it is true that certain of his poems read like rather heavy descriptions in prose tricked out with conventional poeticisms. But it is more convincing to argue that he was essentially a poet who was strengthened by certain valuable prosaic elements in his writing. Lewis' besetting temptation as a poet was an over-fluent lyricism decked with hand-me-down romantic properties, and he needed sobriety of language, unsentimental observation, and the steady rhythm of prosaic speech as a corrective. His poems required the patches on the battle dress as well as the emerald and the mad tormented valley.

Occasionally he wrote hauntingly intense lyrics, such as "Song," subtitled "On seeing dead bodies floating off the Cape":

> The flying fish like kingfishers
> Skim the sea's bewildered crests,
> The whales blow steaming fountains,
> The seagulls have no nests
> Where my lover sways and rests.
>
> (21–25)

He began "To Rilke" on the troopship just before it reached Bombay; he was ill with food poisoning and had dreamed about returning home to find that he had died and his wife had been transformed into a bejeweled blonde. The poem is not one of his best, but it is of considerable psychological interest, since it records Lewis' recognition of India's darkness, his envy for Rilke, who had been granted the gift of silence, and his own need for the simplicity that he had once discovered with his wife in distant Wales.

Lewis was overwhelmed by the immensity of India, by the grinding poverty of its people, and by the way in which patches of brilliant vegetation and the colorful Hindu festivals lend a garish contrast to the monotony of daily existence. He wrote a number of poems that evoke the landscapes he traversed in India and, later, in Burma; in these poems he is seldom content to describe the physical properties of what he saw, but relates the landscapes to the inhabitants or finds in them symbols of the spiritual life that had evolved there. Thus "The Mahratta Ghats" opens with a fierce portrayal of the land burned by drought, where a god has granted the peasants an exiguous dole:

> High on the ghat the new turned soil is red,
> The sun has ground it to the finest red,
> It lies like gold within each horny hand.
> Siva has spilt his seed upon this land.

But before the end of the poem it is the figures in the landscape that have come to occupy the center of the stage; the beggar and the soldier, each of them oppressed and economically enslaved, move hopelessly across the ghat:

> Who is it climbs the summit of the road?
> Only the beggar bumming his dark load.
> Who was it cried to see the falling star?
> Only the landless soldier lost in war.
>
> (22–25)

Lewis is a skillful reporter of the Indian scene, of a village or a Hindu festival, or a funeral, but in spite of his sympathy for the peasants in their wretchedness and squalor he remained a detached observer. He could even view the sufferings of the people in a long perspective, wherein the war is merely a shadow that will pass, while the peasants, exploited by the economic system and at the mercy of nature, represent man's instinct to survive. Such is the moral of "The Peasants":

> Across scorched hills and trampled crops
> The soldiers straggle by.
> History staggers in their wake.
> The peasants watch them die.
>
> (9–12)

In the closing months of his life, Lewis' thoughts turned continually toward death. This may well have been because he broke his jaw playing football and spent some time in the hospital at Poona; there he wrote two poems, about his separation from his wife and about the somber reflections engendered by a spell in hospital. "Burma Casualty," a darker poem, concerns a soldier who, after being wounded in action, has to have his leg amputated and learns to comprehend the realm of darkness.

Yet it would be false to suppose that Lewis was deliberately surrendering himself to death. He believed that his most serious work would be done after he had returned home and that he must come to grips with the details of Welsh life and Welsh thought. His preoccupation with death is understandable: he was tired; he hated the process of war and the separation it brought from everything he loved; like most Europeans he was weighed down by the oppressiveness of India, the passive suffering of its people, the omnipresent stench and panoply of death. It is not surprising that he had a presentiment of his own death, nor that it may sometimes have offered a welcome escape from a world of unease.

In the poems written toward the end of his life

Lewis explored one of the themes that run through the work of Keyes and of Douglas: the conflict between life and death, negation and love. He is explicit about this in a letter to his wife:

And although I am more and more engrossed with the single poetic theme of Life and Death, for there doesn't seem to be any question more directly relevant than this one of what survives of all the beloved, I find myself quite unable to express at once the passion of Love, the coldness of Death (Death is cold) and the fire that beats against resignation, acceptance. Acceptance seems so spiritless, protest so vain. In between the two I live.

(In the Green Tree, p. 16)

The most richly imagined poem to spring from that conflict is "The Jungle." He wrote about it to Robert Graves, who was helping him to prepare a second collection of poems, which was published in 1945 under the title *Ha! Ha! Among the Trumpets*. Part of Lewis' letter is printed in Graves's foreword:

I've felt a number of things deeply out here; perhaps the jungle has moved me more deeply than anything else. . . . but when I wrote a poem about the jungle I found it had become a criticism of the Western world which in a measure I understand, but of the jungle I had said nothing.

It is true that Lewis criticizes the Western world both directly and by stressing the idyllic beauty of the jungle, beside which our urban civilization is mean and drab:

> The patient queues, headlines and slogans flung
> Across a frightened continent, the town
> Sullen and out of work, the little home
> Semi-detached, suburban. . . .
>
> (31–34)

Yet he has said a great deal about the jungle in passages that are among the most vivid and evocative he ever wrote:

> The crocodile slides from the ochre sand
> And drives the great translucent fish
> Under the boughs across the running gravel.
>
> . . .
>
> But we who dream beside this jungle pool
> Prefer the instinctive rightness of the poised
> Pied kingfisher deep darting for a fish
> To all the banal rectitudes of states,
> The dew-bright diamonds on a viper's back

To the slow poison of a meaning lost
And the vituperations of the just.

. . .

The banyan's branching clerestories close
The noon's harsh splendour to a head of light.

(5–7; 37–43; 44–45)

The two final sections of the poem move between meditations on love, death, human responsibility, and the immediacy of the jungle. There is a superb moment when the poet moves away from his concern with elemental love and celebrates the individual's need for human love:

Oh you who want us for ourselves,
Whose love can start the snow-rush in the woods
And melt the glacier in the dark coulisse,
Forgive this strange inconstancy of soul,
The face distorted in a jungle pool
That drowns its image in a mort of leaves.

(64–69)

Lewis seldom uses language so daringly and unerringly. The initial shock of encountering in a poem about the jungle images derived from snowfall and glaciers gives way to a recognition of their rightness. Moreover the employment of uncommon words seems equally well justified. The word "coulisse," besides being the precise geological term required by the context, echoes the sound of "snow" and "glacier" and anticipates the sibilants of the next line. And the phrase "mort of leaves" is an even greater triumph of poetic suggestiveness, for the very rare word "mort," which means a large number, carries with it associations belonging to the French word for death. Lewis seldom equaled the strength and lyrical flow of those few lines.

His own death remains as blurred as the image in the jungle pool. On 5 March 1944 at Goppe Pass in Arakan, Burma, where his regiment had advanced to face the Japanese, Lewis was wounded by a pistol shot and died in the Casualty Clearing Station at Bawli. The vagueness of that account in the official regimental history has led to rumors that he killed himself or was murdered for political reasons (he was the battalion intelligence officer). Nobody has brought forward any evidence to support either of those theories.

Lewis' poetry seldom displays the intellectual force or the hard pulsating clarity that mark the best work of Douglas; and it seldom moves with the lyrical grace and assurance that so often give distinction to Keyes's poems. But his concern for mankind, especially the poor of Wales and of India, his patient exploration of love and death, and his ability, in a handful of poems, to shape his feelings of loneliness and fear into the formal pattern of verse are likely to ensure the survival of the best work that he left behind in *Raiders' Dawn* and *Ha! Ha! Among the Trumpets.*

EPILOGUE

SOME ten years after the war was over Charles Causley wrote "At the British War Cemetery, Bayeux." It is a less solemn, liturgical poem than Laurence Binyon's "For the Fallen," which ever since its publication in September 1914 has been an almost official requiem for those who die in battle. Causley's poem is more lyrical, at times even a refusal to mourn:

On your geometry of sleep
The chestnut and the fir-tree fly,
And lavender and marguerite
Forge with their flowers an English sky.

(9–12)

Yet one notes, in this idyllic stanza, the harsh double meaning of "forge," and in the poem's last two stanzas, Causley's brief dialogue with the dead, he acknowledges the pity of war and the sacrifice of those who died so that the living might be free:

About your easy head my prayers
I said with syllables of clay.
What gift, I asked, shall I bring now
Before I weep and walk away?

Take, they replied, the oak and laurel.
Take our fortune of tears and live
Like a spendthrift lover. All we ask
Is the one gift you cannot give.

(17–24)

SELECTED BIBLIOGRAPHY

JOHN BAYLISS

I. SEPARATE WORKS. *The White Knight* (London, 1945).

POETS OF WORLD WAR II

NORMAN CAMERON

I. Collected Works. *Collected Poems* (London, 1957).

ROY CAMPBELL

I. Separate Works. *Talking Bronco* (London, 1946).

II. Collected Works. *Collected Poems*, 3 vols. (London, 1949; 1957; 1960).

III. Biographical and Critical Sutdies. P. Alexander, *Roy Campbell: A Critical Biography* (London, 1982).

CHARLES CAUSLEY

I. Separate Works. *Farewell, Aggie Weston* (London, 1951); *Survivor's Leave* (London, 1953); *Union Street* (London, 1957).

KEITH DOUGLAS

I. Separate Works. *Alamein to Zem Zem* (London, 1946), prose narrative with app. of poems and author's line drawings, repr. without poems and with intro. by Lawrence Durrell (London, 1966).

II. Selected Works. *Selected Poems of Keith Douglas, J. C. Hall and Norman Nicholson* (London, 1943); T. Hughes, ed., *Selected Poems* (London, 1964).

III. Collected Works. J. Waller and G. S. Fraser, eds., *Collected Poems* (London, 1951); J. Waller, G. S. Fraser, and J. C. Hall, eds., *Collected Poems* (London, 1966), a revision of the 1951 ed.; D. Graham, ed., *Complete Poems* (London, 1978), variant texts for certain poems from 1951 and 1966 eds.

IV. Biographical and Critical Studies. D. Graham, *Keith Douglas 1920–1944: A Biography* (London, 1974); J. Stratford, *The Arts Council Collection of Modern Literary Manuscripts 1963–1972* (London, 1974), contains a description and discussion of the Douglas papers in the British Library.

GAVIN EWART

I. Collected Works. *The Collected Ewart 1933–1980* (London, 1980).

G. S. FRASER

I. Separate Works. *Poems* (Leicester, 1981).

ROY FULLER

I. Separate Works. *The Middle of a War* (London, 1942); *A Lost Season* (London, 1944); *Souvenirs* (London, 1980), autobiography.

II. Collected Works. *Collected Poems* (London, 1962).

BERNARD GUTTERIDGE

I. Separate Works. *The Traveller's Eye* (London, 1948).

HAMISH HENDERSON

I. Separate Works. *Elegies for the Dead in Cyrenaica* (London, 1948).

SIDNEY KEYES

I. Separate Works. *The Iron Laurel* (London, 1942); *The Cruel Solstice* (London, 1943).

II. Collected Works. M. Meyer, ed., *Collected Poems* (London, 1945), with a memoir and notes by Meyer.

III. Biographical Studies. J. Guenther, *Sidney Keyes: A Biographical Enquiry* (London, 1965).

ALUN LEWIS

I. Separate Works. *Raiders' Dawn* (London, 1942); *The Last Inspection* (London, 1943), short stories; *Ha! Ha! Among the Trumpets* (London, 1945), with foreword by R. Graves; *Letters from India* (Cardiff, 1946); *In the Green Tree* (London, 1948), with preface by A. L. Rowse, six unpublished stories and a selection of letters mainly from India.

II. Selected Works. I. Hamilton, ed., *Selected Poetry and Prose* (London, 1966); G. Lewis and J. Hooker, eds., *Selected Poems* (London, 1981), with afterword by J. Hooker; J. Pikoulis, ed., *A Miscellany* (Cardiff, 1982).

EDWARD LOWBURY

I. Separate Works. *Time for Sale* (London, 1961).

II. Selected Works. *Selected Poems* (Aberystwyth, 1978).

JOHN MANIFOLD

I. Selected Works. *Selected Verse* (New York–Toronto, 1946); *Selected Poems* (London, 1948).

F. T. PRINCE

I. Collected Works. *Collected Poems* (London, 1979), Anvil Press ed.; *Collected Poems* (London, 1979), Menard Press ed.

HENRY REED

I. Separate Works. *A Map of Verona* (London, 1946); *Lessons of the War* (New York–London, 1970).

MICHAEL RIVIERE

I. Selected Works. *Selected Poems* (Nitchin, 1983).

ALAN ROSS

I. Separate Works. *Poems 1942–67* (London, 1967); *Open Sea* (London, 1975).

VERNON SCANNELL

I. Collected Works. *New and Collected Poems 1950–1980* (London, 1980).

ANTHOLOGIES

J. Lehmann, ed., *Poems from "New Writing 1936–1946"* (London, 1946); I. Hamilton, ed., *The Poetry of War 1939–1945* (London, 1965); R. Blythe, ed., *Components of the Scene* (London, 1966); B. Gardner, ed., *The Terrible Rain: The War Poets of 1939–1945* (London, 1966); R. Skelton, *Poetry of the Forties* (Harmondsworth, 1968); V. Selwyn, E. de Mauny, I. Fletcher, G. S. Fraser, J. Waller, eds., *Return to Oasis: War Poems and Recollections from the Middle East 1940–1946* (London, 1980), with intro. by L. Durrell.

GENERAL CRITICISM

S. Spender, *Poetry Since 1939* (London, 1946); A. Ross, *Poetry 1945–50* (London, 1951); R. N. Currey, *Poets of the 1939–1945 War* (London, 1960; rev. ed., 1967); N. Davidson, *The Poetry Is in the Pity* (London, 1972); A. Banerjee, *Spirit Above Wars: A Study of the English Poetry of the Two World Wars* (London, 1976); V. Scannell, *Not Without Glory: The Poets of the Second World War* (London, 1976), includes the long ch. "American Poets of the Second World War."